# CONSTITUTIONAL LAW: PRINCIPLES AND POLICY

## CASES AND MATERIALS

CONTEMPORARY LEGAL EDUCATION SERIES

# Constitutional Law: Principles and Policy

CASES AND MATERIALS

**JEROME A. BARRON**

**Professor of Law**
**George Washington University National Law Center**

**C. THOMAS DIENES**

**Professor of Law and Government**
**American University, Washington College of Law**

THE BOBBS-MERRILL COMPANY, INC.
PUBLISHERS
INDIANAPOLIS • NEW YORK

J.A.B. for M.H.B.

———•———

C.T.D. for P.C.D.

# Preface

In this book we have attempted to respond to two problems. The first is that the reach of constitutional law has now extended to virtually every aspect of American life. As a result, the case law and literature in the field is almost without measure. The second problem is that the number of teaching hours given the basic course in constitutional law has in general not been expanded.

In our view, if the basic course book in constitutional law is to be a serviceable teaching tool, its virtues must come from selective editing rather than from encyclopedic scope. We have attempted to edit a concise course book in constitutional law. We have tried both to provide the materials necessary for the basic course in constitutional law and yet to place a particular focus on civil rights including some of the most fertile sources of contemporary constitutional law, the equal protection clause and the first amendment. Although we give rather less in the way of coverage of the taxing and commerce powers, we have striven to confront the student with the issues under those powers which are still lively and in flux. Even in that area, our focus is on the separation of powers and federalism problems which bear so heavily on the development of civil rights and liberties.

We have attempted to approach the enigma of due process from the perspective of social science and also in the light of the problems presented by a new technology. Although we have left to the criminal law teachers the unfolding of the full story of the federalization of state criminal procedure under the aegis of the due process clause, we have given particular and, we hope, novel attention to due process in the noncriminal context in fields like welfare rights, the employment relationship and the rights of the student.

Since we were writing a new teaching tool in constitutional law in the era of Watergate, we have been mindful of those thunderous constitutional events. Accordingly, we have given heavy coverage to the constitutional problems presented by the rise of executive power. In order to develop a concise teaching tool on constitutional law we have had to make choices. But we have made choices which we think reflect the *loci* of the pressure points of constitutional law today. We have not included some of the antique learning about the commerce clause. As a result, we have been able to cover issues such as impoundment, executive privilege and the rise of executive law-making. Similarly, we have devoted entire chapters to topics that, for the moment, appear either to suggest or to preclude new constitutional frontiers such as the right of privacy and state action. We have left less lively topics such as intra-governmental immunities to the constitutional historian.

Finally, the pressures of space have not made it possible to indicate at all times what Justices concurred or dissented with respect to a given case. The "cut-off" date for the manuscript was April 1, 1975. Developments subsequent to that date must be left to future supplements.

Professor Barron wishes to thank for their help with the manuscript, Mary Adamski, Cathy Tafoya, and Ellen Spigt of the secretarial staff at the National Law Center, George Washington University, as well as Jeanetta Cutchens of the staff at Syracuse University College of Law. He would also like to thank Nancy Kaplan of the Syracuse University College of Law, class of 1974, for her research assistance.

Professor Dienes wishes to thank the following students at American University, Washington College of Law, for their research assistance: Judith Catterton, Steven Gordon, Dale Andrews, Patricia Black, Michele Goldfarb, James Kilbreth, Claudia Pabo and Augustus Oliver. He also wishes to thank for their help with the manuscript Rebecca Rhines, Deborah Dill, and Cheryl Meek of the secretarial staff at American University, Washington College of Law.

*Jerome A. Barron*
*C. Thomas Dienes*
*Washington, D. C.*

*March, 1975*

# Table of Contents

# Table of Cases

Principal cases are those with page references in italics.

# Chapter 1

# JUDICIAL REVIEW: INSTRUMENT OF AMERICAN CONSTITUTIONALISM

## A. JUDICIAL REVIEW: THE DOCTRINE AND THE CONTROVERSY

The Doctrine of Judicial Review

### MARBURY v. MADISON
Supreme Court of the United States
5 U.S. (1 Cranch) 137, 2 L. Ed. 60 (1803)

[At the end of the eighteenth century, there were two political parties, the Federalist Party led by President John Adams and Thomas Jefferson's Republican (or Anti-Federalist) Party. Unlike the Federalists, the Republicans favored a limited national government. The presidential election of 1800 saw President Adams defeated and Thomas Jefferson elected. Just before the announcement of the election results, President Adams named John Marshall as Chief Justice of the United States Supreme Court to succeed Oliver Ellsworth. On March 3, 1801, the Senate confirmed the appointment of 42 justices of the peace in the District of Columbia. These commissions were signed and sealed by midnight of March 3rd, when the term of President Adams expired. But the commissions had not yet been delivered and remained in the office of the Acting Secretary of State. After his inauguration, President Jefferson ordered his Secretary of State, James Madison, to deliver 25 of these commissions but to withhold the remainder. Among the 17 who did not receive their commissions were William Marbury and three others who asked the United States Supreme Court for a writ of mandamus to compel Secretary Madison to deliver their commissions. *See* 3 A. BEVERIDGE, THE LIFE OF JOHN MARSHALL 105-156 (1919); 1 C. WARREN, THE SUPREME COURT IN UNITED STATES HISTORY 230-268 (rev. ed. 1937).]

Opinion of the Court [Chief Justice MARSHALL].

At the last term on the affidavits then read and filed with the clerk, a rule was granted in this case, requiring the secretary of state to show cause why a mandamus should not issue, directing him to deliver to William Marbury his commission as a justice of the peace for the county of Washington, in the District of Columbia.

No cause has been shown, and the present motion is for a mandamus. The peculiar delicacy of this case, the novelty of some of its circumstances, and the real difficulty attending the points which occur in it, require a complete exposition of the principles on which the opinion to be given by the court is founded.

. . . .

In the order in which the court has viewed this subject, the following questions have been considered and decided.

1st.   Has the applicant a right to the commission he demands?

2nd.   If he has a right, and that right has been violated, do the laws of his country afford him a remedy?

3d.   If they do afford him a remedy, is a mandamus issuing from this court?

The first object of inquiry is,

1st.   Has the applicant a right to the commission he demands?

. . . .

Mr. Marbury . . . since his commission was signed by the President, and sealed by the Secretary of State, was appointed; and as the law creating the office, gave the officer a right to hold for five years, independent of the executive the appointment was not revocable, but vested in the officer legal rights, which are protected by the laws of his country.

To withhold his commission, therefore, is an act deemed by the court not warranted by law, but violative of a vested legal right.

This brings us to the second inquiry; which is,

2d.   If he has a right, and that right has been violated, do the laws of this country afford him a remedy?

The very essence of civil liberty certainly consists in the right of every individual to claim the protection of the laws, whenever he receives an injury. One of the first duties of government is to afford that protection.

. . . .

The government of the United States has been emphatically termed a government of laws, and not of men. It will certainly cease to deserve this high appellation, if the laws furnish no remedy for the violation of a vested legal right.

If this obloquy is to be cast on the jurisprudence of our country, it must arise from the peculiar character of the case.

. . . .

. . . Is the act of delivering or withholding a commission to be considered as a mere political act, belonging to the executive department alone, for the performance of which entire confidence is placed by our constitution in the supreme executive; and for any misconduct respecting which, the injured individual has no remedy?

That there may be such cases is not to be questioned; but that every act of duty, to be performed in any of the great departments of government, constitutes such a case, is not to be admitted.

. . . .

It follows, then, that the question, whether the legality of an act of the head of a department be examinable in a court of justice or not, must always depend on the nature of that act.

. . . .

By the constitution of the United States, the President is invested with certain important political powers, in the exercise of which he is to use his own discretion, and is accountable only to his country in his political character and to his own conscience. To aid him in the performance of these duties, he is authorized to appoint certain officers, who act by his authority, and in conformity with his orders.

In such cases, their acts are his acts; and whatever opinion may be entertained of the manner in which executive discretion may be used, still there exists, and can exist, no power to control that discretion. The subjects are political. They respect the nation, not individual rights, and being intrusted to the executive, the decision of the executive is exclusive. The application of this remark will be perceived by adverting to the act of congress for establishing the department of foreign affairs. This officer, as his duties were prescribed by that act, is to conform precisely to the will of the President. He is the mere organ by whom that will is communicated. The acts of such an officer, as an officer, can never be examinable by the courts.

But when the legislature proceeds to impose on that officer other duties; when he is directed peremptorily to perform certain acts; when the rights of individuals are dependent on the performance of those acts; he is so far the officer of the law; is amenable to the laws for his conduct; and cannot at his discretion sport away the vested right of others.

The conclusion from this reasoning is, that where the heads of departments are the political or confidential agents of the executive, merely to execute the will of the President, or rather to act in cases in which the executive possesses a constitutional or legal discretion, nothing can be more perfectly clear than that their acts are only politically examinable. But where a specific duty is assigned by law, and individual rights depend upon the performance of that duty, it seems equally clear that the individual who considers himself injured, has a right to resort to the laws of his country for a remedy.

. . . .

It remains to be inquired whether,

3d.　He is entitled to the remedy for which he applies. This depends on,

1st.　The nature of the writ applied for; and,

2d.　The power of this court.

1st.　The nature of the writ.

. . . .

This writ, if awarded, would be directed to an officer of government, and its mandate to him would be, to use the words of Blackstone, "to do a particular thing therein specified, which appertains to his office and duty, and which the court has previously determined, or at least supposes, to be consonant to right and justice." Or, in the words of Lord Mansfield, the applicant, in this case, has a right to execute an office of public concern, and is kept out by possession of that right.

These circumstances certainly concur in this case.

Still, to render the mandamus a proper remedy, the officer to whom it is to be directed, must be one to whom, on legal principles, such writ may be directed; and the person applying for it must be without any other specific and legal remedy.

1st.　With respect to the officer to whom it would be directed. The intimate political relation subsisting between the President of the United States and the heads of departments, necessarily renders any legal investigation of the acts of one of those high officers peculiarly irksome, as well as delicate; and excites some hesitation with respect to the propriety of entering into such investigation. Impressions are often received without much reflection or examination, and it is not wonderful that in such a case as this the assertion, by an individual, of his legal claims in a court of justice, to which claims it is the duty of that court to attend, should at first view be considered by some, as an attempt to intrude into the cabinet, and to intermeddle with the prerogatives of the executive.

It is scarcely necessary for the court to disclaim all pretensions to such jurisdiction. An extravagance, so absurd and excessive, could not have been entertained for a moment. The province of the court is, solely, to decide on the rights of individuals, not to inquire how the executive, or executive officers, perform duties in which they have a discretion. Questions in their nature political, or which are, by the constitution and laws, submitted to the executive, can never be made in this court.

But, if this be not such a question; if, so far from being an intrusion into the secrets of the cabinet, it respects a paper which, according to law, is upon record, and to a copy of which the law gives a right, on the payment of ten cents; if it be no intermeddling with a subject over which the executive can be considered as having exercised any control; what is there in the exalted station of the officer, which shall bar a citizen from asserting, in a court of justice, his legal rights, or shall forbid a court to listen to the claim, or to issue a mandamus directing the performance of a duty, not depending on executive discretion, but on particular acts of congress, and the general principles of law?

. . . .

It is not by the office of the person to whom the writ is directed, but the nature of the thing to be done, that the propriety or impropriety of issuing a mandamus is to be determined. Where the head of a department acts in a case, in which executive discretion is to be exercised; in which he is the mere organ of executive will; it is again repeated, that any application to a court to control, in any respect, his conduct would be rejected without hesitation.

But where he is directed by law to do a certain act affecting the absolute rights of individuals, in the performance of which he is not placed under the particular direction of the President, and the performance of which the President cannot lawfully forbid, and therefore is never presumed to have forbidden; as for example, to record a commission, or a patent for land, which has received all the legal solemnities; or to give a copy of such record; in such cases, it is not perceived on what ground the courts of the country are further excused from the duty of giving judgment that right be done to an injured individual, than if the same services were to be performed by a person not the head of a department.

. . . .

This, then, is a plain case for mandamus, either to deliver the commission, or a copy of it from the record; and it only remains to be inquired,

Whether it can issue from this court.

The act to establish the judicial courts of the United States authorizes the Supreme Court "to issue writs of mandamus in cases warranted by the principles and usages of law, to any courts appointed, or persons holding office, under the authority of the United States."

The secretary of state, being a person holding an office under the authority of the United States, is precisely within the letter of the description, and if this court is not authorized to issue a writ of mandamus to such an officer, it must be because the law is unconstitutional, and therefore absolutely incapable of conferring the authority, and assigning the duties which its words purport to confer and assign.

The constitution vests the whole judicial power of the United States in one Supreme Court, and such inferior courts as congress shall, from time to time, ordain and establish. This power is expressly extended to all cases arising under the laws of the United States; and, consequently, in some form, may be exercised over the present case; because the right claimed is given by a law of the United States.

In the distribution of this power it is declared that "the Supreme Court shall have original jurisdiction in all cases affecting ambassadors, other public ministers and consuls, and those in which a state shall be a party. In all other cases, the Supreme Court shall have appellate jurisdiction."

It has been insisted, at the bar, that as the original grant of jurisdiction, to the Supreme and inferior courts, is general, and the clause, assigning original jurisdiction to the Supreme Court, contains no negative or restrictive words, the power remains to the legislature, to assign original jurisdiction to that court in other cases than those specified in the article which has been recited; provided those cases belong to the judicial power of the United States.

If it had been intended to leave it in the discretion of the legislature to apportion the judicial power between the Supreme and inferior courts according to the will of that body, it would certainly have been useless to have proceeded further than to have defined the judicial power, and the tribunals in which it should be vested. The subsequent part of the section is mere surplusage, is entirely without meaning, if such is to be the construction. If congress remains at liberty to give this court appellate jurisdiction, where the constitution has declared their jurisdiction shall be original; and original jurisdiction where the constitution has declared it shall be appellate; the distribution of jurisdiction, made in the constitution, is form without substance.

Affirmative words are often, in their operation, negative of other objects than those affirmed; and in this case, a negative or exclusive sense must be given to them, or they have no operation at all.

It cannot be presumed that any clause in the constitution is intended to be without effect; and, therefore, such a construction is inadmissible, unless the words require it.

. . . .

When an instrument organizing fundamentally a judicial system, divides it into one supreme, and so many inferior courts as the legislature may ordain and establish; then enumerates its powers, and proceeds so far to distribute them, as to define the jurisdiction of the Supreme Court by declaring the cases in which it shall take original jurisdiction, and that in others it shall take appellate jurisdiction; the plain import of the words seems to be, that in one class of cases its jurisdiction is original, and not appellate; in the other it is appellate, and not original. If any other construction would render the clause inoperative, that is an additional reason for rejecting such other construction, and for adhering to their obvious meaning.

To enable this court, then, to issue a mandamus, it must be shown to be an exercise of appellate jurisdiction, or to be necessary to enable them to exercise appellate jurisdiction.

It has been stated at the bar that the appellate jurisdiction may be exercised in a variety of forms, and that if it be the will of the legislature that a mandamus should be used for that purpose, that will must be obeyed. This is true, yet the jurisdiction must be appellate, not original.

It is the essential criterion of appellate jurisdiction, that it revises and corrects the proceedings in a cause already instituted, and does not create that cause. Although, therefore, a mandamus may be directed to courts, yet to issue such a writ to an officer for the delivery of a paper, is in effect the same as to sustain an original action for that paper, and, therefore, seems not to belong to appellate but to original jurisdiction. Neither is it necessary in such a case as this, to enable the court to exercise its appellate jurisdiction.

The authority, therefore, given to the Supreme Court, by the act establishing the judicial courts of the United States, to issue writs of mandamus to public officers, appears not to be warranted by the constitution; and it becomes necessary to inquire whether a jurisdiction so conferred can be exercised.

The question, whether an act, repugnant to the constitution, can become the law of the land, is a question deeply interesting to the United States; but, happily, not of an intricacy proportioned to its interest. It seems only necessary to recognize certain principles, supposed to have been long and well established, to decide it.

That the people have an original right to establish, for their future government, such principles, as, in their opinion, shall most conduce to their own happiness is the basis on which the whole American fabric has been erected. The exercise of this original right is a very great exertion; nor can it, nor ought it, to be frequently repeated. The principles, therefore, so established, are deemed fundamental. And as the authority from which they proceed is supreme, and can seldom act, they are designed to be permanent.

This original and supreme will organizes the government, and assigns to different departments their respective powers. It may either stop here, or establish certain limits not to be transcended by those departments.

The government of the United States is of the latter description. The powers of the legislature are defined and limited; and that those limits may not be mistaken, or forgotten, the constitution is written. To what purpose are powers limited, and to what purpose is that limitation committed to writing, if these limits may, at any time, be passed by those intended to be restrained? The distinction between a government with limited and unlimited powers is abolished, if those limits do not confine the persons on whom they are imposed, and if acts prohibited and acts allowed, are of equal obligation. It is a proposition too plain to be contested, that the constitution controls any legislative act repugnant to it; or, that the legislature may alter the constitution by an ordinary act.

Between these alternatives there is no middle ground. The constitution is either a superior paramount law, unchangeable by ordinary means, or it is on a level with ordinary legislative acts, and, like other acts, is alterable when the legislature shall please to alter it.

If the former part of the alternative be true, then a legislative act contrary to the constitution is not law: if the latter part be true, then written constitutions are absurd attempts, on the part of the people, to limit a power in its own nature illimitable.

Certainly all those who have framed written constitutions contemplate them as forming the fundamental and paramount law of the nation, and, consequently, the theory of every such government must be, that an act of the legislature, repugnant to the constitution, is void.

This theory is essentially attached to a written constitution, and, is consequently, to be considered, by this court, as one of the fundamental principles of our society. It is not therefore to be lost sight of in the further consideration of this subject.

If an act of the legislature, repugnant to the constitution, is void, does it, notwithstanding its invalidity, bind the courts, and oblige them to give it effect? Or, in other words, though it be not law, does it constitute a rule as operative as if it was a law? This would be to overthrow in fact what was established in theory; and would seem, at first view, an absurdity too gross to be insisted on. It shall, however, receive a more attentive consideration.

It is emphatically the province and duty of the judicial department to say what the law is. Those who apply the rule to particular cases, must of necessity expound and interpret that rule. If two laws conflict with each other, the courts must decide on the operation of each.

So if a law be in opposition to the constitution; if both the law and the constitution apply to a particular case, so that the court must either decide that case conformably to the law, disregarding the constitution; or conformably to the constitution, disregarding the law; the court must determine which of these conflicting rules governs the case. This is of the very essence of judicial duty.

If, then, the courts are to regard the constitution, and the constitution is superior to any ordinary act of the legislature, the constitution, and not such ordinary act, must govern the case to which they both apply.

Those, then, who controvert the principle that the constitution is to be considered, in court, as a paramount law, are reduced to the necessity of maintaining that courts must close their eyes on the constitution, and see only the law.

This doctrine would subvert the very foundation of all written constitutions. It would declare that an act which, according to the principles and theory of our government, is entirely void, is yet, in practice, completely obligatory. It would declare that if the legislature shall do what is expressly forbidden, such act, notwithstanding the express prohibition, is in reality effectual. It would be giving to the legislature a practical and real omnipotence, with the same breath which professes to restrict their powers within narrow limits. It is prescribing limits, and declaring that those limits may be passed at pleasure.

That it thus reduces to nothing what we have deemed the greatest improvement on political institutions, a written constitution, would of itself be sufficient, in America, where written constitutions have been viewed with so much reverence, for rejecting the construction. But the peculiar expressions of the constitution of the United States furnish additional arguments in favour of its rejection.

The judicial power of the United States is extended to all cases arising under the constitution.

Could it be the intention of those who gave this power, to say that in using it the constitution should not be looked into? That a case arising under the constitution should be decided without examining the instrument under which it arises?

This is too extravagant to be maintained.

In some cases, then, the constitution must be looked into by the judges. And if they can open it at all, what part of it are they forbidden to read or to obey?

. . . .

. . . [T]he framers of the constitution contemplated that instrument as a rule for the government of courts, as well as of the legislature.

Why otherwise does it direct the judges to take an oath to support it? This oath certainly applies in an especial manner, to their conduct in their official character. How immoral to impose it on them, if they were to be used as the instruments, and the knowing instruments, for violating what they swear to support!

. . . .

Why does a judge swear to discharge his duties agreeably to the constitution of the United States, if that constitution forms no rule for his government? if it is closed upon him, and cannot be inspected by him?

If such be the real state of things, this is worse than solemn mockery. To prescribe, or to take this oath, becomes equally a crime.

It is also not entirely unworthy of observation, that in declaring what shall be the supreme law of the land, the constitution itself is first mentioned; and not the laws of the United States generally, but those only which shall be made in pursuance of the constitution, have that rank.

Thus, the particular phraseology of the constitution of the United States confirms and strengthens the principle, supposed to be essential to all written constitutions, that a law repugnant to the constitution is void; and that courts, as well as other departments, are bound by that instrument.

The rule must be discharged.

---

## NOTES

1. The distinguished constitutional scholar, Edward S. Corwin says that the court in *Marbury v. Madison* wanted to

make it clear that it thought that President Jefferson should have delivered the commissions to those who had been appointed to office under the previous administration. Yet, says Corwin, the court feared "to invite a snub by actually asserting jurisdiction of the matter." The court says Corwin therefore "took the engaging position of declining to exercise power which the Constitution withheld from it, by making the occasion an opportunity to assert a far more transcendent power." *See* E. CORWIN, THE DOCTRINE OF JUDICIAL REVIEW 9 (1914). Doesn't the structure of the decision in *Marbury* corroborate Professor Corwin's thesis? The "lecture" Marshall gave Jefferson on the right of the justices to have their commissions, and the duty of the President to deliver them was really *dicta*, and unnecessary *dicta* at that, since in the end result, the court had, as Marshall held, no jurisdiction of the cause.

Professors Hart and Wechsler have further developed this theme by asking this question: "Would it be right to describe the parts of Marshall's opinion dealing with Marbury's title to the commission and the propriety of the remedy of mandamus as advisory?" *See* HART AND WECHSLER'S THE FEDERAL COURTS AND THE FEDERAL SYSTEM 81 (2d ed.; P. Bator, P. Mishkin, D. Shapiro, & H. Wechsler, eds., 1973).

2.  Jefferson construed *Marbury v. Madison* as a judicial challenge to executive power. Jefferson viewed the language in *Marbury* on the duty to deliver the commissions as subversive "of the independence of the Executive and Senate within their peculiar departments." The constitutional historian, Charles Warren, chronicles Jefferson's reaction as follows: " 'I found the commissions on the table of the Department of State, on my entrance into office, and I forbade their delivery,' he said. 'Whatever is in the Executive offices is certainly deemed to be in the hands of the President, and in this case, was actually in my hands, because when I countermanded them, there was as yet no Secretary of State'; and his indignation over Marshall's opinion continued hot up to the day of his death." *See* 1 C. WARREN, THE SUPREME COURT IN UNITED STATES HISTORY 243 (1947).

Did Chief Justice Marshall rule in *Marbury v. Madison* that the President and high officers of the executive branch were subject to suit in the courts? This issue arose anew in the famous controversy in 1973 and 1974 in which the special prosecutor and the Senate Select Committee on Presidential Campaign Activities (the Watergate Committee) sought the celebrated tapes. The President's lawyers relying on *Marbury* asserted that the President was immune from suit with regard to the exercise of his discretion. From Warren's account, what do you think was

Jefferson's view on the amenability of the President to judicial process?

Doesn't Marshall's willingness to say that Jefferson should have delivered the commissions suggest that an appropriate court could have submitted the President to judicial process? In a per curiam opinion, Nixon v. Sirica, 487 F.2d 700, 712 (D.C. Cir. 1973), the Court of Appeals made the following response to the contention that executive discretion was judicially unreviewable:

> Finally, the President reminds us that the landmark decisions recognizing judicial power to mandamus Executive compliance with "ministerial" duties also acknowledged that the Executive Branch enjoys an unreviewable discretion in many areas of "political" or "executive" administration. While true, this is irrelevant to the issue of presidential immunity from judicial process. The discretionary-ministerial distinction concerns the nature of the act or omission under review, not the official title of the defendant. No case holds that an act is discretionary merely because the President is the actor. If the Constitution or the laws of evidence confer upon the President the absolute discretion to withhold material subpoenaed by a grand jury, then of course we would vacate, rather than approve with modification, the order entered below. However, this would be because the order touched upon matters within the President's sole discretion, not because the President is immune from process generally. We thus turn to an examination of the President's claim of an absolute discretion to withhold evidence from a grand jury.

**3.** Could Chief Justice Marshall have avoided the constitutional question? Consider the language of § 13 of the Judiciary Act of 1789 providing:

"That the Supreme Court shall have exclusive jurisdiction of all controversies of a civil nature, where a state is a party, except between a state and its citizens; and except also between a state and citizens of other states, or aliens, in which latter case it shall have original but not exclusive jurisdiction. And shall have exclusively all such jurisdiction of suits or proceedings against ambassadors or other public ministers, or their domestics, or domestic servants, as a court of law can have or exercise consistently with the law of nations; and original, but not exclusive jurisdiction of all suits brought by ambassadors or other public ministers, or in which a consul, or vice consul, shall be a party. And the trial of issues of fact in the Supreme Court in all actions at law against citizens of the United States shall be by jury. The

Supreme Court shall also have appellate jurisdiction from the circuit courts and courts of the several states in the cases hereinafter specially provided for; and shall have power to issue writs of prohibition to the district courts, when proceeding as courts of admiralty and maritime jurisdiction, and writs of mandamus, in cases warranted by the principles and usages of law, to any courts appointed, or persons holding office, under the authority of the United States."

4. In a searching and rigorous critique of Marshall's attempt to textually justify the power of judicial review claimed for it by Marshall in *Marbury,* Professor Van Alstyne points out that the actual holding of *Marbury* is not necessarily supportive of a view that the judiciary is supreme in the American constitutional system:

## VAN ALSTYNE, A CRITICAL GUIDE TO MARBURY v. MADISON, 1969 Duke L. J. 1*

. . . .

The point is that Marshall arguably may have begged a critical question, *i.e.,* he failed to acknowledge and thus to answer a question critical to the position he takes. *Assuming that an act repugnant to the Constitution is not a law "in pursuance thereof" and thus must not be given effect as the supreme law of the land, who, according to the Constitution, is to make the determination as to whether any given law is in fact repugnant to the Constitution itself?* Such alleged repugnance is ordinarily not self-demonstrating in most cases, as we well know. Marshall never confronts this question. His substitute question, whether a law repugnant to the Constitution still binds the courts, *assumes* that such "repugnance" has appropriately been determined by those granted such power under the Constitution. It is clear, however, that the supremacy clause itself cannot be the clear textual basis for a claim by the judiciary that this prerogative to determine repugnancy belongs to it.

On its face, the clause does not say by whom or how or at what time it shall be determined whether certain laws of the United States were adopted pursuant to the Constitution. Again, the phrase that only such laws shall be part of the supreme law could mean merely that the people should regard the Constitution with deep concern and that *they* should act to prevent Congress from overstepping the Constitution. It might even imply, moreover, a right of civil disobedience or serve as a written reminder to government of the natural right of revolution against tyrannical government which oversteps the terms of the social compact. Such a construction would be consistent with philosophical writings of the period, consistent with the Declaration of Independence, and consistent also with the view of some antifederalists of the period. As a hortatory reminder to the Government of the ultimate right of the people, however, it clearly does not authorize the Court to make the critical judgment as to which laws, if any, were not made in pursuance of the Constitution.

. . . .

## A SPECIFICATION OF THE HOLDING ON CONSTITUTIONAL REVIEW

*In litigation before the Supreme Court, the Court may refuse to give effect to an act of Congress where the act pertains to the judicial power itself. In deciding whether to give effect to such an act, the Court may determine its decision according to its own interpretation of constitutional provisions which describe the judicial power.*

Thus described, the holding in *Marbury v. Madison* is less remarkable than generally supposed. It is also, however, far more defensible because it draws upon one's sympathy to maintain the Court as a co-ordinate branch of government, and not as a superior branch. It represents a defensive use of constitutional review alone, acquiring considerable support from the concept of *separated* powers. It merely minds the Court's *own* business (*i.e.*, what cases shall originate in the Court, what cases shall be treated on appeal or otherwise). Were the Court to lack *this* capacity, it could scarcely be able to maintain even the ordinary function of *non*constitutional judicial review.

. . . .

It must be conceded, however, that this view of "the holding" is one we bring to the case rather than one which clearly characterizes Marshall's opinion. Even an unhurried rereading of the case is not likely to suggest that Marshall was emphasizing, or limiting himself to, the legitimacy of constitutional review used only defensively in the protection of the balance of judicial power. . . .

It is unsurprising, therefore, that the "holding" has been generally regarded as a broader one which carries at least this far: *In litigation before the Supreme Court, the Court may refuse to give effect to an act of Congress where, in the Court's own view, that act is repugnant to the Constitution.*

. . . .

Even this breadth of holding, however, falls far short of cementing the notion of "judicial supremacy." It does not mean, for instance, that either Congress or the President need defer to Supreme Court interpretations of the Constitution so far as their own deliberations are concerned and so far as the efficacy of their power does not depend upon judicial co-operation.

. . . .

If, at this juncture, it should be thought surprising that *Marbury v. Madison* could sensibly be considered by anyone as authoritatively establishing the doctrine of federal substantive judicial supremacy, however, one need look no further than the Supreme Court itself to find an example of such a view! In *Cooper v. Aaron,* the Court said the following with respect to the exclusiveness of its own constitutional interpretations as applied to state laws and the obligations of state officials:

> This decision [*Marbury v. Madison*] declared the basic principle that the federal judiciary is supreme in the exposition of the law of the Constitution, and that principle has ever since been respected by this Court and the Country as a permanent and indispensable feature of our constitutional system.

---

5. In an influential and controversial essay, Professor Wechsler has attempted to establish a case for an explicit textual justification for the doctrine of judicial review proclaimed by Marshall in *Marbury v. Madison.* In the same essay, Wechsler attempted to suggest an approach to judicial review which he considered indispensable to the appropriate use by the judiciary of a doctrine which might otherwise become a "naked power organ." The reference to Learned Hand in the excerpts below from Professor Wechsler's essay are to Judge Hand's belief that judicial review was a practical necessity of American constitutionalism but not "a logical deduction from the structure of the Constitution." *See* L. HAND, THE BILL OF RIGHTS (1958).

**WECHSLER, TOWARD NEUTRAL PRINCIPLES OF CONSTITUTIONAL LAW, 73 Harv. L. Rev. 1 (1959)\***

I. THE BASIS OF JUDICIAL REVIEW

. . . .

Let me begin by stating that I have not the slightest doubt respecting the legitimacy of judicial review, whether the action called in question in a case which otherwise is proper for adjudi-

---

* Copyright 1959 by The Harvard Law Review Association.

cation is legislative or executive, federal or state. I must address myself to this because the question was so seriously mooted by Judge Hand; and though he answered it in favor of the courts' assumption of the power of review, his answer has overtones quite different from those of the answer I would give.

Judge Hand's position was that "when the Constitution emerged from the Convention in September, 1787, the structure of the proposed government, if one looked to the text, gave no ground for inferring that the decisions of the Supreme Court, and *a fortiori* of the lower courts, were to be authoritative upon the Executive and the Legislature"; that "on the other hand it was probable, if indeed it was not certain, that without some arbiter whose decision should be final the whole system would have collapsed, for it was extremely unlikely that the Executive or the Legislature, having once decided, would yield to the contrary holding of another 'Department,' even of the courts"; that "for centuries it has been an accepted canon in interpretation of documents to interpolate into the text such provisions, though not expressed, as are essential to prevent the defeat of the venture at hand"; that it was therefore "altogether in keeping with established practice for the Supreme Court to assume an authority to keep the states, Congress, and the President within their prescribed powers"; and, finally and explicitly, that for the reason stated "it was not a lawless act to import into the Constitution such a grant of power."

Though I have learned from past experience that disagreement with Judge Hand is usually nothing but the sheerest folly, I must make clear why I believe the power of the courts is grounded in the language of the Constitution and is not a mere interpolation. To do this you must let me quote the supremacy clause, which is mercifully short:

> This Constitution, and the Laws of the United States which shall be made in Pursuance thereof; and all Treaties made, or which shall be made, under the Authority of the United States, shall be the supreme Law of the Land; and the Judges in every State shall be bound thereby, any Thing in the Constitution or Laws of any State to the Contrary notwithstanding.

Judge Hand concedes that under this clause "state courts would at times have to decide whether state laws and constitutions, or even a federal statute, were in conflict with the federal constitution" but he adds that "the fact that this jurisdiction was confined to such occasions, and that it was thought necessary specifically to provide such a limited jurisdiction, looks rather against than in favor of a general jurisdiction."

Are you satisfied, however, to view the supremacy clause in this way, as a grant of jurisdiction to state courts, implying a denial of the power and the duty to all others? This certainly is not its necessary meaning; it may be construed as a mandate to all of officialdom including courts, with a special and emphatic admonition that it binds the judges of the previously independent states. That the latter is the proper reading seems to me persuasive when the other relevant provisions of the Constitution are brought into view.

Article III, section 1 declares that the federal judicial power "shall be vested in one supreme Court, and in such inferior Courts as the Congress may from time to time ordain and establish." This represented, as you know, one of the major compromises of the Constitutional Convention and relegated the establishment *vel non* of lower federal courts to the discretion of the Congress. None might have been established, with the consequence that, as in other federalisms, judicial work of first instance would all have been remitted to state courts. Article III, section 2 goes on, however, to delineate the scope of the federal judicial power, providing that it "shall extend [*inter alia*] to all Cases, in Law and Equity, arising under this Constitution . . ." and, further, that the Supreme Court "shall have appellate jurisdiction" in such cases "with such Exceptions, and under such Regulations as the Congress shall make." Surely this means, as section 25 of the Judiciary Act of 1789 took it to mean, that if a state court passes on a constitutional issue, as the supremacy clause provides that it should, its judgment is reviewable, subject to congressional exceptions, by the Supreme Court, in which event that Court must have no less authority and duty to accord priority to constitutional provisions than the court that it reviews. And such state cases might have encompassed every case in which a constitutional issue could possibly arise, since, as I have said, Congress need not and might not have exerted its authority to establish "inferior" federal courts.

If you abide with me thus far, I doubt that you will hesitate upon the final step. Is it a possible construction of the Constitution, measured strictly as Judge Hand admonishes by the test of "general purpose," that if Congress opts, as it has opted, to create a set of lower courts, those courts in cases falling within their respective jurisdictions and the Supreme Court when it passes on their judgments are less or differently constrained by the supremacy clause than are the state courts, and the Supreme Court when it reviews their judgments? Yet I cannot escape, what is for me the most astonishing conclusion, that this is the precise result of Judge Hand's reading of the text, as distinct from the interpolation he approves on other grounds.

. . . .

Let me repeat what I have thus far tried to say. The courts have both the title and the duty when a case is properly before them to review the actions of the other branches in the light of constitutional provisions, even though the action involves value choices, as invariably action does. In doing so, however, they are bound to function otherwise than as a naked power organ; they participate as courts of law. This calls for facing how determinations of this kind can be asserted to have any legal quality. The answer, I suggest, inheres primarily in that they are—or are obliged to be—entirely principled. A principled decision, in the sense I have in mind, is one that rests on reasons with respect to all the issues in the case, reasons that in their generality and their neutrality transcend any immediate result that is involved. When no sufficient reasons of this kind can be assigned for overturning value choices of the other branches of the Government or of a state, those choices must, of course, survive. Otherwise, as Holmes said in his first opinion for the Court, "a constitution, instead of embodying only relatively fundamental rules of right, as generally understood by all English-speaking communities, would become the partisan of a particular set of ethical or economical opinions. . . ."

---

6. In the essay which follows, Professors Miller and Howell suggest that the principled exercise of judicial review championed by Wechsler is, on the whole, neither desirable nor possible.

## MILLER AND HOWELL, THE MYTH OF NEUTRALITY IN CONSTITUTIONAL ADJUDICATION, 29 U. Chi. L. Rev. 661 (1960)*

Professor Wechsler admits that value choices are inevitable, but diverges on the second point of *how* they are made. What we suggest is that his quest for neutrality is fruitless. In the interest-balancing procedure of constitutional adjudication, neutrality has no place, objectivity is achievable only in part, and impartiality is more of an aspiration than a fact—although certainly possible in some degree. In making choices among competing values, the Justices of the Supreme Court are themselves guided by value preferences. Any reference to neutral or impersonal principles is, accordingly, little more than a call for a return to a mechanistic jurisprudence and for a jurisprudence of nondisclosure as

---

well as an attempted denial of the teleological aspects of any decision, wherever made. The members of the high bench have never adhered to a theory of mechanism, whatever their apologists and commentators may have said, in the judicial decision-making process. Even in the often-quoted assertion by Mr. Justice Roberts about the duty of the Court to lay the statute against the Constitution to ascertain if the one squares with the other, one would indeed have to be naive to believe that this statement in fact described the process. . . .

. . . .

But in saying this—in stating that neutrality or objectivity is essentially impossible of attainment—it should not be inferred that we feel the judge is wholly free and that he does sit kadi-like under a tree dispensing "justice" by whim or caprice. It is one thing to attribute a degree of creativity to the judge and quite another to say that he is at liberty to roam at will.

. . . .

The point emphasized here is that there are no facts apart from a theory, and that, accordingly, a person's view of the facts is unavoidably colored by the nature of that theory. Neutrality, thus, is unattainable in the constitutional adjudicative process, both on the level of (legal) principle and on the level of the facts of the dispute before the Court.

. . . .

The position taken by . . . Wechsler is based on a view of life and the social process in which litigants (and others) are in agreement on the basic essentials—the goal values—and all that remains is the settlement of preferred ways to reach those ends. Put another way, their position is bottomed on a theory of a fundamental harmony of interests of all members of the American community. But that is precisely what may *not* be present in most important constitutional litigation, such as racial relations, where disagreement is over ends or goals and not the means or tactics to attain them; the administration of the criminal law, where an anti-social being is jousting with something called society; and in many of the civil liberty cases, where again the disagreement is over fundamentals. To posit a society with a harmony of interests is to rearticulate a fundamental tenet of the American democracy; to speak otherwise is to question, at least in part, one of the underpinnings of the constitutional order. Nevertheless that, in essence, is what is present here, and serves to explain, at least partially, the counting of votes—as Hart says—of "one up (or down) for civil rights" and so on. To put it in other terms, it is the difference between a Hobbesian view of the social process and that of, say, Burke, Locke or Rousseau.

. . . Compare in this regard, the position of Mr. Justice Douglas, who looks upon the first amendment as the enunciation of absolute principle, with the interest-balancing position of, say, Mr. Justice Frankfurter, who concedes the necessity of value-choice in adjudication. Who, then, is the "activist"; who the exponent of self-restraint? The answer, of course, is that both—plus their colleagues—are activists in the sense that conscious use of decisional power makes it inevitable. Both Douglas and Frankfurter see the Court as a power organ in a social power process, the former desiring to use it affirmatively, the latter more willing to rely on the end-products as they come tumbling out the social decision-making spigot, so long as those results do not unduly upset him. Thus Douglas can, at least in part, be said to hold to a Hobbesian view of the judicial process, with Frankfurter being more a follower in the Burkean or Lockean tradition. The comparison is not exact, but does serve to describe two diverging views of the role of the Court.

. . . .

. . . The *judicial* area is, thus, a *political* battleground—either because, as in the case of the Negro, the legislature is foreclosed to him, or because, as in labor relations, the legislature delegates its responsibility—and there should be little wonder that the results are hailed as victories for one side or another, both by laymen and lawyers. Reason, Hart to the contrary, in these instances, if not in others, is emphatically not "the life of the law"; rather, it is the language of political battle. And the Court *is* a power organ, which aids in the shaping of community values, whether avowedly so as in the hands of a Douglas or whether abashedly so when Frankfurter seeks to convince us that he is an apostle of "self-restraint." Whatever its decision—even a denial of certiorari or taking refuge within the doughy contours of "political questions"—the Court is institutionally a part of a government with affirmative orientation: In a welfare state, it is also concerned with "welfare." The only question is not whether it should be so but whether it should be *outwardly* so, and whether it should try to be so systematically, rather than in a helter-skelter manner.

The role, then, of the Supreme Court in an age of positive government must be that of an active participant in government, assisting in furthering the democratic ideal. Acting at least in part as a "national conscience," the Court should help articulate in broad principle the goals of American society.

---

Do you agree with Miller and Howell that in the "interest-balancing procedure of constitutional adjudication, neutrality has no place"? How would Wechsler respond? Would he not suggest that the "interest-balancing" procedure of constitutional adjudication is only tolerable if it is neutral? On the other hand, isn't there truth in the observations of Miller and Howell that "there are no facts apart from a theory" and that "neutrality" is "unattainable in the constitutional adjudicative process"?

---

7. In the following article, Professor Barron surveys various scholarly reactions to the Supreme Court's failure to take an invariably principled approach to constitutional adjudication. He suggests that since the court in the American system is itself a branch of government, it is inevitable that it should keep an "eye on life" as well as on constitutional principle.

## BARRON, THE AMBIGUITY OF JUDICIAL REVIEW: A RESPONSE TO PROFESSOR BICKEL, 1970 Duke L.J. 591*

. . . .

Increasingly, the use of law in courts to achieve social reform and even social revolution in the United States has undermined the traditional associations the courts have had with the ideals of neutrality, objectivity, and detachment. In his Holmes lecture at Harvard in 1959, Professor Herbert Wechsler said that the Supreme Court should not use political methods but instead neutral principles of constitutional law. It is true, he said, that the approach to politics by most of us is essentially instrumental. But however tolerant we might be of such an approach to politics we expect something else from courts.

How can neutral constitutional principles be developed? Not many would suggest that these principles be gathered from an effort to historically ascertain what the Framers intended by a given phrase in the Constitution. History is as much art as science. Similarly, history is mischievous. Moreover, even if capturing the historical understanding were less elusive a task than it is, obviously we could not be bound by even the most accurate reading of history. The meaning of constitutional language, in a vital and restless constitutionalism such as ours, cannot be deciphered forever by an eighteenth century glossary. Similarly, case law or precedent cannot be a very adequate or productive guide to the development of principles by which to decide new issues presented to courts. Many of the problems presented today

---

either have never been judicially resolved or, if they have arisen in the past, were considered not to be judicially determinable.
. . . .

The Supreme Court has been the most visible example of the use of judicial process as an energizing source of social change. But the Supreme Court's example has been mirrored by lesser courts throughout the country. . . .

Professor Alexander Bickel of Yale, in a more recent Holmes lecture at Harvard in 1969, has suggested that the dominant motif of constitutional interpretation during the life of the Warren Court was the Idea of Progress. In his lecture, Bickel chronicles the disappointing (to him) consequences of the Warren Court's endeavor to achieve social progress through the process of constitutional interpretation.

When courts approach politics, should they use principles which have a life apart from the political problem which is being litigated? If principles are selected to meet the exigencies of a moment we should not be startled to have that principle come back to haunt us. A principle of law should not be created for a specific case but the specific case should be susceptible to a general principle. Certainly, this is classic and beguiling doctrine. It has the impartial sound of justice. But can the problems we really care about be solved without reference to the problems? Is it possible, or desirable, to create principles apart from specific problems? John Dewey condemned for an earlier generation of philosophers the mischief done by the assumption of classical philosophy that the world of thought occupied a separate and higher plane than the world of practical concern.

We see, and we continue to see, both the de-intellectualization of law and a decline in the ideals of impartiality and generality. Judicial integrity in Anglo-American law, in the past, could be defined as the measure of the impartial distance between the problem at hand and the principle applied to resolve it. If even-handed principle is the measure of decision rather than the result to be obtained, reason rather than will shall have prevailed. But judicial integrity is a fragile and subtle thing. Suspicion always endures that it was some submerged preference which in the last analysis really selected the even-handed principle. . . .

Constitutional philosophies have more than superficial resemblance to theological speculation. In the United States, natural law problems are subsumed within the text of the fundamental law itself. They surface in judicial opinions which flesh out constitutional phrases such as due process, liberty, and equal protection.

What usually unites Supreme Court critics is an intrepidly rationalistic approach. They demand a certain standard of judicial performance, a certain deference to the formalisms of constitutional litigation. In that sense they are aestheticians in their criticism. As one of their number, Professor Kurland, puts it, they are Jobbists. They see carved out for the Court a little job, not a large one, but a manageable one, a task capable of standards.

Bickel and Wechsler want to depoliticize the Court. They seek to tame it; they wish its subject-matter to be defined rather than open-ended. Professor Wechsler demands that the Court's doctrines be principled in the sense that they have a logical coherence, a coherence that makes the Court's operations capable of withstanding the rigors of logical analysis. Alexander Bickel's tool for depoliticizing the Court has a quite different emphasis— an emphasis on abstinence.

Wechsler argues for a methodology which transcends politics. Bickel's approach is easier to implement and therefore, not surprisingly, more revolutionary. He doubts that politics can be expelled from constitutional litigation which is conceived in politics. Not content to banish a political approach to constitutional cases, he wants to banish political cases. Bickel doubts the possibility of a "pure" theory of judicial review. Therefore he urges the cultivation of what he calls the passive virtues. [A. BICKEL, THE LEAST DANGEROUS BRANCH (1962)]

Wechsler's approach like most ideal theories is somewhat too ethereal for the real world of American judicial review. But Bickel's critique cuts far deeper. If political cases are to be avoided, the Supreme Court, as the political institution it has become, is challenged root and branch. That challenge requires us to look at what politically the Court does before we can assess the wisdom of such pessimism.

Like the New Critics in literature, Bickel and Wechsler predicate their criticism in the text and structure of judicial literature itself. The difficulty with this approach is that it enormously decreases the role of the Supreme Court in American life. Bickel is really making a radical request: if the great political cases are incapable of principled resolution, then the Court ought to decline decision of such cases. But it is the great political cases which have made the Supreme Court, historically and now, a branch of government.

What is the meaning of this desire for depoliticization? On one level, it is an anguished plea for the self-restraint which, it is argued, ought to animate a formally undemocratic institution. On another level, it reflects a sense of outrage that one's discipline is in the hands of the unworthy. But this aesthetic and intellectual *cri de coeur* is, from a historical point of view, somewhat surprising. The Supreme Court has always played a double-faceted role: a role both political and legal. In cases displaying social tension and ambiguity, it is inevitably a political body. It is this political fact which some critics and some politicians are determined to expel.

. . . .

What in the balance of history does the Court's experience with judicial review actually teach? The Court's political achievement should be weighed with that historical detachment which should be used to assess all social and political institutions. The Court's failures, contemporary and past, should not be used to disparage present and prevent future successes.

Are judicial process and political strategy incongruous? Lon Fuller has written that one of the criteria which operate to place the moral force of a judgment at its maximum is where "the judge confines his decision to the controversy before him and attempts no regulations of the parties' relations going beyond that controversy." This also is the objective of those who seek a principled approach to law.

The price of a possible judicial success is bought at an exchange of briefs and arguments. As against the matching of guns and blood, it is a slight expense. If in addition to that expense some damage is done to the harmony of an aesthetically satisfying constitutional methodology, that again is not an intolerable burden. But critics of the political uses of judicial review are not willing to tolerate the burden. Why? They believe that having yielded the integrity of their craft the political solution may fail as well. Judges in our system do not determine whether slavery can be expanded to the western territories but whether the slave, Dred Scott, shall be returned to his master.

But is there not an approach that lies between choosing a politics indifferent to principle or divorced from life? The Supreme Court is only occasionally a political forum. The Court, like the other branches of government, may occasionally be the means of successful politics. Sometimes it will happen that the Court will have to do what the frankly political branches are unable to do.

The exploitation of a judicial process which cleaves to principle but which has an eye on life is the distinctive contribution of America to politics. The Supreme Court of the United States is not just another high court of a federalist state such as the Supreme Court of Canada. . . .

But the Supreme Court of the United States has had a political role from the beginning. The Court's political weapon is "the law," and particularly the Constitution, just as the weapon of the Congress is the purse, and that of the Executive, its monistic unity. But acknowledgment of the Court's political task is resisted. A stubborn insistence on certainty, the quest for which has been largely abandoned in other disciplines, survives in constitutional law. . . .

Holmes . . . viewed the judicial process itself with a biting realism. In 1896, while still a justice on the Supreme Judicial Court of Massachusetts, he expressed his skepticism: "The true grounds of decision are considerations of . . . social advantage and it is vain to suppose that solutions can be attained merely by logic and the general propositions of law which nobody disputes."

The grievance that Holmes had against the Court of his day was that it had set itself up against popular will and against the future. He thought it inevitable that the Court should reflect contemporary social realities. What he could not fathom was the pretension that it could be otherwise. Holmes is revered by those who have watched with some anxiety the Supreme Court's ascent to a position as a major force for social change. Holmes has been admired by such different men as Mr. Justice Frankfurter and President Nixon. The reason for this appeal is a judicial mind which is not in the service of any ideology but which nevertheless grasps the essence of each passing ideal with trenchancy and detachment. For Holmes it was inevitable that the Court would reflect the dominant politics of the moment.

Usually what is being praised in Holmes is the possession of temperament for judging. When as a Supreme Court Justice he was called to review the case of the Communist, Benjamin Gitlow, he wrote to this friend Harold Laski of the "drool about proletarian dictatorship," but he also wrote in the United States Reports that there was nothing in the Constitution to prevent the dictatorship of the proletariat if that is what the people wanted. For Holmes, neutrality was not a judicial ideal, nor an ideological imperative, it merely was the consequence of a profound skepticism. That the Court should or could transcend the rising ideologies of an epoch was something Holmes as a judge neither expected nor required.

. . . .

Professor Bickel argues that "the Court is the place for principled judgment" or else "its insulation from the political process is inexplicable." It is my suggestion that the political process and the judiciary are not like Hindu castes forever barred from contact with each other in our system. Nor are they assigned

to caste functions which prohibit the assumption of new tasks
or the abandonment of old procedures. Rather the judiciary is
designed to have occasional political uses. The divorcement that
Professor Bickel seeks would remove a forum for social change
too useful and too important to justify limitation of the work
of the Supreme Court to matters always susceptible to and always
governed by principled judgment "disciplined by the method of
reasoning familiar to the discourse of moral philosophy." Such
an approach assigns to the Supreme Court a task at once too
grand and too trivial. Constitutional law of all things should not
be fitted into an atavistic, platonic dichotomy between the real
and the ideal.

Ambiguity should not be thought of as an indication of a new
failure of integrity in the practice of constitutional law. A concern for integrity, both for the survival of the basic political
structure, and for the explication of basic constitutional themes,
free expression and racial equality, are stamped in much of the
contemporary work of the American judiciary, particularly the
Supreme Court and the lower federal courts. In the borderland,
between law and politics, new uses for the corrective capacities
of courts continually arise. But there are uses for uncertainty. As
the public becomes more acquainted with the uses of judicial
process for radical social change, public awareness increases that
the paths a court can travel in decision are not set by a very clear
compass. A new candor arising from the tension in the political
and social order has destroyed the old apparatus of legal and
constitutional certainty. But integrity is apparent amid the rubble.

The enormous resiliency, the constant possibilities for modest
advance and subtle retreat, makes the Court one of the most sensitive sources for social change in the United States.

---

Barron suggests that the very ambiguity of judicial review
is one of the principle institutional weapons of the court. The
implication is that the court's ability to alternate between doctrine and an estimate of the public need is an institutional tool
like the power of Congress to appropriate or the power of the
President to veto. But isn't the crucial distinction that the latter
institutional tools have their source in the Constitution itself?

## B. THE NATURE AND IMPACT OF SUPREME COURT JURISDICTION

### MARTIN v. HUNTER'S LESSEE
Supreme Court of the United States
14 U.S. (1 Wheat.) 304, 4 L. Ed. 97 (1816)

[Lord Fairfax, a citizen of Virginia, willed his Virginia estates to his nephew, Denny Martin, a British subject. After the American Revolution, Virginia in 1789 confiscated lands owned by British subjects. Virginia granted a land patent over the Fairfax devise to David Hunter. Hunter brought an action of ejectment against Martin. The Virginia trial court held for Martin on the basis of the treaties of 1783 and 1794 between the United States and Great Britain, which protected British lands in the United States.

[The Virginia Court of Appeals, however, reversed and held for Hunter on the ground, *inter alia,* that Virginia's title to the land was perfected prior to the enactment of the treaties. In Fairfax's Devisee v. Hunter's Lessee, 11 U.S. (7 Cranch) 603 (1813), the Supreme Court reversed the Virginia Court of Appeals. The mandate of the Supreme Court directed the Virginia Court of Appeals to enter judgment for Martin. But that court refused to obey the Supreme Court's decree on the ground that § 25 of the Judiciary Act of 1789 which conferred appellate jurisdiction on the Supreme Court over the decisions of a state's highest tribunal was unconstitutional.

[The case was brought to the Supreme Court again. In a historic and fundamental decision, Mr. Justice Story, for the court, considered and rejected Virginia's challenge to the paramountcy of the Supreme Court of the United States.]

STORY, J., delivered the opinion of the court:

This is a writ of error from the Court of Appeals of Virginia, founded upon the refusal of that court to obey the mandate of this court, requiring the judgment rendered in this very cause, at February term, 1813, to be carried into due execution. . . .

. . . .

The third article of the constitution is that which must principally attract our attention. . . .

. . . .

Such is the language of the article creating and defining the judicial power of the United States. It is the voice of the whole American people solemnly declared, in establishing one great department of that government which was, in many respects, national, and in all, supreme. It is a part of the very same instrument which was to act not merely upon individuals, but upon states; and to deprive them altogether of the exercise of some powers of sovereignty, and to restrain and regulate them in the exercise of others.

Let this article be carefully weighed and considered. The language of the article throughout is manifestly designed to be mandatory upon the legislature. Its obligatory force is so imperative that Congress could not, without a violation of its duty, have refused to carry it into operation. The judicial power of the United States shall be vested (not may be vested) in one supreme court, and in such inferior courts as Congress may, from time to time, ordain and establish. Could Congress have lawfully refused to create a supreme court, or to vest in it the constitutional jurisdiction? . . . The judicial power must, therefore, be vested in some court, by Congress; and to suppose that it was not an obligation binding on them, but might, at their pleasure, be omitted or declined, is to suppose that, under the sanction of the constitution they might defeat the constitution itself; a construction which would lead to such a result cannot be sound.

. . . .

If, then, it is the duty of Congress to vest the judicial power of the United States, it is a duty to vest the whole judicial power. The language, if imperative as to one part, is imperative as to all. If it were otherwise, this anomaly would exist, that Congress might successively refuse to vest the jurisdiction in any one class of cases enumerated in the constitution, and thereby defeat the jurisdiction as to all; for the constitution has not singled out any class on which Congress are bound to act in preference to others.

The next consideration is as to the courts in which the judicial power shall be vested. It is manifest that a supreme court must be established; but whether it be equally obligatory to establish inferior courts is a question of some difficulty. If Congress may lawfully omit to establish inferior courts, it might follow that in some of the enumerated cases the judicial power could nowhere exist. . . . It would seem, therefore, to follow that Congress are bound to create some inferior courts, in which to vest all that jurisdiction which, under the constitution, is exclusively vested in the United States, and of which the Supreme Court cannot take original cognizance. They might establish one or more inferior courts; they might parcel out the jurisdiction among such courts, from time to time, at their own pleasure. But the whole judicial power of the United States should be, at all times, vested either in an original or appellate form, in some courts created under its authority.

. . . .

It being, then, established that the language of this clause is imperative, the next question is as to the cases to which it shall apply. The answer is found in the constitution itself. The judicial power shall extend to all the cases enumerated in the constitution. As the mode is not limited, it may extend to all such cases, in any form in which judicial power may be exercised. It may, therefore, extend to them in the shape of original or appellate jurisdiction, or both; for there is nothing in the nature of the cases which binds to the exercise of the one in preference to the other.

. . . .

But, even admitting that the language of the constitution is not mandatory, and that Congress may constitutionally omit to vest the judicial power in courts of the United States, it cannot be denied that when it is vested it may be exercised to the utmost constitutional extent.

This leads us to the consideration of the great question as to the nature and extent of the appellate jurisdiction of the United States. We have already seen that appellate jurisdiction is given by the constitution to the Supreme Court in all cases, where it has not original jurisdiction; subject, however, to such exceptions and regulations as Congress may prescribe. It is, therefore, capable of embracing every case enumerated in the constitution, which is not exclusively to be decided by way of original jurisdiction. But the exercise of appellate jurisdiction is far from being limited by the terms of the constitution to the Supreme Court. There can be no doubt that Congress may create a succession of inferior tribunals, in each of which it may vest appellate as well as original jurisdiction. The judicial power is delegated by the constitution in the most general terms, and may, therefore, be exercised by Congress under every variety of form, of appellate or original jurisdiction. And as there is nothing in the constitution which restrains or limits this power, it must, therefore, in all other cases, subsist in the utmost latitude of which, in its own nature, it is susceptible.

As, then, by the terms of the constitution, the appellate jurisdiction is not limited as to the Supreme Court, and as to this court it may be exercised in all other cases than those of which it has original cognizance, what is there to restrain its exercise over state tribunals in the enumerated cases? The appellate power is not limited by the terms of the third article to any particular courts. The words are, "the judicial power (which includes appellate power) shall extend to all cases," etc., and "in all other cases before mentioned the Supreme Court shall have appellate jurisdiction." It is the case, then, and not the court, that gives the jurisdiction. If the judicial power extends to the case, it will be in vain to search in the letter of the constitution for any qualification as to the tribunal where it depends. It is incumbent, then, upon those who assert such a qualification to show its existence by necessary implication. If the text be clear and distinct, no restriction upon its plain and obvious import ought to be admitted, unless the inference be irresistible.

If the constitution meant to limit the appellate jurisdiction to cases pending in the courts of the United States, it would necessarily follow that the jurisdiction of these courts would, in all the cases enumerated in the constitution, be exclusive of state tribunals. How otherwise could the jurisdiction extend to all cases arising under the constitution, laws and treaties of the United States, or to all cases of admiralty and maritime jurisdiction? If some of these cases might be entertained by state tribunals, and no appellate jurisdiction as to them should exist, then the appellate power would not extend to all, but to some, cases. If state tribunals might exercise concurrent jurisdiction over all or some of the other classes of cases in the constitution without control, then the appellate jurisdiction of the United States might, as to such cases, have no real existence, contrary to the manifest intent of the constitution. Under such circumstances, to give effect to the judicial power, it must be construed to be exclusive; and this not only when the casus faederis should arise directly, but when it should arise, incidentally, in cases pending in state courts. This construction would abridge the jurisdiction of such courts far more than has been ever contemplated in any act of Congress.

On the other hand, if, as has been contended, a discretion be vested in Congress to establish, or not to establish, inferior courts at their own pleasure, and Congress should not establish such courts, the appellate jurisdiction of the Supreme Court would have nothing to act upon, unless it could act upon cases pending in the state courts. Under such circumstances it must be held that the appellate power would extend to state courts; for the constitution is peremptory that it shall extend to certain enumerated cases, which cases could exist in no other courts. Any other construction, upon this supposition, would involve this strange contradiction, that a discretionary power vested in Congress, and which they might rightfully omit to exercise, would defeat the absolute injunctions of the constitution in relation to the whole appellate power.

But it is plain that the framers of the constitution did contemplate that cases within the judicial cognizance of the United States not only might but would arise in the state courts, in the exercise of their ordinary jurisdiction. With this view the sixth article declares, that "this constitution, and the laws of the United States which shall be made in pursuance thereof, and all treaties made, or which shall be made, under the authority of the United States, shall be the supreme law of the land, and the judges in every state shall be bound thereby, anything in the constitution or laws of any state to the contrary notwithstanding." It is obvious that this obligation is imperative upon the state judges in their official, and not merely in their private, capacities. From the very nature of their judicial duties they would be called upon to pronounce the law applicable to the case in judgment. They were not to decide merely according to the laws or constitution of the state, but according to the constitution, laws and treaties of the United States—"the supreme law of the land."

. . . .

It must, therefore, be conceded that the constitution not only contemplated, but meant to provide for cases within the scope of the judicial power of the United States, which might yet depend before state tribunals. It was foreseen that in the exercise of their ordinary jurisdiction, state courts would incidentally take cognizance of cases arising under the constitution, the laws and treaties of the United States. Yet to all these cases the judicial power, by the very terms of the constitution, is to extend. It cannot extend by original jurisdiction if that was already rightfully and exclusively attached in the state courts, which (as has been already shown) may occur; it must, therefore, extend by appellate jurisdiction, or not at all. It would seem to follow that the appellate power of the United States must, in such cases, extend to state tribunals; and if in such cases, there is no reason why it should not equally attach upon all others within the purview of the constitution.

. . . .

It is a mistake that the constitution was not designed to operate upon states, in their corporate capacities. It is crowded with provisions which restrain or annul the sovereignty of the states in some of the highest branches of their prerogatives. The tenth section of the first article contains a long list of disabilities and prohibitions imposed upon the states. Surely, when such essential portions of state sovereignty are taken away, or prohibited to be exercised, it cannot be correctly asserted that the constitution does not act upon the states. . . .

Nor can such a right be deemed to impair the independence of state judges. It is assuming the very ground in controversy to assert that they possess an absolute independence of the United States. In respect to the powers granted to the United States, they are not independent; they are expressly bound to obedience by the letter of the constitution; and if they should unintentionally transcend their authority, or misconstrue the constitution, there is no more reason for giving their judgments an absolute and irresistible force than for giving it to the acts of the other co-ordinate departments of state sovereignty.

. . . .

It is further argued that no great public mischief can result from a construction which shall limit the appellate power of the United States to cases in their own courts; first, because state judges are bound by an oath to support the constitution of the United States, and must be presumed to be men of learning and integrity; and, secondly, because Congress must have an unquestionable right to remove all cases within the scope of the judicial power from the state courts to the courts of the United States, at any time before final judgment, though not after final judgment. As to the first reason—admitting that the judges of the state courts are, and always will be, of as much learning, integrity, and wisdom, as those of the courts of the United States (which we very cheerfully admit), it does not aid the argument. It is manifest that the constitution has proceeded upon a theory of its own, and given or withheld powers according to the judgment of the American people, by whom it was adopted. We can only construe its powers, and cannot inquire into the policy or principles which induced the grant of them. The constitution has presumed (whether rightly or wrongly we do not inquire) that state attachments, state prejudices, state jealousies, and state interests, might sometimes obstruct, or control, or be supposed to obstruct or control, the regular administration of justice. . . .

This is not all. A motive of another kind, perfectly compatible with the most sincere respect for state tribunals, might induce the grant of appellate power over their decisions. That motive is the importance, and even necessity of uniformity of decisions throughout the whole United States, upon all subjects within the purview of the constitution. Judges of equal learning and integrity, in different states, might differently interpret a statute, or a treaty of the United States, or even the constitution itself. If there were no revising authority to control these jarring and discordant judgments, and harmonize them into uniformity, the laws, the treaties, and the constitution of the United States would be different in different states, and might, perhaps, never have precisely the same construction, obligation, or efficacy, in any two states. . . .

There is an additional consideration, which is entitled to great weight. The constitution of the United States was designed for the common and equal benefit of all the people of the United States. The judicial power was granted for the same benign and salutary purposes. It was not to be exercised exclusively for the benefit of parties who might be plaintiffs, and would elect the national forum, but also for the protection of defendants who might be entitled to try their rights, or assert their privileges, before the same forum. Yet, if the construction contended for be correct, it will follow, that as the plaintiff may always elect the state court, the defendant, may be deprived of all the security which the constitution intended in aid of his rights. Such a state of things can in no respect be considered as giving equal rights. To obviate this difficulty, we are referred to the power which it is admitted Congress possess to remove suits from state courts to the national courts; and this forms the second ground upon which the argument we are considering has been attempted to be sustained.

. . . [Removal] is always deemed . . . an exercise of appellate, and not of original jurisdiction. If, then, the right of removal be included in the appellate jurisdiction, it is only because it is one mode of exercising that power, and as Congress is not limited by the Constitution to any particular mode, or time of exercising it, it may authorize a removal either before or after judgment. The time, the process, and the manner, must be subject to its absolute legislative control. . . . Precisely the same objections, therefore, exist as to the right of removal before judgment, as after, and both must stand or fall together. Nor, indeed, would the force of the arguments on either side materially vary if the right of removal were an exercise of original jurisdiction. It would equally trench upon the jurisdiction and independence of state tribunals.

. . . .

On the whole, the court are of opinion that the appellate power of the United States does extend to cases pending in the state courts; and that the 25th section of the judiciary act, which authorizes the exercise of this jurisdiction in the specified cases, by a writ of error, is supported by the letter and spirit of the constitution. We find no clause in that instrument which limits this power; and we dare not interpose a limitation where the people have not been disposed to create one.

. . . .

We have not thought it incumbent on us to give any opinion upon the question, whether this court have authority to issue a writ of mandamus to the Court of Appeals to enforce the former judgments, as we do not think it necessarily involved in the decision of this cause.

It is the opinion of the whole court that the judgment of the Court of Appeals of Virginia, rendered on the mandate in this cause, be reversed, and the judgment of the District Court, held at Winchester, be, and the same is hereby affirmed.

[Justice Johnson, concurring:] It will be observed in this case, that the court disavows all intention to decide on the right to issue compulsory process to the state courts; thus leaving us, in my opinion, where the constitution and laws place us—supreme over persons and cases as far as our judicial powers extend, but not asserting any compulsory control over the state tribunals.
. . . .

---

## NOTES

1.  The Virginia Court of Appeals refused to obey the Supreme Court's mandate in *Martin v. Hunter's Lessee* and further declared that § 25 of the Judiciary Act of 1789 was unconstitutional. The opinion of the Virginia judges may be found in Hunter v. Martin, Devisee of Fairfax, 18 Va. (4 Munf.) 11 (1814). Each of four judges rendered separate opinions. Judge Cabell said:

> The constitution of the United States contemplates the independence of both governments and regards the residuary sovereignty of the states, as not less inviolable, than the delegated sovereignty of the United States. It must have been foreseen that controversies would sometimes arise as to the boundaries of the two jurisdictions. Yet the constitution has provided no umpire, has erected no tribunal by which they shall be settled. The omission proceeded, probably, from the belief, that such a tribunal would produce evils greater than those of the occasional collusions which it would be designed to remedy.
> . . . .
>
> If, therefore, I am correct in this position, the appellate jurisdiction of the Supreme Court of the United States (under the constitution), must have reference to the inferior courts of the United States, and not to the state courts. . . . It has been contended that the constitution contemplated only the objects of appeal, and not the tribunals from which the ap-

peal is to be taken; and intended to give to the Supreme Court of the United States appellate jurisdiction in all cases of federal cognizance. But this argument proves too much, and what is utterly inadmissible. It would give appellate jurisdiction, as well over the courts of England or France, as over the State courts; for, although I do not think the state courts are foreign courts in relation to the federal courts, yet I consider them not less independent than foreign courts.

2. The argument of Judge Cabell and the other Virginia Court of Appeals judges who joined in the determination of the Virginia Court of Appeals to defy the decision of the Supreme Court in *Martin v. Hunter's Lessee I* was based fundamentally on the so-called "compact" theory of the Constitution, *i.e.,* the federal constitution was a compact among the states and the parties to that instrument were superior to the federal government which it created.

Professor Corwin chronicling the documentary source of the compact theory states: "The documentary source of this idea, at least in the history of the mischief it worked, was the Virginia Resolution of 1798, of which the author was James Madison, though the Jacob of the transaction was Thomas Jefferson." He notes: "The essential ideas here are two: First, the idea of the constitution as a compact of the States, and secondly, the derivative idea of the right and duty of the individual states under the constitution to interpose the shield of their sovereignty on occasion, between their respective citizens and the national government." Corwin, *National Power and State Interposition, 1787-1861,* 10 Mich. L. Rev. 535, 544 (1911). In what sense was the doctrine of *Martin v. Hunter's Lessee* a body blow to the "compact" theory of the Constitution?

3. What were the arguments used by Justice Story to establish the constitutionality of § 25 of the Judiciary Act? Story hit three now familiar chords in constitutional litigation in his decision in *Martin v. Hunter's Lessee:* constitutional text, constitutional history, and political common sense. Certainly, the practical wisdom of the last of these was irrefutable: "If there were no revising authority to control these jarring and discordant judgments, and harmonize them into uniformity, the laws, the treaties, and the constitution of the United States would be different in different states, and might, perhaps, never have precisely the same construction, obligation, or efficacy in any two states."

Justice Holmes stated a related thought in a later time: "I do not think the United States would come to an end if we lost our power to declare an Act of Congress void. I do think the Union would be imperiled if we could not make that declaration as to the laws of the several states." If Holmes is right, is *Martin* more important than *Marbury v. Madison?*

4. Note that the Supreme Court in *Martin* did not face the question of whether it could order the Virginia Court of Appeals to enforce the Supreme Court's judgment in *Martin*. Instead the court merely reinstated the judgment of the Virginia trial court thus nicely avoiding the question of whether an asserted right to decide cases coming from the state supreme courts also carried with it the power to enforce those decisions. It certainly is a fair implication from Justice Johnson's concurring remarks in *Martin* that he thought the Supreme Court's appellate civil jurisdiction to render decisions in cases coming from the state supreme courts did not necessarily carry with it power to enforce those decisions.

5. The delicacy of the issue of how to treat the defiance of the United States Supreme Court by the Virginia Court of Appeals in *Martin v. Hunter's Lessee* is, of course, indicated in the effort made by the court in its 1816 decision to avoid another confrontation with the Virginia Court of Appeals. The problem of securing compliance with decisions of the Supreme Court has been a recurring one in American constitutional law.

One constitutional scholar has suggested that the court essentially engages in a political estimate of the likelihood of compliance with a decision. This observation, of course, contains an implication that likelihood of compliance affects the substantive content of the Supreme Court decision. The relationship of the Supreme Court's decisional power with what might be called the compliance factor is described by Professor Arthur S. Miller as follows:

"The Supreme Court can issue decrees establishing constitutional duties. Whether it does so or not depends less on its legitimacy or authority than on an implicit evaluation of how given decisions will be received. Holmes and Frankfurter and Hand (and their followers in the profession) would limit judicial creativity to incremental change. The courts would be permitted to legislate only interstitially. They would be confined from molar to molecular motion.

"That, at its best, is a statement of a value judgment or preference. For the Supreme Court to issue norms of general applicability is dependent, not upon a commonly accepted theory of the proper scope of judicial activity, but upon an evaluation, intuitive to be sure, for the Court has no means for the accurate prediction of impact upon the public of its decisions, of how a decision may be received by the American people. Legitimacy ultimately relates as much to current public acceptance as it does to the representative character of the decision-maker. There being no settled conception of what adjudication should consist of, the problem devolves, to put it in its lowest terms, to what the Court can 'get away with.' Or, as it was recently put: 'The turning-point [in Supreme Court activity] came . . . when the court, walking on eggs in the School Segregation Cases, found that its public image was such that it could get away with revolutionary changes . . . in the areas of criminal-law enforcement and reapportionment. . . . Moreover, the court's public image is sustained and fostered each time it has one of the successes. . . . Success begets success; more power begets more power.' Gunnar Myrdal has given a label to this phenomenon, 'the principle of cumulative social causation,' by which he means that social affairs are never in equilibrium but always in flux or in 'process' in an upward or downward cycle. Perhaps an apt analogy is the manner in which the warmaking power has flowed to the President, despite the express constitutional provision to the contrary." Miller, *Toward A Concept of Constitutional Duty*, 1968 Sup. Ct. Rev. 199, 230-231. How does the Supreme Court enforce its mandate?

6. The controversy concerning the power of the Supreme Court to bind state governments is not limited to defiance from the state courts. In Cooper v. Aaron, 358 U.S. 1 (1958), the Supreme Court during the height of the crisis over the integration in the Little Rock public schools was faced with a contention that the governor and legislature of Arkansas were not bound by the Supreme Court's famous decision declaring state mandated school segregation unconstitutional. Brown v. Board of Education, 347 U.S. 483 (1954).

In *Cooper,* the court held that state executives, legislators, and judges were alike bound to obey the decision of the Supreme Court. The court relied on *Marbury* for the proposition that "the federal judiciary is supreme in the exposition of the law of the Constitution" and pointed out that "[e]very state legislator and executive, and judicial officer is solemnly committed by oath taken pursuant to Article VI, cl. 3, to support the Constitution." The court then concluded by asserting that there was a constitutional duty on the part of the members of all the branches of state government to comply with its decisions:

> No state legislator or executive or judicial officer can war against the Constitution without violating his undertaking to support it. Chief Justice Marshall spoke for a unanimous

Court in saying that: "If the legislatures of the several states may, at will, annul the judgments of the courts of the United States, and destroy the rights acquired under those judgments, the constitution itself becomes a solemn mockery. . . ." United States v. Peters, 5 Cranch 115, 136. A Governor who asserts a power to nullify a federal court order is similarly restrained. If he had such power, said Chief Justice Hughes, in 1932, also for a unanimous Court, "it is manifest that the fiat of a state Governor, and not the Constitution of the United States, would be the supreme law of the land; that the restrictions of the Federal Constitution upon the exercise of state power would be but impotent phrases. . . ." Sterling v. Constantin, 287 U.S. 378, 397-398.

7.  In Cohens v. Virginia, 19 U.S. (6 Wheat.) 120 (1821), the issue of whether state courts could successfully defy and deny Supreme Court jurisdiction was raised once again. Congress had authorized the District of Columbia to conduct a lottery. Virginia, on the other hand, forbade lotteries. Virginia prosecuted and convicted two persons for selling District of Columbia lottery tickets in Virginia. The defendants appealed their convictions to the Supreme Court.

Martin v. Hunter's Lessee, 14 U.S. (1 Wheat.) 304 (1816), may have settled the issue that the Supreme Court had appellate jurisdiction of civil cases coming from the state courts. But Cohens raised the issue of whether that settled the matter as far as the criminal jurisdiction of the state supreme courts was concerned. Virginia's argument was that the criminal cases were cases in which a state was a party. Article III of the Constitution gave the Supreme Court original jurisdiction of cases when a state was a party.

The student should reflect that in Marbury the heart of Marshall's reasoning on the invalidity of § 13 of the Judiciary Act of 1789 was that the statute's conferral of mandamus jurisdiction on the Supreme Court was in violation of the Constitution because it unconstitutionally added to the original jurisdiction of the Supreme Court as specified in Art. III. If § 25 of the Judiciary Act was interpreted to give state civil and criminal appellate jurisdiction to the Supreme Court, then was not the conferral of the state criminal jurisdiction on the Supreme Court likewise unconstitutional? Had not the framers impliedly determined that the Supreme Court could take cases in which a state was a party only pursuant to the grant of original jurisdiction?

Incidentally, it has been pointed out that the court did not note in Cohens, but should have, a jurisdictional question which concerned a statutory rather than a constitutional issue: Did § 25 of the Judiciary Act of 1789 in fact grant appellate state criminal jurisdiction to the Supreme Court or did it just confer state civil appellate jurisdiction on the Supreme Court? *See* HART & WECHSLER'S THE FEDERAL COURTS AND THE FEDERAL SYSTEM 456 (2d ed., P. Bator, P. Mishkin, D. Shapiro, & H. Wechsler, eds., 1973).

Marshall held in *Cohens* that state criminal cases like state civil cases came within the appellate jurisdiction of the Supreme Court:

> When we consider the situation of the government of the Union and of a state, in relation to each other; the nature of our constitution; the subordination of the state governments to that constitution; the great purpose for which jurisdiction over all cases arising under the constitution and laws of the United States, is confided to the judicial department; are we at liberty to insert in this general grant, an exception of those cases in which a state may be a party? Will the spirit of the constitution justify this attempt to control its words? We think it will not. We think a case arising under the constitution or laws of the United States, is cognizable in the Courts of the Union, whoever may be the parties to that case.

Although Marshall held that the Supreme Court had jurisdiction of the *Cohens* case, he held against the defendants who were appealing their Virginia convictions. Marshall held that Congress had not intended to authorize the sale of District of Columbia lottery tickets outside the District of Columbia. The decision in *Cohens v. Virginia,* was received with hostility in Virginia. Nevertheless, since Virginia had won on the merits, there was no Supreme Court decision for Virginia to defy even if it had chosen to do so.

Thus, Marshall employed once again in *Cohens* the strategy he had so shrewdly and so successfully used in *Marbury*. The individual case was decided in favor of the anti-Federalists but in the process of so deciding, a rationalization for the decision is asserted which entrenches and establishes the supremacy of federal judicial power.

---

### The Background of Ex parte McCardle

McCardle, a sympathizer with the Southern cause, had published some editorials criticizing the federal military occupation of Mississippi in the Vicksburg, Mississippi Times between October 2 and November 6, 1867. The substance of these editorials resulted in McCardle's arrest and detention by the commanding general of the federal military government in Mississippi. A military commission was convened to try McCardle on charges, among others, of disturbing the peace, inciting insurrection, and impeding reconstruction. McCardle sought a writ of habeas corpus from the federal court and invoked the Act of February 5, 1867 which gave the federal courts jurisdiction to grant writs of habeas corpus in cases where persons were detained in violation of law; the statute also provided for appeal to the United States Supreme Court. The federal court denied the writ, and McCardle appealed to the Supreme Court. McCardle filed his appeal on December 23, 1867. *After* oral argument was heard in the *McCardle* case, Congress, by a bill enacted on March 27, 1868, repealed that part of the Habeas Corpus Act of February 5, 1867 which gave appellate jurisdiction to the Supreme Court. For a detailed historical account of *Ex parte McCardle,* see IV C. FAIRMAN, HISTORY OF THE SUPREME COURT OF THE UNITED STATES: RECONSTRUCTION AND REUNION 1864-88, 433-514 (1971).

Article III, § 2 states that "the Supreme Court shall have appellate Jurisdiction, both as to Law and Fact, with such Exceptions, and under such Regulations as the Congress shall make." Does this provision mean that Congress can repeal the entire appellate jurisdiction of the Supreme Court? Or can Congress merely make exceptions with regard to the court's appellate jurisdiction but not abridge it altogether? Are there any limitations on the nature of such exceptions?

In *Ex parte McCardle,* the Supreme Court upheld the right of Congress to withdraw appellate jurisdiction from the Supreme Court over a pending case. Congress had repealed the statute which gave the court subject matter jurisdiction in *McCardle* and the court acquiesced in the repeal.

Professor Pritchett describes the political background behind the repeal of the Act of 1867 by Congress as follows: "That Court had just declared Lincoln's wartime use of military commissions unconstitutional in *Ex parte Milligan* [71 U.S. (4 Wall.) 2 (1866)], and Congress feared that it would use the *McCardle* appeal to invalidate the Reconstruction legislation. Consequently in March, 1868, the Radical Republicans rushed through Congress, and repassed over the President's veto, a statute repealing the Act of 1867 so far as it granted appeals to the Supreme Court, and withdrawing 'any such jurisdiction by said Supreme Court, on appeals which have been, or may hereafter be taken.'" C. PRITCHETT, THE AMERICAN CONSTITUTIONAL SYSTEMS 130 (2d ed. 1968).

Professor Fairman in his account of *Ex parte McCardle* in *History of the Supreme Court of the United States,* at 486, says that the question Chief Justice Chase wanted to have argued was whether Congress could "oust an appeal already perfected." The Supreme Court ultimately held unanimously, per Chief Justice Chase, that the Supreme Court's jurisdiction had been constitutionally ousted. As you read the *McCardle* case, consider the following question: should federal legislation which deprives the Supreme Court of its undoubted jurisdiction over an appeal in the middle of its consideration of that appeal be regarded as a violation of separation of powers?

### EX PARTE McCARDLE
Supreme Court of the United States
74 U.S. (7 Wall.) 506, 19 L. Ed. 264 (1869)

[Chief Justice CHASE] delivered the opinion of the Court.
. . . .

The first question necessarily is that of jurisdiction; for, if the act of March, 1868, takes away the jurisdiction defined by the act of February, 1867, it is useless, if not improper, to enter into any discussion of other questions.

It is quite true, as was argued by the counsel for the petitioner, that the appellate jurisdiction of this Court is not derived from acts of Congress. It is, strictly speaking, conferred by the Constitution. But it is conferred "with such exceptions and under such regulations as Congress shall make."

It is unnecessary to consider whether, if Congress had made no exceptions and no regulations, this Court might not have exercised general appellate jurisdiction under rules prescribed by itself. For among the earliest acts of the first Congress, at its first session, was the act of September 24th, 1789, to establish the judicial courts of the United States. That act provided for the organization of this Court, and prescribed regulations for the exercise of its jurisdiction.

The source of that jurisdiction, and the limitations of it by the Constitution and by statute, have been on several occasions subjects of consideration here. In the case of Durousseau v. The United States, 6 Cranch 312, particularly, the whole matter was carefully examined, and the Court held, that while "the appellate powers of this Court are not given by the judicial act, but are given by the Constitution," they are, nevertheless, "limited and regulated by that act, and by such other acts as have been passed on the subject." The Court said, further, that the judicial act was an exercise of the power given by the Constitution to Congress "of making exceptions to the appellate jurisdiction of the Supreme Court." "They have described affirmatively," said the Court, "its jurisdiction, and this affirmative description has been understood to imply a negation of the exercise of such appellate power as is not comprehended within it."

The principle that the affirmation of appellate jurisdiction implies the negation of all such jurisdiction not affirmed having been thus established, it was an almost necessary consequence that acts of Congress, providing for the exercise of jurisdiction, should come to be spoken of as acts granting jurisdiction, and not as acts making exceptions to the constitutional grant of it.

The exception to appellate jurisdiction in the case before us, however, is not an inference from the affirmation of other appellate jurisdiction. It is made in terms. The provision of the act of 1867, affirming the appellate jurisdiction of this Court in cases of habeas corpus is expressly repealed. It is hardly possible to imagine a plainer instance of positive exception.

We are not at liberty to inquire into the motives of the legislature. We can only examine into its power under the Constitution; and the power to make exceptions to the appellate jurisdiction of this Court is given by express words.

What, then, is the effect of the repealing act upon the case before us? We cannot doubt as to this. Without jurisdiction the Court cannot proceed at all in any cause. Jurisdiction is power to declare the law, and when it ceases to exist, the only function remaining to the Court is that of announcing the fact and dismissing the cause. And this is not less clear upon authority than upon principle.

. . . .

It is quite clear, therefore, that this Court cannot proceed to pronounce judgment in this case, for it has no longer jurisdiction of the appeal; and judicial duty is not less fitly performed by declining ungranted jurisdiction than in exercising firmly that which the Constitution and the laws confer.

Counsel seem to have supposed, if effect be given to the repealing act in question, that the whole appellate power of the Court, in cases of habeas corpus, is denied. But this is an error. The act of 1868 does not except from that jurisdiction any cases but appeals from Circuit Courts under the act of 1867. It does not affect the jurisdiction which was previously exercised.

The appeal of the petitioner in this case must be

Dismissed for want of jurisdiction.

---

## NOTES

1. The existence of *Ex parte McCardle* as a precedent has served to stimulate repeated congressional efforts to deprive the

Supreme Court of appellate jurisdiction in one or another controversial area where a court decision had met with legislative displeasure.

An illustrative example is the recent effort in Congress to block court-ordered busing of students to effect school integration by attempting to take jurisdiction of such cases away from the federal judiciary.

2. In 1972, Senator Griffin, R. Mich., suggested a statute which would deprive the federal courts, including the Supreme Court, of jurisdiction in cases involving busing. The Griffin amendment is as follows: "No court . . . shall have jurisdiction . . . to issue any order . . . to require that pupils be transported to or from school on the basis of their race, color, religion, or national origin." Senator Griffin believed that just as Art. III, § 2 authorized the repeal by Congress of the Act of 1867, so that constitutional provision authorized removing busing cases from the jurisdiction of the Supreme Court. For one view on the constitutionality of such a proposal, see R. BORK, CONSTITUTIONALITY OF THE PRESIDENT'S BUSING PROPOSALS 7 (1972): "Would the framers have couched a general power to control the Court, to nullify its function as a final interpreter of the law, in the language of 'exceptions' and 'regulations'? Or does that language more probably imply authority over relatively minor problems, matters of detail and convenience?"

Professor Bork makes the following comment about *McCardle*: "*McCardle* is, however, a rather enigmatic precedent. If it stands for the proposition that Congress may take away any category of the Supreme Court's jurisdiction, it obviously is capable of destroying the entire institution of judicial review since *Marbury v. Madison.* So read, there is good reason to doubt *McCardle's* vitality as a precedent today."

3. Professor Bork is not alone in his doubts about the continuing validity of *Ex parte McCardle.* Justice Douglas made a similar observation in dissent in Glidden v. Zdanok, 370 U.S. 530, 605 n. 11 (1962): "There is a serious question whether the McCardle case could command a majority view today." A view of the issue presented in *McCardle* which manifests close allegiance to the text of Art. III but not too much sympathy for separation of powers as a dynamic constitutional concept designed to protect what the federal judiciary has *become* is found in Justice Frankfurter's dissent in National Mut. Ins. Co. v. Tidewater Transfer Co., 337 U.S. 582, 655 (1948): "Congress need not give this Court any appellate power; it may withdraw appellate jurisdiction once conferred and it may do so even while a case is *sub judice.*"

4.   Another administration anti-busing proposal which was designed to contract the jurisdiction of federal courts, enacted as Public Law 93-380, 88 Stat. 517, 20 U.S.C. § 1701, contains a provision which states:

> No court, department or agency of the United States shall, pursuant to section 214, order the implementation of a plan that would require the transportation of any student to a school other than the school closest or next closest to his place of residence which provides the appropriate grade level and type of education for such student.

In proposing the legislation, the Nixon Administration argued that it was not legislation enacted to enforce the fourteenth amendment but rather that it was legislation falling within the area of congressional power over federal court jurisdiction. Former Justice Goldberg has argued that even assuming the proposed legislation to be jurisdictional, the proposals are "constitutionally unsound because congressional power to restrict pre-existing federal court jurisdiction is not limitless." Former Justice Goldberg argued that *McCardle* cannot be viewed as supporting unbounded congressional control over federal court jurisdiction because in *McCardle* the Supreme Court had explicitly pointed out that "it still retained, in addition to its original jurisdiction, discretionary appellate power in habeas corpus proceedings under the Judiciary Act of 1789." *See* Goldberg, *The Administration's Anti-Busing Proposals—Politics Makes Bad Law*, 67 Nw. U.L. Rev. 319, 350-351 (1972). Professor Bickel had taken the position that *McCardle* is "aberrational" and "a fairly narrow holding." *See* Bickel, *What's Wrong With Nixon's Busing Bills?*, The New Republic, April 22, 1972, p. 21. Was the court's reference in *McCardle* to the fact that it still had discretionary appellate power over habeas corpus central to its holding in that case?

5.   Under the Judiciary Act of 1789, a person detained pursuant to federal authority and denied release by the federal circuit court could petition the Supreme Court for habeas corpus. In a case decided two years after *McCardle* it was held that when the Supreme Court issued habeas after the federal court and circuit court had denied it the court was acting in the exercise of its appellate jurisdiction. *See Ex parte* Yerger, 75 U.S. (8 Wall.) 85, 102 (1869).

Viewing *Ex parte Yerger* and *McCardle* together, it has been argued by some commentators that the court in *McCardle* had approved only a limited contraction of the court's appellate jurisdiction in habeas cases. Professor Bernard Schwartz makes clear, for example, that the key point in *McCardle* is that the court did not hold "that Congress could validly oust it of all appellate jurisdiction in habeas corpus cases." *See* B. Schwartz, Constitutional Law, A Textbook 19 (1972). The implication of Professor Schwartz' analysis is that a modest contraction of appellate jurisdiction is permissible but a severe contraction of that jurisdiction is impermissible because it would be a violation of separation of powers. On this theme, see Ratner, *Congressional Power Over the Appellate Jurisdiction of the Supreme Court*, 109 U. Pa. L. Rev. 157, 171-72 (1960). *See also* United States v. Klein, 80 U.S. (13 Wall.) 128 (1872) (Congress cannot withhold jurisdiction where to do so would prescribe a rule of decision in a case). Can Congress eliminate the only effective remedy for vindicating a constitutional right? Do the due process or equal protection provisions limit Congress' power under Art. III, § 2? But on what basis does the degree of legislative interference with the judicial branch affect the question of the constitutionality of the interference?

6.   On December 19, 1972, the controversial Freund Report was issued by Professor Paul Freund, chairman of a seven-person study group appointed by Chief Justice Burger. See Federal Judicial Center Study Group, Report On the Case Load of the Supreme Court (1972) (hereafter called the Freund Report). Among other recommendations, the Freund Report suggested that a National Court of Appeals be established to assume a good part of the appellate jurisdiction now exercised by the Supreme Court of the United States. The Freund Report proposal has been justified by reliance on the same language in Art. III, § 2, on which the repeal act validated in *McCardle* was based. The heart of the proposal has been summarized as follows:

> This new court would have the three-fold function of (1) screening all petitions for certiorari and appeals that at present are filed in the Supreme Court, and certifying or referring to the Supreme Court only those cases that are deemed most review-worthy; (2) denying review in all other cases not deemed worthy of Supreme Court consideration; and (3) retaining certain cases for decision on the merits or receiving from the Supreme Court, for decision on the merits, those cases that involve a "real conflict" between circuits but which otherwise lack sufficient importance to warrant Supreme Court attention. No review or reconsideration by the Supreme Court would be permitted of any case in which the National Court of Appeals had denied certiorari.

Gressman, *The Constitution v. The Freund Report*, 41 Geo. Wash. L. Rev. 951, 957 (1973).

Gressman relies on *McCardle* and *Yerger* for the proposition that legislative exceptions to Supreme Court appellate jurisdiction "have permitted matters essential to the maintenance of national supremacy and uniformity to be adjudicated by the Court in other ways." In Gressman's view, a congressional effort to make a fundamental contraction of the court's appellate jurisdiction would not be justified by *McCardle*. *See also* Freund, *Why We Need the National Court of Appeals*, 59 A.B.A.J. 247, 249, 251 (1973).

---

### The Statutory Basis of Supreme Court Jurisdiction

#### 28 U.S.C. § 1251.　Original jurisdiction

(a) The Supreme Court shall have original and exclusive jurisdiction of:

(1) All controversies between two or more states;

(2) All actions or proceedings against ambassadors or other public ministers of foreign states or their domestics or domestic servants, not inconsistent with the law of nations.

(b) The Supreme Court shall have original but not exclusive jurisdiction of:

(1) All actions or proceedings brought by ambassadors or other public ministers of foreign states or to which consuls or vice consuls of foreign states are parties;

(2) All controversies between the United States and a state;

(3) All actions or proceedings by a state against the citizens of another state or against aliens.

#### 28 U.S.C. § 1254.　Courts of appeals; certiorari; appeal; certified questions

Cases in the courts of appeals may be reviewed by the Supreme Court by the following methods:

(1) By writ of certiorari granted upon the petition of any party to any civil or criminal case, before or after rendition of judgment or decree;

(2) By appeal by a party relying on a state statute held by a court of appeals to be invalid as repugnant to the Constitution, treaties or laws of the United States, but such appeal shall preclude review by writ of certiorari at the instance of such appellant, and the review on appeal shall be restricted to the federal questions presented;

(3) By certification at any time by a court of appeals of any question of law in any civil or criminal case as to which instructions are desired, and upon such certification the Supreme Court may give binding instructions or require the entire record to be sent up for decision of the entire matter in controversy.

#### 28 U.S.C. § 1257.　State courts; appeal; certiorari

Final judgments or decrees rendered by the highest court of a state in which a decision could be had, may be reviewed by the Supreme Court as follows:

(1)  By appeal, where is drawn in question the validity of a treaty or statute of the United States and the decision is against its validity.

(2)  By appeal, where is drawn in question the validity of a statute of any state on the ground of its being repugnant to the Constitution, treaties or laws of the United States, and the decision is in favor of its validity.

(3)  By writ of certiorari, where the validity of a treaty or statute of the United States is drawn in question or where the validity of a State statute is drawn in question on the ground of its being repugnant to the Constitution, treaties or laws of the United States, or where any title, right, privilege or immunity is specially set up or claimed under the Constitution, treaties or statutes of, or commission held or authority exercised under, the United States.

For purposes of this section, the term "highest court of a state" includes the District of Columbia Court of Appeals.

---

The student will note that §§ 1254 and 1257 draw a distinction between obtaining review by appeal and review by certiorari. Technically, the distinction is that if a case falls within the specifications of the statutes providing review by appeal to the Supreme Court, review is a matter of right. Certiorari, on the other hand, is a matter of discretion. In fact, the difference in mode of review has almost become a distinction without a difference. Professor Wright's view on the matter is as follows: "Perhaps the most widely held misconception of the work of the Supreme Court is the notion that appeal is a matter of right, while certiorari is in the discretion of the Court." *See* C. WRIGHT, LAW OF FEDERAL COURTS 493 (2d ed. 1970). Although conceding that one may obtain review more easily by appeal than by certiorari, Professor Wright says that in practice "both modes of review are now essentially discretionary." He explains:

> Some appeals will not be heard because of procedural defects in taking the appeal, or because the case is not one in which appeal will lie, but in most cases the Court summarily affirms, or dismisses the appeal for want of a substantial federal question. Thus while such dispositions represent decisions on the merits, they are of scant comfort to the appellant who has obtained no relief.

Rule 19 of the Revised Rules of the Supreme Court of the United States, as amended to July 30, 1973 states the considerations governing review on certiorari as follows:

> 1.  A review on writ of certiorari is not a matter of right, but of sound judicial discretion, and will be granted only where there are special and important reasons therefor. The following, while neither controlling nor fully measuring the

court's discretion, indicate the character of reasons which will be considered:

(a)  Where a state court has decided a federal question of substance not theretofore determined by this court, or has decided it in a way probably not in accord with applicable decisions of this court.

(b)  Where a court of appeals has rendered a decision in conflict with the decision of another court of appeals on the same matter; or has decided an important state or territorial question in a way in conflict with applicable state or territorial law; or has decided an important question of federal law which has not been, but should be, settled by this court; or has decided a federal question in a way in conflict with applicable decisions of this court; or has so far departed from the accepted and usual course of judicial proceedings, or so far sanctioned such a departure by a lower court, as to call for an exercise of this court's power of supervision.

2.  The same general considerations outlined above will control in respect of petitions for writs of certiorari to review judgments of the Court of Claims, of the Court of Customs and Patent Appeals, or of any other court whose determinations are by law reviewable on writ of certiorari.

Does this adequately explain the considerations involved in the decision not to take a case? The court's control of its workload, the exercise of its discretion in determining which cases to review, is a critical part of Supreme Court decision-making. Like the doctrines that follow it helps define the manner in which the power of judicial review is exercised.

---

## C. CONSTITUTIONAL AND POLICY LIMITATIONS

### The Eleventh Amendment—The Background of Ex Parte Young

1.  In Chisholm v. Georgia, 2 U.S. (2 Dall.) 363, 1 L. Ed. 440 (1793), the Supreme Court held that Art. III permitted a citizen of one state to sue another state in federal court even if the state being sued had not consented to waive sovereign immunity for purposes of the particular litigation. The ratification of the eleventh amendment in 1793 undid the result in *Chisholm*. The eleventh amendment states:

> The Judicial power of the United States shall not be construed to extend to any suit in law or equity, commenced or prosecuted against one of the United States by Citizens of another State, or by Citizens or Subjects of any Foreign State.

Suppose a citizen of a state wishes to sue his own state with regard to a federal claim in a federal court? Suppose further that that state has not waived sovereign immunity regarding such suits by its own citizens? Is the eleventh amendment a bar? Although the text of the eleventh amendment does not speak to this issue, the Supreme Court in Hans v. Louisiana, 134 U.S. 1 (1890), held that the eleventh amendment would bar such a suit. *See generally* Cullison, *Interpretation of the Eleventh Amendment (A Case of the White Knight's Green Whiskers)*, 5 HOUSTON L. REV. 1 (1967).

2. Yet the eleventh amendment has proved to be no road-block to the steady march of federal judicial power proving once again the worldly wisdom of the English bishop, Hoadly, who declared before the King in 1717: "Whoever hath an absolute authority to interpret any written or spoken laws, it is he who is truly the lawgiver, to all intents and purposes, and not the person who first spoke or wrote them."

The case which emasculated the eleventh amendment was *Ex parte* Young, 209 U.S. 123 (1908). Justice Peckham reasoned in *Ex parte Young* that unconstitutional conduct by a state officer should not be considered state action on the ground that the state may never act unconstitutionally. Therefore a suit in a federal court against a state officer acting unconstitutionally was not a suit against the state and the eleventh amendment was not a bar. In this view, the state, like Caesar's wife, is without sin. This reasoning suffices nicely to pierce the obstacle of the eleventh amendment.

But this rationale does produce a logical fallacy. If action by a state officer is not state action for eleventh amendment purposes, then how can it be state action for fourteenth amendment purposes? The substantive constitutional contention in *Ex parte Young* is that the rates the railroads may charge have been set so low by the legislature as to constitute a confiscatory taking of the railroad property. In other words, the contention is that the Minnesota law setting forth the objectionable rates constitutes a deprivation of property without due process of law. However, if Young is not enforcing the statute on behalf of the state for eleventh amendment purposes, how can he be considered as enforcing the statute on behalf of the state for fourteenth amendment purposes? Justice Peckham's response to this problem was not to talk about it.

3. In Scheuer v. Rhodes, 416 U.S. 232 (1974), the personal representatives of the estates of students killed at Kent State sued the Governor, the Adjunct General of the National Guard, various members of the Guard and the university's president for

"intentionally, recklessly, willfully and wantonly" causing the occurrence of illegal acts which resulted in the students' deaths. The court held that the eleventh amendment did not bar a suit against named state officials for allegedly unconstitutional acts which resulted in the death of Kent State students.

4. In Edelman v. Jordan, 415 U.S. 651 (1974), the court held that even in a suit directed against a public official, if relief involves a charge on the general revenues of the state and cannot be distinguished from an award of damages against the state, the eleventh amendment bars the award.

### The "Case" or "Controversy" Requirement

*Marbury v. Madison* sketched a potentially larger power for the Supreme Court of the United States than it has ever cared, or dared, to use. It cannot be overemphasized that the sum of any historical study of judicial review demonstrates that in the main the Supreme Court has declined to use its power of judicial review. One of the principal limitations on judicial review has been the "case" or "controversy" requirement of Art. III. This requirement has been understood to prohibit the Supreme Court from giving advisory opinions on federal constitutional matters. The court may only decide a "flesh and blood" controversy. It cannot reach out to resolve an issue until it comes to the court bearing the battlemarks of actual controversy between two litigants who are adversaries in fact. This, at least, is the theory of the famous *Muskrat* case which follows.

### MUSKRAT v. UNITED STATES
Supreme Court of the United States
219 U.S. 346, 55 L. Ed. 246, 31 S. Ct. 250 (1911)

[Under federal legislation enacted in 1902, certain property was set aside for some Cherokee Indians, although it was to be administered by the federal government. Federal laws, enacted in 1904 and 1906, attempted to enlarge the number of Indians who would share in the property. Also, the duration of the period prohibiting restraints on alienation of the property was lengthened by the 1904 and 1906 federal legislation.

[Indians whose claims derived from the 1902 Act were adversely affected since their property rights were naturally diminished to the extent that they had to share the land with a larger class. Certain Indians whose claims derived from the 1902 Act, among them Muskrat, were authorized by Congress in 1907 to bring suit in the United States Court of Claims in order to obtain a determination of the constitutionality of the 1904 and 1906 Acts.

[What was the constitutional difficulty which concerned Congress? Was the problem that if B was permitted by Congress to share in A's land that this was taking property which was unconstitutional under the fifth amendment unless just compensation were paid to A (Muskrat et al.)?

[The Court of Claims sustained the validity of the Acts and dismissed the petitions.

[In a decision that has since been often cited, the Supreme Court held that the 1907 statute was itself unconstitutional on the ground that it violated the "case" or "controversy" requirement of Art. III.]

Justice DAY delivered the opinion of the Court.

. . . .

The first question in these cases, as in others, involves the jurisdiction of this court to entertain the proceeding, and that depends upon whether the jurisdiction conferred is within the power of Congress, having in view the limitations of the judicial power as established by the Constitution of the United States. [The court quotes Art. III.]

. . . .

It will serve to elucidate the nature and extent of the judicial power thus conferred by the Constitution to note certain instances in which this court has had occasion to examine and define the same.

. . . .

In 1793, by direction of the President, Secretary of State Jefferson addressed to the Justices of the Supreme Court a communication soliciting their views upon the question whether their advice to the executive would be available in the solution of important questions of the construction of treaties, laws of nations and laws of the land, which the Secretary said were often presented under circumstances which *"do not give a cognizance of them to the tribunals of the country."* The answer to the question was postponed until the subsequent sitting of the Supreme Court, when Chief Justice Jay and his associates answered to President Washington that in consideration of the lines of separation drawn by the Constitution between the three departments of government, and being judges of a court of last resort, afforded strong arguments against the propriety of extra-judicially deciding the question alluded to, and expressing the view that the power given by the Constitution to the President of calling on heads of departments for opinions "seems to have been purposely, as well as expressly, united to the executive departments." . . .

. . . .

It therefore becomes necessary to inquire what is meant by the judicial power thus conferred by the Constitution upon this court, and with the aid of appropriate legislation upon the inferior courts of the United States. "Judicial power," says Mr. Justice Miller in his work on the Constitution, "is the power of a court to decide and pronounce a judgment and carry it into effect between persons and parties who bring a case before it for decision." Miller on the Constitution, 314.

As we have already seen by the express terms of the Constitution, the exercise of the judicial power is limited to "cases" and "controversies." Beyond this it does not extend, and unless it is asserted in a case or controversy within the meaning of the Constitution, the power to exercise it is nowhere conferred.

What, then, does the Constitution mean in conferring this judicial power with the right to determine "cases" and "controversies"? A "case" was defined by Mr. Chief Justice Marshall as early as the leading case of Marbury v. Madison, 1 Cranch 137, to be a suit instituted according to the regular course of judicial procedure. And what more, if anything, is meant in the use of the term "controversy"? That question was dealt with by Mr. Justice Field, at the circuit, in the case of In re Pacific Railway Commission, 32 Fed. Rep. 241, 255. Of these terms that learned Justice said:

"The judicial article of the Constitution mentions cases and controversies. The term 'controversies,' if distinguishable at all from 'cases,' is so in that it is less comprehensive than the latter, and includes only suits of a civil nature. By cases and controversies are intended the claims of litigants brought before the courts for determination by such regular proceedings as are established by law or custom for the protection or enforcements of rights, or the prevention, redress, or punishment of wrongs. Whenever the claim of a party under the Constitution, laws, or treaties of the United States takes such a form that the judicial power is capable of acting upon it, then it has become a case. The term implies the existence of present or possible adverse parties whose contentions are submitted to the court for adjudication."

The power being thus limited to require an application of the judicial power to cases and controversies, is the act which undertook to authorize the present suits to determine the constitutional validity of certain legislation within the constitutional authority of the court? This inquiry in the case before us includes the broader question, When may this court, in the exercise of the judicial power, pass upon the constitutional validity of an act of Congress? That question has been settled from the early

history of the court, the leading case on the subject being Marbury
v. Madison, supra.

In that case Chief Justice Marshall, who spoke for the court,
was careful to point out that the right to declare an act of Congress unconstitutional could only be exercised when a proper
case between opposing parties was submitted for judicial determination; that there was no general veto power in the court upon
the legislation of Congress; and that the authority to declare an
act unconstitutional sprung from the requirement that the court,
in administering the law and pronouncing judgment between
the parties to a case, and choosing between the requirements of
the fundamental law established by the people and embodied in
the Constitution and an act of the agents of the people, acting
under authority of the Constitution, should enforce the Constitution as the supreme law of the land. The Chief Justice demonstrated, in a manner which has been regarded as settling the
question, that with the choice thus given between a constitutional
requirement and a conflicting statutory enactment, the plain duty
of the court was to follow and enforce the Constitution as the
supreme law established by the people. . . .

. . . .

Applying the principles thus long settled by the decisions of
this court to the act of Congress undertaking to confer jurisdiction in this case, . . . . [It is] evident that there is neither more nor
less in this procedure than an attempt to provide for a judicial
determination, final in this court, of the constitutional validity of
an act of Congress. Is such a determination within the judicial
power conferred by the Constitution . . .? We think is is not. That
judicial power, as we have seen, is the right to determine actual
controversies arising between adverse litigants, duly instituted in
courts of proper jurisdiction. The right to declare a law unconstitutional arises because an act of Congress relied upon by one or
the other of such parties in determining their rights is in conflict
with the fundamental law. The exercise of this, the most important and delicate duty of this court, is not given to it as a body
with revisory power over the action of Congress, but because the
rights of the litigants in justiciable controversies require the
court to choose between the fundamental law and a law purporting to be enacted within constitutional authority, but in fact
beyond the power delegated to the legislative branch of the Government. This attempt to obtain a judicial declaration of the
validity of the act of Congress is not presented in a "case" or
"controversy," to which, under the Constitution of the United
States, the judicial power alone extends. It is true the United
States is made a defendant to this action, but it has no interest

adverse to the claimants. The object is not to assert a property right as against the Government, or to demand compensation for alleged wrongs because of action upon its part. The whole purpose of the law is to determine the constitutional validity of this class of legislation, in a suit not arising between parties concerning a property right necessarily involved in the decision in question, but in a proceeding against the Government in its sovereign capacity, and concerning which the only judgment required is to settle the doubtful character of the legislation in question. Such judgment will not conclude private parties, when actual litigation brings to the court the question of the constitutionality of such legislation. In a legal sense the judgment could not be executed, and amounts in fact to no more than an expression of opinion upon the validity of the acts in question. Confining the jurisdiction of this court within the limitations conferred by the Constitution, which the court has hitherto been careful to observe, and whose boundaries it has refused to transcend, we think the Congress, in the act of March 1, 1907, exceeded the limitations of legislative authority, so far as it required of this court action not judicial in its nature within the meaning of the Constitution.

Nor can it make any difference that the petitioners had brought suits in the Supreme Court of the District of Columbia to enjoin the Secretary of the Interior from carrying into effect the legislation subsequent to the act of July 1, 1902, which suits were pending when the jurisdictional act here involved was passed. The latter act must depend upon its own terms and be judged by the authority which it undertakes to confer. If such actions as are here attempted, to determine the validity of legislation, are sustained, the result will be that this court, instead of keeping within the limits of judicial power and deciding cases or controversies arising between opposing parties, as the Constitution intended it should, will be required to give opinions in the nature of advice concerning legislative action, a function never conferred upon it by the Constitution, and against the exercise of which this court has steadily set its face from the beginning.

The questions involved in this proceeding as to the validity of the legislation may arise in suits between individuals, and when they do and are properly brought before this court for consideration they, of course, must be determined in the exercise of its judicial functions. For the reasons we have stated, we are constrained to hold that these actions present no justiciable controversy within the authority of the court, acting within the limitations of the Constitution under which it was created. . . .

The judgments will be reversed and the cases remanded to the Court of Claims, with directions to dismiss the petitions for want of jurisdiction. . . .

---

## NOTES

1. Do you think our constitutional tradition would be richer if the Supreme Court had acceded to Secretary of State Jefferson's request to answer the many questions of law with which the Department of State was faced but which were not of the type which were likely to develop into litigation? As the *Muskrat* decision makes clear, Chief Justice Jay reacted negatively to this request on the ground that the Supreme Court must not give advisory opinions. This position has been followed in theory by the Supreme Court to this day. Yet in state jurisdictions whose own constitutions erect no barriers against the rendition of advisory opinions state supreme courts continue to give advisory opinions on proposed state legislation with regard to questions of validity under both state and *federal* constitutions. For example in 1973, the Supreme Judicial Court of Massachusetts declared that a proposed bill by newspapers within the state to require publication of political ads for all candidates running for an office, if the paper published the political ad of one such candidate, was violative of the first amendment. *See* Opinion of the Justices, 298 N.E.2d 829 (Mass. 1973). Is the Supreme Court necessarily without jurisdiction to review an advisory opinion from a state supreme court?

2. Should not a less rigorous definition of the "case" or "controversy" requirement have been arrived at by the court in *Muskrat*? Surely, from the point of view of a reasonable and serviceable definition of the "case or controversy" requirement there is more apparent adversity described in Muskrat's claim that the 1904 and 1906 acts invalidly infringed on his property rights than there is in the Secretary of State's desire to have the Supreme Court do some authoritative legal research for him.

The *Muskrat* fact situation could easily have produced a "case" or "controversy," couldn't it? When someone whose claims derived under the 1904 and 1906 acts went upon Muskrat's land to take possession, Muskrat could sue for ejectment. The issue of the validity of the title would be a "case" or "controversy." Does this possibility of suit make the court's decision in *Muskrat* more or less reasonable?

3. Is the reason the *Muskrat* suit was not a "case" or "controversy" primarily due to the fact that Muskrat had no quarrel

with the federal government, the nominal defendant under the
Act of 1907, but with the new class of Indians who had been given
rights to his property under the Acts of 1904 and 1906. This
new class of Indians should have been the appropriate parties
defendant. Yet even if the Act of 1907 had made this new class
of Indians the parties defendant, there would still not have been
an Art. III "case" or "controversy" violation under the theory
of the *Muskrat* decision. Two things would have had to occur to
make the situation an actual case or controversy. The new class
of Indians would have had to have taken possession of property
claimed by Muskrat and the first class of Indians and Muskrat
would have had to manifest his objection to that possession by
filing a law suit on his own motion.

### The Avoidance of the Disposition of Constitutional Issues

While some limitations on the exercise of judicial review
flow from the jurisdictional provisions of Art. III, others are a
result of the court's own sense of self-restraint, an attempt to
define its proper place within the legal-political system. These
policy parameters on the judicial review power are indicated in
the following case.

### RESCUE ARMY v. MUNICIPAL COURT OF LOS ANGELES
Supreme Court of the United States
331 U.S. 549, 91 L. Ed. 1666, 67 S. Ct. 1409 (1947)

Justice RUTLEDGE delivered the opinion of the Court.

. . . .

From Hayburn's Case, 2 Dall. 409, to . . . the Hatch Act case
decided this term [United Public Workers v. Mitchell] this Court
has followed a policy of strict necessity in disposing of constitutional issues. . . .

The policy, however, has not been limited to jurisdictional
determinations. For, in addition, "the Court [has] developed, for
its own governance in the cases confessedly within its jurisdiction, a series of rules under which it has avoided passing upon a
large part of all the constitutional questions pressed upon it for
decision." Thus, as those rules were listed in support of the
statement quoted, constitutional issues affecting legislation will
not be determined in friendly, nonadversary proceedings; in
advance of the necessity of deciding them; in broader terms than
are required by the precise facts to which the ruling is to be applied; if the record presents some other ground upon which the
case may be disposed of; at the instance of one who fails to show
that he is injured by the statute's operation, or who has availed

himself of its benefits; or if a construction of the statute is fairly possible by which the question may be avoided.

. . . .

. . . Like the case and controversy limitation itself and the policy against entertaining political questions, it [the policy] is one of the rules basic to the federal system and this Court's appropriate place within that structure.

Indeed in origin and in practical effects, though not in technical function, it is a corollary offshoot of the case and controversy rule. And often the line between applying the policy or the rule is very thin. They work, within their respective and technically distinct areas, to achieve the same practical purposes for the process of constitutional adjudication, and upon closely related considerations.

The policy's ultimate foundations, some if not all of which also sustain the jurisdictional limitation, lie in all that goes to make up the unique place and character, in our scheme, of judicial review of governmental action for constitutionality. They are found in the delicacy of that function, particularly in view of possible consequences for others stemming also from constitutional roots; the comparative finality of those consequences; the consideration due to the judgment of other repositories of constitutional power concerning the scope of their authority; the necessity, if government is to function constitutionally, for each to keep within its power, including the courts; the inherent limitations of the judicial process, arising especially from its largely negative character and limited resources of enforcement; withal in the paramount importance of constitutional adjudication in our system.

All these considerations and perhaps others, transcending specific procedures, have united to form and sustain the policy. Its execution has involved a continuous choice between the obvious advantages it produces for the functioning of government in all its coordinate parts and the very real disadvantages, for the assurance of rights, which deferring decision very often entails. On the other hand it is not altogether speculative that a contrary policy, of accelerated decision, might do equal or greater harm for the security of private rights, without attaining any of the benefits of tolerance and harmony for the functioning of the various authorities in our scheme. For premature and relatively abstract decision, which such a policy would be most likely to promote, have their part too in rendering rights uncertain and insecure.

. . . .

## D. THE STANDING LIMITATION: WHO CAN LITIGATE?

Many of the doctrines which the court has developed in connection with the practice of judicial review are intertwined. This is the case, for example, with the "case" or "controversy" requirement and the requirement that a litigant have standing to sue. The standing requirement insists that each litigant in a case have an interest which is legally cognizable.

It should be obvious that the strictness with which the doctrine of standing is approached will have a good deal to do with resolving whether the exercise by the Supreme Court of the doctrine of judicial review is to be on an extended or a limited scale. Rules of standing are thus a means of enforcing the "case" or "controversy" requirement. Professor Jaffe in the course of a discussion of some of the new and relaxed approaches to standing taken by the Warren Court in the sixties identifies at least two social policies behind the "case" or "controversy" requirement:

> The court, not being a representative institution, not having initiating powers and not having a staff for the gathering of information, must rely on the parties and their advocates to frame the problem and to present the opposing considerations relevant to its solution. It is argued that unless the plaintiff is a person whose legal position will be affected by the court's judgment, he cannot be relied on to present a serious, thorough, and complete argument. . . . The second argument for a restrictive definition of case and controversy is that the judicial power—particularly in the constitutional field—is inconsistent with the fundamental premises of a democratic system and has proved to be a block to effective government. Seen in this light, the case or controversy requirement is a device for limiting judicial intervention to the minimum needed for the administration of justice.

Jaffe, *The Citizen as Litigant in Public Actions: The Non-Hohfeldian or Ideological Plaintiff*, 116 U. PA. L. REV. 1033, 1037-1039 (1968).

Reflect on these two policies which are said to underlie the "case" or "controversy" requirement as you read the changing course of the Supreme Court's approach to standing from *Massachusetts v. Mellon* and *Frothingham v. Mellon,* to the present, nearly half a century later.

Professor Jaffe suggests that the "case" or "controversy" requirement serves to "limit judicial intervention to the minimum needed for the administration of justice." But does relaxation of standing, and therefore inevitably, of the "case" or "controversy" requirement automatically expand justice? Is it justice for non-elected judges to be able to set aside statutes, enacted by a democratically elected majority, in circumstances which in the past would not have been judicial questions?

Professor Jaffe says that in his view there is no "compelling" constitutional reason for denying jurisdiction in citizen and taxpayer actions. As you read *Massachusetts v. Mellon* and *Frothingham v. Mellon,* decide whether you agree with this conclusion. Is standing in *Frothingham* a judicial policy choice or a constitutional requirement? Even more fundamental, is what is a constitutional requirement a judicial policy choice?

If standing is relaxed to the point where any federal taxpayer may challenge any federal appropriation on constitutional grounds, hasn't the "case" or "controversy" requirement in Art. III, as interpreted in *Muskrat,* been seriously breached? If it has been breached, hasn't judicial review been impermissibly extended even beyond the ambitious frontiers mapped by Chief Justice Marshall in *Marbury v. Madison?*

---

## MASSACHUSETTS v. MELLON
## FROTHINGHAM v. MELLON
Supreme Court of the United States
262 U.S. 447, 67 L. Ed. 1078, 43 S. Ct. 597 (1923)

Justice SUTHERLAND delivered the opinion of the Court.

. . . Both cases challenge the constitutionality of the Act of November 23, 1921, c. 135, 42 Stat. 224, commonly called the Maternity Act. Briefly, it provides for an initial appropriation and thereafter annual appropriations for a period of five years, to be apportioned among such of the several states as shall accept and comply with its provisions, for the purpose of cooperating with them to reduce maternal and infant mortality and protect the health of mothers and infants. . . .

. . . In the *Massachusetts* case it is alleged that the plaintiff's rights and powers as a sovereign state and the rights of its citizens have been invaded and usurped by these expenditures and acts; and that, although the state has not accepted the act, its constitutional rights are infringed by the passage thereof and the imposition upon the state of an illegal and unconstitutional option either to yield to the federal government a part of its reserved rights or lose the share which it would otherwise be entitled to receive of the moneys appropriated. In the *Frothingham* case plaintiff alleges that the effect of the statute will be to take her property, under the guise of taxation, without due process of law.

We have reached the conclusion that the cases must be disposed of for want of jurisdiction without considering the merits of the constitutional questions.

In the first case, the State of Massachusetts presents no justiciable controversy either in its own behalf or as the representative of its citizens. The appellant in the second suit has no such interest in the subject-matter, nor is any such injury inflicted or threatened, as will enable her to sue.

First. The State of Massachusetts in its own behalf, in effect, complains that the act in question invades the local concerns of the state, and is a usurpation of power, viz.: the power of local self-government reserved to the states.

Probably, it would be sufficient to point out that the powers of the state are not invaded, since the statute imposes no obligation but simply extends an option which the state is free to accept or reject. But we do not rest here. Under Article III, § 2, of the Constitution, the judicial power of the Court extends "to controversies . . . between a State and citizens of another State" and the Court has original jurisdiction "in all cases . . . in which a State shall be party." The effect of this is not to confer jurisdiction upon the Court merely because a state is a party, but only where it is a party to a proceeding of judicial cognizance. Proceedings not of a justiciable character are outside the contemplation of the constitutional grant. . . .

What, then, is the nature of the right of the state here asserted and how is it affected by this statute? . . .

. . . .

In the last analysis, the complaint of the plaintiff state is brought to the naked contention that Congress has usurped the reserved powers of the several states by the mere enactment of the statute, though nothing has been done and nothing is to be done without their consent; and it is plain that that question, as it is thus presented, is political and not judicial in character, and therefore is not a matter which admits of the exercise of the judicial power. . . .

. . . .

It follows that in so far as the case depends upon the assertion of a right on the part of the state to sue in its own behalf we are without jurisdiction. In that aspect of the case we are called upon to adjudicate, not rights of persons or property, not rights of dominion over physical domain, not quasi-sovereign rights actually invaded or threatened, but abstract questions of political power, of sovereignty, of government. No rights of the state falling within the scope of the judicial power have been brought within the actual or threatened operation of the statute. . . .

We come next to consider whether the suit may be maintained by the state as the representative of its citizens. To this the answer is not doubtful. We need not go so far as to say that a state may never intervene by suit to protect its citizens against any form of enforcement of unconstitutional acts of Congress; but we are clear that the right to do so does not arise here. Ordinarily, at least, the only way in which a state may afford protection to its citizens in such cases is through the enforcement of its own criminal statutes, where that is appropriate, or by opening its courts to the injured persons for the maintenance of civil suits or actions. But the citizens of Massachusetts are also citizens of the United States. It cannot be conceded that a state, as parens patriae, may institute judicial proceedings to protect citizens of the United States from the operation of the statutes thereof. While the state, under some circumstances, may sue in that capacity for the protection of its citizens, it is no part of its duty or power to enforce their rights in respect of their relations with the federal government. In that field it is the United States, and not the state, which represents them as parens patriae, when such representation becomes appropriate; and to the former, and not to the latter, they must look for such protective measures as flow from that status.

Second. The attack upon the statute in the *Frothingham* case is, generally, the same, but this plaintiff alleges in addition that she is a taxpayer of the United States; and her contention, though not clear, seems to be that the effect of the appropriation complained of will be to increase the burden of future taxation and thereby take her property without due process of law. The right of a taxpayer to enjoin the execution of a federal appropriation act, on the ground that it is invalid and will result in taxation for illegal purposes, has never been passed upon by this Court. . . . The interest of a taxpayer of a municipality in the application of its moneys is direct and immediate and the remedy by injunction to prevent their misuse is not inappropriate. . . . But the relation of a taxpayer of the United States to the federal government is very different. His interest in the moneys of the Treasury—partly realized from taxation and partly from other sources—is shared with millions of others; is comparatively minute and indeterminable; and the effect upon future taxation, of any payment out of the funds, so remote, fluctuating and uncertain, that no basis is afforded for an appeal to the preventive powers of a court of equity.

The administration of any statute, likely to produce additional taxation to be imposed upon a vast number of taxpayers, the extent of whose several liability is indefinite and constantly changing, is essentially a matter of public and not of individual concern. If one taxpayer may champion and litigate such a cause, then every other taxpayer may do the same, not only in respect of the statute here under review but also in respect of every other appropriation act and statute whose administration requires the outlay of public money, and whose validity may be questioned. The bare suggestion of such a result, with its attendant inconveniences, goes far to sustain the conclusion which we have reached, that a suit of this character cannot be maintained. It is of much significance that no precedent sustaining the right to maintain suits like this has been called to our attention, although, since the formation of the government, as an examination of the acts of Congress will disclose, a large number of statutes appropriating or involving the expenditure of moneys for non-federal purposes have been enacted and carried into effect.

The functions of government under our system are apportioned. To the legislative department has been committed the duty of making laws; to the executive the duty of executing them; and to the judiciary the duty of interpreting and applying them in cases properly brought before the courts. The general rule is that neither department may invade the province of the other and neither may control, direct or restrain the action of the other. We are not now speaking of the merely ministerial duties of officials. We have no power per se to review and annul acts of Congress on the ground that they are unconstitutional. That question may be considered only when the justification for some direct injury suffered or threatened, presenting a justiciable issue, is made to rest upon such an act. Then the power exercised is that of ascertaining and declaring the law applicable to the controversy. It amounts to little more than the negative power to disregard an unconstitutional enactment, which otherwise would stand in the way of the enforcement of a legal right. The party who invokes the power must be able to show not only that the statute is invalid but that he has sustained or is immediately in danger of sustaining some direct injury as the result of its enforcement, and not merely that he suffers in some indefinite way in common with people generally. If a case for preventive relief be presented the court enjoins, in effect, not the execution of the statute, but the acts of the official, the statute notwithstanding. Here the parties plaintiff have no such case. Looking through forms of words to the substance of their complaint, it is merely that officials of the executive department of the government are executing and will execute an act of Congress asserted to be unconstitutional; and this we are asked to prevent. To do so would be not to decide a judicial controversy, but to assume a position of authority over the governmental acts of another and co-equal department, an authority which plainly we do not possess.

No. 24 [*Massachusetts* case], Original, dismissed.

No. 962 [*Frothingham* case] affirmed.

---

## NOTES

1. The *Frothingham* case had established a federal rule of standing for taxpayer suits. This rule differs from the rules of standing established by many states. Thus, in Doremus v. Board of Education, 342 U.S. 429 (1952), two plaintiffs, state and municipal taxpayers, were unable to show that their taxes were affected by the New Jersey statute which they were challenging. The New Jersey statute required some portions from the Old Testament to be read without comment at the opening of each public school day. The state court took the position that standing was present but ruled against the plaintiffs on the merits.

But the Supreme Court dismissed the appeal on the ground that the basis on which standing was conferred by New Jersey was inadequate to evidence a "case or controversy" which is required for the litigation of a case in a federal court. Justice Jackson said in *Doremus:*

> The taxpayer's action can meet this ["case or controversy"] test, but only when it is a good-faith pocketbook action. It is apparent that the grievance which it is sought to litigate here is not a direct dollars-and-cents injury but is a religious difference. If appellants established the requisite special injury necessary to a taxpayer's case or controversy, it would not matter that their dominant inducement to action was more religious than mercenary. It is not a question of motivation but of possession of the requisite financial interest that is, or is threatened to be, injured by the unconstitutional conduct.

2. Don't these remarks of Justice Jackson in *Doremus* at least imply that the Supreme Court could quite legitimately hold, if it chose, that taxpayer suits, whether state or federal, satisfy the case or controversy requirement? Did the court in *Doremus* view denial of standing to federal taxpayers as constitutionally compelled? Do you think Justice Sutherland's holding in *Frothingham* had its base in judicial policy? Did the court in *Frothingham* view its result as constitutionally compelled?

The court's quarrel with the fact situation in *Doremus* was that a good-faith taxpayer's suit was not present. The Bible-reading simply didn't affect the taxes of the plaintiffs. The plaintiffs tried to respond to this argument. In dissent, Justice Douglas, joined by Justices Reed and Burton, said that the Bible-reading statute deflected the public schools "from the education program for which the taxes were raised."

3. Justice Douglas' dissent in *Doremus* set forth many of the same arguments which he made 16 years later when concurring in the decision in Flast v. Cohen, 392 U.S. 83 (1968): (1) Concrete financial injury was not an appropriate yardstick for standing when the first amendment is at issue. (2) All taxpayers, like the shareholders in a corporation, have a general interest in challenging the unlawful actions of their government. (3) Furthermore, the court should, at least, respect the right of the states to allow standing to state taxpayers without a showing of special financial injury. The New Jersey state supreme court had been willing to consider the merits of the *Doremus* case despite its doubts on the standing issue. The Supreme Court should have followed New Jersey's view on standing. If there was standing in a state court on a federal constitutional issue, there should, in Justice Douglas' view, be standing in the ultimate court of appeal for such issues, the United States Supreme Court.

Was the result in *Doremus* constitutionally compelled? Or was the result dictated by stare decisis in the form of the *Frothingham* case? Could the court have distinguished *Frothingham* if it had wanted to? Is there any portion of the *Frothingham* opinion which might be read to support standing for the *Doremus* plaintiffs?

---

### FLAST v. COHEN
Supreme Court of the United States
392 U.S. 83, 20 L. Ed. 2d 947, 88 S. Ct. 1942 (1968)

Chief Justice WARREN delivered the opinion of the Court.

In *Frothingham v. Mellon* this Court ruled that a federal taxpayer is without standing to challenge the constitutionality of a federal statute. That ruling has stood for 45 years as an impenetrable barrier to suits against acts of Congress brought by individuals who can assert only the interest of federal taxpayers. In this case, we must decide whether the *Frothingham* barrier should be lowered when a taxpayer attacks a federal statute on the ground that it violates the Establishment and Free Exercise Clauses of the First Amendment.

. . . .

The gravamen of the appellants' complaint was that federal funds appropriated under the Act were being used to finance instruction in reading, arithmetic, and other subjects in religious schools, and to purchase textbooks and other instructional materials for use in such schools. Such expenditures were alleged to be in contravention of the Establishment and Free Exercise Clauses of the First Amendment. . . .

. . . .

. . . The three-judge court received briefs and heard arguments limited to the standing question, and the court ruled on the authority of *Frothingham* that appellants lacked standing. . . . 271 F. Supp. 1 (1967).

. . . .

Although the barrier *Frothingham* erected against federal taxpayer suits has never been breached, the decision has been the source of some confusion and the object of considerable criticism. The confusion has developed as commentators have tried to determine whether *Frothingham* establishes a constitutional bar to taxpayer suits or whether the Court was simply imposing a rule of self-restraint which was not constitutionally compelled. The conflicting viewpoints are reflected in the arguments made to this Court by the parties in this case. The Government has pressed upon us the view that *Frothingham* announced a constitutional rule, compelled by the Article III limitations on federal court jurisdiction and grounded in considerations of the doctrine of separation of powers. Appellants, however, insist that *Frothingham* expressed no more than a policy of judicial self-restraint which can be disregarded when compelling reasons for assuming jurisdiction over a taxpayer's suit exist. The opinion delivered in *Frothingham* can be read to support either position.
. . .

To the extent that *Frothingham* has been viewed as resting on policy considerations, it has been criticized as depending on assumptions not consistent with modern conditions. For example, some commentators have pointed out that a number of corporate taxpayers today have a federal tax liability running into hundreds of millions of dollars, and such taxpayers have a far greater monetary stake in the Federal Treasury than they do in any municipal treasury. To some degree, the fear expressed in *Frothingham* that allowing one taxpayer to sue would inundate the federal courts with countless similar suits has been mitigated by the ready availability of the devices of class actions and joinder under the Federal Rules of Civil Procedure, adopted subsequent to the decision in *Frothingham*. . . .

The jurisdiction of federal courts is defined and limited by Article III of the Constitution. In terms relevant to the question for decision in this case, the judicial power of federal courts is

constitutionally restricted to "cases" and "controversies." As is
so often the situation in constitutional adjudication, those two
words have an iceberg quality, containing beneath their surface
simplicity submerged complexities which go to the very heart of
our constitutional form of government. Embodied in the words
"cases" and "controversies" are two complementary but somewhat different limitations. In part those words limit the business
of federal courts to questions presented in an adversary context
and in a form historically viewed as capable of resolution through
the judicial process. And in part those words define the role assigned to the judiciary in a tripartite allocation of power to assure that the federal courts will not intrude into areas committed to the other branches of government. Justiciability is the
term of art employed to give expression to this dual limitation
placed upon federal courts by the case-and-controversy doctrine.
. . . .

It is in this context that the standing question presented by
this case must be viewed and that the Government's argument
on that question must be evaluated. As we understand it, the
Government's position is that the constitutional scheme of separation of powers, and the deference owed by the federal judiciary to the other two branches of government within that
scheme, present an absolute bar to taxpayer suits challenging
the validity of federal spending programs. The Government views
such suits as involving no more than the mere disagreement by
the taxpayer "with the uses to which tax money is put." According to the Government, the resolution of such disagreements
is committed to other branches of the Federal Government and
not to the judiciary. Consequently, the Government contends
that, under no circumstances, should standing be conferred on
federal taxpayers to challenge a federal taxing or spending program. An analysis of the function served by standing limitations
compels a rejection of the Government's position.

Standing is an aspect of justiciability and, as such, the problem of standing is surrounded by the same complexities and
vagaries that inhere in justiciability. Standing has been called
one of "the most amorphous [concepts] in the entire domain of
public law." Some of the complexities peculiar to standing problems result because standing "serves, on occasion, as a shorthand
expression for all the various elements of justiciability." In addition, there are at work in the standing doctrine the many subtle
pressures which tend to cause policy considerations to blend
into constitutional limitations.

Despite the complexities and uncertainties, some meaningful
form can be given to the jurisdictional limitations placed on

federal court power by the concept of standing. The fundamental aspect of standing is that it focuses on the party seeking to get his complaint before a federal court and not on the issues he wishes to have adjudicated. The "gist of the question of standing" is whether the party seeking relief has "alleged such a personal stake in the outcome of the controversy as to assure that concrete adverseness which sharpens the presentation of issues upon which the court so largely depends for illumination of difficult constitutional questions." Baker v. Carr, 369 U.S. 186, 204 (1962). In other words, when standing is placed in issue in a case, the question is whether the person whose standing is challenged is a proper party to request an adjudication of a particular issue and not whether the issue itself is justiciable. Thus, a party may have standing in a particular case, but the federal court may nevertheless decline to pass on the merits of the case because, for example, it presents a political question. . . . So stated, the standing requirement is closely related to, although more general than, the rule that federal courts will not entertain friendly suits, or those which are feigned or collusive in nature.

. . . The question whether a particular person is a proper party to maintain the action does not, by its own force, raise separation of powers problems related to improper judicial interference in areas committed to other branches of the Federal Government. Such problems arise, if at all, only from the substantive issues the individual seeks to have adjudicated. Thus, in terms of Article III limitations on federal court jurisdiction, the question of standing is related only to whether the dispute sought to be adjudicated will be presented in an adversary context and in a form historically viewed as capable of judicial resolution. . . . A taxpayer may or may not have the requisite personal stake in the outcome, depending upon the circumstances of the particular case. Therefore, we find no absolute bar in Article III to suits by federal taxpayers challenging allegedly unconstitutional federal taxing and spending programs. . . .

. . . We have noted that, in deciding the question of standing, it is not relevant that the substantive issues in the litigation might be nonjusticiable. However, our decisions establish that, in ruling on standing, it is both appropriate and necessary to look to the substantive issues for another purpose, namely, to determine whether there is a logical nexus between the status asserted and the claim sought to be adjudicated. For example, standing requirements will vary in First Amendment religion cases depending upon whether the party raises an Establishment Clause claim or a claim under the Free Exercise Clause. Such inquiries into the nexus between the status asserted by the litigant and the claim he presents are essential to assure that he is a proper and appropriate party to invoke federal judicial power. Thus, our point of reference in this case is the standing of individuals who assert only the status of federal taxpayers and who challenge the constitutionality of a federal spending program. Whether such individuals have standing to maintain that form of action turns on whether they can demonstrate the necessary stake as taxpayers in the outcome of the litigation to satisfy Article III requirements.

The nexus demanded of federal taxpayers has two aspects to it. First, the taxpayer must establish a logical link between that status and the type of legislative enactment attacked. Thus, a taxpayer will be a proper party to allege the unconstitutionality only of exercises of congressional power under the taxing and spending clause of Art. I, § 8, of the Constitution. It will not be sufficient to allege an incidental expenditure of tax funds in the administration of an essentially regulatory statute. This requirement is consistent with the limitation imposed upon state taxpayer standing in federal courts in Doremus v. Board of Education, 342 U.S. 429 (1952). Secondly, the taxpayer must establish a nexus between that status and the precise nature of the constitutional infringement alleged. Under this requirement, the taxpayer must show that the challenged enactment exceeds specific constitutional limitations imposed upon the exercise of the congressional taxing and spending power and not simply that the enactment is generally beyond the powers delegated to Congress by Art. I, § 8. When both nexuses are established, the litigant will have shown a taxpayer's stake in the outcome of the controversy and will be a proper and appropriate party to invoke a federal court's jurisdiction.

The taxpayer-appellants in this case have satisfied both nexuses to support their claim of standing under the test we announce today. Their constitutional challenge is made to an exercise by Congress of its power under Art. I, § 8, to spend for the general welfare, and the challenged program involves a substantial expenditure of federal tax funds. In addition, appellants have alleged that the challenged expenditures violate the Establishment and Free Exercise Clauses of the First Amendment. Our history vividly illustrates that one of the specific evils feared by those who drafted the Establishment Clause and fought for its adoption was that the taxing and spending power would be used to favor one religion over another or to support religion in general. . . . The Establishment Clause was designed as a specific bulwark against such potential abuses of governmental power, and that clause of the First Amendment operates as a specific constitutional limitation upon the exercise by Congress of the taxing and spending power conferred by Art. I, § 8.

. . . .

We have noted that the Establishment Clause of the First Amendment does specifically limit the taxing and spending power conferred by Art. I, § 8. Whether the Constitution contains other specific limitations can be determined only in the context of future cases. However, whenever such specific limitations are found, we believe a taxpayer will have a clear stake as a taxpayer in assuring that they are not breached by Congress. . . . Under such circumstances, we feel confident that the questions will be framed with the necessary specificity, that the issues will be contested with the necessary adverseness and that the litigation will be pursued with the necessary vigor to assure that the constitutional challenge will be made in a form traditionally thought to be capable of judicial resolution. We lack that confidence in cases such as *Frothingham* where a taxpayer seeks to employ a federal court as a forum in which to air his generalized grievances about the conduct of government or the allocation of power in the Federal System.

While we express no view at all on the merits of appellants' claims in this case, their complaint contains sufficient allegations under the criteria we have outlined to give them standing to invoke a federal court's jurisdiction for an adjudication on the merits.

Reversed.

Justice DOUGLAS, concurring.

While I have joined the opinion of the Court, I do not think that the test it lays down is a durable one for the reasons stated by my Brother Harlan. I think, therefore, that it will suffer erosion and in time result in the demise of *Frothingham v. Mellon*. It would therefore be the part of wisdom, as I see the problem, to be rid of *Frothingham* here and now.

. . . When the Court used substantive due process to determine the wisdom or reasonableness of legislation, it was indeed transforming itself into the Council of Revision which was rejected by the Constitutional Convention. It was that judicial attitude, not the theory of standing to sue rejected in *Frothingham*, that involved "important hazards for the continued effectiveness of the federal judiciary," to borrow a phrase from my Brother Harlan. A contrary result in *Frothingham* in that setting might well have accentuated an ominous trend to judicial supremacy.

But we no longer undertake to exercise that kind of power. Today's problem is in a different setting.

Most laws passed by Congress do not contain even a ghost of a constitutional question. The "political" decisions, as distinguished from the "justiciable" ones, occupy most of the spectrum of congressional action. The case or controversy requirement comes into play only when the Federal Government does something that affects a person's life, his liberty, or his property. The wrong may be slight or it may be grievous. Madison in denouncing state support of churches said the principle was violated when even "three pence" was appropriated to that cause by the Government. It therefore does not do to talk about taxpayers' interest as "infinitesimal." The restraint on "liberty" may be fleeting and passing and still violate a fundamental constitutional guarantee. The "three pence" mentioned by Madison may signal a monstrous invasion by the Government into church affairs, and so on.

The States have experimented with taxpayers' suits and with only two exceptions now allow them. A few state decisions are frankly based on the theory that a taxpayer is a private attorney general seeking to vindicate the public interest. Some of them require that the taxpayer have more than an infinitesimal financial stake in the problem. At the federal level, Congress can of course define broad categories of "aggrieved" persons who have standing to litigate cases or controversies. But, contrary to what my Brother Harlan suggests, the failure of Congress to act has not barred this Court from allowing standing to sue and from providing remedies. The multitude of cases under the Fourth, as well as the Fourteenth Amendment, are witness enough.

The constitutional guide is "cases" or "controversies" within the meaning of § 2 of Art. III of the Constitution. As respects our appellate jurisdiction, Congress may largely fashion it as Congress desires by reason of the express provisions of § 2, Art. III. See Ex parte McCardle, 74 U.S. 506. But where there is judicial power to act, there is judicial power to deal with all the facets of the old issue of standing.

Taxpayers can be vigilant private attorneys general. Their stake in the outcome of litigation may be *de minimus* by financial standards, yet very great when measured by a particular constitutional mandate. My Brother Harlan's opinion reflects the British, not the American tradition of constitutionalism. We have a written Constitution; and it is full of "thou shalt nots" directed at Congress and the President as well as at the courts. And the role of the federal courts is not only to serve as referee between the States and the center but also to protect the individual against prohibited conduct by the other two branches of the Federal Government.

There has long been a school of thought here that the less the judiciary does, the better. It is often said that judicial intrusion should be infrequent, since it is "always attended with a serious evil, namely, that the correction of legislative mistakes comes from the outside, and the people thus lose the political experience, and the moral education and stimulus that come from fighting the question out in the ordinary way, and correcting their own errors"; that the effect of a participation by the judiciary in these processes is "to dwarf the political capacity of the people, and to deaden its sense of moral responsibility." Thayer, John Marshall 106, 107 (1901).

. . . .

The judiciary is an indispensable part of the operation of our federal system. With the growing complexities of government it is often the one and only place where effective relief can be obtained. If the judiciary were to become a super-legislative group sitting in judgment on the affairs of people, the situation would be intolerable. But where wrongs to individuals are done by violation of specific guarantees, it is abdication for courts to close their doors.

. . . .

I would not be niggardly therefore in giving private attorneys general standing to sue. I would certainly not wait for Congress to give its blessing to our deciding cases clearly within our Article III jurisdiction. To wait for a sign from Congress is to allow important Constitutional questions to go undecided and personal liberty unprotected.

There need be no inundation of the federal courts if taxpayers' suits are allowed. There is a wise judicial discretion that usually can distinguish between the frivolous question and the substantial question, between cases ripe for decision and cases that need prior administrative processing, and the like.

. . . .

I would be as liberal in allowing taxpayers standing to object to these violations of the First Amendment as I would in granting standing of people to complain of any invasion of their rights under the Fourth Amendment or the Fourteenth or under any other guarantee in the Constitution itself or in the Bill of Rights.

Justice STEWART, concurring.

I join the judgment and opinion of the Court, which I understand to hold only that a federal taxpayer has standing to assert that a specific expenditure of federal funds violates the Establishment Clause of the First Amendment. Because that clause plainly prohibits taxing and spending in aid of religion, every taxpayer can claim a personal constitutional right not to be taxed for the support of a religious institution. The present case is thus readily distinguishable from Frothingham v. Mellon, 262 U.S. 447, 43 S.Ct. 597, 67 L. Ed. 1078, where the taxpayer did not rely on an explicit constitutional prohibition but instead questioned the scope of the powers delegated to the national legislature by Article I of the Constitution.

. . . .

Justice FORTAS, concurring.

I would confine the ruling in this case to the proposition that a taxpayer may maintain a suit to challenge the validity of a federal expenditure on the ground that the expenditure violates the Establishment Clause. . . .

. . . .

On the other hand, the urgent necessities of this case and the precarious opening through which we find our way to confront it, do not demand that we open the door to a general assault upon exercises of the spending power. The status of taxpayer should not be accepted as a launching pad for an attack upon any target other than legislation affecting the Establishment Clause.

Justice HARLAN, dissenting.

. . . .

It is desirable first to restate the basic issues in this case. The question here is not, as it was not in *Frothingham,* whether "a federal taxpayer is without standing to challenge the constitutionality of a federal statute." It could hardly be disputed that federal taxpayers may, as taxpayers, contest the constitutionality of tax obligations imposed severally upon them by federal statute. Such a challenge may be made by way of defense to an action by the United States to recover the amount of a challenged tax debt, or to a prosecution for willful failure to pay or to report the tax.

. . .

The lawsuits here and in *Frothingham* are fundamentally different. They present the question whether federal taxpayers *qua* taxpayers may, in suits in which they do not contest the validity of their previous or existing tax obligations, challenge the constitutionality of the uses for which Congress has authorized the expenditure of public funds. These differences in the purposes of the cases are reflected in differences in the litigants' interests. An action brought to contest the validity of tax liabilities assessed to the plaintiff is designed to vindicate interests that are personal and proprietary. The wrongs alleged and the relief sought by such a plaintiff are unmistakably private; only secondarily are his interests representative of those of the general population. I take it that the Court, although it does not pause to examine the question, believes that the interests of those who as taxpayers challenge the constitutionality of public expenditures may, at least in certain circumstances, be similar. Yet this assumption is surely mistaken.

The complaint in this case, unlike that in *Frothingham*, contains no allegation that the contested expenditures will in any fashion affect the amount of these taxpayers' own existing or forseeable tax obligations. Even in cases in which such an allegation is made, the suit cannot result in an adjudication either of the plaintiff's tax liabilities or of the propriety of any particular level of taxation. The relief available to such a plaintiff consists entirely of the vindication of rights held in common by all citizens. It is thus scarcely surprising that few of the state courts that permit such suits require proof either that the challenged expenditure is consequential in amount or that it is likely to affect significantly the plaintiff's own tax bill; these courts have at least impliedly recognized that such allegations are surplusage, useful only to preserve the form of an obvious fiction.

Nor are taxpayers' interests in the expenditure of public funds differentiated from those of the general public by any special rights retained by them in their tax payments. The simple fact is that no such rights can sensibly be said to exist. Taxes are ordinarily levied by the United States without limitations of purpose; absent such a limitation, payments received by the Treasury in satisfaction of tax obligations lawfully created become part of the Government's general funds. . . . [T]he United States holds its general funds, not as stakeholder or trustee for those who have paid its imposts, but as surrogate for the population at large. Any rights of a taxpayer with respect to the purposes for which those funds are expended are thus subsumed in, and extinguished by, the common rights of all citizens. To characterize taxpayers' interests in such expenditures as proprietary or even personal either deprives those terms of all meaning or postulates for taxpayers a *scintilla juris* in funds that no longer are theirs.

Surely it is plain that the rights and interests of taxpayers who contest the constitutionality of public expenditures are markedly different from those of "Hohfeldian" plaintiffs,[5] in-

---

[5] The phrase is Professor Jaffe's, adopted, of course, from W. Hohfeld, Fundamental Legal Conceptions (1923). I have here employed the phrases "Hohfeldian" and "non-Hohfeldian" plaintiffs to mark the distinction between the personal and proprietary interests of the traditional plaintiff, and the representative and public interests of the plaintiff in a public action. I

cluding those taxpayer-plaintiffs who challenge the validity of their own tax liabilities. We must recognize that these non-Hohfeldian plaintiffs complain, just as the petitioner in *Frothingham* sought to complain, not as taxpayers, but as "private attorneys-general." The interests they represent, and the rights they espouse, are bereft of any personal or proprietary coloration. They are, as litigants, indistinguishable from any group selected at random from among the general population, taxpayers and nontaxpayers alike. These are and must be, to adopt Professor Jaffe's useful phrase, "public actions" brought to vindicate public rights.

It does not, however, follow that suits brought by non-Hohfeldian plaintiffs are excluded by the "case or controversy" clause of Article III of the Constitution from the jurisdiction of the federal courts. This and other federal courts have repeatedly held that individual litigants, acting as private attorneys-general, may have standing as "representatives of the public interest." The various lines of authority are by no means free of difficulty, and certain of the cases may be explicable as involving a personal, if remote, economic interest, but I think that it is, nonetheless, clear that non-Hohfeldian plaintiffs as such are not *constitutionally* excluded from the federal courts. The problem ultimately presented by this case is, in my view, therefore to determine in what circumstances, consonant with the character and proper functioning of the federal courts, such suits should be permitted. . . .

As I understand it, the Court's position is that it is unnecessary to decide in what circumstances public actions should be permitted, for it is possible to identify situations in which taxpayers who contest the constitutionality of federal expenditures assert "personal" rights and interests, identical in principle to those asserted by Hohfeldian plaintiffs. . . . [F]or reasons that follow, I believe that the Court's position is untenable.

The Court's analysis consists principally of the observation that the requirements of standing are met if a taxpayer has the "requisite personal stake in the outcome" of his suit. This does not, of course, resolve the standing problem; it merely restates it. The Court implements this standard with the declaration that taxpayers will be "deemed" to have the necessary personal interest if their suits satisfy two criteria. . . . The difficulties with these criteria are many and severe, but it is enough for the

_____

am aware that we are confronted here by a spectrum of interests of varying intensities, but the distinction is sufficiently accurate, and convenient, to warrant its use at least for purposes of discussion.

moment to emphasize that they are not in any sense a measurement of any plaintiff's interest in the outcome of any suit. . . .

It is surely clear that a plaintiff's interest in the outcome of a suit in which he challenges the constitutionality of a federal expenditure is not made greater or smaller by the unconnected fact that the expenditure is, or is not, "incidental" to an "essentially regulatory program." . . .

Presumably the Court does not believe that regulatory programs are necessarily less destructive of First Amendment rights, or that regulatory programs are necessarily less prodigal of public funds than are grants-in-aid, for both these general propositions are demonstrably false. . . . Apparently the Court has repudiated the emphasis in *Frothingham* upon the amount of the plaintiff's tax bill, only to substitute an equally irrelevant emphasis upon the form of the challenged expenditure.

The Court's second criterion is similarly unrelated to its standard for the determination of standing. The intensity of a plaintiff's interest in a suit is not measured, even obliquely, by the fact that the constitutional provision under which he claims is, or is not, a "specific limitation" upon Congress' spending powers. Thus, among the claims in *Frothingham* was the assertion that the Maternity Act, deprived the petitioner of property without due process of law. The Court has evidently concluded that this claim did not confer standing because the Due Process Clause of the Fifth Amendment is not a specific limitation upon the spending powers. Disregarding for the moment the formidable obscurity of the Court's categories, how can it be said that Mrs. Frothingham's interests in her suit were, as a consequence of her choice of a constitutional claim, necessarily less intense than those, for example, of the present appellants? I am quite unable to understand how, if a taxpayer believes that a given public expenditure is unconstitutional, and if he seeks to vindicate that belief in a federal court, his interest in the suit can be said necessarily to vary according to the constitutional provision under which he states his claim.

The absence of any connection between the Court's standard for the determination of standing and its criteria for the satisfaction of that standard is not merely a logical ellipsis. Instead, it follows quite relentlessly from the fact that, despite the Court's apparent belief, the plaintiffs in this and similar suits are non-Hohfeldian, and it is very nearly impossible to measure sensibly any differences in the intensity of their personal interests in their suits. The Court has thus been compelled simply to postulate situations in which such taxpayer-plaintiffs will be "deemed" to have the requisite "personal stake and interest." The logical inadequacies of the Court's criteria are thus a reflection of the deficiencies of its entire position. These deficiencies will, however, appear more plainly from an examination of the Court's treatment of the Establishment Clause.

Although the Court does not altogether explain its position, the essence of its reasoning is evidently that a taxpayer's claim under the Establishment Clause is "not merely one of ultra vires," but one which instead asserts "an abridgment of individual religious liberty" and a "governmental infringement of individual rights protected by the Constitution." It must first be emphasized that this is apparently not founded upon any "preferred" position for the First Amendment, nor upon any asserted unavailability of other plaintiffs. The Court's position is instead that, because of the Establishment Clause's historical purposes, taxpayers retain rights under it quite different from those held by them under other constitutional provisions.

. . . I do not suggest that history is without relevance to these questions, or that the use of federal funds for religious purposes was not a form of establishment that many in the 18th century would have found objectionable. I say simply that, given the ultimate obscurity of the Establishment Clause's historical purposes, it is inappropriate for this Court to draw fundamental distinctions among the several constitutional commands upon the supposed authority of isolated dicta extracted from the clause's complex history. In particular, I have not found, and the opinion of the Court has not adduced, historical evidence that properly permits the Court to distinguish, as it has here, among the Establishment Clause, the Tenth Amendment and the Due Process Clause of the Fifth Amendment as limitations upon Congress' taxing and spending powers.

The Court's position is equally precarious if it is assumed that its premise is that the Establishment Clause is in some uncertain fashion a more "specific" limitation upon Congress' powers than are the various other constitutional commands. It is obvious, first, that only in some Pickwickian sense are any of the provisions with which the Court is concerned "specific[ally]" limitations upon spending, for they contain nothing that is expressly directed at the expenditure of public funds. The specificity to which the Court repeatedly refers must therefore arise, not from the provisions' language, but from something implicit in their purposes. But this Court has often emphasized that Congress' powers to spend are coterminous with the purposes for which, and methods by which, it may act, and that the various constitutional commands applicable to the central government, including those implicit both in the Tenth Amendment and in the General Welfare Clause, thus operate as limitations upon spending. I can attach no constitutional significance to the various degrees of specificity with which these limitations appear in the terms or history of the Constitution. . . .

Even if it is assumed that such distinctions may properly be drawn, it does not follow that federal taxpayers hold any "personal constitutional right" such that they may each contest the validity under the Establishment Clause of all federal expenditures. The difficulty, with which the Court never comes to grips, is that taxpayers' suits under the Establishment Clause are not in these circumstances meaningfully different from other public actions. If this case involved a tax specifically designed for the support of religion, as was the Virginia tax opposed by Madison in his Memorial and Remonstrance, I would agree that taxpayers have rights under the religious clauses of the First Amendment that would permit them standing to challenge the tax's validity in the federal courts. But this is not such a case, and appellants challenge an expenditure, not a tax. Where no such tax is involved, a taxpayer's complaint can consist only of an allegation that public funds have been, or shortly will be, expended for purposes inconsistent with the Constitution. The taxpayer cannot ask the return of any portion of his previous tax payments, cannot prevent the collection of any existing tax debt, and cannot demand an adjudication of the propriety of any particular level of taxation. . . .

 . . . .

It seems to me clear that public actions, whatever the constitutional provisions on which they are premised, may involve important hazards for the continued effectiveness of the federal judiciary. Although I believe such actions to be within the jurisdiction conferred upon the federal courts by Article III of the Constitution, there surely can be little doubt that they strain the judicial function and press to the limit judicial authority. There is every reason to fear that unrestricted public actions might well alter the allocation of authority among the three branches of the Federal Government. It is not, I submit, enough to say that the present members of the Court would not seize these opportunities for abuse, for such actions would, even without conscious abuse, go far toward the final transformation of this Court into the Council of Revision which despite Madison's support, was rejected by the Constitutional Convention. I do not doubt that there must be "some effectual power in the government to restrain or correct the infractions" of the Constitution's several commands, but neither can I suppose that such power resides only in the federal courts. We must as judges recall that, as Mr. Justice Holmes wisely observed, the other branches of the Government "are ultimate guardians of the liberties and welfare of the people in quite as great a degree as the courts." The powers of the federal judiciary will be adequate for the great burdens placed upon them only if they are employed prudently, with recognition of the strengths as well as the hazards that go with our kind of representative government.

Presumably the Court recognizes at least certain of these hazards, else it would not have troubled to impose limitations upon the situations in which, and purposes for which, such suits may be brought. Nonetheless, the limitations adopted by the Court are, as I have endeavored to indicate, wholly untenable. This is the more unfortunate because there is available a resolution of this problem that entirely satisfies the demands of the principle of separation of powers. This Court has previously held that individual litigants have standing to represent the public interest, despite their lack of economic or other personal interests, if Congress has appropriately authorized such suits. I would adhere to that principle. Any hazards to the proper allocation of authority among the three branches of the Government would be substantially diminished if public actions had been pertinently authorized by Congress and the President. I appreciate that this Court does not ordinarily await the mandate of other branches of the Government, but it seems to me that the extraordinary character of public actions, and of the mischievous, if not dangerous, consequences they involve for the proper functioning of our constitutional system, and in particular of the federal courts, makes such judicial forbearance the part of wisdom. . . .

. . . .

. . . The question here is not, despite the Court's unarticulated premise, whether the religious clauses of the First Amendment are hereafter to be enforced by the federal courts; the issue is simply whether plaintiffs of an *additional* category, heretofore excluded from those courts, are to be permitted to maintain suits. The recent history of this Court is replete with illustrations . . . that questions involving the religious clauses will not, if federal taxpayers are prevented from contesting federal expenditures, be left "unacknowledged, unresolved, and undecided."

. . . .

---

## NOTES

1. The constitutionality of federal aid to nonpublic schools had been the subject of congressional debate prior to the Supreme Court's decision in *Flast v. Cohen.* There were, for

instance, several attempts by the Senate to attach riders to federal education bills authorizing judicial review by federal citizen-taxpayers "to vindicate the public interest in the observance of the provisions of the first amendment relating to religion." Each time, however, the provision for judicial review was aborted in House-Senate conference. See a discussion of the legislative history in Note, *The Insular Status of the Religion Clauses: The Dilemma of Standing,* 36 GEO. WASH. L. REV. 648, 666-68 (1968).

2. Of the two "religion clauses" in the first amendment, which presents less of a standing problem? Compulsory Bible reading or flag salutes in the schools may invade the religious beliefs of school children and their parents may sue under the free exercise clause by alleging a direct injury to them. But showing direct injury under the establishment clause is another matter.

Suppose Congress passed a law authorizing subsidies for construction of churches and synagogues? Is it not possible that such a program might proceed without directly affecting or injuring any person specifically? Could a taxpayer easily allege that he was "uniquely" injured or affected by such a law?

Under the *Frothingham* rule, federal taxpayers had no standing as taxpayers to raise an establishment clause issue, or any other constitutional issue. But under the free exercise clause, a litigant had standing if he was "uniquely affected" by the challenged action, whether or not he was a taxpayer. In establishment clause cases, a situation could arise where no one person was sufficiently "affected" to be able to sue.

3. After *Flast v. Cohen,* is *Frothingham v. Mellon* still "good law"? In *Flast,* Chief Justice Warren asserted that *Frothingham* still endured. Justice Stewart sought to emphasize *Frothingham's* continuing vitality by narrowly stating the holding of *Flast v. Cohen.* What is a narrow reading of *Flast?* In *Flast,* does the court continue to endorse *Frothingham* and just carve out a single exception to it?

Justice Douglas appeared to believe that most of *Frothingham* was still with us. He urged the court to be "rid of *Frothingham* here and now." If *Frothingham* had been reversed in its entirety, what would the result be—complete judicial review of all federal legislation under which expenditures are made?

Justice Harlan found it difficult to view *Flast* as sufficiently different from *Frothingham* to justify a special rule of standing. Why?

4. Professor Davis has long advocated standing for any party who is aggrieved or injured by administrative action and

challenges that action in the courts. The critical point, argues
Professor Davis, is that the would-be litigant has suffered "injury
in fact," no matter how slight. This requirement could be satisfied, in Davis' view, even by a taxpayer's investment in a federal
spending program.

Professor Davis believes that Justice Harlan misinterpreted
the concept of "private attorney-general" by reading it as a
basis for standing where the plaintiff has no personal interest at
all in the suit. Is this your assessment of Justice Harlan's dissent
in *Flast? See* Davis, *Standing: Taxpayers and Others*, 35 U. Chi.
L. Rev. 601, 611-17, 628-36 (1968).

5. The conventional distinction between allowing state and
municipal taxpayer suits as distinguished from allowing federal
taxpayer suits is that an individual taxpayer's "pocketbook"
injury is a more significant part of total revenues on the state or
municipal level than is the case on the federal level. Obviously,
when we are dealing with corporate taxpayers at the federal
level or even individual taxpayers in populous and wealthy
states like New York and California, the taxpayer's over-all stake
in any given expenditure is also likely to be miniscule.

The state willingness to see taxpayer status as sufficient to
satisfy a standing requirement is obviously based on the view
that it is desirable to provide judicial oversight for state and
local government. Is there any reason that such accountability
should not be desirable at the federal level as well? Or does the
case and controversy requirement of Art. III present a barrier
which is not present on the state or local level?

6. Which of the court's two "nexus" requirements should
be of the greatest help in making standing determinations? What
is the distinction between "specific" and "general" constitutional
prohibitions on the spending power? Why should standing hinge
on whether the constitutional issue raised by a suit is "general"
or "specific"?

7. What are the criteria for standing in a federal taxpayer's
suit after *Flast v. Cohen*? In Protestants & Other Americans United
for Separation of Church & State (P.O.A.U.) v. Watson, 407 F.2d
1264 (D.C. Cir. 1968), the court of appeals attempted to sum up
the impact of *Flast* on the law of standing. There were said to be
four requirements for taxpayer standing in light of *Flast*: 1. The
plaintiff must be a taxpayer in fact. 2. The tax dollars used as a
basis for the suit must be expended in the furtherance of specific
government business. 3. There must be a *substantial* expenditure
involved. 4. This expenditure must exceed the limits imposed
by the establishment clause of the first amendment upon the
taxing and spending power of Congress under Art. I, § 8.

In *P.O.A.U.*, plaintiffs brought suit to enjoin the issuance of a postage stamp commemorating the Christmas holiday. They argued that governmental issuance of such a stamp amounted to official establishment and proselytization of the Christian religion in violation of the first amendment. The federal district court had dismissed the suit for lack of standing on the authority of *Frothingham*. On appeal, the court of appeals deferred decision until the Supreme Court delivered its opinion in *Flast*. When the *Flast* decision was announced the court of appeals reversed and remanded to the federal district court for a determination on (1) whether the plaintiff-organization was in fact a taxpayer, and (2) whether the government expenditure in issuing the Christmas stamp was "substantial."

P.O.A.U. was apparently a non-profit (i.e. non-taxpaying) organization. The court of appeals noted that if the district court so found, P.O.A.U. would lack standing to sue. However, there were two other plaintiffs in the suits who alleged they were taxpayers. Presumably, as to these individual taxpayers there would have been standing.

Did the court of appeals in *P.O.A.U.* read *Flast* too narrowly? Does *Flast* require that the challenged expenditure be "substantial"?

8. The court in *Flast* observed that the government was not concerned about who would challenge appropriations invalid under the establishment clause if federal taxpayer status was an insufficient basis for standing. This was presumably because there were "circumstances under which a taxpayer will be a proper and appropriate party to seek judicial review of federal statutes." Who, if taxpayer status was insufficient, would be a "proper and appropriate party" to seek review? Certainly, no one who would satisfy Justice Harlan's putative Hohfeldian plaintiff.

9. In the oral argument in the Supreme Court in *Flast v. Cohen*, Justice Fortas and Attorney General White became engaged in a discussion as to whether the *Frothingham* case was based on the fourteenth amendment as distinguished from the tenth. From the point of view of the scope that should be given to the *Flast* decision, why is this an important line of inquiry?

10. Professor Davis' analysis of *Flast v. Cohen* (*See* Note 4, *supra*) prompted a reply by another commentator, who argued, in a spoof on the *Flast* case, that *Flast* would eventually be seen as the first step in the abandonment of all standing requirements. *See* Bittker, *The Fictitious Taxpayer: The Federal Taxpayer's Suit Twenty Years After Flast v. Cohen*, 36 U. Chi. L. Rev. 364 (1968). Professor Davis filed a reply, *The Case of the Real Tax-*

*payer: A Reply to Professor Bittker*, 36 U. Chi. L. Rev. 375 (1969). For a further look at the evolution of Professor Davis' views on the Supreme Court's activity in this area, see his article, *The Liberalized Law of Standing*, 37 U. Chi. L. Rev. 450 (1970), which attempts to sum up the cases since *Frothingham*, including two 1970 decisions, *Data Processing* and *Barlow v. Collins*.

11. Association of Data Processing Service Organizations v. Camp, 397 U.S. 150 (1970) concerned whether sellers of data processing services had standing to challenge a ruling of the comptroller of the currency allowing national banks to provide such services. The lower courts in *Data Processing* had denied standing but the Supreme Court reversed.

The lower federal courts had denied standing on the ground that where a private party suffered injury due to loss from a competitor he lacks a legal interest sufficient to maintain a legal action. The lower federal courts had relied for this proposition on Tennessee Electric Power Co. v. TVA, 306 U.S. 118 (1939). The Supreme Court in *Tennessee Electric* had held that private power companies do not have standing to enjoin TVA. The court said the private competitors did not have standing "unless the right involved is a legal right—one of property, one arising out of contract, one protected against tortious invasion, or one founded on a statute which confers a privilege." Justice Douglas writing for the court in *Data Processing* set forth a new approach:

> The "legal interest" test goes to the merits. The question of standing is different. It concerns, *apart from the "case" or "controversy" test,* the question whether the interest sought to be protected by the complainant is arguably within the zone of interests to be protected or regulated by the statute or constitutional guarantee in question. Thus the Administrative Procedure Act grants standing to a person "aggrieved by agency action within the meaning of a relevant statute." 80 Stat. 392. 5 U.S.C. § 702. That interest, at times, may reflect "aesthetic, conservational, and recreational" as well as economic values. . . . A person or a family may have a spiritual stake in first amendment values sufficient to give him standing to raise issues concerning the Establishment Clause and the Free Exercise Clause. . . . We mention these noneconomic values to emphasize that standing may stem from them as well as from the economic injury on which petitioner relies here. Certainly he who is "likely to be financially" injured, may be a reliable private attorney general to litigate the issues of the public interest in the present case. (Emphasis added.)

In *Data Processing,* the statute in question did not in terms protect data processing services against competition from banks. The statute did, however, prohibit bank service corporations from engaging in any activity other than the performance of bank services for banks. In light of the legislative interest behind the statutory prohibition, the court held that for standing purposes the data processing services were within the "zone of interests to be protected by the statute." The "zone of interests" part of the two-fold standing test set forth in *Data Processing* was thus ratified. The other part of the test—whether there was that injury in fact required by Article III—was satisfied because the data processing services would experience economic injury if the banks were in competition against them. *See also* Barlow v. Collins, 397 U.S. 159 (1970), decided on the same day as *Data Processing.*

In both cases, Justice Brennan concurred in the result in the case but dissented from the court's two-fold test for standing. In Brennan's view, the only necessary test for standing was whether there is injury in fact as required by Art. III. The inquiry into whether the party seeking standing came within the "zone of interests" was in his view both unnecessary and incorrect: "By requiring a second, non-constitutional step, the court comes very close to perpetuating the discredited requirement that conditioned standing on a showing by the plaintiff that the challenged governmental action invaded one of his legally protected interests."

12. A major standing suit arose out of a Walt Disney proposal for a multi-million-dollar ski and recreation resort to be built in the Mineral King Valley. The Sierra Club brought suit to block the development. As a basis for standing, the Sierra Club cited its special interest in conservation and wildlife preservation which, it argued, made it, under the Administrative Procedure Act, § 10, "[a] person suffering legal wrong because of agency action or adversely affected or aggrieved by agency action within the meaning of a relevant statute." 5 U.S.C. § 702. Sierra's "relevant statute" was the Forest Service's enabling legislation which charged the Service with preserving and protecting the nation's forests.

The question in *Sierra* was whether a party not alleging any particular interest in the actions of a federal agency had standing to challenge its actions in the federal courts on behalf of the general public interest. The Sierra Club *could* have sued on behalf of its individual members but deliberately chose not to do so. Instead, Sierra sought to make this a test case of public interest litigation. The Supreme Court, 4-3, rejected the Sierra

Club's theory of standing. Sierra Club v. Morton, 405 U.S. 727 (1972).

The court, per Justice Stewart, decided the case in terms of the Administrative Procedure Act. Justice Stewart noted that "[w]here . . . Congress has authorized public officials to perform certain functions according to law, and has provided by statute for judicial review of those actions under certain circumstances, the inquiry as to standing must begin with a determination of whether the statute in question authorizes review at the behest of the plaintiff." He noted that "where a dispute is otherwise justiciable, the question whether the litigant is a 'proper party to request an adjudication of a particular issue,' Flast v. Cohen, . . . is one within the power of Congress to determine."

While recognizing that aesthetic, conservational and recreational values would suffice as injury, Justice Stewart argued that "broadening the categories of injury that may be alleged in support of standing is a different matter from abandoning the requirement that the party seeking review must have himself suffered an injury." He contended that "a mere 'interest in a problem,' no matter how long-standing the interest and no matter how qualified the organization is in evaluating the problem, is not sufficient by itself to render the organization 'adversely affected' or 'aggrieved' within the meaning of the APA."

Justice Douglas, dissenting, noted that "[t]he issue of statutory standing aside, no doubt exists that 'injury in fact' to 'aesthetic' and 'conservational' interests is here sufficiently threatened to satisfy the case or controversy clause." He went on to suggest that "[t]he critical question of 'standing' would be simplified and also put neatly in focus if we fashioned a federal rule that allowed environmental issues to be litigated . . . in the name of the inanimate object about to be despoiled, defaced, or invaded by roads and bulldozers and where injury is the subject of public outrage."

Justice Blackmun, joined by Justice Brennan argued that the court ought to have remanded with directions that Sierra Club be permitted to amend its complaint to allege "injury in fact." Blackmun supported creating an exception in the law of standing to permit "sincere, dedicated, established" organizations to bring actions even where they cannot allege a direct personal interest in the outcome of the suits. Environmental issues, he noted, often touch upon matters of public interest without necessarily affecting any single individual directly. Justice Blackmun asked: "Are we to be rendered helpless to consider and evaluate challenges of this kind because of procedural limitations rooted in traditional concepts of standing?" What should the Sierra

Club do on remand? Does *Sierra Club* suggest that the *Frothing-ham* standing rule has been further eroded? *See* United States v. Students Challenging Regulatory Agency Procedures, 412 U.S. 669 (1973).

**13.** The Burger Court has not shown any inclination to further erode the standing impediments to the public action. In United States v. Richardson, 418 U.S. 166 (1974), the court held, 5-4, per Chief Justice Burger, that a federal taxpayer lacks standing to challenge the constitutionality, under Art. I, § 9, cl. 7, *requiring* a regular accounting of public funds, of a statute which permits the CIA to account for its expenditures "solely on the certificate of the Director. . . ." 50 U. S. C. § 403j(b).

The court said taxpayer standing did not exist for two reasons. First, the suit was not brought to challenge the exercise of the federal taxing or spending power but rather to challenge statutes regulating the CIA. Second, there was no allegation that appropriated funds were being spent in violation of any specific constitutional limitation upon taxing and spending powers. Therefore, the court reasoned there was no logical nexus between the taxpayer's status as a taxpayer and his claim.

Burger stated for the court:

Respondent is seeking "to employ a federal court as a forum in which to air his generalized grievances about the conduct of government." Both *Frothingham* and *Flast* reject that basis for standing.

. . . .

As our society has become more complex, our numbers more vast, our lives more varied, and our resources more strained, citizens increasingly request the intervention of the courts on a greater variety of issues than at any period of our national development. The acceptance of new categories of judicially cognizable injury has not eliminated the basic principle that to invoke judicial power the claimant must have a "personal stake in the outcome," *Baker v. Carr,* or a "particular concrete injury," *Sierra Club,* "or a direct injury," *Ex parte Levitt;* in short, something more than "generalized grievances," *Flast.* Respondent has failed to meet these fundamental tests; accordingly, the judgment of the Court of Appeals is reversed.

An indication that the Burger Court may actually be returning to a pre-*Flast* view of standing is found in Justice Powell's separate concurrence in *Richardson.* Powell concurred specifically on the ground of his dissatisfaction with the "two part 'nexus'" test in *Flast.* Although he "would not overrule *Flast* on its facts,"

Powell said he would not use the rationale of *Flast* to resolve standing problems:

> The ambiguities inherent in the *Flast* "nexus" limitations on federal taxpayer standing are illustrated by this case. There can be little doubt about respondent's fervor in pursuing his case, both within administrative channels and at every level of the federal courts. The intensity of his interest appears to bear no relationship to the fact that, literally speaking, he is not challenging directly a congressional exercise of the taxing and spending power. On the other hand, if the involvement of the taxing and spending power has some relevance, it requires no great leap in reasoning to conclude that the Statements and Accounts Clause, Art. I, § 9, cl. 7, on which the respondent relies, is inextricably linked to that power. And that clause might well be seen as a "specific" limitation on congressional spending. Indeed, it could be viewed as the most democratic of limitations. Thus, although the Court's application of *Flast* to the instant case is probably literally correct, adherence to the *Flast* test in this instance suggests, as does *Flast* itself, that the test is not a sound or logical limitation on standing.

> The lack of real meaning and of principled content in *Flast* "nexus" test renders it likely that it will in time collapse of its own weight, as Mr. Justice DOUGLAS predicted in his concurring opinion in that case. This will present several options for the Court. It may either affirm pre-*Flast*, prudential limitations on federal and citizen taxpayer standing; attempt new doctrinal departures in this area, as would Mr. Justice STEWART; or simply drop standing barriers altogether, as, judging by his concurring opinion in *Flast*, and his dissenting opinion today, would Mr. Justice DOUGLAS. I believe the first option to be the appropriate course, for reasons which may be emphasized by noting the difficulties I see with the other two. And, while I do not disagree at this late date with the *Baker v. Carr* statement of the constitutional indicia of standing, I further believe that constitutional limitations are not the only pertinent considerations.

Justice Powell warned against further "[r]elaxation of standing requirements" which are "directly related to the expansion of judicial power." He argued that it is "inescapable that allowing unrestricted taxpayer or citizen standing would significantly alter the allocation of power at the national level, with a shift away from a democratic form of government." For Justice Powell "[u]nrestrained standing in federal taxpayer or citizen suits would create a remarkably illogical system of judicial supervision of the coordinate branches of the Federal Government." It followed that the court "should limit the expansion of federal taxpayer and citizen standing in the absence of specific statutory authorization to an outer boundary drawn by the *results* in *Flast* and *Baker v. Carr.*"

## SCHLESINGER v. RESERVISTS COMMITTEE TO STOP THE WAR
Supreme Court of the United States
418 U.S. 208, 41 L. Ed. 2d 706, 94 S. Ct. 2962 (1974)

[An organization called Reservists Committee to Stop the War brought a class action to prevent members of Congress from also serving in the Armed Forces Reserve. The Committee asserted that such service violated Art. I, § 6, cl. 2, which provides that "no person holding any office under the United States shall be a member of either House during his continuance in office."

[Reversing the courts below, the Supreme Court held that the Committee did not have standing to sue as citizens or taxpayers.]

Chief Justice BURGER delivered the opinion of the Court.

. . . .

### Citizen Standing

To have standing to sue as a class representative it is essential that a plaintiff must be a part of that class, that is, he must possess the same interest and suffer the same injury shared by all members of the class he represents. In granting respondents standing to sue as representatives of the class of all United States citizens, the District Court therefore necessarily—and correctly—characterized respondents' interest as "undifferentiated" from that of all other citizens.

The only interest all citizens share in the claim advanced by respondents is one which presents injury in the abstract. Respondents seek to have the Judicial Branch compel the Executive Branch to act in conformity with the Incompatibility Clause, an interest shared by all citizens. The very language of respondents' complaint, reveals that it is nothing more than a matter of speculation whether the claimed nonobservance of that clause deprives citizens of the faithful discharge of the legislative duties of Reservist Members of Congress. And that claimed nonobservance, standing alone, would adversely affect only the generalized interest of all citizens in constitutional governance, and that is an abstract injury. The Court has previously declined to treat "generalized grievances" about the conduct of Government as a basis for taxpayer standing. *Flast v. Cohen.* We consider now whether a citizen has standing to sue under such a generalized complaint.

. . . .

. . . [S]tanding to sue may not be predicated upon an interest of the kind alleged here which is held in common by all members of the public, because of the necessarily abstract nature of the injury all citizens share. Concrete injury, whether actual or threatened, is that indispensable element of a dispute which serves in part to cast it in a form traditionally capable of judicial resolution. It adds the essential dimension of specificity to the dispute by requiring that the complaining party have suffered a particular injury caused by the action challenged as unlawful. This personal stake is what the Court has consistently held enables a complainant authoritatively to present to a court a complete perspective upon the adverse consequences flowing from the specific set of facts undergirding his grievance. Such authoritative presentations are an integral part of the judicial process, for a court must rely on the parties' treatment of the facts and claims before it to develop its rules of law. Only concrete injury presents the factual context within which a court, aided by parties who argue within the context, is capable of making decisions.

Moreover, when a court is asked to undertake constitutional adjudication, the most important and delicate of its responsibilities, the requirement of concrete injury further serves the function of insuring that such adjudication does not take place unnecessarily. . . . First, concrete injury removes from the realm of speculation whether there is a real need to exercise the power of judicial review in order to protect the interests of the complaining party.

. . . Second, the discrete factual context within which the concrete injury occurred or is threatened insures the framing of relief no more broad than required by the precise facts to which the court's ruling would be applied. This is especially important when the relief sought produces a confrontation with one of the coordinate branches of the government; here the relief sought would, in practical effect, bring about conflict with two coordinate branches.

To permit a complainant who has no concrete injury to require a court to rule on important constitutional issues in the abstract would create the potential for abuse of the judicial process, distort the role of the Judiciary in its relationship to the Executive and the Legislature and open the Judiciary to an arguable charge of providing "government by injunction."

. . . .

The District Court . . . relied on the fact that the adverse parties sharply conflicted in their interests and views and were supported by able briefs and arguments. [323 F. Supp., at 841.] We have no doubt about the sincerity of respondents' stated objectives and the depth of their commitment to them. But the essence of standing

"is not a question of motivation but of possession of the requisite . . . interest that is, or is threatened to be, injured by the unconstitutional conduct." *Doremus v. Board of Education.* . . .

. . . Respondents' motivation has indeed brought them sharply into conflict with petitioners, but as the Court has noted, motivation is not a substitute for the actual injury needed by the courts and adversaries to focus litigation efforts and judicial decision making. Moreover, the evaluation of the quality of the presentation on the merits was a retrospective judgment that could have properly been arrived at only after standing had been found so as to permit the court to consider the merits. A logical corollary to this approach would be the manifestly untenable view that the inadequacy of the presentation on the merits would be an appropriate basis for denying standing.

Furthermore, to have reached the conclusion that respondents' interests as citizens were meant to be protected by the Incompatibility Clause because the primary purpose of the Clause was to insure independence of each of the branches of the Federal Government, similarly involved an appraisal of the merits before the issue of standing was resolved. All citizens, of course, share equally an interest in the independence of each branch of government. In some fashion, every provision of the Constitution was meant to serve the interests of all. Such a generalized interest, however, is too abstract to constitute a "case or controversy" appropriate for judicial resolution.[16] The proposition that all constitutional provisions are enforceable by any citizen simply because citizens are the ultimate beneficiaries of those provisions has no boundaries.

Closely linked to the idea that generalized citizen interest is a sufficient basis for standing was the District Court's observa-

---

[16] Satisfaction of the *Data Processing* "zone of interest" requirement seemingly relied upon to find citizen standing does not support such standing for two reasons: first, that case involved judicial review under the Administrative Procedure Act of regulatory agency action alleged to have caused private competitive injury; second, *Data Processing* required a showing of injury in fact, in addition to the "zone of interest" requirement. Until a judicially cognizable injury is shown no other inquiry is relevant to consideration of citizen standing.

tion that it was not irrelevant that if respondents could not obtain judicial review of petitioners' action, "then as a practical matter no one can." Our system of government leaves many crucial decisions to the political processes. The assumption that if respondents have no standing to sue, no one would have standing, is not a reason to find standing.

### Taxpayer Standing

. . . .

Here, the District Court, applying the *Flast* holding, denied respondents' standing as taxpayers for failure to satisfy the nexus test. We agree with that conclusion since respondents did not challenge an enactment under Art. I, § 8, but rather the action of the Executive Branch in permitting Members of Congress to maintain their Reserve status.

. . . .

[Reversed and remanded.]

Justice STEWART, concurring.

I agree with the Court that the respondents lack standing to sue either as citizens or taxpayers in this case. Here, unlike *United States v. Richardson,* the respondents do not allege that the petitioners have refused to perform an affirmative duty imposed upon them by the Constitution. Nor can there be taxpayer standing under Flast v. Cohen, 392 U.S. 83, since there is simply no challenge to an exercise of the taxing and spending power.

The Court's judgment in this case is wholly consistent with United States v. SCRAP, 412 U.S. 669. Standing is not today found wanting because an injury has been suffered by many, but rather because *none* of the respondents has alleged the sort of direct, palpable injury required for standing under Art. III. Like the plaintiff in Frothingham v. Mellon, 262 U.S. 447, 43 S. Ct. 597, 67 L. Ed. 1078, the respondents seek only to air what we described in *Flast* as "generalized grievances about the conduct of government." Our prior cases make clear that such abstract allegations cannot suffice to confer Art. III standing, and I therefore join the opinion and judgment of the Court.

Justice DOUGLAS, dissenting.

The requirement of "standing" to sue is a judicially created instrument serving several ends: (1) It protects the status quo by reducing the challenges that may be made to it and to its institutions. . . . Its application in this case serves to make the bureaucracy of the Pentagon more and more immune from the protests of citizens. (2) It sometimes is used to bar from the courts questions which by the Constitution are left to the other two coordinate branches to resolve, *viz.,* the so-called political question. (3) It is at times a way of ridding court dockets whether of abstract questions or questions involving no concrete controversial issue.

. . . .

While respondents have standing as taxpayers, their citizenship also gives them standing to challenge the appropriation acts financing activities of the reservists.

. . . .

The interest of citizens in guarantees written in the Constitution seems obvious. Who other than citizens have a better right to have the Incompatibility Clause enforced? It is their interests that the Incompatibility Clause was designed to protect. The Executive branch under our regime is not a fiefdom or principality competing with the Legislative as another center of power. It operates within a constitutional framework, and it is that constitutional framework that these citizens want to keep intact. That is, in my view, their rightful concern. . . . The "personal stake" in the present case is keeping the Incompatibility Clause an operative force in government by freeing the entanglement of the federal bureaucracy with the Legislative Branch.

. . . .

The interest of the citizen in this constitutional question is of course, common to all citizens. But as we said in United States v. SCRAP, 412 U.S. 669, 687-688 "standing is not to be denied simply because many people suffer the same injury. . . . To deny standing to persons who are in fact injured simply because many others are also injured, would mean that the most injurious and widespread Government actions could be questioned by nobody."

. . . .

Justice MARSHALL, dissenting.

. . . The specific interest which [respondents] asserted, and which they alleged had been infringed by violations of the Incompatibility Clause, though doubtless widely shared, is certainly not a "general interest common to all members of the public." *Ex parte* Levitt, 302 U.S. 633, 634 (1937). Not all citizens desired to have the Congress take all steps necessary to terminate American involvement in Vietnam, and not all citizens who so desired sought to persuade members of Congress to that end.

Respondents nevertheless had a right under the First Amendment to attempt to persuade Congressmen to end the war in Vietnam. And respondents have alleged a right, under the Incompatibility Clause, to have their arguments considered by Congressmen not subject to a conflict of interest by virtue of their positions in the armed forces reserves. Respondents' complaint therefore states, in my view, a claim of direct and concrete injury to a judicially cognizable interest. It is a sad commentary on our priorities that a litigant who contends that a violation of a federal statute has interfered with his aesthetic appreciation of natural resources can have that claim heard by a federal court, see *United States v. SCRAP,* while one who contends that a violation of a specific provision of the United States Constitution has interfered with the effectiveness of expression protected by the First Amendment is turned away without a hearing on the merits of his claim.

. . . .

Justice BRENNAN, dissenting.

The "standing" of a plaintiff to be heard on a claim of invasion of his alleged legally protected right is established, in my view, by his good-faith allegation that "the challenged action has caused him injury in fact." *Barlow v. Collins* (concurring opinion). The Court's further inquiry, in each of these cases, into the connection between "the zone of interests to be protected or regulated by the statute or constitutional guarantee in question," and the "interest sought to be protected by the complainant," is relevant, not to "standing" but, if at all, only to such limitations on exercise of the judicial function as justiciability, see *e.g.,* Baker v. Carr, 369 U.S. 186 (1962), or reviewability, see *e.g.,* Abbott Laboratories v. Gardner, 387 U.S. 136, 140 (1967).

. . . .

. . . I would hold that respondent Reservists Committee and its members have demonstrated sufficient "injury in fact" to maintain their suit. Their allegation that they are injured as taxpayers, while at first glance seeming extraordinarily difficult to prove, is neither impossible nor, on the basis of this record, made in bad faith. If the Secretary of Defense takes a contrary position with regard to either of these requirements, it is open to him to move for summary judgment and compel respondents to establish their position. More stringent requirements, such as the Court's demand that these respondents satisfy *Flast*'s "nexus" requirement, are not appropriate issues for resolution under the rubric of "standing." Since I would find the injury-in-fact requirement met by respondents' taxpayer allegation, I have no occasion to reach the question whether respondent Reservists Committee and its members' allegations of injury to their interests as citizens would be sufficient to confer standing under the circumstances of this case.

. . . .

---

## NOTES

1. In *Flast*, the court indicated that standing was a problem of the "form and context" of the litigation rather than separation of powers. Is this still accurate in light of *Richardson* and *Schlesinger*? Can the citizen in a public action have sufficient adversity to assure full litigation of the issues? According to Chief Justice Burger? According to Justice Powell? According to the dissenters? As you read the materials in the remainder of this chapter, consider whether the concerns raised by separation of powers principles are best handled under standing or other doctrines dealing with when issues are judicially cognizable.

2. *Richardson* and *Schlesinger* place stress on the need for a distinct injury, a requirement which was also emphasized in *Frothingham*. Was this satisfied in *Flast*? In United States v. SCRAP, 412 U.S. 669 (1973), several environmental groups were held to have standing to challenge ICC actions based on their allegation of economic, recreational and aesthetic harm even though the harm was "trivial" and shared by numerous other persons. Is *Richardson* and *Schlesinger* consistent with this position?

3. What is the import of *Flast* after *Richardson* and *Schlesinger*? Has the court returned to the pre-*Flast* rule of standing (*i.e., Frothingham*)? Would *Flast* be decided the same way today?

4. If standing is a problem of Art. III jurisdiction, how can Congress grant standing to citizens qua citizens? Does Congress create a legal right in citizens, the loss of which constitutes legal injury? Does congressional authorization of a citizen's standing merely remove separation of powers impediments?

### Third Party Standing: Raising the Rights of Others

1. In Tileston v. Ullman, 318 U.S. 44 (1943), Tileston, a Connecticut physician, sought a declaratory judgment in state court that the Connecticut law prohibiting the use of contraceptive devices or the giving of advice on their use, was unconstitutional. His complaint alleged that three of his patients had health problems which made pregnancy a threat to their lives, and that the anti-birth control statute deprived them of life without due process of law. The Connecticut law, Tileston alleged, precluded him from offering his patients the medical advice on contraception which their precarious health situations demanded.

The Connecticut court reached the merits of the complaint but upheld the validity of the statute. The appeal to the Supreme Court was dismissed without regard to the merits of the complaint. Tileston was held to lack standing because his suit did not allege any injury to himself. Rather his suit was directed to the constitutional rights of his patients, nonparties to the litigation.

The *Tileston* case enunciated the general rule that a person does not have standing to assert the rights of third parties (*jus tertii*). Had Dr. Tileston framed his complaint differently, he might have satisfied a standing requirement. For instance, he could have alleged that the effect of the Connecticut statute was to infringe upon his liberty to practice medicine since it prohibited him from giving his patients adequate medical care, or he might have claimed a loss of business income. Dr. Tileston was concerned about the health and safety of his patients, not about his potential "pocketbook injury" which the statute might cause. His concern for his patients was simply legally non-cognizable in the contest of constitutional litigation. As far as the Supreme Court was concerned, it was not his fight.

The *Tileston* case was relied on in a recent case, Roe v. Wade, 410 U.S. 113 (1973), in which the Supreme Court dismissed the suit of a Texas physician who sought to challenge the state's anti-abortion statute. Because the plaintiff alleged injury only to his patients, not to himself, the court held that he had no standing to challenge the statute. However, in that same case, individual women directly affected by the abortion statute had brought suit. As a result the individual women plaintiffs had their suits determined on the merits because they were in a position to meet the standing requirement.

2. An important distinction between the third-party standing doctrine involved in these cases and the general standing rules discussed above, lies in the fact that the former is treated as a complementary rule of judicial self-restraint, a "rule of practice." As such, it can be outweighed by competing considerations in a particular case. What are the policies supporting the rule that normally a litigant may not challenge the constitutionality of government action by invoking the rights of others? Is it sufficient that a party is otherwise properly before the court, *i.e.*, once there is personal standing all relevant issues may be litigated?

3. Professor Sedler suggests that the court generally looks to four factors in evaluating the question of *jus tertii*: (1) The interest of the party challenging the government act or statute; (2) The nature of the right asserted; (3) The relationship between

the challenger and the person whose rights he seeks to assert; and (4) The practical limitations upon the ability of those third parties to come forward themselves to vindicate their rights. Sedler, *Standing to Assert Constitutional Jus Tertii in the Supreme Court,* 71 YALE L.J. 599 (1962). *See* Note, *Standing to Assert Constitutional Jus Tertii,* 88 HARV. L. REV. 423 (1974).

4. As to Professor Sedler's fourth factor, consider the case of Barrows v. Jackson, 346 U.S. 249 (1953), in which the Supreme Court granted standing to a white property-owner to contest the constitutionality of judicial enforcement of a restrictive covenant. The property-owner had breached a covenant with neighbors, that they would sell their properties to whites only. The neighbors sued to recover damages, and the property-owner defended on the grounds that for a court to award damages would deny to potential black vendees the equal protection of the laws. The property-owner achieved standing in *Barrows,* although it was not *he* whose right to equal protection was at stake. Rather, the Supreme Court focused on the practical inability of the real parties in interest, black buyers, to bring suit on their own behalf. *See* NAACP v. Alabama, 357 U.S. 449 (1958), recognizing the organization's standing to raise the right of its members to privacy of association.

5. Would a doctor who is convicted for aiding and abetting married persons in violating a criminal statute prohibiting use of contraceptives have standing to raise the rights of privacy of married users? Would a nonphysician, head of a birth control clinic, similarly convicted, have standing? *See* Griswold v. Connecticut, 381 U.S. 479 (1965). If a statute prohibited not the use, but the distribution of contraceptives, would a nonphysician convicted of distributing contraceptives have standing to raise the privacy right of married and non-married users of contraceptives? *See* Eisenstadt v. Baird, 405 U.S. 438 (1972).

## E. THE TIMING LIMITATION: WHEN CAN CONSTITUTIONAL LITIGATION BE BROUGHT?

### Mootness and the Timing of Judicial Review

Just as a case can be brought too early, so it can be brought too late. When an issue that has provoked litigation has been resolved by events, courts may refuse to decide such cases on the basis of mootness. Mootness is one of the many doctrines which concern the timing of judicial review. As the court emphasizes in its per curiam opinion in *DeFunis v. Odegaard,* it is closely intertwined with the "case or controversy" requirement of Art. III. If an issue that brought parties to court has in fact been resolved, then there is not that adversity between them which the case and controversy clause requires.

The celebrated affirmative action-benign quota case, *DeFunis v. Odegaard,* provided a major contemporary illustration of the way the court uses the mootness doctrine. Was the conclusion of the majority in *DeFunis* that the case was moot a matter of constitutional compulsion? Or was it a rationalization seized to avoid a decision in a matter where a majority of the court thought the country was not ready for a clear decision one way or the other? Are doctrines of timing in social policy cases to some extent illustrations, at least in result, of the ways the court has read the nation's pulse?

For an extended discussion of equal protection problems raised by the substantive issues in *DeFunis,* see text, p. 635.

## DEFUNIS v. ODEGAARD
### Supreme Court of the United States
416 U.S. 312, 40 L. Ed. 2d 164, 94 S. Ct. 1704 (1974)

### PER CURIAM

In 1971 the petitioner, Marco DeFunis, applied for admission as a first-year student at the University of Washington Law School, a state-operated institution. The size of the incoming first-year class was to be limited to 150 persons, and the Law School received some 1,600 applications for these 150 places. DeFunis was eventually notified that he had been denied admission. He thereupon commenced this suit in a Washington trial court, contending that the procedures and criteria employed by the Law School Admissions Committee invidiously discriminated against him on account of his race in violation of the Equal Protection Clause of the Fourteenth Amendment to the United States Constitution.

DeFunis brought the suit on behalf of himself alone, and not as the representative of any class, against the various respondents, who are officers, faculty members, and members of the Board of Regents of the University of Washington. He asked the trial court to issue a mandatory injunction commanding the respondents to admit him as a member of the first-year class entering in September of 1971, on the ground that the Law School admissions policy had resulted in the unconstitutional denial of his application for admission. The trial court agreed with his claim and granted the requested relief. DeFunis was, accordingly, admitted to the Law School and began his legal studies there in the fall of 1971. On appeal, the Washington Supreme Court

reversed the judgment of the trial court and held that the Law
School admissions policy did not violate the Constitution. By
this time DeFunis was in his second year at the Law School.

He then petitioned this Court for a writ of certiorari, and
Mr. Justice Douglas, as Circuit Justice, stayed the judgment of
the Washington Supreme Court pending the "final disposition
of the case by this Court." By virtue of this stay, DeFunis has
remained in law school, and was in the first term of his third and
final year when this Court first considered his certiorari petition
in the fall of 1973. Because of our concern that DeFunis' third-
year standing in the Law School might have rendered this case
moot, we requested the parties to brief the question of mootness
before we acted on the petition. In response, both sides contended that the case was not moot. The respondents indicated
that, if the decision of the Washington Supreme Court were permitted to stand, the petitioner could complete the term for which
he was then enrolled but would have to apply to the faculty for
permission to continue in the school before he could register for
another term.[1]

. . . .

In response to questions raised from the bench during the
oral argument, counsel for the petitioner has informed the
Court that DeFunis has now registered "for his final quarter in
law school." Counsel for the respondents have made clear that
the Law School will not in any way seek to abrogate this registration.[2] In light of DeFunis' recent registration for the last
quarter of his final law school year, and the Law School's assurance that his registration is fully effective, the insistent question
again arises whether this case is not moot, and to that question
we now turn.

The starting point for analysis is the familiar proposition
that "federal courts are without power to decide questions that
cannot affect the rights of the litigants before them." The
inability of the federal judiciary "to review moot cases derives
from the requirement of Art. III of the Constitution under
which the exercise of judicial power depends upon the existence

----

[1] By contrast, in their response to the petition for certiorari, the respondents had stated that DeFunis "will complete his third year [of law
school] and be awarded his J.D. degree at the end of the 1973-1974 academic year regardless of the outcome of this appeal."

[2] In their memorandum on the question of mootness, counsel for the
respondents unequivocally stated: "If Mr. DeFunis registers for the spring
quarter under the existing order of this Court during the registration
period from February 20, 1974, to March 1, 1974, that registration would
not be canceled unilaterally by the university regardless of the outcome of
this litigation."

of a case or controversy." Although as a matter of Washington state law it appears that this case would be saved from mootness by "the great public interest in the continuing issues raised by this appeal," the fact remains that under Art. III "[e]ven in cases arising in the state courts, the question of mootness is a federal one which a federal court must resolve before it assumes jurisdiction."

The respondents have represented that, without regard to the ultimate resolution of the issues in this case, DeFunis will remain a student in the law school for the duration of any term in which he has already enrolled. Since he has now registered for his final term, it is evident that he will be given an opportunity to complete all academic and other requirements for graduation, and, if he does so, will receive his diploma regardless of any decision this Court might reach on the merits of this case. In short, all parties agree that DeFunis is now entitled to complete his legal studies at the University of Washington and to receive his degree from that institution. A determination by this Court of the legal issues tendered by the parties is no longer necessary to compel that result, and could not serve to prevent it. DeFunis did not cast his suit as a class action, and the only remedy he requested was an injunction commanding his admission to the Law School. He was not only accorded that remedy, but he now has also been irrevocably admitted to the final term of the final year of the law school course. The controversy between the parties has thus clearly ceased to be "definite and concrete" and no longer "touch[es] the legal relations of parties having adverse legal interests."

It matters not that these circumstances partially stem from a policy decision on the part of the respondent Law School authorities. The respondents, through their counsel, the Attorney General of the State, have professionally represented that in no event will the status of DeFunis now be affected by any view this Court might express on the merits of this controversy. And it has been the settled practice of the Court, in contexts no less significant, fully to accept representations such as these as parameters for decision.

There is a line of decisions in this Court standing for the proposition that the "voluntary cessation of allegedly illegal conduct does not deprive the tribunal of power to hear and determine the case, i.e., does not make the case moot." These decisions and the doctrine they reflect would be quite relevant if the question of mootness here had arisen by reason of a unilateral change in the *admissions procedures* of the Law School. For it was the admissions procedures that were the target of this litigation, and a voluntary cessation of the admissions practices complained of could make this case moot only if it could be said with assurance "that 'there is no reasonable expectation that the wrong will be repeated.' " Otherwise, "[t]he defendant is free to return to his old ways," and this fact would be enough to prevent mootness because of the "public interest in having the legality of the practices settled." But mootness in the present case depends not at all upon a "voluntary cessation" of the admissions practices that were the subject of this litigation. It depends, instead, upon the simple fact that DeFunis is now in the final quarter of the final year of his course of study, and the settled and unchallenged policy of the Law School to permit him to complete the term for which he is now enrolled.

It might also be suggested that this case presents a question that is "capable of repetition, yet evading review," Roe v. Wade, 410 U.S. 113, 125 (1973), and is thus amenable to federal adjudication even though it might otherwise be considered moot. But DeFunis will never again be required to run the gantlet of the Law School's admission process, and so the question is certainly not "capable of repetition" so far as he is concerned. Moreover, just because this particular case did not reach the Court until the eve of the petitioner's graduation from law school, it hardly follows that the issue he raises will in the future evade review. If the admissions procedures of the Law School remain unchanged,[3] there is no reason to suppose that a subsequent case attacking those procedures will not come with relative speed to this Court, now that the Supreme Court of Washington has spoken. This case, therefore, in no way presents the exceptional situation in which [this] doctrine might permit a departure from "[t]he usual rule in federal cases . . . that an actual controversy must exist at stages of appellate or certiorari review, and not simply at the date the action is initiated." Roe v. Wade.

Because the petitioner will complete his law school studies at the end of the term for which he has now registered regardless of any decision this Court might reach on the merits of this litigation, we conclude that the Court cannot, consistently with the limitations of Art. III of the Constitution, consider the substantive constitutional issues tendered by the parties. Accordingly, the judgment of the Supreme Court of Washington is vacated,

_____

[3] In response to an inquiry from the Court, counsel for the respondents has advised that some changes have been made in the admissions procedures "for the applicants seeking admission to the University of Washington law school for the academic year commencing September, 1974." The respondents' counsel states, however, that "[these] changes do not affect the policy challenged by the petitioners . . . in that . . . special consideration still is given to applicants from 'certain ethnic groups.' "

and the cause is remanded for such proceedings as by that Court may be deemed appropriate.

It is so ordered.

Justice BRENNAN, with whom Justice DOUGLAS, Justice WHITE, and Justice MARSHALL concur, dissenting.

I respectfully dissent. Many weeks of the school term remain, and petitioner may not receive his degree despite respondents' assurances that petitioner will be allowed to complete this term's schooling regardless of our decision. Any number of unexpected events—illness, economic necessity, even academic failure—might prevent his graduation at the end of the term. Were that misfortune to befall, and were petitioner required to register for yet another term, the prospect that he would again face the hurdle of the admissions policy is real, not fanciful; for respondents warn that "Mr. DeFunis would have to take some appropriate action to request admission for the remainder of his law school education, and *some discretionary action by the University on such request would have to be taken.*" (Emphasis supplied.) Thus, respondents' assurances have not dissipated the possibility that petitioner might once again have to run the gantlet of the University's allegedly unlawful admissions policy. The Court therefore proceeds on an erroneous premise in resting its mootness holding on a supposed inability to render any judgment that may affect one way or the other petitioner's completion of his law studies. For surely if we were to reverse the Washington Supreme Court, we could insure that, if for some reason petitioner did not graduate this Spring, he would be entitled to re-enrollment at a later time on the same basis as others who have not faced the hurdle of the University's allegedly unlawful admissions policy.

In these circumstances, and because the University's position implies no concession that its admissions policy is unlawful, this controversy falls squarely within the Court's long line of decisions holding that the "[m]ere voluntary cessation of allegedly illegal conduct does not moot a case." Since respondents' voluntary representation to this Court is only that they will permit petitioner to complete this term's studies, respondents have not borne the "heavy burden," of demonstrating that there was not even a "mere possibility" that petitioner would once again be subject to the challenged admissions policy. On the contrary, respondents have positioned themselves so as to be "free to return to [their] old ways."

I can thus find no justification for the Court's straining to rid itself of this dispute. While we must be vigilant to require that litigants maintain a personal stake in the outcome of a controversy to assure that "the questions will be framed with the necessary specificity, that the issues will be contested with the necessary adverseness and that the litigation will be pursued with the necessary vigor to assure that the constitutional challenge will be made in a form traditionally thought to be capable of judicial resolution," there is no want of an adversary contest in this case. Indeed, the Court concedes that, if petitioner has lost his stake in this controversy, he did so only when he registered for the Spring term. But appellant took that action only after the case had been fully litigated in the state courts, briefs had been filed in this Court and oral argument had been heard. The case is thus ripe for decision on a fully developed factual record with sharply defined and fully canvassed legal issues.

Moreover, in endeavoring to dispose of this case as moot, the Court clearly disserves the public interest. The constitutional issues which are avoided today concern vast numbers of people, organizations, and colleges and universities, as evidenced by the filing of twenty-six *amici curiae* briefs. Few constitutional questions in recent history have stirred as much debate, and they will not disappear. They must inevitably return to the federal courts and ultimately again to this Court. Because avoidance of repetitious litigation serves the public interest, that inevitability counsels against mootness determinations, as here, not compelled by the record. Although the Court should, of course, avoid unnecessary decisions of constitutional questions, we should not transform principles of avoidance of constitutional decisions into devices for sidestepping resolution of difficult cases.

. . . .

---

The constitutional law issues raised by the abortion cases are discussed in detail in this text beginning at p. 554. The excerpt from the court's decision in *Roe v. Wade* dealing with mootness is reported here so that the student may compare the court's refusal to declare the issues in *Roe v. Wade* moot with *DeFunis*.

### ROE v. WADE
Supreme Court of the United States
410 U.S. 113, 35 L. Ed. 2d 147, 93 S. Ct. 705 (1973)

Justice BLACKMUN delivered the opinion of the Court.

. . . .

The appellee notes, however, that the record does not disclose that Roe was pregnant at the time of the District Court hearing on May 22, 1970, or on the following June 17 when the court's opinion and judgment were filed. And he suggests that Roe's case must now be moot because she and all other members of her class are no longer subject to any 1970 pregnancy.

The usual rule in federal cases is that an actual controversy must exist at stages of appellate or certiorari review, and not simply at the date the action is initiated.

But when, as here, pregnancy is a significant fact in the litigation, the normal 266-day human gestation period is so short that the pregnancy will come to term before the usual appellate process is complete. If that termination makes a case moot, pregnancy litigation seldom will survive much beyond the trial stage, and appellate review will be effectively denied. Our law should not be that rigid. Pregnancy often comes more than once to the same woman, and in the general population, if man is to survive, it will always be with us. Pregnancy provides a classic justification for a conclusion of nonmootness. It truly could be "capable of repetition, yet evading review."

We, therefore, agree with the District Court . . . that the termination of [Jane Roe's] 1970 pregnancy has not rendered her case moot.

. . . .

---

## NOTES

1. In Singer, *Justiciability and Recent Supreme Court Cases,* 21 ALA. L. REV. 229, 262 (1969), it was observed that the "court is moving, rather rapidly, toward a complete abolition of the mootness doctrine." Does *DeFunis* suggest that the Supreme Court is going to give greater attention to mootness obstacles to constitutional litigation?

Or is *DeFunis* a mootness case only because it promised a refuge from the intractable constitutional issues raised by the merits of the case? But *Roe v. Wade* was a case raising issues of difficulty equal to those presented by *DeFunis* and yet the mootness problem was given short shrift. Is the difference that in *Roe* a clear majority for a particular result was present while such a clear majority might have been lacking in *DeFunis?* In other words, the sport in the Supreme Court's mootness case law may well be *DeFunis* rather than *Roe v. Wade.*

As a doctrinal matter, does it make any sense to say that the litigant in *Roe* might become pregnant again while it was unlikely *DeFunis* would need to go to law school again? On this point it should be noted that the University of Washington School of Law did not concede that *DeFunis* would be allowed to matriculate to the point of graduation.

2.   The implication from Professor Singer's observation about the court's general attitude toward mootness problems is that the court is sometimes cavalier towards jurisdictional-constitutional barriers to judicial review when the court is anxious to rule on a particular constitutional matter. Illustrative of this is the court's decision in North Dakota State Board of Pharmacy v. Snyder's Drug Stores, 414 U.S. 156 (1973), where a unanimous court accepted jurisdiction over an intermediate decision in the absence of the technical finality required by 28 U.S.C. § 1257 which restricts review by the Supreme Court of appeals from the state courts to final judgments.

In *North Dakota State Board of Pharmacy,* the court suggested "that this concept of finality has a 'penumbral' area." In other words, the finality rule can be relaxed where first amendment rights are at issue, or where, if the suitor is forced to wait for a technically final judgment, the right of appeal may be of little use to protect the constitutional right in question. Does the finality rule in 28 USC § 1257 spring from the same textual source in the Constitution as the mootness doctrine, *i.e.* the "case or controversy" requirement of Art. III?

If a case which is either moot or nonfinal is not a true "case or controversy," then on what authority does the court oscillate between enforcing and ignoring these limitations on judicial review?

### Ripeness and the Timing of Judicial Review

## UNITED PUBLIC WORKERS v. MITCHELL
### Supreme Court of the United States
### 330 U.S. 75, 91 L. Ed. 754, 67 S. Ct. 556 (1947)

[In *United Public Workers,* the Supreme Court, 4-3, upheld an attack on the Hatch Act which imposes a ban on the political activities of federal employees. None of the appellants in *United Public Workers,* except one, had violated the provisions of the Act but they wished to engage in political activities forbidden to federal employees by the Act. Therefore, the appellants sought a declaratory judgment on the constitutional limits to regulation of the political activities of government employees. The Court, per Mr. Justice Reed, denied the request for declaratory relief of the appellants who had not yet violated the Hatch Act. With regard to the appellant who had violated the Act and who was being threatened with removal from his job with the Civil Service Commission, the Court held that declaratory relief should obtain.]

Justice REED delivered the opinion of the Court.

. . . .

As is well known the federal courts established pursuant to Article III of the Constitution do not render advisory opinions. For adjudication of constitutional issues, "concrete legal issues, presented in actual cases, not abstractions," are requisite. This is as true of declaratory judgments as any other field. These appellants seem clearly to seek advisory opinions. . . . As these appellants are classified employees, they have a right superior to the generality of citizens, but the facts of their personal interest in their civil rights, of the general threat of possible interference with those rights by the Civil Service Commission under its rules, if specified things are done by appellants, does not make a justiciable case or controversy. Appellants want to engage in "political management and political campaigns," to persuade others to follow appellants' views by discussion, speeches, articles and other acts reasonably designed to secure the selection of appellants' political choices. Such generality of objection is really an attack on the political expediency of the Hatch Act, not the presentation of legal issues. It is beyond the competence of courts to render such a decision.

The power of courts, and ultimately of this Court, to pass upon the constitutionality of acts of Congress arises only when the interests of litigants require the use of this judicial authority for their protection against actual interference. A hypothetical threat is not enough. We can only speculate as to the kinds of political activity the appellants desire to engage in or as to the contents of their proposed public statements or the circumstances of their publication. It would not accord with judicial responsibility to adjudge, in a matter involving constitutionality, between the freedom of the individual and the requirements of public order except when definite rights appear upon the one side and definite prejudicial interferences upon the other.

. . . Should the courts seek to expand their power so as to bring under their jurisdiction ill-defined controversies over constitutional issues, they would become the organ of political theories. Such abuse of judicial power would properly meet rebuke and restriction from other branches. By these mutual checks and balances by and between the branches of government, democracy undertakes to preserve the liberties of the people from excessive concentrations of authority. No threat of interference by the Commission with rights of these appellants appears beyond that implied by the existence of the law and the regulations. . . . [T]he determination of the trial court, that the individual appellants, other than Poole, could maintain this action, was erroneous.

. . . .

--------

## NOTES

1. The Connecticut statute prohibiting the use of birth control devices and advice on their use came under renewed constitutional attack in Poe v. Ullman 367 U.S. 497 (1961). (See this text, p. 93.) In a 5-4 decision, the court dismissed the appeals and declined to adjudicate the question of the constitutionality of the Connecticut statute. A plurality opinion was delivered by Justice Frankfurter, joined by Chief Justice Warren, and Justices Clark and Whittaker.

The appellants, said Frankfurter, had not alleged any immediate threat of prosecution should they proceed to disobey the Connecticut statute in question. Furthermore, even if the complaints contained an allegation of immediate threat of prosecution, "we are not bound to accept as true all that is alleged." The Connecticut law, though on the statute books since 1879, had almost never been enforced through criminal prosecutions. Given this history of non-enforcement, Justice Frankfurter declared the appellants' allegation of fear of prosecution "collide[d] with plausibility." The law, he noted, was widely flouted in Connecticut, where birth control devices "are commonly and notoriously sold in Connecticut drug stores." In his view, Connecticut had nullified the proscriptive force of the statute by deliberately not enforcing the law. It posed no threat and no immediate controversy, and the constitutional challenge to its validity was more hypothetical than real. For these reasons, Justice Frankfurter stated that he thought the case was non-justiciable:

> Justiciability is of course not a legal concept with a fixed content or susceptible of scientific verification. Its utilization is the result of many subtle pressures, including the appropriateness of the issues . . . and the actual hardship to the litigants of denying them the relief sought. Both these factors justify withholding adjudication of the constitutional issues raised under the circumstances and in the manner in which they are now before the Court.

2. Is ripeness an Art. III limitation or a matter of policy? Are the same doctrines involved in *Mitchell* and *Poe*? What would the litigants in *Mitchell* and *Poe* have to do to make their case appropriate for review?

Prematurity and Abstractness

## SOCIALIST LABOR PARTY v. GILLIGAN
Supreme Court of the United States
406 U.S. 583, 32 L. Ed. 2d 317, 92 S. Ct. 1716 (1972)

[The Socialist Labor Party sought a declaratory judgment from a three-judge federal panel that certain sections of the Ohio election law were unconstitutional. The party had brought a similar action in 1968. In that case, Socialist Labor Party v. Rhodes, 393 U.S. 23 (1968), the Court held that the challenged election code provisions violated the fourteenth amendment guarantee of equal protection.

[Following the 1968 Supreme Court decision, Ohio revised much of its election law. The Socialist Labor Party was not satisfied with the changes and brought a second suit in 1970. A three-judge panel was convened to hear the new challenge. The panel struck down as unconstitutional all the pertinent election law provisions except a loyalty oath requirement, which it sustained as valid.

[Both sides to the litigation appealed to the Supreme Court. Meanwhile, the Ohio legislature again revamped the state's election law, modifying those provisions which the three-judge panel had held invalid. All issues in the case were thus mooted, except for the Socialist Labor Party's claim that the Ohio loyalty oath requirement was unconstitutional. Under this provision, an elaborate loyalty oath and disclaimer of subversive activities was established for all political parties seeking access to the ballot except "any political party or group which has had a place on the ballot in each national and gubernatorial election since the year 1900." In other words, the two major national parties, the Democrats and Republicans, were exempt. Only the newer "third" parties were subject to the Ohio election loyalty oath requirement. The Socialist Labor Party, therefore, argued that the law was an unconstitutional denial of equal protection.

[The Supreme Court did not consider this argument on the merits. In a 6-3 decision, delivered by Justice Rehnquist, the Court dismissed the appeal.]

Justice REHNQUIST delivered the opinion of the Court.

. . . .

Appellants did not in their action that came here in 1968 challenge the loyalty oath. Their 1970 complaint respecting the loyalty oath is singularly sparse in its factual allegations. There is no suggestion in it that the Socialist Labor Party has ever refused in the past, or will now refuse, to sign the required oath. There is no allegation of injury that the party has suffered or will suffer because of the existence of the oath requirement.

It is fairly inferable that the absence of such allegations is not merely an oversight in the drafting of a pleading. The requirement of the affidavit under oath was enacted in 1941, and has remained continuously in force since that date. The Socialist Labor Party has appeared on the state ballot since the law's passage, and, unless the state officials have ignored what appear to be mandatory oath provisions, it is reasonable to conclude that the party has in the past executed the required affidavit.

It is axiomatic that the federal courts do not decide abstract questions posed by parties who lack "a personal stake in the outcome of the controversy." Appellants argue that the affidavit requirement violates the First and Fourteenth Amendments, but their pleadings fail to allege that the requirement has in any way affected their speech or conduct, or that executing the oath would impair the exercise of any right that they have as a political party or as members of a political party. They contend that to require it of them but not of the two major political parties denies them equal protection, but they do not allege any particulars that make the requirement other than a hypothetical burden. Finally, they claim that the required affidavit is impermissibly vague and that its enforcement procedures do not comport with due process. But the record before the three-judge District Court, and now before this Court, is extraordinarily skimpy in the sort of proved or admitted facts that would enable us to adjudicate this claim. Since appellants have previously secured a position on the ballot with no untoward consequences, the gravamen of their claim that it injures them remains quite unclear.

In the usual case in which this Court has passed on the validity of similar oath provisions, the party challenging constitutionality was either unable or unwilling to execute the required oath, and in the circumstances of the particular case sustained, or faced the immediate prospect of sustaining, some direct injury as a result of the penalty provisions associated with the oath.

. . . .

The long and the short of the matter is that we know very little more about the operation of the Ohio affidavit procedure as a result of this lawsuit than we would if a prospective plaintiff who had never set foot in Ohio had simply picked this section of the Ohio election laws out of the statute books and filed a complaint in the District Court setting forth the allegedly offending provisions and requesting an injunction against their enforcement. These plaintiffs may well meet the technical requirement of standing, and they may be parties to a case or controversy, but their case has not given any particularity to the effect on them of Ohio's affidavit requirement.

This Court has recognized in the past that even when jurisdiction exists it should not be exercised unless the case "tenders the underlying constitutional issues in clean-cut and concrete form." Rescue Army v. Municipal Court, 331 U.S. 549, 584 (1947). Problems of prematurity and abstractness may well present "insuperable obstacles" to the exercise of the Court's jurisdiction, even though that jurisdiction is technically present.

. . . Notwithstanding the indications that appellants have in the past executed the required affidavit without injury, it is, of course, possible that at some future time they may be able to demonstrate some injury as a result of the application of the provision challenged here. Our adjudication of the merits of such a challenge will await that time. This appeal must be dismissed.

Justice DOUGLAS, with whom Justice BRENNAN and Justice MARSHALL concur, dissenting.

. . . .

---

## NOTES

1. Out of adherence to the policy of avoiding premature resolution of constitutional questions, the court dismissed the appeal on the sole remaining issue, the constitutionality of the Ohio statute requiring third parties to file a loyalty oath to secure a place on the ballot. The court said the record in the case failed to present a concrete, immediate question for judicial resolution. The court dismissed the appeal because of the abstract and speculative posture of the case despite the *presence* of jurisdiction.

If the plaintiffs had standing, and the case met the "case or controversy" requirement of Art. III, what made the case abstract and speculative? Was it the court's concern that there was no certainty either of injury to the plaintiffs or of controversy between the parties?

2. Justice Rehnquist said that the older loyalty oath cases were distinguishable from the instant case because they presented an immediate or threatened injury to the party challenging the oath. The Socialist Labor Party had failed to allege such injury in its complaint. Justice Douglas, dissenting, argued that in the next election in Ohio, the Socialist Labor Party would be faced with the choice of taking the oath or being kept off the ballot. Justice Douglas, unlike the court, was willing to assume for

purposes of deciding the instant case that the Socialist Labor Party would seek a place on the Ohio ballot in the next election, and that the loyalty oath would present a cruel choice at least for the party's officers and individual members.

3. Suppose the Socialist Labor Party had alleged the following in its complaint: (1) Inability in good conscience to comply with the Ohio law; (2) An intention to apply for a place on the ballot in the forthcoming Ohio election; and (3) A fear that Ohio election officials would refuse to give the party access to the ballot if the Ohio law were not complied with. Would the Supreme Court still have declined to decide the appeal?

4. The policy of avoiding the unnecessary resolution of constitutional issues is, of course, concerned with the propriety of the timing of decision. As such it is kind of a specialized ripeness doctrine. Notice that the same factors which relate to making a ripeness determination are also present when making a decision to defer the resolution of unnecessary constitutional issues. The Socialist Labor Party case was premature because the Socialist Labor Party, its officers and members, might decide to file affidavits of loyalty. Similarly if the party and its members decided to file affidavits of loyalty, no controversy with the state of Ohio would ensue and the issue of the constitutional validity of the statute in question, would not be necessary.

5. Is there any problem with the court's order? What is the status of the lower court's holding?

6. See Richardson v. Wright, 405 U.S. 208 (1972) where the court held that judicial review of federal welfare regulations should be deferred pending reprocessing under new regulations of the determinations in dispute. The court reached this conclusion even though the new regulations did not eliminate the alleged constitutional deficiency.

### Justiciability and the Timing of Judicial Review

#### LAIRD v. TATUM
Supreme Court of the United States
408 U.S. 1, 33 L. Ed. 2d 154, 92 S. Ct. 2318 (1972)

[Tatum and other anti-war activists brought suit in federal district court for declaratory and injunctive relief against surveillance being conducted against them by agents of the United States Army. Pursuant to 10 U.S.C. § 331, which authorizes a limited domestic mission for the military in emergency situations, the Army had been called upon by the President to help quell urban riots in 1967-1968. As a preventive measure, the Army initiated a program of domestic surveillance designed to "spot" potential riot situations and, thereby, to avert in advance urban riots and disorders.

[When the facts about the surveillance system, and the storage of the material collected under it in Army data banks at Fort Holabird, Maryland, were revealed in a magazine article, a congressional investigation ensued to inquire into charges that domestic surveillance by the Army was infringing on constitutional rights. Tatum's suit soon followed.]

Chief Justice BURGER delivered the opinion of the Court.

. . . On the basis of the pleadings, the affidavits before the Court, and the oral arguments advanced at the hearing, the District Court granted petitioners' motion to dismiss, holding that there was no justiciable claim for relief.

On appeal, a divided Court of Appeals reversed and ordered the case remanded for further proceedings. We granted certiorari to consider whether, as the Court of Appeals held, respondents presented a justiciable controversy in complaining of a "chilling" effect on the exercise of their First Amendment rights where such effect is allegedly caused, not by any "specific action of the Army against them, (but) only (by) the existence and operation of the intelligence gathering and distributing system, which is confined to the Army and related civilian investigative agencies." 444 F.2d 947, 953. We reverse.

. . . .

In recent years this Court has found in a number of cases that constitutional violations may arise from the deterrent, or "chilling," effect of governmental regulations that fall short of a direct prohibition against the exercise of First Amendment rights. In none of these cases, however, did the chilling effect arise merely from the individual's knowledge that a governmental agency was engaged in certain activities or from the individual's concomitant fear that, armed with the fruits of those activities, the agency might in the future take some *other* and additional action detrimental to that individual. Rather, in each of these cases, the challenged exercise of governmental power was regulatory, proscriptive, or compulsory in nature, and the complainant was either presently or prospectively subject to the regulations, proscriptions, or compulsions that he was challenging.

. . . .

The decisions in these cases fully recognize that governmental action may be subject to constitutional challenge even though it has only an indirect effect on the exercise of First Amendment rights. At the same time, however, these decisions have in no way eroded the "established principle that to entitle a private individual to invoke the judicial power to determine the validity of executive or legislative action he must show that he has sustained or is immediately in danger of sustaining a direct injury as the result of that action . . . ." Ex parte Levitt, 302 U.S. 633, 634 (1937).

The respondents do not meet this test; their claim, simply stated, is that they disagree with the judgments made by the Executive Branch with respect to the type and amount of information the Army needs and that the very existence of the Army's data-gathering system produces a constitutionally impermissible chilling effect upon the exercise of their First Amendment rights. That alleged "chilling" effect may perhaps be seen as arising from respondents' very perception of the system as inappropriate to the Army's role under our form of government, or as arising from respondents' beliefs that it is inherently dangerous for the military to be concerned with activities in the civilian sector, or as arising from respondents' less generalized yet speculative apprehensiveness that the Army may at some future date misuse the information in some way that would cause direct harm to respondents. Allegations of a subjective "chill" are not an adequate substitute for a claim of specific present objective harm or a threat of specific future harm; "the federal courts established pursuant to Article III of the Constitution do not render advisory opinions." United Public Workers of America (C.I.O.) v. Mitchell, 330 U.S. 75.

Stripped to its essentials, what respondents appear to be seeking is a broad-scale investigation, conducted by themselves as private parties armed with the subpoena power of a federal district court and the power of cross-examination, to probe into the Army's intelligence-gathering activities, with the district court determining at the conclusion of that investigation the extent to which those activities may or may not be appropriate to the Army's mission. . . .

Carried to its logical end, this approach would have the federal courts as virtually continuing monitors of the wisdom and soundness of Executive action; such a role is appropriate for the Congress acting through its committees and the "power of the purse"; it is not the role of the judiciary, absent actual present or immediately threatened injury resulting from unlawful governmental action.

We, of course, intimate no view with respect to the propriety or desirability, from a policy standpoint, of the challenged activities of the Department of the Army; our conclusion is a narrow one, namely, that on this record the respondents have not presented a case for resolution by the courts.

. . . Indeed, when presented with claims of judicially cognizable injury resulting from military intrusion into the civilian sector, federal courts are fully empowered to consider claims of those asserting such injury; there is nothing in our Nation's history or in this Court's decided cases, including our holding today, that can properly be seen as giving any indication that actual or threatened injury by reason of unlawful activities of the military would go unnoticed or unremedied.

Reversed.

Justice DOUGLAS, with whom Justice MARSHALL concurs, dissenting.

If Congress had passed a law authorizing the armed services to establish surveillance over the civilian population, a most serious constitutional problem would be presented. There is, however, no law authorizing surveillance over civilians, which in this case the Pentagon concededly had undertaken. The question is whether such authority may be implied. One can search the Constitution in vain for any such authority.

. . . .

The claim that respondents have no standing to challenge the Army's surveillance of them and the other members of the class they seek to represent is too transparent for serious argument. The surveillance of the Army over the civilian sector— a part of society hitherto immune from their control—is a serious charge. It is alleged that the Army maintains files on the membership, ideology, programs, and practices of virtually every activist political group in the country. . . .

Those are the allegations; and the charge is that the purpose and effect of the system of surveillance is to harass and intimidate the respondents and to deter them from exercising their rights of political expression, protest, and dissent "by invading their privacy, damaging their reputations, adversely affecting their employment and their opportunities for employment, and in other ways." Their fear is that "permanent reports of their activities will be maintained in the Army's data bank, and their 'profiles' will appear in the so-called 'Blacklist' and that all of this information will be released to numerous federal and state agencies upon request."

Judge Wilkey, speaking for the Court of Appeals, properly held that this Army surveillance "exercises a *present inhibiting effect* on their full expression and utilization of their First Amendment rights." That is the test. The "deterrent effect" on

First Amendment rights by government oversight marks an unconstitutional intrusion. Or, as stated by Mr. Justice Brennan,
"inhibition as well as prohibition against the exercise of precious
First Amendment rights is a power denied to government." When
refusal of the Court to pass on the constitutionality of an Act
under the normal consideration of forbearance "would itself
have an inhibitory effect on freedom of speech" then the Court
will act.

As stated by the Supreme Court of New Jersey, "there is good
reason to permit the strong to speak for the weak or the timid
in First Amendment matters." Anderson v. Sills, 56 N.J. 210,
220 (1970).

One need not wait to sue until he loses his job or until his
reputation is defamed. To withhold standing to sue until that
time arrives would in practical effect immunize from judicial
scrutiny all surveillance activities regardless of their misuse and
their deterrent effect. . . .

The present controversy is not a remote, imaginary conflict.
Respondents were targets of the Army's surveillance. . . .

. . . .

Justice BRENNAN, with whom Justice STEWART and Justice
MARSHALL join, dissenting.

[These justices agreed with the Court of Appeals that the controversy was a justiciable one. Some excerpts quoted with approval by Justice BRENNAN from Judge Wilkey's opinion for
the Court of Appeals are as follows:]

". . . [U]nder justiciability standards it is the operation of
the system itself which is the breach of the Army's duty toward
[respondents] and other civilians. The case is therefore ripe for
adjudication. Because the evil alleged in the Army intelligence
system is that of overbreadth . . . and because there is no indication that a better opportunity will later arise . . . , the issue can
be considered justiciable at this time. . . .

"To the extent that the Army's argument against justiciability here includes the claim that [respondents] lack standing
to bring this action, we cannot agree. If the Army's system does
indeed derogate First Amendment values, the [respondents] are
persons who are sufficiently affected to permit their complaint
to be heard. The record shows that most if not all of the
[respondents] and/or the organizations of which they are members have been the subject of Army surveillance reports and
their names have appeared in the Army's records. . . . Nor
should the fact that these particular persons are sufficiently un-

inhibited to bring this suit be any ground for objecting to their standing."

Respondents may or may not be able to prove the case they allege. But I agree with the Court of Appeals that they are entitled to try. I would therefore affirm the remand to the District Court for a trial and determination of the issues specified by the Court of Appeals.

## NOTES

1. Perhaps the key to the court's decision was the belief of the majority that the plaintiffs had not really alleged any injury. Did Chief Justice Burger confuse the problem of justiciability with the totally distinct problem of the merits of the case? Burger expressly stated the decision should *not* be interpreted as a disposition on the merits. But did the court in *effect* judge the merits by ruling that the plaintiffs' allegations of first amendment chill *were insufficient to constitute true present injury* to protected interests?

The plaintiffs in *Tatum* were caught in a vicious circle. Without learning more about the Army surveillance program, they could not convince the federal courts that their rights had been infringed sufficiently to present a justiciable controversy. But they could not learn more about the Army surveillance program without the assistance of the compulsory process of the federal courts.

2. In an intriguing footnote, the Chief Justice commented on the related issue of the plaintiffs' *standing* to bring the suit. "Even assuming a justiciable controversy," Burger wrote, it appeared from the record below that the plaintiffs as individuals had not been especially cowed by knowing that Army agents were keeping them under surveillance. Chief Justice Burger said:

> [R]espondents themselves are not chilled, but seek only to represent those "millions" whom they believe are so chilled[;] (they) clearly lack that "personal stake in the outcome of the controversy" essential to standing.

The court of appeals had rejected this argument, holding that the plaintiffs were directly affected by the challenged action:

> [T]hey have standing to seek redress for that alleged injury in court and will provide the necessary adversary interest that is required by the standing doctrine. . . . Nor should the fact that these particular persons are sufficiently uninhibited to bring this suit be any ground for objecting to their standing. 444 F.2d at 954 n. 17.

Should willingness to bring a lawsuit constitute a concession that no standing exists to assert a "chilling effect"?

Notice the distinction set forth by the court of appeals: The crucial issue for standing was whether plaintiffs were so directly affected by the Army's surveillance activities that they could impart a truly adversary tone to the proceedings. If the plaintiffs in *Tatum* had managed to allege at least one specific instance of present unlawful Army action, an illegal wiretap, for instance, on each of their phones, would the Supreme Court still have held the case inappropriate for review?

3. There is another aspect of *Laird v. Tatum* worth noting. Shortly after the decision of the court was announced, the plaintiffs filed a petition for rehearing which asked, *inter alia,* that Justice Rehnquist voluntarily take no part in the case. Before being appointed to the Supreme Court, Justice Rehnquist was an Assistant Attorney General, in which capacity he had testified on behalf of the Executive Branch before a congressional committee investigating the Army surveillance program. In his testimony, he commented briefly upon the *Tatum* case, which was then pending in the lower courts. However, he had taken no direct part in preparing the government's briefs or moving papers.

Because Justice Rehnquist cast a crucial fifth vote for reversal in the *Tatum* case, his participation in the decision was especially upsetting to the plaintiffs. Had he abstained from consideration of the case, the judgment of the court of appeals would probably have been affirmed by a tie vote of the Supreme Court.

The petition for rehearing was denied and Justice Rehnquist took the virtually unprecedented step of issuing a personal memorandum justifying his decision to take part in the case.

## F. SUBJECT MATTER LIMITATIONS: WHAT CAN BE LITIGATED?

### BAKER v. CARR
Supreme Court of the United States
369 U.S. 186, 7 L. Ed. 2d 663, 82 S. Ct. 691 (1962)

Justice BRENNAN delivered the opinion of the Court.

This civil action was brought under 42 U.S.C. §§ 1983 and 1988 to redress the alleged deprivation of federal constitutional rights. The complaint, alleging that by means of a 1901 statute of Tennessee apportioning the members of the General Assembly among the State's 95 counties, "these plaintiffs and others similarly situated, are denied the equal protection of the laws accorded them by the Fourteenth Amendment to the Constitution of the United States by virtue of the debasement of their votes," was dismissed by a three-judge court. . . . The court held that it lacked jurisdiction of the subject matter and also that no claim was stated upon which relief could be granted. . . . We hold that the dismissal was error, and remand the cause to the District Court for trial and further proceedings consistent with this opinion.

. . . .

. . . Tennessee's [state constitutional] standard for allocating legislative representation among her counties is the total number of qualified voters resident in the respective counties, subject only to minor qualifications. Decennial reapportionment in compliance with the constitutional scheme was effected by the General Assembly each decade from 1871 to 1901. . . . In 1901 the General Assembly abandoned separate enumeration in favor of reliance upon the Federal Census and passed the Apportionment Act here in controversy. In the more than 60 years since that action, all proposals in both Houses of the General Assembly for reapportionment have failed to pass.

. . . The relative standings of the counties in terms of qualified voters have changed significantly. It is primarily the continued application of the 1901 Apportionment Act to this shifted and enlarged voting population which gives rise to the present controversy.

. . . [Appellants] seek a declaration that the 1901 statute is unconstitutional and an injunction restraining the appellees from acting to conduct any further elections under it. They also pray that unless and until the General Assembly enacts a valid reapportionment, the District Court should either decree a reapportionment by mathematical application of the Tennessee constitutional formulae to the most recent Federal Census figures, or direct the appellees to conduct legislative elections, primary and general, at large. They also pray for such other and further relief as may be appropriate.

THE DISTRICT COURT'S OPINION AND ORDER OF DISMISSAL

Because we deal with this case on appeal from an order of dismissal granted on appellees' motions, precise identification of the issues presently confronting us demands clear exposition of the grounds upon which the District Court rested in dismissing the case. The dismissal order recited that the court sustained the appellees' grounds "(1) that the Court lacks jurisdiction of the subject matter, and (2) that the complaint fails to state a claim upon which relief can be granted. . . ."

In the setting of a case such as this, the recited grounds embrace two possible reasons for dismissal:

*First:* That the facts and injury alleged, the legal bases invoked as creating the rights and duties relied upon, and the relief sought, fail to come within that language of Article III of the Constitution and of the jurisdictional statutes which define those matters concerning which United States District Courts are empowered to act;

*Second:* That, although the matter is cognizable and facts are alleged which establish infringement of appellants' rights as a result of state legislative action departing from a federal constitutional standard, the court will not proceed because the matter is considered unsuited to judicial inquiry or adjustment.

We treat the first ground of dismissal as "lack of jurisdiction of the subject matter." The second we consider to result in a failure to state a justiciable cause of action. . . .

. . . .

In light of the District Court's treatment of the case, we hold today only (a) that the court possessed jurisdiction of the subject matter; (b) that a justiciable cause of action is stated upon which appellants would be entitled to appropriate relief; and (c) because appellees raise the issue before this Court, that the appellants have standing to challenge the Tennessee apportionment statutes. Beyond noting that we have no cause at this stage to doubt the District Court will be able to fashion relief if violations of constitutional rights are found, it is improper now to consider what remedy would be most appropriate if appellants prevail at the trial.

## JURISDICTION OF THE SUBJECT MATTER

The District Court was uncertain whether our cases withholding federal judicial relief rested upon a lack of federal jurisdiction or upon the inappropriateness of the subject matter for judicial consideration—what we have designated "nonjusticiability." The distinction between the two grounds is significant. In the instance of nonjusticiability, consideration of the cause is not wholly and immediately foreclosed; rather, the Court's inquiry necessarily proceeds to the point of deciding whether the duty asserted can be judicially identified and its reach judicially determined, and whether protection for the right asserted can be judicially molded. In the instance of lack of jurisdiction the cause either does not "arise under" the Federal Constitution,

laws or treaties (or fall within one of the other enumerated categories of Art. III, § 2), or is not a "case or controversy" within
the meaning of that section; or the cause is not one described by
any jurisdictional statute. Our conclusion . . . that this cause
presents no nonjusticiable "political question" settles the only
possible doubt that it is a case or controversy. Under the present
heading of "Jurisdiction of the Subject Matter" we hold only
that the matter set forth in the complaint does arise under the
Constitution and is within 28 U.S.C. § 1343. . . .

. . . .

The appellees refer to *Colegrove v. Green,* 328 U.S. 549, as
authority that the District Court lacked jurisdiction of the subject
matter. Appellees misconceive the holding of that case. The
holding was precisely contrary to their reading of it. . . .

. . . .

We hold that the District Court has jurisdiction of the subject
matter of the federal constitutional claim asserted in the complaint.

. . . .

## JUSTICIABILITY

In holding that the subject matter of this suit was not justiciable, the District Court relied on *Colegrove v. Green* and subsequent *per curiam* cases. . . . We understand the District Court to
have read the cited cases as compelling the conclusion that since
the appellants sought to have a legislative apportionment held
unconstitutional, their suit presented a "political question" and
was therefore nonjusticiable. We hold that this challenge to an
apportionment presents no nonjusticiable "political question."
The cited cases do not hold the contrary.

Of course the mere fact that the suit seeks protection of a
political right does not mean it presents a political question. . . .
Rather, it is argued that apportionment cases, whatever the
actual wording of the complaint, can involve no federal constitutional right except one resting on the guaranty of a republican form of government, and that complaints based on that
clause have been held to present political questions which are
nonjusticiable.

We hold that the claim pleaded here neither rests upon nor
implicates the Guaranty Clause and that its justiciability is
therefore not foreclosed by our decisions of cases involving that
clause. . .

[I]n the Guaranty Clause cases and in the other "political
question" cases, it is the relationship between the judiciary and

the coordinate branches of the Federal Government, and not the federal judiciary's relationship to the States, which gives rise to the "political question."

We have said that "in determining whether a question falls within [the political question] category, the appropriateness under our system of government of attributing finality to the action of the political departments and also the lack of satisfactory criteria for a judicial determination are dominant considerations." Coleman v. Miller, 307 U.S. 433, 454-455. The nonjusticiability of a political question is primarily a function of the separation of powers. Much confusion results from the capacity of the "political question" label to obscure the need for case-by-case inquiry. Deciding whether a matter has in any measure been committed by the Constitution to another branch of government, or whether the action of that branch exceeds whatever authority has been committed, is itself a delicate exercise in constitutional interpretation, and is a responsibility of this Court as ultimate interpreter of the Constitution. To demonstrate this requires no less than to analyze representative cases and to infer from them the analytical threads that make up the political question doctrine. We shall then show that none of those threads catches this case.

*Foreign relations:* There are sweeping statements to the effect that all questions touching foreign relations are political questions. Not only does resolution of such issues frequently turn on standards that defy judicial application, or involve the exercise of a discretion demonstrably committed to the executive or legislature; but many such questions uniquely demand single-voiced statement of the Government's views. Yet it is error to suppose that every case or controversy which touches foreign relations lies beyond judicial cognizance. . . . For example, though a court will not ordinarily inquire whether a treaty has been terminated, since on that question "governmental action . . . must be regarded as of controlling importance," if there has been no conclusive "governmental action" then a court can construe a treaty and may find it provides the answer. . . .

*Dates of duration of hostilities:* Though it has been stated broadly that "the power which declared the necessity is the power to declare its cessation, and what the cessation requires," here too analysis reveals isolable reasons for the presence of political questions, underlying this Court's refusal to review the political department's determination of when or whether a war has ended. Dominant is the need for finality in the political determination, for emergency's nature demands "a prompt and unhesitating obedience," . . . .

*Validity of enactments:* In *Coleman v. Miller* this Court held
that the questions of how long a proposed amendment to the
Federal Constitution remained open to ratification, and what
effect a prior rejection had on a subsequent ratification, were
committed to congressional resolution and involved criteria of
decision that necessarily escaped the judicial grasp. Similar considerations apply to the enacting process: "The respect due to
coequal and independent departments," and the need for finality
and certainty about the status of a statute contribute to judicial
reluctance to inquire whether, as passed, it complied with all
requisite formalities. But it is not true that courts will never
delve into a legislature's records upon such a quest: If the
enrolled statute lacks an effective date, a court will not hesitate
to seek it in the legislative journals in order to preserve the enactment. The political question doctrine, a tool for maintenance of
governmental order, will not be so applied as to promote only
disorder.

. . . .

It is apparent that several formulations which vary slightly
according to the settings in which the questions arise may describe a political question, although each has one or more elements which identifies it as essentially a function of the separation of powers. Prominent on the surface of any case held to
involve a political question is found a textually demonstrable
constitutional commitment of the issue to a coordinate political
department; or a lack of judicially discoverable and manageable
standards for resolving it; or the impossibility of deciding without an initial policy determination of a kind clearly for nonjudicial discretion; or the impossibility of a court's undertaking
independent resolution without expressing lack of the respect
due coordinate branches of government; or an unusual need for
unquestioning adherence to a political decision already made;
or the potentiality of embarrassment from multifarious pronouncements by various departments on one question.

Unless one of these formulations is inextricable from the
case at bar, there should be no dismissal for non-justiciability
on the ground of a political question's presence. The doctrine of
which we treat is one of "political questions," not one of
"political cases." The courts cannot reject as "no law suit" a
bona fide controversy as to whether some action denominated
"political" exceeds constitutional authority. The cases we have
reviewed show the necessity for discriminating inquiry into the
precise facts and posture of the particular case, and the impossibility of resolution by any semantic cataloguing.

But it is argued that this case shares the characteristics of decisions that constitute a category not yet considered, cases concerning the Constitution's guaranty, in Art. IV, § 4, of a republican form of government. . . . We shall discover that Guaranty Clause claims involve those elements which define a "political question," and for that reason and no other, they are nonjusticiable. In particular, we shall discover that the nonjusticiability of such claims has nothing to do with their touching upon matters of state governmental organization.

*Republican form of government:* . . . .

. . . .

Just as the Court has consistently held that a challenge to state action based on the Guaranty Clause presents no justiciable question so has it held, and for the same reasons, that challenges to congressional action on the ground of inconsistency with that clause present no justiciable question. . . .

We come, finally, to the ultimate inquiry whether our precedents as to what constitutes a nonjusticiable "political question" bring the case before us under the umbrella of that doctrine. A natural beginning is to note whether any of the common characteristics which we have been able to identify and label descriptively are present. We find none: The question here is the consistency of state action with the Federal Constitution. We have no question decided, or to be decided, by a political branch of government coequal with this Court. Nor do we risk embarrassment of our government abroad, or grave disturbance at home if we take issue with Tennessee as to the constitutionality of her action here challenged. Nor need the appellants, in order to succeed in this action, ask the Court to enter upon policy determinations for which judicially manageable standards are lacking. Judicial standards under the Equal Protection Clause are well developed and familiar, and it has been open to courts since the enactment of the Fourteenth Amendment to determine, if on the particular facts they must, that a discrimination reflects *no* policy, but simply arbitrary and capricious action.

[B]ecause any reliance on the Guaranty Clause could not have succeeded it does not follow that appellants may not be heard on the equal protection claim which in fact they tender. True, it must be clear that the Fourteenth Amendment claim is not so enmeshed with those political question elements which render Guaranty Clause claims nonjusticiable as actually to present a political question itself. But we have found that not to be the case here.

. . . .

We conclude then that the nonjusticiability of claims resting on the Guaranty Clause which arises from their embodiment of questions that were thought "political," can have no bearing upon the justiciability of the equal protection claim presented in this case. Finally, we emphasize that it is the involvement in Guaranty Clause claims of the elements thought to define "political questions," and no other feature, which could render them nonjusticiable. Specifically, we have said that such claims are not held nonjusticiable because they touch matters of state governmental organization. . . .

[O]nly last Term, in Gomillion v. Lightfoot, 364 U.S. 339, we applied the Fifteenth Amendment to strike down a redrafting of municipal boundaries which effected a discriminatory impairment of voting rights, in the face of what a majority of the Court of Appeals thought to be a sweeping commitment to state legislatures of the power to draw and redraw such boundaries.

· · · ·

We conclude that the complaint's allegations of a denial of equal protection present a justiciable constitutional cause of action upon which appellants are entitled to a trial and a decision. The right asserted is within the reach of judicial protection under the Fourteenth Amendment.

· · · ·

Reversed and remanded.

Justice WHITTAKER did not participate in the decision of this case.

Justice DOUGLAS, concurring.

· · · ·

Justice CLARK, concurring.

· · · ·

Although I find the Tennessee apportionment statute offends the Equal Protection Clause, I would not consider intervention by this Court into so delicate a field if there were any other relief available to the people of Tennessee. But the majority of the people of Tennessee have no "practical opportunities for exerting their political weight at the polls" to correct the existing "invidious discrimination." Tennessee has no initiative and referendum. I have searched diligently for other "practical opportunities" present under the law. I find none other than through the federal courts. The majority of the voters have been caught up in a legislative strait jacket. . . .

· · · ·

Justice STEWART, concurring.

· · · ·

Justice FRANKFURTER, whom Justice HARLAN joins, dissenting.

The Court today reverses a uniform course of decision established by a dozen cases, including one by which the very claim now sustained was unanimously rejected only five years ago. The impressive body of rulings thus cast aside reflected the equally uniform course of our political history regarding the relationship between population and legislative representation—a wholly different matter from denial of the franchise to individuals because of race, color, religion or sex. Such a massive repudiation of the experience of our whole past in asserting destructively novel judicial power demands a detailed analysis of the role of this Court in our constitutional scheme. Disregard of inherent limits in the effective exercise of the Court's "judicial Power" not only presages the futility of judicial intervention in the essentially political conflict of forces by which the relation between population and representation has time out of mind been and now is determined. It may well impair the Court's position as the ultimate organ of "the supreme Law of the Land" in that vast range of legal problems, often strongly entangled in popular feeling, on which this Court must pronounce. The Court's authority—possessed of neither of the purse nor the sword—ultimately rests on sustained public confidence in its moral sanction. Such feeling must be nourished by the Court's complete detachment, in fact and in appearance, from political entanglements and by abstention from injecting itself into the clash of political forces in political settlements.

. . . For this Court to direct the District Court to enforce a claim to which the Court has over the years consistently found itself required to deny legal enforcement and at the same time to find it necessary to withhold any guidance to the lower court how to enforce this turnabout, new legal claim, manifests an odd —indeed an esoteric—conception of judicial propriety. . . . To charge courts with the task of accommodating the incommensurable factors of policy that underlie these mathematical puzzles is to attribute, however flatteringly, omnicompetence to judges. . . .

. . . .

We were soothingly told at the bar of this Court that we need not worry about the kind of remedy a court could effectively fashion once the abstract constitutional right to have courts pass on a state-wide system of electoral districting is recognized as a matter of judicial rhetoric, because legislatures would heed the Court's admonition. This is not only an euphoric hope. It implies a sorry confession of judicial impotence in place of a frank acknowledgment that there is not under our Constitution a judicial remedy for every political mischief, for every undesirable exercise of legislative power. The Framers carefully and with deliberate forethought refused so to enthrone the judiciary. In this situation, as in others of like nature, appeal for relief does not belong here. Appeal must be to an informed, civically militant electorate. In a democratic society like ours, relief must come through an aroused popular conscience that sears the conscience of the people's representatives. In any event there is nothing judicially more unseemly nor more self-defeating than for this Court to make *in terrorem* pronouncements, to indulge in merely empty rhetoric, sounding a word of promise to the ear, sure to be disappointing to the hope.

. . . .

. . . The "political question" principle as applied in *Colegrove* has found wide application commensurate with its function as "one of the rules basic to the federal system and this Court's appropriate place within that structure." Rescue Army v. Municipal Court, 331 U.S. 549, 570. . . .

The *Colegrove* doctrine, in the form in which repeated decisions have settled it, was not an innovation. It represents long judicial thought and experience. From its earliest opinions this Court has consistently recognized a class of controversies which do not lend themselves to judicial standards and judicial remedies. To classify the various instances as "political questions" is rather a form of stating this conclusion than revealing of analysis. . . .

. . . .

The influence of these converging considerations—the caution not to undertake decision where standards meet for judicial judgment are lacking, the reluctance to interfere with matters of state government in the absence of an unquestionable and effectively enforceable mandate, the unwillingness to make courts arbiters of the broad issues of political organization historically committed to other institutions and for whose adjustment the judicial process is ill-adapted—has been decisive of the settled line of cases, reaching back more than a century, which holds that Art. IV, § 4, of the Constitution, guaranteeing to the States "a Republican Form of Government," is not enforceable through the courts. . . .

. . . .

The present case involves all of the elements that have made the Gurantee Clause cases non-justiciable. It is, in effect, a Guarantee Clause claim masquerading under a different label. But it cannot make the case more fit for judicial action that appellants invoke the Fourteenth Amendment rather than Art.

IV, § 4, where, in fact, the gist of their complaint is the same—unless it can be found that the Fourteenth Amendment speaks with greater particularity to their situation. We have been admonished to avoid "the tyranny of labels." . . .

. . . .

. . . Appellants appear as representatives of a class that is prejudiced as a class, in contradistinction to the polity in its entirety. However, the discrimination relied on is the deprivation of what appellants conceive to be their proportionate share of political influence. This, of course, is the practical effect of any allocation of power within the institutions of government. Hardly any distribution of political authority that could be assailed as rendering government nonrepublican would fail similarly to operate to the prejudice of some groups, and to the advantage of others, within the body politic. . . .

What, then, is this question of legislative apportionment? Appellants invoke the right to vote and to have their votes counted. But they are permitted to vote and their votes are counted. They go to the polls, they cast their ballots, they send their representatives to the state councils. Their complaint is simply that the representatives are not sufficiently numerous or powerful—in short, that Tennessee has adopted a basis of representation with which they are dissatisfied. Talk of "debasement" or "dilution" is circular talk. One cannot speak of "debasement" or "dilution" of the value of a vote until there is first defined a standard of reference as to what a vote should be worth. What is actually asked of the Court in this case is to choose among competing bases of representation—ultimately, really, among competing theories of political philosophy—in order to establish an appropriate frame of government for the State of Tennessee and thereby for all of the States of the Union.

In such a matter, abstract analogies which ignore the facts of history deal in unrealities; they betray reason. This is not a case in which a State has, through a device however oblique and sophisticated, denied Negroes or Jews or redheaded persons a vote, or given them only a third or a sixth of a vote. That was *Gomillion v. Lightfoot.* What Tennessee illustrates is an old and still widespread method of representation—representation by local geographical division, only in part respective of population—in preference to others, others, forsooth, more appealing. Appellants contest this choice and seek to make this Court the arbiter of the disagreement. They would make the Equal Protection Clause the charter of adjudication, asserting that the equality which it guarantees comports, if not the assurance of equal weight to every voter's vote, at least the basic conception that representation ought to be proportionate to population, a standard by reference to which the reasonableness of apportionment plans may be judged.

To find such a political conception legally enforceable in the broad and unspecific guarantee of equal protection is to rewrite the Constitution. Certainly, "equal protection" is no more secure a foundation for judicial judgment of the permissibility of varying forms of representative government than is "Republican Form." Indeed since "equal protection of the laws" can only mean an equality of persons standing in the same relation to whatever governmental action is challenged, the determination whether treatment is equal presupposes a determination concerning the nature of the relationship. This, with respect to apportionment, means an inquiry into the theoretic base of representation in an acceptably republican state. For a court could not determine the equal-protection issue without in fact first determining the Republican-Form issue, simply because what is reasonable for equal protection purposes will depend upon what frame of government, basically, is allowed. To divorce "equal protection" from "Republican Form" is to talk about half a question.

The notion that representation proportioned to the geographic spread of population is so universally accepted as a necessary element of equality between man and man that it must be taken to be the standard of a political equality preserved by the Fourteenth Amendment—that it is, in appellants' words "the basic principle of representative government"—is, to put it bluntly, not true. However desirable and however desired by some among the great political thinkers and framers of our government, it has never been generally practiced, today or in the past. . . . Unless judges, the judges of this Court, are to make their private views of political wisdom the measure of the Constitution—views which in all honesty cannot but give the appearance, if not reflect the reality, of involvement with the business of partisan politics so inescapably a part of apportionment controversies—the Fourteenth Amendment, "itself a historical product," provides no guide for judicial oversight of the representation problem.

. . . .

Manifestly, the Equal Protection Clause supplies no clearer guide for judicial examination of apportionment methods than would the Guarantee Clause itself. Apportionment, by its character, is a subject of extraordinary complexity, involving—even after the fundamental theoretical issues concerning what is to be represented in a representative legislature have been fought out or compromised—considerations of geography, demography, electoral convenience, economic and social cohesions or divergencies among particular local groups, communications, the practical effects of political institutions like the lobby and the city machine, ancient traditions and ties of settled usage, respect for proven incumbents of long experience and senior status, mathematical mechanics, censuses compiling relevant data, and a host of others. Legislative responses throughout the country to the reapportionment demands of the 1960 Census have glaringly confirmed that these are not factors that lend themselves to evaluations of a nature that are the staple of judicial determinations or for which judges are equipped to adjudicate by legal training or experience or native wit. And this is the more so true because in every strand of this complicated, intricate web of values meet the contending forces of partisan politics. The practical significance of apportionment is that the next election results may differ because of it. Apportionment battles are overwhelmingly party or intra-party contests. It will add a virulent source of friction and tension in federal-state relations to embroil the federal judiciary in them.

. . . .

Although the District Court had jurisdiction in the very restricted sense of power to determine whether it could adjudicate the claim, the case is of that class of political controversy which, by the nature of its subject, is unfit for federal judicial action. The judgment of the District Court, in dismissing the complaint for failure to state a claim on which relief can be granted, should therefore be affirmed.

Dissenting opinion of Justice HARLAN, whom Justice FRANKFURTER joins.

. . . .

---

### A Comment on Baker v. Carr

1. A revealing example of the way in which the court operates and of the sense of paradox that so often marks its processes is the legislative reapportionment case. In *Baker v. Carr*, the Supreme Court rescued the field of legislative reapportionment from political purgatory and ushered it into the judicial forum. The case can be viewed as an expansion of the court's jurisdiction at the expense of what previously had been the responsibility of the legislature. But from another view, the court's decision that a state's scheme of apportioning representation to its legislature could be litigated in a federal court was not a trespass on

the functions of the legislature at all: It was merely an insistence that legislative responsibilities be discharged.

2. One of the most convenient and conventional principles of American constitutional law has been the political question doctrine. The doctrine could be described as a judicially created self-protective device to shield itself from the unpleasantly political. Resort to the political question doctrine essentially meant that the court would resist the opportunity to make a challenge to the political order. Alternatively, the doctrine could be described as based on jurisdictional considerations.

3. Mr. Justice Brennan's introductory observation in the reapportionment case that the Supreme Court is the "ultimate interpreter of the constitution" is subject to debate. The Supreme Court, before and since, has declined such ultimacy. Several attempts have been made, for example, since the legislative reapportionment case, to challenge the constitutionality of American military involvement in Vietnam. The reaction of the Supreme Court has been consistent: a refusal to accept *cert*. Yet in United States v. Nixon, 418 U.S. 960 (1974), the court reviewed the actions of a sitting President. *See* text, p. 340.

In asserting as Justice Brennan did, such interpretative ultimacy for the court, the richness of judicial review and the remedies that lie within it were exposed. In the legislative reapportionment area, the judiciary did not challenge legislatures so much as get them off the hook. In this sense, the court was completely responsive to the political question doctrine. As John Frank has well said the core of that doctrine is twofold. Responsibility must be divided between the branches of government according to the directives of the constitution but responsibility must be placed somewhere. Frank, *Political Question*, in SUPREME COURT AND SUPREME LAW 36, 46 (E. Cahn ed., 1954).

Malapportionment was long thought to be beyond the resources of judicial resolution because its political subject matter was fraught with the possibility of conflict with other branches of government. Yet in 1964, the Supreme Court turned its back on its own self-created history of abstinence and entered what Justice Frankfurter in Colegrove v. Green, 328 U.S. 549 (1946), called in great distaste the "political thicket." The court declared that the conformance of a state legislature's apportionment to the state constitution could raise an equal protection question under the fourteenth amendment which deserved to be litigated, a question which was, as the lawyers say, justiciable. Malapportionment was rescued from the judicial exile to which it had previously been banished.

4. Justice Frankfurter in his dissent in *Baker v. Carr* assumed that the court's decrees would fall on deaf ears and that the failure of the states and the legislatures to respond to the court's mandates would be subversive of the court. Apportionment was a legislative responsibility and therefore not a duty assigned to the court. By asserting its authority where it had no right to do so, the court would undermine its authority in areas where its responsibility was clear.

On the whole, legislators had remained impassive to the challenge of the "militant electorate." Perhaps the truth of the matter was that the electorate were not that militant and the legislature not that unresponsive. After *Baker v. Carr,* the court's mandate was honored, not defied. Why? Perhaps the opinion is an example of what Eugene Rostow means by the democratic character of judicial review. E. Rostow, THE SOVEREIGN PREROGATIVE: THE SUPREME COURT AND THE QUEST FOR LAW 167-68 (1962).

The court, Rostow wrote, is a teacher in a great national seminar. Sometimes the court teaches badly. Sometimes the court teaches well; and to teach well is occasionally to persuade. So it was that many state legislatures suddenly became persuaded and began to reapportion. The court had provided legislators across the nation with an excuse, an excuse to be disloyal to their own interests. By complying with judicial mandate, legislators had an opportunity to do homage to their better natures by insisting to their constituents and sometimes to themselves that they had no choice. Where legislatures did not reapportion, the lower courts, state and federal, took up the task, on the whole, successfully. The opportunity to say that one cannot help oneself, that one is required to submit to the command of the court, illustrates the manner in which judicial review occasionally arrests *inertia* in the other branches of government. For the discussion of the progeny of *Baker v. Carr,* see this text, pp. 674-75.

5. When *Baker v. Carr* came before the bar of the Supreme Court, Tennessee had not reapportioned its legislature in 60 years. Did this failure violate the fourteenth amendment? The response of the Supreme Court to this issue was a demonstration of the creative capacities within judicial review.

Those who take a disenchanted view of the curative capacities of judges to heal the body politic are much concerned with legitimacy. Gerald Gunther has pointed out, for example, that for Professor Bickel the problem of legitimacy was the real source of his emphasis on an abstinent approach by the Court to its jurisdiction. Gunther, *The Subtle Vices of the "Passive Virtues" —A Comment On Principle and Expediency in Judicial Review,* 64 COLUM. L. REV. 1, 25 (1964). Yet what the court does can be legitimated or authenticated by the mere fact that the court does it. Legitimacy, Carl Friedrich says, arises from the acceptance by those subject to rule of the "rightful title" of those in authority. C. FRIEDRICH, MAN AND HIS GOVERNMENT 237 (1963). In a democracy, he explains, legitimacy is achieved by "an acceptance of the 'rules of the game' laid down in the Constitution."

In *Colegrove v. Green,* Justice Frankfurter in his opinion for the court did not assert that the court had no jurisdiction. Rather he argued that there are some questions which are so political that the court should not litigate them.

Frankfurter had said that the decision would not prove capable of enforcement. In this he was mistaken. Public response to the assertion of judicial review can have the paradoxical effect of setting in motion a process of public acceptance. But not always—as the unfulfilled judicial promise of school desegregation illustrates. Indeed, perhaps it was Frankfurter's witness to public defiance, first active and then passive, of the school segregation case, Brown v. Board of Education, 349 U.S. 294 (1955), which inspired the anxiety he expressed about judicial intervention eight years later in *Baker v. Carr.*

6.   If the "political questions" becomes too rigidly defined, the possibility of needed judicial intervention is often removed. For the view that the merits of an activist approach to judicial review are not inextricably bound up with the political question doctrine and that the doctrine is really functional only in the area of foreign relations, see Scharpf, *Judicial Review and the Political Question: A Functional Analysis,* 75 YALE L.J. 517 (1966). Should the fact that *Baker v. Carr* is possible (that what was not justiciable yesterday may be justiciable tomorrow) cause concern about the reliability and durability of the legal order?

7.   Contingency as a basic element of judicial review is hard doctrine for the received American doctrine of constitutional law to accept. Writing before *Baker v. Carr,* Professor Wechsler valiantly sought to bring a measure of certainty to outline the frontiers of the Supreme Court's jurisdiction. He sought to bring his constitutional philosophy within the historic tradition begun by Marshall's remark in Cohens v. Virginia, 5 U.S. (6 Wheat.) 264 (1821): if the court has jurisdiction it has no jurisdiction to abdicate it. Now to assert adherence to Marshall's admonition would appear to be calling for an expansive view of the jurisdiction of the Supreme Court. But that was not the purpose of the assertion. Professor Wechsler hoped both to depoliticize the court and yet to conform to Marshall's directive in *Cohens v. Virginia.* Cases which comprise the traditional subject matter of litigation should be distinguished from cases which would hurl

the judiciary into areas allocated to other branches of government. Professor Wechsler believes that Marshall's remark in
*Cohens v. Virginia* (that if the court has jurisdiction, it must
decide) must be understood in light of this distinction. In this
view, Marshall was really saying that the court should decline
the resolution of cases when the "Constitution has committed
the issue to another agency of Government than the Courts."
Wechsler, *Toward Neutral Principles of Constitutional Law*, 73
HARV. L. REV. 1, 9 (1959).

In *Baker v. Carr* Justice Brennan sought to express this idea
within his much quoted attempt to summarize the identifying
badges of a "political question." Under his test the case of
*Baker v. Carr* survives the fatal tag "political question" since
what was involved there was not a branch of government coordinate to the Supreme Court, but rather a lesser polity, the legislature of Tennessee.

But the agreement between Professor Wechsler and Justice
Brennan is an agreement of phrase rather than result. For Professor Wechsler suggested that the constitutional commitment
to Congress to "make or alter" state regulations of the "Manner of holding Elections for Senators and Representatives" indicated that Congress alone has the power to draw district
lines or to prescribe the standards to be followed in defining them. In his view therefore, the courts were excluded from
"passing on a constitutional objection to state gerrymanders."
Wechsler, *Toward Neutral Principles of Constitutional Law*, 73
HARV. L. REV. 1, 9 (1959). Yet in the progeny of *Baker v. Carr*,
the attrition of congressional power from lack of use has seen
the courts become just that: the organs for passing on the validity of state imposed gerrymanders.

Legal prophecies even as to matters one might have thought
as legally precise as to what decisions have been textually committed to another branch of government do not have an abiding
meaning. No sure guide has arisen to indicate which branch has
received the "textual commitment" to perform a certain task.

8. Illustrative is the court's landmark decision in United
States v. Nixon, 418 U.S. 960 (1974), discussed in this text, p. 340.
After *United States v. Nixon*, the question as to which branch
of government is the ultimate interpreter of the Constitution,
perhaps, is less open now than it was when Justice Brennan
wrote in *Baker v. Carr*.

Professor Strong has explained the role of the court as final
interpreter of the Constitution in the wake of *United States v.
Nixon* as follows:

In the face of these recent, repeated reassertions by the Supreme Court of the exclusiveness of judicial power to expound the Constitution, how could a lawyer of James D. St. Clair's ability seriously contend in oral argument before the Supreme Court on behalf of President Nixon that "This matter is being submitted to this court for its guidance and judgment with respect to the law. The President, on the other hand, has his obligations under the Constitution."

. . . .

For this nation, however, this issue presumably has been settled. Somehow or other, the courts have come into possession of the authority to resolve constitutional issues with finality. Although the intellectual operation entailed is like that used in the exercise of "judicial review," the function is altogether distinct. Exercise of the power of "constitutional review" places the courts in a relation with the other two branches totally different from that grounding "judicial review."

Strong, *President, Congress, Judiciary: One Is More Equal Than The Others,* 60 A.B.A.J. 1052-1053 (1974).

## NOTES

1. Certain provisions of the Constitution have long been considered judicially unenforceable. Among such constitutional provisions has been "the republican guarantee" clause. Thus, Justice Brennan in *Baker* analyzes the facts of that case to see whether it should be considered as arising under the "guarantee" clause. If the case were to have been so characterized, it would have been nonjusticiable. This immutable cataloguing of any constitutional provision as either justiciable or nonjusticiable has been challenged. Professor Arthur Bonfield lodges the following critique against the tradition of regarding a "guarantee" clause case as unquestionably nonjusticiable:

Neither as a textual or policy matter is the enforcement of the guarantee delegated solely to Congress; nor are there greater difficulties under this provision in defining the criteria necessary for judicial enforcement than there are under the fourteenth amendment. As a result, an issue raised under the guarantee should be deemed "political" solely if it is burdened with some of the other elements Justice Brennan notes. An issue cognizable under the fourteenth amendment, as that in *Baker v. Carr*, must therefore, as a logical proposition, be so under the guarantee.

Bonfield, *Baker v. Carr: 82 Sup. Ct. 691 New Light on the Constitutional Guarantee of Republican Government,* 50 CALIF. L. REV. 245, 252 (1962).

Justice Frankfurter claimed that *Baker v. Carr* was a republican guarantee case masquerading as an equal protection case. The bar to justiciability presented by the guarantee clause was thought to be the fact that the adjudication of a guarantee case would set the courts adrift on a sea of political theory with no constitutionally defined compass. What guide would the Supreme Court have to define what a republican form of government was?

2. Does the now famous statement by Brennan in *Baker v. Carr* of the indicia of a political question automatically bar justiciability of republican guarantee cases? In trying to identify a question as a political one, Brennan suggests that the nonjusticiability of a republican guarantee clause case is due to the fact that these cases concern "political questions." He then suggests that when a constitutional issue involves a textual commitment of the issue to a co-ordinate branch of government, it gives rise to a "political question." Reading Art. IV, § 4, of the Constitution, does the republican guarantee make a textually demonstrable commitment of the issue to Congress?

Among the stigmata of the political question case, we are told is "a lack of judicially discoverable and manageable standards for resolving it." But if the equal protection clause of the fourteenth amendment had never been the subject, as it has, of extensive constitutional adjudication, there would not be any discoverable and manageable standards for resolving equal protection cases either. Until a line of case law has been developed through the process of constitutional adjudication, there is not the same abundance of standards by which to judicially resolve any question turning on the meaning of a constitutional provision. Is not the whole tradition then of the nonjusticiability of the republican guarantee clause the consequence of a triumph of circular reasoning? The republican clause is nonjusticiable precisely because courts refuse to treat cases arising under that clause as justiciable.

## POWELL v. McCORMACK
### Supreme Court of the United States
### 395 U.S. 486, 23 L. Ed. 2d 491, 89 S. Ct. 1944 (1969)

Chief Justice WARREN delivered the opinion of the Court.

In November 1966, Petitioner Adam Clayton Powell, Jr., was duly elected from the 18th Congressional District of New York to serve in the United States House of Representatives for the 90th Congress. However, pursuant to a House resolution, he was not permitted to take his seat. Powell (and some of the voters of his district) then filed suit in Federal District Court, claiming that the House could exclude him only if it found he failed to meet the standing requirements of age, citizenship, and residence contained in Art. I, § 2, of the Constitution—requirements the House specifically found Powell met—and thus had excluded him unconstitutionally. The District Court dismissed petitioners' complaint "for want of jurisdiction of the subject matter." A panel of the Court of Appeals affirmed the dismissal, although on somewhat different grounds, each judge filing a separate opinion. We have determined that it was error to dismiss the complaint and that petitioner Powell is entitled to a declaratory judgment that he was unlawfully excluded from the 90th Congress.

. . . .

## Political Question Doctrine

1.  Textually Demonstrable Constitutional Commitment.
    Respondents maintain that even if this case is otherwise justiciable, it presents only a political question. It is well established that the federal courts will not adjudicate political questions. . . .

    Respondents' first contention is that this case presents a political question because under Art. I, § 5, there has been a "textually demonstrable constitutional commitment" to the House of the "adjudicatory power" to determine Powell's qualifications. Thus it is argued that the House, and the House alone, has power to determine who is qualified to be a member.

    . . . .

    . . . [W]hether there is a "textually demonstrable constitutional commitment of the issue to a coordinate political department of government" and what is the scope of such commitment are questions we must resolve for the first time in this case. For, as we pointed out in *Baker v. Carr,* "[d]eciding whether a matter has in any measure been committed by the Constitution to another branch of government, or whether the action of that branch exceeds whatever authority has been committed, is itself a delicate exercise in constitutional interpretation and is the responsibility of this Court as ultimate interpreter of the Constitution."

    In order to determine the scope of any "textual commitment" under Art. I, § 5, we necessarily must determine the meaning of the phrase to "Be the Judge of the Qualifications of its Own Members." Petitioners argue that the records of the debates during the

Constitutional Convention; available commentary from the post-Convention, pre-ratification period; and early congressional applications of Art. I, § 5, support their construction of the section. Respondents insist, however, that a careful examination of the pre-Convention practices of the English Parliament and American colonial assemblies demonstrates that by 1787, a legislature's power to judge the qualifications of its members was generally understood to encompass exclusion or expulsion on the ground that an individual's character or past conduct rendered him unfit to serve. When the Constitution and the debates over its adoption are thus viewed in historical perspective, argue respondents, it becomes clear that the "qualifications" expressly set forth in the Constitution were not meant to limit the long-recognized legislative power to exclude or expel at will, but merely to establish "standing incapacities," which could be altered only by a constitutional amendment. Our examination of the relevant historical materials leads us to the conclusion that petitioners are correct and that the Constitution leaves the House without authority to *exclude* any person, duly elected by his constituents, who meets all the requirements for membership expressly prescribed in the Constitution.

. . . .

. . . Unquestionably, Congress has an interest in preserving its institutional integrity, but in most cases that interest can be sufficiently safeguarded by the exercise of its power to punish its members for disorderly behavior and, in extreme cases, to expel a member with the concurrence of two-thirds. In short, both the intention of the Framers, to the extent it can be determined, and an examination of the basic principles of our democratic system persuade us that the Constitution does not vest in the Congress a discretionary power to deny membership by a majority vote.

For these reasons, we have concluded that Art. I, § 5, is at most a "textually demonstrable commitment" to Congress to judge only the qualifications expressly set forth in the Constitution. Therefore, the "textual commitment" formulation of the political question doctrine does not bar federal courts from adjudicating petitioners' claims.

## 2. Other Considerations.

Respondents' alternate contention is that the case presents a political question because judicial resolution of petitioners' claim would produce a "potentially embarrassing confrontation between coordinate branches" of the Federal Government. But, as our interpretation of Art. I, § 5, discloses, a determination of petitioner Powell's right to sit would require no more than an interpretation of the Constitution. Such a determination falls within the traditional role accorded courts to interpret the law, and does not involve a "lack of respect due [a] coordinate [branch] of government," nor does it involve an "initial policy determination of a kind clearly for nonjudicial discretion." *Baker v. Carr.* Our system of government requires that federal courts on occasion interpret the Constitution in a manner at variance with the construction given the document by another branch. The alleged conflict that such an adjudication may cause cannot justify the courts' avoiding their constitutional responsibility.

Nor are any of the other formulations of a political question "inextricable from the case at bar." *Baker v. Carr.* Petitioners seek a determination that the House was without power to exclude Powell from the 90th Congress, which, we have seen, requires an interpretation of the Constitution—a determination for which clearly there are "judicially . . . manageable standards." Finally, a judicial resolution of petitioners' claim will not result in "multifarious pronouncements by various departments on one question." For, as we noted in *Baker v. Carr,* it is the responsibility of this Court to act as the ultimate interpreter of the Constitution. Marbury v. Madison, 1 Cranch 137 (1803). Thus, we conclude that petitioners' claim is not barred by the political question doctrine, and, having determined that the claim is otherwise generally justiciable, we hold that the case is justiciable.

. . . .

---

### A Comment on the Powell Case

1. Perhaps there are some constitutional questions over which the Supreme Court is still not the ultimate arbiter. But the demarcation between those issues which federal courts can litigate and those which they cannot litigate is less frozen than ever. The process begun by *Baker v. Carr* and *Powell* shows that. Issues previously considered immune from judicial scrutiny have now been considered appropriate for consideration, *i.e.,* the question of whether the President of the United States must respond to a subpoena. *See* United States v. Nixon, 418 U.S. 960 (1974), this text, p. 340.

2. By the time the court did decide the case on June 16, 1969, the 90th Congress to which Powell had been elected and from which he was excluded had expired. Powell was duly elected by his constituents to the succeeding Congress. As a practical matter, all the court did was to declare that the 90th Congress had acted unconstitutionally in excluding Powell but the

court did not order that his salary be reimbursed, nor did they utter any comment on the effect his conflict with the Congress should have on his seniority.

3. In this skirmish between court and Congress, the court neither fought nor surrendered. The court insisted on its right to decide a constitutional question which Congress denied was within the court's power of interpretation. But the court waited to assert that insistence in such a way and at such a time as it would pose the least possible actual confrontation with the Congress.

The *Powell* case brings to mind many of the things that have been said about American judicial review. It was said that Congressmen in voting to exclude Powell voted as their mail demanded rather than according to their own assessment of the constitutionality of their action. This reinforces the British criticism of American judicial review that the presence of a paternalistic judiciary ready and willing to set aside the action of the legislature encourages legislative irresponsibility. If the decision on qualifications for congressional office rested with Congressmen alone, then Congressmen might more often take a long and independent judgment about the constitutionality of their actions. But this criticism can be turned to advantage.

The possibility of judicial curative action—the contingent aspect of judicial review—curbs both majority action and minority reaction. Is it better that the action of an intolerant or reckless majority can be repealed by a court the majority cannot reach, than to have no organic means of correction other than popular change of heart? Since there is always the possibility in the United States that the majority can be judicially undone, this possibility can and does defuse the intensity of minority reaction.

4. In the *Powell* case, the court might have relied on the political question doctrine. The court could easily have concluded that when a controversy arose between court and Congress and the controversy concerned how Congress should govern itself, such a controversy should be held nonjusticiable. In *Baker v. Carr,* a wedge into the political question doctrine had been maintained by stressing that the state of Tennessee and the federal courts occupied a hierarchical position one to the other. But Congress and the court were *co-equal* branches of government. Surely that was a conflict where it was not wise to assert, or to find out, who was in fact *primus inter pares.*

On the other hand, the court could choose to rely on the case involving Julian Bond's struggle for admission to the Georgia House. In Bond v. Floyd, 385 U.S. 116 (1966), the court held that the Georgia legislature could not add qualifications for its members beyond those textually stipulated in the Georgia constitution. The argument by analogy was clear: just as Georgia could not add qualifications to exclude members from the Georgia House, so Congress could not add new qualifications beyond those appearing in Art. I to exclude members from the U.S. House of Representatives. Although Chief Justice Warren's opinion is consistent with this construction, it does not actually explicitly endorse it.

Wherever ideology is a factor in governmental restraint, the first amendment concern for freedom of expression may overtake the imprecision of language in Art. I with regard to the self-government of Congress for such imprecision is no match, arguably, for the first amendment which speaks so directly to Congress.

Or the court could have chosen to reject both the alternatives of abstinence and that of confrontation and simply held that since Powell had never been admitted to the 90th Congress, he could not be excluded.

5.   The abundance of doctrinal possibilities here should be emphasized because it exposes the many options the Supreme Court had open to it. As it turned out, the court in *Powell* did not choose to abstain from deciding the case, neither did it choose real collision with the Congress. It elected instead what may be called modest confrontation. But the point, for our purposes, is that each of the practical alternatives open to the court was authorized by respectable doctrinal support. These conflicting and intersecting lines of cases and doctrines need not necessarily be regarded as disquieting. The use of doctrine in contemporary American constitutional law is eminently functional.

6.   The U.C.L.A. Law Review devoted a symposium to the *Powell* case. *See Comments on Powell v. McCormack*, 17 U.C.L.A. L. REV. 1 (1969). One of the contributors to the symposium, Professor Dixon, has taken a very critical look at the court's opinion in *Powell*:

> [T]he Court virtually kills the political question concept without saying so. . . . The proper formulation is: Even if there be no "textually demonstrable" (or historically verifiable) *commitment*, should the judiciary proceed to *exercise* the jurisdiction it concededly possesses?

Professor Dixon also says that it is incorrect to think of non-justiciability as an aspect of the separation of powers doctrine:

[T]he nonjusticiability issue centers on a determination of the kinds of things courts can and cannot do effectively. The separation of powers facet of nonjusticiability turns on explicit consideration of action already taken or to be taken by the other branches. But, the mere fact that another branch is materially involved does not itself produce nonjusticiability, as witness the practice of judicial review itself.

Is justiciability in the sense Dixon understands that term present in *Powell?*

Professor Laughlin in the same symposium makes a modified defense of Chief Justice Warren's approach to justiciability in *Powell*:

But in one sense, at least, Chief Justice Warren was eminently correct. A decision that the *Powell* case posed a "political question" would have been a victory for the respondents of equal or greater magnitude than a decision that Powell was properly excluded under Article I, Section 5, for it would have conceded that Congress has unfettered power to exclude members-elect for whatever reason it chooses. Mootness was undoubtedly the only way to actually avoid this issue.

# Chapter 2

## NATIONAL POWER IN THE CONSTITUTIONAL ORDER

*THE DIVISION OF POWERS: PROBLEMS OF FEDERALISM*

---

## A. THE SCOPE OF THE NATIONAL LEGISLATIVE POWER

### The Origins And Rationale of American Federalism

Federalism is not a uniquely American contribution to either constitutional or political theory. It is traceable at least to the Greek city-states and is in use in a number of other countries. See K. WHEARE, FEDERAL GOVERNMENT (4th ed., 1963). Federalism has had a vital influence on the pattern of American constitutional development. As Professor Wechsler has written, "Federalism was the means and price of the formation of the Union. It was inevitable, therefore, that its basic concepts should determine much of our history." Wechsler, *The Political Safeguards of Federalism: The Role of the States in the Composition and Selection of the National Government*, 54 COLUM. L. REV. 543 (1954), SELECTED ESSAYS ON CONSTITUTIONAL LAW 185 (1963).

Why did we adopt a federalist system? What values was it designed to serve? How were these functions of federalism reflected in the political organization established by the Constitution? To what extent do those values persist today? Does the structure of federalism established in 1789 still satisfy modern needs? These are the questions that run through this introduction and the remainder of the chapter.

With the emergence of the new nation, why was a federalist structure adopted rather than a unitary system such as existed in England? At least part of the answer must lie in practical necessity. The geographic dispersion of the American people and the inadequate means of communication led naturally to the emergence of local traditions, interests, and values. Cultural heterogeneity, rather than hegemony, tended further to promote separatism. Economic factors, such as differences in products and forms of economic activity, similarly lent themselves to particularistic interests. And finally the experience of the colonists with Great Britain had generated a fear of centralist tendencies and a desire to preserve local autonomy. See D. MINAR, IDEAS IN POLITICS: THE AMERICAN EXPERIENCE 110-12 (1964).

## The Articles of Confederation

The foundations of our federalist structure, therefore, were laid even before November, 1777, when the Continental Congress adopted the Articles of Confederation and recommended them to the States. Ratified in 1781, the Articles were America's first real attempt to reconcile unity with diversity. But the colonial experience with Great Britain and the dominant belief that government was at best a necessary evil, something to be feared and circumscribed, necessarily determined the course of the new political union.

The Articles of Confederation reflected the colonial faith in state sovereignty as the only viable check on the abuse of centralized power when they pointedly declared that each state retained its "sovereignty, freedom and independence." The Articles were more in the nature of a treaty than a charter for unified government. Congress was denied the power to lay and collect taxes or duties or provide for a uniform currency. It had no regulatory power over interstate or foreign commerce and trade. Each state regardless of its size was entitled to one vote, and the vote of 9 of the 13 states was necessary to enact laws and a unanimous vote was required to amend the Articles. At a time when sectionalism was dominant, legitimate change became impossible.

The Confederation failed. It was increasingly clear that the central government had to be given sufficient powers to govern, at least in those matters in which the states individually were incompetent. But fear of centralized power had not declined. Concern for individual liberty from accumulated power remained. The jealous interest in preserving state sovereignty was widespread. It was this creative tension between efficiency in performing the tasks of government and limiting the abuse of centralized governmental power that dominated the debate over the constitutional allocation of powers between the nation and states.

## James Madison and Federalism

James Madison began his famous tract in THE FEDERALIST, No. 10, with the proposition that "[a]mong the numerous advantages promised by a well constructed Union, none deserves to be more accurately developed than its tendency to break and control the violence of faction." By faction Madison referred to "a number of citizens, whether amounting to a majority or minority of the whole, who are united and actuated by some common impulse of passion, or of interest, adverse to the rights of other citizens, or to the permanent and aggregate interests of the community." Through political arrangements, reasoned

Madison, the dangers of faction might be controlled. Federation, he argued, made possible the governance by a common political authority of a large geographic area possessing multiple factions. The existence of such a pluralism of interests would guard against the accumulation of powers in a constant majority.

### A Modern Perspective

What is the role of the Supreme Court in umpiring the federal system? In exercising the power of judicial review, should the courts give priority to checking abuses of the national power? Or in preserving the division of powers, should the courts give priority instead to maintaining national supremacy against intrusions by the individual states? See Freund, *Umpiring the Federal System*, 54 COLUM. L. REV. 561 (1954), SELECTED ESSAYS 203-217 (1963).

From today's perspective, the concept and role of federalism has undergone great changes since 1789. As social problems grow more complex, as they cross state boundaries, as demands for the rights of national citizenship become more intense, the demand for action by the national government grows. On the other hand, there has been a recent emphasis on returning power to the states through revenue-sharing. The dilemma, however, is essentially the same as it was 184 years ago. "How do we make sure that the powers of government continue to be diffused while at the same time the chores of government are effectively performed." Speech by Senator Muskie cited in Leach, *Intergovernmental Cooperation and American Federalism,* in G. DIETZE, ESSAYS ON THE AMERICAN CONSTITUTION 133 (1964). It has been argued that federalism should be seen as a tool, rather than a rigid set of principles; a tool whose function is to provide for the welfare of the American people by the most efficient means possible. Federalism emerges then not as a static concept but rather as a dynamic instrument for implementing the ends of government. As you read the materials that follow, keep in mind this federalist dilemma: efficiency versus the danger of accumulated power.

---

### The Controversy Over a National Bank

In *McCulloch v. Maryland,* the Supreme Court considered the constitutionality of congressional legislation creating the Second Bank of the United States. In 1791, amidst great controversy, Congress had incorporated the First Bank of the United States with power to issue bank notes, accept private deposits, discount promissory notes and carry on all the usual transactions of a local bank operated for the profit of shareholders. However, the controversy accompanying the creation of the bank was not to dissipate during the years of its operation. "In the minds of much of the public the Bank of the United States was a ruthless and irresponsible institution, controlled by a small group of private bankers for personal profit. The Federal Government held a minor share of stock and held no actual control over the Bank's policies. While much of the antagonism was emotional, and while the bank perhaps received more blame for economic conditions than it deserved, a good deal of the disrepute was justified . . . by poor management and selfish profit-seeking. . . . [T]his central financial institution was also a sharp political issue [since] '[t]he bank was largely under the control of the Federalists who were accused of using it as a political machine and of wielding its great influence for political purposes. . . .' " Plous & Baker, *McCulloch v. Maryland: Right Principle, Wrong Case,* 9 STAN. L. REV. 710, 719 (1957). *See* 1 C. Warren, THE SUPREME COURT IN UNITED STATES HISTORY 499-540 (1922), for a historical treatment of the debate over the bank.

In 1811 the First Bank's charter had been allowed to expire. But on April 10, 1816, the Congress, again over bitter opposition, incorporated the Second Bank of the United States. It was over the constitutionality of this legislation that the battle in *McCulloch* was waged.

---

### McCULLOCH v. MARYLAND
Supreme Court of the United States
17 U.S. (4 Wheat.) 316, 4 L. Ed. 579 (1819)

[Pursuant to its charter, the Second Bank of the United States established a branch bank in Baltimore. On February 11, 1818, the General Assembly of Maryland enacted a statute imposing a tax on the face value of many of the notes issued by banks or their branches located in Maryland but not chartered by the state or alternatively a payment of $15,000 annually.

[When the Baltimore branch of the bank issued notes in contravention of the statute, an action of debt was brought on behalf of the state in the County Court of Baltimore County against McCulloch as cashier of the branch bank to recover the statutory penalty. The Maryland Court of Appeals affirmed judgment against McCulloch and the case came to the Supreme Court on a writ of error. Six counsel, including United States Attorney General William Wirt, Daniel Webster and William Pinckney for the bank and State Attorney General Luther Martin,

Joseph Hopkinson, and Walter Jones for Maryland, argued the case for nine days. Justice Marshall speaking for a unanimous court, including four Republicans, delivered his opinion only three days after argument.]

Chief Justice MARSHALL delivered the opinion of the Court.

. . . .

The first question made in the cause is, has Congress power to incorporate a bank?

. . . .

The power now contested was exercised by the first Congress elected under the present constitution. The bill for incorporating the Bank of the United States did not steal upon an unsuspecting legislature, and pass unobserved. Its principle was completely understood, and was opposed with equal zeal and ability. After being resisted, first in the fair and open field of debate, and afterwards in the executive cabinet, with as much persevering talent as any measure has ever experienced, and being supported by arguments which convinced minds as pure and as intelligent as this country can boast, it became a law. The original act was permitted to expire; but a short experience of the embarrassments to which the refusal to revive it exposed the government, convinced those who were most prejudiced against the measure of its necessity and induced the passage of the present law. It would require no ordinary share of intrepidity to assert that a measure adopted under these circumstances was a bold and plain usurpation, to which the constitution gave no countenance.

These observations belong to the cause; but they are not made under the impression that, were the question entirely new, the law would be found irreconcilable with the constitution.

In discussing this question, the counsel for the state of Maryland have deemed it of some importance, in the construction of the constitution, to consider that instrument not as emanating from the people, but as the act of sovereign and independent states. The powers of the general government, it has been said, are delegated by the states, who alone are truly sovereign; and must be exercised in subordination to the states, who alone possess supreme dominion.

It would be difficult to sustain this proposition. The convention which framed the constitution was indeed elected by the state legislatures. But the instrument, when it came from their hands, was a mere proposal, without obligation, or pretensions to it. It was reported to the then existing Congress of the United States, with a request that it might "be submitted to a convention of delegates, chosen in each state by the people thereof, under the recommendation of its legislature, for their assent and ratification." This mode of proceeding was adopted; and by the convention, by Congress, and by the state legislatures, the instrument was submitted to the people. They acted upon it in the only manner in which they can act safely, effectively, and wisely, on such a subject, by assembling in convention. It is true, they assembled in their several states—and where else should they have assembled? No political dreamer was ever wild enough to think of breaking down the lines which separate the states, and of compounding the American people into one common mass. Of consequence, when they act, they act in their states. But the measures they adopt do not, on that account, cease to be the measures of the people themselves, or become the measures of the state governments.

From these conventions the constitution derives its whole authority. The government proceeds directly from the people; is "ordained and established" in the name of the people; and is declared to be ordained, "in order to form a more perfect union, establish justice, insure domestic tranquility, and secure the blessings of liberty to themselves and to their posterity." The assent of the states, in their sovereign capacity, is implied in calling a convention, and thus submitting that instrument to the people. But the people were at perfect liberty to accept or reject it; and their act was final. It required not the affirmance, and could not be negatived, by the state governments. The constitution, when thus adopted, was of complete obligation, and bound the state sovereignties.

. . . .

The government of the Union, then (whatever may be the influence of this fact on the case), is, emphatically, and truly, a government of the people. In form and in substance it emanates from them. Its powers are granted by them, and are to be exercised directly on them, and for their benefit.

This government is acknowledged by all to be one of enumerated powers. The principle, that it can exercise only the powers granted to it, would seem too apparent to have required to be enforced by all those arguments which its enlightened friends, while it was depending before the people, found it necessary to urge. That principle is now universally admitted. But the question respecting the extent of the powers actually granted, is perpetually arising, and will probably continue to arise, as long as our system shall exist.

. . . .

If any one proposition could command the universal assent of mankind, we might expect it would be this—that the government of the Union, though limited in its powers, is supreme within its sphere of action. This would seem to result necessarily from its nature. It is the government of all; its powers are delegated by all; it represents all, and acts for all. Though any one state may be willing to control its operations, no state is willing to allow others to control them. The nation, on those subjects on which it can act, must necessarily bind its component parts. But this question is not left to mere reason; the people have, in express terms, decided it by saying, "this constitution, and the laws of the United States, which shall be made in pursuance thereof," "shall be the supreme law of the land," and by requiring that the members of the state legislatures, and the officers of the executive and judicial departments of the states shall take the oath of fidelity to it.

The government of the United States, then, though limited in its powers, is supreme; and its laws, when made in pursuance of the constitution, form the supreme law of the land, "anything in the constitution or laws of any state to the contrary notwithstanding."

Among the enumerated powers, we do not find that of establishing a bank or creating a corporation. But there is no phrase in the instrument which, like the articles of confederation, excludes incidental or implied powers; and which requires that everything granted shall be expressly and minutely described. Even the 10th amendment, which was framed for the purpose of quieting the excessive jealousies which had been excited, omits the word "expressly," and declares only that the powers "not delegated to the United States, nor prohibited to the states, are reserved to the states or to the people;" thus leaving the question, whether the particular power which may become the subject of contest, has been delegated to the one government, or prohibited to the other, to depend on a fair construction of the whole instrument. The men who drew and adopted this amendment had experienced the embarrassments resulting from the insertion of this word in the articles of confederation, and probably omitted it to avoid those embarrassments. A constitution, to contain an accurate detail of all the subdivisions of which its great powers will admit, and of all the means by which they may be carried into execution, would partake of the prolixity of a legal code, and could scarcely be embraced by the human mind. It would probably never be understood by the public. Its nature, therefore, requires, that only its great outlines should be marked, its important objects designated, and the minor ingredients which compose those objects be deduced from the nature of the objects themselves. That this idea was entertained by the framers of the American constitution, is not only to be inferred from the nature of the instrument, but from the language. Why else were some of the limitations, found in the ninth section of the 1st article, introduced? It is also, in some degree, warranted by their having omitted to use any restrictive term which might prevent its receiving a fair and just interpretation. In considering this question, then, we must never forget, that it is a constitution we are expounding.

Although, among the enumerated powers of government, we do not find the word "bank" or "incorporation," we find the great powers to lay and collect taxes; to borrow money; to regulate commerce; to declare and conduct a war; and to raise and support armies and navies. The sword and the purse, all the external relations, and no inconsiderable portion of the industry of the nation, are entrusted to its government. It can never be pretended that these vast powers draw after them others of inferior importance, merely because they are inferior. Such an idea can never be advanced. But it may with great reason be contended, that a government, entrusted with such ample powers, on the due execution of which the happiness and prosperity of the nation so vitally depends, must also be entrusted with ample means for their execution. The power being given, it is the interest of the nation to facilitate its execution. It can never be their interest, and cannot be presumed to have been their intention, to clog and embarrass its execution by withholding the most appropriate means. . . . If, indeed, such be the mandate of the constitution, we have only to obey; but that instrument does not profess to enumerate the means by which the powers it confers may be executed; nor does it prohibit the creation of a corporation, if the existence of such a being be essential to the beneficial exercise of those powers. It is, then, the subject of fair inquiry, how far such means may be employed. . . .

. . . .

The government which has a right to do an act, and has imposed on it the duty of performing that act, must, according to the dictates of reason, be allowed to select the means; and those who contend that it may not select any appropriate means, that one particular mode of effecting the object is excepted, take upon themselves the burden of establishing that exception.

. . . .

But the constitution of the United States has not left the right of Congress to employ the necessary means, for the execution of the powers conferred on the government, to general reasoning. To its enumeration of powers is added that of making "all laws which shall be necessary and proper, for carrying into execution the foregoing powers, and all other powers vested by this constitution, in the government of the United States, or in any department [or officer] thereof."

The counsel for the state of Maryland have urged various arguments, to prove that this clause, though in terms a grant of power, is not so in effect; but is really restrictive of the general right, which might otherwise be implied, of selecting means for executing the enumerated powers.

. . . .

But the argument on which most reliance is placed, is drawn from the peculiar language of this clause. Congress is not empowered by it to make all laws, which may have relation to the powers conferred on the government, but such only as may be "necessary and proper" for carrying them into execution. The word "necessary" is considered as controlling the whole sentence, and as limiting the right to pass laws for the execution of the granted powers, to such as are indispensable, and without which the power would be nugatory. That it excludes the choice of means, and leaves to Congress, in each case, that only which is most direct and simple.

Is it true, that this is the sense in which the word "necessary" is always used? Does it always import an absolute physical necessity, so strong that one thing, to which another may be termed necessary, cannot exist without that other? We think it does not. If reference be had to its use, in the common affairs of the world, or in approved authors, we find that it frequently imports no more than that one thing is convenient, or useful, or essential to another. To employ the means necessary to an end, is generally understood as employing any means calculated to produce the end, and not as being confined to those single means, without which the end would be entirely unattainable. . . .

Let this be done in the case under consideration. The subject is the execution of those great powers on which the welfare of a nation essentially depends. It must have been the intention of those who gave these powers, to insure, as far as human prudence could insure, their beneficial execution. This could not be done by confiding the choice of means to such narrow limits as not to leave it in the power of Congress to adopt any which might be appropriate, and which were conducive to the end. This provision is made in a constitution intended to endure for ages to come, and consequently, to be adapted to the various crises of human affairs. To have prescribed the means by which government should, in all future time, execute its powers, would have been to change, entirely, the character of the instrument, and give it the properties of a legal code. It would have been an unwise attempt to provide, by immutable rules, for exigencies which, if foreseen at all, must have been seen dimly, and which can be best provided for as they occur. To have declared that the best means shall not be used, but those alone without which the power given would be nugatory, would have been to deprive the legislature of the capacity to avail itself of experience, to exercise its reason, and to accommodate its legislation to circumstances. If we apply this principle of construction to any of the powers of the government, we shall find it so pernicious in its operation that we shall be compelled to discard it. . . .

. . . .

In ascertaining the sense in which the word "necessary" is used in this clause of the constitution, we may derive some aid from that with which it is associated. Congress shall have power "to make all laws which shall be necessary and proper to carry into execution" the powers of the government. If the word "necessary" was used in that strict and rigorous sense for which the counsel for the state of Maryland contend, it would be an extraordinary departure from the usual course of the human mind, as exhibited in composition, to add a word, the only possible effect of which is to qualify that strict and rigorous meaning; to present to the mind the idea of some choice of means of legislation not straightened and compressed within the narrow limits for which gentlemen contend.

But the argument which most conclusively demonstrates the error of the construction contended for by the counsel for the state of Maryland, is founded on the intention of the convention, as manifested in the whole clause. . . .

. . . 1st.  The clause is placed among the powers of Congress, not among the limitations on those powers.

2d.  Its terms purport to enlarge, not to diminish the powers vested in the government. It purports to be an additional power, not a restriction on those already granted. No reason has been, or can be assigned for thus concealing an intention to narrow the discretion of the national legislature under words which purport to enlarge it. . . .

The result of the most careful and attentive consideration bestowed upon this clause is, that if it does not enlarge, it cannot be construed to restrain the powers of Congress, or to impair the right of the legislature to exercise its best judgment in the selection of measures to carry into execution the constitutional powers of the government. If no other motive for its insertion can be suggested, a sufficient one is found in the desire to remove all doubts respecting the right to legislate on that vast mass of incidental powers which must be involved in the constitution, if that instrument be not a splendid bauble.

We admit, as all must admit, that the powers of the government are limited, and that its limits are not to be transcended. But we think the sound construction of the constitution must allow to the national legislature that discretion, with respect to the means by which the powers it confers are to be carried into execution, which will enable that body to perform the high duties assigned to it, in the manner most beneficial to the people. Let the end be legitimate, let it be within the scope of the constitution, and all means which are appropriate, which are plainly adapted to that end, which are not prohibited, but consist with the letter and spirit of the constitution, are constitutional.

. . . .

If a corporation may be employed indiscriminately with other means to carry into execution the powers of the government, no particular reason can be assigned for excluding the use of a bank, if required for its fiscal operations. To use one, must be within the discretion of Congress, if it be an appropriate mode of executing the powers of government. That it is a convenient, a useful, and essential instrument in the prosecution of its fiscal operations, is not now a subject of controversy. . . .

But, were its necessity less apparent, none can deny its being an appropriate measure; and if it is, the degree of its necessity, as has been very justly observed, is to be discussed in another place. Should Congress, in the execution of its powers, adopt measures which are prohibited by the constitution; or should Congress, under the pretext of executing its powers, pass laws for the accomplishment of objects not entrusted to the government; it would become the painful duty of this tribunal, should a case requiring such a decision come before it, to say that such an act was not the law of the land. But where the law is not prohibited, and is really calculated to effect any of the objects entrusted to the government, to undertake here to inquire into the degree of its necessity, would be to pass the line which circumscribes the judicial department, and to tread on legislative ground. This court disclaims all pretensions to such a power.

. . . .

It being the opinion of the court that the act incorporating the bank is constitutional, and that the power of establishing a branch in the state of Maryland might be properly exercised by the bank itself, we proceed to inquire:

2. Whether the state of Maryland may, without violating the constitution, tax that branch?

That the power of taxation is one of vital importance; that it is retained by the states; that it is not abridged by the grant of a similar power to the government of the Union; that it is to be concurrently exercised by the two governments; are truths which have never been denied. But, such is the paramount character of the constitution that its capacity to withdraw any subject from the action of even this power, is admitted. The states are expressly forbidden to lay any duties on imports or exports, except what may be absolutely necessary for executing their inspection laws. If the obligation of this prohibition must be conceded—if it may restrain a state from the exercise of its taxing power on imports and exports—the same paramount character would seem to restrain, as it certainly may restrain, a state from such other exercise of this power, as is in its nature incompatible with, and repugnant to, the constitutional laws of the Union. A law, absolutely repugnant to another, as entirely repeals that other as if express terms of repeal were used.

On this ground, the counsel for the bank place its claim to be exempted from the power of a state to tax its operations. There is no express provision for the case, but the claim has been sustained on a principle which so entirely pervades the constitution, is so intermixed with the materials which compose it, so interwoven with its web, so blended with its texture, as to be incapable of being separated from it, without rending it into shreds.

This great principle is, that the constitution and the laws made in pursuance thereof are supreme; that they control the constitution and laws of the respective states, and cannot be controlled by them. From this, which may be almost termed an axiom, other propositions are adduced as corollaries, on the truth or error of which, and on their application to this case, the cause has been supposed to depend. These are, 1st. that a power to create implies a power to preserve. 2d. That a power to destroy, if wielded by a different hand, is hostile to, and incompatible with, these powers to create and to preserve. 3d. That where this repugnance exists, that authority which is supreme must control, not yield to that over which it is supreme.

. . . .

The power of Congress to create, and of course to continue, the bank, was the subject of the preceding part of this opinion; and is no longer to be considered as questionable.

That the power of taxing [the bank] by the states may be exercised so as to destroy it, is too obvious to be denied. But taxation is said to be an absolute power, which acknowledges no other limits than those expressly prescribed in the constitution, and like sovereign powers of every other description, is trusted to the discretion of those who use it. But the very terms of this argument admit that the sovereignty of the state, in the article of taxation itself, is subordinate to, and may be controlled by the constitution of the United States. How far it has been controlled by that instrument must be a question of construction. In making this construction, no principle not declared can be admissible, which would defeat the legitimate operations of a supreme government. It is of the very essence of supremacy to remove all obstacles to its action within its own sphere, and so to modify every power vested in subordinate governments as to exempt its own operations from their own influence. This effect need not be stated in terms. It is so involved in the declaration of supremacy, so necessarily implied in it, that the expression of it could not make it more certain. We must, therefore, keep it in view while construing the constitution.

The argument on the part of the state of Maryland, is, not that the states may directly resist a law of Congress, but that they may exercise their acknowledged powers upon it, and that the constitution leaves them this right in the confidence that they will not abuse it.

Before we proceed to examine this argument, and to subject it to the test of the constitution, we must be permitted to bestow a few considerations on the nature and extent of this original right of taxation, which is acknowledged to remain with the states. It is admitted that the power of taxing the people and their property is essential to the very existence of government, and may be legitimately exercised on the objects to which it is applicable, to the utmost extent to which the government may choose to carry it. The only security against the abuse of this power is found in the structure of the government itself. In imposing a tax the legislature acts upon its constituents. This is in general a sufficient security against erroneous and oppressive taxation.

The people of a state, therefore, give to their government a right of taxing themselves and their property, and as the exigencies of government cannot be limited, they prescribe no limits to the exercise of this right, resting confidently on the interest of the legislator, and on the influence of the constituent over their representative, to guard them against its abuse. But the means employed by the government of the Union have no such security, nor is the right of a state to tax them sustained by the same theory. Those means are not given by the people of a

particular state, not given by the constitutents of the legislature, which claim the right to tax them, but by the people of
all the states. They are given by all, for the benefit of all—and
upon theory, should be subjected to that government only
which belongs to all.

. . . .

. . . All subjects over which the sovereign power of a state
extends, are objects of taxation; but those over which it does not
extend, are, upon the soundest principles, exempt from taxation.
This proposition may almost be pronounced self-evident.

The sovereignty of a state extends to everything which exists
by its own authority, or is introduced by its permission; but
does it extend to those means which are employed by Congress
to carry into execution—powers conferred on that body by the
people of the United States? We think it demonstrable that it
does not. Those powers are not given by the people of a single
state. They are given by the people of the United States, to a
government whose laws, made in pursuance of the constitution,
are declared to be supreme. Consequently, the people of a
single state cannot confer a sovereignty which will extend over
them.

. . . .

That the power to tax involves the power to destroy; that the
power to destroy may defeat and render useless the power to
create; that there is a plain repugnance, in conferring on one
government a power to control the constitutional measures of
another, which other, with respect to those very measures, is
declared to be supreme over that which exerts the control, are
propositions not to be denied. But all inconsistencies are to be
reconciled by the magic of the word CONFIDENCE. Taxation, it
is said, does not necessarily and unavoidably destroy. To carry it
to the excess of destruction would be an abuse, to presume
which, would banish that confidence which is essential to all
government.

But is this a case of confidence? Would the people of any one
state trust those of another with a power to control the most insignificant operations of their state government? We know they
would not. Why, then, should we suppose that the people of any
one state should be willing to trust those of another with a power
to control the operations of a government to which they have
confided the most important and most valuable interests? In the
legislature of the Union alone, are all represented. The legislature of the Union alone, therefore, can be trusted by the people
with the power of controlling measures which concern all, in the

confidence that it will not be abused. This, then, is not a case of confidence, and we must consider it as it really is.

If we apply the principle for which the state of Maryland contends, to the constitution generally, we shall find it capable of charging totally the character of that instrument. We shall find it capable of arresting all the measures of the government, and of prostrating it at the foot of the states. The American people have declared their constitution, and the laws made in pursuance thereof, to be supreme; but this principle would transfer the supremacy, in fact, to the states.

. . . .

. . . If the controlling power of the states be established; if their supremacy as to taxation be acknowledged; what is to restrain their exercising this control in any shape they may please to give it? Their sovereignty is not confined to taxation. That is not the only mode in which it might be displayed. The question is, in truth, a question of supremacy; and if the right of the states to tax the means employed by the general government be conceded, the declaration that the constitution, and the laws made in pursuance thereof, shall be the supreme law of the land, is empty and unmeaning declamation.

. . . .

It has also been insisted, that, as the power of taxation in the general and state governments is acknowledged to be concurrent, every argument which would sustain the right of the general government to tax banks chartered by the states, will equally sustain the right of the states to tax banks chartered by the general government.

But the two cases are not on the same reason. The people of all the states have created the general government, and have conferred upon it the general power of taxation. The people of all the states, and the states themselves, are represented in Congress, and, by their representatives, exercise this power. When they tax the chartered institutions of the states, they tax their constituents; and these taxes must be uniform. But, when a state taxes the operations of the government of the United States, it acts upon institutions created, not by their own constituents, but by people over whom they claim no control. It acts upon the measures of a government created by others as well as themselves, for the benefit of others in common with themselves. The difference is that which always exists, and always must exist, between the action of the whole on a part, and the action of a part on the whole—between the laws of a government declared to be supreme, and those of a government which, when in opposition to those laws, is not supreme.

But if the full application of this argument could be admitted, it might bring into question the right of Congress to tax the state banks, and could not prove the right of the states to tax the Bank of the United States.

The court has bestowed on this subject its most deliberate consideration. The result is a conviction that the states have no power, by taxation or otherwise, to retard, impede, burden, or in any manner control the operations of the constitutional laws enacted by Congress to carry into execution the powers vested in the general government. This is, we think, the unavoidable consequence of that supremacy which the Constitution has declared.

We are unanimously of opinion, that the law passed by the legislature of Maryland, imposing a tax on the Bank of the United States, is unconstitutional and void.

This opinion does not deprive the states of any resources which they originally possessed. It does not extend to a tax paid by the real property of the bank, in common with other real property within the state, nor to a tax imposed on the interest which the citizens of Maryland may hold in this institution, in common with other property of the same description throughout the state. But this is a tax on the operations of the bank, and is, consequently, a tax on the operation of an instrument employed by the government of the Union to carry its powers into execution. Such a tax must be unconstitutional.

[Judgment reversed.]

------

## NOTES

1. *Nationalism v. Localism.* The reaction to *McCulloch,* both pro and con, was immediate and intense. *See* 1 C. WARREN, THE SUPREME COURT IN UNITED STATES HISTORY 511-40 (1922); 4 A. BEVERIDGE, THE LIFE OF JOHN MARSHALL 309-39 (1919). While much of the negative opinion was directed at the court's legitimization of the national bank, most critics attacked Marshall's broad nationalist principles. Spencer Roane of Virginia, a strong antagonist of Marshall, writing in the newspapers under the pseudonyms of "Amphictyon" and "Hampden," claimed that Marshall's principles "tend directly to consolidation of the States and to strip them of some of the most important attributes of their sovereignty. If the Congress of the United States should think proper to legislate to the full extent upon the principles now adjudicated by the Supreme Court, it is difficult to say how

small be the remnant of powers left in the hands of the State authorities." 1 C. WARREN, THE SUPREME COURT, at 517.

2. *Broad Interpretation v. Narrow Interpretation.* In defining the delegated powers, should the courts adopt a broad or a narrow construction? The constitutional convention sent the following resolutions, concerning the scope of national powers, which were originally proposed by Randolph, to its Committee of Detail: "Resolved, that the national legislature ought, 1) to possess the legislative rights vested in Congress by the confederation; and 2) moreover, to legislate in all cases for the general interest of the Union, and 3) also in those to which the states are separately incompetent, or 4) in which the harmony of the United States may be interrupted by the exercise of individual legislation." 1 FARRAND, THE RECORDS OF THE FEDERAL CONVENTION OF 1787 131 (1911). The convention consistently rejected attempts to more narrowly define the congressional power. It was the Committee of Detail that changed the language of this resolution into the language of Art. 1, § 8, of the Constitution.

3. *The Constitutional Language.* Are the enumerated powers expressed in Art. 1, § 8, limited to ends or are means also specified? The power to raise armies is a *means* of effectuating the war power. Yet both are expressly provided for. Consider the argument in *McCulloch* of Luther Martin for Maryland: "If, then, the convention has specified some powers, which, being only means to accomplish the ends of government, might have been taken by implication; by what just rule of construction are other sovereign powers, equally vast and important, to be assumed by implication?"

What is the effect of the tenth amendment on this analysis? Marshall uses it to argue for implied powers. The corresponding provision in the Articles of Confederation was phrased in terms of "expressly delegated" powers and Congress rejected an attempt to insert "expressly" into the tenth amendment. ANNALS OF CONGRESS, I, p. 768.

4. *Implied Powers, Limited Government and Federalism.* Is Marshall's theory of implied powers consistent with the principle of limited government? Of federalism? Spencer Roane of Virginia (alias Hampden) had argued that there is no difference between an "*unlimited* grant of power and a grant limited in its terms, but accompanied with *unlimited* means of carrying it into execution." 4 A. BEVERIDGE, THE LIFE OF JOHN MARSHALL, at 316.

Does Marshall provide an adequate standard for limiting Congress' power or is it, in fact, a general grant of legislative power? Is the need for such formal standards lessened by the political realities of our federalist system? Consider again the contention that "[t]he actual extent of central intervention in the governance of our affairs is determined far less by the formal power distribution than by the sheer existence of the states and their political power to influence the action of the national authority. . . ." Wechsler, *The Political Safeguards of Federalism: The Role of the States in the Composition and Selection of the National Government,* 54 COLUM. L. REV. 543 (1954), SELECTED ESSAYS 186 (1963).

5. *The Need for a "Necessary and Proper" Clause.* Hamilton in THE FEDERALIST, No. 33, contended that Congress would still have implied powers if there were no necessary and proper clause. "[I]t may be affirmed with perfect confidence, that the constitutional operation of the intended government would be precisely the same, if [the clause] were entirely obliterated, as if [it] were repeated in every article. [It is] only declaratory of a truth, which would have resulted by necessary and unavoidable implication from the very act of constituting a Federal Government, and vesting it with certain specified powers. . . . What is a power, but the ability or faculty of doing a thing? What is the ability to do a thing but the power of employing the *means* necessary to its execution? What is LEGISLATIVE power but a power of making laws? What are the *means* to execute a legislative power, but LAWS?"

James Madison in THE FEDERALIST, No. 44, states: "Had the Constitution been silent on this head, there can be no doubt that all the particular powers requisite as means of executing the general powers would have resulted to the government, by unavoidable implication." Is there any difference in Hamilton and Madison's approach to the necessary and proper clause? Does the clause itself constitute a grant of powers? If Congress would have implied powers if there were no clause, shouldn't the inclusion of the "necessary and proper" language be read to limit the grant of power?

6. *Inherent Domestic Legislative Powers.* It has been argued that Marshall's approach in *McCulloch* to Congress' power is excessively narrow; that Congress has general, inherent legislative power. *See* W. CROSSKEY, POLITICS AND THE CONSTITUTION IN THE HISTORY OF THE UNITED STATES 380-81 (1953).

7. In Kansas v. Colorado, 206 U.S. 46 (1907), the court dealt with the power of Congress over reclamation of arid lands within a state. In rejecting such power, Justice Brewer also rejected the concept of inherent domestic legislative power. "Turning to the enumeration of powers granted to Congress by the 8th section of the first article of the Constitution, it is enough to say that

no one of them by any implication refers to the reclamation of arid lands. The last paragraph of the section which authorizes Congress to make all laws which shall be necessary and proper for carrying into execution the foregoing powers, and all other powers vested by this Constitution in the Government of the United States, or in any Department or Officer thereof, is not the delegation of a new and independent power, but simply provision for making effective the powers theretofore mentioned. . . . [T]he proposition that there are legislative powers affecting the Nation as a whole which belong to, although not expressed in the grant of powers, is in direct conflict with the doctrine that this is a government of enumerated powers. That this is such a government clearly appears from the Constitution, independently of the Amendment, for otherwise there would be an instrument granting certain specified things made operative to grant other and distinct things. This natural construction of the original body of the Constitution is made absolutely certain by the Tenth Amendment."

8. But the concept of inherent powers is merely a logical derivative of the proposition that a government must have the means necessary for its survival and effectiveness. It would follow that the national government must have all powers which are in their nature national, transcending the capability of the individual states. *Compare* the grant of power in Art. I with the grant of the judicial power in Art. III. With the grant of the executive power in Art. II.

9. It has been argued that if Congress has general legislative power the specification of powers in Art. I, § 8, would be useless. But the specification of these powers could be designed merely to clarify those which are legislative as opposed to executive, *i.e.,* to assure an irreducible minimum of legislative prerogative over subject matters against the executive (royal) prerogative.

Does the tenth amendment preclude such a general legislative power? Note that the amendment does not say "reserved exclusively." Perhaps those powers which are delegated are vested whereas all other powers are concurrent to be exercised jointly by Congress and the states. Whatever the merit of these arguments, (arguments suggested by William Crosskey), they have been generally rejected in theory. Although the courts occasionally use the language of "inherent" domestic legislative power when referring to implied powers, it is generally claimed that in domestic affairs, a constitutional commitment of a power, express or by implication, must be established for congressional legislation.

10. *Legislating Pursuant to Other Constitutional Provisions.* There are numerous express grants of congressional power out-

side Art. I, § 8. *See, e.g.,* Art. I, § 4, recognizing Congress' power
to make or alter regulations for the election of senators and
representatives; Art. III, § 1, giving Congress power to establish
inferior federal courts and to make "exception and regulations"
regarding the appellate jurisdiction of the Supreme Court; Art.
IV, § 1, recognizing Congress' role in assuring full faith and
credit. Similarly, amendments 13, 14, 15, 19, 23, 24, and 26 all
include enabling clauses authorizing congressional legislation.

In addition, Art. I, § 8, cl. 18, empowers Congress "to make all
Laws which shall be necessary and proper for carrying into
Execution . . . all other powers vested by this Constitution in
the Government of the United States, or in any Department or
Officer thereof." While the courts often fail to cite this provision,
they have recognized Congress' implied power to legislate pursuant to other provisions of the Constitution.

11. *Intergovernmental Immunities.* In discussing the validity
of the Maryland tax, Marshall never considers the organizational
structure or the operations of the bank. Joseph Hopkinson,
counsel for the state, raised this question: "Can an institution
. . . purely private, and which disclaims any public character, be
clothed with the power and rights of the government, and demand
subordination from the State government in view of the federal
authority, which it undertakes to wield at its own will and
pleasure? Shall it be private in its direction and interest; public
in its rights and privileges; a trading money-lender in its business; an uncontrolled sovereign in its powers?" *See* Plous & Baker,
*McCulloch v. Maryland: Right Principle, Wrong Case,* 9 STAN.
L. REV. 710 (1957), on the private character of the bank.

Later, in Osborn v. The Bank of the United States, 22 U.S.
(9 Wheat.) 326 (1824), Marshall admitted that a private banking
corporation, even if employed by the national government in the
transaction of its fiscal affairs, would not be exempt from state
taxation. But he rejected the contention that this characterization
applied to the Bank of the United States. "The Bank is not considered as a private corporation, whose principal object is individual trade and individual profit; but as a public corporation,
created for public and national purposes."

Marshall claims that "the power to tax involves the power
to destroy." Is Marshall's opinion limited to discriminatory state
taxes or does it apply to all state taxes on federal instrumentalities? What constitutional provision did the Maryland tax violate?
Would the same constitutional principle require the invalidation
of a federal tax on state instrumentalities?

## B. DEFINING THE COMMERCE POWER: ESTABLISHING THE FOUNDATIONS

Justice Johnson correctly observed in Gibbons v. Ogden 22 U.S. (9 Wheat.) 1 (1824): "[i]f there was any one object riding over every other in the adoption of the Constitution, it was to keep the commercial intercourse among the States free from all invidious and partial restraints." In 1786, James Madison had written "most of our political evils may be traced to our commercial ones. . . ." *See* 1 C. WARREN, THE MAKING OF THE CONSTITUTION 568 (1937). Problems of commerce were of central concern to the constitutional convention.

During the Confederation period, Congress had not been given the power to regulate commerce. While the national government had power to enter into treaties, the inability to enforce such agreements domestically made such a power meaningless. Foreign countries, especially Great Britain, faced with an impotent national government, freely imposed discriminatory trade restrictions on United States' goods and citizens. And interstate commerce fared no better. The states, in an effort to remedy the chaotic condition of their finances following the war, had begun to levy tariffs and imposts not only on foreign goods but on goods coming from or going to sister states. Such action naturally invited retaliation and trade wars were common. And again, the national government lacked power to act. As Madison stated in his "Preface to Debates in the Convention of 1787": "the want of authy. in Congs. to regulate Commerce had produced in foreign nations particularly G.B. a monopolizing policy injurious to the trade of the United States and destructive to their navigation. . . . [the] same want of a general power over Commerce led to an exercise of this power separately, by the States, which not only proved abortive, but engendered rival, conflicting and angry regulation." 3 FARRAND, RECORDS OF THE FEDERAL CONVENTION OF 1787 547 (1911).

Given this situation it is not surprising that there was little debate at the constitutional convention on the question of giving Congress broad powers over commerce. As was stated by Alexander Hamilton in THE FEDERALIST, No. 11, "The importance of the Union, in a commercial life, is one of those points, about which there is least room to entertain a difference of opinion, and which has in fact commanded the most general assent of men, who have any acquaintance with this subject. This applies as well to our intercourse with foreign countries, as with each other."

The commerce clause finally adopted by the convention serves a dual function. It provides both a source of national legislative power and a limit on the power of the states. It is the question of the scope of Congress' power under the clause that is the present subject of inquiry. What is meant by regulating commerce "among the several States?" May Congress regulate local activity if such regulation is "necessary and proper" to the effectuation of its commerce powers? Is the purpose, motive, or intent of Congress relevant in determining the validity of legislation? Can Congress, for example, achieve police power or social welfare objectives through the use of its commerce power? What is the relevance of the tenth amendment? And, if the powers of Congress are to be limited, what is the role of the courts in defining the limits? To what extent is this best left to the political processes? If doctrinal limits are to be fashioned, what considerations should guide the formulation of standards? Again, it is the problem of federalism, the task of assuring efficiency in the performance of governmental functions while checking the abuse of governmental powers, the task of allocating powers between nation and state, that is the focus of concern.

---

### GIBBONS v. OGDEN
Supreme Court of the United States
22 U.S. (9 Wheat.) 1, 6 L. Ed. 23 (1824)

[Livingston and Fulton had received from the New York legislature a monopoly for steamboat navigation within the jurisdictional waters of the state. Ogden was assigned the privilege of operating vessels between New York City and Elizabethtown, New Jersey. He subsequently sought to enjoin Gibbons, who operated under a federal license based on an act of Congress, from trading in the same waters. Gibbons appealed from an affirmance of a decree issuing the injunction.]

Chief Justice MARSHALL delivered the opinion of the Court.

The appellant contends that this decree is erroneous, because the laws which purport to give the exclusive privilege it sustains, are repugnant to the constitution and laws of the United States.

. . . .

The words are: "Congress shall have power to regulate commerce with foreign nations, and among the several states, and with the Indian tribes."

The subject to be regulated is commerce; and our constitution being, as was aptly said at the bar, one of enumeration, and not of definition, to ascertain the extent of the power it becomes necessary to settle the meaning of the word. The counsel for the appellee would limit it to traffic, to buying and selling, or the interchange of commodities, and do not admit that it comprehends navigation. This would restrict a general term, applicable to many objects, to one of its significations. Commerce, undoubtedly, is traffic, but it is something more; it is intercourse. It describes the commercial intercourse between nations, and parts of nations, in all its branches, and is regulated by prescribing rules for carrying on that intercourse. The mind can scarcely conceive a system for regulating commerce between nations, which shall exclude all laws concerning navigation, which shall be silent on the admission of the vessels of the one nation into the ports of the other, and be confined to prescribing rules for the conduct of individuals, in the actual employment of buying and selling, or of barter.

If commerce does not include navigation, the government of the Union has no direct power over that subject, and can make no law prescribing what shall constitute American vessels, or requiring that they shall be navigated by American seamen. Yet this power has been exercised from the commencement of the government, has been exercised with the consent of all, and has been understood by all to be a commercial regulation. All America understands, and has uniformly understood, the word "commerce" to comprehend navigation. It was so understood, and must have been so understood, when the constitution was framed. The power over commerce, including navigation, was one of the primary objects for which the people of America adopted their government, and must have been contemplated in forming it. The convention must have used the word in that sense; because all have understood it in that sense, and the attempt to restrict it comes too late.

. . . .

The word used in the constitution, then, comprehends, and has been always understood to comprehend, navigation within its meaning; and a power to regulate navigation is as expressly granted as if that term had been added to the word "commerce."

To what commerce does this power extend? The constitution informs us, to commerce "with foreign nations, and among the several states, and with the Indian tribes."

It has, we believe, been universally admitted that these words comprehend every species of commercial intercourse between the United States and foreign nations. . . .

If this be the admitted meaning of the word, in its application to foreign nations, it must carry the same meaning throughout the sentence, and remain a unit, unless there be some plain intelligible cause which alters it.

The subject to which the power is next applied, is to commerce "among the several states." The word "among" means intermingled with. A thing which is among others, is intermingled with them. Commerce among the states cannot stop at the external boundary line of each state, but may be introduced into the interior.

It is not intended to say that these words comprehend that commerce which is completely internal, which is carried on between man and man in a state, or between different parts of the same state, and which does not extend to or affect other states. Such a power would be inconvenient, and is certainly unnecessary.

Comprehensive as the word "among" is, it may very properly be restricted to that commerce which concerns more states than one. The phrase is not one which would probably have been selected to indicate the completely interior traffic of a state, because it is not an apt phrase for that purpose; and the enumeration of the particular classes of commerce to which the power was to be extended, would not have been made had the intention been to extend the power to every description. The enumeration presupposes something not enumerated; and that something, if we regard the language or the subject of the sentence, must be the exclusively internal commerce of a state. The genius and character of the whole government seem to be, that its action is to be applied to all the external concerns of the nation, and to those internal concerns which affect the states generally; but not to those which are completely within a particular state, which do not affect other states, and with which it is not necessary to interfere, for the purpose of executing some of the general powers of the government. The completely internal commerce of a state, then, may be considered as reserved for the state itself.

But, in regulating commerce with foreign nations, the power of Congress does not stop at the jurisdictional lines of the several states. It would be a very useless power if it could not pass those lines. The commerce of the United States with foreign nations, is that of the whole United States. Every district has a right to participate in it. The deep streams which penetrate our country in every direction, pass through the interior of almost every state in the Union, and furnish the means of exercising this right. If Congress has the power to regulate it, that power must be exercised whenever the subject exists. If it exists within the states, if a foreign voyage may commence or terminate at a port within a state, then the power of Congress may be exercised within a state.

. . . .

We are now arrived at the inquiry, What is this power?

It is the power to regulate; that is, to prescribe the rule by which commerce is to be governed. This power, like all others vested in Congress, is complete in itself, may be exercised to its utmost extent, and acknowledges no limitations, other than are prescribed in the constitution. These are expressed in plain terms, and do not affect the questions which arise in this case, or which have been discussed at the bar. If, as has always been understood, the sovereignty of Congress, though limited to specified objects, is plenary as to those objects, the power over commerce with foreign nations, and among the several states, is vested in Congress as absolutely as it would be in a single government, having in its constitution the same restrictions on the exercise of the power as are found in the constitution of the United States. The wisdom and the discretion of Congress, their identity with the people, and the influence which their constituents possess at elections, are, in this, as in many other instances, as that, for example, of declaring war, the sole restraints on which they have relied, to secure them from its abuse. They are the restraints on which the people most often rely solely, in all representative governments.

The power of Congress, then, comprehends navigation within the limits of every state in the Union; so far as that navigation may be, in any manner, connected with "commerce with foreign nations, or among the several states, or with the Indian tribes." It may, of consequence, pass the jurisdictional line of New York, and act upon the very waters to which the prohibition now under consideration applies.

. . . .

[Those sections of Chief Justice Marshall's opinion and Justice Johnson's concurrence dealing with the power of the states to regulate the subject matter of interstate commerce are set forth below in text, p. 245.]

---

## NOTES

### What Is "Commerce"?

1. Counsel for the appellant in *Gibbons v. Ogden* argued that commerce should be limited to "traffic, to buying and selling or to the exchange of commodities," and not "navigation." Marshall rejected this argument and gave a broad definition to the term commerce. To accept the appellants' argument would, said Marshall, "restrict a general term, applicable to many objects, to one of its significations. Commerce is undoubtedly traffic, but it is something more—it is intercourse." For the Chief Justice "the word used in the Constitution . . . comprehends, and has been always understood to comprehend, navigation within its meaning. . . ."

Is such a broad definition of the term appropriate? After examining the debates at the Constitutional Convention, one commentator concluded that "[t]he inclusion of the subject-matter 'navigation' within the 'commerce' whose regulation was confided to Congress was thus conspicuously brought to the attention of all concerned at various stages in the formulation and adoption of the Constitution, was never objected to as an erroneous interpretation of the power, and in the upshot won wide acquiescense." Abel, *The Commerce Clause in the Constitutional Convention and in Contemporary Comment*, 25 MINN. L. REV. 432, 456 (1941). In Samuel Johnson's Dictionary of the English Language, the authoritative dictionary of the period, the primary definition of commerce is "intercourse."

2.    Besides navigation and trade, what other activities can be included in the term "commerce"? Since *Gibbons,* commerce has been held to include the transportation of people and goods, whether or not a business transaction is involved (Hoke v. United States, 227 U.S. 308 (1913); United States v. Hill, 248 U.S. 420 (1919); Edwards v. California, 314 U.S. 160 (1941)), communication by means of mail or telegraph; (Western Union Tel. Co. v. Lenroot, 323 U.S. 490 (1945)), traffic in intangibles such as electricity (Electric Bond & Share Co. v. Securities & Exchange Comm'n, 303 U.S. 419 (1938)), lottery tickets (Lottery Case (Champion v. Ames) 188 U.S. 321 (1903)), and information (Associated Press v. United States, 326 U.S. 1 (1945)). *See generally* Carpenter & Mardian, *What Is Commerce?*, 22 SO. CAL. L. REV. 398 (1949). But as will be discussed below, the courts have been reluctant to include manufacturing, production, mining, etc., as a part of "commerce."

3.    In Paul v. Virginia, 75 U.S. (8 Wall.) 168 (1869), the court had held that contracts of insurance were not articles of commerce. But in United States v. South-Eastern Underwriters Ass'n, 322 U.S. 533, 549-50, 553 (1944), the court, declared: "Not only . . . may transactions be commerce though non-commercial; they may be commerce though illegal and sporadic, and though they do not utilize common carriers or concern the flow of anything more tangible than electrons and information. . . . No commercial enterprise of any kind which conducts its activities across state lines has been held to be wholly beyond the regulatory power of Congress under the Commerce Clause. We cannot make an exception of the business of insurance."

4.    Is Chief Justice Marshall's limitation of commerce to "commercial intercourse" proper given the allocation of powers by the Constitutional Convention? If the commerce clause is to serve its functions, is such a limitation viable? In fact, the dis-

tinction has been rejected and commerce covers all species of movement regardless of profit or business motive.

### What Is "Commerce . . . among the several States"?

5. According to Marshall in *Gibbons*, "the word 'among' means intermingled with." Commerce which is among the several states "cannot stop at the external boundary line of each state, but may be introduced into the interior." The term, however, does not comprehend commerce which is "completely internal" and "may very properly be restricted to that commerce which concerns more states than one."

Would this formulation permit Congress to regulate transactions even if there is no movement "between" states? Note that the Constitution does not use the word "interstate commerce." Could Congress regulate even local activity if it "concerns more states than one?" What was it that the Constitutional Convention sought to achieve in its division between federal and state powers, in its allocation of the commerce power to the national government?

6. In The Daniel Ball, 77 U.S. (10 Wall.) 557 (1871), the court held that a vessel operating solely on the waters of Michigan's Grand River, exclusively within Michigan's borders, was nevertheless within the scope of Congress' regulatory powers because the ship "was employed in transporting goods destined for other states or goods brought from without the limits of Michigan and destined to places within that state. . . ." The court concluded that the ship "was employed as an instrument of [commerce between the States]; for whenever a commodity has begun to move as an article of trade from one State to another, commerce in that commodity between the States has commenced. The fact that several different and independent agencies are employed in transporting the commodity, some acting entirely in one State, and some acting through two or more States, does in no respect affect the character of the transaction. To the extent in which each agency acts in that transportation, it is subject to the regulation of Congress."

7. Professor William Crosskey in his iconoclastic work POLITICS AND THE CONSTITUTION IN THE HISTORY OF THE UNITED STATES (1953), considers Marshall's formulation of the constitutional grant far too narrow. Crosskey's thesis is that the commerce clause was designed to cover all gainful activity carried on by the people of the various states. Under this interpretation the commerce power would be all-inclusive and no distinction between intra and interstate commerce could lie. For a more complete

treatment of the Crosskey thesis, see Symposium, 21 U. CHI. L. REV. 1-92 (1953); Symposium, 54 COLUM. L. REV. 439-83 (1954).

8. Whatever the merits of these respective positions, the courts, while using Justice Marshall's language, have frequently adopted a territorial approach to the meaning of the "interstate commerce" clause. The term "among" has become "between" and the courts have required a showing of movement across state lines in order to constitute interstate commerce. As you read the materials below, consider the following: "For if 'among' the states had continued to be construed as covering all commercial transactions affecting more than one state and not merely as transactions 'between' states, there would have been no need for the various 'affectation' doctrines of recent years under which the commerce power has been expanded to reach intrastate activities." Stern, *The Scope of the Phrase Interstate Commerce*, 41 A.B.A.J. 823 (1955), SELECTED ESSAYS 298, 301 (1963).

## What Does the Power to Regulate Mean?

9. What does Chief Justice Marshall mean, when he refers to the regulatory power of Congress as "plenary"? Would it include the power to prohibit or restrict the movement of goods in commerce? *See* text, p. 177. Are there any doctrinal limits on Congress' power over "commerce . . . among the states?" If not, what of the values of limited government? Of federalism? Can political processes provide adequate protection to these values if Marshall's broad interpretation of the commerce clause is accepted?

### Introduction: Framing the Modern Interstate Commerce Power

Little opportunity to apply Chief Justice Marshall's broad organic theory of commerce, or his expansive concept of national power, arose during most of the nineteenth century. Cases arising under the commerce clause presented essentially issues involving the power of the states to regulate the subject matter of interstate commerce. There was little perceived need or demand for positive federal legislation in the still-nascent national economy and hence no opportunity for judicial review of congressional action. But in the latter part of the century, economic conditions changed. It was the era of the great trusts with interlocking components transcending state lines. Cross-continental railroads made state regulation of transportation hopelessly inadequate. Changing economic conditions produced an increasing demand for national intervention.

Congressional action came initially through the Interstate Commerce Act of 1887 and the Sherman Anti-Trust Act of 1890.

But this legislation affected rate fixing practices, contracts, combinations and monopolistic activity which arguably occurred locally and was thus subject to state regulation. And, in the modern era of the positive state, Congress is actively involved in the management of the national economy. The question has been whether Congress' power to regulate "commerce . . . among the States" provided sufficient constitutional nexus to make this legislation effective.

And apart from the problem of the economy, there have been pressing social, moral, health and safety concerns, such as the use of child labor, gambling, obscenity, the white slave traffic, industrial safety, unsafe and impure products. Again, the problems have transcended state lines and the states individually either could not or would not act. Although there was a demand for social reform through federal legislation in the latter part of the nineteenth century, it was during the progressive era in the early twentieth century that the demand for federal intervention became especially intense. And again the national government responded through the enactment of social welfare legislation— the Pure Food and Drug Law of 1906, the Meat Inspection Acts of 1906 and 1907, the White Slave Traffic Act of 1910, and the Child Labor Act of 1916. But this legislation involved some of the most established preserves of state power. Could the commerce clause do the job?

In the modern era, a major concern has been with preserving civil rights and liberties, with assuring equal treatment to citizens generally. When the states separately either could not or would not legislate against discrimination, the demand for federal intervention again arose. The 1964 Civil Rights Act constitutes the most comprehensive modern attempt to legislate equal treatment in this country. But its provisions often involve matters thought by many to lie in the domain of the states, e.g., discrimination in places of public accommodation. Could the commerce clause provide a constitutional nexus for this exercise of national power?

In modern society, local problems increasingly become national problems. Crime does not recognize artificial state boundaries but crime control has been a traditional prerogative of the states. State regulation has proven inadequate to the problems of organized crime, kidnapping, terrorism, etc., which frequently involve a number of jurisdictions. Crime generally adversely affects business conditions and arguably the level of interstate commerce. Again the questions arise: how can these problems be met consistent with the principles and values of federalism? To what extent does the commerce clause provide a jurisdictional nexus for national intervention federalizing criminal law? If the national government may act, is any local crime excluded from potential federal supervision? Are limits to be found through judicial review or political processes?

In each of the above areas, there is a pervasive issue: under what circumstances, if any, can the national government regulate "local" activities pursuant to its power to regulate "commerce . . . among the States"? And in each of the above areas the judiciary was called upon to provide an answer. The next four sections deal with its response to this general problem.

## C. ACHIEVING SOCIAL WELFARE OBJECTIVES THROUGH THE COMMERCE CLAUSE: A NATIONAL POLICE POWER?

The police power has been defined as a power which " 'aims directly to secure and promote the public welfare' by subjecting to restraint or compulsion the members of the community. It is the power by which the government abridges the freedom of action or the free use of property of the individual in order that the [public] welfare . . . may not be jeopardized." Cushman, *The National Police Power Under the Commerce Clause of the Constitution*, 3 MINN. L. REV. 289, 290 (1919), 3 Selected Essays 36, 39 (1938). The Constitution does not grant Congress the power to enact legislation for the national morals, health, safety, and well-being and four resolutions seeking to confer such a power were rejected at the Constitutional Convention. 1 FARRAND, RECORDS OF THE FEDERAL CONVENTION OF 1787 299 (1911); Vol. 2, pp. 25, 26, 367. Consequently, it is arguable that the police power protection is exclusively the responsibility of the states and that the federal government cannot legislate for social welfare objectives.

But with the rapid expansion of the nation and interstate movement in the late nineteenth century, states were increasingly incapable of dealing with interstate problems on a local basis. There was increasing support for the proposition that when the states are incapable of acting because of the national character of a problem, then the federal government, as representative of all the people, must have the power to act. Nevertheless attempts to enact such police power regulations by Congress were rejected. *See, e.g.,* United States v. DeWitt, 76 U.S. (9 Wall.) 41 (1870); Trade-Mark Cases, 100 U.S. (10 Otto) 82 (1879).

Further, in dicta in *McCulloch*, Chief Justice Marshall had indicated that Congress could not "under the pretext of executing its powers, pass laws for the accomplishment of objects not entrusted to the government." But he had also indicated that

Congress possesses not only those powers expressly delegated, but also those necessary and proper to the effectuation of the granted powers and had defined the regulatory power of Congress in extremely broad terms. Could Congress pursuant to its granted power to regulate interstate commerce, legislate to achieve national social welfare objectives which are not within its powers? Could Congress, pursuant to its regulatory powers, *prohibit* the movement in interstate commerce of undesirable objects, not so much because of any tangible harm to commerce itself, but because they are deemed injurious to the national well-being? Could Congress prevent commerce from being used for ends *it* determines to be socially undesirable?

-----

### CHAMPION v. AMES
### (THE LOTTERY CASE)
Supreme Court of the United States
188 U.S. 321, 47 L. Ed. 492, 23 S. Ct. 321 (1903)

[Appellant was arrested and indicted for violation of the Federal Lottery Act of 1895, prohibiting the importation, mailing, or interstate transit of lottery tickets. He appealed from an order of the Circuit Court dismissing a writ of habeas corpus, based on the alleged unconstitutionality of the federal statute. The importance and difficulty of the question presented is suggested by the fact that the case was argued three times before the Supreme Court, and the Court, in upholding the constitutionality of the Act, divided 5-4.]

Justice HARLAN delivered the opinion of the Court.

. . . .

If a state, when considering legislation for the suppression of lotteries within its own limits, may properly take into view the evils that inhere in the raising of money, in that mode, why may not Congress, invested with the power to regulate commerce among the several states, provide that such commerce shall not be polluted by the carrying of lottery tickets from one state to another? In this connection it must not be forgotten that the power of Congress to regulate commerce among the states is plenary, is complete in itself, and is subject to no limitations except such as may be found in the Constitution. What provision in that instrument can be regarded as limiting the exercise of the power granted? What clause can be cited which, in any degree, countenances the suggestion that one may, of right, carry or cause to be carried from one state to another that which will harm the public morals? . . . [S]urely it will not be said to be a part of anyone's liberty, as recognized by the supreme law of the land, that he shall be allowed to introduce into commerce among the states an element that will be confessedly injurious to the public morals.

If it be said that the act of 1895 is inconsistent with the 10th Amendment, reserving to the states respectively, or to the people, the powers not delegated to the United States, the answer is that the power to regulate commerce among the states has been expressly delegated to Congress.

. . . .

---

## NOTES

1. Whatever the merits of the constitutional argument in the *Lottery Case*, it provided the doctrinal foundation for an outpouring of congressional social welfare legislation which was then legitimated by the courts. This included legislation dealing with the white slave traffic (Hoke v. United States, 227 U.S. 308 (1913)), impure food and drugs (Hipolite Egg Co. v. United States, 220 U.S. 45 (1911); Weeks v. United States, 245 U.S. 618 (1918)); shipment of prize fight films (Weber v. Freed, 239 U.S. 325 (1915)). But then came *Hammer v. Dagenhart.*

### HAMMER v. DAGENHART
Supreme Court of the United States
247 U.S. 251, 62 L. Ed. 1101, 38 S. Ct. 529 (1918)

Justice DAY delivered the opinion of the Court.

A bill was filed in the United States district court for the western district of North Carolina by a father in his own behalf and as next friend of his two minor sons, one under the age of fourteen years and the other between the ages of fourteen and sixteen years, employees in a cotton mill at Charlotte, North Carolina, to enjoin the enforcement of the act of Congress intended to prevent interstate commerce in the products of child labor.

The district court held the act unconstitutional and entered a decree enjoining its enforcement. . . .

. . . .

The attack upon the act rests upon three propositions: First. It is not a regulation of interstate and foreign commerce. Second. It contravenes the 10th Amendment to the Constitution. Third. It conflicts with the 5th Amendment to the Constitution.

The controlling question for decision is: Is it within the authority of Congress in regulating commerce among the states to prohibit the transportation in interstate commerce of manufactured goods, the product of a factory in which, within thirty days prior to their removal therefrom, children under the age of fourteen have been employed or permitted to work, or children between the ages of fourteen and sixteen years have been employed or permitted to work more than eight hours in any day, or more than six days in any week, or after the hour of 7 o'clock P. M. or before the hour of 6 o'clock A. M.?

. . . .

In *Gibbons v. Ogden*, Chief Justice Marshall, speaking for this court, and defining the extent and nature of the commerce power, said: "It is the power to regulate,—that is, to prescribe the rule by which commerce is to be governed." In other words, the power is one to control the means by which commerce is carried on, which is directly the contrary of the assumed right to forbid commerce from moving and thus destroy it as to particular commodities. But it is insisted that adjudged cases in this court establish the doctrine that the power to regulate given to Congress incidentally includes the authority to prohibit the movement of ordinary commodities, and therefore that the subject is not open for discussion. The cases demonstrate the contrary. They rest upon the character of the particular subjects dealt with and the fact that the scope of governmental authority, state or national, possessed over them, is such that the authority to prohibit is, as to them, but the exertion of the power to regulate.

[The Court summarized the holdings of the *Lottery Case* and its progeny noted above.]

In each of these instances the use of interstate transportation was necessary to the accomplishment of harmful results. In other words, although the power over interstate transportation was to regulate, that could only be accomplished by prohibiting the use of the facilities of interstate commerce to effect the evil intended.

This element is wanting in the present case. The thing intended to be accomplished by this statute is the denial of the facilities of interstate commerce to those manufacturers in the states who employ children within the prohibited ages. The act in its effect does not regulate transportation among the states, but aims to standardize the ages at which children may be employed in mining and manufacturing within the states. The goods shipped are of themselves harmless. The act permits them to be freely shipped after thirty days from the time of their removal from the factory. When offered for shipment, and before transportation begins, the labor of their production is over, and the mere fact that they were intended for interstate commerce transportation does not make their production subject to Federal control under the commerce power.

. . . .

Over interstate transportation, or its incidents, the regulatory power of Congress is ample, but the production of articles intended for interstate commerce is a matter of local regulation. . . . If it were otherwise, all manufacture intended for interstate shipment would be brought under Federal control to the practical exclusion of the authority of the states,—a result certainly not contemplated by the framers of the Constitution when they vested in Congress the authority to regulate commerce among the states. Kidd v. Pearson, 128 U.S. 1 (1888).

It is further contended that the authority of Congress may be exerted to control interstate commerce in the shipment of child-made goods because of the effect of the circulation of such goods in other states where the evil of this class of labor has been recognized by local legislation, and the right to thus employ child labor has been more rigorously restrained than in the state of production. In other words, that the unfair competition thus engendered may be controlled by closing the channels of interstate commerce to manufacturers in those states where the local laws do not meet what Congress deems to be the more just standard of other states.

There is no power vested in Congress to require the states to exercise their police power so as to prevent possible unfair competition. Many causes may co-operate to give one state, by reason of local laws or conditions, an economic advantage over others. The commerce clause was not intended to give to Congress a general authority to equalize such conditions. In some of the states laws have been passed fixing minimum wages for women; in others the local law regulates the hours of labor of women in various employments. Business done in such states may be at an economic disadvantage when compared with states which have no such regulations; surely, this fact does not give Congress the power to deny transportation in interstate commerce to those who carry on business where the hours of labor and the rate of compensation for women have not been fixed by a standard in the use in other states and approved by Congress.

The grant of power to Congress over the subject of interstate commerce was to enable it to regulate such commerce, and not to give it authority to control the states in their exercise of the police power over local trade and manufacture.

The grant of authority over a purely Federal matter was not intended to destroy the local power always existing and carefully reserved to the states in the 10th Amendment to the Constitution.

Police regulations relating to the internal trade and affairs of the states have been uniformly recognized as within such control. . . .

. . . .

. . . The maintenance of the authority of the states over matters purely local is as essential to the preservation of our institutions as is the conservation of the supremacy of the Federal power in all matters intrusted to the nation by the Federal Constitution.

. . . To sustain this statute would not be, in our judgment, a recognition of the lawful exertion of congressional authority over interstate commerce, but would sanction an invasion by the Federal power of the control of a matter purely local in its character, and over which no authority has been delegated to Congress in conferring the power to regulate commerce among the states.

We have neither authority nor disposition to question the motives of Congress in enacting this legislation. The purposes intended must be attained consistently with constitutional limitations, and not by an invasion of the powers of the states. . . .

. . . The far-reaching result of upholding the act cannot be more plainly indicated than by pointing out that if Congress can thus regulate matters intrusted to local authority by prohibition of the movement of commodities in interstate commerce, all freedom of commerce will be at an end, and the power of the states over local matters may be eliminated, and thus our system of government be practically destroyed.

For these reasons we hold that this law exceeds the constitutional authority of Congress. It follows that the decree of the District Court must be affirmed.

Justice HOLMES, dissenting:

. . . The objection urged against the power is that the states have exclusive control over their methods of production and that Congress cannot meddle with them; and taking the proposition in the sense of direct intermeddling I agree to it and suppose that no one denies it. But if an act is within the powers specifically conferred upon Congress, it seems to me that it is not made any less constitutional because of the indirect effects that it may have, however obvious it may be that it will have those effects; and that we are not at liberty upon such grounds to hold it void.

The first step in my argument is to make plain what no one is likely to dispute,—that the statute in question is within the power expressly given to Congress if considered only as to its immediate effects, and that if invalid it is so only upon some collateral ground. The statute confines itself to prohibiting the carriage of certain goods in interstate or foreign commerce. Congress is given power to regulate such commerce in unqualified terms. It would not be argued today that the power to regulate does not include the power to prohibit. Regulation means the prohibition of something, and when interstate commerce is the matter to be regulated I cannot doubt that the regulations may prohibit any part of such commerce that Congress sees fit to forbid. . . .

The question, then, is narrowed to whether the exercise of its otherwise constitutional power by Congress can be pronounced unconstitutional because of its possible reaction upon the conduct of the states in a matter upon which I have admitted that they are free from direct control. I should have thought that that matter had been disposed of so fully as to leave no room for doubt. I should have thought that the most conspicuous decisions of this court had made it clear that the power to regulate commerce and other constitutional powers could not be cut down or qualified by the fact that it might interfere with the carrying out of the domestic policy of any state.

. . . .

. . . It does not matter whether the supposed evil precedes or follows the transportation. It is enough that, in the opinion of Congress, the transportation encourages the evil. I may add that in the cases on the so-called White Slave Act it was established that the means adopted by Congress as convenient to the exercise of its power might have the character of police regulations. . . .

The notion that prohibition is any less prohibition when applied to things now thought evil I do not understand. But if there is any matter upon which civilized countries have agreed,—far more unanimously than they have with regard to intoxicants and some other matters over which this country is now emotionally aroused,—it is the evil of premature and excessive child labor. I should have thought that if we were to introduce our own moral conceptions where, in my opinion, they do not belong, this was pre-eminently a case for upholding the exercise of all its powers by the United States.

But I had thought that the propriety of the exercise of a power admitted to exist in some cases was for the consideration of Congress alone, and that this court always had disavowed the right to intrude its judgment upon questions of policy or morals. . . .

The act does not meddle with anything belonging to the states. They may regulate their internal affairs and their domestic commerce as they like. But when they seek to send their products across the state line they are no longer within their rights. If there were no Constitution and no Congress their power to cross the line would depend upon their neighbors. Under the Constitution such commerce belongs not to the states, but to Congress to regulate. It may carry out its views of public policy whatever indirect effect they may have upon the activities of the states. Instead of being encountered by a prohibitive tariff at her boundaries, the state encounters the public policy of the United States which it is for Congress to express. The public policy of the United States is shaped with a view to the benefit of the nation as a whole. If, as has been the case within the memory of men still living, a state should take a different view of the propriety of sustaining a lottery from that which generally prevails, I cannot believe that the fact would require a different decision from that reached in *Champion v. Ames*. Yet in that case it would be said with quite as much force as in this that Congress was attempting to intermeddle with the state's domestic affairs. The national welfare as understood by Congress may require a different attitude within its sphere from that of some self-seeking state. It seems to me entirely constitutional for Congress to enforce its understanding by all the means at its command.

Justice McKENNA, Justice BRANDEIS, and Justice CLARKE concur in this opinion.

---

## NOTES

1. Isn't it reasonable that the power to regulate commerce includes some incidental power to prohibit the movement of goods? "[A] modicum of reflection must suffice to show that any regulation whatsoever of commerce necessarily infers some measure of power to prohibit it, since it is the very nature of regulation to lay down terms on which the activity regulated will be permitted and for non-compliance with which it will not be permitted." Corwin, *Congress' Power to Prohibit Commerce: A Crucial Constitutional Issue,* 18 CORNELL L.Q. 477 (1933), 3 SELECTED ESSAYS 103, 104-05 (1938). Further it would seem reasonable that Congress could enact police power-type legislation for the well-being of commercial activity itself, *e.g.,* safety statutes.

2. In sustaining the Mann Act prohibiting the transportation of women and girls across state lines for immoral purposes, the court in Hoke v. United States, 227 U.S. 308 (1913), provided an especially broad statement of Congress' emerging police power: "[S]urely if the facility of interstate transportation can be taken away from the demoralization of lotteries, the debasement of obscene literature, the contagion of diseased cattle or persons, the impurity of food and drugs, the like facility can be taken away from the systematic inticement to and the enslavement in prosti-

tution and the debauchery of women, and more insistently of girls. . . .

"The principle established by the cases is the simple one, when rid of confusing and distracting considerations, that Congress has power over transportation 'among the several States'; that the power is complete in itself, and that Congress, as an incident to it, may adopt not only means necessary but convenient to its exercise, and the means may have the quality of police regulations." *See* Caminetti v. United States, 242 U.S. 470 (1917).

In the *Lottery Case,* Justice Harlan referred to the congressional act as "a regulation of commerce among the several states" and seemed to focus his analysis on the commerce clause itself. *Hoke* changes this focus. The justification for the federal police power regulations in *Hoke* is centered instead in the necessary and proper clause. Does it matter which clause is used?

3. *Prohibition as Interstate Commerce Regulation.* Justice Day for the court in *Hammer* asserts that the power to regulate is "directly the contrary of the assumed right to forbid commerce from moving and thus destroying it as to particular commodities." Mr. Justice Day seeks to distinguish the prior "police power" cases on the basis of "the character of the particular subjects dealt with. . . ." Is the focus of the court on the harmful character of the goods shipped or on a finding that "the use of interstate transportation was necessary to the accomplishment of harmful results?" Why is the character of the *subject* of regulation relevant? What is the constitutional basis for such a limitation on Congress' regulatory power? Should it matter whether the "evil" precedes or follows interstate transportation? Note that Justice Day describes the interstate commerce power in terms of "transportation" rather than "traffic."

Assuming the relevance of the character of the subject, who is to evaluate the harm, the court or Congress? What is the justification for limiting the "plenary" power of Congress to regulate interstate commerce? *See* Powell, *The Child Labor Law, the Tenth Amendment and the Commerce Clause,* 3 SOUTHERN L.Q. 175 (1918), 3 SELECTED ESSAYS 314, 324 (1938), claiming that *Hammer* "is built upon a due process distinction and then unwarrantably transferred to the commerce clause." But, it may be argued that the dissenting opinion of Justice Holmes fails to provide any limitation on the "police power" of Congress.

It has been argued that "[i]t is only because the transportation is necessary to the employment, that the court can urge that the prohibition of the transportation regulates the conditions of employment. If interstate transportation were not necessary to the harmful results of child labor, no employer of children would object when the transportation was forbidden." Powell, *The Child Labor Law*, 3 SELECTED ESSAYS, at 331.

4. *Regulating Interstate Competition.* Justice Day asserts that "[t]he commerce clause was not intended to give Congress a general authority to equalize economic conditions." The court has repeatedly held that a state cannot enact legislation designed to give its producers a competitive advantage against out of state competition. "Why then should not Congress exercise the power which, after all, the Constitution confers upon *it* and not upon the Court, with the same objective in mind, and thereby equalize, if it can, conditions of competition among the states according to *its* view of sound social policy?" Corwin, *Congress' Power to Prohibit Commerce: A Crucial Constitutional Issue*, 18 CORNELL L.Q. 477, 496 (1933), 3 SELECTED ESSAYS 103, 121 (1938).

5. *Effect and Purpose.* The court in *Hammer* concludes that the "effect" of the Child Labor Act is to regulate the age at which children may be employed in production, which occurs prior to transportation, and is "a matter of local regulation." But an improper local "effect" should not obviate an otherwise constitutional regulation. Such a result would hardly be consistent with the supremacy clause.

Justice Day is in fact driven to probe the purpose of the congressional legislation. The attempt of the court in *Hammer* to make the validity of congressional legislation turn on the character of the harm necessitates a probe of purpose.

6. *Dual Federalism and the Tenth Amendment.* Does the police power of the states to regulate production, mining, manufacturing, etc., limit the interstate commerce power of Congress? Is this the effect of the tenth amendment? The doctrine that state powers limit the national power, which has been characterized as "dual federalism," appears to have been accepted as early as the Taney Court. A. MASON, THE SUPREME COURT: PALLADIUM OF FREEDOM 116-18 (1962). Its essentials include: "1. The national government is one of enumerated powers only; 2. Also the purposes which it may constitutionally promote are few; 3. Within their respective spheres the two centers of government are 'sovereign' and hence 'equal'; 4. The relation of the two centers with each other is one of tension rather than collaboration." Corwin, *The Passing of Dual Federalism*, 36 VA. L. REV. 1, 4 (1950).

Note that Justice Day in *Hammer* intruded the word "expressly" into the tenth amendment. The Constitutional Convention twice rejected proposals for such a revision. Compare the court's defense of "dual federalism" in *Hammer* with the first Justice Harlan's treatment of the tenth amendment in the *Lottery Case*. James Madison spoke critically against making the tenth amendment the touchstone of federal legislative power: "Interference with the power of the States was no constitutional criterion of the power of Congress. If the power was not given, Congress could not exercise it; if given, they might exercise it, although it should interfere with the laws, or even the Constitution of the States." ANNALS OF CONGRESS 1897 (1791). A year after *Hammer*, a unan-imous court in Hamilton v. Kentucky Distilleries Co., 251 U.S. 146, 156 (1919), appeared to treat the tenth amendment as a mere residual power: "That the United States lacks the police power, and that this was reserved to the States by the Tenth Amendment, is true. But it is none the less true that when the United States exerts any of the powers conferred upon it by the Constitution, no valid objection can be based upon the fact that such exercise may be attended by the same incidents which attend the exercise by a State of its police power."

Contrary to the dual federalist position, the tenth amendment has been described as a corollary of the supremacy clause in Art. VI, § 2: "[A]ll that the Tenth Amendment signifies is a *specific* recognition of the fact *implied* by Article VI itself, that the States possess certain legislative power. In the exercise of these they may perchance transgress the Constitution, an act of Congress in pursuance thereof, or a treaty made under the authority of the United States. But when this happens, the pertinent provision of the Constitution is no longer the Tenth Amendment, but Article VI, Paragraph 2." E. CORWIN, NATIONAL SUPREMACY: TREATY POWER V. STATE POWER 86 (1913).

**7.** *A Constitutional Vacuum?* There are a number of cases holding that state regulations prohibiting the shipment of com-modities into the state are an unconstitutional interference with Congress' power over interstate commerce. It has been suggested that this principle, when joined to the *Child Labor Case*, estab-lishes that if a state legislature enacts legislation prohibiting the introduction of goods into that state "it is a regulation of inter-state commerce and invalid, whereas if Congress is the enacting body, it is not a regulation of interstate commerce, and invalid. It is difficult to believe that the adoption of the Constitution has left this great void of governmental authority." Gordon, *The Child Labor Law Case,* 32 HARV. L. REV. 45 (1918), 3 SELECTED ESSAYS 51-52 (1938).

As has previously been indicated, a primary motive in the adoption of the commerce clause was the elimination of economic rivalry which characterized the Confederation period. Under the Articles of Confederation, the states had the express right of prohibiting "the exportation or importation of any species of goods or commodities whatever." If the states surrendered this regulatory power doesn't it necessarily follow that Congress must have the power to prevent a vacuum of regulatory power? Sutherland, *The Child Labor Cases and the Constitution,* 8 CORNELL L. REV. 338, 348 (1923).

8. *The Child Labor Tax Case.* Congress sought to circumvent the decision of *Hammer v. Dagenhart* by enacting a statute imposing a prohibitory tax upon manufacturers employing child labor. In Bailey v. Drexel Furniture Co. (The Child Labor Tax Case), 259 U.S. 20 (1922), Justice Taft for eight members of the court, including three out of the four dissenters in *Hammer* (Holmes, Brandeis and McKenna), held the tax unconstitutional. *See* text, p. 226.

## UNITED STATES v. DARBY
Supreme Court of the United States
312 U.S. 100, 85 L. Ed. 609, 61 S. Ct. 451 (1941)

Justice STONE delivered the opinion of the Court.

The two principal questions raised by the record in this case are, *first,* whether Congress has constitutional power to prohibit the shipment in interstate commerce of lumber manufactured by employees whose wages are less than a prescribed minimum or whose weekly hours of labor at that wage are greater than a prescribed maximum, and, *second,* whether it has power to prohibit the employment of workmen in the production of goods "for interstate commerce" at other than prescribed wages and hours. . . .

. . . .

The Fair Labor Standards Act set up a comprehensive legislative scheme for preventing the shipment in interstate commerce of certain products and commodities produced in the United States under labor conditions as respects wages and hours which fail to conform to standards set up by the Act. . . .

. . . .

The indictment charges that appellee is engaged, in the state of Georgia, in the business of acquiring raw materials, which he manufactures into finished lumber with the intent, when manufactured, to ship it in interstate commerce to customers outside the state, and that he does in fact so ship a large part of the lumber so produced. . . .

. . . .

*The prohibition of shipment of the proscribed goods in interstate commerce.* Section 15(a) (1) prohibits, and the indictment charges, shipment in interstate commerce of goods produced for interstate commerce by employes whose wages and hours of employment do not conform to the requirements of the Act. . . . [T]he only question arising under the Commerce Clause with respect to such shipments is whether Congress has the constitutional power to prohibit them.

While manufacture is not of itself interstate commerce the shipment of manufactured goods interstate is such commerce and the prohibition of such shipment by Congress is indubitably a regulation of the commerce. The power to regulate commerce is the power "to prescribe the rule by which commerce is to be governed." *Gibbons v. Ogden.* It extends not only to those regulations which aid, foster and protect the commerce, but embraces those which prohibit it. It is conceded that the power of Congress to prohibit transportation in interstate commerce includes noxious articles, stolen articles, kidnapped persons, and articles such as intoxicating liquor or convict made goods, traffic in which is forbidden or restricted by the laws of the state of destination.

But it is said that the present prohibition falls within the scope of none of these categories; that while the prohibition is nominally a regulation of the commerce its motive or purpose is regulation of wages and hours of persons engaged in manufacture, the control of which has been reserved to the states and upon which Georgia and some of the states of destination have placed no restriction; that the effect of the present statute is not to exclude the prescribed articles from interstate commerce in aid of state regulation . . . , but instead, under the guise of a regulation of interstate commerce, it undertakes to regulate wages and hours within the state contrary to the policy of the state which has elected to leave them unregulated.

The power of Congress over interstate commerce "is complete in itself, may be exercised to its utmost extent, and acknowledges no limitations, other than are prescribed in the Constitution." Gibbons v. Ogden, supra, 9 Wheat. 196. That power can neither be enlarged nor diminished by the exercise or non-exercise of state power. Congress, following its own conception of public policy concerning the restrictions which may appropriately be imposed on interstate commerce, is free to exclude from the commerce articles whose use in the states for which they are destined it may conceive to be injurious to the public health, morals or welfare, even though the state has not sought to regulate their use.

Such regulation is not forbidden invasion of state power merely because either its motive or its consequence is to restrict the use of articles of commerce within the states of destination and is not prohibited unless by other Constitutional provisions. It is no objection to the assertion of the power to regulate interstate commerce that its exercise is attended by the same incidents which attend the exercise of the police power of the states.

The motive and purpose of the present regulation are plainly to make effective the Congressional conception of public policy that interstate commerce should not be made the instrument of competition in the distribution of goods produced under sub-standard labor conditions, which competition is injurious to the commerce and to the states from and to which the commerce flows. The motive and purpose of a regulation of interstate commerce are matters for the legislative judgment upon the exercise of which the Constitution places no restriction and over which the courts are given no control. McCray v. United States, 195 U.S. 27; Sonzinsky v. United States, 300 U.S. 506, 513. . . . Whatever their motive and purpose, regulations of commerce which do not infringe some constitutional prohibition are within the plenary power conferred on Congress by the Commerce Clause. Subject only to that limitation, presently to be considered, we conclude that the prohibition of the shipment interstate of goods produced under the forbidden substandard labor conditions is within the constitutional authority of Congress.

In the more than a century which has elapsed since the decision of *Gibbons v. Ogden,* these principles of constitutional interpretation have been so long and repeatedly recognized by this Court as applicable to the Commerce Clause, that there would be little occasion for repeating them now were it not for the decision of this Court twenty-two years ago in Hammer v. Dagenhart, 247 U.S. 251. In that case it was held by a bare majority of the Court over the powerful and now classic dissent of Mr. Justice Holmes setting forth the fundamental issues involved, that Congress was without power to exclude the products of child labor from interstate commerce. The reasoning and conclusion of the Court's opinion there cannot be reconciled with the conclusion which we have reached, that the power of Congress under the Commerce Clause is plenary to exclude any article from interstate commerce subject only to the specific prohibitions of the Constitution.

*Hammer v. Dagenhart* has not been followed. The distinction on which the decision was rested that Congressional power to prohibit interstate commerce is limited to articles which in themselves have some harmful or deleterious property—a distinction which was novel when made and unsupported by any provision of the Constitution—has long since been abandoned. The thesis of the opinion that the motive of the prohibition or its effect to control in some measure the use or production within the states of the article thus excluded from the commerce can operate to deprive the regulation of its constitutional authority has long since ceased to have force. And finally we have declared "The authority of the federal government over interstate commerce does not differ in extent or character from that retained by the states over intrastate commerce."

The conclusion is inescapable that *Hammer v. Dagenhart,* was a departure from the principles which have prevailed in the interpretation of the commerce clause both before and since the decision and that such vitality, as a precedent, as it then had has long since been exhausted. It should be and now is overruled.

*Validity of the wage and hour requirements.* Section 15(a) (2) and §§ 6 and 7 require employers to conform to the wage and hour provisions with respect to all employees engaged in the production of goods for interstate commerce. As appellee's employees are not alleged to be "engaged in interstate commerce" the validity of the prohibition turns on the question whether the employment, under other than the prescribed labor standards, of employees engaged in the production of goods for interstate commerce is so related to the commerce and so affects it as to be within the reach of the power of Congress to regulate it.

To answer this question we must at the outset determine whether the particular acts charged in the counts which are laid under § 15(a) (2) as they were construed below, constitute "production for commerce" within the meaning of the statute. . . .

Without attempting to define the precise limits of the phrase, we think the acts alleged in the indictment are within the sweep of the statute. The obvious purpose of the Act was not only to prevent the interstate transportation of the proscribed product, but to stop the initial step toward transportation, production with the purpose of so transporting it. Congress was not unaware that most manufacturing businesses shipping their product in interstate commerce make it in their shops without reference to its ultimate destination and then after manufacture select some of it for shipment interstate and some intrastate according to the daily demands of their business, and that it would be practically impossible, without disrupting manufacturing businesses, to restrict the prohibited kind of production to the particular pieces of lumber, cloth, furniture or the like which later move in interstate rather than intrastate commerce.

The recognized need of drafting a workable statute and the well known circumstances in which it was to be applied are persuasive of the conclusion, which the legislative history supports, that the "production for commerce" intended includes at least production of goods, which, at the time of production, the employer, according to the normal course of his business, intends or expects to move in interstate commerce although, through the exigencies of the business, all of the goods may not thereafter actually enter interstate commerce.

There remains the question whether such restriction on the production of goods for commerce is a permissible exercise of the commerce power. The power of Congress over interstate commerce is not confined to the regulation of commerce among the states. It extends to those activities intrastate which so affect interstate commerce or the exercise of the power of Congress over it as to make regulation of them appropriate means to the attainment of a legitimate end, the exercise of the granted power of Congress to regulate interstate commerce. See McCulloch v. Maryland, 4 Wheat. 316, 421.

. . . .

Congress, having by the present Act adopted the policy excluding from interstate commerce all goods produced for the commerce which do not conform to the specified labor standards, it may choose the means reasonably adapted to the attainment of the permitted end, even though they involve control of intrastate activities. Such legislation has often been sustained with respect to powers, other than the commerce power granted to the national government, when the means chosen, although not themselves within the granted power, were nevertheless deemed appropriate aids to the accomplishment of some purpose within an admitted power of the national government. A familiar like exercise of power is the regulation of intrastate transactions which are so commingled with or related to interstate commerce that all must be regulated if the interstate commerce is to be effectively controlled. Shreveport Case, 234 U.S. 342. . . .

We think also that § 15(a) (2), now under consideration, is sustainable independently of § 15(a) (1), which prohibits shipment or transportation of the proscribed goods. As we have said the evils aimed at by the Act are the spread of substandard labor conditions through the use of the facilities of interstate commerce for competition by the goods so produced with those produced under the prescribed or better labor conditions; and the consequent dislocation of the commerce itself caused by the impairment or destruction of local businesses by competition made effective through interstate commerce. The Act is thus directed at the suppression of a method or kind of competition in interstate commerce which it has in effect condemned as "unfair,". . . .

. . . .

Our conclusion is unaffected by the Tenth Amendment. . . . The amendment states but a truism that all is retained which has not been surrendered. There is nothing in the history of its adoption to suggest that it was more than declaratory of the relationship between the national and state governments as it had been established by the Constitution before the amendment or that its purpose was other than to allay fears that the new national government might seek to exercise powers not granted, and that the states might not be able to exercise fully their reserved powers.

From the beginning and for many years the amendment has been construed as not depriving the national government of authority to resort to all means for the exercise of a granted power which are appropriate and plainly adapted to the permitted end. Whatever doubts may have arisen of the soundness of that conclusion they have been put at rest by the decisions under the Sherman Act and the National Labor Relations Act which we have cited.

. . . .

Reversed.

## NOTES

1. *Dual Federalism and the Tenth Amendment.* Justice Stone "had waited nearly five years for an opportunity to read out of constitutional jurisprudence that mainstay of laissez faire— 'dual federalism'—the notion that the Tenth Amendment sets an independent limitation on the powers of Congress. 'I have been thinking for sometime,' he had written Charles A. Beard . . . , 'that the time might be opportune to say something in an opinion about the historic aspects of federal power. I think I shall improve the first opportunity to do something of the kind.' " A. MASON, HARLAN FISKE STONE: PILLAR OF THE LAW 553 (1956). Mason also notes that "Hughes's dismay the year before retirement is reflected in his assignment of the opinion in *U.S. v. Darby,* to Justice Stone. [For Hughes] to uphold the Fair Labor Standards Act of 1938 would be to downgrade the Tenth Amendment to what it has never been for him—'a truism.' Speaking for a unanimous court, Justice Stone ignored Hughes's refinements in the commerce cases decided since 1935, and went all the way back to John Marshall and *Gibbons v. Ogden.*" A. MASON, THE SUPREME COURT: PALLADIUM OF FREEDOM 145 (1962).

Is there anything left of the doctrine of dual federalism after *Darby* or of Chief Justice Marshall's dictum in *McCulloch* that Congress could not "under the pretext of executing its powers, pass laws for the accomplishment of objects not entrusted to the government"?

2. Congress has made frequent use of the police power rationale to fashion an ever-increasing body of federal criminal law based on its commerce powers. Do the police power cases support *any* local regulation or only regulation of interstate commerce itself? If Congress enacts criminal prohibitions on designated interstate traffic, can it legislate against intrastate activity in order to effectuate its prohibitions? *See* text, pp. 217-25.

## D. REGULATING FOR A NATIONAL ECONOMY: LOCAL ACTIVITIES AFFECTING INTERSTATE COMMERCE

While the court has departed from Chief Justice Marshall's broad definition in *Gibbons* of "commerce . . . among the states," the modern commerce power is as broad as Marshall's original conception. Today, Congress' commerce power reaches a whole range of local economic activity as the government seeks to cope with managing our complex national economy. The historical development of this broad-ranging power is discussed in D. ENGDAHL, CONSTITUTIONAL POWER: FEDERAL AND STATE IN A NUTSHELL (1974); P. BENSON, THE SUPREME COURT AND THE COMMERCE CLAUSE, 1937-1970 (1970).

### Streams of Commerce

In part, the transformation has been accomplished by a willingness to define commerce to encompass regulated local activities. For example, in Stafford v. Wallace, 258 U.S. 495 (1922), the court upheld the constitutionality of the Packers and Stockyards Act of 1921 as applied to local dealers in Chicago stockyards. The court spoke of a "stream" or "current" of commerce.

> The stockyards are not a place of rest or final destination. Thousands of head of livestock arrive daily by carload and trainload lots, and must be promptly sold and disposed of and moved out, to give place to the constantly flowing traffic that presses behind. The stockyards are but a throat through which the current flows, and the transactions which occur therein are only incident to this current from the West to the East, and from one state to another. Such transactions cannot be separated from the movement to which they contribute and necessarily take on its character.

It followed that the local activities were only a part of the interstate commerce that Congress could regulate. Citing to its earlier decision in Swift v. United States, 196 U.S. 375 (1905), the court declared:

> The application of the commerce clause of the Constitution in the Swift Case was the result of the natural development of

interstate commerce under modern conditions. It was the inevitable recognition of the great central fact that such streams of commerce from one part of the country to another, which are ever flowing, are in their very essence the commerce among the states and with foreign nations, which historically it was one of the chief purposes of the Constitution to bring under national protection and control. This Court declined to defeat this purpose in respect of such a stream and take it out of complete national regulation by a nice and technical inquiry into the noninterstate character of some of its necessary incidents and facilities, when considered alone and without reference to their association with the movement of which they were an essential but subordinate part.

If Congress could reach activities at the throat, could it similarly regulate activity at the mouth, *e.g.*, production? At the stomach, *e.g.*, sales to the consumer, use of the product?

### The Affectation Doctrine

Even if the court was unwilling to characterize an activity as part of interstate commerce, this did not necessarily negate congressional regulatory power. Some local activities have such a "close and substantial" relation to interstate commerce that their regulation is necessary and proper to foster and protect interstate commerce. *See* Houston, East and West Texas R. Co. v. United States (The Shreveport Case), 234 U.S. 342 (1914). However, the court in reacting to New Deal measures designed to control the economy took a narrow view of this power limiting it to regulation of activities that "directly" affect interstate commerce.

In Carter v. Carter Coal Co., 298 U.S. 238 (1936), for example, Congress' efforts to regulate labor relations in the depressed coal industry through the Bituminous Coal Conservation Act of 1935 was struck down. The court, per Justice Sutherland, rejected efforts to characterize mining as part of interstate commerce—"Mining brings the subject of commerce into existence. Commerce disposes of it." Citing concern for the vitality of federalist principles, Justice Sutherland similarly limited Congress' power to reach local activity to that which "directly" affects interstate commerce.

Whether the effect of a given activity or condition is direct or indirect is not always easy to determine. The word "direct" implies that the activity or condition invoked or blamed shall operate proximately—not mediately, remotely, or collaterally—to produce the effect. It connotes the absence of an efficient intervening agency or condition. And the extent of the effect bears no logical relation to its character. The distinction between a direct and an indirect effect turns, not upon the magnitude of either the cause or the effect, but entirely upon the manner in which the effect has been brought about. If the production by one man of a single ton of coal intended for interstate sale and shipment, and actually so sold and shipped, affects interstate commerce indirectly, the effect does not become direct by multiplying the tonnage, or increasing the number of men employed, or adding to the expense or complexities of the business, or by all combined. It is quite true that rules of law are sometimes qualified by considerations of degree, as the government argues. But the matter of degree has no bearing upon the question here, since that question is not—What is the *extent* of the local activity or condition, or the *extent* of the effect produced upon interstate commerce? but— What is the *relation* between the activity or condition and the effect?

All evils resulting from disruptive labor conditions were "local evils over which the federal government has no legislative control." *See* Schechter Poultry Corp. v. United States, 295 U.S. 495 (1935).

Consider the critique of the man who was to become Mr. Justice Jackson: "[T]hese words [direct-indirect] are not in the Constitution. The majority in [*Carter*], asking [its] non-constitutional question, was able to answer it by simply observing that labor practices in mining must necessarily affect production first, and then interstate commerce. Since there was an intervening effect, the effect on commerce was 'indirect.' And so a national government that has power, through the Federal Trade Commission, to prohibit the giving of prizes with penny candy shipped by the manufacturer from one state to another, was powerless to deal with the causes of critical stoppages in the gigantic bituminous coal industry." R. JACKSON, THE STRUGGLE FOR JUDICIAL SUPREMACY: A STUDY OF A CRISIS IN AMERICAN POWER POLITICS 162-63 (1941).

Under the threat of court-packing, however, the court recanted. In N.L.R.B. v. Jones & Laughlin Steel Corp., 301 U.S. 1 (1937), Justice Roberts and Chief Justice Hughes joined the court's liberal bloc to sustain broad national intervention in the economy. While the court might have applied the stream of commerce doctrine to sustain application of the National Labor Relations Act to the vertically-integrated steel corporation, Chief Justice Hughes instead turned to the broader conception of Congress' commerce power:

The fundamental principle is that the power to regulate
commerce is the power to enact "all appropriate legislation"
for "its protection and advancement" . . . Although activities
may be intrastate in character when separately considered, if
they have such a close and substantial relation to interstate
commerce that their control is essential or appropriate to protect that commerce from burdens and obstructions, Congress
cannot be denied the power to exercise that control. . . .

Noting the "serious effect upon interstate commerce" resulting
from work stoppage in Jones & Laughlin's far-flung activities and
the place of the steel industry in the national economy, the court
sustained Congress' power. The basis had been laid for the
development of the modern affectation doctrine.

See Stern, *The Commerce Clause and the National Economy,
1933-1946,* 59 HARV. L. REV. 645, 883 (1946), SELECTED ESSAYS 218
(1963), for an excellent discussion of the New Deal struggle. *See
United States v. Darby,* text, p. 181, for another example of the
court's retreat from commerce clause activism. *See United States
v. Butler,* text, p. 235 and *Steward Machine Co. v. Davis,* text,
p. 238, on the New Deal controversy over the meaning of the
taxing and spending clause.

### The Modern Affectation Doctrine

**WICKARD v. FILBURN**

Supreme Court of the United States
317 U.S. 111, 87 L. Ed. 122, 63 S. Ct. 82 (1942)

Justice JACKSON delivered the opinion of the Court.

The appellee . . . sought to enjoin enforcement against himself
of the marketing penalty imposed by the amendment of May 26,
1941, to the Agricultural Adjustment Act of 1938, upon that part
of his 1941 wheat crop which was available for marketing in excess of the marketing quota established for his farm. He also
sought a declaratory judgment that the wheat marketing quota
provisions of the Act as amended and applicable to him were
unconstitutional because not sustainable under the Commerce
Clause or consistent with the Due Process Clause of the Fifth
Amendment. . . .

. . . .

The appellee for many years past has owned and operated a
small farm in Montgomery County, Ohio, maintaining a herd of
dairy cattle, selling milk, raising poultry, and selling poultry and
eggs. It has been his practice to raise a small acreage of winter
wheat, sown in the Fall and harvested in the following July; to
sell a portion of the crop; to feed part to poultry and livestock

on the farm, some of which is sold; to use some in making flour for home consumption; and to keep the rest for the following seeding. The intended disposition of the crop here involved has not been expressly stated.

In July of 1940, pursuant to the Agricultural Adjustment Act of 1938, as then amended, there were established for the appellee's 1941 crop a wheat acreage allotment of 11.1 acres and a normal yield of 20.1 bushels of wheat an acre. He was given notice of such allotment in July of 1940, before the Fall planting of his 1941 crop of wheat, and again in July of 1941, before it was harvested. He sowed, however, 23 acres, and harvested from his 11.9 acres of excess acreage 239 bushels, which under the terms of the Act as amended on May 26, 1941, constituted farm marketing excess, subject to a penalty of 49 cents a bushel, or $117.11 in all. The appellee has not paid the penalty and he has not postponed or avoided it by storing the excess under regulations of the Secretary of Agriculture, or by delivering it up to the Secretary. The Committee, therefore, refused him a marketing card, which was, under the terms of Regulations promulgated by the Secretary, necessary to protect a buyer from liability to the penalty and upon its protecting lien.

The general scheme of the Agricultural Adjustment Act of 1938 as related to wheat is to control the volume moving in interstate and foreign commerce in order to avoid surpluses and shortages and the consequent abnormally low or high wheat prices and obstructions to commerce. Within prescribed limits and by prescribed standards the Secretary of Agriculture is directed to ascertain and proclaim each year a national acreage allotment for the next crop of wheat, which is then apportioned to the states and their counties, and is eventually broken up into allotments for individual farms. . . .

. . . .

It is urged that, under the Commerce Clause of the Constitution, Article I, § 8, clause 3, Congress does not possess the power it has in this instance sought to exercise. The question would merit little consideration since our decision in *United States v. Darby*, sustaining the federal power to regulate production of goods for commerce, except for the fact that this Act extends federal regulation to production not intended in any part for commerce but wholly for consumption on the farm. The Act includes a definition of "market" and its derivatives, so that as related to wheat, in addition to its conventional meaning, it also means to dispose of "by feeding (in any form) to poultry or livestock which, or the products of which, are sold, bartered, or exchanged, or to be so disposed of." Hence, marketing quotas not only embrace all that may be sold without penalty but also what may be consumed on the premises. . . .

Appellee says that this is a regulation of production and consumption of wheat. Such activities are, he urges, beyond the reach of Congressional power under the Commerce Clause, since they are local in character, and their effects upon interstate commerce are at most "indirect." In answer the Government argues that the statute regulates neither production nor consumption, but only marketing; and, in the alternative, that if the Act does go beyond the regulation of marketing it is sustainable as a "necessary and proper" implementation of the power of Congress over interstate commerce.

. . . .

The effect of consumption of home-grown wheat on interstate commerce is due to the fact that it constitutes the most variable factor in the disappearance of the wheat crop. Consumption on the farm where grown appears to vary in an amount greater than 20 per cent of average production. The total amount of wheat consumed as food varies but relatively little, and use as seed is relatively constant.

The maintenance by government regulation of a price for wheat undoubtedly can be accomplished as effectively by sustaining or increasing the demand as by limiting the supply. The effect of the statute before us is to restrict the amount which may be produced for market and the extent as well to which one may forestall resort to the market by producing to meet his own needs. That appellee's own contribution to the demand for wheat may be trivial by itself is not enough to remove him from the scope of federal regulation where, as here, his contribution, taken together with that of many others similarly situated, is far from trivial. *United States v. Darby.*

It is well established by decisions of this Court that the power to regulate commerce includes the power to regulate the prices at which commodities in that commerce are dealt in and practices affecting such prices. One of the primary purposes of the act in question was to increase the market price of wheat, and to that end to limit the volume thereof that could affect the market. It can hardly be denied that a factor of such volume and variability as home-consumed wheat would have a substantial influence on price and market conditions. This may arise because being in marketable condition such wheat overhangs the market and, if induced by rising prices, tends to flow into the market and check price increases. But if we assume that it is never marketed, it supplies a need of the man who grew it which would otherwise be reflected by purchasers in the open market. Home-grown wheat in this sense competes with wheat in commerce. The stimulation of commerce is a use of the regulatory function quite as definitely as prohibitions or restrictions thereon. This record leaves us in no doubt that Congress may properly have considered that wheat consumed on the farm where grown, if wholly outside the scheme of regulation, would have substantial effect in defeating and obstructing its purpose to stimulate trade therein at increased prices.

It is said, however, that this Act, forcing some farmers into the market to buy what they could provide for themselves, is an unfair promotion of the markets and prices of specializing wheat growers. It is of the essence of regulation that it lays a restraining hand on the self-interest of the regulated and that advantages from the regulation commonly fall to others. The conflicts of economic interest between the regulated and those who advantage by it are wisely left under our system to resolution by the Congress under its more flexible and responsible legislative process. Such conflicts rarely lend themselves to judicial determination. And with the wisdom, workability, or fairness, of the plan of regulation we have nothing to do.

The statute is also challenged as a deprivation of property without due process of law contrary to the Fifth Amendment, both because of its regulatory effect on the appellee and because of its alleged retroactive effect. . . .

[The Court went on to hold that the application of the statute to the complainant did not violate the Fifth Amendment and reversed the District Court.]

Reversed.

---

### NOTES

1. It has been urged that *Wickard* "completely swept away the old distinction between production and commerce; manufacturing, mining, and agriculture were now considered to be part of commerce and inseparable from it." P. BENSON, THE SUPREME COURT AND THE COMMERCE CLAUSE, 1937-1970 101 (1970). Did *Wickard* expand the concept of commerce or does it reflect the expansion of the powers "necessary and proper" to the effectuation of the commerce power? Compare the following summation of the expansion of Congress' commerce power: "This application of the clause to all business activities which concerns more state[s] than one, and not merely to direct trade and transportation between states, would seem to be precisely what was meant by Marshall's prophetic declaration." Stern, *The Scope of the Phrase Interstate Commerce*, 41 A.B.A.J. 823, 871

(1955), SELECTED ESSAYS 298, 304-05 (1963). Consider also the statement of Justice Rutledge that "the 'affectation' approach was actually a revival of Marshall's 'necessary and proper' doctrine." Mandeville Island Farms, Inc. v. American Crystal Sugar Co., 334 U.S. 219, 232 n. 11 (1948).

2. *Wickard* establishes that Congress may reach local activity if it exerts a "substantial economic effect" on interstate commerce. How important is this limitation given our modern economy? The court in *Wickard* appears willing to accept what in 1935 it had emphatically rejected, *i.e.*, that the interstate and intrastate aspects of the American economy are not distinct, separate and impenetrable and that the tenth amendment does not necessitate the drawing of a fixed line between the state and federal spheres of power. As Robert Stern explains: "It may be true that the application of the principles now approved by the Supreme Court may leave only minor aspects of an economy free from the regulatory power of Congress. The reason for this, however, is not legal but economic." Stern, *Problems of Yesteryear—Commerce and Due Process*, 4 VAND. L. REV. 446, 468 (1951).

3. *Air Pollution.* Pollution control has been a traditional prerogative of the states. But pollution does not respect state boundaries, and the federal government has taken an increasing role in its regulation. *See, e.g.,* The Federal Water Pollution Control Act, 33 U.S.C. § 1251 et seq.; The Federal Clean Air Act, 42 U.S.C. § 1857 et seq. To what extent do the police power cases support such regulation? The "stream of commerce" cases? The affectation doctrine? *See* Edelman, *Federal Air and Water Control: The Application of the Commerce Power to Abate Interstate and Intrastate Pollution*, 33 GEO. WASH. L. REV. 1067 (1965).

4. *No-Fault Insurance.* To what extent is there constitutional support for enactment of the National No-Fault Motor Vehicle Insurance Act? The legislation would afford states an opportunity to enact their own no-fault legislation subject to minimum national standards (Title II). If a state fails to do so, an alternate nationally-defined state no-fault plan would go into effect in that state subject to the state's subsequently developing its own plan.

5. *Energy Legislation.* In 1973, in response to the growing energy crisis, Congress enacted, *inter alia,* an Emergency Petroleum Allocation Act (providing for executive allocation of gasoline supplies) and an Emergency Daylight Savings Time Energy Conservation Act (imposing nation-wide daylight savings time). *See* P-H Energy Controls, ¶¶ 25,451-25,495; 27,401-27,407 (1974). What is the constitutional authority for such legislation? Would

the same rationale that supports earlier Uniform Time Acts support this Emergency Time Act?

**6.** In construing federal legislation regulating commerce, the court has refused to accept the argument that any activity perceptively connected with interstate commerce is itself in interstate commerce. Congress was held not to have used its full commerce power in enacting the Robinson-Patman Act forbidding price discrimination for purchases "in commerce." The court avoided the question of the jurisdictional scope of the Clayton Act by holding that the plaintiff had failed to allege and prove that the apparently local acts involved had adverse effects on the interstate flow of goods as required by the antitrust laws. *Gulf Oil Corp. v. Copp Paving Co.,* — U.S. — (1974). *See* American Radio Ass'n v. Mobile Steamship Ass'n, — U.S. — (1974), holding that a local labor dispute was not "in" or "affecting commerce" as to fall within the exclusive regulatory power of the National Labor Relations Board.

## E. PROTECTING CIVIL RIGHTS THROUGH THE COMMERCE CLAUSE

At common law, an innkeeper impliedly gave a general invitation to all members of the public to enter and use his premises without discrimination. 3 BLACKSTONE, COMMENTARIES ON THE LAWS OF ENGLAND Ch. IX (10th ed. 1787). But since black Americans were considered property, they never received the benefit of these common-law rights. *See* Comment, *Public Accommodations and the Civil Rights Act of 1964,* 19 U. MIAMI L. REV. 456, 459 (1965).

The thirteenth, fourteenth and fifteenth amendments were designed to remove such legal disabilities and Congress sought through legislation, to fashion a sword to give these rights meaning. One such effort came in the Civil Rights Act of 1875 which provided: "that all persons within the jurisdiction of the United States shall be entitled to full and equal enjoyment of the accommodations, advantages, facilities, and privileges of inns, public conveyances on land or water, theaters, or other places of public amusements; subject only to the conditions and limitations established by law, and applicable alike to citizens of every race and color, regardless of any previous condition of servitude." The section was not limited to state action but could be applied even against private discrimination.

But as was to be the fate of much of the Civil War civil rights legislation, the courts undid the congressional handiwork. In the Civil Rights Cases, 109 U.S. 3 (1883), [text, p. 989], the court declared the Act unconstitutional since the fourteenth amendment did not grant Congress power to legislate in the area of private discrimination which was reserved to the states. As has been noted, the court's "decision in the *Civil Rights Cases* was an important stimulus to the enactment of segregation statutes. It gave the assurance the South wanted that the federal government would not intervene to protect the civil rights of Negroes." Franklin, *History of Racial Segregation in the United States,* 5 ANNALS 34 (1956).

Congress was not to legislate again in an effort to eliminate discrimination in public accommodations for 87 years. In the interim, the court struggled with the limitations imposed on direct judicial enforcement of the Civil War amendments by the state action requirement. But the changing attitudes of blacks in the South, manifested through sit-ins, increasing public awareness of the blacks' problem with segregated accommodations, the refusal of restaurants to serve African diplomats along Route 40 between New York and Washington, and the death of President Kennedy, culminated in a demand for new federal intervention. In an attempt to revive the ideal of "freedom and equality for all," Congress passed the Civil Rights Act of 1964, but in doing so, it employed not only the fourteenth amendment guarantees but also the commerce clause.

———

## CIVIL RIGHTS ACT OF 1964, 42 U.S.C. §§ 2000a-2000a-6

### TITLE II—INJUNCTIVE RELIEF AGAINST DISCRIMINATION IN PLACES OF PUBLIC ACCOMMODATION

SEC. 201. (a) All persons shall be entitled to the full and equal enjoyment of the goods, services, facilities, privileges, advantages, and accommodations of any place of public accommodation, as defined in this section, without discrimination or segregation on the ground of race, color, religion, or national origin.

(b) Each of the following establishments which serves the public is a place of public accommodation within the meaning of this title if its operations affect commerce, or if discrimination or segregation by it is supported by State action:

(1) any inn, hotel, motel, or other establishment which provides lodging to transient guests, other than an establishment located within a building which contains not more than five rooms for rent or hire and which is actually occupied by the proprietor of such establishment as his residence;

(2) any restaurant, cafeteria, lunchroom, lunch counter, soda fountain, or other facility principally engaged in selling food for consumption on the premises, including, but not limited to, any such facility located on the premises of any retail establishment; or any gasoline station;

(3) any motion picture house, theater, concert hall, sports arena, stadium or other place of exhibition or entertainment; and

(4) any establishment (A) (i) which is physically located within the premises of any establishment otherwise covered by this subsection, or (ii) within the premises of which is physically located any such covered establishment, and (B) which holds itself out as serving patrons of such covered establishment.

(c) The operations of an establishment affect commerce within the meaning of this title if (1) it is one of the establishments described in paragraph (1) of subsection (b); (2) in the case of an establishment described in paragraph (2) of subsection (b), it serves or offers to serve interstate travelers or a substantial portion of the food which it serves, or gasoline or other products which it sells, has moved in commerce; (3) in the case of an establishment described in paragraph (3) of subsection (b), it customarily presents films, performances, athletic teams, exhibitions, or other sources of entertainment which move in commerce; and (4) in the case of an establishment described in paragraph (4) of subsection (b), it is physically located within the premises of, or there is physically located within its premises, an establishment the operations of which affect commerce within the meaning of this subsection. For purposes of this section, "commerce" means travel, trade, traffic, commerce, transportation, or communication among the several States, or between the District of Columbia and any State, or between any foreign country or any territory or possession and any State or the District of Columbia, or between points in the same State but through any other State or the District of Columbia or a foreign country.

(d) Discrimination or segregation by an establishment is supported by State action within the meaning of this title if such discrimination or segregation (1) is carried on under color of any law, statute, ordinance, or regulation; or (2) is carried on under color of any custom or usage required or enforced by officials of the State or political subdivision thereof; or (3) is required by action of the State or political subdivision thereof.

(e) The provisions of this title shall not apply to a private club or other establishment not in fact open to the public, except to the extent that the facilities of such establishment are made available to the customers or patrons of an establishment within the scope of subsection (b).

SEC. 202. All persons shall be entitled to be free, at any establishment or place, from discrimination or segregation of any kind on the ground of race, color, religion, or national origin, if such discrimination or segregation is or purports to be required by any law, statute, ordinance, regulation, rule, or order of a State or any agency or political subdivision thereof.

SEC. 203. No person shall (a) withhold, deny, or attempt to withhold or deny, or deprive or attempt to deprive, any person of any right or privilege secured by section 201 or 202, or (b) intimidate, threaten, or coerce, or attempt to intimidate, threaten, or coerce any person with the purpose of interfering with any right or privilege secured by section 201 or 202, or (c) punish or attempt to punish any person for exercising or attempting to exercise any right or privilege secured by section 201 or 202.

[§§ 204-207 provide remedies for violation of the rights secured above.]

---

## Senate Hearings on Title II

(Hearings Before the Senate Commerce Committee on S. 1732, 88th Cong., 1st Sess., pts. 1 & 2 (1963))

*Senator Cooper* [*Rep., Ky.*]. I do not suppose that anyone would seriously contend that the administration is proposing legislation, or the Congress is considering legislation, because it has suddenly determined, after all these years, that segregation is a burden on interstate commerce. We are considering legislation because we believe, as the great majority of the people in our country believe, that all citizens have an equal right to have access to goods, services, and facilities which are held out to be available for public use and patronage.

If there is a right to the equal use of accommodations held out to the public, it is a right of citizenship and a constitutional right under the 14th amendment. It has nothing to do with whether a business is in interstate commerce or whether discrimination against individuals places a burden on commerce. It does not depend upon the commerce clause and cannot be limited by that clause, in my opinion as the administration bill would do.

. . . .

If we are going to deal with this question of the use of public accommodations, I think it imperative that Congress should enact legislation which would meet it fully and squarely as a right under the 14th amendment, and not indirectly and partially as the administration's approach would do.

Rights under the Constitution apply to all citizens, and the integrity and dignity of the individual should not be placed on lesser grounds such as the commerce clause.

. . . .

*Senator Prouty* [*Rep., Vt.*]. Mr. Marshall, getting down to the fundamentals, is discrimination the basic evil we think it is, because of its effect on commerce or because of its effect on man and his dignity?

*Mr.* [*Burke*] *Marshall* [*Assistant Attorney General, Civil Rights Division*]. Senator, I think that discrimination is a basic evil because of its effect on people. But it also has an effect on commerce. And Congress has a clear power and responsibility to deal with that effect.

. . . .

*Senator Pastore [Dem., R.I.].* I am a little disturbed about the carefulness we are exercising on both sides here with relation to the inviolability of an opinion of the Supreme Court of 1883. I submit that until it is changed by another opinion of the Supreme Court, or by constitutional amendment, that it is the binding law of the land and we must preserve it.

But is there any constitutional prohibition about Congress taking a second bite at the cherry?

*Mr. Marshall.* No, there isn't, Senator. . . .

*Senator Pastore.* . . . I believe in this bill, because I believe in the dignity of man, not because it impedes our commerce. I don't think any man has the right to say to another man, You can't eat in my restaurant because you have a dark skin; no matter how clean you are, you can't eat at my restaurant.

That deprives a man of his full stature as an American citizen. That shocks me. That hurts me. And that is the reason why I want to vote for this law.

Now, it might well be that I can effect the same remedy through the commerce clause. But I like to feel that what we are talking about is a moral issue, an issue that involves the morality of this great country of ours. And that morality, it seems to me, comes under the 14th amendment, where we speak about immunities and where we speak about equal protection of the law. I would like to feel that the Supreme Court of the United States is given another chance to review it, not under the commerce clause, but under the 14th amendment. . . . Do you see anything wrong in that?

*Mr. Marshall.* Senator, I think it would be a mistake to rely solely on the 14th amendment. This bill, S. 1732, relies on the 14th amendment, and also relies on the commerce clause. I think if it relied solely on the 14th amendment, it might not be held constitutional. I think it would be a disservice to pass a bill that was later thrown out by the Supreme Court.

*Senator Pastore.* I am not being critical of you. I am merely stating my own position. I am saying we are being a little too careful, cagey, and cautious, in debating this question of the 14th amendment. I realize you should bring all of the tools at your disposal and that is what you are doing. You are saying you are not only relying on the 14th amendment, you are relying on the commerce clause as well and you have every right to do that as a good lawyer. All I am saying here is that we have a perfect right to proceed under the 14th amendment and try it again.

## HEART OF ATLANTA MOTEL v. UNITED STATES
Supreme Court of the United States
379 U.S. 241, 13 L. Ed. 2d 258, 85 S. Ct. 348 (1964)

Justice CLARK delivered the opinion of the Court.

This is a declaratory judgment action attacking the constitutionality of Title II of the Civil Rights Act of 1964. . . . A three-judge court . . . sustained the validity of the Act and issued a permanent injunction . . . restraining appellant from continuing to violate the Act. . . . We affirm the judgment.

. . . Appellant owns and operates the Heart of Atlanta Motel which has 216 rooms available to transient guests. The motel is located on Courtland Street, two blocks from downtown Peachtree Street. It is readily accessible to interstate highways 75 and 85 and state highways 23 and 41. Appellant solicits patronage from outside the State of Georgia through various national advertising media, including magazines of national circulation; it maintains over 50 billboards and highway signs within the State, soliciting patronage for the motel; it accepts convention trade from outside Georgia and approximately 75% of its registered guests are from out of State. Prior to passage of the Act the motel had followed a practice of refusing to rent rooms to Negroes, and it alleged that it intended to continue to do so. In an effort to perpetuate that policy this suit was filed.

. . . .

It is admitted that the operation of the motel brings it within the provisions of § 201(a) of the Act and that appellant refused to provide lodging for transient Negroes because of their race or color and that it intends to continue that policy unless restrained.

The sole question posed is, therefore, the constitutionality of the Civil Rights Act of 1964 as applied to these facts. The legislative history of the Act indicates that Congress based the Act on § 5 and the Equal Protection Clause of the Fourteenth Amendment as well as its power to regulate interstate commerce under Art I, § 8, cl 3, of the Constitution.

The Senate Commerce Committee made it quite clear that the fundamental object of Title II was to vindicate "the deprivation of personal dignity that surely accompanies denials of equal access to public establishments." At the same time, however, it noted that such an objective has been and could be readily achieved "by congressional action based on the commerce power of the Constitution." Our study of the legislative record, made in the light of prior cases, has brought us to the conclusion that Congress possessed ample power in this regard, and we have therefore not considered the other grounds relied upon.

This is not to say that the remaining authority upon which it acted was not adequate, a question upon which we do not pass, but merely that since the commerce power is sufficient for our decision here we have considered it alone. Nor is § 201(d) or § 202, having to do with state action, involved here and we do not pass upon either of those sections.

In light of our ground for decision, it might be well at the outset to discuss the *Civil Rights Cases* [text, p. 989], which declared provisions of the Civil Rights Act of 1875 unconstitutional. We think that decision inapposite, and without precedential value in determining the constitutionality of the present Act. Unlike Title II of the present legislation, the 1875 Act broadly proscribed discrimination in "inns, public conveyances on land or water, theaters, and other places of public amusement," without limiting the categories of affected businesses to those impinging upon interstate commerce. In contrast, the applicability of Title II is carefully limited to enterprises having a direct and substantial relation to the interstate flow of goods and people, except where state action is involved. Further, the fact that certain kinds of businesses may not in 1875 have been sufficiently involved in interstate commerce to warrant bringing them within the ambit of the commerce power is not necessarily dispositive of the same question today. Our populace had not reached its present mobility, nor were facilities, goods and services circulating as readily in interstate commerce as they are today. Although the principles which we apply today are those first formulated by Chief Justice Marshall in *Gibbons v. Ogden,* the conditions of transportation and commerce have changed dramatically, and we must apply those principles to the present state of commerce. The sheer increase in volume of interstate traffic alone would give discriminatory practices which inhibit travel a far larger impact upon the Nation's commerce than such practices had on the economy of another day. Finally, there is language in the *Civil Rights Cases* which indicates that the Court did not fully consider whether the 1875 Act could be sustained as an exercise of the commerce power. . . .

. . . .

While the [1964] Act as adopted carried no congressional findings the record of its passage through each house is replete with evidence of the burdens that discrimination by race or color places upon interstate commerce. This testimony included the fact that our people have become increasingly mobile with millions of people of all races traveling from State to State; that Negroes in particular have been the subject of discrimination in transient accommodations, having to travel great distances to secure the same; that often they have been unable to obtain accommodations and have had to call upon friends to put them up overnight; and that these conditions have become so acute as to require the listing of available lodging for Negroes in a special guidebook which was itself "dramatic testimony to the difficulties" Negroes encounter in travel. These exclusionary practices were found to be nationwide, . . . This testimony indicated a qualitative as well as quantitative effect on interstate travel by Negroes. The former was the obvious impairment of the Negro traveler's pleasure and convenience that resulted when he continually was uncertain of finding lodging. As for the latter, there was evidence that this uncertainty stemming from racial discrimination had the effect of discouraging travel on the part of a substantial portion of the Negro community. . . . We shall not burden this opinion with further details since the voluminous testimony presents overwhelming evidence that discrimination by hotels and motels impedes interstate travel.

The power of Congress to deal with these obstructions depends on the meaning of the Commerce Clause. . . .

. . . [T]he determinative test of the exercise of power by the Congress under the Commerce Clause is simply whether the activity sought to be regulated is "commerce which concerns more States than one" and has a real and substantial relation to the national interest. . . .

That the "intercourse" of which Chief Justice [Marshall] spoke included the movement of persons through more States than one was settled as early as 1849, in the Passenger Cases, 7 How 283. . . .

Nor does it make any difference whether the transportation is commercial in character. . . .

The same interest in protecting interstate commerce which led Congress to deal with segregation in interstate carriers and the white-slave traffic has prompted it to extend the exercise of its power to gambling, to criminal enterprises, to deceptive practices in the sale of products, to fraudulent security transactions, to misbranding of drugs, to wages and hours, to members of labor unions, to crop control, to discrimination against shippers, to the protection of small business from injurious price cutting, to resale price maintenance, to professional football, and to racial discrimination by owners and managers of terminal restaurants.

That Congress was legislating against moral wrongs in many of these areas rendered its enactments no less valid. In framing Title II of this Act Congress was also dealing with what it considered a moral problem. But that fact does not detract from the overwhelming evidence of the disruptive effect that racial discrimination has had on commercial intercourse. It was this burden which empowered Congress to enact appropriate legislation, and, given this basis for the exercise of its power, Congress was not restricted by the fact that the particular obstruction to interstate commerce with which it was dealing was also deemed a moral and social wrong.

It is said that the operation of the motel here is of a purely local character. But, assuming this to be true, "[i]f it is interstate commerce that feels the pinch, it does not matter how local the operation which applies the squeeze."

Thus the power of Congress to promote interstate commerce also includes the power to regulate the local incidents thereof, including local activities in both the States of origin and destination, which might have a substantial and harmful effect upon that commerce. One need only examine the evidence which we have discussed above to see that Congress may—as it has—prohibit racial discrimination by motels serving travelers, however "local" their operations may appear.

Nor does the Act deprive appellant of liberty or property under the Fifth Amendment. The commerce power invoked here by the Congress is a specific and plenary one authorized by the Constitution itself. The only questions are: (1) whether Congress had a rational basis for finding that racial discrimination by motels affected commerce, and (2) if it had such a basis, whether the means it selected to eliminate that evil are reasonable and appropriate. If they are, appellant has no "right" to select its guests as it sees fit, free from governmental regulation.

There is nothing novel about such legislation. Thirty-two States now have it on their books either by statute or executive order and many cities provide such regulation. Some of these Acts go back four-score years. It has been repeatedly held by this Court that such laws do not violate the Due Process Clause of the Fourteenth Amendment. . . .

. . . .

We, therefore, conclude that the action of the Congress in the adoption of the Act as applied here to a motel which concededly serves interstate travelers is within the power granted it by the Commerce Clause of the Constitution, as interpreted by this Court for 140 years. It may be argued that Congress could have pursued other methods to eliminate the obstructions it found in interstate commerce caused by racial discrimination. But this is a matter of policy that rests entirely with the Congress not within the courts. How obstructions in commerce may be

removed—what means are to be employed—is within the sound
and exclusive discretion of the Congress. It is subject only to
one caveat—that the means chosen by it must be reasonably
adapted to the end permitted by the Constitution. We cannot
say that its choice here was not so adapted. The Constitution
requires no more.

Affirmed.

[The concurring opinions of Justices BLACK, DOUGLAS and
GOLDBERG follow *Katzenbach v. McClung*.]

---

### KATZENBACH v. McCLUNG
Supreme Court of the United States
379 U.S. 294, 13 L. Ed. 2d 290, 85 S. Ct. 377 (1964)

Justice CLARK delivered the opinion of the Court.

This case was argued with *Heart of Atlanta Motel v United
States*. . . . This complaint for injunctive relief against appellants
attacks the constitutionality of the Act as applied to a restaurant.
The case was heard by a three-judge United States District Court
and an injunction was issued restraining appellants from enforcing the Act against the restaurant. . . . We now reverse the
judgment.

. . . .

Ollie's Barbecue is a family-owned restaurant in Birmingham,
Alabama, specializing in barbecued meats and homemade pies,
with a seating capacity of 220 customers. It is located on a state
highway 11 blocks from an interstate one and a somewhat greater
distance from railroad and bus stations. The restaurant caters to
a family and white-collar trade with a take-out service for Negroes.
It employs 36 persons, two-thirds of whom are Negroes.

In the 12 months preceding the passage of the Act, the restaurant purchased locally approximately $150,000 worth of food,
$69,683 or 46% of which was meat that it bought from a local
supplier who had procured it from outside the State. The District Court expressly found that a substantial portion of the food
served in the restaurant had moved in interstate commerce. The
restaurant has refused to serve Negroes in its dining accommodations since its original opening in 1927, and since July 2, 1964,
it has been operating in violation of the Act. The court below
concluded that if it were required to serve Negroes it would
lose a substantial amount of business.

. . . .

. . . Sections 201(b)(2) and (c) place any "restaurant . . .
principally engaged in selling food for consumption on the

premises" under the Act "if . . . it serves or offers to serve interstate travelers or a substantial portion of the food which it
serves . . . has moved in commerce."

Ollie's Barbecue admits that it is covered by these provisions
of the Act. The Government makes no contention that the
discrimination at the restaurant was supported by the State of
Alabama. There is no claim that interstate travelers frequented
the restaurant. The sole question, therefore, narrows down to
whether Title II, as applied to a restaurant annually receiving
about $70,000 worth of food which has moved in commerce, is a
valid exercise of the power of Congress. The Government has
contended that Congress had ample basis upon which to find
that racial discrimination at restaurants which receive from out
of state a substantial portion of the food served does, in fact, impose commercial burdens of national magnitude upon interstate
commerce. The appellees' major argument is directed to this
premise. They urge that no such basis existed. It is to that question that we now turn.

As we noted in *Heart of Atlanta Motel* both Houses of Congress conducted prolonged hearings on the Act. And, as we said
there, while no formal findings were made, which of course are
not necessary, it is well that we make mention of the testimony
at these hearings the better to understand the problem before
Congress and determine whether the Act is a reasonable and appropriate means toward its solution. The record is replete with
testimony of the burdens placed on interstate commerce by racial
discrimination in restaurants. A comparison of per capita spending by Negroes in restaurants, theaters, and like establishments
indicated less spending, after discounting income differences, in
areas where discrimination is widely practiced. This condition,
which was especially aggravated in the South, was attributed in
the testimony of the Under Secretary of Commerce to racial segregation. This diminutive spending springing from a refusal to
serve Negroes and their total loss as customers has, regardless of
the absence of direct evidence, a close connection to interstate
commerce. The fewer customers a restaurant enjoys the less food
it sells and consequently the less it buys. In addition, the Attorney
General testified that this type of discrimination imposed "an
artificial restriction on the market" and interfered with the flow
of merchandise. In addition, there were many references to discriminatory situations causing wide unrest and having a depres-
sant effect on general business conditions in the respective communities.

Moreover there was an impressive array of testimony that discrimination in restaurants had a direct and highly restrictive

effect upon interstate travel by Negroes. This resulted, it was said, because discriminatory practices prevent Negroes from buying prepared food served on the premises while on a trip, except in isolated and unkept restaurants and under most unsatisfactory and often unpleasant conditions. This obviously discourages travel and obstructs interstate commerce for one can hardly travel without eating. Likewise, it was said, that discrimination deterred professional, as well as skilled, people from moving into areas where such practices occurred and thereby caused industry to be reluctant to establish there.

We believe that this testimony afforded ample basis for the conclusion that established restaurants in such areas sold less interstate goods because of the discrimination, that interstate travel was obstructed directly by it, that business in general suffered and that many new businesses refrained from establishing there as a result of it. . . .

It goes without saying that, viewed in isolation, the volume of food purchased by Ollie's Barbecue from sources supplied from out of state was insignificant when compared with the total foodstuffs moving in commerce. But, as our late Brother Jackson said for the Court in Wickard v Filburn:

> "That appellee's own contribution to the demand for wheat may be trivial by itself is not enough to remove him from the scope of federal regulation where, as here, his contribution, taken together with that of many others similarly situated, is far from trivial."

We noted in *Heart of Atlanta Motel* that a number of witnesses attested to the fact that racial discrimination was not merely a state or regional problem but was one of nationwide scope. Against this background, we must conclude that while the focus of the legislation was on the individual restaurant's relation to interstate commerce, Congress appropriately considered the importance of that connection with the knowledge that the discrimination was but "representative of many others throughout the country, the total incidence of which if left unchecked may well become far-reaching in its harm to commerce." Polish Alliance v Labor Board, 322 U.S. 643, 648 (1944).

With this situation spreading as the record shows, Congress was not required to await the total dislocation of commerce. . . .

. . . Much is said about a restaurant business being local but "even if appellee's activity be local and though it may not be regarded as commerce, it may still, whatever its nature, be reached

by Congress if it exerts a substantial economic effect on interstate commerce. . . ." *Wickard v Filburn.* . . .

. . . .

The appellees contend that Congress has arbitrarily created
a conclusive presumption that all restaurants meeting the criteria
set out in the Act "affect commerce." Stated another way, they
object to the omission of a provision for a case-by-case determination—judicial or administrative—that racial discrimination in a
particular restaurant affects commerce.

But Congress' action in framing this Act was not unprecedented. . . .

Here, as [in *United States v. Darby,* text, p. 181], Congress has
determined for itself that refusals of service to Negroes have imposed burdens both upon the interstate flow of food and upon
the movement of products generally. Of course, the mere fact
that Congress has said when particular activity shall be deemed
to affect commerce does not preclude further examination by
this Court. But where we find that the legislators, in light of the
facts and testimony before them, have a rational basis for finding a chosen regulatory scheme necessary to the protection of
commerce, our investigation is at an end. The only remaining
question—one answered in the affirmative by the court below—
is whether the particular restaurant either serves or offers to
serve interstate travelers or serves food a substantial portion of
which has moved in interstate commerce.

. . . .

Confronted as we are with the facts laid before Congress, we
must conclude that it had a rational basis for finding that racial
discrimination in restaurants had a direct and adverse effect on
the free flow of interstate commerce. . . . We think that Congress
acted well within its power to protect and foster commerce in
extending the coverage of Title II only to those restaurants offering to serve interstate travelers or serving food, a substantial
portion of which has moved in interstate commerce.

The absence of direct evidence connecting discriminatory restaurant service with the flow of interstate food, a factor on which
the appellees place much reliance, is not, given the evidence as
to the effect of such practices on other aspects of commerce, a
crucial matter.

The power of Congress in this field is broad and sweeping;
where it keeps within its sphere and violates no express constitutional limitation it has been the rule of this Court, going
back almost to the founding days of the Republic, not to interfere. The Civil Rights Act of 1964, as here applied, we find to
be plainly appropriate in the resolution of what the Congress

found to be a national commercial problem of the first magnitude. We find it in no violation of any express limitations of the Constitution and we therefore declare it valid.

The judgment is therefore

Reversed.

Justice BLACK, concurring.

. . . .

. . . I recognize that every remote, possible, speculative effect on commerce should not be accepted as an adequate constitutional ground to uproot and throw into the discard all our traditional distinctions between what is purely local, and therefore controlled by state laws, and what affects the national interest and is therefore subject to control by federal laws. I recognize too that some isolated and remote lunchroom which sells only to local people and buys almost all its supplies in the locality may possibly be beyond the reach of the power of Congress to regulate commerce, just as such an establishment is not covered by the present Act. But in deciding the constitutional power of Congress in cases like the two before us we do not consider the effect on interstate commerce of only one isolated, individual, local event, without regard to the fact that this single local event when added to many others of a similar nature may impose a burden on interstate commerce by reducing its volume or distorting its flow.

. . . .

Justice DOUGLAS, concurring.

Though I join the Court's opinions, I am somewhat reluctant to rest solely on the Commerce Clause. My reluctance is not due to any conviction that Congress lacks power to regulate commerce in the interests of human rights. It is rather my belief that the right of people to be free of state action that discriminates against them because of race, like the "right of persons to move freely from State to State" "occupies a more protected position in our constitutional system than does the movement of cattle, fruit, steel and coal across state lines." . . .

. . . .

A decision based on the Fourteenth Amendment would have a more settling effect, making unnecessary litigation over whether a particular restaurant or inn is within the commerce definitions of the Act or whether a particular customer is an interstate traveler. Under my construction, the Act would apply to all customers in all the enumerated places of public accommodation. And that construction would put an end to all obstructionist strategies and finally close one door on a bitter chapter in American history.

. . . .

Justice GOLDBERG, concurring.

I join in the opinions and judgments of the Court, . . .

The primary purpose of the Civil Rights Act of 1964, however, as the Court recognizes, and as I would underscore, is the vindication of human dignity and not mere economics. . . .

. . . .

. . . Congress clearly had authority under both § 5 of the Fourteenth Amendment and the Commerce Clause to enact the Civil Rights Act of 1964.

---

## NOTES

### A Fourteenth Amendment Nexus

1. As the reprinted congressional debate indicates, Congress was torn between a desire to reverse the effect of the *Civil Rights Cases* and the need to assure the constitutionality of the new legislation. The court in the 19th century case had clearly provided an opening when it stated that its "remarks do not apply to those cases in which Congress is clothed with direct plenary power of legislation over the whole subject, accompanied with an expressed or implied denial of such powers to the States, as in the regulation of commerce."

2. Are there any advantages in relying on the fourteenth amendment rather than the commerce clause? As Justices Douglas and Goldberg indicate in their concurring opinions, the fourteenth amendment would seem to provide a more appropriate way of dealing with the problem of racial discrimination. Further, such a nexus would seem to provide broad federal power enabling Congress to legislate against discrimination in public accommodations, thereby eliminating the possible need to prove an interstate commerce nexus in the particular case. On the congressional use of the fourteenth amendment to reach *private* discrimination, *see* text, pp. 1066-78. On the other hand, it is arguable that "[a] decision based on the fourteenth amendment would have a tremendous momentum of principle with potential disruptive consequences for state-federal relationships and implications for judicial power and duty far transcending the immediate controversy—in fact, far beyond issues of racial discrimination or public accommodations." Mishkin, *The Supreme Court, 1964 Term,* 79 HARV. L. REV. 56, 130 (1965).

### The Commerce Clause Nexus

1. Can human beings be objects of commerce? *See* text, p. 272. Is there any limitation on the ability of Congress to use

its granted powers to achieve extraneous social and moral ends over which it cannot regulate? During the Senate committee hearing, Senator Monroney stated: "[M]any of us are worried about the use the interstate clause will have on matters which have been for more than 170 years thought to be within the realm of local control under our dual system of State Federal Government, based on the doctrine that those powers which were not specifically granted to the Federal Government by the Constitution are reserved to the States."

2.   Is the relation of racial discrimination to interstate commerce "far-fetched"? Simson, *Public Accommodations Section of the Civil Rights Bill*, 25 ALA. LAW 305, 306 (1964). Many Southern legislators saw it as a wide avenue upon which federal power could travel, enabling Congress to control local conduct and morals. Conversely, this is the kind of exercise of congressional power envisioned by the fourteenth amendment, § 5. It is no more "potentially intrusive" on local power than the congressional economic regulation discussed in this chapter.

3.   *Police Power.* The court in *Heart of Atlanta* cites a number of the police power cases. Do these cases support the constitutionality of Title II? Is Congress protecting interstate commerce or Black Americans who travel interstate? The public accommodations provision does not prohibit any movement of goods through interstate commerce but seeks to regulate local discrimination. If interstate commerce has begun, does Congress' police power extend to regulation of the goods even after they have reached their destination? Is the theory that Congress can regulate even local activity which has a social or moral effect on interstate commerce, *i.e.*, that interstate commerce should not be used to promote local discrimination? *See* United States v. Sullivan, 332 U.S. 689 (1948), text, p. 217.

4.   *The Affectation Doctrine.* Is congressional power to enact Title II based on the premise that discrimination in public accommodations is an "economic burden" on interstate commerce? Note that the Act does not include specific findings of fact documenting such a burden. During the hearings, Burke Marshall did state that "discrimination burdens Negro interstate travelers and thereby inhibits interstate travel. It artificially restricts the market available for interstate goods and services. It leads to the withholding of patronage by potential customers for such goods and services. It inhibits the holding of conventions and meetings in segregated cities. It interferes with businesses that wish to obtain the services of persons who do not choose to subject themselves to segregation and discrimination. And it restricts business enterprises in their choice of location for offices and

plants, thus preventing the most effective allocation of national resources.

"Clearly, all of these are burdens on interstate commerce and they may therefore be dealt with by the Congress." If discrimination were ended, isn't it probable that whites might be deterred from traveling? From using food which has traveled through interstate commerce? Should such possible consequences be considered in determining the constitutionality of Title II?

5. *The Character of the Interstate Connection.* During the course of the Senate committee hearings, Attorney General Robert F. Kennedy stated: "If the establishment is covered by the commerce clause, then you can regulate; that is correct. . . ." Can Congress regulate racial discrimination in places of public accommodations because they affect interstate commerce or is it necessary that the government show that the racial discrimination itself affects interstate commerce? Burke Marshall, Assistant United States Attorney General, Civil Rights Division, stated: "Let me dispell at the outset a possible misconception. . . . We do not propose to regulate the businesses covered merely because they are engaged in some phase of interstate commerce. Discrimination by the establishments covered in the bill should be prohibited because it is that discrimination itself which adversely affects interstate commerce." On another occasion during the hearing, he stated: "Of course, there are limits on Congressional power under the Commerce Clause. It may be conceded that Congress does not hold the power to regulate all of a man's conduct solely because he has relationship with interstate commerce. What is required is that there be a relationship between interstate commerce and the evil to be regulated. Over the course of the years, various tests have been established for determining whether this relationship exists. The proposed legislation clearly meets these tests." Hearings before the Senate Committee on Commerce on S. 1732, 88th Cong., 1st Sess. (1963).

6. The court in *Katzenbach* has been criticized because in that case "where the connection with interstate commerce appears most tenuous, the court dismissd the issue simply by referring to the analysis in Heart of Atlanta. . . ." Note, *The Civil Rights Act of 1964—Source and Scope of Congressional Power,* 60 Nw. U. L. REV. 574, 578 (1965). Even if you agree with the government's contention that "racial discrimination at restaurants which receive from out of state a substantial portion of the food served does, in fact, impose commercial burdens of national magnitude upon interstate commerce," did Ollie's Barbecue satisfy that "substantiality" test? How does the court handle the *statutory* requirement that a substantial portion of the food travel through com-

merce? Does a restaurant fall under the Act's coverage only when it uses substantial portions of interstate food or does the Act become applicable when it is shown that the restaurant, taken in conjunction with others similarly situated, engages in substantial interstate commerce business? Is *Wickard v. Filburn*, cited by the court, even relevant to this issue? Is the substantial burden on interstate commerce produced by all those who satisfy the statutory standard, *i.e.*, serve a substantial amount of interstate commerce food. *See* Comment, *Regulation of Public Accommodations Via the Commerce Clause—The Civil Rights Act of 1964*, 19 Sw. L.J. 329, 367 (1964), arguing that "[i]f the Court uses the *Wickard v. Filburn* yardstick, every hot dog stand in the country would be covered . . . [since] the mustard obtained through interstate commerce and dispensed by the smallest hot dog stand would, if multiplied by all the hot dog stands in the country, surely affect commerce."

## Applying Title II

1. With the constitutional issue settled, subsequent decisions have dealt with the interpretation of its provisions. *See* C. ANTIEAU, FEDERAL CIVIL RIGHTS ACTS: CIVIL PRACTICE 161-76 (1971). Daniel v. Paul, 395 U.S. 298 (1969), exemplifies the difficulties in utilizing the commerce clause as a constitutional nexus in outlawing discrimination in "public" accomodations. The issue was whether Lake Nixon, a 232-acre amusement and recreation area, was a "public accommodation" within the meaning of Title II.

The court found that a snack bar located on the grounds was covered by Title II because a substantial portion of the food served had moved in interstate commerce and because it served and offered to serve interstate travelers. While admitting the inadequacy of the record regarding the former finding, the court noted that hot dog and hamburger buns and the soft drinks contained ingredients originating in other states. Although no evidence was introduced on the latter finding, the court noted that the Lake Nixon Club had advertised in numerous periodicals and concluded that "it would be unrealistic to assume that none of the 100,000 patrons actually served by the Club each season was an interstate traveler." Since the snack bar was a covered establishment within the scope of Title II, it "automatically brings the entire Lake Nixon facility within the ambit of Title II."

The court also found that Lake Nixon qualified as a "place of entertainment" citing "the overriding purpose of Title II 'to remove the daily affront and humiliation involved in discriminatory denials of access to facilities ostensibly open to the general public.' " It followed that "the statutory language 'place of entertainment' should be given full effect according to its generally accepted meaning and applied to recreational areas."

The court ended by finding that the operations of Lake Nixon "affect commerce" since its customary "sources of entertainment . . . move in commerce." Paddleboats were leased or bought from an out of state company; the juke box and records played were manufactured out of state.

Justice Black, dissenting, argued that such fact-finding, involving the jurisdictional authority of state and nation, must "be met by evidence and judicial findings, not by guesswork, or assumptions, or 'judicial knowledge' of crucially relevant facts, or by unproved probabilities or possibilities."

2.  *Private Clubs.* The statutory exception for private clubs reflects the concern expressed by Justice Goldberg concurring in Bell v. Maryland, 378 U.S. 226, 313 (1964): "Prejudice and bigotry in any form are regrettable, but it is the constitutional right of every person to close his home or club to any person or to choose social intimates and business partners solely on the basis of personal prejudices including race. These and other rights pertaining to privacy and private associations are themselves constitutionally protected liberties." *But see* Comment, *Association, Privacy and the Private Club: The Constitutional Conflict,* 5 HARV. CIV. RTS.—CIV. LIB. L. REV. 460 (1970), arguing that in some circumstances even private clubs should not be immune from antidiscrimination legislation.

Whether a club is private and thereby entitled to these "constitutionally protected liberties" is a factual decision. For an excellent discussion of the public accommodation—private club dichotomy *see* Comment, *Public Accommodations: What Is a Private Club?,* 30 MONT. L. REV. 47 (1968), where the author divides the criteria for determining whether a club is truly private into four groups: (1) membership; (2) reasons for formation; (3) finances; and (4) publicity. Membership, the most frequently emphasized criterion, involves consideration of "(1) admission policies; (2) use of the club by persons other than members or guests; (3) control of the members; and (4) the size of the membership."

## Other Uses of the Commerce Power

1.  *Employment Discrimination.* In Steele v. Louisville & N.R.R., 323 U.S. 192 (1944), the court held that the Railway Labor Act imposed on a union, selected as an exclusive representative, a duty of fair representation. "So long as a labor union

assumes to act as the statutory representative of a craft, it cannot rightly refuse to perform the duty, which is inseparable from the power of representation conferred upon it, to represent the entire membership of the craft. . . . [I]t [requires] the union, in collective bargaining and in making contracts with the carrier, to represent non-union or minority union members of the craft without hostile discrimination, fairly, impartially, and in good faith." Later, the same duty was imposed under the National Labor Relations Act. *See* NLRB v. Local 1367, I.L.A., 368 F.2d 1010 (5th Cir. 1966); Local 12, United Rubber Workers, AFL-CIO v. NLRB, 368 F.2d 12 (5th Cir. 1966). And there has even been a court holding that racial discrimination by an employer acting alone can violate the NLRA. United Packinghouse, Food and Allied Workers International Union, AFL-CIO v. NLRB, 416 F.2d 1126 (D.C. Cir. 1969).

Title VII of the 1964 Civil Rights Act, as amended, declares it to be an "unlawful employment practice" for any employer having 15 or more employees or labor organization engaged in an "industry affecting commerce" to discriminate on the basis of race, color, religion, sex, or national origin. 21 U.S.C. §§ 2000e—2000e-2. "Industry affecting commerce" includes "any activity, business, or industry in commerce or in which a labor dispute would hinder or obstruct commerce or the free flow of commerce and includes any activity or industry 'affecting commerce' within the meaning of the Labor-Management Reporting and Disclosure Act of 1959."

In a Memorandum on Title VII's constitutionality, reprinted in 110 CONG. REC. (Pt. VI) 7210 (April 8, 1964), the Solicitor's Office of the Department of Labor argued: "Since Congress in the exercise of its power over interstate commerce can make it unlawful to discriminate because of union membership and because of [union activity] under [the Fair Labor Standards Act and the National Labor Relations Act], it is clear that Congress also has power to prevent discrimination on the basis of race, color, religion or national origin." *See* New Negro Alliance v. Sanitary Grocery Co., 303 U.S. 552 (1938), supporting this analogy. The Memorandum also contended that it is established that the commerce power "extends to activities affecting commerce in any amount or volume not so minimal or sporadic as to fall within the doctrine of de minimis non curat lex."

2. *Fair Housing Legislation.* Title VIII of the 1968 Civil Rights Act, declaring that "[i]t is the policy of the United States to provide within constitutional limitations, for fair housing throughout the United States," makes it unlawful to discriminate in the sale, rental, financing of housing or in brokerage services

because of race, color, religion, or national origin. The Act was based on both the commerce clause and § 5 of the fourteenth amendment.

In attacking the commerce clause basis of such open housing legislation, Senator Sparkman argued: "Real property is permanent. It does not move. How can it in and of itself become an item in commerce?" 112 Cong. Rec. (Pt. 17) 23028 (Sept. 19, 1966). Senator Thurmond contended: "If [the commerce clause] does indeed authorize Congress to regulate private action dealing with the sale or rental of real property situated within the borders of one State, then there is no field of endeavor which Congress cannot control under the authority granted in this clause." 114 Cong. Rec. (Pt. III) 2718 (Feb. 8, 1968).

But, in support of the legislation, a Memorandum, noting the actual place of the housing industry in our economy and the extent of interstate activity involved, argued: "Discrimination in Housing affects this interstate commerce in several ways. The confinement of Negroes and other minority groups to older homes in ghettos restricts the number of new homes which are built and consequently reduces the amount of building materials and residential financing which moves across state lines. Negroes, especially those in professions or in business, are less likely to change their place of residence to another state when housing discrimination would force them to move their families into ghettos. The result is both to reduce the interstate movement of individuals and to hinder the efficient allocation of labor among the interstate components of the economy." 114 Cong. Rec. (Pt. VI) 9564 (April 10, 1968).

## F. FEDERALIZING CRIME THROUGH THE COMMERCE POWER

As is demonstrated by the *Lottery Case,* text, p. 171, the use of the commerce power to criminalize conduct typically dealt with through state criminal processes is not a modern phenomenon. But there has been an increasing incidence of the federalization of crime using this jurisdictional nexus since the 1930's. As control of criminal behavior has traditionally been considered a prerogative of the states in the exercise of their police power, what do these developments suggest concerning the health of federalism?

### Federalizing Crime Through the Police Power

Until recently, most legislation federalizing crime has involved congressional regulation of interstate traffic itself. As the police power cases indicate, a plenary power to regulate commerce includes the power to prohibit that commerce from being used for socially undesirable ends. Do the examples below support the use of such a rationale to fashion a federal criminal law?

1. *Riot Control.* A rash of disorders inspired Congress to include the following provisions as Title I of the Civil Rights Act of 1968, 18 U.S.C. § 2101:

(a) (1) Whoever travels in interstate or foreign commerce or uses any facility of interstate or foreign commerce, including, but not limited to, the mail, telegraph, telephone, radio, or television, with intent—

(A) to incite a riot; or

(B) to organize, promote, encourage, participate in, or carry on a riot; or

(C) to commit any act of violence in furtherance of a riot; or

(D) to aid or abet any person in inciting or participating in or carrying on a riot or committing any act of violence in furtherance of a riot; and who either during the course of any such travel or use or thereafter performs or attempts to perform any other overt act for any purpose specified in subparagraph (A), (B), (C), (D), of this paragraph—

Shall be fined not more than $10,000, or imprisoned not more than five years, or both.

(b) In any prosecution under this section, proof that the defendant engaged or attempted to engage in one or more of the overt acts described in subparagraph (A), (B), (C), or (D) of paragraph (1) of subsections (a) and (1) have travelled in interstate or foreign commerce, or (2) has use of or used any facility of interstate or foreign commerce, including but not limited to, mail, telegraph, telephone, radio, or television, to communicate with or broadcast to any person or group of persons prior to such overt acts, such travel or use shall be admissible proof to establish that such defendant travelled in or used such facility of interstate or foreign commerce.

Is it proper for the federal government to legislate in this area when all 50 states have criminal penalties covering riots? Former United States Assistant Attorney General Doer suggested otherwise: "[I]ndeed, state and local law enforcement agencies are generally to be commended for the manner in which they have handled the riots. They have acted promptly and vigorously to maintain and restore law and order. They have arrested, prosecuted, and convicted persons who have resorted to violence. . . . [T]here is a real question whether the proposals . . . add materially to existing law enforcement tools." 113 CONG. REC. (Pt. XV) 19366 (July 19, 1967). *See* Note, *The Riot Act of 1968: Congress Rides a Trojan Horse,* 4 GA. L. REV. 359 (1970), for the view that the Act is unconstitutional because the states can effectively control the criminal conduct. For further discussion of the propriety of such legislation see Survey, *Criminal Justice in Extremis: Administration of Justice During the April 1968*

*Chicago Disorder,* 36 U. CHI. L. REV. 455 (1969); Levine, *The Proposed New Federal Criminal Code: A Constitutional and Jurisdictional Analysis,* 39 BROOKLYN L. REV. 1 (1972).

2. *Misbranding Goods.* United States v. Sullivan, 332 U.S. 689 (1948), involved the constitutionality of the Federal Food, Drug and Cosmetic Act of 1938, prohibiting "the doing of any . . . act with respect to, a . . . drug . . . if such act is done while such article is held for sale after shipment in interstate commerce and results in such article being misbranded." It was alleged that properly labeled bottles of sulfathiazole tablets were shipped from Chicago, Illinois, to a consignee in Atlanta, Georgia. Respondent, a Georgia druggist, bought one of these properly labeled bottles in Atlanta and took it to his drug store in Columbus, Georgia, where he removed 12 tablets, placed them in pill boxes which were not properly marked, and resold them. He was indicted and convicted for violating the federal Act. The Circuit Court of Appeals reversed his conviction, interpreting the statutory language " 'while such article is held for sale after shipment in interstate commerce' as though Congress had said 'while such article is held for sale by a person who had himself received it by way of a shipment in interstate commerce.' " The Supreme Court reversed.

Justice Black, for the court, concluded that "the language used by Congress broadly and unqualifiedly prohibits misbranding articles held for sale after shipment in interstate commerce, without regard to how long after the shipment the misbranding occurred, how many intrastate sales had intervened, or who had received the articles at the end of the interstate shipment." Since the purpose of the Act was to safeguard the consumer from dangerous products, its coverage was designed to extend "to articles from the moment of their introduction into interstate commerce all the way to the moment of their delivery to the ultimate consumer." The respondent's conduct thus fell within the statutory prohibition.

As to the contention that the Act as construed was beyond Congress' constitutional power and invades powers reserved to the states, the court held that McDermott v. Wisconsin, 228 U.S. 115 (1913), was controlling. Both cases were said to relate "to the constitutional power of Congress under the commerce clause to regulate the branding of articles that have completed an interstate shipment and are being held for future sales in purely local or intrastate commerce." Justice Frankfurter, joined by Justices Reed and Jackson, dissented on statutory grounds.

In *McDermott,* involving a challenge to the constitutionality of the Pure Food and Drug Act of 1906, the respondents, Wisconsin merchants, had received an interstate shipment of canned goods. They offered the cans for sale in their original packages, labeled in conformity with federal law, but mislabeled according to state law. They appealed their state convictions alleging that the federal law controlled the transaction.

The court unanimously agreed, holding that Congress has "full power to keep the channels of such commerce free from transportation of illicit or harmful articles, to make such as are injurious to the public health outlaws of such commerce, and to bar them from the facilities and privileges thereof. Congress may itself determine the means appropriate to this purpose, and so long as they do no violence to other provisions of the Constitution, it is itself the judge of the means to be employed in exercising the powers conferred upon it in this respect."

There were two factors arguably distinguishing *McDermott.* First, "the possessor of the labeled cans held for sale had himself received them by way of interstate sale and shipment," whereas in *Sullivan,* the possessor had received the goods by way of an intrastate transaction. Second, in *McDermott,* "the labels involved were on the original containers; here [in *Sullivan*] the labels are required to be put on other than the original containers—the boxes to which the tablets were transferred," *i.e.,* the local merchant had to place the federally mandated labels on goods sold intrastate even when he received the goods by way of an intrastate transaction. The *Sullivan* court determined that these distinctions were "not sufficient . . . to detract from the applicability of *McDermott.* . . ." *See* Note, 96 U. PA. L. REV. 710, 711 (1948), contending that *McDermott,* "does not establish as constitutional the regulations upheld in the [*Sullivan*] case."

Was *Sullivan* decided upon a stream of commerce theory? Consider the court's conclusion that the Act extended "to every article that had gone through interstate commerce until it finally reached the ultimate consumer." Is *Sullivan* authority for the proposition that the federal government can regulate the distribution of all goods once they have been "federalized" by entering interstate channels? Where does the stream of commerce end? Where does it begin?

Was the underlying rationale of the *Sullivan* court its belief that the Act was a proper exercise of the police power? The court relied on *McDermott* which cites police power cases and holds, at least in part, that Congress has the power to deny interstate channels to goods which are not properly labeled. What is the significance of the court's failure to take into account economic considerations? Consider the *Sullivan* court's statement that the purpose of the Act was "to insure federal protection until the very moment the article passes into the hands of the consumer by way of interstate transaction. . . ." While the police power cases appear to stress the regulation of interstate commerce itself, does *Sullivan* allow regulation even after interstate commerce has ended?

In *Sullivan,* the court stated that the "question relates to the constitutional power of Congress under the commerce clause to regulate the branding of articles that have completed an interstate shipment and are being held for future sales in purely local or intrastate commerce." Does *Sullivan* establish a non-economic affectation doctrine? The theory appears to be that Congress can regulate local activity appropriate to effectuate other congressional legislation governing interstate commerce. *See* United States v. Darby, 312 U.S. 100 (1941).

The difficulty that most commentators have had with *Sullivan* is its lack of clarity concerning the operative constitutional theory —Stream of commerce? Police power? Affectation?

### Federalizing Crime Through the Affectation Doctrine

Even before *Perez,* the federal government had argued that Congress could federalize local crime without showing any jurisdictional nexus between the local activity and interstate commerce. An example is set forth below.

1.   *Firearms Control.* Title VII of the Omnibus Crime Control and Safe Streets Act provides that "(a) Any person who—(1) has been convicted . . . of a felony . . . and who receives, possesses, or transports in commerce or affecting commerce . . . , any firearm shall be fined not more than $10,000 or imprisoned for not more than 2 years, or both."

United States v. Bass, 404 U.S. 336 (1971), presented the issue whether this provision "banned all possessions and receipts of firearms by convicted felons, and that no connection with interstate commerce had to be demonstrated in individual cases." The government argued that the words "in commerce or affecting commerce" modified only the words "transports" and therefore a convicted felon could be prosecuted for the possession of firearms regardless of his or its connection with interstate commerce.

The court, per Justice Marshall, avoided the constitutional question through statutory interpretation. Justice Marshall concluded that because the Act's "sanctions are criminal and because, under the government's broader reading, the statute would mark a major inroad into a domain traditionally left to the States, we refuse to adopt the broader reading in the absence of a clear direction from Congress." He added that "consistent with our regard for the sensitive relation between federal and state jurisdiction, our reading preserves as an element of all the offenses a requirement suited to federal criminal jurisdiction alone."

Title VII of the Act contains a declaration of findings that "the receipt, possession, or transportation of a firearm by a felon . . . constitutes a burden on commerce or threat affecting the free flow of commerce." While there was little congressional considera-tion of the constitutional issue, there were statements concerning the adverse affect criminal activity had on business. Would this be a sufficient jurisdictional nexus?

18 U.S.C. § 921 et seq., make it a federal offense for unli-censed persons to engage in the business of importing, manu-facturing, or dealing in firearms or ammunition, or in the course of such business to ship, transport, or receive any firearm or ammunition in interstate commerce. In United States v. Nelson, 458 F.2d 556, 559 (5th Cir. 1972), the court examined the legisla-tive history of the Act which unlike that in *Bass* was fairly extensive, and determined that "Congress intended to reach appellant's conduct irrespective of its immediate nexus with commerce." In upholding the constitutionality of the Act, the court stated: "We believe that the acquisition of firearms by convicted felons and persons under indictment for felonies, although arguably intrastate activity, imposes a sufficient burden upon interstate commerce for federal regulation. . . . Therefore, while the Supreme Court in *Bass* impliedly expressed some reser-vations about Congress' power to regulate possession of firearms, we entertain no doubt that it has the power to regulate their acquisition without requiring proof of a nexus with interstate commerce in each individual case."

As you read *Perez*, consider the extent to which it settles the unanswered questions in *Bass*.

### PEREZ v. UNITED STATES
Supreme Court of the United States
402 U.S. 146, 28 L. Ed. 2d 686, 91 S. Ct. 1357 (1971)

Justice DOUGLAS delivered the opinion of the Court.

The question in this case is whether Title II of the Consumer Credit Protection Act, as construed and applied to petitioner, is a permissible exercise by Congress of its powers under the Com-merce Clause of the Constitution.

Petitioner's conviction after trial by jury and his sentence were affirmed by the Court of Appeals, one judge dissenting. . . . We affirm that judgment.

Petitioner is one of the species commonly known as "loan sharks" which Congress found are in large part under the control

of "organized crime." "Extortionate credit transactions" are
defined as those characterized by the use or threat of the use of
"violence or other criminal means" in enforcment. . . .

. . . .

The Commerce Clause reaches, in the main, three categories of
problems. First, the use of channels of interstate or foreign commerce which Congress deems are being misused, as, for example,
the shipment of stolen goods or of persons who have been kid-
naped. Second, protection of the instrumentalities of interstate
commerce, as, for example, the destruction of an aircraft, or
persons or things in commerce, as, for example, thefts from interstate shipments. Third, those activities affecting commerce. It is
with this last category that we are here concerned.

. . . .

. . . [T]he broader view of the Commerce Clause announced
by Chief Justice Marshall had been restored. . . .

. . . .

[I]n *United States v Darby,* the decision sustaining an Act of
Congress which prohibited the employment of workers in the
production of goods "for interstate commerce" at other than
prescribed wages and hours, *a class of activities* was held properly
regulated by Congress without proof that the particular intrastate
activity against which a sanction was laid had an effect on commerce. . . .

That case is particularly relevant here because it involved a
criminal prosecution, a unanimous Court holding that the Act
was "sufficiently definite to meet constitutional demands." Petitioner is clearly *a member of the class* which engages in "extortionate credit transactions" as defined by Congress and the description of that class has the required definiteness.

. . . .

Where the *class of activities* is regulated and that *class* is
within the reach of federal power, the courts have no power "to
excise, as trivial, individual instances" of the class. Maryland v
Wirtz, 392 U.S. 183, 193.

Extortionate credit transactions, though purely intrastate,
may in the judgment of Congress affect interstate commerce. . . .
In the setting of the present case there is a tie-in between local
loan sharks and interstate crime.

The findings by Congress are quite adequate on that ground.
. . .

. . . .

The essence of all these reports and hearings was summarized
and embodied in formal congressional findings. They supplied

Congress with the knowledge that the loan shark racket provides organized crime with its second most lucrative source of revenue, exacts millions from the pockets of people, coerces its victims into the commission of crimes against property, and causes the takeover by racketeers of legitimate businesses.

We have mentioned in detail the economic, financial, and social setting of the problem as revealed to Congress. We do so not to infer that Congress need make particularized findings in order to legislate. We relate the history of the Act in detail to answer the impassioned plea of petitioner that all that is involved in loan sharking is a traditionally local activity. It appears, instead, that loan sharking in its national setting is one way organized interstate crime holds its guns to the heads of the poor and the rich alike and syphons funds from numerous localities to finance its national operations.

Affirmed.

Justice STEWART, dissenting.

. . . [U]nder the statute before us a man can be convicted without any proof of interstate movement, of the use of the facilities of interstate commerce, or of facts showing that his conduct affected interstate commerce. I think the Framers of the Constitution never intended that the National Government might define as a crime and prosecute such wholly local activity through the enactment of federal criminal laws.

In order to sustain this law we would, in my view, have to be able at the least to say that Congress could rationally have concluded that loan sharking is an activity with interstate attributes that distinguish it in some substantial respect from other local crime. But it is not enough to say that loan sharking is a national problem, for all crime is a national problem. It is not enough to say that some loan sharking has interstate characteristics, for any crime may have an interstate setting. And the circumstance that loan sharking has an adverse impact on interstate business is not a distinguishing attribute, for interstate business suffers from almost all criminal activity, be it shoplifting or violence in the streets.

Because I am unable to discern any rational distinction between loan sharking and other local crime, I cannot escape the conclusion that this statute was beyond the power of Congress to enact. The definition and prosecution of local, intrastate crime are reserved to the States under the Ninth and Tenth Amendments.

## NOTES

1. Assuming that Perez is a loanshark linked with organized crime, *how* is interstate commerce affected? Is it enough that local loansharking has an impact on business conditions? Justice Stewart thought this argument proved too much: "[i]nterstate business suffers from all criminal activity. . . ." He also observed: "[S]ince the total economic impact of almost any class of criminal activity substantially injures interstate business, most traditionally local crimes could be federalized under a broad construction of the commerce power." *See* Note, *Constitutional Law—Commerce Power—Mere Possession of Firearms by a Felon, Without Proof of an Effect on Interstate Commerce Is Not Violative of Federal Statute,* 49 Tex. L. Rev. 1106, 1111 (1971).

Is a sufficient "tie-in" found in the financial support organized crime receives from local loansharking? Even so *how* does this affect interstate commerce? Is it fair to classify organized crime with "any class of criminal activity"? One study, entitled The Urban Poor and Organized Crime in 113 Cong. Rec. 24460-64 (1967), attempted to make a distinction: "Ordinary street crime is a national problem—but one which can and should be solved at the local level. But organized crime is a national problem which requires a national solution. . . ." The lower court in *Perez* made the following finding: ". . . loan-sharking is so effective and lucrative because of high-level organization running across state lines, which eliminates competition between money-lenders in metropolitan areas. . . . Loan-sharking activities can persuasively be characterized as generally in or affecting commerce precisely because such practices depend for their full effect on monopoly in metropolitan areas and national, or at least multistate, organization. This provided a logical basis for congressional focus on loan-sharking rather than on a variety of other crimes which may be far more 'local' in nature, *e.g.*, robbery, burglary, larceny." United States v. Perez, 426 F.2d 1073, 1079 (2d Cir. 1970).

If we accept the finding that loan-sharking practices exist due to the nation-wide scope of organized crime, then the federal commerce power could reach all loan-sharking by applying Professor Powell's suggested formula, *i.e.*, that federal power comprehends activity that would not exist if interstate channels were not used or available for use. T. Powell, Vagaries and Varieties in Constitution Interpretation 67-70 (1956).

Consider the suggestion that the regulation of loansharking although it involves criminal penalties, is predominantly an economic measure which, in reality, regulates merely another interstate business—"the unique business of organized crime."

Notes, *Commerce Clause—National Police Power Justified by Economic Impact of Organized Crime*, 46 TUL. L. REV. 829, 834 (1972).

2.  The Extortionate Credit Transaction Act applies to all extortionate credit transactions regardless of amount, relationship between the parties, the number of such transactions made by a co-defendant, or whether the lender is independent or in association with others. Citing *Wickard v. Filburn*, Justice Douglas argues that the test is whether "the *class* of activities regulated" is within the reach of the federal power and not whether individual defendants have the requisite tie-in to interstate commerce. Is *Perez* really analogous to *Wickard v. Filburn*? Filburn was a member of the class whose activities affected interstate commerce. However, Perez was not shown to be a member of the class whose activities related to organized crime. Does *Perez* extend the reaches of the commerce clause farther even than *Wickard v. Filburn*?

Do you agree with the following: "The significance in *Perez*, therefore, is that it is the first case in which the Court upheld federal regulation of a well-defined but possibly over-inclusive class of substantive criminal activity on the grounds that in order to exercise effectively the commerce power over an interstate evil, individual acts unconnected with that evil must also be reached." Stern, *The Commerce Clause Revisited—The Federalization of Intrastate Crime*, 15 ARIZ. L. REV. 271, 279 (1973).

Consider the observation of Representative Eckhardt (Texas): "Should [the Extortionate Credit Transaction Act] become law, [it] would take a long stride by the Federal Government towards occupying the field of general criminal law and towards exercising a general Federal police power; and it would permit prosecution in Federal as well as state courts of a typically State offense." 114 CONG. REC. 1610 (Pt. II) (Jan. 31, 1968).

Following the decision in *Perez*, Senator John McClellan (Arkansas) contended that the case had established the "power of Congress to make legislative findings of the jurisdictional aspects of offenses sufficient to permit conviction, with no requirement that jurisdictional indicia be satisfied in individual prosecutions." McClellan, *Codification, Reform, and Revision: The Challenge of a Modern Federal Criminal Code*, 1971 DUKE L.J. 663, 685.

3.  What is the rationale for such an extension? Does difficulty of proving an interstate nexus in individual cases justify this extension of the affectation doctrine? In fact, *Perez* may merely be an application of the principle that Congress may regulate local activities which are so commingled with interstate com-

merce that all must be regulated if the interstate commerce is to be effectively controlled. As Robert Stern notes: "The principle . . . which emerges in *Perez* is that Congress may regulate local acts which in themselves have no interstate nexus or effect if as a practical matter it is difficult to distinguish such transaction from others which may have some relation to interstate commerce." Stern, *The Commerce Clause Revisited,* 15 ARIZ. L. REV. at 280 (1973).

4. *The Limits of Congressional Power.* Is it desirable to apply the rational basis test to this type of federal legislation? In the area of due process and equal protection, when important rights of the individual are at stake, such as his liberty, courts use a more stringent standard of review.

Perhaps federal intervention should be permissible only when the states individually are incapable of controlling local crime. Or has the distinction between local and national spheres of concern been eroded in this area as it has in economic matters?

Is there any effective judicial limitation remaining on the power of Congress to federalize the law of crimes? Perhaps the increasing number of justices expressing concern with the scope of congressional power suggests that there may still be some limitation. The ultimate limitation remains that suggested by Justice Marshall in *Gibbons v. Ogden:* "[T]he wisdom and the discretion of Congress, their identity with the people, and the influence which their constituents possess at elections, are, in this, as in many other instances, . . . the sole restraint on which they have relied, to secure them from its abuse. They are the restraints on which the people must often rely solely, in all representative governments."

## G. THE TAXING AND SPENDING POWER

Article I, § 8, of the Constitution provides "the Congress shall have power to lay and collect taxes, duties, imposts and excises, to pay the debts and provide for the common defense and general welfare of the United States. . . ." Like the commerce power, the power to tax and spend is plenary. Nevertheless it is necessary to determine the meaning of the granted power and the purposes for which it may be exercised.

In the first section below, the focus will be on the questions which arise when the taxing power is used to achieve regulatory objectives. Can Congress tax for purposes other than the raising of revenue? Can it regulate in otherwise prohibited areas by framing its legislation in the form of a taxing measure? Can it pursue social welfare objectives, normally within the sphere of the state's police power, through the use of the taxing clause? What factors should a court consider in determining whether a law is a "tax" or a regulatory "penalty"? Perhaps, it is proper for a court to probe behind the purported fiscal character of the law to discern its true "regulatory" purpose. Ultimately, the decision characterizing legislation as a tax or a penalty is not a matter of doctrine but a reflection of the currently prevailing judicial values.

In the second section, the focus will be on the purposes for which Congress can spend tax revenues. What is the effect of the general welfare clause in Art. I, § 8? Arguably, it is a separate grant of power to regulate. Or the clause may be read as merely an ancillary reference to the other delegated powers. Or it may envision spending purposes beyond the realm of those delegated powers. What does the term "general welfare" mean? To what extent can Congress condition its spending grants to "induce" or "coerce" compliance from individuals or the states? If a broad interpretation is given the spending provision, is there any judicially meaningful limitation on the exercise of the power? Is a broad interpretation consistent with the principles of federalism? After all, if legal checks prove inadequate, the political process may serve as an effective check on the use of national power.

## 1. When Is A Tax Not A Tax?

### BAILEY v. DREXEL FURNITURE CO. (CHILD LABOR TAX CASE)

Supreme Court of the United States
259 U.S. 20, 66 L. Ed. 817, 42 S. Ct. 449 (1922)

Chief Justice TAFT delivered the opinion of the Court:

This case presents the question of the constitutional validity of the Child Labor Tax Law. . . .

. . . .

The law is attacked on the ground that it is a regulation of the employment of child labor in the states,—an exclusively state function under the Federal Constitution and within the reservations of the 10th Amendment. It is defended on the ground that it is a mere excise tax, levied by the Congress of the United States under its broad power of taxation conferred by § 8, article 1, of the Federal Constitution. We must construe the law and interpret the intent and meaning of Congress from the language of the act. The words are to be given their ordinary meaning unless the context shows that they are differently used. Does this law impose a tax with only that incidental restraint and regulation which a tax must inevitably involve? Or does it regulate by the use of the so-called tax as a penalty? If a tax, it is clearly an excise. If it were an excise on a commodity or other

thing of value we might not be permitted, under previous decisions of this court, to infer, solely from its heavy burden, that the
act intends a prohibition instead of a tax. But this act is more.
It provides a heavy exaction for a departure from a detailed
and specified course of conduct in business. That course of business is that employers shall employ in mines and quarries, children of an age greater than sixteen years; in mills and factories,
children of an age greater than fourteen years; and shall prevent
children of less than sixteen years in mills and factories from
working more than eight hours a day or six days in the week.
If an employer departs from this prescribed course of business,
he is to pay to the government one tenth of his entire net income in the business for a full year. The amount is not to be
proportioned in any degree to the extent or frequency of the
departures, but is to be paid by the employer in full measure
whether he employs five hundred children for a year, or employs
only one for a day. Moreover, if he does not know the child is
within the named age limit, he is not to pay; that is to say, it is
only where he knowingly departs from the prescribed course that
payment is to be exacted. Scienters are associated with penalties,
not with taxes. The employer's factory is to be subject to inspection at any time not only by the taxing officers of the Treasury,
the Department normally charged with the collection of taxes,
but also by the Secretary of Labor and his subordinates, whose
normal function is the advancement and protection of the welfare of the workers. In the light of these features of the act, a
court must be blind not to see that the so-called tax is imposed to
stop the employment of children within the age limits prescribed.
Its prohibitory and regulatory effect and purpose are palpable.
All others can see and understand this. How can we properly
shut our minds to it?

. . . .

The difference between a tax and a penalty is sometimes difficult to define, and yet the consequences of the distinction in the
required method of their collection often are important. Where
the sovereign enacting the law has power to impose both tax and
penalty, the difference between revenue production and mere
regulation may be immaterial; but not so when one sovereign
can impose a tax only, and the power of regulation rests in another. Taxes are occasionally imposed in the discretion of the
legislature on proper subjects with the primary motive of obtaining revenue from them, and with the incidental motive of
discouraging them by making their continuance onerous. They
do not lose their character as taxes because of the incidental
motive. But there comes a time in the extension of the penaliz-

ing features of the so-called tax when it loses its character as such and becomes a mere penalty, with the characteristics of regulation and punishment. Such is the case in the law before us. Although Congress does not invalidate the contract of employment, or expressly declare that the employment within the mentioned ages is illegal, it does exhibit its intent practically to achieve the latter result by adopting the criteria of wrongdoing, and imposing its principal consequence on those who transgress its standard.

. . . .

For the reasons given, we must hold the Child Labor Tax Law invalid, and the judgment of the District Court is affirmed.

Justice CLARKE dissents.

---

## NOTES

1. The first case specifically dealing with the problem of when a tax is not a tax was Veazie Bank v. Fenno, 75 U.S. (8 Wall.) 533 (1869). The court there indicated that the fact that a tax imposes a heavy burden is not determinative that it is a penalty. Is it relevant? Professor Cushman contends that it is not: "How can a court declare a tax to be void because it is too high without subjecting to judicial scrutiny all the many and diverse considerations of public policy and necessity which are the very essence of the legislative function: The courts have wisely refused to assume any such non-judicial duty, and the result is that, assuming that there is no other constitutional objection to it, a tax is valid even though its rate rises to thousand per cent or more." Cushman, *Social and Economic Control through Federal Taxation,* 18 MINN. L. REV. 759 (1934), 3 SELECTED ESSAYS 543, 547 (1938).

As *Fenno* also indicates, Congress can use taxation as a necessary and proper means to carry out its delegated powers. Such a measure is justifiable, however, not on the basis of the taxing clause but as an exercise of one of the other delegated powers.

2. *Regulations Incidental to Producing Revenue.* The judicial deference to congressional judgment in the exercise of its taxing power manifested in *Fenno* continued in a series of later cases discussed in *The Child Labor Tax Case.* In United States v. Doremus, 249 U.S. 86 (1919), the court dealt with the validity of the Harrison Act imposing a $1.00 licensing tax on sellers of narcotic drugs and requiring that all sales be noted on order forms, except those by a physician for medicinal purposes or by pharmacists upon prescription from a physician. While the reve-

nue objectives of the legislation were minimal compared to its regulatory aspects, the court sustained the legislation. The regulation was perceived as a method of assuring the collection of the tax. "Congress, with full power over the subject, short of arbitrary and unreasonable action, which is not to be assumed, inserted these provisions in an act specifically providing for the raising of revenue. Considered of themselves, we think they tend to keep the traffic above-board and subject to inspection by those authorized to collect the revenue. They tend to diminish the opportunity of unauthorized persons to obtain the drugs and sell them clandestinely without paying the tax imposed by the federal law. . . . Congress may have deemed it wise to prevent such possible dealings because of their effect upon the collection of the revenue."

3. *Objective Constitutionality.* "The criterion of 'objective constitutionality,' which may not inaccurately be called the doctrine of 'judicial obtuseness,' permits the Court to uphold any carefully drawn taxing statute designed to promote the social and economic well-being of the Country through regulation or repression by the simple process of keeping the judicial eye discreetly on the portions of the act which spell 'tax' and discreetly off those which spell 'regulation and destruction.' It may be invoked to sustain whatever degree of national police power under the taxing clause the Supreme Court deemed safe and desirable." Cushman, *Social and Economic Control Through Federal Taxation,* 18 MINN. L. REV. 759 (1934), 3 SELECTED ESSAYS at 563.

Judicial deference to the congressional judgment in this area seems to have reached its zenith in this early period in McCray v. United States, 195 U.S. 27 (1904), sustaining a federal tax of 10¢ per pound on colored oleomargarine, which resembles butter, while taxing white oleomargarine at a rate of only 1/4¢ per pound. The legislation, enacted under pressure from the dairy lobby, was quite clearly designed to drive colored oleomargarine off the market by making its price prohibitive. Nevertheless, the court sustained the legislation as a valid taxing measure.

4. *The Penalty Doctrine.* Does Chief Justice Taft inquire into congressional purpose or motive? Does he reject the premise that the validity of a taxing measure is to be determined by its facial characteristics? Is it determinative that a measure is revenue-producing on its face? In short, where does he depart from *McCray?* Corwin argues that the logic of the *Child Labor Tax Case* "makes the Court the supervisor of the *purposes* for which Congress may exercise its constitutional powers. . . . At one stroke a new canon of constitutional interpretation is created and

an out-of-date one revived: legislative motive becomes the test of legislative action; and any effort on the part of Congress to bring within its control matters heretofore falling to the state alone raises the question of valid motive." Corwin, *The Child Labor Decision*, THE NEW REPUBLIC, July 18, 1922, p. 179.

## UNITED STATES v. KAHRIGER
### Supreme Court of the United States
345 U.S. 22, 97 L. Ed. 754, 73 S. Ct. 510 (1953)

Justice REED delivered the opinion of the Court.

The issue raised by this appeal is the constitutionality of the occupational tax provisions of the Revenue Act of 1951 which levy a tax on persons engaged in the business of accepting wagers, and require such persons to register with the Collector of Internal Revenue. The unconstitutionality of the tax is asserted on two grounds. First, it is said that Congress, under the pretense of exercising its power to tax has attempted to penalize illegal intrastate gambling through the regulatory features of the Act, and has thus infringed the police power which is reserved to the states. Secondly, it is urged that the registration provisions of the tax violate the privilege against self-incrimination and are arbitrary and vague, contrary to the guarantees of the Fifth Amendment.

The case comes here on appeal, from the United States District Court for the Eastern District of Pennsylvania, where an information was filed against appellee alleging that he was in the business of accepting wagers and that he willfully failed to register for and pay the occupational tax in question. Appellee moved to dismiss on the ground that the sections upon which the indictment was based were unconstitutional. The District Court sustained the motion on the authority of our opinion in United States v. Constantine, 296 U. S. 287. The court reasoned that while "the subject matter of this legislation so far as revenue purposes is concerned is within the scope of Federal authorities," the tax was unconstitutional in that the information called for by the registration provisions was "peculiarly applicable to the applicant from the standpoint of law enforcement and vice control," and therefore the whole of the legislation was an infringement by the Federal Government on the police power reserved to the states by the Tenth Amendment.

The result below is at odds with the position of the seven other district courts which have considered the matter, and, in our opinion, is erroneous.

In the term following the *Constantine* opinion, this Court pointed out in Sonzinsky v. United States, 300 U. S. 506, at page

513, (a case involving a tax on a "limited class" of objectionable firearms alleged to be prohibitory in effect and "to disclose unmistakably the legislative purpose to regulate rather than to tax"), that the subject of the tax in *Constantine* was "described or treated as criminal by the taxing statute." The tax in the *Constantine* case was a special additional excise tax of $1,000, placed only on persons who carried on a liquor business in violation of state law. The wagering tax with which we are here concerned applies to all persons engaged in the business of receiving wagers regardless of whether such activity violates state law.

The substance of respondent's position with respect to the Tenth Amendment is that Congress has chosen to tax a specified business which is not within its power to regulate. The precedents are many upholding taxes similar to this wagering tax as a proper exercise of the federal taxing power. . . .

Appellee would have us say that because there is legislative history indicating a congressional motive to suppress wagering, this tax is not a proper exercise of such taxing power. . . .

It is conceded that a federal excise tax does not cease to be valid merely because it discourages or deters the activities taxed. Nor is the tax invalid because the revenue obtained is negligible. Appellee, however, argues that the sole purpose of the statute is to penalize only illegal gambling in the states through the guise of a tax measure. As with the above excise taxes which we have held to be valid, the instant tax has a regulatory effect. But regardless of its regulatory effect, the wagering tax produces revenue. As such it surpasses both the narcotics and firearms taxes which we have found valid.

It is axiomatic that the power of Congress to tax is extensive and sometimes falls with crushing effect on businesses deemed unessential or inimical to the public welfare, or where, as in dealings with narcotics, the collection of the tax also is difficult. As is well known, the constitutional restraints on taxing are few. . . .

The difficulty of saying when the power to lay uniform taxes is curtailed, because its use brings a result beyond the direct legislative power of Congress, has given rise to diverse decisions. In that area of abstract ideas, a final definition of the line between state and federal power has baffled judges and legislators.

. . . Where federal legislation has rested on other congressional powers, such as the Necessary and Proper clause or the Commerce clause, this Court has generally sustained the statutes, despite their effect on matters ordinarily considered state concern. When federal power to regulate is found, its exercise is a matter for Congress. Where Congress has employed the taxing clause a greater variation in the decisions has resulted. The division in this Court has been more acute. Without any specific differentiation between the power to tax and other federal powers, the indirect results from the exercise of the power to tax have raised more doubts. . . . It is hard to understand why the power to tax should raise more doubts because of indirect effects than other federal powers.

Penalty provisions in tax statutes added for breach of a regulation concerning activities in themselves subject only to state regulation have caused this Court to declare the enactments invalid. Unless there are provisions, extraneous to any tax need, courts are without authority to limit the exercise of the taxing power. All the provisions of this excise are adapted to the collection of a valid tax.

Nor do we find the registration requirements of the wagering tax offensive. All that is required is the filing of names, addresses, and places of business. This is quite general in tax returns. Such data are directly and intimately related to the collection of the tax and are "obviously supportable as in aid of a revenue purpose." Sonzinsky v. United States, 300 U. S. 506, at page 513. The registration provisions make the tax simpler to collect.

[The Court rejected a self-incrimination argument and a claim that the Act was vague and arbitrary.]

Reversed.

Justice FRANKFURTER, dissenting.

. . . .

What is relevant to judgment here is that, even if the history of this legislation as it went through Congress did not give one the libretto to the song, the context of the circumstances which brought forth this enactment—sensationally exploited disclosures regarding gambling in big cities and small, the relation of this gambling to corrupt politics, the impatient public response to these disclosures, the feeling of ineptitude or paralysis on the part of local law-enforcing agencies—emphatically supports what was revealed on the floor of Congress, namely, that what was formally a means of raising revenue for the Federal Government was essentially an effort to check if not to stamp out professional gambling.

A nominal taxing measure must be found an inadmissible intrusion into a domain of legislation reserved for the States not merely when Congress requires that such a measure is to be enforced through a detailed scheme of administration beyond the obvious fiscal needs, as in the *Child Labor Tax Case*. That is one ground for holding that Congress was unconstitutionally disrespectful of what is reserved to the States. Another basis for deeming such a formal revenue measure inadmissible is presented by this case. In addition to the fact that Congress was concerned with activity beyond the authority of the Federal Government, the enforcing provision of this enactment is designed for the systematic confession of crimes with a view to prosecution for such crimes under State law.

It is one thing to hold that the exception, which the Fifth Amendment makes to the duty of a witness to give his testimony when relevant to a proceeding in a federal court, does not include the potential danger to that witness of possible prosecution in a state court, and, conversely, that the Fifth Amendment does not enable States to give immunity from use in federal courts of testimony given in a State court. It is a wholly different thing to hold that Congress, which cannot constitutionally grapple directly with gambling in the States, may compel self-incriminating disclosures for the enforcement of State gambling laws, merely because it does so under the guise of a revenue measure obviously passed not for revenue purposes. The motive of congressional legislation is not for our scrutiny, provided only that the ulterior purpose is not expressed in ways which negative what the revenue words on their face express and, which do not seek enforcement of the formal revenue purpose through means that offend those standards of decency in our civilization against which due process is a barrier.

I would affirm this judgment.

Justice DOUGLAS, while not joining in the entire opinion, agrees with the views expressed herein that this tax is an attempt by the Congress to control conduct which the Constitution has left to the responsibility of the states.

Justice BLACK, with whom Justice DOUGLAS concurs, dissenting [on the self-incrimination issue].

. . . .

---

## NOTES

### The Effects of Kahriger

1. Is *Kahriger* consistent with the *Child Labor Tax Case*? Is it a return to objective constitutionality? It has been suggested that "[t]he more recent cases indicate a tendency to accept any

'tax' as a real tax so long as it is productive of at least 'some' revenue." D. Engdahl, CONSTITUTIONAL POWER: FEDERAL AND STATE IN A NUTSHELL 130 (1974).

Assuming that factors other than whether the measure is revenue producing are relevant to the constitutional question, what considerations should influence a court? Is any criterion sufficient alone to characterize a measure as a penalty?

2. Compare the modern scope of judicial review in tax cases as reflected in *Kahriger* with that used in the commerce clause cases. As long as a measure is a tax, is there any limit on the motive, purpose, objectives for which Congress may use its taxing power? Is the reserved power of the states any more relevant in this area? Again the final check on legislative abuse of the taxing power is to be found in political processes rather than judicial review.

3. *Self-Incrimination.* Since *Kahriger,* there has been no Supreme Court decision holding a tax measure to be unconstitutional as an impermissible penalty. There has, however, been considerable development of the principle that the privilege against self-incrimination protects persons against prosecution for failure to comply with tax registration provisions.

*Kahriger* had rejected the defendant's contention that making him register for a wagering tax would impermissibly subject him to prosecution for illegal gambling under state law. Fifteen years later this holding was reversed in Marchetti v. United States, 390 U.S. 39 (1968), where the court held that the registration provisions required by the Federal Wagering Tax Laws presented a "real and appreciable" and not merely an "imaginary and unsubstantial" hazard of self-incrimination. "Petitioner was confronted by a comprehensive system of federal and state prohibitions against wagering activities; he was required, on pain of criminal prosecution, to provide information which he might reasonably suppose would be available to prosecuting authorities, and which would surely prove a significant 'link in the chain' of evidence tending to establish his guilt."

It should be noted, however, that in *Marchetti,* the court specifically stated: "The issue before us is *not* whether the United States may tax activities which a state or Congress has declared unlawful. The court has repeatedly indicated that the unlawfulness of an activity does not prevent its taxation, and nothing [in this opinion] is intended to limit or diminish the vitality of those cases." *See* Grosso v. United States, 390 U.S. 62 (1968) (wagering tax), Haynes v. United States, 390 U.S. 85 (1968) (tax on possession of certain kinds of firearms), Leary v. United States, 395 U.S. 6 (1969) (order form requirements of the transfer tax provisions of the Marihuana Tax Act). *See also* United States v. Knox, 396 U.S. 77 (1969) (the filing of false information pursuant to registration requirements is not protected by the self-incrimination guarantee). *Compare* United States v. Freed, 401 U.S. 601 (1971) (upholding constitutionality of revised registration and transfer provisions of the National Firearms Act).

## 2. The National Spending Power

### UNITED STATES v. BUTLER
Supreme Court of the United States
297 U.S. 1, 80 L. Ed. 477, 56 S. Ct. 312 (1936)

Justice ROBERTS delivered the opinion of the Court.

In this case we must determine whether certain provisions of the Agricultural Adjustment Act, 1933, conflict with the Federal Constitution.

. . . .

The Congress is expressly empowered to lay taxes to provide for the general welfare. Funds in the Treasury as a result of taxation may be expended only through appropriation. (Art. I, § 9, cl. 7.) They can never accomplish the objects for which they were collected unless the power to appropriate is as broad as the power to tax. The necessary implication from the terms of the grant is that the public funds may be appropriated "to provide for the general welfare of the United States." These words cannot be meaningless, else they would not have been used. The conclusion must be that they were intended to limit and define the granted power to raise and to expend money. How shall they be construed to effectuate the intent of the instrument?

Since the foundation of the Nation sharp differences of opinion have persisted as to the true interpretation of the phrase. Madison asserted it amounted to no more than a reference to the other powers enumerated in the subsequent clauses of the same section; that, as the United States is a government of limited and enumerated powers, the grant of power to tax and spend for the general national welfare must be confined to the enumerated legislative fields committed to the Congress. In this view the phrase is mere tautology, for taxation and appropriation are or may be necessary incidents of the exercise of any of the enumerated legislative powers. Hamilton, on the other hand, maintained the clause confers a power separate and distinct from those later enumerated, is not restricted in meaning by the grant of them, and Congress consequently has a substantive power to tax and to appropriate, limited only by the requirement that it shall be exercised to provide for the general welfare of the United States. Each contention has had the support of those whose views are entitled to wait. This court has noticed the question, but has never found it necessary to decide which is the true construction. Mr. Justice Story, in his Commentaries, espouses the Hamiltonian position. We shall not review the writings of public men and commentators or discuss the legislative practice. Study of all these leads us to conclude that the reading advocated by Mr. Justice Story is a correct one. While, therefore, the power to tax is not unlimited, its confines are set in the clause which confers it and not in those of § 8 which bestow and define the legislative powers of the Congress. It results that the power of Congress to authorize expenditure of public moneys for public purposes is not limited by the direct grants of legislative power found in the Constitution.

. . . .

That the qualifying phrase must be given effect all advocates of broad construction admit. Hamilton, in his well known Report on Manufactures, states that the purpose must be "general, and not local." Monroe, an advocate of Hamilton's doctrine, wrote: "Have Congress a right to raise and appropriate the money to any and to every purpose according to their will and pleasure? They certainly have not." Story says that if the tax be not proposed for the common defence or general welfare, but for other objects wholly extraneous, it would be wholly indefensible upon constitutional principles. And he makes it clear that the powers of taxation and appropriation extend only to matters of national, as distinguished from local welfare.

. . . .

We are not now required to ascertain the scope of the phrase "general welfare of the United States" or to determine whether an appropriation in aid of agriculture falls within it. Wholly apart from that question, another principle embedded in our Constitution prohibits the enforcement of the Agricultural Adjustment Act. The act invades the reserved rights of the states. It is a statutory plan to regulate and control agricultural production, a matter beyond the powers delegated to the federal government. The tax, the appropriation of the funds raised, and the direction for their disbursement, are but parts of the plan. They are but means to an unconstitutional end. . . .

. . . .

Justice STONE, dissenting [joined by Justices CARDOZO and BRANDEIS].

. . . .

## NOTES

1.  *A Separate Regulatory Power?* The court has consistently held that the general welfare clause in the Preamble is not a separate source of power for any branch of the national government. *See, e.g.,* Jacobson v. Massachusetts, 197 U.S. 11, 22 (1905). But why isn't the General Welfare Clause in Art. I, § 8, when coupled with the necessary and proper clause, a separate source of federal regulatory power? *Compare* 1 W. CROSSKEY, POLITICS AND THE CONSTITUTION IN THE HISTORY OF THE UNITED STATES 501-08 (1953) and J. LAWSON, THE GENERAL WELFARE CLAUSE (1926) with 1 STORY, COMMENTARIES 907-908, 926 (1873).

Is the problem solely one of syntax? "For one thing, it is a fact that in certain early printings of the Constitution the 'common defense and general welfare' clause appears separately paragraphed, while in others it is set off from the 'lay and collect' clause by a semi-colon and not, as modern usage would require, by the less awesome comma. To be sure, the semi-colon may have been due in the first instance to the splattering of a goose quill that needed trimming, for it is notorious that the fate of nations has often turned on just such minute *points.*" E. CORWIN, THE TWILIGHT OF THE SUPREME COURT 153 (1934).

Does the problem lie in federal relationships? In a famous passage, Thomas Jefferson stated: ". . . the laying of taxes is the *power,* and the general welfare the *purpose* for which the power is to be exercised. They [Congress] are not to lay taxes *ad libitum* for any purpose they please; but only to *pay the debts* or *provide for the general welfare of the Union.* In like manner, they are not *to do anything they please,* to provide for the general welfare, but only *to lay taxes* for that purpose. To consider the latter phrase, not as describing the purpose of the first, but as giving a distinct and independent power to do any act they please, which might be for the good of the Union, would render all the preceding and subsequent enumerations of power completely useless. It would reduce the whole instrument to a single phrase, that of instituting a Congress with power to do whatever would be for the good of the United States; and, as they would be the sole judges of the good or evil, it would also be a power to do whatever evil they please." WRITINGS OF THOMAS JEFFERSON 147-49 (Library ed. 1904).

2.  *The Madison-Hamilton Debate.* What are the merits of the positions urged by Hamilton and Madison regarding the purpose of the general welfare clause? Madison argued in Congress that "the terms 'common defense and general welfare,' . . . are not novel terms, first introduced into this Constitution. They are terms familiar in their construction, and well known to the

people of America. They are repeatedly found in the old Articles
of the Confederation where, although they are susceptible of as
great latitude as can be given them by the context here, it was
never supposed or pretended that they conveyed any such power
as is now assigned to them. On the contrary, it was always considered as clear and certain, that the old Congress was limited
to the enumerated powers, and that the enumeration limited
and explained the general terms. I ask the gentlemen themselves,
whether it was ever supposed or suspected that the old Congress
could give away the monies of the States in bounties to encourage agriculture, or for any other purpose they pleased? If such
a power had been possessed by that body, it would have been
much less impotent, or have borne a very different character
from that universally ascribed to it." 2 ANNALS OF CONGRESS 386-
87 (1792). In THE FEDERALIST, No. 41, Madison made the same
argument. *See* Patterson, *The General Welfare Clause*, 30 MINN.
L. REV. 43 (1946), who provides historical support for Madison's
interpretation.

   3.  *Dual Federalism.* The court in *Butler* purports to accept
the Hamiltonian position regarding the purpose of the general
welfare clause. But some have said that the court quoted Hamilton to serve the ends of Madison. The court appears to suggest
that what Congress cannot do directly through regulation, it
cannot do indirectly by spending. The tenth amendment is, purportedly the source of this limiting principle.

STEWARD MACHINE CO. v. DAVIS
Supreme Court of the United States
301 U.S. 548, 81 L. Ed. 1279, 57 S. Ct. 883 (1937)

Justice CARDOZO delivered the opinion of the Court.

   The validity of the tax imposed by the Social Security Act
on employers of eight or more is here to be determined.

   . . . .

   . . . [T]wo propositions must be made out by the assailant.
. . . There must be a showing in the first place that separated
from the credit the revenue provisions are incapable of standing
by themselves. There must be a showing in the second place that
the tax and the credit in combination are weapons of coercion,
destroying or impairing the autonomy of the states. The truth
of each proposition being essential to the success of the assault,
we pass for convenience to a consideration of the second, without
pausing to inquire whether there has been a demonstration of the
first.

   To draw the line intelligently between duress and inducement there is a need to remind ourselves of facts as to the problem

of employment that are now matters of common knowledge. The relevant statistics are gathered in the brief of counsel for the government. Of the many available figures a few only will be mentioned. During the years 1929-1936, when the country was passing through a cyclical depression, the number of the unemployed amounted to unprecedented heights. Often the average was more than 10 million; at times a peak was attained of 16 million or more. Disaster to the bread winner meant disaster to dependents. Accordingly the roll of the unemployed, itself formidable enough, was only a partial roll of the destitute or needy. The fact developed quickly that the states were unable to give the requisite relief. The problem had become national in area and dimensions. There was need of help from the nation if the people were not to starve. It is too late today for the argument to be heard with tolerance that in a crisis so extreme the use of moneys of the nation to relieve the unemployed and their dependents is a use for any purpose narrower than the promotion of the general welfare. [The opinion went on to discuss the enormous expenditure, over $8 billion, from the federal treasury to provide public works employment and other forms of relief.]

. . . .

Who then is coerced through the operation of this statute? Not the taxpayer. He pays in fulfillment of the mandate of the local legislature. Not the state. Even now she does not offer a suggestion that in passing the unemployment law she was affected by duress. For all that appears she is satisfied with her choice, and would be sorely disappointed if it were now to be annulled. The difficulty with the petitioner's contention is that it confuses motive with coercion. "Every tax is in some measure regulatory. To some extent it interposes an economic impediment to the activity taxed as compared with others not taxed." *Sonzinsky v. United States.* In like manner every rebate from a tax when conditioned upon conduct is in some measure a temptation. But to hold that motive or temptation is equivalent to coercion is to plunge the law in endless difficulties. The outcome of such a doctrine is the acceptance of a philosophical determinism by which choice becomes impossible. Till now the law has been guided by a robust common sense which assumes the freedom of the will as a working hypothesis in the solution of its problems. The wisdom of the hypothesis has illustration in this case. Nothing in the case suggests the exertion of a power akin to undue influence, if we assume that such a concept can ever be applied with fitness to the relations between state and nation. Even on that assumption the location of the point at which pressure turns into compulsion, and ceases to be inducement, would be a question of degree—at times, perhaps, of fact. The point had not been reached when Alabama made her choice. We cannot say that she was acting, not of her unfettered will, but under the strain of a persuasion equivalent to undue influence, when she chose to have relief administered under laws of her own making, by agents of her own selection, instead of under federal laws, administered by federal officers, with all the ensuing evils, at least to many minds, of federal patronage and power. There would be a strange irony, indeed, if her choice were now to be annulled on the basis of an assumed duress in the enactment of a statute which her courts have accepted as a true expression of her will. We think the choice must stand.

In ruling as we do, we leave many questions open. We do not say that a tax is valid, when imposed by act of Congress, if it is laid upon the condition that a state may escape its operation through the adoption of a statute unrelated in subject matter to activities fairly within the scope of national policy and power. No such question is before us. In the tender of this credit Congress does not intrude upon fields foreign to its function. The purpose of its intervention, as we have shown, is to safeguard its own treasury and as an incident to that protection to place the states upon a footing of equal opportunity. Drains upon its own resources are to be checked; obstructions to the freedom of the states are to be leveled. It is one thing to impose a tax dependent upon the conduct of the taxpayers, or of the state in which they live, where the conduct to be stimulated or discouraged is unrelated to the fiscal need subserved by the tax in its normal operation, or to any other end legitimately national. The Child Labor Tax Case, 259 U.S. 20, and Hill v. Wallace, 259 U.S. 44, were decided in the belief that the statutes there condemned were exposed to that reproach. It is quite another thing to say that a tax will be abated upon the doing of an act that will satisfy the fiscal need, the tax and the alternative being approximate equivalents. In such circumstances, if in no others, inducement or persuasion does not go beyond the bounds of power. We do not fix the outermost line. Enough for present purposes that wherever the line may be, this statute is within it. Definition more precise must abide the wisdom of the future.

. . . .

*United States v. Butler* is cited by petitioner as a decision to the contrary. . . . The decision was by a divided court, a minority taking the view that the objections were untenable. None of them is applicable to the situation here developed.

(a) The proceeds of the tax in controversy are not earmarked for a special group.

(b)  The unemployment compensation law which is a condition of the credit has had the approval of the state and could not be a law without it.

(c)  The condition is not linked to an irrevocable agreement, for the state at its pleasure may repeal its unemployment law, terminate the credit, and place itself where it was before the credit was accepted.

(d)  The condition is not directed to the attainment of an unlawful end, but to an end, the relief of unemployment, for which nation and state may lawfully co-operate.

. . . .

The judgment is

Affirmed.

[Justice VAN DEVANTER concurred in a dissenting opinion written by Justice SUTHERLAND. Justice BUTLER also delivered a dissenting opinion and Justice McREYNOLDS delivered a separate dissenting opinion.]

---

## NOTES

1.  *Old Age Benefits.* In a companion case to *Steward,* the court, in Helvering v. Davis, 301 U.S. 619 (1937), upheld the payment of old age benefits under Title II of the Social Security Act, financed by taxes on employers and employees (Title VIII). Justice Cardozo for the court found that the provisions did not contravene the tenth amendment: "Congress may spend money in aid of the 'general welfare.' . . . The conception of the spending power advocated by Hamilton and strongly reinforced by Story has prevailed over that of Madison, which has not been lacking in adherents. Yet difficulties are left when the power is conceded. The line must still be drawn between one welfare and another, between particular and general. Where this shall be placed cannot be known through a formula in advance of the event. There is a middle ground or certainly a penumbra in which discretion is at large. The discretion, however, is not confided to the courts."

2.  *The Meaning of "General Welfare."* Hamilton stated that the welfare for which Congress spends must be "general and not local; its operation extending in fact or by possibility throughout the Union, and not being confined to a particular spot." After the Social Security cases, is there any practical limitation on the purposes for which Congress may spend? Even if the immediate effects of a particular project are "local," surely it is likely that the "class" of such projects would have a relation-

ship to the national economy. Is there any subject matter which is the exclusive prerogative of the states?

**3.** *Conditional Grants.* Is it now clear that Congress can, in the exercise of its spending power, condition disbursement upon compliance with stipulations normally within the realm of state power?

In 1974, Congress enacted the Emergency Highway Energy Conservation Act requiring states to limit maximum speeds on any public highway within its jurisdiction to 55 mph as a precondition to receiving highway funds. *See* P-H ENERGY CONTROLS, §§ 27,501-27,502 (1974). Is such legislation constitutional? Is there any limitation on the power of Congress to condition appropriations?

Can a condition be totally unrelated to the subject of the grant? Are the conditions that may be imposed limited to those that are "necessary and proper" to effectuate the spending power? Consider Justice Cardozo's comment in *Steward Machine* that the court was not saying "that a tax is valid . . . if it is laid upon the condition that a State may escape its operation through the adoption of a statute unrelated in subject-matter to activities fairly within the scope of national policy and power." Does this limit the spending power? Is *Helvering v. Davis* consistent?

In Oklahoma v. United States Civil Service Comm'n, 330 U.S. 127 (1947), the court upheld a requirement that state employees comply with Hatch Act provisions regarding partisan political activities as a condition for receiving federal highway funds. The court stated: "While the United States is not concerned and has no power to regulate local political activities as such of state officials, it does have power to fix the terms upon which its money allotments to states shall be disbursed.

"The Tenth Amendment does not forbid the exercise of this power in the way that Congress has proceeded in this case."

**4.** *Cooperative Federalism.* In recent years, increasing emphasis has been placed upon the concept of "Cooperative Federalism," contending that "the National Government and the States are mutually complementary parts of a *single* governmental mechanism all of whose powers are intended to realize the current purposes of government according to their applicability to the problem in hand." The primary method by which this doctrine has been implemented has been the "grants in aid" system whereby "the National Government has held out inducements, primarily of a pecuniary kind, to the States . . . to use their reserved power to support certain objectives of national policy in the field of expenditure. In other words, the greater financial strength of the National Government is joined to the wider coercive powers of the States. Thus since 1911, Congress has voted money to subsidize [projects]; in return for which co-operating States have appropriated equal sums for the same purposes, and have brought their further powers to the support thereof along lines laid down by Congress." Corwin, *The Passing of Dual Federalism*, 36 Va. L. Rev. 1, 19, 20 (1950).

The result has been increasing national involvement in traditionally local matters. In the area of education, health, housing, environmental control, land use, federal moneys and controls are of vital importance. With the rise of revenue sharing, the federal intervention may change both in scope and character.

5. *Civil Rights.* Title VI of the 1964 Civil Rights Act, 42 U.S.C. § 2000d provides "no person in the United States shall, on the ground of race, color, or national origin, be excluded from participation in, be denied the benefits of, or be subjected to discrimination under any program or activity receiving Federal assistance." In the event of a grantee's noncompliance with this mandate, the federal department or agency extending federal financial assistance may terminate or refuse to grant continuing assistance to the offending recipient. (§ 602). As of 1971, this sanction was available in over 400 loan and grant programs including aid to education, hospitals and other health facilities, and highway construction, providing the government with a viable alternative to judicial enforcement of the desegregation mandate.

There has been a natural reluctance to use the potent sanctions of Title VI because of its impact on recipients. The cutoff of benefits to welfare recipients or schools in the ghetto is drastic. It has been suggested, therefore, that the utility of this sanction may depend on the particular program involved. "In the areas of education and health, students and patients do not feel the immediate and full effect of a termination as the welfare recipients, for whom the weekly and monthly welfare grant is frequently the sole source of family income." In any case, the purpose of Title VI is not to withhold funds, but to induce recipients who rely on federal funds to desegregate. "An optimally effective Title VI would convince a recipient that: 1) the recipient needed the funds; 2) funds *would* be withheld; and 3) the recipient would rather comply than lose the funds. An actual cut-off would mean that Title VI had failed, since the particular administrative program would still be subject to discrimination." Comment, *Title VI of the Civil Rights Act of 1964—Implementation and Impact*, 36 Geo. Wash. L. Rev. 824, 843 (1968). On the use of Title VI to achieve desegregation in education, see text, pp. 609.

# Chapter 3

## STATE POWER IN AMERICAN FEDERALISM

### A. STATE POWER TO REGULATE COMMERCE

#### 1. Establishing the Foundations: Exclusive and Concurrent Regulations

Our previous focus has been on the national regulatory power over subjects national and local in character. The focus now turns to the other side of the division of powers, the regulatory power of the state and local governments acting as agents of the state. Again concern is with the scope of power, its sources and the limitations on the exercise of the power arising from the division of powers between the national and state governments.

Some specific limitations on the regulatory power of the states are set forth in Art. I, § 10. Further, some powers are clearly exclusive of state regulation, *e.g.*, the power to declare war or to legislate for the District of Columbia. But does a grant of power to the national government necessarily exclude the existence of a like power in the states? If Congress has not acted, can the states, in the exercise of their police powers, regulate matters charged to the national government, or does the dormant grant of power itself limit the regulatory power of the states? Can the states exercise the granted power itself? What happens if the Congress does legislate in regard to a particular subject— does this necessarily preclude all state regulation? If the Supreme Court has held that certain state regulation is barred by a constitutional grant of power to the national government, can Congress, through legislation, authorize the states to act? Answers to these questions do not flow automatically from a reading of the Constitution, but from a constant re-definition of federal relationships.

GIBBONS v. OGDEN

Supreme Court of the United States

22 U.S. (9 Wheat.) 1, 6 L. Ed. 23 (1824)

[The facts and initial part of the opinion relating to Congress's power to regulate commerce among the states is printed at text, p. 162. In that part of the opinion printed below, Chief Justice Marshall discusses the effect of the constitutional grant of commerce power to the national government and the effect of congressional regulation pursuant thereto on the regulatory power of the states.]

 . . . .

But it has been urged with great earnestness that, although the power of Congress to regulate commerce with foreign nations, and among the several states, be coextensive with the subject itself, and have no other limits than are prescribed in the Constitution, yet the states may severally exercise the same power within their respective jurisdictions. In support of this argument, it is said that they possessed it as an inseparable attribute of sovereignty before the formation of the Constitution, and still retain it, except so far as they have surrendered it by that instrument; that this principle results from the nature of the government, and is secured by the Tenth Amendment; that an affirmative grant of power is not exclusive, unless in its own nature it be such that the continued exercise of it by the former possessor is inconsistent with the grant, and that this is not of that description. The appellant, conceding these postulates, except the last, contends that full power to regulate a particular subject implies the whole power, and leaves no residuum; that a grant of the whole is incompatible with the existence of a right in another to any part of it. . . .

The grant of the power to lay and collect taxes is, like the power to regulate commerce, made in general terms, and has never been understood to interfere with the exercise of the same power by the states; and hence has been drawn an argument which has been applied to the question under consideration. But the two grants are not, it is conceived, similar in their terms or their nature. Although many of the powers formerly exercised by the states are transferred to the government of the Union, yet the state governments remain, and constitute a most important part of our system. The power of taxation is indispensable to their existence, and is a power which, in its own nature, is capable of residing in, and being exercised by, different authorities at the same time. . . . When, then, each government exercises the power of taxation, neither is exercising the power of the other. But when a state proceeds to regulate commerce with foreign nations, or among the several states, it is exercising the very power that is granted to Congress, and is doing the very thing which Congress is authorized to do. There is no analogy, then, between the power of taxation and the power of regulating commerce.

In discussing the question whether this power is still in the states, in the case under consideration, we may dismiss from it the inquiry, whether it is surrendered by the mere grant to

Congress, or is retained until Congress shall exercise the power. We may dismiss that inquiry because it has been exercised, and the regulations which Congress deemed it proper to make are now in full operation. The sole question is, can a state regulate commerce with foreign nations and among the states while Congress is regulating it? . . .

But the inspection laws are said to be regulations of commerce, and are certainly recognized in the Constitution as being passed in the exercise of a power remaining with the states. That inspection laws may have a remote and considerable influence on commerce, will not be denied; but that a power to regulate commerce is the source from which the right to pass them is derived, cannot be admitted. The object of inspection laws is to improve the quality of articles produced by the labor of a country, to fit them for exportation, or it may be for domestic use. They act upon the subject before it becomes an article of foreign commerce, or of commerce among the states, and prepare it for that purpose. They form a portion of that immense mass of legislation which embraces everything within the territory of a state not surrendered to a general government; all which can be most advantageously exercised by the states themselves. Inspection laws, quarantine laws, health laws of every description, as well as laws for regulating the internal commerce of a state, and those which respect turnpike roads, ferries, etc., are component parts of this mass.

. . . [I]f a state, in passing laws on subjects acknowledged to be within its control, and with a view to those subjects, shall adopt a measure of the same character with one which Congress may adopt, it does not derive its authority from the particular power which has been granted, but from some other which remains with the state, and may be executed by the same means. All experience shows that the same measures, or measures scarcely distinguishable from each other, may flow from distinct powers; but this does not prove that the powers themselves are identical. Although the means used in their execution may sometimes approach each other so nearly as to be confounded, there are other situations in which they are sufficiently distinct to establish their individuality.

In our complex system, presenting the rare and difficult scheme of one general government whose action extends over the whole, but which possesses only certain enumerated powers; and of numerous state governments, which retain and exercise all powers not delegated to the Union, contests respecting power must arise. Were it even otherwise, the measures taken by the respective governments to execute their acknowledged powers would often be of the same description, and might sometimes interfere. This, however, does not prove that the one is exercising, or has a right to exercise the powers of the other.

. . . .

It has been contended by the counsel for the appellant that, as the word to "regulate" implies in its nature full power over the thing to be regulated, it excludes, necessarily, the action of all others that would perform the same operation on the same thing. That regulation is designed for the entire result, applying to those parts which remain as they were, as well as to those which are altered. It produces a uniform whole, which is as much disturbed and deranged by changing what the regulating power designs to leave untouched, as that on which it has operated. There is great force in this argument, and the court is not satisfied that it has been refuted. . . .

Since, however, in exercising the power of regulating their own purely internal affairs, whether of trading or police, the States may sometimes enact laws, the validity of which depends on their interfering with and being contrary to, an act of Congress passed in pursuance of the Constitution, the Court will enter upon an inquiry, whether the laws of New York, as expounded by the highest tribunal of that State, have, in their application to this case, come into collision with an Act of Congress, and deprive a citizen of a right to which that act entitles him. Should this collision exist, it will be immaterial whether those laws were passed in virtue of a concurrent power "to regulate commerce with foreign nations and among the several States," or in virtue of a power to regulate their domestic trade and police. In one case and the other, the acts of New York must yield to the law of Congress; and the decision sustaining the privilege they confer, against the right given by a law of the Union, must be erroneous. . . .

[The Court construed the federal legislation to allow a licensee to engage in coastal trade. The New York Act granting a monopoly in navigation therefore, was inconsistent with the rights granted under the federal act, and hence, unconstitutional. The decree below was reversed and the bill dismissed.

[Justice JOHNSON, concurring, contended that the commerce clause gave Congress exclusively power to regulate foreign and interstate commerce thereby excluding any state regulatory power over such commerce.]

———————

## NOTES

### Background to Gibbons

1. In THE FEDERALIST, No. 32, Alexander Hamilton provided the basis for recognition of a concurrent power: "[A]s the plan of the Convention aims only at a partial union or consolidation, the State governments would clearly retain all the rights of sovereignty which they before had, and which were not, by that act, *exclusively* delegated to the United States. This exclusive delegation, or rather this alienation of State sovereignty, would only exist in three cases; where the Constitution in express terms granted an exclusive authority to the Union; where it granted in one instance an authority to the Union, and in another prohibited the States from exercising the like authority; and where it granted an authority to the Union to which a similar authority in the States would be absolutely and totally *contradictory* and *repugnant.*" What the Federalist Papers propagandized, in short, was that the Constitution created "at one and the same time both a consolidated and a federal government—a 'mixed' government." Mann, *The Marshall Court: Nationalization of Private Rights and Personal Liberty from the Authority of the Commerce Clause,* 38 IND. L.J. 117, 193 (1963). Does the failure of the framers to confront directly this issue suggest that the commerce clause was not intended, of its own force, to limit the states?

2. As Chief Justice Marshall notes in *Gibbons,* there were numerous state regulations over various subjects of transportation, trade, and commerce prior to that decision. However, a restrictive view of the meaning of commerce served to prevent legal challenge. *See* Abel, *Commerce Regulation Before Gibbons v. Ogden: Trade and Traffic,* 14 BROOKLYN L. REV. 38, 215 (1947-48). Does the continued existence of state regulation of the subjects of commerce among the states in these early years indicate an understanding that the commerce clause did not disturb state regulatory power?

### Exclusive and Concurrent Powers

1. Daniel Webster, arguing for the appellant in *Gibbons,* relied strongly on the history of the formation of the Constitution, urging that the "very object intended, more than any other" was to divest the states of any power to regulate commerce in its "higher branches" which included the granting of monopolies in trade and navigation. Returning to Hamilton's threefold division in THE FEDERALIST No. 32, Webster argued: "[S]o where the power, or any one subject, is given in general words, like the

power to regulate commerce, the true method of construction would be, to consider of what parts the grant is composed, and which of those, from the nature of the thing, ought to be considered exclusive." While the meaning of the term "higher branches" is unclear, it is certain that Webster was not arguing for an absolutely exclusive commerce power, but rather for a doctrine of selective exclusiveness reflecting the nature of the power as applied to the particular circumstances and against a general concurrent state power over commerce.

William Wirt, his co-counsel, similarly stressed "not that all the commercial powers are exclusive, but that those powers being separated, there are some which are exclusive in their nature; and among them is the power which concerns navigation. . . ." *See* P. BENSON, JR., THE SUPREME COURT AND THE COMMERCE CLAUSE, 1937-1970 15 (1970).

Similarly, respondents' counsel accepted that the court must consider the "nature of the power" but argued that there was "nothing in the nature of the power which renders it exclusive in Congress."

Webster characterized the existing state regulations of transportation, trade, and traffic as "in their general character, rather regulations of police than of commerce, in the Constitutional understanding of that term." Thus, it followed that "quarantine laws, for example, may be considered as affecting commerce; yet they are, in their nature, health laws."

2. Does Chief Justice Marshall accept Webster's argument of selective exclusiveness? Does he accept the contention that the *nature* of the commerce power requires that it be regulated exclusively by Congress? Is Marshall arguing, as has been suggested, that "the commerce power granted to the Congress, unlike the taxing power, is an indivisible unit" and that "as such it is an exclusive power, residing wholly with Congress?" F. RIBBLE, STATE AND NATIONAL POWER OVER COMMERCE 37 (1937). Why is the power to tax any more "divisible" than the power to regulate commerce?

3. Justice Johnson, concurring in *Gibbons,* argued that the power of Congress to regulate commerce among the states is exclusive: "The power of a sovereign state over commerce . . . amounts to nothing more than a power to limit and restrain it at pleasure. And since the power to prescribe the limits to its freedom necessarily implies the power to determine what shall remain unrestrained, it follows that the power must be exclusive; it can reside but in one potentate; and hence, the grant of this power carries with it the whole subject, leaving nothing for the State to act upon." It has been suggested that Johnson's support

for a broad exclusive national power to regulate commerce "out-marshalled Marshall." Morgan, *Mr. Justice William Johnson and the Constitution,* 57 HARV. L. REV. 328, 339 (1944).

## Police Power v. Commerce Regulation

1. What does Chief Justice Marshall mean when he declares that the prior state regulations of trade, transportation, and traffic do not have their source in the power to regulate commerce among the states? To what extent does his distinction turn upon a consideration of the *purpose* of the regulation?

2. Does it matter if the police power or concurrent commerce power rationale is used? Frankfurter concludes: "In *Gibbons v. Ogden,* there begins to emerge a source of authority for state legislation characterized as designed 'to act directly on its system of police.' Because the 'police power' is a response to the dynamic aspects of society, it has eluded attempts at definition. But precisely because it is such a response it is one of the most fertile doctrinal sources for striking an accommodation between local interests and the demands of the commerce clause." F. FRANKFURTER, THE COMMERCE CLAUSE UNDER MARSHALL, TANEY AND WAITE 27 (1937).

3. In Wilson v. The Black Bird Creek Marsh Co., 27 U.S. (2 Pet.) 245 (1829), the court upheld a Delaware law authorizing a company to build a dam across a navigable creek flowing into the Delaware River. Justice Marshall, delivering the opinion of the court, stressed the importance of such state regulation for flood control and health, urging that "[m]easures calculated to produce these objects, provided they do not come into collision with the powers of the general government, are undoubtedly within those which are reserved to the states." Since Congress had not passed any act of relevance, the challenge to the validity of the state legislation rested on its alleged repugnancy to the dormant power to regulate commerce among the several states. Marshall concluded: "We do not think that the act empowering the Black Bird Creek Marsh Company to place a dam across the Creeks, can under all the circumstances of the case, be considered as repugnant to the power to regulate commerce in its dormant state, or as being in conflict with any law passed on the subject."

Is Justice Marshall retreating from his tentative approval of an exclusive commerce power? What does he mean by "under all the circumstances of the case"? Is it relevant that this stream was, according to counsel William Wirt, "one of those sluggish, reptile streams that do not run but creep, and which when wherever it passes, spreads its venom, and destroys the health of all those who inhabit its marshes"?

## COOLEY v. BOARD OF WARDENS OF THE PORT OF PHILADELPHIA
Supreme Court of the United States
53 U.S. (12 How.) 299, 13 L. Ed. 996 (1851)

[Pennsylvania required vessels entering or leaving Philadelphia to have a local pilot for navigating the Delaware River. Cooley's violation of the statute resulted in a monetary judgment against him and the state supreme court affirmed. Cooley appealed, contending that the statute violated the commerce clause.]

Justice CURTIS delivered the opinion of the Court.

. . . .

That the power to regulate commerce includes the regulation of navigation, we consider settled. And when we look to the nature of the service performed by pilots, to the relations which that service and its compensations bear to navigation between the several states, and between the ports of the United States and foreign countries, we are brought to the conclusion, that the regulation of the qualifications of pilots, of the modes and times of offering and rendering their services, of the responsibilities which shall rest upon them, of the powers they shall possess, of the compensation they may demand, and of the penalties by which their rights and duties may be enforced, do constitute regulations of navigation, and consequently of commerce, within the just meaning of this clause of the Constitution.

. . . .

It becomes necessary, therefore, to consider whether this law of Pennsylvania, being a regulation of commerce, is valid.

The Act of Congress of the 7th of August, 1789, § 4, is as follows:

"That all pilots in the bays, inlets, rivers, harbors, and ports of the United States shall continue to be regulated in conformity with the existing laws of the states, respectively, wherein such pilots may be, or with such laws as the states may respectively hereafter enact for the purpose, until further legislative provision shall be made by Congress."

If the law of Pennsylvania, now in question, had been in existence at the date of this act of Congress, we might hold it to have been adopted by Congress, and thus made a law of the United States, and so valid. Because this act does, in effect, give the force of an act of Congress, to the then existing state laws on the subject, so long as they should continue unrepealed by the state which enacted them.

But the law on which these actions are founded, was not enacted till 1803. What effect then can be attributed to so much of the act of 1789 as declares that pilots shall continue to be regulated in conformity "with such laws as the states may respectively hereafter enact for the purpose, until further legislative provision shall be made by Congress"?

If the states were divested of the power to legislate on this subject by the grant of the commercial power to Congress, it is plain this act could not confer upon them power thus to legislate. If the Constitution excluded the states from making any law regulating commerce, certainly Congress cannot regrant, or in any manner reconvey to the states that power. And yet this act of 1789 gives its sanction only to laws enacted by the states. This necessarily implies a constitutional power to legislate; for only a rule created by the sovereign power of a state acting in its legislative capacity, can be deemed a law enacted by a state; and if the state has so limited its sovereign power that it no longer extends to a particular subject, manifestly it cannot, in any proper sense, be said to enact laws thereon. Entertaining these views, we are brought directly and unavoidably to the consideration of the question, whether the grant of the commercial power to Congress did *per se* deprive the states of all power to regulate pilots. This question has never been decided by this court, nor, in our judgment, has any case depending upon all the considerations which must govern this one, come before this court. The grant of commercial power to Congress does not contain any terms which expressly exclude the states from exercising an authority over its subject matter. If they are excluded, it must be because the nature of the power thus granted to Congress requires that a similar authority should not exist in the states. If it were conceded on the one side that the nature of this power, like that to legislate for the District of Columbia, is absolutely and totally repugnant to the existence of similar power in the states, probably no one would deny that the grant of the power to Congress, as effectually and perfectly excludes the states from all future legislation on the subject, as if express words had been used to exclude them. And on the other hand, if it were admitted that the existence of this power in Congress, like the power of taxation, is compatible with the existence of a similar power in the states, then it would be in conformity with the contemporary exposition of the Constitution ("Federalist," No. 32), and with the judicial construction given from time to time by this court, after the most deliberate consideration, to hold that the mere grant of such a power to Congress, did not imply a prohibition on the states to exercise the same power; that it is not the mere existence of such a power, but its exercise by Congress, which may be incompatible with the exercise of the same power by the states, and that the states may legislate in the absence of congressional regulations.

The diversities of opinion, therefore, which have existed on this subject have arisen from the different views taken of the nature of this power. But when the nature of a power like this is spoken of, when it is said that the nature of the power requires that it should be exercised exclusively by Congress, it must be intended to refer to the subjects of that power, and to say they are of such a nature as to require exclusive legislation by Congress. Now, the power to regulate commerce, embraces a vast field, containing not only many, but exceedingly various subjects, quite unlike in their nature; some imperatively demanding a single uniform rule, operating equally on the commerce of the United States in every port; and some, like the subject now in question, as imperatively demanding that diversity, which alone can meet the local necessities of navigation.

Either absolutely to affirm, or deny that the nature of this power requires exclusive regulation by Congress, is to lose sight of the nature of the subjects of this power, and to assert concerning all of them, what is really applicable but to a part. Whatever subjects of this power are in their nature national, or admit only of one uniform system, or plan of regulation, may justly be said to be of such a nature as to require exclusive legislation by Congress. That this cannot be affirmed of laws for the regulation of pilots and pilotage, is plain. The act of 1789 contains a clear and authoritative declaration by the first Congress, that the nature of this subject is such that until Congress should find it necessary to exert its power, it should be left to the legislation of the states; that it is local and not national; that it is likely to be the best provided for, not by one system, or plan of regulations, but by as many as the legislative discretion of the several states should deem applicable to the local peculiarities of the ports within their limits.

Viewed in this light, so much of this act of 1789, as declares that pilots shall continue to be regulated "by such laws as the states may respectively hereafter enact for that purpose," instead of being held to be inoperative, as an attempt to confer on the states a power to legislate, of which the Constitution had deprived them, is allowed an appropriate and important signification. It manifests the understanding of Congress, at the outset of the government, that the nature of this subject is not such as to require its exclusive legislation. The practice of the states, and of the national government, has been in conformity with this declaration, from the origin of the national government to this time; and the nature of the subject when examined, is such as to leave no doubt of the superior fitness and propriety, not to say the absolute necessity, of different systems of regulation drawn from local knowledge and experience, and conformed to local wants. How, then, can we say that, by the mere grant of power to regulate commerce, the states are deprived of all the power to legislate on this subject, because from the nature of the power the legislation of Congress must be exclusive. This would be to affirm that the nature of the power is in any case, something different from the nature of the subject to which, in such case, the power extends, and that the nature of the power necessarily demands, in all cases, exclusive legislation by Congress, while the nature of one of the subjects of that power, not only does not require such exclusive legislation, but may be best provided for by many different systems enacted by the states, in conformity with the circumstances of the ports within their limits. In construing an instrument designed for the formation of a government, and in determining the extent of one of its important grants of power to legislate, we can make no such distinction between the nature of the power and the nature of the subject on which that power was intended practically to operate, nor consider the grant more extensive by affirming of the power, what is not true of its subject now in question.

It is the opinion of a majority of the court that the mere grant to Congress of the power to regulate commerce, did not deprive the states of power to regulate pilots, and that although Congress has legislated on this subject, its legislation manifests an intention, with a single exception, not to regulate this subject, but to leave its regulation to the several states. To these precise questions, which are all we are called on to decide, this opinion must be understood to be confined. It does not extend to the question what other subjects, under the commercial power, are within the exclusive control of Congress, or may be regulated by the states in the absence of all congressional legislation; nor to the general question, how far any regulation of a subject by Congress, may be deemed to operate as an exclusion of all legislation by the states upon the same subject. We decide the precise questions before us, upon what we deem sound principles, applicable to this particular subject in the state in which the legislation of Congress has left it. We go no further.

. . . .

[Judgment affirmed.]

[Justices McLean and Wayne dissented, and Justice Daniel concurred for other reasons.]

## NOTES

1. Is the state enactment in *Cooley* treated as a police power or commerce regulation? Does the meaning of "commerce among the States" remain the same whether federal or state legislation is involved? Does *Cooley* finally reject Marshall's distinction fashioned in *Gibbons* between police and commerce regulation?

2. *Cooley* turns from a consideration of the *nature* of the commerce power to the *subjects* of that power. Is the *Cooley* test adequate for defining the boundaries of national and state power? Referring to Justice Curtis' test, it has been said that it "is well enough for the easy cases at either end of the scale. But there are harder cases not covered by the formula. For some subjects do not imperatively demand either uniformity or diversity of regulatory rules. They will admit of either. . . . In saying that the nature of the power is determined by the nature of the subject over which it is exercised, Mr. Justice Curtis fails to take into account the nature of the regulation." The author goes on to note, however, "[t]hough Mr. Justice Curtis in the *Cooley* case treated his uniformity-diversity dichotomy as a characterization of the subject being regulated, it was not a judgment of any quality inherent in the subject. It was a determination of public policy as to wisdom in choosing between two possible ways of dealing with the subject, nationally or locally." T. POWELL, VAGARIES AND VARIETIES IN CONSTITUTIONAL INTERPRETATION 153, 154, 159 (1956).

Suppose a state imposed a discriminatory tax or regulation on pilotage of interstate commerce? Would pilotage remain a national subject matter? Why is diversity of regulation in *Cooley* of "superior fitness and propriety?" Is Justice Curtis' test, *as applied*, limited to a narrow inquiry into the nature of the subject matter?

3. *Congress or Court?* What is the role of the federal legislation cited in *Cooley*? The court appears to be saying that the congressional finding that the matter can best be handled locally is indicative that uniformity is not required. Is Justice Curtis arguing that congressional intent regarding the character of the subject is determinative? Could Congress authorize state regulation of a subject subsequent to a judicial determination that a subject is national? *See* text, pp. 290-93.

What are the respective roles of Congress and the court in applying the Cooley test? It has been said that when the court "annuls legislation under the theory that the subject demands uniformity of regulation, the only conformity it is in a position to furnish is a uniform lack of regulation" and that the "Court is powerless to promote the cause of uniform positive legislation while Congress is silent." Shenton, *Interstate Commerce During the Silence of Congress*, 23 DICK. L. REV. 78, 118-19 (1919). On the other hand, it has been suggested that *Cooley* has been a tenacious doctrine, partly because it created an "opportunity for the use of judicial discretion in imposing limitations on the power of the states." Sholley, *Negative Implications of the Commerce Clause,* 3 U. CHI. L. REV. 556, 577 (1936). Does a court have the capability to process the kind of data that would be required in determining whether a subject is national or local?

4.  *The Silence of Congress.* Is *Cooley* based upon negative implications drawn from the commerce clause or from an implied meaning drawn from the silence of Congress? Is the conclusion that certain subjects of commerce require national uniformity of regulation a conclusion compelled by the Constitution or de-pendent upon the implied will of Congress?

Should any meaning be implied from the silence of Congress? Thomas Reed Powell's commentary on such an attempt seems apropos. "Now Congress has a wonderful power that only judges and lawyers know about. Congress has a power to keep silent. Congress can regulate interstate commerce just by not doing any-thing about it. Of course, when Congress keeps silent, it takes an expert to know what it means. But the judges are experts. They say that Congress by keeping silent sometimes means that it is keeping silent and sometimes means that it is speaking. If Con-gress keeps silent about the interstate commerce that is not na-tional in character and that may just as well be regulated by the states, then Congress is silently silent, and the state may regulate. But if Congress keeps silent about the kind of commerce that is national in character and ought to be regulated only by Congress, then Congress is silently vocal and says that commerce must be free from state regulation." Powell, *The Still Small Voice of the Commerce Clause,* PROCEEDINGS NAT'L TAX ASS'N 337-39 (1937), 3 SELECTED ESSAYS 931, 932 (1938).

## 2.  Striking the Balance

### *The Struggle for Standards: Direct and Indirect Effects*

Following *Cooley,* the court struggled with the task of form-ulating more adequate standards to reconcile the national and local interests involved. One such formulation sought to define whether a local regulation imposed a "direct" or "indirect" burden on interstate commerce. If the former, it was an un-constitutional interference with the commerce power.

An early effort suggesting the need for a departure from the direct-indirect standard came in a dissenting opinion in Di Santo v. Pennsylvania, 273 U.S. 34 (1927), where the court struck down a state statute requiring that all persons in the business of selling steamship tickets for transportation to or from foreign countries be licensed for a $50.00 fee. The license was granted only upon a showing of good character and fitness, and was revocable for misconduct. The court, did not consider the purpose of the Act, to prevent exploitation of poor immigrants, as relevant. The statute fell because it was an unconstitutional "direct burden" on a well-recognized area of foreign commerce, "regardless of the purpose with which it was passed."

The court nowhere defined why the burden was direct, at least suggesting that the label was little more than a statement of the result. But in a prophetic dissent, Justice Stone suggested a new direction for decision-making.

"The recognition of the power of the states to regulate commerce within certain limits is a recognition that there are matters of local concern which may properly be subject to state regulation and which, because of their local character, as well as their number and diversity, can never be adequately dealt with by Congress. Such regulation, so long as it does not impede the free flow of commerce, may properly be and for the most part has been left to the states by the decisions of this Court.

"In this case the traditional test of the limit of state action by inquiring whether the interference with commerce is direct or indirect seems to me too mechanical, too uncertain in its application, and too remote from actualities, to be of value. In thus making use of the expressions, 'direct' and 'indirect interference' with commerce, we are doing little more than using labels to describe a result rather than any trustworthy formula by which it is reached.

"[I]t seems clear that those interferences not deemed forbidden are to be sustained, not because the effect on commerce is nominally indirect, but because a consideration of all the facts and circumstances, such as the nature of the regulation, its function, the character of the business involved and the actual effect on the flow of commerce, lead to the conclusion that the regulation concerns interests peculiarly local and does not infringe the national interest in maintaining the freedom of commerce across state lines."

The *Di Santo* decision was overruled in California v. Thompson, 313 U.S. 109 (1941).

### a.  Transportation

**SOUTHERN PACIFIC CO. v. ARIZONA ex rel. SULLIVAN**
Supreme Court of the United States
325 U.S. 761, 89 L. Ed. 1915, 165 S. Ct. 1515 (1945)

Chief Justice STONE delivered the opinion of the Court.

The Arizona Train Limit Law makes it unlawful for any person or corporation to operate within the state a railroad train of more than fourteen passenger or seventy freight cars, and authorizes the state to recover a money penalty for each violation of the Act. . . .

. . . .

For a hundred years it has been accepted constitutional doctrine that the commerce clause, without the aid of Congressional legislation, thus affords some protection from state legislation inimical to the national commerce, and that in such cases, where Congress has not acted, this Court, and not the state legislature, is under the commerce clause the final arbiter between the competing demands of state and national interests. . . .

Congress has undoubted power to redefine the distribution of power over interstate commerce. It may either permit the states to regulate the commerce in a manner which would otherwise not be permissible, or exclude state regulation even of matters of peculiarly local concern which nevertheless affect interstate commerce.

But in general Congress has left it to the courts to formulate the rules thus interpreting the commerce clause in its application, doubtless because it has appreciated the destructive consequences to the commerce of the nation if their protection were withdrawn, and has been aware that in their application state laws will not be invalidated without the support of relevant factual material which will "afford a sure basis" for an informed judgment. Meanwhile, Congress has accommodated its legislation, as have the states, to these rules as an established feature of our constitutional system. There has thus been left to the states wide scope for the regulation of matters of local state concern, even though it in some measure affects the commerce, provided it does not materially restrict the free flow of commerce across state lines, or interfere with it in matters with respect to which uniformity of regulation is of predominant national concern.

Hence the matters for ultimate determination here are the nature and extent of the burden which the state regulation of interstate trains, adopted as a safety measure, imposes on interstate commerce, and whether the relative weights of the state and national interests involved are such as to make inapplicable the rule, generally observed, that the free flow of interstate commerce and its freedom from local restraints in matters requiring uniformity of regulation are interests safeguarded by the commerce clause from state interference.

While this Court is not bound by the findings of the state court, and may determine for itself the facts of a case upon which an asserted federal right depends, the facts found by the state trial court showing the nature of the interstate commerce involved, and the effect upon it of the train limit law, are not seriously questioned. Its findings with respect to the need for an effect of the statute as a safety measure, although challenged in some particulars which we do not regard as material to our decision, are likewise supported by evidence. Taken together the findings supply an adequate basis for decision of the constitutional issue.

. . . .

The unchallenged findings leave no doubt that the Arizona Train Limit Law imposes a serious burden on the interstate commerce conducted by appellant. It materially impedes the movement of appellant's interstate trains through that state and interposes a substantial obstruction to the national policy proclaimed by Congress, to promote adequate, economical and efficient railway transportation service. Enforcement of the law in Arizona, while train lengths remain unregulated or are regulated by varying standards in other states, must inevitably result in an impairment of uniformity of efficient railroad operation because the railroads are subjected to regulation which is not uniform in its application. Compliance with a state statute limiting train lengths requires interstate trains of a length lawful in other states to be broken up and reconstituted as they enter each state according as it may impose varying limitations upon train lengths. The alternative is for the carrier to conform to the lowest train limit restriction of any of the states through which its trains pass, whose laws thus control the carriers' operations both within and without the regulating state.

. . . .

If one state may regulate train lengths, so may all the others, and they need not prescribe the same maximum limitation. The practical effect of such regulation is to control train operations beyond the boundaries of the state exacting it because of the necessity of breaking up and reassembling long trains at the nearest terminal points before entering and after leaving the regulating state. The serious impediment to the free flow of commerce by the local regulation of train lengths and the practical necessity that such regulation, if any, must be prescribed by a single body having a nation-wide authority are apparent.

The trial court found that the Arizona law had no reasonable relation to safety, and made train operation more dangerous. Examination of the evidence and the detailed findings makes it clear that this conclusion was rested on facts found which indicate that such increased danger of accident and personal injury as may result from the greater length of trains is more than offset by the increase in the number of accidents resulting from the larger number of trains when train lengths are reduced. . . .

The principal source of danger of accident from increased length of trains is the resulting increase of "slack action" of the train. Slack action is the amount of free movement of one car before it transmits its motion to an adjoining coupled car. . . .

. . . On comparison of the number of slack action accidents in Arizona with those in Nevada, where the length of trains is now unregulated, the trial court found that with substantially the same amount of traffic in each state the number of accidents was relatively the same in long as in short train operations. While accidents from slack action do occur in the operation of passenger trains, it does not appear that they are more frequent or the resulting shocks more severe on long than on short passenger trains. Nor does it appear that slack action accidents occurring on passenger trains, whatever their length, are of sufficient severity to cause serious injury or damage.

As the trial court found, reduction of the length of trains also tends to increase the number of accidents because of the increase in the number of trains. . . .

. . . .

Here we conclude that the state does go too far. Its regulation of train lengths, admittedly obstructive to interstate train operation, and having a seriously adverse effect on transportation efficiency and economy, passes beyond what is plainly essential for safety since it does not appear that it will lessen rather than increase the danger of accident. Its attempted regulation of the operation of interstate trains cannot establish nation-wide control such as is essential to the maintenance of an efficient transportation system, which Congress alone can prescribe. The state interest cannot be preserved at the expense of the national interest by an enactment which regulates interstate train lengths without securing such control, which is a matter of national concern. To this the interest of the state here asserted is subordinate.

. . . .

The contrast between the present regulation and the full train crew laws in point of their effects on the commerce, and the like contrast with the highway safety regulations, in point of the nature of the subject of regulation and the state's interest in it, illustrate and emphasize the considerations which enter into a determination of the relative weights of state and national interests where state regulation affecting interstate commerce is attempted. Here examination of all the relevant factors makes it plain that the state interest is outweighed by the interest of the nation in an adequate, economical and efficient railway transportation service, which must prevail.

Reversed.

[Justices BLACK and DOUGLAS dissented.]

---

## NOTES

1.   Justice Stone's *Di Santo* dissent found fruition in an influential article by Professor Noel T. Dowling, *Interstate Commerce and State Power*, 27 VA. L. REV. 1 (1940), SELECTED ESSAYS 280 (1963), proposing "that in the absence of affirmative consent a Congressional negative will be presumed in the courts against state action which in its effect upon interstate commerce constitutes an unreasonable interference with national interests, the presumption being rebuttable at the pleasure of Congress." He argued that this was not only what the courts were doing in fact but would "involve an avowal that the Court is deliberately balancing national and local interests and making a choice as to which of the two *should* prevail." Arguably *Southern Pacific* is an application of this standard.

2.   What is the function of the *Cooley* subject matter test in the *Southern Pacific* formulation? Is *Cooley* a separate requirement or is it merged into the general balancing of national and state interests? Is *Southern Pacific* an acknowledgment that the *Cooley* test was itself a balancing standard?

3.   *The Barnwell Precedent.*

a.   *The Facts.* In South Carolina State Highway Dep't v. Barnwell Bros., Inc., 303 U.S. 177 (1938), the Supreme Court, per Justice Stone, reversed (7-0) a lower court decision holding a state statute prohibiting use on state highways of trucks whose width exceeded 90 inches, or whose weight including load was over 20,000 pounds unconstitutional. The district court had engaged in extensive fact-finding to determine that the statute had no reasonable relation to the safety of the public using the highway, was unreasonable as a means of preserving the highway, and hence was an unreasonable burden on interstate commerce.

b. *Due Process and the Commerce Clause*. The district court in *Barnwell* had rejected due process claims but had concluded that the commerce clause imposed a more exacting standard of reasonableness than the fourteenth amendment. The Supreme Court, however, held that "[i]n the absence of [congressional] legislation the judicial function, under the Commerce Clause . . . as well as the Fourteenth Amendment, stops with the inquiry whether the state legislature in adopting regulations such as the present has acted within its province, and whether the means chosen are reasonably adapted to the end sought."

The first inquiry was said to be answered by prior decisions "that a state may impose nondiscriminatory regulations with respect to the character of motor vehicles moving in interstate commerce as a safety measure and as a means of securing the economical use of its highways."

In assessing the second criterion, "[w]hen the action of a legislature is within the scope of its power, fairly debatable questions as to reasonableness, wisdom, and propriety are not for the determination of courts, but for the legislative body, on which rests the duty and responsibility of decision" [citing due process cases]. The judicial function was solely "to ascertain upon the whole record whether it is possible to say that the legislative choice is without rational basis." Since the state legislative judgment had adequate support, the fourteenth amendment *and the commerce clause* were satisfied.

Dowling, however, has argued that "the test of reasonableness in interstate commerce cases is not the same as . . . in due process cases. Additional factors are involved. In a sense, a state law must take the hurdle of due process before it comes to the interstate barrier." Consider Justice Stone's comment in *Southern Pacific* that the task of reconciling local and national interests cannot be avoided by "simply invoking the convenient apologetics of the police powers."

c. *Commerce Clause*. As indicated, in *Barnwell* the due process inquiry also resolved the commerce clause issue. Justice Stone specifically stated: "[S]o long as the state action does not discriminate, the burden is one which the Constitution permits because it is an inseparable incident of the exercise of a legislative authority, which, under the Constitution, has been left to the states." A state regulation could be sustained "although it has burdened or impeded interstate commerce," even though it "materially interfere[s]" with such commerce.

Justice Stone did stress that "[f]ew subjects of state regulation are so peculiarly of local concern as is the use of state highways. There are few, local regulations of which is so inseparable from a substantial effect on interstate commerce. Unlike the railroads, local highways are built, owned and maintained by the State or its municipal subdivisions. The State has a primary and immediate concern in their safe and economical administration." But he specifically rejected the court's substituting "their own for the legislative judgment." Protection for national interests was to be found in the politically relevant fact that the state laws affected local interests as well.

Is this consistent with Justice Stone's approach in *Southern Pacific?* What are the proper roles of court and legislature in commerce clause cases in the two opinions? Is Justice Stone's opinion in *Barnwell* consistent with his *Di Santo* dissent? Dowling asks of *Barnwell:* [W]hat had become of the inquiries it suggested for determining whether or not the regulation 'concerns interests peculiarly local and does not infringe the national interest'. Were they thought unnecessary in the Barnwell case because state regulation of motor vehicles had already been sustained? In this respect the case leaves the impression of having been decided on the assumption of validity of a particular kind of regulation rather than a full investigation of the proper balance in the case at hand between the national interest in commerce and the State's interest in its roads." Dowling, *Interstate Commerce and State Power,* 27 VA. L. REV. 1 (1940), SELECTED ESSAYS 280, 286 (1963).

4. *Legislative Facts.* Justice Black is critical of the court's legislative-like fact-finding in *Southern Pacific.* Do courts have the capacity to process such data? Would the problem best be left to congressional judgment with courts deferring until it had spoken? Professor Karst, in *Legislative Facts in Constitutional Litigation,* 1960 SUP. CT. REV. 75, 85, 86 argues: "The assumption seems to be that since ultimate questions of reasonableness are not 'susceptible to solution' wholly on the basis findings of fact, courts are somehow disqualified from deciding them. The assumption ignores centuries of judicial lawmaking when it denies the competency of courts to weigh competing social interests. . . . The alternative to the educated judicial guess . . . is relegation of the issue 'to the category of political questions.' To put it less euphemistically, the alternative is the renunciation of judicial review itself, and acceptance of the intolerable principle that each level or branch of government is the judge of its own powers." *See also* Dowling, *Interstate Commerce and State Power—Revised Version,* 47 COLUM. L. REV. 547 (1947).

**5.** *Discrimination.* In *Barnwell*, Justice Stone states: "The commerce clause, by its own force, prohibits discrimination against interstate commerce, whatever its form or method, and the decisions of this Court have recognized that there is scope for its like operation when state legislation nominally of local concern is in point of fact aimed at interstate commerce, or by its necessary operation is a means of gaining a local benefit by throwing the attendant burdens on those without the state. . . . It was to end these practices that the commerce clause was adopted." Is Justice Stone saying discrimination is *per se* impermissible without balancing? Does it matter if the law is discriminatory in *purpose* or *effect*?

In any case, there has been general agreement on the court that a state law that "discriminates" against interstate commerce is impermissible. The rationale for such treatment is usually based on the historical purpose of the commerce clause to prevent interstate discrimination. But Justice Stone in *Barnwell* suggests a political justification: "Underlying the stated rule has been the thought, often expressed in judicial opinion, that when the regulation is of such a character that its burden falls principally upon those without the state, legislative action is not likely to be subjected to those political restraints which are normally exerted on legislation where it affects adversely some interests within the state." Does this suggest any guidelines in formulating an operational definition of "discrimination"? Does every local regulation favoring local interests against out-of-state interests "discriminate" against interstate commerce?

**6.** *New Directions: Full Train Crews?* In Brotherhood of Locomotive Firemen & Engineers v. Chicago, Rock Island & Pac. R.R., 393 U.S. 129 (1968), the court, per Justice Black, reversed a lower court holding and followed earlier decisions in upholding state full-crew laws. The district court had weighed the competing evidence regarding the safety benefits of such laws concluding that they had "no substantial effect on the safety of operations." Even if they did add "some increment of safety to the operation," the court decided, "such an increment is negligible and not worth the cost." The district court also noted the financial burden of compliance and the burden of adding or removing men at or near the state line.

But Justice Black, in a position reflecting his dissent in *Southern Pacific,* stated: "We think it plain that in striking down the full crew laws on this basis, the District Court indulged in a legislative judgment wholly beyond its limited authority to review state legislation under the Commerce Clause. The evidence as to the need for firemen and other additional crewmen was certainly conflicting and to a considerable extent inconclusive." The conflicting character of the evidence, argued Justice Black, left "little room for doubt that the question of safety in the circumstances of this case is essentially a matter of public policy, and public policy can, under our constitutional system, be fixed only by the people acting through their elected representatives."

Nor did Justice Black find unconstitutional discrimination in mileage exemptions in the laws that effectively freed all of Arkansas' 17 intrastate railroads from coverage, while leaving most of the 11 interstate railroads subject to them, because the "evidence in the record establishes a number of legitimate reasons for the mileage exemption. . . ."

### b.   The Free Flow of Commerce

**BALDWIN v. G.A.F. SEELIG, INC.**
Supreme Court of the United States
294 U.S. 511, 79 L. Ed. 1032, 55 S. Ct. 497 (1935)

[The New York Milk Control Act of 1933 set up a system of minimum prices to be paid by dealers to producers. It included a provision prohibiting sales of milk bought out of state at a price lower than the lawful price set for milk produced within the state. Seelig, a New York City milk dealer, bought milk in Vermont at a below-minimum price which he transported to New York. About 90 per cent was then sold in the original cans in which it was shipped and the remaining ten per cent was bottled and sold. Faced with a requirement that it agree to conform to the New York laws as a condition to receiving a license and threatened with prosecution for trading without a license, Seelig sought to enjoin enforcement of the Act. A three-judge federal court granted relief from enforcement of the Act as applied to goods in their original cans but denied relief as to sales of the bottled milk.]

Justice CARDOZO delivered the opinion of the Court.
. . . .

First.   An injunction was properly granted restraining the enforcement of the Act in its application to sales in the original packages.

New York has no power to project its legislation into Vermont by regulating the price to be paid in that state for milk acquired there. So much is not disputed. New York is equally without power to prohibit the introduction within her territory of milk of wholesome quality acquired in Vermont, whether at high prices or at low ones. This again is not disputed. Accepting those postulates, New York asserts her power to outlaw milk so introduced

by prohibiting its sale thereafter if the price that has been paid
for it to the farmers of Vermont is less than would be owing in
like circumstances to farmers in New York. The importer in that
view may keep his milk or drink it, but sell it he may not.

Such a power, if exerted, will set a barrier to traffic between
one state and another as effective as if customs duties, equal to the
price differential, had been laid upon the thing transported. . . .
Nice distinctions have been made at times between direct and
indirect burdens. They are irrelevant when the avowed purpose of
the obstruction, as well as its necessary tendency, is to suppress or
mitigate the consequences of competition between the states. Such
an obstruction is direct by the very terms of the hypothesis. We
are reminded in the opinion below that a chief occasion of the
commerce clauses was "the mutual jealousies and aggressions of
the States, taking form in customs barriers and other economic
retaliation." Farrand, Records of the Federal Convention, vol. II,
p. 308. If New York, in order to promote the economic welfare
of her farmers, may guard them against competition with the
cheaper prices of Vermont, the door has been opened to rivalries
and reprisals that were meant to be averted by subjecting commerce between the states to the power of the nation.

The argument is pressed upon us, however, that the end to be
served by the Milk Control Act is something more than the economic welfare of the farmers or of any other class or classes. The
end to be served is the maintenance of a regular and adequate
supply of pure and wholesome milk, the supply being put in
jeopardy when the farmers of the state are unable to earn a living
income. Price security, we are told, is only a special form of sanitary security; the economic motive is secondary and subordinate;
the state intervenes to make its inhabitants healthy, and not to
make them rich. On that assumption we are asked to say that
intervention will be upheld as a valid exercise by the state of its
internal police power, though there is an incidental obstruction
to commerce between one state and another. This would be to eat
up the rule under the guise of an exception. Economic welfare is
always related to health, for there can be no health if men are
starving. Let such an exception be admitted, and all that a state
will have to do in times of stress and strain is to say that its
farmers and merchants and workmen must be protected against
competition from without, lest they go upon the poor relief lists
or perish altogether. To give entrance to that excuse would be to
invite a speedy end of our national solidarity. The Constitution
was framed under the dominion of a political philosophy less
parochial in range. It was framed upon the theory that the
peoples of the several states must sink or swim together, and that

in the long run prosperity and salvation are in union and not division.

. . . There is . . . another argument which seeks to establish a relation between the well-being of the producer and the quality of the product. We are told that farmers who are underpaid will be tempted to save the expense of sanitary precautions. This temptation will affect the farmers outside New York as well as those within it. For that reason the exclusion of milk paid for in Vermont below the New York minimum will tend, it is said, to impose a higher standard of quality and thereby promote health. We think the argument will not avail to justify impediments to commerce between the states. There is neither evidence nor presumption that the same minimum prices established by order of the Board for producers in New York are necessary also for producers in Vermont. But apart from such defects of proof, the evils springing from uncared for cattle must be remedied by measures of repression more direct and certain than the creation of a parity of prices between New York and other states. Appropriate certificates may be exacted from farmers in Vermont and elsewhere; milk may be excluded if necessary safeguards have been omitted; but commerce between the states is burdened unduly when one state regulates by indirection the prices to be paid to producers in another, in the faith that augmentation of prices will lift up the level of economic welfare, and that this will stimulate the observance of sanitary requirements in the preparation of the product. The next step would be to condition importation upon proof of a satisfactory wage scale in factory or shop, or even upon proof of the profits of the business. Whatever relation there may be between earnings and sanitation is too remote and indirect to justify obstructions to the normal flow of commerce in its movement between states. One state may not put pressure of that sort upon others to reform their economic standards. If farmers or manufacturers in Vermont are abandoning farms or factories, or are failing to maintain them properly, the legislature of Vermont and not that of New York must supply the fitting remedy.

. . . .

Second.   There was error in refusing an injunction to restrain the enforcement of the Act in its application to milk in bottles to be sold by the importer.

The test of the "original package," which came into our law with Brown v. Maryland, 12 Wheat. 419, is not inflexible and final for the transactions of interstate commerce, whatever may be its validity for commerce with other countries. [See text, p. 293.] There are purposes for which merchandise, transported from another state, will be treated as a part of the general mass of property at the state of destination though still in the original containers. This is so, for illustration, where merchandise so contained is subjected to a non-discriminatory property tax which it bears equally with other merchandise produced within the state. There are other purposes for which the same merchandise will have the benefit of the protection appropriate to interstate commerce, though the original packages have been broken and the contents subdivided. . . . In brief, the test of the original package is not an ultimate principle. It is an illustration of a principle. It marks a convenient boundary and one sufficiently precise save in exceptional conditions. What is ultimate is the principle that one state in its dealings with another may not place itself in a position of economic isolation. Formulas and catchwords are subordinate to this overmastering requirement. Neither the power to tax nor the police power may be used by the state of destination with the aim and effect of establishing an economic barrier against competition with the products of another state or the labor of its residents. Restrictions so contrived are an unreasonable clog upon the mobility of commerce. They set up what is equivalent to a rampart of customs duties designed to neutralize advantages belonging to the place of origin. They are thus hostile in conception as well as burdensome in result. The form of the packages in such circumstances is immaterial, whether they are original or broken. The importer must be free from imposts framed for the very purpose of suppressing competition from without and leading inescapably to the suppression so intended.

The statute here in controversy will not survive that test. . . .
. . . .

---

## NOTES

1. *Impermissible Purpose?* Justice Cardozo says that a burden on interstate commerce is necessarily direct when its "avowed purpose" and "its necessary tendency, is to suppress or mitigate the consequences of competition between the states." Why is this an impermissible purpose? The state may have an interest in protecting its citizens from destructive competition, in assuring fair competition. Is Justice Cardozo saying that such a purpose is equivalent to a discriminatory purpose? Is such a purpose *per se* unconstitutional without the need to balance interests? Perhaps the decision in *Baldwin* would have been altered if the minimum price set for out-of-state milk reflected the costs of transportation. How does the court know the nature of the state's legislative purpose? Is it proper for the court to probe the state's purpose? How do you determine what state purposes are permissi-

ble? *See* D. ENGDAHL, CONSTITUTIONAL POWER: FEDERAL AND STATE IN A NUTSHELL 285 (1974).

2.   The state did offer alternative interests that are permissible, *i.e.*, promoting health and sanitation. Why does the state law still fail? Does the court in *Baldwin* balance the competing interests? Does the court in *Baldwin* reject the alternative state interests? The law was relevant to the state's health interest in protecting the consuming public. Does the existence of the economic purpose negate the alternative purposes? Does it deny the existence of a rational relationship? Suppose there is no alternative way by which the state can effectively pursue its interests?

3.   *Discriminatory Purpose and Effect.* In Dean Milk Co. v. Madison, 340 U.S. 349 (1951), the Supreme Court, per Justice Clark, reversed a state supreme court decision upholding the constitutionality of a Madison, Wisconsin ordinance making it unlawful to sell milk as pasteurized unless it had been processed and bottled at an approved plant within a five-mile radius from the center of the city. The effect of this law was to exclude milk pasteurized at Dean Milk Company's plants in Illinois.

While there were suggestions that the purpose of the ordinance was, in fact, to exclude higher grade milk from outside the Madison milkshed, the court did not rely on a finding of discriminatory purpose. The state court had found that the law furthered health interests by promoting convenient, economical, and efficient plant inspection. But Justice Clark argued that to hold "that the ordinance is valid simply because it professes to be a health measure would mean that the Commerce Clause of itself imposes no limitations on state action other than those laid down by the Due Process Clause, save for the rare instance when a state artlessly discloses an avowed *purpose* to discriminate against interstate goods." (Emphasis added.)

Instead, Justice Clark looked to the character of this local health interest and the available means of protecting it. He began with the premise that "this regulation, like the provision invalidated in *Baldwin v. G.A.F. Seelig, Inc.*, in *practical effect* excludes from distribution in Madison wholesome milk produced and pasteurized in Illinois. . . . In thus erecting an economic barrier protecting a major local industry against competition from without the state, Madison plainly discriminates against interstate commerce. This it cannot do, even in the exercise of its unquestioned power to protect the health and safety of its people, if reasonable nondiscriminatory alternatives, adequate to conserve legitimate local interests, are available [citing *Baldwin*]." And the court noted that this was equally true even though the ordinance also operated against Wisconsin milk outside the Madison milkshed. Is this fact relevant?

In this instance, reasonable and adequate alternatives were available. Madison could use its own inspectors in Dean's plants and charge the costs of such inspections to the importing producers and processors. Or, they could employ the U.S. Public Health Services safety ratings and exclude milk not produced and pasteurized in conformity with their standards.

Based on these findings, Justice Clark concluded: "To permit Madison to adopt a regulation not essential for the protection of local health interests and placing a discriminatory burden on interstate commerce would invite a multiplication of preferential trade areas destructive of the very purpose of the Commerce Clause. Under the circumstances here presented, the regulation must yield to the principle that 'one state in its dealings with another may not place itself in a position of economic isolation.' *Baldwin*."

What is the consequence of a judicial finding that a law purposely discriminates against interstate commerce? That it places a discriminatory burden on interstate commerce? Does the court's approach in *Dean Milk* differ from that used in *Southern Pacific*? *See* Stern, *The Problems of Yesteryear—Commerce and Due Process,* in ESSAYS IN CONSTITUTIONAL LAW 150, 166 (R. McCloskey, ed., 1957).

4. *Less Onerous Alternatives.* In *Dean Milk,* the court stressed the availability of alternative means for achieving valid state interests. As long as the legislative choice of means is rationally related to achieving its permissible goals, what justification is there for additional judicial scrutiny? Should this inquiry into alternatives be limited to "discrimination" cases or should the availability of means less burdensome on national interests be valid for all balancing? However, the court in *Baldwin* did not consider alternative means of achieving the permissible goals of the state.

5. *A Hierachy of Interests?* Some state interests in regulating incoming commerce may be more compelling than others. Consider the deferential treatment accorded highway regulations in *Barnwell. See* Breard v. Alexandria, 341 U.S. 622 (1951), where the court upheld the constitutionality of a "Green River Ordinance" forbidding door to door solicitation of private residences for commercial purposes without the owner's prior consent on the basis of the community's "social welfare" interests.

6. *Baldwin Today.* In Polar Ice Cream & Creamery Co. v. Andrews, 375 U.S. 361 (1964), the court dealt with complex Florida Milk Commission regulations covering milk producer-

distributor relations in the Pensacola area. The regulations would have required, *inter alia,* Polar to accept its total supply of Class I milk from Pensacola producers first at a fixed price substantially below the price at which Polar could obtain Class I milk out of state and would have obliged distributors to take all the milk these local producers might offer.

The Supreme Court, per Justice White, finding that the principles of *Baldwin* remained sound, held that they "justify, indeed require, invalidation as a burden on interstate commerce of that part of the Florida regulatory scheme which reserves to its local producers a substantial share of the Florida milk market." Any economic or health rationale for the laws failed on the principles of *Baldwin* and *Dean Milk.* Nor could the law be justified by asserting that Polar was buying milk at distress prices out of state and selling it at Class I prices locally to the detriment of local producers since this was but another way of asserting that Florida could preempt its local market for its own producers. "[T]he State may not, in the sole interest of promoting the economic welfare of its dairy farmers, insulate the Florida milk industry from competition from other States." To allow Florida to regulate in this manner would create an "unreasonable clog upon the mobility of commerce. They set up what is equivalent to a rampart of customs duties designed to neutralize advantages belonging to the place of origin. They are thus hostile in conception as well as burdensome in result [*Baldwin*]."

## Protecting Personal Mobility

1. As previously indicated, the movement of persons is included in the term "commerce." Thus in Heart of Atlanta Motel, Inc. v. United States, 379 U.S. 241 (1964) and Katzenbach v. McClung, 379 U.S. 294 (1964), text, pp. 200, 204, the commerce clause served as the constitutional nexus for the public accommodations provisions of the 1964 Civil Rights Act. The clause can also be used against state regulations impairing free mobility of citizens.

In Edwards v. California, 314 U.S. 160 (1941), the court used this approach to hold unconstitutional a state statute making it a misdemeanor to bring "into the State any indigent person who is not a resident of the State, knowing him to be an indigent person." Quoting the national common market philosophy of *Baldwin,* Justice Byrnes, for the court, argued that it would be "difficult to conceive of a statute more squarely in conflict with this theory than the [California law]." Its very purpose and immediate effect was to burden interstate commerce. Indigent nonresidents lacked any hope of political redress in the state legislature. While admitting the hardship imposed on California by the influx of migrants, Justice Byrnes contended that the task of providing relief had become a national problem, a shared burden. No state could "isolate itself from difficulties common to all of them by restraining the transportation of persons and property across its borders." Further, prohibition against indigents "is an open invitation to retaliatory measures, and the burdens upon the transportation of such persons become cumulative."

Four justices concurred but on the basis of the fourteenth amendment privileges and immunities clause. For Justice Douglas, joined by Justices Black and Murphy, "the right of persons to move freely from state to state occupies a more protected position in our constitutional system than does the movement of cattle, fruit, steel and coal. . . ." Justice Jackson stated that the "migration of a human being, of whom it is charged that he possesses nothing that can be sold and has no wherewithal to buy, do not fit easily into my notions as to what is commerce. To hold that the measure of his rights is the commerce clause is likely to result eventually either in distorting the commercial law or in denaturing human rights." Under the commerce clause rationale could Congress bar the interstate movement of indigents?

2. *Interstate Discrimination.* Article IV, § 2 provides: "The Citizens of each State shall be entitled to all Privileges and Immunities of Citizens in the several States." While the clause might have served as a broad source of individual rights (see Corfield v. Coryell, 6 Fed. Cas. 546 (No. 3, 230) (4 Wash. C.C.) 371 (1823), text, p. 414), it has been narrowly construed only as a prohibition against discrimination against out-of-state citizens. *See* Paul v. Virginia, 75 U.S. (8 Wall.) 168 (1869).

In Doe v. Bolton, 410 U.S. 179 (1973), the court struck down an abortion residency requirement as violation of Art. IV, § 2. "Just as the Privileges and Immunities Clause . . . protects persons who enter other States to ply their trade . . . , so must it protect persons who enter Georgia seeking the medical services that are available there. . . . A contrary holding would mean that a State could limit to its own residents the general medical care available within its borders. This we could not approve." *See* Toomer v. Witsell, 334 U.S. 385 (1948).

### H. P. HOOD & SONS, INC. v. DU MOND
Supreme Court of the United States
336 U.S. 525, 93 L. Ed. 865, 69 S. Ct. 657 (1949)

Justice JACKSON delivered the opinion of the Court.

This case concerns the power of the State of New York to deny additional facilities to acquire and ship milk in interstate commerce where the grounds of denial are that such limitation upon interstate business will protect and advance local economic interests.

H. P. Hood & Sons, Inc., a Massachusetts corporation, has long distributed milk and its products to inhabitants of Boston. That city obtains about 90% of its fluid milk from states other than Massachusetts. . . . The area in which Hood has been denied an additional license to make interstate purchases has been developed as a part of the Boston milkshed from which both the Hood Company and a competitor have shipped to Boston.

The state courts have held and it is conceded here that Hood's entire business in New York, present and proposed, is interstate commerce. This Hood has conducted for some time by means of three receiving depots, where it takes raw milk from farmers. The milk is not processed in New York but is weighed, tested and, if necessary, cooled and on the same day shipped as fluid milk to Boston. These existing plants have been operated under license from the State and are not in question here as the State has licensed Hood to continue them. The controversy concerns a proposed additional plant for the same kind of operation at Greenwich, New York.

Article 21 of the Agriculture and Markets Law of New York forbids a dealer to buy milk from producers unless licensed to do so by the Commissioner of Agriculture and Markets. . . . [T]he Commissioner may not grant a license unless satisfied . . . "that the issuance of the license will not tend to a destructive competition in a market already adequately served, and that the issuance of the license is in the public interest."

. . . .

The Commissioner found that Hood, if licensed at Greenwich, would permit its present suppliers, at their option, to deliver at the new plant rather than the old ones and for a substantial number this would mean shorter hauls and savings in delivery costs. The new plant also would attract twenty to thirty producers, some of whose milk Hood anticipates will or may be diverted from other buyers. Other large milk distributors have plants within the general area and dealers serving Troy obtain milk in the locality. He found that Troy was inadequately supplied during the preceding short season.

In denying the application for expanded facilities, the Commissioner states his grounds as follows:

"If applicant is permitted to equip and operate another milk plant in this territory, and to take on producers now delivering to plants other than those which it operates, it will tend to reduce the volume of milk received at the plants which lose those producers, and will tend to increase the cost of handling milk in those plants.

"If applicant takes producers now delivering milk to local markets such as Troy, it will have a tendency to deprive such markets of a supply needed during the short season.

"There is no evidence that any producer is without a market for his milk. There is no evidence that any producers not now delivering milk to applicant would receive any higher price, were they to deliver their milk to applicant's proposed plant.

"The issuance of a license to applicant which would permit it to operate an additional plant, would tend to a destructive competition in a market already adequately served, and would not be in the public interest."

Denial of the license was sustained by the Court of Appeals over constitutional objections duly urged under the Commerce Clause. . . .

. . . .

Pennsylvania enacted a law including provisions to protect producers which were very similar to those of this New York Act. A concern which operated a receiving plant in Pennsylvania from which it shipped milk to the New York City market challenged the Act upon grounds thus defined by this Court: "The respondent contends that the act, if construed to require it to obtain a license, to file a bond for the protection of producers, and to pay the farmers the prices prescribed by the Board, unconstitutionally regulates and burdens interstate commerce." *Milk Control Bd. v. Eisenberg Co.* [see Note 3 *infra*]. This Court, specifically limiting its judgment to the Act's provisions with respect to license, bond and regulation of prices to be paid to producers, considered their effect on interstate commerce "incidental and not forbidden by the Constitution, in the absence of regulation by Congress."

The present controversy begins where the *Eisenberg* decision left off. New York's regulations, designed to assure producers a fair price and a responsible purchaser, and consumers a sanitary and modernly equipped handler, are not challenged here but have been complied with. It is only additional restrictions, imposed for the avowed purpose and with the practical effect of curtailing the volume of interstate commerce to aid local economic interests, that are in question here, and no such measures were attempted or such ends sought to be served in the Act before the Court in the *Eisenberg* Case.

Our decision in a milk litigation most relevant to the present controversy deals with the converse of the present situation. Baldwin v. G. A. F. Seelig, Inc., 294 U.S. 511. . . .

. . . .

[The *Baldwin* Court's] distinction between the power of the State to shelter its people from menaces to their health or safety and from fraud, even when those dangers emanate from interstate commerce, and its lack of power to retard, burden or constrict the flow of such commerce for their economic advantage, is one deeply rooted in both our history and our law.

. . . .

Baldwin v. G. A. F. Seelig, Inc. 294 U.S. 511, is an explicit, impressive, recent and unanimous condemnation by this Court of economic restraints on interstate commerce for local economic advantage, but it does not stand alone. This Court consistently has rebuffed attempts of states to advance their own commercial interests by curtailing the movement of articles of commerce, either into or out of the state, while generally supporting their right to impose even burdensome regulations in the interest of local health and safety. As most states serve their own interests best by sending their produce to market, the cases in which this Court has been obliged to deal with prohibitions or limitations by states upon exports of articles of commerce are not numerous. However, in a leading case, West v. Kansas Natural Gas Co. 221 U.S. 229, the Court denied constitutional validity to a statute by which Oklahoma, by regulation of gas companies and pipe lines, sought to restrict the export of natural gas. The Court held that when a state recognizes an article to be a subject of commerce, it cannot prohibit it from being a subject of interstate commerce; that the right to engage in interstate commerce is not the gift of a state, and that a state cannot regulate or restrain it.

. . . .

[The] principle that our economic unit is the Nation, which alone has the gamut of powers necessary to control of the economy, including the vital power of erecting customs barriers against foreign competition, has as its corollary that the states are not separable economic units. As the Court said in *Baldwin v. G. A. F. Seelig, Inc.,* "what is ultimate is the principle that one state in its dealing with another may not place itself in a position of economic isolation." In so speaking it but followed the principle that the state may not use its admitted powers to protect the health and safety of its people as a basis for suppressing competition. In Buck v. Kuykendall, 267 U.S. 307, the Court struck down a state act because, in the language of Mr. Justice Brandeis, "Its primary purpose is not regulation with a view to safety or to conservation of the highways, but the prohibition of competition." The same argument here advanced, that limitation of competition would itself contribute to safety and conservation, and therefore indirectly serve an end permissible to the state, was there declared "not sound." It is no better here. This Court has not only recognized this disability of the state to isolate its own economy as a basis for striking down parochial legislative policies designed to do so, but it has recognized the incapacity of the state to protect its own inhabitants from competition as a reason for sustaining particular exercises of the commerce power of Congress to reach matters in which states were so disabled.

The material success that has come to inhabitants of the states which make up this federal free trade unit has been the most impressive in the history of commerce, but the established interdependence of the states only emphasizes the necessity of protecting interstate movement of goods against local burdens and repressions. We need only consider the consequences if each of the few states that produce copper, lead, high-grade iron ore, timber, cotton, oil or gas should decree that industries located in that state shall have priority. What fantastic rivalries and dislocations and reprisals would ensue if such practices were begun! Or suppose that the field of discrimination and retaliation be industry. May Michigan provide that automobiles cannot be taken out of that State until local dealers' demands are fully met? Would she not have every argument in the favor of such a statute that can be offered in support of New York's limiting sales of milk for out-of-state shipment to protect the economic interests of her competing dealers and local consumers? Could Ohio then pounce upon the rubber-tire industry, on which she has a substantial grip, to retaliate for Michigan's auto monopoly?

Our system, fostered by the Commerce Clause, is that every farmer and every craftsman shall be encouraged to produce by the certainty that he will have free access to every market in the Nation, that no home embargoes will withhold his export, and no foreign state will by customs duties or regulations exclude them. Likewise, every consumer may look to the free competition from every producing area in the Nation to protect him from exploitation by any. Such was the vision of the Founders; such has been the doctrine of this Court which has given it reality.

. . . .

Since the statute as applied violates the Commerce Clause and is not authorized by federal legislation pursuant to that Clause,

it cannot stand. The judgment is reversed and the cause remanded for proceedings not inconsistent with this opinion.

It is so ordered.

Mr. Justice BLACK [joined by Justice MURPHY], dissenting.

. . . .

Justice FRANKFURTER, with whom Justice RUTLEDGE joins,
dissenting.

. . . .

---

## NOTES

### Economic Purposes

1. Justice Clark in Cities Service Gas Co. v. Peerless Oil &
Gas Co., 340 U.S. 179 (1950), stated that "[t]he vice in the regulation invalidated in *Hood* was solely that it denied facilities to a
company in interstate commerce on the articulated ground that
such facilities would divert milk supplies needed by local consumers; in other words, the regulation discriminated against
interstate commerce." Is this an accurate description of the holding in *Hood?* What of the arguments in both dissenting opinions
that a dealer in milk for New York markets would also be denied
a license?

What was the legislative purpose in authorizing the commissioner to deny licenses to avoid "destructive competition in a
market already adequately served"? It has been said that the court
in *Hood* is adopting "the view that the local economic need of a
state could never justify its regulation of interstate commerce."
Notes, *State Regulation of Interstate Commerce—Denial of
License To Ship Milk Held Invalid*, 37 CALIF. L. REV. 667, 668-
69 (1949). Alternatively, economic legislation is only impermissible when enacted for the purpose of protecting local dealers
against out-of-state competition, or for the purpose of denying
access to local markets to foreign dealers. Is *Hood* an application
of *Baldwin* to outgoing commerce?

*Hood* may be based on a finding of impermissible purpose or a
one-sided balancing test. Are state economic justifications suspect?
Is it critical that the state's action in *Hood* is prohibitory and
exclusionary rather than regulatory? If this is balancing, what
of the competing interests? *See* Note, 35 CORNELL L.Q. 211 (1949).

2. Parker v. Brown, 317 U.S. 341 (1943), involved the validity
of California legislation requiring that raisin producers deliver
a substantial portion of their raisin crop to a marketing control
committee as a device for eliminating price competition among
producers. Since 95 per cent of the crop was marketed in interstate commerce, the controls had a substantial impact on interstate commerce.

The court upheld the state law. Justice Stone noted initially that the controls would be constitutional under the "mechanical test" since the regulation applied before "any operation of interstate commerce occurs." But he relied on the principles articulated in his *Di Santo* dissent: "When Congress has not exerted its power under the Commerce Clause, and state regulation of matters of local concern is so related to interstate commerce that it also operates as a regulation of that commerce, the reconciliation of the power thus granted with that reserved to the state is to be attained by the accommodation of the competing demands of the state and national interests involved."

Applying this standard, Justice Stone took judicial notice "that the evils attending the production and marketing of raisins in [California] present a problem local in character and urgently demanding state action for the economic protection of those engaged in one of [the state's] important industries." He went on to stress the extent to which the federal government had itself adopted marketing controls to stabilize agricultural production and had provided assistance to California in administering its program. "In comparing the relative weights of the conflicting local and national interests involved, it is significant that Congress, by its agricultural legislation, has recognized the distressed condition of much of the agricultural production of the United States, and has authorized marketing procedures, substantially like the California prorate program, for stabilizing the marketing of agricultural products.

"[T]he Agricultural Marketing Agreement Act is applicable to raisins only on the direction of the Secretary of Agriculture who, instead of establishing a federal program has, as the statute authorizes, cooperated in promoting the state program and aided it by substantial federal loans. Hence we cannot say that the effect of the state program on interstate commerce is one which conflicts with Congressional policy or is such as to preclude the state from this exercise of this reserve power to regulate domestic agricultural production."

It is clear that California had an "economic purpose" in controlling the supply of raisin prices. The court specifically stated that the law is "for the economic protection of those engaged in one of [California's] important industries." Is *Parker* then inconsistent with *Hood*? If there had been no federal "endorsement" of the California marketing controls, should *Parker* have been decided differently? Consider the assertion that in the absence of such congressional support "it is certainly arguable that the national commercial interest should prevent a state producing most of a commodity distributed throughout the nation from limiting the quantity produced or marketed in order to raise the price to consumers." Stern, *The Problems of Yesteryear—Commerce and Due Process,* 4 VAND. L. REV. 446, 454 (1951).

3.  Milk Control Bd. v. Eisenberg Farm Products, 306 U.S. 346 (1939), discussed in the principal case, upheld the constitutionality of applying a Pennsylvania law requiring milk dealers to be licensed and setting a minimum price to be paid to producers to a New York milk dealer who bought milk from Pennsylvania producers, cooled it in the state and then shipped it to New York for processing and sale.

The court, per Justice Roberts, described the purpose of the statute as designed "to reach a domestic situation in the interest of the welfare of the producers and consumers of milk in Pennsylvania." He then turned to "weighing the nature of the respondent's activities and the propriety of local regulation of them, as disclosed by the record."

Justice Roberts sought to distinguish *Baldwin v. Seelig* as involving a state's attempt to extend its laws into a neighboring state, thereby establishing what amounted to a tariff barrier. In contrast, in the present case, "[t]he commonwealth does not essay to regulate or to restrain the shipment of the respondent's milk into New York or to regulate its sale or the price at which respondent may sell it in New York. . . . Only a small fraction of the milk produced by farmers in Pennsylvania is shipped out of the Commonwealth."

### Retaining Local Assets

1.  Would the regulation in *Hood* be constitutional if it were treated as a device to preserve local assets for domestic use? Justice Jackson stressed an earlier case, West v. Kansas Natural Gas Co., 221 U.S. 229 (1911), where the court had struck down a state's attempt to limit the export of its natural gas, rejecting the theory of a state property right in the commodity. "Gas, when reduced to possession, is his individual property subject to intrastate commerce and interstate commerce." The court went on to dismiss the contention that in the interest of the public welfare, Oklahoma might permit the gas to be sold intrastate while prohibiting its sale interstate. "If the States have such power a singular situation might result. Pennsylvania might keep its coal, the Northwest its timber, the mining States their minerals. And why may not the products of the field be brought within the principle? Thus enlarged, or without that enlargement, an influence on interstate commerce need not be pointed out. To what consequences does such power tend? If one State has it, all States have it; embargo may be retaliated by embargo, and commerce will be

halted at state lines. And yet we have said that 'in matters of foreign and interstate commerce there are no state lines.' In such commerce, instead of the States, a new power appears and a new welfare, a welfare which transcends that of any State." *See* Pennsylvania v. West Virginia, 262 U.S. 553 (1923), rejecting a West Virginia requirement that local needs for scarce natural gas resources be met before out-of-state needs.

2. And in Cities Services Gas Co. v. Peerless Oil & Gas Co., 340 U.S. 179 (1950), the court dealt with a state order requiring Cities Service to take natural gas ratably from Peerless at fixed prices. Ninety per cent of the gas was sent out of state. Justice Clark, for the court in upholding the legislation, argued that "the only requirement [of the commerce clause] consistently recognized has been that the regulation not discriminate against or place an embargo on interstate commerce, that it safeguard an obvious state interest, and that the local interest at stake outweigh whatever national interest there might be in the prevention of state restrictions."

In this instance the legitimate local interest was clear—"A state is justifiably concerned with preventing rapid and uneconomic dissipation of one of its chief natural resources." While recognizing that there was also a strong national interest in natural gas problems, Justice Clark suggested that "it is far from clear that on balance such interest is harmed by the state regulations under attack here. . . . [S]trong arguments have been made that the national interest lies in preserving this limited resource for domestic and industrial uses for which natural gas has no completely satisfactory substitute. . . . Insofar as conservation is concerned, the national interest and the interest of producing states may well tend to coincide. In any event, in the field of this complexity with such diverse interests involved, we cannot say that there is a clear national interest so harmed that the state price fixing orders here employed fall within the ban of the Commerce Clause [citing *Parker v. Brown* and *Eisenberg*]. Nor is it for us to consider whether Oklahoma's unilateral efforts to conserve gas will be fully effective."

## Additional State Interests

1. The court has sustained legislation designed to further a variety of other state interests, *e.g.,* protection of consumers from mislabeled or adulterated goods or from commercial fraud, protection of the public health and safety, elimination of racial discrimination. *See generally,* THE CONSTITUTION OF THE UNITED STATES: ANALYSIS AND INTERPRETATION 258-67 (1973); 2 C. ANTIEAU, MODERN CONSTITUTIONAL LAW §§ 10.37-10.43 (1969).

However, there are limits. In Pike v. Bruce Church, Inc., 397 U.S. 137 (1970), the court invalidated an order, issued under an Arizona statute governing the packaging and shipping of cantaloupes in the state, requiring the company to package its produce in Arizona rather than at its California packaging plant. This would have cost the company an added $200,000.

Justice Stewart, for a unanimous court, defined the standard. "Where the statute regulates even handedly to effectuate a legitimate local public interest, and its effects on interstate commerce are only incidental, it will be upheld unless the burden imposed on such commerce is clearly excessive in relation to the putative local benefits. . . . If a legitimate local purpose is found, then the question becomes one of degree. And the extent of the burden that will be tolerated will of course depend on the nature of the local interest involved, and on whether it could be promoted as well with a lesser impact with interstate activities."

In applying this standard, Justice Stewart argued that Arizona's legitimate interest in having the company's high quality cantaloupes identified as originating in Arizona could not justify the additional cost that would be involved. "The nature of that burden is, constitutionally, more significant than its extent. For the court has viewed with particular suspicion state statutes requiring business operations to be performed in the home State that could more efficiently be performed elsewhere. Even where the State is pursuing a clearly legitimate local interest, this particular burden on commerce has been declared to be virtually per se illegal." The added cost burdens were said to impose a "strait jacket on the appellee company with respect to the allocation of its interstate resources." While a cost burden might be tolerated for a more compelling state interest, "here the State's interest is minimal at best—certainly less substantial than a State's interest in securing employment for its people. If the Commerce Clause forbids a State to require work to be done within its jurisdiction to promote local employment, then surely it cannot permit a State to require a person to go into a local packing business solely for the sake of enhancing the reputation of other producers within its borders."

2. In Allenberg Cotton Co., Inc. v. Pittman, 419 U.S. 20 (1974), the court held that the commerce clause prohibited a state court from refusing to enforce a contract in a suit by an out-of-state dealer unless the dealer had qualified to do business in the state. While the contract was made in Mississippi and called for storage of the goods in the state prior to out-of-state shipment, the goods were viewed as already being in the stream of commerce.

### 3. When Congress Speaks

The previous sections dealt with the negative implications of the dormant commerce clause when Congress has not spoken. In the present section, the focus shifts to consider the consequences when Congress speaks. Congressional legislation may authorize continued state regulation, a subject dealt with in part b of this section. Alternatively, Congress may seek to explicitly exclude continued state regulation over a subject even though such state regulation would be constitutional in the absence of the congressional action. More frequently, Congress may not even address itself to the state power to regulate in the same area or its intent regarding state regulation may be unclear. The latter problems constitute the focus of part a of this section.

### a. Preemption

"Preemption problems arise whenever a state law is asserted to be unenforceable because it is contrary to federal law, as when the state commands conduct which the federal law forbids, or when the federal government forbids state regulation of a field of activity subject to federal superintendence." Hirsch, *Toward a New View of Federal Preemption,* 1972 U. ILL. L.F. 515, 546. As *Gibbons v. Ogden,* text, p. 245, makes clear, a state law which conflicts with a valid federal law must give way under the Art. VI supremacy clause. Further, if Congress, pursuant to its commerce powers expressly excludes state regulation, that is determinative since "the government of the Union though limited in its powers is supreme within its sphere of action." McCulloch v. Maryland, 17 U.S. (4 Wheat.) 159, 199 (1819).

But what if the state law does not directly conflict with federal legislation and Congress does not expressly exclude the states from regulating? What if the state law is inconsistent with the achievement of the federal policy? Or, a more difficult problem—what if the state law appears on its face to be compatible with federal regulation? Does the fact of federal legislation automatically exclude state regulation over the same subject (however that might be defined)? If some concurrent state regulation is permissible, what standard determines the permissible from the impermissible? What is the judicial role in determining these questions of preemption?

---

**BURBANK v. LOCKHEED AIR TERMINAL, INC.**
Supreme Court of the United States
411 U.S. 624, 36 L. Ed. 2d 547, 93 S. Ct. 1854 (1973)

Justice DOUGLAS delivered the opinion of the Court.

. . . .

This suit brought by appellees asked for an injunction against the enforcement of an ordinance adopted by the City Council of Burbank, California, which made it unlawful for a so-called pure jet aircraft to take off from the Hollywood-Burbank Airport between 11 p.m. of one day and 7 a.m. the next day, and making it unlawful for the operator of that airport to allow any such aircraft to take off from that airport during such periods. The only regularly scheduled flight affected by the ordinance was an intrastate flight of Pacific Southwest Airlines originating in Oakland, California, and departing from Hollywood-Burbank Airport for San Diego every Sunday night at 11:30 p.m.

The District Court found the ordinance to be unconstitutional on both Supremacy Clause and Commerce Clause grounds. The Court of Appeals affirmed on the grounds of the Supremacy Clause both as respects pre-emption and as respects conflict. The case is here on appeal. . . . We affirm the Court of Appeals.
. . . .

[The Federal Aviation Act] provides in part, "The United States of America is declared to possess and exercise complete and exclusive national sovereignty in the airspace of the United States. . . ." [T]he Administrator of the Federal Aeronautics Act (FAA) has been given broad authority to regulate the use of the navigable airspace, "in order to insure the safety of aircraft and the efficient utilization of such airspace . . ." and "for the protection of persons and property on the ground. . . ."

The Solicitor General, though arguing against pre-emption, concedes that as respects "airspace management" there is pre-emption. That, however, is a fatal concession, for as the District Court found: "The imposition of curfew ordinances on a nationwide basis would result in a bunching of flights in those hours immediately preceding the curfew. This bunching of flights during these hours would have the twofold effect of increasing an already serious congestion problem and actually increasing, rather than relieving, the noise problem by increasing flights in the period of greatest annoyance to surrounding communities. Such a result is totally inconsistent with the objectives of the federal statutory and regulatory scheme." It also found "[t]he imposition of curfew ordinances on a nationwide basis would cause a serious loss of efficiency in the use of the navigable airspace."

[The Court examined, at length, the legislative history of the Act and the regulations interpreting it and the Noise Control Act of 1972.]

Our prior cases on pre-emption are not precise guidelines in the present controversy, for each case turns on the peculiarities and special features of the federal regulatory scheme in question. Control of noise is of course deep-seated in the police power of the States. Yet the pervasive control vested in EPA and in FAA under the 1972 [Noise Control] Act seems to us to leave no room for local curfews or other local controls. What the ultimate remedy for aircraft noise which plagues many communities and tens of thousands of people is not known. The procedures under the 1972 Act are under way. In addition, the Administrator has imposed a variety of regulations relating to takeoff and landing procedures and runway preferences. The Federal Aviation Act requires a delicate balance between safety and efficiency, and the protection of persons on the ground. Any regulations adopted by the Administrator to control noise pollution must be consistent with the "highest degree of safety." The interdependence of these factors requires a uniform and exclusive system of federal regulation if the congressional objectives underlying the Federal Aviation Act are to be fulfilled.

If we were to uphold the Burbank ordinance and a significant number of municipalities followed suit, it is obvious that fractionalized control of the timing of takeoffs and landings would severely limit the flexibility of the FAA in controlling air traffic flow. The difficulties of scheduling flights to avoid congestion and the concomitant decrease in safety would be compounded. . . . We are not at liberty to diffuse the powers given by Congress to FAA and EPA by letting the States or municipalities in on the planning. If that change is to be made, Congress alone must do it.

Affirmed.

Justice REHNQUIST, with whom Justice STEWART, Justice WHITE, and Justice MARSHALL join, dissenting.

. . . .

## NOTES

1. Congress may include a specific saving clause in its legislation authorizing state regulation or Congress may clearly indicate its intent not to preempt. In Askew v. American Waterways Operators, Inc., 411 U.S. 325 (1973), the court, per Justice Douglas, held that the Federal Water Quality Improvement Act of 1970, providing no-fault liability for clean-up costs incurred by the federal government as a result of oil spills and authorizing the President to issue regulations for the prevention of such spills, did not supersede state laws dealing with liability to the state and private persons from oil spills. The court found no conflict

between the federal and state laws but rather concluded that
they constituted "harmonious parts of an integrated whole." The
Act and accompanying legislative history were said to have clearly
contemplated cooperative action with the states. Justice Douglas
then went on to the constitutional question holding that the
exercise of the state police power was not inconsistent with
Congress' power over admiralty and maritime affairs.

2. It has been suggested that prior to the 1930's, the court
adopted the position "that the *exercise* of federal power was
inherently exclusive of any concurrent state power over any
matter reached by the federal act." Engdahl, *Preemptive Capability of Federal Power,* 45 U. COLO. L. REV. 51, 54 (1973). *See* D.
ENGDAHL, CONSTITUTIONAL POWER: FEDERAL AND STATE IN A NUT-
SHELL 320-27 (1974). *But see* Justice Black's dissent in Campbell
v. Hussey, 368 U.S. 297, 315 (1961), denying that the court has
ever applied an exclusive control doctrine. Would such a doctrine of exclusiveness be compatible with principles of federalism? How would the area—the subject matter—of the federal
legislation be determined? What was the subject of the federal
legislation in *Burbank?* Of the state legislation? In any case, as
*Burbank* makes clear, the exclusiveness approach to preemption
has been abandoned in modern cases.

3. Is the issue in *Burbank* whether Congress intended to
supersede state regulation or whether the existence and operation
of the state law is incompatible with the federal regulation?
Does the court presume negative intent from incompatibility of
operation? Consider the following critique: "By framing the preemption question in terms of specific congressional intent the
Supreme Court has manufactured difficulties for itself. Apart
from the difficult problem of defining which Congress' and which
congressman's intent is relevant, this manner of stating the issues
suggests that the preemption question was consciously resolved
and that only diligent effort is needed to reveal the intended
solution. But Congress, embroiled in controversy over policy
issues, rarely anticipates the possible ramifications of its acts
upon state law. Like the conflict of laws questions which are
inherent in state statutes but seldom articulated, pre-emption
questions are implicit in many federal statutes but remain for
the courts to answer." Note, *Preemption as a Preferential
Ground: A New Canon of Construction,* 12 STAN. L. REV. 208,
209 (1959), SELECTED ESSAYS 310, 310-11 (1963).

4. *The Need for Uniformity.* How does the court in *Burbank*
determine congressional intent? Justice Douglas begins his opinion by quoting the *Cooley* uniformity doctrine. How does that
doctrine apply in preemption cases? Is the theory that the state

regulation would constitute an unreasonable interference with federal regulation? With federal policy?

**5.** *Legislative History.* How important is legislative history in ascertaining the congressional intent in *Burbank*? Should this be the exclusive method for ascertaining congressional intent? Engdahl suggests that "[w]hen their colleagues have seemed too quick to infer an exclusionary congressional intent, some Justices have argued that it is improper to look beyond the legislative history of the federal act. But even inferences drawn from legislative history may vary; and in any event, the court has generally declined to confine itself to that single source of inference." D. ENGDAHL, CONSTITUTIONAL POWER: FEDERAL AND STATE IN A NUT-SHELL 333 (1974).

**6.** *Pervasiveness.* Justice Douglas in *Burbank* places emphasis on the pervasiveness of the federal scheme. This has been an important consideration in a number of preemption cases. In Pennsylvania v. Nelson, 350 U.S. 497 (1956), in holding that the Pennsylvania Sedition Act had been preempted by federal legislation, the majority, per Chief Justice Warren, stressed the numerous federal laws governing sedition such as the Smith Act of 1940, the Internal Security Act of 1950 and the Communist Control Act of 1954. He concluded that " 'the scheme of federal regulation [is] so pervasive as to make reasonable the inference that Congress left no room for the States to supplement it.' . . . We examine these acts only to determine the congressional plan. Looking to all of them in the aggregate, the conclusion is inescapable that Congress has intended to occupy the field of sedition."

**7.** *Federal and State Areas of Interest.* The court in *Nelson* also emphasized that "the federal statutes 'touch a field in which the federal interest is so dominant that the federal system [must] be assumed to preclude enforcement of state laws on the same subject.' " The court cited Hines v. Davidowitz, 312 U.S. 52 (1941), where the court had struck down a 1939 Pennsylvania Alien Registration Act, at least in part because the state law was in the field of international relations which "has been most generally conceded imperatively to demand broad national authority." It followed in *Hines* that "[a]ny concurrent state power that may exist is restricted to the narrowest of limits. . . ." Justice Black noted that "the regulation of aliens is so intimately blended and intertwined with responsibilities of the national government that where it acts and the state also acts on the same subject, 'the act of Congress, or the treaty is supreme, and the law of the state, though enacted in the exercise of its powers not controverted, must yield to it.' " *See* Graham v. Richardson, 403

U.S. 365 (1971), text, pp. 646-48, on alienage regulation. Is the subject of regulation in *Burbank* a matter of predominant national or local interest?

   **8.** *Potential Conflict.* The court in *Nelson* also indicated that "enforcement of state sedition acts presents a serious danger of conflict with the administration of the federal program. Since 1939, in order to avoid hampering of uniformed enforcement of its program by sporadic local prosecution, the federal government has urged local authorities not to intervene in such matters. . . ." The court pointed out that many states had some form of anti-sedition law, some of them "studiously drawn to protect basic rights and others wholly without constitutional safeguard." Noting the warning of Justice Jackson in a like situation in the field of labor-management relations—"A multiplicity of tribunals in a diversity of procedures are quite as apt to produce incompatible or conflicting adjudications as are different rules of substantive law"—the Chief Justice contended that "should the states be permitted to exercise a concurrent jurisdiction in this area, federal enforcement would encounter not only the difficulties mentioned by Mr. Justice Jackson, but the added conflict engendered by different criteria of substantive offenses." He concluded: "We are not unmindful of the risks of compounding punishment which would be created by finding concurrent state power. . . . Without compelling indication to the contrary, we will not assume that Congress intended to permit the possibility of double punishment."

   **9.** *One-Master Theory.* An important criterion in the cases finding federal preemption has been "the fact that Congress has entrusted administration of the . . . policy for the Nation to a centralized administrative agency. . . ." San Diego Bldg. Trades Council v. Garmon, 359 U.S. 236, 242 (1959). One commentator labeling this the "one master" theory explains: "When Congress delegates broad regulatory power to a federal agency without addressing itself to the question of pre-emption in any detail, the court infers that the agency will make all of the regulations which it deems to be required in the field. As a corollary of this principle, the court generally infers that supplementary state regulations are to be pre-empted either because of an inference that the federal agency's failure to establish similar regulations represents an agency judgment that they are not needed or because of the operation of other presumptive considerations such as the need for national uniformity." Hirsch, *Towards a New View of Federal Preemption*, 1972 U. ILL. L.F. 515, 549-50.

   **10.** *Different Purposes.* Is it enough to avoid preemption that federal and state laws have different purposes? Perez v.

Campbell, 402 U.S. 637 (1971), dealt with the effect of the federal
bankruptcy laws on state motor vehicle financial responsibility
statutes which provide for suspension of operator's licenses for
failure to satisfy judgment. Judgment debtors who had been discharged in bankruptcy argued that the federal law superseded
the state law. The Supreme Court in finding that the state law
"frustrated" the operation of the Bankruptcy Act, and hence was
unconstitutional, commented: "We can no longer adhere to the
aberrational doctrine . . . that state law may frustrate the operation of federal law so long as the state legislature in passing its
law had some purpose in mind other than one of frustration.
Apart from the fact that it is at odds with the approach taken in
nearly all our Supremacy Clause cases, such a doctrine would
enable state legislatures to nullify nearly all unwanted federal
legislation by simply publishing a legislative committee report
articulating some state interest or policy—other than frustration
of the federal objective—that would be tangentially furthered by
the proposed state law." Isn't highway regulation an area of
dominant state concern?

11. *A Presumption of Compatibility?* Rehnquist's dissent in
*Burbank* argues that in the absence of a clear intent to the contrary, there should be a presumption against pre-emption. What
would be the rationale for and against such a presumption?

### The Judicial Role

1. As the above cases suggest, preemption is very much
ad hoc decision-making. Each case tends to turn on its own facts
and precedent tends to be of minimal value. The area then is
one of broad judicial discretion.

2. How does judicial decision-making in preemption cases
differ from cases involving the negative implications of the
commerce clause? Is the court really considering congressional
intent or is it "in actuality implementing constitutional principles external to the Supremacy Clause, while nominally deciding the case on the preemption ground." Note, *Preemption as a
Preferential Ground: A New Canon of Construction*, 12 STAN.
L. REV. 208 (1959), SELECTED ESSAYS 310, 317 (1963).

The author contends that "several writers have suggested
that the proper approach is to determine whether the continued
existence of the state law is consistent with the general purpose
of the federal statute by seeking to define the evil Congress
sought to remedy and the method chosen to effectuate its cure.
And, to understand the evil and the remedy the court should
look to the entire text of statute, to its history, and administrative
interpretations, when available.

"Most of the cases appear to have adopted this approach, although lip service is still paid to the specific intent inquiry." SELECTED ESSAYS, at 311-12.

Is it desirable to rationalize the preemption decisions in terms of congressional intent even if they are reached through commerce clause balancing? Is preemption a "preferential ground" of decision?

### b. Legitimizing State Burdens on Commerce

1. In Cooley v. Board of Wardens of Philadelphia, 53 U.S. (12 How.) 318 (1851), the court stated: "If the states were divested of the power to legislate on this subject by the grant of the commercial power to Congress, it is plain [congressional legislation] could not confer upon them power thus to legislate. If the Constitution excluded the states from making any laws regulating commerce, certainly Congress cannot regrant, or in any manner reconvey to the states that power." Does this mean that the commerce power also limits the power of Congress? If Congress has plenary power over interstate commerce as *Gibbons* indicated, is there any limitation on its power to define the subjects of interstate commerce and the mode of their regulation? How could Justice Stone in Southern Pac. Co. v. Arizona, 325 U.S. 761 (1945), text, p. 259, state that Congress has "undoubted" power "to permit the states to regulate the commerce in a manner which would otherwise not be permissible"?

2. In Prudential Insurance Co. v. Benjamin, 328 U.S. 408 (1946), the court dealt with the validity of a three per cent tax imposed on foreign, but not domestic, insurance companies by the state of South Carolina. A long line of decisions had held such discriminatory taxes violative of the commerce clause. Further, two years earlier, in United States v. Southeastern Underwriters Ass'n, 322 U.S. 533 (1944), the court had held that the insurance business was interstate commerce. However, Congress had responded to the *Southeastern Underwriters* decision by passing the McCarran Act providing: "Sec. 1. The Congress hereby declares that the continued regulation and taxation by the several states of the business of insurance is in the public interest, and that silence on the part of Congress shall not be construed to impose any barrier to the regulation or taxation of such business by the several states. Sec. 2(a). The business of insurance and every person engaged therein, shall be subject to the laws of the several states which relate to the regulation or taxation of such business."

The court, per Justice Rutledge, summarized Prudential's claim "[t]hat the commerce clause 'of its own force' and without reference to any action by Congress . . . forbids discriminatory state taxation of interstate commerce. This is to say, in effect, that neither Congress acting affirmatively nor Congress and the states thus acting coordinately can validly impose any regulation which the Court has found or would find to be forbidden by the commerce clause, if laid only by state action taken while Congress' power lies dormant."

But the court rejected any such limitation on the power of Congress when acting alone, and *a fortiori*, when acting with the states. Noting prior court decisions validating congressional revisions of earlier court holdings, Justice Rutledge noted that "[w]henever Congress' judgment has been uttered affirmatively to contradict the Court's previously expressed view that specific action taken by the states in Congress' silence was forbidden by the commerce clause, this body has accommodated its previous judgment to Congress' expressed approval.

"Some part of this readjustment may be explained in ways acceptable on any theory of the commerce clause, and the relations of Congress and the courts toward its functioning. Such explanations, however, hardly go to the root of the matter. For the fact remains that, in these instances, the sustaining of Congress' overriding action has involved something beyond correction of erroneous factual judgment in deference to Congress' presumably better-informed view of the facts, and also beyond giving due deference to its conception of the scope of its power, when it repudiates, just as when its silence is thought to support, the inference that it has forbidden state action."

In the present instance, Congress, through the McCarran Act, "intended to declare, and in effect declared, that uniformity of regulation, and of state taxation, are not required in reference to the business of insurance, by the national public interest, except in the specific respects otherwise specifically provided for. This necessarily was a determination by Congress that state taxes, which in its silence might be held invalid and discriminatory, do not place on interstate insurance business a burden which it is unable generally to bear or should not bear in the competition with local business."

For the court now to strike down the South Carolina tax "would flout the expressly declared policies of both Congress and the states." Congress, acting alone, has plenary power over interstate commerce. "The power of Congress over commerce exercised entirely without reference to coordinated action of the states is not restricted, except as the Constitution expressly provides, by any limitation which forbids it to discriminate against interstate commerce in favor of local trade. Its plenary power

enables Congress not only to promote but also to prohibit interstate commerce, as it has done frequently and for a great variety
of reasons."

While Congress may thus act alone, it also may act "in
conjunction with coordinated action by the states, in which case
limitations imposed by the preservation of their powers become
inoperative and only those designed to forbid action altogether
by any power or combination of powers in our governmental
system remain effective. Here both Congress and South Carolina
have acted, and in complete coordination, to sustain the tax. It
is therefore reinforced by the exercise of all the power of government residing in our scheme."

No limitations arising from the principles of federalism were
thus involved. The limitation proposed by the taxpayer "would
reduce the joint exercise of power by Congress and the states
to achieve common ends and the regulation of our society below
the effective range of either power separately exerted, without
basis in specific constitutional limitation or otherwise in the division itself. We know of no grounding, in either constitutional
experience or spirit, for such a restriction. For great reasons of
policy and history not now necessary to restate, these great
powers were separated. They were not forbidden to cooperate
or by doing so to achieve legislative consequences, particularly
in the great fields of regulating commerce and taxation, which
to some extent at least, neither could accomplish in isolated
exception."

*Prudential Ins. Co. v. Benjamin* indicates that Congress can
legitimate state action that would otherwise violate the commerce clause. If the negative implications on undue state interference with the free flow of commerce arose from presumed
congressional intent, Congress could presumably remove the
barrier. But if it is the Constitution, as interpreted by the court,
that prohibits the state action, how can Congress by ordinary
legislation remove the prohibition? The court in *Benjamin* specifically rejected the view that the question is merely one of Congress' superior fact-finding capabilities. Can the national and state
governments, acting cooperatively, create powers that neither
possesses acting separately? In any case, the court's position in
*Benjamin* would seem fully consistent with the view, expressed
by Professor Wechsler, that the proper function of judicial
review in federalism cases is to check abusive action by the states
rather than exercises of congressional power. *See* Wechsler,
*Political Safeguards of Federalism—The Role of the States in the
Composition and Selection of the National Government,* in

PRINCIPLES, POLITICS AND FUNDAMENTAL LAW 49-82 (1961), SELECTED ESSAYS 185 (1963).

## B.  STATE POWER TO TAX COMMERCE

This section is designed to introduce the student to the problem of state power to tax foreign and interstate commerce. It is not intended, however, to comprehensively cover the topic. First, the subject is too vast and complex to be fully treated in the basic constitutional law course. Second, the field has become an area for specialists. Finally, many of the basic, underlying concepts in the tax area relating to problems of federalism are repetitious of those dealt with in the sections on state power to regulate interstate commerce.

### Foreign Commerce: Imports and Exports

Article I, § 10, cl. 2, of the Constitution provides that "No State shall, without the Consent of the Congress, lay any Impost or Duties on Imports or Exports, except what may be absolutely necessary for executing its inspection Laws. . . ." This tax immunity was born principally of the framers concern that the seaboard states might burden imports with unfair taxes at the expense of the interior states. It also represents a commitment to keep international trade free from diverse local burdens and under national supervision.

The questions raised by this constitutional provision are many. How long does an item remain an import and when does it become an export? Does it matter if an item is imported for the importer's own use or if further sale is contemplated? Should it matter if the imports are being stored for subsequent use or are regularly withdrawn to satisfy operational needs? Can a broad immunity be reconciled with the continuing need of the states for revenue? And if importers of foreign goods are immune, doesn't this discriminate against domestic producers who are subject to local taxes? Is a state prohibited from protecting its domestic production?

### BROWN v. MARYLAND
Supreme Court of the United States
25 U.S. (12 Wheat.) 419, 6 L. Ed. 678 (1827)

[A Maryland law imposed a $50.00 license fee on all importers and wholesalers of foreign goods. Brown was convicted of importing and selling foreign goods without a license, and the Maryland Court of Appeals affirmed.]

Chief Justice MARSHALL delivered the opinion of the Court.

. . . .

1. The first inquiry is into the extent of the prohibition upon states "to lay any imposts or duties on imports or exports."

. . .

. . . .

What, then, is the meaning of the words, "imposts, or duties on imports or exports?"

An impost, or duty on imports, is a custom or a tax levied on articles brought into a country, and is most usually secured before the importer is allowed to exercise his rights of ownership over them, because evasions of the law can be prevented more certainly by executing it while the articles are in its custody. It would not, however, be less an impost or duty on the articles, if it were to be levied on them after they were landed. The policy and consequent practice of levying or securing the duty before, or on entering the port, does not limit the power to that state of things, nor, consequently, the prohibition, unless the true meaning of the clause so confines it. What, then, are "imports"? The lexicons inform us, they are "things imported." If we appeal to usage for the meaning of the word, we shall receive the same answer. They are the articles themselves which are brought into the country. "A duty on imports," then, is not merely a duty on the act of importation, but is a duty on the thing imported. It is not, taken in its literal sense, confined to a duty levied while the article is entering the country, but extends to a duty levied after it has entered the country. . . .

. . . .

. . . Whether the prohibition to "lay imposts, or duties on imports or exports," proceeded from an apprehension that the power might be so exercised as to disturb that equality among the states which was generally advantageous, or that harmony between them which it was desirable to preserve, or to maintain unimpaired our commercial connections with foreign nations, or to confer this source of revenue on the government of the Union, or whatever other motive might have induced the prohibition, it is plain that the object would be as completely defeated by a power to tax the article in the hands of the importer the instant it was landed, as by a power to tax it while entering the port. There is no difference, in effect, between a power to prohibit the sale of an article and a power to prohibit its introduction into the country. The one would be a necessary consequence of the other. No goods would be imported if none could be sold. No object of any description can be accomplished by laying a duty on importation, which may not be accomplished with equal certainty by laying a duty on the thing imported in the hands of the importer. It is obvious, that the same power which imposes a light duty, can impose a very heavy one, one which amounts to a prohibition. Questions of power do not depend on the degree to which it may be exercised. If it may be exercised at all, it must be exercised at the will of those in whose hands it is placed. If the tax may be levied in this form by a state, it may be levied to an extent which will defeat the revenue by impost, so far as it is drawn from importations into the particular state. We are told, that such wild and irrational abuse of power is not to be apprehended, and is not to be taken into view when discussing its existence. . . .

. . . .

These arguments apply with precisely the same force against the whole prohibition. It might, with the same reason be said, that no state would be so blind to its own interests as to lay duties on importation which would either prohibit or diminish its trade. Yet the framers of our constitution have thought this a power which no state ought to exercise. Conceding, to the full extent which is required, that every state would, in its legislation on this subject, provide judiciously for its own interest, it cannot be conceded that each would respect the interest of others. A duty on imports is a tax on the article, which is paid by the consumer. The great importing states would thus levy a tax on the non-importing states, which would not be less a tax because their interest would afford ample security against its ever being so heavy as to expel commerce from their ports.

This would necessarily produce countervailing measures on the part of those states whose situation was less favorable to importation. For this, among other reasons, the whole power of laying duties on imports was, with a single and slight exception, taken from the states. . . .

. . . .

It may be conceded that the words of the prohibition ought not to be pressed to their utmost extent; that in our complex system, the object of the powers conferred on the government of the Union, and the nature of the often conflicting powers which remain in the states must always be taken into view, and may aid in expounding the words of any particular clause. But, while we admit . . . that there must be a point of time when the prohibition ceases, and the power of the state to tax commences; we cannot admit that this point of time is the instant that the articles enter the country. It is, we think, obvious, that this construction would defeat the prohibition.

. . . It is sufficient for the present to say, generally, that when the importer has so acted upon the thing imported, that it has become incorporated and mixed up with the mass of property in the country, it has, perhaps, lost its distinctive character as an import, and has become subject to the taxing power of the state; but while remaining the property of the importer, in his warehouse, in the original form or package in which it was imported, a tax upon it is too plainly a duty on imports to escape the prohibition in the Constitution.

. . . .

This indictment is against the importer, for selling a package of dry goods in the form in which it was imported, without a license. This state of things is changed if he sells them, or otherwise mixes them with the general property of the state, by breaking up his packages, and traveling with them as an itinerant peddler. In the first case, the tax intercepts the import, as an import, in its way to become incorporated with the general mass of property, and denies it the privilege of becoming so incorporated until it shall have contributed to the revenue of the state. It denies to the importer the right of using the privilege which he has purchased from the United States, until he shall have also purchased it from the state. In the last cases, the tax finds the article already incorporated with the mass of property by the act of the importer. He has used the privilege he had purchased, and has himself mixed them up with the common mass, and the law may treat them as it finds them. . . .

. . . .

But if it should be proved, that a duty on the article itself would be repugnant to the Constitution, it is still argued that this is not a tax upon the article, but on the person. The state, [it] is said, may tax occupations, and this is nothing more.

It is impossible to conceal from ourselves that this is varying the form without varying the substance. It is treating a prohibition which is general, as if it were confined to a particular mode of doing the forbidden thing. All must perceive that a tax on the sale of an article, imported only for sale, is a tax on the article itself. It is true the state may tax occupations generally, but this tax must be paid by those who employ the individual, or is a tax on his business. The lawyer, the physician, or the mechanic, must either charge more on the article in which he deals, or the thing itself is taxed through his person. This the state has a right to do, because no constitutional prohibition extends to it. So, a tax on the occupation of an importer is, in like manner, a tax on importation. It must add to the price of the article, and be paid by the consumer, or by the importer himself, in like manner as a direct duty on the article itself would be made. This the state has not a right to do, because it is prohibited by the Constitution.

. . . .

We think, then, that the act under which the plaintiffs in error were indicted, is repugnant to that article of the Constitution which declares that "no State shall lay any impost or duties on imports or exports."

2. Is it also repugnant to that clause in the Constitution which empowers "Congress to regulate commerce with foreign nations, and among the several states, and with the Indian tribes?"

. . . .

If this power reaches the interior of a state, and may be there exercised, it must be capable of authorizing the sale of those articles which it introduces. Commerce is intercourse: one of its most ordinary ingredients is traffic. It is inconceivable, that the power to authorize this traffic, when given in the most comprehensive terms, with the intent that its efficacy should be complete, should cease at the point when its continuance is indispensable to its value. To what purpose should the power to allow importation be given, unaccompanied with the power to authorize a sale of the thing imported? Sale is the object of importation, and is an essential ingredient of that intercourse, of which importation constitutes a part. It is as essential an ingredient, as indispensable to the existence of the entire thing, then, as importation itself. It must be considered as a component part of the power to regulate commerce. Congress has a right, not only to authorize importation, but to authorize the importer to sell.

. . . .

We think, then, that if the power to authorize a sale exists in Congress, the conclusion that the right to sell is connected with the law permitting importation, as an inseparable incident, is inevitable.

If the principles we have stated be correct, the result to which they conduct us cannot be mistaken. Any penalty inflicted on the importer for selling the article in his character of importer, must be in opposition to the Act of Congress which authorizes importation. Any charge on the introduction and incorporation of the articles into and with the mass of property in the country, must be hostile to the power given to Congress to regulate commerce, since an essential part of that regulation, and principal object of it, is to prescribe the regular means for accomplishing that introduction and incorporation.

The distinction between a tax on the thing imported, and on the person of the importer, can have no influence on this part of the subject. It is too obvious for controversy, that they interfere equally with the power to regulate commerce.

It has been contended that this construction of the power to regulate commerce, as was contended in construing the prohibition to lay duties on imports, would abridge the acknowledged power of a state to tax its own citizens, or their property within its territory.

We admit this power to be sacred; but cannot admit that it may be used so as to obstruct the free course of a power given to Congress. We cannot admit that it may be used so as to obstruct or defeat the power to regulate commerce. . . . If the states may tax all persons and property found on their territory, what shall restrain them from taxing goods in their transit through the state from one port to another, for the purpose of re-exportation? The laws of trade authorize this operation, and general convenience requires it. Or what should restrain a state from taxing any article passing through it from one state to another, for the purpose of traffic? or from taxing the transportation of articles passing from the state itself to another, for commercial purposes? These cases are all within the sovereign power of the taxation, but would obviously derange the measures of Congress to regulate commerce, and affect materially the purpose for which that power was given. . . .

It may be proper to add that we suppose the principles laid down in this case to apply equally to importations from a sister state. We do not mean to give any opinion on a tax discriminating between foreign and domestic articles.

. . . .

Reversed.

[Justice THOMPSON delivered a dissenting opinion.]

---

## NOTES

*The Meaning and Scope of the Import and Export Clause*
1. The original package doctrine remains important in defining the immunity of imported goods. Sale, use, or a breaking of the original package ends the immunity. Note, *State Taxation of Imports—When Does an Import Cease To Be an Import?*, 58 HARV. L. REV. 858 (1945). Why shouldn't the constitutional immunity be limited solely to taxes on the act of introducing goods into the country?

2. In Hooven & Allison Co. v. Evatt, 324 U.S. 652 (1945), the court held invalid an Ohio *ad valorem* property tax applied to bales of imported hemp stored in their original bales in a warehouse awaiting use in manufacturing cordage. The court could discern no basis for distinguishing imports for manufacture from those for sale. Is such immunity necessary to serve the purpose of the import-export clause? Isn't this discriminatory against manufacturers using domestic products?

In Youngstown Sheet & Tube Co. v. Bowers, 358 U.S. 534 (1959), the court employed a caveat provided in *Hooven* to uphold another *ad valorem* property tax on imported ore held in bulk and used to satisfy the importer's manufacturing needs. Unlike *Hooven*, the materials were held to have been imported and used to supply the manufacturer's current operating needs and therefore had entered the process of manufacture. "When, after all phases of their importation had ended, they were put to that use and indiscriminate portions of the whole were actually being used to supply daily operating needs, they stood in the same relation to the State as like piles of domestic materials at the same place that were kept for use and used in the same way." Is this decision consistent with the purposes of Art. I, § 10, cl. 2? With the interests of federalism?

3. *Taxing "Exports."* Like the imports problem, it has been necessary to define the point at which items become "exports," immune from state tax. In Empresa Siderurgica, S.A. v. County of Merced, 337 U.S. 154 (1949), the court, in upholding application of a personal property tax on the unshipped portions of a cement plant which had been sold to a foreign purchaser, dismantled and partially shipped, stated: "It is the entrance of the articles into the export stream that marks the start of the process of exportation. Then there is certainty that the goods are headed for their foreign destination and will not be directed to domestic use. Nothing less will suffice." Comment, *Taxation Under the Import-Export Clause*, 47 COLUM. L. REV. 490 (1947). *See* Kosydar v. National Cash Register Co., 417 U.S. 60 (1974), holding that a state may constitutionally impose a personal property tax on machines intended for export where the goods were still in the complete control of the manufacturer at his warehouse.

4. The tax immunity established by the import-export clause applies even to state taxes on imported liquors in spite of the broad state powers recognized in the twenty-first amendment. Department of Revenue v. James B. Beam Distilling Co., 377 U.S. 341 (1964).

## The Original Package Doctrine Domestically

1. The original package doctrine is only a factor to be considered in determining if a state regulation is an impermissible burden on interstate commerce.

2. In the concluding passage of *Brown*, Chief Justice Marshall suggested the application of its principles to interstate commerce. But in Woodruff v. Parham, 75 U.S. (8 Wall.) 123 (1869), the court in upholding a state tax on the sale at auction of goods in their original packages from a sister state, rejected the suggestion. Justice Miller limited the imports clause to foreign commerce, relying on its history and on policy considerations: "The merchant of Chicago who buys his goods in New York and sells at wholesale in the original packages, may have his millions employed in trade for half a lifetime and escape all state, county and city taxes; for all that he is worth is invested in goods which he claims to be protected as imports from New York. Neither the State nor the city which protects his life and property can make him contribute a dollar to support its government, improve its thoroughfares or educate its children. The merchant in a town in Massachusetts, who deals only in wholesale, if he purchase his goods in New York, is exempt from taxation. If his neighbor purchase in Boston, he must pay all the tax which Massachusetts levies with equal justice on the property of all the citizens."

## 2. Domestic Commerce: The Search for a Judicial Role

One of the realities of modern times has been the spiraling need of states and localities for added revenue to meet the increasing demands of their citizens. The result has been a proliferation of taxes from diverse sources—property, net income, gross receipts, sales and use, license, franchise, and the privilege of doing business. The tax formulae in maximizing revenue production and providing benefits to local concerns, often do so at the expense of interstate commerce. Businesses which operate in more than one state are subjected to diverse taxes with conflicting definitions and varying enforcement policies. Attempts to impose this tax liability and the consequent financial and administrative burdens on multistate companies directly challenge the free market philosophy discussed in section A. On the other hand, if interstate business escapes bearing its share of the tax load, local businesses will be put at a competitive disadvantage. The complexities of the taxing system thus challenge the capacity of the courts to reconcile the competing interests. The Constitution provides little guidance and the Congress has been generally silent; as a consequence, the judicial work product in this area leaves much to be desired.

## EVANSVILLE-VANDERBURGH AIRPORT AUTHORITY DIST. v. DELTA AIRLINES

Supreme Court of the United States
405 U.S. 707, 31 L. Ed. 2d 620, 92 S. Ct. 1349 (1972)

Justice BRENNAN delivered the opinion of the Court.

The question is whether a charge by a State or municipality of $1 per commercial airline passenger to help defray the costs of airport construction and maintenance violates the Federal Constitution. Our answer is that, as imposed in these two cases, the charge does not violate the Federal Constitution.

No. 70-99. Evansville-Vanderburgh Airport Authority District [in Indiana] enacted Ordinance No. 33 establishing "a use and service charge of One Dollar ($1.00) for each passenger enplaning any commercial aircraft operated from the Dress Memorial Airport." The commercial airlines are required to collect and remit the charge, less 6% allowed to cover the airlines' administrative costs in doing so. The moneys collected are held by the Airport Authority "in a separate fund for the purpose of defraying the present and future costs incurred by said Airport Authority in the construction, improvement, equipment, and maintenance of said Airport and its facilities for the continued use and future enjoyment by all users thereof."

. . . The [superior] court held that the charge constituted an unreasonable burden on interstate commerce . . . and permanently enjoined enforcement of the ordinance. The Indiana Supreme Court affirmed. . . . We reverse.

No. 70-212. Chapter 391 of the 1969 Laws of New Hampshire, requires every interstate and intrastate "common carrier of passengers for hire by aircraft on a regular schedule" who uses any of New Hampshire's five publicly owned and operated airports to "pay a service charge of one dollar with respect to each passenger enplaning upon its aircraft with a gross weight of 12,500 pounds or more, or a service charge of fifty cents with respect to each passenger enplaning upon its aircraft with a gross weight of less than 12,500 pounds." Fifty percent of the moneys collected are allocated to the State's aeronautical fund and 50% "to the municipalities or the airport authorities owning the public landing areas at which the fees . . . were imposed." The airlines are authorized to pass on the charge to the passenger.

Appellants . . . challenged the constitutionality of the charge as to scheduled commercial flights on the grounds of repugnancy to the Commerce Clause, the Equal Protection Clause of the Fourteenth Amendment and the provisions of the Federal Constitution protecting the right to travel. The Superior Court, without decision, transferred the action to the New Hampshire

Supreme Court, and that court sustained the constitutionality of the statute. . . . We affirm.

We begin our analysis with consideration of the contention of the commercial airlines in both cases that the charge is constitutionally invalid under the Court's decision in Crandall v. Nevada, 73 U.S. 35 (1867). There the Court invalidated a Nevada statute that levied a "tax of one dollar upon every person leaving the State by any railroad, stagecoach, or other vehicle engaged or employed in the business of transporting passengers for hire." The Court approached the problem as one of whether levy of "any tax of that character," whatever its amount, impermissibly burdened the constitutionally protected right of citizens to travel. In holding that it did, the Court reasoned:

"[I]f the State can tax a railroad passenger one dollar, it can tax him one thousand dollars. If one State can do this, so can every other State. And thus one or more States covering the only practicable routes of travel from the east to the west, or from the north to the south, may totally prevent or seriously burden all transportation of passengers from one part of the country to the other."

The Nevada charge, however, was not limited, as are the Indiana and New Hampshire charges before us, to travelers asked to bear a fair share of the costs of providing public facilities that further travel. The Nevada tax applied to passengers traveling interstate by privately owned transportation, such as railroads. Thus the tax was charged without regard to whether Nevada provided any facilities for the passengers required to pay the tax. . . .

. . . .

We therefore regard it as settled that a charge designed only to make the user of state-provided facilities pay a reasonable charge to help defray the costs of their construction and maintenance may constitutionally be imposed on interstate and domestic users alike. The principle that burdens on the right to travel are constitutional only if shown to be necessary to promote a compelling state interest has no application in this context. See Shapiro v. Thompson, 394 U.S. 618 (1969) [text, p. 677]. The facility provided at public expense aids rather than hinders the right to travel. A permissible charge to help defray the cost of the facility is therefore not a burden in the constitutional sense.

The Indiana and New Hampshire Supreme Courts differed in appraising their respective charges in terms of whether the charge was for the use of facilities in aid of travel provided by the public. . . .

In addressing the question, we do not think it particularly important whether the charge is imposed on the passenger himself, to be collected by the airline, or on the airline, to be passed on to the passenger if it chooses. In either case, it is the act of enplanement and the consequent use of runways and other airport facilities that give rise to the obligation. Our inquiry is whether the use of airport facilities occasioned by enplanement is a permissible incident on which to levy these fees, regardless of whether the airline or its passengers bear the formal responsibility for their payment.

Our decisions concerning highway tolls are instructive. . . .

. . . .

[W]hile state or local tolls must reflect a "uniform, fair and practical standard" relating to public expenditures, it is the amount of the tax, not its formula, that is of central concern. At least so long as the toll is based on some fair approximation of use or privilege for use, . . . and is neither discriminatory against interstate commerce nor excessive in comparison with the governmental benefit conferred, it will pass constitutional muster, even though some other formula might reflect more exactly the relative use of the state facilities by individual users.

The Indiana and New Hampshire charges meet those standards. *First,* neither fee discriminates against interstate commerce and travel. While the vast majority of passengers who board flights at the airports involved are traveling interstate, both interstate and domestic flights are subject to the same charges. Furthermore, there is no showing of any inherent difference between these two classes of flights, such that the application of the same fee to both would amount to discrimination against one or the other.

*Second,* these charges reflect a fair if imperfect approximation of the use of facilities for whose benefit they are imposed. We recognize that in imposing a fee on the boarding of commercial flights, both the Indiana and New Hampshire measures exempt in whole or part a majority of the actual number of persons who use facilities of the airports involved. Their number include certain classes of passengers, such as active members of the military and temporary layovers, deplaning commercial passengers, and passengers on noncommercial flights, nonscheduled commercial flights, and commercial flights on light aircraft. Also exempt are nonpassenger users, such as persons delivering or receiving air freight shipments, meeting or seeing off passengers, dining at airport restaurants, and working for employers located on airport grounds. Nevertheless, these exceptions are not wholly unreasonable. Certainly passengers as a class may be distinguished from other airport users, if only because the boarding of flights requires the use of runways and navigational facilities not occasioned by nonflight activities. Furthermore, business users, like shops, restaurants, and private parking concessions do contribute to airport upkeep through rent, a cost that is passed on in part at least to their patrons. And since the visitor who merely sees off or meets a passenger confers a benefit on the passenger himself, his use of the terminal may reasonably be considered to be included in the passenger's fee.

The measures before us also reflect rational distinctions among different classes of passengers and aircraft. Commercial air traffic requires more elaborate navigation and terminal facilities, as well as longer and more costly runway systems, than do flights by smaller private planes. Commercial aviation, therefore, may be made to bear a larger share of the cost of facilities built primarily to meet its special needs, whether that additional charge is levied on a per-flight basis in the form of higher takeoff and landing fees, or as a toll per passenger-use in the form of a boarding fee. In short, distinctions based on aircraft weight or commercial versus private use do not render these charges wholly irrational as a measure of the relative use of the facilities for whose benefit they are levied. Nor does the fact that they are levied on the enplanement of commercial flights, but not deplanement. It is not unreasonable to presume that passengers enplaning at an airport also deplane at the same airport approximately the same number of times. . . .

*Third,* the airlines have not shown these fees to be excessive in relation to costs incurred by the taxing authorities. The record in No. 70-99 shows that in 1965 the Evansville-Vanderburgh Airport Authority paid bond retirement costs of $166,000 for capital improvements at Dress Memorial Airport, but recovered only $9,700 of these costs in the form of airport revenue. The airport's revenues covered only $63,000 of the Authority's $184,-000 bond costs in 1966. $87,000 of $182,000 in 1967, and $65,000 of $178,000 in 1968. The respondents in No. 70-99 have advanced no evidence that a $1.00 boarding fee, if permitted to go into effect, would do more than meet these past, as well as current, deficits. Appellants in No. 70-212 have likewise failed to offer proof of excessiveness.

This omission in No. 70-212 suffices to dispose of the final attack by appellants in that case on the New Hampshire statute. Appellants argue that the statute "on its face belies any legislative intent to impose an exaction based solely on use" because only 50% of its revenue is allocated to the state aeronautical fund while "the remaining fifty percent is allocated to the mu-

nicipalities or airport authorities owning the landing areas at
which the fees were imposed in the form of unrestricted general
revenues." Yet so long as the funds received by local authorities
under the statute are not shown to exceed their airport costs, it
is immaterial whether those funds are expressly earmarked for
airport use. The State's choice to reimburse local expenditures
through unrestricted rather than restricted revenues is not a
matter of concern to these appellants.

We conclude, therefore, that the provisions before us impose valid charges on the use of airport facilities constructed and
maintained with public funds. Furthermore, we do not think
that they conflict with any federal policies furthering uniform
national regulation of air transportation. No federal statute or
specific congressional action or declaration evidences a Congressional purpose to deny or pre-empt state and local power to levy
charges designed to help defray the costs of airport construction
and maintenance. . . .

The commercial airlines argue in these cases that a proliferation of these charges in airports over the country will eventually
follow in the wake of a decision sustaining the validity of the
Indiana and New Hampshire fees, and that this is itself sufficient
reason to adjudge the charges repugnant to the Commerce
Clause. "If such levies were imposed by each airport along a
traveller's route, the total effect on the cost of air transportation
could be prohibitive, the competitive structure of air carriers
could be affected, and air transportation, compared to other forms
of transportation, could be seriously impaired." Brief for appellants in No. 70-212, at 44. The argument relies on Bibb v.
Navajo Freight Lines, Inc., 359 U.S. 520 (1959). . . . But there is no
suggestion that the Indiana and New Hampshire charges do not
in fact advance the constitutionally permissible objective of having
interstate commerce bear a fair share of the costs to the States of
airports constructed and maintained for the purpose of aiding
interstate air travel. In that circumstance, "[a]t least until
Congress chooses to enact a nation-wide rule, the power will not
be denied to the State[s]." Freeman v. Hewit, 329 U. S., at 253.
. . . .

Justice POWELL took no part in the consideration or decision
of these cases.

Justice DOUGLAS, dissenting.

These cases are governed by Crandall v. Nevada, 6 Wall. 35,
18 L.Ed. 744, which must be overruled if we are to sustain the
instant taxes.

. . . .

Heretofore we have held that a tax imposed on a carrier but measured by the number of passengers is no different from a direct exaction upon the passengers themselves, whether or not the carrier is authorized to collect the tax from the passengers. To be sure, getting onto a plane is an intrastate act. But a tax imposed on a local activity that is related to interstate commerce is valid, only if the local activity is not such an integral part of interstate commerce that it cannot be realistically separated from it. . . .

[In the present case,] the step of the enplaning passenger onto the aircraft is but an instant away from and an inseparable part of an interstate flight.

Of course interstate commerce can be made to pay its fair share of the cost of the local government whose protection it enjoys. But though a local resident can be made to pay taxes to support his community, he cannot be required to pay a fee for making a speech or exercising any other First Amendment right. Like prohibitions obtain when licensing is exacted for exercising constitutional rights. Heretofore we have treated the right to participate in interstate commerce in precisely the same way on the theory that the "power to tax the exercise of a privilege is the power to control or suppress its enjoyment." Murdock v. Pennsylvania, 319 U.S. 105, 112. I adhere to that view; federal constitutional rights should neither be "chilled" nor "suffocated."

. . . .

I would affirm the Indiana judgment and reverse New Hampshire's.

---

## NOTES

1. *Due Process.* As a footnote in *Evansville* indicates, before a state can levy a tax, the taxpayer must have acquired a taxable situs in the state. There must be some "definite link, some minimum connection" between the taxpayer and the taxing state in order to satisfy fourteenth amendment due process. A state cannot project its taxing powers beyond its borders. Before it can tax, it must have given something for which it can ask return.

And even if there is some minimal contact, the courts often use the due process clause to demand that the burden imposed by the tax be commensurate with the benefits received by the taxpayer or the demands he makes of the state. The due process question in such cases is whether the state tax is reasonable "in relation to opportunities which it has given, to protection which it has afforded, to benefits which it has conferred. . . . " Wisconsin

v. J. C. Penney Co., 311 U.S. 435 (1940). *See* Hartman, *State Taxation of Interstate Commerce: A Survey and an Appraisal,* 46 VA. L. REV. 1051, 1058-65 (1960).

2. *The Commerce Clause.* While the demands of due process and the commerce clause overlap and the courts often use them interchangeably, they are not identical. Even if the jurisdictional contacts required by due process are satisfied, it remains necessary to determine if the tax imposes impermissible burdens on interstate commerce. *See* Hartman, *State Taxation of Corporate Income from a Multistate Business,* 13 VAND. L. REV. 21, 43 (1959).

In some cases a tax is held unconstitutional because it is a tax *on* interstate commerce itself which the courts argue is solely the prerogative of Congress. But if the states can constitutionally *regulate* interstate commerce itself, why should a tax on interstate commerce be unconstitutional without any consideration of its effects on the free flow of commerce?

Even if the tax is not imposed on interstate commerce itself, it may impose an unconstitutional burden on interstate commerce. While interstate business must pay its way, states may not discriminate against interstate commerce in favor of local interests. (See note 5 *infra*). Alternatively, the tax may subject interstate commerce to a "direct" burden or to an excessive burden when the state interest in levying the tax is compared to the impediment placed on the free flow of commerce. For example, if the imposition of an unapportioned tax would result in the risk or the reality of multiple burdens on interstate commerce from taxation by other states, interstate commerce might be placed in an unfair competitive position with its local competitors.

If people can be articles of commerce as indicated in text, p. 272, is the airport tax in *Evansville* placed on interstate commerce itself? Why isn't it a tax on the *privilege* of engaging in interstate commerce?

Within five months after the *Evansville* decision, some 17 other cities adopted or were considering similar tax levies. AVIATION WEEK & SPACE TECHNOLOGY, Aug. 14, 1972, at 23. Given such a state response, isn't there now a cumulative burden on interstate commerce? Was there a real risk of such a burden when *Evansville* was decided? On the other hand, if the incidence of the tax is on the enplaning passenger, isn't it probable that such passenger would be subjected to such a tax only once or twice during a flight? Is the real burden on the interstate carrier? Airports already pay lease costs as part of overhead which is then passed on to passengers. Isn't the local airport tax, therefore, duplicative of payments already made for benefits received?

The resulting administrative and cost burdens produced a widespread demand for congressional relief which came with passage of a head tax ban bill. The legislation was, however, vetoed by President Nixon on October 27, 1972. *See* Case Comments, *The Airport Cases: A Need for National Uniform Legislation,* 8 NEW ENG. L. REV. 305 (1973).

3. An example of the above two standards, was provided in Standard Pressed Steel Co. v. Washington, — U.S. — (1975), where the court upheld a Washington gross receipts tax imposed on an out-of-state concern, apportioned by the amount of business done in the state. The taxpayer had only one employee in the state, operating out of his home, who consulted with Boeing Aircraft, a buyer, concerning future needs and followed up complaints regarding products. There was no violation of due process since the tax reflected the benefits received by the taxpayer from the taxing state (*i.e.,* the employee made taxpayer's business dealings possible). The tax did not violate the commerce clause since it was apportioned to the activities taxed and thus presented no danger of multiple taxation.

4. *Equal Protection.* Do the tax exemptions recognized by the taxing authority in *Evansville* create equal protection problems? While the classification of individuals or corporations for tax purposes often presents equal protection questions, such a challenge is seldom successful today. Only if the classification is "palpably arbitrary" and "invidious" will the legislation be held unconstitutional. In Lehnhausen v. Lake Shore Auto Parts Co., 410 U.S. 356 (1973), the court, per Justice Douglas, in upholding an Illinois constitutional provision imposing an ad valorem tax on personalty on corporations and similar entities but not on individuals stated: "Where taxation is concerned and no specific federal right, apart from equal protection, is imperiled, the states have large leeway in making classifications and drawing lines which in their judgment produce reasonable systems of taxation."

5. *Discrimination.* Do the tax exemptions recognized by the taxing authority discriminate against interstate commerce?

*Facial Discrimination.* A tax which, on its face, discriminates against out-of-state business is clearly unconstitutional. In Welton v. Missouri, 91 U.S. 275 (1876), the court, per Justice Field, held unconstitutional a Missouri license tax imposed only on peddlers of out-of-state merchandise, not peddlers of Missouri goods. It was the "very object" of the commerce clause grant of power to the general government, argued Justice Field, to protect against "discriminatory state legislation." If the

state power to impose this tax were admitted "all the evils of
discriminating State legislation, favorable to the interests of one
State and injurious to the interests of other states and countries,
which existed previous to the adoption of the Constitution, might
follow . . . from the action of some of the States." He concluded
that the protection of the commerce clause continued "until the
commodity has ceased to be a subject of discriminating legislation by reason of its foreign character."

  *Discrimination in Effect.* Nippert v. Richmond, 327 U.S.
416 (1946), involved the conviction of a solicitor for an out-of-
state merchant for failure to pay a Virginia license tax. While
peddlers for local concerns were also required to pay the tax,
the court, per Justice Rutledge, held that the tax was exclusionary and presented an unconstitutional risk of discrimination against interstate commerce. The difference between interstate and local trade coupled with the "inherent character of
the tax," he argued, made equality of application impossible.
"The tax here in question inherently involves too many probabilities, and we think actualities, for exclusion of or discrimination against interstate commerce, in favor of local competing
business, to be sustained in any application substantially similar
to the present one. *Whether or not it was so intended, those are
its necessary effects.* . . . [W]e cannot be unmindful that these
ordinances lend themselves peculiarly to creating those very
consequences or that in fact this is often if not always the object
of the local commercial influences which induce their adoption.
Provincial interest and local political power are at their maximum
weight in bringing about acceptance of this type of legislation.
With the forces behind it, this is the very kind of barrier the
commerce clause was put in the fundamental law to guard
against." (Emphasis added.)

  Justice Douglas, joined by Justice Murphy, dissenting, argued
that "one who complains that a state tax, though not discriminatory on its face, discriminates against interstate commerce in its
actual operation should be required to come forward with proof
to sustain the charge." Justice Black also dissented without
opinion.

  6. *Subject-Measure Distinctions.* In determining the constitutionality of a state tax, consideration must be given to its
subject and its measure. "Every tax has a nominal subject: The
things or events upon which the power to tax is predicated; and
also a measure: the basis upon which the amount of tax due is
calculated. . . . The basis of measurement determines the economic effect of a tax, the subject is merely an assertion of the
state's right to tax, its only operative significance is to delimit

the class of persons who are to pay the tax." *Developments in the Law: Federal Limitations on State Taxation of Interstate Business,* 75 HARV. L. REV. 953, 960 (1962). This article goes on to suggest that "[c]onstitutionality should depend on the effect upon the open economy of taxing a given class of taxpayers by a given measure."

7. An issue clearly suggested by the material on state taxation is the proper role of the courts and Congress in establishing standards in this area. The extreme complexity of defining the powers of the respective states in taxing the multistate corporation challenges the capacities of an adjudicative body. Justice Frankfurter articulated the problem in his dissent in Northwestern States Portland Cement Co. v. Minnesota, 358 U.S. 450 (1959). "I am not unmindful of the extent to which federal taxes absorb the taxable resources of the Nation, while at the same time the fiscal demands of the States are on the increase. These conditions present far-reaching problems of accommodating federal-state fiscal policy. But a determination of who is to get how much out of the common fund can hardly be made wisely and smoothly through the adjudicatory process. In fact, relying on the courts to solve these problems only aggravates the difficulties and retards proper legislative solution.

"At best, this Court can only act negatively; it can determine whether a specific state tax is imposed in violation of the Commerce Clause. Such decisions must necessarily depend on the application of rough and ready legal concepts. We cannot make a detailed inquiry into the incidents of diverse economic burdens in order to determine the extent to which such burdens conflict with the necessities of national economic life. Neither can we devise appropriate standards for dividing of national revenue on the basis of more or less abstract principles of constitutional law, which cannot be responsive to the subtleties of the interrelated economies of Nation and State.

"The problem calls for solution by devising a congressional policy. Congress alone can provide the full and thorough canvassing of the multitudinous and intricate factors which compose the problem of the taxing freedom of the States and the needed limits on such state taxing power. Congressional committees can make studies and give the claims of the individual States adequate hearing before the ultimate legislative formulation of policy is made by the representatives of all of the States. The solution to these problems ought not to rest on the self-serving determination of the States of what they are entitled to out of the Nation's resources. Congress alone can formulate policies founded upon economic realities, perhaps to be applied to the myriad situation involved by a properly constituted and duly informed administrative agency." For a discussion of the use of legislation and uniform state laws, see Johnson & Visher, *State and Local Government Taxation of Multistate Corporations: A Survey of Legislative Developments,* 3 URBAN LAWYER 1 (1971); Note, *State Taxation of Interstate Business—Looking Toward Federal State Cooperation,* 23 VAND. L. REV. 1317 (1970).

But, if Congress continues to remain silent and uniform laws are not forthcoming, what are the courts to do? Would the problem be better handled through adjudicatory bodies specializing in tax matters? It has been suggested that recent trends have indicated a marked judicial deference to the legislative judgment. "The court early found that the commerce clause impliedly prohibits state regulation of 'national' subjects, and applied a related doctrine to bar taxing measures deemed to impede free trade among the states. But if the Justices, although not without notable exceptions, have given verbal assent to a broad commerce clause policy, few have seemed willing to accept its full implications. Hesitance to interfere with more than a very limited category of state taxing measures has become particularly marked in recent years; it is manifested perhaps as clearly in refusals to review certain cases involving questionable exercises of state taxing power as in the actual legitimation of challenged state taxes." *Developments, Federal Limitations on State Taxation,* 75 HARV. L. REV., at 956.

**8.** *Right to Travel.* The right to travel is considered in text, pp. 677-85. As that discussion indicates, the court has applied a more exacting standard of review to state laws burdening the right to domestic travel, requiring that the state demonstrate that the legalization or a resulting classification is necessary to achieve a compelling state interest. Does *Evansville* apply this standard? Does the state law burden the right to travel? Prior to *Evansville,* four cities that had considered imposing an airport tax concluded that it unconstitutionally burdened the right to travel. Three state courts had found such laws unconstitutional; only New Hampshire courts sustained the tax below. *See* Comment, *Airport "Service Charges" and the Constitutional Barriers to State Taxation of Airport Users,* 43 U. COLO. L. REV. 79 (1971).

# Chapter 4

## EXECUTIVE POWER IN THE CONSTITUTIONAL ORDER: SEPARATION OF POWERS

James Madison in THE FEDERALIST, No. 47, wrote: "No political truth is certainly of greater intrinsic value, or is stamped with the authority of more enlightened patrons of liberty, than that . . . accumulation of all powers, legislative, executive, and judiciary, in the same hands . . . may justly be pronounced the very definition of tyranny." Building on the theoretical writings of Montesquieu and John Locke, and the practical experience of seventeenth-century England, the colonies and the Confederation (where powers were merged in the legislature), the framers undertook to separate the legislative, executive, and judicial powers in the first three articles of the Constitution. *See* Sharp, *The Classical American Doctrine of "The Separation of Powers,"* 2 U. CHI. L. REV. 385 (1935). But would this prevent tyranny? Left to itself, each branch might accumulate power with which to impose its will. Further, total separation, like total merger of powers, might well impair the effective performance of the government's business.

The answer was to reject an absolute separation of governmental functions. While the departments were formally separated, the functions of the branches were mingled and blended. There was created a "government of separated institutions *sharing* powers." R. NEUSTADT, PRESIDENTIAL POWER 33 (1960). This was the system of checks and balances. As Madison explained: "The great security against a gradual concentration of the several powers in the same department consists in giving to those who administer each department the necessary constitutional means and personal motives to resist encroachment on the others. . . . Ambition must be made to counteract ambition." THE FEDERALIST, No. 51. The President, for example, could veto legislation but the Congress could override the veto. The Executive could appoint officials and make treaties, but only with the concurrence of the Senate. The courts might invalidate laws passed by the Congress and signed by the President, but the Executive would appoint the justices with the Senate's approval.

As the above indicates, while the separation of powers principle serves to increase efficiency in government, this is not its only or even primary purpose. As Justice Brandeis said, dissenting in Myers v. United States, 272 U.S. 52, 293 (1926): "The doctrine of the separation of powers was adopted by the Convention of 1787, not to promote efficiency, but to preclude the exercise of arbitrary power. The purpose was, not to avoid friction, but, by means of the inevitable friction incident to the distribution of the governmental powers among three departments, to save the people from autocracy." The task of performing the essential functions of government while preserving this critical function of the separation of powers principle is the central focus of the present chapter.

Throughout this text, consideration has been given to the role of the judiciary in relation to the other branches. In the present chapter, the focus will be on how the separation of powers principle has fared in the interplay of Congress and the executive. To what extent do these two branches exercise "exclusive" and "shared" powers? What principles guide the sharing of powers? Are the governing principles different in the domestic and foreign arenas? To what extent is the distribution of powers between the branches a legal or a political question? What is the role of the judiciary in maintaining separation of powers principles? Is the modified separation of powers principle coupled with checks and balances still effective in modern society? What adaptations have been made, and what lies ahead?

## THE EXECUTIVE POWER

American history has been marked by the expansion of executive power, generally at the expense of Congress. Today the President is Head of State, Chief Legislator, Chief Administrator, Head of Foreign Relations, Commander in Chief, and Head of his Political Party, and a more recent nominee, Chief Prosecutor. But how has this occurred? Corwin notes that the colonists viewed "the executive magistracy" as "the natural enemy, the legislative assembly [as] the natural friend of liberty." E. Corwin, The President, Office and Powers, 1787-1957; History and Analysis of Practice and Opinion 4 (4th ed., 1957). Certainly, fear of the royal prerogative was well established during the colonial period; there was not even a separate executive office during the Confederation. Finally, a review of the powers delegated in Arts. I and II would suggest that the Congress, rather than the President, has the tools for achieving "leadership" in our balanced separation of powers system.

While the framers created a single independent President, who could be re-elected, the vague powers granted only suggest the potential of the institutionalized presidency. Justice Jackson, in his concurring opinion in *Youngstown Sheet & Tube Co. v. Sawyer, infra,* noted "the gap that exists between the President's paper powers and his real powers. The Constitution does not disclose the measure of the actual control wielded by the presidential office. That instrument must be understood as an Eighteenth Century sketch of a government hoped for, not as a blueprint of the Government that is."

Franklin Delano Roosevelt's response to the economic crisis of the Great Depression and the emergency generated by World War II as well as the demands of international relations in modern times did much to shape the modern American presidency. But there have been energetic presidents throughout our history who, responding to the needs of the times, or through personal disposition, have maximized the powers of the executive. Much of the present-day character of separation of powers, then, is a function of the perception and values of the men who have occupied the office. The two excerpts reprinted below provide polar views by two of those occupants.

## THEODORE ROOSEVELT, THE AUTOBIOGRAPHY OF THEODORE ROOSEVELT (W. Andrews ed. 1958)*

The most important factor in getting the right spirit in my Administration, next to the insistence upon courage, honesty, and a genuine democracy of desire to serve the plain people, was my insistence upon the theory that the executive power was limited only by specific restrictions and prohibitions appearing in the Constitution or imposed by the Congress under its constitutional powers.

My view was that every executive officer, and above all every executive officer in high position, was a steward of the people bound actively and affirmatively to do all he could for the people, and not to content himself with the negative merit of keeping his talents undamaged in a napkin. I declined to adopt the view that what was imperatively necessary for the nation could not be done by the President unless he could find some specific authorization to do it. My belief was that it was not only his right but his duty to do anything that the needs of the nation demanded, unless such action was forbidden by the Constitution or by the laws. Under this interpretation of executive power I did and caused to be done many things not previously done by the President and the heads of the departments. I did not usurp power, but I did greatly broaden the use of executive power. In other

---

words, I acted for the public welfare, I acted for the common well-being of all our people, whenever and in whatever manner was necessary, unless prevented by direct constitutional or legislative prohibition. . . .

## WILLIAM H. TAFT, OUR CHIEF MAGISTRATE AND HIS POWERS (1916)*

The true view of the Executive functions is, as I conceive it, that the President can exercise no power which cannot be fairly and reasonably traced to some specific grant of power or justly implied and included within such express grant as proper and necessary to its exercise. Such specific grant must be either in the federal Constitution or in an act of Congress passed in pursuance thereof. There is no undefined residuum of power which he can exercise because it seems to him to be in the public interest, and there is nothing in the Neagle case and its definition of a law of the United States, or in other precedents, warranting such an inference. The grants of Executive power are necessarily in general terms in order not to embarrass the Executive within the field of action plainly marked for him, but his jurisdiction must be justified and vindicated by affirmative constitutional or statutory provision, or it does not exist.

. . . .

My judgment is that the view of . . . Mr. Roosevelt, ascribing an undefined residuum of power to the President is an unsafe doctrine and that it might lead under emergencies to results of an arbitrary character, doing irremediable injustice to private right. The mainspring of such a view is that the Executive is charged with responsibility for the welfare of all the people in a general way, that he is to play the part of a Universal Providence and set all things right, and that anything that in his judgment will help the people he ought to do, unless he is expressly forbidden not to do it. The wide field of action that this would give to the Executive one can hardly limit. . . .

---

## NOTES

1. Judge Pine in the lower court decision in the *Steel Seizure Case,* reprinted below, said that Roosevelt's stewardship theory does not "comport with our recognized theory of government." But consider the argument of John Locke: "Where the legislative and executive power are in distinct hands, as they are in all moderated monarchies and well-framed governments, there the good of society requires that several things should be left to the

---

* Copyright © 1916 by The Columbia University Press. Reprinted by permission.

discretion of him that has the executive power. For the legislature not being able to foresee and provide by law for all that may be useful to the community, the executor of the laws, having the power in his hands, but has, by the common law of nature, a right to make good of it for the good of society, in many cases where the municipal law has given no direction, till the legislative can be conveniently assembled to provide for it; nay, many things there are which the law can by no means provide for, and those must necessarily be left to the discretion of him that has the executive power in his hands, to be ordered by him as the public good and advantage shall require; nay, it is fit that the laws themselves should in some cases give way to the executive power, or rather to this fundamental law of nature and government—viz., that as much as may be all the members of the society are to be preserved." Two TREATISES OF GOVERNMENT, Bk. II, ch. 14, §§ 159-66.

2. *Inherent Power.* Is the stewardship theory premised on inherent presidential powers not dependent on constitutional grant? If such a power is recognized, a question would arise whether it would nevertheless be subject to constitutional limitation. The recognition of inherent powers not subject to constitutional limitation would be inconsistent with the principle that "[n]o man . . . is so high that he is above the law. . . . All the officers of the government . . . are creatures of the law, and are bound to obey it." United States v. Lee, 106 U.S. (16 Otto) 196, 220 (1882). Does it matter whether the subject matter is domestic or foreign?

3. *The Executive Power.* Is Art. II, § 1, vesting the "executive power" in the President, an independent grant of power or only a designation of the office? Is the absence in Art. II of the term "herein granted" significant? How does this compare with the grant of power in Art. III?

If the Art. II provision is a separate grant of power, what is the function of the specific enumeration of powers that follows? It has been argued that the term "vested in the president" means that the powers were vested in one man thus indicating the outcome of the debate at the Constitutional Convention over whether there should be a plural or singular executive and was not intended to vest some unspecified powers in the President. On the other hand, in Myers v. United States, 272 U.S. 52 (1926), involving the President's power to remove government officials, Chief Justice Taft claimed that "[t]he vesting of the executive power in the President was essentially a grant of the power to execute the laws" not subject to qualification by statute, and that the specification was designed to lend emphasis "where emphasis was regarded as appropriate." Further, he noted that the First Congress in debating how the Secretary of the new Department of Foreign Relations might be removed, recognized that the President already had the power of removal, apparently through the "executive power" clause. But Justice Holmes, dissenting in *Myers,* asserted: "The duty of the President to see that the laws are executed is a duty that does not go beyond the laws or require him to achieve more than Congress sees fit to leave within his power."

On the subsequent development of the removal power, see Humphrey's Ex'r v. United States, 295 U.S. 602 (1935); Wiener v. United States, 357 U.S. 349 (1958), the latter drawing "a sharp line of cleavage between officials who were part of the Executive establishment and were thus removable by virtue of the President's constitutional powers, and those who are members of a body 'to exercise its judgment without the leave or hindrance of any other official or any department of the government,' . . . as to whom a power of removal exists only if Congress may fairly be said to have conferred it. This sharp differentiation derives from the difference in function between those who are part of the Executive establishment and those whose tasks require absolute freedom from Executive interference."

4. *In re* Neagle, 135 U.S. 1 (1890), arose from the assignment by the Attorney General of Neagle, a United States marshal, to protect Supreme Court Justice Field whose life had been threatened by one Terry. After Neagle had shot and killed Terry, he sought a writ of habeas corpus on the statutory ground that he had done an act "in pursuance of a law of the United States." Although there was no definite statute authorizing Neagle's action, the court issued the writ. While relying in part on statutes dealing with the powers of federal marshals, Justice Miller used broad language to characterize the executive power. The executive duty, he reasoned, is not limited to the enforcement of acts of Congress or treaties according to their express terms, but instead includes "the rights, duties, and obligations growing out of the Constitution itself, our international relations, and all the protection implied by the nature of the government under the Constitution."

5. *In re* Debs, 158 U.S. 564 (1895), involved an attempt by the Justice Department to enjoin Debs and other strikers from obstructing interstate commerce and the mails. While there was no statutory basis for such an injunction, the court granted it, using language indicative of a broad executive power to act in the public interest: "Every government, entrusted, by the very terms of its being, with powers and duties to be exercised and discharged for the general welfare, has a right to apply to its

own courts for any proper assistance in the exercise of the one and the discharge of the other. . . . [W]henever wrongs complained of are such as affect the public at large, and are in respect of matters which by the Constitution are entrusted to the care of the Nation, and concerning which the Nation owes the duty to all the citizens of securing to them their common rights, then the mere fact that the government has no pecuniary interest in the controversy is not sufficient to exclude it from the courts, or prevent it from taking measures therein to fully discharge those constitutional duties."

As Edward S. Corwin was later to note, "the 'United States' here meant the President. The significance of the Court's choice of terminology is that it was not basing its holding on the duty of the President 'to take care that the laws be faithfully executed,' but on a broader principle—national interest." *The Steel Seizure Case: A Judicial Brick Without Straw*, 53 COLUM. L. REV. 53, 54 (1953). Again, however, it should be noted that the court did use statutes relating to the interstate commerce and postal powers in sustaining the injunction.

6. United States v. Midwest Oil Co., 236 U.S. 459 (1915), represents one of the strongest precedents for broad executive law-making power. Although a congressional statute indicated that public lands were to be closed to public entry when "mineral deposits" were found, President Taft ordered withdrawal of land to prevent depletion of oil reserves. Although there was no direct statutory authorization for such action, the court found power in the continued uncontested usage of the executive. "Both officers, lawmakers and citizens naturally adjust themselves to any long-continued action of the Executive Department—on the presumption that unauthorized acts would not have been allowed to be so often repeated as to crystallize into a regular practice. That presumption is not reasoning in a circle but the basis of a wise and quieting rule that in determining the meaning of a statute or the existence of a power, weight shall be given to the usage itself—even when the validity of the practice is the subject of investigation."

The congressional enactments in this instance were "necessarily general," subject to emergencies and changed conditions justifying executive action. The important element was that Congress had not taken any action "which could, in any way, be construed as a denial of the right of the Executive to make temporary withdrawals of public land in the public interest."

Justice Day, dissenting, argued: "There is nothing in the Constitution suggesting or authorizing such augmentation of executive authority or justifying him in thus acting in aid of a power which the framers of the Constitution saw fit to vest exclusively in the legislative branch of the government."

Can congressional silence in the face of executive action create power? Does silence imply approval? Is *Midwest* actually a case of legislative delegation of power? Does *Midwest* mean that such executive "legislation" is permissible only at the sufferance of Congress? Are Taft's actions as President consistent with his statement concerning presidential power?

## A. THE DOMESTIC ARENA

### 1. Executive Law-Making

There is no question that the modern American President makes as well as executes the law. Operating through the Executive Office, his role in framing legislation and influencing legislative outcomes, added to the veto and threat of veto, is a major factor in his domestic power position vis-a-vis the Congress. Congress, itself, through delegation, regularly vests broad policy-making powers in the executive. And, through the issuance of executive orders and other policy directives, the executive further implements its legislative role. The New Deal, the Square Deal, the New Frontier, the War on Poverty, attest to the domestic law-making role of the modern Chief Executive. He can justifiably be called Legislator-in-Chief. But what is the source of these domestic "legislative" powers of the Executive? To what extent do they depend on constitutional grant? On congressional acquiescence? Independent of congressional authorization, can the executive constitutionally fashion domestic policy? Are there any limitations on executive power to act? Can the executive act only in an emergency? Can Congress override executive law making?

YOUNGSTOWN SHEET & TUBE CO. v. SAWYER
(THE STEEL SEIZURE CASE)
Supreme Court of the United States
343 U.S. 579, 96 L. Ed. 1153, 72 S. Ct. 863 (1952)

Justice BLACK delivered the opinion of the Court.

We are asked to decide whether the President was acting within his constitutional power when he issued an order directing the Secretary of Commerce to take possession of and operate most of the Nation's steel mills. The mill owners argue that the President's order amounts to lawmaking, a legislative function which the Constitution has expressly confided to the Congress and not to the President. The Government's position is that the order was made on findings of the President that his action was necessary to avert a national catastrophe which would inevitably result from a stoppage of steel production, and that in meeting this grave emergency the President was acting within the aggregate of his constitutional powers as the Nation's Chief Executive and the Commander in Chief of the Armed Forces of the United States. . . .

. . . .

. . . [T]he District Court on April 30 issued a preliminary injunction restraining the Secretary from "continuing the seizure and possession of the plants . . . and from acting under the purported authority of Executive Order No. 10340." On the same day the Court of Appeals stayed the District Court's injunction. Deeming it best that the issues raised be promptly decided by this Court, we granted certiorari on May 3 and set the cause for argument on May 12.

. . . .

The President's power, if any, to issue the order must stem either from an act of Congress or from the Constitution itself. There is no statute that expressly authorizes the President to take possession of property as he did here. Nor is there any act of Congress to which our attention has been directed from which such a power can fairly be implied. Indeed, we do not understand the Government to rely on statutory authorization for this seizure. . . .

. . . [T]he use of the seizure technique to solve labor disputes in order to prevent work stoppages was not only unauthorized by any congressional enactment; prior to this controversy, Congress had refused to adopt that method of settling labor disputes. When the Taft-Hartley Act was under consideration in 1947, Congress rejected an amendment which would have authorized such governmental seizures in cases of emergency. . . . Instead, the plan sought to bring about settlements by use of the customary devices of mediation, conciliation, investigation by boards of inquiry, and public reports. In some instances temporary injunctions were authorized to provide cooling-off periods. All this failing, the unions were left free to strike after a secret vote by employees as to whether they wished to accept their employers' final settlement offer.

It is clear that if the President had authority to issue the order he did, it must be found in some provisions of the Constitution. And it is not claimed that express constitutional language grants this power to the President. The contention is that presidential power should be implied from the aggregate of his powers under the Constitution. Particular reliance is placed on provisions in Article II which say that "The executive Power shall be vested in a President . . ."; that "he shall take Care that the Laws be faithfully executed"; and that he "shall be Commander in Chief of the Army and Navy of the United States."

The order cannot properly be sustained as an exercise of the President's military power as Commander in Chief of the Armed Forces. The Government attempts to do so by citing a number of cases upholding broad powers in military commanders engaged in day-to-day fighting in a theater of war. Such cases need not concern us here. Even though "theater of war" be an expanding concept, we cannot with faithfulness to our constitutional system hold that the Commander in Chief of the Armed Forces has the ultimate power as such to take possession of private property in order to keep labor disputes from stopping production. This is a job for the Nation's lawmakers, not for its military authorities.

Nor can the seizure order be sustained because of the several constitutional provisions that grant executive power to the President. In the framework of our Constitution, the President's power to see that the laws are faithfully executed refutes the idea that he is to be a lawmaker. The Constitution limits his functions in the lawmaking process to the recommending of laws he thinks wise and the vetoing of laws he thinks bad. And the Constitution is neither silent nor equivocal about who shall make laws which the President is to execute. . . .

The President's order does not direct that a congressional policy be executed in a manner prescribed by Congress—it directs that a presidential policy be executed in a manner prescribed by the President. . . . The power of Congress to adopt such public policies as those proclaimed by the order is beyond question. It can authorize the taking of private property for public use. It can make laws regulating the relationships between employers and employees, prescribing rules designed to settle labor disputes, and fixing wages and working conditions in certain fields of our economy. The Constitution did not subject this lawmaking power of Congress to presidential or military supervision or control.

It is said that other Presidents without congressional authority have taken possession of private business enterprises in order to settle labor disputes. But even if this be true, Congress has not thereby lost its exclusive constitutional authority to make laws necessary and proper to carry out the powers vested by the Constitution "in the Government of the United States, or any Department or Officer thereof."

The Founders of this Nation entrusted the law-making power to the Congress alone in both good and bad times. It would do no good to recall the historical events, the fears of power and the hopes for freedom that lay behind their choice. Such a review would but confirm our holding that this seizure order cannot stand.

The judgment of the District Court is

Affirmed.

Justice FRANKFURTER, concurring.

. . . .

. . . We must . . . put to one side consideration of what powers the President would have had if there had been no legislation whatever bearing on the authority asserted by the seizure, or if the seizure had been only for a short, explicitly temporary period, to be terminated automatically unless Congressional approval were given. These and other questions, like or unlike, are not now here. I would exceed my authority were I to say anything about them.

. . . .

In adopting the provisions which it did, by the Labor Management Relations Act of 1947, for dealing with a "national emergency" arising out of a breakdown in peaceful industrial relations, Congress was very familiar with Governmental seizure as a protective measure. On a balance of considerations, Congress chose not to lodge this power in the President. It chose not to make available in advance a remedy to which both industry and labor were fiercely hostile. . . .

. . . .

. . . The powers of the President are not as particularized as are those of Congress. But unenumerated powers do not mean undefined powers. The separation of powers built into our Constitution gives essential content to undefined provisions in the frame of our government.

To be sure, the content of the three authorities of government is not to be derived from an abstract analysis. The areas are partly interacting, not wholly disjointed. The Constitution is a framework for government. Therefore the way the framework has consistently operated fairly establishes that it has operated according to its true nature. Deeply embedded traditional ways of conducting government cannot supplant the Constitution or legislation, but they give meaning to the words of a text or supply them. It is an inadmissibly narrow conception of American constitutional law to confine it to the words of the Constitution and to disregard the gloss which life has written upon them. In short, a systematic, unbroken, executive practice, long pursued to the knowledge of the Congress and never before questioned, engaged in by Presidents who have also sworn to uphold the Constitution, making as it were such exercise of power part of the structure of our government, may be treated as a gloss on "executive Power" vested in the President by § 1 of Art. II.

. . . .

Justice Douglas, concurring.

. . . .

. . . The branch of government that has the power to pay compensation for a seizure is the only one able to authorize a seizure or make lawful one that the President has effected. That seems to me to be the necessary result of the condemnation provision in the Fifth Amendment. It squares with the theory of checks and balances expounded by Mr. Justice Black in the opinion of the Court in which I join.

. . . .

Justice Jackson, concurring in the judgment and opinion of the Court.

. . . .

The actual art of governing under our Constitution does not and cannot conform to judicial definitions of the power of any of its branches based on isolated clauses or even single Articles torn from context. While the Constitution diffuses power the better to secure liberty, it also contemplates that practice will integrate the dispersed powers into a workable government. It enjoins upon its branches separateness but interdependence, autonomy but reciprocity. Presidential powers are not fixed but fluctuate, depending upon their disjunction or conjunction with those of Congress. We may well begin by a somewhat over-simplified grouping of practical situations in which a President may doubt, or others may challenge, his powers, and by distinguishing roughly the legal consequences of this factor of relativity.

1. When the President acts pursuant to an express or implied authorization of Congress, his authority is at its maximum, for it includes all that he possesses in his own right plus all that Congress can delegate. In these circumstances, and in these only, may he be said (for what it may be worth) to personify the federal sovereignty. If his act is held unconstitutional under these circumstances, it usually means that the Federal Government as an undivided whole lacks power. A seizure executed by the President pursuant to an Act of Congress would be supported by the strongest of presumptions and the widest latitude of judicial interpretation, and the burden of persuasion would rest heavily upon any who might attack it.

2. When the President acts in absence of either a congressional grant or denial of authority, he can only rely upon his own independent powers, but there is a zone of twilight in which he and Congress may have concurrent authority, or in which its distribution is uncertain. Therefore, congressional inertia, indifference or quiescence may sometimes, at least as a practical matter, enable, if not invite, measures on independent presidential responsibility. In this area, any actual test of power is likely to depend on the imperatives of events and contemporary imponderables rather than on abstract theories of law.

3. When the President takes measures incompatible with the expressed or implied will of Congress, his power is at its lowest ebb, for then he can rely only upon his own constitutional powers minus any constitutional powers of Congress over the matter. Courts can sustain exclusive presidential control in such a case only by disabling the Congress from acting upon the subject. Presidential claim to a power at once so conclusive and preclusive must be scrutinized with caution, for what is at stake is the equilibrium established by our constitutional system.

Into which of these classifications does this executive seizure of the steel industry fit? It is eliminated from the first by admission, for it is conceded that no congressional authorization exists for this seizure. . . .

Can it then be defended under flexible tests available to the second category? It seems clearly eliminated from that class because Congress has not left seizure of private property an open field but has covered it by three statutory policies inconsistent with this seizure. . . . None of these were invoked. . . .

This leaves the current seizure to be justified only by the severe tests under the third grouping, where it can be supported only by any remainder of executive power after subtraction of such powers as Congress may have over the subject. In short, we can sustain the President only by holding that seizure of such strike-bound industries is within his domain and beyond control by Congress. Thus, this Court's first review of such seizures occurs under circumstances which leave presidential power most vulnerable to attack and in the least favorable of possible constitutional postures.

I did not suppose, and I am not persuaded, that history leaves it open to question, at least in the courts, that the executive branch, like the Federal Government as a whole, possesses only delegated powers. The purpose of the Constitution was not only to grant power, but to keep it from getting out of hand. However, because the President does not enjoy unmentioned powers does not mean that the mentioned ones should be narrowed by a niggardly construction. Some clauses could be made almost unworkable, as well as immutable, by refusal to indulge some latitude of interpretation for changing times. . . .

The Solicitor General seeks the power of seizure in three clauses of the Executive Article, the first reading, "The executive Power shall be vested in a President of the United States of America." . . .

. . . I cannot accept the view that this clause is a grant in bulk of all conceivable executive power but regard it as an allocation to the presidential office of the generic powers thereafter stated.

The clause on which the Government next relies is that "The President shall be Commander in Chief of the Army and Navy of the United States. . . ."

. . . [The] argument tendered at our bar [is] that the President having, on his own responsibility, sent American troops abroad derives from that act "affirmative power" to seize the means of producing a supply of steel for them. . . .

I cannot foresee all that it might entail if the Court should indorse this argument. Nothing in our Constitution is plainer than that declaration of a war is entrusted only to Congress. Of course, a state of war may in fact exist without a formal declaration. But no doctrine that the Court could promulgate would seem to me more sinister and alarming than that a President whose conduct of foreign affairs is so largely uncontrolled, and often even is unknown, can vastly enlarge his mastery over the internal affairs of the country by his own commitment of the Nation's armed forces to some foreign venture. . . .

. . . .

The third clause in which the Solicitor General finds seizure powers is that "he shall take Care that the Laws be faithfully executed. . . ." That authority must be matched against words of the Fifth Amendment that "No person shall be . . . deprived of life, liberty or property, without due process of law. . . ." One gives a governmental authority that reaches so far as there is law, the other gives a private right that authority shall go no farther. . . .

The Solicitor General lastly grounds support of the seizure upon nebulous, inherent powers never expressly granted but said to have accrued to the office from the customs and claims of preceding administrations. The plea is for a resulting power to deal with a crisis or an emergency according to the necessities of the case, the unarticulated assumption being that necessity knows no law.

. . . .

In view of the ease, expedition and safety with which Congress can grant and has granted large emergency powers, certainly ample to embrace this crisis, I am quite unimpressed with the argument that we should affirm possession of them without statute. Such power either has no beginning or it has no end. If it exists, it need submit to no legal restraint. I am not alarmed that it would plunge us straightway into dictatorship, but it is at least a step in that wrong direction.

. . . .

Justice BURTON, concurring in both the opinion and judgment of the Court.

. . . .

. . . Does the President, . . . have inherent constitutional power to seize private property which makes congressional action in relation thereto unnecessary? We find no such power available to him under the present circumstances. The present situation is not comparable to that of an imminent invasion or threatened attack. We do not face the issue of what might be the President's constitutional power to meet such catastrophic situations. Nor is it claimed that the current seizure is in the nature of a military command addressed by the President, as Commander-in-Chief, to a mobilized nation waging, or imminently threatened with total war.

The controlling fact here is that Congress, within its constitutionally delegated power, has prescribed for the President specific procedures, exclusive of seizure, for his use in meeting the present type of emergency. . . . Under these circumstances, the President's order of April 8 invaded the jurisdiction of Congress. It violated the essence of the principle of the separation of governmental powers. . . .

Justice CLARK, concurring in the judgment of the Court.

. . . .

. . . In my view . . . the Constitution does grant to the President extensive authority in times of grave and imperative national emergency. In fact, to my thinking, such a grant may well be necessary to the very existence of the Constitution itself. . . . In describing this authority I care not whether one calls it "residual," "inherent," "moral," "implied," "aggregate," "emergency," or otherwise. . . .

I conclude that where Congress has laid down specific procedures to deal with the type of crisis confronting the President, he must follow those procedures in meeting the crisis; but that in the absence of such action by Congress, the President's independent power to act depends upon the gravity of the situation confronting the nation. I cannot sustain the seizure in question because here, . . . , Congress had prescribed methods to be followed by the President in meeting the emergency at hand.

Chief Justice VINSON, with whom Justice REED and Justice MINTON join, dissenting.

[The dissent reviewed post-World War II commitments of the United States leading to the Korean intervention. Emphasizing congressional directives to the Executive to build up our defenses, the Chief Justice noted that "[t]heir successful execution depends upon continued production of steel. . . ." The central fact was "that the Nation's entire basic steel production would have shut down completely if there had been no Government seizure," which "would immediately jeopardize and imperil our national defense." Chief Justice Vinson concluded: "Accordingly, if the President has any power under the Constitution to meet a critical situation in the absence of express statutory authorization, there is no basis whatsoever for criticizing the exercise of such power in this case."]

· · · ·

A review of executive action demonstrates that our Presidents have on many occasions exhibited the leadership contemplated by the Framers when they made the President Commander in Chief, and imposed upon him the trust to "take Care that the Laws be faithfully executed." With or without explicit statutory authorization, Presidents have at such times dealt with national emergencies by acting promptly and resolutely to enforce legislative programs, at least to save those programs until Congress could act. Congress and the courts have responded to such executive initiative with consistent approval.

· · · ·

This is but a cursory summary of executive leadership. But it amply demonstrates that Presidents have taken prompt action to enforce the laws and protect the country whether or not Congress happened to provide in advance for the particular method of execution. At the minimum, the executive actions reviewed herein sustain the action of the President in this case.

· · ·

History bears out the genius of the Founding Fathers, who created a Government subject to law but not left subject to inertia when vigor and initiative are required.

· · · ·

. . . Faced with immediate national peril through stoppage of steel production on the one hand and faced with destruction of the wage and price legislative programs on the other, the President took temporary possession of the steel mills as the only course open to him consistent with his duty to take care that the laws be faithfully executed.

. . . .

. . . The President informed Congress that even a temporary Government operation of plaintiffs' properties was "thoroughly distasteful" to him, but was necessary to prevent immediate paralysis of the mobilization program. Presidents have been in the past, and any man worthy of the Office should be in the future, free to take at least interim action necessary to execute legislative programs essential to survival of the Nation. A sturdy judiciary should not be swayed by the unpleasantness or unpopularity of necessary executive action, but must independently determine for itself whether the President was acting, as required by the Constitution, "to take Care that the Laws be faithfully executed."

. . . .

---

## NOTES

1. *Inherent Executive Powers.* Former Justice Arthur Goldberg has said that the *Steel Seizure Case* rejects the concept of inherent executive power. *See* Goldberg, *The Constitutional Limitations on the President's Powers,* 22 AM. U.L. REV. 667, 675 (1973). The following exchange took place in the lower court between Judge Pine and Assistant Attorney General Holmes Baldridge:

JUDGE PINE: So you contend the Executive has unlimited power in time of an emergency?

MR. BALDRIDGE: He has the power to take such action as is necessary to meet the emergency.

JUDGE PINE: If the emergency is great, it is unlimited, is it?

MR. BALDRIDGE: I suppose if you carry it to its logical conclusion, that is true. But I do want to point out that there are two limitations on the Executive Power. One is the ballot box, and the other is impeachment.

. . . .

JUDGE PINE: And that the Executive determines the emergencies and the Courts cannot even review whether it is an emergency.

MR. BALDRIDGE: That is correct.

. . . .

JUDGE PINE: So, when the sovereign people adopted the Constitution, it enumerated the powers set up in the Constitution but limited the powers of the Congress and limited the powers of the judiciary, but it did not limit the powers of the Executive. Is that what you say?

MR. BALDRIDGE: That is the way we read Article II of the Constitution.

. . . .

It is our position that the President is accountable only to the country, and that the decisions of the President are conclusive.

The White House released a letter repudiating this stand, indicating that the claim to powers justifying the steel seizure was "derived from the Constitution and they are limited, of course, by the provisions of the Constitution. . . ." *See* L. FISHER, PRESIDENT AND CONGRESS, POWER AND POLICY 40 (1972). Before the Supreme Court, the Attorney General stated: "We, of course, do not contend that the President has 'unlimited and unrestrained' power. We contend only that in a situation of national emergency the President has authority *under the Constitution*, and subject to constitutional limitations, to take action of this type necessary to meet the emergency." (Emphasis added.) Does this concede that the President possesses no inherent domestic legislative-like powers?

2. *Concurrent Powers.* What is the holding of *Youngstown*? Do a majority of justices agree with Justice Black that the executive has no domestic legislative-like powers unless granted by Congress? Does it accept the Taft view and reject Roosevelt's perspective on the presidency? Does the majority accept the existence of concurrent legislative power with the executive over some subjects in some cases?

3. *Express and Implied Executive Powers.* Assuming that a majority of justices recognize the existence of a constitutionally based, domestic executive legislative-like power, what is the constitutional source for such power? Must such a constitutional source be expressly provided? Note that there is no necessary and proper clause in Art. II. But consider the argument in THE FEDERALIST, Nos. 33 & 44, in regard to congressional powers, that the very grant of a power necessarily implies a grant of the means necessary to effectuate it. *See* text, pp. 144-60, on implied congressional powers.

   a. *Commander in Chief.* It has been argued "that all the Court agreed that the President's action could not be justified as an exercise of his military power as Commander in Chief of the armed forces. Indeed, the case should serve as a particularly valuable precedent in precluding an extensive interpretation of the President's autonomous military powers as a basis for executive control of the internal economy when the country is not in a state of declared war and not threatened with imminent invasion." Kauper, *The Steel Seizure Case: Congress, the President and the Supreme Court*, 51 MICH. L. REV. 141, 175 (1952), SELECTED ESSAYS, 129, 154 (1963).

   **b.** *Executive Power.* Does the *Steel Seizure Case* settle whether Art. II, § 1, vesting the executive power in the President is itself a separate grant of power, a designation of office, a shorthand reference to the other granted powers?

   **c.** *Executing the Laws.* Professor Kauper also suggests that "[i]n the end, the members of the Court seemed pretty well agreed that whatever constitutional power the President has to take action in a non-military situation, apart from specific authorization by Congress, must rest on the general power stated in Section 3 of Article II that the President 'shall take Care that the Laws be faithfully executed.' " Kauper, *The Steel Seizure Case*, 51 MICH. L. REV., at 175-76, SELECTED ESSAYS, at 154. If Congress has not enacted an applicable law, does this negate any executive power to act under this clause?

   **d.** *Aggregate Residual Power.* Alternatively, perhaps the executive power to act might arise, not from any single grant of power, but from the aggregate of all the granted powers, expressed and implied. "That the president does possess 'residual' or 'resultant' powers over and above, or in consequence of, it's specifically granted powers to take temporary alleviative action in the presence of serious emergency is a proposition to which all but Justices Black and Douglas would probably have assented in the absence of the complicating issue that was created by the president's refusal to follow the procedures laid down in the Taft-Hartley Act." Corwin, *The Steel Seizure Case: A Judicial Brick Without Straw*, 53 COLUM. L. REV. 53, 65 (1953).

   **4.** *Concurrent Powers in the Twilight Zone.* Assuming the existence of some shared domestic lawmaking powers, what rules should govern its exercise? Under what circumstances may the executive act in the absence of congressional authorization? Should the congressional or the executive judgment prevail if a conflict develops? Is the "twilight zone" approach of Justice Jackson to the sharing of powers operational? useful? For a criticism of the approach, see Banks, *Steel, Sawyer and the Executive Power*, 14 U. PITT. L. REV. 467, 528 (1953).

5. *The Meaning of "Emergency."* In his memoirs, President Truman claimed: "It is not very realistic for the Justices to say that comprehensive powers should be available to the President only when a war has been declared or when the country has been invaded. We live in an age when hostilities begin without polite exchanges of diplomatic notes. There are no longer sharp distinctions between combatants and non-combatants, between military targets and the sanctuary of civilian areas; nor can we separate the economic facts from the problems of defense and security." Quoted in A. WESTIN, THE ANATOMY OF A CONSTITUTIONAL LAW CASE: YOUNGSTOWN SHEET & TUBE CO. v. SAWYER 174-75 (1958).

The majority in the *Steel Seizure Case* does not decide whether the emergency would have been inadequate to justify seizure. Can emergency ever create power to act? If there are concurrent powers, what degree of public interest(?), necessity(?), justifies sole executive action? If a President finds severe hunger and malnutrition in a section of the country, can he "legislate" an emergency program without prior congressional authorization? Would actual starvation suffice?

6. *The Judicial Function.* All of the justices appear to accept the *Steel Seizure* dispute as appropriate for judicial review. What is the proper judicial role in resolving such conflicts? Is it proper for a court to examine an executive determination of emergency? Corwin suggests that "[i]t is . . . fairly evident that the Court would never venture to traverse a presidential finding of 'serious' emergency which was prima facie supported by judicially cognizable facts, but would wave aside a challenge to such a finding as raising a 'political' question." *The Steel Seizure Case,* 53 COLUM. L. REV., at 66.

Compare the view that "[t]o constitutional and administrative lawyers, the Steel Seizure case will remain of primary importance as an illustration of the basic principle that, in the American system, assertions of executive power are subject to judicial control." Schwartz, *Inherent Executive Power and the Steel Seizure Case: A Landmark in American Constitutional Law,* 30 CAN. B. REV. 466, 480 (1952).

7. Regardless of the holding of *Youngstown,* the existence of such implied power may be a necessary by-product of our system. "The lessons of history are that Congress, by defaulting in a duty to equip the President with adequate authority by statutory grant to deal with wartime or other emergencies cannot expect in every situation to foreclose him from taking this kind of step. If it is inescapably necessary to protect the public interest and security for the President to act, he will be expected to do so, whether or not Congress has given advance clearance and authorization."

J. Kallenbach, THE AMERICAN CHIEF EXECUTIVE 560 (1966).
Does *Youngstown* involve a legal or a political issue?

8. Corwin poses the question, "What is the lesson of the
Steel Case?" He answers: "Undoubtedly it tends to supplement
presidential emergency power with a power to adopt temporary
remedial legislation when Congress has been, in the judgment of
the President, unduly remiss in taking cognizance of and acting
on a given situation. In other words, the lesson of the case is that,
just as nature abhors a vacuum, so does an age of emergency. Let
Congress see to it, then, that no such vacuum occurs. The best
escape from presidential autocracy in the age we inhabit is not,
in short, judicial review, which can supply only a vacuum, but
timely legislation." E. CORWIN, THE PRESIDENT, OFFICE AND
POWERS 1787-1957; HISTORY AND ANALYSIS OF PRACTICE AND
OPINION 157 (4th ed. 1957).

## Delegation of Legislative Power

1. Much of the executive's legislative role is a product of
conscious legislative delegation of power. Theoretically, law-making power delegated to Congress cannot be redelegated to the
executive—*delegata potestas non potest delegari*. Realistically,
however, Congress must leave some matters to executive discretion
if legislation is to be effective. The executive possesses the continuity, the flexibility, the capacity for day-to-day supervision
and adaptation, the ability to coordinate programs necessary for
implementing the legislative policy. Fisher, *Delegating Power to
the President,* 19 J. PUB. L. 251 (1970). Thus, Louis L. Jaffe
suggests that "legislation and administration are complementary
rather than opposed processes; and . . . delegation is the formal
term and method for their interplay." L. JAFFE, JUDICIAL CON-
TROL OF ADMINISTRATIVE ACTION 34 (1965).

2. The courts at times have sought to overcome this dilemma
by claiming that the executive is merely "filling up details"
within the standards set by Congress. "The permissibility of
delegation thus becomes a matter of definition, with strong
pragmatic overtones." Fisher, *Delegating Power to the President,*
19 J. PUB. L., at 252.

3. A series of New Deal cases took a restrictive view of the
power to delegate. *See* Panama Ref. Co. v. Ryan, 293 U.S. 388
(1935); Schechter Poultry Corp. v. United States, 295 U.S. 495
(1935). Subsequent cases, however, have sustained delegations
having only minimal legislative guidelines. *See, e.g.,* F.P.C. v.
Hope Natural Gas Co., 320 U.S. 591 (1944) ("just and reasonable"
rates for natural gas); National Broadcasting Co. v. United States,
319 U.S. 190 (1943) (licensing of radio communications "as public

convenience, interest or necessity requires"); Yakus v. United States, 321 U.S. 414 (1944) (price fixing authority with maximum prices to be "generally fair and equitable"); Lichter v. United States, 334 U.S. 742 (1948) (recovery of "excessive profits" earned on war contracts).

4. In Amalgamated Meat Cutters and Butcher Workers v. Connally, 337 F. Supp. 737 (D.D.C. 1971), the court refused to enjoin the wage and price freeze controls ordered by President Nixon (Executive Order 11615), pursuant to the Economic Stabilization Act of 1970 (12 U.S.C. § 1904). The union contended that the Act's grant of power to the President "to issue such orders and regulations as he may deem appropriate to stabilize prices, rents, wages, and salaries" was an unconstitutional delegation of legislative power. The court, however, found the controlling principles not in *Schechter, supra,* but in *Yakus, supra.* "Congress is free to delegate legislative authority provided it has exercised 'the essentials of the legislative function'—of determining the basic legislative policy and formulating a rule of conduct. . . . The issue is whether the legislative description of the task assigned 'sufficiently marks the field within which the Administrator is to act so that it may be known whether he has kept within it in compliance with the legislative will.' " The constitutional requirements were thus defined through "concepts of control and accountability." The burden is on the challenging party to show that "there is an absence of standards for the guidance of the Administrator's action, so that it would be impossible in a proper proceeding to ascertain whether the will of Congress has been obeyed."

The court found these conditions satisfied. Prior anti-inflationary controls were seen as providing a "validating context" as to "legislative contours and contemplation." The Act defined a purpose to stabilize the cost of living through the stabilization of wages and prices and specified appropriate means to that end. The court therefore held: "first, that the statute does at least contain a standard of broad fairness in avoiding a gross inequity, —leaving to the future the implementation of that standard; second, that this statute is not unconstitutional as an excessive delegation of power by the legislature to the executive for the limited term of months contemplated by Congress to follow the initiating general freeze." Provision for further executive development of standards and for judicial review were said to blunt "the 'blank check' rhetoric of the plaintiffs."

## 2. Executive Impoundment: Fiscal Integrity or Usurpation?

1. Impoundment involves the withholding or delay in expenditure of congressionally appropriated funds by the execu-

tive. Congress has in fact delegated impoundment authority to the executive through legislation such as the Anti-Deficiency Act, 31 U.S.C. § 665(c), to avoid deficiencies resulting from excessively rapid expenditures or to achieve program savings, or Title VI of the 1964 Civil Rights Act authorizing the withholding of funds from segregated programs. *See* Note, *Impoundment of Funds,* 86 HARV. L. REV. 1505 (1973). Further, the executive argues that impoundment is sanctioned by continued unchallenged usage since at least the time of Jefferson.

However, recently the use of impoundment has changed both quantitatively and qualitatively. Congressional hearings in 1971 indicated that more than ten billion dollars was then being withheld, far more than had ever previously been impounded, affecting a far broader range of governmental programs. Previous impoundments had been principally in the defense arena supported by the President's power as Commander-in-Chief. Recent impoundments have involved domestic programs, especially in the area of social welfare. More important, impoundment has increasingly been used not merely to effectuate economies or prevent program deficiencies but to reflect executive program priorities. It is in this area, where Congress has mandated expenditures in support of a policy that impoundment poses a severe constitutional question. "[A] constitutional issue emerges only when Congress finds a legislative program cancelled or abbreviated because the President considers the purpose unwise, wasteful, or inexpedient. He no longer operates on the basis of legislative authority. On the contrary, he matches his will against that of Congress." Fisher, *Funds Impounded by the President: The Constitutional Issue,* 38 GEO. WASH. L. REV. 124, 125-26 (1969).

2. *The Executive Power.* Can executive impoundment of mandatory funds be justified as an exercise of the "executive power"? Would it be justified to prevent serious inflation? Would *Youngstown* support such executive action? The Department of Justice argues that "[j]ust as Congress has implied power . . . , so does the President have implicit authority—under the executive power clause—in carrying out his constitutional obligations. Impounding funds is one of the most effective means that the President has to maintain fiscal control and to coordinate fiscal policy." *Joint Hearings on S. 373 Before an Ad Hoc Subcomm. on Impoundment of Funds of the Sen. Comm. on Government Operations and the Subcomm. on Separation of Powers of the Sen. Judiciary Comm.,* 93d Cong., 1st Sess. 839 (1973).

Compare the views expressed by then-Assistant Attorney General William H. Rehnquist: "It is in our view extremely difficult to formulate constitutional theory to justify a refusal by the

President to comply with a Congressional directive to spend. It may be argued that the spending of money is inherently an executive function, but the execution of any law is, by definition, an executive function and it seems an anomalous proposition that because the Executive Branch is bound to execute the laws, it is free to decline to execute them." MEMORANDUM RE PRESIDENTIAL AUTHORITY TO IMPOUND FUNDS APPROPRIATED FOR ASSISTANCE TO FEDERALLY IMPACTED SCHOOLS (Dec. 1, 1969).

3. Does the President's duty to faithfully execute the laws support the impoundment of funds? The executive has argued that laws imposing a budget ceiling have made impoundment a constitutional necessity. Thus Deputy Attorney General Sneed argued that the President must "consider all the laws" and that "he is confronted and was confronted in the 1973 budget with laws consisting of appropriation acts, laws consisting of the 1946 Full Employment Act, laws consisting of the debt ceilings, consisting of the Economic Stabilization Act. Above and beyond that, he was looked to by Congress and certainly by the public as one having a very profound responsibility for price stability.

"Now, when we put all that together, the problem is how best to faithfully execute the laws." *1973 Joint Hearings on Impoundment*, at 372. Does this power include authority to harmonize divergent laws into a cohesive program? To decide only when there is a real present conflict between laws? Is there any alternative to impoundment when particular laws conflict with the debt ceiling?

4. *Separation of Powers.* Is impoundment inconsistent with the separation of powers principle? In Sioux Valley Empire Elec. Ass'n Inc. v. Butz, 367 F. Supp. 686, 698 (D.S.D. 1973), Chief Judge Nichol argued that "[t]he power sought to be exercised in the impoundment cases is more all-encompassing than that sought to be exercised in the *Steel Seizure Case*. Indeed, it is by far the most dangerous abdication of legislative power in an age of Congressional acquiescence, for it vests in the executive the very essence of legislative power. If it is conceded that the President has the power to impound Congressionally-appropriated funds to promote sound fiscal policy, who is to determine whether the impoundment was proposed upon the achievement of the Congressional program for which the funds were appropriated? Where impoundment of funds is selective among the various programs, who is to determine the propriety of the President's arrangement of priorities? These questions are unanswerable. Should the power be conceded to the President, the very nucleus of Congressional power would pass to the Executive sphere. The system of checks and balances would be emasculated." But the executive argues

that the separation of powers principle does not mandate absolute separation. Is spending an area of concurrent power? Is impoundment a proper exercise of such concurrent powers?

5. Does Art. I, §§ 8, cl. 1, and 9, cl. 7, give Congress *sole* power to establish spending priorities through appropriation? It has been argued that "[t]he 'intent' of the Founding Fathers also indicates that, at least theoretically, the ultimate authority over all aspects of revenue and expenditure was to rest with the elected representatives of the people. Nowhere in the debate is there any contemplation of budgetary control by the President." Note, *The Impoundment Question—An Overview,* 40 BROOKLYN L. REV. 342, 349-50 (1973). In rebuttal, it is argued that nothing in the appropriations clauses is addressed to spending less than the amount appropriated, *i.e.,* that an appropriation only sets a ceiling on spending and nothing more. *1973 Joint Hearings on Impoundment,* at 374.

6. *Effect on the Veto Power?* Does impoundment constitute a selective or item veto? Or an absolute veto? "If the President refuses to spend appropriated funds, he exercises an absolute veto, since Congress possesses no effective means to override such action. This refusal is contrary to the clear intent of the framers that the President possesses only a qualified veto. If the President delays spending appropriated monies, he exercises a power of suspension rejected by the Constitutional Convention. If the President selects among the provisions of an appropriation bill, he exercises an item veto, a proposal never considered." Note, *Presidential Impoundment: Constitutional Theories and Political Realities,* 61 GEO. L.J. 1295, 1299 (1973). Senator Sam Ervin found this power to effect an item or line veto even more disturbing than the separation of powers problem. "Such a power clearly is prohibited by the Constitution, which empowers the President to veto entire bills only. By impounding appropriated funds, the President is able to modify, reshape, or nullify completely laws passed by the legislative branch, thereby making legislative policy—a power reserved exclusively to the Congress." Such an illegal exercise of the power of his office violates clear constitutional provisions." *1973 Joint Hearings on Impoundment,* at 3.

7. The overwhelming weight of lower court decisions has been against impoundment of mandatory funds. It should be noted, however, that few of these decisions have reached the constitutional issue since the executive frequently decided to release the monies following a judgment that the appropriation was mandatory rather than discretionary. *But see* Sioux Valley Empire Elec. Ass'n, Inc. v. Butz, 367 F. Supp. 686 (D.S.D. 1973). *See also* Local 2677, American Fed'n of Gov't Employees v. Phil-

lips, 358 F. Supp. 60 (D.D.C. 1973), holding illegal the action of the administrator of the O.E.O., acting under presidential directive, in utilizing appropriated funds to phase out the activities of the community action program. The court reasoned that "[a]n administrator's responsibility to carry out the Congressional objectives of a program does not give him the power to discontinue that program, especially in the face of a Congressional mandate that it shall go on."

*See also* Train v. City of New York, — U.S. — (1975), where the court held that the executive lacked statutory authority to withhold funds under the Water Pollution Act of 1972 since Congress had mandated the present expenditure of funds.

8. Does Congress have power to enact legislation limiting the executive discretion to impound? The Department of Justice has argued that "Article II vests 'executive Power' in the President. And Congress may not, by the aggregate effect of its enactment, deprive him of substantial discretion to refrain from spending, where restraint is necessary to prevent ruinous inflation."

Noting "the functional deficiencies of Congress in adequately checking inflationary pressures," Deputy Attorney General Sneed said that "[g]iven these intractable realities, and reading the Constitution as a living document—not a suicide pact—the President's 'executive Power' must be deemed to encompass substantial authority to impound in order to check inflation." He expressed "doubt whether Congress can legislate against impoundment even in the domestic area when to do so results in substantially increasing the rate of inflation. To admit the existence of such power deprives the President of a substantial portion of the 'executive power' vested in him by the Constitution." *1973 Joint Hearings on Impoundment,* at 363, 838.

On the other hand, it is argued that "[t]he congressional power to legislate, override vetos, raise taxes, appropriate funds, and pass laws deemed necessary and proper strongly implies that the Constitution does place the 'power of the purse' with Congress. This power of the purse logically extends beyond the appropriation process, so as to include the execution of appropriations." Levinson & Mills, *Impoundment: A Search for Legal Principles,* 26 U. FLA. L. REV. 191, 195 (1974).

### 3. Executive Privilege: The Need for Information and Confidentiality

During the course of the investigation of the break-in and cover-up of the Democratic National Committee headquarters at Watergate and other misconduct in the 1972 presidential election by the Senate Select Committee on Presidential Campaign Activities (the Watergate Committee), it was learned that President Nixon had recorded numerous presidential conversations on electronic tape. This touched off a new phase of the continuing controversy over the power of the Executive to withhold information from the coordinate branches of the government. Both the congressional committee and the Department of Justice's Special Prosecutor met executive opposition in their efforts to secure access to these tapes.

Dating back to its 1792 investigation of the disastrous St. Clair expedition, Congress has sought, usually with success but sometimes with failure, information from the Executive. Since that time, the Executive has frequently claimed privilege to reject such demands. The modern assertion of a broad executive privilege against congressional demands is suggested by President Eisenhower's order to the Defense Department during the McCarthy-Army hearings in the 1950's:

> Because it is essential to efficient and effective administration that employees of the executive branch be in a position to be completely candid in advising with each other on official matters, and because it is not in the public interest that any of their conversations or communications be disclosed, you will instruct employees of your Department that in all of their appearances before the Subcommittee of the Senate Committee on Government Operation, regarding the inquiry now before it, they are not to testify to any such conversations or communications or to produce any such document or reproductions. This principle must be maintained regardless of who would be benefitted by such disclosures.

> I direct this action so as to maintain the proper separation of powers between the executive and legislative branches of the Government in accordance with my responsibilities and duties under the Constitution. This separation is vital to preclude the exercise of arbitrary power by any branch of the Government.

Similarly, litigation on behalf of or against the Government has spawned demands in the courts for information available only from the Executive.

Does the Executive have power to withhold information for national security? In the "public interest"? To preserve confidentiality? To avoid defaming individuals? Is this merely an evidentiary privilege or is it constitutionally-based? What is its scope and who decides its applicability? Is it an absolute privilege of the Executive? Of the President personally? Is it a conditional privilege subject to judicial or congressional supervision? Can it ever prevail against Congress' need for information in investigating pursuant to its legislative functions? Or in an impeachment inquiry? Can it ever prevail against the grand jury's right "to every man's evidence"?

## UNITED STATES v. NIXON
Supreme Court of the United States
— U.S. —, 41 L. Ed. 2d 231, 94 S. Ct. 3090 (1974)

Chief Justice BURGER delivered the opinion of the Court.

These cases present for review the denial of a motion, filed on behalf of the President of the United States, in the case of United States v. Mitchell et al. (D. C. Crim. No. 74-110), to quash a third-party subpoena *duces tecum* issued by the United States District Court for the District of Columbia, pursuant to Fed. Rule Crim. Proc. 17 (c). The subpoena directed the President to produce certain tape recordings and documents relating to his conversations with aides and advisers. The court rejected the President's claims of absolute executive privilege, of lack of jurisdiction, and of failure to satisfy the requirements of Rule 17 (c). The President appealed to the Court of Appeals. We granted the United States' petition for certiorari before judgment, and also the President's responsive cross-petition for certiorari before judgment, because of the public importance of the issues presented and the need for their prompt resolution.

. . . .

[The Court held that the District Court's order was appealable since the President should not be required to disobey a court order to test its validity nor should a court be required to cite the President in order to invoke review.]

In the District Court, the President's counsel argued that the court lacked jurisdiction to issue the subpoena because the matter was an intra-branch dispute between a subordinate and superior officer of the Executive Branch and hence not subject to judicial resolution. That argument has been renewed in this Court with emphasis on the contention that the dispute does not present a "case" or "controversy" which can be adjudicated in the federal courts. The President's counsel argues that the federal courts should not intrude into areas committed to the other branches of Government. He views the present dispute as essentially a "jurisdictional" dispute within the Executive Branch which he analogizes to a dispute between two congressional committees. Since the Executive Branch has exclusive authority and absolute discretion to decide whether to prosecute a case, it is contended that a President's decision is final in determining what evidence is to be used in a given criminal case. Although his counsel concedes the President has delegated certain specific powers to the Special Prosecutor, he has not "waived nor delegated to the Special Prosecutor the President's duty to claim privilege as to all materials . . . which fall within the President's inherent authority to refuse to disclose to any executive officer." The Special Prosecutor's demand for the items therefore presents, in the view of the President's counsel, a political question . . . since it involves a "textually demonstrable" grant of power under Art. II.

The mere assertion of a claim of an "intra-branch dispute," without more, has never operated to defeat federal jurisdiction; justiciability does not depend on such a surface inquiry. . . .

Our starting point is the nature of the proceeding for which the evidence is sought—here a pending criminal prosecution. It is a judicial proceeding in a federal court alleging violation of federal laws and is brought in the name of the United States as sovereign. Under the authority of Art. II, § 2, Congress has vested in the Attorney General the power to conduct the criminal litigation of the United States Government. It has also vested in him the power to appoint subordinate officers to assist him in the discharge of his duties. Acting pursuant to those statutes, the Attorney General has delegated the authority to represent the United States in these particular matters to a Special Prosecutor with unique authority and tenure. The regulation gives the Special Prosecutor explicit power to contest the invocation of executive privilege in the process of seeking evidence deemed relevant to the performance of these specially delegated duties.

So long as this regulation is extant it has the force of law. . . .

. . . [I]t is theoretically possible for the Attorney General to amend or revoke the regulation defining the Special Prosecutor's authority. But he has not done so. So long as this regulation remains in force the Executive Branch is bound by it, and indeed the United States as the sovereign composed of the three branches is bound to respect and to enforce it. Moreover, the delegation of authority to the Special Prosecutor in this case is not an ordinary delegation by the Attorney General to a subordinate officer: with the authorization of the President, the Acting Attorney General provided in the regulation that the Special Prosecutor was not to be removed without the "consensus" of eight designated leaders of Congress.

The demands of and the resistance to the subpoena present an obvious controversy in the ordinary sense, but that alone is not sufficient to meet constitutional standards. In the constitutional sense, controversy means more than disagreement and conflict; rather it means the kind of controversy courts traditionally resolve. Here at issue is the production or nonproduction of specified evidence deemed by the Special Prosecutor to be relevant and admissible in a pending criminal case. It is sought by one official of the Government within the scope of his express authority; it is resisted by the Chief Executive on the ground of his duty to preserve the confidentiality of the communications of the President. Whatever the correct answer on the merits, these issues are "of a type which are traditionally justiciable." The independent Special Prosecutor with his asserted need for the subpoenaed material in the underlying criminal prosecution is opposed by the President with his steadfast assertion of privilege against disclosure of the material. This setting assures there is "that concrete adverseness which sharpens the presentation of issues upon which the court so largely depends for illumination of difficult constitutional questions." Baker v. Carr, 369 U.S., at 204. Moreover, since the matter is one arising in the regular course of a federal criminal prosecution, it is within the traditional scope of Art. III power.

In light of the uniqueness of the setting in which the conflict arises, the fact that both parties are officers of the Executive Branch cannot be viewed as a barrier to justiciability. It would be inconsistent with the applicable law and regulation, and the unique facts of this case to conclude other than that the Special Prosecutor has standing to bring this action and that a justiciable controversy is presented for decision.

[The Court held that the prosecutor had made a sufficient showing, based on relevancy, admissibility and specificity to require production before trial. The denial of the President's motion to quash the subpoena was held to be consistent with Rule 17 (c) of the Federal Rules of Criminal Procedure.]

Having determined that the requirements of Rule 17 (c) were satisfied, we turn to the claim that the subpoena should be quashed because it demands "confidential conversations between a President and his close advisors that it would be inconsistent with the public interest to produce." The first contention is a broad claim that the separation of powers doctrine precludes judicial review of a President's claim of privilege. The second contention is that if he does not prevail on the claim of absolute privilege, the court should hold as a matter of constitutional law that the privilege prevails over the subpoena *duces tecum*.

In the performance of assigned constitutional duties each branch of the Government must initially interpret the Constitution, and the interpretation of its powers by any branch is due great respect from the others. The President's counsel, as we have noted, reads the Constitution as providing an absolute privilege of confidentiality for all presidential communications. Many decisions of this Court, however, have unequivocally reaffirmed the holding of Marbury v. Madison, 1 Cranch 137 (1803), that "it is emphatically the province and duty of the judicial department to say what the law is."

No holding of the Court has defined the scope of judicial power specifically relating to the enforcement of a subpoena for confidential presidential communications for use in a criminal prosecution, but other exercises of powers by the Executive Branch and the Legislative Branch have been found invalid as in conflict with the Constitution. . . . Since this Court has consistently exercised the power to construe and delineate claims arising under express powers, it must follow that the Court has authority to interpret claims with respect to powers alleged to derive from enumerated powers.

Our system of government "requires that federal courts on occasion interpret the Constitution in a manner at variance with the construction given the document by another branch." *Powell v. McCormack.* . . . Notwithstanding the deference each branch must accord the others, the "judicial power of the United States" vested in the federal courts by Art. III, § 1 of the Constitution can no more be shared with the Executive Branch than the Chief Executive, for example, can share with the Judiciary the veto power, or the Congress share with the Judiciary the power to override a presidential veto. Any other conclusion would be contrary to the basic concept of separation of powers and the checks and balances that flow from the scheme of a tripartite government. We therefore reaffirm that it is "emphatically the province and the duty" of this Court "to say what the law is" with respect to the claim of privilege presented in this case. *Marbury v. Madison.*

In support of his claim of absolute privilege, the President's counsel urges two grounds one of which is common to all governments and one of which is peculiar to our system of separation of powers. The first ground is the valid need for protection of communications between high government officials and those who advise and assist them in the performance of their manifold duties; the importance of this confidentiality is too plain to require further discussion. Human experience teaches that those who expect public dissemination of their remarks may well temper candor with a concern for appearances and for their own interests to the detriment of the decisionmaking process. Whatever the nature of the privilege of confidentiality of presidential communications in the exercise of Art. II powers the privilege can be said to derive from the supremacy of each branch within its own assigned area of constitutional duties. Certain powers and privileges flow from the nature of enumerated powers; the protection of the confidentiality of presidential communications has similar constitutional underpinnings.

The second ground asserted by the President's counsel in support of the claim of absolute privilege rests on the doctrine of separation of powers. Here it is argued that the independence of the Executive Branch within its own sphere, insulates a president from a judicial subpoena in an ongoing criminal prosecution, and thereby protects confidential presidential communications.

However, neither the doctrine of separation of powers, nor the need for confidentiality of high level communications, without more, can sustain an absolute, unqualified presidential privilege of immunity from judicial process under all circumstances. The President's need for complete candor and objectivity from advisers calls for great deference from the courts. However, when the privilege depends solely on the broad, undifferentiated claim of public interest in the confidentiality of such conversations, a confrontation with other values arises. Absent a claim of need to protect military, diplomatic or sensitive national security secrets, we find it difficult to accept the argument that even the very important interest in confidentiality of presidential communications is significantly diminished by production of such material for *in camera* inspection with all the protection that a district court will be obliged to provide.

The impediment that an absolute, unqualified privilege would place in the way of the primary constitutional duty of the Judicial Branch to do justice in criminal prosecutions would plainly conflict with the function of the courts under Art. III. In designing the structure of our Government and dividing and allocating the sovereign power among three coequal branches, the Framers of the Constitution sought to provide a comprehensive system, but the separate powers were not intended to operate with absolute independence. . . . To read the Art. II powers of the President as providing an absolute privilege as against a subpoena essential to enforcement of criminal statutes on no more than a generalized claim of the public interest in confidentiality of nonmilitary and nondiplomatic discussions would upset the constitutional balance of "a workable government" and gravely impair the role of the courts under Art. III.

Since we conclude that the legitimate needs of the judicial process may outweigh presidential privilege, it is necessary to resolve those competing interests in a manner that preserves the essential functions of each branch. The right and indeed the duty to resolve that question does not free the judiciary from according high respect to the representations made on behalf of the President.

The expectation of a President to the confidentiality of his conversations and correspondence, like the claim of confidentiality of judicial deliberations, for example, has all the values to which we accord deference for the privacy of all citizens and added to those values the necessity for protection of the public interest in candid, objective, and even blunt or harsh opinions in presidential decisionmaking. A President and those who assist him must be free to explore alternatives in the process of shaping policies and making decisions and to do so in a way many would be unwilling to express except privately. These are the considerations justifying a presumptive privilege for presidential communications. The privilege is fundamental to the operation of government and inextricably rooted in the separation of powers under the Constitution. In Nixon v. Sirica, 487 F. 2d 700 (1973), the Court of Appeals held that such presidential communications are "presumptively privileged," and this position is accepted by both parties in the present litigation. We agree with Mr. Chief Justice Marshall's observation, therefore, that "in no case of this kind would a court be required to proceed against the President as against an ordinary individual." United States v. Burr, 25 Fed. Cas. 187, 191 (No. 14,694) (CCD Va. 1807).

But this presumptive privilege must be considered in light of our historic commitment to the rule of law. This is nowhere more profoundly manifest than in our view that "the twofold aim [of criminal justice] is that guilt shall not escape or innocence suffer." We have elected to employ an adversary system of criminal justice in which the parties contest all issues before a court of law. The need to develop all relevant facts in the adversary system is both fundamental and comprehensive. The ends of criminal justice would be defeated if judgments were to be founded on a partial or speculative presentation of the facts. The very integrity of the judicial system and public confidence in the system depend on full disclosure of all the facts, within the framework of the rules of evidence. To ensure that justice is done, it is imperative to the function of courts that compulsory process be available for the production of evidence needed either by the prosecution or by the defense.

Only recently the Court restated the ancient proposition of law, albeit in the context of a grand jury inquiry rather than a trial,

" 'that the public . . . has a right to every man's evidence' except for those persons protected by a constitutional, common law, or statutory privilege."

The privileges referred to by the Court are designed to protect weighty and legitimate competing interests. . . .

In this case the President challenges a subpoena served on him as a third party requiring the production of materials for use in a criminal prosecution on the claim that he has a privilege against disclosure of confidential communications. He does not place his claim of privilege on the ground they are military or diplomatic secrets. As to these areas of Art. II duties the courts have traditionally shown the utmost deference to presidential responsibilities. . . . No case of the Court, however, has extended this high degree of deference to a President's generalized interest in confidentiality. Nowhere in the Constitution as we have noted earlier, is there any explicit reference to a privilege of confidentiality yet to the extent this interest relates to the effective discharge of a President's powers, it is constitutionally based.

The right to the production of all evidence at a criminal trial similarly has constitutional dimensions. . . . It is the manifest duty of the courts to vindicate those guarantees and to accomplish that it is essential that all relevant and admissible evidence be produced.

In this case we must weigh the importance of the general privilege of confidentiality of presidential communications in performance of his responsibilities against the inroads of such a privilege on the fair administration of criminal justice.[19] The interest in preserving confidentiality is weighty indeed and entitled to great respect. However we cannot conclude that advisers will be moved to temper the candor of their remarks by the infrequent occasions of disclosure because of the possibility that such conversations will be called for in the context of a criminal prosecution.

On the other hand, the allowance of the privilege to withhold evidence that is demonstrably relevant in a criminal trial would cut deeply into the guarantee of due process of law and gravely impair the basic function of the courts. A President's acknowledged need for confidentiality in the communications of his

---

[19] We are not here concerned with the balance between the President's generalized interest in confidentiality and the need for relevant evidence in civil litigation, nor with that between the confidentiality interest and congressional demands for information, nor with the President's interest in preserving state secrets. We address only the conflict between the President's assertion of a generalized privilege of confidentiality against the constitutional need for relevant evidence to criminal trials.

office is general in nature, whereas the constitutional need for production of relevant evidence in a criminal proceeding is specific and central to the fair adjudication of a particular criminal case in the administration of justice. Without access to specific facts a criminal prosecution may be totally frustrated. The President's broad interest in confidentiality of communications will not be vitiated by disclosure of a limited number of conversations preliminarily shown to have some bearing on the pending criminal cases.

We conclude that when the ground for asserting privilege as to subpoenaed materials sought for use in a criminal trial is based only on the generalized interest in confidentiality, it cannot prevail over the fundamental demands of due process of law in the fair administration of criminal justice. The generalized assertion of privilege must yield to the demonstrated, specific need for evidence in a pending criminal trial.

. . . Here the District Court treated the material as presumptively privileged, proceeded to find that the Special Prosecutor had made a sufficient showing to rebut the presumption and ordered an *in camera* examination of the subpoenaed material. On the basis of our examination of the record we are unable to conclude that the District Court erred in ordering the inspection. Accordingly we affirm the order of the District Court that subpoenaed materials be transmitted to that court. We now turn to the important question of the District Court's responsibilities in conducting the *in camera* examination of presidential materials or communications delivered under the compulsion of the subpoena *duces tecum*.

Enforcement of the subpoena *duces tecum* was stayed pending this Court's resolution of the issues raised by the petitions for certiorari. Those issues now having been disposed of, the matter of implementation will rest with the District Court. "[T]he guard, furnished to [President] to protect him from being harassed by vexatious and unnecessary subpoenas, is to be looked for in the conduct of the [district] court after the subpoenas have issued; not in any circumstances which is to precede their being issued." *United States v. Burr.* Statements that meet the test of admissibility and relevance must be isolated; all other material must be excised. At this stage the District Court is not limited to representations of the Special Prosecutor as to the evidence sought by the subpoena; the material will be available to the District Court. It is elementary that *in camera* inspection of evidence is always a procedure calling for scrupulous protection against any release or publication of material not found by the court, at that stage, probably admissible in evidence and relevant to the issues of the trial for which it is sought. That being true of an ordinary situation, it is obvious that the District Court has a very heavy responsibility to see to it that presidential conversations, which are either not relevant or not admissible, are accorded that high degree of respect due the President of the United States. Mr. Chief Justice Marshall sitting as a trial judge in the *Burr* case was extraordinarily careful to point out that:

> "[I]n no case of this kind would a Court be required to proceed against the President as against an ordinary individual."

Marshall's statement cannot be read to mean in any sense that a President is above the law, but relates to the singularly unique role under Art. II of a President's communications and activities, related to the performance of duties under that Article. Moreover, a President's communications and activities encompass a vastly wider range of sensitive material than would be true of any "ordinary individual." It is therefore necessary in the public interest to afford presidential confidentiality the greatest protection consistent with the fair administration of justice. The need for confidentiality even as to idle conversations with associates in which casual reference might be made concerning political leaders within the country or foreign statesmen is too obvious to call for further treatment. We have no doubt that the District Judge will at all times accord to presidential records that high degree of deference suggested in *United States v. Burr,* and will discharge his responsibility to see to it that until released to the Special Prosecutor no *in camera* material is revealed to anyone. This burden applies with even greater force to excised material; once the decision is made to excise, the material is restored to its privileged status and should be returned under seal to its lawful custodian.

Since this matter came before the Court during the pendency of a criminal prosecution, and on representations that time is of the essence, the mandate shall issue forthwith.

*Affirmed.*

Justice REHNQUIST took no part in the consideration or decision of these cases.

---

## NOTES

### The Precedent

1. *The Burr Litigation.* The Supreme Court in *United States v. Nixon* frequently cites the opinion of Chief Justice Marshall in the trial of Aaron Burr. *See* T. CARPENTER, THE TRIAL OF

COLONEL AARON BURR (1807); D. ROBERTSON, TRIAL OF AARON BURR (1808). Burr sought a private letter written to President Jefferson. Jefferson's counsel, exercising the President's discretion, delivered a copy of the letter excepting confidential parts he deemed not material for the purposes of justice but offering to submit the original to the court for its judgment. United States v. Burr, 25 Fed. Cas. 187, 190 (No. 14,694) (C.C. Va. 1807). Burr, however, argued for an original of the whole letter and contended that relevancy couldn't be determined without disclosing his whole defense which he was not required to do.

Chief Justice Marshall ruled: "That the President of the United States may be subpoenaed and examined as a witness and required to produce any paper in his possession, is not controverted. . . . The President, although subject to the general rules which apply to others, may have sufficient motives for declining to produce a particular paper, and those motives may be such as to restrain the court from enforcing its production . . . I can readily conceive that the President might receive a letter which would be improper to exhibit in public, because of the manifest inconvenience of its exposure. The occasion for demanding it ought, in such a case, be very strong, and to be fully shown to the court before its production could be insisted on. I admit that, in such a case, much reliance must be placed on the declaration of the President; and I do think that a privilege does exist to withhold private letters of a certain description. . . .

"Yet it is a very serious thing, if such letter should contain any information material to the defence, to withhold from the accused the power of making use of it. . . . I cannot precisely lay down any general rule for such a case. Perhaps the court ought to consider the reason which would induce the President to refuse to exhibit such a letter as conclusive on it, unless such letter could be shown to be absolutely necessary in the defence. The President may himself state the particular reason which may have induced him to withhold a paper, and the court would unquestionably allow their full force to those reasons. At the same time, the court could not refuse to pay proper attention to the affidavit of the accused. But on objections being made by the President to the production of a paper, the court would not proceed further in the case without such an affidavit as would clearly shew the paper to be essential to the justice of the case. On the present occasion, the court would willingly hear further testimony on the materiality of the paper required but that is not offered."

Marshall went on to note that Jefferson had not personally determined the need for privilege, concluding: "The propriety of withholding [the paper] must be decided by himself, not by another for him." Jefferson subsequently made a *personal* claim of privilege for the excepted parts "as he deemed ought not to be made public." The letter was never introduced in evidence and no further action was taken in that proceeding.

In subsequent proceedings, the demand for disclosure of the full letter was again made, but the Chief Justice stated that "after such a certificate from the president [claiming privilege] as has been received, I cannot direct the production of those parts of the letter, without a sufficient evidence of their being relevant to the present prosecution." Berger, *The President, Congress, and the Courts,* 83 YALE L.J. 1111, 1120 (1974).

The proper inferences to be drawn from the *Burr* litigation had been a constant source of controversy. *Compare* the use of the case by the majority and dissent in *Nixon v. Sirica* in Note 2 *infra*; R. BERGER, EXECUTIVE PRIVILEGE: A CONSTITUTIONAL MYTH 187-94, 356-61 (1974); Berger, *The President, Congress, and the Courts,* 83 YALE L.J., at 1111-22, *with* Rhodes, *What Really Happened to the Jefferson Subpoenas,* 60 A.B.A.J. 52 (1974). While somewhat indecisive in result, the *Burr* litigation does suggest the degree to which the Executive sought to comply with the demand for information.

2. In Nixon v. Sirica, 487 F.2d 700 (D.C. Cir. 1973), the court, in a *per curiam* opinion, upheld, with modifications, a decision of District Court Chief Judge John Sirica ordering the President to produce certain taped recordings for *in camera* inspection to determine if they were privileged. Then Special Prosecutor Archibald Cox sought the materials, against a claim of executive privilege, on behalf of a grand jury investigating the Watergate break-in and cover-up.

The Court of Appeals initially rejected the President's counsel's argument that the President is absolutely immune from compulsory process of a court, noting that federal courts had frequently assumed that they had power to compel executive officials to produce evidence, *e.g., Youngstown Sheet & Tube Co.,* text, p. 320. To hold that a different rule applies when the President is party to the action would exalt the form of the *Steel Seizure Case* over its substance. "If *Youngstown* still stands, it must stand for the case where the President has himself taken possession and control of the property unconstitutionally seized, and the injunction would be framed accordingly. The practice of judicial review would be rendered capricious—and very likely impotent—if jurisdiction vanished whenever the President personally denoted an Executive action or omission as his own."

Like the Supreme Court in the *Nixon* case, the *per curiam* opinion stressed Justice Marshall's opinion in *Burr* as support for the proposition "that the President's special interest may warrant a careful judicial screening of subpoenas after the President interposes an objection but that some subpoenas will nevertheless be properly sustained by judicial orders of compliance."

Having rejected absolute executive privilege, the court determined "that application of Executive privilege depends on a weighing of the public interest protected by the privilege against the public interest that would be served by disclosure in a particular case." Recognizing the great public interest "in maintaining the confidentiality of conversations that take place in the President's performance of his official duties," the court held such conversation "presumptively privileged." But in this case, the presumption failed given the "strong showing that the subpoenaed tapes contained evidence peculiarly necessary to the carrying out of [the vital functions of the grand jury]—evidence for which no effective substitute is available."

Judge MacKinnon arguing in dissent that "the preservation of the confidentiality of the Presidential decision-making process is of overwhelming importance to the effective functioning of our three branches of government," would have recognized "an absolute privilege for confidential Presidential communications." He asserted that compelled disclosure of the tapes "which contain communications between a President and his most intimate advisors, would endanger seriously the continued efficacy of the Presidential decision-making process."

Judge MacKinnon claimed that the President's communications privilege should be placed on the same footing as that recognized for military or state secrets which, he asserted, "are never subject to disclosure regardless of the weight of countervailing interests." (See Note 3, p. 357, infra.) The national interest was deemed equally strong in both classes of cases. The Burr case, relied on by the majority, was not conclusive for Judge MacKinnon since that involved a criminal trial of an accused claiming a sixth amendment right to compulsory process and Chief Justice Marshall had not made a final disposition of the privilege question even on that issue.

MacKinnon also found support for a constitutional privilege in the separation of powers principle. Whereas "the system of checks and balances begins to operate only at the point 'when [the proceedings of any branch] come forth into action and are ready to affect the whole,' " the separation of powers doctrine "requires that each branch's proceedings, and the motives, views, and principles, which produce those proceedings should be free from the remotest influence, direct or indirect, of either of the other two powers. [2 James Wilson, Works 409-10 (1804)] This doctrine, then, prohibits intrusion in any form by one branch into the decisional processes of an equal and coordinate branch."

Judge Wilkey also dissented: "[T]he basic issue is *who decides* the scope and applicability of the Executive Branch privilege, the Judicial Branch or Executive Branch?" or "Who does the weighing and balancing of conflicting public interests? The District Judge or the President?" The answer to this, he contended, involved separation of powers principles which were ignored by the majority.

Turning to the history of judicial demands for executive papers, Judge Wilkey found the *Burr* case of critical importance, but, he read the case very differently than did the majority. "If we go on *what was actually done*, the *Burr* trials prove that the final 'weighing of the public interest' is done by the Chief Executive. If we go on *what was said* by Marshall, the *Burr* trials leave the ultimate issue of Who finally decides the public interest completely undecided, for Marshall never faced up, even verbally, to a confrontation with the President himself with the issue drawn on the question of separation of powers." *Youngstown*, he argued, "says nothing about *Which Branch Decides* a Constitutional privilege based on separation of powers."

The separation of powers, he argued, rests on a healthy equilibrium of tension which "will be destroyed" if the *per curiam* decision stood. "My colleagues cannot confine the effect of their decision to Richard M. Nixon. The precedent set will inevitably have far-reaching implications on the vulnerability of any Chief Executive to judicial process, not merely at the behest of the Special Prosecutor in the extraordinary circumstances of Watergate, but at the behest of Congress. Congress may have equally plausible needs for similar information." Judgment on the exercise of executive power, Judge Wilkey argued, must rest with the American people. The Constitutional Convention did not "entrust the decision between two conflicting Branches to the third Branch."

3. In Senate Select Committee on Presidential Campaign Activities v. Nixon, 498 F. 2d 725 (D.C. Cir. 1974), the court had an opportunity to apply the holding of *Nixon v. Sirica* to congressional demands for information. The Watergate Committee had issued two subpoenas: (1) For five specified tape recordings of conversations between President Nixon and John Dean; and, (2) for all records concerning the involvement of 25 named persons in any alleged criminal acts in connection with the 1972 presidential election. President Nixon claimed executive privilege, citing the need for confidentiality and the possible prejudi-

cial effects on the Watergate criminal prosecution of public disclosure.

The district court quashed the second subpoena as too vague and conclusory to permit a meaningful response especially given the stringent requirements suggested by *Nixon v. Sirica* when a claim of executive privilege is made. The first subpoena was also quashed. While the district court rejected President Nixon's nonparticularized claim of a confidentiality privilege, its own independent weighing of the competing interests indicated that the public interest in the integrity of the criminal process took priority. The Committee appealed only from the second order. The court of appeals, *en banc,* per Chief Judge Bazelon, unanimously affirmed but on different grounds.

A presidential claim of a need for confidentiality, Chief Judge Bazelon said, is presumptively valid against compelled intrusion by an institution of government. The party seeking the information must make a strong showing of need—"a showing that the responsibilities of that institution cannot responsibly be fulfilled without access to records of the President's deliberations." Only then would the President be obliged to submit subpoenaed materials to the court, together with particularized claims, that would be weighed against the public interest served by disclosure. In this instance, the Watergate Committee had failed to make the requisite showing.

4. *The History of Confrontation.* Proponents of executive privilege place stress on the historical claims of presidents dating back to Washington to withhold information from Congress. *See, e.g.,* THE MEMORANDUM OF ATTORNEY GENERAL WILLIAM P. ROGERS, MEMORANDUMS OF THE ATTORNEY GENERAL, "THE POWER OF THE PRESIDENT TO WITHHOLD INFORMATION FROM CONGRESS," Subcom. on Constitutional Rights of the Sen. Jud. Comm., 85th Cong., 2d Sess. (1958), reprinted at 44 A.B.A.J. 941 (1958). *Compare* R. BERGER, EXECUTIVE PRIVILEGE: A CONSTITUTIONAL MYTH 163-208 (1974); Berger, *Executive Privilege v. Congressional Inquiry,* 12 U.C.L.A. L. REV. 1044 (1965), who reviews the precedents and concludes that they are misinterpreted.

Assuming that presidents have frequently claimed privilege against congressional intrusions successfully, how much weight should be given such precedent? Can custom and usage, uncontested in the courts, establish constitutional principles? Consider the claim that "government is a practical affair intended for practical men. Both officers, lawmakers, and citizens naturally adjust themselves to any long-continued action of the Executive Department—on the presumption that unauthorized acts would not have been allowed to be so often repeated as to crystallize into a regular practice. That presumption is not reasoning in a circle but the basis of a wise and quieting rule that in determining the meaning of a statute for the existence of a power, weight shall be given to the usage itself—even when the validity of the practice is the subject of investigation." United States v. Midwest Oil Co., 236 U.S. 459, 472-73 (1915).

## The Source and Scope of Executive Privilege

1.   Raoul Berger begins his work on executive privilege with the assertion: " 'Executive privilege'—the President's claim of constitutional authority to withhold information from Congress [or the judicial branch]—is a myth. Unlike most myths, the origins of which are lost in the mists of antiquity, 'executive privilege' is a product of the nineteenth century, fashioned by a succession of presidents who created 'precedents' to suit the occasion." EXECUTIVE PRIVILEGE: A CONSTITUTIONAL MYTH 1 (1974).

As the above cases indicate, the President's claim to resist disclosure has been based on evidentiary privilege and on the Constitution, in the separation of powers principle and as implied from express Art. II powers.

a.   *Evidentiary Privilege.* As *Nixon v. Sirica* indicates, executive claims for non-disclosure have usually been based on common law and statute. *See, e.g.,* Environmental Protection Agency v. Mink, 410 U.S. 73 (1973) (recognition of executive privilege for confidential information in the Freedom of Information Act). It has been claimed for military and state secrets, informers' identity, confidential reports and communications. *See* Hardin, *Executive Privilege in the Federal Courts,* 71 YALE L.J. 879 (1962).

There seems to be greater agreement that an evidentiary privilege is conditional and that the opposing interests in a particular case can be weighed by a court. *See, e.g.,* Judge Wilkey, dissenting in *Nixon v. Sirica.* But note Judge MacKinnon, dissenting, who argues for "an absolute evidentiary privilege for conversations and deliberations of a President with his close advisors." Perhaps the fact that the President personally invokes the privilege alters this principle. The President's reply brief in *United States v. Nixon* argued that the issue at stake was "presidential privilege" not just "executive privilege." Should the fact that the case involves communications between the President and his closest advisors alter the principle? Should the privilege be available when the communications relate to criminal misconduct by the officials themselves? In the Watergate Committee's brief in the *Select Committee* case, it was argued: "Considerations of sound policy do not support the privilege here asserted

by the defendant President. We concede an Executive interest
in confidentiality to promote frank discussion. But the occasions
on which it would be necessary to breach that confidentiality in
order to secure crucial evidence on the extent of executive criminality would, we trust, be infrequent. The possibility of occasional inquiry into illegal executive activity can surely have little,
if any, chilling effect on wholly lawful executive deliberations.
And a rule exempting unlawful activities from disclosure would
plainly invite intolerable abuses."

   **b.** *Separation of Powers.* Does the separation of powers
principle support the claim for executive (presidential?) privilege
in domestic matters against judicial demands for information?
Against congressional demands? In resisting the judicial subpoena
in *Nixon v. Sirica,* the President stated, in part, that "[i]n doing
so [he followed] the example of a long line of [his] predecessors
as President of the United States who have consistently adhered
to the position that the President is not subject to compulsory
process from the courts." Arguing that "[t]he independence of
the three Branches of our government is at the very heart of our
Constitutional system," he contended that "[i]t would be wholly
impermissible for the President to seek to compel some particular
action by the courts" and it followed that "[i]t is equally impermissible for the courts to seek to compel some particular action
from the President." He therefore concluded "that it would be
inconsistent with the public interest and with the Constitutional
position of the Presidency to make available recordings of meetings and telephone conversations in which I was a participant
and I must respectfully decline to do so."

   Does the separation of powers principle require an absolute
independence of each of the branches from inquiry or supervision of the others? The ACLU amicus brief in *United States v.
Nixon,* argues that "*no* branch is entirely 'master in its own
house.' Each branch is subject to checks and balance from the
others, and the separation of powers depends on interaction not
isolation."

   **c.** *Implied Powers.* Do the Art. II powers support executive
privilege? "Concededly, the Constitution does not expressly confer upon the President or the Executive Branch the power to
withhold information the disclosure of which is contrary to the
public interest. . . . [But] [t]he same logic which holds that Congress has the power to investigate so that it may effectively exercise its legislative functions, supports the proposition that the
President has the power to withhold information when the use
of that power is necessary to exercise his Executive functions

effectively." Kramer & Marcuse, *Executive Privilege—A Study of the Period 1953-1960—II*, 29 GEO. WASH. L. REV. 827, 899 (1961).

In the President's brief in the *Select Committee* litigation, it was argued that "[t]he § 1 grant of 'executive power' solely to the President is the most obvious and demonstrable source for the heretofore unchallenged right of the President to invoke executive privilege whenever the President deems it appropriate. Such an exercise of executive power is entirely consistent with the unbroken tradition of executive independence from legislative and judicial interference. . . ."

The brief then used Art. II, § 2, empowering the President to require, in writing, the opinions of his principal officers in any subject. "What the Senate Committee does not comprehend, although obvious to the Founding Fathers, is that the power to seek and receive advice would be a useless and empty power if the President could not keep his own counsel free from the review or scrutiny of the courts or the Congress. The very manner in which this inherent § 2 grant was made independent of Congressional interference bears witness to the intent of the Framers of the Constitution to preserve inviolate the confidentiality of the Executive Branch."

The President's counsel then considered Art. II, § 3 which charges the President "from time to time [to] give to the Congress Information of the State of the Union. . . ." It was argued that "[t]his vests in the President, not in the subpoena power of a Senate Committee, the power to determine when and what information he will provide to Congress. The same section imposes on the President the duty 'to take care that the Laws be faithfully executed.' As the President has clearly and forcefully maintained, the meetings and the conversations that the Senate Committee seeks to make public were participated in by the President pursuant to this Constitutional mandate. A performance of this executive duty cannot be brought under legal compulsion."

2. *Absolute v. Conditional Privilege.* In the President's reply brief in *United States v. Nixon,* counsel for the President argued, "that the court's duty and authority of review is complete when it determines that the President of the United States has asserted privilege." Similarly, in the *Select Committee* case, in refusing a congressional subpoena, the President's counsel argued: "[Executive] privilege, inherent as we have demonstrated in the Constitutional grant of executive power, is a matter for Presidential judgment alone. The standards and circumstances that mandate

its use are a function of Presidential judgment. Such judgment cannot be second-guessed and overruled at the caprice of the Senate Committee. Nor can they be evaluated and reviewed by any discernible criteria traditionally utilized by the courts in resolving Constitutional disputes between individuals. . . ." It followed that "[e]ven if [the] Court could somehow acquire the perspective of the Executive Branch and its Chief Officer, which is the perspective from which an invocation of executive privilege is made, the separation of powers inherent in our Constitutional scheme would preclude any review of that initial policy decision. . . . It is submitted that in this . . . duty [to preserve the atmosphere of confidentiality so essential to the proper performance of the Executive's decision-making powers], just as in the area of the conduct of foreign relations, the President is 'accountable in the exercise of (his) discretion only to the people of this country.' Drinan v. Nixon, 364 F. Supp. 853 (D. Mass. 1973)."

3.  *State and Military Secrets.* The court in *United States v. Nixon* specifically indicates that it was not considering a claim of privilege involving foreign affairs or military necessity but suggests such a claim might be treated differently. Should the decision regarding the public interest in these areas be within the sole executive prerogative? *See generally Developments in the Law: the National Security Interest and Civil Liberties,* 85 HARV. L. REV. 1130, 1189-1244 (1972). *See* United States v. Reynolds, 345 U.S. 1 (1953), sustaining a claim of privilege for military secrets in a Federal Tort Claims Act case.

4.  *Congressional Demands.* The principal case deals only with grand jury demands for executive information in criminal matters. The *Select Committee* case, however, suggests that the same principles would be applicable to congressional demands for executive information. *See also* the dissenting opinions in *Nixon v. Sirica* indicating that there was no essential difference in judicial and congressional subpoenas. On the other hand, Special Prosecutor Archibald Cox resisted an attempt by the Watergate Committee to join the Committee and grand jury cases, stating that "the claim of Executive Privilege as against a legislative inquiry raises peculiar problems under the principle of separation of powers and the 'political question' doctrine that are not involved when a Court is asked to rule on the producibility of evidence in a judicial proceeding, including a grand jury investigation. Moreover, the relevant interests which must be weighed when a claim of executive privilege is asserted against Congress are quite different than the interests involved in the grand jury proceeding." Letter from Cox to Judge Sirica, in LEGAL DOCU-

MENTS RELATING TO THE SELECT COMM. ON PRESIDENTIAL CAM-
PAIGN ACTIVITIES, 93 Cong., 1st & 2d Sess. 649-50 (1974).

While the power of Congress to investigate is not specifically authorized in the Constitution, it is established that
"The power of inquiry—with process to enforce it—is an essential and appropriate auxiliary to the legislative function." The
Supreme Court explained: "A legislative body cannot legislate
wisely or effectively in the absence of information respecting the
conditions which the legislation is intended to affect or change;
and where the legislative body does not itself possess the requisite information—which not infrequently is true—recourse must
be had to others who do possess it." McGrain v. Daugherty, 273
U.S. 135, 175 (1927). See Sinclair v. United States, 279 U.S. 263
(1929), both involving congressional investigations arising from
the Teapot Dome scandal. In Watkins v. United States, 354 U.S.
178, 187 (1957), the court stated: "It is unquestionably the duty
of all citizens to cooperate with the Congress in its efforts to
obtain the facts needed for intelligent legislative action. It is
their unremitting obligation to respond to [congressional]
subpoenas."

In the *Select Committee* case, counsel for the committee argued
that Congress needed the information "in deciding the need for
and the form of corrective legislation respecting the conduct of
political campaigns" and "whether legislative regulation of executive involvement in political campaigns is necessary." Why was
this insufficient?

As a matter of policy, are the claims of either the Executive or Congress to be constitutionally preferred? Madison in
THE FEDERALIST, No. 49, said: "Neither the Executive nor the
Legislative can pretend to an exclusive or superior right of
setting the boundaries between their respective powers."

### 4. The Pardon Power

1.   On September 8, 1974, President Ford exercised his power
under Art. II, § 2, to grant "a full, free, and absolute pardon
unto Richard Nixon for all offenses against the United States
which he . . . has committed or may have committed or taken
part in during the period from January 20, 1969, through
August 9, 1974." Some have argued that the pardon does not
extend to a situation where the person pardoned has not yet
been convicted of a crime. *But see Ex parte* Garland, 71 U.S. (4
Wall.) 333 (1867), for a generous view of the presidential pardon
power.

2.   For a recent decision in keeping with that generous view,
*see* Shick v. Reed, — U.S. — (1974), holding that the pardon

power includes authority to impose a condition that commutation of a death penalty to life imprisonment be without possibility of parole. The power was perceived as virtually unlimited, subject only to constitutional restraints.

## B.  THE FOREIGN ARENA

The recent battles over legislative and executive prerogative have not been restricted to the domestic sphere. Until recently, discussion of the constitutional law of foreign relations frequently was limited to federalism issues. *See, e.g.,* Missouri v. Holland, 252 U.S. 416 (1920) (Congress has power to legislate pursuant to the treaty power). But Vietnam has generated a host of questions concerning the allocation of power to commit the United States abroad, with the language of the Constitution and "intent of the framers" being freely used by the combatants.

As will become obvious, the principles governing the separation of powers in the domestic sphere, discussed above, are not fully applicable in the foreign arena. "The foreign relations powers also reflect commitment to Separation and Checks-and-balances but what each branch can do alone, when the other is silent or even in the face of its opposition, is not determined by any 'natural' division. As they have evolved, the foreign relations' powers appear not so much 'separated' as fissured, along jagged lines indifferent to classical categories of governmental powers: some powers and functions belong to the President, some to Congress, some the President-and-Senate; some can be exercised by either the President or the Congress, some require the joint authority of both. Irregular, uncertain divisions render claims of usurpation more difficult to establish and the courts have not been available to adjudicate them." L. HENKIN, FOREIGN AFFAIRS AND THE CONSTITUTION 32 (1972). Further, as indicated above, this is an arena where the courts have been loath to enter, using the political question doctrine to avoid decision. *See* text, p. 119.

### 1.  The Foreign Affairs Power

#### UNITED STATES v. CURTISS-WRIGHT EXPORT CORP.
Supreme Court of the United States
299 U.S. 304, 81 L. Ed. 255, 57 S. Ct. 216 (1936)

[A Joint Resolution of Congress provided in § 1: "[t]hat if the President finds that the prohibition of the sales of arms and munitions of war in the United States to those countries now engaged in armed conflict in the Chaco may contribute to the reestablishment of peace between those countries, and if . . . he makes proclamation to that effect, it shall be unlawful to sell [any arms], except under such limitations and exceptions as the President prescribes. . . ." Section 2 provided penalties for violations.

[The appellees successfully challenged an indictment for conspiracy to sell arms in violation of the Resolution and a subsequent presidential proclamation. The district court held that the Resolution constituted an invalid delegation of legislative power. The case was heard by the Supreme Court on direct appeal.]

Justice SUTHERLAND delivered the opinion of the Court.

. . . .

Whether, if the Joint Resolution had related solely to internal affairs it would be open to the challenge that it constituted an unlawful delegation of legislative power to the Executive, we find it unnecessary to determine. The whole aim of the resolution is to affect a situation entirely external to the United States, and falling within the category of foreign affairs. The determination which we are called to make, therefore, is whether the Joint Resolution, as applied to that situation, is vulnerable to attack under the rule that forbids a delegation of the law-making power. In other words, assuming (but not deciding) that the challenged delegation, if it were confined to internal affairs, would be invalid, may it nevertheless be sustained on the ground that its exclusive aim is to afford a remedy for a hurtful condition within foreign territory?

It will contribute to the elucidation of the question if we first consider the differences between the powers of the Federal government in respect of foreign or external affairs and those in respect of domestic or internal affairs. That there are differences between them, and that these differences are fundamental, may not be doubted.

The two classes of powers are different, both in respect of their origin and their nature. The broad statement that the Federal government can exercise no powers except those specifically enumerated in the Constitution, and such implied powers as are necessary and proper to carry into effect the enumerated powers, is categorically true only in respect to our internal affairs. In that field, the primary purpose of the Constitution was to carve from the general mass of legislative powers *then possessed by the states* such portions as it was thought desirable to vest in the Federal government, leaving those not included in the enumeration still in the states. That this doctrine applies only to powers which the states had, is selfevident. And since the states severally never possessed international powers, such powers could not have been carved from the mass of state powers but obviously were transmitted to the United States from some other source. During the colonial period, those powers were possessed exclusively by and were entirely under the control of the Crown. . . .

As a result of the separation from Great Britain by the colonies, acting as a unit, the powers of external sovereignty passed from the Crown not to the colonies severally, but to the colonies in their collective and corporate capacity as the United States of America. . . .

The Union existed before the Constitution, which was ordained and established among other things to form "a more perfect Union." Prior to that event, it is clear that the Union, declared by the Articles of Confederation to be "perpetual," was the sole possessor of external sovereignty, and in the Union it remained without change save in so far as the Constitution in express terms qualified its exercise. . . .

It results that the investment of the federal government with the powers of external sovereignty did not depend upon the affirmative grants of the Constitution. The powers to declare and wage war, to conclude peace, to make treaties, to maintain diplomatic relations with other sovereignties, if they had never been mentioned in the Constitution, would have vested in the Federal government as necessary concomitants of nationality. Neither the Constitution nor the laws passed in pursuance of it have any force in foreign territory unless in respect of our own citizens and operations of the nation in such territory must be governed by treaties, international understandings and compacts, and the principles of international law. As a member of the family of nations, the right and power of the United States in that field are equal to the right and power of the other members of the international family. Otherwise, the United States is not completely sovereign. The power to acquire territory by discovery and occupation, the power to expel undesirable aliens, the power to make such international agreements as do not constitute treaties in the constitutional sense, none of which is expressly affirmed by the Constitution, nevertheless exist as inherently inseparable from the conception of nationality. This the Court recognized, and in each of the cases cited found the warrant for its conclusions not in the provisions of the Constitution, but in the law of nations.
. . . .

Not only, as we have shown, is the Federal power over external affairs in origin and essential character different from that over internal affairs, but participation in the exercise of the power is significantly limited. In this vast external realm, with its important, complicated, delicate and manifold problems, the President alone has the power to speak or listen as a representative of the nation. He makes treaties with the advice and consent of the Senate; but he alone negotiates. Into the field of negotiation the Senate cannot intrude; and Congress itself is powerless to invade it. . . .

It is important to bear in mind that we are here dealing not alone with an authority vested in the President by an exertion of legislative power, but with such an authority plus the very delicate, plenary and exclusive power of the President as the sole organ of the Federal government in the field of international relations—a power which does not require as a basis for its exercise an act of Congress, but which, of course, like every other governmental power, must be exercised in subordination to the applicable provisions of the Constitution. It is quite apparent that if, in the maintenance of our international relations, embarrassment—perhaps serious embarrassment—is to be avoided and success for our aims achieved, congressional legislation which is to be made effective through negotiation and inquiry within the international field must often accord to the President a degree of discretion and freedom from statutory restriction which would not be admissible were domestic affairs alone involved. Moreover, he, not Congress, has the better opportunity of knowing the conditions which prevail in foreign countries, and especially is this true in time of war. He has his confidential sources of information. He has his agents in the form of diplomatic, consular and other officials. Secrecy in respect of information gathered by them may be highly necessary, and the premature disclosure of it productive of harmful results. Indeed, so clearly is this true that the first President refused to accede to a request to lay before the House of Representatives the instructions, correspondence and documents relating to the negotiation of the Jay Treaty—a refusal the wisdom of which was recognized by the House itself and has never since been doubted. . . .

. . . .

In the light of the foregoing observations, it is evident that this court should not be in haste to apply a general rule which will have the effect of condemning legislation like that under review as constituting an unlawful delegation of legislative power. The principles which justify such legislation find overwhelming support in the unbroken legislative practice which has prevailed almost from the inception of the national government to the present day. . . .

. . . .

We deem it unnecessary to consider, seriatim, the several clauses which are said to evidence the unconstitutionality of the Joint Resolution as involving an unlawful delegation of legislative power. It is enough to summarize by saying that, both upon principle and in accordance with precedent, we conclude there is sufficient warrant for the broad discretion vested in the President to determine whether the enforcement of the statute will have a beneficial effect upon the reestablishment of peace in the affected countries; whether he shall make proclamation to bring the resolution into operation; whether and when the resolution shall cease to operate and to make proclamation accordingly; and to prescribe limitations and exceptions to which the enforcement of the resolution shall be subject.

[The Court went on to hold that the Executive proclamation satisfied the Joint Resolution.]

The judgment of the court below must be reversed and the cause remanded for further proceedings in accordance with the foregoing opinion.

Reversed.

[Justice McREYNOLDS dissented.]

---

## NOTES

### The Sharing of Power

1. Serving as a member of the House of Representatives, John Marshall stated that the "President is sole organ of the nation in its external relations, and is sole representative with foreign nations. Of consequence, the demand of a foreign nation can only be made on him. He possesses the whole Executive power. He holds and directs the force of the nation. Of consequence, any act to be performed by the force of the nation is to be performed through him." 10 ANNALS OF CONGRESS 596, 613-14 (1800).

But where is the constitutional support for such a presidential role? Does Art. II of the Constitution justify such a description of the executive prerogative in foreign affairs? Louis Henkin notes, "A stranger reading the Constitution would get little inkling of such large Presidential authority, . . . What the Constitution says and does not say, then, cannot have determined what the President can and cannot do. The structure of the federal government, the facts of national life, the realities and exigencies of international relations, the practices of diplomacy, have afforded Presidents unique temptations and unique opportunities to acquire unique powers." L. HENKIN, FOREIGN AFFAIRS AND THE CONSTITUTION 37 (1973). What are the respective advantages and disadvantages of Congress and the Executive in dealing in foreign affairs? Can the presidential role be legitimized by the ongoing practices of our government from its beginnings?

2. Justice Sutherland in *Curtiss-Wright* argues for a broad executive prerogative in foreign affairs. Further Locke, Blackstone and Montesquieu, who were all widely read by the framers, characterize foreign relations as an "executive" power. *See* E. CORWIN, THE PRESIDENT: OFFICE AND POWERS 1787-1957 416-18 n. 1 (4th ed. 1957). But consider Alexander Bickel's critique that Sutherland's "grandiose conception, the almost regal conception of the President's independent role in foreign affairs . . . never had any warrant in the constitution, is wrong in theory and unworkable in practice." *Hearings on S. 596 Before the Senate Comm. on Foreign Relations*, 92d Cong., 1st Sess. 26 (1971). *See* Berger, *The Presidential Monopoly of Foreign Relations*, 71 MICH. L. REV. 1 (1972); Kurland, *Impotence of Reticence*, 1968 DUKE L.J. 619; Lofgren, *United States v. Curtiss-Wright Export Corporation: An Historical Reassessment*, 83 YALE L.J. 1 (1973), which are similarly critical of broad claims of sole executive prerogative on foreign affairs. *Compare* Goldwater, *The President's Constitutional Primacy in Foreign Relations and National Defense*, 13 VA. J. INT'L L. 463 (1973).

3. The President has constitutional power to "receive Ambassadors and other public Ministers." Art. II, § 3. Is this merely a ceremonial role or does it confer substantive foreign affairs powers? *See* THE FEDERALIST, No. 69 ["it is more a matter of dignity than of authority."] Does it logically imply an exclusive power to recognize, or alternatively, to decline to recognize or withdraw recognition of foreign nations such as Cuba and China? Does it imply, as Thomas Jefferson wrote in 1790, that "[t]he transaction of business with foreign nations is executive altogether. It belongs, then to the head of that department, except as to such portion of it as are specially submitted to the Senate. Exceptions are to be construed strictly." 5 WRITINGS OF THOMAS JEFFERSON 161-62 (P. Ford, ed. 1894). Edward S. Corwin writes "there is no more securely established principle of constitutional practice than the exclusive right of the President to be the nation's intermediary in dealing with other nations." E. CORWIN, THE PRESIDENT: OFFICE AND POWERS 1787-1957 184 (4th ed. 1957).

4. From these powers of reception, recognition and communication, does it then logically follow that the executive is responsible for the formulation of foreign policy? Compare the contention that "[t]he solid fact is that Congress is the authoritative organ of the government in the determination of foreign

policy. The President is the agent of the Congress, the spokesman of the United States in diplomatic relations. . . ." Testimony of Ruhl J. Bartlett, *Hearings on S. 596 Before the Senate Comm. on Foreign Relations,* 92d Cong., 1st Sess. 19 (1971). Henkin notes "it has sometimes been said that the President has power to conduct foreign relations but not to make foreign policy." But he concludes that "[i]n fact, a President could not conduct foreign relations without thereby making foreign policy. But if the division were feasible and meaningful it is contradicted by what Presidents have done and do daily beyond challenge." L. HENKIN, FOREIGN AFFAIRS AND THE CONSTITUTION 47 (1973). Does the constitutional support for a broad Presidential control of foreign relations lie in the broad, uncertain Art. II grant of the "executive power" to the President, in his duty to take care to see that the laws are faithfully executed or in his powers as Commander-in-Chief?

**5.** *Congressional Powers.* On the other hand, Congress would appear to have the greater prerogative in foreign affairs if only bare constitutional grants of power were considered. In terms of major formal powers, Congress is authorized to regulate foreign commerce, to raise and maintain armies and navies and to declare war. Further, there is the extremely critical power of the purse which is often essential if foreign policy is to be effectuated. And then there are the implied foreign affairs powers, arising either from the inherent powers accompanying statehood or from the necessary and proper clause in relation to Art. I or Art. II express powers.

Apart from these formal powers, Congress also has broad informal controls available if disposed to use them, *e.g.,* riders to legislation, sense resolutions, the formal and informal actions of congressional committees. *See* L. HENKIN, FOREIGN AFFAIRS AND THE CONSTITUTION 86 (1973); R. DAHL, CONGRESS AND FOREIGN POLICY (1950).

**6.** The above suggests the potential for conflict or cooperation in the foreign arena. While some particular powers may be characterized as exclusive, the Constitution establishes a system of shared foreign affairs power.

"[T]he Constitution, considered only for its affirmative grants of powers capable of affecting the issue, is an invitation to struggle for the privilege of directing American Foreign Policy. In such a struggle the President has, it is true, certain great advantages . . . but despite all this, actual *practice* under the Constitution has shown that, while the President is usually in a position to *propose,* the Senate and Congress are often in a technical position at least to *dispose.* The verdict of history, in short, is that the power to determine the substantive content of American Foreign Policy is a divided power, with the lion's share falling usually, though by no means always, to the President." E. CORWIN, THE PRESIDENT, at 171.

Compare the following critique: "The foreign affairs power is vested in the President, while the responsibility to ensure against overaudacious executive ventures abroad remains with the Congress. The plan of the Constitution is thus to confide the power to conduct external relations to the executive department, and at the same time, guard it from serious abuse by placing it under the ultimate superintendence of the legislative branch." 2 B. SCHWARTZ, A COMMENTARY ON THE CONSTITUTION OF THE UNITED STATES: THE POWERS OF GOVERNMENT 100 (1963).

7. *Delegation of Power.* The primary issue in *Curtiss-Wright* involved the power of Congress to delegate power to impose an arms embargo on the President. It is often suggested that the decision indicates that there is little limitation on delegation of foreign affairs powers. *But see* Kent v. Dulles, 357 U.S. 116 (1958), where the court in narrowly interpreting legislation involving passports, stated that if the "right to exit" is to be regulated it "must be pursuant to the law-making functions of the Congress . . . and if that power is delegated, the standards must be adequate to pass scrutiny by the accepted tests."

## The Treaty Power and Executive Agreements

1. *"Advice and Consent."* Article II, § 2, provides that the President shall have power "by and with the Advice and Consent of the Senate, to make Treaties, provided two-thirds present concur." While it was originally intended that the Senate should actively advise the President as an executive counsel in the treaty-making process [THE FEDERALIST, No. 64], this function was aborted almost immediately. Washington actually went to the Senate for advice concerning an Indian treaty, but that was the last occasion of formal consultation. The Senate's subsequent formal role was to be that of potential legislative veto.

2. *Executive Agreements.* Treaties, however, are not the only means by which the United States undertakes international obligations. In fact, in 1971, the nation was party to over 4,000 international agreements other than treaties. Whereas we enter into about 15 new treaties each year, there are about 200 new other international agreements annually. State Department statistics, in *Hearings on S. 596 Before the Senate Committee on Foreign Relations,* 96th Cong., 1st Sess. 58 (1971). The executive agreement, especially since the end of World War II, has increas-

ingly replaced the formal treaty and consequently, the special prerogative of the Senate has been largely abrogated.

Actually, only a small portion of executive agreements are made without some congressional involvement. The Department of State has defined three categories of such agreements: "a. Agreements which are made pursuant to or in accordance with existing legislation or a treaty; b. Agreements which are made subject to Congressional approval or implementation; or c. Agreements which are made under and in accordance with the President's Constitutional power." U.S. DEP'T OF STATE CIRCULAR No. 175, 50 J. INT'L LAW 784 (1956). What is the Constitutional authority for the use of such agreements? *See* United States v. Belmont, 301 U.S. 324 (1937) and United States v. Pink, 315 U.S. 203 (1942), recognizing the legal status of such compacts and their supremacy over inconsistent state law.

## 2. The War Power

A reading of the Constitution on the war powers would, like foreign affairs powers generally, suggest a preponderance of influence in Congress. In addition to the principal power to declare war, Art. I delegates powers to levy and collect taxes for the common defense, to define and punish piracies and felonies committed on the high seas and offenses against the law of nations, to grant letters of marque and reprisal, to make rules governing capture on land and water, to raise and support armies but limiting appropriations to two years, to provide and maintain a navy, to make rules regulating the land and naval forces, to provide for the organization, arming, discipline and calling forth of the militia, as well as the general power to make all laws necessary and proper for carrying into execution these powers and those granted elsewhere in the Constitution. In comparison, the Executive relies principally on the nebulous provision vesting the executive power in the President, the President's role as Commander-in-Chief, his duty to see that the laws are faithfully executed, his power to enter into treaties and the other powers relating to foreign relations.

Nevertheless, it has become increasingly obvious that this specification of powers is not indicative of the present operation of the separation of powers. Today, "war" is seldom formally declared, deployment and use by the Executive of our armed forces in foreign lands is not unusual and the Vietnam episode raises serious questions concerning Congress' continuing role in controlling the war power. Whether this is a product of executive usurpation or congressional atrophy, the result is the same— presidential dominance of the war powers. But what was the original intent of the framers regarding the exercise of these powers? How and why has the executive achieved such dominance in this area? To what extent are the war powers exclusive to a branch and to what extent are they shared?

In 1969, the Senate adopted by a vote of 70-16, a National Commitment Resolution designed to begin a "restoration of the constitutional balance." It began by defining "national commitment" to include the use of our Armed Forces abroad or a promise to assist foreign countries by the use of our Armed Forces or financial resources and provided that "it is the sense of the Senate that a national commitment by the United States results only from affirmative action taken by the Executive and Legislative Branches of the United States Government by means of a treaty, statute, or concurrent resolution of both Houses of Congress specifically providing for such commitment."

In its report on the Resolution, the Senate Foreign Affairs Committee noted: "Our country has come far towards the concentration in its national executive of unchecked powers over foreign relations, particularly over the disposition and use of the Armed Forces. So far has this process advanced that, in the Committee's view, it is no longer accurate to characterize our government, in matters of foreign relations, as one of separated powers checked and balanced against each other. . . ."

Then, on November 7, 1973, Congress passed, over a presidential veto, the War Powers Resolution, reprinted below. Commenting on the proposal, its critics argued that it "rests on heady new perspectives the Senate Foreign Relations Committee has discovered in the necessary and proper clause. Its doctrine would permit a plenipotentiary Congress to dominate the Presidency and the courts as well more completely than the House of Commons governs England; that is, it would permit Congress to amend the Constitution without the inconvenience of consulting the people." The author warned that "[i]ts passage would be a constitutional disaster, depriving the government of the powers it needs most to safeguard the nation in a dangerous and unstable world." Rostow, *Great Cases Make Bad Law: The War Powers Act*, 50 TEX. L. REV. 833, 835, 836 (1972). On the other hand, its proponents argued that "the bill seeks to limit Presidential war-making in the absence of Congressional authorization, leaving the President free to defend the United States and its Armed Forces against sudden attack. The power to wage war, it may be categorically asserted, was vested by the Constitution in Congress, not the President. If this be so, the bill merely seeks to restore the original design. It cannot be unconstitutional to go back to the Constitution." *Testimony of*

*Raoul Berger, War Powers Legislation, 1973, Hearings on S. 440 before the Sen. Comm. on Foreign Relations, 93d Cong., 1st Sess. 5-6 (1973) [1973 Hearings].*

## War Powers Resolution

Public Law 93-148 [H.J. Res. 542], 87 Stat. 555, passed over President's veto November 7, 1973 (50 U.S.C. §§ 1541-48 (Supp. III 1973))

JOINT RESOLUTION Concerning the war powers of Congress and

the President

*Resolved by the Senate and House of Representatives of the United States of America in Congress assembled,*

### SHORT TITLE

SECTION 1. This joint resolution may be cited as the "War Powers Resolution".

### PURPOSE AND POLICY

SEC. 2. (a) It is the purpose of this joint resolution to fulfill the intent of the framers of the Constitution of the United States and insure that the collective judgment of both the Congress and the President will apply to the introduction of United States Armed Forces into hostilities, or into situations where imminent involvement in hostilities is clearly indicated by the circumstances, and to the continued use of such forces in hostilities or in such situations.

(b) Under article I, section 8, of the Constitution, it is specifically provided that the Congress shall have the power to make all laws necessary and proper for carrying into execution, not only its own powers but also all other powers vested by the Constitution in the Government of the United States, or in any department or officer thereof.

(c) The constitutional powers of the President as Commander-in-Chief to introduce United States Armed Forces into hostilities, or into situations where imminent involvement in hostilities is clearly indicated by the circumstances, are exercised only pursuant to (1) a declaration of war, (2) specific statutory authorization, or (3) a national emergency created by attack upon the United States, its territories or possessions, or its armed forces.

### CONSULTATION

SEC. 3. The President in every possible instance shall consult with Congress before introducing United States Armed Forces into hostilities or into situations where imminent involvement in hostilities is clearly indicated by the circumstances, and after every such introduction shall consult regularly with the Congress until United States Armed Forces are no longer engaged in hostilities or have been removed from such situations.

REPORTING

SEC. 4. (a)   In the absence of a declaration of war, in any case in which United States Armed Forces are introduced—

(1)   into hostilities or into situations where imminent involvement in hostilities is clearly indicated by the circumstances;

(2)   into the territory, airspace or waters of a foreign nation, while equipped for combat, except for deployments which relate solely to supply, replacement, repair, or training of such forces; or

(3)   in numbers which substantially enlarge United States Armed Forces equipped for combat already located in a foreign nation;

the President shall submit within 48 hours to the Speaker of the House of Representatives and to the President pro tempore of the Senate a report, in writing, setting forth—

(A)   the circumstances necessitating the introduction of United States Armed Forces;

(B)   the constitutional and legislative authority under which such introduction took place; and

(C)   the estimated scope and duration of the hostilities or involvement.

(b)   The President shall provide such other information as the Congress may request in the fulfillment of its constitutional responsibilities with respect to committing the Nation to war and to the use of United States Armed Forces abroad.

(c)   Whenever United States Armed Forces are introduced into hostilities or into any situation described in subsection (a) of this section, the President shall, so long as such armed forces continue to be engaged in such hostilities or situation, report to the Congress periodically on the status of such hostilities or situation as well as on the scope and duration of such hostilities or situation, but in no event shall he report to the Congress less often than once every six months.

CONGRESSIONAL ACTION

SEC. 5. (a)   Each report submitted pursuant to section 4(a)(1) shall be transmitted to the Speaker of the House of Representatives and to the President pro tempore of the Senate on the same calendar day. Each report so transmitted shall be referred to the Committee on Foreign Affairs of the House of Representatives and to the Committee on Foreign Relations of the Senate for appropriate action. If, when the report is transmitted, the Congress has adjourned sine die or has adjourned for any period in excess of three calendar days, the Speaker of the House of Representatives and the President pro tempore of the Senate, if they deem it advisable (or if petitioned by at least 30 per cent of the membership of their respective Houses) shall jointly request the President to convene Congress in order that it may consider the report and take appropriate action pursuant to this section.

(b)   Within sixty calendar days after a report is submitted or is required to be submitted pursuant to section 4(a)(1), whichever is earlier, the President shall terminate any use of United States Armed Forces with respect to which such report was submitted (or required to be submitted), unless the Congress (1) has declared war or has enacted a specific authorization for such use of United States Armed Forces, (2) has extended by law such sixty-day period, or (3) is physically unable to meet as a result of an armed attack upon the United States. Such sixty-day period shall be extended for not more than an additional thirty days if the President determines and certifies to the Congress in writing that unavoidable military necessity respecting the safety of United States Armed Forces requires the continued use of such armed forces in the course of bringing about a prompt removal of such forces.

(c)   Notwithstanding subsection (b), at any time that United States Armed Forces are engaged in hostilities outside the territory of the United States, its possessions and territories without a declaration of war or specific statutory authorization, such forces shall be removed by the President if the Congress so directs by concurrent resolution.

[Sections 6 & 7 deal with congressional priority procedures for processing joint resolutions or bills pursuant to § 5(b).]

### INTERPRETATION OF JOINT RESOLUTION

SEC. 8. (a)   Authority to introduce United States Armed Forces into hostilities or into situations wherein involvement in hostilities is clearly indicated by the circumstances shall not be inferred—

(1)   from any provision of law (whether or not in effect before the date of the enactment of this joint resolution), including any provision contained in any appropriation Act, unless such provision specifically authorizes the introduction of United States Armed Forces into hostilities or into such situations and states that it is intended to constitute specific statutory authorization within the meaning of this joint resolution; or

(2)   from any treaty heretofore or hereafter ratified unless such treaty is implemented by legislation specifically authorizing the introduction of United States Armed Forces into hostilities or into such situations and stating that it is intended to constitute specific statutory authorization within the meaning of this joint resolution.

(b)   Nothing in this joint resolution shall be construed to require any further specific statutory authorization to permit members of United States Armed Forces to participate jointly with members of the armed forces of one or more foreign countries in the headquarters operations of high-level military commands which were established prior to the date of enactment of this joint resolution and pursuant to the United Nations Charter or any treaty ratified by the United States prior to such date.

372 CONSTITUTIONAL LAW: PRINCIPLES AND POLICIES

(c) For purposes of this joint resolution, the term "introduction of United States Armed Forces" includes the assignment of members of such armed forces to command, coordinate, participate in the movement of, or accompany the regular or irregular military forces of any foreign country or government when such military forces are engaged, or there exists an imminent threat that such forces will become engaged, in hostilities.

(d) Nothing in this joint resolution—

(1) is intended to alter the constitutional authority of the Congress or of the President, or the provisions of existing treaties; or

(2) shall be construed as granting any authority to the President with respect to the introduction of United States Armed Forces into hostilities or into situations wherein involvement in hostilities is clearly indicated by the circumstances which authority he would not have had in the absence of this joint resolution.

. . . .

---

## NOTES

### The Original Understanding

1. To "Declare War." At the Constitutional Convention, there was support for vesting the war power in the President, the Senate, the President and Senate together, and the Congress. The proposed draft vesting the power to "make" war in the legislature was deleted in favor of the congressional power to "declare" war. The debate suggests this was designed, not to enhance executive power, but to prevent "make" from being misconstrued as "conduct" war, which was an executive duty. Does this exclude Congress from making policy regarding the waging of war? The strategies relating to the use and movement of our Armed Forces? Does it limit the power of Congress to terminate a war?

Further, the change was designed to leave the executive with "the power to repel sudden attacks"—that the "executive should be able to repel and not to commence war." 2 FARRAND, THE RECORDS OF THE FEDERAL CONVENTION OF 1787 318-19 (Rev. ed. 1966). Does "sudden attack" include all forms of self-defense? Does it include the threat of sudden attack as well as the reality? Does it include protection of the "Nation's security" in an "emergency" as the state department presently claims? War Powers Legislation Hearings Before the Sen. Comm. on Foreign Relations, 92d Cong., 1st Sess. 488 (1971) [1971 Hearings]. There was clearly support at the Convention for the principle that it should be made difficult to initiate war but made easy to get out of war, which explains why the power was vested in Congress rather than merely the Senate.

The opponents of the war powers legislation don't usually dispute this interpretation but stress instead the framers' intent, after the Confederation experience, to create an independent, vigorous executive. "What emerges from the text, and from the discussions available in THE FEDERALIST in Farrand, in Madison's notes, and in other contemporaneous sources, is a pattern of shared constitutional authority in this vital area, evoking the memory of tyrannies, ancient and modern, much in the minds of the Founding Fathers. It is not an hermetic separation of powers, but a scheme of divided powers—what Hamilton called an intermixture of powers, the only effective way to prevent a monopoly of power in any one branch of government." Rostow, *Great Cases Make Bad Law*, 50 TEX. L. REV., at 847.

2. *Commander-in-Chief.* Alexander Hamilton wrote in THE FEDERALIST No. 69: "The president is to be commander-in-chief of the army and navy of the United States. In this respect, his authority would be nominally the same with that of the king of Great Britain, but in substance much inferior to it. It would amount to nothing more than the supreme command and direction of the military and naval forces, as first general and admiral of the confederacy while that of the British king extends to the *declaring* of war, and to the *raising* and *regulating* of fleets and armies, all which, by the Constitution under consideration, would appertain to the legislature."

Professor Corwin, in commenting on the Hamilton perspective, states: "Rendered freely, this appears to mean that in any war in which the United States becomes involved—one presumably declared by Congress—the President will be top general and top admiral of the forces provided by Congress, so that no one can be put over him or be authorized to give him orders in the direction of the said forces; but otherwise he will have no powers that any high military or naval commander not also President might not have." E. CORWIN, THE PRESIDENT, OFFICE AND POWERS 1787-1957 228 (4th ed. 1957). Similarly, Professor Henkin notes: "[G]enerals and admirals even when they are 'first', do not determine the political purposes for which troops are to be used; they command them in the execution of policy made by others." He concludes that "[t]here is little evidence that the Framers intended more than to establish in the President civilian command of the forces for wars declared by Congress (or when the United States was attacked). . . ." L. HENKIN, FOREIGN AFFAIRS AND THE CONSTITUTION 50-51 (1973).

3. *Other Sources of Executive Power.* Does the vesting of the "Executive power" in Art. II, the President's foreign affairs power, or the concept of inherent power support the presidential

claim for discretion in initiating hostilities without congressional authorization? Madison and James Wilson agreed that "executive powers . . . do not include the rights of war and peace. . . ." 1 FARRAND, THE RECORDS OF THE FEDERAL CONVENTION OF 1787 70 (1966). As indicated in note 1, the framers certainly considered and rejected vesting the power to declare war in the President because it was "too dangerous."

4.   There is also a question as to what constitutes the "war" that Congress may declare. The term may be used in an international law sense. This would exclude a wide range of self-help measures short of juridicial war. But if the President is empowered to employ the Armed Forces in all situations short of juridicial war, Congress' power to declare "war" would be relatively meaningless. Even Rostow, an opponent of legislative attempts to curtail the executive war power, rejects this conclusion, arguing that "[t]he Constitutional pattern is, and should be, more complex than any such formula." Rostow, *Great Cases Make Bad Law*, 50 TEX. L. REV., at 851.

What is the alternative? Should "war" be defined quantitatively reflecting the level of intensity of the engagement? It has been suggested that "the meaning of 'war' in the context of the constitutional allocation of power to use force in foreign relations must be determined with reference to the purpose of the war-declaring clause: to safeguard the United States against unchecked executive decisions to commit the country to a trial of force." Note, *Congress, the President and the Power to Commit Forces to Combat*, 81 HARV. L. REV. 1771, 1774-75 (1968). Does the meaning of the term "war" affect Congress' power? Alexander Bickel argued: "There is utterly no reason to think that Congress has only the megapower to declare war in the exact terms of the constitutional clause that authorizes declarations of war and mini- or intermediate power to commit the country to something less than a declared war. Congress . . . has the power to do anything that is necessary and proper to carry out the functions conferred upon it, and upon any other department or officer of the government. If, in the conditions of our day, it is necessary to carry out the power to declare war by taking measures short of a declaration of war, everything in the scheme of government set up by the Constitution indicates that Congress has the needed authority." *The Constitution and the War*, 54 COMMENTARY 49, 52-53 (July, 1972).

## The Precedent for Executive Prerogative

Opponents of the congressional restriction of executive war powers argue principally from custom and usage. But again, there is substantial disagreement as to the proper interpretation of historical events. *Compare, e.g.,* R. BERGER, EXECUTIVE PRIV-ILEGE: A CONSTITUTIONAL MYTH 75-88 (1974); F. Wormuth, *The Vietnam War: The President Versus the Constitution,* in 2 THE VIETNAM WAR AND INTERNATIONAL LAW (R. Falk ed. 1969), and Berger, *War-Making by the President,* 121 U. PA. L. REV. 29, 54-69 (1972), with Office of Legal Advisor, U. S. Dept. of State, *The Legality of United States Participation in Vietnam,* reprint-ed in 75 YALE L.J. 1085 (1966); Ratner, *The Coordinated War-making Power—Legislative, Executive and Judicial Roles,* 44 S. CALIF. L. REV. 461 (1971); Rostow, *Great Cases Make Bad Law,* 50 TEX. L. REV., at 851-70.

1. *Nineteenth Century Practice.* A majority of the incidents of sole presidential use of our Armed Forces occurred during the nineteenth century. But it is noted that "[m]ost of them were not actions that involved conflicts with foreign states; rather, the bulk involved the protection of individuals, police actions against pirates or actions against primitive peoples. Furthermore, the United States did not have a significant standing army during peacetime until after 1945, and the President was limited in the military actions that he could take by the need to approach Congress to ask for any increase in the size of the armed forces." *Indochina: The Constitutional Crisis,* Memorandum prepared at Yale Law School, printed in 116 CONG. REC. 15410 (1970) [Yale Paper].

Does this suggest a qualitative distinction in the use of force, *i.e.,* between "important" uses of military force requiring a congressional role and "unimportant" interventions where the President may act alone? But who is to judge importance? While these incidents may seem relatively minor by present-day stand-ards, were they necessarily so unimportant when they occurred?

Nineteenth century practice also suggested a new justification for presidential intervention beyond the sudden attack theory—the neutrality theory of interposition. Most of the incidents in-volved troop landings to protect American lives and property abroad while retaining a neutral posture between conflicting interests. Note, 81 HARV. L. REV., at 1788.

2. *Twentieth Century Practice.* Beginning in the early twen-tieth century, the neutrality theory gave way to an interventionist policy against foreign states, especially in the Caribbean, in furtherance of American foreign policy. Presidential use of the Armed Forces without congressional sanction went relatively un-contested by the Congress. It has been suggested that the opera-tions tended to be minor affairs and that "it is possible to con-clude that 'war' in the sense of article I, section 8, requiring

congressional sanction, does not include interventions to maintain order in weak countries where a severe contest at arms with another nation is not likely to result. Under such a 'quantitative' definition of war, there was no infringement of Congress' power to initiate major conflicts." Note, 81 HARV. L. REV., at 1790. *But see* Monaghan, *Presidential War-Making,* 50 B.U.L. REV. 19, 26-27 (1970).

Any attempt at quantitative distinctions fails when consideration is given to the Korean "police action" taken without congressional authorization and with little congressional dissent. While consideration was given to having a post hoc resolution endorsing the action, the executive believed this to be unnecessary. In 1951, Secretary of State, Dean Acheson, testifying before Congress, explained: "Not only has the President the authority to use the Armed Forces in carrying out the broad foreign policy of the United States and implementing treaties, but it is equally clear that this authority may not be interfered with by the Congress in the exercise of powers which it has under the Constitution." Acheson added that "[w]e are in a position in the world today where the argument as to who has the power to do this, that, or the other thing, is not exactly what is called for from America in this very critical hour." *Hearing Before the Sen. Comms. on Foreign Relations and Armed Services,* 82d Cong., 1st Sess. 993 (1951).

Following the precedent set in the Korean war, President Eisenhower intervened in Formosa and the Middle East, President Kennedy acted in the Cuban Missile Crisis of 1962 and President Johnson sent marines to the Dominican Republic in 1965. While congressional resolutions supporting presidential action in these instances were adopted, there is little doubt that the presidents did not consider such support constitutionally necessary.

Does "repel sudden attack" mean the same thing today as it did in 1787? Is it feasible to distinguish between offensive and defensive use of the armed forces? Has the need for swift and decisive action made congressional control of the war power no longer feasible? *See* Ratner, *The Coordinated War-Making Power —Legislative, Executive, and Judicial Roles,* 44 S. CALIF. L. REV. 461, 466-69 (1971).

3.  *Vietnam.* Professor Alexander Bickel stated that "[t]he decisions of 1965 may have differed only in degree from earlier stages in this process of growth [of executive war power]. But there comes a point when a difference of degree achieves the magnitude of a difference in kind. The decisions of 1965 amounted to an all but explicit transfer of the power to declare

war from Congress, where the Constitution lodged it, to the President, on whom the framers refused to confer it." *The Constitution and the War*, 54 COMMENTARY 49, 50-51 (July 1972). *See 1971 Hearings* 551-53.

## The War Powers Debate

1. As the above suggests, much of the debate on the War Powers legislation has been a matter of constitutional methodology. Proponents stress the intent of the framers and opponents emphasize presidential usage and custom and the dynamic character of constitutional growth.

Alexander Bickel distinguished between growth in the great open-ended provisions of the Constitution, principally the Bill of Rights and the fourteenth amendment and "the stability of structural arrangements, the binding nature of the rules of the game, which may be changed only by express amendment." It follows, he argued, that "[t]here is a crucial difference, therefore, between extending the President's war-making power by another degree, and leaping over the brink to a change in kind, to an explicit, notorious, inexpiable alteration of the original structure." *The Constitution and the War*, 54 COMMENTARY 49, 53 (July 1972). The Senate Foreign Relations Committee in its 1973 War Powers Report similarly argued that "the notion of a 'single' living 'Constitution' ceases to make sense when it is taken as license for nullifying the Constitution's intent—or at least some part of it." S. REP. No. 220, 93d Cong., 1st Sess. 9 (1973).

2. Is the War Powers Resolution an unconstitutional infringement on presidential power? The position of the State Department was "that the description and allocation of war powers in the Constitution intentionally and wisely left the great questions of war and peace in specific cases to be resolved through fundamental political processes in which both the President and Congress participate." It contended that "the proposed legislation would alter this fundamental constitutional scheme. . . . It would either expand or encroach on the underlying constitutional powers thought to be elaborated, a revision which in any event cannot be properly accomplished absent a constitutional amendment." Statement of Charles N. Brower, Acting Legal Advisor, Dept. of State, *1973 Hearings*, 52.

Alexander Bickel, however, argued that the necessary and proper clause is constitutionally determinative. He admitted that "[t]here is a substantial area of exclusive Presidential power, which Congress cannot disturb," but he contended that the resolution "touches upon [it] only to affirm it." He argued that the real issue went to the allocation of powers in the twilight zone, the treatment of Justice Jackson's second and third zones. *See* text, p. 325. "The issue is the authority of Congress, in exercise of the legislative function, to recapture power that under the Constitution properly read belongs to Congress, although Presidents have of late exercised it independently of Congress, and to render certain a distribution of powers within the 'zone of twilight' which has in the past been uncertain. This authority of Congress may be viewed as existing in any case, because in general, Congress has the residual power . . . to do anything that perfects or clarifies or declares the structure and operation of the Government or aids its function. But the necessary and proper clause confirms the existence of this authority and frees it from any possible doubt." *1973 Hearings,* at 19, 20.

Could Congress legislate regarding the President's use of force to reply to sudden attack? Can Congress seek to control the deployment of our military forces? Could Congress prevent the President from taking action to assure the safety of our troops once they have been engaged? Couldn't any President intent on continuing hostilities justify his future actions as a "winding down" process?

**3.** *Delegation Problems.* Professor Francis Wormuth argues that the Formosa, Middle-East and Tonkin Gulf Resolutions were all impermissible delegations of legislative war power. "[T]he invocation of a conditional declaration of war changes the legal status of the nation itself. It changes the status and relations of the nation in an international order whose significant details, perhaps even its major outlines, change from month to month or day to day. The posture of international affairs in the future cannot be known to Congress at the time the resolution is passed. If Congress makes a contingent declaration of war, it is not determining policy for the future; it is casting dice." He concludes that "[t]he attempt of Congress to transfer its power and responsibility to make war to the President is constitutionally unauthorized and destroys the political system envisioned by the framers." *The Viet Nam War: The President Versus the Constitution,* reprinted in part in *Documents,* at 142. Is the War Powers Resolution subject to the same criticism?

**4.** Apart from the question of constitutionality of the War Powers Resolution, consider its efficacy in resolving the basic issues of the dispute over war powers.

**a.** Does the War Powers Resolution provide an answer to the critical question of when a President can unilaterally initiate hostilities? An earlier draft of the bill (the Javits Bill) specified the occasions for executive initiative, *e.g.,* to repel armed attack on the United States or its Armed Forces, to "forestall direct and imminent threat of such attack." In support of such a specification, Alexander Bickel claimed that it was "a full implementation of the Constitutional grants to the President. . . ." He added "[m]oreover, as a matter of effective drafting, it seems to me impossible to state with any clarity what is reserved to Congress without stating first what belongs to the President. . . . It can be done without saying anything about Presidential power, but it is my strong conviction that it could not be done nearly as well." *1973 Hearings,* at 21.

But the specification was deleted in conference. Senator Fulbright explained that it would "go too far in the direction of executive prerogative. . . . The danger here is that these provisions could be construed as sanctioning a pre-emptive, or first strike attack solely on the President's own judgment. . . . The provision authorizing the President to 'forestall the direct and imminent threat' of an attack could also be used to justify actions such as the Cambodian intervention of 1971, both of which were explained as being necessary to forestall attacks on American forces." S. Rep. No. 220, 93d Cong., 1st Sess. 33 (1973). Does the present resolution meet Senator Fulbright's concerns?

**b.** What is meant by "national emergency" in § 2 (c)? What is the import of § 3 and § 8 (d)? Are these provisions too open-ended? Do they too closely confine executive discretion? Does the Resolution draw a qualitative or a quantitative distinction between hostilities?

Under what circumstances should the executive seek congressional sanction before committing U.S. Armed Forces abroad? A second part of the Yale Paper, reprinted in 116 Cong. Rec. S. 7591-S. 7593 (daily ed. May 21, 1970), using Justice Jackson's "twilight zone" analysis looked to the respective competencies of each branch and "the probable internal consequences of external actions" and concluded: " (1) When a decision in foreign or military affairs demands speed and decisiveness, there is a presumption that it is within the exclusive power of the President. (2) *All other decisions* are within the power of Congress. Some of that congressional power is in the twilight zone and held concurrently with the President. But when the decision entails a significant commitment of the nation's human, physical, and moral resources, there is a presumption of constitutional exclusivity. The presumption can be rebutted: The President can unilaterally commit a significant amount of the nation's human, physical, and moral resources; but he can do so *only if* there is a *clear need* for speed and decisiveness."

The Harvard Note suggests: "Instead of assuming that the President may deploy American forces as he sees fit and only in the exceptional case need he seek congressional approval, the presumption should be that congressional collaboration is the general rule wherever the use of the military is involved, with Presidential initiative being reserved for the exceptional case." 81 HARV. L. REV., at 1789. Why shouldn't the presumption lie with the executive who represents a national constituency?

c. How might the War Powers Resolution have affected the handling of the post-World War II military interventions? Given the Gulf of Tonkin Resolution, would it have stopped Vietnam? Is it only a symbolic reaffirmation of Congress's war power? Is it likely to be effective in curtailing future presidential military initiatives? Former Under-Secretary of State Nicholas Katzenbach testified: "One hopes and prays that we can avoid future Vietnams; but I doubt that this legislation would be an important part of that process. Of necessity, the language is broad and the President who wishes to exploit its ambiguities has plenty of scope to do so. And he could, in my view, almost always create the public support which would give him the political license to do so.

"This problem is aggravated by the fact that to the extent the President claims authority greater than that given in this legislation he may simply ignore its strictures. In that way it could inadvertently become the vehicle for expanding rather than restating Presidential power. And certainly there are Presidential statements today, and in the past, which suggest that in the President's view he has power somewhat greater than that provided for in this legislation." *1973 Hearings,* at 24.

d. Suppose a President concludes that the Resolution is an unconstitutional condition on his powers. May he constitutionally disobey it? What remedy would be available? Cut-off of funds? Impeachment? Would the issue be justiciable? "A political question, in the broader sense, is a question which is confined to some other branch for determination. Here you have two branches, neither of which can conclusively determine a boundary dispute between them. . . . The arbiter must be the courts; anything else is unthinkable." Statement of Raoul Berger in *1973 Hearings,* at 27. All efforts to secure a Supreme Court ruling on the constitutionality of the Vietnam War failed. *See e.g.,* Mora v. McNamara, 389 U.S. 934 (1967); Velvel v. Nixon, 396 U.S. 1042 (1970); Holtzman v. Schlesinger, 414 U.S. 1304 (1973). *See generally* A. D'AMATO & R. O'NEILL, THE JUDICIARY AND VIETNAM (1972).

## C.  THE ULTIMATE REMEDY: IMPEACHMENT

On August 9, 1974, Richard Nixon resigned as thirty-seventh President of the United States. He gave as his reason the erosion of his political base and that the purpose of the constitutional processes had been satisfied. Only two weeks earlier the House Judiciary Committee had voted out three articles charging obstruction of justice, abuse of power, and failure to comply with congressional subpoenas. By the time of the resignation, House impeachment was considered certain and Senate conviction was becoming increasingly probable.

Only once, in the 1867 case of Andrew Johnson, had the House of Representatives impeached a President and then the Senate failed to convict. Only 12 other federal officials have been impeached; and only four of these cases ended in Senate conviction and removal from office. The infrequent use of this ultimate weapon in the separation of powers largely explains the confusion surrounding the application of the constitutional provisions dealing with impeachment.

"The President, Vice President and all civil Officers of the United States, shall be removed from Office on Impeachment for, and Conviction of, Treason, Bribery, or other high Crimes and Misdemeanors." Art. II, § 4.

"The House of Representatives . . . shall have the sole Power of Impeachment." Art. I, § 2, cl. 5.

"The Senate shall have the sole Power to try all Impeachments. When sitting for that Purpose, they shall be on Oath or Affirmation. When the President of the United States is tried, the Chief Justice shall preside: And no Person shall be convicted without the Concurrence of two thirds of the Members present." Art. I, § 3, cl. 6.

"Judgment in Cases of Impeachment shall not extend further than to removal from Office, and disqualification to hold and enjoy any Office of Honor, Trust, or Profit under the United States: But the party convicted shall nevertheless be liable and subject to Indictment, Trial, Judgment and Punishment, according to Law." Art. I, § 3, cl. 7.

"The President shall have Power to grant Reprieves and Pardons for Offenses against the United States, except in Cases of Impeachment." Art. II, § 2, cl. 1.

"Trial of all Crimes, except in Cases of Impeachment, shall be by Jury. . . ." Art. III, § 2, cl. 3.

The most critical and hotly contested of the issues generated by these provisions involves the grounds for impeachment. Are "high Crimes and Misdemeanors" limited to criminal offenses? Is impeachment solely a political judgment? Does it include serious neglect in supervising officials of the executive branch who commit criminal acts relevant to their office? Does it reach any "maladministration"? Does it include serious wrongdoing short of criminal action? The selections below reflect the continuing debate.

THE BROAD VIEW OF IMPEACHMENT ["Constitutional Grounds for Presidential Impeachment," Rept. by the Staff of the Impeachment Inquiry, House Comm. on the Judiciary, 93d Cong., 2d Sess. 22-27 (1974)]

. . . .

. . . The impeachment of a President must occur only for reasons at least as pressing as those needs of government that give rise to the creation of criminal offenses. But this does not mean that the various elements of proof, defenses, and other substantive concepts surrounding an indictable offense control the impeachment process. Nor does it mean that state or federal criminal codes are necessarily the place to turn to provide a standard under the United States Constitution. Impeachment is a constitutional remedy. The framers intended that the impeachment language they employed should reflect the grave misconduct that so injures or abuses our constitutional institutions and form of government as to justify impeachment.

This view is supported by the historical evidence of the constitutional meaning of the words "high Crimes and Misdemeanors." . . . It establishes that the phrase "high Crimes and Misdemeanors"—which over a period of centuries evolved into the English standard of impeachable conduct—has a special historical meaning different from the ordinary meaning of the terms "crimes" and "misdemeanors." "High misdemeanors" referred to a category of offenses that subverted the system of government. Since the fourteenth century the phrase "high Crimes and Misdemeanors" had been used in English impeachment cases to charge officials with a wide range of criminal and non-criminal offenses against the institutions and fundamental principles of English government.

There is evidence that the framers were aware of this special, noncriminal meaning of the phrase "high Crimes and Misdemeanors" in the English law of impeachment. Not only did Hamilton acknowledge Great Britain as "the model from which [impeachment] has been borrowed," but George Mason referred in the debates to the impeachment of Warren Hastings, then pending before Parliament. Indeed, Mason, who proposed the phrase "high Crimes and Misdemeanors," expressly stated his intent to encompass "[a]ttempts to subvert the Constitution."

The published records of the state ratifying conventions do not reveal an intention to limit the grounds of impeachment to criminal offenses. . . .

The post-convention statements and writings of Alexander Hamilton, James Wilson, and James Madison—each a participant in the Constitutional Convention—show that they regarded impeachment as an appropriate device to deal with offenses against constitutional government by those who hold civil office, and not a device limited to criminal offenses. . . .

The American experience with impeachment, . . . reflects the principle that impeachable conduct need not be criminal. Of the thirteen impeachments voted by the House since 1789, at least ten involved one or more allegations that did not charge a violation of criminal law.

Impeachment and the criminal law serve fundamentally different purposes. Impeachment is the first step in a remedial process—removal from office and possible disqualification from holding future office. The purpose of impeachment is not personal punishment; its function is primarily to maintain constitutional government. Furthermore, the Constitution itself provides that impeachment is no substitute for the ordinary process of criminal law since it specifies that impeachment does not immunize the officer from criminal liability for his wrongdoing.

The general applicability of the criminal law also makes it inappropriate as the standard for a process applicable to a highly specific situation such as removal of a President. The criminal law sets a general standard of conduct that all must follow. It does not address itself to the abuses of presidential power. In an impeachment proceeding a President is called to account for abusing powers that only a President possesses.

Other characteristics of the criminal law make criminality inappropriate as an essential element of impeachable conduct. While the failure to act may be a crime, the traditional focus of criminal law is prohibitory. Impeachable conduct, on the other hand, may include the serious failure to discharge the affirmative duties imposed on the President by the Constitution. Unlike a criminal case, the cause for the removal of a President may be based on his entire course of conduct in office. In particular situations, it may be a course of conduct more than individual acts that has a tendency to subvert constitutional government.

To confine impeachable conduct to indictable offenses may well be to set a standard so restrictive as not to reach conduct that might adversely affect the system of government. Some of the most grievous offenses against our constitutional form of government may not entail violations of the criminal law.

If criminality is to be the basic element of impeachable conduct, what is the standard of criminal conduct to be? Is it to be criminality as known to the common law, or as divined from the Federal Criminal Code, or from an amalgam of State criminal statutes? If one is to turn to State statutes, then which of those of the States is to obtain? If the present Federal Criminal Code is to be the standard, then which of its provisions are to apply? If there is to be new Federal legislation to define the criminal standard, then presumably both the Senate and the President will take part in fixing that standard. How is this to be accomplished without encroachment upon the constitutional provision that "the sole power" of impeachment is vested in the House of Representatives?

A requirement of criminality would be incompatible with the intent of the framers to provide a mechanism broad enough to maintain the integrity of constitutional government. Impeachment is a constitutional safety valve; to fulfill this function, it must be flexible enough to cope with exigencies not now foreseeable. Congress has never undertaken to define impeachable offenses in the criminal code. Even respecting bribery, which is specifically identified in the Constitution as grounds for impeachment, the federal statute establishing the criminal offense for civil officers generally was enacted over seventy-five years after the Constitutional Convention.

In sum, to limit impeachable conduct to criminal offenses would be incompatible with the evidence concerning the constitutional meaning of the phrase "high Crimes and Misdemeanors" and would frustrate the purpose that the framers intended for impeachment. State and federal criminal laws are not written in order to preserve the nation against serious abuse of the presidential office. But this is the purpose of the constitutional provision for the impeachment of a President and that purpose gives meaning to "high Crimes and Misdemeanors."

. . . .

While it may be argued that some articles of impeachment have charged conduct that constituted crime and thus that criminality is an essential ingredient, or that some have charged conduct that was not criminal and thus that criminality is not essential, the fact remains that in the English practice and in several of the American impeachments the criminality issue was not raised at all. The emphasis has been on the significant effects of the conduct—undermining the integrity of office, disregard of constitutional duties and oath of office, arrogation of power, abuse of the governmental process, adverse impact on the system of government. . . .

Not all presidential misconduct is sufficient to constitute grounds for impeachment. There is a further requirement—

substantiality. In deciding whether this further requirement has been met, the facts must be considered as a whole in the context of the office, not in terms of separate or isolated events. Because impeachment of a President is a grave step for the nation, it is to be predicated only upon conduct seriously incompatible with either the constitutional form and principles of our government or the proper performance of constitutional duties of the presidential office.

---

THE NARROW VIEW OF IMPEACHMENT [Submitted to the House Judiciary Comm. by Attorneys for the President, Feb. 28, 1974, Weekly Comp. of Pres. Docs., Vol. 10, No. 8, pp. 270-83]

[President Nixon's lawyers examined the English precedent on the use of impeachment, arguing that it had been used "for crimes committed against the laws relative to the individual's official position" and as a weapon for achieving parliamentary supremacy. In the latter instance, "[t]he old criminal process was distorted and turned into a weapon to remove ministers and judges for supporting policies disliked by the Commons, although even here the criminal nature of impeachment was so obvious that criminal language was still used to support such political impeachments."]

[T]he Framers, in the light of English experience, circumscribed and limited the old remedy against office holders who failed to obey the laws. They felt impeachment was a necessary check on a President who might commit a crime, but they did not want to see the vague standards of the English system that made impeachment a weapon to achieve parliamentary supremacy.

The amount of time the Framers spent on defining impeachable offenses certainly makes this clear. The whole clause is circumscribed by limits. It is limited to holders of public office. Narrow and technical language is used. . . .

. . . .

To argue that the President may be impeached for something less than a criminal offense, with all the safeguards that definition implies, would be a monumental step backwards into all those old English practices that our Constitution sought to eliminate. American impeachment was not designed to force a President into surrendering executive authority (Congress has more than adequate legislative authority under the Constitution and the amendment process to redirect any administrative policy) but to check overtly criminal actions as they are defined by the law. The centuries of political, religious, and personal misuse of criminal process, whether impeachment, bill of attainder,

Star Chamber or common law judges overbroadly defining treason, were a precedent the Framers rejected with both blood and ink.

. . . .

In our attempt to understand what constitutes an impeachable offense we must, of course, look to the intent of the Framers as demonstrated by their statements at the Convention.

. . . .

It is evident from the actual debate and from the events leading up to it that Morris' remark that "An election of every four years will prevent maladministration," expressed the will of the Convention. Thus, the impeachment provision adopted was designed to deal exclusively with indictable criminal conduct. The relevant constitutional debates support nothing to the contrary.

One further point should be mentioned. The Convention rejected all non-criminal definitions of impeachable offenses. Terms like "mal-practice," "neglect of duty," "removeable by Congress on application by a majority of the executives of the several states," and "misconduct" were all considered and discarded by the Framers. To distort the clear meaning of the phrase "Treason, bribery, or other high crimes and misdemeanors" by including non-indictable conduct would thus most certainly violate the Framers' intent.

. . . .

"Treason" is a crime defined by the Constitution and statute. "Bribery" is a crime defined by statute. Both "treason" and "bribery" were common law crimes. That "crime" means criminal offense is obvious, as is the fact that a "misdemeanor" is "generally used in contradistinction to felony, misdemeanors comprehending all indictable offenses which do not amount to felony." *Black's Law Dictionary* 1150. And in common parlance a misdemeanor is considered a crime by lawyers, judges, defendants, and the general public. . . . Further, it is obvious that the word "high" modifies "misdemeanors" as well as "crimes," as it would be illogical to conclude that one could be impeached for only *high* crimes but for *any* misdemeanors. This is further evidenced by the use of the word "and" rather than "or" before "misdemeanors." If considered in its present day context, the purpose of the inclusion of the word "misdemeanor" is to include lesser *criminal* offenses that are not felonies. But if considered in its common law context, it is meant to exclude non-criminal actions fitting into the broad category of maladministration. At the Convention the phrase "other high crimes and misdemeanors" was adopted because it had a technical meaning more narrow in scope than "maladministration." The latter term was specifically rejected in the debates as it was thought of as an unwise and dangerous invitation to make overly broad interpretations.

. . . .

That an impeachable offense is limited to criminal conduct is clear not only from the explicit meaning of the actual words utilized, but also from the criminal context of the terms utilized in the other phrases of the Constitution concerning impeachment. Such terms as "to try," "convicted," "pardons for offenses . . . except . . . impeachment," "conviction of . . . ," "trial of all crimes except . . . impeachment, shall be by jury," "the party convicted," are all terms limited in context to criminal matters.

. . . .

. . . Moreover, considerations of sound and sensible public policy, which demand stability in our form of government, assist us in understanding the intent of the Framers that a President may not be impeached for anything short of criminal conduct. The constitutional proscription against bills of attainder, the prohibition against *ex post facto* laws, the requirements of due process, and the separation of powers preclude the use of any other standard.

. . . .

. . . [T]he Framers, having in mind the difference in tenure, distinguished between the President and judges concerning the standard to be employed for an impeachment. Otherwise the "good Behavior" clause is a nullity as there is no other constitutional method for the removal of a federal judge.

. . . .

. . . [O]ne must review the four methods provided by the United States Constitution for the removal of a President. First, after a President has served his first term in office, he may be removed through defeat at the polls when he seeks reelection. Second, after a President serves a second term he will automatically be removed at the end of that term by the operation of the twenty-second amendment. Third, if a President cannot discharge the powers and duties of his office he may be replaced through the procedures set forth in the recently adopted twenty-fifth amendment. Lastly, under Article II, section 4, a President may be impeached and removed from office upon conviction for "Treason, Bribery, or other high Crimes and Misdemeanors." In sum, the clear language of the Constitution recognizes a distinction between a President who may be removed from office by various methods and a judge who may only be removed by impeachment. This distinction is of paramount importance in determining for what substantive offenses a President can be held accountable in an impeachment proceeding. In arriving at that conclusion, we can look for guidance to the impeachment trial of President Andrew Johnson. In the 187-year history of the United States, it has been the only impeachment of a President and for that reason alone it is an important precedent.

. . . .

The acquittal of President Johnson over a century ago strongly indicates that the Senate has refused to adopt a broad view of "other high crimes and misdemeanors" as a basis for impeaching a President. The most salient lesson to be learned from the Johnson trial is that impeachment of a President should be resorted to only for cases of the gravest kind—the commission of a crime named in the Constitution or a criminal offense against the laws of the United States. If there is any doubt as to the gravity of an offense or as to a President's conduct or motives, the doubt should be resolved in his favor. This is the necessary price for having an independent Executive.

. . . .

Those who seek to broaden the impeachment power invite the use of power "as a means of crushing political adversaries or ejecting them from office." 1 A. De Tocqueville, *Democracy in America* 114-115 (P. Bradley ed., 1945). The acceptance of such an invitation would be destructive to our system of government, and to the fundamental principle of separation of powers inherent in the very structure of the Constitution. If, as some have asserted, there is no appeal from the ultimate judgment of Congress, the moral responsibility of Congress is underscored in exercising its awesome power under the impeachment clause so as not to impair other provisions of the Constitution. The Framers never intended that the impeachment clause serve to dominate or destroy the executive branch of government. In their wisdom, they provided adequate and proper methods for change. The misuse of the impeachment clause was not one of them.

---

## NOTES

1. *The Framer's Intent.* At the Convention, George Mason objected to limiting impeachable offenses to treason and bribery: "Why is the provision restrained to Treason and bribery only? Treason as defined in the Constitution will not reach many great and dangerous offenses. . . . Attempts to subvert the Consti-

tution may not be Treason as above defined. . . ." When James Madison objected to Mason's proposal to add "maladministration" as being so vague as to be equivalent to tenure at the Senate's pleasure, he substituted "high crimes and misdemeanors." 2 FARRAND, THE RECORDS OF THE FEDERAL CONVENTION OF 1787 550 (1966).

Madison in the Convention debate on impeachment said he "thought it indispensable that some provision should be made for defending the Community against the incapacity, negligence or perfidy of the Chief Magistrate." 2 FARRAND, THE RECORDS OF THE FEDERAL CONVENTION OF 1787 65 (1966). And, in the debate over executive removal power in the First Congress, Madison stated "I think it absolutely necessary that the President should have the power of removing from office; it will make him, in a peculiar manner, responsible for [subordinates] conduct, and subject him to impeachment himself, if he suffers them to perpetrate with impunity high crimes or misdemeanors against the United States, or neglects to superintend their conduct, so as to check their excesses." 1 ANNALS OF CONG. 372-73 (1789).

In THE FEDERALIST, No. 65, Alexander Hamilton, in discussing the Senate's role in the impeachment process, stated: "The subject of its jurisdiction are those offenses which proceed from the misconduct of public men, or in other words, from the abuse or violation of some public trust. They are of a nature which may with peculiar propriety be denominated POLITICAL as they relate chiefly to injuries done immediately to the society itself." See THE FEDERALIST, No. 70.

2. *The Political Impeachment.* The political approach is exemplified by then-Congressman Gerald Ford's statement in 1970 during his unsuccessful attempt to initiate impeachment proceedings against Justice William O. Douglas: "What, then, is an impeachable offense? The only honest answer is that an impeachable offense is whatever a majority of the House of Representatives considers it to be at a given moment in history; conviction results from whatever offense or offenses two-thirds of the [Senate] considers to be sufficiently serious to require removal of the accused from office." 116 CONG. REC. H. 3113-14 (daily ed. April 15, 1970). A Justice Department memorandum, "Legal Aspects of Impeachment: An Overview," February, 1974, contended that "the 'political power' positions are not supported by pertinent historical sources. . . ." How does the political power position differ from the position of the staff of the House Judiciary Committee? Which is preferable as a matter of policy?

3. The Memorandum of President Nixon's lawyers stresses the criminal law language used in the impeachment provisions

of the Constitution. Raoul Berger argues that the criminal law language was borrowed from English precedent; that the framers were unable to fashion a new vocabulary during the short life of the convention; but that this in no way detracted from their objective of providing for removal even for non-indictable wrongs. Berger, *The President, Congress, and the Courts*, 83 YALE L.J. 1111, 1144-45 (1974). *Compare* Art. III, § 3, cl. 3, and the sixth amendment provisions relating to jury trial—do they provide any guidance on whether impeachment is limited to indictable crimes?

If presidential impeachment is limited to criminal offenses, what is the purpose of the provisions relating to indictment? Would this create double jeopardy problems? Would all criminal offenses be punishable? Are there any criminal offenses that would not be impeachable offenses that would immunize a president from any punishment?

4. Raoul Berger, a leading proponent of the position that the term high crimes and misdemeanors is not limited to criminal conduct argues that at the time of the convention, the term had a technical meaning derived from English precedent that was both limited and noncriminal in the sense of general criminal law. A President can be impeached, he argues, for "great" "political" acts such as misapplication of funds, abuse of official power, neglect of duty, encroachment on or contempt of the legislative prerogative, and corruption. R. BERGER, IMPEACHMENT: THE CONSTITUTIONAL PROBLEMS 70 (1973). Could a President who murdered his wife be impeached under this standard? What is the meaning of "great" and "political"? Are these terms sufficiently limited to protect the separation of powers? Would income tax fraud be an impeachable offense?

Compare the position of Irving Brant who, arguing almost entirely from the language of the Constitution, concludes that only serious criminal acts and willful violations of an oath of office justify impeachment. IMPEACHMENT: TRIALS AND ERRORS (1972). Is there anything in the constitutional language suggesting that violation of an oath of office is a basis for impeachment? The Watergate cover-up? Would this include such matters as the abuse of power? For a comparison of the two works, see Books Noted, 25 STAN. L. REV. 908 (1973).

Charles Black similarly suggests that the term high crimes and misdemeanors "in the constitutional sense ought to be held to be those offenses which are rather obviously wrong, whether or not 'criminal,' and which so seriously threaten the order of political society as to make pestilent and dangerous the continuance in power of their perpetrator." IMPEACHMENT: A HANDBOOK (1974).

## Indictment and Impeachment

5. In the aftermath of Watergate, a Grand Jury sought to indict President Nixon as a co-conspirator in the resulting cover-up. Special Prosecutor Leon Jaworski told the Grand Jury that there was substantial doubt that a President could be indicted prior to impeachment. But he added that the President could be named by the Grand Jury as an unindicted co-conspirator which it did. In subsequent litigation involving executive privilege (see text, pp. 340-48), the President's lawyers argued that the Grand Jury action was illegal and must be expunged. The Supreme Court avoided the issue.

Is a President immune from indictment prior to impeachment? Does he have the equivalent of the express constitutional immunity provided for legislative acts in Art. I, § 6? Would it then follow that the grand jury action was unconstitutional? In short, what is the effect of Art. I, § 3, cl. 4? *See* Gravel v. United States, 408 U.S. 606 (1972); United States v. Brewster, 408 U.S. 501 (1972); Doe v. McMillan, 412 U.S. 306 (1973); Reinstein & Silverglate, *Legislative Privilege and the Separation of Powers*, 86 HARV. L. REV. 1113 (1973), on constitutional immunity for "legislative acts."

6. In United States v. Isaacs, 493 F.2d 1124 (7th Cir. 1974), the court rejected the contention that a federal judge was immune from indictment prior to impeachment. The court noted that the purpose of Article I, § 3, cl. 4, "may be to assure that after impeachment a trial on criminal charges is not foreclosed by the principle of double jeopardy, or may be to differentiate the provision of the Constitution from the English practice of impeachment." The court concluded that "whatever immunities or privileges the Constitution confers for the purpose of assuring independence of the co-equal branches of government they do not exempt the members of those branches 'from the operation of the ordinary criminal laws.' Criminal conduct is not part of the necessary functions performed by public officials. Punishment for that conduct will not interfere with the legitimate operations of a branch of government. Historically, the impeachment process has proven to be cumbersome and fraught with political overtones." Should a different rule be applicable to the President?

# *Chapter 5*

## SUBSTANTIVE LIMITS ON GOVERNMENTAL POWER: THE SEARCH FOR FOURTEENTH AMENDMENT STANDARDS

### INTRODUCTION

We now turn from consideration of the division of governmental power to the limitation on governmental power. In the age of massive government, the task of securing individual rights and autonomy becomes especially difficult. Further, fundamental constitutional rights often compete with each other and must be reconciled, *e.g.*, the demands of liberty and equality, the prohibition against discrimination and the right of free association, privacy and free speech and press. There is the problem of accommodating the principle of majoritarian democracy with sufficient protection for minority rights. Questions arise whether constitutional guarantees impose only negative prohibitions or also affirmative duties on government and whether the provisions are addressed only to government officials or whether they apply also to private individuals or power aggregates in general. And, in each instance, it is necessary to consider the proper role of the courts, legislature, and executive in resolving these problems. Issues such as these will occupy the remainder of this text.

Although we tend to think of constitutional rights and liberties in terms of the various constitutional amendments, there are, in fact a number of guarantees in the body of the original document. Article 1, § 9, prohibits the suspension of the writ of habeas corpus except in cases of rebellion or invasion. Article 1, §§ 9 and 10, prohibit either the state or federal government from passing bills of attainder or ex post facto laws. Article 3, § 2, guarantees trial by jury in criminal cases except in cases of impeachment. The requirements for a conviction of treason are specifically enumerated in Article 3, § 3. Article 6, § 2, prohibits the use of religious tests as a qualification for public office. Article 4, § 2, guarantees to citizens of each state all the privileges and immunities of the citizens in the several states.

Further, as was stressed earlier in the text, the separation and division of power, with provision for checks and balances, is itself a vital means of preventing the abuse of governmental power. By defining the powers of government, and denying those not granted, the government is theoretically limited in the demands it can make of the individual. Indeed, the Framers at the 1787 convention placed such reliance on the principle of limited government achieved through enumerated powers that they defeated attempts to include a specification of individual rights. For example, it was argued that there was no need for a guarantee of freedom of speech since Congress lacked the power to enact a law that regulated speech. In fact, it was argued that specification of rights might suggest the existence of powers that had not been delegated. Further, the diversity of social and political interests in the new republic, the size of the polity, the mobility of its citizens, would all serve to secure liberty. On the other hand, state constitutions specifically guaranteed individual rights and there was a history of written guarantees in England, such as Magna Carta, the Petition of Right and the Bill of Rights.

The state ratifying conventions produced a demand for inclusion of such a specification as the price of ratification. On June 8, 1789, James Madison presented a proposed set of amendments to the newly formed House of Representatives. From these came the first ten amendments, the Bill of Rights, which became part of the Constitution on December 15, 1791. Today the states debate the addition of the twenty-seventh amendment on women's rights.

The focus of this chapter will be on the early implementation and failure to implement these guarantees through adjudication. In Chapter 13, consideration will be given Congress' power to promote individual liberty through legislation implementing the constitutional amendments. The concern of the present chapter is principally on the early search for *substantive* limitations on federal and state governmental power imposed by the due process clause of the fifth amendment and the guarantees set forth in the first section of the fourteenth amendment. In Chapters 6 and 7, the focus will turn to *procedural* guarantees available to the individual who confronts governmental power in criminal and civil proceedings. In Chapters 8-11, we will return to the problem of substantive restraints on the use of governmental power with a consideration of the right of privacy and the development of the equal protection and first amendment guarantees.

## A.  THE HISTORICAL PRELUDE

### NATURAL AND VESTED RIGHTS: UNWRITTEN LIMITATIONS ON GOVERNMENTAL POWER

1.  *The Declaration of Independence.* When a question involving limitation on governmental power arises today, the initial reaction is to look for some potentially controlling constitutional provision. In the early days of the Republic, however, recourse was frequently made to the "unwritten law" ordained by "nature and nature's God." A general acceptance of this limitation on government in the seventeenth and eighteenth century is suggested in the Declaration of Independence. *See generally* C. BECKER, THE DECLARATION OF INDEPENDENCE (1922).

The Declaration proceeds from the premise that it is a "self-evident truth" that "all men are created equal" and endowed with God-given, inalienable rights to life, liberty, and the pursuit of happiness. To these might be added the rights of property and conscience. 3 C. ROSSITER, THE SEEDTIME OF THE REPUBLIC 108 (1953). This is the philosophy of "natural rights." While influentially discussed in Locke's Second Treatise on Government, its origins are traceable to ancient Greece and Rome. *See* E. CORWIN, LIBERTY AGAINST GOVERNMENT 10-57 (1948); Corwin, *The "Higher Law" Background of American Constitutional Law*, 42 HARV. L. REV. 149, 165 (1928). It is questionable that the designated rights were all viewed as equally inalienable, since some were partially surrendered as a consequence of living in civil society. Nevertheless, there was acceptance that there are limits on the claims that government can make on an individual that are not dependent on human laws and constitutions but belong naturally to all persons.

But if a government abuses its power and contravenes this higher authority, what is the remedy? The answer of the Declaration was revolution. A more temperate alternative is judicial invalidation. In Dr. Bonham's Case, 8 Co. 113b, 118a, Lord Coke stated: "And it appears in our books, that in many cases, the common law will controul Acts of Parliament, and sometimes adjudge them to be utterly void: For when an Act of Parliament is against common right and reason, or repugnant, or impossible to be performed, the common law will controul it, and adjudge such Act to be void. . . ." And as indicated above, judicial review is part of the American legal framework.

2.  *Judicial Review Based on Natural Rights.* An early example of judicial implementation of this natural rights philosophy came in Calder v. Bull, 3 U.S. (3 Dall.) 386 (1798), involving the validity of a Connecticut law overturning a probate court decree

and granting a new hearing to certain claimants under a will. The legislation was attacked as an ex post facto law prohibited by Art. I, § 10. While the court held that the constitutional provision applied only to penal, not civil legislation, Justice Samuel Chase, commented on the limitations of governmental power arising from the social compact.

"I cannot subscribe to the omnipotence of a state legislature, or that it is absolute and without control; although its authority should not be expressly restrained by the Constitution, or fundamental law of the state. The people of the United States erected their constitutions or forms of government, to establish justice, to promote the general welfare, to secure the blessings of liberty, and to protect their persons and property from violence. The purposes for which men enter into society will determine the nature and terms of the social compact; and as they are the foundation of the legislative power, they will decide what are proper objects of it. The nature, and ends of legislative power will limit the exercise of it. This fundamental principle flows from the very nature of our free republican governments, that no man should be compelled to do what the laws do not require; nor to refrain from acts which the laws permit. There are acts which the federal, or state legislature cannot do, without exceeding their authority. There are certain vital principles in our free republican governments, which will determine and overrule an apparent and flagrant abuse of legislative power; as to authorize manifest injustice by positive law; or to take away that security for personal liberty, or private property, for the protection whereof the government was established. An act of the legislature (for I cannot call it a law), contrary to the great first principles of the social compact, cannot be considered a rightful exercise of legislative authority. The obligation of a law, in governments established on express compact, and on republican principles, must be determined by the nature of the power on which it is founded."

Justice Iredell, in a separate opinion, admitted that "some speculative jurists have held, that a legislative act against natural justice must, in itself, be void" but he rejected the power of a court, in the absence of any constitutional restraints, to declare the law void. Quoting Sir William Blackstone, Justice Iredell argued, that "[I]t has been the policy of all the American states, which have, individually, framed their state constitutions, since the Revolution, and of the people of the United States, when they framed the Federal Constitution, to define with precision the objects of the legislative power, and to restrain its exercise within marked and settled boundaries. If any act of Congress, or of the legislature of a state, violates those constitutional provisions, it is undoubtedly void." On the other hand, he contended that if "the legislature of the Union, or the legislature of any member of the Union shall pass a law, within the general scope of their constitutional power, the court cannot pronounce it to be void, merely because it is, in their judgment, contrary to the principles of natural justice. The ideas of natural justice are regulated by no fixed standard: the ablest and the purest men have differed upon the subject; and all that the court could properly say, in such an event, would be, that the legislature (possessed of an equal right of opinion) had passed an act which, in the opinion of the judges, was inconsistent with the abstract principles of natural justice. . . ."

Which opinion do you think has the better of the argument? It has been suggested that "[i]n the last analysis, the law of nature is nothing more or less than the popular conception of justice and right. Jefferson's use of it as a justification for revolution is less troublesome than its use by Chase as a basis for judicial review. A revolution will occur only when a group, powerful enough to overthrow the government, demands a change. But may the application of an unwritten law be left to a court with safety? . . . To give [a court] such discretion is to give [it] a veto power over legislative enactments." Howe, *The Meaning of "Due Process of Law" Prior to the Adoption of the Fourteenth Amendment*, 18 CALIF. L. REV. 583, 591 (1930). As you read the materials below, consider which opinion has emerged victorious, in form and in fact.

In any case, the natural rights philosophy was to dominate judicial decision-making through much of the early nineteenth century. And, in the process, the courts fashioned what has been called "the basic doctrine of American constitutional law," the doctrine of vested rights.

**3.** *The Doctrine of Vested Rights.* This doctrine, "setting out with the assumption that the property right is fundamental, treats any law impairing *vested rights,* whatever its intention, as a bill of pains and penalties, and so, void." Corwin, *The Basic Doctrine of American Constitutional Law,* 12 MICH. L. REV. 243, 255 (1914). *See generally,* E. CORWIN, LIBERTY AGAINST GOVERNMENT (1948).

The shield erected around property rights from legislative attack is said by Corwin to have "represented the essential spirit and point of view of the founders of American Constitutional Law, who saw before them the same problem that had confronted the Convention of 1787, namely, the problem of harmonizing majority rule with minority rights, or more specifically, the republican institutions with the security of property, contracts, and commerce." Corwin, *The Basic Doctrine of American Constitutional Law,* 12 MICH. L. REV. 276.

In the light of its animus in favor of property, it is not surprising that critics of the doctrine of vested rights viewed it as a bulwark of aristocracy. On the other hand, James Madison, in his Essay on Property, suggested a broader meaning to the right of property: "This term means 'that dominion which one man claims and exercises over the external things of the world, in exclusion of every other individual.' But in its larger and juster meaning, it embraces everything to which a man may attach a value and may have a right; and which leaves to everyone else the like advantage. In the former sense, a man's land, or merchandise, or money is called his property. In the latter sense, a man has property in his opinions and a free communication of them. He has a property of peculiar value in his religious opinions, and in the profession and practice dictated by them. He has a property dear to him in the safety and liberty of his person. He has equal property in the free use of his faculties and free choice of the objects on which to employ them. In a word, as a man is said to have a right to his property, he may be equally said to have a property in his right."

Madison to the contrary, the doctrine of vested rights was used by the courts principally as a bulwark of economic property interests against state legislative intrusion. But if the doctrine was to provide a secure base even for economic interests, it needed a constitutional nexus rather than the vagaries of natural rights jurisprudence.

## FIFTH AMENDMENT DUE PROCESS

The fifth amendment guarantees that no person shall be deprived of life, liberty or property without due process of law. Could this provision provide a safe constitutional nexus for the doctrine of vested rights?

1. *Origins of the Due Process Clause.* The due process principle derives from the "law of the land" clause in Ch. 29 of Magna Carta, providing that "no freeman shall be taken, imprisoned, disseized, outlawed, or in any way destroyed, nor will we proceed against him or prosecute him, except by the lawful judgment of his peers, and by the law of the land." Later, Ch. 3 of 28 Edw. III (1355), guaranteed that "no man of what state or condition he be, shall be put out of his lands or tenements, nor taken, nor imprisoned, nor disinherited, nor put to death, without he be brought to answer by due process of law." This assurance was reaffirmed in the Petition of Right.

The guarantee in one form or the other found its way into most early state constitutions. While the two clauses came to be used interchangeably, American courts, unlike their English counterparts, treated the clause as a restriction not only on the King or executive and the judiciary but also on the legislature. Murray v. Hoboken Land & Improvement Co., 59 U.S. (18 How.) 272 (1856). There is serious question, however, that either phrase was originally intended to provide a substantive, rather than a procedural, limitation on governmental power. "To the lay mind the term 'due process of law' suggests at once a form of trial, with the result that if it limits the legislature at all, it is only when that body is delineating the *process* whereby the legislative will is to be applied to specific cases; and a little research soon demonstrates that the lay mind is probably right so far as the history of the matter is concerned." E. CORWIN, THE TWILIGHT OF THE SUPREME COURT: A HISTORY OF OUR CONSTITUTIONAL THEORY 68-69 (1934). *See* E. CORWIN, LIBERTY AGAINST GOVERNMENT 91 (1948); Corwin, *The Doctrine of Due Process of Law Before the Civil War*, 24 HARV. L. REV. 366, 370-73 (1911).

2. *State Due Process Guarantees.* While early state cases rejected attempts to read their "law of the land" or "due process" guarantees as a sanctuary for the doctrine of vested rights, the principle gradually found acceptance. Wynehamer v. People, 13 N.Y. (3 Kernan) 378 (1856), described by Corwin as providing "a new starting point in the history of due process of law" (E. CORWIN, LIBERTY AGAINST GOVERNMENT 102 (1948)), involved a New York penal statute forbidding the sale and storage of intoxicating liquors except for medicinal or sacramental purposes. The New York Court of Appeals held the act violative of the due process of law clause of the state constitution.

Judge Comstock for the court, citing Blackstone for "the sanctity of private property, as against theories of public good," argued that "in a government like ours theories of public good or public necessity may be so plausible, or even so truthful, as to command popular majority. But whether truthful or plausible merely, and by whatever numbers they are assented to, there are some absolute private rights beyond their reach, and among these the constitution places the right of property."

Noting "the great danger in attempting to define the limits" of the natural rights philosophy which had previously been used to protect property, Judge Comstock saw no necessity for deciding the question on this basis. The necessary substantive restraint on legislative power was found in the due process guarantee. "The true interpretation of these constitutional phrases is, that where rights are acquired by the citizen under the existing law, there is no power in any branch of the government to take them away . . . where rights of property are admitted to exist, the Legislature cannot say they shall exist no longer. . . ."

Judge Johnson, dissenting, branded the majority opinion as judicial usurpation arguing that protection of citizens' rights from legislative abuse lay "in their reserved power of changing . . . the representatives of the legislative sovereignty; and to that final and ultimate tribunal should all such errors and mistakes in legislation be referred for correction." The majority's use of the due process guarantee placed property rights over all other rights, independent of the powers of government. "A government which does not possess the power to make all needful regulations with respect to internal trade and commerce, to impose such restrictions upon it as may be deemed necessary for the good of all, and even to prohibit and suppress entirely any particular traffic which is found to be injurious and demoralizing in its tendencies and consequences, is no government."

3. *Fifth Amendment Due Process.* At almost the same time as *Wynehamer,* the U.S. Supreme Court was giving fifth amendment due process a substantive content in dicta in the infamous *Dred Scott* decision, Scott v. Sanford, 60 U.S. (19 How.) 393 (1857). Although the case was decided on the ground that Dred Scott, being a "free Negro of African descent," was not entitled to sue as "citizen" of the United States, the court also considered the constitutionality of the Missouri compromise. Congress had no power to prohibit slavery in specified areas, Chief Justice Taney stated, because the "powers over person and property . . . are not only not granted to Congress, but are in express terms denied, and they are forbidden to exercise them." He explained this "express" limitation as follows: "[A]n act of Congress which deprives a citizen of the United States of his liberty or property, merely because he came himself or brought his property into a particular Territory of the United States, and who had committed no offense against the laws, could hardly be dignified with the name of due process of law." It followed that "if the constitution recognizes the right of property of the master in a slave, and makes no distinction between that description of property and other property owned by a citizen, no tribunal, acting under the authority of the United States, whether it be legislative, executive, or judicial, has a right to draw such a distinction, or deny to it the benefit of the provisions and guarantees which have been provided for the protection of private property against the encroachments of the government." On Taney's extraordinary use of the fifth amendment due process clause, see C. SWISHER, ROGER B. TANEY 508 (1935); Harris, *Chief*

*Justice Taney: Prophet of Reform and Reaction,* 10 VAND. L. REV. 227, 251-55 (1957).

**4.    *The Bill of Rights as a Limit on State Legislative Power.*** Neither of the above decisions, however, established the critical proposition that the fifth amendment due process guarantee was available to litigants challenging state legislation intruding on their property rights. In fact, the court early rejected the use of the Bill of Rights as a limitation on the use of state governmental power. In Barron v. Mayor & City Council of Baltimore, 32 U.S. (7 Pet.) 243 (1833), Chief Justice Marshall, reasoning that "[t]he constitution was ordained and established by the people of the United States for themselves, for their own government, and not for the government of the individual states" and that "the limitations on power, if expressed in general terms, are naturally, and, we think, necessarily, applicable to the government created by the instrument," held that "the fifth amendment must be understood as restraining the power of the general government, not as applicable to the states."

In addition to this argument based on the nature of the federal Constitution, Marshall also argued that "had the framers of these amendments intended [the Bill of Rights] to be limitations on the powers of the state governments, they would have imitated the framers of the original constitution, and have expressed that intention." He noted specifically that Art. I, §§ 9 and 10, particularly indicate whether they are to operate on the national or state government.

Finally, he turned to the historical origin of the Bill of Rights. "But it is universally understood, it is a part of the history of the day, that the great revolution which established the constitution of the United States was not effected without immense opposition. Serious fears were extensively entertained that those powers which the patriot statesmen, who then watched over the interests of our country, deemed essential to union, and to the attainment of those invaluable objects for which union was sought, might be exercised in a manner dangerous to liberty. In almost every convention by which the constitution was adopted, amendments to guard against the abuse of power were recommended. These amendments demanded security against the apprehended encroachments of the general government—not against those of the local governments. In compliance with a sentiment thus generally expressed, to quiet fears thus extensively entertained, amendments were proposed by the required majority in Congress, and adopted by the states. These amendments contain no expression indicating an intention to apply them to the state governments. This court cannot so apply them."

Before the Civil War, then, those seeking protection for their vested economic property rights, and a fortiori, for their broader "property" interests in rights, from offensive state legislation, had to look either to state constitutions or to principles of natural justice. Federal constitutional protection was generally unavailable. The aftermath of the Civil War, however, was to provide new potential tools for limiting state regulatory power.

## B.  PRIVILEGES AND IMMUNITIES: THE CONCEPT THAT FAILED

The fourteenth amendment became part of the Constitution on July 28, 1868. Section 1 recognized citizenship based on birth or naturalization and extended protection against state denial of the privileges or immunities of United States citizens or of due process of law or equal protection of the laws to any person. But what did these guarantees mean and what was the purpose of the amendment? What did it add to the guarantees of the thirteenth amendment passed in 1865? Was it intended to protect individual freedom against state interference—a constitutional nexus for the natural rights of man? Was it a protection for economic and commercial interests from intrusive state regulation —the doctrine of vested rights—re-constitutionalized? Did it make the guarantees of the Bill of Rights applicable to the states? And in any case, what were the respective functions of the various guarantees of the section? The history of the amendment remains clouded and uncertain and subject to varying interpretations, and the present section will set forth some of the directions that fourteenth amendment interpretation has travelled.

It might have been expected that the court's initial venture into answering the above questions would involve the rights of newly-freed Blacks. Instead, the first significant fourteenth amendment case arose out of a grant of a right to engage in the slaughtering of cattle.

### SLAUGHTER-HOUSE CASES
Supreme Court of the United States
83 U.S. (16 Wall.) 36, 21 L. Ed. 394 (1873)

[A Louisiana statute incorporated a company with a 25-year monopoly to engage in the slaughtering business within a 1,154 square-mile area in and around New Orleans. This suit was brought by butchers injured by the grant challenging its constitutionality.]

Justice MILLER delivered the opinion of the Court. . . .
. . . .

It may, therefore, be considered as established, that the authority of the legislature of Louisiana to pass the present statute is ample, unless some restraint in the exercise of that power be found in the Constitution of that State or in the [thirteenth and fourteenth] amendments to the Constitution of the United States.
. . .
. . . .

The plaintiffs in error . . . , allege that the statute is a violation of the Constitution of the United States in these several particulars:

That it creates an involuntary servitude forbidden by the 13th article of amendment;

That it abridges the privileges and immunities of citizens of the United States;

That it denies to the plaintiffs the equal protection of the laws; and,

That it deprives them of their property without due process of law; contrary to the provisions of the 1st section of the 14th article of amendment.

This court is thus called upon for the first time to give construction to these articles.
. . . .

. . . [N]o one can fail to be impressed with the one pervading purpose found in them all, lying at the foundation of each, and without which none of them would have been even suggested; we mean the freedom of the slave race, the security and firm establishment of that freedom, and the protection of the newly made freemen and citizen from the oppressions of those who had formerly exercised unlimited dominion over him. . . .

We do not say that no one else but the negro can share in this protection. Both the language and spirit of these articles are to have their fair and just weight in any question of construction. Undoubtedly, while negro slavery alone was in the mind of the Congress which proposed the 13th article, it forbids any other kind of slavery, now or hereafter. . . . And so, if other rights are assailed by the states which properly and necessarily fall within the protection of these articles, that protection will apply though the party interested may not be of African descent. But what we do say, and what we wish to be understood, is, that in any fair and just construction of any section or phrase of these amendments, it is necessary to look to the purpose which we have said was the pervading spirit of them all, the evil which they were designed to remedy, and the process of continued addition to the Constitution until that purpose was supposed to be accomplished, as far as constitutional law can accomplish it.

The 1st section of the 14th article, to which our attention is more specially invited, opens with a definition of citizenship— not only citizenship of the United States, but citizenship of the states. No such definition was previously found in the Constitution, nor had any attempt been made to define it by act of Congress. . . .

. . . .

. . . It declares that persons may be citizens of the United States without regard to their citizenship of a particular state, and it overturns the *Dred Scott* decision by making all persons born within the United States and subject to its jurisdiction citizens of the United States. That its main purpose was to establish the citizenship of the negro can admit of no doubt.

The next observation is more important in view of the arguments of counsel in the present case. It is that the distinction between citizenship of the United States and citizenship of a state is clearly recognized and established. Not only may a man be a citizen of the United States without being a citizen of a state, but an important element is necessary to convert the former into the latter. He must reside within the state to make him a citizen of it, but it is only necessary that he should be born or naturalized in the United States to be a citizen of the Union.

It is quite clear, then, that there is a citizenship of the United States and a citizenship of a state, which are distinct from each other and which depend upon different characteristics or circumstances in the individual.

We think this distinction and its explicit recognition in this Amendment of great weight in this argument, because the next paragraph of this same section, which is the one mainly relied on by the plaintiffs in error, speaks only of privileges and immunities of citizens of the United States, and does not speak of those of citizens of the several states. The argument, however, in favor of the plaintiffs, rests wholly on the assumption that the citizenship is the same and the privileges and immunities guaranteed by the clause are the same.

. . . It is a little remarkable, if this clause was intended as a protection to the citizen of a state against the legislative power of his own state, that the words "citizen of the state" should be left out when it is so carefully used, and used in contradistinction to "citizens of the United States" in the very sentence which precedes it. It is too clear for argument that the change in phraseology was adopted understandingly and with a purpose.

Of the privileges and immunities of the citizens of the United States, and of the privileges and immunities of the citizen of the state, and what they respectively are, we will presently consider; but we wish to state here that it is only the former which are placed by this clause under the protection of the Federal Constitution, and that the latter, whatever they may be, are not intended to have any additional protection by this paragraph of the Amendment.

If, then, there is a difference between the privileges and immunities belonging to a citizen of the United States as such, and those belonging to the citizen of the state as such, the latter must rest for their security and protection where they have heretofore rested; for they are not embraced by this paragraph of the Amendment.

. . . .

In the Constitution of the United States [Art. IV, § 2, provides:], The citizens of each state shall be entitled to all the privileges and immunities of citizens of the several states.

. . . .

Fortunately we are not without judicial construction of this clause of the Constitution. The first and the leading case on the subject is that of *Corfield v. Coryell,* decided by Mr. Justice Washington in the circuit court for the district of Pennsylvania in 1823. 4 Wash. C. C. 371.

"The inquiry," he says, "is, what are the privileges and immunities of citizens of the several states? We feel no hesitation in confining these expressions to those privileges and immunities which are fundamental; which belong of right to the citizens of all free governments, and which have at all times been enjoyed by citizens of the several states which compose this Union, from the time of their becoming free, independent, and sovereign. What these fundamental principles are, it would be more tedious than difficult to enumerate." "They may all, however, be comprehended under the following general heads: protection by the government, with the right to acquire and possess property of every kind, and to pursue and obtain happiness and safety, subject, nevertheless, to such restraints as the government may prescribe for the general good of the whole."

. . . The description, when taken to include others not named, but which are of the same general character, embraces nearly every civil right for the establishment and protection of which organized government is instituted. They are, in the language of Judge Washington, those rights which are fundamental. Throughout his opinion, they are spoken of as rights belonging to the individual as a citizen of a state. They are so spoken of in the constitutional provision which he was construing. And they have always been held to be the class of rights which the state governments were created to establish and secure.

. . . .

The constitutional provision . . . did not create those rights, which it called privileges and immunities of citizens of the states. It threw around them in that clause no security for the citizen of the state in which they were claimed or exercised. Nor did it profess to control the power of the state governments over the rights of its own citizens.

Its sole purpose was to declare to the several states, that whatever those rights, as you grant or establish them to your own citizens, or as you limit or qualify, or impose restrictions on their exercise, the same, neither more nor less, shall be the measure of the rights of citizens of other states within your jurisdiction.

It would be the vainest show of learning to attempt to prove by citations of authority, that up to the adoption of the recent Amendments, no claim or pretense was set up that those rights depended on the Federal government for their existence or protection, beyond the very few express limitations which the Federal Constitution imposed upon the states—such, for instance, as the prohibition against *ex post facto* laws, bills of attainder, and laws impairing the obligation of contracts. But with the exception of these and a few other restrictions, the entire domain of the privileges and immunities of citizens of the states, as above defined, lay within the constitutional and legislative power of the states, and without that of the Federal government. Was it the purpose of the 14th Amendment, by the simple declaration that no state should make or enforce any law which shall abridge the privileges and immunities of citizens of the United States, to transfer the security and protection of all the civil rights which we have mentioned, from the states to the Federal government? And where it is declared that Congress shall have the power to enforce that article, was it intended to bring within the power of Congress the entire domain of civil rights heretofore belonging exclusively to the states?

All this and more must follow, if the proposition of the plaintiffs in error be sound. For not only are these rights subject to the control of Congress whenever in its discretion any of them are supposed to be abridged by state legislation, but that body may also pass laws in advance, limiting and restricting the exercise of legislative power by the states, in their most ordinary and usual functions, as in its judgment it may think proper on all such subjects. And still further, such a construction . . . would constitute this court a perpetual censor upon all legislation of the states, on the civil rights of their own citizens, with authority to nullify such as it did not approve as consistent with those rights, as they existed at the time of the adoption of this Amendment. The argument, we admit, is not always the most conclusive which is drawn from the consequences urged against the adoption of a particular construction of an instrument. But when, as in the case before us, these consequences are so serious, so far reaching and pervading, so great a departure from the structure and spirit of our institutions; when the effect is to fetter and degrade the state governments by subjecting them to the control of Congress, in the exercise of powers heretofore universally conceded to them of the most ordinary and fundamental character; when in fact it radically changes the whole theory of the relations of the state and Federal governments to each other and of both these governments to the people; the argument has a force that is irresistible, in the absence of language which expresses such a purpose too clearly to admit of doubt.

We are convinced that no such results were intended by the Congress which proposed these amendments, nor by the legislatures of the states, which ratified them.

Having shown that the privileges and immunities relied on in the argument are those which belong to citizens of the states as such, and that they are left to the state governments for security and protection, and not by this article placed under the special care of the Federal government, we may hold ourselves excused from defining the privileges and immunities of citizens of the United States which no state can abridge, until some case involving those privileges may make it necessary to do so.

But lest it should be said that no such privileges and immunities are to be found if those we have been considering are excluded, we venture to suggest some which owe their existence to the Federal government, its national character, its Constitution, or its laws.

One of these is well described in the case of Crandall v. Nevada, 6 Wall. 36. It is said to be the right of the citizen of this great country, protected by implied guaranties of its Constitution, "to come to the seat of government to assert any claim he may have upon that government, to transact any business he may have with it, to seek its protection, to share its offices, to engage in administering its functions. He has the right of free access to its seaports, through which all operations of foreign commerce are conducted, to the sub-treasuries, land-offices, and courts of justice in the several states." . . .

Another privilege of a citizen of the United States is to demand the care and protection of the Federal government over his life,

liberty, and property when on the high seas or within the jurisdiction of a foreign government. . . . The right to peaceably
assemble and petition for redress of grievances, the privilege of
the writ of habeas corpus, are rights of the citizen guaranteed by
the Federal Constitution. The right to use the navigable waters
of the United States, however they may penetrate the territory of
the several states, and all rights secured to our citizens by treaties
with foreign nations, are dependent upon citizenship of the
United States, and not citizenship of a state. One of these privileges is conferred by the very article under consideration. It is
that a citizen of the United States can, of his own volition, become
a citizen of any state of the Union by a bona fide residence
therein, with the same rights as other citizens of that state. To
these may be added the rights secured by the 13th and 15th articles of Amendment, and by the other clause of the Fourteenth,
next to be considered.

But it is useless to pursue this branch of the inquiry, since we
are of opinion that the rights claimed by these plaintiffs in error,
if they have any existence, are not privileges and immunities of
citizens of the United States within the meaning of the clause of
the 14th Amendment under consideration.

. . . .

The argument has not been much pressed in these cases that
the defendant's charter deprives the plaintiffs of their property
without due process of law, or that it denies to them the equal
protection of the law. . . .

We are not without judicial interpretation, therefore, both
state and national, of the meaning of [the due process] clause.
And it is sufficient to say that under no construction of that provision that we have ever seen, or any that we deem admissible,
can the restraint imposed by the state of Louisiana upon the
exercise of their trade by the butchers of New Orleans be held
to be a deprivation of property within the meaning of that
provision.

"Nor shall any state deny to any person within its jurisdiction
the equal protection of the laws."

In the light of the history of these amendments, and the
pervading purpose of them, which we have already discussed, it
is not difficult to give a meaning to this clause. The existence of
laws in the states where the newly emancipated negroes resided,
which discriminated with gross injustice and hardship against
them as a class, was the evil to be remedied by this clause, and by
it such laws are forbidden.

If, however, the states did not conform their laws to its
requirements, then by the 5th section of the article of amendment

Congress was authorized to enforce it by suitable legislation. We doubt very much whether any action of a state not directed by way of discrimination against the negroes as a class, or on account of their race, will ever be held to come within the purview of this provision. It is so clearly a provision for that race and that emergency, that a strong case would be necessary for its application to any other. But as it is a state that is to be dealt with, and not alone the validity of its laws, we may safely leave that matter until Congress shall have exercised its power, or some case of state oppression, by denial of equal justice in its courts, shall have claimed a decision at our hands. We find no such case in the one before us, and we do not deem it necessary to go over the argument again, as it may have relation to this particular clause of the Amendment.

. . . .

Affirmed.

Justice FIELD, dissenting:

. . . .

. . . The counsel of the plaintiffs in error . . . contend that "wherever a law of a state, or a law of the United States, makes a discrimination between classes of persons, which deprive the one class of their freedom or their property, or which makes a caste of them to subserve the power, pride, avarice, vanity, or vengence of others," there involuntary servitude exists within the meaning of the 13th Amendment.

It is not necessary in my judgment, for the disposition of the present case in favor of the plaintiffs in error, to accept as entirely correct this conclusion of counsel. It, however, finds support in the act of Congress known as the civil rights act, which was framed and adopted upon a construction of the 13th Amendment, giving to its language a similar breadth. . . . Its 1st section declares that all persons born in the United States, and not subject to any foreign power, excluding Indians not taxed, are "citizens of the United States," and that "such citizens, of every race and color, without regard to any previous condition of slavery, or involuntary servitude, except as a punishment for crime, whereof the party shall have been duly convicted, shall have the same right in every state and territory in the United States to make and enforce contracts, to sue, be parties, and give evidence, to inherit, purchase, lease, sell, hold, and convey real and personal property, and to full and equal benefit of all laws and proceedings for the security of persons and property, as enjoyed by white citizens."

This legislation was supported upon the theory that citizens of the United States as such were entitled to the rights and privileges enumerated, and that to deny to any such citizen equality in these rights and privileges with others was, to the extent of the denial, subjecting him to an involuntary servitude. . . .

. . . .

. . . The provisions of the Fourteenth Amendment, which is properly a supplement to the thirteenth, cover, in my judgment, the case before us, and inhibit any legislation which confers special and exclusive privileges like these under consideration. The Amendment was adopted to obviate objections which had been raised and pressed with great force to the validity of the civil rights act, and to place the common rights of the American citizens under the protection of the National government. . . .

. . . .

. . . A citizen of a state is now only a citizen of the United States residing in that state. The fundamental rights, privileges, and immunities which belong to him as a free man and as a free citizen, now belong to him as a citizen of the United States, and are not dependent upon his citizenship of any state. . . .

The Amendment does not attempt to confer any new privileges or immunities upon citizens or to enumerate or define those already existing. It assumes that there are such privileges and immunities which belong of right to citizens as such, and ordains that they shall not be abridged by state legislation. If this inhibition has no reference to privileges and immunities of this character, but only refers, as held by the majority of the court in their opinion, to such privileges and immunities as were before its adoption specially designated in the Constitution or necessarily implied as belonging to citizens of the United States, it was a vain and idle enactment, which accomplished nothing, and most unnecessarily excited Congress and the people on its passage. With privileges and immunities thus designated no state could ever have interfered by its laws, and no new constitutional provision was required to inhibit such interference. The supremacy of the Constitution and the laws of the United States always controlled any state legislation of that character. But if the Amendment refers to the natural and inalienable rights which belong to all citizens, the inhibition has a profound significance and consequence.

What, then, are the privileges and immunities which are secured against abridgement by state legislation?

In the 1st section of the civil rights act Congress has given its interpretation to these terms, or at least has stated some of the rights which, in its judgment, these terms include, . . . the right "to move and enforce contracts, to sue, be parties and give evidence; to inherit, purchase, lease, sell, hold, and convey real personal property, and to full and equal benefit of all laws and proceedings for the security of person and property." That act, it is true, was passed before the 14th Amendment, but the Amendment was adopted, . . . to obviate objections to the act, or, speaking more accurately, I should say, to obviate objections to legislation of a similar character, extending the protection of the national government over the common right of all citizens of the United States. Accordingly, after its ratification Congress re-enacted the act under the belief that whatever doubts may have previously existed of its validity, they were removed by the Amendment [May 31, 1870].

The terms "privileges and immunities" are not new in the Amendment; they were in the Constitution before the Amendment was adopted. They are found in the 2d section of the 4th article. [The language from *Corfield v. Coryell, supra* is quoted.] The privileges and immunities designated are those which of right belong to the citizens of all free governments. Clearly among these must be placed the right to pursue a lawful employment in a lawful manner, without other restraint than such as equally affects all persons. . . .

. . . .

What the clause in question did for the protection of the citizens of one state against hostile and discriminating legislation of other states, the 14th Amendment does for the protection of every citizen of the United States against hostile and discriminating legislation, against him in favor of others whether they reside in the same or in different states. If, under the 4th article of the Constitution, equality of privileges and immunities is secured between citizens of different states, under the 14th Amendment the same equality is secured between citizens of the United States.

. . . .

I am authorized by Chief Justice CHASE, Justice SWAYNE and Justice BRADLEY, to state that they concur with me in this dissenting opinion.

Justice BRADLEY, dissenting.

. . . .

. . . [I]n my judgment, the right of any citizen to follow whatever lawful employment he chooses to adopt (submitting himself to all lawful regulations) is one of his most valuable rights, and one which the legislature of a state cannot invade, whether restrained by its own Constitution or not.

. . . .

. . . [L]ife, liberty, and property . . . are the fundamental rights which can only be taken away by due process of law, and which can only be interfered with, or the enjoyment of which can only be modified, by lawful regulations necessary or proper for the mutual good of all; and these rights, I contend, belong to the citizens of every free government.

For the preservation, exercise and enjoyment of these rights the individual citizen, as a necessity, must be left free to adopt such calling, profession or trade as may seem to him most conducive to that end. Without this right he can not be a freeman. This right to choose one's calling is an essential part of that liberty which it is the object of the government to protect; and a calling, when chosen, is a man's property and right. Liberty and property are not protected where these rights are arbitrarily assailed.

. . . .

In my view, a law which prohibits a large class of citizens from adopting a lawful employment, or from following a lawful employment previously adopted, does deprive them of liberty as well as property, without due process of law. Their right of choice is a portion of their liberty; their occupation is their property. Such a law also deprives those citizens of the equal protection of the laws, contrary to the last clause of the section.

. . . .

Justice SWAYNE, dissenting.

. . . .

. . . It is necessary to enable the government of the nation to secure to every one within its jurisdiction the rights and privileges enumerated, which, according to the plainest considerations of reason and justice and the fundamental principles of the social compact, all are entitled to enjoy. Without such authority any government claiming to be national is glaringly defective. The construction adopted by the majority of my brethren is, in my judgment, much too narrow. It defeats by a limitation not anticipated, the intent of those by whom the instrument was framed and of those by whom it was adopted. . . .

. . . .

---

## NOTES

### An Abolitionist Perspective

1. It has been suggested that "[t]he three much-discussed clauses of § 1 of the 14th amendment were the product of and perhaps took their meaning, application, and significance from a

popular and primarily lay movement, which was moral, ethical, religious, revivalist rather than legal in character." J. TEN-BROEK, EQUAL UNDER LAW 116 (1965). The reference is to the abolitionist movement whose adherents constituted a major segment of the Joint Committee on Reconstruction of the 39th Congress that formulated the fourteenth amendment.

2.  The thesis continues that for the abolitionist, the three clauses of the amendment were part of an overlapping trilogy. "The Federal Government, it was at first assumed, then argued, had not only the *power,* but the *duty* to protect the fundamental rights of life, liberty, and property wherever and whenever those rights were abridged, either by state action or by flagrant state inaction. To buttress further the double comity clause—due process safeguard, and to give fullest possible expression to underlying Lockean ideas of human equality and of the universal need for legal protection, the antislavery theorists also developed and repeatedly employed in their arguments the equal protection concept derived from the 'all men are created equal' premise in the Declaration of Independence. By this third concept the users meant first, the citizen's right to *protection,* secondly, his right to *equality* of *protection*; these two related rights were also among his rights as a 'person' as well as among his most precious 'privileges and immunities as a *citizen of the United States'*." Graham, *Early Antislavery Backgrounds of the Fourteenth Amendment,* II, 1950 WIS. L. REV. 610, 659.

Thus, the fourteenth amendment was "a meeting ground of constitutional and natural rights." Its guarantees "were required by justice. They were indispensable to liberty. They were what governments were instituted to protect and to protect equally by laws. They were the privileges and immunities of the United States. They were the natural and inherent rights of all men." J. TENBROEK, EQUAL UNDER LAW, at 128.

3.  It was the duty of Congress to protect these fundamental rights. "While section 1 of the fourteenth amendment was thus declaratory and confirmatory, section 5 corrected the one great constitutional defect, the one pressing want which years of systematic violation of men's natural rights are demonstrated. It gave Congress power to protect those rights." J. TENBROEK, EQUAL UNDER LAW, at 233.

4.  *The Comity Clause.* Both the majority and dissents refer to Art. IV, § 2. As previously indicated (text, p. 273), the clause had become merely a bar against interstate discrimination. In fact, Justice Field had written the opinion in Paul v. Virginia, 75 U.S. (8 Wall.) 168 (1869), establishing this con-

struction. Is his dissent in *Slaughter-House* consistent with such an interpretation of the comity clause?

Does Justice Washington's analysis of the clause in *Corfield v. Coryell*, which was widely accepted at the time, suggest a broader meaning to Art. IV, § 2—a constitutional acceptance of fundamental rights binding on the states? For an assertion that this was precisely the import of Art. IV, § 2, see Antieau, *Paul's Perverted Privileges or the True Meaning of the Privileges and Immunities Clause of Article Four,* 9 WM. & MARY L. REV. 1 (1967). The author argues that "the privileges and immunities of the Fourteenth Amendment were to be those of the original Constitution —the Fourth Article—that is, the basic, fundamental rights of free men.

"The language employed by the Congress in the Fourteenth Amendment was so chosen, not to identify or create new rights, but to make it certain that the rights therein referred to were not deemed attributes of state citizenship, and not to be defined by any state."

5. *Legislative Guidelines.* The Civil Rights Act of 1866 began with a clause similar to that in the fourteenth amendment, § 1, overruling *Dred Scott.* The Act then went on to describe the rights that belong to such citizens in broad terms. While it was argued that the thirteenth amendment supported this legislation, the fourteenth amendment was designed to remove any doubt of its constitutionality. Does this Act then indicate the meaning of the guarantees of the fourteenth amendment, § 1? TenBroek suggests that both dealt with the "great natural rights of men. . . ." EQUAL UNDER LAW, at 232. What would be the status of political rights, *e.g.,* voting, under such a definition? Would it cover a right to desegregated education, to decent housing, to interracial marriage?

6. *Slavery vs. Freedom.* The passage of the 1866 legislation pursuant to the thirteenth amendment suggests, as Justice Bradley's dissent in *Slaughter-House* indicates, that that amendment had a far broader meaning than the abolition of slavery. In the debate on the legislation, Senator Howard said of the thirteenth amendment, "its intention was to make him the opposite of a slave, to make him a free man. And what are the attributes of a free man according to the universal understanding of the American people? Is a free man to be deprived of the right of acquiring property, the right of having a family, a wife, children, home? 36 CONG. GLOBE 504 (1866) .

### The Slaughter-House Reaction

1. *Federalism or Revolution.* Why does the majority in *Slaughter-House* reject the abolitionist construction of the thir-

teenth and fourteenth amendments? Is Justice Miller's argument based on a counter-reading of history? On textual exegesis? On competing value and policy choices?

Justice Miller argues that the framers could not have intended to restructure the American federal system in order to provide federal protection for civil rights. See 2 C. WARREN, THE SUPREME COURT IN UNITED STATES HISTORY 542-46 (1937), who agrees with this conclusion. *Compare* Edward Corwin's assessment:

"The debates in Congress on the amendment leave one in little doubt of the intention of its framers to nationalize civil liberty in the United States, primarily for the benefit of the freedmen, to be sure, but incidentally for the benefit of all. This would be done, it was calculated, by converting State citizenship and its privileges and immunities into privileges and immunities of national citizenship. Then by section 5 of the amendment, which empowers Congress to enforce its other provisions by 'appropriate legislation,' that body would be made the ultimate authority in delimiting the entire sphere of private rights in relation to the powers of the States, leaving to the Supreme Court an intermediate role in this respect." LIBERTY AGAINST GOVERNMENT 118-19 (1948).

2. Does the dissent adopt the abolitionist perspective? The doctrine of economic vested rights? Justices Field and Bradley were later to be the leading proponents of economic laissez-faire —limitation of government's ability to regulate vested economic property interests through the due process clause. Text, pp. 417-27. To what extent do their *Slaughter-House* dissents reflect this economic protectionism which was so strongly urged on the court in *Slaughter-House* by the counsel opposing the monopolies, ex-Justice John A. Campbell? *See* B. TWISS, LAWYERS AND THE CONSTITUTION: HOW LAISSEZ-FAIRE CAME TO THE SUPREME COURT 56-57 (1962). *See generally* Graham, *The "Conspiracy Theory" of the Fourteenth Amendment*, 47 YALE L.J. 371 (1938). It should be noted, however, that both justices included substantial discussion of civil and political rights other than economic property rights. Field, for example, argued that the fourteenth amendment was intended "to give practical effect to the Declaration of 1776 of inalienable rights, rights which are the gift of the Creator, which law does not confer, but only recognizes. . . ."

## The Continuing Debate

1. *The Incorporation Controversy.* In recent times a major debate has been waged regarding whether the fourteenth amendment was designed to incorporate the Bill of Rights and to make them applicable to the states. *See* text, Ch. 6. Does the aboli-

tionist perspective suggest that only the "fundamental" rights of the Bill of Rights were intended to be incorporated? *See* TEN-BROEK, EQUAL UNDER LAW, at 238-39. Compare the view that the amendment was intended to include the entire Bill of Rights and a great deal more, including "the whole spectrum of rights embraced in such phrases as 'natural rights,' 'fundamental rights,' 'the rights of man,' 'God-given rights' and so forth, and in such documents as the Declaration of Independence, the Preamble to the Constitution, and the Bill of Rights. In throwing together this miscellany of philosophical and historical antecedents, the interpreters of the amendments followed the example of the abolitionists of an earlier generation." H. Commager, *Historical Background of the Fourteenth Amendment*, in THE FOURTEENTH AMENDMENT: Centennial Volume 14, 24 (B. Schwartz ed. 1970).

2. But as Chief Justice Earl Warren suggested in Brown v. Board of Education, 347 U.S. 483, 489 (1954), the history of the fourteenth amendment is "[a]t best, . . . inconclusive." It has been suggested that all a legal scholar or historian can hope to glean from the historical background of the Civil War amendments is the "spirit" which gave them life and that a precise meaning of the words can never be determined. H. Commager, *Historical Background,* at 14. Thus Justice Brennan, concurring and dissenting in Oregon v. Mitchell, 400 U.S. 112, 278 (1970) (text, p. 1095), concluded that the "record left by the framers of the 14th amendment . . . is . . . too vague and imprecise," and that the amendment therefore remains "capable of being interpreted by future generations in accordance with the vision and needs of those generations."

### The Consequences of Slaughter-House

1. Whatever the historical purpose of the privileges and immunities clause, it has been rendered virtually useless by judicial interpretation. There have been occasional attempted resurrections. *See, e.g.,* Colgate v. Harvey, 296 U.S. 404 (1935) (state statute held to abridge the privilege of a citizen to lend money, trade and make contracts), overruled in Madden v. Kentucky, 309 U.S. 83 (1940); Hague v. C.I.O., 307 U.S. 496 (1939), where a minority of the court argued that the right to peaceably assemble to discuss federal rights was a privilege of national citizenship, the majority using a due process rationale.

Recently, there have been strong indications that the right to travel interstate is a privilege of national citizenship. *See* text, pp. 677-85. *See generally* Kurland, *The Privileges and Immunities Clause: "Its Hour Come Round At Last"?,* 1972 WASH. U.L.Q. 405, 415-20. Early indication of such a guarantee was provided in

Crandall v. Nevada, 73 U.S. (6 Wall.) 35 (1867); Edwards v. California, 314 U.S. 160 (1941) (Douglas, J. & Jackson, J., concurring).

2. Is the failure of the privileges clause as a source of the "fundamental" rights perhaps a fortunate, if accidental occurence? Note that the due process and equal protection clauses extend to "persons" rather than "citizens." The former, but not the latter, includes aliens and corporations. Further, "[a] relationship between government and the governed that turns on citizenship can always be dissolved or denied. Citizenship is a legal construct, an abstraction, a theory. No matter what safeguards it may be equipped with, it is at best something that was given, and given to some and not to others, and it can be taken away. It has always been easier, it always will be easier, to think of someone as a non-citizen and to decide that he is a non-person which is the point of the *Dred Scott* case." Bickel, *Citizenship in the American Constitution*, 15 ARIZ. L. REV. 369, 387 (1973).

3. The failure of privileges and immunities, is not in fact a source of modern concern. The reason is that the broader functions it might have served are accomplished through other provisions. *See* Kurland, *The Privileges or Immunities Clause: "Its Hour Come Round at Last"?*, 1972 WASH. U.L.Q. 405, 414-15.

But if the guarantees of personal liberty were ultimately to be achieved through other means, the disposition in the years following *Slaughter-House* was towards protection of economic interests. The Doctrine of Vested Rights and economic laissez-faire were given a constitutional nexus and Justices Field and Bradley had their revenge.

## C. THE RISE AND FALL OF SUBSTANTIVE DUE PROCESS

### 1. The Path To Lochner

In the years following *Slaughter-House,* the constitutional protection of the liberty and property right to contract for employment, free of governmental interference, remained a minority position. For the time being, the police power of the state continued to receive judicial recognition. But the demands of the expanding industrialism for freedom from governmental restraint could not be denied. The social context was being revised. "Due process was fashioned from the most respectable ideological stuff of the later nineteenth century. The ideas out of which it was shaped were in full accord with the dominant thought of the age. They were an aspect of common sense, a standard of economic orthodoxy, a test of straight thinking and sound opinion. In the domain of thought their general attitude was on the present. In philosophy it was individualism; in government, laissez-faire; in economics, the natural law of supply and demand; in law, the freedom of contract. The system of thought had possessed every other discipline; it had in many a domain reshaped the law to its teachings." Hamilton, *The Path of Due Process of Law,* 48 ETHICS 269, 294-95 (1938).

In 1878, the American Bar Association was formed and "became a sort of juristic sewing circle for mutual education in the gospel of laissez-faire." E. CORWIN, LIBERTY AGAINST GOVERNMENT 138 (1948). In the states, the judiciary produced an increasing supply of legal precedent for protecting liberty of contract. *See* B. TWISS, LAWYERS AND THE CONSTITUTION: HOW LAISSEZ-FAIRE CAME TO THE SUPREME COURT 63-92 (1962). And the composition of the Supreme Court itself slowly began to mirror the corporations whose interests it was ultimately to serve. As Justice Samuel F. Miller complained: "It is vain to contend with judges who have been at the bar the advocates for 40 years of railroad companies, and all the forms of associated capital, when they are called upon to decide cases where such interests are in contest. All their training, all their feeling are from the start in favor of those who need no such influence." Quoted in C. FAIRMAN, MR. JUSTICE MILLER AND THE SUPREME COURT 374 (1939).

### LOCHNER v. NEW YORK
Supreme Court of the United States
198 U.S. 45, 49 L. Ed. 937, 25 S. Ct. 539 (1905)

[Lochner was convicted of violating a New York statute prohibiting employers from employing workers in bakeries and confectionaries more than 60 hours per week or ten hours per day. His conviction was affirmed by the New York Court of Appeals.]

Justice PECKHAM delivered the opinion of the Court.

. . . .

The statute necessarily interferes with the right of contract between the employer and employes, concerning the number of hours in which the latter may labor in the bakery of the employer. The general right to make a contract in relation to his business is part of the liberty of the individual protected by the Fourteenth Amendment of the federal Constitution. Allgeyer v. Louisiana, 165 U.S. 578. . . . The right to purchase or to sell labor is part of the liberty protected by this amendment, unless there are circumstances which exclude the right. There are, however, certain powers, existing in the sovereignty of each state in the Union, somewhat vaguely termed police powers, the exact

description and limitation of which have not been attempted by
the courts. Those powers, broadly stated, and without, at present,
any attempt at a more specific limitation, relate to the safety, *powers of the states*
health, morals and general welfare of the public. Both property
and liberty are held on such reasonable conditions as may be
imposed by the governing power of the state in the exercise of
those powers, and with such conditions the Fourteenth Amendment was not designed to interfere.

. . . .

It must, of course, be conceded that there is a limit to the
valid exercise of the police power by the state. There is no
dispute concerning this general proposition. . . . In every case
that comes before this Court, therefore, where legislation of this
character is concerned, and where the protection of the federal
Constitution is sought, the question necessarily arises: [Is this a
fair, reasonable, and appropriate exercise of the police power
of the state, or is it an unreasonable, unnecessary, and arbitrary
interference with the right of the individual to his personal liberty, or to enter into those contracts in relation to labor which
may seem to him appropriate or necessary for the support of
himself and his family?] Of course the liberty of contract relating
to labor includes both parties to it. The one has as much right
to purchase as the other to sell labor.

[This is not a question of substituting the judgment of the
court for that of the legislature. If the act be within the power
of the state it is valid, although the judgment of the court might
be totally opposed to the enactment of such a law.) But the
question would still remain: Is it within the police power of the
state? and that question must be answered by the Court.

. . [Viewed in the light of a purely labor law, with no reference whatever to the question of health, we think that a law like
the one before us involves neither the safety, the morals, nor the
welfare, of the public, and that the interest of the public is not
in the slightest degree affected by such an act.] The law must be
upheld, if at all, as a law pertaining to the health of the individual
engaged in the occupation of a baker. It does not affect any other
portion of the public than those who are engaged in that occupation. Clean and wholesome bread does not depend upon
whether the baker works but ten hours per day or only sixty
hours a week. The limitation of the hours of labor does not come
within the police power on that ground.

It is a question of which of two powers or rights shall prevail,
—the power of the state to legislate or the right of the individual
to liberty of person and freedom of contract. The mere assertion
that the subject relates, though but in a remote degree, to the

public health, does not necessarily render the enactment valid. The act must have a more direct relation, as a means to an end, and the end itself must be appropriate and legitimate, before an act can be held to be valid which interferes with the general right of an individual to be free in his person and in his power to contract in relation to his own labor.

. . . .

We think the limit of the police power has been reached and passed in this case. There is, in our judgment, no reasonable foundation for holding this to be necessary or appropriate as a health law to safeguard the public health, or the health of the individuals who are following the trade of a baker. If this statute be valid, and if, therefore, a proper case is made out in which to deny the right of an individual, *sui juris,* as employer or employe, to make contracts for the labor of the latter under the protection of the provisions of the federal Constitution, there would seem to be no length to which legislation of this nature might not go. . . .

We think that there can be no fair doubt that the trade of a baker, in and of itself, is not an unhealthy one to that degree which would authorize the legislature to interfere with the right to labor, and with the right of free contract on the part of the individual, either as employer or employe. . . . Some occupations are more healthy than others, but we think there are none which might not come under the power of the legislature to supervise and control the hours of working therein, if the mere fact that the occupation is not absolutely and perfectly healthy is to confer that right upon the legislative department of the government. It might be safely affirmed that almost all occupations more or less affect the health. There must be more than the mere fact of the possible existence of some small amount of unhealthiness to warrant legislative interference with liberty. . . .

It is also urged, pursuing the same line of argument, that it is to the interest of the state that its population should be strong and robust, and therefore any legislation which may be said to tend to make people healthy must be valid as health laws, enacted under the police power. If this be a valid argument and a justification for this kind of legislation, it follows that the protection of the federal Constitution from undue interference with liberty of person and freedom of contract is visionary, wherever the law is sought to be justified as a valid exercise of the police power. Scarcely any law but might find shelter under such assumptions, and conduct, properly so called, as well as contract, would come under the restrictive sway of the legislature. . . . We do not believe in the soundness of the views which uphold this law. On the contrary, we think that such a law as this, although passed in the assumed exercise of the police power, and as relating to the public health, or the health of the employes named, is not within that power, and is invalid. The act is not, within any fair meaning of the term, a health law, but is an illegal interference with the rights of individuals, both employers and employes, to make contracts regarding labor upon such terms as they may think best, or which they may agree upon with the other parties to such contracts. Statutes of the nature of that under review, limiting the hours in which grown and intelligent men may labor to earn their living, are mere meddlesome interferences with the rights of the individual, and they are not saved from condemnation by the claim that they are passed in the exercise of the police power and upon the subject of the health of the individual whose rights are interfered with, unless there be some fair ground, reasonable in and of itself, to say that there is material danger to the public health, or to the health of the employes, if the hours of labor are not curtailed. . . .

. . . .

This interference on the part of the legislatures of the several states with the ordinary trades and occupations of the people seems to be on the increase. . . .

. . . .

. . . It is impossible for us to shut our eyes to the fact that many of the laws of this character, while passed under what is claimed to be the police power for the purpose of protecting the public health or welfare, are, in reality, passed from other motives. . . .

. . . It seems to us that the real object and purpose were simply to regulate the hours of labor between the master and his employes (all being men, *sui juris*), in a private business, not dangerous in any degree to morals, or in any real and substantial degree to the health of the employes. Under such circumstances the freedom of master and employe to contract with each other in relation to their employment, and in defining the same, cannot be prohibited or interfered with, without violating the federal Constitution. . . .

. . . .

*Reversed.*   overruled legislation of a state

Justice HARLAN, with whom Justice WHITE and Justice DAY concurred, dissenting:

. . . .

Justice HOLMES, dissenting.

. . . .

This case is decided upon an economic theory which a large part of the country does not entertain. If it were a question whether I agreed with that theory, I should desire to study it further and long before making up my mind. But I do not conceive that to be my duty, because I strongly believe that my agreement or disagreement has nothing to do with the right of a majority to embody their opinions in law. It is settled by various decisions of this court that state constitutions and state laws may regulate life in many ways which we as legislators might think as injudicious, or if you like as tyrannical, as this, and which, equally with this, interfere with the liberty to contract. . . . The Fourteenth Amendment does not enact Mr. Herbert Spencer's Social Statics. . . . [A] constitution is not intended to embody a particular economic theory, whether of paternalism and the organic relation of the citizen to the state or of laissez faire. It is made for people of fundamentally differing views, and the accident of our finding certain opinions natural and familiar, or novel, and even shocking, ought not to conclude our judgment upon the question whether statutes embodying them conflict with the Constitution of the United States.

General propositions do not decide concrete cases. The decision will depend on a judgment or intuition more subtle than any articulate major premise. But I think that the proposition just stated, if it is accepted, will carry us far toward the end. Every opinion tends to become a law. I think that the word "liberty," in the Fourteenth Amendment, is perverted when it is held to prevent the natural outcome of a dominant opinion, unless it can be said that a rational and fair man necessarily would admit that the statute proposed would infringe fundamental principles as they have been understood by the traditions of our people and our law. It does not need research to show that no such sweeping condemnation can be passed upon the statute before us. A reasonable man might think it a proper measure on the score of health. Men whom I certainly could not pronounce unreasonable would uphold it as a first instalment of a general regulation of the hours of work. Whether in the latter aspect it would be open to the charge of inequality I think it unnecessary to discuss.

------

## NOTES

1. *Liberty of Contract. Lochner* completed the merger of the concepts of liberty and property in a due process-based "liberty of contract." *Lochner* proceeds on a doubtful assumption of equality of bargaining power between employer and em-

ployees, between two "persons" one of whom happens to be a corporation. Professor Arthur S. Miller argues that "[t]he Court considered the power of the individual worker to be equal to the power of the employer—even though that employer was a collectivity, a corporation, and a person in law only by application of a transparent legal fiction—an assumption that is difficult to explain except on grounds of willful blindness or, perhaps, of a complete lack of knowledge of the facts of industrial life. . . . The entire Court at that time did not recognize that the *collective* nature of economic endeavor had created an entirely new social milieu in which ancient doctrines of individualism and of freedom had to operate. They failed to see that freedom could be limited by centers of economic power—the corporation—as well as by government." A. MILLER, THE SUPREME COURT AND AMERICAN CAPITALISM 57-58, 59-60 (1968).

*[handwritten margin note: no equal power between employer and employee]*

2. *The Public Interest.* Why isn't the public "in the slightest degree affected" by the hours a baker works? Professor, later Justice, Felix Frankfurter noted that "[t]he underlying assumption was, of course, that industry presented only contract relations between individuals. That industry is part of society, the relation of business to the community, was naturally enough lost sight of in the days of pioneer development and free land." *Hours of Labor and Realism in Constitutional Law,* 29 HARV. L. REV. 353, 363 (1916).

3. The Holmes dissent in *Lochner* has justly received long standing acclaim. How does he define the error of the majority? Is it an error in assessing the facts concerning the bakery business? Is it an error in legal reasoning? Does the error, for Justice Holmes, lie in the economic values of the majority? Or in the judicial function in judging the validity of legislation under the due process clause?

4. Is the burden of proof on the state or on the challenging party in *Lochner?* Is the legislation presumed valid? Justice Peckham claimed not to be "substituting the judgment of the Court for that of the legislature." Is this accurate? It has been urged that judges are after all human beings and "it requires minds of unusual intellectual disinterestedness, detachment, and imagination to escape from the too easy tendency to find lack of power where one is convinced of lack of wisdom." Frankfurter, *Hours of Labor and Realism in Constitutional Law,* 29 HARV. L. REV., at 363.

5. *The Proper Function of the Court.* What should be the role of the courts in reviewing social and economic legislation? It has been urged that "[e]ven where the social undesirability of the law may be convincingly urged, invalidation of the law by

*Courts should not act as the legislature*

a court debilitates popular democratic government. Most laws dealing with economic and social problems are matters of trial and error. . . . [E]ven if a law is found wanting on trial, it is better that its defects should be demonstrated and removed than that the law should be aborted by judicial fiat. Such an assertion of judicial power deflects responsibility from those on whom in a democratic society it ultimately rests—the people." A.F.L. v. American Sash & Door Co., 335 U.S. 538, 553 (1949) (Frankfurter, J., concurring). Learned Hand similarly urged deference to the legislative judgment in socio-economic questions since "the whole matter is yet to such an extent experimental that no one can with justice apply to the concrete problems the yardstick of abstract economic theory. We do not know, and we cannot for a long time learn, what are the total results of such 'meddlesome interference with the rights of the individual.' . . . [T]he legislature, with its paraphernalia of committee and commission, is the only public representative really fitted to experiment." Hand, *Due Process of Law and the Eight-Hour Day,* 21 HARV. L. REV. 495, 507-08 (1908).

6. *The Significance of Lochner.* A modern commentator on *Lochner* suggests that its great significance "lies in the fact that it was the focal point in a judicial move to fasten on the country by constitutional exegesis unsanctioned by the Constitution a pattern of economic organization believed by the Court to be essential to the fullest development of the nation's economy. Without appreciation of this dimension of *Lochner,* the lesson of this episode in constitutional history, however read, will be lost for evaluation of other instances where pressures build to induce the Court to discover in the Constitution what is not there but arguably ought to be in furtherance of fundamental postulates of political and social organization." Strong, *The Economic Philosophy of Lochner: Emergence, Embrasure and Emasculation,* 15 ARIZ. L. REV. 419 (1973).

*the Court read into the Constitution to find a basis for Lochner*

### 2. Lochner Applied

*protection of weaker party*

1. In the early twentieth century, the movement to reform evils generated by the factory system and industrial concentration—the Progressive Era—generated a mass of state and federal reform legislation. Unionization sought to provide greater equality of bargaining power between employees and employers. But *Lochner* characterized the judicial response. "Courts continued to ignore newly arisen social needs. They applied complacently 18th century conceptions of the liberty of the individual and of the sacredness of private property. . . . [T]he strain became dangerous: the constitutional limitations were invoked to stop

the natural vent of legislation. In the course of relatively few years, hundreds of statutes which embodied attempts (often very crude) to adjust legal rights to the demands of social justice were nullified by the court, on the grounds that the statutes violated the constitutional guarantees of liberty or property." Brandeis, *The Living Law*, 10 ILL. L. REV. 461, 464 (1916). *See* R. JACKSON, THE STRUGGLE FOR JUDICIAL SUPREMACY 50 (1941).

2.  In Adair v. United States, 208 U.S. 161 (1908), the court struck down a federal law which made it a criminal offense for an interstate carrier to discharge an employee simply because of his membership in a labor union. The first Justice Harlan, who had dissented in *Lochner,* wrote the majority opinion premised on the "liberty of contract" guarantee of the fifth amendment. "[I]t is not within the functions of government . . . to compel any person in the course of his business and against his will to accept or retain the personal services of another, or to compel any person, against his will, to perform personal services for another. . . . [T]he employer and the employee have equality of right, and any legislation that disturbs that equality is an arbitrary interference with the liberty of contract which no government can legally justify in a free land." Justice Holmes in dissent argued that the law "simply prohibits the more powerful party to exact certain undertakings, or to threaten dismissal or unjustly discriminate on certain grounds against those already employed."

*equality of both parties*

*control of stronger party*

Professor Swindler comments on the essential difference between Harlan and Holmes: "Harlan, looking at the word 'liberty,' saw the whole spectrum of political freedoms which made up the heritage of the nineteenth century; Holmes, looking at the phrase 'liberty of contract,' saw the word 'contract' as an instrument of economic strategy in the emerging corporate society of the twentieth century. For Harlan, 'liberty' was a universal; for Holmes, in an economic context it was relative, and to make a categorical imperative of a political concept when applied to a technical economic concept was to become entrapped by doctrines in which the word 'has been stretched to its extreme.'" W. SWINDLER, COURT AND CONSTITUTION IN THE TWENTIETH CENTURY—THE OLD LEGALITY 1889-1932 117 (1969).

3.  Seven years after *Adair,* the court in Coppage v. Kansas, 236 U.S. 1 (1915), invalidated a similar state law. Justice Pitney, for the majority, recognized the inequality of bargaining position between employer and employee. "No doubt, wherever the right of private property exists, there must and will be inequalities of fortune; and thus it naturally happens that parties negotiating about a contract are not equally unhampered about circumstances." Nevertheless, as *Adair* had recognized, the constitutional

guarantee of liberty of contract allowed the parties to determine the conditions of employment. "[T]he Fourteenth Amendment recognizes 'liberty' and 'property' as co-existent human rights, and debars the States from any unwarranted interference with either."

Justice Holmes in dissent urged the court to overrule both *Adair* and *Lochner,* arguing that "in present conditions a workman not unnaturally may believe that only by belonging to a union can he secure a contract that shall be fair to him. . . . If that belief, whether right or wrong, <u>may be held by a reasonable man</u>, it seems to me that it may be enforced by law in order to establish the equality of position between the parties in which liberty of contract begins."

*help employee to ensure equality*

4. In Adkins v. Children's Hosp., 261 U.S. 525 (1923), *Lochner* was again applied to invalidate a District of Columbia minimum wage law for women. Justice Sutherland, writing for the majority, while recognizing that there is "no such thing as absolute freedom of contract," stressed that "freedom of contract is, nevertheless, the general rule and restraint the exception."

Again, Justice Holmes dissented, challenging the expansion of the innocuous concept of liberty into a dogma of "liberty of contract"—["Contract is not specially mentioned in the text that we have to construe. It is merely an example of doing what you want to do, embodied in the word liberty.] But pretty much all law consists in forbidding men to do some things that they want to do, and contract is no more exempt from law than other acts. . . . This statute does not compel anybody to pay anything. It simply forbids employment at rates below those fixed as the minimum requirement of health and right living. . . . In short, the law in its character and operation is like hundreds of so-called police laws that have been upheld."

*the court adjusts to allow for equality and freedom*

5. It should not be assumed, however, that there were no deviations from the *Allgeyer-Lochner-Adair-Coppage* line of decision. "The tendency in the United States towards equality, early noted by DeTocqueville, had by 1900 become sufficiently strong . . . that the Court could not invalidate all efforts of legislatures to rectify imbalances in economic power. Its power . . . was never complete. Some countervailing tendencies in judicial decisions may be seen in the early twentieth century. . . ." Nevertheless the author notes that "[t]hese cases, however, are aberrations; they reveal that the principle of substantive due process had begun slowly to erode about as soon as it had been created out of the whole cloth by the intellectual heirs of Mr. Justice Field." A. MILLER, THE SUPREME COURT AND AMERICAN CAPITALISM 61-62 (1968).

In Muller v. Oregon, 208 U.S. 412 (1908), the court unanimously upheld a state maximum hour law for women, reasoning that a "woman's physical structure and the performance of maternal functions place her at a disadvantage in the struggle for subsistence" and that "because healthy mothers are essential to vigorous offspring, the physical well-being of woman becomes an object of public interest and care in order to preserve the strength and vigor of the race." The court thus took "judicial cognizance" of considerations which made woman *sui generis,* so that "she is properly placed in a class by herself, and like legislation is not necessary for men and could not be sustained [as in *Lochner*]."

## The Origins of the Brandeis Brief

Perhaps more important than the decision in *Muller* was the manner in which these premises were established. Louis Brandeis submitted a brief containing a mass of socio-economic data on the harm to women from excessive hours of employment. "For the first time the arguments and briefs breathed the air of reality. . . . [T]he support of legislation by an array of facts which established the *reasonableness* of the legislative action, however it may be with its wisdom—laid down a new technique for counsel charged with the responsibility of arguing such constitutional questions, and an obligation upon courts to insist upon such method of argument before deciding the issue, surely, at least, before deciding the issue adversely to the legislature." Frankfurter, *Hours of Labor and Realism in Constitutional Law,* 29 HARV. L. REV. 353, 364-65 (1916).

6. Again, in 1917, with Felix Frankfurter submitting a two-volume "Brandeis Brief," the court in Bunting v. Oregon, 243 *overruled* U.S. 426 (1917), sustained an Oregon law establishing a ten-hour *Lochner* day for male workers. No reference was made to *Lochner* which was clearly contrary precedent. Simply, the statute was a real health measure and therefore a proper exercise of the police power of the state.

How do you explain *Muller* and *Bunting* in light of *Lochner*? And how do you explain *Adkins* in light of *Muller* and *Bunting*? Are minimum wage and maximum hour laws different in purpose? For various attempts to explain the inconsistencies, see Strong, *The Economic Philosophy of Lochner: Emergence, Embrasure, and Emasculation,* 15 ARIZ. L. REV. 419, 438 (1973); Rodes, *Due Process and Social Legislation in the Supreme Court —a Post Mortem,* 33 NOTRE DAME L. REV. 5 (1957); Powell, *The Judiciality of Minimum-Wage Legislation,* 37 HARV. L. REV. 545 (1924).

## 3.  The Court Abdicates: The Fall of Economic Substantive Due Process

### NEBBIA v. NEW YORK
Supreme Court of the United States
291 U.S. 502, 78 L. Ed. 940, 54 S. Ct. 505 (1934)

[Nebbia was convicted for selling two quarts of milk below the minimum price set by a milk control board acting under a 1933 state law. The Court of Appeals affirmed.]

Justice ROBERTS delivered the opinion of the Court.

. . . .

*private vs. public interest*

Under our form of government the use of property and the making of contracts are normally matters of private and not of public concern. The general rule is that both shall be free of governmental interference. But neither property rights nor contract rights are absolute; for government cannot exist if the citizen may at will use his property to the detriment of his fellows, or exercise his freedom of contract to work them harm. Equally fundamental with the private right is that of the public to regulate it in the common interest. . . .

. . . .

*means related to end*

The Fifth Amendment, in the field of federal activity, and the Fourteenth, as respects state action, do not prohibit governmental regulation for the public welfare. They merely condition the exertion of the admitted power, by securing that the end shall be accomplished by methods consistent with due process. And the guaranty of due process, as has often been held, demands only that the law shall not be unreasonable, arbitrary or capricious, and that the means selected shall have a real and substantial relation to the object sought to be attained. It results that a regulation valid for one sort of business, or in given circumstances, may be invalid for another sort, or for the same business under other circumstances, because the reasonableness of each regulation depends upon the relevant facts.

. . . .

The milk industry in New York has been the subject of longstanding and drastic regulation in the public interest. . . . In the light of the facts the order appears not to be unreasonable or arbitrary, or without relation to the purpose to prevent ruthless competition from destroying the wholesale price structure on which the farmer depends for his livelihood, and the community for an assured supply of milk.

But we are told that because the law essays to control prices it denies due process. Notwithstanding the admitted power to correct existing economic ills by appropriate regulation of business, even though an indirect result may be a restriction of the

freedom of contract or a modification of charges for services or
the price of commodities, the appellant urges that direct fixation
of prices is a type of regulation absolutely forbidden. . . . [ The
argument runs that the public control of rates or prices is per se *standard*
unreasonable and unconstitutional, save as applied to businesses *for regula-*
affected with a public interest; that a business so affected is one *tion of a*
in which property is devoted to an enterprise of a sort which the *business*
public itself might appropriately undertake, or one whose owner
relies on a public grant or franchise for the right to conduct the
business, or in which he is bound to serve all who apply; in short,
such as is commonly called a public utility; or a business in its
nature a monopoly. ]The milk industry, it is said, possesses none of
these characteristics, and, therefore, not being affected with a
public interest, its charges may not be controlled by the state. . . .

. . . .

[It is clear that there is no closed class or category of businesses
affected with a public interest, and the function of courts in the
application of the Fifth and Fourteenth Amendments is to determine in each case whether circumstances vindicate the challenged
regulation as a reasonable exertion of governmental authority
or condemn it as arbitrary or discriminatory.] The phrase
"affected with a public interest" can, in the nature of things,
mean no more than that an industry, for adequate reason, is subject to control for the public good. In several of the decisions of
this Court wherein the expressions "affected with a public interest," and "clothed with a public use," have been brought forward as the criteria of the validity of price control, it has been
admitted that they are not susceptible of definition and form an
unsatisfactory test of the constitutionality of legislation directed
at business practices or prices. These decisions must rest, finally,
upon the basis that the requirements of due process were not met
because the laws were found arbitrary in their operation and
effect. But there can be no doubt that upon proper occasion
and by appropriate measures the state may regulate a business
in any of its aspects, including the prices to be charged for the
products or commodities it sells.

So far as the requirement of due process is concerned, and in
the absence of other constitutional restriction, a state is free to
adopt whatever economic policy may reasonably be deemed to
promote public welfare, and to enforce that policy by legislation
adapted to its purpose. [The courts are without authority either
to declare such policy, or, when it is declared by the legislature,
to override it.] If the laws passed are seen to have a reasonable
relation to a proper legislative purpose, and are neither arbitrary
nor discriminatory, the requirements of due process are satisfied,

and judicial determination to that effect renders a court functus officio. . . . [And it is equally clear that if the legislative policy be to curb unrestrained and harmful competition by measures which are not arbitrary or discriminatory it does not lie with the courts to determine that the rule is unwise. With the wisdom of the policy adopted, with the adequacy or practicability of the law enacted to forward it, the courts are both incompetent and unauthorized to deal.] The course of decision in this Court exhibits a firm adherence to these principles. . . .

*the court adheres to the state legislation*

. . . If the law-making body within its sphere of government concludes that the conditions or practices in an industry make unrestricted competition an inadequate safeguard of the consumer's interests, produce waste harmful to the public, threaten ultimately to cut off the supply of a commodity needed by the public or portend the destruction of the industry itself, appropriate statutes passed in an honest effort to correct the threatened consequences may not be set aside because the regulation adopted fixes prices reasonably deemed by the legislature to be fair to those engaged in the industry and to the consuming public. And this is especially so where, as here, the economic maladjustment is one of price, which threatens harm to the producer at one end of the series and the consumer at the other. The Constitution does not secure to anyone liberty to conduct his business in such fashion as to inflict injury upon the public at large, or upon any substantial group of the people. Price control, like any other form of regulation, is unconstitutional only if arbitrary, discriminatory or demonstrably irrelevant to the policy the legislature is free to adopt, and hence an unnecessary and unwarranted interference with individual liberty.

Tested by these considerations we find no basis in the due process clause of the Fourteenth Amendment for condemning the provisions of the Agriculture and Markets Law here drawn into question.

The judgment is

Affirmed.

[Justice McReynolds joined by Justices Van Devanter, Sutherland and Butler, dissented.]

---

## NOTES

1. *Nebbia* did not mark so abrupt a turning point as proponents of the New Deal would have liked. Between 1934 and 1937, the court continued to invalidate a substantial part of President Roosevelt's program. Further, the *Lochner* line of

cases had never been formally overruled. Nevertheless, the rationale of Justice Roberts in *Nebbia,* the changing composition of the court and the country, and the demands of the New Deal assured the ultimate demise of *Lochner's* economics. Simply, its nineteenth century laissez-faire principles did not meet twentieth century needs. With *Nebbia,* the court began a march that was to end, not with judicial review of the reasonableness of economic legislation characterized by restraint and deference to the legislative judgment, but with total judicial abdication. *See* McCloskey, *Economic Due Process and the Supreme Court: An Exhumation and Reburial,* 1962 SUP. CT. REV. 34.

2.  A definitive change came in West Coast Hotel Co. v. Parrish, 300 U.S. 379 (1937), sustaining a state minimum wage law. The court, per Chief Justice Hughes, overruled *Adkins* and accepted Justice Holmes' approach to the "liberty" guarantee. "The Constitution does not speak of freedom of contract. It speaks of liberty and prohibits the deprivation of liberty without due process of law. In prohibiting that deprivation, the Constitution does not recognize an absolute and uncontrollable liberty. . . . [T]he liberty safeguarded is liberty in a social organization which requires the protection of law against the evils which menace the health, safety, morals and welfare of the people. Liberty under the Constitution is thus necessarily subject to the restraints of due process, and regulation which is reasonable in relation to its subject and is adopted in the interests of the community is due process.

"This essential limitation of liberty in general governs freedom of contract in particular."

The Chief Justice asked: "What can be closer to the public interest than the health of women and their protection from unscrupulous and overreaching employers?" He stated that the protection of women is a legitimate purpose for state legislation and the requirement that a "minimum wage fairly fixed in order to meet the very necessities of existence" is a proper means to that end. Further, "[t]he exploitation of a class of workers who are in an unequal position with respect to bargaining power and are thus relatively defenceless against the denial of a living wage is not only detrimental to their health and well being but casts a direct burden for their support upon the community. . . . The community is not bound to provide what is in effect a subsidy for unconscionable employers. The community may direct its law-making power to correct the abuse which springs from our selfish disregard of the public interest." It was now Justice Sutherland, joined by Justices Van Devanter, McReynolds and Butler who dissented on the principles of *Adkins.*

Any suspicion that *Parrish* might represent only judicial solicitude for the alleged needs of women was dispelled in United States v. Darby, 312 U.S. 100 (1941), upholding the minimum wage and maximum hour provisions of the Fair Labor Standards Act, declaring "it is no longer open to question that the fixing of a minimum wage is within the legislative power and that the bare fact of its exercise is not a denial of due process. . . ."

3. In subsequent years, decisions distinguished and overruled almost all of the court's earlier laissez-faire holdings on state and federal regulation in the economic sphere. In Lincoln Fed. Labor Union v. Northwestern Iron & Metal Co., 335 U.S. 525 (1949), the court, per Justice Black, refused to follow *Adair* and *Coppage* and held constitutional a clause which forbade discrimination against nonunion employees. Justice Black declared, "This court, beginning at least as early as 1934, when the *Nebbia* case was decided, has steadily rejected the due process philosophy enunciated in the *Adair-Coppage* line of cases. In doing so, it has consciously returned closer and closer to the earlier constitutional principle that states have power to legislate against what are bound to be injurious practices in their internal commercial and business affairs, so long as their laws do not run afoul of some specific federal constitutional prohibition, or of some valid federal law. . . . Under this constitutional doctrine, the due process clause is no longer to be so broadly construed that the Congress and state legislatures are put in a strait jacket when they attempt to suppress business and industrial conditions which they regard as offensive to the public welfare."

4. Justice Black's opinion in Ferguson v. Skrupa, 372 U.S. 726 (1962), holding constitutional a Kansas law making it unlawful for anyone to engage in the business of debt-adjusting, except as incident to the practice of law, spelled "the last rites for the economic philosophy of *Lochner*." Strong, *The Economic Philosophy of Lochner: Emergence, Embrasure and Emasculation,* 15 Ariz. L. Rev., at 454. In upholding the law, Justice Black declared, "Under the system of government created by our Constitution, it is up to legislatures, not courts, to decide on the wisdom and utility of legislation. There was a time when the Due Process Clause was used by this Court to strike down laws which were thought unreasonable, that is, unwise or incompatible with some particular economic or social philosophy. . . .

"The doctrine that prevailed in *Lochner, Coppage, Adkins* . . . has long since been discarded. We have returned to the original constitutional proposition that courts do not substitute their social and economic beliefs for the judgment of legislative bodies, who are elected to pass laws. . . .

"In face of our abandonment of the use of the 'vague contours' of the Due Process Clause to nullify laws which a majority of the Court believed to be economically unwise, . . . [w]e conclude that the Kansas legislature was free to decide for itself that legislation was needed to deal with the business of debt adjusting. Unquestionably, there are arguments showing that the business of debt adjusting has social utility, but such arguments are properly addressed to the legislature, not to us. . . . Whether the legislature takes for its textbook Adam Smith, Herbert Spencer, Lord Keynes, or some other is no concern of ours. The Kansas debt adjusting statute may be wise or unwise. But relief, if any be needed, lies not with us but with the body constituted to pass laws for the State of Kansas." *See* Day-Brite Lighting, Inc. v. Missouri, 342 U.S. 421 (1952); Williamson v. Lee Optical Co., 348 U.S. 483 (1955).

5.    The Burger Court has as little sympathy for using the due process clause to invalidate state economic legislation as that revealed by the court in *Ferguson*. In fact, the Burger Court expressly overruled one of the leading remaining substantive due process precedents, Liggett Co. v. Baldridge, 278 U.S. 105 (1928). *Liggett* had held that a Pennsylvania statute requiring that 100 per cent of the stock of a pharmaceutical corporation be owned by pharmacists violated due process. In North Dakota State Board of Pharmacy v. Snyder's Drug Stores, Inc., 414 U.S. 156 (1973), involving a North Dakota law requiring that pharmacies be operated by pharmacists in good standing or by a corporation or association predominantly controlled by pharmacists, Justice Douglas, for a unanimous court, rejected the state supreme court's reliance on *Liggett*. "The *Liggett* case was a creation at war with the earlier constitutional view of legislative power, Munn v. Illinois, 94 U.S. 113, and opposed to our more recent decisions. . . . The *Liggett* case, being a derelict in the stream of the law, is hereby overruled."

6.    The deference displayed by the Supreme Court in due process review of state economic regulation is also applied to review of state taxation. In Pittsburgh v. Alco Parking Corp., 417 U.S. 369 (1974), a unanimous court, per Justice White, upheld an extremely burdensome 20 per cent gross receipts tax on parking garages. This had the effect of giving a competitive advantage to public garages, which had broad immunities under the law. A tax is not violative of due process, stated Justice White, "because it renders a business unprofitable" or even if it is "so

excessive as to bring about the destruction of a particular business." The act is unconstitutional only if it is " 'so arbitrary as to compel the conclusion that it does not involve an exertion of the taxing power, but constitutes, in substance and effect, the direct exertion of a different and forbidden power, as, for example, the confiscation of property.' " If the act amounted to an uncompensated taking of property, it would be unconstitutional. But the courts will not infer the use of a forbidden power from the fact that a tax appears excessive or even threatens the destruction of a business.

**7.** The standard by which the court presently purports to judge the validity of economic regulation was set forth in United States v. Carolene Products Co., 304 U.S. 144 (1938): "[T]he existence of facts supporting the legislative judgment is to be presumed, for regulatory legislation affecting ordinary commercial transactions is not to be pronounced unconstitutional unless in the light of the facts made known or generally assumed it is of such character as to preclude the assumption that it rests upon some rational basis within the knowledge and experience of the legislators." Application of this standard has not resulted in holding economic legislation unconstitutional under the due process clause since the time of the New Deal.

Is the court fulfilling its proper role in reviewing such legislation under the due process clause? Professor McCloskey has argued that the court "should reassert its claim to reexamine the reasonableness of economic legislation" and "begin to apply a modest but real version of the rational-basis standard in economic fields that are not intrinsically inaccessible to the judicial power." *See* McCloskey, *Economic Due Process and the Supreme Court: An Exhumation and Reburial*, 1962 SUP. CT. REV., at 60.

# Chapter 6

## THE BILL OF RIGHTS, LAW ENFORCEMENT AND TECHNOLOGY: CONSTITUTIONAL PRINCIPLES AND THE CRIMINAL PROCESS

---

### A. METHODOLOGY IN CONSTITUTIONAL LAW: THE CONTINUING SEARCH FOR AN OBJECTIVE DUE PROCESS

> The quality of a nation's civilization can be largely measured by the methods it uses in the enforcement of its criminal laws.
>
> Justice Walter Schaefer*

As we have seen, judicial reaction to the active use of the due process clause to strike down social and economic legislation resulted in a wariness of using the guarantee as a basis for decisions. But as economic "substantive due process" adjudication waned, "procedural due process" became the new center of gravity for constitutional litigation. Economic laissez-faire gave way to the protection of personal liberty. In the era of the Warren Court, judicial superintendence of the criminal justice system took on a special importance.

A new constitutional debate arose:

Should the due process clause of the fourteenth amendment be interpreted as making the Bill of Rights binding on the states? If the answer was no, and the due process clause of the fourteenth amendment had a meaning of its own, how was the definition of that independent meaning to be developed? The famous *Palko* case represents an early attempt to grapple with this problem.

Palko v. Connecticut, 302 U.S. 319 (1937) involved the validity under the fourteenth amendment of a Connecticut statute permitting criminal appeals by the state. Palko had been tried once, found guilty and sentenced to life imprisonment. Following appeal by the state, Palko was brought to trial again. Palko objected without success that he had been twice placed in jeopardy for the same offense. Nevertheless, he was convicted again and this time he was sentenced to death.

---

* Former Justice, Supreme Court of Illinois in *Federalism and State Criminal Procedure*, 70 HARV. L. REV. 1, 26 (1956).

On appeal, Palko argued that if the federal government had twice tried him for the same offense the double jeopardy clause of the fifth amendment would have invalidated the second trial. Cardozo summarized and rejected Palko's argument: "We have said that in appellant's view the fourteenth amendment is to be taken as embodying the prohibitions of the fifth. His thesis is even broader. Whatever would be a violation of the original bill of rights (Amendments I to VIII) if done by the federal government is now equally unlawful by force of the fourteenth amendment if done by a state. There is no such general rule."

Cardozo conceded that some of the values protected in the Bill of Rights, *i.e.*, freedom of expression, the free exercise of religion, the right of peaceable assembly, and the right of one accused of crime to the benefit of counsel, were also protected by the fourteenth amendment. But this was so, not "by force of the specific pledges of particular amendments" but because these values "have been found to be implicit in the concept of ordered liberty." In Cardozo's view, the double jeopardy complained of by Palko did not offend the "concept of ordered liberty." Freedom from double jeopardy was not a privilege and immunity of federal citizenship carried over to the states through the privileges and immunities clause of the fourteenth amendment. It was true that some such rights have been carried over to the states by "a process of absorption." Illustrative was freedom of thought and expression. But the Bill of Rights did not govern this situation:

> The state is not attempting to wear the accused out by a multitude of cases with accumulated trials. It asks no more than this, that the case against him shall go on until there shall be a trial free from the corrosion of substantial error. . . . This is not cruelty at all. . . .

> The conviction of appellant is not in derogation of any privileges or immunities that belong to him as a citizen of the United States.

But the essential problem endured: Was it possible to provide meaningful judicial review in the field of individual liberties without having decision turn on the subjective reaction of the judicial mind to the wisdom of legislation. Or as one commentator phrased it: "Is there a 'rationalizing principle' that serves to give 'proper order' to these adjudications?" Kadish, *Methodology and Criteria on Due Process Adjudication: A Survey and Criticism*, 66 YALE L.J. 319, 320 (1957), SELECTED ESSAYS 522, 523 (1963).

The inherent and insoluble ambiguity of judicial constitutional interpretation is reflected by the disappointment inherent in attempts at resolution of what are essentially problems of moral and ethical choice. Twenty years ago, in *Adamson v. California,* Justice Frankfurter and Justice Black each wrote separate opinions: Frankfurter wrote a concurrence, Black, a dissent. The issue between them was whether the California procedure which permits an adverse inference to be taken against an accused by his failure to take the stand violated the due process clause of the fourteenth amendment. What matters for our purposes is not the different results that each of these men reached with regard to the issue at hand but rather what united them and what divided them. What united them was a common passion for objectivity, and a common quest for a doctrinal barometer by which to ascertain when the heavy hand of judicial review should be exerted against a state law. Both Black and Frankfurter agreed that the desired test should be one which would transcend the individual preference of judges.

---

### ADAMSON v. CALIFORNIA
Supreme Court of the United States
332 U.S. 46, 91 L. Ed. 1903, 67 S. Ct. 1672 (1947)

[Adamson was convicted in a California state court by a jury for murder in the first degree. Under the California procedure which was atypical even at that time, if a defendant failed to explain or to deny evidence against him, that failure could be commented upon by the court and counsel and be considered by court and jury. The defendant Adamson failed to testify and the District Attorney commented on that failure. Adamson contended that his privilege against self-incrimination had thereby been infringed.

[The court, per Justice Reed, easily disposed of Adamson's claim that the privilege against self-incrimination guaranteed by the fifth amendment was applicable to state action by reason of the privileges and immunities clause of the fourteenth amendment. The force of precedent was clearly against such a claim. *Slaughter-House Cases,* 83 U.S. (16 Wall.) 36 (1873).

[Adamson had also claimed that his right to a fair trial, protected by the due process clause of the fourteenth amendment, had been infringed. If he did take the stand, he would be subject to cross-examination about his prior criminal record for the purpose of impeaching his credibility. Disclosure of the prior criminal record might well prejudice his case in the instant proceeding. This, he contended, would violate due process.

[The court, however, rejected the claim, again stressing precedent. *Twining v. New Jersey*, 211 U.S. 78 (1908). The due process clause of the fourteenth amendment while guaranteeing fair trial did not "draw all the rights of the federal Bill of Rights under its protection." There was nothing unfair in requiring a defendant to choose between leaving adverse evidence unanswered or responding, thereby subjecting himself to impeachment through disclosure of a prior criminal record. This was viewed as a dilemma facing any defendant. Therefore, "a state may control such a situation in accordance with its own ideas of the most efficient administration of criminal justice" without violating due process.

[Justice Frankfurter, although agreeing in the result, wrote a separate opinion in which he developed his position that the due process clause of the fourteenth amendment should not be defined by mechanical reference to the Bill of Rights. In an influential concurrence which governed due process adjudication for nearly a decade and a half, Frankfurter detailed his position that the due process clause of the fourteenth amendment had an independent potency and meaning apart from the Bill of Rights.]

Justice FRANKFURTER, concurring.

. . . .

. . . Only a technical rule of law would exclude from consideration that which is relevant, as a matter of fair reasoning, to the solution of a problem. Sensible and just-minded men, in important affairs of life, deem it significant that a man remains silent when confronted with serious and responsible evidence against himself which it is within his power to contradict. The notion that to allow jurors to do that which sensible and right-minded men do every day violates the "immutable principles of justice" as conceived by a civilized society is to trivialize the importance of "due process." . . .

For historical reasons a limited immunity from the common duty to testify was written into the Federal Bill of Rights, and I am prepared to agree that, as part of that immunity, comment on the failure of an accused to take the witness stand is forbidden in federal prosecutions. It is so, of course, by explicit act of Congress. But to suggest that such a limitation can be drawn out of "due process" in its protection of ultimate decency in a civilized society is to suggest that the Due Process Clause fastened fetters of unreason upon the States. . . .

Between the incorporation of the Fourteenth Amendment into the Constitution and the beginning of the present membership of the Court—a period of 70 years—the scope of that Amendment was passed upon by 43 judges. Of all these judges only one, who may respectfully be called an eccentric exception, ever indicated the belief that the Fourteenth Amendment was a shorthand summary of the first eight Amendments theretofore limiting only the Federal Government, and that due process incorporated those eight Amendments as restrictions upon the powers of the States.

*Court's view— not encompassing Bill of Rights*

. . .

The short answer to the suggestion that the . . . [due process clause] was a way of saying that every State must thereafter initiate prosecutions through indictment by a grand jury, must have a trial by a jury of twelve in criminal cases, and must have a trial by such a jury in common law suits where the amount in controversy exceeds twenty dollars, is that it is a strange way of saying it. It would be extraordinarily strange for a Constitution to convey such specific commands in such a roundabout and inexplicit way. . . . Those reading the English language with the meaning which it ordinarily conveys, those conversant with the political and legal history of the concept of due process, those sensitive to the relations of the States to the central government as well as the relation of some of the provisions of the Bill of Rights to the process of justice, would hardly recognize the Fourteenth Amendment as a cover for the various explicit provisions of the first eight Amendments. Some of these are enduring reflections of experience with human nature, while some express the restricted views of Eighteenth-Century England regarding the best methods for the ascertainment of facts. The notion that the Fourteenth Amendment was a covert way of imposing upon the States all the rules which it seemed important to Eighteenth-Century statesmen to write into the Federal Amendments, was rejected by judges who were themselves witnesses of the process by which the Fourteenth Amendment became part of the Constitution.

. . . .

Indeed, the suggestion that the Fourteenth Amendment incorporates the first eight Amendments as such is not unambiguously urged. Even the boldest innovator would shrink from suggesting to more than half the States that they may no longer initiate prosecutions without indictment by grand jury, or that thereafter all the States of the Union must furnish a jury of 12 for every case involving a claim above $20. There is suggested merely a selective incorporation of the first eight Amendments into the Fourteenth Amendment. Some are in and some are out, but we are left in the dark as to which are in and which are out. Nor are we given the calculus for determining which go in and which stay out. If the basis of selection is merely that those provisions of the first eight Amendments are incorporated which commend themselves to individual justices as indispensable to the dignity and happiness of a free man, we are thrown back to a merely subjective test. The protection against unreasonable search and seizure might have primacy for one judge, while trial by a jury of 12 for every claim above $20 might appear to another as an ultimate need in a free society. In the history of thought "natural law" has a much longer and much better founded meaning and justification than such subjective selection of the first eight Amendments for incorporation into the Fourteenth. If all that is meant is that due process contains within itself certain minimal standards which are "of the very essence of a scheme of ordered liberty," Palko v. Connecticut, 302 U.S. 319, putting upon this Court the duty of applying these standards from time to time, then we have merely arrived at the insight which our predecessors long ago expressed. . . .

It may not be amiss to restate the pervasive function of the Fourteenth Amendment in exacting from the States observance of basic liberties. . . . The Amendment neither comprehends the specific provisions by which the founders deemed it appropriate to restrict the federal government nor is it confined to them. The Due Process Clause of the Fourteenth Amendment has an independent potency, precisely as does the Due Process Clause of the Fifth Amendment in relation to the Federal Government. It ought not to require argument to reject the notion that due process of law meant one thing in the Fifth Amendment and another in the Fourteenth. The Fifth Amendment specifically prohibits prosecution of an "infamous crime" except upon indictment; it forbids double jeopardy; it bars compelling a person to be a witness against himself in any criminal case; it precludes deprivation of "life, liberty, or property, without due process of law." Are Madison and his contemporaries in the framing of the Bill of Rights to be charged with writing into it a meaningless clause? To consider "due process of law" as merely a shorthand statement of other specific clauses in the same amendment is to attribute to the authors and proponents of this Amendment ignorance of, or indifference to, a historic conception which was one of the great instruments in the arsenal of constitutional freedom which the Bill of Rights was to protect and strengthen.

A construction which gives to due process no independent function but turns it into a summary of the specific provisions of the Bill of Rights would, as has been noted, tear up by the roots much of the fabric of law in the several States, and would deprive the States of opportunity for reforms in legal process designed for extending the area of freedom. It would assume that no other abuses would reveal themselves in the course of time than those which had become manifest in 1791. Such a view not only disregards the historic meaning of "due process." It leads inevitably to a warped construction of specific provisions of the Bill of Rights to bring within their scope conduct clearly condemned by due process but not easily fitting into the pigeon-holes of the specific provisions. It seems pretty late in the day to suggest that a phrase so laden with historic meaning should be given an improvised content consisting of some but not all of the provisions of the first eight Amendments, selected on an undefined basis, with improvisation of content for the provisions so selected.

And so, when, as in a case like the present, a conviction in a State court is here for review under a claim that a right protected by the Due Process Clause of the Fourteenth Amendment has been denied, the issue is not whether an infraction of one of the specific provisions of the first eight Amendments is disclosed by the record. The relevant question is whether the criminal proceedings which resulted in conviction deprived the accused of the due process of law to which the United States Constitution entitled him. Judicial review of that guaranty of the Fourteenth Amendment inescapably imposes upon this Court an exercise of judgment upon the whole course of the proceedings in order to ascertain whether they offend those canons of decency and fairness which express the notions of justice of English-speaking peoples even toward those charged with the most heinous offenses. These standards of justice are not authoritatively formulated anywhere as though they were prescriptions in a pharmacopoeia. But neither does the application of the Due Process Clause imply that judges are wholly at large. The judicial judgment in applying the Due Process Clause must move within the limits of accepted notions of justice and is not to be based upon the idiosyncrasies of a merely personal judgment. The fact that judges among themselves may differ whether in a particular case a trial offends accepted notions of justice is not disproof that general rather than idiosyncratic standards are applied. An important safeguard against such merely individual judgment is an alert deference to the judgment of the State court under review.

Justice BLACK, dissenting.

. . . .

This decision reasserts a constitutional theory spelled out in Twining v. New Jersey, 211 U.S. 78, that this Court is endowed by the Constitution with boundless power under "natural law" periodically to expand and contract constitutional standards to conform to the Court's conception of what at a particular time constitutes "civilized decency" and "fundamental principles of liberty and justice." Invoking this *Twining* rule, the Court concludes that although comment upon testimony in a federal court would violate the Fifth Amendment, identical comment in a state court does not violate today's fashion in civilized decency and fundamentals and is therefore not prohibited by the Federal Constitution as amended.

. . . I would not reaffirm the *Twining* decision. I think that decision and the "natural law" theory of the Constitution upon which it relies, degrade the constitutional safeguards of the Bill of Rights and simultaneously appropriate for this Court a broad power which we are not authorized by the Constitution to exercise. . . . My reasons for believing that the *Twining* decision should not be revitalized can best be understood by reference to the constitutional, judicial, and general history that preceded and followed the case. . . .

. . . .

. . . In my judgment [the Amendment's] history conclusively demonstrates that the language of the first section of the Fourteenth Amendment, taken as a whole, was thought by those responsible for its submission to the people, and by those who opposed its submission, sufficiently explicit to guarantee that thereafter no state could deprive its citizens of the privileges and protections of the Bill of Rights. Whether this Court ever will, or whether it now should, in the light of past decisions, give full effect to what the Amendment was intended to accomplish is not necessarily essential to a decision here. However that may be, our prior decisions, including *Twining,* do not prevent our carrying out that purpose, at least to the extent of making applicable to the states, not a mere part, as the Court has, but the full protection of the Fifth Amendment's provision against compelling evidence from an accused to convict him of crime. And I further contend that the "natural law" formula which the Court uses to reach its conclusion in this case should be abandoned as an incongruous excrescence on our Constitution. I believe that formula to be itself a violation of our Constitution, in that it subtly conveys to courts, at the expense of legislatures, ultimate power over public policies in fields where no specific provision of the Constitution limits legislative power. And my belief seems to be in accord with the views expressed by this Court, at least for the first two decades after the Fourteenth Amendment was adopted. . . .

I cannot consider the Bill of Rights to be an outworn 18th Century "strait jacket" as the *Twining* opinion did. Its provisions may be thought outdated abstractions by some. And it is true that they were designed to meet ancient evils. But they are the same kind of human evils that have emerged from century to century wherever excessive power is sought by the few at the expense of the many. In my judgment the people of no nation can lose their liberty so long as a Bill of Rights like ours survives and its basic purposes are conscientiously interpreted, enforced and respected so as to afford continuous protection against old, as well as new, devices and practices which might thwart those purposes. I fear to see the consequences of the Court's practice of substituting its own concepts of decency and fundamental justice for the language of the Bill of Rights as its point of departure in interpreting and enforcing that Bill of Rights. If the choice must be between the selective process of the *Palko* decision applying some of the Bill of Rights to the States, or the *Twining* rule applying none of them, I would choose the *Palko* selective process. But rather than accept either of these choices. I would follow what I believe was the original purpose of the Fourteenth Amendment to extend to all the people of the nation the complete protection of the Bill of Rights. To hold that this Court can determine what, if any, provisions of the Bill of Rights will be enforced, and if so to what degree, is to frustrate the great design of a written Constitution.

Conceding the possibility that this Court is now wise enough to improve on the Bill of Rights by substituting natural law concepts for the Bill of Rights. I think the possibility is entirely too speculative to agree to take that course. I would therefore hold in this case that the full protection of the Fifth Amendment's proscription against compelled testimony must be afforded by California. This I would do because of reliance upon the original purpose of the Fourteenth Amendment.

It is an illusory apprehension that literal application of some or all of the provisions of the Bill of Rights to the States would unwisely increase the sum total of the powers of this Court to invalidate state legislation. The Federal Government has not been harmfully burdened by the requirement that enforcement of federal laws affecting civil liberty conform literally to the Bill of Rights. Who would advocate its repeal? It must be conceded, of course, that the natural-law-due-process formula, which the Court today reaffirms, has been interpreted to limit substantially this Court's power to prevent state violations of the individual civil liberties guaranteed by the Bill of Rights. But this formula also has been used in the past and can be used in the future, to license this Court, in considering regulatory legislation, to roam at large in the broad expanses of policy and morals and to trespass, all too freely, on the legislative domain of the States as well as the Federal Government.

Since Marbury v. Madison, 1 Cranch 137, 2 L.Ed. 60, was decided, the practice has been firmly established for better or worse, that courts can strike down legislative enactments which violate the Constitution. This process, of course, involves interpretation, and since words can have many meanings, interpretation obviously may result in contraction or extension of the original purpose of a constitutional provision thereby affecting policy. But to pass upon the constitutionality of statutes by looking to the particular standards enumerated in the Bill of Rights and other parts of the Constitution is one thing; to invalidate statutes because of application of "natural law" deemed to be above and undefined by the Constitution is another. "In the one instance, courts proceeding within clearly marked constitutional boundaries seek to execute policies written into the Constitution; in the other they roam at will in the limitless area of their own beliefs as to reasonableness and actually select policies, a responsibility which the Constitution entrusts to the legislative representatives of the people." Federal Power Commission v. Natural Gas Pipeline Co., 315 U.S. 575, 599, 601, n. 4.

Justice DOUGLAS joins in this opinion.

. . . .

Justice MURPHY, with whom Justice RUTLEDGE concurs, dissenting.

While in substantial agreement with the views of Mr. Justice BLACK, I have one reservation and one addition to make.

I agree that the specific guarantees of the Bill of Rights should be carried over intact into the first section of the Fourteenth Amendment. But I am not prepared to say that the latter is entirely and necessarily limited by the Bill of Rights. Occasions may arise where a proceeding falls so far short of conforming to fundamental standards of procedure as to warrant constitutional condemnation in terms of a lack of due process despite the absence of a specific provision in the Bill of Rights.

That point, however, need not be pursued here inasmuch as the Fifth Amendment is explicit in its provision that no person shall be compelled in any criminal case to be a witness against himself. That provision, as Mr. Justice BLACK demonstrates, is a constituent part of the Fourteenth Amendment.

. . . .

Much can be said pro and con as to the desirability of allowing comment on the failure of the accused to testify. But policy arguments are to no avail in the face of a clear constitutional command. This guarantee of freedom from self-incrimination is grounded on a deep respect for those who might prefer to remain silent before their accusers.* . . .

. . . .

---

## A COMMENT ON METHOD IN DUE PROCESS ADJUDICATION

Justice Frankfurter thought any abiding judicial interpretation of the due process clause of the fourteenth amendment had to meet two requirements. First, the judicial interpretation had to be a dynamic one, capable of changing with a maturing (or declining?) sense of decency. It would not and could not, he said, be imprisoned within the confines of a fixed formula. Second, the judicial interpretation had to be infused by an awareness that any judicial test which diminished state independence had to be used with reluctance.

The test for invalidity was admittedly an awesome one: the procedure was to be invalidated when it offended the fundamental standards of decency. But what are these standards and how are they ascertained? Frankfurter answered that they were to be found in "accepted notions of justice of English-speaking peoples."

Justice Black in Griswold v. Connecticut, 381 U.S. 479, 519 (1965), commented that "the scientific miracles of this age have not yet produced a gadget which the Court can use to determine what traditions are rooted in the [collective] conscience of our people." The court, he noted, lacked a Gallup poll. Is it possible to objectively determine social values? There has been some nascent effort to empirically investigate the moral feelings of the community. *See* Cohen, Robson & Bates, *Ascertaining the Moral Sense of the Community,* 8 J. LEGAL ED. 137 (1955). *See also* Barton & Mendlovitz, *The Experience of Injustice as a Research Problem,* 13 J. LEGAL ED. 24 (1960); Kadish, *Methodology and Criteria in Due Process Adjudication: A Survey and a Criticism,* 66 YALE L.J., at 319, SELECTED ESSAYS, at 544-59, for further consideration of the valuation problem.

Kadish suggests that the courts have referred to four sources of guidance: "(1) the opinions of the progenitors and architects of American institutions; (2) the implicit opinions of the policy-making organs of state governments; (3) the explicit opinions of other American courts that have evaluated the fundamentality of a given mode of procedure; or, (4) the opinions of other countries

---

* In Malloy v. Hogan, 378 U.S. 1 (1964), the court held that the fifth amendment privilege against self-incrimination was applicable to the states through the due process guarantee. The specific holding in *Adamson* was overruled in Griffin v. California, 380 U.S. 609 (1965).

in the Anglo-Saxon tradition 'not less civilized than our own' as reflected in their statutes, decisions and practices." Kadish, *Methodology and Criteria,* 66 YALE L.J., at 328, SELECTED ESSAYS, at 530. Do these criteria provide greater objectivity? Does the Bill of Rights have any relevance in defining the content of due process?

Does actual legal practice necessarily comport with the "notions of justice" of the people? In any case, why should the content of due process be determined by reference to what is the prevailing practice? Consider Justice Walter Schaefer's warning that "it is easy indeed to get used to a particular procedural system. What is familiar tends to become what is right." Schaefer, *Federalism and State Criminal Procedure,* 70 HARV. L. REV. 1, 7 (1956). *See* Henkin, *"Selective Incorporation" in the Fourteenth Amendment,* 73 YALE L.J. 74, 78 (1963). Does all of the above reveal a studied federal judicial deference to decisions made elsewhere in the legal system?

It is probably a mistake to assume that Frankfurter's resolution of due process issues is necessitated by his methodology. Reference to civilized standards of decency, to "shocking the conscience" of the court, are words deliberately chosen not to perform a task but to transmit a message. The message is that the task of deciding whether to invalidate state law must be exercised with restraint. Private predilection at least at the subconscious level cannot be winnowed out. Therefore only in the clearest cases, *i.e.,* offenses to fundamental decency, should the fourteenth amendment be construed to permit federal invalidation of state law.

Thus Frankfurter's theory although it professes to provide the methodology for an objective constitutional interpretation is really animated by the idea that such objectivity is not possible. It represents a determination to tolerate as much state criminal procedure as possible. If the independent theory of due process is understood in this way, then, it becomes clear why all the attention to ferreting out the "standards of the English-speaking people" is somewhat disingenuous.

For Justice Black, this flexible approach to due process was unacceptable. Civilized standards of decency were too unconfined. How could we have an objective constitutional interpretation given such an obscure guide? For him, Frankfurter's conception was natural law, leaving judicial judgment at large, and therefore intolerably unpredictable. As Black interpreted the matter, the history and text of the Constitution led to a single conclusion and conception. The first eight amendments were intended to be incorporated into the due process clause of the fourteenth and thereby binding the states. Due process did not have, as Frankfurter taught, an independent potency. The exorbitant price for such an independent approach to the fourteenth was its imprecision. To Frankfurter this, of course, was a virtue because it demonstrated at the first level of disposition the "non-Euclidean" character of the problems presented to the court. To Black this imprecision was the undermining vice of the whole Frankfurter theory of due process, for in the end, Justice Black prophesied, what would be applied were the values of the judges themselves.

To Justice Black the history of the fourteenth amendment indicated the appropriate solution. The fourteenth incorporated the first eight amendments, nothing more or less. These values were too important to be trusted to the risk of alternative enforcement or subordination on the basis of a judicial assessment of what the national consensus then was with regard to each of them.

It should be noted that there is no textual support for the Black position. In fact, it has been argued that the fourteenth amendment due process clause in restating identically only a single provision of the Bill of Rights, could not have been intended to serve as a short-hand expression for all of the Bill of Rights. *Contra:* Powell v. Alabama, 287 U.S. 45, 65-67 (1932). *See* Henkin, *"Selective Incorporation" in the Fourteenth Amendment,* 73 YALE L.J. 74, 78 (1963).

Further, the accuracy of Justice Black's reading of history, set forth in a lengthy appendix to *Adamson,* has been the subject of considerable dispute. *Compare* H. FLACK, THE ADOPTION OF THE FOURTEENTH AMENDMENT (1908); Crosskey, *Charles Fairman, "Legislative History," and the Constitutional Limitations on State Authority,* 22 U. CHI. L. REV. 1 (1954), with Fairman, *Does the Fourteenth Amendment Incorporate Bill of Rights? Original Understanding,* 2 STAN. L. REV. 5 (1949); Morrison, *Does the Fourteenth Amendment Incorporate Bill of Rights? Judicial Interpretation,* 2 STAN. L. REV. 140 (1949). *See generally,* Commager, HISTORICAL BACKGROUND OF THE FOURTEENTH AMENDMENT, IN THE FOURTEENTH AMENDMENT: A CENTURY IN AMERICAN LAW & LIFE 14 (B. Schwartz ed. 1970); Kelly, *Clio and the Court: An Illicit Love Affair,* 1965 SUP. CT. REV. 119, 132-34.

As a methodological approach, Justice Black's promised certainty in due process interpretation by resort to the cryptic and often uninterpreted phrases of the first eight amendments seems certain to provide for the subjective value preferences of the judge, a result Justice Black abhors. What is the meaning of unreasonable search and seizure? Double jeopardy? Cruel and unusual punishment? What is a confession? When does the right to counsel attach? These questions cannot be answered by simple recourse to the language of the Bill of Rights. No matter how passionate Justice Black's pleas for literal constitutional interpretation, his impulses have been reformist and ethical; his search for the objective by resort to the "specifics" in the Bill of Rights was to prove illusory.

Is there an equally severe problem in that Justice Black's approach *limits* the definition of due process to the text of the Bill of Rights? *See* the Murphy-Rutledge dissent in *Adamson*.

If due process adjudication involves judicial value predispositions, understanding of the process involves inquiry into the relation of those values to decisional behavior. Social scientists have employed increasingly complex techniques in an effort to probe judicial behavior. *See, e.g.,* W. MURPHY & J. TANENHAUS, THE STUDY OF PUBLIC LAW 116-78 (1972); J. GROSSMAN & J. TANENHAUS, FRONTIERS OF JUDICIAL RESEARCH (1968); G. SCHUBERT, JUDICIAL BEHAVIOR (1964); Symposium, *Social Science Approaches to the Judicial Process,* 79 HARV. L. REV. 1551 (1966).

While the Cardozo-Frankfurter "flexible" approach dominated due process decision-making for a decade and a half, it was to suffer a demise. But its replacement was not to be Justice Black's "total incorporation" methodology, but a process of "selective incorporation," a gradual process of inclusion and exclusion of the Bill of Rights. The next sections survey this transition. No attempt is made in this book to provide a new treatise on criminal procedure—the emphasis is on constitutional methodology.

It has been argued that: "Try as one might to avoid the phrase, 'ordered liberty' or something much like it remains as the principle of selection, to determine which specifics are 'incorporated,' and which are not. . . . That judgment of selection is as likely to be 'subjective' as is the application of the traditional standard." Henkin, *"Selective Incorporation" in the Fourteenth Amendment,* 73 YALE L.J. 74, 82 (1963) . As you read the cases, consider what standard governs selection under the selective incorporation doctrine. Have the ends desired by Justice Black been achieved using the language of Cardozo and Frankfurter? If a guarantee is "incorporated," must it apply in exactly the same way to the states as it does the federal government?

## B.  THE MARCH OF DUE PROCESS: FEDERALIZING THE STATE CRIMINAL PROCESS

### 1.  Search and Seizure

#### a.  Due Process and the Exclusionary Rule

In constitutional law, more than for most areas of dispute in the history of ideas, it is possible to chart, to use Santayana's phrase, the winds of doctrine. In the area of due process adjudication, the Frankfurter approach was first to prevail.

An initial area of controversy focused on the applicability to the states of the guarantee against unreasonable search and seizures in the fourth amendment. What is to be done when the police illegally search and seize evidence and then seek to introduce it as evidence in the subsequent criminal prosecution? It may well be relevant and trustworthy evidence of guilt, but can the courts give effect to such police activity?

In Wolf v. Colorado, 338 U.S. 25 (1949), Justice Frankfurter, speaking for the court, declared that "the security of one's privacy against arbitrary intrusion by the police—which is at the core of the fourth amendment—is basic to a free society." Since this was a "basic right," implicit in "the concept of ordered liberty," it was binding on the states through the due process clause.

But while it would violate due process "were a State to affirmatively sanction such police incursion into privacy," the remedies, "the ways of enforcing such a basic right," were viewed as raising "questions of a different order."

*Wolf* thus raised the important question of whether a right protected by the due process clause of the fourteenth amendment should be enforced in the same way a similar or equivalent right is enforced against the federal government under the Bill of Rights. In 1914 the Supreme Court had held that evidence secured by federal agents through an illegal search and seizure was inadmissible in a federal prosecution. Weeks v. United States, 232 U.S. 383 (1914). This was the famous exclusionary rule. But Justice Black, concurring in *Wolf,* argued that *Weeks* was based on the general supervisory powers of the Supreme Court. The exclusionary rule was perceived as a judicially-created rule of evidence, not as a constitutional command of the fourth amendment itself. Hence, there was no basis for "incorporation."

*rule of evidence constitutional command*

Justice Frankfurter in *Wolf* relied again on the principle that the requirements of due process were to be determined not by "a tidy formula" but by "a gradual and empiric process of 'inclusion and exclusion.' " While the right of privacy was basic, the manner of its enforcement was subject "to varying solutions which spring from an allowable range of judgment on issues not susceptible of quantitative solution." Justice Frankfurter noted especially that other English-speaking jurisdictions and the majority of the states had rejected the exclusionary rule of *Weeks.* Reliance on alternative methods for enforcing the basic right of privacy, therefore, could not be viewed as falling below the "minimal standards assured by the Due Process Clause." The states were not required as a constitutional matter to use the exclusionary rule. Justice Murphy, dissenting, criticized this approach by saying: "I cannot believe that we should decide due process questions by simply taking a poll of the rules in various jurisdictions, even if we follow the '*Palko*' test." Why did the "*Palko*" test encourage an analysis of whether there was a consensus among the states vis-a-vis a particular constitutional problem? *See* text, p. 435.

It has been suggested that *Wolf* contained the seeds of its own destruction. While recognizing the existence of a federal right, it provided no federal remedy. Allen, *Federalism and the Fourth Amendment: A Requiem for Wolf,* 1961 SUP. CT. REV. 1, 5. Frankfurter suggested the force of local opinion, the remedies of private action and the internal discipline of the police would suffice. Justice Murphy's answer was that the "alternative to the rule of exclusion" was "no sanction at all." Does an argument for the practical need for the exclusionary rule serve to make a case for its constitutional compulsion? In any case, the Frankfurter approach to due process adjudication had achieved majority recognition.

But did *Wolf* mean that the states were completely free from federal judicial review in admitting illegally seized evidence?

While Justice Frankfurter dealt with the abstract issue in *Wolf* and had failed to consider the facts relating to the police intrusion, he had suggested the existence of "minimal standards" of decency binding on the states. But what were the standards? Rochin v. California, 342 U.S. 165 (1952), sought to provide an answer.

In *Rochin,* the California police in a narcotics raid broke into the defendant's apartment. They saw the defendant swallow two morphine capsules. They, then, took him to a hospital where a doctor "forced an enemic solution through a tube into the defendant's stomach." This stomach-pumping produced vomiting yielding the capsules which were subsequently used as evidence leading to his conviction for possession of narcotics.

*shocks the conscience standard for judging action*

The Supreme Court, per Justice Frankfurter, set aside the conviction on the ground that the evidence used to support Rochin's conviction was obtained by means which violated the due process clause of the fourteenth amendment. The behavior of the police was "conduct that shocks the conscience." The methods used were "too close to the rack and the screw to permit of constitutional differentiation."

Justice Frankfurter analogized the exclusion of such illegally seized evidence to the exclusion of coerced confessions. Both were instances "of the general requirement that states in their prosecutions respect certain decencies of civilized conduct."

Coerced confessions are not excluded only because of their "unreliability" but because they "offend the community's sense of fair play and decency." Similarly, to sanction the brutal conduct involved in this case would be "to afford brutality the cloak of law" and by thus discrediting the law, would "brutalize the temper of a society."

Again Justice Frankfurter defended this "flexible" approach to the meaning of due process. This process did not leave judges at large: ["In each case due process of law requires an evaluation based on a disinterested inquiry pursued in the spirit of science, on a balanced order of facts exactly and fairly stated, on the detached consideration of conflicting claims, . . . on a judgment not ad hoc and episodic but duly mindful of reconciling the needs both of continuity and of change in a progressive society."]

*rational, individual consideration*

Justice Black concurred on the ground that the states, by reason of the fourteenth amendment, were bound to obey the fifth amendment command that "no person . . . shall be compelled in any criminal case to be a witness against himself." Still he felt a need to protest the majority's approach to the meaning of due process. While acknowledging that the majority purported to reject reliance on the judges' own conscience, he still could discover no "avenues of investigation . . . to discover 'canons' of conduct so universally favored that this Court should write them into the Constitution." As Justice Douglas, concurring, noted, the seized evidence would probably be admissible in a majority of states. For Justice Black, the "accordion-like qualities of this [Frankfurter] philosophy must inevitably imperil all the individual liberty safeguards specifically enumerated in the Bill of Rights."

The Frankfurter methodology had carried the day but it did not bring certainty.

Two years after *Rochin*, the court decided Irvine v. California, 347 U.S. 128 (1954). The police had made a number of illegal entries into the petitioner's home for the purpose of installing a concealed microphone and moving it to the bedroom and bedroom closet. The evidence secured through the eavesdropping was then used to convict the petitioner of gambling offenses.

Justice Jackson in an opinion joined by three other justices, castigated the police behavior as a flagrant violation of the fundamental right of privacy recognized as binding on the states by *Wolf*. But *Wolf* had also established that the fourteenth amendment did not require exclusion of evidence obtained by illegal search and seizure. Nor was *Rochin* controlling—"However obnoxious are the facts in the case before us, they do not involve coercion, violence or brutality to the person, but rather a trespass

*Wolf recognized right of privacy at state level but didn't demand exclusion of evidence*

to property, plus eavesdropping." The court's conscience, as a majority matter, was not shocked. While inviting the states to "reconsider their evidentiary rules," *Wolf* was still deemed persuasive.

Justice Clark reluctantly provided the fifth vote. In an opinion which was a portent of his switch in *Mapp,* he stated his belief that *Wolf* was wrongly decided. Nor was he enamored of the case-by-case shock the conscience approach: "this makes for such uncertainty and unpredictability that it would be impossible to foretell—other than by guesswork—just how brazen the invasion of the intimate privacies of one's home must be in order to shock itself into the protective arms of the Constitution." The test provided no effective deterrent against illegal police activity. While he felt bound by the *Wolf* precedent, he expressed hope that "strict adherence" might produce the converts needed for its extinction.

*[handwritten margin note: shock the conscience standard does not deter police action]*

Justice Frankfurter dissented since "what is decisive here, as in *Rochin,* is additional aggravating conduct which the Court finds repulsive." What Justice Frankfurter witnessed in *Irvine* was the inability of his test to do the work he had set for it. The court had said the accused in *Irvine* had not been the victim of physical coercion and therefore *Rochin* did not apply. This wrote Frankfurter, misses the point. His colleagues were attempting to capture the ineluctable. "In the *Wolf* Case, the Court rejected one absolute. In *Rochin* it rejected another." "Due process," he wrote, is not "a mechanical yardstick," and "does not afford mechanical answers." The point was that the conviction of Irvine had been obtained by "methods which offend the elementary standards of justice." He had not, he wrote indignantly, assayed a rule for *ad hoc* application in *Rochin.* He thought there was a "general principle" at stake in both *Rochin* and *Irvine*; his colleagues did not.

Frankfurter's experience in *Irvine* demonstrated the folly of hoping to extrapolate general principles which could yield conclusions apart from subjective reaction. *Irvine* reduced itself to the fear that the illegal installation of a concealed microphone in the bedroom of the accused was something that could not be tolerated constitutionally because for him, Felix Frankfurter, such behavior was intolerable. Justice Jackson's majority opinion revealed that for him that which concededly distasteful was not yet sufficiently distasteful to be unconstitutional.

The hopelessness of the quest for objectivity by the Frankfurter approach to due process, revealed in *Irvine,* was further demonstrated by the case of Breithaupt v. Abram, 352 U.S. 432

(1957). In *Breithaupt,* the court held, during the reign of the Frankfurter theory of due process, that to take a blood test of a drunken driver while he is unconscious did not offend elementary principles of justice. Blood tests performed "under the protective eye of a physician" had become routine. Against the interest of the individual in his inviolable personality "must be set the interests of society in the scientific determination of intoxication, one of the great causes of the mortal hazards of the road."

Chief Justice Warren, joined by Justice Black and Justice Douglas, dissented on the ground that *Breithaupt* could not be distinguished from *Rochin.* But Justice Frankfurter, the author of *Rochin,* joined the majority holding that convictions resting on a blood test taken from an unconscious suspect did not violate the due process clause. How would you distinguish *Breithaupt* from *Rochin*? Is it that there was no compulsion in *Breithaupt*?

Justice Douglas, joined by Justice Black, dissenting said on this point: "Under our system of government, police cannot compel people to furnish the evidence necessary to send them to prison. Yet there is compulsion here, following the violation by the police of the sanctity of the unconscious man." For Justice Douglas, the practice was "repulsive."

In 1962, the Supreme Court in Mapp v. Ohio, 367 U.S. 643 (1961), reversed *Wolf v. Colorado* and at last applied the exclusionary rule to state criminal procedure. As you read *Mapp,* ask yourself the following questions: What is the court's textual basis in the constitution for the exclusionary rule? Is the doctrinal basis for *Mapp* an incorporationist approach or does it rely on the theory that the due process clause has an independent potency of its own? Note that the court in *Mapp* discusses the change in factual circumstances since *Wolf.* How important are these changed facts to the court's decision?

## MAPP v. OHIO
### Supreme Court of the United States
### 367 U.S. 643, 6 L. Ed. 2d 1081, 81 S. Ct. 1684 (1961)

Justice CLARK delivered the opinion of the Court.

Appellant stands convicted of knowingly having had in her possession and under her control certain lewd and lascivious books, pictures, and photographs in violation of § 2905.34 of Ohio's Revised Code. [T]he Supreme Court of Ohio found that her conviction was valid though "based primarily upon the introduction in evidence of lewd and lascivious books and pictures unlawfully seized during an unlawful search of defendant's home."

. . . .

At the trial no search warrant was produced by the prosecution, nor was the failure to produce one explained or accounted for. [The Ohio Supreme Court, affirming the conviction, recognized that] "There is in the record, considerable doubt as to whether there ever was any warrant for the search of defendant's home." . . . [B]ut the court found determinative the fact that the evidence had not been taken "from defendant's person by the use of brutal or offensive physical force against defendant."

The State says that even if the search were made without authority, or otherwise unreasonably, it is not prevented from using the unconstitutionally seized evidence at trial, citing Wolf v. People of State of Colorado, 338 U.S. 25 (1949). . . . On this appeal, . . . it is urged once again that we review that holding.[3]

Seventy-five years ago, in Boyd v. United States, 116 U.S. 616, 630 (1886), considering the Fourth and Fifth Amendments as running "almost into each other" on the facts before it, this Court held that the doctrines of those Amendments

> "apply to all invasions on the part of the government and its employes of the sanctity of a man's home and the privacies of life. It is not the breaking of his doors, and the rummaging of his drawers, that constitutes the essence of the offence; but it is the invasion of his indefeasible right of personal security, personal liberty and private property. . . ."

. . . .

The Court in *Wolf* first stated that "[t]he contrariety of views of the States" on the adoption of the exclusionary rule of *Weeks* was "particularly impressive." . . . While in 1949, prior to the *Wolf* case, almost two-thirds of the States were opposed to the use of the exclusionary rule, now, despite the *Wolf* case, more than half of those since passing upon it, by their own legislative or judicial decision, have wholly or partly adopted or adhered to the *Weeks* rule. Significantly, among those now following the rule is California, which, according to its highest court, was "compelled to reach that conclusion because other remedies have completely failed to secure compliance with the constitutional provisions. . . ." People v. Cahan, 44 Cal.2d 434, 445, 282 P.2d 905, 911 (1955). In connection with this California case, we note that the second basis elaborated in *Wolf* in support of its failure to enforce the exclusionary doctrine against the States was that

*Other reme-*
*dies do not*
*deter police*
*action as*
*the exper-*
*ience of the*
*states*
*shows*

---

[3] Other issues have been raised on this appeal but, in the view we have taken of the case, they need not be decided. Although appellant chose to urge what may have appeared to be the surer ground for favorable disposition and did not insist that Wolf be overruled, the *amicus curiae,* who was also permitted to participate in the oral argument, did urge the Court to overrule Wolf.

"other means of protection" have been afforded "the right to privacy." The experience of California that such other remedies have been worthless and futile is buttressed by the experience of other States. The obvious futility of relegating the Fourth Amendment to the protection of other remedies has, moreover, been recognized by this Court since *Wolf.* See Irvine v. People of State of California, 347 U.S. 128, 137 (1954).

Likewise, time has set its face against what *Wolf* called the "weighty testimony" of People v. Defore, 242 N.Y. 13, 150 N.E. 585 (1926). There Justice (then Judge) Cardozo, rejecting adoption of the *Weeks* exclusionary rule in New York, had said that "[t]he Federal rule as it stands is either too strict or too lax." However, the force of that reasoning has been largely vitiated by later decisions of this Court. These include the recent discarding of the "silver platter" doctrine which allowed federal judicial use of evidence seized in violation of the Constitution by state agents, Elkins v. United States [364 U.S. 206 (1960)]; the relaxation of the formerly strict requirements as to standing to challenge the use of evidence thus seized, . . . Jones v. United States, 362 U.S. 257 (1960); and finally, the formulation of a method to prevent state use of evidence unconstitutionally seized by federal agents, Rea v. United States, 350 U.S. 214 (1956). . . .

*tightening of regulations on evidence given to States by federal when obtained in unlawful search*

It, therefore, plainly appears that the factual considerations supporting the failure of the *Wolf* Court to include the *Weeks* exclusionary rule when it recognized the enforceability of the right to privacy against the States in 1949, while not basically relevant to the constitutional consideration, could not, in any analysis, now be deemed controlling.

*✳ factual considerations altered*

Some five years after *Wolf,* in answer to a plea made here Term after Term that we overturn its doctrine on applicability of the *Weeks* exclusionary rule, this Court indicated that such should not be done until the States had "adequate opportunity to adopt or reject the [*Weeks*] rule." Irvine v. People of State of California [347 U.S. 128 (1954)]. . . . Today we once again examine *Wolf*'s constitutional documentation of the right to privacy free from unreasonable state intrusion, and, after its dozen years on our books, are led by it to close the only courtroom door remaining open to evidence secured by official lawlessness in flagrant abuse of that basic right, reserved to all persons as a specific guarantee against that very same unlawful conduct. We hold that all evidence obtained by searches and seizures in violation of the Constitution is, by that same authority, inadmissible in a state court.

Since the Fourth Amendment's right of privacy has been declared enforceable against the States through the Due Process

Clause of the Fourteenth, it is enforceable against them by the same sanction of exclusion as is used against the Federal Government. Were it otherwise, then just as without the *Weeks* rule the assurance against unreasonable federal searches and seizures would be "a form of words," valueless and undeserving of mention in a perpetual charter of inestimable human liberties, so too, without that rule the freedom from state invasions of privacy would be so ephemeral and so neatly severed from its conceptual nexus with the freedom from all brutish means of coercing evidence as not to merit this Court's high regard as a freedom "implicit in 'the concept of ordered liberty.' " . . . The right to privacy, when conceded operatively enforceable against the States, was not susceptible of destruction by avulsion of the sanction upon which its protection and enjoyment had always been deemed dependent [in the federal courts] under the *Boyd, Weeks* and *Silverthorne* cases. Therefore, in extending the substantive protections of due process to all constitutionally unreasonable searches—state or federal—it was logically and constitutionally necessary that the exclusion doctrine—an essential part of the right to privacy—be also insisted upon as an essential ingredient of the right newly recognized by the *Wolf* case. In short, the admission of the new constitutional right by *Wolf* could not consistently tolerate denial of its most important constitutional privilege, namely, the exclusion of the evidence which an accused had been forced to give by reason of the unlawful seizure. To hold otherwise is to grant the right but in reality to withhold its privilege and enjoyment. . . .

Indeed, we are aware of no restraint, similar to that rejected today, conditioning the enforcement of any other basic constitutional right. The right to privacy, no less important than any other right carefully and particularly reserved to the people, would stand in marked contrast to all other rights declared as "basic to a free society." Wolf v. Colorado, 338 U.S. at page 27. This Court has not hesitated to enforce as strictly against the States as it does against the Federal Government the rights of free speech and of a free press, the rights to notice and to a fair, public trial, including, as it does, the right not to be convicted by use of a coerced confession, however logically relevant it be, and without regard to its reliability. And nothing could be more certain that that when a coerced confession is involved, "the relevant rules of evidence" are overridden without regard to "the incidence of such conduct by the police," slight or frequent. Why should not the same rule apply to what is tantamount to coerced testimony by way of unconstitutional seizure of goods, papers, effects, documents, etc.? We find that, as to the Federal

*[margin note: other rights enforced upon the states; why not privacy and exclusionary rule?]*

Government, the Fourth and Fifth Amendments and, as to the States, the freedom from unconscionable invasions of privacy and the freedom from convictions based upon coerced confessions do enjoy an "intimate relation" in their perpetuation of "principles of humanity and civil liberty [secured] . . . only after years of struggle." Bram v. United States, 168 U.S. 532, 543-544 (1897). They express "supplementing phases of the same constitutional purpose—to maintain inviolate large areas of personal privacy." Feldman v. United States, 322 U.S. 487, 489-490 (1944). The philosophy of each Amendment and of each freedom is complementary to, although not dependent upon, that of the other in its sphere of influence—the very least that together they assure in either sphere is that no man is to be convicted on unconstitutional evidence.

. . . .

Federal-state cooperation in the solution of crime under constitutional standards will be promoted, if only by recognition of their now mutual obligation to respect the same fundamental criteria in their approaches. . . . Denying shortcuts to only one of two cooperating law enforcement agencies tends naturally to breed legitimate suspicion of "working arrangements" whose results are equally tainted.

*promote federal-state co-operation*

There are those who say, as did Justice (then Judge) Cardozo, that under our constitutional exclusionary doctrine "[t]he criminal is to go free because the constable has blundered." People v. Defore, 242 N.Y. at page 21, 150 N.E. at page 587. In some cases this will undoubtedly be the result. . . . The criminal goes free, if he must, but it is the law that sets him free. Nothing can destroy a government more quickly than its failure to observe its own laws, or worse, its disregard of the charter of its own existence. . . . Nor can it lightly be assumed that, as a practical matter, adoption of the exclusionary rule fetters law enforcement. Only last year this Court expressly considered that contention and found that "pragmatic evidence of a sort" to the contrary was not wanting. *Elkins v. United States.* The Court [in *Elkins*] noted that

> "The federal courts themselves have operated under the exclusionary rule of *Weeks* for almost half a century; yet it has not been suggested either that the Federal Bureau of Investigation has thereby been rendered ineffective, or that the administration of criminal justice in the federal courts has thereby been disrupted. Moreover, the experience of the states is impressive. . . . The movement towards the rule of exclusion has been halting but seemingly inexorable."

*exclusionary rule will not hinder police*

The ignoble shortcut to conviction left open to the State tends to destroy the entire system of constitutional restraints on which the liberties of the people rest. Having once recognized that the right to privacy embodied in the Fourth Amendment is enforceable against the States, and that the right to be secure against rude invasions of privacy by state officers is, therefore, constitutional in origin, we can no longer permit that right to remain an empty promise. Because it is enforceable in the same manner and to like effect as other basic rights secured by the Due Process Clause, we can no longer permit it to be revocable at the whim of any police officer who, in the name of law enforcement itself, chooses to suspend its enjoyment. Our decision, founded on reason and truth, gives to the individual no more than that which the Constitution guarantees him, to the police officer no less than that to which honest law enforcement is entitled, and, to the courts, that judicial integrity so necessary in the true administration of justice.

. . . .

Reversed and remanded.

Justice BLACK, concurring.

. . . .

I am still not persuaded that the Fourth Amendment, standing alone, would be enough to bar the introduction into evidence against an accused of papers and effects seized from him in violation of its commands. For the Fourth Amendment does not itself contain any provision expressly precluding the use of such evidence, and I am extremely doubtful that such a provision could properly be inferred from nothing more than the basic command against unreasonable searches and seizures. Reflection on the problem, however, in the light of cases coming before the Court since *Wolf*, has led me to conclude that when the Fourth Amendment's ban against unreasonable searches and seizures is considered together with the Fifth Amendment's ban against compelled self-incrimination, a constitutional basis emerges which not only justifies but actually requires the exclusionary rule.

The close interrelationship between the Fourth and Fifth Amendments, as they apply to this problem, has long been recognized and, indeed, was expressly made the ground for this Court's holding in *Boyd v. United States*. There the Court fully discussed this relationship and declared itself "unable to perceive that the seizure of a man's private books and papers to be used in evidence against him is substantially different from compelling him to be a witness against himself." It was upon this ground that Mr. Justice Rutledge largely relied in his dissenting opinion in the *Wolf* case. And, although I rejected the argument at that time, its force has, for me at least, become compelling with the more thorough understanding of the problem brought on by recent cases. . . .

. . . .

. . . As I understand the Court's opinion in this case, we again [as in *Irvine*] reject the confusing "shock-the-conscience" standard of the *Wolf* and *Rochin* cases and, instead, set aside this state conviction in reliance upon the precise, intelligible and more predictable constitutional doctrine enunciated in the *Boyd* case. . . .

Justice DOUGLAS concurring.

. . . .

Without judicial action making the exclusionary rule applicable to the States, *Wolf v. Colorado* in practical effect reduced the guarantee against unreasonable searches and seizures to "a dead letter." . . .

. . . I believe that this is an appropriate case in which to put an end to the asymmetry which *Wolf* imported into the law. . . .

. . . .

Memorandum of Justice STEWART.

Agreeing fully with Part I of Mr. Justice HARLAN's dissenting opinion, I express no view as to the merits of the constitutional issue which the Court today decides. I would, however, reverse the judgment in this case, because I am persuaded that the provision . . . of the Ohio Revised Code, upon which the petitioner's conviction was based, is, in the words of Mr. Justice HARLAN, not "consistent with the rights of free thought and expression assured against state action by the Fourteenth Amendment."

Justice HARLAN, whom Justice FRANKFURTER and Justice WHITTAKER join, dissenting.

. . . .

## THE CONTINUING CONTROVERSY: THE EXCLUSIONARY RULE

Debate over the merits of the exclusionary rule has not subsided since *Mapp.* Unlike many other types of evidence that are obtained through an unlawful search and seizure it is not objectionable because it is unreliable nor even because it might unduly prejudice the defendant. The evidence is inadmissible solely because it has been obtained illegally. Critics and proponents of the exclusionary rule alike agree that its immediate consequence is generally that a guilty defendant goes free. What purpose does it serve to let the "criminal go free because the constable has blundered"? People v. Defore, 242 N.Y. 13, 21, 150 N.E. 585 (1926).

## The Deterrent Effect of the Exclusionary Rule

*justifica-*
*tion of ex-*
*clusionary*
*rule: de-*
*terrence*

1. The persistent justification offered for the rule has been that it serves to deter unlawful police conduct both in the short run by making it clear that if criminal prosecutions are to succeed police must obey the law and in the long run by stigmatizing police misconduct in the eyes of both law enforcement officials themselves and the general public. But does the exclusionary rule in fact function as a deterrent to unlawful searches and seizures?

*no basis*
*showing*
*that ex-*
*clusionary*
*rule is*
*effective*

The court in *Mapp* concludes that experience teaches that remedies other than the exclusionary rule have failed to protect fourth amendment rights. But the court points to no positive experience showing that the exclusionary rule *is* an effective remedy. No empirical data is offered to prove that the rule is the only, the best, or indeed any deterrent to illegal searches and seizures. It is interesting to note that seven years before *Mapp* the court had suggested the absence of such empirical evidence: "What actual experience teaches we do not know. Our cases evidence the fact that the federal rule of exclusion and our reversal of conviction for its violation are not sanctions which put an end to illegal searches and seizures by federal officers. . . . The extent to which the practice was curtailed, if at all, is doubtful. . . . There is no reliable evidence known to us that inhabitants of those states which exclude the evidence suffer less from lawless searches and seizures, than those states that admit it." Irvine v. California, 347 U.S. 128, 135 (1954).

2. It is not easy to measure the deterrent value of the exclusionary rule. Not surprisingly, the police do not keep records of the incidence of unlawful searches and seizures before and after the rule. More indirect methods of measuring the effect of the rule may not adequately account for the host of variables which determine police conduct. Dallin Oaks in his exhaustive study of existing empirical evidence concludes that the data provides little support for the claim that the exclusionary rule in fact discourages illegal searches, but falls short of establishing that it does not. Oaks, *Studying Exclusionary Rule in Search and Seizure*, 37 U. CHI. L. REV. 665, 667, 709 (1970). What of the rule's long range deterrent effect? Is it possible that the moral and educative influence of the law will eventually cause police to reevaluate their own behavior and voluntarily conform to the constitutional norms? But even the underlying logic of the rule has been criticized.

**3.** The rule is directed principally against police activity, yet the immediate impact of the suppression of evidence is felt by the prosecutor and not by the police. Is it reasonable to assume that the police will make fewer illegal searches because it impairs the ability of the prosecutor to obtain convictions? Chief Justice Burger has suggested that "the suppression doctrine vaguely assumes that law enforcement is a monolithic governmental enterprise," and that it "misconstrues the relationship between prosecutors and police." Bivens v. Six Unknown Named Agents of Federal Bureau of Narcotics, 403 U.S. 388, 416 (1971) (Burger, J., dissenting).

*[handwritten margin note: controlling action of prosecutor, also?]*

**4.** Even assuming that police are completely unresponsive to the problems of prosecution, might they not still be motivated to refrain from illegal searches merely by the knowledge that the fruits of a previous search have been nullified by the rule? According to Burger in *Bivens*: "Policemen do not have the time, inclination, or training to read and grasp the nuances of the appellate opinions that ultimately define the standards of conduct they are to follow." 403 U.S. at 417. *See* LaFave, *Improving Police Performance Through the Exclusionary Rule —Part I: Current Police and Local Court Practices*, 30 Mo. L. REV. 391 (1965). The lack of clarity and the long delay between the original police action and judicial review militate against the rule's deterrent value. But police in their capacity as government witnesses are no strangers to the judicial process. Are they not in fact acutely aware of the outcome of "bad" searches? And even if it were accurate to say that ineffective channels of communication between police, prosecutors and courts tend to minimize the effectiveness of the exclusionary rule, this does not mean to say the rule is devoid of deterrent effect.

**5.** It has been suggested that the logic of the rule is defective in that it assumes that all police searches are conducted with an eye towards prosecution and conviction. In fact police frequently have no desire to prosecute or convict. Most illegal searches and seizures tend to be concentrated in only a few types of crimes, primarily what are known as "victimless crimes," *i.e.* gambling, narcotics, prostitution, liquor. There is some indication that with respect to these offenses police are less likely to be interested in convictions. *See* L. TIFFANY, D. MCINTYRE & D. ROTENBERG, DETECTION OF CRIME: STOPPING AND QUESTIONING, SEARCH AND SEIZURE, AND ENCOURAGEMENT AND ENTRAPMENT 95, 183-99 (1967). Further, illegally seized evidence may contribute to successful prosecutions if the defendant pleads guilty.

**6.** The doctrine is a "mechanically inflexible response to widely varying degrees of police error. . . ." Bivens v. Six

Unknown Named Federal Narcotics Agents, 403 U.S. 388, 418 (1971) (Burger, J., dissenting). [The rule makes no distinctions between blatant police misconduct and honest mistakes.]

7. Use of the rule may forestall the development of better methods of controlling police behavior.

*no punish-*
*ment of*
*unlawful*
*police ac-*
*tion*

8. "Rejection of the evidence does nothing to punish the wrongdoing official, while it may, and likely will, release the wrongdoing defendant. It deprives society of its remedy against one lawbreaker because he has been pursued by another. It protects one against whom incriminating evidence is discovered, but does nothing to protect innocent persons who are the victims of illegal but fruitless searches." Irvine v. California, 347 U.S. 128, 136 (1954).

But consider Judge Traynor's statement: "It is seriously misleading, however, to suggest that wholesale release of the guilty is a consequence of the exclusionary rule. It is a large assumption that the police have invariably exhausted the possibilities of obtaining evidence legally when they have relied upon illegally obtained evidence. It is more rational to assume the opposite when the offer of illegally obtained evidence becomes routine." Traynor, *Mapp v. Ohio at Large in the Fifty States*, 1962 DUKE L.J. 319, 322.

## Negative Effects of the Exclusionary Rule

Criticism of the exclusionary rule ranges from the view that it does nothing at all to the view that it is the most serious impediment to effective law enforcement. Some of the negative consequences of the rule which have been suggested are:

1. It increases the incidence of police perjury and the falsification of police reports. There is some evidence that to avoid the rule police "slant" the facts on the manner in which evidence was obtained. F. GRAHAM, THE SELF-INFLICTED WOUND 136-37 (1970); J. SKOLNICK, JUSTICE WITHOUT TRIAL: LAW ENFORCEMENT IN DEMOCRATIC SOCIETY 212-15 (1966).

2. Hearings on motions to suppress evidence are time-consuming and divert attention from the critical question of guilt or innocence. A criminal prosecution is "at least an indirect and awkward forum for inquiring into the behavior of some other person, a police officer, with a view to punishing him or creating some deterrent against similar conduct in the future." Oaks, *Studying the Exclusionary Rule*, 37 U. CHI. L. REV., at 743.

3. The rule destroys respect for the law because it provides the public with the spectacle of the courts letting the guilty free on a "technicality." *See* Barrett, *Exclusion of Evidence Obtained*

*by Illegal Searches—A Comment on People vs. Cahan,* 43 CALIF.
L. REV. 565, 589 (1955).

4. If police are unable to obtain convictions they may resort
to extrajudicial controls, such as harassment.

5. Police may in some circumstances deliberately overstep
legal boundaries to immunize a criminal from prosecution.
People v. DeFore, 242 N.Y. 13, 23-24, 150 N.E. 585 (1926).

## ✳ *Alternative Remedies*

The *Mapp* court assumed that there was no viable alternative to the exclusionary rule. But is this true today? Illegal police
conduct may itself be subject to criminal prosecution. But prosecutors are reluctant to prosecute and juries are reluctant to convict police officers. Police misconduct may also be tortious. Further, federal damage actions are available for constitutional
wrongs by state officers (42 U.S.C. §§ 1983, 1985 (3)) and by federal officers (Bivens v. Six Unknown Named Fed. Narcotics
Agents, 403 U.S. 388 (1971)). But again, even if the immunity
defense is overcome, how likely is it that a jury will find against
a police officer and in favor of an accused or convicted criminal?
And if judgment is obtained how probable is it that it will be
satisfied?

## *The Normative Justification for the Exclusionary Rule*

Advocates of the exclusionary rule maintain that regardless
of deterrence considerations, the rule is necessary to maintain
judicial integrity. Courts should not condone illegal practices by
accepting its fruits. *See* Thompson, *Unconstitutional Search and
Seizure and the Myth of Harmless Error,* 42 NOTRE DAME L.
457, 461 (1967); Plumb, *Illegal Enforcement of the Law,* 24
CORNELL L.Q. 337, 377-79 (1939); Oaks, *Studying the Exclusionary
Rule,* 37 U. CHI. L. REV., at 668-69.

### b. Electronic Surveillance and Eavesdropping: A New Technology and an Eighteenth Century Bill of Rights

What the ancients knew as "eavesdropping" we now call
"electronic surveillance"; but to equate the two is to treat
man's first gunpowder on the same level as the nuclear bomb.
Electronic surveillance is the greatest leveler of human privacy
ever known. How most forms of it can be held "reasonable"
within the meaning of the Fourth Amendment is a mystery.
To be sure, the Constitution and the Bill of Rights are not
to be read as covering only the technology known in the 18th
Century. . . . At the same time the concepts of privacy which

the Founders enshrined in the Fourth Amendment vanish completely when we slavishly allow an all-powerful government, proclaiming law and order, efficiency, and other benign purposes, to penetrate all the walls and doors which men need to shield them from the pressures of a turbulent life around them and give them the health and strength to carry on. United States v. White, 401 U.S. 745, 756 (1971) (Douglas, J., dissenting).

The technological revolution and the sophisticated electronic surveillance and detection devices it has fostered pose new threats to privacy and challenge the adequacy of traditional search and seizure standards. Electronic equipment is more than just a new medium for carrying out old government surveillance objectives. "Electronic aids add a wholly new dimension to eavesdropping. They make it more penetrating, more indiscriminate, more truly obnoxious to a free society." Lopez v. United States, 373 U.S. 427, 466 (1963) (Brennan, J., dissenting). Tagging and bugging transmitters capable of being secreted in three buttons on a suit, radio pills for tagging, highly sensitive laser microphones, high-powered television eyes conjure up visions of Orwell's 1984. *See* A. MILLER, THE ASSAULT ON PRIVACY: COMPUTERS, DATA BANKS AND DOSSIERS (1971); A. WESTIN, PRIVACY AND FREEDOM (1967); Book Review, 6 HOUSTON L. REV. 200 (1968).

But is data collection through the use of an electronic listening device a "search" within the meaning of the fourth amendment? Are conversations overheard and transcribed through the use of such devices "seizures" subject to the exclusionary rule? What is the applicable criteria of "reasonableness"?

## A Question of Trespass?

The initial Supreme Court approach to the problem of applying fourth amendment standards to electronic surveillance was set forth in Olmstead v. United States, 277 U.S. 438 (1928). The prosecution of Olmstead for conspiracy to violate the National Prohibition Act was based in large measure on evidence obtained by intercepting telephone conversations by means of wiretapping. A closely divided Court (5-4) held that wiretapping was not a search and seizure within the meaning of the fourth amendment. Chief Justice Taft, for the court, concluded that the fourth amendment only protects material things—persons, houses, papers and effects being tangible objects. What was seized in *Olmstead* was not tangible evidence but telephone messages, "secured by the use of the sense of hearing and that only." The case involved no physical trespass on Olmstead's property. There was no entry into his house or office. "The reasonable view is that one who installs in his house a telephone instrument with connecting wires intends to project his voice to those quite outside, and that the wires beyond his house and messages while passing over them are not within the protection of the Fourth Amendment."

But must there be both physical evidence and a physical trespass to either the defendant's home or person? It is not clear whether the court in *Olmstead* believed both criteria were essential to invoke the fourth amendment. If the court had found that telephone conversations were protected "effects," would it have mattered that their seizure involved no physical trespass?

*physical trespass — physical evidence standard*

Brandeis in his dissent in *Olmstead* indicated that he viewed neither element as controlling. To him wiretapping was a serious threat to personal liberty. "As a means of espionage, writs of assistance and general warrants are but puny instruments of tyranny and oppression when compared with wiretapping." The court's emphasis on trespass and tangible evidence placed an unduly literal construction on the fourth amendment.

The protection guaranteed by the Amendments is much broader in scope. The makers of our Constitution, undertook to secure conditions favorable to the pursuit of happiness. The framers recognized the significance of man's spiritual nature of his feelings and of his intellect. They knew that only a part of the pain, pleasure and satisfactions of life are to be found in material things. They sought to protect Americans in their beliefs and their sensations. . . .

The makers of our Constitution conferred, as against the government, the right to be let alone—the most comprehensive of rights and the right most valued by civilized men. To protect that right, every unjustifiable intrusion by the government upon the privacy of the individual, whatever the means employed, must be deemed a violation of the Fourth Amendment. And the use, as evidence in a criminal proceeding, of facts ascertained by such intrusion must be deemed a violation of the Fifth. . . .

Decency, security and liberty alike demand that government officials shall be subjected to the same rules of conduct that are commands to the citizen. In a government of laws, existence of the government will be imperiled if it fails to observe the law scrupulously. Our government is the potent, the omnipresent teacher. For good or for ill, it teaches the whole people by its example. Crime is contagious. If the government becomes a lawbreaker, it breeds contempt for law; it invites every man to become a law unto himself; it invites

anarchy. To declare that in the administration of the criminal law the end justifies the means—to declare that the government may commit crimes in order to secure the conviction
of a private criminal—would bring terrible retribution.
Against that pernicious doctrine this court should resolutely
set its face.

Justice Holmes, dissenting, similarly concluded that "it is a less
evil that some criminals should escape than that the government
should play an ignoble part."

The distinctions laid down by the majority in *Olmstead* were
too limiting and too nice to endure. It was the broader dissenting
view that was ultimately to prevail. *See generally* Scoular, *Wiretapping and Eavesdropping Constitutional Development From
Olmstead to Katz,* 12 ST. LOUIS L.J. 513 (1968).

At the same time, the courts were undermining the doctrinal
foundations of *Olmstead*. There was a gradual judicial recognition that nontangible evidence is within the purview of the fourth
amendment. *See* Goldman v. United States, 316 U.S. 129 (1942);
Silverman v. United States, 365 U.S. 505 (1961); Wong Sun v.
United States, 371 U.S. 471 (1963). Other cases established that
actual physical trespass is not a prerequisite to violation of the
fourth amendment. *See, e.g.,* Jones v. United States, 362 U.S.
257 (1960); Chapman v. United States, 365 U.S. 610 (1961);
Lanza v. New York, 370 U.S. 139 (1962). It was only a matter of
time until *Olmstead* itself would be rejected.

### *Berger v. New York: Fourth Amendment Warrants for Eavesdropping?*

A major step toward overruling *Olmstead* came in Berger v.
New York, 388 U.S. 41 (1967), holding the New York statute
providing warrant procedures for electronic eavesdropping to be
unconstitutional on its face. The language of the statute was
found to be "too broad in its sweep resulting in a trespassory
intrusion into a constitutionally protected area."

The court, *contra Olmstead,* recognized that electronic eavesdropping involved a search and seizure to be judged by demanding
fourth amendment warrant standards. "The need for particularity
and evidence of reliability in the showing required when judicial
authorization of a search is sought is especially great in the case
of eavesdropping" since "[b]y its very nature eavesdropping involves an intrusion on privacy that is broad in scope." In the
present case, the statutory requirements failed to satisfy the
constitutional standards. It did not require particularized belief
that an offense has been or is being committed or that the

conversations to be seized be particularly described. Further, a single showing of probable cause would suffice to justify searches over a two-month period or even longer if "in the public interest." Also, the statute made no provision for termination of the search once the desired conversation was seized. Finally, the statutory scheme, dependent on secrecy, made no provision for notice as required for conventional warrants "nor does it overcome this defect by requiring some showing of special facts." The court added that "[s]uch a showing of exigency . . . would appear more important in eavesdropping, with its inherent dangers, than that required when conventional procedures of search and seizure are utilized."

Professor Ralph Spritzer questions whether it is possible to "reconcile the inherent character of an electronic surveillance with the condition that [a] warrant describe with particularity 'the things to be seized.' " Spritzer, *Electronic Surveillance by Leave of the Magistrate: The Case in Opposition*, 118 U. PA. L. REV. 169 (1969). He suggests that electronic surveillance is necessarily akin to the general search which the fourth amendment was designed to prevent. Does *Berger* accept this position? Is electronic eavesdropping necessarily inconsistent with the notice requirement? *Compare* Burpo, *Electronic Surveillance by Leave of the Magistrate: The Case for the Prosecution*, 38 TENN. L. REV. 14 (1970), who argues that "electronic surveillance is entirely permissible so long as real safeguards are present that comport with the spirit of the Fourth Amendment."

### Katz v. United States: The Constitutional Standards

*Olmstead* was interred in Katz v. United States, 389 U.S. 347 (1967), holding that non-trespassory electronic surveillance is subject to the fourth amendment. Katz had been convicted of transmitting wagering information by telephone in violation of federal law, using evidence of telephone conversations overheard by FBI agents. The conversations were intercepted by electronic listening and recording devices attached by the agents to the outside of a public telephone booth from which Katz placed calls. The Supreme Court reversed the Court of Appeals affirmance of the conviction.

Justice Stewart, writing for the court, rejected the contention that the fourth amendment resolution depended on whether a public telephone booth is a "constitutionally protected place." "For the Fourth Amendment protects people, not places. What a person knowingly exposes to the public even in his home or office, is not a subject of Fourth Amendment protection. . . .

But what he seeks to preserve as private, even in an area accessible to the public, may be constitutionally protected."

What is important, then, is whether there is an expectation of privacy in a given place under given circumstances. A person in a telephone booth seeks to exclude not the "intruding eye" but the "uninvited ear." He expects that his words "will not be broadcast to the world."

The lack of any physical penetration of the telephone booth was seen as immaterial. "[A]lthough a closely divided Court supposed in *Olmstead* that surveillance without any trespass and without seizure of any material object fell outside the ambit of the Constitution we have since departed from the narrow view on which that decision rests. . . . We conclude that the underpinning of *Olmstead* and *Goldman* have been so eroded by our subsequent decisions that the 'trespass' doctrine there enunciated can no longer be regarded as controlling. The Government's activities in electronically listening to and recording the petitioner's words violated the privacy upon which he justifiably relied while using the telephone booth and thus constituted a 'search and seizure' within the meaning of the Fourth Amendment. The fact that the electronic device employed to achieve that end did not happen to penetrate the wall of the booth can have no constitutional significance."

Having concluded that the wiretap did constitute a search and seizure, the court went on to consider whether its use complied with the constitutional standards of reasonableness. While recognizing that surveillance must be tested by fourth amendment standards, the court also established that not all surveillance is unconstitutional. While it was clear that there had been no search warrant, the court accepted that "this surveillance was so narrowly circumscribed that a duly authorized magistrate, properly notified of the need for such investigation, specifically informed of the basis on which it was to proceed, and clearly apprised of the precise intrusion it would entail, could constitutionally have authorized, with appropriate safeguards, the very limited search and seizure that the Government asserts in fact took place." But the court was not persuaded that because the federal agents exercised restraint in the scope and duration of their search and may well have been able to establish the probable cause required for antecedent judicial sanction, that the search was constitutional. " '[S]earches conducted outside the judicial process, without prior approval by judge or magistrate, are *per se* unreasonable under the Fourth Amendment—subject only to a few specifically established and well-delineated exceptions.' " A post hoc showing of probable cause will not justify a warrantless search. None of the established exceptions applied and the court was unwilling to create a new exception to cover this type of case. The wiretap therefore involved an unreasonable search and seizure; the fruits of it should have been held to be inadmissible. Katz's conviction was overturned.

The fourth amendment protected Katz's conversations because he was "justified" in relying on the privacy of his communications while he was in a public telephone booth. What does the court mean by justifiable reliance? Would Katz have been equally justified in relying on such privacy if he had left the door to the booth open? Suppose there had been no booth at all enclosing the telephone? Justice Harlan, concurring in *Katz*, suggests that justifiable reliance is really "a twofold requirement, first that a person have exhibited an actual (subjective) expectation of privacy and, second, that the expectation be one that society is prepared to recognize as 'reasonable.' Thus a man's home is, for most purposes, a place where he expects privacy, but objects, activities, or statements that he exposes to the 'plain view' of outsiders are not 'protected' because no intention to keep them to himself has been exhibited. On the other hand, conversations in the open would not be protected against being overheard, for the expectation of privacy under the circumstances would be unreasonable."

Does the first of Justice Harlan's two-fold test suggest some sort of waiver or estoppel theory, *i.e.*, one cannot claim a privacy right if his actions indicate indifference to privacy? *See The Supreme Court, 1967 Term*, 82 HARV. L. REV. 63, 187 (1968). Kitch suggests the following hypothetical: "Suppose that instead of speaking in a public telephone booth, Katz had gone with a friend for a walk in a deserted section of a public park to discuss his illegal activities, but that that area of the park had been extensively covered by sensitive microphones so that police officers could listen to the conversation." He asked "[w]ould Katz have 'justifiably' relied on the privacy afforded by the park's seclusion?" Kitch, *Katz v. United States: The Limits of the Fourth Amendment*, 1968 SUP. CT. REV. 133, 139.

Justice Black, dissenting, concluded that no type of eavesdropping falls within the fourth amendment which is concerned only with the idea of "tangible things." It is not the court's function "to rewrite the Amendment in order to bring it into harmony with the times."

Justice Black noted that *Katz* "differs sharply" from *Berger* since it "removes the doubts about state power in this field and abates to a large extent the confusion and near-paralyzing effect of the *Berger* holding." Justices Harlan and White who had dissented in Berger, joined the Stewart opinion in *Katz*. What in Stewart's opinion explains this reaction?

## Title III and National Security Surveillance

In 1968 Congress passed Title III of the Omnibus Crime Control and Safe Streets Act (18 U.S.C. §§ 2510-2520), which authorizes the use of electronic surveillance by federal and state officials for certain selected crimes and details the conditions and requirements to be met for its use. Reflecting *Berger* and *Katz*, wiretapping is generally permitted only by court order pursuant to a detailed and particularized application meeting specified requirements.

The Act does, however, contain a proviso excepting measures taken by the President to:

> protect the Nation against actual or potential attack or other hostile acts of a foreign power, to obtain foreign intelligence information deemed essential to the security of the United States, or to protect national security information against foreign intelligence activities. Nor shall anything contained in this Chapter be deemed to limit the constitutional power of the President to take such measures as he deems necessary to protect the United States against the overthrow of the Government by force or other unlawful means, or against any other clear and present danger to the structure or existence of the Government. [18 U.S.C. § 2511 (3)].

In *Katz*, the court noted the question "[w]hether safeguards other than prior authorization by a magistrate would satisfy the Fourth Amendment in a situation involving national security is a question not presented by this case." Nevertheless, Justice White, concurring, had commented that the court "should not require the warrant procedure and the magistrate's judgment if the President of the United States or his chief legal officer, the Attorney General, has considered the requirements of national security and authorized electronic surveillance as reasonable." This had drawn a concurring opinion from Justice Douglas, arguing that "[s]ince spies and saboteurs are [as] entitled to the protection of the Fourth Amendment" as those suspected of other crimes, adequate fourth amendment protection could not be provided if "the President and Attorney General assume both the position of adversary-and-prosecutor and disinterested, neutral magistrate."

Can "national security" serve as an exception to the warrant requirement for electronic surveillance? Part of the answer came in United States v. United States Dist. Court, 407 U.S. 297 (1972). The government argued that a wiretap was authorized despite the lack of prior judicial approval, by 18 U.S.C. § 2511(3) or by reason of the executive power. Defendants were charged with conspiracy to destroy government property and the wiretap was said to have been conducted pursuant to the President's authority to conduct domestic security surveillance. But the court held that 18 U.S.C. § 2511(3) is essentially neutral, conferring no power on the President but merely providing that such power as the President has under the Constitution shall go undisturbed.

Does the President have the constitutional power to order surveillance in domestic security cases without first obtaining a warrant? The court balanced the competing interests and decided he did not. "Fourth Amendment protections become the more necessary when the targets of official surveillance may be those suspected of unorthodoxy in their political beliefs. The danger to political dissent is acute where the Government attempts to act under so vague a concept as the power to protect 'domestic security'. . . . [P]rivate discourse, no less than open discourse, is essential to a free society."

The court found "pragmatic force [in] the Government's position." It noted the Government's contention that such surveillance is normally for intelligence-gathering rather than for evidence to support a specific prosecution and hence should be judged by different standards, that courts lack competency to make findings of probable cause in such cases and that prior judicial authorization would impair "[s]ecrecy [which] is the essential ingredient in data-gathering. . . ." But none of this was found sufficient to justify exemption of national security surveillance from judicial supervision. "Official surveillance, whether its purpose be criminal investigation or ongoing intelligence gathering, risks infringement of constitutionally protected privacy of speech. Security surveillances are especially sensitive because of the inherent vagueness of the domestic security concept, the necessarily broad and continuing nature of intelligence gathering, and the temptation to utilize such surveillances to oversee political dissent. We recognize, as we have before, the constitutional basis of the President's domestic security role, but we think it must be exercised in a manner compatible with the Fourth Amendment."

Title III was held not to empower the Executive Assistant to the Attorney General to authorize applications for wiretap orders in United States v. Giordano, 416 U.S. 505 (1974). Congress was said to have intended suppression of wiretap evidence "where there is failure to satisfy any of those statutory requirements that directly and substantially implement the congressional intention to limit the use of intercept procedures to those situations clearly calling for employment of this extraordinary investigative device." Misidentification of the official authorizing the wiretap, however, does not require suppression under Title III. United States v. Chavez, 416 U.S. 562 (1974).

## 2. The Right to Trial by Jury: The Triumph of Selective Incorporation?

### DUNCAN v. LOUISIANA
Supreme Court of the United States
391 U.S. 145, 20 L. Ed. 2d 491, 88 S. Ct. 1444 (1968)

Justice WHITE delivered the opinion of the Court.

Appellant, Gary Duncan, was convicted of simple battery [which under Louisiana law] . . . is a misdemeanor, punishable by two years' imprisonment and a $300 fine. Appellant sought trial by jury, but because the Louisiana Constitution grants jury trials only in cases in which capital punishment or imprisonment at hard labor may be imposed, the trial judge denied the request. Appellant was convicted and sentenced to serve 60 days in the parish prison and pay a fine of $150. Appellant . . . [alleges] that the Sixth and Fourteenth Amendments to the United States Constitution secure the right to jury trial in state criminal prosecutions where a sentence as long as two years may be imposed. . . .

. . . .

. . . In resolving conflicting claims concerning the meaning of this spacious language [of the due process clause], the Court has looked increasingly to the Bill of Rights for guidance; many of the rights guaranteed by the first eight Amendments to the Constitution have been held to be protected against state action by the Due Process Clause of the Fourteenth Amendment. . . .

The test for determining whether a right extended by the Fifth and Sixth Amendments with respect to federal criminal proceedings is also protected against state action by the Fourteenth Amendment has been phrased in a variety of ways in the opinions of this Court. The question has been asked whether a right is among those " 'fundamental principles of liberty and justice which lie at the base of all our civil and political institutions,' " Powell v. State of Alabama, 287 U.S. 45, 67 (1932); whether it is "basic in our system of jurisprudence," In re Oliver, 333 U.S. 257, 273 (1948); and whether it is "a fundamental right, essential to a fair trial," Gideon v. Wainwright, 372 U.S. 335, 343-344 (1963); Malloy v. Hogan, 378 U.S. 1, 6 (1964); Pointer v. State of Texas, 380 U.S. 400, 403 (1965). The claim before us is that the right to trial by jury guaranteed by the Sixth Amendment meets these tests. The position of Louisiana, on the other hand, is that the Constitution imposes upon the States no duty to give a jury trial in any criminal case, regardless of the seriousness of the crime or the size of the punishment which may be imposed. Because we believe that trial by jury in criminal cases is fundamental to the American scheme of justice, we hold that the Fourteenth Amendment guarantees a right of jury trial in all criminal cases which—were they to be tried in a federal court— would come within the Sixth Amendment's guarantee.[14] Since we consider the appeal before us to be such a case, we hold that the Constitution was violated when appellant's demand for jury trial was refused.

-----

[14] In one sense recent cases applying provisions of the first eight amendments to the States represent a new approach to the "incorporation" debate. Earlier the Court can be seen as having asked, when inquiring into whether some particular procedural safeguard was required of a State, if a civilized system could be imagined that would not accord the particular protection. For example, Palko v. Connecticut, 302 U.S. 319, 325 (1937), stated: "The right to trial by jury and the immunity from prosecution except as the result of an indictment may have value and importance. Even so, they are not of the very essence of a scheme of ordered liberty. . . . Few would be so narrow or provincial as to maintain that a fair and enlightened system of justice would be impossible without them." The recent cases, on the other hand, have proceeded upon the valid assumption that state criminal processes are not imaginary and theoretical schemes but actual systems bearing virtually every characteristic of the common-law system that has been developing contemporaneously in England and in this country. The question thus is whether given this kind of system a particular procedure is fundamental—whether, that is, a procedure is necessary to an Anglo-American regime of ordered liberty. It is this sort of inquiry that can justify the conclusions that state courts must exclude evidence seized in violation of the Fourth Amendment, Mapp v. Ohio, 367 U.S. 643 (1961); that state prosecutors may not comment on a defendant's failure to testify, Griffin v. California, 380 U.S. 609 (1965); and that criminal punishment may not be imposed for the status of narcotics addiction, Robinson v. California, 370 U.S. 660 (1962). Of immediate relevance for this case are the Court's holdings that the States must comply with certain provisions of the Sixth Amendment, specifically that the States may not refuse a speedy trial, confrontation of witnesses, and the assistance, at state expense if necessary, of counsel. Of each of these determinations that a constitutional provision originally written to bind the Federal Government should bind the States as well it might be said that the limitation in question is not necessarily fundamental to fairness in every criminal system that might be imagined but is fundamental in the context of the criminal processes maintained by the American States.

When the inquiry is approached in this way the question whether the States can impose criminal punishment without granting a jury trial appears quite different from the way it appeared in the older cases opining that States might abolish jury trial. See, e.g., Maxwell v. Dow, 176 U.S. 581 (1900). A criminal process which was fair and equitable but used no juries is easy to imagine. It would make use of alternative guarantees and protections which would serve the purposes that the jury serves in the English and American systems. Yet no American State has undertaken to construct such a system. Instead, every American State, including Louisiana, uses the jury extensively, and imposes very serious punishments only after a trial at which the defendant has a right to a jury's verdict. In every State, including Louisiana, the structure and style of the criminal process—the supporting framework and the subsidiary procedures—are of the sort that naturally complement jury trial, and have developed in connection with and in reliance upon jury trial.

The history of trial by jury in criminal cases has been frequently told. It is sufficient for present purposes to say that by the time our Constitution was written, jury trial in criminal cases had been in existence in England for several centuries and carried impressive credentials traced by many to Magna Carta. Its preservation and proper operation as a protection against arbitrary rule were among the major objectives of the revolutionary settlement which was expressed in the Declaration and Bill of Rights of 1689. . . .

Jury trial came to America with English colonists, and received strong support from them. . . .

The constitutions adopted by the original States guaranteed jury trial. Also, the constitution of every State entering the Union thereafter in one form or another protected the right to jury trial in criminal cases.

Even such skeletal history is impressive support for considering the right to jury trial in criminal cases to be fundamental to our system of justice, an importance frequently recognized in the opinions of this Court. . . .

Jury trial continues to receive strong support. The laws of every State guarantee a right to jury trial in serious criminal cases; no State has dispensed with it; nor are there significant movements underway to do so. . . .

We are aware of prior cases in this Court in which the prevailing opinion contains statements contrary to our holding today that the right to jury trial in serious criminal cases is a fundamental right and hence must be recognized by the States as part of their obligation to extend due process of law to all persons within their jurisdiction. Louisiana relies especially on Maxwell v. Dow, 176 U.S. 581 (1900); Palko v. Connecticut, 302 U.S. 319 (1937); and Snyder v. Massachusetts, 291 U.S. 97 (1934). None of these cases, however dealt with a State which had purported to dispense entirely with a jury trial in serious criminal cases. *Maxwell* held that no provision of the Bill of Rights applied to the States—a position long since repudiated—and that the Due Process Clause of the Fourteenth Amendment did not prevent a State from trying a defendant for a noncapital offense with fewer than 12 men on the jury. It did not deal with a case in which no jury at all had been provided. In neither *Palko* nor *Snyder* was jury trial actually at issue. . . . Perhaps because the right to jury trial was not directly at stake, the Court's remarks about the jury in *Palko* and *Snyder* took no note of past or current developments regarding jury trials, did not consider its purposes and functions, attempted no inquiry into how well it was performing its job, and did not discuss possible distinctions between civil and crim-

[margin annotations:]

trial by jury historically supported as necessary

thus, is fundamental to our system of justice

dicta rather than ratio decidendi (analogy rather than basic principle for decision) what the Court said previously about jury trials was irrelevant because this had not been the main issue of these cases.

inal cases. In *Malloy v. Hogan, supra,* the Court rejected Palko's discussion of self-incrimination clause. Respectfully, we reject the prior dicta regarding jury trial in criminal cases.

The guarantees of jury trial in the Federal and State Constitutions reflect a profound judgment about the way in which law should be enforced and justice administered. [A right to jury trial is granted to criminal defendants in order to prevent oppression by the Government.] Those who wrote our constitutions knew from history and experience that it was necessary to protect against unfounded criminal charges brought to eliminate enemies and against judges too responsive to the voice of higher authority. The framers of the constitutions strove to create an independent judiciary but insisted upon further protection against arbitrary action. [Providing an accused with the right to be tried by a jury of his peers gave him an inestimable safeguard against the corrupt or overzealous prosecutor and against the compliant, biased, or eccentric judge.] If the defendant preferred the common-sense judgment of a jury to the more tutored but perhaps less sympathetic reaction of the single judge, he was to have it. [Beyond this, the jury trial provisions in the Federal and State Constitutions reflect a fundamental decision about the exercise of official power —a reluctance to entrust plenary powers over the life and liberty of the citizen to one judge or to a group of judges.] Fear of unchecked power, so typical of our State and Federal Governments in other respects, found expression in the criminal law in this insistence upon community participation in the determination of guilt or innocence. The deep commitment of the Nation to the right of jury trial in serious criminal cases as a defense against arbitrary law enforcement qualifies for protection under the Due Process Clause of the Fourteenth Amendment, and must therefore be respected by the States.

Of course jury trial has "its weaknesses and the potential for misuse." We are aware of the long debate, especially in this century, among those who write about the administration of justice, as to the wisdom of permitting untrained laymen to determine the facts in civil and criminal proceedings. Although the debate has been intense, with powerful voices on either side, most of the controversy has centered on the jury in civil cases. Indeed, some of the severest critics of civil juries acknowledge that the arguments for criminal juries are much stronger. In addition, at the heart of the dispute have been express or implicit assertions that juries are incapable of adequately understanding evidence or determining issues of fact, and that they are unpredictable, quixotic, and little better than a roll of dice. Yet, the most recent and exhaustive study of the jury in criminal cases concluded that juries do understand the evidence and come to sound conclusions in most of the cases presented to them and that when juries differ with the result at which the judge would have arrived, it is usually because they are serving some of the very purposes for which they were created and for which they are now employed.

The State of Louisiana urges that holding that the Fourteenth Amendment assures a right to jury trial will cast doubt on the integrity of every trial conducted without a jury. Plainly, this is not the import of our holding. Our conclusion is that in the American States, as in the federal judicial system, a general grant of jury trial for serious offenses is a fundamental right, essential for preventing miscarriages of justice and for assuring that fair trials are provided for all defendants. We would not assert, however, that every criminal trial—or any particular trial—held before a judge alone is unfair or that a defendant may never be as fairly treated by a judge as he would be by a jury. Thus we hold no constitutional doubts about the practices, common in both federal and state courts, of accepting waivers of jury trial and prosecuting petty crimes without extending a right to jury trial. However, the fact is that in most places more trials for serious crimes are to juries than to a court alone; a great many defendants prefer the judgment of a jury to that of a court. Even where defendants are satisfied with bench trials, the right to a jury trial very likely serves its intended purpose of making judicial or prosecutorial unfairness less likely.[30]

----

[30] Louisiana also asserts that if due process is deemed to include the right to jury trial, States will be obligated to comply with all past interpretations of the Sixth Amendment, an amendment which in its inception was designed to control only the federal courts and which throughout its history has operated in this limited environment where uniformity is a more obvious and immediate consideration. In particular, Louisiana objects to application of the decisions of this Court interpreting the Sixth Amendment as guaranteeing a 12-man jury in serious criminal cases. Thompson v. State of Utah, 170 U.S. 343 (1898); as requiring a unanimous verdict before guilt can be found, Maxwell v. Dow, 176 U.S. 581, 586 (1900); and as barring procedures by which crimes subject to the Sixth Amendment jury trial provision are tried in the first instance without a jury but at the first appellate stage by de novo trial with a jury, Callan v. Wilson, 127 U.S. 540, 557 (1888). It seems very unlikely to us that our decision today will require widespread changes in state criminal processes. First, our decisions interpreting the Sixth Amendment are always subject to reconsideration, a fact amply demonstrated by the instant decision. In addition, most of the States have provisions for jury trials equal in breadth to the Sixth Amendment, if that amendment is construed, as it has been, to permit the trial of petty crimes and offenses without a jury. Indeed, there appear to be only four States in which juries of fewer than 12 can be used without the defendant's consent for offenses carrying a maximum penalty of greater than one year. Only in Oregon and Louisiana can a less-than-unanimous jury convict for an offense with a maximum penalty greater than one year. However 10 States authorize first-stage trials without

Louisiana's final contention is that even if it must grant jury trials in serious criminal cases, the conviction before us is valid and constitutional because here the petitioner was tried for simple battery and was sentenced to only 60 days in the parish prison. We are not persuaded. It is doubtless true that there is a category of petty crimes or offenses which is not subject to the Sixth Amendment jury trial provision and should not be subject to the Fourteenth Amendment jury trial requirement here applied to the States. Crimes carrying possible penalties up to six months do not require a jury trial if they otherwise qualify as petty offenses, Cheff v. Schnackenberg, 384 U.S. 373 (1966). But the penalty authorized for a particular crime is of major relevance in determining whether it is serious or not and may in itself, if severe enough, subject the trial to the mandates of the Sixth Amendment. . . .

. . . .

. . . We need not, however, settle in this case the exact location of the line between petty offenses and serious crimes. It is sufficient for our purposes to hold that a crime punishable by two years in prison is, based on past and contemporary standards in this country, a serious crime and not a petty offense. Consequently, appellant was entitled to a jury trial and it was error to deny it.

The judgment below is reversed and the case is remanded for proceedings not inconsistent with this opinion.

Justice BLACK, with whom Justice DOUGLAS joins, concurring.

. . . With this holding I agree for reasons given by the Court. I also agree because of reasons given in my dissent in Adamson v. People of State of California, 332 U.S. 46. . . .

Justice FORTAS, concurring.

. . . .

. . . [A]lthough I agree with the decision of the Court, I cannot agree with the implication, that the tail must go with the hide: that when we hold, influenced by the Sixth Amendment, that "due process" requires that the States accord the right of jury trial for all but petty offenses, we automatically import all of the ancillary rules which have been or may hereafter be developed incidental to the right to jury trial in the federal courts. I see no reason whatever, for example, to assume that our decision today should require us to impose federal requirements such as unanimous verdicts or a jury of 12 upon the States. We may well conclude that these and other features of federal jury practice

---

juries for crimes carrying lengthy penalties; these States give a convicted defendant the right to a *de novo* trial before a jury in a different court. . . .

are by no means fundamental—that they are not essential to due process of law—and that they are not obligatory on the States.

I would make these points clear today. Neither logic nor history nor the intent of the draftsmen of the Fourteenth Amendment can possibly be said to require that the Sixth Amendment or its jury trial provision be applied to the States together with the total gloss that this Court's decisions have supplied. The draftsmen of the Fourteenth Amendment intended what they said, not more or less: that no State shall deprive any person of life, liberty, or property without due process of law. It is ultimately the duty of this Court to interpret, to ascribe specific meaning to this phrase. There is no reason whatever for us to conclude that, in so doing, we are bound slavishly to follow not only the Sixth Amendment but all of its bag and baggage, however securely or insecurely affixed they may be by law and precedent to federal proceedings. To take this course, in my judgment, would be not only unnecessary but mischievous because it would inflict a serious blow upon the principle of federalism. [The Due Process Clause commands us to apply its great standard to state court proceedings to assure basic fairness. It does not command us rigidly and arbitrarily to impose the exact pattern of federal proceedings upon the 50 States. On the contrary, the Constitution's command, in my view, is that in our insistence upon state observance of due process, we should, so far as possible, allow the greatest latitude for state differences.] It requires, within the limits of the lofty basic standards that it prescribes for the States as well as the Federal Government, maximum opportunity for diversity and minimal imposition of uniformity of method and detail upon the States. Our Constitution sets up a federal union, not a monolith.

*federal standards need not be placed as a whole on the states* [margin annotation]

This Court has heretofore held that various provisions of the Bill of Rights . . . "are all to be enforced against the States under the Fourteenth Amendment according to the same standards that protect those rights against federal encroachment." Malloy v. Hogan, 378 U.S. 1, 10 (1964). But unless one adheres slavishly to the incorporation theory, body and substance, the same conclusion need not be superimposed upon the jury trial right. I respectfully but urgently suggest that it should not be. Jury trial is more than a principle of justice applicable to individual cases. It is a system of administration of the business of the State. While we may believe (and I do believe) that the right of jury trial is fundamental, it does not follow that the particulars of according that right must be uniform. We should be ready to welcome state variations which do not impair—indeed, which may advance—the theory and purpose of trial by jury.

*individual state variations* [margin annotation]

Justice HARLAN, whom Justice STEWART joins, dissenting.

. . . .

Today's Court still remains unwilling to accept the total incorporationists' view of the history of the Fourteenth Amendment. This, if accepted, would afford a cogent reason for applying the Sixth Amendment to the States. The Court is also, apparently, unwilling to face the task of determining whether denial of trial by jury in the situation before us, or in other situations, is fundamentally unfair. Consequently, the Court has compromised on the ease of the incorporationist position, without its internal logic. It has simply assumed that the question before us is whether the Jury Trial Clause of the Sixth Amendment should be incorporated into the Fourteenth, jot-for-jot and case-for-case, or ignored. Then the Court merely declares that the clause in question is "in" rather than "out."

. . . .

In sum, there is a wide range of views on the desirability of trial by jury, and on the ways to make it most effective when it is used; there is also considerable variation from State to State in local conditions such as the size of the criminal caseload, the ease or difficulty of summoning jurors, and other trial conditions bearing on fairness. We have before us, therefore, an almost perfect example of a situation in which the celebrated dictum of Mr. Justice Brandeis should be invoked. It is, he said,

> "one of the happy incidents of the federal system that a single courageous state may, if its citizens choose, serve as a laboratory. . . ." New State Ice Co. v. Liebmann, 285 U.S. 262, 280, 311 (dissenting opinion).

This Court, other courts, and the political process are available to correct any experiments in criminal procedure that prove fundamentally unfair to defendants. That is not what is being done today: instead, and quite without reason, the Court has chosen to impose upon every State one means of trying criminal cases; it is a good means, but it is not the only fair means, and it is not demonstrably better than the alternatives States might devise.

I would affirm the judgment of the Supreme Court of Louisiana.

———————

### NOTES

1. *The Due Process Inquiry.* The *Duncan* majority admits that jury trial is not "of the very essence of ordered liberty" and that "a fair and enlightened system of justice" is possible without

the guarantee. But the court utilizes a new due process standard, asking whether jury trial is "fundamental to the American scheme of justice." Does the new test limit due process to the Bill of Rights?

How do you determine if the test is satisfied? Does the test significantly alter the nature of the due process inquiry? Does it involve anything more than an assessment of the historical use of jury trial in this country? Does it turn on the importance of the role presently played by the jury trial in the American system?

Perhaps part of the fundamental character of the jury arises from its central legal function as a fact-finding institution. Broeder, *The Functions of the Jury: Facts or Fictions?*, 21 U. Chi. L. Rev. 386, 387 (1954). But the aspect of trial by jury which is most emphasized is its political function as "an inestimable safeguard against the corrupt or overzealous prosecutor and against the compliant, biased or eccentric judge." Duncan v. Louisiana, 391 U.S. at 156. Or as was said in Baldwin v. New York, 399 U.S. 66 (1970): "[T]he primary purpose of the jury is to prevent the possibility of oppression by the government; the jury interposes between the accused and the accuser the judgment of laymen who are less tutored perhaps than a judge or panel of judges, but who at the same time are less likely to function or appear as but another arm of the Government which has proceeded against him." *See* Note, *Trial by Jury in Criminal Cases*, 69 Colum. L. Rev. 419 (1969), which places stress on the jury as a political institution.

**2.** *Jury Nullification.* Justice Harlan, dissenting in *Duncan* contends that the original political value of jury trial, *i.e.*, checking a tyrannous judiciary, has largely disappeared. If true, does the jury still serve important political values? Does the fundamental political role of the jury lie in its capacity to "nullify" laws by refusing to enforce harsh laws or mitigating their severity by not fully enforcing them? H. Kalven & H. Zeisel, The American Jury 310-312, 433 (1966). If so, is it desirable to achieve flexibility in the law by providing an institutional mechanism for undermining it?

**3.** *Understanding Jury Behavior.* It is now common in the jury trial cases for the justices, both majority and dissent, to draw support from social science studies of the jury. See H. Kalven & H. Zeisel, The American Jury (1966); Simon & Marshall, *The Jury System*, in The Rights of the Accused 218-30 (S. Nagel ed. 1972); Erlanger, *Jury Research in America*, 4 Law & Soc. Rev. 345 (1970), for a discussion of the findings of the various studies. The major finding of the American jury study was the degree of similarity between juror verdicts and the decision the judges claim they would have reached. Of what relevance, if any, is such a finding to the issue in *Duncan?*

In terms of jury performance, the data tends to show "that the jury understands its task, wants to and does perform it competently, and believes that the experience was worthwhile." SIMON & MARSHALL, THE JURY SYSTEM, at 220.

4. *Petty Offenses.* In *Duncan,* the court indicated that defendants accused of "serious offenses" as opposed to "petty offenses" must be accorded the right to trial by jury. Using "objective criteria" such as the severity of the maximum authorized penalty, the court held that a two-year maximum was sufficiently serious.

In Baldwin v. New York, 399 U.S. 66 (1970), the court, per Justice White, joined by Justices Brennan and Marshall, held "that no offense can be deemed 'petty' for purposes of the right to trial by jury where imprisonment for more than six months is authorized." Looking to " 'the existing laws and practices in the nation,' " the court found that only New York City would not grant jury trial for an offense carrying a maximum sentence in excess of six months. "This near uniform judgment of the Nation" reflecting a "fundamental decision about the exercise of official power" provided the governing criterion for what is a serious offense.

## DILUTING THE BILL OF RIGHTS: RISKS OF SELECTIVE INCORPORATION?

*Duncan* holds that the sixth amendment with "all of its bag and baggage" is applicable to the states. The court had previously recognized on numerous occasions that the sixth amendment guarantee includes "a trial by jury as understood and applied at common law, and includes all the essential elements as they were recognized in this country and England when the Constitution was adopted. . . . Those elements were—(1) that the jury should consist of twelve men, neither more nor less; (2) that the jury be in the presence or under the superintendence of a judge . . . and (3) that the verdict be unanimous." Patton v. United States, 281 U.S. 276, 288 (1930). But the court in *Duncan* had also noted that "decisions interpreting the Sixth Amendment are always subject to reconsideration."

### The Twelve-Member Jury

In Thompson v. Utah, 170 U.S. 343 (1898), the court had concluded that the "jury" referred to in the sixth amendment was a jury "constituted, as it was at common law, of twelve persons, neither more nor less." *See* Patton v. United States, 281 U.S. 276, 288 (1930). But in Williams v. Florida, 399 U.S. 78 (1970), the court characterized this language as unnecessary to the *Thompson* decision and considered anew "whether the constitutional guarantee of a trial by 'jury' necessarily requires trial by exactly twelve persons, rather than some lesser number—in this case six [as permitted by Florida law in all but capital cases]."

Justice White, for the court, affirmed the lower court's rejection of the petitioner's sixth amendment claim, holding that "the 12-man panel is not a necessary ingredient of 'trial by jury,' and that respondent's refusal to impanel more than six members provided for by Florida law did not violate petitioner's Sixth Amendment rights as applied to the State through the Fourteenth Amendment." He concluded that the fact that the common-law jury consisted of twelve members was "an historical accident, unrelated to the great purposes which gave use to the jury in the first place."

Accepting the political purpose of the jury as defined in *Duncan,* Justice White reasoned "[g]iven this purpose, the essential feature of a jury obviously lies in the interposition between the accused and his accuser of the common-sense judgment of a group of laymen, and in the community participation and shared responsibility which results from that group's determination of guilt or innocence." But he went on to argue that "[t]he performance of this role is not a function of the particular number of the body which makes up the jury. To be sure, the number should probably be large enough to promote group deliberation, free from outside attempts at intimidation, and to provide a fair possibility for obtaining a representative cross section of the community. But we find little reason to think that these goals are in any meaningful sense less likely to be achieved when the jury numbers six, than when it numbers twelve—particularly if the requirement of unanimity is retained. And, certainly the reliability of the jury as a factfinder hardly seems likely to be a function of its size."

In support of this conclusion, Justice White contended that "neither currently available evidence nor theory suggests that the 12-man jury is necessarily more advantageous to the defendant than a jury composed of fewer members." Nor did the possibility of securing a broader cross-section of the community through the use of the larger number of jurors impress Justice White. He found such a concern to be "unrealistic." Whatever the relative merits of large and small juries, he argued, decision was to be left to Congress and the state legislatures, although he did indicate that there was some minimum number necessary to constitute a "jury."

Is there any meaningful difference between the expected performance of a six versus a twelve-member jury? Hans Zeisel notes that "[t]he jury system is predicated on the insight that people see and evaluate things differently. It is one function of the jury to bring these divergent perceptions and evaluations to trial process." Zeisel, . . . *And Then There Were None: The Diminution of the Federal Jury*, 38 U. Chi. L. Rev. 710, 715 (1971).

But another study has suggested that the quality of deliberation of a six-member jury is higher than that of the 12-member group. Note, *Reducing the Size of Juries*, 5 U. Mich. J. L. Reform 87, 99-106 (1971) and Note, *An Empirical Study of Six and Twelve Member Jury Decision-Making Process*, 6 U. Mich. J. L. Reform 671 (1972). And there is empirical evidence that the size of the jury does not affect trial outcomes. Bermant & Coppock, *Outcomes of Six- and Twelve-Member Jury Trials: An Analysis of 128 Civil Cases in the State of Washington*, 48 Wash. L. Rev. 593 (1973); Note, *Six-Member and Twelve-Member Juries: An Empirical Study of Trial Results*, 6 U. Mich. J.L. Reform 671 (1973); Note, *An Empirical Study of Six- and Twelve-Member Jury Decision-Making Processes*, 6 U. Mich. J.L. Reform 712 (1973).

Justice Harlan concurred in the *Williams* decision but castigated the "selective incorporationist" approach by which it was reached. "The decision evinces . . . a recognition that the 'incorporationist' view of the Due Process Clause of the Fourteenth Amendment which underlay *Duncan* . . . must be tempered to allow the States more elbow room in ordering their own criminal systems." While he agreed with the need to accommodate the demands of federalism, he rejected accomplishing this "by diluting constitutional protections within the federal system itself. . . . Tempering the rigor of *Duncan* should be done forthrightly, by facing up to the fact that at least in this area the 'incorporation' doctrine does not fit well with our federal structure, and by the same token that *Duncan* was wrongly decided."

Justice Harlan argued that prior to *Williams*, "it would have been unthinkable to suggest that the Sixth Amendment's right to a trial by jury is satisfied by a jury of six, or less. . . ." He rejected the majority's "cutting the umbilical cord that ties the form of the jury to the past" since "[t]he right to a trial by jury . . . has no enduring meaning apart from historical form." In contrast to the historical model of jury trial, "[t]he Court's elaboration of what is required provides no standard and vexes the meaning of the right to a jury trial in federal courts, as well as state courts, by uncertainty." He asked "[c]an it be doubted that a

unanimous jury of 12 provides a greater safeguard than a majority of six."

For Harlan, the decisions in *Baldwin* and *Williams* "demonstrate[d] a constitutional schizophrenia born of the need to cope
with national diversity under the constraints of the incorporation
doctrine." They represented the failure of the incorporationist
approach.

Justice Black, joined by Justice Douglas concurred in Justice
White's disposition of the sixth amendment issue and sought to
counter Justice Harlan's critique of the incorporation doctrine.
They rejected the assertion that *Williams* represented an attempt
to reconcile the incorporation methodology with the demands of
federalism, contending that the court would have reached the
same result had the question arisen in federal court before *Duncan*. "Today's decision is in no way attributable to any desire to
dilute the Sixth Amendment in order more easily to apply it to
the States, but follows solely as a necessary consequence of our
duty to reexamine prior decisions to reach the correct constitutional meaning in each case." Previous decisions requiring a
12-man jury, they argued, were based on an improper interpretation of the sixth amendment.

Only Justice Marshall dissented in *Williams,* citing the authority of *Thompson v. Utah* and 70 years of unbroken precedent.

### The Unanimous Jury

The question whether a "conviction of a crime by less than a
unanimous jury violates the right to trial by jury in criminal
cases specified by the Sixth Amendment and made applicable to
the States by the Fourteenth" was decided in Apodaca v. Oregon,
406 U.S. 404 (1972). Again, there was substantial precedent that
unanimity was an essential requirement for sixth amendment
jury trial. *See, e.g.,* Patton v. United States, 281 U.S. 276 (1930).
But in a plurality opinion by Justice White, joined by Chief
Justice Burger and Justices Blackmun and Rehnquist, the court
held that the sixth amendment did not require unanimity. The
decisive vote, however, was cast by Justice Powell, who concluded
that the sixth amendment did require unanimity but that this
element should not be imposed on the states as a part of fourteenth amendment due process. Hence, it would appear that a
majority of the court would hold unanimity to be constitutionally
required for federal jury trial but not for state jury trials.

Justice White's opinion in *Apodaca* mirrors *Williams.* After
finding "[t]he origins of the unanimity rule . . . shrouded in
obscurity" and the "intent of the framers" to be indeterminable,

he turned to "the function served by the jury in contemporary society." While " 'the essential feature of a jury obviously lies in the interposition between the accused and the accuser of the commonsense judgment of a group of laymen,' " he concluded that "[a] requirement of unanimity . . . does not materially contribute to the exercise of this commonsense judgment." While admitting that requiring unanimity could produce hung juries where non-unanimity would result in convictions or acquittals, he concluded that "the interest of the defendant in having the judgment of his peers interposed between himself and the officers of the State who prosecute and judge him is equally well served."

Justice White also rejected the claim that the sixth amendment jury trial provision "should be held to require a unanimous jury verdict in order to give substance to the reasonable doubt standard otherwise mandated by the Due Process Clause." Simply, the reasonable doubt guarantee is a mandate of due process and "the Sixth Amendment does not require proof beyond a reasonable doubt at all." Is this an adequate answer?

Finally, Justice White rejected the contention "that unanimity is a necessary precondition for effective application of the cross-section requirement because a rule permitting less than unanimous verdicts will make it possible for convictions to occur without the acquiescence of minority elements within the community." This erroneously assumed, stated the Justice, that "every distinct voice in the community has a right to be represented on every jury and a right to prevent conviction of a defendant in any case." In fact, all that is constitutionally forbidden is the "systematic exclusion of identifiable segments of the community"; it is a right to participate in the legal process but not to block convictions. Further, the Court believed that membership on a jury would provide representation of alternative views even though they might ultimately be rejected—"We cannot assume that the majority of the jury will refuse to weigh the evidence and reach a decision upon rational grounds, just as it must now do in order to obtain unanimous verdicts, or that a majority will deprive a man of his liberty on the basis of prejudice when a minority is presenting a reasonable argument in favor of acquittal."

In a companion case, Johnson v. Louisiana, 406 U.S. 356 (1972), the appellant had been convicted by a 9 to 3 verdict authorized by Louisiana law. Since the trial had taken place prior to *Duncan* which had been held not to have retroactive effect (DeStefano v. Woods, 392 U.S. 631 (1968)), a sixth amendment claim was not available. Appellant contended, however, *inter alia*, that the less than unanimous jury conviction violated his due process rights. His claims were rejected by the Louisiana courts and the Supreme Court affirmed 5-4.

Justice Powell concurred in *Johnson* and *Apodaca*. As indicated above, in *Apodaca* he concluded "in accord with both history and precedent, that the Sixth Amendment requires a unanimous jury verdict to convict in a federal criminal trial." But he provided the decisive vote against unanimity as a constitutional requirement for state jury trials since he did not think "that all of the elements of jury trial within the meaning of the Sixth Amendment are necessarily embodied in or incorporated into the Due Process Clause of the Fourteenth Amendment." The critical question for Justice Powell was "whether unanimity is in fact so fundamental to the essentials of jury trial ['viewed in the context of the basic Anglo-American jurisprudential system common to the States'] that this particular requirement of the Sixth Amendment is necessarily binding on the States under the Due Process Clause of the Fourteenth Amendment."

Justice Blackmun, concurring, was unable to find the 9-3 system "constitutionally offensive," Powell warned that "a system employing a 7-5, rather than a 9-3 or 75% minimum would afford . . . great difficulty." He noted, however, that Justice White had pointed out that the approved system required a "substantial majority of the jury." But consider the claim made in Justice Stewart's dissent that "there is nothing in the reasoning of the Court's opinion that would stop it from approving verdicts by 8-4 or even 7-5."

Justices Brennan, Douglas, Marshall and Stewart dissented in both cases and each wrote a separate opinion.

Douglas noted that the civil rights protected by the Bill of Rights "in cold reality touch mostly the lower castes of our society" and he asked "[a]re we giving the States the power to experiment in diluting their civil rights?" Further, he saw the unanimity rule as necessary to the proper effectuation of the reasonable doubt standard. He asked: "Suppose a jury begins with the substantial minority but then in the process of deliberation a sufficient number changes to reach the required 9:3 or 10:2 for a verdict. Is not there still a lingering doubt about that verdict? Is it not clear that the safeguard of unanimity operates in this context to make it far more likely that guilt is established beyond a reasonable doubt?" The "law and order" judicial mood was seen as lowering the "barricades of liberty" and Justice Douglas asked where it would stop. "Would the Court relax the standard of reasonable doubt still further by resorting to eight to four verdict or even majority rule?" In light of *Williams*, would it permit three to two or two to one convictions? "Is the next step the elimination of the presumption of innocence?" Such changes, he argued, must be achieved by constitutional amendment since "[t]he vast restructuring of American law which is entailed in today's decision is for political not for judicial action."

Justice Brennan, dissenting, questioned whether the majority of jurors could be relied on to give adequate weight to minority views. If, on entering the jury room, there is a majority available to reach a verdict "these jurors in the majority will have nothing but their own common sense to restrain them from returning a verdict before they have fairly considered the positions of jurors who would reach a different conclusion."

Consider the claim of Hans Zeisel that it is statistically demonstrable that "a majority verdict requirement is far more effective in nullifying the potency of minority viewpoints than is the outright reduction of a jury to a size equivalent to the majority that is allowed to agree on a verdict." Zeisel, . . . *And Then There Were None,* 38 U. CHI. L. REV., at 722.

In assessing the relation of the unanimity requirement to the reasonable doubt standard, does Justice White adequately consider the social value of maximizing certainty in jury decisions? Consider the emphasis on this value in *In re* Winship, 397 U.S. 358, 364 (1970): "[T]he use of the reasonable-doubt standard is indispensible to command the respect and confidence of the community in applications of the Criminal law. It is critical that the moral force of the criminal law not be diluted by a standard of proof that leaves people in doubt whether innocent men are being condemned." Given this premise, it has been argued that "[a] dissenting minority of two, three, or more in itself suggests to the popular mind the existence of a reasonable doubt and impairs public confidence in the criminal justice system." Note, 51 N. CAR. L. REV. 134, 140 (1972).

# *Chapter 7*

## DUE PROCESS IN THE NONCRIMINAL CONTEXT: SOME NEW CONSTITUTIONAL FRONTIERS

### A. WELFARE RIGHTS AND "THE NEW PROPERTY"

"The institution called property guards the troubled boundary between individual man and the state. It is not the only guardian; many other institutions, laws, and practices serve as well. But in a society that chiefly values material well-being, the power to control a particular portion of that well-being is the very foundation of individuality." Reich, *The New Property*, 73 YALE L.J. 733 (1964).

In 1964, Charles Reich wrote a seminal article detailing the emergence of a "new property" in the form of government largesse. The rise in government awards of money, benefits, services, contracts, franchises and licenses means that individuals are increasingly dependent on their relationship to government. With the emergence of this "new property," new legal doctrine governing the emerging relationships between government and individuals is being fashioned. A vital part of this legal development involves the concept of "entitlement" and the processes required to safeguard it. *See* Reich, *Individual Rights and Social Welfare: The Emerging Legal Issues*, 74 YALE L.J. 1245 (1965); *The Law of The Planned Society*, 75 YALE L.J. 1227 (1966).

### GOLDBERG v. KELLY
Supreme Court of the United States
397 U.S. 254, 25 L. Ed. 2d 287, 90 S. Ct. 1011 (1970)

Justice BRENNAN delivered the opinion of the Court.

The question for decision is whether a State which terminates public assistance payments to a particular recipient without affording him the opportunity for an evidentiary hearing prior to termination denies the recipient procedural due process in violation of the Due Process Clause of the Fourteenth Amendment.

. . . .

The constitutional issue to be decided, therefore, is the narrow one whether the Due Process Clause requires that the recipient be afforded an evidentiary hearing *before* the termination of benefits. The District Court held that only a pre-termination evidentiary hearing would satisfy the constitutional command, and rejected the argument of the state and city officials that the combination of the post-termination "fair hearing" with the informal pre-termination review disposed of all due process claims. The Court said: "While post-termination review is relevant, there is one overpowering fact which controls here. By hypothesis, a welfare recipient is destitute, without funds or assets. . . . Suffice it to say that to cut off a welfare recipient in the face of . . . 'brutal need' without a prior hearing of some sort is unconscionable, unless overwhelming considerations justify it." Kelly v. Wyman, 294 F. Supp. 893, 899, 900 (1968). The Court rejected the argument that the need to protect the public's tax revenues supplied the requisite "overwhelming consideration." "Against the justified desire to protect public funds must be weighed the individual's overpowering need in this unique situation not to be wrongfully deprived of assistance. . . . While the problem of additional expense must be kept in mind, it does not justify denying a hearing meeting the ordinary standards of due process. Under all the circumstances, we hold that due process requires an adequate hearing before termination of welfare benefits, and the fact that there is a later constitutionally fair proceeding does not alter the result." Although state officials were party defendants in the action, only the City of New York appealed. . . .

Appellant does not contend that procedural due process is not applicable to the termination of welfare benefits. Such benefits are a matter of statutory entitlement for persons qualified to receive them.[8] Their termination involves state action that adjudi-

---

[8] It may be realistic today to regard welfare entitlements as more like "property" than a "gratuity." Much of the existing wealth in this country takes the form of rights which do not fall within traditional common-law concepts of property. It has been aptly noted that

"[s]ociety today is built around entitlement. The automobile dealer has his franchise, the doctor and lawyer their professional licenses, the worker his union membership, contract, and pension rights, the executive his contract and stock options; all are devices to aid security and independence. Many of the most important of these entitlements now flow from government: subsidies to farmers and businessmen, routes for airlines and channels for television stations; long term contracts for defense, space, and education; social security pensions for individuals. Such sources of security, whether private or public, are no longer regarded as luxuries or gratuities; to the recipients they are essentials, fully deserved, and in no sense a form of charity. It is only the poor whose entitlements, although recognized by public policy, have not been effectively enforced." Reich, Individual Rights and Social Welfare: The Emerging Legal Issues, 74 Yale L.J. 1245, 1255 (1965). See also Reich, The New Property, 73 Yale L.J. 733 (1964).

cates important rights. The constitutional challenge cannot be answered by an argument that public assistance benefits are "a 'privilege' and not a 'right.' " Relevant constitutional restraints apply as much to the withdrawal of public assistance benefits as to disqualification for unemployment compensation; or to denial of a tax exemption; or to discharge from public employment. The extent to which procedural due process must be afforded the recipient is influenced by the extent to which he may be "condemned to suffer grievous loss," and depends upon whether the recipient's interest in avoiding that loss outweighs the governmental interest in summary adjudication. . . .

It is true, of course, that some governmental benefits may be administratively terminated without affording the recipient a pre-termination evidentiary hearing. But we agree with the District Court that when welfare is discontinued, only a pre-termination evidentiary hearing provides the recipient with procedural due process. For qualified recipients, welfare provides the means to obtain essential food, clothing, housing, and medical care. Thus the crucial factor in this context—a factor not present in the case of the blacklisted government contractor, the discharged government employee, the taxpayer denied a tax exemption, or virtually anyone else whose governmental largesse is ended—is that termination of aid pending resolution of a controversy over eligibility may deprive an *eligible* recipient of the very means by which to live while he waits. Since he lacks independent resources, his situation becomes immediately desperate. His need to concentrate upon finding the means for daily subsistence, in turn, adversely affects his ability to seek redress from the welfare bureaucracy.

Moreover, important governmental interests are promoted by affording recipients a pre-termination evidentiary hearing. From its founding the Nation's basic commitment has been to foster the dignity and well-being of all persons within its borders. We have come to recognize that forces not within the control of the poor contribute to their poverty. This perception, against the background of our traditions, has significantly influenced the development of the contemporary public assistance system. Welfare, by meeting the basic demands of subsistence, can help bring within the reach of the poor the same opportunities that are available to others to participate meaningfully in the life of the community. At the same time, welfare guards against the societal malaise that may flow from a widespread sense of unjustified frustration and insecurity. Public assistance, then, is not mere charity, but a means to "promote the general Welfare, and secure the Blessings of Liberty to ourselves and our Posterity."

The same governmental interests which counsel the provision of welfare, counsel as well its uninterrupted provision to those eligible to receive it; pre-termination evidentiary hearings are indispensable to that end.

Appellant does not challenge the force of these considerations but argues that they are outweighed by countervailing governmental interests in conserving fiscal and administrative resources. These interests, the argument goes, justify the delay of any evidentiary hearing until after discontinuance of the grants. Summary adjudication protects the public fisc by stopping payments promptly upon discovery of reason to believe that a recipient is no longer eligible. Since most terminations are accepted without challenge, summary adjudication also conserves both the fisc and administrative time and energy by reducing the number of evidentiary hearings actually held.

We agree with the District Court, however, that these governmental interests are not overriding in the welfare context. The requirement of a prior hearing doubtless involves some greater expense, and the benefits paid to ineligible recipients pending decision at the hearing probably cannot be recouped, since these recipients are likely to be judgment-proof. But the State is not without weapons to minimize these increased costs. Much of the drain on fiscal and administrative resources can be reduced by developing procedures for prompt pre-termination hearings and by skillful use of personnel and facilities. Indeed, the very provision for a post-termination evidentiary hearing in New York's Home Relief program is itself cogent evidence that the State recognizes the primacy of the public interest in correct eligibility determinations and therefore in the provision of procedural safeguards. Thus, the interest of the eligible recipient in uninterrupted receipt of public assistance, coupled with the State's interest that his payments not be erroneously terminated, clearly outweighs the State's competing concern to prevent any increase in its fiscal and administrative burdens. . . .

We also agree with the District Court, however, that the pre-termination hearing need not take the form of a judicial or quasi-judicial trial. We bear in mind that the statutory "fair hearing" will provide the recipient with a full administrative review. Accordingly, the pre-termination hearing has one function only: to produce an initial determination of the validity of the welfare department's grounds for discontinuance of payments in order to protect a recipient against an erroneous termination of his benefits. Thus, a complete record and a comprehensive opinion, which would serve primarily to facilitate judicial review and to guide future decisions, need not be provided at the pre-termination stage. We recognize, too, that both welfare authorities and recipients have an interest in relatively speedy resolution of questions of eligibility, that they are used to dealing with one another informally, and that some welfare departments have very burdensome caseloads. These considerations justify the limitation of the pre-termination hearing to minimum procedural safeguards, adapted to the particular characteristics of welfare recipients, and to the limited nature of the controversies to be resolved. We wish to add that we, no less than the dissenters, recognize the importance of not imposing upon the States or the Federal Government in this developing field of law any procedural requirements beyond those demanded by rudimentary due process.

. . . The hearing must be "at a meaningful time and in a meaningful manner." In the present context these principles require that a recipient have timely and adequate notice detailing the reasons for a proposed termination, and an effective opportunity to defend by confronting any adverse witnesses and by presenting his own arguments and evidence orally. These rights are important in cases such as those before us, where recipients have challenged proposed terminations as resting on incorrect or misleading factual premises or on misapplication of rules or policies to the facts of particular cases.

We are not prepared to say that the seven-days notice currently provided by New York City is constitutionally insufficient *per se,* although there may be cases where fairness would require that a longer time be given. Nor do we see any constitutional deficiency in the content or form of the notice. New York employs both a letter and a personal conference with a caseworker to inform a recipient of the precise questions raised about his continued eligibility. Evidently the recipient is told the legal and factual bases for the Department's doubts. This combination is probably the most effective method of communicating with recipients.

The city's procedures presently do not permit recipients to appear personally with or without counsel before the official who finally determines continued eligibility. Thus a recipient is not permitted to present evidence to that official orally, or to confront or cross-examine adverse witnesses. These omissions are fatal to the constitutional adequacy of the procedures.

The opportunity to be heard must be tailored to the capacities and circumstances of those who are to be heard. It is not enough that a welfare recipient may present his position to the decision maker in writing or second-hand through his caseworker. Written submissions are an unrealistic option for most recipients, who lack the educational attainment necessary to write effectively and who cannot obtain professional assistance. Moreover, written submissions do not afford the flexibility of oral presentations; they do not permit the recipient to mold his argument to the issues the decision maker appears to regard as important. Particularly where credibility and veracity are at issue, as they must be in many termination proceedings, written submissions are a wholly unsatisfactory basis for decision. The second-hand presentation to the decision maker by the caseworker has its own deficiencies; since the caseworker usually gathers the facts upon which the charge of ineligibility rests, the presentation of the recipient's side of the controversy cannot safely be left to him. Therefore a recipient must be allowed to state his position orally. Informal procedures will suffice; in this context due process does not require a particular order of proof or mode of offering evidence.

In almost every setting where important decisions turn on questions of fact, due process requires an opportunity to confront and cross-examine adverse witnesses. . . . Welfare recipients must therefore be given an opportunity to confront and cross-examine the witnesses relied on by the department.

"The right to be heard would be, in many cases, of little avail if it did not comprehend the right to be heard by counsel." Powell v. Alabama, 287 U.S. 45, 68-69 (1932). We do not say that counsel must be provided at the pre-termination hearing, but only that the recipient must be allowed to retain an attorney if he so desires. Counsel can help delineate the issues, present the factual contentions in an orderly manner, conduct cross-examination, and generally safeguard the interests of the recipient. We do not anticipate that this assistance will unduly prolong or otherwise encumber the hearing. Evidently HEW has reached the same conclusion.

Finally, the decision maker's conclusion as to a recipient's eligibility must rest solely on the legal rules and evidence adduced at the hearing. To demonstrate compliance with this elementary requirement, the decision maker should state the reasons for his determination and indicate the evidence relied on, though his statement need not amount to a full opinion or even formal findings of fact and conclusions of law. And, of course, an impartial decision maker is essential. We agree with the District Court that prior involvement in some aspects of a case will not necessarily bar a welfare official from acting as a decision maker. He should not, however, have participated in making the determination under review.

Affirmed.

Justice BLACK, dissenting.

In the last half century the United States, along with many, perhaps most, other nations of the world, has moved far towards becoming a welfare state, that is, a nation that for one reason or another taxes its most affluent people to help support, feed, clothe and shelter its less fortunate citizens. The result is that today more than nine million men, women, and children in the United States receive some kind of state or federally financed public assistance in the form of allowances or gratuities, generally paid them periodically, usually by the week, month, or quarter. Since these gratuities are paid on the basis of need, the list of recipients is not static, and some people go off the lists and others are added from time to time. These ever-changing lists put a constant administrative burden on the Government and it certainly could not have reasonably anticipated that this burden would include the additional procedural expense imposed by the Court today.

. . . .

. . . Doubtless some draw relief checks from time to time who know they are not eligible, either because they are not actually in need or for some other reason. Many of those who thus draw undeserved gratuities are without sufficient property to enable the Government to collect back from them any money they wrongfully receive. But the Court today holds that it would violate the Due Process Clause of the Fourteenth Amendment to stop paying those people weekly or monthly allowances unless the Government first affords them a full "evidentiary hearing" even though welfare officials are persuaded that the recipients are not rightfully entitled to receive a penny under the law. In other words, although some recipients might be on the lists for payment wholly because of deliberate fraud on their parts, the Court holds that the Government is helpless and must continue, until after an evidentiary hearing, to pay money that it does not owe, never has owed, and never could owe. I do not believe there is any provision in our Constitution that should thus paralyze the Government's efforts to protect itself against making payments to people who are not entitled to them.

. . . .

. . . Today's balancing act requires a "pre-termination evidentiary hearing," yet there is nothing that indicates what tomorrow's balance will be. Although the majority attempts to bolster its decision with limited quotations from prior cases, it is obvious that today's result depends neither on the language of the Constitution itself or the principles of other decisions, but solely on the collective judgment of the majority as to what would be a fair and humane procedure in this case.

. . . .

The procedure required today as a matter of constitutional law finds no precedent in our legal system. Reduced to its simplest terms, the problem in this case is similar to that frequently encountered when two parties have an ongoing legal relationship which requires one party to make periodic payments to the other. Often the situation arises where the party "owing" the money stops paying it and justifies his conduct by arguing that the recipient is not legally entitled to payment. The recipient can, of course, disagree and go to court to compel payment. But I know of no situation in our legal system in which the person alleged to owe money to another is required by law to continue making payments to a judgment-proof claimant without the benefit of any security or bond to insure that these payments can be recovered if he wins his legal argument. Yet today's decision in no way obligates the welfare recipient to pay back any benefits wrongfully received during the pretermination evidentiary hearings or post any bond, and in all "fairness" it could not do so. These recipients are by definition too poor to post a bond or to repay the benefits which, as the majority assumes, must be spent as received to insure survival.

The Court apparently feels that this decision will benefit the poor and needy. In my judgment the eventual result will be just the opposite. While today's decision requires only an administrative, evidentiary hearing, the inevitable logic of the approach taken will lead to constitutionally imposed, time-consuming delays of a full adversary process of administrative and judicial review. In the next case the welfare recipients are bound to argue that cutting off benefits before judicial review of the agency's decision is also a denial of due process. Since, by hypothesis, termination of aid at that point may still "deprive an *eligible* recipient of the very means by which to live while he waits" I would be surprised if the weighing process did not compel the conclusion that termination without full judicial review would be unconscionable. After all, at each step, as the majority seems to feel, the issue is only one of weighing the Government's pocketbook against the actual survival of the recipient, and surely that balance must always tip in favor of the individual. Similarly today's decision requires only the opportunity to have the benefit of counsel at the administrative hearing, but it is difficult to believe that the same reasoning process would not require the appointment of counsel, for otherwise the right to counsel is a meaningless one since these people are too poor to hire their own advocates. Thus the end result of today's decision may well be that the Government, once it decides to give welfare benefits, cannot reverse that decision until the recipient has had the benefits of full administrative and judicial review, including, of course, the opportunity to present his case to this Court. Since this process will usually entail a delay of several years, the inevitable result of such a constitutionally imposed burden will be that the Government will not put a claimant on the rolls initially until it has made an exhaustive investigation to determine his eligibility. While this Court will perhaps have insured that no needy person will be taken off the rolls without a full "due process" proceeding, it will also have insured that many will never get on the rolls, or at least that they will remain destitute during the lengthy proceedings followed to determine initial eligibility.

For the foregoing reasons I dissent from the Court's holding. The operation of a welfare state is a new experiment for our Nation. For this reason, among others, I feel that new experiments in carrying out a welfare program should not be frozen into our constitutional structure. It should be left, as are other legislative determinations, to the Congress and the legislatures which the people elect to make our laws.

[Justice Stewart and Chief Justice Burger, joined by Justice Black, wrote separate dissenting opinions, which appeared in the companion case to *Kelly*, Wheeler v. Montgomery, 397 U.S. 280 (1970). Justice Stewart wrote a one-paragraph dissent noting that the "question . . . is a close one; . . ." but providing no further explanation.]

---

## NOTES

1. A number of cases have rejected the application of due process standards to welfare, characterizing benefits as a matter of "privilege" rather than "right." The dichotomy has increasingly been criticized and rejected. *See, e.g.*, Wieman v. Updegraff, 344 U.S. 183, 191-92 (1952); Schware v. Board of Bar Examiners, 353 U.S. 232, 239 n. 5 (1957); Sherbert v. Verner, 374 U.S. 398, 401 (1963); Van Alstyne, *The Demise of the Right-Privilege Distinction in Constitutional Law*, 81 HARV. L. REV. 1439 (1968); Comment, *Withdrawal of Public Welfare: The Right to a Prior Hearing*, 76 YALE L.J. 1234 (1967). Does *Goldberg v. Kelly* explicitly reject the "right-privilege" dichotomy? Does the court actually characterize welfare benefits as a right? It has been contended that Justice Brennan found welfare to be a new property right which "affords to welfare that greater presumption of inviolability that attends more traditional forms of property. The

burden is on the state to show functionally that the 'overriding demands' of the public interest require that the welfare recipient suffer diminution of his 'property.' " *See* Christensen, *Of Prior Hearings and Welfare as "New Property,"* 3 CLEARINGHOUSE REV. 334, 335 (1970).

2. *Kelly* may be saying that there is a "property" interest in welfare benefits. Must interest asserted involve "life, liberty and property" for due process to apply? Newman, *The Process of Prescribing "Due Process,"* 49 CALIF. L. REV. 215, 218 (1961), argues that " 'life, liberty or property' should be treated as a description of *all legal interests.*"

Of what importance is Justice Brennan's emphasis on the "statutory entitlement" of an eligible person to welfare? In Bell v. Burson, 402 U.S. 535 (1971), a Georgia statute, providing for suspension of the motor vehicle registration and the driver's license of an uninsured motorist involved in an accident unless security were posted and excluding any consideration of fault at a pre-suspension hearing, was held violative of procedural due process since it did not provide a prior hearing for the determination of whether there existed a reasonable possibility of an adverse judgment. Justice Brennan, writing for the court in *Burson,* held that due process standards should be applied to such a procedure since: "Once licenses are issued, as in petitioner's case, their continued possession may become essential in the pursuit of a livelihood. Suspension of issued licenses thus involves state action that adjudicates important interests of the licensees. In such cases the licenses are not to be taken away without that procedural due process required by the Fourteenth Amendment. . . . This is but an application of the general proposition that relevant constitutional restraints limit state power to terminate an entitlement whether the entitlement is denominated a 'right' or a 'privilege.' "

3. *See* O'Neil, *Of Justice Delayed and Justice Denied: The Welfare Prior Hearing Cases,* 1970 SUP. CT. REV. 161, for an excellent analysis of *Kelly* and its implications. Professor O'Neil suggests that there is a two-fold dimension to the new emphasis on entitlement: "First, the very use of this terminology may indicate that some kinds of government benefits rank higher than others on a still unannounced priority list. . . . Second, there is a lurking implication that claims to procedural due process may require a firmer basis than claims of substantive rights."

4. Does *Kelly* lend any support to a claim for a substantive right to welfare benefits? Richardson v. Belcher, 404 U.S. 78 (1971), rejects the claim that "an expectation interest in public benefits [disability payments] confer[s] a contractual right to receive the expected amounts." The court distinguished *Kelly*

as involving procedural rights. "But there is no controversy over procedure in the present case, and the analogy drawn in *Goldberg* between social welfare and 'property,' cannot be stretched to impose a constitutional limitation on the power of Congress to make substantive changes in the law of entitlements to public benefits."

5. *Kelly* rejects the view that pre-termination hearings are always required when governmental benefits are discontinued. What process is due in a particular context, "depends upon whether the recipient's interest in avoiding . . . loss outweighs the governmental interest in summary adjudication." Can such differing interests be "objectively" balanced? Is it a proper function of the judiciary to engage in such balancing? *Kelly* never had to confront the initial question of whether the welfare recipient has a constitutional right to a formal hearing since there was a statutory right to a "fair hearing." Rather, the question became one of timing. Is there a constitutional right to a hearing? What factors are balanced in *Kelly* in determining whether due process requires a prior hearing?

6. What guarantees must be afforded at welfare pre-termination hearings? Professor O'Neil comments that "the overriding interest of both beneficiary and system in the adversary process is the achievement of accuracy and fairness. The requirement of notice and the opportunity for confrontation combine to deter erroneous agency action and to avert the certainly harmful, sometimes irreversible, consequences of error. Other interests also served by the adversary process are secondary though not unimportant." O'Neil, *Of Justice Delayed*, 1970 SUP. CT. REV., at 190. Can these objectives be achieved without the appointment of counsel? See the dissenting opinion of Justice Black in *Kelly* on the issue of right to appointed counsel. Why isn't a complete record and a comprehensive opinion required to assure fairness? How "involved" in the case may the decision-maker be before due process is violated?

7. Is *Goldberg v. Kelly* applicable to the reduction of welfare benefits? In Daniel v. Goliday, 398 U.S. 73 (1970), the court in a *per curiam* opinion, noted that *Kelly* had not reached this issue and concluded: "We think that the bearing of those decisions on the treatment of benefit reductions should be determined in the first instance by the District Court on a record developed by the parties with specific attention to that issue." In Hunt v. Edmunds, 328 F. Supp. 468, 476 (D. Minn. 1971), the court concluded that "[t]he concept of 'brutal need' is not limited to termination or suspension, but may as well be applicable to reductions, at least a substantial one such as here." *Kelly* was also controlling since "the issue underlying the determination

to reduce is of such a nature here that affording plaintiffs an
opportunity to be heard on the facts before a reduction is ordered
might affect the decision to be made." *See* Dooley & Goldberg,
*The Search for Due Process in the Administration of Social Wel-
fare Programs,* 47 N. DAK. L. REV. 209 (1971).

### Nonwelfare Public Assistance Proceedings

1.  To what extent does due process mandate particular
procedures in other public assistance proceedings? In Richardson
v. Perales, 402 U.S. 389 (1971), the court was concerned with the
due process requirements applicable to medical reports in a
Social Security hearing to determine the validity of a disability
claim. The court held that written medical evidence alone was
sufficient to support a finding of nondisability despite the hearsay
character of such evidence, the absence of any cross-examination
and the presence of opposing nonhearsay medical testimony in
support of the claim. The court stressed that the claimant had
failed to exercise his opportunity to subpoena the examining
physicans. *Kelly* was distinguished since: "We are not concerned
with termination of disability benefits once granted. Neither are
we concerned with a change of status without notice. . . . Further,
the spectre of questionable credibility and veracity is not present;
there is professional disagreement with medical conclusions, to be
sure, but there is no attack here upon the doctor's credibility or
veracity. *Kelly* affords little comfort to the claimant."

2.  In Richardson v. Wright, 405 U.S. 208 (1972), the court
declined to consider the applicability of *Kelly* to the suspension
and termination of disability benefit payments under the Social
Security Act because, prior to oral argument, the Social Security
Administration had adopted new suspension and termination
procedures. The Court remanded the case to the Social Security
Administration, without comment on the merits, concluding
that: "In the context of a comprehensive complex administrative
program, the administrative process must have a reasonable
opportunity to evolve procedures to meet needs as they arise."
*See* text, p. 109.

### Some Recent "New Property" Cases

1. As Bell v. Burson, 402 U.S. 535 (1971), text, p. 498,
suggests, *Kelly* is applicable to denials of other entitlements.
California Dep't of Human Resources v. Java, 402 U.S. 121
(1971), involved the validity of withholding unemployment
compensation benefits pending an employer's appeal. California
sought to distinguish *Kelly* on grounds that "welfare is based on
need; unemployment insurance is not." Although the court de-

cided the case on statutory grounds, Justice Douglas, concurring, rejected the alleged distinction arguing that "history makes clear that the thrust of the scheme for unemployment benefits was to take care of the need of displaced workers, pending a search for other employment." Like *Goldberg,* "the requirements of procedural due process protect the payment of benefits owing the displaced employee. . . ." *See* Crow v. California Dep't of Human Resources, 325 F. Supp. 1314 (N.D. Cal. 1970), holding that unemployment compensation may not be terminated without a hearing.

    2.  *Kelly* has also been extended to public housing evictions. *See, e.g.,* Escalera v. New York City Housing Authority, 425 F.2d 853 (2d Cir.), *cert. denied,* 400 U.S. 853 (1970).

## B.  RIGHT TO USE AND POSSESS PROPERTY: CONSTITUTIONALIZING THE CONSUMER CREDIT RELATIONSHIP

    Consumer credit, like government largesse, plays an increasingly important role in our economy. And as is true in the new property context, the citizen often has a vital stake in the legal procedures governing the credit process. In this area as in so many others, legal institutions are being called upon to define the meaning and scope of the due process guarantee in a field where, previously, it had not been a major consideration.

    Among the new questions raised by application of the Constitution to the credit process are these: Does the purchaser of goods under a conditional sales contract have a "property interest" within the meaning of the due process guarantee? If it is property, does a temporary dispossession of goods, pending adjudication of default, constitute a deprivation? What is constitutionally required before a person can waive his rights to notice and hearing in a cognovit note? How much weight is to be given to the state interest in assuring collectability of debts, in promoting the extension of credit, in avoiding burdensome administrative proceedings? These are only indicative of the kinds of concerns involved. *See* Note, 68 Mich. L. Rev. 986 (1970).

    Some answers were provided in Sniadach v. Family Finance Corp., 395 U.S. 337 (1969). A state statutory procedure permitting garnishment of an employee's wages without notice and an opportunity to be heard, subject to being "unfrozen" if the wage earner won on the merits, was held to violate due process. Justice Douglas' opinion for the court stressed that the wage earner was deprived of the enjoyment of wages—"a specialized type of property presenting distinct problems in our economic system"—even the temporary loss of which "may impose tremendous hardship on wage earners with families to support." Such a summary procedure "may as a practical matter drive a wage-earning family to the wall." Further, the debt often turns out to be fraudulent, thereby intensifying the injustice. There was no indication in the facts that "special protection to a state or creditor interest" was present.

Justice Harlan concurred in a separate opinion, emphasizing that wages constitute property within the meaning of the due process guarantee which embodies "concepts [of fundamental fairness] which are part of the Anglo-American legal heritage."

Justice Black dissented in an opinion again reflecting his rejection of the "due process philosophy which brought on President Roosevelt's Court fight." The decision, argued Justice Black, reflected only the majority's conclusion that this garnishment procedure is "bad state policy," a determination only the state legislature, and not the court, has the power to make. Further, the petitioner did not claim to have suffered any of the injustices or deprivations that might be occasioned by some garnishment provisions. The court, argued Justice Black, should respect the state court's policy of not anticipating controversies.

**FUENTES v. SHEVIN**
Supreme Court of the United States
407 U.S. 67, 32 L. Ed. 2d 556, 92 S. Ct. 1983 (1972)

Justice STEWART delivered the opinion of the Court.

We here review the decisions of two three-judge federal district courts that upheld the constitutionality of Florida and Pennsylvania laws authorizing the summary seizure of goods or chattels in a person's possession under a writ of replevin. Both statutes provide for the issuance of writs ordering state agents to seize a person's possessions, simply upon the *ex parte* application of any other person who claims a right to them and posts a security bond. Neither statute provides for notice to be given to the possessor of the property, and neither statute gives the possessor an opportunity to challenge the seizure at any kind of prior hearing. . . .

The primary question in the present cases is whether these state statutes are constitutionally defective in failing to provide for hearings "at a meaningful time." . . . The issue is whether procedural due process in the context of these cases requires an opportunity for a hearing *before* the State authorizes its agents to seize property in the possession of a person upon the application of another.

The constitutional right to be heard is a basic aspect of the duty of government to follow a fair process of decision-making when it acts to deprive a person of his possessions. The purpose of this requirement is not only to ensure abstract fair play to the individual. Its purpose, more particularly, is to protect his use and possession of property from arbitrary encroachment—to minimize substantially unfair or mistaken deprivations of property, a danger that is especially great when the State seizes goods simply upon application of and for the benefit of a private party. So viewed, the prohibition against the deprivation of property without due process of law reflects the high value, embedded in our constitutional and political history, that we place on a person's right to enjoy what is his, free of governmental interference.

The requirement of notice and an opportunity to be heard raises no impenetrable barrier to the taking of a person's possessions. But the fair process of decision-making that it guarantees works, by itself, to protect against arbitrary deprivation of property. For when a person has an opportunity to speak up in his own defense, and when the State must listen to what he has to say, substantively unfair and simply mistaken deprivations of property interests can be prevented. . . .

If the right to notice and a hearing is to serve its full purpose, then, it is clear that it must be granted at a time when the deprivation can still be prevented. At a later hearing, an individual's possessions can be returned to him if it was unfairly or mistakenly taken in the first place. Damages may even be awarded to him for the wrongful deprivation. But no later hearing and no damage award can undo the fact that the arbitrary taking that was subject to the right of procedural due process has already occurred. . . .

This is no new principle of constitutional law. The right to a prior hearing has long been recognized by this Court under the Fourteenth and Fifth Amendments. Although the Court has held that due process tolerates variances in the *form* of a hearing "appropriate to the nature of the case," . . . the Court has traditionally insisted that, whatever its form, opportunity for that hearing must be provided before the deprivation at issue takes effect. . . .

The Florida and Pennsylvania prejudgment replevin statutes fly in the face of this principle. To be sure, the requirements that a party seeking a writ must first post a bond, allege conclusorily that he is entitled to specific goods, and open himself to possible liability in damages if he is wrong, serve to deter wholly unfounded applications for a writ. But those requirements are hardly a substitute for a prior hearing, for they test no more than the strength of the applicant's own belief in his rights.[13] . . . Because of the understandable, self-interested fallibility of litigants, a court does not decide a dispute until it has had an opportunity to hear both sides—and does not generally take even tentative action until it has itself examined the support for the plaintiff's position. The Florida and Pennsylvania statutes do not even require the official issuing a writ of replevin to do that much.

. . . .

The right to a prior hearing, of course, attaches only to the deprivation of an interest encompassed within the Fourteenth Amendment's protection. In the present cases, the Florida and Pennsylvania statutes were applied to replevy chattels in the appellants' possession. The replevin was not cast as a final judgment; most, if not all, of the appellants lacked full title to the chattels; and their claim even to continued possession was a matter in dispute. Moreover, the chattels at stake were nothing more than an assortment of household goods. Nonetheless, it is clear that the appellants were deprived of possessory interests in those chattels that were within the protection of the Fourteenth Amendment.

A deprivation of a person's possessions under a prejudgment writ of replevin, at least in theory, may be only temporary. The Florida and Pennsylvania statutes do not require a person to wait until a post-seizure hearing and final judgment to recover what has been replevied. Within three days after the seizure, the statutes allowing him to recover the goods if he, in return, surrenders other property—a payment necessary to secure a bond in double the value of the goods seized from him. But it is now well settled that a temporary, nonfinal deprivation of property is nonetheless a "deprivation" in the terms of the Fourteenth Amendment. Both *Sniadach* and *Bell* involved takings of property pending a final judgment in an underlying dispute. In both cases, the challenged statutes included recovery provisions, allowing the defendants to post security to quickly regain the property taken from them. Yet the Court firmly held that these were deprivations of property that must be preceded by a fair hearing.

The present cases are no different. When officials of Florida or Pennsylvania seize one piece of property from a person's possession and then agree to return it if he surrenders another,

---

[13] They may not even test that much. For if an applicant for the writ knows that he is dealing with an uneducated, uninformed consumer with little access to legal help and little familiarity with legal procedures, there may be a substantial possibility that a summary seizure of property—however unwarranted—may go unchallenged, and the applicant may feel that he can act with impunity.

they deprive him of property whether or not he has the funds, the knowledge and the time needed to take advantage of the recovery provision. The Fourteenth Amendment draws no bright lines around three-day, 10-day or 50-day deprivations of property. Any significant taking of property by the State is within the purview of the Due Process Clause. While the length and consequent severity of a deprivation may be another factor to weigh in determining the appropriate form of hearing, it is not decisive of the basic right to a prior hearing of some kind.

The appellants who signed conditional sales contracts lacked full legal title to the replevied goods. The Fourteenth Amendment's protection of "property," however, has never been interpreted to safeguard only the rights of undisputed ownership. Rather, it has been read broadly to extend protection to "any significant property interest," including statutory entitlements.

The appellants were deprived of such an interest in the replevied goods—the interest in continued possession and use of the goods. They had acquired this interest under the conditional sales contracts that entitled them to possession and use of the chattels before transfer of title. In exchange for immediate possession, the appellants had agreed to pay a major financing charge beyond the basic price of the merchandise. Moreover, by the time the goods were summarily repossessed, they had made substantial installment payments. Clearly, their possessory interest in the goods, dearly bought and protected by contract, was sufficient to invoke the protection of the Due Process Clause.

. . . It is enough to invoke the procedural safeguards of the Fourteenth Amendment that a significant property interest is at stake, whatever the ultimate outcome of a hearing on the contractual right to continued possession and use of the goods.

. . . .

We hold that the Florida and Pennsylvania prejudgment replevin provisions work a deprivation of property without due process of law insofar as they deny the right to a prior opportunity to be heard before chattels are taken from their possessor. Our holding, however, is a narrow one. We do not question the power of a State to seize goods before a final judgment in order to protect the security interests of creditors so long as those creditors have tested their claim to the goods through the process of a fair prior hearing. The nature and form of such prior hearings, moreover, are legitimately open to many potential variations and are a subject, at this point, for legislation—not adjudication. Since the essential reason for the requirement of a prior hearing is to prevent unfair and mistaken deprivations of property, however, it is axiomatic that the hearing must provide a real test. . . .

Justice POWELL and Justice REHNQUIST did not participate in the consideration or decision of these cases.

Justice WHITE, with whom THE CHIEF JUSTICE and Justice BLACKMUN join, dissenting.

Because the Court's opinion and judgment improvidently, in my view, call into question important aspects of the statutes of almost all the States governing secured transactions and the procedure for repossessing personal property, I must dissent for the reasons which follow.

. . . .

. . . I would not construe the Due Process Clause to require the creditors to do more than they have done in these cases to secure possession pending final hearing. Certainly, I would not ignore, as the Court does, the creditor's interest in preventing further use and deterioration of the property in which he has substantial interest. Surely under the Court's own definition, the creditor has a "property" interest as deserving of protection as that of the debtor. At least the debtor, who is very likely uninterested in a speedy resolution that could terminate his use of the property, should be required to make those payments, into court or otherwise, upon which his right to possession is conditioned. Cf. Lindsay v. Normet, 405 U.S. 56 (1972).

. . . The Court's rhetoric is seductive, but in end analysis, the result it reaches will have little impact and represents no more than ideological tinkering with state law. It would appear that creditors could withstand attack under today's opinion simply by making clear in the controlling credit instruments that they may retake possession without a hearing, or, for that matter, without resort to judicial process at all. Alternatively, they need only give a few days' notice of a hearing, take possession if hearing is waived or if there is default; and if hearing is necessary merely establish probable cause for asserting that default has occurred. It is very doubtful in my mind that such a hearing would in fact result in protections for the debtor substantially different from those the present laws provide. On the contrary, the availability of credit may well be diminished or, in any event, the expense of securing it increased.

None of this seems worth the candle to me. The procedure which the Court strikes down is not some barbaric hang-over from bygone days. The respective rights of the parties in secured transactions have undergone the most intensive analysis in recent years. The Uniform Commercial Code, which now so pervasively governs the subject matter with which it deals, provides in Art. 9, § 9-503, that:

"Unless otherwise agreed a secured party has on default the right to take possession of the collateral. In taking possession a secured party may proceed without judicial process if this can be done without breach of peace or may proceed by action. . . ."

Recent studies have suggested no changes in Art. 9 in this respect. See Permanent Editorial Board for the Uniform Commercial Code, Review Committee for Article 9 of the Uniform Commercial Code, Final Report, § 9-503 (April 25, 1971). I am content to rest on the judgment of those who have wrestled with these problems so long and often and upon the judgment of the legislatures that have considered and so recently adopted provisions that contemplate precisely what has happened in these cases.

---

## NOTES

1. *The Meaning of Due Process.* Is the possession and use of all forms of property interests now established as "property" within the meaning of due process guarantee? Does the due process guarantee extend to an "expectation" of receiving property even though title has not yet been transferred? Is every dispossession, no matter how temporary, a deprivation within the meaning of the due process guarantee?

2. *Scope of Due Process.* Why is a *prior* hearing required in *Sniadach*? It has been said that *Sniadach* failed to consider the competing state and creditor interests. Notes, 68 MICH. L. REV. 986, 995-98 (1970). In Randone v. Appellate Dep't of Superior Court, 5 Cal. 3d 536, 96 Cal. Rptr. 709, 488 P.2d 13 (1971), the court stated that "the hardship imposed on the debtor by the attachment of his 'necessities of life' is so severe that we do not believe that a creditor's private interest is ever sufficient to permit imposition of such deprivation before notice and a hearing on the validity of the creditor's claim."

How important is the debtor's interest in *Fuentes v. Shevin*? What are the state and private creditor's interests? In *Randone,* the court stated: "the greater the deprivation an individual will suffer by an attachment of property, the greater the public urgency must be to justify the imposition of that loss on an individual, and the more substantial the procedural safeguards that must be afforded when such notice and hearing are required." In *Sniadach* and *Fuentes,* the court defines certain "extraordinary situations" justifying summary deprivation of property. Would any of the stated reasons justify preadjudicatory deprivation of the "necessities of life"? Does *Fuentes* involve such necessities?

In both *Sniadach* and *Fuentes,* the dissent accuses the majority of legislating their ideological preferences into law. Do you agree?

What procedures would be constitutionally required in a prior hearing? If the hearing is to be "meaningful," does an indigent have a right to appointed counsel?

3. *Prejudgment Attachment Generally.* What other property interests would require an adjudicatory proceeding prior to attachment or garnishment? In Larson v. Fetherston, 44 Wis. 2d 712, 172 N.W.2d 20 (1969), the court held unconstitutional a preadjudication garnishment of a bank account, commenting: "[C]learly, a due process violation should not depend upon the type of property being subjected to the procedure." 172 N.W.2d at 23. *Compare* the following: "The application of the court's reasoning in *Sniadach* to other forms of prejudgment attachment and garnishment should result in a finding of a denial of due process only in isolated instances, such as those involving the attachment and removal of personal property essential to the defendant, or those involving the garnishment of intangible assets which the defendant needs in order to purchase daily necessities." Note, 68 MICH. L. REV. 986, 1004 (1970). Does *Fuentes* reject this limitation?

Can a lien attach to realty, encumbering its alienability, prior to adjudication? *See* Note, 68 MICH. L. REV. 986, 1000 (1970), for an affirmative response, emphasizing that the debtor retains the possession and use of the property. *See also* Black Watch Farms Inc. v. Dick, 323 F. Supp. 100, 102 (D. Conn. 1971), holding that a "real property attachment is not a final proceeding, nor is it unduly harsh. Therefore, due process is satisfied by the subsequent plenary hearing in the main action."

4. *Waiver.* In D. H. Overmyer Co. v. Frick Co., 405 U.S. 174 (1972), discussed at length in *Fuentes,* the court held that the waiver of notice and hearing provisions in a cognovit note are not *per se* violative of due process. The court limited itself to the facts noting: "our holding, of course, is not controlling precedent for facts of other cases. For example, where the contract is one of adhesion, where there is great disparity in bargaining power, and where the debtor receives nothing for the cognovit provision, other legal consequences may ensue."

What must be shown in order to establish waiver? In *Overmyer,* the court stated: "Even if, for present purposes, we assumed that the standard for waiver in a corporate-property-right case of this kind is the same standard applicable to waiver in a criminal proceeding, that is, that it be voluntary, knowing, and intelligently made . . . that standard was fully satisfied here." It was not necessary, therefore, to define the standards for civil cases. Does *Fuentes* help in identifying the governing waiver standard in civil cases?

Is the fact that waiver is not demonstrable on the face of the contract dispositive? Do you agree with Justice White, dissenting in *Fuentes,* that "creditors could withstand attack under today's opinion simply by making it clear in the controlling credit instruments that they may retake possession without a hearing, or, for that matter, without resort to the judicial process at all"?

## MITCHELL v. W. T. GRANT CO.
Supreme Court of the United States
416 U.S. 600, 40 L. Ed. 2d 406, 94 S. Ct. 1895 (1974)

Justice WHITE delivered the opinion of the Court.

In this case, a state trial judge in Louisiana ordered the sequestration of personal property on the application of a creditor who had made an installment sale of the goods to petitioner and whose affidavit asserted delinquency and prayed for sequestration to enforce a vendor's lien under state law. The issue is whether the sequestration violated the Due Process Clause of the Fourteenth Amendment because it was ordered *ex parte,* without prior notice or opportunity for a hearing.

. . . .

Petitioner's basic proposition is that because he had possession of and a substantial interest in the sequestered property, the Due Process Clause of the Fourteenth Amendment necessarily forbade the seizure without prior notice and opportunity for a hearing. In the circumstances presented here, we cannot agree.

. . . .

Plainly enough, this is not a case where the property sequestered by the court is exclusively the property of the defendant debtor. The question is not whether a debtor's property may be seized by his creditors, *pendente lite,* where they hold no present interest in the property sought to be seized. The reality is that both seller and buyer had current, real interests in the property, and the definition of property rights is a matter of state law. Resolution of the due process question must take account not only of the interests of the buyer of the property but those of the seller as well.

. . . .

Petitioner asserts that his right to a hearing before his possession is in any way disturbed is nonetheless mandated by a long line of cases in this Court, culminating in Sniadach v.

Family Finance Corp., 395 U.S. 337 (1969) and Fuentes v. Shevin, 407 U.S. 67 (1972). . . .

. . . In *Sniadach,* the Court . . . observed that garnishment was subject to abuse by creditors without valid claims, a risk minimized by the nature of the security interest here at stake and the protections to the debtor offered by Louisiana procedure. Nor was it apparent in *Sniadach* with what speed the debtor could challenge the validity of the garnishment, and obviously the creditor's claim could not rest on the danger of destruction of wages, the property seized, since their availability to satisfy the debt remained within the power of the debtor who could simply leave his job. The suing creditor in *Sniadach* had no prior interest in the property attached, and the opinion did not purport to govern the typical case of the installment seller who brings a suit to collect an unpaid balance and who does not seek to attach wages pending the outcome of the suit but to repossess the sold property on which he had retained a lien to secure the purchase price. . . . [W]e are convinced that *Fuentes* was decided against a factual and legal background sufficiently different from that now before us and that it does not require the invalidation of the Louisiana sequestration statute, either on its face or as applied in this case.

The Florida law under examination in *Fuentes* authorized repossession of the sold goods without judicial order, approval or participation. A writ of replevin was employed, but it was issued by the court clerk. As the Florida law was perceived by this Court, "[t]here is no requirement that the applicant make a convincing showing before the seizure"; the law required only "the bare assertion of the party seeking the writ that he is entitled to one" as a condition to the clerk's issuance of the writ. The Court also said that under the statute the defendant-buyer would "eventually" have an opportunity for a hearing, "as the defendant in the trial of the court action for repossession. . . ." The Pennsylvania law was considered to be essentially the same as that of Florida except that it did "not require that there *ever* be opportunity for a hearing on the merits of the conflicting claims to possession of the replevied property." . . .

The Louisiana sequestration statute followed in this case mandates a considerably different procedure. A writ of sequestration is available to a mortgage or lien holder to forestall waste or alienation of the property, but different from the Florida and Pennsylvania systems, bare conclusionary claims of ownership or lien will not suffice under the Louisiana statute. [The statute] authorizes the writ "only when the nature of the claim and the amount thereof, if any, and the grounds relied upon for the issuance of the writ clearly appear from specific facts" shown by verified petition or affidavit. Moreover, in the parish where this case arose, the requisite showing must be made to a judge and judicial authorization obtained. Mitchell was not at the unsupervised mercy of the creditor and court functionaries. The Louisiana law provides for judicial control of the process from beginning to end. This control is one of the measures adopted by the State to minimize the risk that the *ex parte* procedure will lead to a wrongful taking. It is buttressed by the provision that should the writ be dissolved there are "damages for the wrongful issuance of a writ" and for attorneys' fees "whether the writ is dissolved on motion or after trial on the merits."

The risk of wrongful use of the procedure must also be judged in the context of the issues which are to be determined at that proceeding. . . . In Louisiana, . . . the facts relevant to obtaining a writ of sequestration are narrowly confined. . . . [D]ocumentary proof is particularly suited for questions of the existence of a vendor's lien and the issue of default. There is thus far less danger here that the seizure will be mistaken and a corresponding decrease in the utility of an adversary hearing which will be immediately available in any event.

Of course, as in *Fuentes,* consideration of the impact on the debtor remains. Under Louisiana procedure, however, the debtor, Mitchell, was not left in limbo to await a hearing that might or might not "eventually" occur, as he was under the statutory schemes before the Court in *Fuentes.* Louisiana law expressly provides for an immediate hearing and dissolution of the writ "unless the plaintiff proves the grounds upon which the writ was issued."

To summarize, the Louisiana system seeks to minimize the risk of error of a wrongful interim possession by the creditor. The system protects the debtor's interest in every conceivable way, except allowing him to have the property to start with, and this is done in pursuit of what we deem an acceptable arrangement *pendente lite* to put the property in the possession of the party who furnishes protection against loss or damage to the other pending trial on the merits.

The court must be sensitive to the possible consequences, already foreseen in antiquity, of invalidating this state statute. Doing so might not increase private violence, but self-help repossession could easily lessen protections for the debtor.[13] Here,

---

[13] The advisability of requiring prior notice and hearing before repossession has been under study for several years. . . .

. . . [T]he principal question yet to be satisfactorily answered is the impact of prior notice and hearing on the price of credit, and more particu-

the initial hardship to the debtor is limited, the seller has a strong interest, the process proceeds under judicial supervision and management and the prevailing party is protected against all loss. . . .

[Affirmed.]

Justice POWELL, concurring.

In sweeping language, Fuentes v. Shevin, 407 U.S. 67 (1972), enunciated the principle that the constitutional guarantee of procedural due process requires an adversary hearing before an individual may be temporarily deprived of any possessory interest in tangible personal property, however brief the dispossession and however slight his monetary interest in the property. The Court's decision today withdraws significantly from the full reach of that principle, and to this extent I think it fair to say that the *Fuentes* opinion is overruled.

. . . .

. . . To the extent that the *Fuentes* opinion established a Procrustean rule of a prior adversary hearing, it marked a significant departure from past teachings as to the meaning of due process. . . . The *Fuentes* opinion sounded a potential death knell for a panoply of statutes in the commercial field. This fact alone justifies a re-examination of its premises. The Court today reviews these at length, and I join its opinion because I think it represents a reaffirmation of the traditional meaning of procedural due process.

Justice STEWART, with whom Justice DOUGLAS and Justice MARSHALL concur, dissenting.

. . . .

The deprivation of property in this case is identical to that at issue in *Fuentes,* and the Court does not say otherwise. Thus, under *Fuentes,* due process of law permits Louisiana to effect this deprivation only after notice to the possessor and opportunity for a hearing. Because I would adhere to the holding of *Fuentes,* I dissent. . . .

. . . .

[JUSTICE BRENNAN also dissented on the basis of *Fuentes.*]

---

## NOTES

1. *Mitchell* left the status of *Fuentes* uncertain. While Justice White purported to distinguish the cases on factual

---

larly, of the mix of procedural requirements necessary to minimize the cost.
. . .

We indicate no view whatsoever on the desirability of one or more of the proposed reforms. The uncertainty evident in the current debate suggests caution in the adoption of an inflexible constitutional rule. . . .

grounds, both the concurring and dissenting opinions in *Mitchell* could find no basis for distinction.

2. In North Georgia Finishing, Inc. v. Di-Chem, Inc., — U.S. — (1975), the court, per Justice White, held 6-3, that a Georgia garnishment statute violated due process. *Mitchell* was distinguished; *Fuentes* was applied.

The Georgia statute permitted a writ of garnishment to be issued by a court clerk, without judicial participation, on an affidavit of the creditor or his attorney which "need contain only conclusory allegations," and the posting of bond. The garnishment could be dissolved only by the defendant debtor's filing of a security bond. There was no "probable cause" hearing, nor apparently, any hearing unless the defendant posted the bond. These considerations were held to make *Fuentes*, rather than *Mitchell*, the applicable precedent. The fact that, in this case, the garnishment involved a bank account of a commercial dealer did not serve to distinguish *Fuentes* since "the probability of irreparable injury [to property interests] is sufficiently great so that some procedures are necessary to guard against the risk of initial errors."

## C. CONSTITUTIONALIZING THE EMPLOYMENT RELATIONSHIP IN THE PUBLIC SECTOR

Charles Reich has argued that public employment itself is a form of "the new property." Reich, *The New Property*, 73 YALE L.J., at 733, 734. An increasing number of citizens are either directly employed by government or are dependent on government action, *e.g.*, licenses, for their job and their status. Further, the citizen's "liberty," his freedom to act in the community, is vitally influenced by his employment situation.

Oliver Wendell Holmes, in a case involving dismissal of a policeman, once said: "The petitioner may have a constitutional right to talk politics, but he has no constitutional right to be a policeman." McAuliffe v. Mayor of New Bedford, 155 Mass. 216, 220, 29 N.E. 517 (1892). But with the continuing demise of the right-privilege dichotomy, the crucial issue for the future is the extent to which the employment interest may be burdened by government action without affording due process guarantees.

### BOARD OF REGENTS v. ROTH
Supreme Court of the United States
408 U.S. 564, 33 L. Ed. 2d 548, 92 S. Ct. 2701 (1971)

Justice STEWART delivered the opinion of the Court.

In 1968 the respondent, David Roth, was hired for his first teaching job as assistant professor of political science at Wisconsin State University-Oshkosh. He was hired for a fixed term of one academic year. The notice of his faculty appointment specified that his employment would begin on September 1, 1968, and would end on June 30, 1969. The respondent completed that term. But he was informed that he would not be rehired for the next academic year.

The respondent had no tenure rights to continued employment. Under Wisconsin statutory law a state university teacher can acquire tenure as a "permanent" employee only after four years of year-to-year employment. Having acquired tenure, a teacher is entitled to continued employment "during efficiency and good behavior." A relatively new teacher without tenure, however, is under Wisconsin law entitled to nothing beyond his one-year appointment. There are no statutory or administrative standards defining eligibility for re-employment. State law thus clearly leaves the decision whether to rehire a nontenured teacher for another year to the unfettered discretion of University officials.

The procedural protection afforded a Wisconsin State University teacher before he is separated from the University corresponds to his job security. As a matter of statutory law, a tenured teacher cannot be "discharged except for cause upon written charges" and pursuant to certain procedures. A nontenured teacher, similarly, is protected to some extent *during* his one-year term. Rules promulgated by the Board of Regents provide that a nontenured teacher "dismissed" before the end of the year may have some opportunity for review of the "dismissal." But the Rules provide no real protection for a nontenured teacher who simply is not re-employed for the next year. He must be informed by February first "concerning retention or non-retention for the ensuing year." But "no reason for non-retention need be given. No review or appeal is provided in such case."

In conformance with these Rules, the President of Wisconsin State University-Oshkosh informed the respondent before February 1, 1969, that he would not be rehired for the 1969-1970 academic year. He gave the respondent no reason for the decision and no opportunity to challenge it at any sort of hearing.

The respondent then brought this action in a federal district court alleging that the decision not to rehire him for the next year infringed his Fourteenth Amendment rights. He attacked the decision both in substance and procedure. First, he alleged that the true reason for the decision was to punish him for certain statements critical of the University administration, and that it therefore violated his right to freedom of speech. Second, he

alleged that the failure of University officials to give him notice
of any reason for nonretention and an opportunity for a hearing
violated his right to procedural due process of law.

The District Court granted summary judgment for the respondent on the procedural issue, ordering the University officials
to provide him with reasons and a hearing. 310 F.Supp. 972. The
Court of Appeals, with one judge dissenting, affirmed this partial
summary judgment. 446 F.2d 806. The only question presented to
us at this stage in the case is whether the respondent had a
constitutional right to a statement of reasons and a hearing on the
University's decision not to rehire him for another year. We hold
that he did not.

The requirements of procedural due process apply only to
the deprivation of interests encompassed within the Fourteenth
Amendment's protection of liberty and property. When protected
interests are implicated the right to some kind of prior hearing is
paramount. But the range of interests protected by procedural
due process is not infinite.

The District Court decided that procedural due process
guarantees apply in this case by assessing and balancing the
weights of the particular interests involved. It concluded that the
respondent's interest in re-employment at the Wisconsin State
University-Oshkosh outweighed the University's interest in denying him re-employment summarily. Undeniably, the respondent's
re-employment prospects were of major concern to him—concern
that we surely cannot say was insignificant. And a weighing
process has long been a part of any determination of the *form*
of hearing required in particular situations by procedural due
process. But, to determine whether due process requirements
apply in the first place, we must look not to the "weight" but to
the *nature* of the interest at stake. We must look to see if the
interest is within the Fourteenth Amendment's protection of
liberty and property.

"Liberty" and "property" are broad and majestic terms.
They are among the "[g]reat [constitutional] concepts . . . purposely left to gather meaning from experience. . . . [T]hey relate to
the whole domain of social and economic fact, and the statesmen
who founded this Nation knew too well that only a stagnant
society remains unchanged." For that reason the Court has fully
and finally rejected the wooden distinction between "rights" and
"privileges" that once seemed to govern the applicability of
procedural due process rights. The Court has also made clear
that the property interests protected by procedural due process
extend well beyond actual ownership of real estate, chattels, or
money. By the same token, the Court has required due process

protection for deprivations of liberty beyond the sort of formal constraints imposed by the criminal process.

Yet, while the Court has eschewed rigid or formalistic limitations on the protection of procedural due process, it has at the same time observed certain boundaries. For the words "liberty" and "property" in the Due Process Clause of the Fourteenth Amendment must be given some meaning.

"While this court has not attempted to define with exactness the liberty . . . guaranteed [by the Fourteenth Amendment], the term has received much consideration, and some of the included things have been definitely stated. Without doubt, it denotes not merely freedom from bodily restraint but also the right of the individual to contract, to engage in any of the common occupations of life, to acquire useful knowledge, to marry, establish a home and bring up children, to worship God according to the dictates of his own conscience, and generally to enjoy those privileges long recognized . . . as essential to the orderly pursuit of happiness by free men." Meyer v. Nebraska, 262 U.S. 390, 399. In a Constitution for a free people, there can be no doubt that the meaning of "liberty" must be broad indeed.

There might be cases in which a State refused to re-employ a person under such circumstances that interests in liberty would be implicated. But this is not such a case.

The State, in declining to rehire the respondent, did not make any charge against him that might seriously damage his standing and associations in his community. It did not base the nonrenewal of his contract on a charge, for example, that he had been guilty of dishonesty, or immorality. Had it done so, this would be a different case. For "[w]here a person's good name, reputation, honor, or integrity is at stake because of what the government is doing to him, notice and an opportunity to be heard are essential." Wisconsin v. Constantineau, 400 U.S. 433, 437 [additional citations omitted]. In such a case, due process would accord an opportunity to refute the charge before University officials. In the present case, however, there is no suggestion whatever that the respondent's interest in his "good name, reputation, honor or integrity" is at stake.

Similarly, there is no suggestion that the State, in declining to re-employ the respondent, imposed on him a stigma or other disability that foreclosed his freedom to take advantage of other employment opportunities. The State, for example, did not invoke any regulations to bar the respondent from all other public employment in State universities. Had it done so, this, again, would be a different case. . . .

To be sure, the respondent has alleged that the nonrenewal of his contract was based on his exercise of his right to freedom of speech. But this allegation is not now before us. The District Court stayed proceedings on this issue, and the respondent has yet to prove that the decision not to rehire him was, in fact, based on his free speech activities.

Hence, on the record before us, all that clearly appears is that the respondent was not rehired for one year at one University. It stretches the concept too far to suggest that a person is deprived of "liberty" when he simply is not rehired in one job but remains as free as before to seek another. Cafeteria Workers v. McElroy [367 U.S. 886 (1961)].

The Fourteenth Amendment's procedural protection of property is a safeguard of the security of interests that a person has already acquired in specific benefits. These interests—property interests—may take many forms.

. . . .

Certain attributes of "property" interests protected by procedural due process emerge from [prior] decisions. To have a property interest in a benefit, a person clearly must have more than an abstract need or desire for it. He must have more than a unilateral expectation of it. He must, instead, have a legitimate claim of entitlement to it. It is a purpose of the ancient institution of property to protect those claims upon which people rely in their daily lives, reliance that must not be arbitrarily undermined. It is a purpose of the constitutional right to a hearing to provide an opportunity for a person to vindicate those claims.

Property interests, of course, are not created by the Constitution. Rather they are created and their dimensions are defined by existing rules or understandings that stem from an independent source such as state law—rules or understandings that secure certain benefits and that support claims of entitlement to those benefits. Thus the welfare recipients in Goldberg v. Kelly, had a claim of entitlement to welfare payments that was grounded in the statute defining eligibility for them. The recipients had not yet shown that they were, in fact, within the statutory terms of eligibility. But we held that they had a right to a hearing at which they might attempt to do so.

Just as the welfare recipients' "property" interest in welfare payments was created and defined by statutory terms, so the respondent's "property" interest in employment at the Wisconsin State University-Oshkosh was created and defined by the terms of his appointment. Those terms secured his interest in employment up to June 30, 1969. But the important fact in this case is that they specifically provided that the respondent's employment was

to terminate on June 30. They did not provide for contract renewal absent "sufficient cause." Indeed, they made no provision
for renewal whatsoever.

Thus the terms of the respondent's appointment secured
absolutely no interest in re-employment for the next year. They
supported absolutely no possible claim of entitlement to re-
employment. Nor, significantly, was there any state statute or University rule or policy that secured his interest in re-employment or
that created any legitimate claim to it.[16] In these circumstances,
the respondent surely had an abstract concern in being rehired,
but he did not have a *property* interest sufficient to require the
University authorities to give him a hearing when they declined
to renew his contract of employment.

Our analysis of the respondent's constitutional rights in this
case in no way indicates a view that an opportunity for a hearing
or a statement of reasons for nonretention would, or would not,
be appropriate or wise in public colleges and universities. For it
is a written Constitution that we apply. Our role is confined to
interpretation of that Constitution.

We must conclude that the summary judgment for the respondent should not have been granted, since the respondent has
not shown that he was deprived of liberty or property protected
by the Fourteenth Amendment. . . .

[Reversed and remanded.]

Justice POWELL took no part in the decision of this case.

Justice DOUGLAS, dissenting.

. . . .

. . . [W]here "important interests" of the citizen are implicated they are not to be denied or taken away without Due
Process. *Bell v. Burson* involved a driver's license. . . . We should
now add that nonrenewal of a teacher's contract, whether or not
he has tenure, is an entitlement of the same importance and
dignity.

Cafeteria & Restaurant Workers v. McElroy, 367 U.S. 886, is
not opposed. It held that a cook employed in a cafeteria in a
military installation was not entitled to a hearing prior to the
withdrawal of her access to the facility. Her employer was prepared to employ her at another of its restaurants, the withdrawal

---

[16] To be sure, the respondent does suggest that most teachers hired on
a year-to-year basis by the Wisconsin State University-Oshkosh are, in fact,
rehired. But the District Court has not found that there is anything approaching a "common law" of re-employment, see *Perry v. Sindermann,* so strong as
to require University officials to give the respondent a statement of reasons
and a hearing on their decision not to rehire him.

was not likely to injure her reputation, and her employment opportunities elsewhere were not impaired. The Court held that the very limited individual interest in this one job did not outweigh the Government's authority over an important federal military establishment. Nonrenewal of a teacher's contract is tantamount in effect to a dismissal and the consequences may be enormous. Nonrenewal can be a blemish that turns into a permanent scar and effectively limits any chance the teacher has of being rehired as a teacher at least in his State.

If this nonrenewal implicated the First Amendment, then Roth was deprived of constitutional rights because his employment was conditioned on a surrender of First Amendment rights; and apart from the First Amendment he was denied due process when he received no notice and hearing of the adverse action contemplated against him. Without a statement of the reasons for the discharge and an opportunity to rebut those reasons—both of which were refused by petitioners—there is no means short of a lawsuit to safeguard the right not to be discharged for the exercise of First Amendment guarantees.

. . . .

Justice MARSHALL dissenting.

. . . .

This Court has long maintained that "the right to work for a living in the common occupations of the community is of the very essence of the personal freedom and opportunity that it was the purpose of the [Fourteenth] Amendment to secure." Truax v. Raich, 239 U.S. 33, 41 (1915). It has also established that the fact that an employee has no contract guaranteeing work for a specific future period does not mean that as the result of action by the government he may be "discharged at any time, for any reason or for no reason." *Truax v. Raich.*

In my view, every citizen who applies for a government job is entitled to it unless the government can establish some reason for denying the employment. This is the "property" right that I believe is protected by the Fourteenth Amendment and that cannot be denied "without due process of law." And it is also liberty—liberty to work—which is the "very essence of the personal freedom and opportunity" secured by the Fourteenth Amendment.

This Court has often had occasion to note that the denial of public employment is a serious blow to any citizen. Thus, when an application for public employment is denied or the contract of a government employee is not renewed, the government must say why, for it is only when the reasons underlying government action are known that citizens feel secure and protected against arbitrary government action.

Employment is one of the greatest, if not the greatest, benefits that governments offer in modern-day life. When something as valuable as the opportunity to work is at stake, the government may not reward some citizens and not others without demonstrating that its actions are fair and equitable. And it is procedural due process that is our fundamental guarantee of fairness, our protection against arbitrary, capricious, and unreasonable government action.

. . . .

. . . I would . . . hold that respondent was denied due process when his contract was not renewed and he was not informed of the reasons and given an opportunity to respond.

It may be argued that to provide procedural due process to all public employees or prospective employees would place an intolerable burden on the machinery of government. The short answer to that argument is that it is not burdensome to give reasons when reasons exist. Whenever an application for employment is denied, an employee is discharged, or a decision not to rehire an employee is made, there should be some reason for the decision. It can scarcely be argued that government would be crippled by a requirement that the reason be communicated to the person most directly affected by the government's action.

Where there are numerous applicants for jobs, it is likely that few will choose to demand reasons for not being hired. But, if the demand for reasons is exceptionally great, summary procedures can be devised that would provide fair and adequate information to all persons. As long as the government has a good reason for its actions it need not fear disclosure. It is only where the government acts improperly that procedural due process is truly burdensome. And that is precisely when it is most necessary.

It might also be argued that to require a hearing and a statement of reasons is to require a useless act, because a government bent on denying employment to one or more persons will do so regardless of the procedural hurdles that are placed in its path. Perhaps this is so, but a requirement of procedural regularity at least renders arbitrary action more difficult. Moreover, proper procedures will surely eliminate some of the arbitrariness that results not from malice, but from innocent error. . . . When the government knows it may have to justify its decisions with sound reasons, its conduct is likely to be more cautious, careful, and correct.

. . . .

[Justice BRENNAN's dissent follows *Perry v. Sindermann*.]

## PERRY v. SINDERMANN
Supreme Court of the United States
408 U.S. 593, 33 L. Ed. 2d 570, 92 S. Ct. 2694 (1972)

Justice STEWART delivered the opinion of the Court.

From 1959 to 1969 the respondent, Robert Sindermann, was a teacher in the state college system of the State of Texas. After teaching for two years at the University of Texas and for four years at San Antonio Junior College, he became a professor of Government and Social Science at Odessa Junior College in 1965. He was employed at the college for four successive years, under a series of one-year contracts. He was successful enough to be appointed, for a time, the cochairman of his department.

During the 1968-1969 academic year, however, controversy arose between the respondent and the college administration. The respondent was elected president of the Texas Junior College Teachers Association. In this capacity, he left his teaching duties on several occasions to testify before committees of the Texas Legislature, and he became involved in public disagreements with the policies of the college's Board of Regents. In particular, he aligned himself with a group advocating the elevation of the college to four-year status—a change opposed by the Regents. And, on one occasion, a newspaper advertisement appeared over his name that was highly critical of the Regents.

Finally, in May 1969, the respondent's one-year employment contract terminated and the Board of Regents voted not to offer him a new contract for the next academic year. The Regents issued a press release setting forth allegations of the respondent's insubordination. But they provided him no official statement of the reasons for the nonrenewal of his contract. And they allowed him no opportunity for a hearing to challenge the basis of the nonrenewal.

The respondent then brought this action in a federal district court. He alleged primarily that the Regents' decision not to rehire him was based on his public criticism of the policies of the college administration and thus infringed his right to freedom of speech. He also alleged that their failure to provide him an opportunity for a hearing violated the Fourteenth Amendment's guarantee of procedural due process. The petitioners—members of the Board of Regents and the president of the college—denied that their decision was made in retaliation for the respondent's public criticism and argued that they had no obligation to provide a hearing. On the basis of these bare pleadings and three brief affidavits filed by the respondent, the District Court granted summary judgment for the petitioners. It concluded that the respondent had "no cause of action against the [petitioners] since his contract of employment terminated May 31, 1969, and Odessa Junior College has not adopted the tenure system."

The Court of Appeals reversed the judgment of the District Court. Sindermann v. Perry, 430 F.2d 939. First, it held that, despite the respondent's lack of tenure, the nonrenewal of his contract would violate the Fourteenth Amendment if it in fact was based on his protected free speech. Since the actual reason for the Regents' decision was "in total dispute" in the pleadings, the court remanded the case for a full hearing on this contested issue of fact. Second, the Court of Appeals held that, despite the respondent's lack of tenure, the failure to allow him an opportunity for a hearing would violate the constitutional guarantee of procedural due process if the respondent could show that he had an "expectancy" of re-employment. It, therefore, ordered that this issue of fact also be aired upon remand. . . .

The first question presented is whether the respondent's lack of a contractual or tenure right to re-employment, taken alone, defeats his claim that the nonrenewal of his contract violated the First and Fourteenth Amendments. We hold that it does not.

For at least a quarter century, this Court has made clear that even though a person has no "right" to a valuable governmental benefit and even though the government may deny him the benefit for any number of reasons, there are some reasons upon which the government may not act. It may not deny a benefit to a person on a basis that infringes his constitutionally protected interests—especially, his interest in freedom of speech. For if the government could deny a benefit to a person because of his constitutionally protected speech or associations, his exercise of those freedoms would in effect be penalized and inhibited. This would allow the government to "produce a result which [it] could not command directly." Speiser v. Randall, 357 U.S. 513, 526. Such interference with constitutional rights is impermissible.

. . . [W]e have applied the principle to denials of public employment. We have applied the principle regardless of the public employee's contractual or other claim to a job.

. . . .

In this case, of course, the respondent has yet to show that the decision not to renew his contract was, in fact, made in retaliation for his exercise of the constitutional right of free speech. The District Court foreclosed any opportunity to make this showing when it granted summary judgment. Hence, we cannot now hold that the Board of Regents' action was invalid.

But we agree with the Court of Appeals that there is a genuine dispute as to "whether the college refused to renew the teaching contract on an impermissible basis—as a reprisal for the exercise of constitutionally protected rights." The respondent has alleged that his nonretention was based on his testimony before legislative committees and his other public statements critical of the Regents' policies. And he has alleged that this public criticism was within the First and Fourteenth Amendment's protection of freedom of speech. Plainly, these allegations present a *bona fide* constitutional claim. . . .

For this reason we hold that the grant of summary judgment against the respondent, without full exploration of this issue, was improper.

The respondent's lack of formal contractual or tenure security in continued employment at Odessa Junior College, though irrelevant to his free speech claim, is highly relevant to his procedural due process claim. But it may not be entirely dispositive.

We have held today in *Board of Regents v. Roth,* that the Constitution does not require opportunity for a hearing before the nonrenewal of a nontenured teacher's contract, unless he can show that the decision not to rehire him somehow deprived him of an interest in "liberty" or that he had a "property" interest in continued employment, despite the lack of tenure or a formal contract. In *Roth* the teacher had not made a showing on either point to justify summary judgment in his favor.

Similarly, the respondent here has yet to show that he has been deprived of an interest that could invoke procedural due process protection. As in *Roth,* the mere showing that he was not rehired in one particular job, without more, did not amount to a showing of a loss of liberty. Nor did it amount to a showing of a loss of property.

But the respondent's allegations—which we must construe most favorably to the respondent at this stage of the litigation—do raise a genuine issue as to his interest in continued employment at Odessa Junior College. He alleged that this interest, though not secured by a formal contractual tenure provision, was secured by a no less binding understanding fostered by the college administration. In particular, the respondent alleged that the college had a *de facto* tenure program, and that he had tenure under that program. He claimed that he and others legitimately relied upon an unusual provision that had been in the college's official Faculty Guide for many years:

> "*Teacher Tenure*: Odessa College has no tenure system. The Administration of the College wishes the faculty member to feel that he has permanent tenure as long as his teaching services are satisfactory and as long as he displays a cooperative attitude toward his co-workers and his superiors, and as long as he is happy in his work."

Moreover, the respondent claimed legitimate reliance upon guidelines promulgated by the Coordinating Board of the Texas College and University System that provided that a person, like himself, who had been employed as a teacher in the state college and university system for seven years or more has some form of job tenure. Thus the respondent offered to prove that a teacher, with his long period of service, at this particular State College had no less a "property" interest in continued employment than a formally tenured teacher at other colleges and had no less a procedural due process right to a statement of reasons and a hearing before college officials upon their decision not to retain him.

We have made clear in *Roth*, that "property" interests subject to procedural due process protection are not limited by a few rigid, technical forms. Rather, "property" denotes a broad range of interests that are secured by "existing rules or understandings." A person's interest in a benefit is a "property" interest for due process purposes if there are such rules or mutually explicit understandings that support his claim of entitlement to the benefit and that he may invoke at a hearing.

A written contract with an explicit tenure provision clearly is evidence of a formal understanding that supports a teacher's claim of entitlement to continued employment unless sufficient "cause" is shown. Yet absence of such an explicit contractual provision may not always foreclose the possibility that a teacher has a "property" interest in re-employment. For example, the law of contracts in most, if not all, jurisdictions long has employed a process by which agreements, though not formalized in writing, may be "implied." Explicit contractual provisions may be supplemented by other agreements implied from "the promisor's words and conduct in the light of the surrounding circumstances." And, "[t]he meaning of [the promisor's] words and acts is found by relating them to the usage of the past."

A teacher, like the respondent, who has held his position for a number of years, might be able to show from the circumstances of this service—and from other relevant facts—that he has a legitimate claim of entitlement to job tenure. Just as this Court has found there to be a "common law of a particular industry or of a particular plant" that may supplement a collective-bargaining agreement, United Steelworkers v. Warrior & Gulf Nav. Co., 363 U.S. 574, 579, so there may be an unwritten "common law" in a particular university that certain employees shall have the equivalent of tenure. This is particularly likely in a college or university, like Odessa Junior College, that has no explicit tenure system even for senior members of its faculty, but that nonetheless may have created such a system in practice.

In this case, the respondent has alleged the existence of rules
and understandings, promulgated and fostered by state officials,
that may justify his legitimate claim of entitlement to continued
employment absent "sufficient cause." We disagree with the Court
of Appeals insofar as it held that a mere subjective "expectancy"
is protected by procedural due process, but we agree that the
respondent must be given an opportunity to prove the legitimacy
of his claim of such entitlement in light of "the policies and practices of the institution." Proof of such a property interest would
not, of course, entitle him to reinstatement. But such proof would
obligate college officials to grant a hearing at his request, where he
could be informed of the grounds for his nonretention and challenge their sufficiency.

Therefore, while we do not wholly agree with the opinion of
the Court of Appeals, its judgment remanding this case to the
District Court is affirmed.

Affirmed.

Justice POWELL took no part in the decision of this case.

Justice BRENNAN, with whom Justice DOUGLAS joins, dissenting
[in *Roth*] and dissenting in part in [*Perry*].

Although I agree with Part I of the Court's opinion in [*Perry*],
I also agree with my Brother MARSHALL that "respondent[s]
[were] denied due process when [their] contract[s] [were] not
renewed and [they were] not informed of the reasons and
given an opportunity to respond." . . .

Justice MARSHALL, dissenting in part.

. . . .

## NOTES

1. *Right vs. Privilege.* Is there a constitutionally protected
"right" in governmental employment? The recognition of constitutional protection has been severely hampered by acceptance
of the view that due process does not apply since employment
is a "privilege," not a "right." In Crenshaw v. United States, 134
U.S. 99, 108 (1890), it was said that government employment is
a privilege "revocable by the sovereignty at will." And in
Bailey v. Richardson, 182 F.2d 46 (D.C. Cir. 1950), aff'd, by an
equally divided court, 341 U.S. 918 (1951), the Court of Appeals
analogized governmental and private employment, deeming both
to be held at the suffrance of the employer. "If removal be at
will, of what purpose would process be? To hold office at the will

of the superior and to be removable therefrom only by constitutional due process of law are opposite and inherently conflicting laws. Due process of law is not applicable unless one is being deprived of something to which he has a right." But as has been indicated, text, pp. 497-98, the right-privilege dichotomy has been increasingly rejected. Does the right-privilege dichotomy have a greater credibility in the employment context?

*Compare* Justice Jackson in Butler v. White, 83 F. 578, 586 (C.C.D. W.Va. 1897), *rev'd on other grounds,* 171 U.S. 379 (1898): "Has he [the government employee] not a material interest in the possession of office and the salary attached to it? If he has such an interest in the office and emoluments, is there not a right which should be recognized and protected by the law in the employment of it?" *See* Chaturvedi, *Legal Protection Available to Federal Employees Against Wrongful Dismissal,* 63 Nw. U.L. Rev. 287, 321-22 (1968), for a view which seems to accept employment as a property right. *But see* Cafeteria & Restaurant Workers Union v. McElroy, 367 U.S. 886 (1961), rejecting the claim that a short-order cook had a right to notice and a hearing before termination of her employment at a gun factory.

2. *Due Process Methodology.* While eschewing the right-privilege dichotomy, the court in *Roth* and *Sindermann* rejects a balancing of interests to determine if a hearing is constitutionally required. Balancing is appropriate for determining the *form* of a hearing but not the *right* to a hearing. The latter requires a determination of whether the state is denying a "property" or "liberty" interest. Some lower courts, in addition to the lower court in *Roth,* appear to have balanced interests to determine if a hearing is constitutionally required. *See* Drown v. Portsmouth School Dist., 435 F.2d 1182 (1st Cir. 1970) *cert. denied,* 402 U.S. 972 (1971) (teacher has right to notice, including a detailed statement of reasons, but not a hearing). Roumani v. Leestamper, 330 F. Supp. 1248 (D. Mass. 1971) (court balances concluding teacher has right to statement of reasons and hearing). *But see* Ferguson v. Thomas, 430 F.2d 852 (5th Cir. 1970), Lucas v. Chapman, 430 F.2d 945 (5th Cir. 1970) (both holding teacher has "expectancy of reemployment" and hence, a right to minimal due process).

Does the court in *Roth* and *Sindermann* "balance" for the purpose of defining "property" and "liberty"? The court may have retreated from the conceptualistic right-privilege dichotomy only to create a new conceptualism, the determination of whether the interest is "property" or "liberty." *See* Van Alstyne, *The Constitutional Rights of Teachers and Professors,* 1970 Duke L.J. 841, 863, suggesting that "one's status in the public sector is *itself* a form of 'liberty' or 'property' " and Justice Marshall's dissent in *Roth* taking a broad view of the meaning of the due process clause.

3.   *Liberty Interests.* How does the court define "liberty" and what are the sources of its definition? Justice Marshall, dissenting in *Board of Regents v. Roth*, says it must include liberty to work, "which is the 'very essence of the personal freedom and opportunity' secured by the Fourteenth Amendment." Justice Stewart does suggest in *Board of Regents v. Roth* that "liberty" would be involved if a failure to reappoint "imposed . . . a stigma or other disability that preclosed his [the teacher's] freedom to take advantage of other employment opportunities," but the record disclosed no evidence of such an impact. *Compare* Justice Douglas' observation in his dissent in *Board of Regents v. Roth*: "Nonrenewal can be a blemish that turns into a permanent scar and effectively limits any chance the teacher has of being rehired as a teacher at least in his State." Is the problem, then, only one of proving adverse impact from dismissal? Is it sufficient that dismissal *burdens* the teacher's ability to secure subsequent employment as a teacher? Is the hardship lessened by the ability of teachers to bargain collectively to establish the terms of their contract? *See generally* Wellington & Winter, *The Limits of Collective Bargaining in Public Employment,* 78 YALE L.J. 1107 (1969).

Justice Stewart also notes in *Roth* that where the teacher's " 'good name, reputation, honor or integrity' is at stake," due process would require a hearing. In Wisconsin v. Constantineau, 400 U.S. 433 (1971), the court held unconstitutional a statute permitting certain officials to forbid by posting the sale or gift of intoxicating liquors to persons who by excessive drinking produce certain described conditions or exhibit specified traits such as exposing themselves or their families "to want" or becoming "dangerous to the peace" of the community. Such posting, without notice or hearing to the individual affected, was held violative of due process since: "Where a person's good name, reputation, honor, or integrity are at stake because of what the government is doing to him, notice and an opportunity to be heard are essential." Is it sufficient if the charges made upon dismissal injure professional reputation? Doesn't dismissal of a teacher even without reasons carry social stigma? Is the "liberty" interest in employment limited to the capacity to obtain *future* employment?

4.   *Property Interests.* The Supreme Court apparently accepts the premise that dismissal of a tenured teacher or of a nontenured teacher during the contract term involves denial of a "property" interest. What does the court mean by "property"? And what does the court mean by a "legitimate claim of entitlement"? Is the

source of a teacher's entitlement now solely state law as claimed
in Chief Justice Burger's concurrence? Note that Justice Stewart
says that property interests are defined by rules or understanding
"that stem from an independent source *such as* state law."
(Emphasis added.) But the court's emphasis on the state law of
contracts would seem to support the Chief Justice's assertion. If
the Chief Justice is correct, is abstention the appropriate response
for federal courts in the future?

What was the source of Sindermann's entitlement? What does
the court mean that a "common law of reemployment" existed
within the college? If a teacher has not completed a required
waiting period for tenure, can he nevertheless seek to establish
*de facto* tenure?

Consider the divergence among the Justices in Arnett v.
Kennedy, 416 U.S. 134 (1974), rejecting the claim of a nonproba-
tionary civil service employee to a full-trial type hearing prior
to dismissal. While a majority of the justices recognized the
existence of a property interest arising from applicable federal
statutes, a majority felt that due process was satisfied by the
procedures provided.

5. *Substantive and Procedural Rights.* In Slochower v. Board
of Higher Educ., 350 U.S. 551 (1956), a tenured teacher was
dismissed under a statute without notice or hearing, for invoking
his privilege against self-incrimination while testifying before a
legislative committee. This was held to violate due process since
no inference of guilt could be drawn from the constitutionally-
protected refusal to answer. In Connell v. Higginbotham, 403
U.S. 207 (1971), the appellant, an elementary school teacher for
four months, was dismissed without notice or hearing, for refusing
to sign a state loyalty oath. Again this was held unconstitutional
since part of the oath "falls within the ambit of decisions of this
Court proscribing summary dismissal from public employment
without hearing or inquiry required by due process" and therefore could not stand. *See* Pickering v. Board of Educ., 391
U.S. 563 (1968), dealing with the "unconstitutional conditions"
doctrine.

The court in *Roth* and *Perry* reaffirms that government "may
not deny a benefit to a person on a basis that infringes his constitutionally protected interests—especially, his interest in free
speech." In fact, in *Perry*, the court held that the district court's
grant of summary judgment without affording the teacher to
establish his free speech clauses was improper. But Justice
Douglas in *Roth*, quoting the lower court, argues that such
substantive protection "is useless without procedural safeguards."
What is the effect of *Roth* on *Slochower, Higginbotham*, etc.? How

is the teacher to know and prove that the reasons for his dismissal were improper if denied a pre-termination hearing? Professor Van Alstyne, *The Constitutional Rights of Teachers and Professors,* 1970 Duke L.J. 841, 859-60, indicates the realistic impediments to vindicating protected rights through post-termination litigation: "Faculty members are not litigious by nature, the costs of formal controversy are high and usually must be borne personally, the burden of proof—often exceedingly difficult to carry —falls upon the plaintiff-teacher, and the ordinary case may not reach judgment for months or even years after the plaintiff has been separated from his job. In addition, the teacher must face the practical recognition that the extra-legal hazards of such litigation are themselves quite great: to sue and to lose establishes a public record against oneself as a teacher and may further prejudice one's chances for employment or advancement. To sue and to win will not permit one actually to resume teaching at the institution in most instances, and it will almost certainly spread upon the public record whatever evidence of the plaintiff's shortcomings the defending institution can muster—thereby warning other institutions which may be chary of seemingly irascible professors who sue their employer and 'launder their linen' in public places."

6. *The Scope of Due Process.* If an academic property or liberty interest is denied by the state, what procedures are constitutionally required? Apparently, a statement of reasons and an opportunity to "challenge their sufficiency" is always required. Does due process require access to personnel files, which often contain confidential communication from persons not connected with the school? Will a hearing be constitutionally sufficient if conducted by a "rank and tenure" committee who made the original decision to dismiss? Who has the burden of proof and burden of going forward with the evidence? The lower court in *Roth* held that the burden is on the teacher but is this correct if the employee has a "property" or "liberty" interest? Is there a right to call witnesses, to confrontation and cross-examination of adverse witnesses, to be represented by counsel or have counsel appointed, to have a transcript? *See* Van Alstyne, *The Constitutional Rights of Teachers and Professors,* 1970 Duke L.J. 841, 864-74; *Report of Committee A on Academic Freedom and Tenure, Procedural Standards in the Renewal or Nonrenewal of Faculty Appointments,* 56 A.A.U.P. Bull. 21 (1970).

7. Justice Douglas, dissenting in *Roth,* notes that: "There may not be a constitutional right to continued employment if private schools and colleges are involved." Is the action of officials at a private school "state action" within the meaning of the

fourteenth amendment due process clause? *See Developments in the Law: Academic Freedom,* 81 HARV. L. REV. 1045, 1056-64 (1968), discussing the utility of the various theories of state action.

**8.** *Professionals and Nonprofessionals.* Again, is there a constitutionally meaningful difference between the employment interest of a professional and nonprofessional? Is such a distinction consistent with "the new property" approach? And what job categories qualify as professional? What is the status of an engineer, a legal secretary, a librarian, a police officer?

## D. THE DUE PROCESS RIGHTS OF THE STUDENT

The academic environment has proven an increasingly fertile area for students claiming denials of procedural due process. While recognition of the right-privilege dichotomy, judicial reluctance to intervene in the sensitive area of school-student relationships and acceptance that schools act *in loco parentis* have impeded legal change, litigation is now rampant. Challenges have been directed at school procedures governing expulsion, suspension, denial of degrees, probation, denial of privileges, and even review of academic performance. The cases involve elementary, secondary, college and professional schools.

**GOSS v. LOPEZ**

Supreme Court of the United States

— U.S. —, 42 L. Ed. 2d 725, 95 S. Ct. 729 (1975)

Justice WHITE delivered the opinion of the Court.

. . . .

The nine named appellees, each of whom alleged that he or she had been suspended from public high school in Columbus for up to 10 days without a hearing pursuant to [Ohio law] § 3313.66, filed an action against the Columbus Board of Education and various administrators of the CPSS [Columbus Public School System] under 42 U.S.C. § 1983. The complaint sought a declaration that § 3313.66 was unconstitutional in that it permitted public school administrators to deprive plaintiffs of their rights to an education without a hearing of any kind, in violation of the procedural due process component of the Fourteenth Amendment. It also sought to enjoin the public school officials from issuing future suspensions pursuant to § 3313.66 and to require them to remove references to the past suspensions from the records of the students in question.

. . . .

On the basis of this evidence, the three-judge court declared that plaintiffs were denied due process of law. . . .

. . . .

. . . We affirm.

At the outset, appellants contend that because there is no constitutional right to an education at public expense, the Due Process Clause does not protect against expulsions from the public school system. This position misconceives the nature of the issue and is refuted by prior decisions. . . .

. . . .

. . . Having chosen to extend the right to an education to people of appellees' class generally, Ohio may not withdraw that right on grounds of misconduct absent fundamentally fair procedures to determine whether the misconduct has occurred.

Although Ohio may not be constitutionally obligated to establish and maintain a public school system, it has nevertheless done so and has required its children to attend. . . . Among other things, the State is constrained to recognize a student's legitimate entitlement to a public education as a property interest which is protected by the Due Process Clause and which may not be taken away for misconduct without adherence to the minimum procedures required by that clause.

The Due Process Clause also forbids arbitrary deprivations of liberty. . . . School authorities here suspended appellees from school for periods of up to 10 days based on charges of misconduct. If sustained and recorded, those charges could seriously damage the students' standing with their fellow pupils and their teachers as well as interfere with later opportunities for higher education and employment. It is apparent that the claimed right of the State to determine unilaterally and without process whether that misconduct has occurred immediately collides with the requirements of the Constitution.

Appellants proceed to argue that even if there is a right to a public education protected by the Due Process Clause generally, the clause comes into play only when the State subjects a student to a "severe detriment or grievous loss." The loss of 10 days, it is said, is neither severe nor grievous and the Due Process Clause is therefore of no relevance. . . . The Court's view has been that as long as a property deprivation is not *de minimus,* its gravity is irrelevant to the question whether account must be taken of the Due Process Clause. A 10-day suspension from school is not *de minimis* in our view and may not be imposed in complete disregard of the Due Process Clause.

. . . .

. . . At the very minimum, . . . students facing suspension and the consequent interference with a protected property interest must be given *some* kind of notice and afforded *some* kind of hearing. . . .

. . . .

The difficulty is that our schools are vast and complex. Some modicum of discipline and order is essential if the educational function is to be performed. Events calling for discipline are frequent occurrences and sometimes require immediate, effective action. Suspension is considered not only to be a necessary tool to maintain order but a valuable educational device. The prospect of imposing elaborate hearing requirements in every suspension case is viewed with great concern, and many school authorities may well prefer the untrammeled power to act unilaterally, unhampered by rules about notice and hearing. But it would be a strange disciplinary system in an educational institution if no communication was sought by the disciplinarian with the student in an effort to inform him of his defalcation and to let him tell his side of the story in order to make sure that an injustice is not done. . . .

We do not believe that school authorities must be totally free from notice and hearing requirements if their schools are to operate with acceptable efficiency. Students facing temporary suspension have interests qualifying for protection of the Due Process Clause, and due process requires, in connection with a suspension of 10 days or less, that the student be given oral or written notice of the charges against him and, if he denies them, an explanation of the evidence the authorities have and an opportunity to present his side of the story. The clause requires at least these rudimentary precautions against unfair or mistaken findings of misconduct and arbitrary exclusion from school.

There need be no delay between the time "notice" is given and the time of the hearing. In the great majority of cases the disciplinarian may informally discuss the alleged misconduct with the student minutes after it has occurred. We hold only that, in being given an opportunity to explain his version of the facts at this discussion, the student first be told what he is accused of doing and what the basis of the accusation is. Lower courts which have addressed the question of the *nature* of the procedures required in short suspension cases have reached the same conclusion. Since the hearing may occur almost immediately following the misconduct, it follows that as a general rule notice and hearing should precede removal of the student from school. We agree with the District Court, however, that there are recurring situations in which prior notice and hearing cannot be insisted upon.

Students whose presence poses a continuing danger to persons or property or an ongoing threat of disrupting the academic process may be immediately removed from school. In such cases, the necessary notice and rudimentary hearing should follow as soon as practicable, as the District Court indicated.

In holding as we do, we do not believe that we have imposed procedures on school disciplinarians which are inappropriate in a classroom setting. Instead we have imposed requirements which are, if anything, less than a fair-minded school principal would impose upon himself in order to avoid unfair suspensions. . . .

We stop short of construing the Due Process Clause to require, countrywide, that hearings in connection with short suspensions must afford the student the opportunity to secure counsel, to confront and cross-examine witnesses supporting the charge or to call his own witnesses to verify his version of the incident. Brief disciplinary suspensions are almost countless. To impose in each such case even truncated trial type procedures might well overwhelm administrative facilities in many places and, by diverting resources, cost more than it would save in educational effectiveness. Moreover, further formalizing the suspension process and escalating its formality and adversary nature may not only make it too costly as a regular disciplinary tool but also destroy its effectiveness as part of the teaching process.

We should also make it clear that we have addressed ourselves solely to the short suspension, not exceeding 10 days. Longer suspensions or expulsions for the remainder of the school term, or permanently, may require more formal procedures. Nor do we put aside the possibility that in unusual situations, although involving only a short suspension, something more than the rudimentary procedures will be required.

. . . .

Affirmed.

Justice POWELL, with whom THE CHIEF JUSTICE, Justice BLACKMUN, and Justice REHNQUIST join, dissenting.

. . . .

In prior decisions, this Court has explicitly recognized that school authorities must have broad discretionary authority in the daily operation of public schools. This includes wide latitude with respect to maintaining discipline and good order. . . . It can hardly seriously be claimed that a school principal's decision to suspend a pupil for a single day would "directly and sharply implicate basic constitutional values."

. . . Until today, and except in the special context of the First Amendment issue in [Tinker v. Des Moines Community

School Dist. 393 U.S. 503 (1969), text, p. 823], the educational
rights of children and teenagers in the elementary and secondary
schools have not been analogized to the rights of adults or to
those accorded college students. Even with respect to the First
Amendment, the rights of children have not been regarded as
"coextensive with those of adults."

. . . .

One of the more disturbing aspects of today's decision is its
indiscriminate reliance upon the judiciary, and the adversary
process, as the means of resolving many of the most routine
problems arising in the classroom. In mandating due process procedures the Court misapprehends the reality of the normal teach-
er-pupil relationship. There is an ongoing relationship, one in
which the teacher must occupy many roles—educator, adviser,
friend and, at times, parent-substitute. It is rarely adversary in
nature except with respect to the chronically disruptive or in-
subordinate pupil whom the teacher must be free to discipline
without frustrating formalities.

. . . .

------------

## NOTES

1.  The leading case until *Lopez* had been Dixon v. Alabama
State Bd. of Educ., 294 F.2d 150 (5th Cir.), *cert. denied*, 368 U.S.
930 (1961), holding that due process requires notice and a hearing
before expulsion of a student from a tax-supported college. In
considering the competing interests, the court stressed that
"[w]ithout sufficient education the plaintiffs would not be able
to earn an adequate livelihood, to enjoy life to the fullest or to
fulfill as completely as possible the duties and responsibilities
of good citizens." Expulsion could impair the student's ability
to complete his education at any other institution. It is, in short,
an interest of "extremely great value." On the other side, "[i]n
the disciplining of college students there are no considerations of
immediate danger to the public, or of peril to the national
security, which should prevent the Board from exercising at
least the fundamental principles of fairness. . . ."

Fairness was held to require notice specifying the grounds for
expulsion and a hearing, before expulsion, embodying "the rudi-
ments of an adversary proceeding." This would include the names
of adverse witnesses and a report on their claims, an opportunity
for the student to present evidence on his behalf, access to a
report on the results and findings based on substantial evidence.

But the court in *Dixon* did not hold that the facts warranted
a "full dress judicial hearing" since "[s]uch a hearing, with the

attending publicity and disturbance of college activities, might be detrimental to the college's educational atmosphere and impractical to carry out." How viable are these considerations for denying a trial-type hearing in the context of expulsion?

2. Consider the following: "it is now evident that expulsion or exclusion from college may, in the long run, disadvantage an individual at least as much as a single infraction of a criminal statute. There should be no surprise, therefore that students are entitled at least to a similar degree of due process as a suspected pickpocket." Van Alstyne, *The Student as University Resident,* 45 DENVER L.J. 497, 595 (1968).

*Compare:* "In the case of irrevocable expulsion for misconduct, the process is not punitive or deterrent in the criminal law sense, but the process is rather the determination that the student is unqualified to continue as a member of the educational community. Even then, the disciplinary process is not equivalent to the criminal law processes of federal and state criminal law. For, while the expelled student may suffer damaging effects, sometimes irreparable, to his educational, social, and economic future, he or she may not be imprisoned, fined, disenfranchised, or subjected to probationary supervision. The attempted analogy of student discipline to criminal proceedings against adults and juveniles is not sound." General Order on Judicial Standards of Procedure and Substance, 45 F.R.D. 133, 142 (W.D. Mo. 1968).

3. The dissent in *Goss* contended that there was no analytically sound distinction between suspension and the myriad other disciplinary and academic decisions (*e.g.,* grading, promotion, placement) made by school authorities. Does *Goss* suggest that grading judgments by teachers in public schools should be subject to due process review? Perhaps, the answer lies in the fact that the student who does not like his grade is still, after all, in school. Arguably, there has been much less transgression on the student's liberty and property interests.

It has been argued "[i]n the lesser disciplinary procedures, including but not limited to guidance counseling, reprimand, suspension of social or academic privileges, probation, restriction to campus and dismissal with leave to apply for readmission, the lawful aim of discipline may be teaching in performance of a lawful mission of the institution. The nature and procedures of the disciplinary process in such cases should not be required to conform to federal processes of criminal law, which are far from perfect, and designed for circumstances and ends unrelated to the academic community. By judicial mandate to impose upon the academic community in student discipline the intricate, time consuming, sophisticated procedures, rules and safeguards of criminal law would frustrate the teaching process and render the institutional control impotent." General Order on Judicial Standards of Procedure and Substance, 45 F.R.D. 133, 142 (W.D. Mo. 1968). Do you agree?

4. Should elementary and secondary students be afforded the same due process rights as college students? Consider the following: "The need for procedural fairness in the state's dealing with college students' rights to public education, where in many instances students are adults and have already attained at least a high school diploma, should be no greater than the need for such fairness when one is dealing with the expulsion or suspension of juveniles from the public schools. . . . These children emerge in the main, from the quagmire of urban poverty and the vast social distortions which now infect the inner city. . . . For most of these children perhaps, the one state conferred benefit which they have of greatest monetary value is the right which has been given them by state law to attend public schools without charge." Madera v. Board of Educ. of the City of New York, 267 F. Supp. 356, 373-74 (S.D.N.Y. 1967). On the rights of secondary school students, see generally, Butler, *The Public High School Student's Constitutional Right to a Hearing*, 5 CLEARINGHOUSE REV. 431 (1971); Abbott, *Due Process and Secondary School Dismissals*, 20 CASE WEST. L. REV. 378 (1969).

5. Application of due process norms to private institutions has been impeded by the "state action" requirement. But "state action has so far expanded and the presence of government so far penetrated in educational finances that few colleges are likely to be found immune from the reach of the Fourteenth Amendment." Van Alstyne, *The Judicial Trend Toward Academic Freedom*, 20 U. FLA. L. REV. 290, 291 (1968). There is some indication that the applicability of the guarantee may vary with the size of the institution. *Compare* Powe v. Miles, 407 F.2d 73 (2d Cir. 1968), *with* Brown v. Strickler, 422 F.2d 1000 (6th Cir. 1970). It has been suggested that private school students can assert state claims cast in terms of contractual or fiduciary duties together with their federal claims. Lucas, *The Rights of Students*, in THE RIGHTS OF AMERICANS 572, 587 (N. Dorsen ed. 1971).

6. The Supreme Court has ruled that federal courts have jurisdiction to entertain suits for liability against school board members brought by students on due process grounds. Woods v. Strickland, — U.S. — (1975).

# Chapter 8

## SUBSTANTIVE DUE PROCESS REVISITED: THE RIGHT TO PRIVACY

In Chapter 5, consideration was given to the rise and fall of substantive economic due process. As was indicated in the last two chapters, at the same time that economic due process rose and waned the fourteenth amendment was being fashioned into an effective tool for the protection of procedural rights from state abuse. And just as due process was used to hold the states to certain procedural standards in criminal and civil cases, it also became a vehicle for substantive protection of personal rights. Appeal was not made to the clause as a guarantee against arbitrary invasions of liberty or property but as a source of other constitutional guarantees. Thus, in the first amendment area, the due process clause became the conduit whereby the substantive limits mandated by the guarantees of free speech, press and assembly, freedom of belief and association, free exercise of religion and freedom from state establishment of religion were applied to state action. See text, Chapters 10 and 11. In the present chapter, the focus will be on the fashioning of a right of privacy that serves as a substantive restraint on the legislative power of the states.

But what of the disclaimers of judicial activism, the deference to state legislative policy judgment, and the judicial abdication in substantive matters described in Chapter 5. If the court adopts an active policy of review to overturn state legislation burdening free speech or privacy, isn't it doing essentially what was done in *Lochner*? But if the court employs an interventionist policy for procedural review should substantive review be handled any differently? Should the majority be free to impose its will through state legislation subject only to political and procedural checks?

Is there any reason that substantive due process challenges should be treated differently in cases involving property rights and economic liberty (as in *Lochner*) than in cases involving other personal rights and liberties like privacy or free speech? Should it matter whether the asserted due process right is specifically enumerated elsewhere in the Constitution? What standards are to be used in determining whether a particular asserted substantive right is part of "the liberty" guaranteed by the due process clause? If a right is applicable to the states as part of due process liberty, is the right absolute or are there circumstances in which the state may burden the right? Will a showing that the legislation is a reasonable means of achieving a permissible state purpose suffice for constitutionality, *i.e.*, what is the appropriate standard of judicial review? These are the issues that have challenged the judges in dealing with the "new substantive due process."

### GRISWOLD v. CONNECTICUT
Supreme Court of the United States
381 U.S. 479, 14 L. Ed. 2d 510, 85 S. Ct. 1678 (1965)

Justice DOUGLAS delivered the opinion of the Court.

Appellant Griswold is Executive Director of the Planned Parenthood League of Connecticut. Appellant Buxton is a licensed physician and a professor at the Yale Medical School who served as Medical Director for the League at its Center in New Haven—a center open and operating from November 1 to November 10, 1961, when appellants were arrested.

They gave information, instruction, and medical advice to *married persons* as to the means of preventing conception. They examined the wife and prescribed the best contraceptive device or material for her use. Fees were usually charged, although some couples were serviced free.

The statutes whose constitutionality is involved in this appeal are §§ 53-32 and 54-196 of the General Statutes of Connecticut (1958 rev.). The former provides:

"Any person who uses any drug, medicinal article or instrument for the purpose of preventing conception shall be fined not less than fifty dollars or imprisoned not less than sixty days nor more than one year or be both fined and imprisoned."

Section 54-196 provides:

"Any person who assists, abets, counsels, causes, hires or commands another to commit any offense may be prosecuted and punished as if he were the principal offender."

The appellants were found guilty as accessories and fined $100 each, against the claim that the accessory statute as so applied violated the Fourteenth Amendment. . . . The Supreme Court of Errors affirmed that judgment.

[The Court initially held that the appellants had "standing to raise the constitutional rights of the married people with whom they had a professional relationship."]

Coming to the merits, we are met with a wide range of questions that implicate the Due Process Clause of the Fourteenth

Amendment. Overtones of some arguments suggest that Lochner v. New York, 198 U.S. 45, should be our guide. But we decline that invitation. . . . We do not sit as a super-legislature to determine the wisdom, need, and propriety of laws that touch economic problems, business affairs, or social conditions. This law, however, operates directly on an intimate relation of husband and wife and their physician's role in one aspect of that relation.

The association of people is not mentioned in the Constitution nor in the Bill of Rights. The right to educate a child in a school of the parents' choice—whether public or private or parochial—is also not mentioned. Nor is the right to study any particular subject or any foreign language. Yet the First Amendment has been construed to include certain of those rights.

By Pierce v. Society of Sisters [268 U.S. 510 (1925)], the right to educate one's children as one chooses is made applicable to the States by the force of the First and Fourteenth Amendments. By Meyer v. Nebraska [262 U.S. 390 (1923)], the same dignity is given the right to study the German language in a private school. In other words, the State may not, consistently with the spirit of the First Amendment, contract the spectrum of available knowledge. The right of freedom of speech and press includes not only the right to utter or to print, but the right to distribute, the right to receive, the right to read and freedom of inquiry, freedom of thought, and freedom to teach—indeed the freedom of the entire university community. Without those peripheral rights the specific rights would be less secure. And so we reaffirm the principle of the *Pierce* and the *Meyer* cases.

. . . In other words, the First Amendment has a penumbra where privacy is protected from governmental intrusion. In like context, we have protected forms of "association" that are not political in the customary sense but pertain to the social, legal, and economic benefit of the members. NAACP v. Button, 371 U.S. 415, 430-431. . . .

. . . The right of "association," like the right of belief, is more than the right to attend a meeting; it includes the right to express one's attitudes or philosophies by membership in a group or by affiliation with it or by other lawful means. Association in that context is a form of expression of opinion; and while it is not expressly included in the First Amendment its existence is necessary in making the express guarantees fully meaningful.

The foregoing cases suggest that specific guarantees in the Bill of Rights have penumbras, formed by emanations from those guarantees that help give them life and substance. Various guarantees create zones of privacy. The right of association contained in the penumbra of the First Amendment is one . . . . The

Third Amendment in its prohibition against the quartering of soldiers "in any house" in time of peace without the consent of the owner is another facet of that privacy. The Fourth Amendment explicitly affirms the "right of the people to be secure in their persons, houses, papers, and effects, against unreasonable searches and seizures." The Fifth Amendment in its Self-Incrimination Clause enables the citizen to create a zone of privacy which government may not force him to surrender to his detriment. The Ninth Amendment provides: "The enumeration in the Constitution, of certain rights, shall not be construed to deny or disparage others retained by the people."

. . . .

We have had many controversies over these penumbral rights of "privacy and repose." See, e.g., Breard v. Alexandria, 341 U.S. 622, 626, 644; Public Utilities Comm'n v. Pollak, 343 U.S. 451; Monroe v. Pape, 365 U.S. 167; Skinner v. Oklahoma, 316 U.S. 535, 541. These cases bear witness that the right of privacy which presses for recognition here is a legitimate one.

The present case, then, concerns a relationship lying within the zone of privacy created by several fundamental constitutional guarantees. And it concerns a law which, in forbidding the *use* of contraceptives rather than regulating their manufacture or sale, seeks to achieve its goals by means having a maximum destructive impact upon that relationship. Such a law cannot stand in light of the familiar principle, so often applied by this Court, that a "governmental purpose to control or prevent activities constitutionally subject to state regulation may not be achieved by means which sweep unnecessarily broadly and thereby invade the area of protected freedoms." NAACP v. Alabama, 377 U.S. 288, 307. Would we allow the police to search the sacred precincts of marital bedrooms for telltale signs of the use of contraceptives? The very idea is repulsive to the notions of privacy surrounding the marriage relationship.

We deal with a right of privacy older than the Bill of Rights —older than our political parties, older than our school system. Marriage is a coming together for better or for worse, hopefully enduring, and intimate to the degree of being sacred. It is an association that promotes a way of life, not causes; a harmony in living, not political faiths; a bilateral loyalty, not commercial or social projects. Yet it is an association for as noble a purpose as any involved in our prior decisions.

Reversed.

Justice GOLDBERG, whom THE CHIEF JUSTICE and Justice BRENNAN join, concurring.

I agree with the Court that Connecticut's birth-control law unconstitutionally intrudes upon the right of marital privacy, and I join in its opinion and judgment. Although I have not accepted the view that "due process" as used in the Fourteenth Amendment incorporates all of the first eight Amendments, I do agree that the concept of liberty protects those personal rights that are fundamental, and is not confined to the specific terms of the Bill of Rights. My conclusion that the concept of liberty is not so restricted and that it embraces the right of marital privacy though that right is not mentioned explicitly in the Constitution[1] is supported both by numerous decisions of this Court, referred to in the Court's opinion, and by the language and history of the Ninth Amendment. In reaching the conclusion that the right of marital privacy is protected, as being within the protected penumbra of specific guarantees of the Bill of Rights, the Court refers to the Ninth Amendment. I add these words to emphasize the relevance of that Amendment to the Court's holding.

. . . .

This Court, in a series of decisions, has held that the Fourteenth Amendment absorbs and applies to the States those specifics of the first eight amendments which express fundamental personal rights. The language and history of the Ninth Amendment reveal that the Framers of the Constitution believed that there are additional fundamental rights, protected from governmental infringement, which exist alongside those fundamental rights specifically mentioned in the first eight constitutional amendments.

The Ninth Amendment . . . is almost entirely the work of James Madison. It was introduced in Congress by him and passed the House and Senate with little or no debate and virtually no change in language. It was proffered to quiet expressed fears that a bill of specifically enumerated rights could not be sufficiently broad to cover all essential rights and that the specific mention of certain rights would be interpreted as a denial that others were protected.

. . . .

While this Court has had little occasion to interpret the Ninth Amendment, "[i]t cannot be presumed that any clause in the constitution is intended to be without effect." . . . The Ninth Amendment to the Constitution may be regarded by some as a recent discovery and may be forgotten by others, but since 1791 it

---

[1] . . . This Court, . . . has never held that the Bill of Rights or the Fourteenth Amendment protects only those rights that the Constitution specifically mentions by name. . . .

has been a basic part of the Constitution which we are sworn to uphold. To hold that a right so basic and fundamental and so deep-rooted in our society as the right of privacy in marriage may be infringed because that right is not guaranteed in so many words by the first eight amendments to the Constitution is to ignore the Ninth Amendment and to give it no effect whatsoever. Moreover, a judicial construction that this fundamental right is not protected by the Constitution because it is not mentioned in explicit terms by one of the first eight amendments or elsewhere in the Constitution would violate the Ninth Amendment, which specifically states that "[t]he enumeration in the Constitution, of certain rights, shall not be *construed* to deny or disparage others retained by the people." (Emphasis added.)

A dissenting opinion suggests that my interpretation of the Ninth Amendment somehow "broaden[s] the powers of this Court." With all due respect, I believe that it misses the import of what I am saying. I do not take the position of my Brother Black in his dissent in Adamson v. California, 332 U.S. 46, 68, that the entire Bill of Rights is incorporated in the Fourteenth Amendment, and I do not mean to imply that the Ninth Amendment is applied against the States by the Fourteenth. Nor do I mean to state that the Ninth Amendment constitutes an independent source of rights protected from infringement by either the States or the Federal Government. Rather, the Ninth Amendment shows a belief of the Constitution's authors that fundamental rights exist that are not expressly enumerated in the first eight amendments and an intent that the list of rights included there not be deemed exhaustive. As any student of this Court's opinions knows, this Court has held, often unanimously, that the Fifth and Fourteenth Amendments protect certain fundamental personal liberties from abridgment by the Federal Government or the States. The Ninth Amendment simply shows the intent of the Constitution's authors that other fundamental personal rights should not be denied such protection or disparaged in any other way simply because they are not specifically listed in the first eight constitutional amendments. I do not see how this broadens the authority of the Court; rather it serves to support what this Court has been doing in protecting fundamental rights.

Nor am I turning somersaults with history in arguing that the Ninth Amendment is relevant in a case dealing with a *State's* infringement of a fundamental right. While the Ninth Amendment—and indeed the entire Bill of Rights—originally concerned restrictions upon *federal* power, the subsequently enacted Fourteenth Amendment prohibits the States as well from abridging fundamental personal liberties. And, the Ninth Amendment, in indicating that not all such liberties are specifically mentioned in the first eight amendments, is surely relevant in showing the existence of other fundamental personal rights, now protected from state, as well as federal, infringement. In sum, the Ninth Amendment simply lends strong support to the view that the "liberty" protected by the Fifth and Fourteenth Amendments from infringement by the Federal Government or the States is not restricted to rights specifically mentioned in the first eight amendments.

In determining which rights are fundamental, judges are not left at large to decide cases in light of their personal and private notions. Rather, they must look to the "traditions and [collective] conscience of our people" to determine whether a principle is "so rooted [there] . . . as to be ranked as fundamental." "Liberty" also "gains content from the emanations of . . . specific [constitutional] guarantees" and "from experience with the requirements of a free society."

*[handwritten margin note: test of fundamental rights]*

I agree fully with the Court that, applying these tests, the right of privacy is a fundamental personal right, emanating "from the totality of the constitutional scheme under which we live." . . .

. . . .

The entire fabric of the Constitution and the purposes that clearly underlie its specific guarantees demonstrate that the rights to marital privacy and to marry and raise a family are of similar order and magnitude as the fundamental rights specifically protected.

. . . .

The logic of the dissents would sanction federal or state legislation that seems to me even more plainly unconstitutional than the statute before us. Surely the Government, absent a showing of a compelling subordinating state interest, could not decree that all husbands and wives must be sterilized after two children have been born to them. Yet by their reasoning such an invasion of marital privacy would not be subject to constitutional challenge because, while it might be "silly," no provision of the Constitution specifically prevents the Government from curtailing the marital right to bear children and raise a family. While it may shock some of my Brethren that the Court today holds that the Constitution protects the right of marital privacy, in my view it is far more shocking to believe that the personal liberty guaranteed by the Constitution does not include protection against such totalitarian limitation of family size, which is at complete variance with our constitutional concepts. Yet, if upon a showing of a slender basis of rationality, a law outlawing voluntary birth control by married persons is valid, then, by the same reasoning, a law requiring compulsory birth control also would seem to be valid. In my view, however, both types of law would unjustifiably intrude upon rights of marital privacy which are constitutionally protected.

In a long series of cases this Court has held that where fundamental personal liberties are involved, they may not be abridged by the States simply on a showing that a regulatory statute has some rational relationship to the effectuation of a proper state purpose. . . .

*purpose of statute does not justify infringement of liberty*

Although the Connecticut birth-control law obviously encroaches upon a fundamental personal liberty, the State does not show that the law serves any "subordinating [state] interest which is compelling" or that it is "necessary . . . to the accomplishment of a permissible state policy." The State, at most, argues that there is some rational relation between this statute and what is admittedly a legitimate subject of state concern—the discouraging of extra-marital relations. It says that preventing the use of birth-control devices by married persons helps prevent the indulgence by some in such extra-marital relations. The rationality of this justification is dubious, particularly in light of the admitted widespread availability to all persons in the State of Connecticut, unmarried as well as married, of birth-control devices for the prevention of disease, as distinguished from the prevention of conception. But, in any event, it is clear that the state interest in safeguarding marital fidelity can be served by a more discriminately tailored statute, which does not, like the present one, sweep unnecessarily broadly, reaching far beyond the evil sought to be dealt with and intruding upon the privacy of all married couples. The State of Connecticut does have statutes, the constitutionality of which is beyond doubt, which prohibit adultery and fornication. These statutes demonstrate that means for achieving the same basic purpose of protecting marital fidelity are available to Connecticut without the need to "invade the area of protected freedoms."

Finally, it should be said of the Court's holding today that it in no way interferes with a State's proper regulation of sexual promiscuity or misconduct. . . .

. . . .

Justice HARLAN, concurring in the judgment.

. . . .

In my view, the proper constitutional inquiry in this case is whether this Connecticut statute infringes the Due Process Clause of the Fourteenth Amendment because the enactment violates basic values "implicit in the concept of ordered liberty,"

Palko v. Connecticut, 302 U.S. 319, 325. For reasons stated at length in my dissenting opinion in *Poe v. Ullman,* I believe that it does. While the relevant inquiry may be aided by resort to one or more of the provisions of the Bill of Rights, it is not dependent on them or any of their radiations. The Due Process Clause of the Fourteenth Amendment stands, in my opinion, on its own bottom.

. . . .

Justice WHITE, concurring in the judgment.

. . . .

. . . [T]he clear effect of these statutes, as enforced, is to deny disadvantaged citizens of Connecticut, those without either adequate knowledge or resources to obtain private counseling, access to medical assistance and up-to-date information in respect to proper methods of birth control. In my view, a statute with these effects bears a substantial burden of justification when attacked under the Fourteenth Amendment. [Citing equal protection and freedom of association cases.]

An examination of the justification offered, however, cannot be avoided by saying that the Connecticut anti-use statute invades a protected area of privacy and association or that it demeans the marriage relationship. [The nature of the right invaded is pertinent, to be sure, for statutes regulating sensitive areas of liberty do, under the cases of this court require "strict scrutiny," Skinner v. Oklahoma, 316 U.S. 535, 541, and "must be viewed in the light of less drastic means for achieving the same basic purpose." Shelton v. Tucker, 364 U.S. 479, 488. [ "Where there is a significant encroachment upon personal liberty, the State may prevail only upon showing a subordinating interest which is compelling."] Bates v. Little Rock, 361 U.S. 516, 524. But such statutes, if reasonably necessary for the effectuation of a legitimate and substantial state interest, and not arbitrary or capricious in application, are not invalid under the Due Process Clause.

*the state's interest must be compelling*

. . . There is no serious contention that Connecticut thinks the use of artificial or external methods of contraception immoral or unwise in itself, or that the anti-use statute is founded upon any policy of promoting population expansion. Rather, the statute is said to serve the State's policy against all forms of promiscuous or illicit sexual relationships, be they premarital or extramarital, concededly a permissible and legitimate legislative goal.

Without taking issue with the premise that the fear of conception operates as a deterrent to such relationships in addition to the criminal proscriptions Connecticut has against such conduct, I wholly fail to see how the ban on the use of contraceptives by married couples in any way reinforces the State's ban on illicit sexual relationships. . . .

. . . I find nothing in this record justifying the sweeping scope of this statute, with its telling effect on the freedoms of married persons, and therefore conclude that it deprives such persons of liberty without due process of law.

Justice BLACK, with whom Justice STEWART joins, dissenting.
. . . .

The Court talks about a constitutional "right of privacy" as though there is some constitutional provision or provisions forbidding any law ever to be passed which might abridge the "privacy" of individuals. But there is not. There are, of course, guarantees in certain specific constitutional provisions which are designed in part to protect privacy at certain times and places with respect to certain activities. Such, for example, is the Fourth Amendment's guarantee against "unreasonable searches and seizures." But I think it belittles that Amendment to talk about it as though it protects nothing but "privacy." . . . The average man would very likely not have his feelings soothed any more by having his property seized openly than by having it seized privately and by stealth. He simply wants his property left alone. And a person can be just as much, if not more, irritated, annoyed and injured by an unceremonious public arrest by a policeman as he is by a seizure in the privacy of his office or home.

One of the most effective ways of diluting or expanding a constitutionally guaranteed right is to substitute for the crucial word or words of a constitutional guarantee another word or words more or less flexible and more or less restricted in meaning. . . . "Privacy" is a broad, abstract and ambiguous concept which can easily be shrunken in meaning but which can also, on the other hand, easily be interpreted as a constitutional ban against many things other than searches and seizures. . . . I like my privacy as well as the next one, but I am nevertheless compelled to admit that government has a right to invade it unless prohibited by some specific constitutional provision. For these reasons I cannot agree with the Court's judgment and the reasons it gives for holding this Connecticut law unconstitutional.
. . . .

. . . Our Court certainly has no machinery with which to take a Gallup Poll. And the scientific miracles of this age have not yet produced a gadget which the Court can use to determine what traditions are rooted in the "[collective] conscience of our people." Moreover, one would certainly have to look far beyond the language of the Ninth Amendment to find that the Framers

vested in this Court any such awesome veto powers over lawmaking, either by the States or by the Congress. Nor does anything
in the history of the Amendment offer any support for such a
shocking doctrine. . . . That Amendment was passed, not to
broaden the powers of this Court or any other department of
"the General Government," but, as every student of history
knows, to assure the people that the Constitution in all its provisions was intended to limit the Federal Government to the
powers granted expressly or by necessary implication. . . . This
fact is perhaps responsible for the peculiar phenomenon that for
a period of a century and a half no serious suggestion was ever
made that the Ninth Amendment, enacted to protect state powers
against federal invasion, could be used as a weapon of federal
power to prevent state legislatures from passing laws they consider
appropriate to govern local affairs. Use of any such broad,
unbounded judicial authority would make of this Court's members a day-to-day constitutional convention.

. . . .

Justice STEWART, who Justice BLACK joins, dissenting.

. . . As a practical matter, the law is obviously unenforceable, except in the oblique context of the present case. As a
philosophical matter, I believe the use of contraceptives in the
relationship of marriage should be left to personal and private
choice, based upon each individual's moral, ethical, and religious
beliefs. As a matter of social policy, I think professional counsel
about methods of birth control should be available to all, so
that each individual's choice can be meaningfully made. But we
are not asked in this case to say whether we think this law is
unwise, or even asinine. We are asked to hold that it violates
the United States Constitution. And that I cannot do.

. . . .

What provision of the Constitution, then, does make this state
law invalid? The Court says it is the right of privacy "created by
several fundamental constitutional guarantees." With all deference, I can find no such general right of privacy in the Bill of
Rights, in any other part of the Constitution, or in any case ever
before decided by this Court.

. . . .

---

## NOTES

### Avoiding the Lochner Precedent

1. Justice Douglas wrote many of the post-New Deal decisions repudiating *Lochner*. What is his justification, then, for the
interventionist approach adopted in *Griswold*? In Poe v. Ullman,

367 U.S. 497 (1961) (text, p. 105), where the court avoided the question decided in *Griswold* on justiciability grounds, Justice Douglas, dissenting, had said "the error of the old Court, as I see it, was not in entertaining inquiries concerning the constitutionality of social legislation but in applying the standards that it did. . . . Social legislation dealing with business and economic matters touches no particularized prohibition of the Constitution, unless it be the provision of the Fifth Amendment that private property should not be taken for public use without just compensation. If it is free of the latter guarantee it has wide scope for application. Some go so far as to suggest that whatever the majority in the legislatures says goes . . . that there is no other standard of constitutionality. That reduces the legislative power to sheer voting strength and the judicial function to a matter of statistics. . . ."

2.  *The Standard of Review.* The members of the majority in *Griswold* not only rejected the judicial deference characteristic of economic due process, but required a showing of more than mere rationality in order to sustain state legislation. In Poe v. Ullman, 367 U.S. 497 (1961), Justice Harlan, dissenting, stated: "The statute must pass a more rigorous constitutional test than that going merely to the plausibility of its underlying rationale. This enactment involves what, by common understanding throughout the English-speaking world, must be granted to be a most fundamental aspect of 'liberty,' the privacy of the home in its most basic sense, and it is this which requires that the statute be subjected to 'strict scrutiny.' " What must the state establish in order to satisfy this "strict scrutiny"?

3.  What is the justification for such a different standard of review? Can substantive personal rights be meaningfully distinguished from substantive economic rights? Aren't economic resources vital to the maintenance of personal rights? Justice Frankfurter observed, "There is truth behind the familiar contrast between rights of property and rights of man. But certainly in some of its aspects property is a function of personality, and conversely the free range of the human spirit becomes shriveled and constrained under economic dependence. Especially in a civilization like ours . . . a sharp division between property rights and human rights largely falsifies reality." F. FRANKFURTER, MR. JUSTICE HOLMES AND THE SUPREME COURT 74 (2d ed. 1961).

On the other hand, compare the following view: "The different approach utilized by the courts in cases involving personal, individual liberties reflects in part the judicial sensitivity to the importance of the interests involved. It is highly questionable for a political system which purports to exalt human values to treat

alleged violations of these interests in the same manner as challenges to the validity of ordinary economic controls. If we do
purport to follow a hierarchy of values, our legal policy must
be fashioned in such a way as to reflect these differences. The
elevation of human values over economic values in constitutional
adjudication is a logical manifestation of this principle. To
blandly throw basic human needs and aspirations into the same
mix as business and industrial concerns goes far to vindicate the
accusations of those critics of our system who claim we have
distorted value priorities. For the courts to abdicate their responsibility to protect scrupulously these basic human needs, while
other institutions of government are increasingly perceived as
being closed to reform, is to invite chaos." C. T. DIENES, LAW,
POLITICS AND BIRTH CONTROL 179 (1972). *See* Cox, *The Role of
the Supreme Court in American Society,* 50 MARQ. L. REV. 575,
584 (1967).

4. Can the differing standards of review be justified on the
basis of differing judicial capability? "[T]he special scrutiny
employed for laws affecting personal human liberties has reflected
an assessment by the court of its competence viz-a-viz the legislature to decide complex social, economic, technical issues as
opposed to those involving basic human freedoms guaranteed by
the Constitution. Whereas legislatures usually have the capability
for marshalling the intelligence necessary for effective policy formulation in the former area, the courts generally possess a greater
insulation and the capacity for commitment to long-range principles vital to the preservation of personal guarantees. As has
been noted: 'Knowledge about civil and individual rights, unlike
some economic data, is neither so technical nor so esoteric as to
lie beyond the legitimate cognizance of the court.' [Tussman &
Tenbroek, *The Equal Protection of the Laws,* 37 CALIF. L. REV.
341, 373 (1949).]" C. T. DIENES, LAW, POLITICS AND BIRTH CON-
TROL 180 (1972).

5. Does reliance on independent constitutional rights such
as privacy, held to be embodied in due process "liberty," avoid
the pitfalls of *Lochner?* Is the court any less of a super-legislature?
Is the constitutional decision more "objective" than the subjectivity involved in determining that a law is an arbitrary and unreasonable interference with economic liberty and property rights?

6. Admitting the propriety of judicial intervention when a
separate constitutional right embodied within the "liberty"
guarantee is infringed, should this be limited to explicit constitutional rights? It has been suggested that in his *Griswold*
opinion, Justice Douglas "wishes to avoid on the one hand the
'natural law' principle which involves selecting rights includable

in the due process clause of the 14th Amendment—a process that he and Justice Black had sought to avoid by demanding full incorporation of the Bill of Rights. At the same time, he wants to circumvent the limitations posed by Black's insistence that only those rights specified in the Bill of Rights or other provisions of the Constitution are protected.[What results is a modified 'natural law' yielding a body of rights whose content is suggested by specific constitutional provisions but whose scope and content are not restricted to, or by, the enumerated rights."]Beaney, *The Griswold Case and the Expanding Right to Privacy*, 1966 WIS. L. REV. 979, 982. Does Justice Douglas succeed in avoiding natural law jurisprudence, or is his opinion an updated version of Justice Chase's opinion in *Calder v. Bull* [text, p. 395]? Professor Kauper stated: "Notwithstanding . . . Justice Douglas' protestations, *Griswold* marked a significant revival of natural rights thinking, whatever the formal argument employed by the majority." *The Higher Law and the Rights of Man in a Revolutionary Society*, 18 U. MICH. L. QUAD. NOTES 9, 14 (Winter, 1974).

7. The dilemma between the desire to avoid having the court sit as a super-legislature while providing some judicially reviewable limit on the use of legislative power can be seen in a historical perspective. "Hitler's popularity among the German people, public support of the Un-American Activities Committee and the McCarthy hearings, ancient racial wrongs, recurring state censorship statutes . . . all these brought about a certain amount of revisionism in our ideas about the Supreme Court. . . . [W]e academics had poked fun at Mr. Justice Peckham for asking with dismay [in *Lochner*], 'are we all . . . at the mercy of legislative majorities?' . . . Upon some of us who had been votaries of unreviewed majoritarianism, there had suddenly burst fearful demonstrations that unrestricted majorities could be as tyrannical as wicked oligarchs." Sutherland, *Privacy in Connecticut*, 64 MICH. L. REV. 197, 284 (1965).

## The Right of Privacy

1. What is the constitutional basis for a right of privacy? Prior to *Griswold*, the privacy concept had been used in tort law. *See* W. PROSSER, LAW OF TORTS 802-18 (4th ed. 1971); Warren & Brandeis, *The Right to Privacy*, 4 HARV. L. REV. 193 (1890); Bloustein, *Privacy as an Aspect of Human Dignity: An Answer to Dean Prosser*, 39 N.Y.U. L. REV. 962 (1964). Privacy interests also found expression in search and seizure and self-incrimination cases.

2. As indicated above, Justice Douglas' opinion reflects his total incorporation approach to the meaning of the due process

clause. The concept of penumbras whereby constitutional rights are fashioned on the basis of the specific guarantees has received both acclaim and criticism. One of the authors of this text has argued in support that ["the court has frequently recognized peripheral 'rights' or 'interests' not specifically guaranteed, but necessary to effectuate the primary right.] That these derived rights previously had a greater degree of propinquity to a particular guarantee does not belie recognition that the right to be let alone is pervasive to the constitutional scheme and vital to the exercise of the enumerated guarantees. It is this flexibility of the constitutional guarantees that permits the instrument to be adjusted to social realities, to become a living constitution. While the language of the Douglas opinion might be considered ambiguous, the decision itself is grounded on the prior behavior of the courts and provides the flexibility requisite for constitutional adjustment to social change." C. T. DIENES, LAW, POLITICS AND BIRTH CONTROL 174 (1972).

3.   What is the function of the ninth amendment according to Justice Goldberg? Is it a source of the right of privacy? It has been said that "the ninth amendment is only a rule of construction applicable to the entire Constitution; it is a guidepost at the end of the Bill of Rights reminding courts of the existence of other rights not specifically enumerated. It is emphatically not the source of these rights, nor is it a vehicle for protecting them. Rather, it points to other parts of the Constitution—particularly the due process clauses of the fifth and fourteenth amendments—as the contexts within which unenumerated rights are to be determined, and the means by which they are to be protected." Note, *The Uncertain Renaissance of the Ninth Amendment,* 33 U. CHI. L. REV. 814, 815 (1966).

*Ninth amendment as reminder of rights, not as source.*

How does Justice Goldberg determine that the right of marital privacy is such an enumerated right? Are such rights derived by analogy to the express rights? Is there any difference between Justice Douglas' and Justice Goldberg's approach to the meaning of due process liberty? To the meaning of the Bill of Rights provisions to be incorporated? *See* Franklin, *The Ninth Amendment as Civil Law Method and Its Implications for a Republican Form of Government: Griswold v. Connecticut; South Carolina v. Katzenbach,* 40 TUL. L. REV. 487 (1966).

## The Scope of the Right of Privacy

Assuming the existence of a constitutional right of privacy, what are its conceptual boundaries? Does *Griswold* provide guidelines for growth of the constitutional right? Is Justice Brandeis' definition of privacy in *Olmstead,* quoted by Justice Goldberg,

an adequate guide to future decisions? Consider the following
definition offered by Allen F. Westin in his excellent socio-legal
study of the privacy right. "Privacy is the claim of individuals,
groups, or institutions to determine for themselves when, how,
and to what extent information about them is communicated to
others. . . . Privacy is the voluntary and temporary withdrawal
of a person from the general society by physical or psychological
means, either in a state of solitude or small-group intimacy, or,
when among larger groups, in a condition of anonymity or
reserve." A. WESTIN, PRIVACY AND FREEDOM 7 (1967). *See* A.
MILLER, THE ASSAULT ON PRIVACY (1971).

How do the justices in the *Griswold* majority determine that
the right of privacy covers the use of contraceptives by married
couples? Is the right limited to use of contraceptives or does it
include a right of access to contraceptives? Is the right recognized
in *Griswold* limited to marriage and familial privacy? Does it
include all matters relating to sex? To the use of one's own body?
To all matters relating to one's personality?

1.  In Stanley v. Georgia, 394 U.S. 557 (1969), the court
struck down a conviction based on possession of obscene materials in one's own home, citing the first amendment and the
right to privacy. The privacy discussion emphasized the home
as a critical locus of privacy and the realm of beliefs and thoughts
as essential parts of the "right to be let alone." *See* Katz, *Privacy
and Pornography: Stanley v. Georgia*, 1969 SUP. CT. REV. 203.
*But see* Paris Adult Theatre, Inc. v. Slaton, 413 U.S. 49 (1973),
treating *Stanley* as emphasizing privacy in the home rather than
privacy in the realm of ideas and thought.

2.  Does *Griswold* encompass the decision whether or not to
be sterilized? In Hathaway v. Worcester City Hosp., 475 F.2d 701
(1st Cir. 1973), the Court of Appeals held that the right to decide
to be sterilized was fundamental, and that the state could not
unreasonably interfere with it.

3.  Challenges to state fornication, sodomy, adultery and
cohabitation laws have arisen frequently since *Griswold*. Some
judges indicated a willingness to use *Griswold* to strike down
state interference with adult private consensual sexual behavior.
*See* Lovisi v. Slayton, 363 F. Supp. 620 (E.D. Va. 1973) (Merhige,
J.). Most of the courts, however, have tended to follow Justice
Goldberg's suggestions in *Griswold* limiting the applicability of
the privacy right.

4.  One hard-hit group seeking protection of the new privacy
right are homosexuals. *See* Baker v. Nelson, 291 Minn. 310, 191
N.W.2d 185 (1971) (en banc), appeal dismissed, 409 U.S. 810
(1972), rejecting the right of homosexuals to marry. Can the

state deny homosexuals benefits available to others? *See* Acanfora v. Board of Educ., 359 F. Supp. 843 (D. Md. 1973), applying *Griswold* on behalf of homosexual rights. *See also* Mindel v. United States Civil Serv. Comm'n, 312 F. Supp. 485 (N.D. Cal. 1970); Fisher v. Snyder, 346 F. Supp. 396 (D. Neb. 1972), *aff'd on other grounds,* 476 F.2d 375 (8th Cir. 1973), applying *Griswold* on behalf of employees discharged because of "immoral" activities.

5.   Thus far, claims that the right to privacy protects a person smoking marijuana in his or her own home have generally been unavailing. *See, e.g.,* Miller v. State, 458 S.W.2d 680 (Tex. Crim. App. 1970); Commonwealth v. Leis, 355 Mass. 189, 243 N.E.2d 898 (1969). Some cases have suggested, however, that there might be a right to private possession of marijuana for use distinguishable from possession for sale. *See* United States v. Kiffer, 477 F.2d 349 (2d Cir. 1973), *cert. denied,* 414 U.S. 831 (1973); United States v. Maiden, 355 F. Supp. 743 (D. Conn. 1973).

6.   Nontraditional families have often been disfavored by a variety of local laws, particularly zoning ordinances. An area will be zoned for "single family dwellings" with family defined as one or more persons related by blood, adoption, or marriage, thereby excluding groups of nonrelated persons. In Village of Belle Terre v. Boraas, 416 U.S. 1 (1974), Justice Douglas, for the court, rejected an equal protection challenge to such anti-commune zoning ordinances. *See* text, p. 707. Justice Marshall in dissent argued that "the choice of household companions—of whether a person's 'intellectual and emotional needs' are best met by living with family, friends, professional associates, or others—involves deeply personal considerations as to the kind and quality of intimate relationships within the home. That decision surely falls within the ambit of the right to privacy protected by the Constitution."

7.   If *Griswold* is read to protect the right of married couples to use contraceptives, the constitutionality of statutes limiting access to contraceptives, especially for unmarried persons, would remain in doubt. In Eisenstadt v. Baird, 405 U.S. 438 (1972) [text, p. 709], the court struck down a Massachusetts statute which, while allowing distribution of contraceptives to married persons by medical personnel, prohibited their distribution to unmarried persons. While the case was decided on equal protection grounds, the opinion indicated that the right of privacy recognized in *Griswold* could not be limited to married couples: "[A]lthough, 'we need not and do not' decide the 'important question' of whether such a prohibition 'conflicts with fundamental human rights,' whatever the rights of the individual to access to contraceptives may be, the rights must be the same for the married and the unmarried alike. If under *Griswold* the distribution of contra-

ceptives to married persons cannot be prohibited, a ban on distribution to unmarried persons would be equally impermissible. It is true that in *Griswold* the right of privacy in question inhered in the marital relationship. Yet the marital couple is not an independent entity with a mind and heart of its own, but an association of two individuals, each with a separate intellectual and emotional makeup. If the right of privacy means anything, it is the right of the individual, married or single, to be free from unwarranted governmental intrusion into matters so fundamentally affecting a person as the decision whether to bear or beget a child." Is this language from *Baird* only a logical extension of *Griswold?*

## ROE v. WADE
### Supreme Court of the United States
### 410 U.S. 113, 35 L. Ed. 2d 147, 93 S. Ct. (1973)

Justice BLACKMUN delivered the opinion of the Court.

This Texas federal appeal and its Georgia companion, Doe v. Bolton, 410 U.S. 179, present constitutional challenges to state criminal abortion legislation. The Texas statutes under attack here are typical of those that have been in effect in many States for approximately a century. . . .

. . . .

Our task, of course, is to resolve the issue by constitutional measurement, free of emotion and of predilection. We seek earnestly to do this, and, because we do, we have inquired into, and in this opinion place some emphasis upon, medical and medical-legal history and what that history reveals about man's attitudes toward the abortion procedure over the centuries. . . .

The Texas statutes . . . make it a crime to "procure an abortion," as therein defined, or to attempt one, except with respect to "an abortion procured or attempted by medical advice for the purpose of saving the life of the mother." . . .

. . . .

Jane Roe, a single woman . . . sought a declaratory judgment that the Texas criminal abortion statutes were unconstitutional on their face, and an injunction restraining the defendant from enforcing the statutes.

Roe alleged that she was unmarried and pregnant; that she wished to terminate her pregnancy by an abortion "performed by a competent, licensed physician, under safe, clinical conditions"; that she was unable to get a "legal" abortion in Texas because her life did not appear to be threatened by the continuation of her pregnancy; and that she could not afford to travel to another jurisdiction in order to secure a legal abortion under safe conditions. . . .

[The District Court held, on the merits, that the Texas statutes were unconstitutionally vague and constituted an overbroad infringement of the plaintiffs' Ninth Amendment rights, but denied the injunction on the abstention grounds. The disposition of the claims of the other litigants is omitted since the Supreme Court, on the basis of justiciability, standing and abstention, held that only Jane Roe was a proper litigant.]

It perhaps is not generally appreciated that the restrictive criminal abortion laws in effect in a majority of States today are of relatively recent vintage. Those laws, general proscribing abortion or its attempt at any time during pregnancy except when necessary to preserve the pregnant woman's life, are not of ancient or even of common-law origin. Instead, they derive from statutory changes effected, for the most part, in the latter half of the 19th century.

[Justice Blackmun's extensive review of ancient attitudes towards abortion, the Hippocratic oath, the common law, the English statutory law and American law and the positions of medical and legal professional associations is omitted.]

Three reasons have been advanced to explain historically the enactment of criminal abortion laws in the 19th century and to justify their continued existence.

It has been argued occasionally that these laws were the product of a Victorian social concern to discourage illicit sexual conduct. Texas, however, does not advance this justification in the present case, and it appears that no court or commentator has taken the argument seriously. . . .

A second reason is concerned with abortion as a medical procedure. When most criminal abortion laws were first enacted, the procedure was a hazardous one for the woman. . . .

Modern medical techniques have altered this situation. Appellants and various amici refer to medical data indicating that abortion in early pregnancy, this is, prior to the end of the first trimester, although not without its risk, is now relatively safe. Mortality rates for women undergoing early abortions, where the procedure is legal, appear to be as low as or lower than the rates for normal childbirth. Consequently, any interest of the State in protecting the woman from an inherently hazardous procedure, except when it would be equally dangerous for her to forgo it, has largely disappeared. Of course, important state interests in the area of health and medical standards do remain.

The State has a legitimate interest in seeing to it that abortion, like any other medical procedure, is performed under circumstances that insure maximum safety for the patient. This interest obviously extends at least to the performing physician and his staff, to the facilities involved, to the availability of after-care, and to adequate provision for any complication or emergency that might arise. The prevalence of high mortality rates at illegal "abortion mills" strengthens, rather than weakens, the State's interest in regulating the conditions under which abortions are performed. Moreover, the risk to the woman increases as her pregnancy continues. Thus, the State retains a definite interest in protecting the woman's own health and safety when an abortion is proposed at a late stage of pregnancy.

The third reason is the State's interest—some phrase it in terms of duty—in protecting prenatal life. Some of the argument for this justification rests on the theory that a new human life is present from the moment of conception. The State's interest and general obligation to protect life then extends, it is argued, to prenatal life. Only when the life of the pregnant mother herself is at stake, balanced against the life she carries within her, should the interest of the embryo or fetus not prevail. Logically, of course, a legitimate state interest in this area need not stand or fall on acceptance of the belief that life begins at conception or at some other point prior to live birth. In assessing the State's interest, recognition may be given to the less rigid claim that as long as at least *potential* life is involved, the State may assert interests beyond the protection of the pregnant woman alone.

Parties challenging state abortion laws have sharply disputed in some courts the contention that a purpose of these laws, when enacted, was to protect prenatal life. . . . [T]hey claim that most state laws were designed solely to protect the woman. Because medical advances have lessened this concern, at least with respect to abortion in the early pregnancy, they argue that with respect to such abortions the laws can no longer be justified by any state interest. . . .

It is with these interests, and the weight to be attached to them, that this case is concerned.

The Constitution does not explicitly mention any right of privacy. In a line of decisions, the Court has recognized that a right of personal privacy, or a guarantee of certain areas or zones of privacy, does exist under the Constitution. . . .

This right of privacy, whether it be founded in the Fourteenth Amendment's concept of personal liberty and restrictions upon state action, as we feel it is, or, as the District Court determined, in the Ninth Amendment's reservation of rights to the people, is broad enough to encompass a woman's decision whether or not to terminate her pregnancy. The detriment that the State would

impose upon the pregnant woman by denying this choice altogether is apparent. Specific and direct harm medically diagnosable
even in early pregnancy may be involved. Maternity, or additional offspring, may force upon the woman a distressful life and
future. Psychological harm may be imminent. Mental and physical health may be taxed by child care. There is also the distress,
for all concerned, associated with the unwanted child, and there
is the problem of bringing a child into a family already unable,
psychologically and otherwise, to care for it. In other cases, as
in this one, the additional difficulties and continuing stigma of
unwed motherhood may be involved. All these are factors the
woman and her responsible physician necessarily will consider
in consultation.

On the basis of elements such as these, appellant and some
amici argue that the woman's right is absolute and that she
is entitled to terminate her pregnancy at whatever time, in
whatever way, and for whatever reason she alone chooses.
With this we do not agree. . . . The Court's decisions recognizing a right of privacy also acknowledge that some state
regulation in areas protected by that right is appropriate. As
noted above, a State may properly assert important interests in
safeguarding health, in maintaining medical standards, and in
protecting potential life. At some point in pregnancy, these respective interests become sufficiently compelling to sustain regulation
of the factors that govern the abortion decision. The privacy
right involved, therefore, cannot be said to be absolute. In fact,
it is not clear to us that the claim asserted by some amici that
one has an unlimited right to do with one's body as one pleases
bears a close relationship to the right of privacy previously articulated in the Court's decisions. The Court has refused to recognize an unlimited right of this kind in the past. Jacobson v.
Massachusetts, 197 U.S. 11 (1905) (vaccination); Buck v. Bell,
274 U.S. 200 (1927) (sterilization).

We, therefore, conclude that the right of personal privacy
includes the abortion decision, but that this right is not unqualified and must be considered against important state interests in
regulation.

. . . .

Where certain fundamental "rights" are involved, the Court
has held that regulation limiting these rights may be justified
only by a "compelling state interest," [citing equal protection
and first amendment cases], and that legislative enactments must
be narrowly drawn to express only the legitimate state interests
at stake.

. . . .

The appellee and certain amici argue that the fetus is a "person" within the language and meaning of the Fourteenth Amendment. In support of this, they outline at length and in detail the well-known facts of fetal development. If this suggestion of personhood is established, the appellant's case, of course, collapses, for the fetus' right to life is then guaranteed specifically by the Amendment. . . . On the other hand, the appellee conceded on the reargument that no case could be cited that holds that a fetus is a person within the meaning of the Fourteenth Amendment.

The Constitution does not define "person" in so many words. [The Court reviews all references to "person" in the Constitution.] But in nearly all these instances, the use of the word is such that it has application only postnatally. None indicates, with any assurance, that it has any possible prenatal application.

All this, together with our observation, that throughout the major portion of the 19th century prevailing legal abortion practices were far freer than they are today, persuades us that the word "person," as used in the Fourteenth Amendment, does not include the unborn. . . .

This conclusion, however, does not of itself fully answer the contentions raised by Texas, and we pass on to other considerations.

The pregnant woman cannot be isolated in her privacy. She carries an embryo and, later, a fetus, if one accepts the medical definitions of the developing young in the human uterus. The situation therefore is inherently different from marital intimacy, or bedroom possession of obscene material, or marriage, or procreation, or education, with which *Eisenstadt, Griswold, Stanley, Loving, Skinner, Pierce,* and *Meyer* were respectively concerned. . . .

Texas urges that, apart from the Fourteenth Amendment, life begins at conception and is present throughout pregnancy, and that, therefore, the State has a compelling interest in protecting that life from and after conception. We need not resolve the difficult question of when life begins. When those trained in the respective disciplines of medicine, philosophy, and theology are unable to arrive at any consensus, the judiciary, at this point in the development of man's knowledge, is not in a position to speculate as to the answer.

. . . .

In view of all this, we do not agree that, by adopting one theory of life, Texas may override the rights of the pregnant woman that are at stake. We repeat, however, that the State does have an important and legitimate interest in preserving and pro-

tecting the health of the pregnant woman, whether she be a resident of the State or a nonresident who seeks medical consultation
and treatment there, and that it has still *another* important and
legitimate interest in protecting the potentiality of human life.
These interests are separate and distinct. Each grows in substantiality as the woman approaches term and, at a point during pregnancy, each becomes "compelling."

*[margin note: changes in the compelling interests of the state]*

With respect to the State's important and legitimate interest
in the health of the mother, the "compelling" point, in the light
of present medical knowledge, is at approximately the end of the
first trimester. This is so because of the now-established medical
fact, that until the end of the first trimester mortality in abortion
may be less than mortality in normal childbirth. It follows that,
from and after this point, a State may regulate the abortion procedure to the extent that the regulation reasonably relates to the
preservation and protection of maternal health. Examples of permissible state regulation in this area are requirements as to the
qualifications of the person who is to perform the abortion; as
to the licensure of that person; as to the facility in which the
procedure is to be performed, that is, whether it must be a hospital or may be a clinic or some other place of less-than-hospital
status; as to the licensing of the facility; and the like.

This means, on the other hand, that, for the period of pregnancy prior to this "compelling" point, the attending physician,
in consultation with his patient, is free to determine, without
regulation by the State, that, in his medical judgment, the
patient's pregnancy should be terminated. If that decision is
reached, the judgment may be effectuated by an abortion free of
interference by the State.

With respect to the State's important and legitimate interest
in potential life, the "compelling" point is at viability. This is
so because the fetus then presumably has the capability of meaningful life outside the mother's womb. State regulation protective
of fetal life after viability thus has both logical and biological
justifications. If the State is interested in protecting fetal life
after viability, it may go so far as to proscribe abortion during
that period, except when it is necessary to preserve the life or
health of the mother.

Measured against these standards . . . of the Texas Penal Code,
. . . sweeps too broadly. The statute makes no distinction between
abortions performed early in pregnancy and those performed
later, and it limits to a single reason, "saving" the mother's life,
the legal justification for the procedure. The statute, therefore,
cannot survive the constitutional attack made upon it here.

*[margin note: broadness of statue]*

This conclusion makes it unnecessary for us to consider the additional challenge to the Texas statute asserted on grounds of vagueness.

. . . .

In Doe v. Bolton, 410 U.S. 179, procedural requirements contained in one of the modern abortion statutes are considered. That opinion and this one, of course, are to be read together.

This holding, we feel, is consistent with the relative weights of the respective interests involved, with the lessons and examples of medical and legal history, with the lenity of the common law, and with the demands of the profound problems of the present day. The decision leaves the State free to place increasing restrictions on abortion as the period of pregnancy lengthens, so long as those restrictions are tailored to the recognized state interests. The decision vindicates the right of the physician to administer medical treatment according to his professional judgment up to the points where important state interests provide compelling justifications for intervention. Up to those points, the abortion decision in all its aspects is inherently, and primarily, a medical decision, and basic responsibility for it must rest with the physician. If an individual practitioner abuses the privilege of exercising proper medical judgment, the usual remedies, judicial and intra-professional, are available.

. . . .

Justice DOUGLAS, concurring [in Doe v. Bolton, noted text, p. 565, and in Roe v. Wade].

While I join the opinion of the Court [except on the abstention issue], I add a few words.

. . . .

The Ninth Amendment obviously does not create federally enforceable rights. It merely says, "The enumeration in the Constitution, of certain rights, shall not be construed to deny or disparage others retained by the people." But a catalogue of these rights includes customary, traditional, and time-honored rights, amenities, privileges, and immunities that come within the sweep of "the Blessings of Liberty" mentioned in the preamble to the Constitution. Many of them, in my view, come within the meaning of the term "liberty" as used in the Fourteenth Amendment.

First is the autonomous control over the development and expression of one's intellect, interests, tastes, and personality.

These are rights protected by the First Amendment and, in my view, they are absolute, permitting of no exceptions. The

Free Exercise Clause of the First Amendment is one facet of this constitutional right. The right to remain silent as respects one's own beliefs, is protected by the First and the Fifth. The First Amendment grants the privacy of first-class mail. All of these aspects of the right of privacy are rights "retained by the people" in the meaning of the Ninth Amendment.

*Second is freedom of choice in the basic decisions of one's life respecting marriage, divorce, procreation, contraception, and the education and upbringing of children.*

These rights, unlike those protected by the First Amendment, are subject to some control by the police power. These rights are "fundamental," and we have held that in order to support legislative action the statute must be narrowly and precisely drawn and that a "compelling state interest" must be shown in support of the limitation.[4]

. . . .

*Third is the freedom to care for one's health and person, freedom from bodily restraint or compulsion, freedom to walk, stroll, or loaf.*

These rights, though fundamental, are likewise subject to regulation on a showing of "compelling state interest." . . .

. . . .

. . . [A] woman is free to make the basic decision whether to bear an unwanted child. Elaborate argument is hardly necessary to demonstrate that childbirth may deprive a woman of her

---

[4] My Brother Stewart, writing in Roe v. Wade, supra, says that our decision in Griswold reintroduced substantive due process that had been rejected in Ferguson v. Skrupa [text, p. 432]. Skrupa involved legislation governing a business enterprise; and the Court in that case, as had Mr. Justice Holmes on earlier occasions, rejected the idea that "liberty" within the meaning of the Due Process Clause of the Fourteenth Amendment was a vessel to be filled with one's personal choices of values, whether drawn from the laissez faire school, from the socialistic school, or from the technocrats. Griswold involved legislation touching on the marital relation and involving the conviction of a licensed physician for giving married people information concerning contraception. There is nothing specific in the Bill of Rights that covers that item. Nor is there anything in the Bill of Rights that in terms protects the right of association or the privacy in one's association. Yet we found those rights in the periphery of the First Amendment. Other peripheral rights are the right to educate one's children as one chooses, and the right to study the German language. These decisions, with all respect, have nothing to do with substantive due process. One may think they are not peripheral to other rights that are expressed in the Bill of Rights. But that is not enough to bring into play the protection of substantive due process.

There are, of course, those who have believed that the reach of due process in the Fourteenth Amendment included all of the Bill of Rights but went further. Such was the view of Mr. Justice Murphy and Mr. Justice Rutledge. See Adamson v. California, [text, p. 437]. Perhaps they were right; but it is a bridge that neither I nor those who joined the Court's opinion in Griswold crossed.

preferred lifestyle and force upon her a radically different and undesired future. For example, rejected applicants under the Georgia statute are required to endure the discomforts of pregnancy; to incur the pain, higher mortality rate, and aftereffects of childbirth; to abandon educational plans; to sustain loss of income; to forgo the satisfactions of careers; to tax further mental and physical health in providing child care; and, in some cases, to bear the lifelong stigma of unwed motherhood, a badge which may haunt, if not deter, later legitimate family relationships.

. . . .

Justice STEWART, concurring.

In 1963, this Court, in *Ferguson v. Skrupa* [text, p. 432], purported to sound the death knell for the doctrine of substantive due process. . . .

Barely two years later, in Griswold v. Connecticut, 381 U.S. 479, the Court held a Connecticut birth control law unconstitutional. In view of what had been so recently said in *Skrupa,* the Court's opinion in *Griswold* understandably did its best to avoid reliance on the Due Process Clause of the Fourteenth Amendment as the ground for decision. Yet, the Connecticut law did not violate any provision of the Bill of Rights, nor any other specific provision of the Constitution. So it was clear to me then, and it is equally clear to me now, that the *Griswold* decision can be rationally understood only as a holding that the Connecticut statute substantively invaded the "liberty" that is protected by the Due Process Clause of the Fourteenth Amendment. As so understood, *Griswold* stands as one in a long line of pre-*Skrupa* cases decided under the doctrine of substantive due process, and I now accept it as such.

. . . .

Clearly, therefore, the Court today is correct in holding that the right asserted by Jane Roe is embraced within the personal liberty protected by the Due Process Clause of the Fourteenth Amendment.

It is evident that the Texas abortion statute infringes that right directly. Indeed, it is difficult to imagine a more complete abridgment of a constitutional freedom than that worked by the inflexible criminal statute now in force in Texas. The question then becomes whether the state interests advanced to justify this abridgment can survive the "particularly careful scrutiny" that the Fourteenth Amendment here requires.

. . . I think the Court today has thoroughly demonstrated that [the] state interests cannot constitutionally support the broad abridgment of personal liberty worked by the existing Texas law. . . .

Justice WHITE, with whom Justice REHNQUIST joins, dissenting [in *Doe v. Bolton,* noted *infra,* and *Roe v. Wade*].

. . . .

. . . I find nothing in the language or history of the Constitution to support the Court's judgment. The Court simply fashions and announces a new constitutional right for pregnant mothers and, with scarcely any reason or authority for its action, invests that right with sufficient substance to override most existing state abortion statutes. The upshot is that the people and the legislatures of the 50 States are constitutionally disentitled to weigh the relative importance of the continued existence and development of the fetus, on the one hand, against a spectrum of possible impacts on the mother, on the other hand. As an exercise of raw judicial power, the Court perhaps has authority to do what it does today; but in my view its judgment is an improvident and extravagant exercise of the power of judicial review that the Constitution extends to this Court.

. . . .

Justice REHNQUIST, dissenting.

. . . .

. . . I have difficulty in concluding, as the Court does, that the right of "privacy" is involved in this case. Texas, by the statute here challenged, bars the performance of a medical abortion by a licensed physician on a plaintiff such as Roe. A transaction resulting in an operation such as this is not "private" in the ordinary usage of that word. Nor is the "privacy" that the Court finds here even a distant relative of the freedom from searches and seizures protected by the Fourth Amendment to the Constitution, which the Court has referred to as embodying a right to privacy.

If the Court means by the term "privacy" no more than that the claim of a person to be free from unwanted state regulation of consensual transactions may be a form of "liberty" protected by the Fourteenth Amendment, there is no doubt that similar claims have been upheld in our earlier decisions on the basis of that liberty. I agree with the statement of Mr. Justice Stewart in his concurring opinion that the "liberty," against deprivation of which without due process the Fourteenth Amendment protects, embraces more than the rights found in the Bill of Rights. But that liberty is not guaranteed absolutely against deprivation, only against deprivation without due process of law. The test traditionally applied in the area of social and economic legislation is whether or not a law such as that challenged has a rational relation to a valid state objective. The Due Process Clause of the Fourteenth Amendment undoubtedly does place a limit, albeit a broad one, on legislative power to enact laws such as this. If the Texas statute were to prohibit an abortion even where the mother's life is in jeopardy, I have little doubt that such a statute would lack a rational relation to a valid state objective. . . . But the Court's sweeping invalidation of any restrictions on abortion during the first trimester is impossible to justify under that standard, and the conscious weighing of competing factors that the Court's opinion apparently substitutes for the established test is far more appropriate to a legislative judgment than to a judicial one.

The Court eschews the history of the Fourteenth Amendment in its reliance on the "compelling state interest" test. But the Court adds a new wrinkle to this test by transposing it from the legal considerations associated with the Equal Protection Clause of the Fourteenth Amendment to this case arising under the Due Process Clause of the Fourteenth Amendment. Unless I misapprehended the consequences of this transplanting of the "compelling state interest test," the Court's opinion will accomplish the seemingly impossible feat of leaving this area of the law more confused than it found it.

While the Court's opinion quotes from the dissent of Mr. Justice Holmes in Lochner v. New York, 198 U.S. 45 (1905), the result it reaches is more closely attuned to the majority opinion of Mr. Justice Peckham in that case. As in *Lochner* and similar cases applying substantive due process standards to economic and social welfare legislation, the adoption of the compelling state interest standard will inevitably require this Court to examine the legislative policies and pass on the wisdom of these policies in the very process of deciding whether a particular state interest put forward may or may not be "compelling." The decision here to break pregnancy into three distinct terms and to outline the permissible restrictions the State may impose in each one, for example, partakes more of judicial legislation than it does of a determination of the intent of the drafters of the Fourteenth Amendment.

*[margin handwritten note: legislative action in determining compelling interests]*

The fact that a majority of the States reflecting, after all, the majority sentiment in those States, have had restrictions on abortions for at least a century is a strong indication, it seems to me, that the asserted right to an abortion is not "so rooted in the traditions and conscience of our people as to be ranked as fundamental," Snyder v. Massachusetts, 291 U.S. 97 (1934). Even today, when society's views on abortion are changing, the very existence of the debate is evidence that the "right" to an abortion is not so universally accepted as the appellants would have us believe.

. . . .

In DOE V. BOLTON, 410 U.S. 179 (1973), the court dealt with the constitutionality of the Georgia abortion statutes, similar to that adopted by about one-fourth of the states, based on the ALI Modern Penal Code. The law made abortion a crime except where performed by a licensed physician when "based upon his best clinical judgment . . . an abortion is necessary" because continued pregnancy would be dangerous to the life of the mother or would seriously and permanently injure her health; or, if the fetus would very likely be born with grave, permanent mental or physical defects; or, if the pregnancy resulted from rape. Georgia also imposed a residency and various other procedural requirements. A three-judge district court held that the three specified conditions for abortion unconstitutionally restricted rights of privacy and "personal liberty." But it held that the state interest in protecting health and the potentiality of life justified state procedural regulations regarding "the manner of performance as well as the quality of the final decision to abort."

The Court, per Justice Blackmun, upheld the substantive abortion provision as modified by the district court against the claim that the provision was left unconstitutionally vague. The best clinical judgment of the physician, argued Justice Blackmun, is no longer restricted but "may be exercised in the light of all factors—physical, emotional, psychological, familial, and the woman's age—relevant to the well-being of the patient. All these factors may relate to health. This allows the attending physician the room he needs to make his best medical judgment. And it is room that operates for the benefit, not the disadvantage, of the pregnant woman."

The court, however, reversed the district court's holding that three challenged procedural requirements were constitutional. First, a requirement that only hospitals accredited by the J.A.C.H. (Joint Commission on Accreditation of Hospitals) could perform abortions was found not " 'based on differences that are reasonably related to the purposes of the Act in which it is found,' " since non-abortion surgery at non-accredited hospitals was permitted if other state regulations were satisfied. While the state may, after the first trimester, impose relevant licensing requirements, the state had failed to show that only *hospitals* could provide adequate care. "We feel compelled to agree with appellants that the State must show more than it has in order to prove that only the full resources of a licensed hospital, rather than those of some other appropriately licensed institution, satisfy these health interests. We hold that the hospital requirement of the Georgia law, because it fails to exclude the first trimester of pregnancy, is also invalid."

Second, the Court held unconstitutional a requirement that an abortion be approved by hospital staff committee. "Viewing the Georgia statute as a whole, we see no constitutionally justifiable pertinence in the structure for the advance approval by the abortion committee. With regard to the protection of potential life, the medical judgment is already completed prior to the committee stage, and review by a committee once removed from diagnosis is basically redundant. We are not cited to any other surgical procedure made subject to committee approval as a matter of state criminal law. The woman's right to receive medical care in accordance with her licensed physician's best judgment and the physician's right to administer it are substantially limited by this statutorily imposed overview. And the hospital itself is otherwise fully protected." Justice Blackmun therefore concluded "[t]o ask more serves neither the hospital nor the State." In dicta, he noted that "a physician or any other employee [of a hospital] has the right to refrain, for moral or religious reasons, from participating in the abortion procedure" and that "the hospital is free not to admit a patient for an abortion."

Third, a requirement that the performing physician's judgment be confirmed by the examination of two other licensed physicians was also struck down. The judgment of the woman's physician, licensed by the state and subject to disciplinary proceedings, Justice Blackmun concluded, was sufficient. No other medical or surgical procedure required such confirmation. "Required acquiescence by co-practitioners has no rational connection with a patient's needs and unduly infringes on the physician's right to practice."

Finally, the court held that the residency requirement violated the Art. IV, § 2, privileges and immunities guarantee, since it would permit a state to limit to residents, without justification, the general medical care available. *See* text p. 273.

The court also concluded that its disposition of the procedural claims disposed of a challenge to the Georgia system as violative of equal protection on grounds that it discriminates against the poor.

---

## NOTES

1. The court in *Roe* again adopts the more stringent standard of review in judging the constitutionality of the state legislation. It has been noted: "What is unusual about *Roe* is that the liberty involved is accorded a far more stringent protection, so stringent that a desire to preserve the fetus' existence is unable to overcome it—a protection more stringent, I think it

fair to say, than that the present Court accords the freedom of the press explicitly guaranteed by the First Amendment." Ely, *The Wages of Crying Wolf: A Comment on Roe v. Wade,* 82 YALE L.J. 920, 935 (1973). The justification for departing from the rationality standard, as in *Griswold,* turns on the determination that the fundamental right of privacy is burdened by the state abortion law.

2. Justice Blackmun asserts that the privacy right "is broad enough to encompass a woman's decision whether or not to terminate her pregnancy." What is the Court's basis for this determination? Is it anything more than a reflection of the substantive values of the justices? *See* Wheeler & Kovar, *Roe v. Wade: The Right of Privacy Revisited,* 21 U. KAN. L. REV. 527 (1973), for an attempt to fashion an analytic model which would encompass the abortion decision.

3. Supporters of *Roe* have argued that it is only an "incremental development in constitutional doctrine"—"The couples' right to decide whether to have a family is the very same right as that established and protected in the cases dealing with contraception; considerations identical to those that justify protecting the broader class require careful scrutiny of regulations concerning abortion." This is based on the contention that privacy involves a sphere of interests: "At the core of this sphere is the right of the individual to make for himself—except where a very good reason exists for placing the decision in society's hands—the fundamental decisions that shape family life: whom to marry; whether and when to have children; and with what values to rear those children." Heymann & Barzelay, *The Forest and the Trees: Roe v. Wade and Its Critics,* 53 BOSTON U.L. REV. 765, 772, 775, 777 n. 61 (1973). Does *Roe* stand for the proposition that there is a constitutional right of a woman to control her own body? That there is a generic right of privacy in sexual matters?

4. A critic of *Roe* has argued that "the Supreme Court appeared to go out of its way to distinguish *Griswold* from the abortion cases, treating it as just one of the many cases that recognize the right of privacy. Both *Griswold* and *Baird* studiously avoided discussion of the possible claims that any putative child could make on behalf of anticontraception legislation. Yet it is precisely the claims of the fetus and its status to assert them that raise the greatest difficulty in the abortion cases. In the end, therefore, it does seem fruitless to look to *Griswold* for either guidance or authority. Any reliance upon it would require the rationalization of two difficult decisions instead of one." Epstein, *Substantive Due Process By Any Other Name: The Abortion Cases,* 1973

SUP. CT. REV. 159, 169-70. Do the abortion cases turn on the claims of the fetus and its status to assert them?

*No Con-stitution al basis for Roe*

5. Critics of *Roe* contend that the decision represents a "quantum jump" from *Griswold* and *Baird*. "What is frightening about *Roe* is that this super-protected right [of the woman to choose an abortion] is not inferable from the language of the Constitution, the framers' thinking respecting the specific problem in issue, any general value derivable from the provisions they included, or the nation's governmental structure. Nor is it explainable in terms of the unusual political impotence of the group judicially protected vis-a-vis the interest that legislatively prevailed over it." Ely, *The Wages of Crying Wolf,* 82 YALE L.J., at 935-37.

Similarly Professor Tribe argues that: "One of the most curious things about *Roe* is that, behind its own verbal smoke-screen, the substantive judgment on which it rests is nowhere to be found." Tribe, *Supreme Court 1972 Term, Foreword: Toward a Model of Roles in the Due Process of Life and Law,* 87 HARV. L. REV. 1, 7 (1973).

6. Why doesn't the state have a compelling interest in the potentiality of life prior to viability? Why not at quickening or at conception? Is it relevant that a fetus is not a "person" for due process purposes? Why doesn't the state have a compelling interest in maternal health justifying regulation during the first trimester?

7. Professor Kauper suggested that "[e]ven more strikingly than *Griswold* is [*Roe's*] affirmation of the classic notion that the liberty secured under the due process clause protects the so-called fundamental rights which the Court articulates by a natural rights process type of reasoning. . . . This is the Declaration of Independence all over again." *The Higher Law and the Rights of Man in a Revolutionary Society,* 18 U. MICH. L. QUAD. Notes 9, 14 (Winter, 1974).

8. Does *Roe* provide any assistance in defining the conceptual boundaries of the privacy right? Is it possible to distinguish state control of homosexuality, marijuana use, and private sexual activity generally?

# Chapter 9

## THE MEANING OF EQUAL PROTECTION

### A. FASHIONING THE CONCEPTS: TRADITIONAL EQUAL PROTECTION

[The courts have established that only "unreasonable" classifications violate the Equal Protection guarantee.] But this principle merely states a conclusion. The questions raised are manifold: How is the "reasonableness" of a classification to be determined? Reasonable in relation to what? To what extent may the state deviate from perfection in classification? Suppose we are dealing with a state law which bars women from all occupations requiring that employees lift over 30 pounds. How would you determine if such a law violates equal protection?

#### RAILWAY EXPRESS AGENCY v. NEW YORK
Supreme Court of the United States
336 U.S. 106, 93 L. Ed. 533, 69 S. Ct. 463 (1949)

Justice Douglas delivered the opinion of the Court.

Section 124 of the Traffic Regulations of the City of New York promulgated by the Police Commissioner provides:

"No person shall operate, or cause to be operated, in or upon any street an advertising vehicle; provided that nothing herein contained shall prevent the putting of business notices upon business delivery vehicles, so long as such vehicles are engaged in the usual business or regular work of the owner and not used merely or mainly for advertising."

Appellant is engaged in a nation-wide express business. It operates about 1,900 trucks in New York City and sells the space on the exterior sides of these trucks for advertising. That advertising is for the most part unconnected with its own business. It was convicted in the magistrate's court and fined. . . . The Court of Appeals affirmed. . . .

[The Court held that the regulations do not violate due process.]

The question of equal protection of the laws is pressed more strenuously on us. It is pointed out that the regulation draws the line between advertisements of products sold by the owner of the truck and general advertisements. It is argued that unequal treatment on the basis of such a distinction is not justified by the aim and purpose of the regulation. . . .

. . . The local authorities may well have concluded that those who advertise their own wares on their trucks do not present the same traffic problem in view of the nature or extent of the advertising which they use. It would take a degree of omniscience which we lack to say that such is not the case. If that judgment is correct, the advertising displays that are exempt have less incidence on traffic than those of appellants.

We cannot say that that judgment is not an allowable one. Yet if it is, <u>the classification has relation to the purpose for which it is made</u> and does not contain the kind of discrimination against which the Equal Protection Clause affords protection. It is by such practical considerations based on experience rather than by theoretical inconsistencies that the question of equal protection is to be answered. And the fact that New York City sees fit to eliminate from traffic this kind of distraction but does not touch what may be even greater ones in a different category, such as the vivid displays on Times Square, is immaterial. It is no requirement of equal protection that all evils of the same genus be eradicated or none at all.

*a law need not solve all problems to be valid*

. . . .

Affirmed.

Justice RUTLEDGE acquiesces in the Court's opinion and judgment, *dubitante* on the question of equal protection of the laws.

Justice JACKSON, concurring.

. . . .

My philosophy as to the relative readiness with which we should resort to these two clauses [due process and equal protection] is almost diametrically opposed to the philosophy which prevails on this Court. While claims of denial of equal protection are frequently asserted, they are rarely sustained. But the Court frequently uses the due process clause to strike down measures taken by municipalities to deal with activities in their streets and public places which the local authorities consider to create hazards, annoyances or discomforts to their inhabitants. And I have frequently dissented when I thought local power was improperly denied.

The burden should rest heavily upon one who would persuade us to use the due process clause to strike down a substantive law or ordinance. Even its provident use against municipal regulations frequently disables all government—state, municipal and federal —from dealing with the conduct in question because the requirement of due process is also applicable to State and Federal Governments. Invalidation of a statute or an ordinance on due process grounds leaves ungoverned and ungovernable conduct which many people find objectionable.

Invocation of the equal protection clause, on the other hand, does not disable any governmental body from dealing with the subject at hand. It merely means that the prohibition or regulation must have a broader impact. I regard it as a salutary doctrine that cities, states and the Federal Government must exercise their powers so as not to discriminate between their inhabitants except upon some reasonable differentiation fairly related to the object of regulation. . . .

. . . .

The question in my mind comes to this. Where individuals contribute to an evil or danger in the same way and to the same degree, may those who do so for hire be prohibited, while those who do so for their own commercial ends but not for hire be allowed to continue? I think the answer has to be that the hireling may be put in a class by himself and may be dealt with differently than those who act on their own. But this is not merely because such a discrimination will enable the lawmaker to diminish the evil. That might be done by many classifications, which I should think wholly unsustainable. It is rather because there is a real difference between doing in self-interest and doing for hire, so that it is one thing to tolerate action from those who act on their own and it is another thing to permit the same action to be promoted for a price.

. . . .

Of course, this appellant did not hold itself out to carry or display everybody's advertising, and its rental of space on the sides of its trucks was only incidental to the main business which brought its trucks into the streets. But it is not difficult to see that, in a day of extravagant advertising more or less subsidized by tax deduction, the rental of truck space could become an obnoxious enterprise. While I do not think highly of this type of regulation, that is not my business, and in view of the control I would concede to cities to protect citizens in quiet and orderly use for their proper purposes of the highways and public places, I think the judgment below must be affirmed.

———————

**NOTES**

1. How do the majority and Justice Jackson deal with the classification in *REA*? Is it a question of justifying an under-inclusive classification? Alternatively, the majority may be arguing

that the law is not underinclusive in relation to its safety purpose.
If the former, is the underinclusion justifiable? If the latter,
shouldn't the court examine the legislative fact-finding to determine if the safety hazard posed by the two classes of truckers is the
same? Who has the burden of proof on the constitutional question? *See* Tussman & TenBroek, *The Equal Protection of the
Laws,* 37 CALIF. L. REV. 341 (1949), SELECTED ESSAYS 789 (1963),
and *Developments in the Law—Equal Protection,* 82 HARV. L.
REV. 1065, 1076-87 (1969), for excellent discussions of the traditional standards for equal protection review.

Applicable principles were defined in Lindsley v. Natural
Carbonic Gas Co., 220 U.S. 61 (1911): "1. The equal protection
clause of the Fourteenth Amendment does not take from the
State the power to classify in the adoption of police laws, but
admits of the exercise of a wide scope of discretion in that regard,
and avoids what is done only when it is without any reasonable
basis and therefore is purely arbitrary. 2. A classification having
some reasonable basis does not offend against that clause merely
because it is not made with mathematical nicety or because in
practice it results in some inequality. 3. When the classification
in such a law is called in question, if any state of facts reasonably
can be conceived that would sustain it, the existence of that
state of facts at the time the law was enacted must be assumed.
4. One who assails the classification in such a law must carry
the burden of showing that it does not rest upon any reasonable
basis, but is essentially arbitrary."

2.   *Probing Legislative Purposes.* If a court inquires into the
reasonableness of the relationship of a classification to a permissible state purpose, it is necessary for it to determine the existence of a permissible purpose. In Goesaert v. Cleary, 335 U.S.
464 (1948), the court, per Justice Frankfurter, held constitutional
under the equal protection clause, a Michigan statute excluding
women from being licensed as bartenders while excepting wives
and daughters of male owners of bars.

*[margin note: the purpose of a classification must be examined]*

Justice Frankfurter began with the premise that Michigan
could constitutionally exclude *all women* from working at a bar.
While the social and legal position of women had changed, the
state could draw "a sharp line between the sexes," especially in
the area of liquor control, an area of historic state legislative
regulation. "The Constitution does not require legislatures to
reflect sociological insight, or shifting social standards, anymore
than it requires them to keep abreast of the latest scientific
standards."

Nevertheless, Justice Frankfurter noted, the state "cannot
play favorites among women without rhyme or reason." The Con-

stitution prevents "irrational discrimination as between persons
or groups of persons in the incidence of a law." Justice Frankfurter countered, however, that "the Constitution does not require situations 'which are different in fact or opinion to be
treated in law as though they were the same.'] Tigner v. Texas,
310 U.S. 141 (1940). Since bartending by women, may, in the
allowable legislative judgment, give rise to moral and social *legislature*
problems against which it may devise preventive measures, the *to giving*
legislature need not go to the full length of prohibition, if it *protection*
believes that as to a defined group of females other factors are *to women*
operating which either eliminate or reduce the moral and social
problems otherwise calling for prohibition. Michigan evidently
believes that the oversight assured through ownership of a bar
by a barmaid's husband or father minimizes hazards that may
confront a barmaid without such protecting oversight. This Court
is certainly not in a position to gainsay such belief by the Michigan legislature. If it is entertainable, as we think it is, Michigan
has not violated its duties to afford equal protection of the laws."

Justice Rutledge, joined by Justices Douglas and Murphy,
dissenting, argued that "[t]he statute arbitrarily discriminates
between male and female owners of liquor establishments. . . .
A female owner may neither work as a barmaid herself or employ
her daughter in that position, even if a man is always present in
the establishment to keep order. This inevitable result of the
classification belies the assumption that the statute was motivated by a legislative solicitude for the moral and physical well-
being of women who, but for the law, would be employed as
barmaids since there could be no other conceivable justification
for such discrimination against women owners of liquor establishments, the statute should be held invalid as a denial of equal
protection."

3. Assuming that the statute in *Goesaert v. Cleary* has a
public welfare purpose, is the classification rationally related to
it? Note that the male owner need not be present under the statute when his spouse or daughter are bartending. Is it underinclusive? Overinclusive? Would such an infirmity be justifiable?

4. Between 1930 and 1970, only one case involving economic
regulation was held unconstitutional under the equal protection
clause. In Morey v. Doud, 354 U.S. 457 (1957), the court struck
down an Illinois statute regulating currency exchanges selling
money orders but excepting those issuing money orders of the
United States Post Office, American Express Co., Postal Telegraph
Co., and Western Union Telegraph Co. Only the exception for
American Express was challenged on appeal. The state argued
that the purpose of the Act's provisions was to protect the public

when dealing with currency exchanges and that since American Express was an enterprise of unquestioned solvency and high financial standing, the legislative exception was reasonable.

But the court, per Justice Burton, determined that the Act's provisions "make it clear that the statute was intended to afford the public *continuing* protection. The discrimination in favor of the American Express Company does not conform to this purpose." He concluded: "Taking all of these factors in conjunction —the remote relationship of the statutory classification to the Act's purpose or to business characteristics, and the creation of a closed class by the singling out of money orders of a named company, with accompanying economic advantages—we hold that the application of the Act to appellees deprives them of equal protection of the laws. . . ."

Justice Frankfurter, joined by Justice Harlan, dissented, arguing that the Illinois legislature could rationally conclude that American Express had "the necessary safeguards for solvency and reliability in issuing money orders and redeeming them." As for the majority's consideration of the remote contingencies that might imperil continuing protection, Justice Frankfurter argued "[w]hat is this but to deny a State the right to legislate on the basis of circumstances that exist because a State may not in speculatively different circumstances that may never come to pass have such a right? Surely there is time enough to strike down legislation when its constitutional justification is gone." For the dissent, "[t]he vital fact is that the American Express Co. is decisively different from those money order issuers that are within the regulatory scheme." He continued: "Sociologically one may think what one may of the State's recognition of the special financial position obviously enjoyed by the American Express Co. Whatever one may think is none of this Court's business. [In applying the Equal Protection Clause, we must be fastidiously careful to observe the admonition that we do not 'sit as superlegislature.'"]

Does the majority opinion satisfy the standards defined in *Lindsley*? Was there any reason for departing from those standards?

## B.  NEW DIMENSIONS FOR EQUAL PROTECTION

In most equal protection cases, the traditional standard of review described in the above section, characterized by its extreme judicial deference, applies. But should all classifications be judged by the same standard? [If a law imposes special hardships on minorities or burdens the exercise of critical rights should the judiciary defer to the legislative judgment?] During

the Warren years, the court increasingly found occasion to depart
from the rationality standard in favor of a stricter scrutiny of
governmental classifications. The quest for greater equality became rapidly a primary value in constitutional adjudication. In
justifying classifications involving "suspect" traits or burdening
the exercise of "fundamental" rights, the state is required to
show that the classification is *necessary* to a *compelling* state
interest. The ordinary presumption of constitutionality no longer
obtains and the very invocation of the heightened standard of
review tends to determine the result.

But what classifying traits are "suspect" and when is an
interest "fundamental"? Is the former limited to race classifications which have been historically disfavored? Does the equal
protection clause impose affirmative duties on government to
remedy inequalities in our society? Does the latter concept encompass all "important" interests, however determined? Only
constitutional rights? All constitutional rights?

1.  **Suspect Classifications**

    a.  *Racial Classifications: Malign and Benign*

(1) *Discrimination Through Law and Its Administration: Problems of Rule,*
    *Purpose and Effect*

### LOVING v. VIRGINIA
Supreme Court of the United States
388 U.S. 1, 18 L. Ed. 2d 1010, 87 S. Ct. 1817 (1967)

Chief Justice WARREN delivered the opinion of the Court.

This case presents a constitutional question never addressed
by this Court: whether a statutory scheme adopted by the State
of Virginia to prevent marriages between persons solely on the
basis of racial classifications violates the Equal Protection and
Due Process Clauses of the Fourteenth Amendment. For reasons
which seem to us to reflect the central meaning of those constitutional commands, we conclude that these statutes cannot stand
consistently with the Fourteenth Amendment.

In June 1958, two residents of Virginia, Mildred Jeter, a
Negro woman, and Richard Loving, a white man, were married
in the District of Columbia pursuant to its laws. Shortly after
their marriage, the Lovings returned to Virginia and established
their marital abode in Caroline County. . . .

[They were subsequently convicted of violating Virginia's ban
on interracial marriages. The State Supreme Court of Appeals
upheld the law and affirmed the convictions.]

In upholding the constitutionality of these provisions in the
decision below, the Supreme Court of Appeals of Virginia re-

ferred to its 1955 decision in Naim v. Naim, 197 Va. 80, 87 S.E. 2d 749 . . . [that the State's legitimate purposes were "to preserve the racial integrity of its citizens," and to prevent "the corruption of blood," "a mongrel breed of citizens," and "the obliteration of racial pride," obviously an endorsement of the doctrine of White Supremacy. The court also reasoned that marriage has traditionally been subject to state regulation without federal intervention, and, consequently, the regulation of marriage should be left to exclusive state control by the Tenth Amendment.]

While the state court is no doubt correct in asserting that marriage is a social relation subject to the State's police power, the State does not contend in its argument before this Court that its powers to regulate marriage are unlimited notwithstanding the commands of the Fourteenth Amendment. . . .

Because we reject the notion that the mere "equal application" of a statute containing racial classifications is enough to remove the classifications from the Fourteenth Amendment's proscription of all invidious racial discriminations, [we do not accept the State's contention that these statutes should be upheld if there is any possible basis for concluding that they serve a rational purpose.] The mere fact of equal application does not mean that our analysis of these statutes should follow the approach we have taken in cases involving no racial discrimination. . . . [In ✳ these cases, involving distinctions not drawn according to race, the Court has merely asked whether there is any rational foundation for the discriminations, and has deferred to the wisdom of the state legislatures.] In the case at bar, however, we deal with statutes containing racial classifications, and the fact of equal application does not immunize the statute from the very heavy burden of justification which the Fourteenth Amendment has traditionally required of state statutes drawn according to race.

. . . .

. . . We have rejected the proposition that the debates in the Thirty-ninth Congress or in the state legislatures which ratified the Fourteenth Amendment supported the theory advanced by the State, that the requirement of equal protection of the laws is satisfied by penal laws defining offenses based on racial classifications so long as white and Negro participants in the offense were similarly punished. McLaughlin v. State of Florida, 379 U.S. 184 (1964).

. . . .

There can be no question but that Virginia's miscegenation statutes rest solely upon distinctions drawn according to race. The statutes proscribe generally accepted conduct if engaged in by members of different races. Over the years, this Court has consistently repudiated "[d]istinctions between citizens solely because of their ancestry" as being "odious to a free people whose institutions are founded upon the doctrine of equality." Hirabayashi v. United States, 320 U.S. 81, 100 (1943). At the very least, the Equal Protection Clause demands that racial classifications, especially suspect in criminal statutes, be subjected to the "most rigid scrutiny," Korematsu v. United States, 323 U.S. 214, 216 (1944), and, if they are ever to be upheld, [they must be shown to be necessary to the accomplishment of some permissible state objective,] independent of the racial discrimination which it was the object of the Fourteenth Amendment to eliminate. Indeed, two members of this Court have already stated that they "cannot conceive of a valid legislative purpose . . . which makes the color of a person's skin the test of whether his conduct is a criminal offense." *McLaughlin v. Florida* (Stewart, J., joined by Douglas, J., concurring).

There is patently no legitimate overriding purpose independent of invidious racial discrimination which justifies this classification. The fact that Virginia prohibits only interracial marriages involving white persons demonstrates that the racial classifications must stand on their own justification, as measures designed to maintain White Supremacy. [We have consistently denied the constitutionality of measures which restrict the rights of citizens on account of race. There can be no doubt that restricting the freedom to marry solely because of racial classifications violates the central meaning of the Equal Protection Clause.]

These statutes also deprive the Lovings of liberty without due process of law in violation of the Due Process Clause of the Fourteenth Amendment. The freedom to marry has long been recognized as one of the vital personal rights essential to the orderly pursuit of happiness by free men.    *due process*

Marriage is one of the "basic civil rights of man," fundamental to our very existence and survival. *Skinner v. State of Oklahoma*. To deny this fundamental freedom on so unsupportable a basis as the racial classifications embodied in these statutes, classifications so directly subversive of the principle of equality at the heart of the Fourteenth Amendment, is surely to deprive all the State's citizens of liberty without due process of law. The Fourteenth Amendment requires that the freedom of choice to marry not be restricted by invidious racial discriminations. Under our Constitution, the freedom to marry or not marry, a person of

another race resides with the individual and cannot be infringed
by the State.

. . . .

Reversed.

---

## NOTES

### The Argument From History

Virginia argued that historically it was not the intent of the
framers of the fourteenth amendment to upset the miscegenation
laws which were common at the time. See text, pp. 402-17, on the
historical debate on the meaning of the fourteenth amendment.
Similarly, Professor Bickel concludes: "the obvious conclusion
to which the evidence . . . easily leads is that section 1 of the
14th Amendment, like section 1 of the Civil Rights Act of 1866,
carried out the relatively narrow objective of the Moderates, and
hence, as originally understood, was meant to apply neither to
jury service, nor suffrage, nor antimiscegenation statutes, nor
segregation." Bickel, *The Original Understanding and the Segregation Decision,* 69 HARV. L. REV. 1 (1955), SELECTED ESSAYS 853,
892 (1963). Assuming the framers did not intend to eliminate
miscegenation laws, what effect should this have on a present day
court judging their constitutionality?

Bickel goes on to speculate that the historical meaning of the
amendment may be more subtle. "But may it not be that the
Moderates and the Radicals reached a compromise permitting
them to go to the country with language which they could, where
necessary, defend against damaging alarms raised by the opposition, but which at the same time was sufficiently elastic to permit
reasonable future advances?" Under this interpretation, the "future effect" of the amendment "was left to future determination."
Is this what Chief Justice Warren means in *Loving* when he labels
the history inconclusive?

### The Social Science Argument

In oral argument in *Loving,* Justice Harlan asked, assuming
that the argument is rejected that as a matter of history the fourteenth amendment was supposed to leave state restraints on interracial marriage intact, what then would be the constitutional
status of Virginia's statute under contemporary fourteenth amendment principles? The question really provided an opportunity to
choose between two quite different means of disposing of constitutional litigation: either the route of analyzing the strands of
contemporary constitutional doctrine or the route of inquiry into
social science studies on the status of interracial marriage. When

we ask for a conclusion about contemporary fourteenth amendment principles, are we asking about judicial precedent or are we asking for the most scientific estimate of which of several competing approaches is more socially desirable?

The Assistant Attorney General for Virginia, in responding to Justice Harlan's question, pointed to a copious volume on the lectern entitled INTERMARRIAGE-INTERFAITH, INTERRACIAL, INTER-ETHNIC, by Dr. Albert I. Gordon. The sense of the data collected in the book was that children of mixed marriages suffered greater difficulties, psychological or otherwise, than children of more homogeneous unions. In other words, Virginia was saying that social science techniques indicated the psychological undesirability of interracial marriage. *See* Brown v. Board of Educ., 347 U.S. 483 (1954), for the converse use of social science evidence to support civil rights arguments. In fact, among the many amici briefs filed in *Loving,* there was much reliance on the social sciences. One is struck with the way in which social science authorities were used as equivalents of legal precedents. Lists of articles and books were strung together like so many string citations of conventional cases.

The Supreme Court of Appeals for Virginia, however, rejected reliance on such arguments: "A decision by this Court reversing [precedents] upon considerations of such text writers would be judicial legislation in the raw sense of that term. Such arguments are properly addressable to the legislature, which enacted the law in the first place, and not to this Court, whose prescribed role in the separated powers of government is to adjudicate, and not to legislate." Loving v. Virginia, 206 Va. 924, 147 S.E.2d 78 (1966).

Nor did the Supreme Court rely on the social science material to justify its conclusion. Why was this factor ignored in the court's opinion? Because the social science footnote in *Brown v. Board of Educ.* [see text, pp. 601-03] had occasioned so much controversy? Is judicial procedure generally inadequate to handle social science material? Should judicial decision reflect such data?

The ethical neutrality proclaimed for social science data is doubtful. But, assuming such neutrality, social science data presents a particularly difficult problem for constitutional litigation. Law is normative but social science data presumably is not normative at all. "Concerned with ordering men's conduct in accordance with certain standards, values, and societal goals, the legal system is a descriptive and normative one dealing with 'ought to be.' Much scientific knowledge, on the other hand, is purely descriptive; its 'laws' seek not to control or judge the phenomena of the real world, but to describe and explain them in neutral terms."

Korn, *Law, Fact and Science in the Courts,* 66 COLUM. L. REV.
1080, 1093-94 (1966). What is the proper relationship between the
normative legal judgment and the allegedly non-normative data?

### The Legal Argument: Equal Protection
### Race as a Suspect Classifying Trait?

1. What is the rationale for departing from the traditional
standard of equal protection review when a law, on its face, classifies on the basis of race? The rationale used necessarily affects the
extent to which similar treatment will be accorded other classifying traits. If the special treatment is accorded solely because of
the historical purpose of the fourteenth amendment, race might
be the only classifying trait triggering the more active standard
of review. *See* text, pp. 646-65, on other "suspect" traits.

On the other hand, could the special treatment afforded racial
classifications be functionally justified given the special needs for
judicial protection of "insular minorities" who are denied effective representation through ordinary political processes? *See*
United States v. Carolene Prod. Co., 304 U.S. 144, 152 n. 4
(1938); M. HARRINGTON, THE OTHER AMERICA 14 (1962). Judge
Skelly Wright in Hobson v. Hansen, 269 F. Supp. 401, 507-08
(D.D.C. 1967), *aff'd sub nom.,* Smuck v. Hobson, 408 F.2d 175
(D.C. Cir. 1969), stated: "[T]hese groups are not always assured
of a full and fair hearing through the ordinary political processes,
not so much because of the chance of outright bias, but because
of the abiding danger that the power structure—a term which
need carry no disparaging or abusive overtones—may incline to
pay little heed to even the deserving interests of a politically
voiceless and invisible minority. These considerations impel a
closer judicial surveillance and review of administrative judgments adversely affecting racial minorities and the poor, than
would otherwise be necessary."

2. *Per Se Invalidity?* If race classifications are so onerous,
should they be *per se* impermissible rather than suspect? Should
"invidious racial discrimination" be *per se* impermissible? *See*
text, pp. 635-46, on "benign" classifications.

In Strauder v. West Virginia, 100 U.S. 303 (1880), the court,
in overturning as violative of the equal protection guarantee the
murder conviction of a Black when Blacks were excluded by state
law from jury service, asserted that the fourteenth amendment
established that "the law in the States shall be the same for the
Black as for the White; that all persons, whether colored or white,
shall stand equal before the laws of the States, and in regard to
the colored race, for whose protection the amendment was primarily designed, that no discrimination shall be made against

them by law because of their color." The amendment was said to imply "a positive immunity, or right, most valuable to the colored race,—the right to exemption from unfriendly legislation against them distinctively as colored,—exemption from legal discrimination, implying inferiority in civil society, lessening the security of their enjoyment of the rights which others enjoy, and discriminations which are steps toward reducing them to the conditions of a subject race."

3. [Loving raises the question of whether race as a classifying trait could ever be justified. Are racial classifications, while not per se impermissible in theory, necessarily invalid in fact?] In Tancil v. Woolls, 379 U.S. 19 (1964), the court, per curiam, affirmed a lower court decree striking down a civil law requiring separate racial voting, property, and tax records but sustaining a law requiring racial designation on divorce decrees. Could racial classifications in criminal laws ever be justified? See Korematsu v. United States, 323 U.S. 214 (1944) (internment of American citizens of Japanese descent, while suspect, was upheld by "pressing public necessity").

### The Occasions for Active Review

1. *Discriminatory Legal Rules: Facial Discrimination.* Is the court's departure from the traditional standard of review in *Loving* based on a finding that the state legislature had the *purpose* of discriminating against Blacks? Suppose the state argued that the classification was designed to assure an educated, interested jury? [Is the departure based on a holding that, regardless of legislative purpose, a law that classifies on a racial basis is "suspect."]

Legislation may specifically visit a burden on a racial minority. But more frequently, the legislation appears neutral on its face. In *Loving* the state argued that the law applied equally to Whites and Blacks alike. Why does this argument fail? How does the court know that these laws constitute "invidious racial discrimination"?

2. *Disproportionate Impact.* If a law is facially neutral, both overtly and covertly, but produces a discriminatory impact, should this alone trigger the more stringent standard of review? For example, if a law results in Blacks being under-represented on a jury, should this, in itself, require compelling justification? Should any disproportionate impact suffice or must it be "substantial"? See text, pp. 587-92, on administrative impact.

Considering the pervasiveness of differential impact of laws, would such a rule be unworkable? It has been suggested that "[t]he 'impact' of a law generally has had little or no constitutional significance independent of a suspect operative rule. For example, although rules classifying persons on the basis of . . . race are suspect, the demand for an extraordinary justification is not triggered . . . by enactment and enforcement of criminal laws that may disproportionately burden particular ethnic minorities. It would be both impracticable and undesirable to require decisionmakers to assure that all decisions have an equal effect . . . on all races." Brest, *Palmer v. Thompson: An Approach to the Problem of Unconstitutional Legislative Motive,* 1971 SUP. CT. REV. 95, 110.

If such a standard were adopted, would it require racial balancing? A rule of proportionate representation of races on juries, in schools, in electoral districts, employment categories? Would it require legislators to consider race in order to avoid the heightened burden of justification? *See generally* Ely, *Legislative and Administrative Motivation in Constitutional Law,* 79 YALE L.J. 1205, 1255-61 (1970) and the material in text, pp. 593-646 on affirmative legislative duties under the equal protection clause.

3.   Hunter v. Erickson, 393 U.S. 385 (1969), involved the constitutionality of an amendment to the city charter of Akron, Ohio, preventing the city council from implementing any ordinance dealing with racial, religious, or ancestral discrimination in housing without the approval of the majority of voters of Akron.

The court, per Justice White, held the amendment unconstitutional, reasoning that while "the law on its face treats Negro and White . . . in an identical manner, the reality is that the law's impact falls on the minority. The majority needs no protection against discrimination and if it did, the referendum might be bothersome but no more than that." Justice White characterized the amendment as an "explicitly racial classification" adding that "[b]ecause the core of the 14th Amendment is the prevention of meaningful and unjustified official distinctions based on race . . ., classifications are constitutionally suspect. . . ." Since the city could not meet the "far heavier burden of justification," the law failed.

Justice Harlan, joined by Justice Stewart, concurring, argued that the provision "has the clear purpose of making it more difficult for certain racial and religious minorities to achieve legislation that is in their interest. Since the Charter Amendment is *discriminatory on its face,* Akron must 'bear a far heavier burden of justification' than is required in the normal case. . . . and Akron has failed to sustain this burden." (Emphasis added.) Is *Hunter* a case of covert rule discrimination or discriminatory impact?

## PALMER v. THOMPSON
Supreme Court of the United States
403 U.S. 217, 29 L. Ed. 2d 438, 91 S. Ct. 1940 (1971)

Justice BLACK delivered the opinion of the Court.

In 1962 the city of Jackson, Mississippi, was maintaining five public parks along with swimming pools, golf links, and other facilities for use by the public on a racially segregated basis. Four of the swimming pools were used by whites only and one by Negroes only. Plaintiffs brought an action in the United States District Court seeking a declaratory judgment that this state-enforced segregation of the races was a violation of the Thirteenth and Fourteenth Amendments, and asking an injunction to forbid such practices. After hearings the district court entered a judgment declaring that enforced segregation denied equal protection of the laws but it declined to issue an injunction. The Court of Appeals affirmed, and we denied certiorari. The city proceeded to desegregate its public parks, auditoriums, golf course, and the city zoo. However, the city council decided not to try to operate the public swimming pools on a desegregated basis. Acting in its legislative capacity, the council surrendered its lease on one pool and closed four which it owned. A number of Negro citizens of Jackson then filed this suit to force the city to reopen the pools and operate them on a desegregated basis. The District Court found that the closing was justified to preserve peace and order and because the pools could not be operated economically on an integrated basis. It held the city's action did not deny black citizens equal protection of the laws. The Court of Appeals sitting *en banc* affirmed, six out of 13 judges dissenting. That court rejected the contention that since the pools had been closed either in whole or in part to avoid desegregation the city council's action was a denial of equal protection of the laws. We granted certiorari to decide that question. We affirm.

. . . The question . . . is whether this closing of the pools is state action that denies "the equal protection of the laws" to Negroes. . . .

. . . .

Petitioners have . . . argued that respondents' action violates the Equal Protection Clause because the decision to close the pools was motivated by a desire to avoid integration of the races. But no case in this Court has held that a legislative act may violate equal protection solely because of the motivations of the men who voted for it. . . .

. . . First, it is extremely difficult for a court to ascertain the motivation, or collection of different motivations, that lie behind a legislative enactment. Here, for example, petitioners have argued that the Jackson pools were closed because of ideological opposition to racial integration in swimming pools. Some evidence in the record appears to support this argument. On the other hand the courts below found that the pools were closed because the city council felt they could not be operated safely and economically on an integrated basis. There is substantial evidence in the record to support this conclusion. It is difficult or impossible for any court to determine the "sole" or "dominant" motivation behind the choices of a group of legislators. Furthermore, there is an element of futility in a judicial attempt to invalidate a law because of the bad motives of its supporters. If the law is struck down for this reason, rather than because of its facial content or effect, it would presumably be valid as soon as the legislature or relevant governing body repassed it for different reasons.

It is true there is language in some of our cases interpreting the Fourteenth and Fifteenth Amendments which may suggest that the motive or purpose behind a law is relevant to its constitutionality. Griffin v. Prince Edward County [377 U.S. 218 (1964)]; Gomillion v. Lightfoot, 364 U.S. 339, 347 (1960). But the focus in those cases was on the actual effect of the enactments, not upon the motivation which led the States to behave as they did. In *Griffin,* . . . the State was in fact perpetuating a segregated public school system by financing segregated "private" academies. And in *Gomillion* the Alabama Legislature's gerrymander of the boundaries of Tuskegee excluded virtually all Negroes from voting in town elections. Here the record indicates only that Jackson once ran segregated public swimming pools and that no public pools are now maintained by the city. Moreover, there is no evidence in this record to show that the city is now covertly aiding the maintenance and operation of pools which are private in name only. It shows no state action affecting blacks differently from whites.

Petitioners have argued strenuously that a city's possible motivations to ensure safety and save money cannot validate an otherwise impermissible state action. This proposition is of course true. Citizens may not be compelled to forgo their constitutional rights because officials fear public hostility or desire to save money. But the issue here is whether black citizens in Jackson *are* being denied their constitutional rights when the city has closed the public pools to black and white alike. Nothing in the history or the language of the Fourteenth Amendment nor in any of our prior cases persuades us that the closing of the Jackson swimming pools to all its citizens constitutes a denial of "the equal protection of the laws."

[The Court's discussion of a claimed Thirteenth Amendment violation is omitted.]

It has not been so many years since it was first deemed proper and lawful for cities to tax their citizens to build and operate swimming pools for the public. Probably few persons, prior to this case, would have imagined that cities could be forced by five lifetime judges to construct or refurbish swimming pools which they choose not to operate for any reason, sound or unsound. Should citizens of Jackson or any other city be able to establish in court that public, tax-supported swimming pools are being denied to one group because of color and supplied to another, they will be entitled to relief. But that is not the case here.

The judgment is affirmed.

Chief Justice BURGER, concurring.

. . . .

. . . To hold, as petitioner would have us do, that every public facility or service, once opened, constitutionally "locks in" the public sponsor so that they may not be dropped would plainly discourage the expansion and enlargement of needed services in the long run.

. . . .

Justice BLACKMUN, concurring.

. . . .

I remain impressed with the following factors: (1) No other municipal recreational facility in the city of Jackson has been discontinued. . . . (2) The pools are not part of the city's educational system. They are a general municipal service of the nice-to-have but not essential variety, and they are a service, perhaps a luxury, not enjoyed by many communities. (3) The pools had operated at a deficit. It was the judgment of the city officials that these deficits would increase. (4) I cannot read into the closing of the pools an official expression of inferiority toward black citizens, . . . and certainly on this record I cannot perceive this to be a "fact" or anything other than speculation. Furthermore, the alleged deterrent to relief, said to exist because of the risk of losing other public facilities, is not detectable here in the face of the continued and desegregated presence of all other recreational facilities provided by the city of Jackson. . . .

*luxury vs necessity (Griffin)?*

. . . .

[Justices DOUGLAS, WHITE, BRENNAN and MARSHALL, dissented.]

---

## NOTES

1. The court, in *Palmer*, characterizes *Griffin* as based on effect rather than purpose but the language of Justice Black in

that case certainly challenges his characterization in *Palmer:* "[T]he record in the present case could not be clearer that Prince Edward's public schools were closed and private schools operated in their place with state and county assistance, for one reason, and one reason only: to insure through measures taken by the county and State, that White and Colored children in Prince Edward County would not, under any circumstances, go to the same school. Whatever non-racial grounds might support a State's allowing a county to abandon public schools, the object must be a constitutional one, and grounds of race and opposition to desegregation do not qualify as constitutional."

In Reitman v. Mulkey, 387 U.S. 369 (1967), text, p. 1015, the court affirmed the state court determination that the "purpose and intent" of the state constitutional amendment in question was to authorize private racial discrimination. Approval was given to the state court's examination of the "purpose, scope and operative effect" of the provision; its "immediate objective," its "ultimate impact" and its "historical context and other conditions existing prior to its enactment." Doesn't this suggest approval of an inquiry into purpose?

In Gomillion v. Lightfoot, 364 U.S. 339 (1960), the court characterized impermissible legislative restructuring of city boundaries as "tantamount for all practical purposes to a mathematical demonstration, that the legislation is solely concerned with segregating Whites and Colored voters by fencing Negro citizens out of town." Why is there a reluctance to probe legislative purpose? Is there a meaningful difference between purpose and motive?

2.   If a purpose to racially segregate is clearly established, what effect should this have? [Ely argues that proof of impermissible motive should require only proof by the government of some legitimate, rational basis for the different treatment.] Ely, *Legislative and Administrative Motivation*, 79 YALE L.J., at 1261-75, 1281-84. Brest, however, rejects this approach contending that proof of racial purpose should require either that the objective be held per se invalid or, if suspect, that the state establish an extraordinary justification. Brest, *Palmer v. Thompson*, 1971 SUP. CT. REV., at 135-36.

## The Palmer Rationale

1.   Would the pool closings involved in *Palmer*, even if partially racially motivated, be justifiable given the state's concern over violence and economy? The court on a number of occasions has indicated that the fear of violence will not justify state maintenance of segregation. *See* Watson v. Memphis, 373 U.S. 526

(1963); Cooper v. Aaron, 358 U.S. 1 (1958). Similarly, the court has stated that "vindication of conceded constitutional rights cannot be made dependent upon any theory that it is less expensive to deny than to afford them." Watson v. City of Memphis, 373 U.S. 526, 537 (1963).

But are these prior education discrimination cases distinguishable? If a non-essential service, *e.g.*, recreational facilities, is gratuitously provided by government, should it be subject to less stringent equal protection requirements? ✳

## YICK WO v. HOPKINS
### Supreme Court of the United States
118 U.S. 356, 30 L. Ed. 220, 6 S. Ct. 1064 (1886)

[The city and county of San Francisco enacted the following ordinance: "It shall be unlawful, from and after the passage of this order, for any person or persons to establish, maintain, or carry on a laundry within the corporate limits of the city and county of San Francisco without having first obtained the consent of the board of supervisors, except the same be located in a building constructed either of brick or stone." Yick Wo, a Chinese alien who has operated a laundry in the same building for 22 years, was convicted for doing business without such consent and was imprisoned for nonpayment of the $10.00 fine. The Supreme Court of California denied his petition for a writ of habeas corpus. It was admitted that of the 320 laundries in the city 240 were owned by Chinese aliens, that 310, as was Yick Wo's, were constructed of wood, as was Yick Wo's and that 200 Chinese who had applied for laundry licenses had been denied them, while all applications by persons who were not Chinese had been granted.]

Justice MATTHEWS delivered the opinion of the Court.

. . . .

. . . In the present cases, we are not obliged to reason from the probable to the actual, and pass upon the validity of the ordinances complained of, as tried merely by the opportunities which their terms afford, of unequal and unjust discrimination in their administration. For the cases present the ordinances in actual operation, and the facts shown establish an administration directed so exclusively against a particular class of persons as to warrant and require the conclusion, that, whatever may have been the intent of the ordinances as adopted, they are applied by the public authorities charged with their administration, and thus representing the state itself, with a mind so unequal and oppressive as to amount to a practical denial by the state of that equal protection of the laws which is secured to the petitioners, as to all other persons, by the broad and benign provisions of the Fourteenth Amendment to the Constitution of the United States. Though the <u>law itself be fair on its face</u> and impartial in appearance, yet, <u>if it is applied and administered</u> by public authority <u>with an evil eye and an unequal hand</u>, so as practically to make unjust and illegal discriminations between persons in similar circumstances, material to their rights, <u>the denial of equal justice is still within the prohibition</u> of the Constitution. . . .

The present cases, as shown by the facts disclosed in the record, are within this class. It appears that both petitioners have complied with every requisite, deemed by the law or by the public officers charged with its administration, necessary for the protection of neighboring property from fire, or as a precaution against injury to the public health. No reason whatever, except the will of the supervisors, is assigned why they should not be permitted to carry on, in the accustomed manner, their harmless and useful occupation, on which they depend for a livelihood. And while this consent of the supervisors is withheld from them and from two hundred others who have also petitioned, all of whom happen to be Chinese subjects, eighty others, not Chinese subjects, are permitted to carry on the same business under similar conditions. The fact of this discrimination is admitted. No reason for it is shown, and the conclusion cannot be resisted, that no reason for it exists except hostility to the race and nationality to which the petitioners belong, and which in the eye of the law is not justified. The discrimination is, therefore, illegal, and the public administration which enforces it is a denial of the equal protection of the laws and a violation of the Fourteenth Amendment of the Constitution. The imprisonment of the petitioners is, therefore, illegal, and they must be discharged. . . .

---

## NOTES

1. If an administrator establishes a policy that, on its face, segregates racially, it would seem clear that at least the compelling interest standard should be applicable. But more frequently, administrative action appears neutral on its face. The issue, then, once again revolves around whether the plaintiff must prove discriminatory administrative purpose, whether the courts will probe for racial purpose, the evidentiary techniques available to the plaintiff, and the burden of justification on the defendant.

2. *Selective Enforcement of Penal Laws.* There has been some question whether *Yick Wo* even applies to the activities of penal law enforcement officials. If a person is charged with violating prostitution laws, should she be able to escape conviction by showing that the law is selectively enforced on even a purposeful

racial basis? Should she escape the effect of violating valid criminal laws because of discriminatory actions of some police or prosecutors? Should it matter that her business, unlike Yick Wo's, is illegal? Would your answer be different if this was not a "victimless crime"? *See* Givelber, *The Application of Equal Protection Principles to Selective Enforcement of the Criminal Law*, 1973 U. ILL. L.F. 88; Note, 61 COLUM. L. REV. 1103, 1106-12 (1961).

**3.** In Snowden v. Hughes, 321 U.S. 1 (1944), the court dismissed the petitioner's equal protection claim for failure to prove intentional administrative discrimination. "The unlawful administration by state officers of a state statute fair on its face, resulting in its unequal application to those who are entitled to be treated alike, is not a denial of equal protection unless there is shown to be present in it an element of intentional or purposeful discrimination."

Similarly in a civil suit in which the appellant claimed that he had been denied equal protection since his property had been assessed at full value by the tax board while other property was assessed at one-third value, the court indicated that mere errors of judgment do not constitute discrimination—"intentional violation of the essential principle of practical uniformity" is required. Sunday Lake Iron Co. v. Township of Wakefield, 247 U.S. 350 (1918). *See also* Mackay Tel. & Cable Co. v. Little Rock, 250 U.S. 94 (1919) (license tax on utility deemed reasonable and not intentionally excessive).

**4.** *The Underlying Rationale.* Should purpose or intent to discriminate be required? How do you prove purpose? It is argued that a more active standard of review would impair necessary administrative discretion, would encourage going outside normal appeals processes and thus generate a flood of litigation burdening the courts, and would undermine the legislative policy involved in otherwise racially neutral statutes. Do the courts have the capability to review the values and data involved in the administrative decision-making? Should the state be required to demonstrate a compelling justification whenever administration results in discriminatory application of an otherwise neutral law?

**5.** *Discriminatory Impact.* Judge Skelly Wright has stated "[T]he complaint that analytically no violation of equal protection vests unless the inequalities stem from a deliberately discriminatory plan is simply false. Whatever the law once was, it is a testament to our maturing concept of equality that, with the help of Supreme Court decisions in the last decade, we now firmly recognize that the arbitrary quality of thoughtlessness can be as disastrous and unfair to private rights and the public interest as

the perversity of a willful scheme." Hobson v. Hansen, 269 F.
Supp. 401, 497 (D.D.C. 1967), aff'd sub nom. Smuck v. Hobson,
408 F.2d 175 (D.C. Cir. 1969). See Hawkins v. Shaw, Mississippi,
437 F.2d 1286 (5th Cir. 1971), aff'd en banc 461 F.2d 1171 (5th
Cir. 1972); Norwalk CORE v. Norwalk Redevelopment Agency,
395 F.2d 920, 931 (2d Cir. 1968). See generally Horowitz, *Unsep-
arate but Unequal—The Emerging Fourteenth Amendment Issue
in Public School Education,* 13 U.C.L.A. L. REV. 1147, 1152
(1966); Dimond, *School Segregation in the North: There is But
One Constitution,* 7 HARV. CIV. RTS.-CIV. LIB. L. REV. 1, 8
(1972).

6. If a court does not require proof of discriminatory *purpose,* should statistical racial disparity establish a fourteenth
amendment violation? Should it shift the burden of proof to the
state to establish that the discriminatory impact is necessary to a
compelling government interest?

In Hawkins v. Shaw, Mississippi, 437 F.2d 1286 (5th Cir.
1971), aff'd en banc 461 F.2d 1171 (5th Cir. 1972), the court, per
Judge Tuttle, held that the provision of various municipal services in a discriminatory manner based on race violated the equal
protection guarantee. Starting from the premise that "figures
speak and when they do, courts listen," the court held that the
appellants proof of qualitative and quantitative disparities in the
level and nature of services provided in White and Black neighborhoods established a prima facie case of racial discrimination.
Judge Tuttle went on to hold that "[i]n a civil rights suit alleging
racial discrimination in contravention of the 14th Amendment,
actual intent or motive need not be directly proved," citing the
quote from Hobson v. Hansen, *supra.* He then concluded: "Having determined that no compelling state interest can possibly
justify the discriminatory *results* of Shaw's administration of
municipal services, we conclude that a violation of equal protection has occurred."

Sitting en banc, the circuit court accepted the rationale of
its panel, adding that "the facts before us squarely and certainly
support the reasonable and logical inference that there was here
neglect involving clear overtones of racial discrimination in the
administration of governmental affairs of the Town of Shaw
resulting in the evils which characterize an intentional and purposeful disregard of the principle of equal protection of the
laws."

Judge Roney, joined by Judges Simpson and Clark, dissented
from this manner of using the prima facie technique: "The Court
verbalizes no more for the statistical data submitted by plaintiffs
then that it presented a prima facie case of racial discrimination
but then it treats that prima facie case as conclusive proof of a

racial classification violative of the Equal Protection Clause which
defendants must justify by a compelling state interest. . . . Thus
the Court entirely forecloses the defendant's opportunity to
disprove the prima facie <u>case of racial discrimination by a preponderance of the evidence.</u> The law is clear that before the
government action here should have to be justified by a showing
of compelling state interest in order to withstand the impact of
the Equal Protection Clause, there must first be a finding that the
action discriminated against citizens because of their race.

"To my mind the En Banc Court, by adopting the position
of the original panel, [has converted the compelling interest
doctrine into a standard of evidence and procedure that has
despoiled the processes of law and could well obliterate the truth
in a given case.] <u>It has confused prima facie evidence of racial
classification,</u> which is related to the problems of shifting burdens
of proof and evidence, <u>with a prima facie case of the denial of
equal protection, which</u> in racial cases <u>requires justification by a
compelling state interest,</u> or put another way, which requires a
showing that the condition that results in the 'unequal protection'
achieves a <u>compelling state purpose.</u>" *See generally* Fessler &
Haar, *Beyond the Wrong Side of the Tracks: Municipal Services
in the Interstices of Procedure,* 6 HARV. CIV. RTS.-CIV. LIB. L.
REV. 441 (1971).

7.   In Jefferson v. Hackney, 406 U.S. 535 (1972), the appellants challenged a Texas welfare scheme whereby Aid to Families
with Dependent Children (AFDC) recipients received benefits
equal to only 75 per cent of their estimated need while recipients
in other welfare categories received 95 or 100 per cent of need.
They demonstrated that AFDC in Texas is disproportionately
composed of Blacks and Mexican-Americans.

The court, per Justice Rehnquist, refused to find any basis
for an equal protection claim in these facts. "As the statistics
cited in the footnote demonstrate, the number of minority members in all categories is substantial. The basic outlines of eligibility for the various categorical grants are established by Congress, not by the states; given the heterogeneity of the Nation's
population, it would be only an infrequent coincidence that the
racial composition of each grant class was identical to that of the
others. The acceptance of appellants' constitutional theory would
render suspect each difference in treatment among the grant
classes, however lacking in racial motivation and however otherwise rational the treatment might be. Few legislative efforts to
deal with the difficult problems posed by current welfare programs could survive such scrutiny, and we do not find it required
by the Fourteenth Amendment."

Justice Rehnquist then applied the traditional standard of review, concluding that "[s]ince budgetary constraints do not allow the payment of the full standard of need for all welfare recipients, the State may have concluded that the aged and infirmed are the least able of the categorical grant recipients to bear the hardships of inadequate standard of living. While different policy judgments are of course possible, it is not irrational for the State to believe that the young are more adaptable than the sick and elderly, especially because the latter have less hope of improving their situation in the years remaining to them. Whether or not one agrees with this state determination, there is nothing in the Constitution which forbids it."

Justice Marshall, joined by Justices Brennan and Stewart, dissenting on statutory grounds, did not reach the constitutional issue directly, but indicated their dissent from the majority's treatment of the problem. "If I were to face this question, I would certainly have more difficulty with it than either the District Court did or than this court seems to. The record contains the numerous statements by state officials to the effect that AFDC is funded at a lower level than other programs because it is not a politically popular program. There is also evidence of a stigma that seemingly attaches to AFDC recipients and no others . . . yet, both the District Court and this Court have little difficulty in concluding that the fact that AFDC is politically unpopular and the fact that AFDC recipients are disfavored by the state and its citizens have nothing whatsoever to do with the racial make up of the program. This conclusion is neither so apparent, nor so correct in my view.

"Moreover, because I find that each one of the State's reasons for treating AFDC differently from the other programs dissolves under close scrutiny . . . I am not at all certain who should bear the burden of proof on the question of racial discrimination, nor am I sure that the 'traditional' standard of review would govern the case as the court holds. . . [Percentages themselves are certainly not conclusive, but at some point a showing that state action has a devastating impact on the lives of minority racial groups must be relevant."] Justice Douglas, dissenting on statutory grounds, did not reach the constitutional issue.

See Whitcomb v. Chavis, 403 U.S. 124 (1971) (showing of under-representation of Blacks in a multimember district held not violative of equal protection); Mayor of Philadelphia v. Educational Equality League, 415 U.S. 605 (1974) (proof held inadequate to establish "a prima facie case of racial discrimination").

(2)  *Discrimination in Education: An Affirmative Duty to Equalize?*

(a)  Establishing the Foundations: Plessy and Brown

By the late nineteenth century, the Negro was being subjected to a new form of slavery in the form of Jim Crow segregation. Denied political equality by restrictive voting laws, Negroes were now relegated to social inferiority by state law. "In bulk and detail as well as in effectiveness of enforcement, the segregation codes were comparable with the black codes of the old regime, though the laxity that mitigated the harshness of the black codes was replaced by a rigidity that was more typical of the segregation code. That code lent the sanction of law to a racial ostracism that extended to churches and schools, to housing and jobs, to eating and drinking. Whether by law or by custom, that ostracism extended to virtually all forms of public transportation, to sports and recreations, to hospitals, orphanages, prisons, and asylums, and ultimately to funeral homes, morgues, and cemeteries." C. VANN WOODWARD, THE STRANGE CAREER OF JIM CROW 7 (2d ed. 1966). But in Strauder v. West Virginia, 100 U.S. 303 (1880), the Supreme Court had said that the fourteenth amendment conferred "the right to exemption from unfriendly legislation against [Negroes] distinctively as colored. . . ."

In Plessy v. Ferguson, 163 U.S. 537 (1896), the court considered these apparently inconsistent legal commands in the context of a statute requiring "equal but separate" railway accommodations for whites and blacks, concluding:

"The object of the [Fourteenth] Amendment was undoubtedly to enforce the absolute equality of the two races before the law, but, in the nature of things, it could not have been intended to abolish distinctions based upon color, or to enforce social, as distinguished from political, equality, or a commingling of the two races upon terms unsatisfactory to either. Laws permitting, and even requiring, their separation, in places where they are liable to be brought into contact, do not necessarily imply the inferiority of either race to the other, and have been generally, if not universally, recognized as within the competency of the state legislatures in the exercise of their police power. . . .

. . . .

"We consider the underlying fallacy of the plaintiffs's argument to consist in the assumption that the enforced separation of the two races stamps the colored race with a badge of inferiority. If this be so, it is not by reason of anything found in the act, but solely because the colored race chooses to put that construction upon it. . . . The argument also assumes that social prejudices may be overcome by legislation, and that equal rights cannot be secured to the negro except by an enforced commingling of the two races. We cannot accept this proposition. If the two races are to meet upon terms of social equality, it must be the result of natural affinities, a mutual appreciation of each other's merits, and a voluntary consent of individuals. . . ."

. . . .

In dissent, Justice Harlan argued:

" . . . [I]n view of the Constitution, in the eye of the law, there is in this country no superior, dominant, ruling class of citizens. There is no caste here. Our Constitution is color-blind, and neither knows nor tolerates classes among citizens. In respect of civil rights, all citizens are equal before the law."

## From Plessy to Brown

*there was never equality in the separate facilities*

1.  There is little discussion in *Plessy* regarding the "equal" facet of separate but equal. In fact, there was little equality even in tangible resources between black and white schools. "In 1915 South Carolina spent $23.76 on the average white child in public school, $2.91 on the average Negro child. As late as 1931, six southeastern states . . . spent less than a third as much per Negro public-school pupil as per white child. Ten years later spending for the Negro had risen only forty-four per cent of the white figure. At the time of the 1954 decision the South as a whole was spending $165 a year for the average white pupil, $115 for the Negro." A. LEWIS, PORTRAIT OF A DECADE: The Second American Revolution 17 (1964). In the early twentieth century, the Court did nothing to give meaning to the "equality" principle.

2.  In Missouri *ex rel.* Gaines v. Canada, 305 U.S. 337 (1938), the court held unconstitutional a Missouri plan whereby the state provided a law school for whites and financed legal education for Negroes in other states. Chief Justice Hughes reasoned that Missouri must give equal protection of the laws in its own jurisdiction. "By the operation of the laws of Missouri a privilege has been created for white law students which is denied to Negroes by reason of their race. The white resident is afforded legal education within the State; the Negro resident having the same qualifications is refused it there and must go outside the State to obtain it. That is a denial of the equality of legal right to the enjoyment of the privilege which the State has set up, and the provision for the payment of tuition fees in another State does not remove the discrimination. . . ."

3.  In 1950, the court decided two cases that went far in undermining state-imposed educational segregation regardless of the equality and tangible facilities. McLaurin v. Oklahoma Regents for Higher Education, 339 U.S. 637 (1950), held that Negro

graduate students who were consigned to certain desks in the classroom and special areas of the library and cafeteria were not being afforded their "present and personal right" to equal protection of the laws. Such restrictions "handicapped" McLaurin "in his pursuit of effective graduate education" since they "impair and inhibit his ability to study, to engage in discussions and exchange views with other students, and, in general, to learn his profession."

In Sweatt v. Painter, 339 U.S. 629 (1950), again avoiding the "broader issues," the court found inequality even though the state maintained separate law schools for Negroes and whites within the state. Numerous inequalities and tangible resources were noted including many difficult of measurement such as the reputation of the faculty, the experience of the administrators, the influence of alumni and community standing. But the court went on to even more intangible features, noting the difference between the segregated schools in opportunity for "the interplay of ideas and the exchange of views with which the law is concerned." *See* Sipuel v. Board of Regents, 332 U.S. 631 (1948). It was becoming virtually impossible for state segregated schools to meet the equality mandate. The stage was set for *Brown v. Board of Education.*

## BROWN v. BOARD OF EDUCATION
Supreme Court of the United States
347 U.S. 483, 98 L. Ed. 873, 74 S. Ct. 686 (1954)

Chief Justice WARREN delivered the opinion of the Court.

These cases come to us from the States of Kansas, South Carolina, Virginia and Delaware. . . .

In each of the cases, minors of the Negro race, through their legal representatives, seek the aid of the courts in obtaining admission to the public schools of their community on a nonsegregated basis. In each instance, they have been denied admission to schools attended by white children under laws requiring or permitting segregation according to race. . . .

The plaintiffs contend that segregated public schools are not "equal" and cannot be made "equal," and that hence they are deprived of the equal protection of the laws. Because of the obvious importance of the question presented, the Court took jurisdiction. Argument was heard in the 1952 Term, and reargument was heard this Term on certain questions propounded by the Court.

Reargument was largely devoted to the circumstances surrounding the adoption of the Fourteenth Amendment in 1868. . . . This discussion and our own investigation convince us that, although these sources cast some light, it is not enough to resolve the problem with which we are faced. At best, they are inconclusive. The most avid proponents of the post-War Amendments undoubtedly intended them to remove all legal distinctions among "all persons born or naturalized in the United States." Their opponents, just as certainly, were antagonistic to both the letter and the spirit of the Amendments and wished them to have the most limited effect. What others in Congress and state legislatures had in mind cannot be determined with any degree of certainty.

. . . .

In the first cases in this Court construing the Fourteenth Amendment, decided shortly after its adoption, the Court interpreted it as proscribing all state-imposed discriminations against the Negro race. The doctrine of "separate but equal" did not make its appearance in this Court until 1896 in the case of *Plessy v. Ferguson,* involving not education but transportation. American courts have since labored with the doctrine for over half a century. . . .

. . . Our decision, therefore, cannot turn on merely a comparison of these tangible factors in the Negro and white schools involved in each of the cases. We must look instead to the effect of segregation itself on public education.

In approaching this problem, we cannot turn the clock back to 1868 when the Amendment was adopted, or even to 1896 when *Plessy v. Ferguson* was written. We must consider public education in the light of its full development and its present place in American life throughout the Nation. Only in this way can it be determined if segregation in public schools deprives these plaintiffs of the equal protection of the laws.

*time and changes*

Today, education is perhaps the most important function of state and local governments. Compulsory school attendance laws and the great expenditures for education both demonstrate our recognition of the importance of education to our democratic society. It is required in the performance of our most basic public responsibilities, even service in the armed forces. It is the very foundation of good citizenship. Today it is a principal instrument in awakening the child to cultural values, in preparing him for later professional training, and in helping him to adjust normally to his environment. In these days, it is doubtful that any child may reasonably be expected to succeed in life if he is denied the opportunity of an education. Such an opportunity, where the state has undertaken to provide it, is a right which must be made available to all on equal terms.

We come then to the question presented: Does segregation of children in public schools solely on the basis of race, even though the physical facilities and other "tangible" factors may be equal, deprive the children of the minority group of equal educational opportunities? We believe that it does.

In *Sweatt v. Painter,* in finding that a segregated law school for Negroes could not provide them equal educational opportunities, this Court relied in large part on "those qualities which are incapable of objective measurement but which make for greatness in a law school." . . . Such considerations apply with added force to children in grade and high schools. To separate them from others of similar age and qualifications solely because of their race generates a feeling of inferiority as to their status in the community that may affect their hearts and minds in a way unlikely ever to be undone. The effect of this separation on their educational opportunities was well stated by a finding in the Kansas case by a court which nevertheless felt compelled to rule against the Negro plaintiffs:

*separation implies inferiority.*

"Segregation of white and colored children in public schools has a detrimental effect upon the colored children. The impact is greater when it has the sanction of the law; for the policy of separating the races is usually interpreted as denoting the inferiority of the Negro group. A sense of inferiority affects the motivation of a child to learn. Segregation with the sanction of law, therefore, has a tendency to retard the educational and mental development of Negro children and to deprive them of some of the benefits they would receive in a racially integrated school system."

*inferiority affect motivation and learning*

Whatever may have been the extent of psychological knowledge at the time of *Plessy v. Ferguson,* this finding is amply supported by modern authority.[11] Any language in *Plessy v. Ferguson* contrary to this finding is rejected.

We conclude that in the field of public education the doctrine of "separate but equal" has no place. Separate educational facilities are inherently unequal. Therefore, we hold that the plaintiffs and others similarly situated for whom the actions have been brought are, by reason of the segregation complained of, deprived of the equal protection of the laws guaranteed by the Fourteenth

[11] K.B. Clark, Effect of Prejudice and Discrimination on Personality Development (Midcentury White House Conference on Children and Youth, 1950); Witmer and Kotinsky, Personality in the Making (1952), c. VI; Deutscher and Chein, The Psychological Effects of Enforced Segregation: A Survey of Social Science Opinion, 26 J.Psychol. 259 (1948); Chein, What are the Psychological Effects of Segregation Under Conditions of Equal Facilities?, 3 Int.J. Opinion and Attitude Res. 229 (1949); Brameld, Educational Costs, in Discrimination and National Welfare (McIver, ed., 1949), 44-48; Frazier, The Negro in the United States (1949), 674-681. And see generally Myrdal, An American Dilemma (1944).

Amendment. This disposition makes unnecessary any discussion whether such segregation also violates the Due Process Clause of the Fourteenth Amendment.

Because these are class actions, because of the wide applicability of this decision, and because of the great variety of local conditions, the formulation of decrees in these cases presents problems of considerable complexity. On reargument, the consideration of appropriate relief was necessarily subordinated to the primary question—the constitutionality of segregation in public education. We have now announced that such segregation is a denial of the equal protection of the laws. In order that we may have the full assistance of the parties in formulating decrees, the cases will be restored to the docket, and the parties are requested to present further argument. . . .

It is so ordered.

---

## NOTES

### The Holding of Brown

1. While *Brown I* is clearly a landmark decision, there is substantial disagreement as to what the court held and the basis for its holding. As you consider the various alternatives, consider the political position of the court at the time: ("The Court knew, of course, that its judgment would have an unparalleled impact on the daily lives of a very substantial portion of the population and that the response to many of those affected would be in varying degrees hostile. It was necessary, therefore, if ever it had been, to exert to the utmost the prestige, the oracular authority of the institution. To this end, it was desirable that the Court speak unanimously, with one voice from the deep. And the less said, the less chance of internal disagreement. By the same token, it was wise to present as small a target as possible to marksmen on the outside.") Bickel, *The Original Understanding and the Segregation Decision*, 69 HARV. L. REV. 1, 2 (1955), SELECTED ESSAYS 853-54 (1963).

*Brown I: education only?*

2. *An Emphasis on Education?* Does the court hold simply that state-imposed racial segregation in *education* is unconstitutional? Is the decision based on the fundamental character of education and the harm to the child from race segregation in this context? Immediately after *Brown I,* the court issued a series of *per curiam* decisions holding state-imposed segregation in various public facilities unconstitutional on the basis of *Brown I. See, e.g.,* Mayor of Baltimore v. Dawson, 350 U.S. 877 (1955) (beaches); Holmes v. Atlanta, 355 U.S. 879 (1955) (municipal golfcourses); Gayle v. Browder, 352 U.S. 903 (1956) (buses); New Orleans City

Park Improvement Ass'n v. Detiege, 358 U.S. 54 (1958) (parks). Do these decisions flow logically from *Brown* if it is based on the place of education in our society?

3. *An Emphasis on Race?* Does *Brown* hold that state-imposed *racial* segregation, regardless of the context, is violative to equal protection? Is *Plessy* overruled? Is the court adopting the dissent of Justice Harlan in *Plessy*? Is the court saying that racial classifications are *per se* impermissible? If so, is the fact-finding of harm necessary to the decision?

4. In Bolling v. Sharpe, 347 U.S. 497 (1954), a companion case to *Brown*, the court held that the educational segregation laws of the District of Columbia violated the due process clause of the fifth amendment—"discrimination may be so unjustifiable as to be violative of due process." Chief Justice Warren for a unanimous court, began with the premise that "[c]lassifications based solely upon race must be scrutinized with particular care since they are contrary to our traditions and hence constitution-ally suspect. . . . Liberty under law extends to the full range of conduct which the individual is free to pursue, and it cannot be restricted except for a proper governmental objective." Applying this standard, the Chief Justice concluded: "Segregation in public education is not reasonably related to any proper governmental objective and thus it imposes on Negro children of the District of Columbia a burden that constitutes an arbitrary deprivation of their liberty in violation of the Due Process Clause." Is the lack of a reasonable relation assumed in *Brown*?

*[handwritten margin note: classifications — due process]*

5. Professor Herbert Wechsler contends that *Brown* is not a principled decision, *i.e.,* "one that rests on reasons with respect to all the issues in the case, reasons that in their generality and their neutrality transcend any immediate result that is involved." Wechsler, *Toward Neutral Principles of Constitutional Law*, 73 HARV. L. REV. 1 (1959). He argues "the problem [with *Brown*] strictly in the reasoning of the opinion, an opinion which is often read with less fidelity by those who praise it than by those by whom it is condemned." How would you characterize the holding in *Brown*? Does it yield "neutral principles"? *See* Pollak, *Racial Discrimination and Judicial Integrity: A Reply to Professor Wechsler*, 108 U. PA. L. REV. 1 (1959), SELECTED ESSAYS 819 (1963); Wright, *Professor Bickel, The Scholarly Tradition and the Supreme Court*, 84 HARV. L. REV. 769 (1971).

6. Wechsler argues that "the question posed by state-enforced segregation is not one of discrimination at all. Its human and its constitutional dimensions lie entirely elsewhere, in the denial by the state of freedom to associate, a denial that impinges in the same way on any groups or races that may be involved."

*[handwritten margin note: liberty should have been argued on association rather than equal protection]*

## The Basis of Brown

An alternative way of approaching the above question is to consider the material that the Chief Justice uses in *Brown* in arriving at his holding. What are the respective roles of history, precedent, social science data, ethical judgment and social change?

1. *History*. The first question presented by the court for reargument was addressed to the history of the fourteenth amendment. The court in *Brown* found the history of the fourteenth amendment inconclusive regarding the status of racial segregation in education. It has been argued that since separate schools were common at the time that the fourteenth amendment was drafted, it could not have been intended to upset the system of segregated schools. On the other hand, it has been said "that it was accepted virtually unanimously by all who supported the fourteenth amendment that it required equal schools and that a very large number of its supporters thought that the amendment forbade segregated schools." Frank & Munro, *The Original Understanding of "Equal Protection of the Laws,"* 1972 WASHINGTON U.L.Q. 381, 467. As previously indicated [text, p. 578], Alexander Bickel has suggested that the fourteenth amendment, § 1, implemented "the relatively narrow objectives of the moderates," and therefore was not intended to apply to segregated education, but that the language of the amendment was left sufficiently flexible to accommodate future growth. Bickel, *The Original Understanding and the Segregation Decision,* 69 HARV. L. REV. 1 (1955), SELECTED ESSAYS 853 (1973).

Assuming that the framers of the fourteenth amendment did not intend the equal protection guarantee to apply to segregated education, what effect should be given to this intent today? Justice Douglas was later to argue "notions of what constitutes equal treatment for purposes of the Equal Protection Clause *do* change." Harper v. Virginia State Bd., 383 U.S. 663, 669 (1966). On the other hand, Justice Harlan adopted the view of one of the members of the 39th Congress which proposed the fourteenth amendment: "Every Constitution embodies the principles of its framers. It is a transcript of their minds. If its meaning in any place is open to doubt, or if words are used which seem to have no fixed signification, we cannot err if we turn to the framers; and their authority increases in proportion to the evidence which they have left on the question." Oregon v. Mitchell, 400 U.S. 112, 154 (1970) (Harlan J., concurring in part and dissenting in part).

In a proposed redraft of the *Brown* opinion, Professor Louis H. Pollak agrees that the history of the fourteenth amendment does not disclose any intent on the part of the framers to end educational segregation but asserts that this is not dispositive: "For one thing, it is familiar constitutional history that this court has progressively brought within the ambit of the fourteenth amendment many issues and many litigants probably not contemplated by those who framed and ratified the amendment. Moreover, and of more immediate moment, we read the history of the amendment as contemplating an essentially dynamic development by Congress and this Court of the liberties outlined in such generalized terms in the amendment." Pollak, *Racial Discrimination and Judicial Integrity: A Reply to Professor Wechsler*, 108 U. PA. L. REV. 1 (1959), SELECTED ESSAYS 819, 837 (1963).

2.   *Social Science*. The Chief Justice's statement that "separate educational facilities are inherently unequal," his comments on the effects of segregation on the child and his citation in footnote 11 of social science authorities have received extensive commentary. *See generally*, A. DAVID, THE UNITED STATES SUPREME COURT AND THE USES OF SOCIAL SCIENCE DATA chs. IV & V (1973); P. ROSEN, THE SUPREME COURT AND SOCIAL SCIENCE chs. 7-9 (1972). At the trial, social scientists were used by the NAACP as expert witnesses. *See* Greenberg, *Social Scientists Take the Stand: A Review and Appraisal of Their Testimony in Litigation*, 54 MICH. L. REV. 953 (1956). The Virginia and South Carolina courts rejected such evidence while the Delaware and Kansas courts accepted it. The NAACP brief to the Supreme Court contained an extensive social science appendix signed by 35 distinguished social scientists, concluding that "enforced segregation is psychologically detrimental to the members of the segregated group." Reprinted in 37 MINN. L. REV. 427 (1953). In oral argument, the social science findings were described by Robert Carter, one of the plaintiff's attorneys as "the heart of our case." Thurgood Marshall similarly contended that the social science witnesses "stand in the record as unchallenged as experts in their field, and I think we have arrived at the stage where the courts do give credence to the testimony of people who are experts in their fields."

3.   How important a role did the social science evidence play in the decision in *Brown*? Is it only used to rebut *Plessy's* questionable fact-finding? Would the decision have been the same even if no empirical evidence had been provided? Kenneth Clark, a social psychologist who played a leading role in *Brown* contends: "The role of social science in the Brown decision was crucial, in the Court's opinion, in supplying persuasive evidence that segregation itself means inequality." K. Clark, *The Social Scientists, The Brown Decision and Contemporary Confusion*, in ARGUMENT: THE ORAL ARGUMENT BEFORE THE SUPREME

COURT IN BROWN V. BOARD OF EDUCATION OF TOPEKA, 1952-55 (L. Friedman, ed., 1969).

4. The "scientific" character of these social science studies has been both challenged and defended. *Compare* Garfinkel, *Social Science Evidence and the School Segregation Cases*, 21 J. POLITICS 37 (1959); Clark, *The Desegregation Cases: Criticism of the Social Scientist's Role*, 5 VILL. L. REV. 224 (1959); Van Den Haag, *Social Science Testimony in the Desegregation Cases—A Reply to Professor Kenneth Clark*, 6 VILL. L. REV. 69 (1960). *See generally*, P. ROSEN, THE SUPREME COURT AND SOCIAL SCIENCE, at chs. 8 and 9.

5. What should be the role of such evidence in constitutional adjudication? Is such a Brandeis brief questionable when used to *attack* rather than *support* legislation? Isn't it possible to marshal experts and social science data on any side of a question? Would it be relevant if the presumption of constitutionality of legislation would be inapplicable?

Suppose a court were to find that Professor Arthur Jensen is correct that "genetic factors are strongly implicated in the average Negro-White intelligence difference." *How Much Can We Boost IQ and Scholastic Achievement?*, 39 HARV. EDUC. REV. 1 (1969). Consider the findings of the Coleman Report that school desegregation is not likely without more, to have a great effect on a child's achievement. HEW, OFFICE OF EDUC. EQUALITY OF EDUCATIONAL OPPORTUNITY 295-316 (1966). *See* U.S. COMMISSION ON CIVIL RIGHTS, RACIAL ISOLATION IN THE PUBLIC SCHOOLS (1967), emphasizing the importance of racial factors in educational development. *See generally* F. Mosteller and D.P. Moynihan, eds., ON EQUALITY OF EDUCATIONAL OPPORTUNITY (1972). In one lower court decision, the court did allow non-legal data purporting to show that desegregation would be educationally disadvantageous to black children. Stell v. Savannah-Chatham County Bd. of Educ., 220 F. Supp. 667 (S.D. Ga. 1963).

Compare the following two views: "The Brown decision was actually more than a legal attack on legislation predicated on racism. In broader cultural terms Chief Justice Warren's opinion symbolized the confrontation between mythology and empiricism. In the context of judicial discourse legal rationality in the Brown case was formally and deliberately expressed as empiricism, rejecting the ideology and mythology implicitly contained in the Plessy case." P. ROSEN, THE SUPREME COURT AND SOCIAL SCIENCE, at 156. On the other hand, Edmund Cahn warns: "I would not have the constitutional rights of Negroes—or of other Americans —rest on any such flimsy foundation as some of the scientific demonstrations in these records. . . . [S]ince the behavioral sciences are

so very young, imprecise, and changeable, their findings have an
uncertain expectancy of life. Today's sanguine assertion may be
cancelled by tomorrow's new revelation—or new technical fad.
It is one thing to use the current scientific findings, however
ephemeral they may be, in order to ascertain whether the legislature has acted reasonably in adopting some scheme of social or
economic regulation; deference here is not so much to the findings as to the legislature. It would be quite another thing to have
our fundamental rights rise, fall, or change along with the latest
fashion of psychological literature." *Jurisprudence,* 30 N.Y.U. L.
Rev. 150, 157-58, 167 (1955).

   6. *Ethical Choice.* Professor Edmund Cahn concludes that
the decision could properly rest on "the most familiar and universally accepted standards of right and wrong." *Jurisprudence,* 30
N.Y.U. L. Rev., at 159. Similarly it has been suggested that ["[i]f
desegregation decisions are to be stable, consistent, and manageable, courts have little choice but to rely on ethical principles. The
cases can be explained only by reference to such principles."]
Yudof, *Equal Educational Opportunity and the Courts,* 51 Tex. L.
Rev. 411, 446 (1973). Is *Brown* ultimately a question of ethics, a
subjective judgment of how our society should be run? Of an egalitarian ethic? It has been argued: "Throughout the history of
American constitutional development may be found recurring
evidence of the fact that Supreme Court Justices have been motivated by value preferences in reaching decisions. At no time have
they resorted to neutrality or impersonality of principle in making
choices between competing alternatives." Miller & Howell, *The
Myth of Neutrality in Constitutional Adjudication,* 27 U. Chi.
L. Rev. 661, 671-72 (1960).

### (b)  Making Brown Work: Judicial and Administrative Implementation

#### BROWN v. BOARD OF EDUCATION
Supreme Court of the United States
349 U.S. 294, 99 L. Ed. 1083, 75 S. Ct. 753 (1955)

Chief Justice WARREN delivered the opinion of the Court.

   These cases were decided on May 17, 1954. The opinions of
that date, declaring the fundamental principle that racial discrimination in public education is unconstitutional, are incorporated herein by reference. All provisions of federal, state,
or local law requiring or permitting such discrimination must
yield to this principle. There remains for consideration the
manner in which relief is to be accorded.

   . . . .

   Full implementation of these constitutional principles may
require solution of varied local school problems. School au-

thorities have the primary responsibility for elucidating, assessing, and solving these problems; courts will have to consider whether the action of school authorities constitutes good faith implementation of the governing constitutional principles. Because of their proximity to local conditions and the possible need for further hearings, the courts which originally heard these cases can best perform this judicial appraisal. Accordingly, we believe it appropriate to remand the cases to those courts.

In fashioning and effectuating the decrees, the courts will be guided by equitable principles. [Traditionally, equity has been characterized by a practical flexibility in shaping its remedies and by a facility for adjusting and reconciling public and private needs.] These cases call for the exercise of these traditional attributes of equity power. At stake is the personal interest of the plaintiffs in admission to public schools as soon as practicable on a nondiscriminatory basis. To effectuate this interest may call for elimination of a variety of obstacles in making the transition to school systems operated in accordance with the constitutional principles set forth in our May 17, 1954, decision. Courts of equity may properly take into account the public interest in the elimination of such obstacles in a systematic and effective manner. But it should go without saying that the vitality of these constitutional principles cannot be allowed to yield simply because of disagreement with them.

While giving weight to these public and private considerations, the courts will require that the defendants make a prompt and reasonable start toward full compliance with our May 17, 1954, ruling. Once such a start has been made, the courts may find that additional time is necessary to carry out the ruling in an effective manner. The burden rests upon the defendants to establish that such time is necessary in the public interest and is consistent with good faith compliance at the earliest practicable date. To that end, the courts may consider problems related to administration, arising from the physical condition of the school plant, the school transportation system, personnel, revision of school districts and attendance areas into compact units to achieve a system of determining admission to the public schools on a nonracial basis, and revision of local laws and regulations which may be necessary in solving the foregoing problems. They will also consider the adequacy of any plans the defendants may propose to meet these problems and to effectuate a transition to a racially nondiscriminatory school system. During this period of transition, the courts will retain jurisdiction of these cases.

The judgments below, except that in the Delaware case, are accordingly reversed and remanded to the District Courts to take

such proceedings and enter such orders and decrees consistent
with this opinion as are necessary and proper to admit to public
schools on a racially nondiscriminatory basis with all deliberate
speed the parties to these cases. . . .

---

## NOTES

1. [In *McLaurin* and earlier segregation cases, the right to
equal protection had been treated as a "personal and present
right."] The unusual character of the *Brown II* decree is noted by
Professor Bickel. "In the vast majority of cases—barring those
that are dismissed outright as not suitable for adjudication—the
normal and expected judgment of the Court is a crisp and specific writing which tells one of the parties exactly what he must
do, such as pay a judgment, deliver certain real estate, cease from
doing something, or, indeed, go to jail. The equivalent in these
cases would have been a decree ordering the named children,
and perhaps, since these were class actions, all children in the five
school districts effected, who were similarly situated, to be admitted forthwith to the white schools of their choice. The question is, why should the Court not have issued such a decree?
Indeed, one might have asked whether the Court could do other
than issue such a decree?" A. BICKEL, THE LEAST DANGEROUS
BRANCH: THE SUPREME COURT AT THE BAR OF POLITICS 247
(1962).

*specific ruling in Brown II?*

2. *Personal and Group Rights.* Is the right recognized in
*Brown* a personal right or a right of Blacks as a class? Assuming
even delayed relief is an adequate remedy for the group, what of
the individual litigants who graduate before desegregation? If a
policy such as benign quotas works for the benefit of the class,
does this then justify denial of the claims of black individuals
who suffer because of the quota? Consider the language of the
court in United States v. Jefferson County Bd. of Educ., 372
F.2d 836, 868 (5th Cir. 1966): "The gradual transition the
Supreme Court authorized was to allow the states time to solve
the administration problems inherent in that changeover. No
delay would have been necessary if the right at issue in Brown
had been only the right of individual Negro plaintiffs to admission
to a white school. Moreover, the delay of one year in deciding
Brown II and the gradual remedy Brown II fashioned can be
justified only on the ground that the 'personal and present' right
of the individual plaintiffs must yield to the overriding right of
Negroes as a class to a completely integrated public education."
Consider the later explanation of Chief Justice Warren in an
interview: "In these days . . . you'll find a lot of people who are

*judgement for a class rather than an individual*

*Setting the standard for wide-spread application*

saying . . . that they should have said, 'These people must be allowed to go to this school.' Well, if they had, it was the opinion, my opinion and most of us, that it would have solved nothing. We would have one or two Negroes go to a white school, but that would be all there was to it. [So we treated it as a class action, so that everyone in the same situation as they were would be treated in the same manner judicially."] Earl Warren, 1891-1974, The Washington Post, July 14, 1974, p. C3.

**3.** *"With All Deliberate Speed."* (a) In a brief for the CIO as amicus curiae in *Brown I,* Arthur Goldberg stated: "If the policy of non-discrimination or non-segregation is put into effect concurrently with its announcement, and if it is enforced with firmness and decisiveness, there is every likelihood that the policy would be generally accepted and that any substantial degree of inter-racial friction will be avoided." On the other hand, he argued, " 'gradual adjustment' to a new policy of non-segregation or non-discrimination is apt to work less well. Long drawn out discussion of a contemplated ultimate end of segregation or discrimination may serve only to exacerbate racial tensions. Division along racial lines may harden and people may be led to take more extreme and adamant stands than they would have if the issue had been disposed of promptly, once and for all."

**4.** While the court had the equitable power to fashion a suitable remedy appropriate to the case, why did they adopt this formula? Whereas *Brown I* was met with fervid hostility in the South, *Brown II* was well-received and even cheered in a southern state legislature. Wasn't delay an open invitation to resistance and evasion? Or, as Alexander Bickel asserts, is it likely that "[t]he system would have worked no differently, no matter what was the form of the Supreme Court's decree"? Bickel, *The Decade of School Desegregation: Progress and Prospects,* 64 COLUM. L. REV. 193, 201 (1964).

Chief Justice Warren in the interview referred to above noted that the phrase "with all deliberate speed" was used in English admiralty. He explained: "But it was suggested that that would be a way to proceed in the case because we realize that under our federal system there were so many blocks preventing an immediate solution of the thing in reality, that the best we could look for would be a progression of action, and to keep it going, in a proper manner, we adopted that phrase, 'all deliberate speed.' " Earl Warren, 1891-1974, The Washington Post, July 14, 1974, p. C3.

*Resistance to Brown: The Early Judicial Response*

The *Brown* decision did not end school segregation. The neighborhood school in the North and the dual system of schools in the South, the heritage of enforced segregation, tended to recreate, or leave intact, sometimes fortuitously, sometimes deliberately, the fact of school segregation, even if the law forbade it. In the border states and especially in the District of Columbia, the dual system did begin to erode. But the story in the South generally was one of massive resistance. Individuals were forced to litigate the applicability of *Brown* in district after district. Through a variety of strategies, the South sought to discourage litigants and resist court decrees to desegregate. As the laws in the books requiring a dual school system were eliminated, they were replaced by new devices designed to achieve the same end. A decade after *Brown,* only 1.17 percent of black children in the 11 states of the old Confederacy attended school with whites.

1. *Response to Violence: Cooper v. Aaron.* A gradual plan of desegregation formulated by the School Board of Little Rock, Arkansas, and approved by the district court stimulated state constitutional amendment and legislation designed to thwart desegregation. When the school board persisted, Governor Orval Faubus declared the local high school in Little Rock "off limits" to colored students and sent in the Arkansas National Guard to enforce his order. While the district court ordered the governor and national guard to desist, mob action successfully prevented black children from entering school until President Eisenhower (whose own support for *Brown* was questionable) sent in federal troops.

In Cooper v. Aaron, 358 U.S. 1 (1958), the court rejected an effort by local school officials to delay implementing the desegregation plan because of the public hostility. Each member of the Supreme Court signed an opinion unanimously reaffirming *Brown* as well as "the basic principle that the federal judiciary is supreme in the exposition of the law of the Constitution . . . as a permanent and indispensable feature of our constitutional system." It necessarily followed that the interpretation of the fourteenth amendment enunciated in *Brown* was the supreme law of the land. The constitutional rights there recognized were "not to be sacrificed or yielded to the violence and disorder which have followed upon the actions of the Governor and Legislature. . . . [L]aw and order are not here to be preserved by depriving the Negro children of their constitutional rights. . . .

"The constitutional rights of children not to be discriminated against in school admission on grounds of race or color declared by this court in the Brown case can neither be nullified openly and directly by state legislators or state executive or judicial officers, nor nullified indirectly by them through evasive schemes for segregation whether attempted 'ingeniously or ingenuously.' "

**2.** *Pupil Assignment Laws.* A common device used by southern districts was the pupil placement laws whereby children could be assigned to schools usually on the basis of "objective" factors such as intelligence, academic fitness, or psychological capacity. While the child could challenge the action in court, this would require exhaustion of administrative remedies. *See* Orleans Parish School Bd. v. Bush, 242 F.2d 156 (5th Cir. 1957), *cert. denied,* 354 U.S. 921 (1957), in striking down such a law. *See generally* Meador, *The Constitution and the Assignment of Pupils to Public Schools,* 45 VA. L. REV. 517 (1959).

**3.** *Transfer Plans.* Closely allied to the assignment plans were provisions allowing a child assigned to a school where he would be in a racial minority to transfer to a school where his race would be in the majority. In Goss v. Board of Educ., 373 U.S. 683 (1963), the court, in striking down such a transfer provision, noted that they were racially motivated and "inevitably lead toward segregation of the students by race."

✳ **4.** *Closing the Schools.* Prince Edward County, Virginia, one of the affected communities under the *Brown* decision, acting under a state law making continuation of public schools a matter of local option, closed its public education system rather than desegregate. State and local funds, however, were subsequently provided to segregated private schools established for whites.

In Griffin v. County School Bd. of Prince Edward County, 377 U.S. 218, (1964), the court, per Justice Black, held that this violated the equal protection guarantee. While there is no constitutional requirement that counties as counties be treated alike, the record made it clear "that Prince Edward's public schools were closed and private schools operated in their place with state and county assistance, for one reason, and one reason only: To insure, through measures taken by the county and the State that white and colored children in Prince Edward County would not, under any circumstances, go to the same school. Whatever non-racial grounds might support a State's allowing a county to abandon public schools, the object must be a constitutional one, and grounds of race and opposition to desegregation do not qualify as constitutional."

In remanding the case, Justice Black noted that an "injunction against paying tuition grants and giving tax credits while public schools remain closed is appropriate and necessary since those grants and tax credits have been essential parts of the county's program, successful thus far, to deprive petitioners of the same advantages of a public school education enjoyed by children in every other part of Virginia. For the same reasons, the district court may, if necessary to prevent further racial dis-

crimination, require the Supervisors to exercise the power that
is theirs to levy taxes to raise funds adequate to reopen, operate,
and maintain without racial discrimination a public school system
in Prince Edward county like that operated in other counties in
Virginia."

In closing, Justice Black noted that "[t]he time for more
'deliberate speed' has run out, and that phrase can no longer
justify denying these Prince Edward County school children their
constitutional rights to an education equal to that afforded by the
public schools in the other parts of Virginia."

Why could Jackson, Mississippi close its swimming pools following a desegregation order (*Palmer v. Thompson*, text, p. 583)
given the *Griffin* holding? Does *Griffin* turn on a finding of unconstitutional purpose? Does *Griffin* stand for a broad principle
that municipal benefits must be made available to all citizens
without discrimination? Is the judicial remedy appropriate? Or
is this, as Professor Kurland suggests, "one of the many factual
situations that compels the Court to resort to unbecoming and
unfortunate methods for assuring that its will be done." Kurland,
*Supreme Court 1963 Term, Foreword: Equal in Origin and Equal
in Title to the Legislative and Executive Branches of the Government,* 78 HARV. L. REV. 143, 158 (1964).

## The Administrative Era

A decade of judicial enforcement had done little in making
*Brown* work. Added impetus towards this end came with the passage of the Civil Rights Act of 1964. Title IV authorized the Office
of Education to give technical and financial assistance to local
school systems in desegregating. Further, it empowered the Attorney General upon complaint, to institute a federal civil suit in
the name of the United States (§ 407). Title VI, 42 U.S.C.
§ 20000d, of the Act provided that: "No person . . . shall, on the
ground of race, color, or national origin, be excluded from
participation in, be denied the benefits of, or be subjected to
discrimination under any program or activity receiving Federal
assistance." Financial grants were to be terminated if this guarantee were violated. The importance of this sanction was enhanced
by the passage of the Elementary and Secondary Education Act of
1965, channeling large sums of federal money into state and local
educational systems.

Between 1964 and the 1968-69 school year, over 120 school
districts were denied federal funds. The percentage of black
children in schools having more than one-half white students
increased to 20.3 per cent in the 11 southern states. H. HOROWITZ
& K. KARST, LAW, LAWYERS, AND SOCIAL CHANGE 352 (1969);

SOUTHERN REGIONAL COUNCIL, THE FEDERAL RETREAT IN SCHOOL DESEGREGATION 1 (1969). *See generally* G. ORFIELD, THE RECONSTRUCTION OF SOUTHERN EDUCATION (1969).

### (c)  Redefining the Fourteenth Amendment Right to Equal Protection: An Affirmative Duty to Integrate?

1.  In Briggs v. Elliott, 132 F. Supp. 776 (E.D. S.C. 1955), the court stated that "[t]he Constitution . . . does not require integration. It merely forbids [segregation]." But in United States v. Jefferson County Bd. of Educ., 372 F.2d 836 (5th Cir. 1966), *aff'd en banc,* 380 F.2d 385 (5th Cir. 1967), *cert. denied,* 389 U.S. 840 (1967), the court, per Judge Wisdom, equated desegregation and integration and spoke in terms of an affirmative duty imposed by the fourteenth amendment. "If *Brown I* left any doubt as to the affirmative duty of states to furnish a fully integrated education to Negroes as a class, *Brown II* resolved that doubt. . . . The two *Brown* decisions established equalization of educational opportunities as a high priority goal for all of the states and compelled 17 states, which by law had segregated public schools, to take affirmative action, to reorganize their schools into a unitary, non-racial system."

But wouldn't this violate the color blind principle urged by Justice Harlan dissenting in *Plessy?* Certainly it forces governmental officials to consider race in making decisions.

*Jefferson* reflected the class-based right approach of *Brown II* and rejected the claim that the fourteenth amendment is satisfied if the personal rights of the individual Negro are not denied. But is it merely a clarification and restatement of *Brown I* and *Brown II* or is it a major step in redefining the fourteenth amendment right? Is the constitutional guarantee a negative command to the states not to segregate on the basis of race—to admit Negroes to schools on a non-racial basis—or an affirmative duty to integrate? What is the operative effect of the difference?

2.  *Freedom of Choice.* Southern school districts, seeking federal aid while avoiding desegregation, increasingly adopted "freedom of choice" plans which allowed a pupil to choose his own public school. New Kent County, Virginia, which had been de jure segregated prior to *Brown,* adopted such a plan in 1965. Nevertheless, by 1968 no white children were in the Negro school and 85 per cent of the black children in the system were still in the all-Negro school. In Green v. County School Bd. of New Kent County, 391 U.S. 430 (1968), the court held the plan unconstitutional.

Justice Brennan, for the court, framed the question as "whether, under all the circumstances here, respondent School

Board's adoption of a 'freedom-of-choice' plan which allows a pupil to choose his own public school constitutes adequate compliance with the Board's responsibilities 'to achieve a system of determining admission to the public schools on a non-racial basis.' "

In answering the question, Justice Brennan found that "the State acting through the local school board and school officials organized and operated a dual system, part 'white' and part 'Negro.' " But this was precisely what *Brown I & II* had held must be eliminated—"school boards operating such school systems were *required* by *Brown II* 'to affectuate a transition to a racially non-discriminatory school system.' "

Justice Brennan contended that, under *Brown II* school boards "then operating state-compelled dual systems were nevertheless clearly charged with the affirmative duty to take whatever steps might be necessary to convert to a unitary system in which racial discrimination would be eliminated root and branch." This did not mean that " 'freedom-of-choice' can have no place in such a plan. We do not hold that a 'freedom-of-choice' plan might of itself be unconstitutional, although that argument has been urged upon us. Rather, all we decide today is that in desegregating a dual system a plan utilizing 'freedom-of-choice' is not an end in itself." It is a permissible plan, only if "it offers real promise of aiding a desegregation program to effectuate conversion of a state-imposed dual system to a unitary, non-racial system there might be no objection to allowing such a device to prove itself an operation. On the other hand, if there are reasonably available other ways, such as zoning, promising speedier and more effective conversion to unitary, non-racial school systems, 'freedom-of-choice' must be held unacceptable."

Applying these standards to the New Kent School Board Plan, Justice Brennan concluded: "The Board must be required to formulate a new plan and, in light of other courses which appear open to the Board, such as zoning, fashion steps which promise realistically to convert promptly to a system without the 'white' school, but just schools."

Does Justice Brennan correctly state the issue to which he provides an answer? What is the meaning of *Brown* according to *Jefferson*? According to *Green*? Must a school system adopt the "best" plan? "Best" according to what criteria? Perhaps the formerly de jure segregated school system is being required to achieve a higher level of racial mixture than would have been achieved had there been no de jure segregation. What is the justification for using integration as a remedy? Is it punitive? Is it necessary to assure actual desegregation? To redress the psychological harm that was done by de jure segregation? *See* Goodman, *De Facto School Segregation: A Constitutional and Empirical Analysis*, 60 CALIF. L. REV. 275, 285-90 (1972). *See also* Monroe v. Board of Comm'rs, 391 U.S. 450 (1968), where the court struck down a plan permitting free transfer wherever space was available since "it patently operates as a device to allow resegregation." The fear that white students would leave the school system altogether was deemed insufficient justification.

**3.** *Immediate Desegregation.* In the summer of 1969, the federal government in an unusual position, requested a delay in implementing desegregation orders in 30 Mississippi school districts. While the Fifth Circuit granted the request, the Supreme Court in Alexander v. Holmes County Bd. of Educ., 396 U.S. 19 (1969), reversed *per curiam,* stating: "Continued operation of segregated schools under a standard of allowing 'all deliberate speed' for desegregation is no longer constitutionally permissible. Under explicit holdings of this Court the obligation of every school district is to terminate dual school systems at once and to operate now and hereafter only unitary schools." The Court of Appeals was to make its order effective immediately. While the school systems were operating under this order, the district court might hear and consider objections. *See also* Carter v. West Feliciana Parish School Bd., 396 U.S. 290 (1970), where the court required integration even in the middle of a school year.

## SWANN v. CHARLOTTE-MECKLENBURG BD. OF EDUC.
### Supreme Court of the United States
402 U.S. 1, 28 L. Ed. 2d 554, 91 S. Ct. 1267 (1971)

[The cases arose from attempts to desegregate the metropolitan Charlotte, North Carolina, school district, having a racial composition of approximately 71 per cent white and 29 per cent Negro. After finding several Board plans unacceptable, the district court appointed its own expert. It subsequently approved a modified Board plan for secondary schools but accepted its expert's plan, involving zoning, pairing and grouping, and the consequent busing of pupils resulting in student bodies of between nine and 38 per cent Negro throughout the system, for elementary schools. The Court of Appeals affirmed as to the secondary schools but held that the elementary school plan would place an unreasonable burden on the Board and the system's pupils. On remand, the district court identified three acceptable alternative plans and ordered its expert's plan to remain in effect if the Board failed to accept one of the three. The Board "acquiesced" in the expert's plan.]

Chief Justice BURGER delivered the opinion of the Court.

. . . .

This case and those argued with it arose in states having a long history of maintaining two sets of schools in a single school system deliberately operated to carry out a governmental policy to separate pupils in schools solely on the basis of race. That was what *Brown v. Board of Education* was all about. These cases present us with the problem of defining in more precise terms than heretofore the scope of the duty of school authorities and district courts in implementing *Brown I* and the mandate to eliminate dual systems and establish unitary systems at once. . . .

. . . .

The objective today remains to eliminate from the public schools all vestiges of state-imposed segregation. . . .

. . . .

We turn . . . to the problem of defining with more particularity the responsibilities of school authorities in desegregating a state-enforced dual school system in light of the Equal Protection Clause. Although the several related cases before us are primarily concerned with problems of student assignment, it may be helpful to begin with a brief discussion of other aspects of the process.

In *Green,* we pointed out that existing policy and practice with regard to faculty, staff, transportation, extracurricular activities, and facilities were among the most important indicia of a segregated system. Independent of student assignment, where it is possible to identify a "white school" or a "Negro school" simply by reference to the racial composition of teachers and staff, the quality of school buildings and equipment, or the organization of sports activities, a *prima facie* case of violation of substantive constitutional rights under the Equal Protection Clause is shown.

When a system has been dual in these respects, the first remedial responsibility of school authorities is to eliminate invidious racial distinctions. With respect to such matters as transportation, supporting personnel, and extracurricular activities, no more than this may be necessary. Similar corrective action must be taken with regard to the maintenance of buildings and the distribution of equipment. In these areas, normal administrative practice should produce schools of like quality, facilities, and staffs. Something more must be said, however, as to faculty assignment and new school construction.

In the companion *Davis* case, the Mobile school board has argued that the Constitution requires that teachers be assigned on a "color blind" basis. It also argues that the Constitution prohibits district courts from using their equity power to order assignment of teachers to achieve a particular degree of faculty desegregation. We reject that contention.

. . . .

The construction of new schools and the closing of old ones is one of the most important functions of local school authorities and also one of the most complex. They must decide questions of location and capacity in light of population growth, finances, land values, site availability, through an almost endless list of factors to be considered. The result of this will be a decision which, when combined with one technique or another of student assignment, will determine the racial composition of the student body in each school in the system. Over the long run, the consequences of the choices will be far reaching. People gravitate toward school facilities, just as schools are located in response to the needs of people. The location of schools may thus influence the patterns of residential development of a metropolitan area and have important impact on composition of inner city neighborhoods.

In the past, choices in this respect have been used as a potent weapon for creating or maintaining a state-segregated school system. . . . Upon a proper showing a district court may consider this in fashioning a remedy.

In ascertaining the existence of legally imposed school segregation, the existence of a pattern of school construction and abandonment is thus a factor of great weight. In devising remedies where legally imposed segregation has been established, it is the responsibility of local authorities and district courts to see to it that future school construction and abandonment is not used and does not serve to perpetuate or re-establish the dual system. When necessary, district courts should retain jurisdiction to assure that these responsibilities are carried out.

The central issue in this case is that of student assignment, and there are essentially four problem areas:

. . . .

(1)  Racial Balances or Racial Quotas.

. . . We do not reach in this case the question whether a showing that school segregation is a consequence of other types of state action, without any discriminatory action by the school authorities, is a constitutional violation requiring remedial action by the school desegregation decree. This case does not present that question and we therefore do not decide it.

Our objective in dealing with the issues presented by these cases is to see that school authorities exclude no pupil of a racial minority from any school, directly or indirectly, on account of race; it does not and cannot embrace all the problems of racial

prejudice, even when those problems contribute to disproportionate racial concentrations in some schools.

In this case it is urged that the District Court has imposed a
racial balance requirement of 71%-29% on individual schools. . . .

[The District Court opinion] contains intimations that the
"norm" is a fixed mathematical racial balance reflecting the pupil
constituency of the system. If we were to read the holding of the
District Court to require, as a matter of substantive constitutional right, any particular degree of racial balance or mixing,
that approach would be disapproved and we would be obliged to
reverse. The constitutional command to desegregate schools does
not mean that every school in every community must always
reflect the racial composition of the school system as a whole.

. . . .

[But, in this case] the use made of mathematical ratios was
no more than a starting point in the process of shaping a remedy,
rather than an inflexible requirement. . . . As we said in *Green,*
a school authority's remedial plan or a district court's remedial
decree is to be judged by its effectiveness. Awareness of the racial
composition of the whole school system is likely to be a useful
starting point in shaping a remedy to correct past constitutional
violations. In sum, the very limited use made of mathematical
ratios was within the equitable remedial discretion of the District Court.

*(2) One-Race Schools.*

The record in this case reveals the familiar phenomenon that
in metropolitan areas minority groups are often found concentrated in one part of the city. In some circumstances certain
schools may remain all or largely of one race until new schools
can be provided or neighborhood patterns change. Schools all or
predominately of one race in a district of mixed population will
require close scrutiny to determine that school assignments are
not part of state-enforced segregation.

In light of the above, it should be clear that the existence of
some small number of one-race, or virtually one-race, schools
within a district is not in and of itself the mark of a system which
still practices segregation by law. . . . The court should scrutinize
such schools, and the burden upon the school authorities will be
to satisfy the court that their racial composition is not the result
of present or past discriminatory action on their part.

An optional majority-to-minority transfer provision has long
been recognized as a useful part of every desegregation plan.
Provision for optional transfer of those in the majority racial
group of a particular school to other schools where they will be
in the minority is an indispensable remedy for those students

willing to transfer to other schools in order to lessen the impact
on them of the state-imposed stigma of segregation. In order to
be effective, such a transfer arrangement must grant the transferring student free transportation and space must be made available in the school to which he desires to move. . . .

   *(3)  Remedial Altering of Attendance Zones.*
   . . . .

   Absent a constitutional violation there would be no basis for
judicially ordering assignment of students on a racial basis. All
things being equal, with no history of discrimination, it might
well be desirable to assign pupils to schools nearest their homes.
But all things are not equal in a system that has been deliberately
constructed and maintained to enforce racial segregation. The
remedy for such segregation may be administratively awkward,
inconvenient and even bizarre in some situations and may impose burdens on some; but all awkwardness and inconvenience
cannot be avoided in the interim period when remedial adjustments are being made to eliminate the dual school systems.
   . . . .

   In this area, we must of necessity rely to a large extent, as
this Court has for more than 16 years, on the informed judgment
of the district courts in the first instance and on courts of appeals.
   We hold that the pairing and grouping of non-contiguous
school zones is a permissible tool and such action is to be considered in light of the objectives sought. . . .

   *(4)  Transportation of Students.*
   . . . No rigid guidelines as to student transportation can be
given for application to the infinite variety of problems presented
in thousands of situations. Bus transportation has been an integral
part of the public education system for years, and was perhaps
the single most important factor in the transition from the one-
room schoolhouse to the consolidated school. Eighteen million
of the nation's public school children, approximately 39% were
transported to their schools by bus in 1969-1970 in all parts of
the country.
   The importance of bus transportation as a normal and accepted tool of educational policy is readily discernible in this
and the companion case. . . .
   . . . .

   An objection to transportation of students may have validity
when the time or distance of travel is so great as to risk either
the health of the children or significantly impinge on the educational process. . . .
   . . . On the facts of this case, we are unable to conclude that
the order of the District Court is not reasonable, feasible and

workable. However, in seeking to define the scope of remedial power or the limits on remedial power of courts in an area as sensitive as we deal with here, words are poor instruments to convey the sense of basic fairness inherent in equity. Substance, not semantics, must govern, and we have sought to suggest the nature of limitations without frustrating the appropriate scope of equity.

At some point, these school authorities and others like them should have achieved full compliance with this Court's decision in *Brown I*. The systems will then be "unitary" in the sense required by our decisions in *Green* and *Alexander*.

It does not follow that the communities served by such systems will remain demographically stable, for in a growing, mobile society, few will do so. Neither school authorities nor district courts are constitutionally required to make year-by-year adjustments of the racial composition of student bodies once the affirmative duty to desegregate has been accomplished and racial discrimination through official action is eliminated from the system. This does not mean that federal courts are without power to deal with future problems; but in the absence of a showing that either the school authorities or some other agency of the State has deliberately attempted to fix or alter demographic patterns to affect the racial composition of the schools, further intervention by a district court should not be necessary.

For the reasons herein set forth, the judgment of the Court of Appeals is affirmed as to those parts in which it affirmed the judgment of the District Court....

. . . .

---

## NOTES

1. Professor Owen Fiss suggests that *Swann* took four additional steps beyond previous segregation cases: (1) "[E]ven if geographic proximity, not race, were the basis for [school attendance] zones and thus for assignments, the Board's duty to convert to a 'unitary non-racial school system' would not be satisfied." What is the rationale for preventing school districts from using a neutral assignment policy? (2) The recognition of an evidentiary presumption that past discrimination causally related to present segregation. "The school board will also have to show that its past discriminatory conduct—involving racial designation of schools, site selection, and determination of school size—is not a link in the causal chain producing the segregation. This will be very difficult to do, and the difficulty of overcoming a presumption will tend to accentuate the fact that gives rise to it, namely,

the segregated patterns, and this will be reflected in the board's assignment policies. Greater attention will be paid to the segregated patterns." (3) The Court said that a district must do everything possible to eliminate these patterns of segregation. Integration is not merely a value to be considered; in the hierarchy of values "integration assumes a role of paramount importance." (4) *Swann* "validates the use of race in student assignments when the goal is integration rather than segregation." Fiss, *The Charlotte-Mecklenburg Case—Its Significance for Northern School Desegregation*, 38 U. CHI. L. REV. 697, 699-703 (1971). Is it now clear that the equal protection clause does not command a color-blind constitution? *See* text, pp. 635-46, on preferential treatment (benign racial classifications).

2. *The Right Involved.* In *Swann*, Chief Justice Burger said that "the greatest possible degree of actual desegregation" must be the goal. What does this mean? If there is a plan that would yield a student racial mixture more closely mirroring the racial composition of the community must it be used? Must a de jure school system achieve a greater degree of racial mixture than would have been obtained if it had never intentionally segregated? Is there now a right to an "integrated education"?

In a companion case to *Swann*, the court dealt with a desegregation plan from Mobile, Alabama which used unified geographic zones and provided for no busing, leaving some all-black schools. Chief Justice Burger stated that " 'neighborhood school zoning,' whether based strictly on home-to-school distance or on 'unified geographic zones,' is not the only constitutionally permissible remedy; nor is it *per se* adequate to meet the remedial responsibilities of local boards. Having once found a violation, the district judge or school authorities should make every effort to achieve the greatest possible degree of actual desegregation, taking into account the practicalities of the situation. A district court may and should consider the use of all available techniques. . . . The measure of any desegregation plan is its effectiveness." Since the district courts had failed to consider the use of busing and alternative zoning, the case was remanded. Davis v. Board of School Comm'rs, 402 U.S. 33 (1971).

3. The possibility that *Swann* might demand the use of all reasonable means available to achieve the best racial mix is also suggested by Wright v. Council of Emporia, 407 U.S. 451 (1972). The Court, per Justice Stewart, rejected an attempt of the town of Emporia to withdraw from the county school system which had been ordered to desegregate, holding "that a new school district may not be created where its effect would be to impede the process of dismantling a dual system."

No finding was made that Emporia had itself intentionally segregated or that its withdrawal was racially motivated, but the city had been part of the single county educational unit during the entire time that the dual school system was maintained. The court rejected reliance on the "benign" motivation of the city in withdrawing. Justice Stewart emphasized that "[u]nder the principles of *Green* and *Monroe*, . . . a proposal must be judged according to whether it hinders or furthers the process of school desegregation. If the proposal would impede the dismantling of the dual system, then a district court, in the exercise of its remedial discretion may enjoin it from being carried out."

In this instance, data indicated that a system including both Emporia and the county would have a racial composition of 34 per cent white and 66 per cent Negro. If Emporia withdrew and maintained its own system it would have 48 per cent white and 52 per cent Negro while the county would be 28 per cent white and 72 per cent Negro. "We need not and do not hold that this disparity in the racial composition of the two systems would be a sufficient reason, standing alone, to enjoin the creation of the separate school district. The fact that a school board's desegregation plan leaves some disparity in racial balance among various schools in the system does not alone make that plan unacceptable." But the court found more. "In the first place, the District Court found that if Emporia were allowed to withdraw from the existing system, it 'may be anticipated that the proportion of whites in county schools may drop as those who can register in white academies,' . . . while some whites might return to the city schools from the private schools in which they had previously enrolled." Further, "the significance of any racial disparity in this case is enhanced by the fact that the two formerly all-white schools are located within Emporia, while all the schools located in the surrounding counties were formerly all-Negro. The record further reflects that the school buildings in Emporia are better-equipped and are located on better sites than are those in the county." Finally, Justice Stewart emphasized "[t]he timing of Emporia's action" which came in reaction to a court's desegregation order. He concluded: "Given the totality of the circumstances, we hold that the District Court was justified in its conclusion that Emporia's establishment of a separate system would actually impede the process of dismantling the existing dual system."

4.  Chief Justice Burger, joined by Justices Blackmun, Powell and Rehnquist, dissenting in *Wright*, (the first dissents registered in educational desegregation cases since *Brown*) argued, that "the proposed arrangement [resulting from Emporia's withdrawal]

would completely eliminate all traces of state-imposed segregation." It would thus achieve a unitary school system. While the
Chief Justice recognized "that the racial ratios of the two school
systems would differ," he argued that "the elimination of such
disparities is not the mission of desegregation." As in the present
case "[o]bsession with such minor statistical differences reflects
the gravely mistaken view that a plan providing more consistent
racial ratios is somehow more unitary than one which tolerates a
lack of racial balance. Since the goal is to dismantle dual school
systems rather than to reproduce in each classroom a microcosmic
reflection of the racial proportions of a given geographical area,
there is no basis for saying that a plan providing a uniform racial
balance is more effective or constitutionally preferred. School authorities may wish to pursue that goal as a matter of policy, but
we have made it plain that it is not constitutionally mandated."

5.  In a companion case, United States v. Scotland Neck City
Bd. of Educ., 407 U.S. 484 (1972), a unanimous court upheld an
order enjoining implementation of a state statute creating a new
school district for Scotland Neck, North Carolina, out of the larger
Halifax county school district which was then under a desegregation order. The Halifax district was 78 per cent Negro. If
withdrawal were permitted, the Scotland Neck Schools would be
57 per cent white and the remaining county schools would be
89 per cent Negro. The court found the disparity in racial composition "substantial" and implementation of the state statute therefore "would have the effect of impeding the disestablishment of
the dual school system. . . ." Fear of white flight "cannot . . .
be accepted as a reason for achieving anything less than complete
uprooting of the dual public school system." Chief Justice Burger,
joined by Justices Blackmun, Powell and Rehnquist, concurred.

6.  *Second Generation Segregation.* If *Swann* and its predecessors suggest the ultimate demise of southern dual school systems, they have spawned a "second generation" of problems now
plaguing the lower courts: "dismissal or demotion of black
school principals and teachers as integration progresses and their
jobs are to be given to whites; expulsions of black students for
disciplinary reasons; the use of provocative symbols (the Con-
federate flag, the singing of 'Dixie'); segregation within individual
schools based on test and ability grouping; and the rise of private
schools in which whites can escape desegregation." Glazer, *Is
Busing Necessary?*, 53 COMMENTARY 39 (March, 1972). The "one-
way busing" of Black children has also generated litigation. *See*
D. KIRP & M. YUDOF, EDUCATIONAL POLICY AND THE LAW: CASES
AND MATERIALS 430-33 (1974).

**7.** *Anti-busing Legislation.* On August 23, 1974, President Ford signed the Equal Educational Opportunities Act of 1974. After a finding of facts, the Act declares that its purpose is to specify appropriate remedies for the orderly elimination of the last vestiges of dual-school systems but provides that it is "not intended to modify or diminish the authority of the courts of the United States to enforce fully the fifth and fourteenth amendments to the Constitution of the United States." (§ 203(b)) Various unlawful practices denying equal educational opportunity on account of race, color, sex, or national origin, are specified but it is declared that failure to attain a balance of students on the basis of race, color, sex, or national origin (§ 205), and neutral assignment of students on a neighborhood basis (§ 206) do not constitute denials of equal protection.

The critical sections on remedies indicate that only "essential" remedies are to be used (§ 213), establish a priority list of remedies (§ 214), and in § 215, in addition to dealing with resegregation of desegregated districts declare:

(a) No court, department or agency of the United States shall, . . . order the implementation of a plan that would require the transportation of any student to a school other than the school closest or next closest to his place of residence which provides the appropriate grade level and type of education for such a student.

(b) No court, department, or agency of the United States shall require directly or indirectly the transportation of any student if such transportation poses a risk to the health of such student or constitutes a significant impingement on the educational process with respect to such student.

Provision is made for seeking to reopen desegregation proceedings and for intervention in ongoing proceedings when "the time or distance of travel is so great as to risk the health of the student or significantly impinge on his or her educational process." (§ 218.) Appropriated federal funds are not to be used for busing (§ 420) and a prior legislative stay on lower court orders requiring busing for achieving a balance of students with respect to race, sex, religion or socio-economic status pending appeal is continued until June 30, 1978 (§ 253). No busing order is to go into effect during a school year (§ 258).

Is the Act constitutional as an exercise of Congress' power over Art. III jurisdiction? *See* text, pp. 39-46. As an exercise of Congress' power under the fourteenth amendment to enforce the equal protection guarantee "by appropriate legislation"? *See* text, pp. 1085-1101.

### (d)   The Court Looks North: Challenging De Facto Segregation

While the desegregation of southern schools has met with at least some limited success, school segregation in the North has only intensified. Today education in the North is more racially segregated than in the South. In 1970, HEW reported that 57.6 per cent of Black students in 32 northern and western states attended class in schools 80-100 per cent minority compared with only 39.4 per cent in 11 southern states.

But if education in the North is as segregated as in the South, its causes have been more difficult to isolate. While many jurisdictions had statutes requiring dual school systems, most had been eliminated before *Brown*. In many northern areas, however, racial segregation in education can be traced to intentionally discriminatory school board policies involving gerrymandered school attendance zones, transfer policies, school construction and closing policies. But in other instances, educational segregation appears to be a product of following what seems to be a racially neutral school attendance policy in the context of increasing residential racial segregation.

These differing forms of educational segregation may even exist in different schools in the same school district. The question of whether such distinctions are constitutionally relevant is the focus of the present section. More particularly, does the equal protection clause impose an affirmative duty on the state to equalize only when there is a showing of intentional school board action to racially segregate? Is the state constitutionally responsible for segregated education regardless of the source of that segregation? If intent is to be constitutionally required, rather than merely relying on discriminatory effect, how is intent to be determined? What is the effect of showing intentional discrimination in part of a school system? The court was afforded an opportunity to deal with these questions in *Keyes v. School District No. 1.*

### KEYES v. SCHOOL DIST. NO. 1
Supreme Court of the United States
413 U.S. 189, 37 L. Ed. 2d 548, 93 S. Ct. 2686 (1973)

Justice BRENNAN delivered the opinion of the Court.

[T]he gravamen of this action, brought in June 1969 in the District Court for the District of Colorado by parents of Denver school children, is that respondent School Board alone, by use of various techniques such as the manipulation of student attendance zones, school site selection and a neighborhood school policy, created or maintained racially or ethnically (or both racially and ethnically) segregated schools throughout the school district, entitling petitioners to a decree directing desegregation of the entire school district.

. . . .

[W]here plaintiffs prove that the school authorities have carried out a systematic program of segregation affecting a substantial portion of the students, schools, teachers and facilities within the school system, it is only common sense to conclude that there exists a predicate for a finding of the existence of a dual school system. Several considerations support this conclusion. First, it is obvious that a practice of concentrating Negroes in certain schools by structuring attendance zones or designating "feeder" schools on the basis of race has the reciprocal effect of keeping other nearby schools predominantly white. Similarly, the practice of building a school . . . to a certain size and in a certain location, "with conscious knowledge that it would be a segregated school," has a substantial reciprocal effect on the racial composition of other nearby schools. So also, the use of mobile classrooms, the drafting of student transfer policies, the transportation of students, and the assignment of faculty and staff, on racially identifiable bases, have the clear effect of earmarking schools according to their racial composition, and this, in turn, together with the elements of student assignment and school construction, may have a profound reciprocal effect on the racial composition of residential neighborhoods within a metropolitan area, thereby causing further racial concentration within the schools. . . .

. . . .

. . . [W]e hold that a finding of intentionally segregative school board actions in a meaningful portion of a school system, as in this case, creates a presumption that other segregated schooling within the system is not adventitious. It establishes, in other words, a prima facie case of unlawful segregative design on the part of school authorities, and shifts to those authorities the burden of proving that other segregated schools within the system are not also the result of intentionally segregative actions. This is true even if it is determined that different areas of the school district should be viewed independently of each other because, even in that situation, there is high probability that where school authorities have effectuated an intentionally segregative policy in a meaningful portion of the school system, similar impermissible considerations have motivated their actions in other areas of the system. We emphasize that the differentiating factor between *de jure* segregation and so-called *de facto* segregation to which we referred in *Swann* is *purpose* or *intent* to segregate. Where school authorities have been found to have practiced purposeful segregation in part of a school system, they may be expected to oppose system-wide desegregation, as did the respondents in this case, on the ground that their purposefully segregative actions were isolated and individual events, thus leaving plaintiffs with the burden of proving otherwise. But at that point where an intentionally segregative policy is practiced in a meaningful or significant segment of a school system, as in this case, the school authorities can not be heard to argue that plaintiffs have proved only "isolated and individual" unlawfully segregative actions. In that circumstance, it is both fair and reasonable to require that the school authorities bear the burden of showing that their actions as to other segregated schools within the system were not also motivated by segregative intent.

. . . .

In discharging that burden, it is not enough, of course, that the school authorities rely upon some allegedly logical, racially neutral explanation for their actions. Their burden is to adduce proof sufficient to support a finding that segregative intent was not among the factors that motivated their actions. . . . We reject any suggestion that remoteness in time has any relevance to the issue of intent. If the actions of school authorities were to any degree motivated by segregative intent and the segregation resulting from those actions continues to exist, the fact of remoteness in time certainly does not make those actions any less "intentional."

This is not to say, however, that the prima facie case may not be met by evidence supporting a finding that a lesser degree of segregated schooling in the core city area would not have resulted even if the Board had not acted as it did. . . . [I]f respondent School Board cannot disprove segregative intent, it can rebut the prima facie case only by showing that its past segregative acts did not create or contribute to the current segregated condition of the core city schools.

The respondent School Board invoked at trial its "neighborhood school policy" as explaining racial and ethnic concentrations within the core city schools, arguing that since the core city area population had long been Negro and Hispano, the concentrations were necessarily the result of residential patterns and not of purposefully segregative policies. We have no occasion to consider in this case whether a "neighborhood school policy" of itself will justify racial or ethnic concentrations in the absence of a finding that school authorities have committed acts constituting *de jure* segregation. It is enough that we hold that the mere assertion of such a policy is not dispositive where, as in this case, the school authorities have been found to have practiced *de jure* segregation in a meaningful portion of the school system by techniques that indicate that the "neighborhood school" concept has not been maintained free of manipulation. . . .

Justice WHITE took no part in the decision of this case.

Justice POWELL concurring in part and dissenting in part.

. . . .

. . . I concur in the Court's position that the public school authorities are the responsible agency of the State, and that if the affirmative duty doctrine is sound constitutional law for Charlotte, it is equally so for Denver. I would not, however, perpetuate the *de jure/de facto* distinction nor would I leave to petitioners the initial tortuous effort of identifying "segregative acts" and deducing "segregatory intent." I would hold, quite simply, that where segregated public schools exist within a school district to a substantial degree, there is a prima facie case that the duly constituted public authorities (I will usually refer to them collectively as the "school board") are sufficiently responsible to impose upon them a nationally applicable burden to demonstrate they nevertheless are operating a genuinely integrated school system.

The principal reason for abandonment of the *de jure/de facto* distinction is that, in view of the evolution of the holding in *Brown I* into the affirmative duty doctrine, the distinction no longer can be justified on a principled basis. In decreeing remedial requirements for the Charlotte/Mecklenburg school district, *Swann* dealt with a metropolitan, urbanized area in which the basic causes of segregation were generally similar to those in all sections of the country, and also largely irrelevant to the existence of historic, state-imposed segregation at the time of the *Brown* decision. Further, the extension of the affirmative duty concept to include compulsory student transportation went well beyond the mere remedying of that portion of school segregation for which former state segregation laws were ever responsible. Moreover, as the Court's opinion today abundantly demonstrates, the facts deemed necessary to establish *de jure* discrimination present problems of subjective intent which the courts cannot fairly resolve.

. . . .

Justice REHNQUIST, dissenting.

. . . .

. . . [I]n a school district the size of Denver's, it is quite conceivable that the school board might have engaged in the racial gerrymandering of the attendance boundary between two particular schools in order to keep one largely Negro and Hispano, and the other largely Anglo, as the District Court found to have been the fact in this case. Such action would have deprived affected minority students who were the victims of such gerrymandering of their constitutional right to equal protection of the law. But if the school board had been even-handed in its drawing of the attendance lines for other schools in the district, minority students required to attend other schools within the district would have suffered no such deprivation. It certainly would not reflect normal English usage to describe the entire district as "segregated" on such a state of facts, and it would be a quite unprecedented application of principles of equitable relief to determine that if the gerrymandering of one attendance zone were proven, particular racial mixtures could be required by a federal district court for every school in the district.

. . . [U]nless the Equal Protection Clause of the Fourteenth Amendment now be held to embody a principle of "taint," found in some primitive legal systems but discarded centuries ago in ours, such a result can only be described as the product of judicial fiat.

. . . .

---

## NOTES

**1.** The term *de jure* segregation is misleading if it is limited to formal legal rules of racial segregation. It now encompasses any form of intentional state segregation mandated by law or by public policy, and this occurs in the north as well as in the south. In Taylor v. Board of Educ., 294 F.2d 36 (2d Cir. 1961), *cert. denied,* 368 U.S. 940 (1961), the court found an equal protection violation in the creation and perpetuation of gerrymandered school boundary lines and discriminatory transfer provisions which fostered racial segregation. *See* Kaplan, *Segregation Litigation and the Schools—Part I: The New Rochelle Experience,* 58 Nw. U.L. Rev. 1 (1963).

**2.** While *Keyes* did not eliminate the de facto-de jure dichotomy, it does appear to have facilitated establishing system-wide de jure segregation in the north. As Justice Powell's partial concurrence indicates, a major difficulty in attacking school segregation in the north has been the problem of proving intent. Does *Keyes* significantly relax this burden? What is the justification for giving a system-wide remedy on the basis of a showing of intentional segregation in a substantial part of the system?

What is meant by a "substantial" or "meaningful" part of a school system?

3. *Reciprocal Effects.* What does Justice Brennan mean by "reciprocal effects"? How does de jure segregation in one school or part of a district affect other schools in the immediate locality? Schools at a long distance from the locus of the infection? Does de jure educational segregation affect residential racial composition? How important is the racial composition of schools in selecting a residence? Can it affect district-wide residential patterns?

*Presumed Intent.* Even if the school board overcomes the first hurdle, it still must overcome the presumption that all other segregation in the district is de jure. Is proof of localized de jure segregation relevant to a finding of system-wide intentional segregation? What if the de jure acts are remote in time or done by a different board? Is the use of the presumption justified by the difficulty of proving system-wide segregatory intent? By the superior access of the school board to the facts? *See* Case Comment, *Keyes v. School District No. 1: Unlocking the Northern Schoolhouse Doors,* 9 HARV. CIV. RTS.-CIV. LIB. L. REV. 124, 135-142 (1974).

How does a board establish that "segregative intent was not among the factors that motivated their actions"? Why isn't it sufficient to prove an alternative explanation for the segregation? Is the presumption in *Keyes* analogous to that used in *Swann* in regard to one-race schools?

4. *Harmful Effects.* Proponents of an affirmative state duty to remedy *de facto* segregation begin with the premise in *Brown I* that "[s]eparate educational facilities are inherently unequal" and stress its discussion of the "detrimental effect upon the colored children" of racial segregation. They argue that the harm is the same regardless of the cause of the racial disparity. Professor Frank Goodman warns: "In the *de facto* situation, the alleged harmful effects on Negro children arise in the context of a state policy—the preservation of neighborhood schools—that has a proper governmental objective, and the harmful effects are not self-evident nor judicially noticeable; the challengers of social segregation must therefore face the burden of proving these effects. The findings in *Brown,* based on the conclusory opinions of social scientists unsupported by actual data, merely raise possibilities of harm, but do not sustain this burden of proof. Thus, . . . the findings of harm in *Brown* are largely irrelevant to the issue of *de facto* segregation." Goodman, *De Facto School Segregation: A Constitutional and Empirical Analysis,* 60 CALIF. L. REV. 275, 283 (1972).

This need for empirical support results in briefs and argument citing a mass of social science data designed to show that racial segregation, whatever its source, creates feelings of inferiority in black children, impairs their learning processes, and generates racist attitudes and behavior in the community. *See* U.S. COMM'N ON CIVIL RIGHTS, RACIAL ISOLATION IN THE SCHOOLS 100-114 (1967). *See generally* Goodman, *De Facto School Segregation: A Constitutional and Empirical Analysis,* 60 CALIF. L. REV., at 400-35; Bell, *School Litigation Strategies for the 1970's: New Phases in the Continuing Quest for Equality Schools,* 1970 WIS. L. REV. 257, 264-289.

In Hobson v. Hansen, 269 F. Supp. 401 (D.D.C. 1967), *aff'd sub nom.* Smuck v. Hobson, 408 F.2d 175 (D.C. Cir. 1969), Judge Skelly Wright provided a leading judicial condemnation of racial segregation, whatever its source. He included the following as findings of fact. "1. Racially and socially homogeneous schools damage the minds and spirits of all children who attend them—the Negro, the White, the poor and the affluent—and block the attainment of the broader goals of democratic education, whether the segregation occurs by law or by fact. 2. The scholastic achievement of the disadvantaged child, Negro and White is strongly related to the racial and socio-economic composition of the student body of his school. A racially and socially integrated school environment increases the scholastic achievement of the disadvantaged child of whatever race." He added that "segregation in the schools precludes the kind of social encounter between Negroes and Whites which is an indispensable attribute of education for mature citizenship in an interracial and democratic society." *See* Note, *Hobson v. Hansen: Judicial Supervision of the Color Blind School Board,* 81 HARV. L. REV. 1511 (1968). Is there a right to equal educational opportunity? *See* People v. San Diego Unified School Dist., 19 Cal. App. 3d 252, 96 Cal. Rptr. 658 (1971).

**5.** Courts rejecting attacks on *de facto* segregation stress the lack of state responsibility and hence the lack of a constitutional duty to remedy racial imbalance in schools absent a showing of intent. They contend that *Brown I* rested not on the finding of harm to Black children from educational segregation, but on the state's use of race to classify persons. *See* Deal v. Cincinnati Bd. of Educ., 369 F.2d 55 (6th Cir. 1966).

#### (e)  Interdistrict Desegregation

Prior to the decision in *Milliken v. Bradley,* reprinted below, the attorney for the plaintiff had predicted that *Bradley* would be the *Brown* of the North. BBC-TV Documentary, "Deep

South . . . Deep North." In fact, the decision may be more
analogous to *Plessy v. Ferguson*. For the first time, a majority
of the Supreme Court rejected the desegregation claims of Black
children. As a result, the effective desegregation of northern-style
segregated metropolitan schools has been made far more difficult.

Metropolitan Detroit resembles many of the big cities of the
North. Whites have increasingly left the central city for the
suburbs leaving a predominantly black city surrounded by predominantly white enclaves. Any attempt to eliminate substantial
racial imbalance in even a de jure segregated city is doomed to
failure unless the surrounding jurisdictions can be joined in
fashioning a remedy. But how far can the courts go in ignoring
jurisdictional boundaries? Is the state the proper defendant or
the local district? Is it enough to show de jure segregation in
each of the adjoining school districts? Must some joint action
by local actors be shown? If an intradistrict constitutional wrong
is established, what remedies are available? These are some of
the questions the court examined in *Milliken v. Bradley*.

## MILLIKEN v. BRADLEY
Supreme Court of the United States
418 U.S. 717, 39 L. Ed. 2d 107, 94 S. Ct. 3112 (1974)

[A class action was brought by the local NAACP Branch
against various State and local officials claiming that the Detroit
Public School System was de jure segregated and seeking implementation of a plan that would eliminate "the racial identity
of every school in the [Detroit] system and . . . maintain now
and hereafter a unitary non-racial school system." The District
Court found that "Government action and inaction at all levels,
Federal, State and Local, have combined, with those of private
organizations, such as lending institutions and real estate associations and brokerage firms, to establish and to maintain the pattern
of residential segregation throughout the Detroit Metropolitan
area." The School Board's use of optional attendance zones in
transitional areas, its drawing of attendance lines rejecting boundaries that would result in significantly greater desegregation, its
use of discriminatory busing, its selecting of school sites and
construction of schools having a segregative effect had a "natural,
probable, foreseeable and actual effect" of facilitating white flight
and promoting segregation. Further, the State Legislature had
failed to provide funds for transportation of students within
Detroit while providing such funds for mostly white suburbs,
had, through Act 48, delayed a Detroit School Board desegregation
plan and adopted free choice-neighborhood school plans which
"had as their purpose and effect the maintenance of segregation";
and, with local boards had condoned at least one instance of

busing Black children from an over-crowded suburban school to a Black school in Detroit. The court also held the State responsible vicariously for the acts of the Detroit School Board.

[After allowing limited intervention by outlying school districts, the District Court concluded that there was State action, that the Detroit-only desegregation plans would only make Detroit more identifiably Black and increase white flight and hence "would not accomplish desegregation within the corporate geographical limits of the city," that school district lines "are simply matters of political convenience and may not be used to deny Constitutional rights," defined a desegregation area of Detroit and 53 suburban school districts, appointed a panel to fashion "an effective desegregation plan" based on 15 clusters each containing part of the Detroit system and two or more suburban districts, designed to "achieve the greatest degree of actual desegregation to the end that, upon implementation, no school, grade or classroom [would be] substantially disproportionate to the overall racial composition," and ordered the Detroit Board of Education to purchase or lease at least 295 school buses under an interim plan for 1972-73.

[The Court of Appeals, en banc, generally affirmed but remanded, ordering the lower court to allow affected suburban districts to be heard regarding the scope and implementation of the remedy and to postpone any order to purchase any buses until it was appropriate. 484 F.2d 215 (6th Cir. 1973).]

Chief Justice BURGER delivered the opinion of the Court.

We granted certiorari in these consolidated cases to determine whether a federal court may impose a multidistrict, areawide remedy to a single district *de jure* segregation problem absent any finding that the other included school districts have failed to operate unitary school systems within their districts, absent any claim or finding that the boundary lines of any affected school district were established with the purpose of fostering racial segregation in public schools, absent any finding that the included districts committed acts which effected segregation within the other districts, and absent a meaningful opportunity for the included neighboring school districts to present evidence or be heard on the propriety of a multidistrict remedy or on the question of constitutional violations by those neighboring districts.

. . . .

Viewing the record as a whole, it seems clear that the District Court and the Court of Appeals shifted the primary focus from a Detroit remedy to the metropolitan area only because of their conclusion that total desegregation of Detroit would not produce the racial balance which they perceived as desirable. Both courts

proceeded on an assumption that the Detroit schools could not
be truly desegregated—in their view of what constituted desegregation—unless the racial composition of the student body of each
school substantially reflected the racial composition of the population of the metropolitan area as a whole. The metropolitan
area was then defined as Detroit plus 53 of the outlying school
districts. . . .

. . . .

. . . The clear import of . . . *Swann* is that desegregation,  ⟩ *numeri-*
in the sense of dismantling a dual school system, does not re-   *cal balance*
quire any particular racial balance in each "school, grade or
classroom."

Here the District Court's approach to what constituted "actual
desegregation" raises the fundamental question, not presented
in *Swann,* as to the circumstances in which a federal court may
order desegregation relief that embraces more than a single school
district. [The court's analytical starting point was its conclusion
that school district lines are no more than arbitrary lines on a
map "drawn for political convenience." Boundary lines may be
bridged where there has been a constitutional violation calling
for inter-district relief but, the notion that school district lines
may be casually ignored or treated as a mere administrative    *state law-*
convenience is contrary to the history of public education in    *local con-*
our country. No single tradition in public education is more    *trol*
deeply rooted than local control over the operation of schools;
local autonomy has long been thought essential.] . . .

. . . .

Of course, no state law is above the Constitution. School district lines and the present laws with respect to local control, are
not sacrosanct and if they conflict with the Fourteenth Amendment federal courts have a duty to prescribe appropriate remedies. . . . But our prior holdings have been confined to violations and remedies within a single school district. We therefore
turn to address, for the first time, the validity of a remedy mandating cross-district or inter-district consolidation to remedy a
condition of segregation found to exist in only one district.

[The controlling principle consistently expounded in our holdings is that the scope of the remedy is determined by the nature
and extent of the constitutional violation.] Before the boundaries
of separate and autonomous school districts may be set aside
by consolidating the separate units for remedial purposes or by
imposing a cross-district remedy, it must first be shown that
there has been a constitutional violation within one district
that produces a significant segregative effect in another district.
Specifically it must be shown that racially discriminatory acts
of the state or local school districts, or of a single school district

have been a substantial cause of inter-district segregation. Thus an inter-district remedy might be in order where the racially discriminatory acts of one or more school districts caused racial segregation in an adjacent district, or where district lines have been deliberately drawn on the basis of race. In such circumstances an inter-district remedy would be appropriate to eliminate the inter-district segregation directly caused by the constitutional violation. Conversely, without an inter-district violation and inter-district effect, there is no constitutional wrong calling for an inter-district remedy.

The record before us, voluminous as it is, contains evidence of *de jure* segregated conditions only in the Detroit schools; indeed, that was the theory on which the litigation was initially based and on which the Detroit Court took evidence. With no showing of significant violation by the 53 outlying school districts and no evidence of any inter-district violation or effect, the court went beyond the original theory of the case as framed by the pleadings and mandated a metropolitan area remedy. To approve the remedy ordered by the court would impose on the outlying districts, not shown to have committed any constitutional violation, a wholly impermissible remedy based on a standard not hinted at in *Brown I* and *II* or any holding of this Court.

. . . .

The constitutional right of the Negro respondents residing in Detroit is to attend a unitary school system in that district. Unless petitioners drew the district lines in a discriminatory fashion, or arranged for White students residing in the Detroit district to attend schools in Oakland and Macomb Counties, they were under no constitutional duty to make provisions for Negro students to do so. The view of the dissenters . . . can be supported only by drastic expansion of the constitutional right itself, an expansion without any support in either constitutional principle or precedent.

*like Plessy— equal, but may be separate*

. . . .

We conclude that the relief ordered by the District Court and affirmed by the Court of Appeals was based upon an erroneous standard and was unsupported by record evidence that acts of the outlying districts affected the discrimination found to exist in the schools of Detroit. Accordingly, the judgment of the Court of Appeals is reversed and the case is remanded for further proceedings consistent with this opinion leading to prompt formulation of a decree directed to eliminating the segregation found to exist in Detroit city schools, a remedy which has been delayed since 1970.

Reversed and remanded.

Justice MARSHALL, with whom Justice DOUGLAS, Justice BRENNAN, and Justice WHITE join, dissenting.

. . . .

[S]everal factors in this case coalesce to support the District Court's ruling that it was the State of Michigan itself, not simply the Detroit Board of Education, which bore the obligation of curing the condition of segregation within the Detroit city schools. The actions of the State itself directly contributed to Detroit's segregation. Under the Fourteenth Amendment, the State is ultimately responsible for the actions of its local agencies. And finally, given the structure of Michigan's educational system, Detroit's segregation cannot be viewed as the problem of an independent and separate entity. Michigan operates a single state-wide system of education, a substantial part of which was shown to be segregated in this case.

*ultimately the duty of the State not her than district*

. . . .

After examining three plans limited to the city of Detroit, the District Court correctly concluded that none would eliminate root and branch the vestiges of unconstitutional segregation. . . .

. . . .

The rippling effects on residential patterns caused by purposeful acts of segregation do not automatically subside at the school district border. With rare exceptions, these effects naturally spread through all the residential neighborhoods within a metropolitan area. See *Keyes*. . . .

. . . .

The majority asserts, however, that involvement of outlying districts would do violence to the accepted principle that "the nature of the violation determines the scope of the remedy." . . . To read this principle as barring a District Court from imposing the only effective remedy for past segregation and remitting the court to a patently ineffective alternative is, in my view, to turn a simple commonsense rule into a cruel and meaningless paradox. Ironically, by ruling out an inter-district remedy, the only relief which promises to cure segregation in the Detroit public schools, the majority flouts the very principle on which it purports to rely.

*cross-district remedy only solution.*

Nor should it be of any significance that the suburban school districts were not shown to have themselves taken any direct action to promote segregation of the races. Given the State's broad powers over local school districts, it was well within the State's powers to require those districts surrounding the Detroit school district to participate in a metropolitan remedy. The State's duty should be no different here than in cases where it is shown that certain of a State's voting districts are malapportioned in violation of the Fourteenth Amendment. . . .

. . . .

## NOTES

1. In Bradley v. School Board of Richmond, 338 F. Supp. 67 (E.D. Va. 1972), Judge Mehrige ordered consolidation of the predominantly black Richmond school system with two adjoining predominantly suburban school systems. The Court of Appeals reversed, 462 F.2d 1058 (4th Cir. 1972), holding: "Because we think the last vestiges of state-imposed segregation have been wiped out in the public schools of the [three jurisdictions involved] and unitary school systems achieved, and because it is not established that the racial composition of the schools in the City of Richmond and the counties is the result of invidious State action, we conclude there is no constitutional violation and that, therefore, the district judge exceeded his power of intervention."

The Supreme Court in reviewing *Bradley* split 4 to 4, Justice Powell abstaining, thus leaving the Court of Appeals decision standing. 412 U.S. 92, *rehearing denied,* 414 U.S. 834 (1973).

2. *Rights and Remedies.* Is the problem in *Milliken v. Bradley* one of constitutional rights or remedies? Are the lower court opinions concerned with remedying de jure segregation in Detroit or with remedying the racial imbalance, de jure or de facto, between adjoining school districts?

3. *The State as Defendant.* The plaintiffs in *Milliken v. Bradley* sought to distinguish the *Richmond* decision on grounds that no consolidation was ordered by the Michigan district court and that Michigan recognized state, rather than local, control of education. Are these distinctions constitutionally relevant? *See* Comment, *Interdistrict Segregation: Finding a Violation of the Equal Protection Clause,* 23 AM. U.L. REV. 785 (1974). Regardless of the structure of the educational system, isn't the equal protection clause a command running to the states? In Reynolds v. Sims, 377 U.S. 533, 575 (1964), the court said: "Political subdivisions of states—counties, cities, or whatever—never were and never have been considered as sovereign entities. Rather they have been traditionally regarded as subordinate governmental instrumentalities created by the State to assist in the carrying out of state governmental functions."

4. *Maintaining Political Boundaries.* In fashioning a remedy, how much weight should be given to established political boundary lines? As the dissent in *Milliken v. Bradley* notes, in reappor-

tionment cases such as *Reynolds v. Sims,* racial gerrymander cases such as Gomillion v. Lightfoot, 364 U.S. 339 (1960), and de-annexation cases such as *Wright v. Council of Emporia* and *United States v. Scotland Neck,* text, pp. 618, 620, the court did not feel bound by jurisdictional lines in fashioning remedies. Judge Skelly Wright similarly noted that "no state-created political lines can protect the state against the constitutional command of equal protection for its citizens or relieve the state from the obligation of providing educational opportunities for its Negro slum children equal to those provided for its white children in the affluent suburbs." Wright, *Public School Desegregation: Legal Remedies for De Facto Segregation,* 40 N.Y.U. L. REV. 285, 306 (1965). *See* Comment, *Comprehensive Metropolitan Planning: A Reinterpretation of Equal Educational Opportunity,* 67 Nw. U.L. REV. 388, 392-93 (1972).

Is there any reason for different treatment of political boundary lines in the interdistrict segregation cases? Are the policy problems in requiring common action by different jurisdictions too complex for the district courts?

5.  *The Future of Interdistrict Litigation.* After *Milliken v. Bradley* how can interdistrict segregation be attacked? Must you show purposeful segregation between school districts? Intent (in the tort sense) to segregate between districts? Substantial segregative effect of local decisions in adjoining areas? Must there be "joint interaction" as required by the Fourth Circuit in the *Richmond* decision?

In order to make the requisite showing, are the principles fashioned in *Keyes,* text, p. 622, applicable? If so, de jure segregation established for part of the state-wide system creates a presumption that segregation in at least adjoining school districts is de jure. Aren't "reciprocal effects" between districts likely? Are school districts more separate and distinct than the parts of a single school district?

In the absence of the requisite showing is there any remedy for the racially concentrated city school districts even if de jure segregation within the district is demonstrated? What is the import of *Milliken v. Bradley* for those advocating desegregation as the preferred goal? Does it strengthen the case of those who argue for separate, racially identifiable, community controlled schools?

(3)  *Benign Quotas, Preferential Treatment and Affirmative Action — The Next Phase?*

As the cases in the previous section indicate, the courts today frequently require the use of racial classifications in fashioning remedies for de jure segregation. On the other hand, the first Justice Harlan in *Plessy v. Ferguson*, text, p. 593, said that the Constitution is color-blind and there have been judicial indications that racial classifications might be per se impermissible. How is this need to use racial factors to equalize to be reconciled with the desire to avoid public decisions made on racial grounds? To what extent may race be considered for "benign" state purposes? How is a classification determined to be benign? Can the state give preference to racial minorities in distributing benefits? Can racial quotas be used in an effort to achieve and stabilize desegregation?

In 1971, Marco DeFunis, a white applicant, sought and was denied admission to the University of Washington Law School. The law school had 1,601 applications for 155 places. While other factors were considered, primarily on the basis of a Predicted First Year Average (PFYA), some applicants were summarily accepted or rejected while others were held for further screening. However, Blacks, Chicanos, Filipinos and American Indians below the statistical cut-off point were not summarily rejected. They were given separate consideration. While no acceptance quotas for these minorities were used, a certain percentage of minority applicants, some with lower PFYA's than rejected non-minority students, were virtually guaranteed acceptance.

While DeFunis was placed on a waiting list, he was ultimately rejected. He brought action alleging that the University's policy of preferential treatment for racial minorities denied him equal protection. While the Supreme Court was ultimately to hold the case moot, text, p. 96, the judicial opinions rendered and legal arguments made provide a valuable insight into the challenging issues involved.

## DEFUNIS v. ODEGAARD
### 82 Wash. 2d 11, 507 P.2d 1169 (1973)

[Neill, J., delivered the opinion of the Court.]

. . . .

It has been suggested that the less strict "rational basis" test should be applied to the consideration of race here, since the racial distinction is being used to redress the effects of past discrimination; thus, because the persons normally stigmatized by racial classifications are being benefited, the action complained of should be considered "benign" and reviewed under the more permissive standard. However, the minority admissions policy is certainly not benign with respect to nonminority students who are displaced by it.

The burden is upon the law school to show that its consideration of race in admitting students is necessary to the accomplishment of a compelling state interest.

It can hardly be gainsaid that the minorities have been, and
are, grossly underrepresented in the law schools—and consequently
in the legal profession—of this state and this nation. We believe
the state has an overriding interest in promoting integration in
public education. In light of the serious underrepresentation of
minority groups in the law schools, and considering that minority
groups participate on an equal basis in the tax support of the law
school, we find the state interest in eliminating racial imbalance
within public legal education to be compelling.

Plaintiff contends, however, that any discrimination in this
case has been de facto, rather than de jure. Thus, reasons plaintiff, since the law school itself has not actively discriminated
against minority applicants, it may not attempt to remedy racial
imbalance in the law school student body, and, consequently,
throughout the legal profession. We disagree.

*de facto remedy for de jure situation*

. . . .

Significantly, this case does not present for review a court
order imposing a program of desegregation. Rather, the minority
admissions policy is a voluntary plan initiated by school authorities. Therefore, the question before us is not whether the Fourteenth Amendment *requires* the law school to take affirmative
action to eliminate the continuing effects of de facto segregation;
the question is whether the Constitution *permits* the law school
to remedy racial imbalance through its minority admissions
policy. . . .

The de jure-de facto distinction is not controlling in determining the constitutionality of the minority admissions policy
voluntarily adopted by the law school. Further, we see no reason
why the state interest in eradicating the continuing effects of
past racial discrimination is less merely because the law school
itself may have previously been neutral in the matter.

The state also has an overriding interest in providing *all* law
students with a legal education that will adequately prepare them
to deal with the societal problems which will confront them upon
graduation. As the Supreme Court has observed, this cannot be
done through books alone. . . .

. . . The educational interest of the state in producing a
racially balanced student body at the law school is compelling.

Finally, the shortage of minority attorneys—and, consequently,
minority prosecutors, judges and public officials—constitutes an
undeniably compelling state interest. If minorities are to live

within the rule of law, they must enjoy equal representation within our legal system.

*relationship between state interest and classification*

Once a constitutionally valid state interest has been established, it remains for the state to show the requisite connection between the racial classification employed and that interest. The consideration of race in the law school admissions policy meets the test of necessity here because racial imbalance in the law school and the legal profession is the evil to be corrected, and it can only be corrected by providing legal education to those minority groups which have been previously deprived.

. . . .

There remains a further question as to the <u>scope of the classification</u>. . . . <u>The classification</u> used by defendants <u>does not include all racial minorities, but only four</u> (Blacks, Chicanos, Indians and Philippine Americans). However, the purpose of the racial classification here is to give special consideration to those racial minority groups which are underrepresented in the law schools and legal profession, and which cannot secure proportionate representation if strictly subjected to the standardized mathematical criteria for admission to the law school.

*law or policy need not correct all evils*
*(REA)*

In selecting minority groups for special consideration, the law school sought to identify those groups most in need of help. . . . The state may identify and correct the most serious examples of racial imbalance, even though in so doing it does not provide an immediate solution to the entire problem of equal representation within the legal system.

We hold that the minority admissions policy of the law school, and the denial by the law school of admission to plaintiff, violate neither the equal protection clause of the fourteenth amendment to the United States Constitution nor Article 1, § 12 of the Washington State Constitution.

FINLEY, HAMILTON, STAFFORD, WRIGHT and UTTER, JJ., and TUTTLE, J. pro tem., concur.

HALE, Chief Justice (dissenting).

. . . .

---

AMICUS BRIEF OF ANTI-DEFAMATION LEAGUE OF B'NAI B'RITH, in DEFUNIS v. ODEGAARD 416 U.S. 312 (1974), by Alexander Bickel and Philip Kurland.

## ARGUMENT

. . . The size of the class [at the University of Washington Law School] was fixed within approximately five places. There was no suggestion that class size was expandable. Minority and majority applicants, as those terms were defined by the law school, went through separate, segregated admission procedures. . . . The most desirable students were chosen within each of the two groups. But the candidates in one group were never considered in competition for the places allotted to the other group. The number of places allotted to minority applicants was changed from year to year by as inconspicuous a decision as possible. But a quota is no less a quota because it is not labelled as such or because it is subject to annual adjustment.

The use of the quota system—the segregation of two groups of applicants by race with admission for each group limited to its assigned numbers—makes it clear that this is not simply a case where race was used as one among many factors to determine admission. Instead, the law school used race as the criterion for imposing entirely separate admissions procedures. The class that entered the University of Washington Law School in 1971 was in fact two classes, distinguished in terms of racial attributes, one of "minority" students and the other of "majority" students, recognized and chosen as such by the University. To the extent that a place was assigned to one group, it was inaccessible to a student from the other group. What was demonstrated by the law school here was not a form of integration of races but rather a form of segregation of the races.

Never, since this Court struck down what Mr. Roy Wilkins has called a "zero quota" (N. Y. Post, 3 March 1973) in Brown v. Board of Education, 347 U.S. 483 (1954), has a racial quota been approved by this Court. Both proponents and opponents of integration have recognized such quotas as *per se* violations of the Equal Protection Clause that cannot be justified. That is why respondents try to assert that what is involved here is not a "quota." For a quota is not merely a racial classification. It is an attribution of status—of caste—fixed by race. A quota necessarily legislates not equality, but a governmental rule of racial differences without regard to an individual's attributes or merits.

. . . .

It is our position that a racial classification that takes the form of a racial quota, as in this case, is unconstitutional *vel non*, because racial quotas are anathema to the concept of individual freedom. But we submit that even if a racial quota does not fall into a special invalid category of its own giving rise to an irrebuttable presumption of violation of the Fourteenth Amendment, the racial classification here cannot be validly imposed within the limits of the Equal Protection Clause.

. . . .

Not since Hirabayashi v. United States, 320 U.S. 81 (1943), and Korematsu v. United States, 323 U.S. 214 (1944), has this Court permitted the use of race as a factor for classification, except to cure an earlier illegally imposed racial discrimination. And even in those cases in which this Court has sanctioned such limited cognizance of a racial factor, the use of the racial factor has been condoned only to assure the elimination of the illegal discrimination and never as a tool for "reverse discrimination" of the kind sought to be justified by the Washington Supreme Court here.

. . . .

It is argued that the racial quotas adopted by the law school here are not "invidious" because their purpose was "benign." But respondents' purpose in effecting its racial quota system is irrelevant. It is not the purpose but the effect of a racial classification that commands its invalidation. This is a lesson that this Court has continuously declared. . . .

The Supreme Court of Washington conceded that "the minority admissions policy is certainly not benign with respect to nonminority students who are displaced by it." Since it is the "nonminority student" who is the victim of this invalid racial classification, that should suffice to dispose of the argument of the benign nature of the racial classification. But there is even reason to doubt that State court's notion that the evil of a racial quota does not stigmatize the "minority student" who gains admission under such circumstances. For there is certainly the great possibility of that consequence, especially where, as under the law school's admissions program, the lower admission standards for "minority students" were such a well-publicized element.

Indeed, a racial quota is always stigmatizing and invidious, particularly when it is applied to areas concerned with intellectual competency and capacity. . . . A racial quota is derogatory to those it is intended to benefit and depriving of those from whom is taken what is "given" to the minority. A beneficent quota is invidious as it is patronizing.

. . . .

. . . The evidence is . . . clear that defendants did not give preferential treatment to "deprived students" who were not blacks, Chicanos, Indians, or Filipinos.

There is nothing in this record that shows that membership in one of the four minority races correlates with such deprivation. Indeed, a member of one of the favored minorities was to be treated as "culturally deprived" so far as the law school was concerned, even if he came from a highly intellectual and cultured family. Moreover, if a correlation could be made that showed

※

every member of the four racial minorities to fall into the cate- *disadvan-*
gory of culturally and educationally deprived, the classification *taged of*
would still be invalid for underinclusiveness because it would *other races*
fail to include culturally and economically deprived persons who *(including*
are not members of these four racial minorities. *whites?)*

. . . .

In this case the State . . . made only a token effort to shoulder
the heavy burden of proving a compelling state interest in racial
discrimination. Even if the minimal proof accepted by the Supreme Court of Washington could qualify under a rational
means test, it cannot meet the compelling state interest test. The
substitution of the lower quantum of proof is explicitly forbidden
by a consistent line of cases in this Court dealing with racial
classifications.

. . . .

Obviously, as the compelling state interest cases already cited
reveal, this Court is not the place to examine the alternatives
that might permit the State to bring more of the culturally deprived members of racial minorities into the law school on an
equal footing with other students. Affirmative action programs,
not quotas are the requirements of national policy. . . . This
case, however, involves no legitimate affirmative action, but a
racial quota. . . . [S]o-called affirmative action programs that are
not circumscribed in terms consistent with the Equal Protection
Clause collapse into the very evil they seek to cure.

. . . .

---

### DEFUNIS v. ODEGAARD
Supreme Court of the United States
416 U.S. 312, 40 L. Ed. 2d 164, 94 S. Ct. 1704 (1974)

(The per curiam opinion of the Court is reported at text,
p. 96.)

(DOUGLAS, J., dissenting.)

. . . .

The consideration of race as a measure of an applicant's
qualification normally introduces a capricious and irrelevant
factor working an invidious discrimination. Once race is a starting
point educators and courts are immediately embroiled in competing claims of different racial and ethnic groups that would make
difficult manageable standards consistent with the Equal Protection Clause. "The clear and central purpose of the Fourteenth
Amendment was to eliminate all official state sources of invidious
racial discrimination in the States." *Loving, supra,* 388 U.S. at
10. The law school's admissions policy cannot be reconciled with

that purpose, unless cultural standards of a diverse rather than a homogeneous society are taken into account. The reason is that professional persons, particularly lawyers, are not selected for life in a computerized society. The Indian who walks to the beat of Chief Seattle of the Muckleshoot Tribe in Washington has a different culture than Examiners at Law Schools.

The key to the problem is the consideration of each application *in a racially neutral way*. Since LSAT reflects questions touching on cultural backgrounds, the admissions committee acted properly in my view in setting minority applications apart for separate processing. These minorities have cultural backgrounds that are vastly different from the dominant Caucasian. [A] test sensitively tuned for most applicants would be wide of the mark for many minorities.

The melting pot is not designed to homogenize people, making them uniform in consistency. . . .

. . . .

. . . [A]t least as respects Indians, Blacks, and Chicanos—as well as those from Asian cultures—I think a separate classification of these applicants is warranted, lest race be a subtle force in eliminating minority members because of cultural differences.

Insofar as LSAT tests reflect the dimensions and orientation of the Organization Man they do a disservice to minorities. I personally know that admissions tests were once used to eliminate Jews. How many other minorities they aim at I do not know. My reaction is that the presence of an LSAT test is sufficient warrant for a school to put racial minorities into a separate class in order better to probe their capacities and potentials.

This does not mean that a separate LSAT test be designed for minority racial groups, although that might be a possibility. The merits of the present controversy cannot in my view be resolved on this record. A trial would involve the disclosure of hidden prejudices, if any, against certain minorities and the manner in which substitute measurements of one's talents and character were employed in the conventional tests. I could agree with the majority of the Washington Supreme Court only, if on the record, it could be said that the law school's selection was racially neutral. The case, in my view, should be remanded for a new trial to consider, *inter alia*, whether the established LSAT tests should be eliminated so far as racial minorities are concerned.

. . . The reason for the separate treatment of minorities as a class is to make more certain that racial factors do not militate *against an applicant or on his behalf.*

There is no constitutional right for any race to be preferred. . . . A DeFunis who is white is entitled to no advantage by reason of that fact; nor is he subject to any disability, no matter his race or color. Whatever his race, he had a constitutional right to have his application considered on its individual merits in a racially neutral manner.

. . . .

The reservation of a proportion of the law school class for members of selected minority groups is fraught with similar dangers, for one must immediately determine which groups are to receive such favored treatment and which are to be excluded, the proportions of the class that are to be allocated to each, and even the criteria by which to determine whether an individual is a member of a favored group. There is no assurance that a common agreement can be reached, and first the schools, and then the courts, will be buffeted with the competing claims. . . .

. . . .

The key to the problem is consideration of such applications *in a racially neutral way.* Abolition of the LSAT test would be a start. . . . Interviews with the applicant and others who know him is a time-honored test. Some schools currently run summer programs in which potential students who likely would be by-passed under conventional admissions criteria are given the opportunity to try their hand at law courses, and certainly their performance in such programs could be weighed heavily. There is, moreover, no bar to considering an individual's prior achievements in light of the racial discrimination that barred his way, as a factor in attempting to assess his true potential for a successful legal career. Nor is there any bar to considering on an individual basis, rather than according to racial classifications, the likelihood that a particular candidate will more likely employy his legal skills to service communities that are not now adequately represented than will competing candidates. . . .

*alternatives*

The argument is that a "compelling" state interest can easily justify the racial discrimination that is practiced here. To many "compelling" would give members of one race even more than *pro rata* representation. . . . The State, however, may not proceed by racial classification to force strict population equivalencies for every group in every occupation, overriding individual preferences. The Equal Protection Clause commands the elimination of racial barriers, not their creation in order to satisfy our theory as to how society ought to be organized. The purpose of the University of Washington cannot be to produce Black lawyers for Blacks, Polish lawyers for Poles, Jewish lawyers for Jews, Irish lawyers for the Irish. It should be to produce good lawyers for

Americans and not to place First Amendment barriers against anyone. That is the point at the heart of all our school desegregation cases, from *Brown v. Board of Education* through *Swann v. Charlotte-Mecklenburg Board of Educ.* A segregated admissions process creates suggestions of stigma and caste no less than a segregated classroom, and in the end it may produce that result despite its contrary intentions. One other assumption must be clearly disapproved, that Blacks or Browns cannot make it on their individual merit. That is a stamp of inferiority that a State is not permitted to place on any lawyer.

*stigma of minority admissions*

If discrimination based on race is constitutionally permissible when those who hold the reins can come up with "compelling" reasons to justify it, then constitutional guarantees acquire an accordionlike quality. . . . It may well be that racial strains, racial susceptibility to certain diseases, racial sensitiveness to environmental conditions that other races do not experience may in an extreme situation justify differences in racial treatment that no fairminded person would call "invidious" discrimination. Mental ability is not in the category. All races can compete fairly at all professional levels. So far as race is concerned, any state sponsored preference to one race over another in that competition is in my view "invidious" and violative of the Equal Protection Clause.

. . . .

We would have a different case if the suit were one to displace the applicant who was chosen in lieu of DeFunis. What the record would show concerning his potentials would have to be considered and weighed. The educational decision, provided proper guidelines were used, would reflect an expertise that courts should honor. The problem is not tendered here because the physical facilities were apparently adequate to take DeFunis in addition to the others. My view is only that I cannot say by the tests used and applied he was invidiously discriminated against because of his race.

I cannot conclude that the admissions procedure of the Law School of the University of Washington that excluded DeFunis is violative of the Equal Protection Clause of the Fourteenth Amendment. The judgment of the Washington Supreme Court should be vacated and the case remanded for a new trial.

———

## NOTES

1. *Benign Quotas in Housing.* Suppose a public housing project sells houses according to a predetermined racial ratio for the expressed purpose of establishing a stable desegregated residential environment. The ratio is not proportionate to the repre-

sentation of minorities in the community but is based on the percentage of minority residents that the white majority would tolerate before moving out. This is the "benign quota." It is based on the premise that an "invasion-succession" phenomenon exists whereby, as a previously all-white neighborhood begins to desegregate, a "tipping-point" is reached when whites will begin to emigrate and the neighborhood will resegregate. By setting rigid racial percentages, the "tipping-point" would never be reached.

Are such benign quotas constitutional? What standard of review should be used? Does the quota in the hypothetical differ significantly from that used in *DeFunis? See generally* Hughes, *The Right of Special Treatment,* in THE RIGHTS OF AMERICANS: WHAT THEY ARE—WHAT THEY SHOULD BE 94 (Dorsen ed. 1971); Hellerstein, *The Benign Quota, Equal Protection, and "The Rule in Shelley's Case",* 17 RUTGERS L. REV. 531 (1963); Bittker, *The Case of the Checker-Board Ordinance: An Experiment in Race Relations,* 71 YALE L.J. 1387 (1962); Kaplan, *Equal Justice in an Unequal World: Equality for the Negro—The Problem of Special Treatment,* 61 Nw. U.L. REV. 363 (1966).

**2.** *Affirmative Action in Employment.* Can private employers be compelled to hire a prescribed percentage of minorities as a precondition to obtaining federal contracts? Executive Order 11246, as interpreted, requires government contractors to take "affirmative action" to assure "full and equal employment." This requires a determination of labor categories in which minorities are "under-utilized," the development of a comprehensive plan for achieving defined hiring goals at stated times, and audits designed to determine if a good faith effort is being made to meet these goals. 41 C.F.R. § 60-2.1 *et seq.* Is this a benign quota? Does such a program violate the fourteenth amendment?

**3.** How relevant to the *DeFunis* problem are the cases recognizing race as a basis for remedying de jure segregation? For remedying de facto segregation? In Lau v. Nichols, 414 U.S. 563 (1974), the Supreme Court, per Justice Douglas, held that Title VI of the 1964 Civil Rights Act required the San Francisco school system to take affirmative action to provide English language instruction to Chinese-speaking minority students. The case was remanded to determine appropriate relief. Justice Stewart joined by the Chief Justice and Justice Blackmun stressed HEW guidelines interpreting Title VI to require affirmative action to aid linguistically deprived children. Justice Blackmun, joined by Chief Justice Burger, emphasized that a substantial number of children were involved. Is there an equal protection right to a bilingual education? *See* Grubb, *Breaking the Language Barrier:*

*The Right to a Bilingual Education,* 9 HARV. CIV. RTS.-CIV. LIB. L. REV. 52 (1974).

### b.    Alienage and Nationality Classifications

1. As Yick Wo v. Hopkins, 118 U.S. 356 (1886), text, 587, indicates, an alien is a "person," protected by the equal protection guarantee. *See* Truax v. Raich, 239 U.S. 33 (1915) (Arizona law requiring employers of five or more workers to hire not less than 80 per cent citizens held violative of the equal protection guarantee). While the fourteenth amendment may have been intended for the special protection of Blacks, the language is not so limited (see Wong Wing v. United States, 163 U.S. 228 (1896) holding that the fifth amendment applies to aliens). Similarly, citizens who are treated differently from other citizens because of their ancestry can claim the protection of the guarantee. Korematsu v. United States, 323 U.S. 214 (1945). As was said in Strauder v. West Virginia, 100 U.S. 303 (1880), "If a law should be passed excluding all naturalized Celtic Irishmen, would there be any doubt of its inconsistency with the spirit of the [fourteenth] Amendment?"

But even if the guarantee is applicable, what standard of review should be used? If the special treatment accorded race classifications is based on historical considerations, must all other classifications be judged by traditional standards? If we are to depart from traditional review, what is the justification? Can alienage or nationality classifications be analogized to race?

2. In Graham v. Richardson, 403 U.S. 365 (1971), the court, per Justice Blackmun, struck down a 15-year residency requirement for aliens as a pre-condition for eligibility for welfare benefits. Justice Blackmun declared "that classifications based on alienage, like those based on nationality or race, are inherently suspect and subject to close judicial scrutiny. Aliens as a class are a prime example of a single 'discrete and insular' minority . . . for whom such heightened judicial solicitude is appropriate." Justice Blackmun went on to conclude "that a State's desire to preserve limited welfare benefits for its own citizens (the special interest doctrine) is inadequate to justify . . . restricting benefits to citizens and long time resident aliens." *See* Sugarman v. Dougall, 413 U.S. 634 (1973), striking down a New York citizenship requirement for all competitive civil service positions as "neither narrowly confined nor precise in its application" and *In re* Griffiths, 413 U.S. 717 (1973), striking down a Connecticut court rule restricting admission to the bar to citizens of the United States since the state failed to show that the classification was

"necessary to the accomplishment of its purpose or the safeguarding of its interests."

3. What is the rationale for using strict scrutiny in judging
alienage classifications? Justice Rehnquist wrote a separate dissent
for both *Sugarman* and *Griffiths* attacking the use of the more
stringent standard of review. He argued first that "there is no
language used in the Amendment, or any historical evidence as
to the intent of the Framers, which would suggest the slightest
degree that it was intended to render alienage a 'suspect' classification, that it was designed in any way to protect 'discreet and
insular minorities' other than racial minorities, or that it would
in any way justify the result reached by the Court in these two
cases." He noted the frequent references in the Constitution
differentiating between aliens and citizens, including the provisions in the fourteenth amendment, § 1.

Noting the questionable origins of the "discrete and insular
minorities" rationale in the *Carolene Products* footnote, Justice
Rehnquist criticized its value as a "constitutional reason" for
using a different standard of review: "Our society, consisting of
over 200 million individuals of multitudinous origins, customs,
tongues, beliefs, and cultures is, to say the least, diverse. It would
hardly take extraordinary ingenuity for a lawyer to find 'insular
and discrete,' minorities at every turn in the road. Yet unless the
Court can precisely define and constitutionally justify both the
terms and analysis it uses, these decisions today stand for the
proposition that the Court can choose a 'minority' it 'feels'
deserves 'solicitude' and thereafter prohibit the states from classifying that 'minority' differently from the 'majority.' I cannot find,
and the Court does not cite, any constitutional authority for such
a 'ward of the Court' approach to equal protection."

Nor, Justice Rehnquist argued, could alienage and race be
analogized as classifications based on an unalterable status since
"there is a marked difference between a status or condition such
as illegitimacy, national origin, or race, which cannot be altered
by an individual and the 'status' of the [alien] cases. There is
nothing in the record indicating that their status as aliens cannot
be changed by their affirmative acts." *But see,* Comment, *State
Discrimination Against Mexican Aliens,* 38 GEO. WASH. L. REV.
1091, 1102 (1970), on the difficulty in removing oneself from the
alienage classification. Is it desirable to require aliens to become
citizens in order to avoid discrimination? Are classifications based
on the "status" of illegitimacy suspect? *See* text, p. 714.

Justice Rehnquist found especially disturbing "the intimation
if not the statement, that [native born and especially naturalized
citizens] are really not any different from aliens." He asserted that

"[i]f citizenship is not 'special,' the Court has wasted a great deal of effort in the past." Is citizenship, like race, generally a "neutral" factor in classifying, irrelevant to most legitimate governmental purposes?

### c. Sex Classifications: "All [Persons] Are Created Equal"

In Reed v. Reed, 404 U.S. 71 (1971), the court, per Chief Justice Burger, unanimously struck down an Idaho law giving males a preference over females as administrators of estates. The appellant's brief had argued "that designation of sex as a suspect classification is overdue, is the only wholly satisfactory standard for dealing with the claim in this case, and should be the starting point for assessing that claim. Nonetheless . . . it should be apparent that the reasonable relation test also must yield a conclusion in favor of the appellant."

Chief Justice Burger framed the question as: "Whether the difference in the sex of competing applicants for letters of administration bears a rational relationship to a state objective that is sought to be advanced. . . ." Relying entirely on traditional equal protection cases as precedent, the court nevertheless found that the statute violated equal protection. While the state interest in reducing the work load of probate courts was deemed "not without some legitimacy," the state's manner of advancing that interest did not satisfy equal protection standards. "To give a mandatory preference to members of either sex over members of the other, merely to accomplish the elimination of hearings on the merits, is to make the very kind of arbitrary legislative choice forbidden by the Equal Protection Clause of the Fourteenth Amendment; and whatever may be said as to the positive values of avoiding intra-family controversy, the choice in this context may not lawfully be mandated solely on the basis of sex." Persons within the various classes of relationship to the intestate were similarly situated. "By providing dissimilar treatment for men and women who are thus similarly situated, the challenged section violates the Equal Protection Clause."

### FRONTIERO v. RICHARDSON
Supreme Court of the United States
411 U.S. 677, 36 L. Ed. 2d 583, 93 S. Ct. 1764 (1973)

Justice BRENNAN announced the judgment of the Court in an opinion in which Justice DOUGLAS, Justice WHITE, and Justice MARSHALL join.

The question before us concerns the right of a female member of the uniformed services to claim her spouse as a "dependent" for the purposes of obtaining increased quarters allowances and medical and dental benefits on an equal footing with male members. Under these statutes, a serviceman may claim his wife as a "dependent" without regard to whether she is in fact dependent upon him for any part of her support. A servicewoman, on the other hand, may not claim her husband as a "dependent" under these programs unless he is in fact dependent upon her for over one-half of his support. Thus, the question for decision is whether this difference in treatment constitutes an unconstitutional discrimination against servicewomen in violation of the Due Process Clause of the Fifth Amendment. A three-judge District Court for the Middle District of Alabama, one judge dissenting, rejected this contention and sustained the constitutionality of the provisions of the statutes making this distinction. 341 F.Supp. 201 (1972).

. . . We reverse.

. . . In essence, appellants asserted that the discriminatory impact of the statutes is two-fold: first, as a procedural matter, a female member is required to demonstrate her spouse's dependency, while no such burden is imposed upon male members; and second, as a substantive matter, a male member who does not provide more than one-half of his wife's support receives benefits, while a similarly situated female member is denied such benefits. Appellants therefore sought a permanent injunction against the continued enforcement of these statutes and an order directing the appellees to provide Lieutenant Frontiero with the same housing and medical benefits that a similarly situated male member would receive. . . .

*[margin note: procedural and substantive]*

. . . .

At the outset, appellants contend that classifications based upon sex, like classifications based upon race, alienage, and national origin, are inherently suspect and must therefore be subjected to close judicial scrutiny. We agree and, indeed, find at least implicit support for such an approach in our unanimous decision only last Term in Reed v. Reed, 404 U.S. 71.

. . . .

. . . [T]he Court [in Reed] held the statutory preference for male applicants unconstitutional. In reaching this result, the Court implicitly rejected appellee's apparently rational explanation of the statutory scheme, and concluded that, by ignoring the individual qualifications of particular applicants, the challenged statute provided "dissimilar treatment for men and women who are . . . similarly situated." . . . This departure from "traditional" rational basis analysis with respect to sex-based classifications is clearly justified.

There can be no doubt that our Nation has had a long and unfortunate history of sex discrimination. Traditionally, such discrimination was rationalized by an attitude of "romantic paternalism" which, in practical effect, put women not on a pedestal, but in a cage. . . .

As a result of notions such as these, our statute books gradually became laden with gross, stereotypical distinctions between the sexes and, indeed, throughout much of the 19th century the position of women in our society was, in many respects, comparable to that of blacks under the pre-Civil War slave codes. Neither slaves nor women could hold office, serve on juries, or bring suit in their own names, and married women traditionally were denied the legal capacity to hold or convey property or to serve as legal guardians of their own children. And although blacks were guaranteed the right to vote in 1870, women were denied even that right—which is itself "preservative of other basic civil and political rights"—until adoption of the Nineteenth Amendment half a century later.

It is true, of course, that the position of women in America has improved markedly in recent decades. Nevertheless, it can hardly be doubted that, in part because of the high visibility of the sex characteristic, women still face pervasive, although at times more subtle, discrimination in our educational institutions, on the job market and, perhaps most conspicuously, in the political arena.

Moreover, since sex, like race and national origin, is an immutable characteristic determined solely by the accident of birth, the imposition of special disabilities upon the members of a particular sex because of their sex would seem to violate "the basic concept of our system that legal burdens should bear some relationship to individual responsibility. . . ." Weber v. Aetna Casualty & Surety Co., 406 U.S. 164, 175 (1972) [text, p. 716]. And what differentiates sex from such nonsuspect statutes as intelligence or physical disability, and aligns it with the recognized suspect criteria, is that the sex characteristic frequently bears no relation to ability to perform or contribute to society. As a result, statutory distinctions between the sexes often have the effect of invidiously relegating the entire class of females to inferior legal status without regard to the actual capabilities of its individual members.

We might also note that, over the past decade, Congress has itself manifested an increasing sensitivity to sex-based classifications. In Tit. VII of the Civil Rights Act of 1964, for example, Congress expressly declared that no employer, labor union, or other organization subject to the provisions of the Act shall discriminate against any individual on the basis of "race, color, religion, *sex,* or national origin." Similarly, the Equal Pay Act of 1963 provides that no employer covered by the Act "shall discriminate . . . between employees on the basis of sex." And § 1 of the Equal Rights Amendment, passed by Congress on March 22, 1972, and submitted to the legislatures of the States for ratification, declares that "[e]quality of rights under the law shall not be denied or abridged by the United States or by any State on account of sex." Thus, Congress has itself concluded that classifications based upon sex are inherently invidious, and this conclusion of a coequal branch of Government is not without significance to the question presently under consideration.

With these considerations in mind, we can only conclude that classifications based upon sex, like classifications based upon race, alienage, or national origin, are inherently suspect, and must therefore be subjected to strict judicial scrutiny. Applying the analysis mandated by that stricter standard of review, it is clear that the statutory scheme now before us is constitutionally invalid.

. . . .

[T]he Government concedes that the differential treatment accorded men and women under these statutes serves no purpose other than mere "administrative convenience." In essence, the *govern-mental purpose unproven and un-related* Government maintains that, as an empirical matter, wives in our society frequently are dependent upon their husbands, while husbands rarely are dependent upon their wives. Thus, the Government argues that Congress might reasonably have concluded that it would be both cheaper and easier simply conclusively to presume that wives of male members are financially dependent upon their husbands, while burdening female members with the task of establishing dependency in fact.[22]

The Government offers no concrete evidence, however, tending to support its view that such differential treatment in fact saves the Government any money. In order to satisfy the demands of strict judicial scrutiny, the Government must demonstrate, for example, that it is actually cheaper to grant increased benefits with respect to *all* male members, than it is to determine which male members are in fact entitled to such benefits and to grant increased benefits only to those members whose wives actually meet the dependency requirement. Here, however, there is substantial evidence that, if put to the test, many of the wives of male members would fail to qualify for benefits. And in light of the fact that the dependency determination with respect to the hus-

---

[22] It should be noted that these statutes are not in any sense designed to rectify the effects of past discrimination against women. . . .

bands of female members is presently made solely on the basis of affidavits rather than through the more costly hearing process, the Government's explanation of the statutory scheme is, to say the least, questionable.

In any case, our prior decisions make clear that, although efficacious administration of governmental programs is not without some importance, "The Constitution recognizes higher values than speed and efficiency." Stanley v. Illinois, 405 U.S. 645, 656 (1972) [text, p. 724]. And when we enter the realm of "strict judicial scrutiny," there can be no doubt that "administrative convenience" is not a shibboleth, the mere recitation of which dictates constitutionality. On the contrary, any statutory scheme which draws a sharp line between the sexes, *solely* for the purpose of achieving administrative convenience, necessarily commands "dissimilar treatment for men and women who are . . . similarly situated," and therefore involves the "very kind of arbitrary legislative choice forbidden by the [Constitution]. . . ." *Reed v. Reed.* We therefore conclude that, by according differential treatment to male and female members of the uniformed services for the sole purpose of achieving administrative convenience, the challenged statutes violate the Due Process Clause of the Fifth Amendment insofar as they require a female member to prove the dependency of her husband.

Reversed.

Justice STEWART concurs in the judgment, agreeing that the statutes before us work an invidious discrimination in violation of the Constitution. *Reed v. Reed.*

Justice REHNQUIST dissents for the reasons stated by Judge Rives in his opinion for the District Court, Frontiero v. Laird, 341 F.Supp. 201 (1972).

Justice POWELL, with whom the CHIEF JUSTICE and Justice BLACKMUN join, concurring in the judgment.

I agree that the challenged statutes constitute an unconstitutional discrimination against service women in violation of the Due Process Clause of the Fifth Amendment, but I cannot join the opinion of Mr. Justice BRENNAN. . . . It is unnecessary for the Court in this case to characterize sex as a suspect classification, with all of the far-reaching implications of such a holding. *Reed v. Reed,* which abundantly supports our decision today, did not add sex to the narrowly limited group of classifications which are inherently suspect. In my view, we can and should decide this case on the authority of *Reed* and reserve for the future any expansion of its rationale.

There is another, and I find compelling, reason for deferring a general categorizing of sex classifications as invoking the strictest test of judicial scrutiny. The Equal Rights Amendment, which if adopted will resolve the substance of this precise question, has been approved by the Congress and submitted for ratification by the States. If this Amendment is duly adopted, it will represent the will of the people accomplished in the manner prescribed by the Constitution. By acting prematurely and unnecessarily, as I view it, the Court has assumed a decisional responsibility at the very time when state legislatures, functioning within the traditional democratic process, are debating the proposed Amendment. It seems to me that this reaching out to pre-empt by judicial action a major political decision which is currently in process of resolution does not reflect appropriate respect for duly prescribed legislative processes.

*Supreme Court over-powering Congress with regards to ERA.*

There are times when this Court, under our system, cannot avoid a constitutional decision on issues which normally should be resolved by the elected representatives of the people. But democratic institutions are weakened, and confidence in the restraint of the Court is impaired, when we appear unnecessarily to decide sensitive issues of broad social and political importance at the very time they are under consideration within the prescribed constitutional processes.

## NOTES

1. *Reed Redefined?* The majority and concurring opinions in *Frontiero* give different interpretations to *Reed*. Which is more accurate? While *Reed* uses the terminology of traditional equal protection, Professor Gunther suggests that this may be misleading. "It is difficult to understand [the *Reed*] result without an assumption that some special sensitivity to sex as a classifying factor entered into the analysis. Clear priority classifications are plainly relevant to the State's interest in reducing administrative disputes. Even if the requirement be that the means bear a 'significant relationship' to the state's purpose, or contribute substantially to its achievement, the test would seem to have been met in *Reed*. Only by importing some special suspicion of sex-related means from the new equal protection area can the result be made entirely persuasive. Yet application of new equal protection criteria is precisely what *Reed v. Reed* purported to avoid." Gunther, *Supreme Court 1971 Term, Foreword: In Search of Evolving Doctrine on a Changing Court: A Model for a Newer Equal Protection,* 86 HARV. L. REV. 1, 34 (1972).

2. *Discrimination Against Males.* Should laws discriminating against males be treated as suspect? In Kahn v. Shevin, 416 U.S. 351 (1974), the court, per Justice Douglas, affirmed a Florida Su-

preme Court decision upholding a state law granting a property tax exemption to female widows but not male widowers. Citing data indicating that women working full time earned a 1972 median income only 57.9 per cent of the male median—6 points lower than in 1955—Justice Douglas argued that "[t]here can be no dispute that the financial difficulties confronting the lone woman . . . exceed those facing the man. Whether from overt discrimination or from the socialization process of a male dominated culture, the job market is inhospitable to the woman seeking any but the lowest paid jobs. . . . While the widower can usually continue in the occupation which preceded his spouse's death, in many cases the widow will find herself suddenly forced into a job market with which she is unfamiliar, and in which, because of her former economic dependency, she will have fewer skills to offer." [Thus, Florida's law " 'rest[s] upon some ground of difference having a fair and substantial relation to the object of the legislation.' "] *Frontiero* was distinguishable since the present case dealt "with a state tax law reasonably designed to further the state policy of cushioning the financial impact of spousal loss upon the sex for whom that loss imposes a disproportionately heavy burden." Justice Douglas accused the dissent of using the "Equal Protection Clause as a vehicle for reinstating notions of substantive due process that have been repudiated." He noted that "[g]ender has never been rejected as an impermissible classification in all instances," citing Muller v. Oregon, 208 U.S. 412 (1908), upholding a state maximum hour regulation for women.

Justice Brennan, joined by Justice Marshall, dissented, arguing that a legislative classification that distinguishes potential beneficiaries solely by reference to their gender-based status as widows or widowers, like classifications based upon race, alienage, and national origin, must be subjected to "judicial scrutiny, because it focuses upon generally immutable characteristics over which individuals have little or no control, and also because gender-based classifications too often have been inexcusably utilized to stereotype and stigmatize politically powerless segments of society. See *Frontiero v. Richardson.* . . ." While the statute served the compelling interest of achieving greater equality for a needy segment of society, it was over-inclusive in including widows with no need of assistance. Justice White also dissented.

**3.** *When Is a Classification Sex-Based?* In Geduldig v. Aiello, 417 U.S. 484 (1974), the court reversed the district court and upheld a California disability insurance program which exempted from coverage any work loss resulting from normal pregnancy. Justice Stewart, for the Court, found no discrimination with re-

spect to the persons or groups eligible for participation. "There is
no evidence in the record that the selection of the risk insured by
the program worked to discriminate against any definable group
or class in terms of the aggregate risk protection derived by that
group or class from the program. There is no risk from which
men are protected and women are not. Likewise, there is no risk
from which women are protected and men are not." In a footnote,
sex discrimination cases were distinguished since the insurance
program, "does not exclude anyone from benefit eligibility because of gender but merely removes one physical condition —
pregnancy — from the list of compensable disabilities. While it
is true that only women can become pregnant, it does not follow
that every legislative classification concerning pregnancy is a
sex-based classification like those considered in *Reed* and
*Frontiero*. Normal pregnancy is an objectively identifiable physical condition with unique characteristics. Absent a showing that
distinctions involving pregnancy are mere pretexts designed to
effect an invidious discrimination against the members of one
sex or the other, lawmakers are constitutionally free to include or
exclude pregnancy from the coverage of legislation such as this
on any reasonable basis, just as with respect to any other physical
condition." The two classes were not men and women but
"pregnant women and non-pregnant persons," the latter class
including both males and females.

The challenge, then, was solely to the under-inclusiveness of
the set of risks insured. The line drawn, however, was rationally
supportable since a totally comprehensive program "would be
substantially more costly than the present program and would
inevitably require State subsidy, a higher rate of employee contribution, a lower scale of benefits for those suffering insured
disabilities, or some combination of these measures." The state
had a legitimate interest in avoiding these results and "there is
nothing in the Constitution . . . that requires the State to subordinate or compromise its legitimate interests solely to create a
more comprehensive social insurance program than it already
has."

Justice Brennan, joined by Justices Douglas and Marshall,
dissenting, argued that "by singling out for less favorable treatment a gender-linked disability peculiar to women, the State has
created a double standard for disability compensation: a limitation is imposed upon the disabilities for which women workers
may recover, while men receive full compensation for all disabilities suffered, including those that affect only or primarily their
sex. . . . In affect, one set of rules is applied to females and
another to males. Such dissimilar treatment of men and women,

on the basis of physical characteristics inextricably linked to one sex, inevitably constitutes sex discrimination." He warned that the majority's decision "threatens to return men and women to a time when 'traditional' equal protection analysis sustained legislative classifications that treated differently members of a particular sex solely because of the sex." Since any state interest in fiscal integrity was insufficient and could have been satisfied by less drastic means, the law should be held unconstitutional.

4.   The court (5-4) has rejected a fifth amendment due process challenge to a federal statutory scheme requiring discharge of male military officers passed over twice for promotion after nine years of service and of female officers after 13 years of service. Schlesinger v. Ballard, — U.S. — (1975). Justice Stewart, for the court, distinguished *Reed* and *Frontiero* on grounds that there "the challenged classifications based on sex were premised on over-broad generalizations that could not be tolerated under the Constitution." In enacting this federal statute, "Congress may . . . quite *rationally* have believed that women line officers had less opportunity for promotion that did their male counterpart, and that a longer period of tenure for women officers would, therefore, be consistent with the goal to provide women officers with single 'fair and equitable career advancement programs.' " (Emphasis added.)

*See* Taylor v. Louisiana, — U.S. — (1975), where the court held unconstitutional a state statute which placed women on petit jury roles only if they indicated the desire to be included as violative of sixth and fourteenth amendment right to have juries drawn from a representative cross-section of the community.

5.   *Equal Rights Amendment.* On March 22, 1972, 49 years after it was first introduced, the Senate completed congressional approval of an equal rights amendment.

Section 1.   Equality of rights under the law shall not be denied or abridged by the United States or by any State on account of sex.

Section 2.   The Congress shall have the power to enforce, by appropriate legislation, the provisions of this article.

Section 3.   The Amendment shall take effect two years after the date of ratification.

It has been stated: "The fundamental legal principle underlying the Equal Rights Amendment . . . is that the law must deal with particular attributes of individuals, not with a classification based on the broad and impermissible attribute of sex." Brown, Emerson, Falk & Freedman, *The Equal Rights Amendment: A Constitutional Basis for Equal Rights for Women,* 80 YALE L.J. 871, 893

(1971). Proponents of the measure argue that it would make sex classifications per se impermissible with two exceptions, *i.e.,* personal privacy and physical characteristics unique to one sex. S. REP. No. 92-689, SEN. COMM. ON THE JUDICIARY, 92d CONG., 2d SESS. (1972).

Is a constitutional amendment needed or desirable in light of statutory and judicial developments? Is a per se rule desirable? Does the amendment embody such a per se rule? Would men as well as women be protected? Are the two areas of exception sufficiently precise? What would be the effect of the law on protective labor laws, family support laws, military service? What would be the status of benign, compensatory treatment designed to correct past discriminatory treatment? *See generally* R. GINSBURG, THE CONSTITUTIONAL ASPECTS OF SEX-BASED DISCRIMINATION 107-16 (1974); *Equal Rights for Women: A Symposium on the Proposed Constitutional Amendment,* 6 HARV. CIV. L. REV. 215 (1971).

### d. Wealth Classifications; Due Process or Equal Protection; Suspect Classification or Fundamental Right?

1. In Griffin v. Illinois, 351 U.S. 12 (1956), the court reviewed an Illinois law which provided appeal as a matter of right in criminal cases and required that the defendant provide the appellate court with a bill of exceptions or report of trial proceedings certified by the trial judge. While the state conceded that it was sometimes impossible to satisfy this requirement without a transcript of the proceedings, Illinois furnished free trial transcripts only to indigents condemned to death. All other defendants had to pay a fee. The court held this unconstitutional using both equal protection and due process reasoning.

Justice Black in a plurality opinion, joined by Justices Douglas, Clark, and Chief Justice Warren, concluded that "[i]n criminal trials a State can no more discriminate on account of poverty than on account of religion, race, or color. Plainly the ability to pay costs in advance bears no rational relationship to a defendant's guilt or innocence and could not be used as an excuse to deprive a defendant of a fair trial." Justice Black could find "no meaningful distinction between a rule which would deny the poor the right to defend themselves in a trial court and one which effectively denies the poor an adequate appellate review accorded to all who have money enough to pay the cost in advance." While a state need not provide appellate review, if it does so, it cannot "do so in a way that discriminates against some convicted defendants on account of their poverty. . . . Consequently at all stages of the proceedings the Due Process and Equal Protection

Clauses protect persons like petitioners from invidious discrimination." In a frequently quoted passage, Justice Black stated: "There can be no equal justice where the kind of trial a man gets depends on the amount of money he has. Destitute defendants must be afforded as adequate appellate review as defendants who have money enough to buy transcripts."

### DOUGLAS v. CALIFORNIA
Supreme Court of the United States
372 U.S. 353, 9 L. Ed. 2d 811, 83 S. Ct. 814 (1963)

Justice DOUGLAS delivered the opinion of the Court.
. . . .

. . . In Griffin v. Illinois, 351 U.S. 12, . . . the right to a free transcript on appeal was an issue. Here the issue is whether or not an indigent shall be denied the assistance of counsel on appeal. In either case the evil is the same: discrimination against the indigent. . . .

In spite of California's forward treatment of indigents, under its present practice the type of an appeal a person is afforded in the District Court of Appeals hinges upon whether or not he can pay for the assistance of counsel. If he can the appellate court passes on the merits of his case only after having the full benefit of written briefs and oral argument by counsel. If he cannot the appellate court is forced to prejudge the merits before it can even determine whether counsel should be provided. At this stage in the proceedings only the barren record speaks for the indigent, and, unless the printed pages show that an injustice has been committed, he is forced to go without a champion on appeal. Any real chance he may have had of showing that his appeal has hidden merit is deprived him when the court decides on an *ex parte* examination of the record that the assistance of counsel is not required.

We are not here concerned with problems that might arise from the denial of counsel for the preparation of a petition for discretionary or mandatory review beyond the stage in the appellate process at which the claims have once been presented by a lawyer and passed upon by an appellate court. We are dealing only with the *first appeal,* granted as a matter of right to rich and poor alike, from a criminal conviction. We need not now decide whether California would have to provide counsel for an indigent seeking a discretionary hearing from the California Supreme Court after the District Court of Appeal had sustained his conviction, or whether counsel must be appointed for an indigent seeking review of an appellate affirmance of his conviction in this Court by appeal as of right or by petition for a writ of certiorari which lies within the Court's discretion. But it is appropriate to observe that a State can, consistently with the Fourteenth Amendment, provide for differences so long as the result does not amount to a denial of due process or an "invidious discrimination." Absolute equality is not required; lines can be and are drawn and we often sustain them. Goesaert v. Cleary, 335 U.S. 464. But where the merits of *the one and only appeal* an indigent has as of right are decided without benefit of counsel, we think an unconstitutional line has been drawn between rich and poor.

When an indigent is forced to run this gantlet of a preliminary showing of merit, the right to appeal does not comport with fair procedure. . . .There is lacking that equality demanded by the Fourteenth Amendment where the rich man, who appeals as of right, enjoys the benefit of counsel's examination into the record, research of the law, and marshalling of arguments on his behalf, while the indigent, already burdened by a preliminary determination that his case is without merit, is forced to shift for himself. The indigent, where the record is unclear or the errors are hidden, has only the right to a meaningless ritual, while the rich man has a meaningful appeal.

. . . .

Justice CLARK dissenting.

. . . .

Justice HARLAN, whom Justice STEWART joins, dissenting.

. . . .

Laws such as these do not deny equal protection to the less fortunate for one essential reason: the Equal Protection Clause does not impose on the States "an affirmative duty to lift the handicaps flowing from differences in economic circumstances." To so construe it would be to read into the Constitution a philosophy of leveling that would be foreign to many of our basic concepts of the proper relations between government and society. The State may have a moral obligation to eliminate the evils of poverty, but it is not required by the Equal Protection Clause to give to some whatever others can afford.

. . . .

The real question in this case, I submit, and the only one that permits of satisfactory analysis, is whether or not the state rule, as applied in this case is consistent with the requirements of fair procedure guaranteed by the Due Process Clause. Of course, in considering this question, it must not be lost sight of that the State's responsibility under the Due Process Clause is to provide justice for all. Refusal to furnish criminal indigents with some things that others can afford may fall short of constitutional standards of fairness. The problem before us is whether this is such a case.

. . . .

---

## NOTES

1. *De Jure and De Facto Discrimination.* Justice Harlan in *Douglas* states that the Equal Protection Clause prohibits discrimination between rich and poor *"as such."* What does he mean? Should there be a difference in judicial handling of wealth classifications depending on whether they are de jure or de facto? It has been noted that "the nature of dollar discrimination is such that it is most likely to emerge in the context of apparently good-faith governmental decisions. Whenever the state charges for its benefits, taxes, fails to provide full advocative assistance to an individual whose welfare turns upon the outcome of a state proceeding, or dispenses education or other social advantage in a way more suited to those of social and economic means, it has involved itself in an economic discrimination of de facto sort. Even in the racial area, the constitutional status of such de facto situations is far from clear." Sager, *Tight Little Islands: Exclusionary Zoning, Equal Protection, and the Indigent*, 21 STAN. L. REV. 767, 786 (1969).

2. Are *Griffin* and *Douglas* applications of the suspect classification approach? Does the remedy afforded, *i.e.*, provision of the service involved to the indigent while fees are required of others, suggest that the cases do turn on discrimination against the poor? Professor Michelman, however, argues that "a little reflection will show that it makes at least as much sense to speak of an obligation on the part of organized society to ensure that everyone's just wants are fulfilled—which obligation is, in these instances, carried out by free provision to those and only to those who cannot satisfy their just wants out of their means. Moreover, the common practice of limiting special assistance to those claiming indigency or inability to afford a lawyer, rather than employing a graduated schedule of partial subsidies geared to ability to pay, suggests strongly that fulfillment of just wants exhausts the system's concern." Michelman, *Foreword: On Protecting the Poor Through the Fourteenth Amendment*, 83 HARV. L. REV. 7, 26 (1969).

3. The *Griffin-Douglas* decisions spawned a mass of subsequent decisions in criminal cases which tended to implement and extend its principles. *See* Williams v. Illinois, 399 U.S. 235 (1970); Tate v. Short, 401 U.S. 395 (1971); Mayer v. Chicago, 404 U.S. 189 (1971). *But see* Ross v. Moffitt, 417 U.S. 600, (1974), holding

that a state need not provide free counsel to indigents for discretionary appeals.

## JAMES v. VALTIERRA
Supreme Court of the United States
402 U.S. 137, 28 L. Ed. 2d 678, 91 S. Ct. 1331 (1971)

Justice BLACK delivered the opinion of the Court.

. . . The Article [XXXIV of the California Constitution] provided that no low-rent housing project should be developed, constructed or acquired in any manner by a state public body until the project was approved by a majority of those voting at a community election.

The present suits were brought by citizens of San Jose, California, and San Mateo County, localities where housing authorities could not apply for federal funds because low-cost housing proposals had been defeated in referendums. . . . A three-judge court held that Article XXXIV denied the plaintiffs equal protection of the laws and it enjoined its enforcement. 313 F. Supp. 1 (N.D. Cal. 1970). . . . For the reasons that follow, we reverse.

. . . .

While the District Court cited several cases of this Court, its chief reliance plainly rested on *Hunter v. Erickson* [text, p. 582]. . . . The court below erred in relying on *Hunter* to invalidate Article XXXIV. Unlike the case before us, *Hunter* rested on the conclusion that Akron's referendum law denied equal protection by placing "special burdens on racial minorities within the governmental process." . . .

Unlike the Akron referendum provision, it cannot be said that California's Article XXXIV rests on "distinctions based on race." The Article requires referendum approval for any low-rent public housing project, not only for projects which will be occupied by a racial minority. And the record here would not support any claim that a law seemingly neutral on its face is in fact aimed at a racial minority. Cf. Gomillion v. Lightfoot, 364 U.S. 339 (1960). The present case could be affirmed only by extending *Hunter,* and this we decline to do.

California's entire history demonstrates the repeated use of referendums to give citizens a voice on questions of public policy. A referendum provision was included in the first state constitution and referendums have been a commonplace occurrence in the State's active political life. Provisions for referendums demonstrate devotion to democracy, not to bias, discrimination, or prejudice. Nonetheless, appellees contend that Article XXXIV denies them equal protection because it demands a mandatory referendum while many other referendums only take place upon citizen initiative. They suggest that the mandatory nature of the Article XXXIV referendum constitutes unconstitutional discrimination because it hampers persons desiring public housing from achieving their objective when no such roadblock faces other groups seeking to influence other public decisions to their advantage. But of course a lawmaking procedure that "disadvantages" a particular group does not always deny equal protection. Under any such holding, presumably a State would not be able to require referendums on any subject unless referendums were required on all, because they would always disadvantage some group. And this Court would be required to analyze governmental structures to determine whether a gubernatorial veto provision or a filibuster rule is likely to "disadvantage" any of the diverse and shifting groups that make up the American people.

No special disadvantage for minorities because of referendum

Furthermore, an examination of California law reveals that persons advocating low-income housing have not been singled out for mandatory referendums while no other group must face that obstacle. Mandatory referendums are required for approval of state constitutional amendments, for the issuance of general obligation long-term bonds by local governments, and for certain municipal territorial annexations. . . .

The people of California have also decided by their own vote to require referendum approval of low-rent public housing projects. This procedure ensures that all the people of a community will have a voice in a decision which may lead to large expenditures of local governmental funds for increased public services and to lower tax revenues. It gives them a voice in decisions that will affect the future development of their own community. This procedure for democratic decision-making does not violate the constitutional command that no State shall deny to any person "the equal protection of the laws."

The judgment of the three-judge court is reversed and the case is remanded for dismissal of the complaint.

Reversed.

Justice DOUGLAS took no part in the consideration or decision of this case.

Justice MARSHALL, whom Justice BRENNAN and Justice BLACKMUN join, dissenting.

Appears neutral on face, but not in fact.

. . . The article explicitly singles out low-income persons to bear its burden. Publicly assisted housing developments designed to accommodate the aged, veterans, state employees, persons of moderate income, or any class of citizens other than the poor, need not be approved by prior referenda.

In my view, Article 34 on its face constitutes invidious discrimination which the Equal Protection Clause of the Fourteenth

Amendment plainly prohibits. "The States, of course, are prohibited by the Equal Protection Clause from discriminating
between 'rich' and 'poor' *as such* in the formulation and application of their laws." Douglas v. California, 372 U.S. 353 (1963).
(Mr. Justice Harlan, dissenting). Article 34 is neither "a law of
general applicability that may affect the poor more harshly than
it does the rich," *ibid,* nor an "effort to redress economic imbalances," *ibid.* It is rather an explicit classification on the basis
of poverty—a suspect classification which demands exacting judicial scrutiny.

The Court, however, chooses to subject the article to no
scrutiny whatsoever and treats the provision as if it contained a
totally benign, technical economic classification. . . . It is far too
late in the day to contend that the Fourteenth Amendment
prohibits only racial discrimination; and to me, singling out
the poor to bear a burden not placed on any other class of
citizens tramples the values that the Fourteenth Amendment was
designed to protect.

I respectfully dissent.

----

### NOTES
#### *The Meaning of Valtierra*

1. What standard of review does the *Valtierra* majority adopt?
Couldn't the California law be read as a racial measure? The
lower court had said: "Although Article XXXIV does not specifically require a referendum for low income projects which will
be predominantly occupied by Negroes or other minority group,
the Equal Protection Clause is violated if a 'special burden' is
placed on those groups by operation of the challenged provision,
if the reality is that the law's impact falls on the minority."

The majority gives no consideration to wealth as a classifying
trait. *See* Comment, *James v. Valtierra: Housing Discrimination
by Referendum?,* 39 U. Chi. L. Rev. 115, 122 (1971). Is there a
wealth classification involved in the case? Is the wealth classification de jure or de facto? Consider the view that "the crucial
distinction as the *majority saw it* [in *Valtierra*], was . . . between
*de jure* race classifications and *de facto* wealth classifications.
When combined with the right to low income housing, *de
facto* wealth discriminations were simply insufficient to merit
strict scrutiny. The latter evaluation would confirm the hypothesis
that in cases where a purposeful wealth discrimination was not
clear in the Court's eyes and where a defense of pricing was
present, the Court has always sought to insure equal access to

some interests and not to others." Comments, *The Evolution of Equal Protection—Education, Municipal Services, and Wealth,* 7 HARV. CIV. RTS.-CIV. LIB. L. REV. 105, 145-46 (1972).

**2.** Is *Valtierra* inconsistent with *Griffin-Douglas*? Arguably the critical factor in distinguishing the cases is the nature of the interest involved, *i.e.,* housing is not of the same stature as fair trials and effective appeals in assuring criminal justice or voting. *See* text, pp. 669-70, on the relation of suspect classifications and fundamental rights.

**3.** Consider the following possible explanation of *Valtierra.* "Of course, one might merely throw up his hands in desperation, arguing that the Burger Court is effectively undermining the egalitarianism of the Warren era. Certainly, the present Court has shown little interest in exploring new avenues of constitutional adjudication and has manifested a far more restrained attitude towards civil liberties claims than its predecessor. To assume that the legal distinctions set forth . . . are the real explanations for a case like *Valtierra* is to ignore the political reality that a power shift in the dominant constitutional philosophy in the Court is well under way." Dienes, *The Progeny of Comstockery—Birth Control Laws Return to Court,* 21 AM. U.L. REV. 1, 107-08 (1971).

**4.** It has been noted that "there is no evidence that the framers [of the fourteenth amendment] were concerned with the distribution of income." Winter, *Poverty, Economic Equality, and the Equal Protection Clause,* 1972 SUP. CT. REV. 41, 98. Discrimination based on wealth was common during the nineteenth century and there is no legislative history supporting the view that the fourteenth amendment was intended to protect the poor as a class. How critical is this factor? Again consider the general language used in the fourteenth amendment.

*wealth classifications equal to racial classifications*

**5.** Do wealth classifications impose a stigma equivalent to racial classifications? It has been argued that there is "considerable evidence that much of American life is organized around a class structure, and that those on the bottom—regardless of their race or ethnic background—are regarded with considerable contempt by those on top." Note, *Exclusionary Zoning and Equal Protection,* 84 HARV. L. REV. 1645, 1655 (1971). *See* E. Banfield, THE UNHEAVENLY CITY: THE NATURE AND THE FUTURE OF OUR URBAN CRISES, 63, 75-76 (1970); *The Supreme Court, 1970 Term,* 85 HARV. L. REV. 3, 40, 129 (1971). On the other hand, it is argued by Professor Winter that the poor are not even an identifiable class—"there is no transcendant income line below which is poverty. The fact is that any person who has less material income than someone else will feel deprived. [T]he poverty problem is a relative inequality problem rather than some sort of absolute affliction." *Poverty,* 1972 SUP. CT. REV., at 98-99.

## 2. Fundamental Rights and Interests

As the previous section on wealth discrimination suggests, concern for inequalities may involve not only the basis on which persons receive benefits or suffer deprivations by law but also the character of the deprivations suffered and the importance of the interests affected by the classification. A fee charged for admission to state recreation facilities may pass constitutional muster even though a fee charged as a pre-condition to voting might fail. Since total social and political equality is impossible and analysis is not to be limited solely to the basis of the classifications, consideration must be given to the character of the inequalities to be tolerated and the character of the inequalities to be mitigated. *See* J. RAWLS, A THEORY OF JUSTICE (1971); Michelman, *Foreword: On Protecting the Poor Through the Fourteenth Amendment,* 83 HARV. L. REV. 7 (1969).

In Skinner v. Oklahoma *ex rel.* Williamson, 316 U.S. 535 (1942), the court struck down a state law providing for sexual sterilization of persons convicted more than twice of felonies involving moral turpitude. While Justice Stone, concurring, urged the use of due process to invalidate the Act, Justice Douglas for the majority, held it violative of equal protection. Among the inequalities in the Act, Justice Douglas emphasized the fact that larceny but not embezzlement was included, even though "the nature of the two crimes is intrinsically the same and they are punishable in the same manner." While purporting to "give Oklahoma that large deference which [previous equal protection cases] requires," Justice Douglas, emphasized that the court was "dealing here with legislation which involves one of the basic civil rights of man. Marriage and procreation are fundamental to the very existence and survival of the race." Simply, the case "touches a sensitive and important area of human rights." In such cases, "strict scrutiny of the classification which a State makes . . . is essential. . . ."

### a. Protecting the Franchise

#### HARPER v. VIRGINIA STATE BD. OF ELECTIONS
Supreme Court of the United States
383 U.S. 663, 16 L. Ed. 2d 169, 86 S. Ct. 1079 (1966)

Justice DOUGLAS delivered the opinion of the Court.

These are suits by Virginia residents to have declared unconstitutional Virginia's poll tax. The three-judge District Court, . . . dismissed the complaint. . . .

While the right to vote in federal elections is conferred by Art. I, § 2, of the Constitution, the right to vote is nowhere expressly mentioned. It is argued that the right to vote in state elections is implicit, particularly by reason of the First Amendment and that it may not constitutionally be conditioned upon the payment of a tax or fee. We do not stop to canvass the relation between voting and political expression. For it is enough to say that once the franchise is granted to the electorate, lines may not be drawn which are inconsistent with the Equal Protection Clause of the Fourteenth Amendment. . . .

We conclude that a State violates the Equal Protection Clause of the Fourteenth Amendment whenever it makes the affluence of the voter or payment of any fee an electoral standard. Voter qualifications have no relation to wealth nor to paying or not paying this or any other tax. Our cases demonstrate that the Equal Protection Clause of the Fourteenth Amendment restrains the States from fixing voter qualifications which invidiously discriminate. . . .

. . . .

. . . For to repeat, wealth or fee paying has, in our view no relation to voting qualifications; the right to vote is too precious, too fundamental to be so burdened or conditioned.

Reversed.

Justice BLACK, dissenting.

. . . A study of our cases shows that this Court has refused to use the general language of the Equal Protection Clause as though it provided a handy instrument to strike down state laws which the Court feels are based on bad governmental policy. The equal protection cases carefully analyzed boil down to the principle that distinctions drawn and even discriminations imposed by state laws do not violate the Equal Protection Clause so long as these distinctions and discriminations are not "irrational," "irrelevant," "unreasonable," "arbitrary," or "invidious." . . . State poll tax legislation can "reasonably," "rationally" and without an "invidious" or evil purpose to injure anyone be found to rest on a number of state policies including (1) the State's desire to collect its revenue, and (2) its belief that voters who pay a poll tax will be interested in furthering the State's welfare when they vote. Certainly it is rational to believe that people may be more likely to pay taxes if payment is a prerequisite to voting. And if history can be a factor in determining the "rationality" of discrimination in a state law, then whatever may be our personal opinion, history is on the side of "rationality" of the State's poll tax policy. Property qualifications existed in the Colonies and were continued by many States after the Constitution was adopted. . . .

. . . .

The Court denies that it is using the "natural-law-due-process formula." . . . I find no statement in the Court's opinion, however, which advances even a plausible argument as to why the alleged discriminations which might possibly be effected by Virginia's poll tax law are "irrational," "unreasonable," "arbitrary," or "invidious" or have no relevance to a legitimate policy which the State wishes to adopt. . . . I can only conclude that the primary, controlling, predominate, if not the exclusive reason for declaring the Virginia law unconstitutional is the Court's deep-seated hostility and antagonism, which I share, to making payment of a tax a prerequisite to voting.

. . . .

Justice HARLAN, whom Justice STEWART joins, dissenting.

. . . .

The Equal Protection Clause prevents States from arbitrarily treating people differently under their laws. Whether any such differing treatment is to be deemed arbitrary depends on whether or not it reflects an appropriate differentiating classification among those affected; the clause has never been thought to require equal treatment of all persons despite differing circumstances. The test evolved by this Court for determining whether an asserted justifying classification exists is whether such a classification can be deemed to be founded on some rational and otherwise constitutionally permissible state policy. This standard reduces to a minimum the likelihood that the federal judiciary will judge state policies in terms of the individual notions and predilections of its own members, and until recently it has been followed in all kinds of "equal protection" cases.

*Reynolds v. Sims,* among its other breaks with the past, also marked a departure from these traditional and wise principles. Unless its "one man, one vote" thesis of state legislative apportionment is to be attributed to the unsupportable proposition that "Equal Protection" simply means indiscriminate equality, it seems inescapable that what *Reynolds* really reflected was but this Court's own views of how modern American representative government should be run. For it can hardly be thought that no other method of apportionment may be considered rational.

. . . In substance the Court's analysis of the equal protection issue goes no further than to say that the electoral franchise is "precious" and "fundamental," and to conclude that "[t]o introduce wealth or payment of a fee as a measure of a voter's qualifications is to introduce a capricious or irrelevant factor." These are of course captivating phrases, but they are wholly inadequate to satisfy the standard governing adjudication of the equal protection issue: Is there a rational basis for Virginia's poll tax as a voting qualification? I think the answer to that question is undoubtedly "yes."

. . . .

Property and poll-tax qualifications, very simply, are not in accord with current egalitarian notions of how a modern democracy should be organized. It is of course entirely fitting that legislatures should modify the law to reflect such changes in popular attitudes. However, it is all wrong, in my view, for the Court to adopt the political doctrines popularly accepted at a particular moment of our history and to declare all others to be irrational and invidious, barring them from the range of choice by reasonably minded people acting through the political process. It was not too long ago that Mr. Justice Holmes felt impelled to remind the Court that the Due Process Clause of the Fourteenth Amendment does not enact the laissez-faire theory of society, Lochner v. New York, 198 U.S. 45. The times have changed, and perhaps it is appropriate to observe that neither does the Equal Protection Clause of that Amendment rigidly impose upon America an ideology of unrestrained egalitarianism.

I would affirm the decision of the District Court.

---

## NOTES

1. *Suspect Classification?* Is *Harper* a suspect classification case? Are poll taxes racially discriminatory? Do they classify on the basis of wealth? Is it a problem of de jure or de facto classification? Would *Harper* bar a fee for voting graduated by ability to pay? Consider Professor Michelman's assertion: "Nowhere in *Harper* is there any occasion for inference that the poor are, in any more general sense, a judicially favored class or that de facto wealth discriminations are generally disfavored." Michelman, *Foreword: On Protecting the Poor Through the Fourteenth Amendment,* 83 HARV. L. REV. 7, 25 (1969).

2. *Fundamental Interest?* Does *Harper* turn on the importance of the interest which is burdened, *i.e.*, on what is lost? Is there any justification for singling out classifications affecting certain interests for more stringent review? Are some interests more important than others? Consider the claim that the active standard of review provides, "[t]he Court with a means to inform us as to which rights and principles it considers basic and indispensable. Some symbolic ranking of the multitude of claims

pressed in a democracy may be necessary in order to sustain the polity as a meaningful experience." Casper, *Apportionment and the Right to Vote: Standards of Judicial Scrutiny*, 1973 SUP. CT. REV. 1, 31. Does the court have special competence in determining what are critical personal interests?

3. *Voting as Fundamental.* Is voting a fundamental right? Is it a constitutional right? In Wesberry v. Sanders, 376 U.S. 1, 17 (1964), Justice Black said: "Other rights, even the most basic, are illusory if the right to vote is undermined." Consider also the language of the court in Reynolds v. Sims, 377 U.S. 533, 561-62 (1964), that "the right to exercise the franchise in a free and unimpaired manner is preservative of other basic civil and political rights. . . ." It has been suggested that voting has a special relation to first amendment rights. "Voting is the institutionalized means for the people to express their consent, and it is, therefore, the continuous process by which the people participate in the legitimization of government and in the peaceable assembly and association of individuals in the body politic. The assembly of votes together is a means of association, involving elements of speech, assembly and petition and demonstrating the cognate nature of these rights and their function, in practice, of giving effect to political expression." Cocanower & Rich, *Residency Requirements for Voting*, 12 ARIZ. L. REV. 477, 508 (1970). This perspective suggests that "[a]ny restriction on a person's ability to participate in a political process must be carefully scrutinized in a society where basic decisions are made and gain acceptability through the political mechanisms of a representative democracy." *Developments in the Law—Equal Protection*, 82 HARV. L. REV. 1065, 1129 (1969).

4. *Suspect Classifications and Fundamental Interests.* But in Lassiter v. Northampton County Bd. of Elections, 360 U.S. 45 (1959), the court upheld state literacy requirements for voting against equal protection attack in the absence of any showing of discriminatory use of the test. Justice Douglas for the majority spoke of the "broad powers [of the states] to determine the conditions under which the right of suffrage may be exercised. . . ." He suggested that "[r]esidence requirements, age, previous criminal record . . . are obvious examples indicating factors" which a state might consider in determining voter qualification. And he concluded that "[t]he ability to read and write likewise has some relation to standards designed to promote intelligent use of the ballot." *See* Oregon v. Mitchell, text, pp. 1099-1100, on the use of literacy tests.

Would imposition of a poll tax *on indigents* promote the state interests cited by the dissent in *Harper?* It is certainly arguable that the majority rationale does not support invalidation of the poll tax but only its application to indigents. Why then is a poll tax an impermissable qualification on voting? The court in *Harper* is not saying all qualifications on the franchise are impermissible but rather that they are subject to strict scrutiny. What standard of review would be applied in determining the validity of charging an indigent a fee for a driver's license? What is the relation of the classifying trait and the character of the interest involved in determining the standard of review? *See Developments in the Law—Equal Protection,* 82 HARV. L. REV. 1065, 1120-21 (1969).

## KRAMER v. UNION FREE SCHOOL DIST.
Supreme Court of the United States
395 U.S. 621, 23 L. Ed. 2d 583, 89 S. Ct. 1886 (1969)

Chief Justice WARREN delivered the opinion of the Court.

In this case we are called on to determine whether § 2012 of the New York Education Law is constitutional. The legislation provides that in certain New York school districts residents who are otherwise elegible to vote in state and federal elections may vote in the school district election only if they (1) own (or lease) taxable real property within the district, or (2) are parents (or have custody of) children enrolled in the local public schools. Appellant, a bachelor who neither owns nor leases taxable real property, filed suit in federal court claiming that § 2012 denied him equal protection. . . . With one judge dissenting, a three-judge District Court dismissed appellant's complaint. Finding that § 2012 does violate the Equal Protection Clause of the Fourteenth Amendment, we reverse.

. . . .

. . . All members of the community have an interest in the quality and structure of public education, appellant says, and he urges that "the decisions taken by the local boards . . . may have grave consequences to the entire population." Appellant also argues that the level of property taxation affects him, even though he does not own property, as property tax levels affect the price of goods and services in the community.

We turn therefore to question whether the exclusion is necessary to promote a compelling state interest. First appellees argue that the State has a legitimate interest in limiting the franchise in school district elections to "members of the community of interest"—those "primarily interested in such elections." Second, appellees urge that the State may reasonably and permissibly conclude that "property taxpayers" (including lessees of taxable property who share the tax burden through rent payments) and parents of the children enrolled in the district's schools are those "primarily interested" in school affairs.

. . . .

We need express no opinion as to whether the State in some circumstances might limit the exercise of the franchise to those "primarily interested" or "primarily affected." Of course, we therefore do not reach the issue of whether these particular elections are of the type in which the franchise may be so limited. For, assuming *arguendo* that New York legitimately might limit the franchise in these school district elections to those "primarily interested in school affairs," close scrutiny of the § 2012 classifications demonstrates that they do not accomplish this purpose with sufficient precision to justify denying appellant the franchise.

Whether classifications allegedly limiting the franchise to those resident citizens "primarily interested" deny those excluded equal protection of the law depends, *inter alia,* on whether all those excluded are in fact substantially less interested or affected than those the statute includes. In other words, the classifications must be tailored so that the exclusion of appellant and members of his class is necessary to achieve the articulated state goal. Section 2012 does not meet the exacting standard of precision we require of statutes which selectively distribute the franchise. The classifications in § 2012 permit inclusion of many persons who have, at best, a remote and indirect interest, in school affairs and on the other hand, exclude others who have a distinct and direct interest in the school meeting decisions.

Nor do appellees offer any justification for the exclusion of seemingly interested and informed residents—other than to argue that the § 2012 classifications include those "whom the State could understandably deem to be the most intimately interested in actions taken by the school board," and urge that "the task . . . balancing the interest of the community in the maintenance of orderly school district elections against the interest of any individual in voting in such elections should clearly remain with the legislature." But the issue is not whether the legislative judgments are rational. A more exacting standard obtains. The issue is whether the § 2012 requirements do in fact sufficiently further a compelling state interest to justify denying the franchise to appellant and members of his class. The requirements of § 2012 are not sufficiently tailored to limiting the franchise to those "primarily interested" in school affairs to justify the denial of the franchise to appellant and members of his class.

The judgment . . . is therefore reversed. . . .

. . . .

Justice STEWART with whom Justice BLACK, and Justice HAR-
LAN join, dissenting.

. . . .

---

## NOTES

1. Any doubt left by *Harper* that voting is a "fundamental
right" requiring strict judicial scrutiny and a more exacting
standard of state justification is dispelled by *Kramer.* Is the fact
that *Kramer* deals with a special purpose rather than a general
purpose election as in *Harper* relevant in determining the proper
mode of review? Should the presumption of constitutionality
apply in such a case? It has been argued that the conflict of interest argued in legislative apportionment cases as a basis for rejecting the presumption of constitutionality is not equally applicable
in cases like *Kramer,* since "the determinations concerning the
qualifications and circumstances for voting are not made by the
same governmental entity affected by the substantive content of
those decisions. Voter qualifications for school districts in New
York are the province of the state legislature and not the school
districts." Lee, *Mr. Herbert Spencer and the Bachelor Stock
Broker: Kramer v. Union Free School District No. 15,* 15 ARIZ.
L. REV. 457, 463 (1973).

2. Is it permissible to limit the franchise to those "primarily
interested"? "Although the Court did not make the point, it is
the central tenet of democracy that all citizens are in some fashion
'interested' in the affairs of their government. When a state purports to distinguish its citizens as to degrees of electoral 'interest,'
democratic values must call that effort into serious question."
*The Supreme Court, 1968 Term,* 83 HARV. L. REV. 7, 79 (1969).

Assuming that a state has a compelling interest in limiting
the franchise to those "primarily interested," is it possible to draw
precise lines in defining this class? How is "interest" to be measured? Is it subjective? Objective? Is the concern with comparative
interest among citizens or with the interest of the particular
complaining class in the election? Are property tests ever a permissible basis for measuring interest?

In determining whether even to use strict scrutiny, should
the Court first consider whether "it may not be appropriate to
give the disenfranchised citizen political influence in the unit or
decision in question because he is not affected by that unit or
decision to the same degree. . . . [A] restriction on the franchise
in an election involving a local government unit the activities of
which have varying degrees of impact may be a less serious violation of the interest in representative government than severe mal-

apportionment of districts in a general governing unit." Note, *Salyer Land Co. v. Tulare Lake Basin Water Storage District (93 Sup. Ct. 1224): Opening the Floodgates in Local Special Government Elections,* 72 MICH. L. REV. 868, 879 (1974). Or is the mere fact that the franchise is not extended to the class represented by the litigant itself sufficient to impose the heavy burden of justification?

5. In Phoenix v. Kolodziejski, 399 U.S. 204 (1970), the court, per Justice White, held that equal protection is violated when a state restricts the franchise to property owners in elections to approve the issuance of general obligation municipal improvement bonds, even though the bonds were to be serviced primarily through property taxes. Justice White noted: "All residents of Phoenix, property owners and nonproperty owners alike, have a substantial interest in the public facilities and the services available in the city and will be substantially affected by the ultimate outcome of the bond election at issue in this case. Presumptively, when all citizens are affected in important ways by a government decision subject to a referendum, the Constitution does not permit weighted voting or the exclusion of otherwise qualified citizens from the franchise." Further, other city revenues could be used to retire the bonds. But even if this were not the case, Justice White reasoned, "[a] significant part of the ultimate burden of each year's tax on rental property will very likely be borne by the tenant rather than the landlord since . . . the landlord will treat the property tax as a business expense and normally will be able to pass all or a large part of this cost on to the tenant in the form of a higher rent." Similarly, property taxes on commercial property, "[w]ill be treated as a cost of doing business and will normally be reflected in the prices of goods and services. . . ." *See* Ciprano v. Houma, 395 U.S. 701 (1969).

6. But in *Salyer Land Co. v. Tulare Lake Basin Water Storage Dist.,* 410 U.S. 719 (1973), the court, per Justice Rehnquist, upheld a law permitting only landowners to vote in water storage district general elections and apportioning votes in those elections according to the assessed valuation of land. The court concluded that the water storage district "by reason of its special limited purpose and of the disproportionate effect of its activities on landowners as a group" was an exception to the *Kramer* requirements.

Although recognizing that the water district was vested with some typical governmental powers, *e.g.,* sovereign immunity, eminent domain powers, Justice Rehnquist argued that, apart from its distribution of water, it provided "no other general public services such as schools, housing, transportation, utilities, road or anything else of the type ordinarily financed by a munici-

pal body." He went on to argue that "not only does the district
not exercise what might be thought of as 'normal governmental'
authority, but its actions disproportionately affects landowners.
All of the costs of district projects are assessed against land by
assessors in proportion to the benefits received." Thus there was
"no way that the economic burdens of district operations can
fall on residents *qua* residents, and the operations of the districts
primarily effect the land within their boundaries."

Applying the traditional equal protection standards, Justice
Rehnquist reasoned that "landowners as a class were to bear the
entire burden of the district's costs, and the State could conclude
that they to the exclusion of residents should be charged with
responsibility for its operation." Turning to the exclusion of
lessees, Justice Rehnquist found justification in the short term
character of the lessees' interests and their ability to bargain for a
right to vote at the time that the lease was negoiated. Finally,
" 'the benefits and burden to each landowner in the district are in
proportion to the assessed value of the land' " the court could not
say that the weighted vote provisions were not rationally based.
Justice Douglas, joined by Justices Brennan and Marshall, dissented, arguing that the activities of the district in irrigation,
water storage, the building of levees, and flood control are "important governmental functions" which "implicate the entire
community." Are all special district elections exempted from the
*Kramer* requirement? *See* Note, 72 MICH. L. REV., at 883-84
(1974).

7.    Consider also recent developments in the reapportionment
area. In Mahan v. Howell, 410 U.S. 315 (1973), for example, the
court permitted a 16.4 per cent variation from numerical equality
in a state apportionment scheme in order to maintain historic
political boundaries. And in White v. Regester, 412 U.S. 755
(1973), a 9.9 per cent variation was permitted without even
requiring justification. In Gaffney v. Cummings, 412 U.S. 735
(1973), the court stated: "It is now time to recognize . . . that
minor deviations from mathematical equality among state legislative districts are insufficient to make out a prima facie case . . . so
as to require justification by the State." The court has, however,
been more stringent in applying one-man, one-vote principles to
congressional districting. *See, e.g.,* White v. Weiser, 412 U.S. 783
(1973).

The court has sustained multi-member districts against the
claim that they *per se* violate equal protection, stating that in
each case "the challenger [must] carry the burden of proving that
multi-member districts unconstitutionally operate to dilute or
cancel the voting strength of racial or political elements." Whit-

comb v. Chavis, 403 U.S. 124 (1971). However, a lower court holding that multi-member districting schemes did invidiously exclude blacks and Mexican-Americans was upheld. *See* White v. Regester, 412 U.S. 755 (1973). In Gordon v. Lance, 403 U.S. 1 (1971), the court upheld a requirement of 60 per cent approval in bond and tax elections. *See* Casper, *Apportionment and the Right to Vote: Standards of Judicial Scrutiny,* 1973 SUP. CT. REV. 1.

On the voting rights of prisoners and ex-felons, see Richardson v. Ramirez, 418 U.S. 24 (1974); O'Brien v. Skinner, 414 U.S. 524 (1974); McDonald v. Board of Election Comm'rs, 394 U.S. 802 (1969).

### Residency and Durational Residency Requirements

1. The Supreme Court has not clearly and directly held that bona fide residency requirements for voting are constitutional. But the court has frequently indicated the validity of such requirements. *See* Kramer v. Union Free School Dist. No. 15; Carrington v. Rash, 380 U.S. 89 (1965); Pope v. Williams, 193 U.S. 621 (1904). In Dunn v. Blumstein, 405 U.S. 330 (1972), for example, the court stated: "An appropriately defined and uniformly applied requirement of bona fide residence may be necessary to preserve the basic conception of a political community, and therefore could withstand close constitutional scrutiny." Are such requirements necessary in order to identify voters so as to prevent fraud? To promote a more intelligent vote? To assure a voter's membership and interest in the community? Macleod & Wilberding, *State Voting Residency Requirements and Civil Rights,* 38 GEO. WASH. L. REV. 93 (1969). *See* Evans v. Cornman, 398 U.S. 419 (1970), holding that residents of the National Institutes of Health, a federal enclave in Maryland, could not constitutionally be denied the franchise on non-residency grounds since such persons, "have a stake equal to that of other Maryland residents" and therefore, "they are entitled under the Fourteenth Amendment to protect that stake by exercising the equal right to vote."

2. *Durational Residency.* A requirement that a person be a resident of the state for a year and of the county for three months was held violative of equal protection in Dunn v. Blumstein, 405 U.S. 330 (1972). Justice Marshall, for the court, used the strict scrutiny standard of review because, "[b]y denying some citizens the right to vote, such laws deprive them of 'a fundamental political right,' . . . preservative of all rights" and because such a durational residency requirement, "directly impinges on the exercise of a second fundamental personal right, the right to travel." *See* text, p. 683. The fact that the vote was denied while

travel was only penalized was deemed irrelevant to the decision. Therefore, "durational residence laws must be measured by a strict equal protection test: they are unconstitutional unless the State can demonstrate that such laws are '*necessary* to promote a *compelling* governmental interest.' "

Using this standard, the court considered the state interests in assuring the "purity of the ballot box" and having "knowledgeable voters." While admitting that "the prevention of fraud is a legitimate and compelling government goal," the court found it impossible to view durational residency requirements as necessary to achieve that state interest. "Fixing a constitutionally acceptable period is surely a matter of degree. It is sufficient to note here that 30 days appears to be an ample period of time for the State to complete whatever administrative tasks are necessary to prevent fraud—and a year, or three months, too much." The use of a conclusive presumption, rather than individualized inquiry, to assure bona fide residence was deemed too drastic a means of achieving the state interest.

Similarly, the use of such conclusive presumption to assure knowledgeable voters was, "much too crude," and the relationship between the state interest in an informed electorate and durational residency requirements was "too attenuated." Justice Marshall explained: "The classifications created by durational residence requirements obviously permit any long time resident to vote regardless of his knowledge of the issues—and obviously many long time residents do not have any. On the other hand, the classifications bar from the franchise many other, admittedly new, residents who have become at least minimally, and often fully, informed about the issues. . . ." Does this reasoning apply equally to bona fide residence requirements? *See The Supreme Court, 1971 Term, Foreword: In Search of Evolving Doctrine on a Changing Court: A Model for a Newer Equal Protection,* 86 HARV. L. REV. 1, 109 (1972). *See generally* Cocanower & Rich, *Residency Requirements for Voting,* 12 ARIZ. L. REV. 477 (1970).

Chief Justice Burger, dissenting, argued that "some lines must be drawn. To challenge such lines by the 'compelling state interest' standard is to condemn them all. So far as I am aware, no state law has ever satisfied this seemingly insurmountable standard, and I doubt one ever will, for it demands nothing less than perfection."

In the 1970 Voting Rights Act, Congress banned state durational residency requirements and imposed a 30-day minimum registration closing requirement for presidential and vice-presidential elections. *See Oregon v. Mitchell,* text, pp. 1100-1101.

**3.** But one year later, in Marston v. Lewis, 410 U.S. 679 (1973), the court, per curiam, upheld Arizona's 50-day durational voting residency requirement and 50-day voter registration cut-off requirement. Noting the frequency of mistakes by volunteer registrars and the close timing of primaries and general elections, the court found, "a recent and amply justifiable [state] judgment that 50 days rather than 30 is necessary to promote the State's important interest in accurate voter lists. The Constitution is not so rigid that that determination and others like it may not stand." Justice Marshall, dissented, arguing that *Dunn* indicated that a 30-day residency requirement "provided the State with 'an ample period of time . . . to complete whatever administrative tasks are necessary to prevent fraud' in the process of voter registration." He accepted the district court's conclusion that the state had failed to meet its "heavy burden" of justification "in light of reasonably available and less restrictive alternatives." *See* Burns v. Fortson, 410 U.S. 686 (1973), discussed *infra*.

**4.** On the use of registration requirements as a condition for voting, see Kusper v. Pontikes, 414 U.S. 51 (1973); Rosario v. Rockefeller, 410 U.S. 752 (1973); Burns v. Fortson, 410 U.S. 686 (1973). The state may not constitutionally "lock" the voter into a party affiliation. It may not "substantially restrict" the freedom to associate with a party of one's choice. But a limited registration period is a valid means of assuring an orderly election, free from fraud.

### b. The Right to Travel

### SHAPIRO v. THOMPSON

Supreme Court of the United States
394 U.S. 618, 22 L. Ed. 2d 600, 89 S. Ct. 1322 (1969)

Justice BRENNAN delivered the opinion of the Court.

These three appeals were restored to the calendar for re-argument. Each is an appeal from a decision of a three-judge District Court holding unconstitutional a State or District of Columbia statutory provision which denies welfare assistance to residents of the State or District who have not resided within their jurisdictions for at least one year immediately preceding their applications for such assistance. We affirm the judgments of the District Courts in the three cases.

. . . .

There is no dispute that the effect of the waiting-period requirement in each case is to create two classes of needy resident families indistinguishable from each other except that one is composed of residents who have resided a year or more, and the second of residents who have resided less than a year, in the jurisdiction. On the basis of this sole difference the first class is granted and the second class is denied welfare aid upon which may depend the ability of the families to obtain the very means to subsist—food, shelter, and other necessities of life. In each case, the District Court found that appellees met the test for residence in their jurisdictions, as well as all other eligibility requirements except the requirement of residence for a full year prior to their applications. On reargument, appellees' central contention is that the statutory prohibition of benefits to residents of less than a year creates a classification which constitutes an invidious discrimination denying them equal protection of the laws. We agree. The interests which appellants assert are promoted by the classification either may not constitutionally be promoted by government or are not compelling governmental interests.

Primarily, appellants justify the waiting-period requirement as a protective device to preserve the fiscal integrity of state public assistance programs. It is asserted that people who require welfare assistance during their first year of residence in a State are likely to become continuing burdens on state welfare programs. Therefore, the argument runs, if such people can be deterred from entering the jurisdiction by denying them welfare benefits during the first year, state programs to assist longtime residents will not be impaired by a substantial influx of indigent newcomers.

. . . .

We do not doubt that the one-year waiting period device is well suited to discourage the influx of poor families in need of assistance. An indigent who desires to migrate, resettle, find a new job, start a new life will doubtless hesitate if he knows that he must risk making the move without the possibility of falling back on state welfare assistance during his first year of residence, when his need may be most acute. But the purpose of inhibiting migration by needy persons into the State is constitutionally impermissible.

This Court long ago recognized that the nature of our Federal Union and our constitutional concepts of personal liberty unite to require that all citizens be free to travel throughout the length and breadth of our land uninhibited by statutes, rules, or regulations which unreasonably burden or restrict this movement. . . .

We have no occasion to ascribe the source of this right to travel interstate to a particular constitutional provision. [See United States v. Guest, text, p. 1066.] . . .

Thus, the purpose of deterring the in-migration of indigents cannot serve as justification for the classification created by the one-year waiting period, since that purpose is constitutionally impermissible. . . .

Alternatively, appellants argue that even if it is impermissible for a State to attempt to deter the entry of all indigents, the challenged classification may be justified as a permissible state attempt to discourage those indigents who would enter the State solely to obtain larger benefits. We observe first that none of the statutes before us is tailored to serve that objective. Rather, the class of barred newcomers is all-inclusive, lumping the great majority who come to the State for other purposes with those who come for the sole purpose of collecting higher benefits. . . .

More fundamentally, a State may no more try to fence out those indigents who seek higher welfare benefits than it may try to fence out indigents generally. Implicit in any such distinction is the notion that indigents who enter a State with the hope of securing higher welfare benefits are somehow less deserving than indigents who do not take this consideration into account. But we do not perceive why a mother who is seeking to make a new life for herself and her children should be regarded as less deserving because she considers, among others factors, the level of a State's public assistance. Surely such a mother is no less deserving than a mother who moves into a particular State in order to take advantage of its better educational facilities.

Appellants argue further that the challenged classification may be sustained as an attempt to distinguish between new and old residents on the basis of the contribution they have made to the community through the payment of taxes. We have difficulty seeing how long-term residents who qualify for welfare are making a greater present contribution to the State in taxes than indigent residents who have recently arrived. . . . Appellants' reasoning would logically permit the State to bar new residents from schools, parks, and libraries or deprive them of police and fire protection. Indeed it would permit the State to apportion all benefits and services according to the past tax contributions of its citizens. The Equal Protection Clause prohibits such an apportionment of state services.

. . . .

In sum, neither deterrence of indigents from migrating to the State nor limitation of welfare benefits to those regarded as contributing to the State is a constitutionally permissible state objective.

Appellants next advance as justification certain administrative and related governmental objectives allegedly served by the waiting-period requirement. They argue that the requirement (1) facilitates the planning of the welfare budget; (2) provides an objective test of residency; (3) minimizes the opportunity for recipients fraudulently to receive payments from more than one jurisdiction; and (4) encourages early entry of new residents into the labor force.

. . . .

We conclude . . . that appellants in these cases do not use and have no need to use the one-year requirement for the governmental purposes suggested. Thus, even under traditional equal protection tests a classification of welfare applicants according to whether they have lived in the State for one year would seem irrational and unconstitutional. But, of course, the traditional criteria do not apply in these cases. Since the classification here touches on the fundamental right of interstate movement, its constitutionality must be judged by the stricter standard of whether it promotes a *compelling* state interest. Under this standard, the waiting period requirement clearly violates the Equal Protection Clause.

[The Court held that the Social Security Act had not approved use of such waiting periods.]

The waiting-period requirement in the District of Columbia Code . . . violates the Due Process Clause of the Fifth Amendment. . . .

Affirmed.

Chief Justice WARREN, with whom Justice BLACK joins, dissenting.

. . . .

Justice HARLAN, dissenting.

. . . .

The "compelling interest" doctrine, which today is articulated more explicitly than ever before, constitutes an increasingly significant exception to the long-established rule that a statute does not deny equal protection if it is rationally related to a legitimate governmental objective. The "compelling interest" doctrine has two branches. The branch which requires that classifications based upon "suspect" criteria be supported by a compelling interest apparently had its genesis in cases involving racial classifications, which have . . . been regarded as inherently "suspect." The criterion of "wealth" apparently was added to the list of "suspects" as an alternative justification for the rationale in *Harper v. Virginia Bd. of Elections*. . . . The criterion of political allegiance may have been added in Williams v. Rhodes, 393 U.S. 23, (1968). Today the list apparently has been further enlarged to include classifications based upon recent interstate movement, and perhaps those based upon the exercise of *any* constitutional right. . . .

I think that this branch of the "compelling interest" doctrine is sound when applied to racial classifications, for historically the Equal Protection Clause was largely a product of the desire to eradicate legal distinctions founded upon race. . . .

The second branch of the "compelling interest" principle is even more troublesome. For it has been held that a statutory classification is subject to the "compelling interest" test if the result of the classification may be to affect a "fundamental right," regardless of the basis of the classification. . . .

*[margin note: fundamental right]*

I think this branch of the "compelling interest" doctrine particularly unfortunate and unnecessary. It is unfortunate because it creates an exception which threatens to swallow the standard equal protection rule. Virtually every state statute affects important rights. This Court has repeatedly held, for example, that the traditional equal protection standard is applicable to statutory classifications affecting such fundamental matters as the right to pursue a particular occupation, the right to receive greater or smaller wages or to work more or less hours, and the right to inherit property. Rights such as these are in principle indistinguishable from those involved here, and to extend the "compelling interest" rule to all cases in which such rights are affected would go far toward making this Court a "super-legislature." This branch of the doctrine is also unnecessary. When the right affected is one assured by the federal Constitution, any infringement can be dealt with under the Due Process Clause. But when a statute affects only matters not mentioned in the federal Constitution and is not arbitrary or irrational, I must reiterate that I know of nothing which entitles this Court to pick out particular human activities, characterize them as "fundamental," and give them added protection under an unusually stringent equal protection test.

*[margin note: giving added protection to so called "fundamental" rights creates super-legislature of the court.]*

. . . If the issue is regarded purely as one of equal protection, then for the reasons just set forth this nonracial classification should be judged by ordinary equal protection standards. . . .

. . . [A] legislature might rationally find that the imposition of a welfare residence requirement would aid in the accomplishment of at least four valid governmental objectives. It might also find that residence requirements have advantages not shared by other methods of achieving the same goals. In light of this undeniable relation of residence requirements to valid legislative aims, it cannot be said that the requirements are "arbitrary" or "lacking in rational justification." Hence, I can find no objection to these residence requirements under the Equal Protection Clause of the Fourteenth Amendment or under the analogous standard embodied in the Due Process Clause of the Fifth Amendment.

The next issue, which I think requires fuller analysis than that deemed necessary by the Court under its equal protection rationale, is whether a one-year welfare residence requirement amounts to an undue burden upon the right of interstate travel. . . .

The initial problem is to identify the source of the right to travel asserted by the appellees. . . .

. . . .

Opinions of this Court and of individual Justices have suggested four provisions of the Constitution as possible sources of a right to travel enforceable against the federal or state governments: the Commerce Clause; the Privileges and Immunities Clause of Art. IV, § 2; the Privileges and Immunities Clause of the Fourteenth Amendment; and the Due Process Clause of the Fifth Amendment. . . .

. . . .

*fundamental rights must be stated in Constitution*

. . . I conclude that the right to travel interstate is a "fundamental" right which, for present purposes, should be regarded as having its source in the Due Process Clause of the Fifth Amendment.

The next questions are: (1) To what extent does a one-year residence condition upon welfare eligibility interfere with this right to travel?; and (2) What are the governmental interests supporting such a condition? . . . The number or proportion of persons who are actually deterred from changing residence by the existence of these provisions is unknown. If one accepts evidence put forward by the appellees, to the effect that there would be only a miniscule increase in the number of welfare applicants were existing residence requirements to be done away with, it follows that the requirements do not deter an appreciable number of persons from moving interstate.

Against this indirect impact on the right to travel must be set the interests in imposing residence conditions. . . .

---

## NOTES

1. *The Right to Travel.* While the right to travel was specifically recognized in the Articles of Confederation, it is not mentioned in the Constitution. Nevertheless, the court has consistently recognized its existence. *See* Z. CHAFEE, THREE HUMAN

RIGHTS IN THE CONSTITUTION OF 1787 (1956); Boudin, *The Constitutional Right to Travel*, 56 COLUM. L. REV. 47 (1956). But, as in *Shapiro,* the Court has not specified its source. It has been suggested that "[t]he common thread running through all opinions and discussions on the right to travel is the belief that the right is inherent in the concept of the Federal Union. While this concept may be implicit in the commerce clause and the privileges and immunities clauses, no specific clause in the Constitution created the Federal Union." Note, *Shapiro v. Thompson: Travel, Welfare and the Constitution,* 44 N.Y.U. L. Rev. 989, 999 (1969). *See* Note, *Residence Requirements after Shapiro v. Thompson,* 70 COLUM L. REV. 134, 137-39 (1970).

Does *Shapiro* hold that the right to travel is an independent and fundamental constitutional guarantee? Does the decision rest on the importance of the welfare interests at stake? On a right to welfare? Why didn't the court strike down the requirement on right to travel grounds alone without invoking the equal protection clause? It has been suggested that "[b]y invalidating the residence requirement on equal protection grounds, rather than on right to travel grounds alone, the *Shapiro* decision must ultimately be viewed in terms of the benefit underlying the unconstitutional classification." Note, 44 N.Y.U. L. REV., at 1003.

2. In *Dunn v. Blumstein,* text, p. 675, the court struck down a one-year durational residency requirement for voting. But a 50-day durational residency requirement for voting was subsequently upheld. Marston v. Lewis, 410 U.S. 679 (1973). In Starns v. Malkerson, 326 F. Supp. 234 (D. Minn. 1970), aff'd 401 U.S. 935 (1971), the court summarily affirmed the lower court decision upholding Minnesota's one-year durational residency requirement for receiving in-state tuition benefits and in Vlandis v. Kline, 412 U.S. 441 (1973), text, p. 725, the court again indicated that not all durational residency requirements are constitutional. On a number of occasions, the court has indicated that bona fide residence requirements are constitutional. Yet all of these burden the right to travel.

Is the compelling state interest standard applicable for such burdens? How do you distinguish between permissible and impermissible waiting periods? Does it turn on the value of the interest lost as a result of the requirement? Is *Shapiro* a suspect classification or a fundamental rights case? What is the classifying trait? Wealth? Recent interstate movement?

3. The court considered the applicability of *Shapiro* to a one-year durational residency requirement as a condition to an indigent's receiving non-emergency hospital or medical care at public expense in Memorial Hosp. v. Maricopa County, 415 U.S.

250 (1973). Justice Marshall, for the majority, found *Shapiro* to be controlling and held that the state failed to demonstrate a compelling state interest for burdening the right to interstate travel.

In explaining the scope of *Shapiro*, Justice Marshall noted that the right of travel was involved there only in the limited sense of a right to migrate "with an intent to settle and abide." Not all residency requirements were invalidated even though "a *bona fide* residence requirement would burden the right to travel, if travel meant merely movement." The court in *Shapiro* had not even declared durational residency requirements per se unconstitutional but held that they may not be "penalties" upon the constitutional right to travel. While the "amount of impact required to give rise to the compelling state interest test was not made clear" in *Shapiro*, the court looked at two factors: first, "whether the waiting period would deter migration"; second, the extent to which the residency requirement served to penalize the exercise of the right to travel.

While admitting that there was no evidence of anyone being deterred from migrating by the durational residency requirement in this case, Justice Marshall contended such deterrence was not improbable. In any case, he argued, deterrence was not determinative, since *Dunn* and *Shapiro* established that a "penalty" on the exercise of the right to travel must be justified by a compelling state interest. What was a "penalty" turned on the interest burdened—durational residency requirements for tuition benefits, for example, had not been struck down. Justice Marshall concluded: "Whatever the ultimate parameters of the *Shapiro* penalty analysis, it is at least clear that medical care is as much a 'basic necessity of life' to an indigent as welfare assistance. And, government privileges or benefits necessary to basic sustenance have often been viewed as being of greater constitutional significance than less essential forms of governmental entitlements."

Following lines of analysis similar to those in *Shapiro*, Justice Marshall rejected asserted state interests in fiscal integrity, preserving the quality of services provided and preserving the public support for public facilities, and various administrative objectives, such as facilitating the determination of bona fide residence, preventing fraud and promoting budget predictability, as insufficient to satisfy the heavy burden of justification.

4. But, in Sosna v. Iowa, — U.S. — (1975), the court held 6-3 that a one-year residency requirement for divorce in Iowa is constitutional. Distinguishing *Shapiro*, *Dunn* and *Maricopa County* as involving laws justified only by administrative and budgetary considerations, Justice Rehnquist for the majority held

"that the state interest in requiring that those who seek a divorce from its courts be genuinely attached to the state, as well as a desire to insulate divorce decrees from the likelihood of collateral attack, requires a different resolution of the constitutional issue presented. . . ." He further stressed that the appellant in the present case was not irretrievably foreclosed from obtaining what she sought but was merely delayed. The court similarly rejected a contention that failure to provide an individualized determination of residency violated the fourteenth amendment due process guarantee. *See* text, pp. 721-29. Does the Iowa law impose a "penalty" on the right of interstate travel? Has the court abandoned the compelling interest standard in travel cases?

### c. Access to Justice

#### (1) Access to Criminal Justice

### DOUGLAS v. CALIFORNIA
Supreme Court of the United States
372 U.S. 353, 9 L. Ed. 2d 811, 83 S. Ct. 814 (1963)

[*Douglas* is reprinted in text, p. 658.]

---

### NOTES

1. As indicated in text, p. 660, *Griffin-Douglas* and their progeny involve not only wealth discrimination but important interests of the individual. The cases "can easily be explained as belonging to a family which treats as meriting special support the interest in strong opposition to the state's prosecutorial thrust." Michelman, *Foreword: On Protecting the Poor Through the Fourteenth Amendment,* 83 HARV. L. REV. 7, 25 (1969).

2. If special recognition is given to the interest involved in *Griffin-Douglas* is there any way of distinguishing interests such as education, housing, or medical services? It has been suggested that "basic legal services are not of the same order, in our theory of government, as basic medical services. The provision of applied justice is an essential function of the state even under the most conservative political theory." The authors argue that "[w]e cannot conceive of a man as truly a citizen if he is too poor to have access to the courts. We can, however, conceive of him as truly a citizen if he is too poor to receive adequate medical care." They conclude: "Equal access to the processes of law is embedded in our Constitution and in every democratic constitution, as a necessary element in the relationship between the citizen and his government." Willcox & Bloustein, *The Griffin Case—Poverty and the Fourteenth Amendment,* 43 CORNELL L.Q. 1, 16-17 (1957).

**3.** If we recognize the interest in *Griffin-Douglas* must we also recognize pre-trial and post-conviction interests as fundamental? Is the concern in these cases access to criminal justice or the quality of that access? Is the degree of state involvement in the area important? Consider the argument that "the greater the government preemption of the private market and the fewer the substitutes available, the more likely it should be that a particular right should be labeled fundamental. Where the government has a true economic monopoly, fundamentality might even be presumed." Wheeler, *In Defense of Economic Equal Protection,* 22 U. KAN. L. REV. 1, 11 (1973).

### (2)  Access to Civil Justice

#### BODDIE v. CONNECTICUT
Supreme Court of the United States
401 U.S. 371, 28 L. Ed. 2d 113, 91 S. Ct. 780 (1971)

Justice HARLAN delivered the opinion of the Court.

Appellants, welfare recipients residing in the State of Connecticut, brought this action in the federal district court for the District of Connecticut on behalf of themselves and others similarly situated, challenging, as applied to them, certain state procedures for the commencement of a litigation, including requirements for payment of court fees and costs for service of process [costs averaged $60.00] that restrict their access to the courts in their effort to bring an action for divorce.

. . . .

[A three-judge court denied declaratory and injunctive relief.] We now reverse. Our conclusion is that, given the basic position of the marriage relationship in this society's hierarchy of values and the concomitant state monopolization of the means for legally dissolving this relationship, due process does prohibit the State from denying, solely because of inability to pay, access to its courts to individuals who seek judicial dissolution of their marriages.

. . . .

Reversed.

----

### NOTES

**1.**  *Costs of Litigation.* If fees cannot be used to deny access to the indigent seeking a divorce, what is the status of the other costs of litigation, *e.g.,* court reporters, judgment and execution fees, security bonds, witness fees, costs of briefs, investigation expenses? *See* Note, *Indigent Access to Civil Courts: The Tiger*

*Is at the Gates*, 26 VAND. L. REV. 25, 26-29 (1973); Note, *Litigation Costs: The Hidden Barrier to the Indigent*, 56 GEO. L.J. 516, 517 (1968). Is the problem solely one of access or the ability to meaningfully litigate a claim?

2. *A Right of Access?* Some commentators read *Boddie* as recognizing a right of access to the courts as a fundamental right. *See, e.g.*, LaFrance, *Constitutional Law Reform for the Poor: Boddie v. Connecticut*, 1971 DUKE L.J. 487, 536-37; Abram, *Access to the Judicial Process*, 6 GA. L. REV. 247, 255 (1972). Do the principles relied on by Justice Harlan suggest such a right? What are the values served by civil litigation. Professor Michelman suggests that litigation promotes dignity values (the potential loss a person might suffer if denied an opportunity to vindicate his claims), deterrence values (a means for constraining undesirable social behavior), participation values (a means of exerting influence, expressing one's needs and desires), and effectuation values (a means of realizing one's own interests and needs). Michelman, *The Supreme Court and Litigation Access Fees: The Right to Protect One's Rights—Part I*, 1973 DUKE L.J. 1153, 1172-77. *See* Abram, *Access to the Judicial Process*, 6 GA. L. REV. at 248-251. Is access a right "preservative of all other rights"? Is it analogous to the first amendment? *See* Goodpaster, *The Integration of Equal Protection, Due Process Standards, and the Indigent's Right of Free Access to the Courts*, 56 IOWA L. REV. 223 (1970).

3. Any possibility for an early broadening of *Boddie* into a right of access, suffered a severe setback in two recent Burger Court decisions.

a. In United States v. Kras, 409 U.S. 434 (1973), the court 5-4, per Justice Blackmun, held that a provision of the Bankruptcy Act imposing a $50.00 fee did not violate due process or equal protection protected by the fifth amendment. *Boddie* was distinguished. First the petitioner's "alleged interest in the elimination of his debt burden, and in obtaining his desired new start in life, although important . . . does not rise to the same constitutional level" since "[i]f Kras is not discharged on bankruptcy, his position will not be materially altered in any constitutional sense. Gaining or not gaining a discharge will effect no change with respect to basic necessities." It followed that "no fundamental interest . . . is gained or lost depending on the availability of a discharge of bankruptcy." Further, "the government's control over the establishment, enforcement, or dissolution of debts [is not] nearly so exclusive as Connecticut's control over the marriage relationship in Boddie." Justice Blackmun argued that "[h]owever unrealistic the remedy may be in a particular situation, a debtor, in theory, and often in actuality, may adjust his debts by negotiated agreement with his creditors." Therefore, that "[g]overnment's role with respect to the private commercial relationship is qualitatively and quantitatively different than its role in the establishment, enforcement, and dissolution of marriage."

Nor did the filing fee requirement deny equal protection. "Bankruptcy is hardly akin to free speech or marriage or to those other rights . . . that the Court has come to regard as fundamental and that demand the lofty requirement of a compelling governmental interest before they may be significantly regulated." Further, it does not "touch upon what has been said to be the suspect criteria of race, nationality, or alienage." Rather, Justice Blackmun reasoned "bankruptcy legislation is in the area of economics and social welfare." And, following the court's rationale in *Dandridge v. Williams,* text, p. 690, "the applicable standard, in measuring the propriety of Congress' classification, is that of rational justification." The rational basis for requiring fees was deemed "readily apparent" in Congress' desire to "make the system self-sustaining and paid for by those who use it rather than by tax revenues drawn from the public at large."

b. Less than two months later, the court again distinguished *Boddie.* In Ortwein v. Schwab, 410 U.S. 656 (1973), an indigent petitioner challenged a $25.00 fee as a pre-condition to his ability to appeal to the courts from a welfare agency's reduction of his state old-age assistance benefits. The court held, *per curiam,* that there was "no fundamental interest" involved since the interest of the indigent in increased welfare payments "has far less constitutional significance than the interest of the *Boddie* appellants." Moreover, judicial appeal was not exclusive because the state had provided administrative hearings. "The hearings provide a procedure, not conditioned on payment of any fee, through which appellants have been able to seek redress. This court has long recognized that, even in criminal cases, due process does not require a State to provide an appellate system."

Relying on *Kras* for the proposition that appeal from welfare payment reduction involves "economics and social welfare," the court applied the requirement of rationality in determining the equal protection issue. The state's interest in offsetting the expense of the court system was deemed reason enough for the fee.

Justices Stewart, Douglas, Brennan and Marshall each separately dissented. Justice Douglas noted that the present case was even stronger than *Kras* in justifying an invalidation of the fee because it dealt "not with appellate review of a judicial determination, but with *initial access* to the courts for review of an adverse administrative determination."

c.  What do *Kras* and *Ortwein* do to the claim of a right of access in civil cases? What kinds of cases might still require waiver of fee requirements—custody suits, adoptions, guardianship, housing eviction proceedings?

4.  *State Monopolization.* Justice Harlan in *Boddie* stressed that the *plaintiff* in a divorce action, like a civil *defendant* generally, is "forced to settle" through the use of judicial proceedings. Is this a valid analogy? Do all civil defendants lack alternatives to judicial resolution? Does "monopolization" serve to distinguish divorce plaintiffs from other civil litigants? From the litigants in *Kras*? In *Schwab*?

Is there any basis in the monopoly notion for distinguishing among civil plaintiffs as in *Kras* and *Schwab*? Justice Black, dissenting from a denial of certiorari in Meltzer v. Buck Le Craw & Co., 402 U.S. 954 (1971), argued that if *Boddie* was binding, it could not be meaningfully limited to divorce plaintiffs. How much flexibility does an indigent have in resolving his disputes without litigation? *See* Goodpaster, *The Integration of Equal Protection, Due Process Standards and the Indigent's Right of Free Access to the Courts,* 56 IOWA L. REV., at 234-36.

5.  *Fundamental Interests.* Justice Harlan emphasizes that *Boddie* involved a "fundamental interest." Is this an independent ground for the decision or is "monopolization" also required? Justice Black has argued that "the right to seek a divorce is simply not very 'fundamental' in the hierarchy of disputes. Marriage is one of the cornerstones of our civilized society . . . and since *Boddie* held that the right to a divorce was 'fundamental,' I can only conclude that almost every other kind of legally enforceable right is also fundamental to our society." Meltzer v. Buck Le Craw & Co., 402 U.S. 954, 957. Isn't the interest in vindicating any legal right of "fundamental" importance to the individual?

6.  *Due Process or Equal Protection?* Justice Harlan ignores the equal protection rationale developed in the *Griffin-Douglas* line of cases. As indicated in those decisions and *Harper* and *Shapiro,* Justice Harlan consistently expressed his preference for a due process analysis. Is he using procedural or substantive due process? *See* Comment, *Indigents' Access to Civil Courts,* 4 COLUM. HUM. RTS. L. REV. 267, 297 (1972); Note, *Indigent Access to Civil Courts: The Tiger Is at the Gates,* 26 VAND. L. REV. 25, 41 (1973). Which rationale is preferable? *See* LaFrance, *Constitutional Law Reform for the Poor: Boddie v. Connecticut,* 1971 DUKE L.J., at 528.

## C.  THE RETREAT FROM ACTIVISM

While the Warren Court clearly broke new ground in equal protection doctrine, the revolution was only in a nascent stage when the personnel of the court began to change. With the emergence of the Burger Court, the trend towards expanding the domain of the strict standard of review was halted. Not that there was direct reversal of the precedent. Rather, fine distinctions were drawn and opportunities to extend the governing principles were rejected. The judicial value structure that had provided the impetus for the new directions based on social meliorism was now in the minority on the court.

In the present section, the focus will be on this change of direction and the reasons given for limiting the new equal protection. In examining the cases, consider whether the strict scrutiny standard might have been applied and how the opinion and decision would have been framed. To what extent do the decisions rest on reasoned analysis? On different valuations? What do the decisions suggest for the future growth of equal protection? What new doctrinal principles are being fashioned?

### 1.  Equality in the Welfare System

**DANDRIDGE v. WILLIAMS**

Supreme Court of the United States

397 U.S. 471, 25 L. Ed. 2d 491, 90 S. Ct. 1153 (1970)

Justice STEWART delivered the opinion of the Court.

. . . [Maryland] computes the standard of need for each eligible family based on the number of children in the family and the circumstances under which the family lives. In general, the standard of need increases with each additional person in the household, but the increments become proportionately smaller. The regulation here in issue imposes upon the grant that any single family may receive an upper limit of $250 per month in certain counties including Baltimore City, and of $240 per month elsewhere in the State. The appellees all have large families, so that their standards of need as computed by the State substantially exceed the maximum grants that they actually receive under the regulation. The appellees urged in the District Court that the maximum grant limitation operates to discriminate against them merely because of the size of their families, in violation of the Equal Protection Clause of the Fourteenth Amendment. . . .

[The majority held that the maximum grant does not violate the Social Security Act.]

. . . The District Court, while apparently recognizing the validity of at least some of these state concerns, nonetheless held that the regulation "is invalid on its face for overreaching,"—that it violates the Equal Protection Clause "[b]ecause it cuts too broad a swath on an indiscriminate basis as applied to the entire group of AFDC eligibles to which it purports to apply, . . . ."

If this were a case involving government action claimed to violate the First Amendment guarantee of free speech, a finding of "overreaching" would be significant and might be crucial. For when otherwise valid governmental regulation sweeps so broadly as to impinge upon activity protected by the First Amendment, its very overbreadth may make it unconstitutional. But the concept of "overreaching" has no place in this case. For here we deal with state regulation in the social and economic field, not affecting freedoms guaranteed by the Bill of Rights, and claimed to violate the Fourteenth Amendment only because the regulation results in some disparity in grants of welfare payments to the largest AFDC families. For this Court to approve the invalidation of state economic or social regulation as "overreaching" would be far too reminiscent of an era when the Court thought the Fourteenth Amendment gave it power to strike down state laws "because they may be unwise, improvident, or out of harmony with a particular school of thought." Williamson v. Lee Optical of Oklahoma, Inc., 348 U.S. 483, 488. That era long ago passed into history.

In the area of economics and social welfare, a State does not violate the Equal Protection Clause merely because the classifications made by its laws are imperfect. . . .

To be sure, the cases cited, and many other enunciating this fundamental standard under the Equal Protection Clause, have in the main involved state regulation of business or industry. The administration of public welfare assistance, by contrast, involves the most basic economic needs of impoverished human beings. We recognize the dramatically real factual difference between the cited cases and this one, but we can find no basis for applying a different constitutional standard. It is a standard that has consistently been applied to state legislation restricting the availability of employment opportunities. Goesaert v. Cleary, 335 U.S. 464; Kotch v. Board of River Port Pilot Com'rs, 330 U.S. 552. And it is a standard that is true to the principle that the Fourteenth Amendment gives the federal courts no power to impose upon the States their views of wise economic or social policy.

Under this long-established meaning of the Equal Protection Clause, it is clear that the Maryland maximum grant regulation is constitutionally valid. We need not explore all the reasons that the State advances in justification of the regulation. It is enough that a solid foundation for the regulation can be found in the State's legitimate interest in encouraging employment and in avoiding discrimination between welfare families and the families of the working poor. By combining a limit on the recipient's grant with permission to retain money earned, without reduction in the amount of the grant, Maryland provides an incentive to seek gainful employment. And by keying the maximum family AFDC grants to the minimum wage a steadily employed head of a household receives, the State maintains some semblance of an equitable balance between families on welfare and those supported by an employed breadwinner.

It is true that in some AFDC families there may be no person who is employable. It is also true that with respect to AFDC families whose determined standard of need is below the regulatory maximum, and who therefore receive grants equal to the determined standard, the employment incentive is absent. But the Equal Protection Clause does not require that a State must choose between attacking every aspect of a problem or not attacking the problem at all. It is enough that the State's action be rationally based and free from invidious discrimination. The regulation before us meets that test.

We do not decide today that the Maryland regulation is wise, that it best fulfills the relevant social and economic objectives that Maryland might ideally espouse, or that a more just and humane system could not be devised. Conflicting claims of morality and intelligence are raised by opponents and proponents of almost every measure, certainly including the one before us. But the intractable economic, social, and even philosophical problems presented by public welfare assistance programs are not the business of this Court. The Constitution may impose certain procedural safeguards upon systems of welfare administration. But the Constitution does not empower this Court to second-guess state officials charged with the difficult responsibility of allocating limited public welfare funds among the myriad of potential recipients.

The judgment is reversed.

[The concurring opinions of Justice BLACK, joined by the Chief Justice and Justice HARLAN, all of whom joined the majority opinion, are omitted. Justice DOUGLAS dissented on statutory grounds, not reaching the constitutional issues. Justice MARSHALL, joined by Justice BRENNAN dissented on both statutory and constitutional grounds.]

## NOTES

1.  Justice Marshall, in dissent, criticizes "the Court's emasculation of the Equal Protection Clause as a constitutional principle applicable to the area of social welfare administration" and asserts that "the Court's decision today is wholly without precedent." What is the effect of *Dandridge* on the development of the new equal protection? One reviewer compares the impact of *Dandridge* to that of *Nebbia v. New York,* text, p. 428. "Just as *Nebbia v. New York* ended the stewardship of substantive due process in the reign of Laissez-Faire economics, *Dandridge* halted equal protection's expanding role as the rationalizing legal premise of Roosevelt liberalism." Note, *The Decline and Fall of the New Equal Protection: A Polemical Approach,* 58 VA. L. REV. 1489, 1500 (1972).

Has egalitarianism as a primary judicial value run its course? An author of this text, commenting on the decision and Justice Marshall's concern stated: "Justice Marshall's evaluation may actually be an understatement of the potential implications of the Court's emasculation of equal protection—the consequences may go well beyond the confines of welfare administration. The character of the court's approach to equal protection adjudication, especially when contrasted with its benign treatment of procedural due process in welfare cases in *Goldberg v. Kelly,* [text, p. 489], decided only two weeks earlier, coupled with the block identity of the Justices in the majority and dissent, portends evil days for those who see in the equal protection clause the tool for refashioning American society to more fully realize that vaguely-defined value, equality." Dienes, *To Feed the Hungry: Judicial Retrenchment in Welfare Adjudication,* 58 CALIF. L. REV. 555, 591-92 (1970).

2.  *Fundamental Rights.* Other than Justice Stewart's references to "overreaching" and the First Amendment, there is only minimal reference to suspect traits or fundamental interests by the majority. Aren't there any fundamental rights burdened by the maximum grant? Is there a "right to procreate"? *See Skinner v. Oklahoma,* text, p. 665. It has been argued that "[t]here are a number of precedents which suggest that basic guarantees were at stake. For example, courts have recognized the maintenance of a viable marital and familial relationship as derivative of basic constitutional guarantees requiring judicial protection. . . . [T]he *Williams* Court might have considered the impact of the maximum grant on such interests as the right to privacy in the marital relationship (where a viable marriage exists), the freedom to choose family size, and the interest in maintaining a harmonious marital union. Similarly, the effect of the provision

to induce the disillusion of the parent-child relationship as the price of adequate funds for subsistence and to place further strains on familial stability in the family already struggling to maintain itself against the disruptive effects of poverty also deserves judicial cognizance. If the state cannot interfere with these guarantees directly, it should not be permitted to do so through indirect means." Dienes, *To Feed the Hungry*, 58 CALIF. L. REV., at 596. What of the more general right of privacy recognized in *Griswold, Baird,* and *Roe*? Is there a right to welfare? Is there any suspect classification created by the maximum grant?

3. *Fundamental Interests.* Apart from whether the interests burdened by the maximum grant are constitutional *rights* (see text, pp. 706-07), they are different in character from the interests in the business and economic regulation and tax cases. Nor is the court's approach in *Dandridge* consistent with its language in *Shapiro v. Thompson,* text, p. 677, criticizing the effect of the classification involved as denying "food, shelter, and the other necessities of life." *See* Goldberg v. Kelly, 397 U.S. 254, 262 n. 8 (1970) and Rothstein v. Wyman, 303 F. Supp. 339 (S.D. N.Y. 1969), on the importance of the welfare interest.

4. *Traditional Equal Protection.* Justice Marshall, dissenting, argued that the maximum grant classification does not satisfy even traditional equal protection. How would you evaluate the Maryland law using traditional rational basis standards? *See* Dienes, *To Feed the Hungry*, 58 CALIF. L. REV., at 604-14. The various justifications offered by Maryland can be summarized as the "principle of less benefits," *i.e.,* assuring that welfare is of less benefit to the individual than pursuing behavior favored by the state such as employment or fertility control. It has been argued that "[u]nderlying all of these alleged interests appears to be the questionable assumption that people *want* to be on welfare and *prefer* receiving government assistance rather than working, an assumption characterizing the history of welfare administration under the poor laws." Dienes, *To Feed the Hungry*, 58 CALIF. L. REV., at 607. *See* Reinstein, *The Welfare Cases: Fundamental Rights, the Poor, and the Burden of Proof in Constitutional Litigation*, 44 TEMPLE L.Q. 1, 29-36 (1970).

5. *Dandridge* became the critical precedent in Richardson v. Belcher, 404 U.S. 78 (1971), in upholding the Social Security Act's reduction of social security benefits for those receiving workman's compensation but not for those receiving tort awards. *See also* Jefferson v. Hackney, 406 U.S. 535 (1972), text, p. 591, upholding differentials in the percentage of need met for recipients in AFDC vis-à-vis other welfare categories.

## 2. Educational Financing: A Right to Education?

Denial of equal educational opportunity may arise not only from racial discrimination but also from fiscal disparities between educational districts. Some commentators argue that government has an affirmative duty to equalize educational output and see increased inputs as a primary tool to this end. Others argue that inequalities in resource inputs into education is a denial of equal educational opportunity apart from any proof that the educational product will be markedly improved. In any case, litigation aimed at ending fiscal disparities among school districts and within school districts has mushroomed during the 60's and 70's.

The problem arises from traditional reliance on the property tax for the bulk of the local share of educational revenues. Since the taxable property wealth of districts varies greatly so also does the resources available per child. "For example, in California, per pupil expenditures for Emery Unified and Newark Unified school districts, both in Alameda County, were $2,223 and $616 respectively. In New Jersey, 14 districts with a total of 13,391 students spent less than $700 per pupil while 16 districts with 29,653 pupils spent more than $1,500 per pupil. In New York, two Long Island school districts within 10 miles of each other spent $2,078 and $1,189 respectively per pupil." Glickstein & Want, *Inequality in School Financing: The Role of the Law,* 25 STAN. L. REV. 335, 337 (1973).

Tax resources for education, however, are not only a product of district wealth but the rate (the effort) at which the property is taxed. A property-poor district must tax itself at a higher rate to yield the dollars produced from a lower tax rate in a property-rich district. "Because for the poor district each dollar above [the state aid] represents a much greater tax sacrifice (rate) than for the richer one, spending per pupil is highly correlated with, and obviously influenced by, local resources." Coons, Clune & Sugarman, *A First Appraisal of Serrano,* 2 YALE REV. OF LAW & SOC. ACTION 111, 112-13 (1971). Further, poor persons often lack the means to devote a larger share of their limited income to education even if they so desired.

Nor do state sharing techniques eliminate this disparity in resources. First, nationally state aid supplies only about one-half of local expenditures. Further, such aid may be no more than a flat grant to each district merely exacerbating wealth differentials. Finally, even when it is "equalizing," formulas for measuring financial need often are inadequate. *See* Levin, *Alternatives to the Present System of School Finance: Their Problems and Prospects,* 61 GEO. L.J., 845, 887 (1973). Resources available for education, then, continue to reflect the property wealth of the district. But the question is whether this presents a constitutional problem.

A major breakthrough in litigation strategy came with publication of J. Coons, S. Sugarman, and W. Clune, PRIVATE WEALTH AND PUBLIC EDUCATION (1970), which focused on inequality of *inputs* and argued that "the quality of education may not be a function of wealth other than the wealth of the state as a whole." This thesis found expression in a rash of successful lawsuits led by Serrano v. Priest, 96 Cal. Rptr. 601, 487 P.2d 1241 (1971), holding that the California financing system "conditions the full entitlement to [education] on wealth, classifies its recipients on the basis of their collective affluence and makes the quality of a child's education depend upon the resources of his school district and ultimately upon the pocketbook of his parents. We find that such a financing system as presently constituted is not necessary to the attainment of any compelling state interest. Since it does not withstand the requisite 'strict scrutiny' it denies to the plaintiffs and others similarly situated the equal protection of the laws." By August, 1972, over 50 lawsuits in more than 30 states were under way. U.S. COMM'N ON CIVIL RIGHTS, INEQUALITY IN SCHOOL FINANCING: THE ROLE OF THE LAW 52-77 (1972). *See School Finance Litigation: A Strategy Session*, 2 YALE REV. OF LAW & SOC. ACTION 149 (1971). Then came *Rodriguez.*

### SAN ANTONIO INDEPENDENT SCHOOL DIST. v. RODRIGUEZ
Supreme Court of the United States
411 U.S. 1, 36 L. Ed. 2d 16, 93 S. Ct. 1278 (1973)

Justice POWELL delivered the opinion of the Court.

This suit attacking the Texas system of financing public education was initiated by Mexican-American parents . . . [as] a class action on behalf of school children throughout the State who are members of minority groups or who are poor and reside in school districts having a low property tax base. . . .

. . . .

. . . The District Court held that the Texas system discriminates on the basis of wealth in the manner in which education is provided for its people. [337 F. Supp. 280]. Finding that wealth is a "suspect" classification and that education is a "fundamental" interest, the District Court held that the Texas system could be sustained only if the State could show that it was premised upon some compelling state interest. On this issue the court concluded that "[n]ot only are defendants unable to demonstrate compelling state interests . . . they fail even to establish a reasonable basis for these classifications."

. . . .

The wealth discrimination discovered by the District Court in this case, and by several other courts that have recently struck down school financing laws in other States, is quite unlike any of the forms of wealth discrimination heretofore reviewed by this Court. . . .

. . . .

. . . Even a cursory examination . . . demonstrates that neither of the two distinguishing characteristics of wealth classifications can be found here. First, in support of their charge that the system discriminates against the "poor," appellees have made no effort to demonstrate that it operates to the peculiar disadvantage of any class fairly definable as indigent, or as composed of persons whose incomes are beneath any designated poverty level. Indeed, there is reason to believe that the poorest families are not necessarily clustered in the poorest property districts. . . .

Second, neither appellees nor the District Court addressed the fact that, unlike each of the foregoing cases, lack of personal resources has not occasioned an absolute deprivation of the desired benefit. . . .

[A second theory] might be characterized as a theory of relative or comparative discrimination based on family income. Appellees sought to prove that a direct correlation exists between the wealth of families within each district and the expenditures therein for education. That is, along a continuum, the poorer the family the lower the dollar amount of education received by the family's children.

. . . .

If, in fact, these correlations could be sustained, then it might be argued that expenditures on education—equated by appellees to the quality of education—are dependent on personal wealth. Appellees' comparative discrimination theory would still face serious unanswered questions, including whether a bare positive correlation or some higher degree of correlation is necessary to provide a basis for concluding that the financing system is designed to operate to the peculiar disadvantage of the comparatively poor, and whether a class of this size and diversity could ever claim the special protection accorded "suspect" classes. These questions need not be addressed in this case, however, since appellees' proof fails to support their allegations or the District Court's conclusions.

. . . .

This brings us, then, to the third way in which the classification scheme might be defined—*district* wealth discrimination. Since the only correlation indicated by the evidence is between district property wealth and expenditures, it may be argued that discrimination might be found without regard to the individual income characteristics of district residents. . . .

However described, it is clear that appellees' suit asks this Court to extend its most exacting scrutiny to review a system that allegedly discriminates against a large, diverse, and amorphous class, unified only by the common factor of residence in districts that happen to have less taxable wealth than other districts. The system of alleged discrimination and the class it defines have none of the traditional indicia of suspectness: the class is not saddled with such disabilities, or subjected to such a history of purposeful unequal treatment, or relegated to such a position of political powerlessness as to command extraordinary protection from the majoritarian political process.

We thus conclude that the Texas system does not operate to the peculiar disadvantage of any suspect class. But in recognition of the fact that this Court has never heretofore held that wealth discrimination alone provides an adequate basis for invoking strict scrutiny, appellees have not relied solely on this contention. They also assert that the State's system impermissibly interferes with the exercise of a "fundamental" right and that accordingly the prior decisions of this Court require the application of the strict standard of judicial review. It is this question— whether education is a fundamental right, in the sense that it is among the rights and liberties protected by the Constitution— which has so consumed the attention of courts and commentators in recent years.

. . . .

. . . The importance of a service performed by the State does not determine whether it must be regarded as fundamental for purposes of examination under the Equal Protection Clause. . . .

. . . .

Education, of course, is not among the rights afforded explicit protection under our Federal Constitution. Nor do we find any basis for saying it is implicitly so protected. . . . It is appellees' contention, however, that education is distinguishable from other services and benefits provided by the State because it bears a peculiarly close relationship to other rights and liberties accorded protection under the Constitution. Specifically, they insist that education is itself a fundamental personal right because it is essential to the effective exercise of First Amendment freedoms and to intelligent utilization of the right to vote. In asserting a nexus between speech and education, appellees urge that the right to speak is meaningless unless the speaker is capable of articulating his thoughts intelligently and persuasively. . . . Likewise, they argue that the corollary right to receive information becomes little more than a hollow privilege when the recipient has not been taught to read, assimilate, and utilize available knowledge.

. . . .

We need not dispute any of these propositions. . . . Yet we have never presumed to possess either the ability or the authority to guarantee to the citizenry the most *effective* speech or the most *informed* electoral choice. That these may be desirable goals of a system of freedom of expression and of a representative form of government is not to be doubted. . . . But they are not values to be implemented by judicial intrusion into otherwise legitimate state activities.

Even if it were conceded that some identifiable quantum of education is a constitutionally protected prerequisite to the meaningful exercise of either right, we have no indication that the present levels of educational expenditure in Texas provide an education that falls short. . . . [T]hat argument provides no basis for finding an interference with fundamental rights where only relative differences in spending levels are involved and where . . . no charge fairly could be made that the system fails to provide each child with an opportunity to acquire the basic minimal skills necessary for the enjoyment of the rights of speech and of full participation in the political process.

Furthermore, the logical limitations on appellees' nexus theory are difficult to perceive. How, for instance, is education to be distinguished from the significant personal interests in the basics of decent food and shelter? Empirical examination might well buttress an assumption that the ill-fed, ill-clothed, and ill-housed are among the most ineffective participants in the political process and that they derive the least enjoyment from the benefits of the First Amendment. If so appellees' thesis would cast serious doubt on the authority of *Dandridge v. Williams,* and *Lindsey v. Normet.*

. . . In one further respect we find this a particularly inappropriate case in which to subject state action to strict judicial scrutiny. . . . Each of our prior cases involved legislation which "deprived," "infringed," or "interfered" with the free exercise of some such fundamental personal right or liberty. A critical distinction between those cases and the one now before us lies in what Texas is endeavoring to do with respect to education. . . . Every step leading to the establishment of the system Texas utilizes today—including the decisions permitting localities to tax and expend locally, and creating and continuously expanding the state aid—was implemented in an effort to *extend* public education and to improve its quality. Of course, every reform that benefits some more than others may be criticized for what its fails to accomplish. But we think it plain that, in substance, the thrust of the Texas system is affirmative and reformatory and, therefore, should be scrutinized under judicial principles sensitive to the nature of the State's efforts and to the rights reserved to the States under the Constitution.

. . . .

We need not rest our decision, however, solely on the inappropriateness of the strict-scrutiny test. A century of Supreme Court adjudication under the Equal Protection Clause affirmatively supports the application of the traditional standard of review, which requires only that the State's system be shown to bear some rational relationship to legitimate state purposes. This case represents . . . a direct attack on the way in which Texas has chosen to raise and disburse state and local tax revenues. . . . In so doing, appellees would have the Court intrude in an area in which it has traditionally deferred to state legislatures.

. . .

. . . .

In sum, to the extent that the Texas system of school finance results in unequal expenditures between children who happen to reside in different districts, we cannot say that such disparities are the product of a system that is so irrational as to be invidiously discriminatory. . . . One also must remember that the system here challenged is not peculiar to Texas or to any other State. In its essential characteristics the Texas plan for financing public education reflects what many educators for a half century have thought was an enlightened approach to a problem for which there is no perfect solution. We are unwilling to assume for ourselves a level of wisdom superior to that of legislators, scholars, and educational authorities in 50 States, especially where the alternatives proposed are only recently conceived and nowhere yet tested. . . .

. . . .

These practical considerations, of course, play no role in the adjudication of the constitutional issues presented here. But they serve to highlight the wisdom of the traditional limitations on this Court's function. . . .

Reversed.

[Justice STEWART's concurring opinion, and the dissenting opinions of Justice BRENNAN and Justice WHITE, joined by Justices, DOUGLAS and BRENNAN, are omitted.]

Justice MARSHALL, with whom Justice DOUGLAS concurs, dissenting.

. . . .

. . . We sit . . . not to resolve disputes over educational theory but to enforce our Constitution. It is an inescapable fact that if one district has more funds available per pupil than another district, the former will have greater choice in educational planning than will the latter. In this regard, I believe the question of discrimination in educational quality must be deemed to be an objective one that looks to what the State provides its children, not to what the children are able to do with what they receive. . . .

. . . .

At the very least, in view of the substantial interdistrict disparities in funding and in resulting educational inputs shown by appellees to exist under the Texas financing scheme, the burden of proving that these disparities do not in fact affect the quality of children's education must fall upon the appellants. Cf. Hobson v. Hansen, 327 F.Supp. 844, 860-861 (D.C.D.C. 1971). . . .

. . . .

Alternatively, the appellants and the majority may believe that the Equal Protection Clause cannot be offended by substantially unequal state treatment of persons who are similarly situated so long as the State provides everyone with some unspecified amount of education which evidently is "enough." The basis for such a novel view is far from clear. . . .

Even if the Equal Protection Clause encompassed some theory of constitutional adequacy, discrimination in the provision of educational opportunity would certainly seem to be a poor candidate for its application. Neither the majority nor appellants informs us how judicially manageable standards are to be derived for determining how much education is "enough" to excuse constitutional discrimination. . . .

. . . [W]hile on its face the Texas scheme may merely discriminate between local districts, the impact of that discrimination falls directly upon the children whose educational opportunity is dependent upon where they happen to live. . . .

. . . .

I believe it is sufficient that the over-arching form of discrimination in this case is between the school children of Texas on the basis of the taxable property wealth of the districts in which they happen to live. . . . [A]s the District Court concluded, . . . "the quality of public education may not be a function of wealth, other than the wealth of the state as a whole." Under such a principle, the children of a district are excessively advantaged if that district has more taxable property per pupil than the average amount of taxable property per pupil considering the State as a whole. By contrast, the children of a district are disadvantaged if that district has less taxable property per pupil than the state average. . . . Whether this discrimination, against the school children of property poor districts, inherent in the Texas financing scheme is violative of the Equal Protection Clause is the question to which we must now turn.

. . . .

To begin, I must once more voice my disagreement with the Court's rigidified approach to equal protection analysis. The Court apparently seeks to establish today that equal protection cases fall into one of two neat categories which dictate the appropriate standard of review—strict scrutiny or mere rationality. But this Court's decisions in the field of equal protection defy such easy categorization. A principled reading of what this Court has done reveals that it has applied a spectrum of standards in reviewing discrimination allegedly violative of the Equal Protection Clause. This spectrum clearly comprehends variations in the degree of care with which the Court will scrutinize particular classifications, depending, I believe, on the constitutional and societal importance of the interest adversely affected and the recognized invidiousness of the basis upon which the particular classification is drawn. I find in fact that many of the Court's recent decisions embody the very sort of reasoned approach to equal protection analysis for which I previously argued. . . . *Dandridge v. Williams* (dissenting opinion).

I therefore cannot accept the majority's labored efforts to demonstrate that fundamental interests, which call for strict scrutiny of the challenged classification, encompass only established rights which we are somehow bound to recognize from the text of the Constitution itself. To be sure, some interests which the Court has deemed to be fundamental for purposes of equal protection analysis are themselves constitutionally protected rights. . . . But it will not do to suggest that the "answer" to whether an interest is fundamental for purposes of equal protection analysis is *always* determined by whether that interest "is a right . . . explicitly or implicitly guaranteed by the Constitution."

. . . .

. . . The task in every case should be to determine the extent to which constitutionally guaranteed rights are dependent on interests not mentioned in the Constitution. As the nexus between the specific constitutional guarantee and the nonconstitutional interest draws closer, the nonconstitutional interest becomes more fundamental and the degree of judicial scrutiny

applied when the interest is infringed on a discriminatory basis
must be adjusted accordingly. . . .

. . . In the context of economic interests, we find that discriminatory state action is almost always sustained for such interests are generally far removed from constitutional guarantees.
. . . But the situation differs markedly when discrimination
against important individual interests with constitutional implications and against particularly disadvantaged or powerless
classes is involved. The majority suggests, however, that a variable
standard of review would give this Court the appearance of a
"superlegislature." I cannot agree. Such an approach seems to
me a part of the guarantees of our Constitution and of the historic experiences with oppression of and discrimination against
discrete, powerless minorities which underlie that Document. In
truth, the Court itself will be open to the criticism raised by
the majority so long as it continues on its present course of
effectively selecting in private which cases will be afforded special
consideration without acknowledging the true basis of its action.
. . .

. . . [I]f the discrimination inherent in the Texas scheme is
scrutinized with the care demanded by the interest and classification present in this case, the unconstitutionality of that scheme
is unmistakable.

. . . [T]he Court concludes that public education is not constitutionally guaranteed. It is true that this Court has never
deemed the provision of free public education to be required by
the Constitution. . . . Nevertheless, the fundamental importance
of education is amply indicated by the prior decisions of this
Court, by the unique status accorded public education by our
society, and by the close relationship between education and
some of our most basic constitutional values.

. . . .

. . . It is this very sort of intimate relationship between a
particular personal interest and specific constitutional guarantees
that has heretofore caused the Court to attach special significance,
for purposes of equal protection analysis, to individual interests
such as procreation and the exercise of state franchise.

. . . The factors just considered, including the relationship between education and the social and political interests enshrined
within the Constitution, compel us to recognize the fundamentality of education and to scrutinize with appropriate care
the basis for state discrimination affecting equality of educational
opportunity in Texas' school districts—a conclusion which is only
strengthened when we consider the character of the classification
in this case.

. . . This Court has frequently recognized that discrimination on the basis of wealth may create a classification of a suspect character and thereby call for exacting judicial scrutiny. . . .

. . . .

[*Harper,*] *Griffin* and *Douglas* refute the majority's contention that we have in the past required an absolute deprivation before subjecting wealth classifications to strict scrutiny. . . .

. . . .

. . . [District wealth] bears no relationship whatsoever to the interest of Texas school children in the educational opportunity afforded them by the State of Texas. Given the importance of that interest, we must be particularly sensitive to the invidious characteristics of any form of discrimination that is not clearly intended to serve it, as opposed to some other distinct state interest. Discrimination on the basis of group wealth may not, to be sure, reflect the social stigma frequently attached to personal poverty. Nevertheless, insofar as group wealth discrimination involves wealth over which the disadvantaged individual has no significant control, it represents in fact a more serious basis of discrimination than does personal wealth. . . .

The disability of the disadvantaged class in this case extends as well into the political processes upon which we ordinarily rely as adequate for the protection and promotion of all interests.
. . .

. . . .

The nature of our inquiry into the justifications for state discrimination is essentially the same in all equal protection cases: We must consider the substantiality of the state interests sought to be served, and we must scrutinize the reasonableness of the means by which the State has sought to advance its interests. . . .

. . . .

At the outset, I do not question that local control of public education, as an abstract matter, constitutes a very substantial state interest. . . . But I need not now decide how I might ultimately strike the balance were we confronted with the situation where the State's sincere concern for local control inevitably produced educational inequality. For on this record, it is apparent that the State's purported concern with local control is offered primarily as an excuse rather than as a justification for interdistrict inequality.

. . . .

. . . In fact, the Texas scheme produces precisely the opposite result. Local school districts cannot choose to have the best education in the State by imposing the highest tax rate.

Instead, the quality of the educational opportunity offered by any particular district is largely determined by the amount of taxable property located in a district—a factor over which local voters can exercise no control.

. . . .

Nor does the District Court's decision necessarily eliminate local control of educational funding. . . . Both centralized and decentralized plans for educational funding not involving such interdistrict discrimination have been put forward. . . .

. . . .

---

## NOTES

### *Wealth Discrimination*

1. *Identifying the Discrimination.* Justice Powell argues that there is inadequate evidence of a general correlation between individual wealth and the property wealth of a district. Poor people may live in property-rich districts, especially those with heavy commercial or industrial concentrations. Nonpoor persons may live in property-poor districts. Justice Marshall, dissenting, indicated that, in fact, in Texas, the correlation existed in about 20 per cent—rather than ten per cent—of the districts. Would this be a general correlation? Isn't it enough that there is some correlation? Is it necessary to show an identifiable class or, as Justice Marshall asserts, is it enough that "the basis of the discrimination is clearly identifiable. . . ." Would it be sufficient to show a correlation within a single district?

2. Even if Justice Powell's initial concern was overcome, what of his assertion that there must be total inability to pay and the deprivation must be absolute. Was this required in prior wealth discrimination cases? Compare the view that the "assertion that the strict scrutiny cases always involve absolute, not relative, deprivation of a benefit ignores significant prior case law. . . . [T]he view that the strict scrutiny test is based on this notion is inconsistent with holding a poll tax of $1.50 invalid in toto although the discrimination extended only to a small portion of the electorate; and also with the criminal procedure cases in which there was no question of the right to appeal but rather of the adequacy of that right when transcripts or counsel are not financially available to the poor to better effectuate the right." Richards, *Equal Opportunity and School Financing: Towards a Moral Theory of Constitutional Adjudication*, 41 U. CHI. L. REV. 32, 61 (1973). *See* Wheeler, *In Defense of Economic Equal Protection*, 22 KAN. L. REV. 1, 13 (1973).

3. In a post-*Rodriguez* commentary, Professor Clune seeks to demonstrate that such a class is "politically insular." He asserts "that given any substantial pattern of injury to poor people's children, the political situation of the injured poor is exactly the same as if only the poor were injured." He provides a series of arguments designed to show "that the poor receive a special kind and degree of injury and are less able to compensate for it; that the potential political allies of the poor are themselves helpless; and, that the poor are a historically identified target of majority manipulation in the politics of school finance, so that the claims of the poor for reform are dealt with as a special category." Clune, *Wealth Discrimination in School Finance*, 68 Nw. U.L. Rev. 651, 670-75 (1973).

## Fundamental Rights

1. *Rodriguez* clearly establishes that the importance of the interest is, in itself, insufficient to trigger the new equal protection. Rather, a constitutional right must be established. In *Serrano*, the court held that education was fundamental, arguing "first, education is a major determinant of an individual's chances for economic and social success in our competitive society; second, education is a unique influence on a child's development as a citizen and his participation in political and community life. . . . [E]ducation is the lifeline of both the individual and society." Why does the *Rodriguez* Court reject this rationale?

2. Is Justice Powell saying that constitutional rights must be specifically enumerated? What were the constitutional rights in *Griffin* and *Douglas*? What was the constitutional source for the right to privacy recognized in *Roe v. Wade*, text, p. 554, in which Justice Powell concurred? *See* Tribe, *Foreword: Toward a Model of Roles in the Due Process of Life and Law*, 87 Harv. L. Rev. 1, 42-44 (1973), attempting to distinguish *Roe* and *Rodriguez*. Professor Goodpaster has argued: "Had the same rationale been applied when the rights of privacy, procreation or travel were being thrust as being fundamental constitutional rights, they probably would not have qualified." Goodpaster, *The Constitution and Fundamental Rights*, 15 Ariz. L. Rev. 479, 502 (1973).

3. Justice Powell emphasizes that Texas provides a "minimum education" to its children. Does this suggest that there is a right to a "minimum education"? Is this sufficient to meet the demand for "equal educational opportunity"? Professor Clune notes: "Unfortunately, the enlightened guarantee of minimum skills is perfectly consistent with conscious denial of anything greater, especially of that level of competence which begins to be politically and economically competitive." Clune, *Wealth*

*Discrimination In School Finance,* 68 Nw. U.L. Rev. 651, 660 (1973).

4.  Professor Kurland argues that while "one must agree that education is a fundamental function of local government" it is also true that "no less can be said about health services, police and fire services, water supply, public housing, parks and recreational facilities, transportation . . . and what have you." And he warns that "Statewide equality is not consistent with local authority; national equality is not consistent with state power." Kurland, *Equal Educational Opportunity: The Limits of Constitutional Jurisprudence Undefined,* 35 U. Chi. L. Rev. 583, 589-90 (1968). Can education be distinguished from other state services?

5.  Could the court's decision regarding education have been any different considering its decision in *Dandridge v. Williams,* text, p. 690? It has been argued: "Subsistence benefits are at least as important to the individual and society as education. . . . While education has a more universal effect upon society than does the right of indigents to receive subsistence benefits, there is certainly nothing more universal than the need of all men to receive those basics that insure their daily existence." Comment, *Educational Financing, Equal Protection of the Laws and The Supreme Court,* 70 Mich. L. Rev. 1324 (1972). Does the implication of the state in producing the inequalities adequately distinguish education from other "fundamental interests"? *See* Coons, Clune & Sugarman, Private Wealth and Public Education 7 (1970).

## Limited Equal Protection Review After Rodriguez

What is the effect of *Rodriguez* on the development or equal protection generally? On the recognition of further fundamental rights for equal protection review? *See The Supreme Court, 1972 Term,* 87 Harv. L. Rev. 1, 113-14 (1973).

1.  A zoning ordinance limiting occupancy of one-family dwelling places to traditional families or groups of not more than two unrelated persons was upheld in Village of Belle Terre v. Boraas, 416 U.S. 1 (1973), against claims that it violated the rights to travel, privacy, association and equal protection. The Second Circuit had held the statute unconstitutional by rejecting the two tier approach in favor of "a more flexible and equitable approach, which permits consideration to be given to evidence of the nature of the rights adversely affected and the governmental interest urged in support of it." 476 F.2d 806 (2d Cir. 1973). But Justice Douglas, for the majority, rejected all of the respondent's theories, characterized the law as involving "social and economic legislation" and applied the traditional

rational basis test. He saw the measure as a form of aesthetic zoning. "A quiet place where yards are wide, people few, and motor vehicles restricted are legitimate guidelines in a land use project addressed to family needs. . . . The police power . . . is ample to lay out zones where family values, youth values, and the blessings of quiet seclusion and clean air make the area a sanctuary for people." The limitation of families to *two* unrelated persons was dismissed by noting that "every line drawn by a legislature leaves some out that might well have been included. That exercise of discretion, however, is a legislative not a judicial function."

Justice Marshall, dissenting, argued that the limitation on unrelated households to two persons, while placing no limitations on households of related individuals, "burdens the students' rights of association and privacy guaranteed by the First and Fourteenth Amendments." Applying "strict equal protection scrutiny," he reasoned that "Belle Terre imposes upon those who deviate from the community norm in their choice of living companions significantly greater restrictions than are applied to residential groups who are related by blood or marriage, and comprise the established order within the community. The town has, in effect, acted to fence out those individuals whose choice of lifestyle differs from that of its current residents." While admitting the community's interest in aesthetic zoning, he found the means chosen both over- and under-inclusive and contended that they could be "as effectively achieved by means of an ordinance that did not discriminate on the basis of constitutionally protected choices of lifestyle."

2. In Marshall v. United States, 414 U. S. 417 (1974), the court (6-3), per Chief Justice Burger, upheld a provision of the Narcotics Rehabilitation Act of 1966 disqualifying individuals with two prior felony convictions from taking advantage of the rehabilitative benefits of the Act. Following the logic of the Court of Appeals that "there is no 'fundamental right' to rehabilitatation from narcotic addiction at public expense," the court applied a rational basis standard of review. Congress could rationally conclude that an addict with a multiple-felony record is less likely to benefit from rehabilitative treatment, might present an impediment to the treatment of others, and could be a greater threat to society upon release.

## D. THE SEARCH FOR ALTERNATIVES

### 1. Newer Equal Protection

The cases in the previous section suggest that the Burger Court, while not directly overturning the new equal protection where established, will not be amenable to its further expansion. But this does not necessarily mean application of traditional review marked by extreme judicial deference. Nonreview remains a questionable alternative when critical interests of individuals are involved or when classifications disadvantage discrete classes needing judicial recognition and protection. The possibility remains of fashioning new standards of review, of developing alternatives to both traditional and the new equal protection.

### a.   Using the Newer Equal Protection

#### EISENSTADT v. BAIRD
Supreme Court of the United States
405 U.S. 438, 31 L. Ed. 2d 349, 92 S. Ct. 1029 (1972)

Justice BRENNAN delivered the opinion of the Court.

Appellee William Baird was convicted in the Massachusetts Superior Court first, for exhibiting contraceptive articles in the course of delivering a lecture on contraception to a group of students at Boston University and, second, for giving a young woman a package of Emko vaginal foam at the close of his address.[1] . . . On appeal, however, the Court of Appeals for the First Circuit vacated the dismissal and remanded the action with directions to grant the writ discharging Baird. 429 F.2d 1398 (1970). . . . We affirm.

. . . The statutory scheme [§§ 21, 21A] distinguishes among three distinct classes of distributees—*first,* married persons may obtain contraceptives to prevent pregnancy, but only from doctors or druggists on prescription; *second,* single persons may not obtain contraceptives from anyone to prevent pregnancy; and, *third,* married or single persons may obtain contraceptives from anyone to prevent not pregnancy, but the spread of disease. . . .

The legislative purposes that the statute is meant to serve are not altogether clear. . . .

. . . [T]he goals of deterring premarital sex and regulating the distribution of potentially harmful articles cannot reasonably be regarded as legislative aims of §§ 21 and 21A. And we hold that the statute, viewed as a prohibition on contraception *per se,* violates the rights of single persons under the Equal Protection Clause of the Fourteenth Amendment.

. . . .

. . . The question for our determination in this case is whether there is some ground of difference that rationally explains the

---

[1] The Court of Appeals below described the recipient of the foam as "an unmarried adult woman." However, there is no evidence in the record about her marital status.

different treatment accorded married and unmarried persons under Massachusetts General Laws c. 272, §§ 21 and 21A.[7] For the reasons that follow, we conclude that no such ground exists.

[First, the Court considered the State's purpose "to discourage premarital sexual intercourse."] [W]e cannot agree that the deterrence of premarital sex may reasonably be regarded as the purpose of the Massachusetts law.

It would be plainly unreasonable to assume that Massachusetts has prescribed pregnancy and the birth of an unwanted child as punishment for fornication, which is a misdemeanor. . . . Aside from the scheme of values that assumption would attribute to the State, it is abundantly clear that the effect of the ban on distribution of contraceptives to unmarried persons has at best a marginal relation to the preferred objective. . . . Even on the assumption that the fear of pregnancy operates as a deterrent to fornication, the Massachusetts statute is . . . so riddled with exceptions that deterrence of premarital sex cannot reasonably be regarded as its aim.

Moreover, §§ 21 and 21A on their face have a dubious relation to the State's criminal prohibition on fornication. . . . We find it hard to believe that the legislature adopted a statute carrying a five-year penalty for its possible, obviously by no means fully effective, deterrence of the commission of a ninety-day misdemeanor. . . . The very terms of the State's criminal statutes coupled with the *de minimis* effect of §§ 21 and 21A in deterring fornication, thus compel the conclusion that such deterrence cannot reasonably be taken as the purpose of the ban on distribution of contraceptives to unmarried persons.

[The Court next considers the health purpose concluding:] If health were the rationale of § 21A, the statute would be both discriminatory and overbroad. . . . "If there is need to have a physician prescribe (and a pharmacist dispense) contraceptives, that need is as great for unmarried persons as for married persons." . . . Furthermore, we must join the Court of Appeals in noting that not all contraceptives are potentially dangerous. As a result, if the Massachusetts statute were a health measure, it would not only invidiously discriminate against the unmarried, but also be overbroad with respect to the married. . . .

---

[7] Of course, if we were to conclude that the Massachusetts statute impinges upon fundamental freedoms under *Griswold,* the statutory classification would have to be not merely *rationally related* to a valid public purpose but *necessary* to the achievement of a *compelling* state interest. But just as in *Reed v. Reed,* we do not have to address the statute's validity under that test because the law fails to satisfy even the more lenient equal protection standard.

. . . We conclude, accordingly, that, despite the statute's superficial earmarks as a health measure, health, on the face of the statute, may no more reasonably be regarded as its purpose than the deterrence of premarital sexual relations.

Third. If the Massachusetts statute cannot be upheld as a deterrent to fornication or as a health measure, may it, nevertheless, be sustained simply as a prohibition on contraception? . . . [W]hatever the rights of the individual to access to contraceptives may be, the rights must be the same for the unmarried and the married alike.

If under *Griswold* the distribution of contraceptives to married persons cannot be prohibited, a ban on distribution to unmarried persons would be equally impermissible. It is true that in *Griswold* the right of privacy in question inhered in the marital relationship. Yet the marital couple is not an independent entity with a mind and heart of its own, but an association of two individuals each with a separate intellectual and emotional make-up. If the right of privacy means anything, it is the right of the *individual,* married or single, to be free from unwarranted governmental intrusion into matters so fundamentally affecting a person as the decision whether to bear or beget a child. See Stanley v. Georgia, 394 U.S. 557 (1969). See also Skinner v. Oklahoma ex rel. Williamson, 316 U.S. 535 (1942); Jacobson v. Massachusetts, 197 U.S. 11, 29 (1905).

On the other hand, if *Griswold* is no bar to a prohibition on the distribution of contraceptives, the State could not, consistently with the Equal Protection Clause, outlaw distribution to unmarried but not to married persons. In each case the evil, as perceived by the State, would be identical, and the underinclusion would be invidious. . . . We hold that by providing dissimilar treatment for married and unmarried persons who are similarly situated, Massachusetts General Laws c. 272, §§ 21 and 21A, violate the Equal Protection Clause. . . .

Affirmed.

Justice POWELL and Justice REHNQUIST took no part in the consideration or decision of this case.

[Justice DOUGLAS' concurring opinion based on freedom of expression is omitted.]

Justice WHITE, with whom Justice BLACKMUN joins, concurring in the result.

. . . .

Because this case can be disposed of on the basis of settled constitutional doctrine, I perceive no reason for reaching the novel constitutional question whether a State may restrict or forbid the distribution of contraceptives to the unmarried.

Chief Justice BURGER, dissenting.

. . . .

---

## NOTES

1. *Alternative Rationale.* What alternative lines of decision were available to the court in *Baird?* Would the right of privacy cover the claims involved? Would it be necessary to argue for a right to use contraceptives? To have access to contraceptives? It could be argued that the law burdened a fundamental right of a doctor to practice his profession. *See* C. T. DIENES, LAW, POLITICS, AND BIRTH CONTROL 228-32 (1972); Dienes, *The Progeny of Comstockery—Birth Control Laws Return to Court,* 21 AM. U.L. REV. 1, 75-86, 109 (1971). Similarly, the suspect classification doctrine could be invoked since the poor and racial minorities are especially subject to excess fertility, which is not a matter of choice and is primarily due to a lack of access to effective contraceptives. Does it matter constitutionally that the burden of the Massachusetts law falls principally on the married poor and married nonwhites who lack access to medical services? Is the Massachusetts law a discriminatory sex classification? *See* Dienes, *The Progeny of Comstockery,* 21 AM. U.L. REV., at 109-17.

Does *Baird* suggest that any criminal prohibition on the use of contraceptives by unmarried persons would be held unconstitutional? What is the status of access to contraceptives—or bans on the distribution of contraceptives—after *Baird?* After *Roe v. Wade?*

2. Why does the Massachusetts statute violate equal protection? It has been urged that the *Baird* opinion "suggests that the decisive question [in applying the rational basis standard] is how courts formulate the legislative purpose against which the rationality of the statutory classification is to be tested." Note, *Legislative Purpose, Rationality, and Equal Protection,* 82 YALE L.J. 123, 124 (1972). The history of the Massachusetts laws suggests that originally the purpose was to proscribe contraceptives as such for all persons but that 1966 amendments were aimed at discouraging illicit sex while promoting public health and greater personal freedom for married persons. *See* C. T. DIENES, LAW, POLITICS and BIRTH CONTROL 44-46, 200-09, 247 (1972); Dienes, *The Progeny of Comstockery,* 21 AM. U.L. REV., at 3-44. Justice Brennan appears to be saying either that the asserted state interest in discouraging illicit sex or protecting public health is impermissible or that they aren't *really* the state purposes. Why does the

legislation fail under the imputed purpose to curb the use of contraceptives? Is the problem in the relation of the classification to the purpose?

How is the legislative purpose to be determined? Is it arguable that Justice Brennan oversimplifies the complex of purposes behind the legislation? "The legislature's overall purpose might have been defined as follows: to discourage premarital sex by making contraceptives harder to obtain to the extent that this would not increase the risk of venereal disease; to provide for the medical supervision of the distribution of contraceptives to the extent that this would not increase the availability of contraceptives to the unmarried; and to discourage the use of contraceptives to the extent that this would not interfere with the private behavior of married persons." Note, 82 YALE L.J., at 127.

**3.** One of the authors has commented on the majority opinion in *Baird* as follows: "What is demanded is that state legislation be narrowly drawn and applied to further its actual interest in health or morals. It is the sweeping governmental intrusion into private matters of individual choice that is condemned. Indeed, the opinions invite the state legislature to clarify its vital objectives and more carefully delineate what interferences with individual liberty are necessary to effectuate them—only then is it possible to determine if the benefits are worth the cost." C. T. DIENES, LAW, POLITICS AND BIRTH CONTROL 251-52 (1972).

## Fashioning a Newer Equal Protection

**1.** In an important article, Professor Gerald Gunther has suggested that the court may be in the process of fashioning a "newer equal protection." He cites recent cases which "found bite in the equal protection clause after explicitly voicing the traditionally toothless minimal scrutiny standard" and which suggest that "[a]fter the years in which the strict scrutiny—invalidation and minimal scrutiny—non-intervention correlations were virtually perfect, the pattern had suddenly become unsettled. After an era during which the 'mere rationality' requirement symbolized virtual judicial abdication, the Court—following personnel changes in a non-interventionist direction—has suddenly found repeated occasion to intervene on the basis of the deferential standard."

Professor Gunther suggests a model for the development of this "old equal protection with new bite" which "would view equal protection as a means-focused, relatively narrow, preferred ground of decision in a broad range of cases. Stated most simply, it would have the Court take seriously a constitutional requirement that has never been formally abandoned: that legislative purposes have substantial basis in actuality, not merely in conjecture. Moreover, it would have the Justices gauge the reasonableness of questionable means on the basis of materials that are offered to the Court rather than resorting to rationalizations created by perfunctory judicial hypothesizing."

Does *Baird* fit this model? Is it possible or desirable for the court to avoid extensive concern with legislative ends? Should the court limit itself solely to the state's proffered purposes? Is it proper to probe whether they represent real purposes? What if some of the purposes are impermissible and others are permissible? What if the impermissible purpose is primary? Can a court avoid the subjective value preferences in equal protection review?

2.  Whatever the merits of the Gunther model, *Reed* and *Baird* do indicate that the court is willing to strike down legislation using at least the language of traditional equal protection.

In United States Dept. of Agriculture v. Moreno, 413 U.S. 528 (1973), the court, per Justice Brennan, struck down § 3(e) of the Food Stamp Act which, with certain exceptions, excludes from participation in the program any household containing an individual who is unrelated to any other member of the household as violative of equal protection. The classification was said to be "clearly irrelevant to the declared purpose of the Act to safeguard the health and well-being of the Nation's population and raise levels of nutrition among low-income households." Nor did it "rationally further some [other] legitimate governmental interest."

Justice Douglas applied a strict scrutiny standard to the provision since he found that it curtailed the right to associate "to combat the common foe of hunger." Justice Rehnquist, joined by the Chief Justice, dissenting, argued that "the limitation which Congress enacted could, in the judgment of reasonable men, conceivably deny food stamps to members of households which have been formed solely for the purpose of taking advantage of the Food Stamp program. . . . [T]his was a permissible congressional decision quite consistent with the underlying policy of the Act."

### b.  Illegitimacy Classifications: The Search for Standards

1.  A major breakthrough toward recognizing a meaningful equal protection guarantee for illegitimates came in Levy v. Louisiana, 391 U.S. 68 (1968). The court, per Justice Douglas, held unconstitutional Louisiana's Wrongful Death Act which prevented an illegitimate child from recovering for the death

of his mother. While recognizing the traditional deference in applying the equal protection clause accorded state social and economic legislation, Justice Douglas stated that "[the state] may not draw a line which constitutes an invidious discrimination against a particular class. . . . Though the test has been variously stated, the end result is whether the line drawn is a rational one."

But Justice Douglas went on to stress that "[H]owever that might be, we have been extremely sensitive when it comes to basic civil rights (*Skinner v. Oklahoma*, text. p. 665; *Harper v. Virginia State Bd. of Elections*, text, p. 665) and have not hesitated to strike down an invidious classification even though it had history and tradition on its side. . . . The rights asserted here involve the intimate, familial relationship between a child and his own mother. . . .

"Legitimacy or illegitimacy of birth has no relation to the nature of the wrong allegedly inflicted on the mother. These children, though illegitimate, were dependent on her; she cared for them and nurtured them; they were indeed hers in the biological and the spiritual sense; in her death they suffered wrong in the sense that any dependent would."

2. Labine v. Vincent, 401 U.S. 532 (1971), involved a Louisiana law barring illegitimate children from sharing equally with legitimate children in the estates of their fathers who died intestate, even though the children were acknowledged. Such "natural children" could inherit by will, or succeed to the estate of their father "to the exclusion only of the State." Unacknowledged children could not claim by intestate succession and had only a limited ability to be beneficiaries under a will. A legitimated or adopted child was treated as any legitimate child. The court, per Justice Black, upheld the law.

Justice Black rejected the view that *Levy* meant that "a state can never treat an illegitimate child differently from legitimate offspring." *Levy* was limited to cases "where the State had created an insurmountable barrier to [the] illegitimate child." In the present case, Justice Black argued, the father could have executed a will, could have legitimated the child by marrying her mother, or in an acknowledgment of paternity, he could have stated his desire to legitimate the little girl.

While the Justices might not agree with the policy choices of the state legislature, Justice Black argued, this was not a basis for invalidation of the law. "[T]he power to make rules to establish, protect, and strengthen family life as well as to regulate the disposition of property left in Louisiana by a man dying there is committed by the Constitution of the United States and the people of Louisiana to the legislature of that State. Absent a specific constitutional guarantee, it is for that legislature, not the life-tenured judges of this Court to select from among possible laws." Justice Black, therefore, concluded "that in the circumstances presented in this case, there is nothing in the vague generalities of the Equal Protection and Due Process Clauses which empower this Court to nullify the deliberate choices of the elected representatives of the people of Louisiana."

In a cryptic footnote, Justice Black added: "Even if we were to apply the 'rational basis' test to the Louisiana intestate succession statute, that statute clearly has a rational basis in view of Louisiana's interest in promoting family life and of directing the disposition of property left within the State." What standard was the court applying? Did the majority, as claimed by the dissent, "resort to the startling measure of simply excluding . . . illegitimate children from the protection of the Clause, in order to uphold the untenable and discredited moral prejudice of bygone centuries which vindictively punished not only the illegitimates' parents, but also the helpless, and innocent, children. Based upon such a premise, today's decision cannot even pretend to be a principled decision."

Justice Brennan in dissent, charged that "for reasons not articulated, the Court refuses to consider in this case whether there is any reason at all, or any basis whatever, for the difference in treatment that Louisiana accords to publicly acknowledged illegitimates and to legitimate children."

### WEBER v. AETNA CASUALTY & SURETY CO.
Supreme Court of the United States
406 U.S. 164, 31 L. Ed. 2d 768, 92 S. Ct. 1400 (1972)

Justice POWELL delivered the opinion of the Court.

The question before us . . . concerns the right of dependent unacknowledged, illegitimate children to recover under Louisiana workmen's compensation laws benefits for the death of their natural father on an equal footing with his dependent legitimate children. We hold that Louisiana's denial of equal recovery rights to dependent unacknowledged illegitimates violates the Equal Protection Clause of the Fourteenth Amendment. . . .

. . . .

Both the statute in *Levy* and the statute in the present case involve state-created compensation schemes, designed to provide close relatives and dependents of a deceased a means of recovery for his often abrupt and accidental death. . . . Given the similarities in the origins and purposes of these two statutes, and the similarity of Louisiana's pattern of discrimination in recovery rights, it would require a disregard of precedent and the principles of *stare decisis* to hold that *Levy* did not control the facts of the case before us. It makes no difference that illegitimates are not so absolutely or broadly barred here as in *Levy;* the discrimination remains apparent.

Having determined that *Levy* is the applicable precedent we briefly reaffirm here the reasoning which produced that result. The tests to determine the validity of state statutes under the Equal Protection Clause have been variously expressed, but this Court requires, at a minimum, that a statutory classification bear some rational relationship to a legitimate state purpose. Though the attitude given state economic and social regulation is necessarily broad, when state statutory classifications approach sensitive and fundamental personal rights, this Court exercises a stricter scrutiny. The essential inquiry in all the foregoing cases is, however, inevitably a dual one: What legitimate state interest does the classification promote? What fundamental personal rights might the classification endanger?

The Louisiana Supreme Court emphasized strongly the State's interest in protecting "legitimate family relationships," and the regulation and protection of the family unit has indeed been a venerable state concern. We do not question the importance of that interest; what we do question is how the challenged statute will promote it. . . . [It cannot] be thought here that persons will shun illicit relations because the offspring may not one day reap the benefits of workmen's compensation.

It may perhaps be said that statutory distinctions between the legitimate and illegitimate reflect closer family relationships in that the illegitimate is more often not under care in the home of the father nor even supported by him. The illegitimate, so this argument runs, may thus be made less eligible for the statutory recoveries and inheritances reserved for those more likely to be within the ambit of familial care and affection. Whatever the merits elsewhere of this contention, it is not compelling in a statutory compensation scheme where dependency on the deceased is a prerequisite to anyone's recovery, and where the acknowledgment so necessary to equal recovery rights may be unlikely to occur or legally impossible to effectuate even where the illegitimate child may be nourished and loved.

Finally, we are mindful that States have frequently drawn arbitrary lines in workmen's compensation and wrongful death statutes to facilitate potentially difficult problems of proof. Nothing in our decision would impose on state court systems a greater burden in this regard. By limiting recovery to dependents of the deceased, Louisiana substantially lessens the possible problems of locating illegitimate children and of determining uncertain claims of parenthood. Our decision fully respects Louisiana's choice on this matter. It will not expand claimants for workmen's compensation beyond those in a direct blood and dependency relationship with the deceased and avoids altogether diffuse questions of affection and affinity which pose difficult probative problems. Our ruling requires equality of treatment between two classes of persons the genuineness of whose claims the State might in any event be required to determine.

The state interest in legitimate family relationships is not served by the statute; the state interest in minimizing problems of proof is not significantly disturbed by our decision. The inferior classification of dependent unacknowledged illegitimates bears, in this instance, no significant relationship to those recognized purposes of recovery which workmen's compensation statutes commendably serve.

The status of illegitimacy has expressed through the ages society's condemnation of irresponsible liaisons beyond the bonds of marriage. But visiting this condemnation on the head of an infant is illogical and unjust. Moreover, imposing disabilities on the illegitimate child is contrary to the basic concept of our system that legal burdens should bear some relationship to individual responsibility or wrongdoing. Obviously, no child is responsible for his birth and penalizing the illegitimate child is an ineffectual —as well as an unjust—way of deterring the parent. Courts are powerless to prevent the social opprobrium suffered by these hapless children, but the Equal Protection Clause does enable us to strike down discriminatory laws relating to status of birth where —as in this case—the classification is justified by no legitimate state interest, compelling or otherwise.

Reversed and remanded.

Justice REHNQUIST, dissenting.

. . . .

I certainly do not regard the Court's decision as an unreasonable drawing of the line between *Levy* and *Labine,* and would not feel impelled to dissent if I regarded *Levy* as rightly decided. I do not so regard it.

---

## NOTES

### Post-Weber Developments

1. In Gomez v. Perez, 409 U.S. 535 (1973), the court, per curiam, struck down a Texas statute granting legitimate children paternal support while denying it to illegitimates. Citing *Weber,* the court held "that once a State posits a judicially en-

forceable right on behalf of children to needed support from their natural fathers there is no constitutionally sufficient justification for denying such an essential right to a child simply because her natural father has not married her mother. For a state to do so is 'illogical and unjust.' " While recognizing "the lurking problems with respect to proof of paternity," the court said that they cannot "be made into an impenetrable barrier that works to shield otherwise invidious discrimination." No mention was made of *Labine v. Vincent.*

2. In New Jersey Welfare Rights Organization v. Cahill, 411 U.S. 619 (1973), the court, per curiam, held that a welfare provision defining eligible "households" so as to limit the eligibility of illegitimate children violated equal protection. "[B]enefits extended under the . . . program are as indispensable to the health and well-being of illegitimate children as to those who are legitimate."

3. In Jimenez v. Weinberger, 414 U.S. 1061 (1973), the court upheld, per Burger, C.J., a provision of the Social Security Act providing that certain illegitimate children, who cannot qualify for benefits under any other provision of the Act, may obtain benefits if, but only if, the disabled wage-earner parent is shown to have contributed to the child's support or to have lived with him prior to the parent's disability. The court avoided deciding whether a classification based on illegitimacy was "suspect" relying instead on the holding of *Weber.*

### Selecting a Standard of Review

1. *Suspect Classifications.* Should status classifications based on illegitimacy be treated as suspect? It has been argued that "[s]uch discriminations are imposed without regard to an individual's actions or capacities and affect persons who have no more control over their birth status than the black man has over the color of his skin. . . . Classifications based on status of birth are also similar to racial classifications in that illegitimates share with nonwhite Americans a history of widespread private discrimination reinforced and institutionalized by legal disabilities. They too are second class citizens in a society in which illegitimacy has been described as a 'psychic catastrophe.' Illegitimates suffer from psychological and social handicaps closely comparable to those which result from racial discrimination. . . . Finally, like nonwhites, illegitimates constitute a class that is a 'discrete and insular' minority peculiarly susceptible to prejudice which tends to 'curtail the operation of those political processes ordinarily to be relied upon to protect minorities. . . .' Indeed the stigma of 'bastardy' in American society is so strong that illegitimates may

be even more disabled than nonwhites from forming a political force to affect changes on a social or legislative level." Gray & Rudovsky, *The Court Acknowledges the Illegitimate: Levy v. Louisiana and Glona v. American Guarantee & Liability Insurance Co.*, 118 U. PA. L. REV. 1, 6-7 (1969).

If *Weber* is based on a suspect classification rationale, isn't *Labine* necessarily overruled? The court's avoidance of the suspect classification issue in *Jimenez* suggests that the issue remains undecided.

2. *Fundamental Rights.* Do the above cases turn on the fundamental nature of the right burdened by an illegitimacy classification? What is the asserted fundamental right and what makes it "fundamental"? In *Weber*, Justice Powell asserts that a fundamental right is involved, but is his analysis framed in compelling interest terms? If *Weber* is based on a fundamental rights rationale, is *Labine* necessarily overruled? "Perhaps the greatest shortcoming of the *Weber* decision . . . was its imprecise identification of exactly which equal protection standard should apply. . . . If the Court had clearly identified the 'fundamental right' involved as the right of a child to a *relationship with his father* and to receive the usual incidents of care and support, *Weber* could not have been so easily distinguished from *Labine*. *Weber* involved an unacknowledged illegitimate child while *Labine* involved an acknowledged one. Assuming that a relationship with a father *is* a fundamental right, *Labine* would unavoidably have to have been overruled because the *same* fundamental right would be present in that case. . . ." The author concludes: "While the *Weber* Court makes reference to terms such as 'fundamental right' and 'compelling state interest,' one may indeed wonder if the Court really meant to invoke the 'compelling state interest' doctrine at all. As Mr. Justice Rehnquist observed, if there is a fundamental right involved, what is it?" Note, *A Decision on Illegitimacy: A Quest for Equality*, 34 U. PITT. L. REV. 472, 482-83 (1973).

3. *Weber* may be an application of traditional equal protection. *Weber* does not recognize the presumption of validity accorded legislation nor does the court manifest the deference characteristic of traditional review. While each of the statutes in question in the above illegitimacy cases involve some particular state purposes, there are some recurring interests urged on behalf of the state. Consider the rationality of employing legitimacy classifications to achieve the possible state interests. For some, *Weber* may be an example of the "newer equal protection."

## 2. Irrebuttable Presumptions: Due Process or Equal Protection

In his dissent in *Jimenez v. Weinberger,* Justice Rehnquist argued that the majority opinion paid homage "to the still novel, and I think unsupportable theory, that 'irrebuttable presumptions' violate due process." His reference was to a series of recent decisions striking down state acts on grounds that the rule declared, categorically and conclusively presumes the existence of a fact relevant to the state's purpose, even though this presumption may be wrong in particular cases, without affording any opportunity for individuals affected to challenge the presumption.

These cases often were argued not on due process but rather on equal protection grounds. The possibility arises, then, that the emerging doctrine may provide an alternative to equal protection analysis. As you read the following cases, consider the alternative lines of decision available to the court. If equal protection or substantive due process had been used, how would the case have been decided? How would the opinion have been structured? How does the conclusive presumption doctrine compare with equal protection? Is it merely substantive due process in new clothes? What is the court's role vis-à-vis the legislature when the doctrine is used? Is it any more than an alternative form of terminology for reaching a desired result?

### CLEVELAND BD. OF EDUC. v. LaFLEUR
Supreme Court of the United States
414 U.S. 632, 39 L. Ed. 2d 52, 94 S. Ct. 791 (1974)

Justice STEWART delivered the opinion of the Court.

. . . .

Jo Carol LaFleur and Ann Elizabeth Nelson are junior high school teachers employed by the Board of Education of Cleveland, Ohio. Pursuant to a rule first adopted in 1952, the school board requires every pregnant school teacher to take a maternity leave without pay, beginning five months before the expected birth of her child. . . . The teacher on maternity leave is not promised re-employment after the birth of the child; she is merely given priority in reassignment to a position for which she is qualified. Failure to comply with the mandatory maternity leave provisions is grounds for dismissal.

. . . .

The petitioner, Susan Cohen, was employed by the School Board of Chesterfield County, Virginia. That school board's maternity leave regulation requires that a pregnant teacher leave work at least four months prior to the expected birth of her child. Notice in writing must be given to the school board at least six months prior to the expected birth date. A teacher on maternity leave is declared re-eligible for employment when she submits written notice from a physician that she is physically fit for re-employment, and when she can give assurances that care of the child will cause minimal interferences with her job responsibilities. The teacher is guaranteed re-employment no later than the first day of the school year following the date upon which she is declared re-eligible.

. . . .

This Court has long recognized that freedom of personal choice in matters of marriage and family life is one of the liberties protected by the Due Process Clause of the Fourteenth Amendment. . . .

By acting to penalize the pregnant teacher for deciding to bear a child, overly restrictive maternity leave regulations can constitute a heavy burden on the exercise of these protected freedoms. Because public school maternity leave rules directly affect "one of the basic civil rights of man," *Skinner v. Oklahoma,* the Due Process Clause of the Fourteenth Amendment requires that such rules must not needlessly, arbitrarily, or capriciously impinge upon this vital area of a teacher's constitutional liberty. The question before us in these cases is whether the interests advanced in support of the rules of the Cleveland and Chesterfield County School Boards can justify the particular procedures they have adopted.

The school boards in these cases have offered two essentially overlapping explanations for their mandatory maternity leave rules. First, they contend that the firm cut-off dates are necessary to maintain continuity of classroom instruction, since advance knowledge of when a pregnant teacher must leave facilitates the finding and hiring of a qualified substitute. Secondly, the school boards seek to justify their maternity rules by arguing that at least some teachers become physically incapable of adequately performing certain of their duties during the latter part of pregnancy. By keeping the pregnant teacher out of the classroom during these final months, the maternity leave rules are said to protect the health of the teacher and her unborn child, while at the same time assuring that students have a physically capable instructor in the classroom at all times.

. . . .

We thus conclude that the arbitrary cut-off dates embodied in the mandatory leave rules before us have no rational relationship to the valid state interest of preserving continuity of instruction. As long as the teacher is required to give substantial advance notice of her condition, the choice of firm dates later in pregnancy would serve the boards' objectives just as well, while

imposing a far lesser burden on the women's exercise of constitutionally protected freedom.

. . . .

The mandatory termination provisions of the Cleveland and
Chesterfield County rules surely operate to insulate the classroom
from the presence of potentially incapacitated pregnant teachers.
But the question is whether the rules sweep too broadly. That
question must be answered in the affirmative, for the provisions
amount to a conclusive presumption that every pregnant teacher
who reaches the fifth or sixth month of pregnancy is physically
incapable of continuing. There is no individualized determination by the teacher's doctor—or the school board's—as to any
particular teacher's ability to continue at her job. The rules
contain an irrebuttable presumption of physical incompetency,
and that presumption applies even when the medical evidence
as to an individual woman's physical status might be wholly to
the contrary.

. . . .

These principles control our decision in the cases before us.
While the medical experts in these cases differed on many points,
they unanimously agreed on one—the ability of any particular
pregnant woman to continue at work past any fixed time in her
pregnancy is very much an individual matter. . . . Thus, the
conclusive presumption embodied in these rules is neither "necessarily nor universally true," and is violative of the Due Process
Clause.

. . . .

While it might be easier for the school boards to conclusively
presume that all pregnant women are unfit to teach past the
fourth or fifth month or even the first month, of pregnancy, administrative convenience alone is insufficient to make valid what
otherwise is a violation of due process of law. The Fourteenth
Amendment requires the school boards to employ alternative
administrative means, which do not so broadly infringe upon
basic constitutional liberty, in support of their legitimate goals.

. . . .

In addition to the mandatory termination provisions, both
the Cleveland and Chesterfield County rules contain limitations
upon a teacher's eligibility to return to work after giving birth.
Again, the school boards offer two justifications for the return
rules—continuity of instruction and the desire to be certain that
the teacher is physically competent when she returns to work. As
is the case with the leave provisions, the question is not whether
the school board's goals are legitimate, but rather whether the

particular means chosen to achieve those objectives unduly infringe upon the teachers' constitutional liberty.

. . . .

. . . [W]e conclude that the Cleveland return rule, insofar as it embodies the three months ago provision, is wholly arbitrary and irrational, and hence violates the Due Process Clause of the Fourteenth Amendment. The age limitation serves no legitimate state interest, and unnecessarily penalizes the female teacher for asserting her right to bear children.

We perceive no such constitutional infirmities in the Chesterfield County rule. In that school system, the teacher becomes eligible for reemployment upon submission of a medical certificate from her physician; return to work is guaranteed no later than the beginning of the next school year following the eligibility determination. The medical certificate is both a reasonable and narrow method of protecting the school board's interest in teacher fitness, while the possible deferring of return until the next school year serves the goal of preserving continuity of instruction. In short, the Chesterfield County rule manages to serve the legitimate state interests here without employing unnecessary presumptions that broadly burden the exercise of protected constitutional liberty.

. . . .

Justice DOUGLAS concurs in the result.

Justice POWELL, concurring in the result.

I concur in the Court's result, but I am unable to join its opinion. In my view these cases should not be decided on the ground that the mandatory maternity leave regulations impair any right to bear children or create an "irrebuttable presumption." It seems to me that equal protection analysis is the appropriate frame of reference.

. . . .

Justice REHNQUIST, with whom the Chief Justice joins, dissenting.

. . . .

---

## NOTES

### Prior Use of the Doctrine

1. Stanley v. Illinois, 405 U.S. 645 (1972), held unconstitutional an Illinois statutory scheme whereby the children of unmarried fathers upon the death of the mother were declared dependents without any hearing on parental fitness and without any proof of neglect, even though such hearing and proof were

required before the state assumed custody of children of married
or divorced parents and unwed mothers. Peter Stanley claimed
that the taking of his three illegitimate children under this
statute denied him equal protection.

Although the Illinois courts had never considered the due
process issue, the Supreme Court, per Justice White, held that
"as a matter of due process of law, Stanley was entitled to a
hearing on his fitness as a parent before his children were taken
from him and that by denying him a hearing and extending it to
all other parents whose custody of their children is challenged
the State denied Stanley the equal protection of the law guaranteed by the Fourteenth Amendment." The court also held the
procedure contrary to equal protection.

Turning initially to the interest of the father, Justice White
stated that "the private interest here, that of a man in the children
he has sired and raised undeniably warrants deference and, absent a powerful countervailing interest, protection." In this instance, the state did have an important interest in protecting the
welfare of the minor and strengthening family ties whenever
possible by removing neglected children from their parents "but
we are here not as to evaluate the legitimacy of the state end,
but rather to determine whether the means used to achieve these
ends are constitutionally defensible." First, "the State registers
no gain towards its declared goal when it separates children
from the custody of fit parents. Indeed, if Stanley is a fit father,
the State spites its own articulated goal when it needlessly separates him from his family." Further, even if it were true that
most unmarried fathers are unsuitable and neglectful parents
"all unmarried fathers are not in this category; some are wholly
suited to have custody of their children." Nothing is in the record
which indicates that Stanley is or was neglectful. "Given the
opportunity to make his case, Stanley may have been seen to be
deserving of custody of his offsprings. Had this been so, the
State's statutory policy would have been furthered by leaving
custody in him."

2. In Vlandis v. Kline, 412 U.S. 441 (1973), the court dealt
with a Connecticut statute providing that nonresident students
at the time of admission to the state university would be conclusively presumed to remain nonresidents for tuition purposes
during the time they remained a student. Appellees possessed
Connecticut drivers licenses, car registrations, voters registrations, etc., but were conclusively presumed nonresident.

The court, per Justice Stewart, held that the state is "forbidden by the Due Process Clause to deny an individual the resident
rates on the basis of the permanent and irrebuttable presumption

726    CONSTITUTIONAL LAW: PRINCIPLES AND POLICIES

of non-residence, when that presumption is not necessarily or universally true in fact, and when the State has reasonable alternative means of making the crucial determination. Rather, standards of due process require that the State allow an individual the opportunity to present evidence showing that he is a bona fide resident entitled to the in-state rates. Since [the statute] precluded the appellees from ever rebutting the presumption that they were non-residents of Connecticut, that statute operated to deprive them of a significant amount of their money without due process of law."

The court considered the alleged state interests in presuming the critical fact were inadequate.

Chief Justice Burger, joined by Justice Rehnquist, dissented, claiming that the majority opinion seeks "to accomplish a transference of the elusive and arbitrary 'compelling state interest' concept into the orbit of the Due Process Clause. The Court categorizes the Connecticut statutory classification as a 'permanent and irrebuttable presumption'; it explains that this 'presumption' leads to unseemly results in this and other isolated cases; and it relies upon the State's stop-gap guidelines for determining bona fide residency to demonstrate that 'the state has reasonable alternative means of making the crucial determination.' This is the language of strict scrutiny. We ought not try to correct 'unseemly results' of state statute by resorting to constitutional adjudication."

Justice Rehnquist, joined by Chief Justice Burger and Justice Douglas, dissented, arguing that the majority opinion adopts "a highly theoretical analysis that relies heavily on notions of substantive due process that have been authoritatively repudiated by subsequent decisions of the Court."

3.   U. S. Dep't of Agriculture v. Murry, 413 U.S. 508 (1973), held unconstitutional (5-4) § 5(b) of the Food Stamp Act of 1964, as amended, providing that "[a]ny household which includes a member who has reached his 18th birthday and who is claimed as a dependent child for Federal income purposes by a taxpayer who is not a member of an eligible household, shall be ineligible to participate in any food stamp program . . . during the tax period such dependency is claimed and for a period of one year after the expiration of such tax period."

Justice Douglas, for the court, said that the provision, generated by congressional concern over non-needy households, college students, and children of wealthy parents, participating in the food stamp program, "creates a conclusive presumption that the 'tax dependent's' household is not needy and has access to nutritional adequacy." Such a presumption, he asserted, is contrary to fact. "Tax dependency in a prior year seems to have no relation to the 'need' of the dependent in the following year." But even if it did, "the deduction taken for the benefit of the parent in the prior year is not a rational measure of a need of a different household with whom the child of the tax deducting parent lives and rests on an irrebuttable presumption often contrary to fact." Justice Douglas therefore concluded that the presumption "lacks critical ingredients of due process found wanting in *Vlandis v. Kline; Stanley v. Illinois;* and *Bell v. Burson.*"

Justice Rehnquist, joined by Chief Justice Burger and Justice Powell, dissenting, argued that "Congress has not in any reasoned sense of that word employed a conclusive presumption." Instead, "it had simply made a legislative decision that certain abuses which it conceived to exist in the program as previously administered were of sufficient seriousness to warrant the substantive limitation which it enacted. . . ." Thus, the issue did not involve the law of evidence, but "the extent to which the Fifth Amendment permits this Court to invalidate such a determination by Congress." For the dissent, "the challenged provision for the Food Stamp Act has a legitimate purpose and cannot be said to lack any rational basis. . . . To be sure, there may be no perfect correlation between the fact that a tax payer is part of a household which has income exceeding food stamp eligibility standard and his provision of enough support to raise his dependent's household above such standards. But there is some correlation, and the provision is, therefore, not irrational. *Dandridge v. Williams.*"

### The Due Process Standard

4. Is the new doctrine a form of procedural or substantive due process? Justice Rehnquist dissenting in *Vlandis* argued that the irrebuttable presumption approach is equivalent to substantive due process. *See* Sewell, *Conclusive Presumption and/or Substantive Due Process of Law,* 27 OKLA. L. REV. 151 (1974), who reviews the historical use of substantive due process and concludes that "the conclusive presumption doctrine rests on clear substantive due process underpinnings." *See* Note, *Conclusive Presumption Doctrine: Equal Process or Due Protection?* 72 MICH. L. REV. 800, 824 (1974).

5. On the other hand, Justice Marshall, concurring in *Vlandis,* rejects the substantive due process characterization. Similarly, it has been argued that "[s]tatutory presumption-due process reasoning does not question the right of the state to infringe upon a protected interest but only requires that the individual be given an opportunity to prove that he is not within the purview of the presumption. . . . Because the right to a fair

hearing is a procedural right, the irrebuttable presumption analysis is a procedural due process approach entailing neither the opprobrium nor the pitfalls which have been connected with the substantive due process doctrine." Note, *Irrebuttable Presumptions As An Alternative to Strict Scrutiny from Rodriguez to LaFleur,* 62 GEO. L.J. 1173, 1198-99 (1974).

### Due Process or Equal Protection?

6. *LaFleur* was argued solely on equal protection grounds. How would you analyze the case using equal protection methodology? Does the mandatory leave policy serve a rational basis? Does the existence of alternative means of realizing the state interests negate rationality? What argument might be made for using the compelling interest standard of review? What result would be arrived at in the *Vlandis* and *Murry* cases if equal protection analysis is used?

7. How does the irrebuttable presumption approach differ from equal protection? It has been suggested that "[i]rrebuttable presumption analysis represents a hybrid, if not simply a confusion, of the scrutiny usually applied to each of . . . two processes [of classifying individuals in accordance with legislative purposes]. The cases involve challenges by individuals who belong to classes which have been disadvantaged by a legislative enactment. The concern of the Court is not whether the complainants do in fact belong to the group disadvantaged by the classification, but rather whether the individuals disadvantaged by the classification have been accurately grouped with respect to the statutory purpose. In *LaFleur,* for example, the inquiry is not whether the plaintiffs were in fact past five months of pregnancy, but rather whether teachers in that classification are indeed unfit. This concern with classificatory accuracy resembles the concern of equal protection analysis." Note, *The Irrebuttable Presumption Doctrine in the Supreme Court,* 87 HARV. L. REV. 1534, 1547 (1974). Does it matter which approach is used to reach a desired result?

8. Why does the court use the irrebuttable presumption approach rather than equal protection? Could it be "because equal protection precedent would have led to sustaining the legislation"? Note, 72 MICH. L. REV., at 830. Is the new doctrine simply a way for certain members of the court to strike down burdensome legislation in the social welfare area without resorting to the confused doctrines of equal protection?

### The Limits of the Doctrine

9. The school board policy in *LaFleur* could be phrased as a rule that a teacher cannot teach past five months pregnancy, or,

alternatively, that any teacher past five months pregnancy is presumed unfit to teach. In determining the scope of due process review, should it matter which form is used? How did the court in *LaFleur* determine that the school board policy embodied a presumption of unfitness? How did the court in *Stanley*, *Vlandis* and *Murry* determine that the rule embodied a presumption? Is Chief Justice Burger correct that every statute that classifies can be construed to create an irrebuttable presumption?

# *Chapter 10*

# FREEDOM OF EXPRESSION

---

## A. THE RATIONALE OF FIRST AMENDMENT PROTECTION: SOME DOCTRINAL TOOLS

### 1. The Origins and Development of First Amendment Doctrine

Supreme Court consideration of the specific protection afforded by the first amendment against governmental legislation or action restrictive of freedom of expression did not really begin until after World War I. The introduction of conscription in the United States in World War I plus the resulting American alliance with Czarist Russia provoked a reaction from communist and radical groups in the United States. The activities of these groups insofar as they defied the Espionage Act of 1917 provoked the beginning of modern first amendment law in the Supreme Court.

The Espionage Act prohibited making false statements directed at interfering with the prosecution of the war. The Act also forbade the obstruction of recruiting or the encouragement of insubordination in the armed services. Radical discontent with conscription precipitated a confrontation between government and socialist dissidents which required the Supreme Court to elaborate on the scope of first amendment protection. This was the background behind Schenck v. United States, 249 U.S. 47 (1919).

Schenck, General Secretary of the Socialist Party, along with other defendants, had mailed leaflets to draft-age men. The leaflets asserted that the draft was in violation of the thirteenth amendment. Further, the leaflets were deemed by the government to encourage obstruction of the draft.

Schenck and his associates were indicted and convicted for violation of the Espionage Act. On review to the Supreme Court, the conviction was affirmed. In *Schenck,* the court gave judicial approval to a federal legislative restraint on expression. Yet *Schenck* is considered one of the seminal cases in first amendment law. The opinion, written by Justice Oliver Wendell Holmes, bore the earmarks of his judicial opinion writing: clarity, eloquence and creative analysis. Holmes permanently affected first amendment law by his decision in *Schenck.*

731

*clear and present danger*

In *Schenck*, Holmes set forth the embryo of the clear and present danger doctrine, a doctrine which represented one of the early serious efforts on the part of the court to reconcile the conflicting claims of national security and freedom of expression. Holmes tried to give a large bite to the scope of first amendment protection but he was not prepared to treat the first amendment as an absolute value. In *Schenck* in 1919, Holmes sketched the outline for the clear and present danger doctrine as follows:

> We admit that in many places and in ordinary times the defendants in saying all that was said in the circular would have been within their constitutional rights. But the character of every act depends upon the circumstances in which it is done. The most stringent protection of free speech would not protect a man in falsely shouting fire in a theatre and causing a panic. It does not even protect a man from an injunction against uttering words that may have all the effect of force. *The question in every case is whether the words used are used in such circumstances and are of such a nature as to create a clear and present danger that they will bring about the substantive evils that Congress has a right to prevent.* It is a question of proximity and degree. (Emphasis added.)

Another idea that has continued to have force in first amendment law which is found in *Schenck* is that in war-time a claim for first amendment protection is necessarily diminished:

> When a nation is at war many things that might be said in time of peace are such a hindrance to its effort that their utterance will not be endured so long as men fight and that no Court should regard them as protected by any constitutional right. It seems to be admitted that if an actual obstruction of the recruiting service were proved, liability for words that produced that effect might be enforced.

Justice Black, who is perhaps Justice Holmes' only peer as an influence on modern first amendment law later attempted to make the touchstone of first amendment protection depend on whether "speech" or "action" was being regulated. In his view, "speech" had absolute protection. *See generally*, BLACK, THE BILL OF RIGHTS 865 (1960). "Action," on the other hand, was subject to reasonable regulation. A systematic study of the whole range of first amendment problems which proceeds from this analysis is found in T. EMERSON, THE SYSTEM OF FREEDOM OF EXPRESSION (1973). An illustration of the relative modernity of the speech-action dichotomy is found in *Schenck* where Holmes uses the terms speech and action interchangeably: "If the act (speaking, or circulating a paper,) its tendency and the intent with which it is done are the same, we perceive no ground for saying that success alone warrants making the act a crime. . . ."

*Schenck* raises a question that still is a matter of bitter controversy: If congressional abridgement of speech and press is prohibited without qualification in the first amendment, what justification can be there for imposition of judge-made qualification to the plain meaning of the amendment? Professor Alexander Meiklejohn attacked the clear and present danger doctrine because it was designed to permit what he believed the first amendment forbade, *i.e.,* governmental restriction of political speech. *See* A. MEIKLEJOHN, FREE SPEECH: AND ITS RELATION TO SELF-GOVERNMENT 29 (1948).

*congressional vs judicial action* [handwritten margin note]

In the late 1940's when Congress was once again set forth on imposing some restrictions on freedom of expression the debate on whether the first amendment permitted any such legislation resumed. In a review of Meiklejohn's FREE SPEECH: AND ITS RELATION TO SELF-GOVERNMENT, Professor Zechariah Chafee defended the utility of the clear and present danger doctrine as a basis for resolving such problems and criticized Meiklejohn's absolutist approach which Chafee summarized as follows:

> No matter how terrible and immediate the dangers may be, he keeps saying, the First Amendment will not let Congress or anybody else in the Government try to deal with Communists who have not yet committed unlawful acts. It is hopeless to use reasoning like this in order to win votes against the Mundt-Nixon Bill. Such a view may be courageous, but it won't work.

*See* Chafee, Book Review, 62 HARV. L. REV. 891, 894 (1949).

For Chafee, Meiklejohn's pleas for absolute first amendment protection, although perhaps admirable as a theoretical ideal, were bound to founder on the harsh shores of political reality. Chafee wrote:

> The true alternative to Holmes' view of the First Amendment was not at all the perfect immunity for public discussion which Mr. Meiklejohn desires. It was no immunity at all in the face of legislation.

It is worth noting that Professor Meiklejohn's view of absolute first amendment protection was less encompassing than might appear. In Meiklejohn's view, the language to emphasize in the first amendment is "freedom of speech." Abridgment of speech *per se* is not prohibited. Meiklejohn concludes that it is "public" speech which is absolutely protected. "Private" speech, "speech" not concerning public affairs or political criticism, is a lower species of speech and not protected by the first amendment but rather by the due process clause of the fifth amendment. In Meiklejohn's analysis, "public" speech was absolutely protected by the first amendment whereas "private" speech is protected by virtue of the due process clause of the fifth amendment against unreasonable restriction.

### ABRAMS v. UNITED STATES
Supreme Court of the United States
250 U.S. 616, 63 L. Ed. 1173, 40 S. Ct. 17 (1919)

[In the same year in which *Schenck* was decided, the Court came down with another influential decision in the free speech area. Again the influential decision was authored by Holmes, but this time Holmes was in dissent. But the words of his dissent, particularly insofar as they set forth the famous marketplace of ideas theory of freedom of expression are still quoted long after the majority opinion by Justice Clarke has been forgotten.

[Abrams, along with others had published pamphlets attacking the special American expeditionary force sent to Russia to defeat the new Communist revolutionary government of Russia. The Supreme Court held that the publication and distribution of the pamphlet during the war was not protected by the first amendment.]

Justice HOLMES, dissenting.

. . . .

I never have seen any reason to doubt that the questions of law that alone were before this Court in the Cases of *Schenck, Frohwerk* and *Debs* were rightly decided. I do not doubt for a moment that by the same reasoning that would justify punishing persuasion to murder, the United States constitutionally may punish speech that produces or is intended to produce a clear and imminent danger that it will bring about forthwith certain substantive evils that the United States constitutionally may seek to prevent. The power undoubtedly is greater in time of war than in time of peace because war opens dangers that do not exist at other times.

But as against dangers peculiar to war, as against others, the principle of the right to free speech is always the same. *It is only the present danger of immediate evil or an intent to bring it about that warrants Congress in setting a limit to the expression of opinion where private rights are not concerned.* [Emphasis added.] Congress certainly cannot forbid all effort to change the mind of the country. Now nobody can suppose that the surreptitious publishing of a silly leaflet by an unknown man, without more, would present any immediate danger that its opinions would hinder the success of the government arms or have any appreciable tendency to do so. . . .

. . . .

In this case sentences of twenty years imprisonment have been imposed for the publishing of two leaflets that I believe the defendants had as much right to publish as the Government has to publish the Constitution of the United States now vainly invoked by them. Even if I am technically wrong and enough can be squeezed from these poor and puny anonymities to turn the color of legal litmus paper; I will add, even if what I think the necessary intent were shown; the most nominal punishment seems to me all that possibly could be inflicted, unless the defendants are to be made to suffer not for what the indictment alleges but for the creed that they avow—a creed that I believe to be the creed of ignorance and immaturity when honestly held, as I see no reason to doubt that it was held here but which, although made the subject of examination at the trial, no one has a right even to consider in dealing with the charges before the Court.

Persecution for the expression of opinions seems to me perfectly logical. If you have no doubt of your premises or your power and want a certain result with all your heart you naturally express your wishes in law and sweep away all opposition. To allow opposition by speech seems to indicate that you think the speech impotent, as when a man says that he has squared the circle, or that you do not care wholeheartedly for the result, or that you doubt either your power or your premises. But when men have realized that time has upset many fighting faiths, [they may come to believe even more than they believe the very foundations of their own conduct that the ultimate good desired is better reached by free trade in ideas—that the best test of truth is the power of the thought to get itself accepted in the competition of the market, and that truth is the only ground upon which their wishes safely can be carried out.] That at any rate is the theory of our Constitution. It is an experiment, as all life is an experiment. Every year if not every day we have to wager our salvation upon some prophecy based upon imperfect knowledge. While that experiment is part of our system I think that we should be eternally vigilant against attempts to check the expression of opinions that we loathe and believe to be fraught with death, unless they so imminently threaten immediate interference with the lawful and pressing purposes of the law that an immediate check is required to save the country. I wholly disagree with the argument of the Government that the First Amendment left the common law as to seditious libel in force. History seems to me against the notion. I had conceived that the United States through many years had shown its repentance for the Sedition Act of 1798, by repaying fines that it imposed. Only the emergency that makes it immediately dangerous to leave the correction of evil counsels to time warrants making any exception to the sweeping command, "Congress shall make no law abridging the freedom of speech." Of course I am speaking only of expressions of opinion and exhortations, which were all that were uttered here, but I regret that I cannot put into more impressive words my belief that in their conviction upon this indictment the defendants were deprived of their rights under the Constitution of the United States.

Justice BRANDEIS concurs with the foregoing opinion.

_____

## NOTES

1. Holmes' marketplace of ideas theory was not, of course, a new idea in Anglo-American political theory. In a sense, the marketplace of ideas theory represented the application of Social Darwinism to ideas just as earlier Social Darwinism had been applied to economic theory.

The marketplace of ideas justification for a rationale for free expression did not, of course, arise full blown from Holmes' pen but rose out of deep currents in British political thought. English poet and political thinker, John Milton, writing in the seventeenth century, advocated the same laissez-faire clash of ideas extolled by Holmes in *Abrams:* "And though all the winds of doctrine were let loose to play upon the earth, so truth be in the field, we do injuriously by licensing and prohibiting to misdoubt her strength. Let her and Falsehood grapple; who ever knew truth put to the worse in a free and open encounter?" MILTON, AREOPAGITICA 58 (Jebb, ed.; Cambridge University Press, 1918).

The English political economist John Stuart Mill expressed similar ideas in the nineteenth century. The student should compare Holmes' observation in *Abrams* that "the best test of truth is the power of the thought to get itself accepted in the competition of the market" with the following passage from Mill: "But the peculiar evil of silencing the expression of an opinion is, that it is robbing the human race; posterity as well as the existing generation; those who dissent from the opinion, still more than those who hold it. If the opinion is right, they are deprived of the opportunity of exchanging error for truth; if wrong, they lose, what is almost as great a benefit, the clearer perception and livelier impression of truth, produced by its collision

with error." MILL, UTILITARIANISM, LIBERTY AND REPRESENTA-
TIVE GOVERNMENT 104 (Lindsay ed. 1951).

2. Holmes remarked in *Abrams* that he disagreed with the
argument made by the government in that case that the "First
Amendment left the common law as to seditious libel in force."
This is a reference to the enactment in 1798, seven years after the
ratification of the constitution, a constitution which contained a
first amendment, of the Alien and Sedition Acts. The Sedition
Act of 1798 prohibited the publication of "false, scandalous, or
malicious" criticism of the Government, Congress or the President
designed to bring established governmental authority into "contempt, or disrepute." The Act was never tested in the Supreme
Court. In 1801, President Jefferson, an antagonist of the Federal-
ist-inspired legislation designed to strike at his Democrat-Republi-
can Party's sympathy for revolutionary France, allowed the
legislation to lapse.

For some, the failure to re-enact the Act, and the repayment
by the Government of the fines imposed under the Act justified
Holmes' conclusion that the weight of history was against the
notion that the first amendment and the Sedition Act could co-
exist. For others, the passage of the Act so soon after the enactment of the first amendment illustrates that the framers and their
contemporaries had not understood the first amendment as placing an absolute restraint on governmental restrictions on political
expression. *See* Berns, *Freedom of the Press and the Alien and
Sedition Laws: A Reappraisal,* 1970 S. CT. REV. 109.

Holmes' view expressed in dissent in *Abrams* that the Alien
and Sedition Act was unconstitutional was endorsed by the
majority of the Supreme Court nearly half a century later in
New York Times v. Sullivan, 376 U.S. 254 (1964), where the
Court said: "Although the Sedition Act was never tested in this
Court, the attack upon its validity has carried the day in the court
of history."

3. The marketplace of ideas theory set forth by Holmes in
*Abrams* has increasingly been subject to attack. The philosopher
of the radical left, Herbert Marcuse, has launched the following
attack against the marketplace of ideas theory: "Different opinions and 'philosophies' can no longer compete peacefully for
adherence and persuasion on rational grounds. The 'marketplace
of ideas' is organized and delimited by those who determine the
national and individual interest." *See* MARCUSE, REPRESSIVE TOL-
ERANCE IN WOLFF, MOORE AND MARCUSE, A CRITIQUE OF PURE
TOLERANCE 110 (1965).

The view of freedom of expression or protecting the process
of dialogue which prohibits any governmental effort to influence

that dialogue has been called "repressive tolerance" by Marcuse. For Marcuse, this tolerance in the interchange of ideas is permitted only because it is ineffective to change the status quo. The marketplace of ideas in Marcuse's view is a travesty: "The result is an objective contradiction between the economic and political structure on the one side, and the theory and practice of toleration on the other."

Marcuse believes that the free discussion of ideas is an illusion, that the marketplace of ideas is so distorted by economic reality that the dissenting idea or viewpoint really does not have a fair chance: "Under the rule of monopolistic media—themselves the mere instruments of economic and political power—a mentality is created from which right and wrong, true and false are predefined whenever they affect the vital interests of the society."

What is a tolerance which is not repressive? Marcuse distinguishes "liberating tolerance" from "repressive tolerance": "Liberating tolerance, then, would mean intolerance against movements from the right, and tolerance of movements from the left."

Compare Marcuse's endorsement of a communication policy, or free speech in theory, which is ideologically predisposed toward "precensorship" with Professor Bork's plea for a neutral approach to first amendment problems: "Constitutional protection should be accorded only to speech that is explicitly political. . . . Moreover, within that category of speech we ordinarily call political, there should be no constitutional obstruction to laws making criminal any speech that advocates forcible overthrow of the government or the violation of any law." Bork, *Neutral Principles and Some First Amendment Problems*, 47 IND. L.J. 1, 20 (1971).

Professor Bork continues his analysis as follows: "Speech advocating forcible overthrow of the government contemplates a group less than a majority seizing control of the monopoly power of the state when it cannot gain its ends through speech and political activity. Speech advocating violent overthrow is thus not 'political speech'. . . . It is not political speech because it violates constitutional truths about processes and because it is not aimed at a new definition of political truth by a legislative majority. Violent overthrow of government breaks the premises of our system concerning the ways in which truth is defined, and yet those premises are the only reasons for protecting political speech. It follows that there is no constitutional reason to protect speech advocating forcible overthrow." *Id.* at 31.

Is Bork's "neutral" approach to first amendment problems really any more "neutral" than Marcuse's? Marcuse sees a

"liberating tolerance" as one which represses groups and views
on the Right end of the political spectrum but which nurtures
and propagandizes for groups on the Left end of the political
spectrum. Bork says that speech which is protected by the first
amendment is speech which does not transgress "constitutional
truths" about what should be the established processes of government. Arguably, the Holmesian marketplace of ideas is more truly
"neutral" because the only ideology entertained by this view is
an attachment to a process which keeps the exchange of opinion
free from governmentally-imposed restraints or burdens.

The marketplace of ideas has been attacked not on the ground
that the impartiality and inclusiveness of its reach should be
resisted but on the ground that the abiding difficulty with the
marketplace of ideas approach to first amendment theory is that
the theory simply has no actual or working counterpart in the
reality of the contemporary mass media.

4. Professor Barron has argued that the marketplace of
ideas is a romantic concept: "Our constitutional theory is in the
grip of a romantic conception of free expression, a belief that the
'marketplace of ideas' is freely accessible. But if ever there were a
self-operating marketplace of ideas, it has long ceased to exist."
See Barron, Access To The Press—A New First Amendment
Right, 80 HARV. L. REV. 1641 (1967). The reasons for the romantic quality of the marketplace theory are described as follows:

"There is inequality in the power to communicate ideas just
as there is inequality in economic bargaining power; to recognize
the latter and deny the former is quixotic. The 'marketplace of
ideas' has rested on the assumption that protecting the right of
expression is equivalent to providing for it. But changes in the
communications industry have destroyed the equilibrium in
that marketplace. While it may still have been possible in 1925
to believe with Justice Holmes that every idea is 'acted on unless some other belief outweighs it or some failure of energy stifles
the movement at its birth,' it is impossible to believe that now.
Yet the Holmesian theory is not abandoned even though the
advent of radio and television has made even more evident that
philosophy's unreality. A realistic view of the first amendment
requires recognition that a right of expression is somewhat thin
if it can be exercised only at the sufferance of the managers of
mass communications."

## 2. The Test of "Reasonableness"

### GITLOW v. NEW YORK
Supreme Court of the United States
268 U.S. 652, 69 L. Ed. 1138, 45 S. Ct. 625 (1925)

[Gitlow, a member of the left-wing of the Socialist Party, was indicted and convicted under New York's criminal anarchy statute for publishing a radical "manifesto." The New York Criminal Anarchy statute forbade the publication of material advocating or "teaching the duty, necessity, or propriety of over-throwing or overturning organized government by force or violence." Gitlow's Manifesto had criticized the approach of the moderate socialists in seeking to obtain political power through democratic processes. Gitlow, instead, advocated mass strikes by the proletariat. On review, the Supreme Court affirmed Gitlow's conviction. Although the Court used the vocabulary of clear and present danger in *Gitlow,* it actually employed a "reasonableness" test to evaluate the constitutionality of New York's criminal anarchy statute. The Court simply asked: Was there a reasonable basis which justified the enactment of the statute by the legislature?

[Since it is a rare piece of legislation for which human ingenuity can not offer some rational justification, this approach provides little indeed in the way of protection to freedom of speech and press. Nevertheless, Justice Sanford's majority opinion in *Gitlow,* despite its use of the discredited reasonableness test for the resolution of first amendment cases, was of enduring significance for first amendment law since for the first time, by way of a casual dictum, a majority of the Supreme Court held that the due process clause of the fourteenth amendment protected the states from abridging freedom of speech and of the press.]

Justice SANFORD delivered the opinion of the Court.

. . . .

For present purposes we may and do assume that freedom of speech and of the press—which are protected by the First Amendment from abridgment by Congress—are among the fundamental personal rights and "liberties" protected by the due process clause of the Fourteenth Amendment from impairment by the States. . . .

. . . .

We cannot hold that the present statute is an arbitrary or unreasonable exercise of the police power of the State unwarrantably infringing the freedom of speech or press; and we must and do sustain its constitutionality.

This being so it may be applied to every utterance—not too trivial to be beneath the notice of the law—which is of such a character and used with such intent and purpose as to bring it within the prohibition of the statute. . . . In other words, when the legislative body has determined generally, in the constitutional exercise of its discretion, that utterances of a certain kind involve such danger of substantive evil that they may be punished, the question whether any specific utterance coming within the prohibited class is likely, in and of itself, to bring about the substantive evil, is not open to consideration. It is sufficient that the statute itself be constitutional and that the use of the language comes within its prohibition.

It is clear that the question in such cases is entirely different from that involved in those cases where the statute merely prohibits certain acts involving the danger of substantive evil, without any reference to language itself, and it is sought to apply its provisions to language used by the defendant for the purpose of bringing about the prohibited results. There, if it be contended that the statute cannot be applied to the language used by the defendant because of its protection by the freedom of speech or press, it must necessarily be found, as an original question, without any previous determination by the legislative body, whether the specific language used involved such likelihood of bringing about the substantive evil as to deprive it of the constitutional protection. In such case it has been held that the general provisions of the statute may be constitutionally applied to the specific utterance of the defendant if its natural tendency and probable effect was to bring about the substantive evil which the legislative body might prevent. And the general statement in the *Schenck Case*, that the "question in every case is whether the words used are used in such circumstances and are of such a nature as to create a clear and present danger that they will bring about the substantive evils,"—upon which great reliance is placed in the defendant's argument—was manifestly intended, as shown by the context, to apply only in cases of this class, and has no application to those like the present, where the legislative body itself has previously determined the danger of substantive evil arising from utterances of a specified character.

. . . .

And finding, for the reasons stated, that the statute is not in itself unconstitutional, and that it has not been applied in the present case in derogation of any constitutional right, the judgment of the Court of Appeals is

Affirmed.

Justice HOLMES, dissenting.

Justice BRANDEIS and I are of opinion that this judgment should be reversed. . . .

. . . Every idea is an incitement. It offers itself for belief and if believed it is acted on unless some other belief outweighs it or some failure of energy stifles the movement at its birth. The only difference between the expression of an opinion and an incitement in the narrower sense is the speaker's enthusiasm for the result. Eloquence may set fire to reason. But whatever may be thought of the redundant discourse before us it had no chance of starting a present conflagration. If in the long run the beliefs expressed in proletarian dictatorship are destined to be accepted by the dominant forces of the community, the only meaning of free speech is that they should be given their chance and have their way.

. . . .

---

## NOTES

1. Justice Sanford approached the clear and present danger test by assuming that if the legislature had determined specified expression was prohibited because its expression would create a clear and present danger, the only task remaining for a court would be to inquire into whether that legislative determination was "reasonable." This approach, of course, made the court a rubber stamp for the legislature and deprived the clear and present danger doctrine of serving as an effective judicial tool for keeping the scope of governmental regulation of expression to a minimum.

2. As has been mentioned, Sanford's crippling "reasonableness" approach to the clear and present danger test was abandoned by the court. The approach to clear and present danger which has survived is the formulation of that doctrine provided by Holmes and Brandeis. The formulation found in the case which follows, the classic statement of the clear and present danger doctrine set forth in the concurring opinion of Justice Brandeis in Whitney v. California, has in fact come to be considered the most sensitive rendition of the doctrine. The Brandeis formulation is designed to give as much scope to freedom of expression as it is possible for a non-absolutist test, such as clear and present danger, to provide.

### 3. The Clear and Present Danger Doctrine

#### WHITNEY v. CALIFORNIA
Supreme Court of the United States
274 U.S. 357, 71 L. Ed. 1095, 47 S. Ct. 641 (1927)

[*Whitney v. California* was an example of still another first amendment case in the Supreme Court where what has endured is not the opinion of the Court but the separate opinion of a Justice who did not join the reasoning of the Court's opinion.

[*Whitney v. California* arose out of the following facts. Anita Whitney attended a Communist Party Convention in California where she was elected an alternate member of the Party's state executive committee. She was indicted and convicted under the California Criminal Syndicalism Act. Criminal Syndicalism was defined under the law "as any doctrine, advocating, teaching . . . unlawful methods of terrorism as a means of accomplishing a change in industrial ownership or control, or effecting any political change."

[Whitney argued that although it turned out that the majority of delegates attending the convention favored violence as a means of securing political change, she did not favor such activity nor did she intend that the Communist Labor Party of California be used to engage in such activity.

[The Court rejected her defense on the ground that she was raising issues of fact which had been found against her by the lower court and which the Supreme Court, as an appellate court, could not re-open for consideration. The Court affirmed her conviction declaring that acting in concert was a greater threat to the public order than the expressions or acts of individuals acting separately.

[Brandeis's concurrence follows:]

Justice BRANDEIS, concurring.

Miss Whitney was convicted of the felony of assisting in organizing, in the year 1919, the Communist Labor Party of California, of being a member of it, and of assembling with it. These acts are held to constitute a crime, because the party was formed to teach criminal syndicalism. The statute which made these acts a crime restricted the right of free speech and of assembly theretofore existing. The claim is that the statute, as applied, denied to Miss Whitney the liberty guaranteed by the Fourteenth Amendment.

The felony which the statute created is a crime very unlike the old felony of conspiracy or the old misdemeanor of unlawful assembly. The mere act of assisting in forming a society for teaching syndicalism, of becoming a member of it, or assembling with others for that purpose is given the dynamic quality of crime. There is guilt although the society may not contemplate immediate promulgation of the doctrine. Thus the accused is to be punished, not for attempt, incitement or conspiracy, but for a step in preparation, which, if it threatens the public order at all, does so only remotely. The novelty in the prohibition introduced is that the statute aims, not at the practice of criminal syndicalism, nor even directly at the preaching of it, but at association with those who propose to preach it.

Despite arguments to the contrary which had seemed to me persuasive, it is settled that the due process clause of the Fourteenth Amendment applies to matters of substantive law as well as to matters of procedure. Thus all fundamental rights comprised within the term liberty are protected by the federal Constitution from invasion by the states. The right of free speech, the right to teach and the right of assembly are, of course, fundamental rights. These may not be denied or abridged. But, although the rights of free speech and assembly are fundamental, they are not in their nature absolute. Their exercise is subject to restriction, if the particular restriction proposed is required in order to protect the state from destruction or from serious injury, political, economic or moral. That the necessity which is essential to a valid restriction does not exist unless speech would produce, or is intended to produce, a clear and imminent danger of some substantive evil which the state constitutionally may seek to prevent has been settled.

*legislative determinism of clear and present danger*

It is said to be the function of the Legislature to determine whether at a particular time and under the particular circumstances the formation of, or assembly with, a society organized to advocate criminal syndicalism constitutes a clear and present danger of substantive evil; and that by enacting the law here in question the Legislature of California determined that question in the affirmative. Compare *Gitlow v. New York*. The Legislature must obviously decide, in the first instance, whether a danger exists which calls for a particular protective measure. But where a statute is valid only in case certain conditions exist, the enactment of the statute cannot alone establish the facts which are essential to its validity. Prohibitory legislation has repeatedly been held invalid, because unnecessary, where the denial of liberty involved was that of engaging in a particular business. The powers of the courts to strike down an offending law are no less when the interests involved are not property rights, but the fundamental personal rights of free speech and assembly.

*no standard to decide on clear and present danger*

This court has not yet fixed the standard by which to determine when a danger shall be deemed clear; how remote the danger may be and yet be deemed present; and what degree of evil shall be deemed sufficiently substantial to justify resort to abridgment of free speech and assembly as the means of protection. To reach sound conclusions on these matters, we must bear in mind why a state is, ordinarily, denied the power to prohibit dissemination of social, economic and political doctrine which a vast majority of its citizens believes to be false and fraught with evil consequence.

Those who won our independence believed that the final end of the state was to make men free to develop their faculties, and that in its government the deliberative forces should prevail over the arbitrary. They valued liberty both as an end and as a means. They believed liberty to be the secret of happiness and courage to be the secret of liberty. They believed that freedom to think as you will and to speak as you think are means indispensable to the discovery and spread of political truth; that without free speech and assembly discussion would be futile; that with them, discussion affords ordinarily adequate protection against the dissemination of noxious doctrine; that the greatest menace to freedom is an inert people; that public discussion is a political duty; and that this should be a fundamental principle of the American government. They recognized the risks to which all human institutions are subject. But they knew that order cannot be secured merely through fear of punishment for its infraction; that it is hazardous to discourage thought, hope and imagination; that fear breeds repression; that repression breeds hate; that hate menaces stable government; that the path of safety lies in the opportunity to discuss freely supposed grievances and proposed remedies; and that the fitting remedy for evil counsels is good ones. Believing in the power of reason as applied through public discussion, they eschewed silence coerced by law—the argument of force in its worst form. Recognizing the occasional tyrannies of governing majorities, they amended the Constitution so that free speech and assembly should be guaranteed.

Fear of serious injury cannot alone justify suppression of free speech and assembly. Men feared witches and burnt women. It is the function of speech to free men from the bondage of irrational fears. To justify suppression of free speech there must be reasonable ground to fear that serious evil will result if free speech is practiced. There must be reasonable ground to believe that the danger apprehended is imminent. There must be reasonable ground to believe that the evil to be prevented is a serious one. Every denunciation of existing law tends in some measure to increase the probability that there will be violation of it. Condonation of a breach enhances the probability. Expressions of approval add to the probability. Propagation of the criminal state of mind by teaching syndicalism increases it. Advocacy of law-breaking heightens it still further. But even advocacy of violation, however reprehensible morally, is not a justification for denying free speech where the advocacy falls short of incitement and there is nothing to indicate that the advocacy would be immediately acted on. The wide difference between advocacy and incitement, between preparation and attempt, between assembling and conspiracy, must be borne in mind. In order to support a finding of clear and present danger it must be shown either that immediate serious violence was to be expected or was advocated, or that the past conduct furnished reason to believe that such advocacy was then contemplated.

Those who won our independence by revolution were not cowards. They did not fear political change. They did not exalt order at the cost of liberty. To courageous, self-reliant men, with confidence in the power of free and fearless reasoning applied through the processes of popular government, no danger flowing from speech can be deemed clear and present, unless the incidence of the evil apprehended is so imminent that it may befall before there is opportunity for full discussion. If there be time to expose through discussion the falsehood and fallacies, to avert the evil by the processes of education, the remedy to be applied is more speech, not enforced silence. Only an emergency can justify repression. Such must be the rule if authority is to be reconciled with freedom. Such, in my opinion, is the command of the Constitution. It is therefore always open to Americans to challenge a law abridging free speech and assembly by showing that there was no emergency justifying it.

Moreover, even imminent danger cannot justify resort to prohibition of these functions essential to effective democracy, unless the evil apprehended is relatively serious. . . . The fact that speech is likely to result in some violence or in destruction of property is not enough to justify its suppression. There must be the probability of serious injury to the State. Among free men, the deterrents ordinarily to be applied to prevent crime are education and punishment for violations of the law, not abridgment of the rights of free speech and assembly.

. . . .

. . . Whenever the fundamental rights of free speech and assembly are alleged to have been invaded, it must remain open to a defendant to present the issue whether there actually did exist at the time a clear danger, whether the danger, if any, was imminent, and whether the evil apprehended was one so substantial as to justify the stringent restriction interposed by the

Legislature. The legislative declaration, like the fact that the statute was passed and was sustained by the highest court of the State, creates merely a rebuttable presumption that these conditions have been satisfied.

Whether in 1919, when Miss Whitney did the things complained of, there was in California such clear and present danger of serious evil, might have been made the important issue in the case. She might have required that the issue be determined either by the court or the jury. She claimed below that the statute as applied to her violated the federal Constitution; but she did not claim that it was void because there was no clear and present danger of serious evil, nor did she request that the existence of these conditions of a valid measure thus restricting the rights of free speech and assembly be passed upon by the court or a jury. On the other hand, there was evidence on which the court or jury might have found that such danger existed. I am unable to assent to the suggestion in the opinion of the court that assembling with a political party, formed to advocate the desirability of a proletarian revolution by mass action at some date necessarily far in the future, is not a right within the protection of the Fourteenth Amendment. In the present case, however, there was other testimony which tended to establish the existence of a conspiracy, on the part of members of the International Workers of the World, to commit present serious crimes, and likewise to show that such a conspiracy would be furthered by the activity of the society of which Miss Whitney was a member. Under these circumstances the judgment of the State court cannot be disturbed.

. . . .

Justice HOLMES joins in this opinion.

------------

## NOTES

1. A critical approach to the Holmes-Brandeis view in *Gitlow* and *Whitney* is found in Bork, *Neutral Principles And Some First Amendment Problems*, 47 IND. L.J. 1, 23 (1971). Bork argues that the law "should have been built on Justice Sanford's majority opinions in Gitlow and Whitney." Against the Brandeis-Holmes view which has prevailed, Bork lodges the following criticism: "Justice Holmes' dissent in *Gitlow* and Justice Brandeis' concurrence in *Whitney* insisted that the Court must also find that, as Brandeis put it, the speech would produce, or is intended to produce, a clear and imminent danger of some substantive evil which the state constitutionally may seek to prevent. Neither of them ex-

plained why the danger must be 'clear and imminent' . . . before a particular instance of speech could be punished." Is this criticism really just?

2. The reason for asking whether a danger was imminent was clearly stated by Brandeis. Brandeis said: "Only an emergency can justify repression." In Brandeis' view, the implicit assumption of the first amendment is that free discussion is curative in nature. In this view, the best antidote to expression inimical to the processes of a free society is more discussion. Only when the danger is so immediate that discussion cannot be relied on to perform its redeeming and curative role is repression justified. This formulation of the clear and present danger doctrine of course does not satisfy the absolutist view of the first amendment, any more than it satisfies those who, like Professor Bork (and Justice Sanford in *Gitlow* and *Whitney*) believe that a legislative determination proscribing certain classes of expression should be upheld if deemed to be reasonable. Professor Bork defends Justice Sanford's opinions for the Court: "The legislatures had struck at speech not aimed at the discovery and spread of political truth but aimed rather at destroying the premises of our political system and the means by which we define political truth. *There is no value that judges can independently give such speech in opposition to a legislative determination.*" *Id.* at 32. (Emphasis added.)

Notice that Bork conceives the matter of deciding whether certain speech is aimed at "destroying the premises of our political system" as a legislative task. Note further that Bork's test, although professedly neutral, is arguably predisposed toward preservation of the existing governmental order. Certainly the test calls for the formulation at least of some hypothesis concerning "the premises of our political system." What are these premises? Brandeis, on the other hand, would not remove any category of expression from first amendment protection on such a basis. The ideological neutrality of Brandeis' first amendment position is limited only by the exception he makes for the emergency situation. Further, in Brandeis' view the ultimate arbiter of the existence of an emergency is the judiciary.

Brandeis believed that the courts should decide the imminence of danger. This preference for consigning the ultimate determination, as to whether repression of expression is ever justified, to the judiciary rather than to the legislature is still another major ground of difference between the Brandeis-Holmes view and the Sanford-Bork view. The quarrel over the branch of government appropriate to define the reach of first amendment protection of course shifts the battle to the larger and perennial

battleground over the wisdom of an extended concept of judicial
review. On the one hand, the argument is that if a Bill of Rights
does not ever serve to curb a legislative majority against legislative wishes, what purpose does a Bill of Rights serve? The argument is the familiar one that the very purpose of constitutionalism is to occasionally set aside legislation desired by the majority.
On the other hand, the argument is that in a democratic society
judicial invalidation of a legislative determination that certain
speech is inimical "to the premises of our political system" is
neither neutral nor democratically arrived at. Perhaps a skeptic
like Holmes, or a libertarian like Brandeis, would suggest that
the only assumption that the first amendment makes is that there
are no inviolable "premises" in "our political system."

*judicial review*

Justice Brandeis' opinion in *Whitney* is no less an attempt
to provide a rationale for first amendment protection than was
Holmes' dissent in *Abrams*. It has been suggested that the Brandeis opinion in *Whitney* hit at a rationale not recognized by
Holmes in his earlier dissents. Brandeis, like Holmes, had recognized the indispensability of exposing citizens, the individual
decision makers in a democracy, with the broadest spectrum of
competing ideas. But Brandeis uniquely emphasized in *Whitney*
another goal of first amendment protection, the "public order"
function. Consider the following:

"The relationship between constitutional assurance of an
opportunity to communicate ideas and the integrity of the public
order was appreciated by . . . Brandeis. . . . If freedom of expression cannot be secured because entry into the communication
media is not free but is confined as a matter of discretion by a
few private hands, the sense of the justice of existing institutions,
which freedom of expression is designed to assure, vanishes from
some section of our population as surely as if access to the media
were restricted by the government.

*public order*

"Justice Brandeis in his seminal opinion in *Whitney*—one of
the few efforts of a Supreme Court Justice to go beyond the
banality of the 'marketplace of ideas'—also stressed the intimacy
of the relationship between the goals of a respect for public order
and the assurance of free expression. For Brandeis one of the
assumptions implicit in the guarantee of free expression is that
. . . the path of safety lies in the opportunity to discuss freely
supposed grievances and proposed remedies. . . ."

Barron, *Access to the Press—A New First Amendment Right*, 80
HARV. L. REV. 1641 (1967).

### 4. The Doctrine Of Prior Restraint

In Near v. Minnesota, 283 U.S. 697 (1931), the court made it clear that the first amendment provides two modes of protection: freedom from subsequent punishment and freedom from prior restraint. The former freedom protects expression once it has managed to secure public expression. The latter freedom provides protection for expression so that it should not be officially suppressed in advance of expression. In *Near,* the court said that the first amendment granted protection against prior restraints vis-à-vis both state and federal governments. But the court asserted that freedom from prior restraint was not absolutely protected. Justification for some prior restraint could be predicated, said Chief Justice Hughes, on three different grounds: (1) national security in time of war; (2) where the "primary requirements of decency were involved"; (3) where the "security of the community life" requires protection "against incitements to acts of violence and the overthrow by force of orderly government."

## THE PENTAGON PAPERS CASE: AN INTRODUCTION

A controversial, well-publicized and difficult prior restraint case was the now famous Pentagon Papers fracas. A former Pentagon employee, Dr. Daniel Ellsberg, had a change of heart about the merit of American involvement in the Vietnam war. Ellsberg turned over a secret classified government report which formed a record of American involvement in war in Vietnam. In June, 1971, the New York Times decided to publish these papers which became known as the Pentagon papers.

The United States Government sought a temporary restraining order prohibiting the publication of the papers which was granted by the United States District Court for the Southern District of New York. But the court refused a permanent injunction. The United States Court of Appeals for the Second Circuit then reversed the lower federal court and held that the Times should be restrained from publishing pending a government showing that prohibition of the papers placed the national security in jeopardy. The United States Court of Appeals for the District of Columbia refused to grant the government's request to restrain publication of the papers by the Washington Post. As you consider each of nine separate opinions, ask yourself whether the cause of freedom from prior restraint has been advanced or set back as a result of the decisions.

## NEW YORK TIMES CO. v. UNITED STATES
Supreme Court of the United States
403 U.S. 713, 29 L. Ed. 2d 822, 91 S. Ct. 2140 (1971)

PER CURIAM.

We granted certiorari, in these cases in which the United States seeks to enjoin the New York Times and the Washington Post from publishing the contents of a classified study entitled "History of U.S. Decision-Making Process on Viet Nam Policy."

"Any system of prior restraints of expression comes to this Court bearing a heavy presumption against its constitutional validity." Bantam Books, Inc. v. Sullivan, 372 U.S. 58, 70 (1963). The Government "thus carries a heavy burden of showing justification for the imposition of such a restraint." Organization for a Better Austin v. Keefe, 401 U.S. [415] (1971). The District Court for the Southern District of New York in the *New York Times* case, and the District Court for the District of Columbia and the Court of Appeals for the District of Columbia Circuit in the *Washington Post* case held that the Government had not met that burden. We agree.

The judgment of the Court of Appeals for the District of Columbia Circuit is therefore affirmed. The order of the Court of Appeals for the Second Circuit is reversed, and the case is remanded with directions to enter a judgment affirming the judgment of the District Court for the Southern District of New York. The stays entered June 25, 1971, by the Court are vacated. The judgments shall issue forthwith.

So ordered.

---

## THE OPINIONS OF THE JUSTICES IN THE PENTAGON PAPERS CASE

Following this short per curiam opinion, each of the Justices of the Supreme Court filed an opinion. Those opinions are summarized below.

## 1. JUSTICE BLACK'S OPINION

The government's position in the principal case, said Justice Black, constituted a "bold and dangerously far reaching contention that the courts should take it upon themselves to 'make' a law abridging freedom of the press in the name of equity, presidential power and national security." He appeared to reject any theory that "inherent Presidential power" had become an additional exception to the general freedom from prior restraint. Are the exceptions to the prior restraint doctrine set forth in

*Near* dependent for implementation on codification of these exceptions in a *statute?* Justice Black made it clear that even if publication had been authorized by statute, he would have found such a statute invalid. Why?

Justice Black said with dismay that "some of my Brethren are apparently willing to hold that the publication of news may sometimes be enjoined." But this is, rather astringently expressed to be sure, the essence of the doctrine of *Near v. Minnesota.*

In *Near,* Chief Justice Hughes conceded that first amendment protection "even as to previous restraint is not absolutely unlimited. But the exception has been recognized only in exceptional cases." Further, Chief Justice Hughes observed: "No one would question but that a government might prevent actual obstruction of its recruiting service or the publication of the sailing dates of transports or the number and location of troops."

The government in the *Pentagon Papers Case* had relied on national security as a justification for enjoining publication. Justice Black rejected the justification saying that the word "security" was too broad and vague a term to utilize as an exception to first amendment protection.

## 2.  JUSTICE DOUGLAS' OPINION

While Justice Douglas asserted that "the First Amendment . . . leaves . . . no room for governmental restraint on the press," he appeared in some respects to part company with Justice Black over the extent of protection the first amendment freedom from prior restraint grants the press. Douglas emphasized that no existing federal legislation authorized a press restraint or publication. It may be argued that Douglas' emphasis on the lack of statutory authorization for the injunctive relief sought by the government suggests that for Douglas the situation might have been altered if there had been a statute explicitly covering the case.

## 3.  JUSTICE BRENNAN'S OPINION

Justice Brennan stated that "the First Amendment stands as an absolute bar to the imposition of judicial restraints in circumstances of the kind presented by these cases." Brennan then says that there is a "single extremely narrow class of cases in which the First Amendment's bar on prior judicial restraint may be overridden." Brennan says the case law indicates this occurs when the nation "is at war." But even if the "present world situation" were equivalent, "only governmental allegation and proof that publication must inevitably, directly and immediately cause the occurrence of an event kindred to imperiling the safety of a transport already at sea can support the issuance of an interim restraining order." Brennan would provide a freedom from prior restraint which is almost, but not quite, absolute. This approach certainly finds authoritative support in the emphasis by Chief Justice Hughes in *Near* that exceptions to the doctrine of freedom from prior restraint were exceptional. Is this a restatement of the clear and present danger doctrine?

## 4. JUSTICE STEWART'S OPINION

Stewart thought Congress could not and should not unduly transgress on the discretion and privacy the President believed necessary for the conduct of international affairs and negotiations: "The responsibility must be where the power is. If the Constitution gives the Executive a large degree of unshared power in the conduct of foreign affairs and the maintenance of our national defense, then under the Constitution the Executive must have the largely unshared duty to determine and preserve the degree of internal security necessary to exercise that power successfully."

Does Stewart's view leave the constitutional validity of a classification system for documents too far outside the range of public inquiry? Is the classification system that this view of executive prerogative or inherent Presidential power permits itself an invalid prior restraint?

Despite Stewart's sympathy for the need for some confidentiality on the part of the Executive in the conduct of international affairs, it should be remembered that Stewart joined the majority opinion and held that the publication of the Pentagon Papers could not be enjoined. His reasons for reaching this result follow:

"This is not to say that Congress and the courts have no role to play. Undoubtedly Congress has the power to enact specific and appropriate criminal laws to protect government property and preserve government secrets. Congress has passed such laws, and several of them are of very colorable relevance to the apparent circumstances of these cases. And if a criminal prosecution is instituted, it will be the responsibility of the courts to decide the applicability of the criminal law under which the charge is brought. Moreover, if Congress should pass a specific law authorizing civil proceedings in this field, the courts would likewise have the duty to decide the constitutionality of such a law as well as its applicability to the facts proved.

"But in the cases before us we are asked neither to construe specific regulations nor to apply specific laws. We are asked, instead, to perform a function that the Constitution gave to the Executive, not the Judiciary. We are asked, quite simply, to prevent the publication by two newspapers of material that the Executive Branch insists should not, in the national interest, be published. I am convinced that the Executive is correct with respect to some of the documents involved. But I cannot say that disclosure of any of them will surely result in direct, immediate, and irreparable damage to our Nation or its people. That being so, there can under the First Amendment be but one judicial resolution of the issues before us. I join the judgments of the Court."

Is the separation of powers doctrine the basis for Stewart's conclusion that in these circumstances, the courts should not enjoin what the legislature has not in terms prohibited? Note that Stewart does not make the absence of legislation the dispositive factor as an absolute matter. He suggests that the court could enjoin publication if publication threatened "irreparable damage" to the nation. But if the court acted in that situation would it not still be "performing a function that the Constitution gave to the Executive"?

## 5.   JUSTICE WHITE'S OPINION

Justice White announced his disagreement with the view that "in no circumstances would the First Amendment permit an injunction about publishing information about government plans or operations."

White disagreed with both camps of absolutists: Those who saw no limits to inherent Presidential power, on the one hand, and those who saw no limits to the scope of first amendment protection on the other. White rejected the government's position that there existed inherent presidential power which authorized injunction of a publication by the press on the ground the publication presented a "grave and irreparable" threat to the public interest. He based his conclusion on two factors: The absence of a statute permitting a prior restraint, and the failure of the government to show the kind of necessity required to justify a prior restraint in the absence of legislation.

Justice White does suggest that if the publishers had violated existing federal legislation by publishing the Pentagon Papers (and he implies they might have), the publishers might under the first amendment, be punished *subsequent* to publication:

> What is more, terminating the ban on publication of the relatively few sensitive documents the Government now seeks to suppress does not mean that the law either requires or invites newspapers or others to publish them or that they will be immune from criminal action if they do. *Prior re-*

*straints require an unusually heavy justification under the
First Amendment; but failure by the government to justify
prior restraints does not measure its constitutional entitlement
to a conviction for criminal publication. That the government
chose to proceed by injunction does not mean that it could
not successfully proceed in another way.* (Emphasis added.)

## 6. JUSTICE MARSHALL'S OPINION

For Marshall the issue was not, as the government contended,
whether the first amendment barred a court from prohibiting a
newspaper from publishing material whose publication jeopardized the national security. The issue he said was more fundamental: "The issue is whether this Court or the Congress has the
power to make law."

Marshall like Stewart appeared to think that the separation
of powers prevented judicial issuance of an injunction in these
circumstances: "It would, however, be utterly inconsistent with
the concept of separation of power for this Court to use its power
of contempt to prevent behavior that Congress has specifically
declined to prohibit." For Marshall what was crucial was that
"Congress had specifically rejected legislation that would have
clearly given the President the power he seeks here and made
the current activity of the newspapers unlawful."

If Congress had given the President the authority to enjoin
the press where warranted by an extreme national security emergency, would such a statute have been consistent with the first
amendment? Marshall did not say. Since the court was not really
required to reach this point, the *Pentagon Papers Case* provides
less in the way of an authoritative first amendment decision than
its pro-press result might suggest.

## THE DISSENTING OPINIONS

## 7. CHIEF JUSTICE BURGER'S DISSENT

In the early part of Burger's opinion he made clear that for
him the first amendment was not an absolute: "Only those who
view the First Amendment as an absolute in all circumstances—
a view I respect, but reject—can find such a case as this to be
simple or easy."

Burger complained that the cases had proceeded in such haste
through the courts that no judge who has passed on the case has
known all the facts of the case. As a result, Burger said: "only
those judges to whom the First Amendment is absolute and
permits of no restraint in any circumstances or for any reason,
are really in a position to act."

Burger argued that the Times had had "unauthorized possession of the documents for three to four months, during which it has had its expert analysts studying them, presumably digesting them and preparing the material for publication." In these circumstances, Burger asked: "Would it have been unreasonable, since the newspaper could anticipate the government's objections to release of secret material, to give the government an opportunity to review the entire collection and determine whether agreement could be reached on publication?"

On the question of the Times refusal to allow the government to examine the Pentagon Papers in its possession on the ground of protecting its sources, Burger made the following caustic observation:

> Interestingly the *Times* explained its refusal to allow the government to examine its own purloined documents by saying in substance this might compromise *their* sources and informants! The *Times* thus asserts a right to guard the secrecy of its sources while denying that the Government of the United States has that power.

Perhaps the most interesting aspect of Burger's opinion was his apparent belief that the President contained inherent power to classify documents and shield them from public scrutiny.

> With respect to the question of inherent power of the Executive to classify papers, records and documents as secret, or otherwise unavailable for public exposure, and to secure aid of the courts for enforcement, there may be an analogy with respect to this Court. No statute gives this Court express power to establish and enforce the utmost security measures for the secrecy of our deliberations and records. Yet I have little doubt as to the inherent power of the Court to protect the confidentiality of its internal operations by whatever judicial measures may be required."

Burger apparently did not believe that either the doctrine of separation of power or the strictures of the first amendment served to destroy justification for a classification system on the basis of inherent Presidential power.

A major theme of Burger's dissent was a protest against the Times' position that it was the absolute trustee of the public's right to know. For him, the same factor which prevented the first amendment from being an absolute made it unacceptable that the press should be the ultimate arbiter of whether a governmental claim of privacy or confidentiality should be respected. In a quarrel between the press and the government, where the facts were unclear, and the case had to be resolved between the right asserted by the press of the public's right to know and the right asserted by the Executive to keep documents secret, the new Chief Justice chose the Executive.

## 8. JUSTICE BLACKMUN'S DISSENT

Justice Blackmun began his dissent with a protest that the government and the courts had been given far less time to arrive at accommodation between the public's right to know and the national security than had the New York Times.

Consistent with this beginning, Blackmun made it very clear that for him the first amendment was not an absolute. One of the functions of the Pentagon Papers legal drama was that it revealed that Burger and Blackmun were not disciples of Justice Black's first amendment teachings. Blackmun apparently considered the first amendment and the President's power to conduct foreign relations to be constitutional values of equal status:

> The First Amendment, after all, is only one part of an entire Constitution. Article II of the great document vests in the Executive Branch primary power over the conduct of foreign affairs and places in that branch the responsibility for the Nation's safety. Each provision of the Constitution is important, and I cannot subscribe to a doctrine of unlimited absolutism for the First Amendment at the cost of downgrading other provisions. First Amendment absolutism has never commanded a majority of this Court.

What is necessary to reconcile the conflict between these competing constitutional values, Blackmun says, is "properly developed standards, of the broad right of the press to print and of the very narrow of the Government to prevent." Blackmun felt these standards would be more likely to have resulted from a "schedule permitting the orderly presentation of evidence from both sides" rather than, as was actually the case, on the basis of "inadequately developed and largely assumed facts."

Blackmun concluded his dissent with an admonition that if harm resulted to the nation from publication of the Papers in controversy the fault would lie with the press:

> . . . [I]f, with the Court's action today, these newspapers proceed to publish the critical documents and there results therefrom "the death of soldiers, the destruction of alliances, the greatly increased difficulty of negotiation with our enemies, the inability of our diplomats to negotiate," to which list I might add the factors of prolongation of the war and of further delay in the freeing of United States prisoners, then the

Nation's people will know where the responsibility for these sad consequences rests.

## 9.  JUSTICE HARLAN'S DISSENT

Justice Harlan expressed the view that the haste with which the Supreme Court had considered the *Pentagon Papers Case* had obscured the resolution of fundamental constitutional questions presented by the case:

1.  Whether the Attorney General is authorized to bring these suits in the name of the United States. This question involves as well the construction and validity of a singularly opaque statute—the Espionage Act, 18 U.S.C. § 793 (e).

2.  Whether the First Amendment permits the federal courts to enjoin publication of stories which would present a serious threat to national security. See Near v. Minnesota, ex rel. Olson, 283 U.S. 697 (1931) (dictum).

3.  Whether the threat to publish highly secret documents is of itself a sufficient implication of national security to justify an injunction on the theory that regardless of the contents of the documents harm enough results simply from the demonstration of such a breach of secrecy.

4.  Whether the unauthorized disclosure of any of these particular documents would seriously impair the national security.

5.  What weight should be given to the opinion of high officers in the Executive Branch of the Government with respect to questions 3 and 4.

6.  Whether the newspapers are entitled to retain and use the documents notwithstanding the seemingly uncontested facts that the documents, or the originals of which they are duplicates, were purloined from the Government's possession and that the newspapers received them with knowledge that they had been feloniously acquired.

7.  Whether the threatened harm to the national security or the Government's possessory interest in the documents justifies the issuance of an injunction against publication in light of—

a. The strong First Amendment policy against prior restraints on publication;

b. The doctrine against enjoining conduct in violation of criminal statutes; and

c. The extent to which the materials at issue have apparently already been otherwise disseminated.

In Harlan's view, the power "to evaluate the 'pernicious' influence of premature disclosure" was lodged to some extent in the inherent power of the Executive. However, unlike Burger, Harlan clearly assigned a role to the judiciary in reviewing an initial executive determination against disclosure.

Harlan's suggested judicial procedure for weighing whether an executive determination to prohibit disclosure of documents is constitutionally permissible does not appear to require the government to turn over the documents to the court. If that is true, how does the judiciary satisfy itself that the subject matter of the documents lies within the proper compass of the President's foreign relations power?

A fair assessment of Harlan's dissent would appear to be that a claim of Presidential secrecy for Executive papers should come with a presumption in favor of respecting the claim at least as against a first amendment claim for their exposure as long as the subject matter of the documents was in the area of foreign relations. Harlan's view in this sense permits first amendment protection to be qualified by the President's power over foreign relations. Is a justification for this position that a claim for exposure of documents is a far more attentuated first amendment claim than where something that has been independently gathered is being denied publication?

## 5. The Preferred Position

In 1938, Chief Justice Stone in an opinion for the court enunciated the standard for judicial review of federal economic legislation as follows: "regulatory legislation affecting ordinary commercial transactions is not to be pronounced unconstitutional unless in the light of the facts made known or generally assumed it is of such character as to preclude the assumption that it rests upon some rational basis within the knowledge and experience of the legislators." United States v. Carolene Products Co., 304 U.S. 144, 152 (1938).

At the suggestion of his law clerk, Chief Justice Stone included a footnote which suggested that in cases raising issues such as first amendment matters the standard of judicial review could be more stringent. Footnote 4, in *Carolene Products,* became one of the most famous footnotes in American constitutional law. The footnote launched a constitutional idea: the doctrine of a preferred position for the first amendment in judicial review. The preferred position theory has stimulated both respect and controversy in Supreme Court opinions. Yet it has to this day failed to win sufficient and consistent enough support to become accepted doctrine. The text of footnote 4 in *Carolene Products, inter alia,* provides:

There may be narrower scope for operation of the presumption of constitutionality when legislation appears on its
face to be within a specific prohibition of the Constitution,
such as those of the first ten amendments, which are deemed
equally specific when held to be embraced within the Fourteenth.

It is unnecessary to consider now whether legislation which
restricts those political processes which can ordinarily be
expected to bring about repeal of undesirable legislation, is
to be subjected to more exacting judicial scrutiny under the
general prohibitions of the Fourteenth Amendment than are
most other types of legislation.

---

## NOTES

**1.** Should we read the footnote in *Carolene Products* as
saying that as a general proposition economic legislation will
have the benefit of a presumption of constitutionality but that
legislation that infringes on constitutional guarantees of individual liberty will carry with it a presumption of invalidity?

Notice that Stone in his footnote does not speak of a presumption of invalidity but instead uses more careful language. Legislation falling within a "specific" prohibition "of the first ten
amendments" should be given "narrower scope"; *perhaps,* legislation restricting the legislative process should be subjected to
"more exacting judicial scrutiny."

**2.** Whether the use in subsequent constitutional adjudication
made of a preferred position for the first amendment in judicial
review was justified by its statement in *Carolene Products,* Judge
Learned Hand has asserted that Chief Justice Stone had no wish
to exchange a dying substantive due process which had been
built upon property rights for a new one built around individual
liberties:

"Even before Justice Stone became Chief Justice it began to
seem as though, when 'personal rights' were in issue, something
strangely akin to the discredited attitude towards the Bill of
Rights of the old apostles of the institution of property was
regaining recognition. . . . [B]ut the fact remained that in the
name of the Bill of Rights the courts were upsetting statutes which
were plainly compromises between conflicting interests, each of
which had more than a merely plausible support in reason. . . .
[H]e (Stone) would not be content with what to him was an
opportunistic reversion at the expense of his conviction as to the
powers of a court. He could not understand how the principle

(of limited judicial review) which he all along supported, could mean that, when concerned with interests other than property, the courts should have a wider latitude for enforcing their own predilections, than when they were concerned with property itself." Hand, *Chief Justice Stone's Conception of the Judicial Function*, 46 COLUM. L. REV. 696, 698 (1946).

**3.** Professor Freund, in an article quoting and stressing the above passage from Judge Hand's paper on Chief Justice Stone, is cautious in his appraisal of the "preferred position" theory. Professor Freund implies that too vigorous an indulgence by the courts in the invalidation of legislation on a preferred position basis could easily revive the discredited approach to judicial review marked by Lochner v. New York, 198 U.S. 45 (1905):

"It has been suggested that legislation restricting liberty of contract is designed to enlarge the effective freedom of one group by limiting the freedom of another, while restrictions on freedom of expression have no such compensating effect. . . . But if the Court is to judge the validity of a restraint by its effect in enlarging the freedom of a group, the way will unfortunately be open for a return to the era of the judicial veto on social legislation. It will hardly do to depend on the judgment of the Court regarding the liberating economic effects, for example, of legislation directed against chain stores or against the closed shop or the open shop. It would be but a short step from the *Social Statics* of Herbert Spencer to the social ecstatics of the judges." *See* Freund, *The Supreme Court and Civil Liberties*, 4 VAND. L. REV. 533, 548 (1951), SELECTED ESSAYS, 449, 462 (1963).

**4.** Whatever Chief Justice Stone intended, judicial review today has its greatest vitality in the area of individual liberties. The wealth of contemporary first amendment case law collected in this chapter is testimony to that. The year 1938 and the *Carolene Products* case, with its twin statements on the presumption of validity for economic legislation and of a more searching judicial scrutiny for legislation infringing individual liberties and minority rights, are almost perfect benchmarks for demarcating the death of the old economic due process whose content was protection of property rights, see text, pp. 417-34, and the rise of a new due process, enforced by the incorporation doctrine, text, Chapter 6, whose content focused on the protection of individual liberties. For a rigorous critique of the preferred position doctrine, which catalogs the Supreme Court's use of the doctrine in first amendment cases, see Justice Frankfurter's concurring opinion in Kovacs v. Cooper, 336 U.S. 77 (1949).

**6.   Clear and Present Danger: Failure In Crisis**

### DENNIS v. UNITED STATES
Supreme Court of the United States
341 U.S. 494, 95 L. Ed. 1137, 71 S. Ct. 857 (1951)

Chief Justice VINSON announced the judgment of the Court and an opinion in which Justice REED, Justice BURTON and Justice MINTON join.

Petitioners were indicted in July, 1948, for violation of the conspiracy provisions of the Smith Act during the period of April, 1945, to July, 1948. . . . A verdict of guilty as to all the petitioners was returned by the jury on October 14, 1949. The Court of Appeals affirmed the convictions. 183 F.2d 201. We granted certiorari, limited to the following two questions: (1) Whether either § 2 or § 3 of the Smith Act, inherently or as construed and applied in the instant case, violates the First Amendment and other provisions of the Bill of Rights; (2) whether either § 2 or § 3 of the Act, inherently or as construed and applied in the instant case, violates the First and Fifth Amendments because of indefiniteness.

Sections 2 and 3 of the Smith Act provide as follows:

"Sec. 2.

"(a)   It shall be unlawful for any person—

"(1)   to knowingly or willfully advocate, abet, advise, or teach the duty, necessity, desirability, or propriety of overthrowing or destroying any government in the United States by force or violence, or by the assassination of any officer of any such government;

. . . .

"(3)   to organize or help to organize any society, group, or assembly of persons who teach, advocate, or encourage the overthrow or destruction of any government in the United States by force or violence; or to be or become a member of, or affiliate with, any such society, group, or assembly of persons, knowing the purposes thereof.

. . . .

"Sec. 3.   It shall be unlawful for any person to attempt to commit, or to conspire to commit, any of the acts prohibited by the provisions of this title."

The indictment charged the petitioners with wilfully and knowingly conspiring (1) to organize as the Communist Party of the United States of America a society, group and assembly of persons who teach and advocate the overthrow and destruction of the Government of the United States by force and violence, and (2) knowingly and wilfully to advocate and teach the duty and necessity of overthrowing and destroying the Government of the United States by force and violence. The indictment further alleged that § 2 of the Smith Act proscribes these acts and that any conspiracy to take such action is a violation of § 3 of the Act.

. . . Our limited grant of the writ of certiorari has removed from our consideration any question as to the sufficiency of the evidence to support the jury's determination that petitioners are guilty of the offense charged. Whether on this record petitioners did in fact advocate the overthrow of the Government by force and violence is not before us, and we must base any discussion of this point upon the conclusions stated in the opinion of the Court of Appeals, which treated the issue in great detail. That court held that the record amply supports the necessary finding of the jury that petitioners, the leaders of the Communist Party in this country, . . . intended to initiate a violent revolution whenever the propitious occasion appeared. . . .

. . . .

The obvious purpose of the statute is to protect existing Government, not from change by peaceable, lawful and constitutional means, but from change by violence, revolution and terrorism. That it is within the *power* of the Congress to protect the Government of the United States from armed rebellion is a proposition which requires little discussion. Whatever theoretical merit there may be to the argument that there is a "right" to rebellion against dictatorial governments is without force where the existing structure of the government provides for peaceful and orderly change. We reject any principle of governmental helplessness in the face of preparation for revolution, which principle, carried to its logical conclusion, must lead to anarchy. No one could conceive that it is not within the power of Congress to prohibit acts intended to overthrow the Government by force and violence. The question with which we are concerned here is not whether Congress has such *power*, but whether the *means* which it has employed conflict with the First and Fifth Amendments to the Constitution.

One of the bases for the contention that the means which Congress has employed are invalid takes the form of an attack on the face of the statute on the grounds that by its terms it prohibits academic discussion of the merits of Marxism-Leninism, that it stifles ideas and is contrary to all concepts of a free speech and a free press. . . .

The very language of the Smith Act negates the interpretation which petitioners would have us impose on that Act. It is directed at advocacy, not discussion. Thus, the trial judge properly charged the jury that they could not convict if they found that petitioners did "no more than pursue peaceful studies and discussions or teaching and advocacy in the realm of ideas." He further charged that it was not unlawful "to conduct in an American college and university a course explaining the philosophical theories set forth in the books which have been placed in evidence." Such a charge is in strict accord with the statutory language, and illustrates the meaning to be placed on those words. Congress did not intend to eradicate the free discussion of political theories, to destroy the traditional rights of Americans to discuss and evaluate ideas without fear of governmental sanction. Rather Congress was concerned with the very kind of activity in which the evidence showed these petitioners engaged.

But although the statute is not directed at the hypothetical cases which petitioners have conjured, its application in this case has resulted in convictions for the teaching and advocacy of the overthrow of the Government by force and violence, which, even though coupled with the intent to accomplish that overthrow, contains an element of speech. For this reason, we must pay special heed to the demands of the First Amendment marking out the boundaries of speech.

. . . .

The rule we deduce from [prior] cases is that where an offense is specified by a statute in nonspeech or nonpress terms, a conviction relying upon speech or press as evidence of violation may be sustained only when the speech or publication created a "clear and present danger" of attempting or accomplishing the prohibited crime, e.g., interference with enlistment. The dissents, we repeat, in emphasizing the value of speech, were addressed to the argument of the sufficiency of the evidence.

. . . .

Although no case subsequent to Whitney and Gitlow has expressly overruled the majority opinions in those cases, there is little doubt that subsequent opinions have inclined toward the Holmes-Brandeis rationale. . . .

[N]either Justice Holmes nor Justice Brandeis ever envisioned that a shorthand phrase should be crystallized into a rigid rule to be applied inflexibly without regard to the circumstances of each case. Speech is not an absolute, above and beyond control by the legislature when its judgment, subject to review here, is that certain kinds of speech are so undesirable as to warrant criminal sanction. Nothing is more certain in modern society than the principle that there are no absolutes, that a name, a phrase, a standard has meaning only when associated with the considerations which gave birth to the nomenclature. To those who would paralyze our Government in the face of impending threat by encasing it in a semantic straitjacket we must reply that all concepts are relative.

In this case we are squarely presented with the application of the "clear and present danger" test, and must decide what that phrase imports. . . . Overthrow of the Government by force and violence is certainly a substantial enough interest for the Government to limit speech. Indeed, this is the ultimate value of any society, for if a society cannot protect its very structure from armed internal attack, it must follow that no subordinate value can be protected. If, then, this interest may be protected, the literal problem which is presented is what has been meant by the use of the phrase "clear and present danger" of the utterances bringing about the evil within the power of Congress to punish.

Obviously, the words cannot mean that before the Government may act, it must wait until the *putsch* is about to be executed, the plans have been laid and the signal awaited. If Government is aware that a group aiming at its overthrow is attempting to indoctrinate its members and to commit them to a course whereby they will strike when the leaders feel the circumstances permit, action by the Government is required. . . . a sufficient evil for Congress to prevent. The damage which such attempts create both physically and politically to a nation makes it impossible to measure the validity in terms of the probability of success, or the immediacy of a successful attempt. In the instant case the trial judge charged the jury that they could not convict unless they found that petitioners intended to overthrow the Government "as speedily as circumstances would permit." This does not mean, and could not properly mean, that they would not strike until there was certainty of success. What was meant was that the revolutionists would strike when they thought the time was ripe. We must therefore reject the contention that success or probability of success is the criterion.

The situation with which Justices Holmes and Brandeis were concerned in *Gitlow* was a comparatively isolated event, bearing little relation in their minds to any substantial threat to the safety of the community. . . . They were not confronted with any situation comparable to the instant one—the development of an apparatus designed and dedicated to the overthrow of the Government, in the context of world crisis after crisis.

Chief Judge Learned Hand, writing for the majority below, interpreted the phrase as follows: "In each case [courts] must ask whether the gravity of the 'evil,' discounted by its improbability, justifies such invasion of free speech as is necessary to avoid the danger." 183 F.2d at 212. We adopt this statement of the rule. As articulated by Chief Judge Hand, it is as succinct and inclusive as any other we might devise at this time. It takes into consideration those factors which we deem relevant, and relates their significances. More we cannot expect from words.

Likewise, we are in accord with the court below, which affirmed the trial court's finding that the requisite danger existed. The mere fact that from the period 1945 to 1948 petitioners' activities did not result in an attempt to overthrow the Government by force and violence is of course no answer to the fact that there was a group that was ready to make the attempt. The formation by petitioners of such a highly organized conspiracy, with rigidly disciplined members subject to call when the leaders, these petitioners, felt that the time had come for action, coupled with the inflammable nature of world conditions, similar uprisings in other countries, and the touch-and-go nature of our relations with countries with whom petitioners were in the very least ideologically attuned, convince us that their convictions were justified on this score. And this analysis disposes of the contention that a conspiracy to advocate, as distinguished from the advocacy itself, cannot be constitutionally restrained, because it comprises only the preparation. It is the existence of the conspiracy which creates the danger. If the ingredients of the reaction are present, we cannot bind the Government to wait until the catalyst is added.

. . . .

We hold that §§ 2(a) (1), 2(a) (3) and 3 of the Smith Act, do not inherently, or as construed or applied in the instant case, violate the First Amendment and other provisions of the Bill of Rights, or the First and Fifth Amendments because of indefiniteness. Petitioners intended to overthrow the Government of the United States as speedily as the circumstances would permit. Their conspiracy to organize the Communist Party and to teach and advocate the overthrow of the Government of the United States by force and violence created a "clear and present danger" of an attempt to overthrow the Government by force and violence. They were properly and constitutionally convicted for violation of the Smith Act. The judgments of conviction are affirmed.

Affirmed.

Justice CLARK took no part in the consideration or decision of this case.

Justice FRANKFURTER, concurring in affirmance of the judgment.

. . . .

. . . Absolute rules would inevitably lead to absolute exceptions, and such exceptions would eventually corrode the rules.
The demands of free speech in a democratic society as well as
the interest in national security are better served by candid and
informed weighing of the competing interests, within the confines
of the judicial process, than by announcing dogmas too inflexible for the non-Euclidian problems to be solved.

But how are competing interests to be assessed? Since they
are not subject to quantitative ascertainment, the issue necessarily
resolves itself into asking, who is to make the adjustment?—who
is to balance the relevant factors and ascertain which interest is
in the circumstances to prevail? Full responsibility for the choice
cannot be given to the courts. Courts are not representative
bodies. They are not designed to be a good reflex of a democratic
society. Their judgment is best informed, and therefore most
dependable, within narrow limits. Their essential quality is
detachment, founded on independence. History teaches that the
independence of the judiciary is jeopardized when courts become
embroiled in the passions of the day and assume primary responsibility in choosing between competing political, economic and
social pressures.

Primary responsibility for adjusting the interests which compete in the situation before us of necessity belongs to the Congress. The nature of the power to be exercised by this Court has
been delineated in decisions not charged with the emotional
appeal of situations such as that now before us. We are to set
aside the judgment of those whose duty it is to legislate only if
there is no reasonable basis for it. We are to determine whether
a statute is sufficiently definite to meet the constitutional requirements of due process, and whether it respects the safeguards
against undue concentration of authority secured by separation
of power. . . .

. . . .

Justice BLACK, dissenting.

. . . .

Justice DOUGLAS, dissenting.

. . . .

The vice of treating speech as the equivalent of overt acts of a
treasonable or seditious character is emphasized by a concurring
opinion, which by invoking the law of conspiracy makes speech
do service for deeds which are dangerous to society. The doctrine
of conspiracy has served divers and oppressive purposes and in
its broad reach can be made to do great evil. But never until
today has anyone seriously thought that the ancient law of conspiracy could constitutionally be used to turn speech into sedi-

tious conduct. Yet that is precisely what is suggested. I repeat that we deal here with speech alone, not with speech *plus* acts of sabotage or unlawful conduct. Not a single seditious act is charged in the indictment. To make a lawful speech unlawful because two men conceive it is to raise the law of conspiracy to appalling proportions. That course is to make a radical break with the past and to violate one of the cardinal principles of our constitutional scheme.

. . . .

There comes a time when even speech loses its constitutional immunity. Speech innocuous one year may at another time fan such destructive flames that it must be halted in the interests of the safety of the Republic. That is the meaning of the clear and present danger test. When conditions are so critical that there will be no time to avoid the evil that the speech threatens, it is time to call a halt. Otherwise, free speech which is the strength of the Nation will be the cause of its destruction.

---

## NOTES

1. Does Vinson really follow the old "reasonableness" test of Justice Sanford in *Gitlow*?

Notice Frankfurter's attack on the clear and present danger doctrine. Do you agree with him that the doctrine was an "inflexible dogma supporting 'uncritical libertarian generalities.' "?

Justice Jackson, concurring, took the position that the clear and present danger test was designed for domestic subversion but not for a case like *Dennis* which involved Communist Party leaders controlled by a foreign power. What rebuttal would you make to this contention?

Justice Black in dissent criticized any test which sustained laws "suppressing freedom of speech and press on the basis of Congress' or our own notions of mere 'reasonableness.' "

2. Vinson said he agreed with the test used by Judge Learned Hand in the court of appeals which was "whether the gravity of the 'evil,' discounted by its improbability, justifies such invasion of free speech as is necessary to avoid the danger." Do you think Vinson's application of clear and present danger is, in fact, the same as Hand's formulation of the doctrine?

Vinson was certain that the clear and present danger test, thus understood, did not mean that government action is prohibited "until the putsch is about to be executed." Vinson denied "success or probability of success" was appropriate in applying the clear and present danger test. Operating from these premises Vinson was driven to set aside the factor of time in applying the clear and present danger test.

3. Frankfurter's long concurrence in *Dennis* argues for a balancing approach for cases where the values of freedom of expression and national security are in conflict. As articulated, this appears to be a rational and dispassionate approach.

But Frankfurter intends the balancing to be done by the Congress rather than by the court. What difference does it make? It is Congress which has passed the law which is under attack as violative of the first amendment. If the congressional determination is to be upheld on the theory that the congressional balancing decision should be respected, there is no place for judicial review. Unless it can be said Congress engaged in no balancing process whatever, the congressional determination controls. Frankfurter extolls his approach as implementing the popular or democratic will and as causing no lasting damage to civil liberties. Frankfurter says in *Dennis* on this point: "But it is relevant to remind that in sustaining the power of Congress in a case like this nothing irrevocable is done. The democratic process at all events is not impaired or restricted. Power and responsibility remain with the people and immediately with their representatives. All the Court says is that Congress was not forbidden by the Court to pass this enactment and that a prosecution under it may be brought against a conspiracy such as the one before us."

Are majoritarianism and constitutionalism necessarily synonymous? The purpose behind constitutional limitations such as the Bill of Rights, after all, is to protect certain values from destruction by a legislative majority. In this sense, a basic American constitutional goal is limitation of majority will. Therefore, it is somewhat anomalous if majority preference, as expressed in a statute, is given too heavy a weight in evaluating whether such a statute violates a constitutional limitation such as the first amendment.

4. The favorable result in *Dennis* encouraged the government to continue its program of criminal prosecution of Communists under the Smith Act. The target now broadened to reach not just the Party leaders but the smaller-fry in the Party leadership as well. Attempts by persons convicted as a result of these prosecutions to win Supreme Court review failed in the years immediately following *Dennis*. Finally, in 1955, the court granted certiorari in the case of Yates v. United States, 354 U.S. 298 (1957). The decision in the case revealed that the court had engaged in one of its more celebrated somersaults.

Although *Yates* was professedly a case involving judicial construction of the Smith Act rather than a case involving direct interpretation of the first amendment, the court in *Yates* had clearly narrowed the scope of *Dennis*. A key passage in *Yates* is found in this excerpt from Justice Harlan's opinion for the court:

> We are thus faced with the question whether the Smith Act prohibits advocacy and teaching of forcible overthrow as an abstract principle, divorced from any effect to instigate action to that end, so long as such advocacy or teaching is engaged in with evil intent. We hold that it does not.
>
> The distinction between advocacy of abstract doctrine and advocacy directed at promoting unlawful action is one that has been consistently recognized in the decisions of this Court. . . .

An embarrassing question was whether the distinction between "advocacy of abstract doctrine" and "advocacy directed at promoting unlawful action" had been recognized in *Dennis*. Justice Harlan in *Yates* preferred to read *Dennis* as if distinction had been honored there:

> The Government's reliance on this Court's decision in *Dennis* is misplaced. . . . It is true that at one point in the late Chief Justice's opinion it is stated that the Smith Act "is directed at advocacy, not discussion." . . . [B]ut it is clear that the reference was to advocacy of action, not ideas, for in the very next sentence the opinion emphasizes that the jury was properly instructed that there could be no conviction for "advocacy in the realm of ideas." The two concurring opinions in that case likewise emphasized the distinction with which we are concerned.

Harlan in *Yates* stated the *Dennis* holding anew:

> The essence of the *Dennis* holding was that indoctrination of a group in preparation for future violent action, as well as exhortation to immediate action, by advocacy found to be directed to "action for the accomplishment" of forcible over-throw, to violence "as a rule or principle of action," and employing "language of incitement," . . . is not constitutionally protected when the group is of sufficient size and cohesiveness, is sufficiently oriented towards action, and other circumstances are such as reasonable to justify apprehension that action will occur.

Justice Clark believed that *Dennis* and *Yates* were inconsistent. The charge to the jury of the trial judge in *Yates* was in his view correct. Clark did not agree that *Dennis* required, as

Harlan put it in *Yates,* that the jury be told that the Smith Act "does not denounce advocacy in the sense of preaching abstractly the forcible overthrow of the government."

Dissenting, Justice Clark made the following caustic comments about the Harlan statement in *Yates* on the "essence of *Dennis*":

> I have read this statement over and over but do not seem to grasp its meaning for I see no resemblance between it and what the respected Chief Justice wrote in *Dennis,* nor do I find any such theory in the concurring opinions. As I see it, the trial judge charged in essence all that was required under *Dennis* opinions, whether one takes the view of the Chief Justice or of those concurring in the judgment.

The key development in *Yates* was that it precluded the idea that advocacy of abstract doctrine could be punishable consistent with the first amendment. Advocacy of action, as defined by Harlan in *Yates,* alone was punishable. In this view, *Yates* was considered a welcome advance by libertarians over *Dennis.*

### 7.  The Resurrection of Clear and Present Danger

#### BRANDENBURG v. OHIO
Supreme Court of the United States
395 U.S. 444, 23 L. Ed. 2d 430, 89 S. Ct. 1827  (1969)

PER CURIAM.

The appellant, a leader of a Ku Klux Klan group, was convicted under the Ohio Criminal Syndicalism statute for "advocat[ing] . . . the duty, necessity, or propriety of crime, sabotage, violence, or unlawful methods of terrorism as a means of accomplishing industrial or political reform" and for "voluntarily assembl[ing] with any society, group, or assemblage of persons formed to teach or advocate the doctrines of criminal syndicalism." Ohio Rev. Code Ann. § 2923.13. . . .

. . . .

The Ohio Criminal Syndicalism Statute was enacted in 1919. From 1917 to 1920, identical or quite similar laws were adopted by 20 States and two territories. In 1927, this Court sustained the constitutionality of California's Criminal Syndicalism Act, the text of which is quite similar to that of the laws of Ohio. *Whitney v. California.* The Court upheld the statute on the ground that, without more, "advocating" violent means to effect political and economic change involves such danger to the security of the State that the State may outlaw it. . . . But *Whitney* has been thoroughly discredited by later decisions. See Dennis v. United States, 341 U.S. 494 (1951). These later decisions have fashioned the principle that the constitutional guarantees of free speech and free press do not permit a State to forbid or proscribe advocacy of the use of force or of law violation except where such advocacy is directed to inciting or producing imminent lawless action and is likely to incite or produce such actions. . . . A statute which fails to draw this distinction impermissibly intrudes upon the freedoms guaranteed by the First and Fourteenth Amendments. It sweeps within its condemnation speech which our Constitution has immunized from governmental control. . . .

Measured by this test, Ohio's Criminal Syndicalism Act cannot be sustained. The Act punishes persons who "advocate or teach the duty, necessity, or propriety" of violence "as a means of accomplishing industrial or political reform"; or who publish or circulate or display any book or paper containing such advocacy; or who "justify" the commission of violent acts "with intent to exemplify, spread or advocate the propriety of the doctrines of criminal syndicalism"; or who "voluntarily assemble" with a group formed "to teach or advocate the doctrines of criminal syndicalism." Neither the indictment nor the trial judge's instructions to the jury in any way refined the statute's bald definition of the crime in terms of mere advocacy not distinguished from incitement to imminent lawless action.

Accordingly, we are here confronted with a statute which, by its own words and as applied, purports to punish mere advocacy and to forbid, on pain of criminal punishment, assembly with others merely to advocate the described type of action. Such a statute falls within the condemnation of the First and Fourteenth Amendments. The contrary teaching of *Whitney v. California,* cannot be supported, and that decision is therefore overruled.

Reversed.

Justice BLACK, concurring.

I agree with the views expressed by Mr. Justice DOUGLAS in his concurring opinion in this case that the "clear and present danger" doctrine should have no place in the interpretation of the First Amendment. I join the Court's opinion, which, as I understand it, simply cites Dennis v. United States, 341 U.S. 494 (1951), but does not indicate any agreement on the Court's part with the "clear and present danger" doctrine on which *Dennis* purported to rely.

Justice DOUGLAS, concurring.

While I join the opinion of the Court, I desire to enter a *caveat.*

. . . .

Though I doubt if the "clear and present danger" test is congenial to the First Amendment in time of a declared war, I am certain it is not reconcilable with the First Amendment in days of peace.

. . . .

. . . I see no place in the regime of the First Amendment for any "clear and present danger" test, whether strict and tight as some would make it, or free-wheeling as the Court in *Dennis* rephrased it.

When one reads the opinions closely and sees when and how the "clear and present danger" test has been applied, great misgivings are aroused. First, the threats were often loud but always puny and made serious only by judges so wedded to the *status quo* that critical analysis made them nervous. Second, the test was so twisted and perverted in *Dennis* as to make the trial of those teachers of Marxism an all-out political trial which was part and parcel of the cold war that has eroded substantial parts of the First Amendment.

Action is often a method of expression and within the protection of the First Amendment.

Suppose one tears up his own copy of the Constitution in eloquent protest to a decision of this Court. May he be indicted?

Suppose one rips his own Bible to shreds to celebrate his departure from one "faith" and his embrace of atheism. May he be indicted?

. . . .

The line between what is permissible and not subject to control and what may be made impermissible and subject to regulation is the line between ideas and overt acts.

The example usually given by those who would punish speech is the case of one who falsely shouts fire in a crowded theatre.

This is, however, a classic case where speech is brigaded with action. They are indeed inseparable and a prosecution can be launched for the overt acts actually caused. Apart from rare instances of that kind, speech is, I think, immune from prosecution. Certainly there is no constitutional line between advocacy of abstract ideas as in *Yates* and advocacy of political action as in *Scales*. The quality of advocacy turns on the depth of the conviction; and government has no power to invade that sanctuary of belief and conscience.

---

## NOTES

1. Why did the Supreme Court issue its *Brandenburg* decision as an anonymous per curiam opinion? Further, in purporting

to summarize and clarify 50 years' worth of free speech doctrine, why did *Brandenburg* spend only one brief paragraph on this issue?

One wholly new question which *Brandenburg* appeared to raise was the constitutional importance, if any, of the actual, objective danger posed by advocacy of political ideology. The per curiam opinion summarized past decisions by saying that legislative proscription of advocacy is not constitutional *except* [1] where such advocacy is directed to inciting or producing imminent lawless action *and* [2] is likely to incite or produce such action. The court thus established a two-part test. One, the subjective intent of the speaker; the other, the objective likelihood that the speaker will succeed in carrying out that intent.

2. Professor Linde contends that the "imminence" and "likelihood" of unlawful action had not been relevant in previous first amendment cases. In Linde's estimation, the *Yates* (text, p. 769) and *Scales* (text, p. 784) decisions (which did not mention the phrase, "clear and present danger") stand for the proposition that the deliberate incitement to commission of unlawful actions was outside first amendment protection and therefore subject to proscription, regardless of the imminence or probability of the unlawful actions. Linde, *"Clear and Present Danger" Re-examined: Dissonance in the Brandenburg Concerto*, 22 STAN. L. REV. 1163 (1970). If, for instance, "imminence" had been of constitutional significance when the court decided the *Dennis* case in 1951, would the convictions have stood?

3. If proscription of free speech is to be judged, as *Brandenburg* suggests, by the actual danger posed by the advocacy, does this not render useless an examination of the statute on its face? Under such a standard of review, Professor Linde points out that a criminal anarchy statute "might well be unconstitutional now but might be constitutional in the light of diverse events in 1945, in 1951, in 1957, and in 1961, perhaps not in 1966, but again in 1968." Is such a result necessarily objectionable? If the American system of judicial review amounts to a continuous constitutional convention, isn't the situation Linde describes inevitable?

4. Professor Frank Strong describes the *Dennis* outcome this way: "In the hour of its greatest test, against the tough opponent of national security at mid-twentieth century, the rule of clear and present danger lost its bid for general acceptance as a requirement that for state or federal restriction of speech to be valid it must be shown that a legitimate objective of government is imminently and substantially imperiled." Strong, *Fifty*

*Years of "Clear and Present Danger": From Schenck to Branden-burg—And Beyond,* 1969 SUP. CT. REV. 41, 52.

In *Dennis,* Professor Strong points out, the court's watering-down of the "clear and present danger" test made it roughly equivalent to the "balancing-of-interests" test which Justice Frankfurter had been advocating all along. If the original "clear and present danger" test was roughly analogous to Justice Black's "preferred freedom" doctrine, we can see how far the first amendment theory strayed between *Schenck* and *Brandenburg. See* 1969 SUP. CT. REV., at 64-68.

### 8. The Balancing Test: Legislative Investigations and Government Employment

1. Watkins was prosecuted under 2 U.S.C. § 192 for contempt of Congress for refusing to answer questions "pertinent to the questions under inquiry." Although willing to testify on other matters, Watkins refused to say whether or not certain persons he knew were or had been members of the Communist Party. He refused to plead the fifth amendment but said he would not answer questions about persons who had long since severed their associations with the Communist movement. On review of his contempt conviction, the Supreme Court, per Chief Justice Warren, reversed. Watkins v. United States, 354 U.S. 178 (1957).

From the point of view of first amendment rights, the crucial aspect of the court's opinion in *Watkins* was the holding that the questions propounded to a witness by a legislative investigating committee must meet a high standard of pertinency. The reference to pertinency, of course, came from the reference in the federal congressional contempt statute, 2 U.S.C. § 192, that questions asked of a witness be "pertinent" to the inquiry. The court held that the "pertinency" required by 2 U.S.C. § 192 demanded the same precision and clarity which the due process clause of the fifth amendment required in any criminal offense. By insisting that the federal contempt statute forbade "vagueness" in propounding questions to a witness called before a committee of Congress, the scope of legislative investigation committees was confined with resultant benefit to the exercise of first amendment rights through a diminution of the pressure put on those rights by untrammeled interrogation of the past politics and associations of witnesses.

There is a fundamental problem with the technique employed by the court in *Watkins.* The court attempts to curb the power of legislative investigation committees by insisting on pertinency and specific and explicit grants of legislative authority to investigating committees. But doesn't this leave first amendment rights in this area to the mercy of the expert draftsman? In other words, suppose the legislative investigating committee's authorizing resolution was precise? Suppose, further, that the question propounded but refused answer was clearly related to the subject of legislative inquiry? And suppose, finally, that the motive behind the unanswered questions was not for information dedicated to some legislative end but to expose and, hopefully, to punish some unpopular group, person, or idea? In other words, did *Watkins* give abiding protection to infringement on first amendment rights by legislative investigating committees? The case that put the *Watkins* approach to the test of durability in this regard was Barenblatt v. United States, 360 U.S. 109 (1959).

2.  In Barenblatt v. United States, 360 U.S. 109 (1959), the court, per Justice Harlan, reviewed petitioner's contempt conviction for refusing to answer certain questions of a subcommittee of the House Un-American Activities Committee. Justice Harlan recognized that "the First Amendment in some circumstances protects an individual from being compelled to disclose his associational relationships." Nevertheless, "the protections of the First Amendment, unlike a proper claim of the privilege against self-incrimination under the Fifth Amendment, do not afford a witness the right to resist inquiry in all circumstances. Where First Amendment rights are asserted to bar governmental interrogation resolution of the issue always involves a balancing by the courts of the competing private and public interests at stake in the particular circumstances shown."

Purporting to balance the interests, the court stressed Congress' "wide power to legislate in the field of Communist activity in this Country, and to conduct appropriate investigations in aid thereof" which "[i]n the last analysis . . . rests on the right of self-preservation, 'the ultimate value of any society.' *Dennis v. United States*. . . ." Investigatory power of such activity was not "denied Congress solely because the field of education is involved."

In regard to opposing interests, Justice Harlan argued that "the record is barren of other factors which in themselves might sometimes lead to the conclusion that the individual interests at stake were not subordinate to those of the state. There is no indication in this record that the Subcommittee was attempting to pillory witnesses. Nor did petitioner's appearance as a witness follow from indiscriminate dragnet procedures, lacking in probable cause for belief that he possessed information which might be helpful to the Subcommittee. And the relevancy of the questions put to him by the Subcommittee is not open to doubt." Justice Harlan therefore concluded "that the balance between the individual and the governmental interests here at stake must be struck in favor of the latter, and that therefore the provisions of the First Amendment have not been offended."

Justice Black, joined by Chief Justice Warren and Justice Douglas, dissenting, accepted that "a law which primarily regulates conduct but which might also indirectly affect speech can be upheld if the effect on speech is minor in relation to the need for control of the conduct." But he did not agree "that laws directly abridging First Amendment freedoms can be justified by a congressional or judicial balancing process."

However, even if interests were to be balanced, Justice Black argued that the majority ignored its own test. "At most it balances the right of the Government to preserve itself, against Barenblatt's right to refrain from revealing Communist affiliations. Such a balance, however, mistakes the factors to be weighed. In the first place, it completely leaves out the real interest in Barenblatt's silence, the interest of the people as a whole in being able to join organizations, advocate causes and make political 'mistakes' without later being subjected to governmental penalties for having dared to think for themselves. It is this right, the right to error politically, which keeps us strong as a Nation."

Further, Justice Black was unable to accept the national security rationale of the majority. "That notion rests on the unarticulated premise that this Nation's security hangs upon its power to punish people because of what they think, speak or write about, or because of those with whom they associate for political purposes." Instead the first amendment establishes "that the only constitutional way our Government can preserve itself is to leave its people the fullest freedom to praise, criticize or discuss, as they see fit, all governmental policies and to suggest, if they desire, that even its most fundamental postulates are bad and should be changed. . . ."

Finally, Justice Black argued that "Barenblatt's conviction violates the Constitution because the chief aim, purpose and practice of the House Un-American Activities Committee, as disclosed by its many reports, is to try witnesses and punish them because they are or had been Communists and because they refuse to admit or deny Communist affiliations." But, Justice Black argued "[i]t is the protection from arbitrary punishment through the right to a judicial trial with all . . . safeguards which over the years has distinguished America from lands where drum-head courts and other similar 'tribunals' deprive the weak and the unorthodox of life, liberty and property without due process of law."

**3.** Does the following formula make any sense to you?

*Barenblatt* is to *Watkins*

as

*Yates* is to *Dennis*

but in reverse.

In both case sequences, the court retreated from a previous position, more perhaps because of a quasi-political sensitivity to the popular reaction to the previous decision, than to any felt need to reconsider legal doctrine which had previously been announced. This use of doctrine to suit political realities again reveals the court as a political as well as a legal institution. Since under Art. III, the "Judges of the Supreme and inferior Courts shall hold their Offices during good Behaviour. . . .", should Justices who enjoy what is essentially life tenure be influenced by shifting political currents? *Compare,* for example, the militant anti-Communism of the *Dennis* period, the early 'fifties, with the more relaxed liberalism exemplified by *Yates* in the late 'fifties. Similarly, why was the adverse conservative reaction to *Watkins* in 1957 so swiftly followed by capitulation in *Barenblatt* in 1959? Or is it not fair to say that one finds in *Barenblatt* a much more responsive and sympathetic view of Congress' power to investigate and less concerned approach to freedom of association as evidenced by *Barenblatt*?

**4.** Reading Harlan's opinion in *Barenblatt,* which amendment would you say is absolute for Harlan? Although Lloyd Barenblatt could have used the fifth amendment, he expressly disclaimed reliance on it in preference to the first amendment. Barenblatt was truly a martyr to an absolutist view of the first amendment. Do you think Barenblatt and his counsel were justified in feeling that the *Watkins* decision supported the first amendment claim?

Black says the court poses the issue as the government's right of self-preservation against Barenblatt's right to refrain from revealing Communist affiliations. The real issue, he says, is the government's interest in its security against the constitutionally protected rights of association and expression. If "balancing" is capable of such different interpretations, is it not fairly useless as a test for constitutional adjudication? Or as Laurent Frantz put it: "How is the judge to convert balancing into something that does not merely give him back whatever answer he feeds into it?" *See* Frantz, *Is the First Amendment Law?—A Reply to Professor Mendelson*, 51 CALIF. L. REV. 729 (1963).

Frantz criticized the "balancing" test for its gross imprecision: "Which 'interest' is the judge to balance against which? It is obvious that if he balances Mr. Barenblatt's personal interests against 'national self-preservation' he will get one result. If he balances the Committee's desire to verify Mr. Crowley's testimony against freedom of speech, and also assumes that an important public interest is at stake in the latter, he will get another. So it appears to be very difficult for him to identify the 'interests' without predetermining the result. The difficulty is emphasized by the ease with which Justice Black, while continuing to protest 'balancing,' demonstrates that, for him, it would produce an opposite result. He simply trims the asserted governmental interest to more moderate size, puts a more generalized (and therefore weightier) free speech interest on the other side of the scales, and there you are. Anyone can do it. And anyone can reverse it just as easily by the opposite process."

*Compare:* Mendelson, *On the Meaning of the First Amendment: Absolutes in the Balance*, 50 CALIF. L. REV. 821 (1962); *The First Amendment and the Judicial Process: A Reply to Mr. Frantz*, 17 VAND. L. REV. 479 (1964).

5. Reading *Watkins* and *Barenblatt* together must we conclude that so long as the technical requirements of "pertinency" as defined by Chief Justice Warren in *Watkins* are met, the clash of an individual's exercise of first amendment rights and a congressional investigative committee's request for compulsory testimony will nearly always result in a victory for the congressional committee and the subordination of the first amendment claim? As Justice Harlan conceives the "balancing" test, is it possible for a first amendment claim asserted by an individual ever to prevail against a governmental claim for self-preservation?

It may be argued that there is more left to the "pertinency" requirement than too close a focus on the facts of *Barenblatt* betrays. After all, in an investigation of education, questions were asked of an educator concerning himself. It may be said that here we are in the very matrix of a "pertinent" question but questions farther afield are still safely kept at bay by *Watkins*. Do you agree?

6. Although in *Barenblatt*, congressional power to investigate was upheld, the investigative powers of state legislatures were curtailed in Gibson v. Florida Legislative Investigation Comm., 372 U.S. 539 (1963).

Goldberg, J., speaking for the court in *Gibson* said:

"Significantly, the parties are in substantial agreement as to the proper test to be applied to reconcile the competing claims of government and individual and to determine the propriety of the Committee's demands . . . it is an essential prerequisite to the validity of an investigation which intrudes into the area of constitutionally protected rights of speech, press, association and petition that the State convincingly show a substantial relation between the information sought and a subject of overriding and compelling state interest. Absent such a relation between the N.A.A.C.P. and conduct in which the State may have a compelling regulatory concern, the Committee has not 'demonstrated so cogent an interest in obtaining and making public' the membership information sought to be obtained as to 'justify the substantial abridgment of associational freedom which such disclosures will effect.' Bates v. Little Rock [361 U.S. 516 (1960)].

. . . .

"[I]t is not alleged Communists who are the witnesses before the Committee and it is not discovery of their membership in that party which is the object of the challenged inquiries. Rather, it is the N.A.A.C.P. itself which is the subject of the investigation, and it is its local president, the petitioner, who was called before the Committee and held in contempt because he refused to divulge the contents of its membership records. There is no suggestion that the Miami branch of the N.A.A.C.P. or the national organization with which it is affiliated were, or are, themselves subversive organizations. . . .

". . . [W]e are asked to find a compelling and subordinating state interest which must exist if essential freedoms are to be curtailed or inhibited. This we cannot do. The respondent Committee has laid no adequate foundation for its direct demands upon the officers and records of a wholly legitimate organization for disclosure of its membership; the Committee has neither demonstrated nor pointed out any threat to the State by virtue of the existence of the N.A.A.C.P. or the pursuit of its activities or the minimal associational ties of the 14 asserted Communists. The strong associational interest in maintaining the privacy of membership lists of groups engaged in the constitutionally protected free trade in ideas and beliefs may not be substantially infringed upon such a slender showing as here made by the respondent. While, of course, all legitimate organizations are the beneficiaries of these protections, they are all the more essential here, where the challenged privacy is that of persons espousing beliefs already unpopular with their neighbors and the deterrent and 'chilling' effect on the free exercise of constitutionally enshrined rights of free speech, expression, and association are consequently the more immediate and substantial. . . ."

7.    In De Gregory v. Attorney General, 383 U.S. 825 (1966), state investigating power was curbed on the authority of *Gibson*. In 1964, De Gregory testified that he had no knowledge or affiliation with Communist activities since 1957 but he refused to respond to questions concerning Communist activities prior to 1957. For his refusal to respond to a lawfully authorized investigation into subversive activities in New Hampshire by the state attorney general, De Gregory was held in contempt. The Supreme Court, per Douglas, J., held that New Hampshire had acted unconstitutionally. The Supreme Court held that there was no showing of "overriding and compelling state need" as required by *Gibson:*

> The information being sought was historical, not current. Lawmaking at the investigatory stage may properly probe historic events for any light that may be thrown on present conditions and problems. But the First Amendment prevents the Government from using the power to investigate enforced by the contempt power to probe at will and without relation to existing need. The present record is devoid of any evidence that there is any Communist movement in New Hampshire. . . . There is thus absent that (required) "nexus" between petitioner and subversive activities in New Hampshire. . . .

Protesting that the majority was passing judgment on the wisdom of the investigation, contrary to *Barenblatt*, Justice Harlan, with whom Stewart and White joined, dissented. Harlan said: "I cannot say as a constitutional matter that inquiry into the current operations of the local Communist Party could not be advanced by knowledge of its operations a decade ago."

## GOVERNMENT EMPLOYMENT, NATIONAL SECURITY AND THE FIRST AMENDMENT—THE *ROBEL* CASE

A first amendment case which, on the merits, appeared appropriate for resolution by a "balancing" type analysis was United States v. Robel, 389 U.S. 258 (1967). In *Robel*, the Supreme Court invalidated a provision of the Subversive Activities Control Act of 1950, § 5(a)(1)(D), which prohibited members of communist-action organizations under a final order to register from engaging in "any employment in any defense facility."

The court refused to read the elements of active membership and specific intent into the provision to save the statute as the court had done with the membership clause of the Smith Act. *See* text, pp. 783-86. The court instead said the case was governed by Aptheker v. Secretary of State, 378 U.S. 500 (1964), where the court held that the clarity and precision of the provision at issue made it impossible to narrow its indiscriminate scope. Accordingly in *Robel*, the court held § 5(a)(1)(D) invalid "because that statute sweeps indiscriminately across all types of associations with communist-action groups, without regard to the quality and degree of membership."

The court agreed that a basis under the war power could be ascribed to the offending provision. The case, therefore, presented a clash between the exercise of constitutionally authorized legislative power and an individual's assertion of a first amendment right. The court declined to utilize the "balancing" test to resolve this clash. Chief Justice Warren expressed the holding of the court as follows:

> Our decision today simply recognizes that, when legitimate legislature concerns are expressed in a substantial burden on protected First Amendment activities, congress must achieve its goal by means which have a "less drastic" impact on the continued vitality of First Amendment freedoms.

Chief Justice Warren explained in a footnote the court's refusal to use a balancing approach rationale as follows:

"It has been suggested that this case should be decided by 'balancing' the governmental interests expressed in § 5(a)(1)(D) against the First Amendment rights asserted by the appellee. This we decline to do. We recognize that both interests are substantial, but we deem it inappropriate for this Court to label one as being more important or more substantial than the other. Our inquiry is more circumscribed. Faced with a clear conflict between a federal statute enacted in the interests of national security and an individual's exercise of his First Amendment rights, we have confined our analysis to whether Congress has adopted a constitutional means in achieving its concededly legitimate legislative goal. In making this determination we have found it necessary to measure the validity of the means adopted by Congress against both the goal it has sought to achieve and the specific prohibitions of the First Amendment. But we have in no way 'balanced' those respective interests. We have ruled only that the Constitution requires that the conflict between congressional power and individual rights be accommodated by legislation drawn more narrowly to avoid the conflict.

There is, of course, nothing novel in that analysis. Such a course of adjudication was enunciated by Chief Justice Marshall when he declared: 'Let the end be legitimate, let it be within the scope of the constitution, and all means which are appropriate, which are plainly adapted to that end, which are not prohibited, but which consist with the letter and spirit of the constitution, are constitutional.' *McCulloch v. State of Maryland,* 4 Wheat. 316, 421, 4 L.Ed. 579 (emphasis added). In this case, the means chosen by Congress are contrary to the 'letter and spirit' of the First Amendment."

---

## NOTES

1. One of the particularly baffling aspects of constitutional law is the difficulty in being able to predict when a particular constitutional doctrine will be selected by the court to become the operational major premise of a case and when it will not. In *Robel,* the court deliberately eschewed the "balancing" test for a far more limited mode of measuring the relative strengths of competing constitutional values and used an alternative means test.

2. Is the reason that the court declined to use the "balancing" test in *Robel* attributable to the fact that *federal* legislation was at issue? As it was, *Robel* is a very rare example of the use of judicial review to invalidate a provision of a *federal* statute on the basis of the first amendment.

9. Freedom of Association for Social and Political Action: Another Context for the Balancing Test?

a. *The Communist Party Cases and Freedom of Association*

In June, 1961, the Supreme Court decided three cases, Communist Party of the United States v. Subversive Activities Control Bd., 367 U.S. 1 (1961); Scales v. United States, 367 U.S. 203 (1961); and Noto v. United States, 367 U.S. 290 (1961), which upheld national security laws and took a narrow view of the first amendment guarantee of freedom of association. The three cases involved federal legislation directed at the American Communist Party and its members, *i.e.,* the Smith Act of 1940, as amended, and the Subversive Activities Control Act of 1950. 18 U.S.C. § 2385; 50 U.S.C. § 781 *et seq.* The Communist Party and several individual members challenged the federal laws on a variety of constitutional grounds, including a claim that the laws restrained political activity and advocacy in violation of the first amendment. The majority of the court turned down that argument and all others raised against the constitutional validity of the national security legislation.

The Communist Party cases arose out of legislation enacted by Congress at the height of popular feeling against Communism. The cases wound their way through years of litigation, and finally reached the Supreme Court for adjudication in 1961, long after the anti-Communist feeling had died down. Nevertheless, the court exercised extreme deference to the "findings" made in 1950. The *Scales* decision is indicative of the court's deference.

Scales v. United States, 367 U.S. 203 (1961) concerned a constitutional challenge to the federal statute which had been the focal point of the *Dennis* case, the Smith Act. This law included a membership clause (18 U.S.C. § 2385) which made it a felony for any person to be a member of an organization which advocated the forceful overthrow of the government, knowing the purposes of the organization. The obvious target was the Communist Party. The petitioner, Scales, was an official of the Communist Party who had been sentenced to six years in prison under the membership clause. Scales brought his appeal on first and fifth amendment grounds.

In upholding the Smith Act membership clause, the court, per Justice Harlan, virtually rewrote the membership clause, reading into it several narrowing elements which Congress itself had not seen fit to include. For instance, the statute did not say that in order to satisfy the membership clause's "knowing" element, a Party member need exhibit a specific mental intent to advocate illegal actions. The statute was silent on this point. The court, however, held that the statute was only to be enforced if an element of specific intent on the defendant's part to advocate illegal acts could be shown, beyond mere intent to advocate abstract doctrine. Thus, Justice Harlan wrote, Scales's membership in the Communist Party was not constitutionally protected at all, and first amendment considerations were irrelevant, since there was evidence that Scales had had a specific intent to advocate illegal acts.

Since the membership clause of the Smith Act provided for penalties of up to 20 years' imprisonment and a fine of up to $20,000, Justice Black, in dissent, accused the majority of establishing an *ex post facto* law. Justice Black said that if Congress had intended to make specific illegal intent an element of the membership clause offense, it would have written it into the statute. By implying additional and uncalled-for language into the membership clause, he said, the court violated due process.

Furthermore, Justice Black asserted, the result in *Scales* demonstrated the bankruptcy of the "balancing of interests" approach to first amendment freedoms. He charged that the court had " 'balanced' away the protections of the first amendment," by applying a test under which almost any act of government suppression could be upheld. The court, he said, was adopting, without critical analysis, the legislative judgments of Congress. Congress "found" that the activities of subversive organizations posed an overriding threat to the national interest. The court, Black argued, merely accepted this political judgment by the Congress. Then, in bootstrap fashion, it took this "national interest" and balanced it against the "individual interest" of the petitioner. Naturally, the national interest appeared subordinating. This method of balancing-of-interests, said Justice Black, would invariably come down on the side of the governmental interest, so long as the Congress was alert enough to couch its national security legislation in suitably crisis-oriented "findings." If the court as here, refused to analyse those "findings," then Congress, not the court, would become the arbiter of first amendment freedoms. To Justice Black, this was anathema.

Justice Douglas also dissented in *Scales,* saying the result put a serious and sinister light on a once-comic observation by Mark Twain: "It is by the goodness of God that in our country we have those three unspeakably precious things: freedom of speech, freedom of conscience, and the prudence never to practice either one of them."

---

### NOTES

1.  Section 6 of the Subversive Activities Control Act of 1950 had prohibited registrants from applying for passports. In Aptheker v. Secretary of State, 378 U.S. 500 (1964), the Supreme Court, per Justice Goldberg, held § 6 unconstitutional on its face. In a 6-3 decision, the court ruled that freedom to travel was a fundamental right of all citizens, embodied in the first amendment freedom of association, which the government could not abridge without meeting constitutional tests. Section 6, said the court, on its face applied to all registrants, whether or not they were active participants in a subversive organization; whether or not they were personally committed to the organization's goals and purpose; and whether or not the passport being sought was related to a national security interest.

Notice that in *Aptheker* the Supreme Court refused to follow the example of the *Scales* decision three years earlier. The court in *Scales* had construed the statute to imply a narrow focus and specific illegal intent on the part of the accused. In *Aptheker,* the court took the words of § 6 on their face value and declined to provide a savings construction.

Justice Clark, joined by Justice Harlan and Justice White, dissented in *Aptheker.* He read § 6 as valid on its face, a rational exercise of governmental power to meet a threat to national security, and therefore not a denial of due process under the fifth amendment. He did not believe the first amendment was pertinent.

2. Under the pressure of *Aptheker* and other cases, the Congress in 1968 repealed § 7 of the Subversive Activities Control Act of 1950, requiring registration by the party, its members and officers and filing of detailed information. In its place, the Congress instituted voluntary registration for members of "Communist-action" organizations and withdrew penalties for failure to register. Registration of the party and its officers was retained.

In repealing the compulsory registration requirements which had been unsuccessfully fought in the *Subversive Activities Control Board* case, Congress appeared primarily concerned about the fifth amendment, rather than the first amendment problems entailed by § 7. Undoubtedly, too, the Congress of 1968 entertained fewer fears of Communist subversion than had the Congress of 1950. While the 1968 legislative history shows efforts by the House Un-American Activities Committee to reiterate the "findings" of the 1950 Act, the record also contains dissenting remarks by congressmen deploring anti-Communist hysteria and citing first and fifth amendment grounds for rejecting the 1950 Act altogether.

Thus, the Congress after 18 years did what the Supreme Court had refused to do. It assessed the 1950 Act in its political context and applied critical analysis to the "findings" which formed the underpinning for its provisions. Do you think that the Supreme Court, in the 1961 cases, failed to carry its responsibilities? Or was its deference to the legislative determination the proper approach to such a delicate political issue?

### b. First Amendment Freedom to Associate for Social and Political Action

Before the advent of student sit-ins and of Northern civil rights workers into the Deep South, the movement for racial equality in the South was led by local organizations such as state chapters of the National Association for the Advancement of Colored People (NAACP). The NAACP, incorporated in New York State, had affiliates in various Southern communities, which worked tirelessly in the civil rights struggle. The Alabama chapter of the NAACP, for example, was active in support of the Montgomery bus boycott of 1956. The boycott, which became a pivotal event in the civil rights movement, was organized by the late Rev. Dr. Martin Luther King, Jr., then a young minister of a black church in Montgomery.

NAACP support of this and other civil rights efforts incurred the wrath of Alabama state officials. In 1956, state attorney general John Patterson moved against the Alabama chapter of the NAACP in an attempt to drive it from the state. Patterson's effort culminated in a landmark Supreme Court decision, NAACP v. Alabama *ex rel.* Patterson, 357 U.S. 449 (1958). In this case, the court unanimously ruled that the NAACP could not be compelled to disclose to the state the names of its Alabama members. To compel disclosure, said the court, per Justice Harlan, would violate the first amendment guarantee of freedom of association, applicable to the states through the due process clause of the fourteenth amendment. Justice Harlan's opinion affirmed the right to associate for the advancement of social and political beliefs, however unpopular or controversial. However, the decision in *NAACP v. Alabama* did not provide automatic immunity from state inquiry into social action organizations. The test applied involved a balancing-of-interests approach which other cases might well follow in the future (and in fact did).

In *NAACP v. Alabama,* the Supreme Court reasoned that there was a link between the first amendment freedom of association and the individual's right to privacy: "Inviolability of privacy in group association may in many circumstances be indispensable to preservation of freedom of association, particularly where a group espouses dissident beliefs." In its challenge to the membership registration requirement of the Subversive Activities Control Act in the Communist Party Cases, the party had argued that the holding in *NAACP v. Alabama* should be applied to protect the party against forced disclosure of its membership. Why did the court reject this argument? Do you think its rejection was consistent with Justice Harlan's approach in *NAACP v. Alabama?*

One clue to a difference between the two cases is found in the *NAACP* opinion itself. An earlier Supreme Court decision, Bryant v. Zimmerman, 278 U.S. 63 (1928) had upheld a New York law requiring registration of Ku Klux Klan members. Naturally, the state of Alabama relied upon *Bryant* in its own case before the court. But Justice Harlan distinguished *Bryant* on the ground that the Ku Klux Klan was an organization dedicated to unlawful acts and violence. Should the *NAACP* Court have distinguished *Bryant* or overruled it? Do you think the distinction is justified? Isn't it likely that groups espousing dissident beliefs may be regarded by legislatures and courts as prone to unlawful acts and therefore vulnerable to forced disclosure of membership? Isn't this precisely the constitutional danger the court sought to avoid in *NAACP v. Alabama?* The NAACP was not a respectable organization in the minds of state officials of Alabama, but it was viewed more positively by the members of the court. Is this a proper basis on which to protect one organization but not another?

### c.  Freedom of Association and Loyalty Oaths

### COLE v. RICHARDSON

Supreme Court of the United States
405 U.S. 676, 31 L. Ed. 2d 593, 92 S. Ct. 1332 (1972)

Chief Justice BURGER delivered the opinion of the Court.

In this appeal we review the decision of the three-judge District Court holding a Massachusetts loyalty oath unconstitutional, 300 F. Supp. 1321.

The appellee, Richardson, was hired as a research sociologist by the Boston State Hospital. The appellant is superintendent of the hospital. Soon after she entered on duty Mrs. Richardson was asked to subscribe to the oath required of all public employees in Massachusetts. The oath is as follows:

"I do solemnly swear (or affirm) that I will uphold and defend the Constitution of the United States of America and the Constitution of the Commonwealth of Massachusetts and that I will oppose the overthrow of the government of the United States of America or of this Commonwealth by force, violence or by any illegal or unconstitutional method."

Mrs. Richardson informed that hospital's personnel department that she could not take the oath as ordered because of her belief that it was in violation of the United States Constitution. Approximately 10 days later appellant Cole personally informed Mrs. Richardson that under state law she could not continue as an employee of the Boston State Hospital unless she subscribed to the oath. Again she refused. On November 25, 1968, Mrs. Richardson's employment was terminated and she was paid through that date.

. . . .

We conclude that the Massachusetts oath is constitutionally permissible. . . .

A review of the oath cases in this Court will put the instant oath into context. We have made clear that neither federal nor state governments may condition employment on taking oaths which impinge rights guaranteed by the First and Fourteenth Amendments respectively, as for example those relating to political beliefs. Nor may employment be conditioned on an oath that one has not engaged, or will not engage, in protected speech activities such as the following: criticizing institutions of government; discussing political doctrine that approves the overthrow of certain forms of government; and supporting candidates for political office. Keyishian v. Board of Regents, 385 U.S. 589 (1967); Baggett v. Bullitt, 377 U.S. 360 (1964). Employment may not be conditioned on an oath denying past, or abjuring future, associational activities within constitutional protection; such protected activities include membership in organizations having illegal purposes unless one knows of the purpose and shares a specific intent to promote the illegal purpose. Whitehill v. Elkins, 389 U.S. 54 (1967); Keyishian v. Board of Regents, *supra;* Elfbrandt v. Russell, 384 U.S. 11 (1966). . . . Concern for vagueness in the oath cases has been especially great because uncertainty as to an oath's meaning may deter individuals from engaging in constitutionally protected activity conceivably within the scope of the oath.

. . . .

Several cases recently decided by the Court stand out among our oath cases because they have upheld the constitutionality of oaths, addressed to the future, promising constitutional support in broad terms. . . .

. . . .

The District Court in the instant case properly recognized that the first clause of the Massachusetts oath, in which the individual swears to "uphold and defend" the constitutions of the United States and the Commonwealth, is indistinguishable from the oaths this Court has recently approved. Yet the District Court applied a highly literalistic approach to the second clause to strike it down. We view the second clause of the oath as essentially the same as the first.

The second clause of the oath contains a promise to "oppose the overthrow of the government of the United States of America or of this Commonwealth by force, violence or by any illegal or unconstitutional method." The District Court sought to give a dictionary meaning to this language and found "oppose" to raise the specter of vague, undefinable responsibilities actively to combat a potential overthrow of the government. That reading of the oath understandably troubled the court because of what it saw as vagueness in terms of what threats would constitute sufficient danger of overthrow to require the oathgiver to actively oppose overthrow, and exactly what actions he would have to take in that respect.

But such a literal approach to the second clause is inconsistent with the Court's approach to the "support" oaths. One could make a literal argument that "support" involves nebulous, undefined responsibilities for action in some hypothetical situations. . . . We have rejected such rigidly literal notions and recognized that the purpose leading legislatures to enact such oaths, just as the purpose leading the Framers of our Constitution to include the two explicit constitutional oaths, was not to create specific responsibilities but to assure that those in positions of public trust were willing to commit themselves to live by the constitutional processes of our system. . . . Here the second clause does not require specific action in some hypothetical or actual situation. Plainly "force, violence or . . . any illegal or unconstitutional method" modifies "overthrow" and does not commit the oath taker to meet force with force. Just as the connotatively active word "support" has been interpreted to mean simply a commitment to abide by our constitutional system, the second clause of this oath is merely oriented to the negative implication of this notion; it is a commitment not to use illegal and constitutionally unprotected force to change the constitutional system. The second clause does not expand the obligation of the first; it simply makes clear the application of the first clause to a particular issue. Such repetition, whether for emphasis or cadence, seems to be wont with authors of oaths. That the second clause may be redundant is no ground to strike it down; we are not charged with correcting grammar but with enforcing a constitution.

The purpose of the oath is clear on its face. We cannot presume that the Massachusetts legislature intended by its use of such general terms as "uphold," "defend," and "oppose" to impose obligations of specific, positive action on oath takers. Any such construction would raise serious questions whether the oath was so vague as to amount to a denial of due process.

Nor is the oath as interpreted void for vagueness. As Mr. Justice Harlan pointed out in his opinion on our earlier consideration of this case, the oath is "no more than an amenity." It is punishable only by a prosecution for perjury and, since perjury is a knowing and willful falsehood, the constitutional vice of punishment without fair warning cannot occur here. Nor here is there any problem of the punishment inflicted by mere prosecution. There has been no prosecution under this statute since its 1948 enactment, and there is no indication that prosecutions have been planned or begun. The oath "triggered no serious pos-

sibility of prosecution" by the Commonwealth. Were we confronted with a record of actual prosecutions or harassment
through threatened prosecutions, we might be faced with a different question. Those who view the Massachusetts oath in terms
of an endless "parade of horribles" would do well to bear in
mind that many of the hazards of human existence that can be
imagined are circumscribed by the classic observation of Mr. Justice Holmes, when confronted with the prophecy of dire consequences of certain judicial action, that it would not occur "while
this Court sits."

Appellee mounts an additional attack on the Massachusetts
oath program in that it does not provide for a hearing prior to
the determination not to hire the individual based on the refusal
to subscribe to the oath. All of the cases in this Court which
require a hearing before discharge for failure to take an oath
involved impermissible oaths. . . . In the circumstances of those
cases only by holding a hearing, showing evidence of disloyalty,
and allowing the employee an opportunity to respond might the
State develop a permissible basis for concluding that the employee
was to be discharged.

Since there is no constitutionally protected right to overthrow
a government by force, violence, or illegal or unconstitutional
means, no constitutional right is infringed by an oath to abide
by the constitutional system in the future. Therefore there is no
requirement that one who refuses to take the Massachusetts
oath be granted a hearing for the determination of some other
fact before being discharged.

The judgment of the District Court is reversed and the case
is remanded for further proceedings consistent with this opinion.

Justice POWELL and Justice REHNQUIST took no part in the
consideration or decision in this case.

Justice DOUGLAS, dissenting.

. . . .

Justice MARSHALL, with whom Justice BRENNAN joins, dissenting.

. . . .

It is the second half of the oath to which I object. I find the
language . . . to be impermissibly vague and overbroad.

. . . .

I would also strike down the second half of this oath as an
overbroad infringement of protected expression and conduct.

The Court's prior decisions represent a judgment that simple
affirmative oaths of support are less suspect and less evil than
negative oaths requiring a disaffirmance of political ties, group
affiliations, or beliefs.

Yet, I think that it is plain that affirmative oaths of loyalty, no less than negative ones, have odious connotations and that they present dangers. We have tolerated support oaths as applied to all government employees only because we view these affirmations as an expression of "minimal loyalty to the Government." Such oaths are merely indications by the employee "in entirely familiar and traditional language that he will endeavor to perform his public duties lawfully."

It is precisely because these oaths are minimal, requiring only that nominal expression of allegiance "which, by the common law, every citizen was understood to owe his sovereign that they have been sustained." That they are minimal intrusions into the freedom of government officials and employees to think, speak, and act makes them constitutional; it does not mean that greater intrusions will be tolerated. On the conrary, each time this Court has been faced with an attempt by government to make the traditional support oath more comprehensive or demanding, it has struck the oath down.

When faced with an "imminent clear and present danger," governments may be able to compel citizens to do things which would ordinarily be beyond their authority to mandate. But, such emergency governmental power is a far cry from compelling every state employee in advance of any such danger to promise in any and all circumstances to conform speech and conduct to opposing an "overthrow" of the government. The Constitution severely circumscribes the power of government to force its citizens to perform symbolic gestures of loyalty. Since the overbreadth of the oath tends to infringe areas of speech and conduct which may be protected by the Constitution, I believe that it cannot stand.

. . . .

---

## NOTES

1. The state of Washington had argued in Baggett v. Bullitt, 377 U.S. 360 (1964), that both it and the state employees taking the oaths knew very well what the statutory language meant and against what sort of conduct it was aimed. Justice White replied: "It will not do to say that a prosecutor's sense of fairness and the Constitution would prevent a successful perjury prosecution for some of the activities seemingly embraced within the sweeping statutory definitions. The hazard nevertheless remains. . . . Well-intentioned prosecutors and judicial safeguards do not neutralize the vice of a vague law." Compare this reasoning with that advanced by Chief Justice Burger eight years later in *Cole*

*v. Richardson.* Justice White concurred in *Cole,* on the ground that the word "oppose" in the oath was not unconstitutionally vague. He did not expressly endorse, however, the reasoning of the court's opinion which distinguished standards of review on the basis of enforcement patterns.

2. It has been suggested that the Supreme Court's invalidation of loyalty oath statutes has not and could not have had much of an impact. State courts, for instance, could satisfy the holding in Elfbrandt v. Russell, 384 U.S. 11 (1966), by reading into their state loyalty oath laws a requirement of knowing membership-plus-support for unlawful aims. And where, as in *Elfbrandt,* the membership clause of an oath is struck down, state courts could invoke the principle of severability and hold that their loyalty oath laws, minus their membership clauses, are still valid. *See* Israel, *Elfbrandt v. Russell: The Demise of the Oath?,* 1966 SUP. CT. REV. 193, 245-47.

Has the Supreme Court decided to beat a strategic retreat on loyalty oath cases and to henceforth construe them with deference to the desire of the legislatures to "do something" about loyalty oaths? If so, does this decision mark a total break in the loyalty oath cases? Even in the name of pragmatism, is such a sharp departure justifiable?

3. In his dissenting opinion in *Cole v. Richardson,* Justice Marshall called for an analysis of the Massachusetts statutory language, similar to that employed in *Baggett, Elfbrandt,* and *Keyishian.* What, for instance, does "oppose" or "overthrow" mean in the context of the Massachusetts oath, he asked? What are the standards to be used in delimiting the responsibilities which each oath-taker or affirmant assumes?

4. What is difficult to assess is the over-all impact of the Massachusetts loyalty oath in *Cole v. Richardson.* The court stressed that there had been no prosecution under the Massachusetts law since its enactment in 1948. Chief Justice Burger pointed out those who envision a "parade of horribles" should reflect on the fact that the court can always take corrective action. An issue which arises as a result of *Cole* is whether a statute will now survive a vagueness attack if no record of actual prosecution or harassment is demonstrated. Is this an amendment to the vagueness doctrine, a kind of constitutional vagueness-desuetude doctrine?

5. Are "positive" oaths less immediately vulnerable constitutionally as applied to state or federal government employees than are "negative" oaths? Professor Thomas I. Emerson suggests "positive" oaths applied to private employees are no different in effect than disclaimer or negative oaths. Selection is based

on a decision to use the oath to avoid hiring the nonconformist. It should be noted that Professor Emerson anticipated and rebutted Chief Justice Burger's non-enforcement argument vis-à-vis positive oaths in *Cole v. Richardson*. Professor Emerson states: "The fact that positive oaths are rarely enforced does not save them. For either the cautious or the conscientious, the impact is the same." *See* T. EMERSON, THE SYSTEM OF FREEDOM OF EXPRESSION 245 (1970).

### d.    Free Speech and Association and the Bar Admission Cases

In Schware v. Board of Bar Examiners, 353 U.S. 232 (1957) the court found a due process violation in the refusal in 1953 of the New Mexico Board of Bar Examiners to admit the applicant, Schware, to its bar. The Board based its determination on some pre-1940 activities of Schware: "the use of aliases . . . former connection with subversive organizations, and his record of arrests." The Board had argued that admission to the bar was a privilege not a right and the requirements of procedural due process therefore did not obtain. The court, per Justice Black, declined to "enter into a discussion, whether the practice of law is a 'right' or 'privilege.'" However, the court did say that the "practice of law is not a matter of the State's grace." Denial of admission to the bar could not be constitutionally based on insufficient grounds. If the grounds for denial of admission were insufficient then the state had acted unreasonably and due process was offended. The ancient vintage of the demerits against Schware plus his "forceful showing of good moral character" in the intervening years led the court to conclude that the New Mexico Board of Bar Examiners had offended due process.

In the same year that it decided *Schware,* the court decided Konigsberg v. State Bar, 353 U.S. 252 (1957) (Konigsberg I). Konigsberg had passed the California bar but was denied admission on two grounds: (1) failure to show good moral character; (2) failure to show that he did not advocate overthrow of the government. Konigsberg refused on first amendment grounds at hearings before the Committee of Bar Examiners in California to answer questions concerning his political associations and beliefs. A majority of the court in *Konigsberg I* took the position that Konigsberg had been denied admission because of a finding by the Committee that he had failed to meet the requisite showing of good moral character and loyalty. On that basis, the Committee's conclusion was reversed on the ground that it was not warranted by the evidence.

After the *Konigsberg I* decision, the Bar Committee again held hearings and Konigsberg once again refused to say whether he was a member of the Communist Party. Konigsberg did testify that he did not believe in violent overthrow of the government, and that he had never knowingly been a member of any organization advocating violent overthrow. The Committee refused to admit Konigsberg to the bar on the ground that "his refusals to answer had obstructed a full investigation into his qualifications." This time, the Supreme Court, per Harlan, J., 5-4, affirmed the determination of the California Committee of Bar Examiners that Konigsberg should be denied admission. Konigsberg v. State Bar of California, 366 U.S. 36 (1961) (Konigsberg II).

Justice Harlan said for the court: "We think it clear that the Fourteenth Amendment's protection against arbitrary state action does not forbid a State from denying admission to a bar applicant so long as he refuses to provide unprivileged answers to questions having a substantial relevance to his qualifications."

With respect to Konigsberg's argument that he was privileged not to answer questions dealing with Communist party membership on the basis of the rights of free speech and association, the court disagreed. First, the court emphasized that those rights had not been granted absolute protection. In the case of regulatory statutes not aimed at controlling speech but incidentally limiting speech, the government interest has traditionally not been subordinated to the assertion of the first amendment right so long as a "weighing of the governmental interest involved" justified its primacy. Harlan said in such cases that the court has always upheld "rules compelling disclosure of prior association" when the rules serve as "an incident of the informed exercise of a valid governmental function."

The "balancing" exercise whereby free speech and association rights were subordinated to the "governmental interest" in a bar admission case was described by Justice Harlan for the court as follows: "With more particular reference to the present context of a state decision as to character qualifications, it is difficult, indeed, to imagine a view of the constitutional protections of speech and association which would automatically and without consideration of the extent of the deterrence of speech and association and the importance of the state function, exclude all reference to prior speech or association on such issues as character, purpose, credibility, or intent."

Harlan said the "use of illegal means" to change the form of State or Federal government "was not an unimportant consideration in determining the fitness of applicants for membership in a profession in whose hands so largely lies the safekeeping of this country's legal and political institutions."

The court relied on cases subordinating the speech and association rights of public employees "to the State's interest in ascertaining the fitness of the employee for the post he holds . . . Beilan v. Board of Public Educ., 357 U.S. 399 [1958], Garner v. Board of Public Works, 341 U.S. 716 [1951]. With respect to this same question of Communist Party membership, we regard the State's interest in having lawyers who are devoted to the law in its broadest sense, including not only its substantive provisions, but also its procedures for orderly change, as clearly sufficient to outweigh the minimal effect upon free association occasioned by compulsory disclosure in the circumstances here presented. . . ."

As you read the cases which follow, *Baird, Stolar* and *Wadmond,* ask yourself whether *Konigsberg II* has been fatally undermined? Is admission to the bar considered to be a privilege by a majority on the Supreme Court?

### e.  The Bar Admission Cases of 1971: Wadmond, Baird and Stolar

1.  In Law Students Civil Rights Research Council v. Wadmond, 401 U.S. 154 (1971), the court, per Justice Stewart, rejected 5-4, a challenge to New York's admission procedure.

New York's Rule 9406 directing character committees not to admit an applicant unless he can furnish proof that he "believes in the form of the government of the United States and is loyal to such government" was upheld because authoritative construction of the rule was narrow and responsive to protected freedoms, *i.e.,* "the form of government of the United States" and the "government" referred solely to the Constitution. This requirement of proof was related to the oath applicants had to take prior to being admitted to the bar. The oath, said the court, merely required an applicant to swear that he would "support the United States and New York Constitutions."

There was a question in the form, Question 26a, asking whether an applicant had ever "organized or helped to organize" or had become a member of any organization or group which "during the period of your membership or association, you knew was teaching or advocating" violent overthrow of the government. If the answer to that question was in the affirmative, then Question 26(b) had to be answered: "(D)id you, during the period of such membership or association, have the specific intent to further the aims of such organization or group of persons to overthrow or overturn the government of the United States or any state or any political subdivision thereof by force, violence, or any unlawful means?"

The Court read Question 26 as whole and held it to be constitutional: "Question 26 is precisely tailored to conform to the relevant decisions of this Court. Our cases establish that inquiry into associations of the kind referred to is permissible under the limitations carefully observed here. We have held that knowing membership in an organization advocating the overthrow of the Government by force or violence, on the part of one sharing the specific intent to further the organization's illegal goals, may be made criminally punishable. *Scales*. It is also well settled that Bar Examiners may ask about Communist affiliations as preliminary to further inquiry into the nature of the association and may exclude an applicant for refusal to answer. *Konigsberg, II*."

2.  In Baird v. State Bar of Arizona, 401 U.S. 1 (1971), the court held that the Arizona bar admissions committee could not deny admission to an applicant who refused to answer the following question on the application form.

Question 27: "Are you or have you ever been a member of the Communist Party or any organization that advocated overthrow of the United States government by force or violence?"

Arizona had said that it was entitled to demand an answer to question 27 on the following grounds:

"Unless we are to conclude that one who truly and sincerely *believes* in the overthrow of the United States Government by force and violence is also qualified to practice law in our Arizona Courts, then an answer to the question is indeed appropriate. The Committee again emphasized that a mere answer of 'yes' would not lead to an automatic rejection of the application. It would lead to an investigation and interrogation as to whether the applicant presently holds the view that a violent overthrow of the United States Government is something to be sought after. If the answer to this inquiry was 'yes' then indeed we would reject the application and recommend against admission."

Justice Black, for the court, joined in by Douglas, Brennan and Marshall said:

"The First Amendment's protection of association prohibits a State from excluding a person from a profession or punishing him solely because he is a member of a particular political organization or because he holds certain beliefs. . . . Similarly, when a State attempts to make inquiries about a person's beliefs or association, its power is limited by the First Amendment. Broad and sweeping state inquiries into these protected areas, as Arizona has engaged in here, discourage citizens from exercising rights protected by the Constitution. . . .

"Of course, Arizona has a legitimate interest in determining whether petitioner has the qualities of character and the professional competence requisite to the practice of law. But here . . . petitioner has already supplied the Committee with extensive personal and professional information to assist its determination. . . . And whatever justification may be offered, a State may not inquire about a man's views or associations solely for the purpose of withholding a right or benefit because of what he believes. . . . Clearly Arizona has engaged in such questioning here.

"The practice of law is not a matter of grace, but of right for one who is qualified by his learning and his moral character."

Justice Stewart supplied the crucial fifth vote supporting the court's decision holding Question 27 to be an infringement of the fifth amendment. Stewart said Question 27 went beyond "simple inquiry to present a past Communist Party membership" but inquired into membership in any organization advocating violent overthrow. Such inquiry must be limited to "knowing membership to satisfy the First and Fourteenth Amendments." Citing *Wadmond*. Note that Question 26(b) in *Wadmond* meets a specific intent requirement. Further, Stewart said that the Arizona bar admission committee had stated that it would deny admission to an applicant if it found "applicant's beliefs . . . objectionable."

Suppose a bar committee writes its questions inquiring into present and past political associations with the requisite concern for specific intent? Suppose further the committee is careful to say that one will be denied admission because of his political associations or beliefs?

What the *Wadmond* case reveals is that it is still entirely possible to require a detailed statement from the bar applicant of every past political or group association and yet satisfy the technical requirements of first amendment law. But the fact that the bar committee can cast its dragnet into the applicant's past still permits "broad and sweeping inquiries" into protected first amendment areas and thus serves to "discourage citizens from exercising rights protected by the Constitution. . . ."

Finally, although Justice Black in his plurality opinion for the court in *Baird* called the "practice of law" a "right," this view has not yet gained a majority in the court. Stewart did not espouse this view in his separate concurrence in *Baird*. The advantages that would flow to the bar candidate from viewing the practice of law as a right and the fact that a majority of his brethren were not yet minded to take such a view were discussed by Justice Black in his dissent in *Wadmond* as follows:

When it seeks to deprive a person of the right to practice law, a State must accord him the same rights as when it seeks to deprive him of other property. Perhaps almost anyone would be stunned if a State sought to take away a man's house because he failed to prove his loyalty or refused to answer questions about his political beliefs. But it seems to me that New York is attempting to deprive people of the right to practice law for precisely these reasons, and the Court is approving its actions.

3. In *In re* Stolar, 401 U.S. 23 (1971), the court held that petitioner could not, consistently with the first amendment, be required to answer the following questions on the application form for admission to the Ohio Bar:

"12(g). State whether you have been, or presently are . . . a member of any organization which advocates the overthrow of the Government of the United States by force. . . ."

The court held that the same lack of specific intent which invalidated a similar question in *Baird* invalidated 12(g).

The Ohio form also contained two questions which ferreted deeply into the associational activities of the bar admission applicant: "13. List the names and addresses of all clubs, societies or organizations of which you are or have been a member. . . ."

"7. List the names and addresses of all clubs, societies or organizations of which you are or have become a member since registering as a law student."

The court, per Justice Black, joined by Douglas, Brennan and Marshall, said concerning questions 13 and 7:

> [The] committee frankly suggests that the listing of an organization which it felt "espoused illegal aims" would cause it to "investigate further." Law students who know they must survive this screening process before practicing their profession are encouraged to protect their future by shunning unpopular or controversial organizations.

The committee asserted it had a legitimate interest in knowing "whether an applicant has belonged to an organization," which has "espoused illegal aims" and whether the applicant shares such aims. But Justice Black disagreed with the legitimacy of this interest because the first amendment prevented denial of admission to the bar "solely because of the applicant's membership in an organization" or "solely because he personally . . . 'espouses illegal aims.'"

With respect to the state's alleged interest in inquiring into past associational activities in order to identify persons who could furnish requisite information concerning the applicant's qualifications, the court stated:

Undoubtedly, Ohio has a legitimate interest in determining whether an applicant has "the qualities of character and the professional competence requisite to the practice of law."

However, Stolar was "already a member in good standing of the New York Bar" and had supplied the committee with extensive personal and professional information as well as numerous character references to enable it to make the necessary investigation and determination.

### 10.   The Speech-Action Test and the Right To Assemble and Petition For Grievances

#### THE "FIGHTING WORDS" DOCTRINE

1.   Chaplinsky v. New Hampshire, 315 U.S. 568 (1942), involved the prosecution of a Jehovah's Witness, who distributed pamphlets on the streets of Rochester, New Hampshire. Citizens complained to the City Marshal that Chaplinsky was denouncing all religion as a "racket." Although the Marshal did tell the irate citizens Chaplinsky was lawfully engaged, he also warned Chaplinsky that the crowd was restless.

Chaplinsky made this statement to the Marshal outside City Hall: "You are a God-damned racketeer and a damned fascist and the whole government of Rochester are Fascists or agents of Fascists." He was prosecuted under a New Hampshire statute which forbade "addressing any offensive, derisive or annoying word to any other person who is lawfully in any street or other public place, nor call him by any offensive or derisive name. . . ."

The state supreme court put a gloss on the statute. Only those words were forbidden which had a "direct tendency to cause acts of violence by the persons to whom, individually, the remark is addressed." This gave birth to "fighting words" as a first amendment doctrine. The Supreme Court endorsed the New Hampshire Supreme Court's statement of the new doctrine: "The word 'offensive' is not to be defined in terms of what a particular addressee thinks. . . . The test is what men of common intelligence would understand to be words likely to cause an average addressee to fight. . . . The English language has a number of words and expressions which by general consent are 'fighting words' when said without a disarming smile. . . . Such words, as ordinary men know, are likely to cause a fight. . . .

"The statute, as construed, does no more than prohibit the face-to-face words plainly likely to cause a breach of the peace by the speaker—including 'classical fighting words', words in current use less 'classical' but equally likely to cause violence, and other disorderly words, including profanity, obscenity and threats."

The Supreme Court observed: "Argument is unnecessary to demonstrate that the appellations 'damned racketeer' and 'damned Fascist' are epithets likely to provoke the average person to retaliation, and thereby cause a breach of the peace."

2. The "fighting words" doctrine has endured. In *Gooding* v. *Wilson,* 405 U.S. 518 (1972), the court once more endorsed the doctrine:

> Our decisions since *Chaplinsky* have continued to recognize state power constitutionally to punish "fighting words" under carefully drawn statutes not also susceptible of application to protected expression, Cohen v. California, 403 U.S., at 20; Bachellar v. Maryland, 397 U. S. 564, 567 (1970). We reaffirm that proposition today.

But *Gooding* illustrates that the court is zealous to keep the "fighting words" doctrine within very limited boundaries. *Gooding* involved a Georgia statute punishing the use of "opprobrious words or abusive language, tending to cause a breach of the peace." The lower federal courts, exercising habeas corpus jurisdiction, held that the Georgia statute was unconstitutionally vague and broad and set aside the conviction.

Justice Brennan delivered the opinion of the court:

"Appellant argues that the Georgia appellate courts have by construction limited the proscription of § 26-6303 to 'fighting' words, as the New Hampshire Supreme Court limited the New Hampshire statute. . . . Neither the District Court nor the Court of Appeals so read the Georgia decisions. . . . We have, however, made our own examination of the Georgia cases, both those cited and others discovered in research. That examination brings us to the conclusion, in agreement with the courts below, that the Georgia appellate decisions have not construed [the statute] to be limited in application, as in *Chaplinsky,* to words that 'have a direct tendency to cause acts of violence by the person to whom, individually, the remark is addressed.'

"The dictionary definitions of 'opprobrious' and 'abusive' give them greater reach than 'fighting' words. Webster's Third New International Dictionary (1961) defined 'opprobrious' as 'conveying or intended to convey disgrace,' and 'abusive' as including 'harsh insulting language.' Georgia appellate decisions have construed [the statute] to apply to utterances that, although within these definitions, are not 'fighting' words as *Chaplinsky* defines them. . . .

"Georgia appellate decisions construing the reach of 'tending to cause a breach of the peace' underscore that [the statute] is not limited, as appellant argues, to words that 'naurally tend to provoke violent resentment.'

"This definition makes it a 'breach of peace' merely to speak words offensive to some who hear them, and so sweeps too broadly. . . .

"Unlike the construction of the New Hampshire statute by the New Hampshire Supreme Court, the Georgia appellate courts have not construed [the statute] 'so as to avoid all constitutional difficulties.' "

Chief Justice Burger, dissenting, stated:

If words are to bear their common meaning, and are to be considered in context, rather than dissected with surgical precision using a semantical scalpel, this statute has little potential for application outside the realm of "fighting words" which this Court held beyond the protection of the First Amendment in *Chaplinsky*. . . .

Justice Blackmun, with whom the Chief Justice joined, similarly contended:

For me, Chaplinsky v. New Hampshire, 315 U.S. 568 (1942), was good law when it was decided and deserves to remain as good law now. . . . But I feel that by decisions such as this one and, indeed, Cohen v. California, 403 U.S. 15 (1971), the Court, despite its protestations to the contrary, is merely paying lip service to *Chaplinsky*. As the appellee states in a footnote to his brief, p. 14, "Although there is no doubt that the state can punish 'fighting words' this appears to be about all that is left of the decision in *Chaplinsky*." If this is what the overbreadth doctrine means, and if this is what it produces, it urgently needs reexamination. The Court has painted itself into a corner from which it, and the States, can extricate themselves only with difficulty.

3.  In Lewis v. New Orleans, 415 U.S. 130 (1974), a New Orleans ordinance making it unlawful "to curse or revile or to use obscene or opprobrious language toward or with reference to" a police officer acting in the performance of his duties was held overbroad and facially invalid. The Louisiana Supreme Court stated that the ordinance was limited to "fighting words" but the Supreme Court held that the statute reached further and extended to words "conveying or intended to convey disgrace."

Appellant and her husband were following a police patrol car that was carrying their young son after his arrest. The boy's

mother said to a police officer: "(Y)ou god damn m.f. police—
I am going to the Superintendent of police about this." Appellant's husband testified as follows: The police officer said: "(L)et
me see your god damned license." Appellant's wife was then
alleged to have said: "Officer I want to find out about my son."
The officer was alleged to have replied: "(Y)ou get in the car
woman. Get your black ass in the god damned car or I will show
you something."

Justice Brennan delivered the opinion of the court:

"But § 49-7 plainly has a broader sweep than the constitutional definition of 'fighting words' announced in *Chaplinsky v. New Hampshire* and reaffirmed in *Gooding v.
Wilson,* namely, '. . . those [words] which by their very utterance inflict injury or tend to incite an immediate breach
of the peace.' That the Louisiana Supreme Court contemplated
a broader reach of the ordinance is evident from its emphasis
upon the City's justification for regulation of 'the conduct of
any person towards a member of the city police while in the
actual performance of his duty. . . . Permitting the cursing or
reviling of or using obscene or opprobrious words to a police
officer while in the actual performance of his duty would be
unreasonable and basically incompatible with the officer's activities and the place where such activities are performed.'

"At the least, the proscription of the use of 'opprobrious
language,' embraces words that do not 'by their very utterance
inflict injury or tend to incite an immediate breach of the peace.'
That was our conclusion as to the word 'opprobrious' in the
Georgia statute held unconstitutional in *Gooding v. Wilson,*
where we found that the common dictionary definition of that
term embraced words 'conveying or intended to convey disgrace'
and therefore that the word was not limited to words which
'by their very utterance inflict injury or tend to invite an immediate breach of the peace.' The same conclusion is compelled
as to the reach of the word in § 49-7, for we find nothing in the
opinion of the Louisiana Supreme Court that makes any meaningful attempt to limit or properly define—as limited by *Chaplinsky* and *Gooding*—'opprobrious,' or indeed any other term
in § 49-7. In that circumstance it is immaterial whether the words
appellant used might be punishable under a properly limited
statute.

. . . .

"In sum, § 49-7 punishes only spoken words. It can therefore
withstand appellant's attack upon its facial constitutionality only
if, as authoritatively construed by the Louisiana Supreme Court,

it is not susceptible of application to speech, although vulgar or
offensive, that is protected by the First and Fourteenth Amendments. . . . Since § 49-7, as construed by the Louisiana Supreme
Court, is susceptible of application to protected speech, the section is constitutionally overbroad and therefore is facially invalid."

Justice Powell, concurring in the result, stated

"Quite apart from the ambiguity inherent in the term 'opprobrious,' words may or may not be 'fighting words' depending
upon the circumstances of their utterance. It is unlikely, for
example, that the words said to have been used here would have
precipitated a physical confrontation between the middle-aged
woman who spoke them and the police officer in whose presence
they were uttered. The words may well have conveyed anger and
frustration without provoking a violent reaction from the officer.
Moreover, as noted in my previous concurrence, a properly trained
officer may reasonably be expected to 'exercise a higher degree
of restraint' than the average citizen, and thus be less likely to
respond belligerently to 'fighting words.' "

Justice Blackmun, with whom the Chief Justice and Justice
Rehnquist join, dissenting, argued:

. . . .

"Overbreadth and vagueness in the field of speech, as the
present case and *Gooding* indicate, have become result-oriented
rubberstamps attuned to the easy and imagined self-assurance
that 'one man's vulgarity is another's lyric.'

. . . .

"In the interest of the arrested person who could become
the victim of police overbearance, and in the interest of the
officer, who must anticipate violence and who, like the rest of
us, is fallibly human, legislatures have enacted laws of the kind
challenged in this case to serve a legitimate social purpose and to
restrict only speech that is 'of such slight social value as a step
to truth that any benefit that may be derived from [it] is clearly
outweighed by the social interest in order and morality.' *Chaplinsky.* In such circumstances we should stay our hand and not
yield to the absolutes of doctrine."

## THE HOSTILE AUDIENCE PROBLEM

1.   In Feiner v. New York, 340 U.S. 315 (1951), a speaker was
interrupted by a policeman who demanded that he stop because
his remarks in derogation of the President, the Mayor of Syracuse,
and the American Legion, which incurred both approval and
hostility from his audience, appeared to be about to cause a fight.

When the speaker refused to stop, he was arrested for disturbing the peace. The Supreme Court upheld Feiner's conviction against a contention that the arrest violated free speech.

*Feiner* is often thought to exemplify the "hostile audience" problem: If a speaker angers a crowd to the point that either the physical security of the speaker or a public disorder is likely, who should the police arrest? The speaker or the crowd? Is it relevant that the speaker is not inciting to violence? If the audience outnumbers the police, does logistics become constitutional law? If the crowd is many and menacing, and the police are few, are the police constitutionally justified in carrying away the speaker? Compare the various responses of the Justices to this question in the excerpts which follow.

Chief Justice Vinson, speaking for the Court, affirmed Feiner's conviction:

"Petitioner was thus neither arrested nor convicted for the making or the content of his speech. Rather, it was the reaction which it actually engendered.

. . . .

"We are well aware that the ordinary murmurings and objections of a hostile audience cannot be allowed to silence a speaker, and are also mindful of the possible danger of giving overzealous police officials complete discretion to break up otherwise lawful public meetings.

. . . .

"But we are not faced here with such a situation. It is one thing to say that the police cannot be used as an instrument for the suppression of unpopular views, and another to say that, when as here the speaker passes the bounds of argument or persuasion and undertakes incitement to riot, they are powerless to prevent a breach of the peace."

Justice Frankfurter wrote a single opinion in which he concurred in the result in *Feiner* as well as the results in Kunz v. New York, 340 U.S. 290 (1951), and Niemotko v. Maryland, 340 U.S. 268 (1951). The core of Frankfurter's analysis of the "hostile audience" problem is found in the following statement:

"Where the conduct is within the allowable limits of free speech, the police are peace officers for the speaker as well as for his hearers. But the power effectively to preserve order cannot be displaced by giving a speaker complete immunity. Here, there were only two police officers present for 20 minutes. They interfered only when they apprehended imminence of violence. It is not a constitutional principle that, in acting to preserve order, the police must proceed against the crowd, whatever its size and temper, and not against the speaker.

"It is true that breach-peace statutes, like most tools of government, may be misused. . . . But the possibility of misuse is not alone a sufficient reason to deny New York the power here asserted or so limit it by constitutional construction as to deny its practical effect."

Justice Black vigorously dissented in *Feiner:*

"As to the existence of a dangerous situation on the street-corner, it seems far-fetched to suggest that the 'facts' show any imminent threat of riot or uncontrollable disorder.

. . . .

"Moreover, assuming that the 'facts' did indicate a critical situation, I reject the implication of the Court's opinion that the police had no obligation to protect petitioner's constitutional right to talk. The police of course have power to prevent breaches of the peace. But if, in the name of preserving order, they ever can interfere with a lawful public speaker, they first must make all reasonable efforts to protect him. Here the police did not even pretend to try to protect petitioner. According to the officers' testimony, the crowd was restless but there is no showing of any attempt to quiet it. . . . Their duty was to protect petitioner's right to talk, even to the extent of arresting the man who threatened to interfere. Instead, they shirked that duty and acted only to suppress the right to speak.

. . . .

"Here the petitioner was 'asked' then 'told' then 'commanded' to stop speaking, but a man making a lawful address is certainly not required to be silent merely because an officer directs it. Petitioner was entitled to know why he should cease doing a lawful act. Not once was he told. I understand that people in authoritarian countries must obey arbitrary orders. I had hoped there was no such duty in the United States."

2. A companion case to *Feiner* was Kunz v. New York, 340 U.S. 290 (1951). Kunz, an ordained Baptist minister, had obtained a permit to hold religious meetings on New York City streets. The permit was revoked because Kunz's speeches denounced other religious groups such as Jews and Catholics. These speeches resulted in revocation of Kunz's permit. Kunz was unsuccessful in obtaining a new permit because his earlier one had been revoked. Kunz was convicted for holding a religious meeting on the street without a permit. The Supreme Court, per Chief Justice Vinson, reversed:

Disapproval of the 1948 permit application by the police commissioner was justified by the New York courts on the ground that a permit had previously been revoked "for good reasons." It is noteworthy that there is no mention in the ordinance of reasons for which such a permit application can be refused.

. . . .

We have here, then, an ordinance which gives an administrative official discretionary power to control in advance the rights of citizens to speak on religious matters on the streets of New York. As such, the ordinance is clearly invalid as a prior restraint on the exercise of First Amendment rights.

Justice Jackson dissented in *Kunz* because in his view *Feiner* and *Kunz* were inconsistent. Jackson reasoned that to hold that *Kunz* need not comply with the permit procedure for speaking on the streets in New York and to hold at the same time that a policeman may stop a speech on his own assessment that the speaker's words threatened the public order made no sense:

Of course, emergencies may arise with or without the permit system. A speaker with a permit may go beyond bounds and incite violence, or a mob may undertake to break up an unauthorized and properly conducted meeting. In either case, the policeman on the spot must make the judgment as to what measures will most likely avoid violent disorders. But those emergencies seem less likely to occur with the permit system than if every man and his adversary take the law in their own hands.

In Justice Jackson's dissent in *Kunz* he lodged the following critique against the court's practice of invalidating licensing laws in the realm of first amendment rights when those laws provided insufficient guidance as to the standard to be utilized on granting or denying a license:

"It is suggested that a permit for a street meeting could be required if the ordinance would prescribe precise standards for its grant or denial. . . . As this case exemplifies, local acts are struck down, not because in practical application they have actually invaded anyone's protected freedoms, but because they do not set up standards which would make such invasion impossible.

. . . .

"Of course, standards for administrative action are always desirable, and the more exact the better. But I do not see how this Court can condemn municipal ordinances for not setting forth comprehensive First Amendment standards. This Court never has announced what those standards must be, it does not say what they are, and it is not clear that any majority could agree on them. In no field are there more numerous individual opinions among the Justices. The Court as an institution not infrequently disagrees with its former self or relies on distinctions that are not very substantial. . . . It seems hypercritical to strike down local laws on their faces for want of standards when we have no standards."

*See* Coates v. Cincinnati, 402 U.S. 611 (1971), striking down an ordinance making it a crime for "three or more persons to assemble . . . on any of the sidewalks . . . and there conduct themselves in a manner annoying to persons passing by" as "vague and overbroad."

### PICKETS, PARADES AND DEMONSTRATIONS AS POLITICAL PROTEST: MORE ON THE SPEECH PLUS PROBLEM
### ADDERLEY v. FLORIDA
Supreme Court of the United States
385 U.S. 39, 17 L. Ed. 2d 149, 87 S. Ct. 242 (1966)

Justice BLACK delivered the opinion of the Court.

Petitioners, Harriett Louise Adderley and 31 other persons, were convicted . . . on a charge of "trespass with a malicious and mischievous intent" upon the premises of the county jail contrary to § 821.18 of the Florida statutes. . . . Petitioners, apparently all students of the Florida A. & M. University in Tallahassee, had gone from the school to the jail about a mile away, along with many other students, to "demonstrate" at the jail their protests of arrests of other protesting students the day before, and perhaps to protest more generally against state and local policies and practices of racial segregation, including segregation of the jail. The county sheriff, legal custodian of the jail and jail grounds, tried to persuade the students to leave the jail grounds. When this did not work, he notified them that they must leave, that if they did not leave he would arrest them for trespassing, and that if they resisted he would charge them with that as well. Some of the students left but others, including petitioners, remained and they were arrested. On appeal the convictions were affirmed by the Florida Circuit Court and then by the Florida District Court of Appeal, 175 So. 2d 249. . . .

Petitioners have insisted from the beginning of this case that it is controlled by and must be reversed because of our prior cases of Edwards v. South Carolina, 372 U.S. 229, and Cox v. Louisiana, 379 U.S. 536, 559 [Cox I & II]. We cannot agree.

. . . In *Edwards,* the demonstrators went to the South Carolina State Capitol grounds to protest. In this case they went to the jail. Traditionally, state capitol grounds are open to the public. Jails, built for security purposes, are not. The demonstrators at the South Carolina Capitol went in through a public driveway and as they entered they were told by state officials that they had a right as citizens to go through the State House grounds as long as they were peaceful. Here the demonstrators entered the jail grounds through a driveway used only for jail purposes and without warning to or permission from the sheriff. More importantly, South Carolina sought to prosecute its State Capitol demonstrators by charging them with the common-law crime of breach of the peace. This Court in *Edwards* took pains to point out at length the indefinite, loose, and broad nature of this charge. . . . The South Carolina breach-of-the-peace statute was thus struck down as being so broad and all-embracing as to jeopardize speech, press, assembly and petition. . . . And it was on this same ground of vagueness that in *Cox v. Louisiana,* the Louisiana breach-of-the-peace law used to prosecute Cox was invalidated.

The Florida trespass statute under which these petitioners were charged cannot be challenged on this ground. It is aimed at conduct of one limited kind, that is, for one person or persons to trespass upon the property of another with a malicious and mischievous intent. There is no lack of notice in this law, nothing to entrap or fool the unwary.

Petitioners seem to argue that the Florida trespass law is void for vagueness because it requires a trespass to be "with a malicious and mischievous intent. . . ." But these words do not broaden the scope of trespass so as to make it cover a multitude of types of conduct as does the common-law breach-of-the-peace charge. On the contrary, these words narrow the scope of the offense. The trial court charged the jury as to their meaning and petitioners have not argued that this definition, set out below,[2] is not a reasonable and clear definition of the terms. The use of these terms in the statute, instead of contributing to uncertainty and misunderstanding, actually makes its meaning more understandable and clear.

. . . .

---

[2] ". . . The word 'malicious' means that the wrongful act shall be done voluntarily, unlawfully and without excuse or justification. The word 'malicious' that is used in these affidavits does not necessarily allege nor require the State to prove that the defendant had actual malice in his mind at the time of the alleged trespass. Another way of stating the definition of 'malicious' is that sense by 'malicious' is meant the act was done knowingly and willfully and without any legal justification.

" 'Mischievous,' which is also required, means that the alleged trespass shall be inclined to cause petty and trivial trouble, annoyance and vexation to others in order for you to find that the alleged trespass was committed with mischievous intent."

. . . [On the basis of the evidence] the jury was authorized to find that the State had proven every essential element of the crime, as it was defined by the state court. That interpretation is, of course, binding on us, leaving only the question of whether conviction of the state offense, thus defined, unconstitutionally deprives petitioners of their rights to freedom of speech, press, assembly or petition. We hold it does not. The sheriff, as jail custodian, had power, as the state courts have here held, to direct that this large crowd of people get off the grounds. There is not a shred of evidence in this record that this power was exercised, or that its exercise was sanctioned by the lower courts, because the sheriff objected to what was being sung or said by the demonstrators or because he disagreed with the objectives of their protest. The record reveals that he objected only to their presence on that part of the jail grounds reserved for jail uses. There is no evidence at all that on any other occasion had similarly large groups of the public been permitted to gather on this portion of the jail grounds for any purpose.[6] Nothing in the Constitution of the United States prevents Florida from even-handed enforcement of its general trespass statute against those refusing to obey the sheriff's order to remove themselves from what amounted to the curtilage of the jailhouse. The State, no less than a private owner of property, has power to preserve the property under its control for the use to which it is lawfully dedicated. For this reason there is no merit to the petitioners' argument that they had a constitutional right to stay on the property, over the jail custodian's objections, because this "area chosen for the peaceful civil rights demonstration was not only 'reasonable' but also particularly appropriate. . . ." Such an argument has as its major unarticulated premise the assumption that people who want to propagandize protests or views have a constitutional right to do so whenever and however and wherever they please. That concept of constitutional laws was vigorously and forthrightly rejected [Cox I & II]. We reject it again. The United States Constitution does not forbid a State to control the use of its own property for its own lawful nondiscriminatory purpose.

---

[6] In [Cox I] the Court emphasized: "It is, of course, undisputed that appropriate, limited discretion, under properly drawn statutes or ordinances, concerning the time, place, duration, or manner of use of the streets for public assemblies may be vested in administrative officials, provided that such limited discretion is 'exercised with "uniformity of method of treatment upon the facts of each application, free from improper or inappropriate considerations and from unfair discrimination" . . . [and with] a "systematic, consistent and just order of treatment, with reference to the convenience of public use of the highways. . . ."' "

These judgments are

Affirmed.

Justice Douglas, with whom The Chief Justice, Justice
Brennan, and Justice Fortas concur, dissenting.

[First Amendment rights] are preferred rights of the Constitution, made so by reason of that explicit guarantee and what
Edmond Cahn in Confronting Injustice (1966) referred to as
"The Firstness of the First Amendment." With all respect, therefore, the Court errs in treating the case as if it were an ordinary
trespass case or an ordinary picketing case.

The jailhouse, like an executive mansion, a legislative chamber, a courthouse, or the statehouse itself (*Edwards v. South Carolina*) is one of the seats of government, whether it be the Tower
of London, the Bastille, or a small county jail. And when it
houses political prisoners or those who many think are unjustly
held, it is an obvious center for protest. The right to petition
for the redress of grievances has an ancient history and is not
limited to writing a letter or sending a telegram to a congressman; it is not confined to appearing before the local city council,
or writing letters to the President or Governor or Mayor. Conventional methods of petitioning may be, and often have been,
shut off to large groups of our citizens. Legislators may turn deaf
ears; formal complaints may be routed endlessly through a bu-
reaucratic maze; courts may let the wheels of justice grind very
slowly. Those who do not control television and radio, those who
cannot afford to advertise in newspapers or circulate elaborate
pamphlets may have only a more limited type of access to public
officials. Their methods should not be condemned as tactics of
obstruction and harassment as long as the assembly and petition
are peaceable, as these were.

There is no question that petitioners had as their purpose a
protest against the arrest of Florida A. & M. students for trying
to integrate public theatres. . . . The fact that no one gave a
formal speech, that no elaborate handbills were distributed, and
that the group was not laden with signs would seem to be immaterial. Such methods are not the sine qua non of petitioning for
the redress of grievances. The group did sing "freedom" songs.
And history shows that a song can be a powerful tool of protest.
See Cox v. Louisiana, 379 U.S. 536. There was no violence; no
threat of violence; no attempted jail break; no storming of a
prison; no plan or plot to do anything but protest. . . . Finally,
the fact that some of the protestants may have felt their cause so
just that they were willing to be arrested for making their protest
outside the jail seems wholly irrelevant. A petition is nonetheless
a petition, though its futility may make martyrdom attractive.

We do violence to the First Amendment when we permit this "petition for redress of grievances" to be turned into a trespass action. It does not help to analogize this problem to the problem of picketing. Picketing is a form of protest usually directed against private interests. I do not see how rules governing picketing in general are relevant to this express constitutional right to assemble and to petition for redress of grievances. In the first place the jailhouse grounds were not marked with "NO TRESPASSING!" signs, nor does respondent claim that the public was generally excluded from the grounds. Only the sheriff's fiat transformed lawful conduct into an unlawful trespass. To say that a private owner could have done the same if the rally had taken place on private property is to speak of a different case, as an assembly and a petition for redress of grievances run to government, not to private proprietors.

The Court forgets that prior to this day our decisions have drastically limited the application of state statutes inhibiting the right to go peacefully on public property to exercise First Amendment rights. . . .

. . . Would the case be any different if, as is common, the demonstration took place outside a building which housed both the jail and the legislative body? I think not.

There may be some public places which are so clearly committed to other purposes that their use for the airing of grievances is anomalous. There may be some instances in which assemblies and petitions for redress of grievances are not consistent with other necessary purposes of public property. A noisy meeting may be out of keeping with the serenity of the statehouse or the quiet of the courthouse. No one, for example, would suggest that the Senate gallery is the proper place for a vociferous protest rally. And in other cases it may be necessary to adjust the right to petition for redress of grievances to the other interests inhering in the uses to which the public property is normally put. But this is quite different from saying that all public places are off limits to people with grievances. And it is farther yet from saying that the "custodian" of the public property in his discretion can decide when public places shall be used for the communication of ideas, especially the constitutional right to assemble and petition for redress of grievances. For to place such discretion in any public official, be he the "custodian" of the public property or the local police commissioner, is to place those who assert their First Amendment rights at his mercy. It gives him the awesome power to decide whose ideas may be expressed and who shall be denied a place to air their claims and petition their government. Such power is out of step with all our decisions prior to today where we have insisted that before a First Amendment right may be curtailed under the guise of a criminal law, any evil that may be collateral to the exercise of the right, must be isolated and defined in a "narrowly drawn" statute lest the power to control excesses of conduct be used to suppress the constitutional right itself.

. . . .

---

## NOTES

1. In Edwards v. South Carolina, 372 U.S. 229 (1963), the court rejected attempts to cast mass picketing accompanied by singing, speeches, clapping, etc. on statehouse grounds as "fighting words." Instead, the demonstration was characterized as "an exercise of [first amendment] rights in their most pristine and classic form." *See* Brown v. Louisiana, 383 U.S. 131 (1966) (breach of peace conviction for peaceful sit-in at a public library reversed). *Compare* Justice Goldberg's statement in Cox v. Louisiana, 379 U.S. 536 (1965) (Cox I): "We emphatically reject the notion . . . that the First and Fourteenth Amendments afford the same kind of freedom to those who would communicate ideas by conduct such as patrolling, marching and picketing on streets and highways as these amendments afford to those who communicate ideas by pure speech." Which approach is adopted in *Adderley*?

2. Professor Kalven suggests three basic principles are involved in the "public forum cases": "First, that in an open democratic society the streets, the parks, and other public places are an important facility for public discussion and political process. They are in brief a public forum that the citizen can commandeer; the generosity and empathy with which such facilities are made available is an index of freedom. Second, that only confusion can result from distinguishing sharply between 'speech pure' and 'speech plus.' And, third, that what is required is in effect a set of Robert's Rules of Order for the new uses of the public forum, albeit the designing of such rules poses a problem of formidable practical difficulty." Kalven, *The Concept of the Public Forum: Cox v. Louisiana*, 1965 SUP. CT. REV. 1.

3. Can time, place and manner regulations be meaningfully distinguished from government controls on the content of *speech*? Should different constitutional standards be applied? Can public protest ever be completely barred from the streets? If there are alternative forums available?

4. The "public forum" question was also at issue in cases involving protests at shopping centers (text, pp. 1027-1042) and

in cases involving access to the media (text, pp. 869-92) and advertising on public vehicles (text, pp. 888-92).

## WALKER v. BIRMINGHAM
Supreme Court of the United States
388 U.S. 307, 18 L. Ed. 2d 1210, 87 S. Ct. 1824 (1967)

[*Walker v. Birmingham,* was an important case in the first amendment litigation that arose out of the Negro civil rights protest movement of the sixties. Eight black ministers, including the late Martin Luther King, led civil rights marches in Birmingham on Easter, 1963 in defiance of an *ex parte* restraining order banning all marches, parades, sit-ins or other demonstrations in violation of the Birmingham parade ordinance. The petitioners were held in contempt for violating the *ex parte* order. The state courts held that petitioners could not violate the injunction and later challenge its validity. The Supreme Court, per Justice Stewart, affirmed the conviction, 5-4. Justices Warren, Douglas, Brennan and Fortas dissented. All but Fortas wrote a separate dissent.]

Justice STEWART delivered the opinion of the Court.

. . . .

The generality of the language contained in the Birmingham parade ordinance upon which the injunction was based would unquestionably raise substantial constitutional issues concerning some of its provisions. The petitioners, however, did not even attempt to apply to the Alabama courts for an authoritative construction of the ordinance. Had they done so, those courts might have given the licensing authority granted in the ordinance a narrow and precise scope. . . .

The breadth and vagueness of the injunction itself would also unquestionably be subject to substantial constitutional question. But the way to raise that question was to apply to the Alabama courts to have the injunction modified or dissolved. The injunction in all events clearly prohibited mass parading without a permit, and the evidence shows that the petitioners fully understood that prohibition when they violated it.

. . . .

This case would arise in quite a different constitutional posture if the petitioners, before disobeying the injunction, had challenged it in the Alabama courts, and had been met with delay or frustration of their constitutional claims. But there is no showing that such would have been the fate of a timely motion to modify or dissolve the injunction. There was an interim of two days between the issuance of the injunction and the Good Friday march. The petitioners give absolutely no explanation of why they did not make some application to the state court during that period. The injunction had issued *ex parte;* if the court had been presented with the petitioners' contentions, it might well have dissolved or at least modified its order in some respects. If it had not done so, Alabama procedure would have provided for an expedited process of appellate review. It cannot be presumed that the Alabama courts would have ignored the petitioners' constitutional claims. Indeed, these contentions were accepted in another case by an Alabama appellate court that struck down on direct review the conviction under this very ordinance of one of these same petitioners.

. . . .

. . . [P]recedents clearly put the petitioners on notice that they could not bypass orderly judicial review of the injunction before disobeying it. Any claim that they were entrapped or misled is wholly unfounded, a conclusion confirmed by evidence in the record showing that when the petitioners deliberately violated the injunction they expected to go to jail.

The rule of law that Alabama followed in this case reflects a belief that in the fair administration of justice no man can be judge in his own case, however exalted his station, however righteous his motives, and irrespective of his race, color, politics, or religion. This Court cannot hold that the petitioners were constitutionally free to ignore all the procedures of the law and carry their battle to the streets. One may sympathize with the petitioners' impatient commitment to their cause. But respect for judicial process is a small price to pay for the civilizing hand of law which alone can give abiding meaning to constitutional freedom.

Affirmed.

Chief Justice WARREN, whom Justice BRENNAN and Justice FORTAS join, dissenting.

. . . The Court . . . holds that petitioners may . . . be convicted and sent to jail because the patently unconstitutional ordinance was copied into an injunction—issued *ex parte* without prior notice or hearing on the request of the Police Commissioner—forbidding all persons having notice of the injunction to violate the ordinance without any limitation of time. I dissent because I do not believe that the fundamental protections of the Constitution were meant to be so easily evaded, or that "the civilizing hand of judicial process" would be hampered in the slightest by enforcing the First Amendment in this case.

. . . .

. . . It has never been thought that violation of a statute indicated such a disrespect for the legislature that the violator always must be punished even if the statute was unconstitutional. On the contrary, some cases have required that persons seeking to challenge the constitutionality of a statute first violate it to establish their standing to sue. Indeed, it shows no disrespect for law to violate a statute on the ground that it is unconstitutional and then to submit one's case to the courts with the willingness to accept the penalty if the statute is held to be valid.

. . . .

. . . The only circumstance that the court can find to justify anything other than a *per curiam* reversal is that Commissioner Connor had the foresight to have the unconstitutional ordinance included in an *ex parte* injunction issued without notice or hearing or any showing that it was impossible to have notice or a hearing, forbidding the world at large (insofar as it knew of the order) to conduct demonstrations in Birmingham without the consent of the city officials. This injunction was such potent magic that it transformed the command of an unconstitutional statute into an impregnable barrier, challengeable only in what likely would have been protracted legal proceedings and entirely superior in the meantime even to the United States Constitution.

. . . .

---

## NOTES

1. In Shuttlesworth v. Birmingham, 394 U.S. 147 (1969), the court, per Stewart, J., overturned the conviction of Shuttlesworth who led 52 people in a protest march without a permit as required by a Birmingham licensing ordinance. He had been informed that no license would be issued under the ordinance which required that licenses be issued unless the City Commission concluded that "the public welfare, peace, safety, health, decency, good order, morals or convenience require that it be refused."

While the ordinance as subsequently construed by the Alabama Supreme Court "would pass Constitutional muster," Justice Stewart reasoned it was impossible to know its limited construction at the time of the protest and the conviction, therefore, could not stand. Justice Stewart also held that Shuttlesworth's failure to test the licensing statute was not determinative: "[O]ur decisions have made clear that a person faced with such an unconstitutional licensing law may ignore it, and engage with impunity in the exercise of the right of free expression for which the law purports to require a license."

Justice Harlan, concurring, emphasized that there were no expedited procedures available for testing the validity of the ordinance. If there were such procedures, should protesters be required to exhaust them? Does it matter if a law is facially unconstitutional or unconstitutional as applied? *See* Poulos v. New Hampshire, 345 U.S. 395 (1953). Is *Shuttleworth* inconsistent with *Walker? See generally* Blasi, *Prior Restraints on Demonstrations,* 68 MICH. L. REV. 1481 (1970); Monaghan, *First Amendment "Due Process,"* 83 HARV. L. REV. 518 (1970).

**2.** Does obedience to the rule of law as exemplified in a state court injunction occupy a preferred position superior to the exercise of first amendment rights? The court said that the Birmingham, Alabama ordinance at issue in *Walker* was clearly unconstitutional. The constitutional infirmity of the ordinance was that it conferred unbridled discretion on the city commissioners. If the ordinance was so unconstitutional, why was it necessary to obey the lower court order until a higher court could rule on the invalidity of the statute?

Is the rule of law more seriously threatened if an unconstitutional court rule is disobeyed than if an unconstitutional statute or ordinance is disobeyed? It should be remembered that in Thornhill v. Alabama, 310 U.S. 88 (1940), Justice Murphy said that a statute setting up an invalid licensing procedure inhibitory of first amendment rights need not be complied with despite the fact that no court had yet ruled on the invalidity of the statute: "One who might have had a license for the asking may therefore call into question the whole scheme of licensing when he is prosecuted for failure to procure it."

**3.** *Walker v. Birmingham* was given new vitality in a controversial decision of the Fifth Circuit, United States v. Dickinson, 465 F.2d 496 (5th Cir. 1972), *cert. den.* 409 U.S. 1046 (1973). The convictions for contempt of two Baton Rouge reporters were upheld. The case arose out of a federal district court proceeding to determine whether the federal court should abstain from deciding a case where it was alleged that a VISTA worker was being unconstitutionally prosecuted on a groundless charge of having conspired to murder the Mayor of New Orleans.

The judge issued a so-called "gag order" to the reporters "that no report of the testimony taken in the case today shall be made in any newspaper or by radio or television, or by any other news media." The two reporters defied the order and were held in contempt. On appeal, the Fifth Circuit held that the "gag order" was a violation of the first amendment but affirmed the conviction on the basis of the doctrine set forth in *Walker*: even in the realm of first amendment litigation a void but nonfrivolous judicial order must be obeyed.

## 11.  "Symbolic" Speech

### DRAFT-CARD BURNING AND THE BACKGROUND OF THE *O'BRIEN* CASE

In West Virginia State Bd. of Educ. v. Barnette, 319 U.S. 624 (1943), Justice Jackson in his eloquent way recognized for the court that action could sometimes be the most effective form of symbolic speech:

> There is no doubt that . . . the (compulsory) flag salute is a form of utterance. Symbolism is a primitive but effective way of communicating ideas. The use of an emblem or flag to symbolize some system, idea, institution, or personality, is a short cut from mind to mind.

Suppose we assume that speech should have full first amendment protection but that action should not. On which side of the speech-action line should symbolic speech be placed? Symbols have been given first amendment protection by the Supreme Court in the past. In Stromberg v. California, 283 U.S. 359 (1931), the Supreme Court struck down on first amendment grounds a state statute that prohibited "the display of a red flag as a symbol of opposition by peaceful and legal means to organized government."

The widespread bitterness about American military participation in Vietnam, and the accompanying hostility to the military draft which made that participation possible, re-opened the difficult question of the constitutional status to be accorded symbolic speech. Draft-card burning was one militant form of symbolism engaged in by some draft-age youths in the sixties as a means to express their disapproval of American involvement in Vietnam. A 1965 Amendment to the Universal Military Service and Training Act forbade the knowing destruction or mutilation of a draft card. Nevertheless, draft cards were burned. In a prosecution following one such burning, the defendant sought to use symbolic speech as a complete first amendment defense to his prosecution for draft card burning.

### UNITED STATES v. O'BRIEN
Supreme Court of the United States
391 U.S. 367, 20 L. Ed. 2d 672, 88 S. Ct. 1673 (1968)

Chief Justice WARREN delivered the opinion of the Court.

On the morning of March 31, 1966, David Paul O'Brien and three companions burned their Selective Service registration certificates on the steps of the South Boston Courthouse. A sizeable crowd, including several agents of the Federal Bureau of Investigation, witnessed the event. Immediately after the burning, members of the crowd began attacking O'Brien and his companions. An FBI agent ushered O'Brien to safety inside the courthouse. After he was advised of his right to counsel and to silence, O'Brien stated to FBI agents that he had burned his registration certificate because of his beliefs, knowing that he was violating federal law. He produced the charred remains of the certificate, which, with his consent, were photographed.

For this act, O'Brien was indicted, tried, convicted, and sentenced in the United States District Court for the District of Massachusetts. He did not contest the fact that he had burned the certificate. He stated in argument to the jury that he burned the certificate publicly to influence others to adopt his antiwar beliefs, as he put it, "so that other people would reevaluate their positions with Selective Service, with the armed forces, and reevaluate their place in the culture of today, to hopefully consider my position."

. . . .

By [a] 1965 Amendment, Congress added to § 12(b)(3) of the 1948 [Universal Military Training and Service] Act the provision here at issue, subjecting to criminal liability not only one who "forges, alters, or in any manner changes" but also one who "knowingly destroys, [or] knowingly mutilates" a certificate. We note at the outset that the 1965 Amendment plainly does not abridge free speech on its face, and we do not understand O'Brien to argue otherwise. Amended § 12(b)(3) on its face deals with conduct having no connection with speech. It prohibits the knowing destruction of certificates issued by the Selective Service System, and there is nothing necessarily expressive about such conduct. The Amendment does not distinguish between public and private destruction, and it does not punish only destruction engaged in for the purpose of expressing views. . . .

O'Brien nonetheless argues that the 1965 Amendment is unconstitutional in its application to him, and is unconstitutional as enacted because what he calls the "purpose" of Congress was "to suppress freedom of speech." We consider these arguments separately.

O'Brien first argues that the 1965 Amendment is unconstitutional as applied to him because his act of burning his registration certificate was protected "symbolic speech" within the First Amendment. His argument is that the freedom of expression which the First Amendment guarantees includes all modes of "communication of ideas by conduct," and that his conduct is within this definition because he did it in "demonstration against the war and against the draft."

We cannot accept the view that an apparently limitless variety of conduct can be labelled "speech" whenever the person engaging in the conduct intends thereby to express an idea. However, even on the assumption that the alleged communicative element in O'Brien's conduct is sufficient to bring into play the First Amendment, it does not necessarily follow that the destruction of a registration certificate is constitutionally protected activity. This Court has held that when "speech" and "nonspeech" elements are combined in the same course of conduct, a sufficiently important governmental interest in regulating the nonspeech element can justify incidental limitations on First Amendment freedoms. To characterize the quality of the governmental interest which must appear, the Court has employed a variety of descriptive terms: compelling; substantial; subordinating; paramount; cogent; strong. Whatever imprecision inheres in these terms, we think it clear that a governmental regulation is sufficiently justified if it is within the constitutional power of the government; if it furthers an important or substantial governmental interest; if the governmental interest is unrelated to the suppression of free expression; and if the incidental restriction on alleged First Amendment freedom is no greater than is essential to the furtherance of that interest. We find that the 1965 Amendment to § 462(b) (3) of the Universal Military Training and Service Act meets all of these requirements, and consequently that O'Brien can be constitutionally convicted for violating it.

. . . .

1.  The registration certificate serves as proof that the individual described thereon has registered for the draft. The classification certificate shows the eligibility classification of a named but undescribed individual. . . .

2.  The information supplied on the certificates facilitates communication between registrants and local boards, simplifying the system and benefiting all concerned. . . .

3.  . . . The smooth functioning of the system requires that local boards be continually aware of the status and whereabouts of registrants, and the destruction of certificates deprives the system of a potentially useful notice device.

4.  The regulatory scheme involving Selective Service certificates includes clearly valid prohibitions against the alteration, forgery or similar deceptive misuse of certificates. . . .

The many functions performed by Selective Service certificates establish beyond doubt that Congress has a legitimate and substantial interest in preventing their wanton and unrestrained destruction and assuring their continuing availability by punishing people who knowingly and wilfully destroy or mutilate them.

. . .

. . . .

We think it apparent that the continuing availability to each registrant of his Selective Service certificates substantially furthers the smooth and proper functioning of the system that Congress has established to raise armies. We think it also apparent that the Nation has a vital interest in having a system for raising armies that functions with maximum efficiency and is capable of easily and quickly responding to continually changing circumstances. For these reasons, the Government has a substantial interest in assuring the continuing availability of issued Selective Service certificates.

It is equally clear that the 1965 Amendment specifically protects this substantial governmental interest. We perceive no alternative means that would more precisely and narrowly assure the continuing availability of issued Selective Service certificates than a law which prohibits their wilful mutilation or destruction. The 1965 Amendment prohibits such conduct and does nothing more. In other words, both the governmental interest and the operation of the 1965 Amendment are limited to the non-communicative aspect of O'Brien's conduct. The governmental interest and the scope of the 1965 Amendment are limited to preventing a harm to the smooth and efficient functioning of the Selective Service System. When O'Brien deliberately rendered unavailable his registration certificate, he wilfully frustrated this governmental interest. For this noncommunicative impact of his conduct, and for nothing else, he was convicted.

The case at bar is therefore unlike one where the alleged governmental interest in regulating conduct arises in some measure because the communication allegedly integral to the conduct is itself thought to be harmful. . . .

In conclusion, we find that because of the Government's substantial interest in assuring the continuing availability of issued Selective Service certificates, because amended § 462(b) is an appropriately narrow means of protecting this interest and condemns only the independent noncommunicative impact of conduct within its reach, and because the noncommunicative impact of O'Brien's act of burning his registration certificate frustrated the Government's interest, a sufficient governmental interest has been shown to justify O'Brien's conviction.

. . . .

. . . This disposition makes unnecessary consideration of O'Brien's claim that the Court of Appeals erred in affirming his conviction on the basis of the nonpossession regulation.

It is so ordered.

Justice MARSHALL took no part in the consideration or decision of these cases.

[Justice DOUGLAS dissented on the ground that the basic but undecided constitutional issue in the case was whether conscription was unconstitutional in the absence of a declaration of war.]

---

## NOTES

1. Chief Justice Warren's test in *O'Brien* arguably is just another form of the balancing test frequently used in speech plus cases. Is Warren's "balancing" test particularly weighted in favor of the government?

2. The court distinguishes the *Stromberg* case from *O'Brien* on the ground that there the statute was aimed in terms of suppressing communication. Suppose the 1965 Amendment had made criminal the destruction or mutilation of a draft card as a means of "expressing opposition to the Vietnam War." Same result? Notice O'Brien's lawyers tried to show that the congressional motivation was aimed at suppressing communication. Why wasn't legislative intent behind the 1965 Amendment more seriously considered by the court?

### THE BACKGROUND OF *TINKER v. DES MOINES COMMUNITY SCHOOL DISTRICT:* A VICTORY FOR "SYMBOLIC SPEECH"?

In December 1965, a group of adults and public school students in Des Moines, Iowa decided to wear black armbands during the Christmas holidays in order to dramatize their opposition to the Vietnam War. The principals of the Des Moines public schools then announced a policy prohibiting the wearing of armbands and providing for suspension of such a student until he removed the armband. Three public school children, two high school students and a junior high student, were all suspended until they desisted from wearing armbands.

Relying on 42 U.S.C. § 1983, the fathers of the children went to federal court to enjoin the Des Moines school authorities for disciplining their children. The federal district court dismissed the complaint, and the federal court of appeals, sitting *en banc*, was equally divided on appeal and, therefore, the lower court opinion was affirmed.

In an influential opinion, the Supreme Court reversed.

After calling the wearing of an "armband" a symbol, Justice Fortas said that such a practice was "akin to 'pure speech' which, we have repeatedly held, is entitled to comprehensive protection under the First Amendment." As you read Fortas' opinion, ask yourself whether the court's designation in *Tinker* of the wearing of armbands as "symbolic speech" really won for this practice "comprehensive protection under the First Amendment." Is *Tinker* a triumph for the extension of first amendment protection to "symbolic speech" or does the case illustrate instead still another balancing test which tries to accommodate the legitimate interests of the state with the assertion by individuals of first amendment rights?

### TINKER v. DES MOINES SCHOOL DIST.
Supreme Court of the United States
393 U.S. 503, 21 L. Ed. 2d 731, 89 S. Ct. 733 (1969)

Justice FORTAS delivered the opinion of the Court.

. . . .

The District Court recognized that the wearing of an armband for the purpose of expressing certain views is the type of symbolic act that is within the Free Speech Clause of the First Amendment. As we shall discuss, the wearing of armbands in the circumstances of this case was entirely divorced from actually or potentially disruptive conduct by those participating in it. It was closely akin to "pure speech" which, we have repeatedly held, is entitled to comprehensive protection under the First Amendment.

First Amendment rights, applied in light of the special characteristics of the school environment, are available to teachers and students. It can hardly be argued that either students or teachers shed their constitutional rights to freedom of speech or expression at the schoolhouse gate. This has been the unmistakable holding of this Court for almost 50 years. . . .

. . . On the other hand, the Court has repeatedly emphasized the need for affirming the comprehensive authority of the States and of school officials, consistent with fundamental constitutional safeguards, to prescribe and control conduct in the schools. Our problem lies in the area where students in the exercise of First Amendment rights collide with the rules of the school authorities.

The problem posed by the present case does not relate to regulation of the length of skirts or the type of clothing, to hair style, or deportment. It does not concern aggressive, disruptive action or even group demonstrations. Our problem involves direct, primary First Amendment rights akin to "pure speech."

The school officials banned and sought to punish petitioners for a silent, passive expression of opinion, unaccompanied by any disorder or disturbance on the part of petitioners. There is here no evidence whatever of petitioners' interference, actual or nascent, with the schools' work or of collision with the rights of other students to be secure and to be let alone. Accordingly, this case does not concern speech or action that intrudes upon the work of the schools or the rights of other students.

Only a few of the 18,000 students in the school system wore the black armbands. Only five students were suspended for wearing them. There is no indication that the work of the schools or any class was disrupted. Outside the classrooms, a few students made hostile remarks to the children wearing armbands, but there were no threats or acts of violence on school premises.

The District Court concluded that the action of the school authorities was reasonable because it was based upon their fear of a disturbance from the wearing of the armbands. But, in our system, undifferentiated fear or apprehension of disturbance is not enough to overcome the right to freedom of expression. Any departure from absolute regimentation may cause trouble. Any variation from the majority's opinion may inspire fear. Any word spoken, in class, in the lunchroom, or on the campus, that deviates from the views of another person may start an argument or cause a disturbance. . . .

In order for the State in the person of school officials to justify prohibition of a particular expression of opinion, it must be able to show that its action was caused by something more than a mere desire to avoid the discomfort and unpleasantness that always accompany an unpopular viewpoint. Certainly where there is no finding and no showing that engaging in of the forbidden conduct would "materially and substantially interfere with the requirements of appropriate discipline in the operation of the school," the prohibition cannot be sustained.

. . . .

. . . [T]he action of the school authorities appears to have been based upon an urgent wish to avoid the controversy which might result from the expression, even by the silent symbol of armbands, of opposition to this Nation's part in the conflagration in Vietnam. It is revealing, in this respect, that the meeting at which the school principals decided to issue the contested regulation was called in response to a student's statement to the journalism teacher in one of the schools that he wanted to write an article on Vietnam and have it published in the school paper. (The student was dissuaded.)

It is also relevant that the school authorities did not purport to prohibit the wearing of all symbols of political or controversial significance. The record shows that students in some of the schools wore buttons relating to national political campaigns, and some even wore the Iron Cross, traditionally a symbol of Nazism. The order prohibiting the wearing of armbands did not extend to these. Instead, a particular symbol—black armbands worn to exhibit opposition to this Nation's involvement in Vietnam—was singled out for prohibition. Clearly, the prohibition of expression of one particular opinion, at least without evidence that it is necessary to avoid material and substantial interference with schoolwork or discipline, is not constitutionally permissible.

In our system, state-operated schools may not be enclaves of totalitarianism. School officials do not possess absolute authority over their students. Students in school as well as out of school are "persons" under our Constitution. They are possessed of fundamental rights which the State must respect, just as they themselves must respect their obligations to the State. In our system, students may not be regarded as closed-circuit recipients of only that which the State chooses to communicate. They may not be confined to the expression of those sentiments that are officially approved. In the absence of a specific showing of constitutionally valid reasons to regulate their speech, students are entitled to freedom of expression of their views. . . .

. . . .

. . . The principal use to which the schools are dedicated is to accommodate students during prescribed hours for the purpose of certain types of activities. Among those activities is personal intercommunication among the students. This is not only an inevitable part of the process of attending school; it is also an important part of the educational process. A student's rights, therefore, do not embrace merely the classroom hours. When he is in the cafeteria, or on the playing field, or on the campus during the authorized hours, he may express his opinions, even on controversial subjects like the conflict in Vietnam, if he does so without "materially and substantially interfer[ing] with the requirements of appropriate discipline in the operation of the school" and without colliding with the rights of others. But conduct by the student, in class or out of it, which for any reason—whether it stems from time, place, or type of behavior—materially disrupts classwork or involves substantial disorder or invasion of the rights of others is, of course, not immunized by the constitutional guarantee of freedom of speech.

Under our Constitution, free speech is not a right that is given only to be so circumscribed that it exists in principle but not in fact. Freedom of expression would not truly exist if the right could be exercised only in an area that a benevolent government has provided as a safe haven for crackpots. The Constitution says that Congress (and the States) may not abridge the right to free speech. This provision means what it says. We properly read it to permit reasonable regulation of speech-connected activities in carefully restricted circumstances. But we do not confine the permissible exercise of First Amendment rights to a telephone booth or the four corners of a pamphlet, or to supervised and ordained discussion in a school classroom.

If a regulation were adopted by school officials forbidding discussion of the Vietnam conflict, or the expression by any student of opposition to it anywhere on school property except as part of a prescribed classroom exercise, it would be obvious that the regulation would violate the constitutional rights of students, at least if it could not be justified by a showing that the students' activities would materially and substantially disrupt the work and discipline of the school. In the circumstances of the present case, the prohibition of the silent, passive "witness of the armbands," as one of the children called it, is no less offensive to the Constitution's guarantees.

. . . .

Reversed and remanded.

Justice BLACK, dissenting.

. . . .

Assuming that the Court is correct in holding that the conduct of wearing armbands for the purpose of conveying political ideas is protected by the First Amendment, the crucial remaining questions are whether students and teachers may use the schools at their whim as a platform for the exercise of free speech—"symbolic" or "pure"—and whether the courts will allocate to themselves the function of deciding how the pupils' school day will be spent. While I have always believed that under the First and Fourteenth Amendments neither the State nor the Federal Government has any authority to regulate or censor the content of speech, I have never believed that any person has a right to give speeches or engage in demonstrations where he pleases and when he pleases. . . .

. . . .

## NOTES

1. *Tinker* recognizes a right of free expression for public school students on public school premises so long as there is no "material disruption of classwork," "substantial disorder," or "invasion of the rights of others." The difficulty with such a test arises out of the inherent imprecision of a test which depends on an estimate as to whether something will or will not "materially" disrupt normal school operations.

Fortas stressed that the federal district court had made no finding that the school authorities had acted out of anticipation of disruption and concluded that "avoidance of controversy" rather than fear of disruption was the basis of the armband-ban. Yet in dissent Justice Black gave a definition to "disruption" which would appear to embrace anything which distracts students from their studies.

Although Fortas denied that "anticipation of disruption" did take place in *Tinker,* he did appear to approve restriction of the expression where the school authorities in fact *do* anticipate such disruption. Does not permitting restriction of expression by school authorities on the basis of anticipation of disruption involve an invalid prior restraint?

2. A first amendment issue related to the problem of *Tinker* is the question of the extent of the power of public school authorities to regulate student appearance. Should a student be able to claim a constitutional right to wear long hair or dress in a particular way as a means of self-expression? As a retained ninth amendment right?

3. Sometimes even when a particular controversial message involves no incitement to action, the state will try to treat such speech as "offensive conduct." In Cohen v. California, 403 U.S. 15 (1971), pure speech designed to symbolize political protest, which the state tried to punish as impermissible conduct, was given first amendment protection. A defendant had been convicted for disturbing the peace when he walked through a Los Angeles courthouse wearing a jacket carrying the words "Fuck the draft." The Supreme Court reversed the conviction. The court, per Justice Harlan, deemed the words on the jacket as unlikely to cause a violent reaction. The court also held that the states could not, under the first amendment, remove an offensive word from the public vocabulary.

The state contended that it could excise as "offensive conduct" a particular scurrilous epithet from the public discourse. Justice Harlan rejected this: "(T)he principle contended for by the State seems inherently boundless. How is one to distinguish this from any other offensive word? Surely the State has no right to cleanse public debate to the point where it is grammatically palatable to the most squeamish among us. Yet no readily ascertainable general principle exists for stopping short of that result were we to affirm the judgment below. For, while the particular four-letter word being litigated here is perhaps more distasteful than most others of its genre, it is nevertheless often true that one man's vulgarity is another's lyric. Indeed, we think it is largely because governmental officials cannot make principled distinctions in this area that the Constitution leaves matters of taste and style so largely to the individual."

*Cohen* was an ideal case to set forth, as Professor Emerson has long advocated, a doctrine of full first amendment protection for pure expression. This the court declined to do. Justice Harlan observed that the first and fourteenth amendments "have never been thought to give absolute protection." Even though the first amendment interest was protected in *Cohen*, Justice Harlan kept the door clearly open to an application of a balancing test which would go against the first amendment claim: "It is, in sum, our judgment that, absent a more particularized and com- pelling reason for its actions, the State may not, consistently with the First and Fourteenth Amendments, make the simple public display here involved of this single four-letter expletive a criminal offense. Because that is the only arguably sustainable rationale for the conviction here at issue, the judgment below must be reversed."

Justice Blackmun dissented in *Cohen*, joined by Chief Justice Burger, and *mirabile dictu*, Justice Black. Blackmun said that Cohen's antic was "mainly conduct and little speech."

On the basis of *Cohen*, it would appear that it may be said that among Supreme Court justices what constitutes "speech" or "action" depends on the eye of the beholder. To say that the epithet on Cohen's sweater is "mainly conduct" is merely to call for application of a conclusion, *i.e.*, the affirmance of a conviction.

If the speech-action dichotomy has any merit, it derives from at least a superficial objectivity and some possibility for ease of application, *i.e.*, pure "speech" merits full first amendment pro- tection while "action" is capable of some regulation. Such an analysis would appear to work in *Cohen* (and incidentally yield the same result as that which in fact obtained).

Is the expression-versus-disruption test of *Tinker* a more sensitive and useful test? In *Tinker*, the first amendment claim is protected as long as the normal activities of the site of the exercise of the first amendment right are not unduly disrupted. In *Tinker* and *Cohen*, both school and courthouse were able to function. Harlan emphasized in *Cohen* that the message on the sweater appeared to invoke neither anger nor interest by onlookers in the courthouse. Blackmun said Cohen's sweater should have been considered "fighting words." Is the indifference in the courthouse to the epithet on Cohen's sweater the reason that the court did not consider the message on his sweater "fighting words"?

4. The court demonstrated anew its coolness for the symbolic speech doctrine as a means of resolving problems such as the constitutional validity of statutes punishing flag demonstration in Smith v. Goguen, 415 U.S. 566 (1974). In *Goguen,* the Supreme Court invalidated a provision of the Massachusetts flag misuse statute which subjected to criminal liability anyone who publicly "treats contemptuously" the flag of the United States. Goguen was convicted for wearing a small United States flag sewn to the seat of his trousers. The Supreme Court ruled that the statute was unconstitutionally vague.

Justice White, concurring, belittled the vagueness objection to the statute and attempted to do that which the court declined to do, to confront the first amendment symbolic speech problem presented by the case:

"I am also confident that the statute was not vague with respect to the conduct for which Goguen was arrested and convicted. It should not be beyond the reasonable comprehension of anyone who would conform his language to the law to realize that sewing a flag on the seat of his pants is contemptuous of the flag. . . .

. . . .

"[I]t must be recalled that respondent's major argument is that wearing a flag patch on his trousers was conduct that 'clearly expressed an idea, albeit unpopular or unpatriotic, about the flag or about the country it symbolizes.'

. . . .

"The unavoidable inquiry, therefore, becomes whether the 'treats contemptuously' provision of the statute, as applied in this case, is unconstitutional under the First Amendment. That Amendment, of course, applies to speech and not to conduct without substantial communicative intent and impact. Even though particular conduct may be expressive and is understood to be of this nature, it may be prohibited if necessary to further a nonspeech interest of the Government that is within the power of the Government to implement. *United States v. O'Brien."*

Justice White made it clear that statutes, state or federal, proscribing mutilation, defacement or burning of the flag designed solely to protect the physical integrity of the flag "without regard to whether such conduct might provoke violence" were constitutional. In White's view, the Massachusetts statute went beyond protection of the physical integrity of the flag but it also punished the "expression of contempt for the flag." A conviction on such a basis was punishment for "communicating ideas about the flag unacceptable to the controlling majority in the legislature."

Such a basis for conviction violated the first amendment, according to Justice White, for the following reasons:

"Neither the United States nor any State may require any individual to salute or express favorable attitudes towards the flag. West Virginia State Board of Education v. Barnette, 319 U.S. 624 (1943). It is also clear under our cases that disrespectful or contemptuous spoken or written words about the flag may not be punished consistently with the First Amendment. Street v. New York, 394 U.S. 576 (1969). Although neither written nor spoken, an act may be sufficiently communicative to invoke the protection of the First Amendment, Tinker v. Des Moines Independent Community School District, 393 U.S. 503 (1969), and may not be forbidden by law except incidental to preventing unprotected conduct or unless the communication is itself among those that falls outside the protection of the First Amendment. In *O'Brien*, the Court sustained a conviction for draft card burning, although admittedly the burning was itself expressive. There, destruction of draft cards, whether communicative or not, was found to be inimical to important governmental considerations. . . . It would be difficult to believe that the conviction in *O'Brien* would have been sustained had the statute proscribed only contemptuous burning of draft cards.

"Any conviction under the 'treats contemptuously' provision of the Massachusetts statute would suffer from the same infirmity. This is true of Goguen's conviction. And if it be said that the conviction does not violate the First and Fourteenth Amendments because Goguen communicated nothing at all by his conduct and did not intend to do so, there would then be no evidentiary basis whatsoever for convicting him of being 'contemptuous' of the flag. I concur in the Court's judgment."

Justice Blackmun, joined by Chief Justice Burger, dissented on the ground that the Massachusetts Court had limited the conviction to protecting the physical integrity of the flag.

Justice Rehnquist, also joined by the Chief Justice, filed a separate dissent. One observation of Rehnquist's serves to summarize this section of the text thus far:

The issue of the application of the First Amendment to expressive conduct, of "symbolic speech," is undoubtedly a difficult one, and in cases dealing with the United States flag it has unfortunately been expounded only in dissents and concurrences.

Rehnquist said further:

I have difficulty seeing how Goguen could be found by a jury to have treated the flag contemptuously by his act and still not to have expressed any idea at all. There are, therefore, in my opinion, at least marginal elements of "symbolic speech" in Goguen's conduct as reflected by this record.

He was unable to "accept the conclusion that the Massachusetts statute must be invalidated for punishing only some conduct that impairs the flag's physical integrity," reasoning:

". . . Massachusetts metes out punishment to anyone who publicly mutilates, tramples, or defaces the flag, regardless of his motive or purpose. It also punishes the display of any 'words, figures, advertisements or designs' on the flag, or the use of a flag in a parade as a receptacle for depositing or collecting money. Likewise prohibited is the offering or selling of any article on which is engraved a representation of the United States flag.

"The variety of these prohibitions demonstrates that Massachusetts has not merely prohibited impairment of the physical integrity of the flag by those who would cast contempt upon it, but equally by those who would seek to take advantage of its favorable image in order to facilitate any commercial purpose, or those who would seek to convey any message at all by means of imprinting words or designs on the flag. These prohibitions are broad enough that it can be fairly said that the Massachusetts statute is one essentially designed to preserve the physical integrity of the flag, and not merely to punish those who would infringe that integrity for the purpose of disparaging the flag as a symbol.

. . . .

"He was simply prohibited from impairing the physical integrity of a unique national symbol which has been given content by generations of his and our forebears, a symbol of which he had purchased a copy. I believe Massachusetts had a right to enact this prohibition."

Is White saying that a statute which punishes a contemptuous attitude toward the flag is not permissible under the first amendment but that a statute which punishes impairment of the physical integrity of the flag is constitutionally valid? If this is the first amendment approval which White is advocating, it would not appear to have much to do with a doctrine of protection for symbolic speech. Note that although White reads *Tinker* to provide first amendment protection for an act "neither written nor spoken," he then says that such a "communicative" act may be forbidden by law if "incidental to preventing unprotected conduct or unless the communication is itself among those that fall outside the protection of the First Amendment." Is this a pointless definition of symbolic speech? As White conceives it, isn't symbolic speech just a way of describing a particular kind of first amendment "balancing" problem?

Justice Rehnquist appears to think there is no first amendment infirmity with the Massachusetts statute because Massachusetts sought to ban all impairments on the integrity of the flag whether physical in character or "for the purpose of disparaging the flag as a symbol." But does this inclusive interpretation of the Massachusetts statute prove the neutrality of the Massachusetts statute with regard to ideas? The anti-establishment views of those who wear the flag on the seat of their pants are certainly censored by Rehnquist's view of the Massachusetts statute. The fact is that the Massachusetts statute, so interpreted, rejects the political position represented by those who use contempt for the flag as a symbol of their politics. How is the Massachusetts statute, insofar as it affects those who use contempt for the flag as a symbol of political protest, redeemed because Massachusetts is also willing to punish those who impair the integrity of the flag out of mindless mischief?

5.   In Spence v. Washington, 418 U.S. 505 (1974), Spence was convicted for displaying an American flag upside down from his apartment in Seattle. In a per curiam opinion, the Supreme Court reversed.

The court held the application of the flag misuse statute to Spence's display of the flag in his apartment window was unconstitutional. The court stressed four reasons for reaching its results: (1) The flag was privately owned; (2) the flag was displayed on private property; (3) the record contained no proof of any breach of the peace; and (4) that the state and the Washington Supreme Court had both conceded that "appellant engaged in a form of communication."

The court said it agreed with the observation in *O'Brien* that "an apparent limitless variety of conduct should not be labeled 'speech' whenever the person engaging in the conduct intends thereby to express an idea." Nevertheless, in *Spence,* "the nature of appellant's activity, combined with the factual context and environment in which it was undertaken, lead to the conclusion that he engaged in a form of protected expression."

The court also said:

"On this record there can be little doubt that appellant communicated through the use of symbols. The symbolism included not only the flag but also the superimposed peace symbol.

. . . .

"It may be noted, further, that this was not an act of mindless nihilism. Rather, it was a pointed expression of anguish by appellant about the then current domestic and foreign affairs of his government. An intent to convey a particularized message was present, and in the surrounding circumstances the likelihood was great that the message would be understood by those who viewed it.

"We are confronted then with a case of prosecution for the expression of an idea through activity. . . .

"We are brought, then, to the state court's thesis that Washington has an interest in preserving the national flag as an unalloyed symbol of our country. . . . Presumably, this interest might be seen as an effort to prevent the appropriation of a revered national symbol by an individual, interest group, or enterprise where there was a risk that association of the symbol with a particular product or viewpoint might be taken erroneously as evidence of governmental endorsement. Alternatively, it might be argued that the interest asserted by the state court is based on the uniquely universal character of the national flag as a symbol. . . .

"But we need not decide in this case whether the interest advanced by the court below is valid. We assume *arguendo* that it is. The statute is nonetheless unconstitutional as applied to appellant's activity. There was no risk that appellant's acts would mislead viewers into assuming that the Government endorsed his viewpoint. To the contrary, he was plainly and peacefully protesting the fact that it did not. Appellant was not charged under the desecration statute, . . . nor did he permanently disfigure the flag or destroy it. . . . Given the protected character of his expression and in light of the fact that no interest the State may have in preserving the physical integrity of a privately-owned flag was significantly impaired on these facts, the conviction must be invalidated."

Justice Douglas concurred stating that he believed defendant's conduct constituted "symbolic speech" to which he would apparently give full first amendment protection.

Justice Rehnquist dissented, joined by Chief Justice Burger and Justice White:

". . . [The State] presumably cannot punish criticism of the flag, or the principles for which it stands, anymore than it could punish criticism of this country's policies or ideas. But the statute in this case demands no such allegiance. Its operation does not depend upon whether the flag is used for communicative purposes; upon whether a particular message is deemed commercial or political; upon whether the use of the flag is respectful or contemptuous; or upon whether any particular segment of the State's citizenry might applaud or oppose the intended message. It simply withdraws a unique national symbol from the roster of materials that may be used as a background for communications. Since I do not believe the Constitution prohibits Washington from making that decision, I dissent."

## 12. The Commercial Speech Doctrine

1. In Valentine v. Chrestensen, 316 U.S. 52 (1942), the Supreme Court unanimously held that commercial speech was outside the ambit of the first amendment and therefore subject to regulation by government.

The difficulty in *Chrestensen* was whether a municipal anti-litter ordinance could constitutionally be enforced against the exhibitor of a submarine who criticized the police commissioner on the back of his advertising handbill. The federal court of appeals, in affirming the injunction against the provision, was troubled by the prospect of allowing an exception for the regulation of commercial speech to contract without establishing clear perimeters for the area of expression protected by the first amendment. But the Supreme Court did not really resolve the problem of how to give a sufficiently precise definition to commercial speech. The court instead stressed that Chrestensen printed his noncommercial message solely to evade the law. The court's evaluation of Chrestensen's subjective intent, in other words, deprived him of first amendment protection. Chrestensen's first amendment claim was seen as a mere ploy to escape a municipal ordinance.

2. *Valentine v. Chrestensen* has sown the seeds of a constitutional doctrine of increasing significance: the theory that the first amendment does not protect "purely" commercial speech. Is there such a thing as "purely commercial speech"? Some commentators have argued that every advertisement contains an implicit noncommercial message, *i.e.*, the expression of social, political and economic values such as materialism, consumerism, even capitalism. *See* Black, *He Cannot Choose But Hear: The Plight of The Captive Auditor*, 53 COLUM. L. REV. 960 (1953).

3. A high-water mark for the commercial speech doctrine with respect to the electronic media was Capital Broadcasting Co. v. Mitchell, 333 F. Supp. 582 (D.D.C. 1971), where the federal court held that 15 U.S.C. § 1335 making it unlawful to advertise cigarettes in any electronic medium was constitutional. One of the specific grounds of decision was the concept that product advertising merited less first amendment protection than other modes

of expression. The Supreme Court affirmed the decision without opinion. Capital Broadcasting v. Kleindienst, 405 U.S. 1000 (1972).

### PITTSBURGH PRESS CO. v. PITTSBURGH COMM'N ON HUMAN RELATIONS
Supreme Court of the United States
413 U.S. 376, 37 L. Ed. 2d 669, 93 S. Ct. 2553 (1973)

Justice POWELL delivered the opinion of the Court.

The Human Relations Ordinance of the City of Pittsburgh (the "Ordinance") has been construed ↛below by the courts of Pennsylvania as forbidding newspapers to carry "help-wanted" advertisements in sex-designated columns except where the employer or advertiser is free to make hiring or employment referral decisions on the basis of sex. We are called upon to decide whether the Ordinance as so construed violates the freedoms of speech and of the press guaranteed by the First and Fourteenth Amendments. . . .

. . . .

Respondents rely principally on the argument that this regulation is permissible because the speech is commercial speech unprotected by the First Amendment. The commercial speech doctrine is traceable to the brief opinion in Valentine v. Chrestensen. . . .

. . . If a newspaper's profit motive were determinative, all aspects of its operations—from the selection of news stories to the choice of editorial position—would be subject to regulation if it could be established that they were conducted with a view toward increased sales. Such a basis for regulation clearly would be incompatible with the First Amendment.

The critical feature of the advertisement in *Valentine v. Chrestensen* was that, in the Court's view, it did no more than propose a commercial transaction, the sale of admission to a submarine. . . . In the crucial respects, the advertisements in the present record resemble the *Chrestensen* . . . advertisement. None expresses a position on whether, as a matter of social policy, certain positions ought to be filled by members of one or the other sex, nor does any of them criticize the Ordinance or the Commission's enforcement practices. Each is no more than a proposal of possible employment. The advertisements are thus classic examples of commercial speech.

But Pittsburgh Press contends that *Chrestensen* is not applicable, as the focus in this case must be, upon the exercise of editorial judgment by the newspaper as to where to place the advertisement rather than upon its commercial content. The

Commission made a finding of fact that Pittsburgh Press defers in every case to the advertiser's wishes regarding the column in which a want-ad should be placed. It is nonetheless true, however, that the newspaper does make a judgment whether or not to allow the advertiser to select the column. We must therefore consider whether this degree of judgmental discretion by the newspaper with respect to a purely commercial advertisement is distinguishable, for the purposes of First Amendment analysis, from the content of the advertisement itself. Or, to put the question differently, is the conduct of the newspaper with respect to the employment want-ad entitled to a protection under the First Amendment which the Court held in *Chrestensen* was not available to a commercial advertiser?

Under some circumstances, at least, a newspaper's editorial judgments in connection with an advertisement take on the character of the advertisement and, in those cases, the scope of the newspaper's First Amendment protection may be affected by the content of the advertisement. In the context of a libelous advertisement, for example, this Court has held that the First Amendment does not shield a newspaper from punishment for libel when with actual malice it publishes a falsely defamatory advertisement. *New York Times v. Sullivan* [text. p. 841.] Assuming the requisite state of mind, then, nothing in a newspaper's editorial decision to accept an advertisement changes the character of the falsely defamatory statements. The newspaper may not defend a libel suit on the ground that the falsely defamatory statements are not its own.

. . . .

As for the present case, we are not persuaded that either the decision to accept a commercial advertisement which the advertiser directs to be placed in a sex-designated column or the actual placement there lifts the newspaper's actions from the category of commercial speech. By implication at least, an advertiser whose want-ad appears in the "Jobs—Male Interest" column is likely to discriminate against women in his hiring decisions. Nothing in a sex-designated column heading sufficiently dissociates the designation from the want-ads placed beneath it to make the placement severable for First Amendment purposes from the want-ads themselves. The combination, which conveys essentially the same message as an overtly discriminatory want-ad, is in practical effect an integrated commercial statement.

Pittsburgh Press goes on to argue that if this package of advertisement and placement is commercial speech, then commercial speech should be accorded a higher level of protection than *Chrestensen* and its progeny would suggest. Insisting that the exchange of information is as important in the commercial realm as in any other, the newspaper here would have us abrogate the distinction between commercial and other speech.

Whatever the merits of this contention may be in other contexts, it is unpersuasive in this case. Discrimination in employment is not only commercial activity, it is *illegal* commercial activity under the Ordinance. We have no doubt that a newspaper constitutionally could be forbidden to publish a want-ad proposing a sale of narcotics or soliciting prostitutes. Nor would the result be different if the nature of the transaction were indicated by placement under columns captioned "Narcotics for Sale" and "Prostitutes Wanted" rather than stated within the four corners of the advertisement.

. . . .

. . . Any First Amendment interest which might be served by advertising an ordinary commercial proposal and which might arguably outweigh the governmental interest supporting the regulation is altogether absent when the commercial activity itself is illegal and the restriction on advertising is incidental to a valid limitation on economic activity.

It is suggested, in the brief of an *amicus curiae,* that apart from other considerations, the Commission's order should be condemned as a prior restraint on expression. . . .

The present order does not endanger arguably protected speech. Because the order is based on a continuing course of repetitive conduct, this is not a case in which the Court is asked to speculate as to the effect of publication. Cf. *New York Times v. United States* [text, p. 841]. Moreover, the order is clear and sweeps no more broadly than necessary. And because no interim relief was granted, the order will not have gone into effect until it was finally determined that the actions of Pittsburgh Press were unprotected.

We emphasize that nothing in our holding allows government at any level to forbid Pittsburgh Press to publish and distribute advertisements commenting on the Ordinance, the enforcement practices of the Commission, or the propriety of sex preferences in employment. Nor, *a fortiori,* does our decision authorize any restriction whatever, whether of content or layout, on stories or commentary originated by Pittsburgh Press, its columnists, or its contributors. On the contrary, we reaffirm unequivocally the protection afforded to editorial judgment and to the free expression of views on these and other issues, however controversial. We hold only that the Commission's modified order, narrowly drawn to prohibit placement in sex-designated columns of advertisements for nonexempt job opportunities, does not infringe the First Amendment rights of Pittsburgh Press.

Affirmed.

Chief Justice BURGER, dissenting.

Despite the Court's efforts to decide only the most narrow question presented in this case, the holding represents, for me, a disturbing enlargement of the "commercial speech" doctrine. Valentine v. Chrestensen, 316 U.S. 52 (1942), and a serious encroachment on the freedom of press guaranteed by the First Amendment. It also launches the courts on what I perceive to be a treacherous path of defining what layout and organizational decisions of newspapers are "sufficiently associated" with the "commercial" parts of the papers as to be constitutionally unprotected and therefore subject to governmental regulation. . . .

To my way of thinking, Pittsburgh Press has clearly acted within its protected journalistic discretion in adopting this arrangement of its classified advertisements. . . . I believe the First Amendment freedom of press includes the right of a newspaper to arrange the content of its paper, whether it be news items, editorials or advertising, as it sees fit. . . .

The Court's conclusion that the Commission's cease and desist order does not constitute a prior restraint gives me little reassurance. . . .

. . . .

Justice DOUGLAS, dissenting.

. . . .

. . . I believe that Pittsburgh Press by reason of the First Amendment may publish what it pleases about any law without censorship or restraint by Government. The First Amendment does not require the press to reflect any ideological or political creed reflecting the dominant philosophy, whether transient or fixed. It may use its pages and facilities to denounce a law and urge its repeal or at the other extreme denounce those who do not respect its letter and spirit.

Commercial matter, as distinguished from news, was held in Valentine v. Chrestensen, 316 U.S. 52, not to be subject to First Amendment protection. My views on that issue have changed since 1942, the year *Valentine* was decided. *As I have stated on earlier occasions I believe that commercial materials also have First Amendment protection.* (Emphasis added.) . . .

. . . .

. . . I would let any expression in that broad spectrum flourish, unrestrained by Government, unless it was an integral part of action—the only point which in the Jeffersonian philosophy marks the permissible point of governmental intrusion.

I therefore dissent from affirmance of this judgment.

Justice STEWART, with whom Mr. Justice DOUGLAS joins, dissenting.

. . . .

Justice BLACKMUN, dissenting.

. . . .

---

## NOTES

1. Doesn't *Pittsburgh Press* vividly expose the limitations of the commercial speech doctrine? A hierarchy of expression may be a reasonable approach to take to resolve difficult issues in first amendment adjudication. Perhaps in those situations where what is dominant or exclusive is not an "idea" but the "leer of the sensualist" or commercial self-aggrandizement, the first amendment should not be available as a shield for the cynical. But has the court adequately defined commercial speech? Has it provided an objective calculus for identifying this particular genus of expression?

2. Suppose the *Pittsburgh Press* had contended that the want-ad plus its placement in a sex-designated column conveyed "essentially the same message as an overtly discriminating want-ad." Suppose further the *Press* said that as a matter of belief and sound policy it endorsed the right to discriminate on the basis of sex? Would the court have still concluded that this "package of advertisement and placement" was "commercial speech"?

If the *Press* had vigorously defended its sex-designated classified columns on the basis of ideological conviction, then the court would have been presented with a choice between the equality protected by the fourteenth amendment and the free expression protected by the first amendment.

Is there not a danger in an area where a particular viewpoint (such as sex discrimination) is considered by enlightened opinion to be particularly benighted that the matter will be shielded from careful judicial appraisal? Can the reality of underlying constitutional valves in conflict too easily be submerged by a too ready willingness to over-apply the commercial speech label?

3. Burger wrote the opinion for the unanimous court in the Florida right of reply case, *Miami Herald Publishing Co. v. Tornillo*, text, p. 881, where he made the following observations: "The choice of material to go into a newspaper, and the decisions made as to limitations on the size of the paper, and content,

and treatment to public issue and public officials—whether fair or unfair constitutes the exercise of editorial control and judgment. It has yet to be demonstrated how governmental regulation of this crucial process can be exercised consistent with First Amendment guarantees of a free press as they evolved to this time." Chief Justice Burger dissented in the *Pittsburgh Press Case* on the specific ground that the Pittsburgh ordinance was an invasion of editorial discretion in the area of newspaper content and layout. Yet, in *Tornillo,* Burger quoted an excerpt from Powell's opinion in *Pittsburgh Press* insisting that the decision "did not authorize any restriction of content or layout." Do you think Burger has changed his mind about *Pittsburgh Press?*

4.  Chief Justice Burger says that *Pittsburgh Press* was a disturbing enlargement of *Valentine v. Chrestensen.* Is the enlargement found in the fact that in *Pittsburgh Press* the commercial speech doctrine is extended to what Burger considers to be journalistic discretion? Note that Burger says that even assuming the content of commercial advertisements can be restricted by the states, he would stop at extending such a doctrine to newspaper layouts.

## B.  SOME SPECIFIC PROBLEMS IN DEFINING FIRST AMENDMENT PROTECTION

### 1.  The Constitutionalization of Libel And Privacy

#### a.  The New York Times v. Sullivan Doctrine And Its Progeny

The *New York Times* case posed the question whether the first amendment permitted a law of libel. The court took a half-way position. It did not hold that the law of libel was unconstitutional but it did say that the central meaning of the first amendment was to encourage robust and vigorous criticism of government. If the press had to live in fear of severe libel judgments, criticism of government would be stilled or lessened. To avoid this the Supreme Court revolutionized the law of libel and created the now famous public law of libel. Under the facts and holding of the case where elected public officials are involved, libel judgments will be permissible only when the libel has been published with actual malice.

The result of the decision was to give the press an incentive to engage in the criticism of elected public officials. The court did not concern itself with the question of whether elected public officials would have an opportunity to respond to criticism. Apparently, the court's assumption was that an elected public official would always be able to get space in the press to voice his side of a dispute. Was this a reasonable assumption?

## NEW YORK TIMES CO. v. SULLIVAN
Supreme Court of the United States
376 U.S. 254, 11 L. Ed. 2d 686, 84 S. Ct. 710 (1964)

Justice BRENNAN delivered the opinion of the Court.

We are required for the first time in this case to determine the extent to which the constitutional protections for speech and press limit a State's power to award damages in a libel action brought by a public official against critics of his official conduct.

Respondent L. B. Sullivan is one of the three elected Commissioners of the City of Montgomery, Alabama. He testified that he was "Commissioner of Public Affairs and the duties are supervision of the Police Department, Fire Department, Department of Cemetery and Department of Scales." . . . A jury in the Circuit Court of Montgomery County awarded him damages of $500,000, the full amount claimed, against all the petitioners, and the Supreme Court of Alabama affirmed.

Respondent's complaint alleged that he had been libeled by statements in a full-page advertisement that was carried in the New York Times on March 29, 1960. Entitled "Heed Their Rising Voices," . . . .

. . . .

Of the 10 paragraphs of text in the advertisement, the third and a portion of the sixth were the basis of respondent's claim of libel. They read as follows:

Third paragraph:

"In Montgomery, Alabama, after students sang 'My Country, 'Tis of Thee' on the State Capitol steps, their leaders were expelled from school, and truckloads of police armed with shotguns and tear-gas ringed the Alabama State College Campus. When the entire student body protested to state authorities by refusing to re-register, their dining hall was padlocked in an attempt to starve them into submission."

Sixth paragraph:

"Again and again the Southern violators have answered Dr. King's peaceful protests with intimidation and violence. They have bombed his home almost killing his wife and child. They have assaulted his person. They have arrested him seven times— for 'speeding,' 'loitering' and similar 'offenses.' And now they have charged him with 'perjury'—a *felony* under which they would imprison him for *ten years*. . . ."

Although neither of these statements mentions respondent by name, . . . [r]espondent and six other Montgomery residents testified that they read some or all of the statements as referring to him in his capacity as Commissioner.

It is uncontroverted that some of the statements contained in the two paragraphs were not accurate descriptions of events which occurred in Montgomery. . . .

. . . .

In affirming the judgment [against the New York Times], the Supreme Court of Alabama sustained the trial judge's rulings and instructions in all respects. . . . In sustaining the trial court's determination that the verdict was not excessive, the court said that malice could be inferred from the Times' "irresponsibility" in printing the advertisement while "the Times in its own files had articles already published which would have demonstrated the falsity of the allegations in the advertisement"; from the Times' failure to retract for respondent while retracting for the Governor, whereas the falsity of some of the allegations was then known to the Times and "the matter contained in the advertisement was equally false as to both parties"; and from the testimony of the Times' Secretary that, apart from the statement that the dining hall was padlocked, he thought the two paragraphs were "substantially correct." . . . It rejected petitioners' constitutional contentions with the brief statements that "The First Amendment of the U. S. Constitution does not protect libelous publications" and "The Fourteenth Amendment is directed against State action and not private action."

. . . We reverse the judgment. We hold that the rule of law applied by the Alabama courts is constitutionally deficient for failure to provide the safeguards for freedom of speech and of the press that are required by the First and Fourteenth Amendments in a libel action brought by a public official against critics of his official conduct. We further hold that under the proper safeguards the evidence presented in this case is constitutionally insufficient to support the judgment for respondent.

. . . .

Respondent relies heavily, as did the Alabama courts, on statements of this Court to the effect that the Constitution does not protect libelous publications. Those statements do not foreclose our inquiry here. None of the cases sustained the use of libel laws to impose sanctions upon expression critical of the official conduct of public officials. . . .

. . . .

[W]e consider this case against the background of a profound national commitment to the principle that debate on public issues should be uninhibited, robust, and wide-open, and that it may well include vehement, caustic, and sometimes unpleasantly sharp attacks on government and public officials. The present advertisement, as an expression of grievance and protest on one of the major public issues of our time, would seem clearly to qualify for the constitutional protection. The question is whether it forfeits that protection by the falsity of some of its factual statements and by its alleged defamation of respondent.

Authoritative interpretations of the First Amendment guarantees have consistently refused to recognize an exception for any test of truth, whether administered by judges, juries, or administrative officials—and especially not one that puts the burden of proving truth on the speaker. . . .

That erroneous statement is inevitable in free debate, and that it must be protected if the freedoms of expression are to have the "breathing space" that they "need . . . to survive," [has been previously recognized].

. . . .

Injury to official reputation affords no more warrant for repressing speech that would otherwise be free than does factual error. Where judicial officers are involved, this Court has held that concern for the dignity and reputation of the courts does not justify the punishment as criminal contempt of criticism of the judge or his decision. Bridges v. California, 314 U.S. 252. This is true even though the utterance contains "half truths" and "misinformation." Such repression can be justified, if at all, only by a clear and present danger of the obstruction of justice. If judges are to be treated as "men of fortitude, able to thrive in a hardy climate," surely the same must be true of other government officials, such as elected city commissioners. Criticism of their official conduct does not lose its constitutional protection merely because it is effective criticism and hence diminishes their official reputations.

If neither factual error nor defamatory content suffices to remove the constitutional shield from criticism of official conduct, the combination of the two elements is no less inadequate. This is the lesson to be drawn from the great controversy over the Sedition Act of 1798, which first crystallized a national awareness of the central meaning of the First Amendment. . . .

Although the Sedition Act was never tested in this Court, the attack upon its validity has carried the day in the court of history. . . .

. . . .

What a State may not constitutionally bring about by means of a criminal statute is likewise beyond the reach of its civil law of libel. The fear of damage awards under a rule such as that invoked by the Alabama courts here may be markedly more inhibiting than the fear of prosecution under a criminal statute. . . . The judgment awarded in this case—without the need for any proof of actual pecuniary loss—was one thousand times greater than the maximum fine provided by the Alabama criminal statute, and one hundred times greater than that provided by the Sedition Act. And since there is no double-jeopardy limitation applicable to civil lawsuits, this is not the only judgment that may be awarded against petitioners for the same publication.[18] Whether or not a newspaper can survive a succession of such judgments, the pall of fear and timidity imposed upon those who would give voice to public criticism is an atmosphere in which the First Amendment freedoms cannot survive. . . .

The state rule of law is not saved by its allowance of the defense of truth. A defense for erroneous statements honestly made is no less essential here than was the requirement of proof of guilty knowledge which, in Smith v. California, 361 U.S. 147, we held indispensable to a valid conviction of a bookseller for possessing obscene writings for sale. . . .

A rule compelling the critic of official conduct to guarantee the truth of all his factual assertions—and to do so on pain of libel judgments virtually unlimited in amount—leads to a comparable "self-censorship." Allowance of the defense of truth, with the burden of proving it on the defendant, does not mean that only false speech will be deterred. Even courts accepting this defense as an adequate safeguard have recognized the difficulties of adducing legal proofs that the alleged libel was true in all its factual particulars. Under such a rule, would-be critics of official conduct may be deterred from voicing their criticism, even though it is believed to be true and even though it is in fact true, because of doubt whether it can be proved in court or fear of the expense of having to do so. They tend to make only statements which "steer far wider of the unlawful zone." The rule thus dampens the vigor and limits the variety of public debate. It is inconsistent with the First and Fourteenth Amendments.

The constitutional guarantees require, we think, a federal rule that prohibits a public official from recovering damages for a defamatory falsehood relating to his official conduct unless

---

[18] The Times states that four other libel suits based on the advertisement have been filed against it by others who have served as Montgomery City Commissioners and by the Governor of Alabama; that another $500,000 verdict has been awarded in the only one of these cases that has yet gone to trial; and that the damages sought in the other three total $2,000,000.

he proves that the statement was made with "actual malice"—
this is, with knowledge that it was false or with reckless disregard
of whether it was false or not. . . .

. . . .

Such a privilege for criticism of official conduct is appropriately analogous to the protection accorded a public official when
*he* is sued for libel by a private citizen. In Barr v. Matteo, 360
U.S. 564, 575, this Court held the utterance of a federal official
to be absolutely privileged if made "within the outer perimeter"
of his duties. The States accord the same immunity to statements
of their highest officers, although some differentiate their lesser
officials and qualify the privilege they enjoy. But all hold that
all officials are protected unless actual malice can be proved.
The reason for the official privilege is said to be that the threat
of damage suits would otherwise "inhibit the fearless, vigorous,
and effective administration of policies of government" and
"dampen the ardor of all but the most resolute, or the most
irresponsible, in the unflinching discharge of their duties." Analogous considerations support the privilege for the citizen-critic of
government. It is as much his duty to criticize as it is the official's
duty to administer. See *Whitney v. California* (concurring opinion of Mr. Justice Brandeis). As Madison said, "the censorial
power is in the people over the Government, and not in the
Government over the people." It would give public servants an
unjustified preference over the public they serve, if critics of
official conduct did not have a fair equivalent of the immunity
granted to the officials themselves.

We conclude that such a privilege is required by the First
and Fourteenth Amendments.

We hold today that the Constitution delimits a State's power
to award damages for libel in actions brought by public officials
against critics of their official conduct. Since this is such an
action, the rule requiring proof of actual malice is applicable.
While Alabama law apparently requires proof of actual malice
for an award of punitive damages, where general damages are
concerned malice is "presumed." Such a presumption is inconsistent with the federal rule. . . . Since the trial judge did not
instruct the jury to differentiate between general and punitive
damages, it may be that the verdict was wholly an award of one
or the other. But it is impossible to know, in view of the general verdict returned. Because of this uncertainty, the judgment
must be reversed and the case remanded.

Since respondent may seek a new trial, we deem that considerations of effective judicial administration require us to re-

view the evidence in the present record to determine whether it could constitutionally support a judgment for respondent. This Court's duty is not limited to the elaboration of constitutional principles; we must also in proper cases review the evidence to make certain that those principles have been constitutionally applied. This is such a case, particularly since the question is one of alleged trespass across "the line between speech unconditionally guaranteed and speech which may legitimately be regulated." In cases where that line must be drawn, the rule is that we "examine for ourselves the statements in issue and the circumstances under which they were made to see . . . whether they are of a character which the principles of the First Amendment, as adopted by the Due Process Clause of the Fourteenth Amendment, protect." We must "make an independent examination of the whole record," so as to assure ourselves that the judgment does not constitute a forbidden intrusion on the field of free expression.

Applying these standards, we consider that the proof presented to show actual malice lacks the convincing clarity which the constitutional standard demands, and hence that it would not constitutionally sustain the judgment for respondent under the proper rule of law. The case of the individual petitioners requires little discussion. Even assuming that they could constitutionally be found to have authorized the use of their names on the advertisement, there was no evidence whatever that they were aware of any erroneous statements or were in any way reckless in that regard. The judgment against them is thus without constitutional support.

As to the Times, we similarly conclude that the facts do not support a finding of actual malice. [The Court's review of the evidence is omitted.]

. . . .

We also think the evidence was constitutionally defective in another respect: it was incapable of supporting the jury's finding that the allegedly libelous statements were made "of and concerning" respondent. . . .

. . . .

This proposition has disquieting implications for criticism of governmental conduct. . . . The present proposition would sidestep this obstacle by transmuting criticism of government, however impersonal it may seem on its face, into personal criticism, and hence potential libel, of the officials of whom the government is composed. . . . Raising as it does the possibility that a good-faith critic of government will be penalized for his criticism, the proposition relied on by the Alabama courts strikes at the very center of the constitutionally protected area of free expression. We hold that such a proposition may not constitutionally be utilized to establish that an otherwise impersonal attack on governmental operations was a libel of an official responsible for those operations. Since it was relied on exclusively here, and there was no other evidence to connect the statements with respondent, the evidence was constitutionally insufficient to support a finding that the statements referred to respondent.

The judgment of the Supreme Court of Alabama is reversed and the case is remanded to that court for further proceedings not inconsistent with this opinion.

Reversed and remanded.

Justice BLACK, with whom Justice DOUGLAS joins, concurring.

. . . I base my vote to reverse on the belief that the First and Fourteenth Amendments not merely "delimit" a State's power to award damages to "a public official against critics of his official conduct" but completely prohibit a State from exercising such a power. The Court goes on to hold that a State can subject such critics to damages if "actual malice" can be proved against them. "Malice," even as defined by the Court, is an elusive, abstract concept, hard to prove and hard to disprove. The requirement that malice be proved provides at best an evanescent protection for the right critically to discuss public affairs and certainly does not measure up to the sturdy safeguard embodied in the First Amendment. Unlike the Court, therefore, I vote to reverse exclusively on the ground that the Times and the individual defendants had an absolute, unconditional constitutional right to publish in the Times advertisement their criticisms of the Montgomery agencies and officials. . . .

The half-million-dollar verdict does give dramatic proof, however, that state libel laws threaten the very existence of an American press virile enough to publish unpopular views on public affairs and bold enough to criticize the conduct of public officials. . . .

. . . .

---

## NOTES

1. In *New York Times v. Sullivan*, Justice Brennan cites the profound national commitment to "uninhibited, robust, and wide-open" debate on public issues. If support for unfettered

discussion is so unequivocal, why isn't the first amendment privilege absolute?

Suppose the Supreme Court had established an absolute privilege for "public statements" like the ad in the *New York Times* case but then allowed state courts to determine for themselves what a "public statement" was? It is not difficult to see how a court, bent on limiting the impact of the *New York Times* rule, could establish a very narrow definition for "public statement" which might well afford protection for fewer defendants than before. As one academic critic has said: "This would not be the first time that a rule fashioned to achieve a measure of liberality would live to become an instrument of restraint." *See* Berney, *Libel and the First Amendment—A New Constitutional Privilege,* 51 VA. L. REV. 1 (1965).

**2.** Justice Brennan in *New York Times v. Sullivan* placed great reliance on an early state case involving libel and freedom of the press, Coleman v. MacLennan, 78 Kan. 711, 98 P. 281 (1908). In *Coleman,* the court enunciated its view that "the history of all liberty, religious, political, and economic, teaches that undue restrictions merely excite and inflame, and that social progress is best facilitated, the social welfare is best preserved, and social justice is best promoted in the presence of the least necessary restraint." Accordingly, *Coleman* held that the common law privilege of fair comment should include privilege for false statements as well as true, providing they were made in good faith. This rule was the leading minority view among the states; the majority of the states, however, adhered to the traditional common law rule that the fair comment privilege extended only to true statements and that publication of a false statement would leave the publisher wide open to an action for libel. The *New York Times* rule, of course, does not protect calculated falsehood. Is there any difference between the first amendment-based *New York Times* rule and the *Coleman* rule with regard to protection of untrue statements?

**3.** Professor Kalven, in an article published shortly after the *New York Times* decision was announced, predicted that the case might well mark a shift in the Supreme Court's entire approach to the issue of free speech. Kalven, *The New York Times Case: A Note on "The Central Meaning of the First Amendment",* 1964 SUP. CT. REV. 191. Kalven believes that the court took the opportunity in *New York Times* to restate that "central meaning"—a quote from Justice Brennan's opinion—in terms of the old criminal offense of seditious libel.

The court, in *New York Times* according to Professor Kalven, formulated a "crucial syllogism": "The central meaning of the

[First] Amendment is that seditious libel cannot be made the subject of governmental sanction. The Alabama rule on fair comment [under which the Times was found guilty] is closely akin to making seditious libel an offense. The Alabama rule therefore violated the central meaning of the Amendment." What is the "governmental sanction" being discussed here? Alabama did not convict the Times of the criminal offense of seditious libel, *i.e.* criticizing the public officials of Montgomery, Alabama.

4. Professor Kalven thinks that there was method in the court's decision to use the *New York Times* case as an opportunity for a fundamental restatement of the first amendment. By re-affirming the primary right of citizens to freely criticize their government, he argues that the court has carved out an area of expression which is "off-limits" to governmental interference or sanction except under the most crucial emergency circumstances. Any attempt by the government, direct or indirect, to impinge on this "off-limits" area would then be presumed to violate the first amendment. Such a formulation is, to say the least, at odds with the balancing tests by which the Supreme Court has often viewed free speech issues in the past. Kalven suggested in 1964 that the *New York Times* decision might well mark the end for the "clear and present danger" test and other "balancing of interests" standards of review of free speech cases. Has this prediction come true? Or was it premature? Doesn't the de-termination of what is "malice" under *New York Times* still constitute a "balancing of interests" test?

5. As Justice Brennan pointed out in *New York Times,* the facts of the case concerned "one of the major public issues of our time"—the civil rights struggle. Professor Kalven suggests that the court was "compelled by the political realities of the case to decide it in favor of the New York Times." He suggests that the *New York Times* rule itself and the explanation of free speech doctrine accompanying it was developed by the court in order to justify the politically-ordained result. If "political reali-ties" can be the impetus to a "new meaning" for the first amend-ment, might this not operate, in a given political context, to restrict civil liberties as well as to expand them? Could it be that in the *New York Times* case, political realities coincided with, rather than dictated, the result? If the court had been con-cerned with nothing more than political realities, why didn't it reverse for insufficient evidence, and avoid the first amendment issue entirely?

Might not a self-censorship argument in a *Times* situation cut both ways? An attorney who represented Dr. Linus Pauling in his unsuccessful libel action against a metropolitan news-paper views the *New York Times* rule as an instrument of restraint upon the free exchange of ideas: "Those persons best qualified to add something of value to the marketplace of ideas will be constrained by fear of irresponsible ad hominem attacks. The result is an expansion of freedom to libel at the expense of free-dom of speech." *See* Green, *The New York Times Rule: Judicial Overkill*, 12 VILL. L. REV. 730 (1967).

Much the same argument was presented to the Kansas Court in the *Coleman* case of 1908: If the fair comment privilege was extended to false statements about public officials, honorable men would no longer choose to seek public office for fear of being libeled without any means of defending themselves. The *Coleman* court rejected this argument as unfounded. Do you believe that the quality of those seeking public office will be adversely affected by the fact that office holders are now being subject to criticism which in the past would have constituted actionable defamation?

**6.** The common law itself granted absolute privilege, against defamation actions, to judges and attorneys in the courtroom, and to legislators in legislative chambers. In such cases, the in-jured reputation of the individual was considered subordinate to the public's need for office-holders and judicial servants to perform their duties without fear of legal retribution—and this privilege was preserved by the common law even where the de-fendant had acted *with malice*. In the case of Barr v. Matteo, 360 U.S. 564 (1959), the Supreme Court extended this absolute privilege to federal officials. In *New York Times,* the court analogizing from *Barr,* viewed the "citizen-critic" of govern-ment as an individual acting in a quasi-public capacity. If gov-ernment officials enjoy an absolute privilege, shouldn't their "citizen-critics" enjoy some privilege as well? *See Miami Herald v. Tornillo,* text, p. 881. *See* Hanson, *The Right to Know: Fair Comment, Twentieth Century,* 12 VILL. L. REV. 725 (1967).

**7.** If encouragement of "uninhibited, robust and wide-open" debate on public issues is the operating premise of the court's opinion in *New York Times,* why didn't the court take steps to assure debate? But shouldn't the court have imposed some ob-ligation on the press to assure that the debate which the court considered so important actually transpired? If the press is to be freer from libel suits than ever before in the interest of pro-moting searing social criticism, shouldn't individuals or groups attacked in the press have some right of reply in the same forum? In such circumstances, does the first amendment require a right of reply? In Barron, *Access to the Press—A New First Amend-*

*ment Right,* 80 HARV. L. REV. 1641 (1967), the view is expressed
that it was precisely in terms of assuring debate in the press,
the *raison d'etre* of the *New York Times v. Sullivan* decision,
that the case was a failure. *See* text, p. 879.

8.   The *New York Times* case soon spawned a considerable
progeny. *See* Garrison v. Louisiana, 379 U.S. 64 (1964) (*Times*
rule applies to criminal libel); Rosenblatt v. Baer, 383 U.S. 75
(1966) (*Times* applies to nonelected public officials); Curtis Publishing Co. v. Butts and Associated Press v. Walker, 388 U.S. 130
(1967) (majority of justices hold *Times* standards applicable to
public figures); St. Amant v. Thompson, 390 U.S. 727 (1968)
("reckless disregard" defined as "serious doubts as to the truth of
[the] publication"); Monitor Patriot Co. v. Roy, 401 U.S. 265
(1971) (a charge of criminal conduct is relevant to an official's or
candidate's fitness for office for purposes of applying the *Times*
rule.)

### b.   The New York Times v. Sullivan Doctrine, The Right of Privacy, And The First Amendment

In Time, Inc. v. Hill, 385 U.S. 374 (1967), the Supreme Court
made it clear that the first amendment interest in vigorous and
robust public discussion was going to affect the law of privacy as
well as the law of libel. In the *Hill* case, a suit based on New
York's right of privacy statute was brought against *Life* magazine
by a family whose experience as hostages of three escaped con-
victs was falsely exploited by *Life* magazine. The Hills won a
verdict for $50,000 compensatory damages and $25,000 punitive
damages which was later cut on retrial to $25,000 compen-
satory damages and no punitive damages. The Supreme Court
reversed, holding that the *New York Times* doctrine should be
applied to the New York privacy statute to redress false reports
of matters of public interest. The court held that in such actions
the *New York Times* standard of actual malice should be applied.
In other words, the plaintiff must prove that defendant had published the report with reckless disregard of the truth or falsity
of what was said. Since the proof would conceivably be interpreted as supporting a jury finding of negligent misstatement by
the magazine or of reckless disregard of truth, the Supreme Court
ordered a new trial. Is it a fair assumption that under *Time v.
Hill* and *New York Times v. Sullivan* negligent misstatement
alone is insufficient to support a libel recovery where the facts
of the case command application of the *New York Times* doctrine?

But how do the facts of *Time v. Hill* accommodate themselves
to the public official-public figure context of the *New York Times*

doctrine? Are the members of the Hill family public figures? If they were, they were such only after *Life* had publicized them. Does this mean that any private person is a public figure if he brings a suit for invasion of his right of privacy? After all, a privacy plaintiff will only be written about if he is newsworthy. Moreover, if newsworthiness is the touchstone of the qualified privilege conferred by the *New York Times* doctrine in privacy cases, doesn't this give even a wider berth to the press than did the "public figure" standard?

Justices Black and Douglas concurred in reversing the judgment but repeated their dislike for the *New York Times* actual malice test on the ground that it gave insufficient protection to freedom of the press from assaults by way of damage judgments in libel and privacy actions.

Justice Harlan concurred in the result but dissented from the court's holding that the New York right of privacy case should be adjudicated pursuant to the actual malice standard of liability.

Justice Fortas argued in dissent: "But I do not believe that whatever is in words, however much of an aggression it may be upon individual rights, is beyond the reach of the law, no matter how heedless of others' rights—how remote from public purpose, how reckless, irresponsible, and untrue it may be. I do not believe that the First Amendment precludes effective protection of the right of privacy—or, for that matter, an effective law of libel."

---

## NOTES

1. *Time, Inc. v. Hill* arose under a New York statute enabling individuals to recover damages for invasion of privacy where the defendant had appropriated plaintiff's name or likeness for commercial purposes. New York case law had grafted a privilege onto the statute barring suit where the press had appropriated plaintiff's name or likeness in the course of reporting newsworthy events. Only if the press account contained false or inaccurate information could the plaintiff bring a cause of action for invasion of privacy under the New York law. It is anomalous to begin with that the Hills should have brought suit for commercial appropriation, and false light (to defeat the newsworthy privilege) since their real grievance was more akin to the original formulation of the privacy tort, public disclosure of private facts. Furthermore, had not Life Magazine embellished the news story with some flattering, though inaccurate details, the Hills would have been barred by the newsworthy privilege from asserting a cause of action entirely.

2. Even some proponents of the *New York Times* rule in its original, 1964 context of libel law, reacted to *Hill* with dismay. Nimmer, *The Right to Speak from Times to Time: First Amendment Theory Applied to Libel and Misapplied to Privacy*, 56 CALIF. L. REV. 935 (1968). Professor Nimmer argues that the libel suit and the privacy suit are concerned with fundamentally different interests and that the first amendment has no place in pure privacy cases. The defamation action aims at restoring or defending the plaintiff's public reputation. (If that reputation is a matter of public importance, is it therefore protected by the first amendment?) The privacy action essentially seeks compensation for the outright destruction by the press of the plaintiff's right to keep his private life to himself.

3. Because the New York courts made newsworthiness the key to the privilege, the Supreme Court was brought face to face with an idea Justice Douglas had stated in the earlier case of *Rosenblatt v. Baer*. Public interest in an issue has more first amendment significance than the particular status of the plaintiff. Before *Hill*, the court had conditioned the first amendment privilege upon the plaintiff's own status as a public official presumably because of such an official's opportunity for access to the media for rebuttal, reply, and even counter-defamation against his press critics. Justice Douglas, on the other hand, had argued that right of reply was not the key issue because the first amendment's protection was geared to the public's right to know rather than to the ability of the defamed plaintiff to defend his individual reputation.

The *Hill* decision, because of the curious way in which the issue arose under New York law, framed the legal issue in terms of newsworthiness rather than plaintiff status, almost prematurely, from the standpoint of the development of law. Only after *Hill*, in the *Butts* and *Walker* cases, did the court propound an extension of *New York Times* to cover public figures generally. Not until 1971, in *Rosenbloom v. Metromedia*, noted below, did the majority conclusively adopt Justice Douglas' position and hold that a private citizen caught up (even involuntarily) in events of public interest must meet the *New York Times* actual malice standard before he may recover in an action for defamation. Thus, the right of privacy problem of *Hill* was gobbled up by the *Times* case. Professor Kalven has suggested that *Hill* came out of turn and should logically have been decided after *Butts* and *Walker* had expanded the *Times* rule to public figures. But, paradoxically, he believes that the strange sequence of decisions came out for the best. (Why?) *See* Kalven, *The Reasonable Man and the First Amendment: Hill, Butts, and Walker,* 1967 Sup. Ct. Rev. 267.

4. Did the court in *Hill* accept the newsworthiness test of the New York statute and elevate it to the level of a first amendment privilege in privacy cases, or did it stop short of that? One scholar has observed that *Hill* does not make newsworthiness the "final answer to the right of personal privacy." In this view, the principle of *Hill* is consistent with an individual's cause of action for invasion of privacy where the information divulged is not relevant to the matter of public interest at hand. *See* Pedrick, *Publicity and Privacy: Is It Any of Our Business?* 20 U. Toronto L.J. 391 (1970). Dean Pedrick's test asks: Does this publicity belong in public? "That, at least, would have been seen as the critical question had the [Hill] case not arisen under the distorting New York statute." But is Pedrick's proposed solution any more practical than Nimmer's suggestion that we simply remove privacy actions from first amendment protection? Administrative convenience aside, how would either standard or test provide guidance to potential defendants? Does it matter?

5. For further discussion of the modern power of the news media and the question of whether immunity from suit is something they need or deserve, see Merin, *Libel and the Supreme Court,* 11 Wm. & Mary L. Rev. 371, 423 (1969). Calling the court's approach "legal overkill," Merin emphasizes the near-immunity from libel and privacy suits extended to corporate news media. He scores the majority for insensitivity to human values and terms the *Times* rule "a constitutional procrustean bed onto which all other values are forced, even if they have to be cut or stretched to fit."

6. Justice Harlan also pointed out that the *Hill* case was not analogous to the problem of seditious libel which was such an impetus to the formulation of the *New York Times* rule. Certainly, on its facts, the *Hill* facts were far removed from criticism of government officials. Can you discern a thread connecting *Hill* to the seditious libel issue? Is the underlying principle or strategy of *Hill* reminiscent of *New York Times?* Professor Kalven perceives an important, though latent connection between the two decisions. Professor Nimmer and others maintain that *Hill* was a break with *New York Times* and not in conformance with its principles.

c.   *Extending the Times Doctrine to the Public Issue*

1. With Rosenbloom v. Metromedia, 403 U.S. (1971), the *New York Times* rule came full circle. Discarding the public

official-public figure standard, the court held that in the interest
of wide-open and robust debate of public issues, the actual malice
rule must apply even to private citizens caught up in events of
public or general interest. In effect, the court took up Justice
Douglas' position in the earlier *Rosenblatt* case. Douglas had
argued then that the first amendment privilege should hinge on
whether the issue was of public interest, not on the status of the
plaintiff.

Of great importance in evaluating *Rosenbloom*, is the fact
that the opinion of the court did *not* receive the endorsement
of a majority of the Justices. It was merely a *plurality* opinion. In
all, there were five separate opinions filed in the case, and they
are strikingly different.

a.  The court's plurality opinion, consisting of Justices Brennan, Burger, and Blackmun extended the *New York Times* rule to
private citizens thrust into the public eye by involvement in news
events. The actual malice standard was applied to public issues
involving private figures. Furthermore, the decision made it absolutely clear that the *New York Times* doctrine applied to the
broadcast media as well as the print media.

b.  Justice Black, *concurring* in the result (which affirmed
the Third Circuit's holding that Rosenbloom could not recover
against Metromedia), reiterated his position that the first amendment privilege was absolute and that any form of libel or defamation action against the news media was automatically unconstitutional.

c.  Justice White, *concurring* in the result, declined to reach
the broad constitutional issue at all. White argued that under
Pennsylvania libel law the news media had a first amendment
privilege to report the activities of local law enforcement agencies, *i.e.*, the police raid on Rosenbloom's home. Absent proof of
malice, Justice White agreed that the private citizen arrested in
the raid had no cause of action for either defamation or invasion
of privacy.

The two dissenting opinions demonstrated growing disen-
chantment with the apparently uncontainable growth of the
*New York Times* rule beyond its original fact situation and
philosophical justification.

d.  Justice Harlan made three points: (1) The press has a
first amendment privilege to report news events in which private
citizens are involved. (2) However, the scope of protection afforded by the first amendment to the press in such cases should be
less than that provided by the *New York Times*, and a private
plaintiff like Rosenbloom should recover on a showing of negli-

gence rather than actual malice. (3) To further protect the press
against punitive suit, damages in such actions should be governed by traditional negligence standards. The presumption of
general damages should be abolished. The plaintiff should recover damages for actual harm done and should recover punitive
damages, at a reasonable level, only on showing of actual malice.

e.   Justice Marshall, joined by Stewart, agreed with Harlan
that damages should be limited to actual losses. Marshall went
further than Harlan by arguing that punitive damages should be
abolished altogether. Finally, Marshall urged that the states be permitted to set their own standards of fault, so long as they did
not impose absolute (strict) liability on the press.

2.   This court's position in *Rosenbloom* is very similar to that
of the late Professor Alexander Meiklejohn, a noted constitutional
scholar who advocated a distinction be drawn between public and
private speech. *See* A. MEIKLEJOHN, FREE SPEECH: AND ITS RELA-
TION TO SELF-GOVERNMENT (1948). Meiklejohn argued that the first
amendment protected only "public speech" and protected it absolutely. Outside the ambit of first amendment, however, was the
field of "private speech," which had only fifth amendment protection and therefore was subject to regulation and restriction by
federal and state governments.

Applying this principle to the *Rosenbloom* holding, a private
citizen who becomes involved, willingly or not, in a matter of
general or public interest is barred by the first amendment from
asserting a cause of action against the news media absent proof
of actual malice. Note that this is not completely consistent with
Professor Meiklejohn's thesis, since the first amendment privilege
is defeasible by proof of malice. Professor Meiklejohn, and Justice Black, argued for an absolute first amendment privilege, but
as we have seen the court was not willing to go this far.

3.   Note that the *Rosenbloom* holding does not leave the
lives of private citizens entirely open to media publicity. Justice
Brennan's opinion expressly reserved comment on what, if any,
constitutional standards apply to defamation concerning a person's
activities not *within* the area of public or general interest. The
boundaries of public interest and rightful privacy were to await
delineation in further cases. It was significant, however, that the
court in *Rosenbloom* was not prepared to sanction a press-created
standard of public interest under which anything published becomes *ipso facto,* a matter of first amendment privilege.

4.   Even though the media is privileged to report, even
inaccurately, details of a person's life as it relates to matters of
public interest, may a cause of action still lie for invasion of

privacy? Conceivably, the methods by which the press secures information (which it is privileged to publish), may constitute a tort. Where reporters gain access to a person's private home by impersonating police officers, may the plaintiff recover for invasion of privacy even if he cannot recover for defamatory publication?

5. *Rosenbloom* incorporates *Time, Inc. v. Hill* into the *New York Times* line of cases. With reference to *Hill*, Professor Bloustein had argued that publication of the names of private individuals could still be deemed irrelevant to the reporting of public interest events. *See* Bloustein, *Privacy, Tort Law and The Constitution: Is Warren and Brandeis' Tort Petty and Constitutional As Well*, 46 Tex. L. Rev. 650 (1968). Consider the position of the Hill family. In 1952, when the actual news event occurred, would publication of their names in news stories have been newsworthy? Years later, when a fictionalized account of the episode was the subject of a theatre review in *Life* magazine, was publication of the family's true name still newsworthy? Justice White dealt with the relevance issue in *Rosenbloom* when he wrote that the press had a first amendment privilege to report the police raid as a matter of public interest and that the person involved or affected (*i.e.* arrested) in the raid could not be spared from public view.

Possibly, the issue of relevance must be decided by the courts case by case. Where the private individual's involvement in public events is immediate and timely, there can be little doubt after *Rosenbloom* that the first amendment privilege will apply. If *Hill* had been decided after *Rosenbloom*, do you think the court would have been more sympathetic to the plaintiff's privacy argument? *See* Kalven, *The Reasonable Man and the First Amendment: Hill, Butts and Walker*, 1967 Sup. Ct. Rev. 267.

6. The plurality opinion for the court in *Rosenbloom* encouraged the enactment of right of reply legislation by the states. *See* Barron, *Access to the Press—A New First Amendment Right*, 80 Harv. L. Rev. 1641 (1967); *Miami Herald v. Tornillo*, text, p. 881. Was *Rosenbloom* concerned with a right of reply to defamation while *Tornillo* was concerned with a right of reply in a non-defamation political candidate context?

The efficacy of right-of-reply statutes and other counter-access remedies for persons defamed or exploited by media publicity has been questioned. *See The Supreme Court, 1970 Term*, 85 Harv. L. Rev. 3, 227 (1971).

7. After *Rosenbloom* was the key to first amendment privilege the status of the plaintiff, or the "newsworthiness" of the issue? Does the progression of cases from *New York Times v.*

*Sullivan* to *Time v. Hill* to *Rosenbloom* support a conclusion that the key to first amendment privilege is "newsworthiness" rather than the status of the libel plaintiff (*i.e.* elected public official, nonelected public official, public figure).

### d. Halting the Advance of the Times Doctrine

### GERTZ v. ROBERT WELCH, INC.
Supreme Court of the United States
418 U.S. 323, 35 L. Ed. 2d 585, 94 S. Ct. 2997 (1974)

Justice POWELL delivered the opinion of the Court.

. . . .

In 1968 a Chicago policeman named Nuccio shot and killed a youth named Nelson. The state authorities prosecuted Nuccio for the homicide and ultimately obtained a conviction for murder in the second degree. The Nelson family retained petitioner Elmer Gertz, a reputable attorney, to represent them in civil litigation against Nuccio.

Respondent publishes American Opinion, a monthly outlet for the views of the John Birch Society. Early in the 1960's the magazine began to warn of a nationwide conspiracy to discredit local law enforcement agencies and create in their stead a national police force capable of supporting a communist dictatorship. As part of the continuing effort to alert the public to this assumed danger, the managing editor of American Opinion commissioned an article on the murder trial of officer Nuccio. For this purpose he engaged a regular contributor to the magazine. In March of 1969 respondent published the resulting article under the title "FRAME-UP: Richard Nuccio And The War On Police." The article purports to demonstrate that the testimony against Nuccio at his criminal trial was false and that his prosecution was part of the communist campaign against the police.

In his capacity as counsel for the Nelson family in the civil litigation, petitioner attended the coroner's inquest into the boy's death and initiated actions for damages, but he neither discussed officer Nuccio with the press nor played any part in the criminal proceeding. Notwithstanding petitioner's remote connection with the prosecution of Nuccio, respondent's magazine portrayed him as an architect of the "frame-up." According to the article, the police file on petitioner took "a big, Irish cop to lift." The article stated that petitioner had been an official of the "Marxist League for Industrial Democracy, originally known as the Intercollegiate Socialist Society, which has advocated the violent seizure of our government." It labelled Gertz a "Leninist" and a "Communist-fronter." It also stated that Gertz had been an officer of the National Lawyers Guild, described as a communist organization that "probably did more than any other outfit to plan the Communist attack on the Chicago police during the 1968 Democratic convention."

These statements contained serious inaccuracies. . . .

The managing editor of American Opinion made no effort to verify or substantiate the charges against petitioner. . . .

Petitioner filed a diversity action for libel in the United States District Court for the Northern District of Illinois. He claimed that the falsehoods published by respondent injured his reputation as a lawyer and a citizen. . . .

[Following a jury verdict, the district court entered judgment for respondent Robert Welch, Inc.]

Petitioner appealed to contest the applicability of the *New York Times* standard to this case. . . . The Court of Appeals . . . affirmed 471 F. 2d 801 (1972). For the reasons stated below, we reverse.

The principal issue in this case is whether a newspaper or broadcaster that publishes defamatory falsehoods about an individual who is neither a public official nor a public figure may claim a constitutional privilege against liability for the injury inflicted by those statements.

. . . .

We begin with the common ground. Under the First Amendment there is no such thing as a false idea. However pernicious an opinion may seem, we depend for its correction not on the conscience of judges and juries but on the competition of other ideas. But there is no constitutional value in false statements of fact. Neither the intentional lie nor the careless error materially advances society's interest in "uninhibited, robust, and wide-open" debate on public issues. *New York Times Co. v. Sullivan.* They belong to that category of utterances which "are no essential part of any exposition of ideas, and are of such slight social value as a step to truth that any benefit that may be derived from them is clearly outweighed by the social interest in order and morality." *Chaplinsky v. New Hampshire.*

Although the erroneous statement of fact is not worthy of constitutional protection, it is nevertheless inevitable in free debate. . . . Our decisions recognize that a rule of strict liability that compels a publisher or broadcaster to guarantee the accuracy of his factual assertions may lead to intolerable self-censorship. Allowing the media to avoid liability only by proving the truth of all injurious statements does not accord adequate protection to First Amendment liberties. . . .

The need to avoid self-censorship by the news media is, however, not the only societal value at issue. If it were, this Court would have embraced long ago the view that publishers and broadcasters enjoy an unconditional and indefeasible immunity from liability for defamation. Such a rule would indeed obviate the fear that the prospect of civil liability for injurious falsehood might dissuade a timorous press from the effective exercise of First Amendment freedoms. Yet absolute protection for the communications media requires a total sacrifice of the competing value served by the law of defamation.

. . . .

The *New York Times* standard defines the level of constitutional protection appropriate to the context of defamation of a public person. Those who, by reason of the notoriety of their achievements or the vigor and success with which they seek the public's attention, are properly classed as public figures and those who hold governmental office may recover for injury to reputation only on clear and convincing proof that the defamatory falsehood was made with knowledge of its falsity or with reckless disregard for the truth. This standard administers an extremely powerful antidote to the inducement to media self-censorship of the common law rule of strict liability for libel and slander. And it exacts a correspondingly high price from the victims of defamatory falsehood. Plainly many deserving plaintiffs, including some intentionally subjected to injury, will be unable to surmount the barrier of the *New York Times* test. . . .

. . . .

. . . For the reasons stated below, we conclude that the state interest in compensating injury to the reputation of private individuals requires a different rule should obtain with respect to them.

. . . .

. . . The first remedy of any victim of defamation is self-help —using available opportunities to contradict the lie or correct the error and thereby to minimize its adverse impact on reputation. Public officials and public figures usually enjoy significantly greater access to the channels of effective communication and hence have a more realistic opportunity to counteract false statements than private individuals normally enjoy.[9] Private individuals are therefore more vulnerable to injury, and the state interest in protecting them is correspondingly greater.

---

[9] Of course, an opportunity for rebuttal seldom suffices to undo harm of defamatory falsehood. Indeed, the law of defamation is rooted in our experience that the truth rarely catches up with a lie. But the fact that the self-help remedy of rebuttal, standing alone, is inadequate to its task does not mean that it is irrelevant to our inquiry.

More important than the likelihood that private individuals will lack effective opportunities for rebuttal, there is a compelling normative consideration underlying the distinction between public and private defamation plaintiffs. An individual who decides to seek governmental office must accept certain necessary consequences of that involvement in public affairs. He runs the risk of closer public scrutiny than might otherwise be the case. And society's interest in the officers of government is not strictly limited to the formal discharge of official duties. As the Court pointed out in Garrison v. Louisiana, 379 U.S. 64, 77 (1964), the public's interest extends to "anything that might touch on an official's fitness for office. . . ."

. . . Hypothetically, it may be possible for someone to become a public figure through no purposeful action of his own, but the instances of truly involuntary public figures must be exceedingly rare. For the most part those who attain this status have assumed roles of especial prominence in the affairs of society. Some occupy positions of such persuasive power and influence that they are deemed public figures for all purposes. More commonly, those classed as public figures have thrust themselves to the forefront of particular public controversies in order to influence the resolution of the issues involved. In either event, they invite attention and comment.

Even if the foregoing generalities do not obtain in every instance, the communications media are entitled to act on the assumption that public officials and public figures have voluntarily exposed themselves to increased risk of injury from defamatory falsehoods concerning them. No such assumption is justified with respect to a private individual. He has not accepted public office nor assumed an "influential role in ordering society." *Curtis Publishing Co. v. Butts* (opinion of Warren, C. J.). He has relinquished no part of his interest in the protection of his own good name, and consequently he has a more compelling call on the courts for redress of injury inflicted by defamatory falsehood. Thus, private individuals are not only more vulnerable to injury than public officials and public figures; they are also more deserving of recovery.

For these reasons we conclude that the States should retain substantial latitude in their efforts to enforce a legal remedy for defamatory falsehood injurious to the reputation of a private individual. The extension of the *New York Times* test proposed by the *Rosenbloom* plurality would abridge this legitimate state interest to a degree that we find unacceptable. And it would occasion the additional difficulty of forcing state and federal judges to decide on an *ad hoc* basis which publications address issues of "general or public interest" and which do not—to determine, in the words of Mr. Justice MARSHALL, "what information is relevant to self-government." *Rosenbloom v. Metromedia, Inc.* We doubt the wisdom of committing this task to the conscience of judges. Nor does the Constitution require us to draw so thin a line between the drastic alternatives of the *New York Times* privilege and the common law of strict liability for defamatory error. The "public or general interest" test for determining the applicability of the *New York Times* standard to private defamation actions inadequately serves both of the competing values at stake. On the one hand, a private individual whose reputation is injured by defamatory falsehood that does concern an issue of public or general interest has no recourse unless he can meet the rigorous requirements of *New York Times*. This is true despite the factors that distinguish the state interest in compensating private individuals from the analogous interest involved in the context of public persons. On the other hand, a publisher or broadcaster of a defamatory error which a court deems unrelated to an issue of public or general interest may be held liable in damages even if it took every reasonable precaution to ensure the accuracy of its assertions. And liability may far exceed compensation for any actual injury to the plaintiff, for the jury may be permitted to presume damages without proof of loss and even to award punitive damages.

We hold that, so long as they do not impose liability without fault, the States may define for themselves the appropriate standard of liability for a publisher or broadcaster of defamatory falsehood injurious to a private individual. This approach provides a more equitable boundary between the competing concerns involved here. It recognizes the strength of the legitimate state interest in compensating private individuals for wrongful injury to reputation, yet shields the press and broadcast media from the rigors of strict liability for defamation. At least this conclusion obtains where, as here, the substance of the defamatory statement "makes substantial danger to reputation apparent." . . .

. . . [Further] we hold that the States may not permit recovery of presumed or punitive damages, at least when liability is not based on a showing of knowledge of falsity or reckless disregard for the truth.

. . . The largely uncontrolled discretion of juries to award damages where there ˙is no loss unnecessarily compounds the potential of any system of liability for defamatory falsehood to inhibit the vigorous exercise of First Amendment freedoms. Additionally, the doctrine of presumed damages invites juries to punish unpopular opinion rather than to compensate individuals for injury sustained by the publication of a false fact. More to the point, the States have no substantial interest in securing for plaintiffs such as this petitioner gratuitous awards of money damages far in excess of any actual injury.

. . . It is necessary to restrict defamation plaintiffs who do not prove knowledge of falsity or reckless disregard for the truth to compensation for actual injury. We need not define "actual injury," as trial courts have wide experience in framing appropriate jury instructions in tort action. Suffice it to say that actual injury is not limited to out-of-pocket loss. Indeed, the more customary types of actual harm inflicted by defamatory falsehood include impairment of reputation and standing in the community, personal humiliation, and mental anguish and suffering. Of course, juries must be limited by appropriate instructions, and all awards must be supported by competent evidence concerning the injury, although there need be no evidence which assigns an actual dollar value to the injury.

We also find no justification for allowing awards of punitive damages against publishers and broadcasters held liable under state-defined standards of liability for defamation. . . . Like the doctrine of presumed damages, jury discretion to award punitive damages unnecessarily exacerbates the danger of media self-censorship, but, unlike the former rule, punitive damages are wholly irrelevant to the state interest that justifies a negligence standard for private defamation actions. They are not compensation for injury. Instead, they are private fines levied by civil juries to punish reprehensible conduct and to deter its future occurrence. In short, the private defamation plaintiff who establishes liability under a less demanding standard than that stated by *New York Times* may recover only such damages as are sufficient to compensate him for actual injury.

Notwithstanding our refusal to extend the *New York Times* privilege to defamation of private individuals, respondent contends that we should affirm the judgment below on the ground that petitioner is either a public official or a public figure. There is little basis for the former assertion. . . .

Respondent's characterization of petitioner as a public figure raises a different question. That designation may rest on either of two alternative bases. In some instances an individual may achieve such pervasive fame or notoriety that he becomes a public figure for all purposes and in all contexts. More commonly, an individual voluntarily injects himself or is drawn into a particular public controversy and thereby becomes a public figure for a limited range of issues. In either case such persons assume special prominence in the resolution of public questions.

Petitioner has long been active in community and professional affairs. He has served as an officer of local civil groups and of various professional organizations, and he has published several books and articles on legal subjects. Although petitioner was consequently well-known in some circles, he had achieved no general fame or notoriety in the community. None of the prospective jurors called at the trial had ever heard of petitioner prior to this litigation, and respondent offered no proof that this response was atypical of the local population. We would not lightly assume that a citizen's participation in community and professional affairs rendered him a public figure for all purposes. Absent clear evidence of general fame or notoriety in the community, and pervasive involvement in the affairs of society, an individual should not be deemed a public personality for all aspects of his life. It is preferable to reduce the public figure question to a more meaningful context by looking to the nature and extent of an individual's participation in the particular controversy giving rise to the defamation.

In this context it is plain that petitioner was not a public figure. He played a minimal role at the coroner's inquest, and his participation related solely to his representation of a private client. He took no part in the criminal prosecution of officer Nuccio. Moreover, he never discussed either the criminal or civil litigation with the press and was never quoted as having done so. He plainly did not thrust himself into the vortex of this public issue, nor did he engage the public's attention in an attempt to influence its outcome. We are persuaded that the trial court did not err in refusing to characterize petitioner as a public figure for the purpose of this litigation.

We therefore conclude that the *New York Times* standard is inapplicable to this case and that the trial court erred in entering judgment for respondent. Because the jury was allowed to impose liability without fault and was permitted to presume damages without proof of injury, a new trial is necessary. We reverse and remand for further proceedings in accord with this opinion.

It is so ordered.

Justice BLACKMUN, concurring.

. . . .

The Court was sadly fractionated in *Rosenbloom*. A result of that kind inevitably leads to uncertainty. I feel that it is of profound importance for the Court to come to rest in the defamation area and to have a clearly defined majority position that eliminates the unsureness engendered by *Rosenbloom's* diversity.

If my vote were not needed to create a majority, I would adhere to my prior view. A definitive ruling, however, is paramount.

For these reasons, I join the opinion and the judgment of the Court.

Justice BRENNAN, dissenting.

. . . .

. . . Matters of public or general interest do not "suddenly become less so merely because a private individual is involved or because in some sense the individual did not 'voluntarily' choose to become involved." See *Times, Inc. v. Hill.*

. . . .

. . . I reject the argument that my *Rosenbloom* view improperly commits to judges the task of determining what is and what is not an issue of "general or public interest."[3] I noted in *Rosenbloom* that performance of this task would not always be easy. But surely the courts, the ultimate arbiters of all disputes concerning clashes of constitutional values, would only be performing one of their traditional functions in undertaking this duty. . . . The public interest is necessarily broad; any residual self-censorship that may result from the uncertain contours of the "general or public interest" concept should be of far less concern to publishers and broadcasters than that occasioned by state laws imposing liability for negligent falsehood.

. . . I would affirm the judgment of the Court of Appeals.

Justice WHITE, dissenting.

. . . .

. . . [T]he Court, in a few printed pages, has federalized major aspects of libel law by declaring unconstitutional in important respects the prevailing defamation law in all or most of the 50 States. . .

. . . .

. . . Under the new rule the plaintiff can lose, not because the statement is true, but because it was not negligently made.

---

[3] . . . Parenthetically, my Brother WHITE argues that the Court's view and mine will prevent a plaintiff—unable to demonstrate some degree of fault —from vindicating his reputation by securing a judgment that the publication was false. This argument overlooks the possible enactment of statutes, not requiring proof of fault, which provide for an action or retraction or for publication of a court's determination of falsity if the plaintiff is able to demonstrate that false statements have been published concerning his activities. Cf., Note, Vindication of the Reputation of a Public Official, 80 Harv. L. Rev. 1730, 1739-1747 (1967). Although it may be that questions could be raised concerning the constitutionality of such statutes, certainly nothing I have said today (and, as I read the Court's opinion, nothing said there) should be read to imply that a private plaintiff unable to prove fault, must inevitably be denied the opportunity to secure a judgment upon the truth or falsity of statements published about him. Cf. *Rosenbloom v. Metromedia, Inc.*

So too, the requirement of proving special injury to reputation before general damages may be awarded will clearly eliminate the prevailing rule, worked out over a very long period of time, that, in the case of defamations not actionable *per se,* the recovery of general damages for injury to reputation may also be had if some form of material or pecuniary loss is proved. Finally, an inflexible federal standard is imposed for the award of punitive damages. No longer will it be enough to prove ill will and an attempt to injure.

These are radical changes in the law and severe invasions of the prerogatives of the States. They should at least be shown to be required by the First Amendment or necessitated by our present circumstances. Neither has been demonstrated.

. . . .

I fail to see how the quality or quantity of public debate will be promoted by further emasculation of state libel laws for the benefit of the news media. If anything, this trend may provoke a new and radical imbalance in the communications process. Cf. Barron, Access to the Press—A New First Amendment Right, 80 Harv. L. Rev. 1641, 1657 (1967). It is not at all inconceivable that virtually unrestrained defamatory remarks about private citizens will discourage them from speaking out and concerning themselves with social problems. This would turn the First Amendment on its head. David Riesman, writing in the midst of World War II on the fascists' effective use of defamatory attacks on their opponents, commented: "Thus it is that the law of libel, with its ecclesiastic background and domestic character, its aura of heart-balm suits and crusading nineteenth-century editors, becomes suddenly important for modern democratic survival." Riesman, Democracy and Defamation: Fair Game and Fair Comment I, 42 Col. L. Rev. 1085, 1088 (1942).

This case ultimately comes down to the importance the Court attaches to society's "pervasive and strong interest in preventing and redressing attacks upon reputation." *Rosenblatt v. Baer.* From all that I have seen, the Court has miscalculated and denigrates that interest at a time when escalating assaults on individuality and personal dignity counsel otherwise. At the very least, the issue is highly debatable, and the Court has not carried its heavy burden of proof to justify tampering with state libel laws.[43]

---

[43] With the evisceration of the common law libel remedy for the private citizen, the Court removes from his legal arsenal the most effective weapon to combat assault on personal reputation by the press establishment. The David and Goliath nature of this relationship is all the more accentuated by the Court's holding today in *The Miami Herald Publishing Co. v. Tornillo*

[The dissenting opinions of Chief Justice BURGER and Justice DOUGLAS are omitted.]

. . . .

---

## NOTES

1. In *Gertz,* the court rejected the extension of the *New York Times* doctrine to publications concerning matters of "general or public interest." A fundamental reason for this rejection was that the court was persuaded that the opportunity for self-help rebuttal was far less available to private figures than is the case with public figures.

The court's assessment of the opportunity for reply on the part of the libel plaintiff thus appears to be crucial to whether the *New York Times* rule may be invoked by the libel defendant. *Gertz* was decided on the same day as *Miami Herald v. Tornillo,* see text, p. 881. *Tornillo* rejected the efficacy of right of reply legislation as a means of making an accommodation between the *New York Times v. Sullivan* doctrine and its broad protection for media criticism and the ability of those criticized to respond. Taking the two cases together, do you agree with the court's implicit assumption that damages rather than reply as a remedy for defamation is less inhibitory of freedom of the press?

Unwilling to uphold a mandatory right of reply and yet fearful that self-help rebuttal would be inadequate for private figures, the court retreated from the continuous inflation of *New York Times v. Sullivan.* The new *Rosenbloom* doctrine was set aside: the status of the plaintiff rather than the content of the publication was to be the touchstone for application of the *New York Times* doctrine.

The focal point of inquiry of the public law of libel now is not whether the publication in question involves a "public issue" but rather whether the libel plaintiff is a public or a private person. In the latter event, the *New York Times* standard could not be available to the libel defendant. What standards would apply in such a case?

2. Justice Brennan authored the plurality opinion in *Rosenbloom* with its sympathetic reference to right of reply legislation as a way both to extend the *New York Times v. Sullivan* doctrine to a still larger area of defamation law and yet to assure some opportunity to individuals to counter adverse criticism in the

---

[text, p. 881], which I have joined, that an individual criticized by a newspaper's editorial is precluded by the First Amendment from requiring that newspaper to print his reply to that attack. . . .

media. Brennan said nothing in *Tornillo* to explain his surprising willingness to invalidate right of reply legislation. But in his dissent in *Gertz v. Welch,* Brennan did cite, apparently with some continuing approval, the text and footnote from his plurality opinion for the court in *Rosenbloom,* which favored right of reply legislation.

Justice Brennan suggested that the fact that the libel plaintiff is not going to be able to recover damages unless he can show lack of care on the part of the libel defendant need not mean that a libel plaintiff of whom something is printed that is in fact false will be without a remedy. He suggested two remedies: (1) compulsory statutes not requiring proof of fault which would provide for retraction; (2) statutes compelling publication of a court's determination of falsity if the plaintiff can show that a false statement was in fact made.

On the basis of Brennan's dissent in *Gertz,* is it fair to conclude that he thinks mandatory reply statutes limited to defamation are valid despite *Tornillo?* Note that Brennan in *Tornillo* concurred specially to declare his view that retraction statutes were constitutional.

3.   In a "false light" invasion of privacy case which is significant, mainly, because it was decided after Gertz v. Welch, 418 U.S. 323 (1974), the court did not extend the rationale of *Gertz* to the privacy area. Cantrell v. Forest City Publishing Co., — U.S. — (1974). The court in *Cantrell* cleaved to the rationale of Time, Inc. v. Hill, 385 U.S. 374 (1967). The court explained that no objection was made by any of the parties to the use by the trial judge of the "actual malice" standard in his instructions to the jury. The court, therefore, said there was no occasion to consider whether *Time, Inc. v. Hill*-type privacy cases should be released from conformance to the "actual malice" standard of New York Times v. Sullivan, 376 U.S. 255 (1964). What would be the nature of an argument that *Time, Inc. v. Hill* is inconsistent with *Gertz?*

4.   Another individual right of privacy versus free press clash is Cohn v. Cox Broadcasting Co., — U.S. — (1975), where the Supreme Court upheld the right of the press to report facts disclosed in a court trial and in court records open to the public. In news broadcasts of a rape trial, an Atlanta television station reported the name of a rape victim who died as a result of the incident. Georgia law made it a crime to publish the name of a rape victim. The name of the girl was obtained by a television news reporter from a clerk of the court who gave the news reporter a copy of the indictment. On the basis of the statute, the

girl's father brought an action for invasion of his privacy. The state supreme court held that a cause of action for damages for invasion of privacy was legally cognizable in these circumstances. The broadcaster contended that recognition of such a cause of action violated the first and fourteenth amendments.

In a decision carefully limited to the facts, the Supreme Court, per White, J., reversed:

> At the very least, the First and Fourteenth Amendments will not allow exposing the press to liability for truthfully publishing information released to the public in official court records. If there are privacy interests to be protected in judicial proceedings, the States must respond by means which avoid public documentation or other exposure of private information. Their political institutions must weigh the interests in privacy with the interests of the public to know and of the press to publish. Once true information is disclosed in public court documents open to public inspection, the press cannot be sanctioned for publishing it.

The court refused to rule on the contention of the media that accurate publication of information cannot constitutionally be punished by either civil or criminal actions for invasion of privacy. The court also said:

> We mean to imply nothing about any constitutional questions which might arise from a state policy not allowing access by the public and press to various kinds of official records, such as records of juvenile-court proceedings.

2. Access to and for Free Expression: Problems of An Affirmative View of First Amendment Protection

### a.  A Right of Access to the Electronic Media?

RED LION BROADCASTING CO. v. FCC

Supreme Court of the United States
395 U.S. 367, 23 L. Ed. 2d 371, 89 S. Ct. 1794 (1969)

Justice WHITE delivered the opinion of the Court.

The Federal Communications Commission has for many years imposed on radio and television broadcasters the requirement that discussion of public issues be presented on broadcast stations, and that each side of those issues must be given fair coverage. This is known as the fairness doctrine, which originated very early in the history of broadcasting and has maintained its present outlines for some time. It is an obligation whose content has been defined in a long series of FCC rulings in particular cases, and which is distinct from the statutory requirement of § 315

of the Communications Act that equal time be allotted all qualified candidates for public office. . . .

. . . .

The broadcasters challenge the fairness doctrine and its specific manifestations in the personal attack and political editorial
rules on conventional First Amendment grounds, alleging that
the rules abridge their freedom of speech and press. Their contention is that the First Amendment protects their desire to use
their allotted frequencies continuously to broadcast whatever
they choose, and to exclude whomever they choose from ever
using that frequency. No man may be prevented from saying or
publishing what he thinks, or from refusing in his speech or
other utterances to give equal weight to the views of his opponents. This right, they say, applies equally to broadcasters.

. . . .

. . . It would be strange if the First Amendment, aimed at
protecting and furthering communications, prevented the Government from making radio communication possible by requiring licenses to broadcast and by limiting the number of licenses
so as not to overcrowd the spectrum.

. . . No one has a First Amendment right to a license or to
monopolize a radio frequency; to deny a station license because
"the public interest" requires it "is not a denial of free speech."
National Broadcasting Co. v. United States, 319 U.S. 190, 227
(1943).

. . . There is nothing in the First Amendment which prevents
the Government from requiring a licensee to share his frequency
with others and to conduct himself as a proxy or fiduciary with
obligations to present those views and voices which are representative of his community and which would otherwise, by necessity,
be barred from the airwaves.

This is not to say that the First Amendment is irrelevant to
public broadcasting. On the contrary, it has a major role to play
as the Congress itself recognized in § 326, which forbids FCC
interference with "the right of free speech by means of radio
communication." Because of the scarcity of radio frequencies, the
Government is permitted to put restraints on licensees in favor of
others whose views should be expressed on this unique medium.
But the people as a whole retain their interest in free speech by
radio and their collective right to have the medium function
consistently with the ends and purposes of the First Amendment.
It is the right of the viewers and listeners, not the right of the
broadcasters, which is paramount. It is the purpose of the First
Amendment to preserve an uninhibited marketplace of ideas in

which truth will ultimately prevail, rather than to countenance monopolization of that market, whether it be by the Government itself or a private licensee. . . . It is the right of the public to receive suitable access to social, political, esthetic, moral, and other ideas and experiences which is crucial here. That right may not constitutionally be abridged either by Congress or by the FCC.

. . . .

Nor can we say that it is inconsistent with the First Amendment goal of producing an informed public capable of conducting its own affairs to require a broadcaster to permit answers to personal attacks occurring in the course of discussing controversial issues, or to require that the political opponents of those endorsed by the station be given a chance to communicate with the public. Otherwise, station owners and a few networks would have unfettered power to make time available only to the highest bidders, to communicate only their own views on public issues, people and candidates, and to permit on the air only those with whom they agreed. There is no sanctuary in the First Amendment for unlimited private censorship operating in a medium not open to all. "Freedom of the press from governmental interference under the First Amendment does not sanction repression of that freedom by private interests."

. . . .

. . . [I]f present licensees should suddenly prove timorous, the Commission is not powerless to insist that they give adequate and fair attention to public issues. It does not violate the First Amendment to treat licensees given the privilege of using scarce radio frequencies as proxies for the entire community, obligated to give suitable time and attention to matters of great public concern. To condition the granting or renewal of licenses on a willingness to present representative community views on controversial issues is consistent with the ends and purposes of those constitutional provisions forbidding the abridgment of freedom of speech and freedom of the press. Congress need not stand idly by and permit those with licenses to ignore the problems which beset the people or to exclude from the airways anything but their own views of fundamental questions. . . .

. . . .

---

## NOTES

1. For some the *Red Lion* case heralded the advent of an affirmative interpretation of the first amendment. In other words, the first amendment had two dimensions. It forbade government

from inhibiting expression but it, in some circumstances, mandated government to provide for expression. This view has been stated as follows: "*Red Lion* launches the Supreme Court on the path of an affirmative approach to freedom of expression that emphasizes the positive dimension of the First Amendment. In fact, the access-for-ideas rationale practically replaces the original legal justification for broadcast regulation—that broadcasting is a limited access medium." *See* Barron, *Access—The Only Choice For the Media?*, 48 TEXAS L. REV. 766 (1970).

The same commentator saw the *Red Lion* case as presenting a challenge and a contradiction to the doctrine of *New York Times v. Sullivan:* "It was the essential philosophy of *New York Times v. Sullivan* that a free press, engaged in public debate, should not have to live in fear of prohibitive libel judgments. But what is the purpose of free debate? It is free so that there shall really be free debate within the nation. If that is true, then a necessary step to securing debate should have been to require newspapers to provide the subjects of their attacks with an opportunity for reply. This would have been a fair price to extract for the new relative freedom from libel judgments. In many cases the same corporations or families own both television stations and newspapers, yet the responsibilities of these same people in the newspaper field are far less. Does not *Red Lion* present a sharp contrast to *New York Times v. Sullivan?* In reason, does it not seem absurd that both decisions could be correct? One of them, since it fails to provide the vital supplement of right to reply is in error, and that one is *New York Times v. Sullivan. . . .*"

COLUMBIA BROADCASTING SYSTEM, INC. v. DEMOCRATIC
NAT'L COMM.

Supreme Court of the United States
412 U.S. 94, 36 L. Ed. 2d 772, 93 S. Ct. 2080 (1973)

Chief Justice BURGER delivered the opinion of the Court (Parts I, II, and IV) together with an opinion (Part III) in which Justice STEWART and Justice REHNQUIST joined.

. . . .

In two orders announced the same day, the Federal Communications Commission ruled that a broadcaster who meets his public obligation to provide full and fair coverage of public issues is not required to accept editorial advertisements. A divided Court of Appeals reversed the Commission, holding that a broadcaster's fixed policy of refusing editorial advertisements violates the First Amendment; the court remanded the cases to the Commission to develop procedures and guidelines for administering a First Amendment right of access. Business Executives' Move

For Vietnam Peace v. FCC, 146 U.S.App.D.C. 181, 450 F.2d 642 (1971).

The complainants in these actions are the Democratic National Committee (DNC) and the Business Executives' Move for Vietnam Peace (BEM), a national organization of businessmen opposed to United States involvement in the Vietnam conflict. In January 1970, BEM filed a complaint with the Commission charging that radio station WTOP in Washington, D. C., had refused to sell it time to broadcast a series of one-minute spot announcements expressing BEM views on Vietnam. WTOP, in common with many but not all broadcasters, followed a policy of refusing to sell time for spot announcements to individuals and groups who wished to expound their views on controversial issues. WTOP took the position that since it presented full and fair coverage of important public questions, including the Vietnam conflict, it was justified in refusing to accept editorial advertisements. WTOP also submitted evidence showing that the station had aired the views of critics of our Vietnam policy on numerous occasions. BEM challenged the fairness of WTOP's coverage of criticism of that policy, but it presented no evidence in support of that claim.

Four months later, in May 1970, the DNC filed with the Commission a request for a declaratory ruling:

> "That under the First Amendment to the Constitution and the Communications Act, a broadcaster may not, as a general policy, refuse to sell time to responsible entities, such as DNC, for the solicitation of funds and for comment on public issues."

DNC claimed that it intended to purchase time from radio and television stations and from the national networks in order to present the views of the Democratic Party and to solicit funds.

. . . .

. . . Congress has affirmatively indicated in the Communications Act that certain journalistic decisions are for the licensee, subject only to the restrictions imposed by evaluation of its overall performance under the public interest standard. . . .

. . . .

. . . [I]t would be anomalous for us to hold, in the name of promoting the constitutional guarantees of free expression, that the day-to-day editorial decisions of broadcast licensees are subject to the kind of restraints urged by respondents. To do so in the name of the First Amendment would be a contradiction. Journalistic discretion would in many ways be lost to the rigid limitations that the First Amendment imposes on government. Application of such standards to broadcast licensees would be antithetical to the very ideal of vigorous, challenging debate on issues of public interest. Every licensee is already held accountable for the totality of its performance of public interest obligations.

The concept of private, independent broadcast journalism, regulated by government to assure protection of the public interest, has evolved slowly and cautiously over more than 40 years and has been nurtured by processes of adjudication. That concept of journalistic independence could not co-exist with a reading of the challenged conduct of the licensee as governmental action. Nor could it exist without administrative flexibility to meet changing needs and the swift technological developments. We therefore conclude that the policies complained of do not constitute governmental action violative of the First Amendment.

There remains for consideration the question whether the "public interest" standard of the Communications Act requires broadcasters to accept editorial advertisements or, whether, assuming governmental action, broadcasters are required to do so by reason of the First Amendment. . . . Many of those policies, as the legislative history makes clear, were drawn from the First Amendment itself; the "public interest" standard necessarily invites reference to First Amendment principles. Thus, the question before us is whether the various interests in free expression of the public, the broadcaster and the individual require broadcasters to sell commercial time to persons wishing to discuss controversial issues. . . .

At the outset we reiterate what was made clear earlier that nothing in the language of the Communications Act or its legislative history compels a conclusion different from that reached by the Commission. As we have seen, Congress has time and again rejected various legislative attempts that would have mandated a variety of forms of individual access. That is not to say that Congress' rejection of such proposals must be taken to mean that Congress is opposed to private rights of access under all circumstances. Rather, the point is that Congress has chosen to leave such questions with the Commission, to which it has given the flexibility to experiment with new ideas as changing conditions require. In this case, the Commission has decided that on balance the undesirable effects of the right of access urged by respondents would outweigh the asserted benefits. The Court of Appeals failed to give due weight to the Commission's judgment on these matters.

The Commission was justified in concluding that the public interest in providing access to the marketplace of "ideas and experiences" would scarcely be served by a system so heavily weighted in favor of the financially affluent, or those with access to wealth. Even under a first-come-first-served system, proposed by the dissenting Commissioner in these cases, the views of the affluent could well prevail over those of others, since they would have it within their power to purchase time more frequently. Moreover, there is the substantial danger, as the Court of Appeals acknowledged, that the time allotted for editorial advertising could be monopolized by those of one political persuasion.

These problems would not necessarily be solved by applying the Fairness Doctrine, to editorial advertising. If broadcasters were required to provide time, free when necessary, for the discussion of the various shades of opinion on the issue discussed in the advertisement, the affluent could still determine in large part the issues to be discussed. Thus, the very premise of the Court of Appeals' holding—that a right of access is necessary to allow individuals and groups the opportunity for self-initiated speech — would have little meaning to those who could not afford to purchase time in the first instance.

. . . .

Nor can we accept the Court of Appeals' view that every potential speaker is "the best judge" of what the listening public ought to hear or indeed the best judge of the merits of his or her views. All journalistic tradition and experience is to the contrary. For better or worse, editing is what editors are for; and editing is selection and choice of material. That editors—newspaper or broadcast—can and do abuse this power is beyond doubt, but that is not reason to deny the discretion Congress provided. Calculated risks of abuse are taken in order to preserve higher values. The presence of these risks is nothing new; the authors of the Bill of Rights accepted the reality that these risks were evils for which there was no acceptable remedy other than a spirit of moderation and a sense of responsibility—and civility—on the part of those who exercise the guaranteed freedoms of expression.

It was reasonable for Congress to conclude that the public interest in being informed requires periodic accountability on the part of those who are entrusted with the use of broadcast frequencies, scarce as they are. In the delicate balancing historically followed in the regulation of broadcasting Congress and the Commission could appropriately conclude that the allocation of journalistic priorities should be concentrated in the licensee rather than diffused among many. This policy gives the public some assurance that the broadcaster will be answerable if he fails to meet their legitimate needs. No such accountability attaches to the private individual, whose only qualifications for using the broadcast facility may be abundant funds and a point of view. To agree that debate on public issues should be "robust, and wide-open" does not mean that we should exchange "public trustee" broadcasting, with all its limitations, for a system of self-appointed editorial commentators.

. . . .

By minimizing the difficult problems involved in implementing such a right of access, the Court of Appeals failed to come to grips with another problem of critical importance to broadcast regulation and the First Amendment—the risk of an enlargement of government control over the content of broadcast discussion of public issues. This risk is inherent in the Court of Appeals remand requiring regulations and procedures to sort out requests to be heard—a process involving the very editing that licensees now perform as to regular programming. Although the use of a public resource by the broadcast media permits a limited degree of Government surveillance, as is not true with respect to private media, the Government's power over licensees, as we have noted, is by no means absolute and is carefully circumscribed by the Act itself.

Under a constitutionally commanded and government supervised right-of-access system urged by respondents and mandated by the Court of Appeals, the Commission would be required to oversee far more of the day-to-day operations of broadcasters' conduct, deciding such questions as whether a particular individual or group has had sufficient opportunity to present its viewpoint and whether a particular viewpoint has already been sufficiently aired. Regimenting broadcasters is too radical a therapy for the ailment respondents complain of.

Under the Fairness Doctrine the Commission's responsibility is to judge whether a licensee's overall performance indicates a sustained good faith effort to meet the public interest in being fully and fairly informed. The Commission's responsibilities under a right-of-access system would tend to draw it into a continuing case-by-case determination of who should be heard and when. Indeed, the likelihood of Government involvement is so great that it has been suggested that the accepted constitutional principles against control of speech content would need to be relaxed with respect to editorial advertisement. To sacrifice First Amendment protections for so speculative a gain is not warranted, and it was well within the Commission's discretion to construe the Act so as to avoid such a result.[21]

The Commission is also entitled to take into account the reality that in a very real sense listeners and viewers constitute a "captive audience." . . . It is no answer to say that because we tolerate pervasive commercial advertisement we can also live with its political counterparts.

. . . .

Reversed.

[Note: The dissenting opinion of Justice BRENNAN, joined by Justice MARSHALL is omitted. The state action portion of Justice Brennan's opinion is discussed in this text, p. 1050.]

---

## NOTES

**1.** A discussion of the state action aspects of *CBS* is found in the text, pp. 1048-1051.

**2.** Has the whole movement for a constitutional right of access to the broadcast media been mortally wounded by the *CBS* case? Is *CBS* the death knell for such a right at least for the lifespan of the Burger Court?

In answer to this question, it must be noted that the court's restatement of the fairness doctrine is very similar to the language of the access concept. The essence of Burger's decision for the court in *CBS* is clear: access is not necessary because the fairness doctrine is an adequate vehicle to require affirmative efforts on the part of broadcasters to ferret out controversial issues of public importance. As described by Chief Justice Burger, the fairness doctrine is not a mechanical rule which requires balanced presentation of issues whenever triggered by the arbitrary espousal of the licensee. The fairness doctrine is described as requiring an affirmative effort to seek out and present the whole spectrum of controversial issues of public importance. Is not the first amendment significance of the *CBS* re-affirmation of the fairness doctrine that the court, at least with regard to the broadcast media, still recognizes a theory of first amendment interpretation which imposes affirmative obligations on "private" broadcasters? In other words, the positive dimension to first amendment interpretation symbolized by *Red Lion* is still left intact after *CBS*.

---

[21] DNC has urged in this Court that we at least recognize a right of our national parties to purchase airtime for the purpose of discussing public issues. We see no principled means under the First Amendment of favoring access by organized political parties over other groups and individuals.

3. In his spirited dissent in *CBS*, Justice Douglas lodges a determined attack on any first amendment theory which gives government an affirmative role to implement first amendment goals of free expression and free discussion. Douglas said both the fairness doctrine and the public broadcasting system are unconstitutional. Why? Justice Douglas did not participate in *Red Lion* but Justice Black did. Black like Douglas has been among the foremost defenders of the classic first amendment position that government should not be involved with free expression. Why did Black join in the court's unanimous decision in *Red Lion* when Douglas, in retrospect in *CBS*, says *Red Lion* should have been decided the other way?

4. Justice Brennan in dissent in *CBS* thought the massive governmental regulation of broadcasting so intertwined the activities of "private broadcasters" with government as to suffuse broadcasters with the first amendment obligations we demand of government.

To the great emphasis on journalistic discretion which a rule forbidding a ban on selling editorial advertising is supposed to threaten, Justice Brennan says journalistic discretion, if it is unaccompanied by no access obligations, may perpetuate as much censorship as it is supposed to thwart. In fact, Brennan points out that the briefs to the Court demonstrate that private censorship by the networks is a continuing reality: "The briefs of the broadcaster-petitioners in this case illustrate the type of 'journalistic discretion' licensees now exercise in this regard. Thus ABC suggests that it would refuse to air those views which it considers 'scandalous' or 'crackpot', while CBS would exclude those issues as 'insignificant' or 'trivial'. Similarly, NBC would bar speech that strays 'beyond the bounds of normally accepted taste' and WTOP would protect the public from subjects that are 'slight, parochial or inappropriate.' "

Does the application of an eighteenth century conception of freedom of the press to network programming policies make sense?

5. Chief Justice Burger fears the effects of requiring television time to be for hire for ideas. The networks and the FCC fear this too. Is what we really have a delegation of censorship? The dichotomy between private and public action is being exploited to permit a power of censorship to corporate power which is, at least, theoretically not available to governmental power.

6. Isn't the result in *CBS* to some extent an inversion of Valentine v. Chrestensen, 316 U.S. 52 (1942). In *Chrestensen*, the court held that a lesser measure of protection is owing to commercial speech, but doesn't *CBS* give higher protection to com-

mercial speech? It is public or political speech that is discriminated against by the refusal of the networks as a policy to sell time for the dissemination of social and political ideas.

Furthermore, doesn't the result in *CBS* turn the preferred position theory upside down? Public or political speech has no claims to network time. Indeed, a blanket restriction on the sale of such time was held by the court to be permissible under the first amendment. Are the first amendment implications of the result of *CBS* completely answered by saying that the networks are private not public and, therefore, not subject to first amendment requirements?

### b.   A Right of Access to the Print Media?

BARRON, *ACCESS TO THE PRESS—A NEW FIRST AMENDMENT RIGHT,* 80 Harv. L. Rev. 1641 (1967).*

. . . .

## NEW WINDS OF CONSTITUTIONAL DOCTRINE: THE IMPLICATIONS FOR A RIGHT TO BE HEARD

### A.   New York Times Co. v. Sullivan: A Lost Opportunity

The potential of existing law to support recognition of a right of access has gone largely unnoticed by the Supreme Court. Judicial blindness to the problem of securing access to the press is dramatically illustrated by *New York Times Co. v. Sullivan,* one of the latest chapters in the romantic and rigid interpretation of the first amendment. . . .

The constitutional armor which *Times* now offers newspapers is predicated on the "principle that debate on public issues should be uninhibited, robust, and wide-open, and that it may well include vehement, caustic, and sometimes unpleasantly sharp attacks on government and public officials." But it is paradoxical that although the libel laws have been emasculated for the benefit of defendant newspapers where the plaintiff is a "public official," the Court shows no corresponding concern as to whether debate will in fact be assured. The irony of *Times* and its progeny lies in the unexamined assumption that reducing newspaper exposure to libel litigation will remove restraints on expression and lead to an "informed society." But in fact the decision creates a new imbalance in the communications process. Purporting to deepen the constitutional guarantee of full expression, the actual effect of the decision is to perpetuate the freedom of a few in a manner adverse to the public interest in uninhibited debate. Unless the

---

*Times* doctrine is deepened to require opportunities for the public figure to reply to a defamatory attack, the *Times* decision will merely serve to equip the press with some new and rather heavy artillery which can crush as well as stimulate debate.

. . . .

The law of libel is not the only threat to first amendment values; problems of equal moment are raised by judicial inattention to the fact that the newspaper publisher is not the only addressee of first amendment protection. Supreme Court efforts to remove the press from judicial as well as legislative control do not necessarily stimulate and preserve that "multitude of tongues" on which "we have staked . . . our all." What the Court has done is to magnify the power of one of the participants in the communications process with apparently no thought of imposing on newspapers concomitant responsibilities to assure that the new protection will actually enlarge and protect opportunities for expression.

If financial immunization by the Supreme Court is necessary to ensure a courageous press, the public officials who fall prey to such judicially reinforced lions should at least have the right to respond or to demand retraction in the pages of the newspapers which have published charges against them. The opportunity for counterattack ought to be at the very heart of a constitutional theory which supposedly is concerned with providing an outlet for individuals "who wish to exercise their freedom of speech even though they are not members of the press." If no such right is afforded or even considered, it seems meaningless to talk about vigorous public debate.

By severely undercutting a public official's ability to recover damages when he has been defamed, the *Times* decision would seem to reduce the likelihood of retractions since the normal mitigation incentive to retract will be absent. For example, the *Times* failed to print a retraction as requested by Sullivan even though an Alabama statute provided that a retraction eliminates the jury's ability to award punitive damages. On the other hand, *Times* was a special case and the Court explicitly left open the question of a public official's ability to recover damages if there were a refusal to retract. . . .

Although the Court did not foreclose the possibility of allowing public officials to recover damages for a newspaper's refusal to retract, its failure to impose such a responsibility represents a lost opportunity to work out a more relevant theory of the first amendment. Similarly, the Court's failure to require newspapers to print a public official's reply ignored a device which could further first amendment objectives by making debate meaningful and responsive. Abandonment of the romantic view of the first amendment would highlight the importance of giving constitutional status to these responsibilities of the press.

However, even these devices are no substitute for the development of a general right of access to the press. A group that is not being attacked but merely ignored will find them of little use. Indifference rather than hostility is the bane of new ideas and for that malaise only some device of more general application will suffice. It is true that Justice Brennan, writing for the Court in *Times,* did suggest that a rigorous test for libel in the public criticism area is particularly necessary where the offending publication is an "editorial advertisement," since this is an "important outlet for the promulgation of information and ideas by *persons who do not themselves have access to publishing facilities* —who wish to exercise their freedom of speech *even though they are not members of the press."* This statement leaves us at the threshold of the question of whether these individuals—the "nonpress"—should have a right of access secured by the first amendment: should the newspaper have an obligation to take the editorial advertisement? As Justice Brennan appropriately noted, newspapers are an important outlet for ideas. But currently they are outlets entry to which is granted at the pleasure of their managers. The press having been given the *Times* immunity to promote public debate, there seems little justification for not enforcing coordinate responsibility to allocate space equitably among ideas competing for public attention. And, some quite recent shifts in constitutional doctrine may at last make feasible the articulation of a constitutionally based right of access to the media.

### MIAMI HERALD PUBLISHING CO. v. TORNILLO
Supreme Court of the United States
418 U.S. 241, 39 L. Ed. 2d 1, 94 S. Ct. 2831 (1974)

Chief Justice BURGER delivered the opinion of the Court.

The issue in this case is whether a state statute granting a political candidate a right to equal space to reply to criticism and attacks on his record by a newspaper, violates the guarantees of a free press.

In the fall of 1972, appellee, Executive Director of the Classroom Teachers Association, apparently a teachers' collective-bargaining agent, was a candidate for the Florida House of Representatives. On September 20, 1972, and again on September 29, 1972, appellant printed editorials critical of appellee's candidacy. In response to these editorials appellee demanded that appellant print verbatim his replies, defending the role of the Classroom

Teachers Association and the organization's accomplishments for the citizens of Dade County. Appellant declined to print the appellee's replies, and appellee brought suit in Circuit Court, Dade County, seeking declaratory and injunctive relief and actual and punitive damages in excess of $5,000. The action was premised on Florida Statute § 104.38, a "right of reply" statute which provides that if a candidate for nomination or election is assailed regarding his personal character or official record by any newspaper, the candidate has the right to demand that the newspaper print, free of cost to the candidate, any reply the candidate may make to the newspaper's charges. The reply must appear in as conspicuous a place and in the same kind of type as the charges which prompted the reply, provided it does not take up more space than the charges. Failure to comply with the statute constitutes a first-degree misdemeanor.

. . . .

Appellant contends the statute is void on its face because it purports to regulate the content of a newspaper in violation of the First Amendment. Alternatively it is urged that the statute is void for vagueness since no editor could know exactly what words would call the statute into operation. It is also contended that the statute fails to distinguish between critical comment which is and is not defamatory.

The appellee and supporting advocates of an enforceable right of access to the press vigorously argue that Government has an obligation to ensure that a wide variety of views reach the public. The contentions of access proponents will be set out in some detail. It is urged that at the time the First Amendment to the Constitution was enacted in 1791 as part of our Bill of Rights the press was broadly representative of the people it was serving. While many of the newspapers were intensely partisan and narrow in their views, the press collectively presented a broad range of opinions to readers. Entry into publishing was inexpensive; pamphlets and books provided meaningful alternatives to the organized press for the expression of unpopular ideas and often treated events and expressed views not covered by conventional newspapers. A true marketplace of ideas existed in which there was relatively easy access to the channels of communication.

Access advocates submit that although newspapers of the present are superficially similar to those of 1791 the press of today is in reality very different from that known in the early years of our national existence. In the past half century a communications revolution has seen the introduction of radio and television into our lives, the promise of a global community through the use of communications satellites, and the spectre of a "wired" nation by means of an expanding cable television network with two-way capabilities. The printed press, it is said, has not escaped the effects of this revolution. Newspapers have become big business and there are far fewer of them to serve a larger literate population. Chains of newspapers, national newspapers, national wire and news services, and one-newspaper towns, are the dominant features of a press that has become noncompetitive and enormously powerful and influential in its capacity to manipulate popular opinion and change the course of events. Major metropolitan newspapers have collaborated to establish news services national in scope. Such national news organizations provide syndicated "interpretative reporting" as well as syndicated features and commentary, all of which can serve as part of the new school of "advocacy journalism."

The elimination of competing newspapers in most of our large cities, and the concentration of control of media that results from the only newspaper being owned by the same interests which own a television station and a radio station, are important components of this trend toward concentration of control of outlets to inform the public.

The result of these vast changes has been to place in a few hands the power to inform the American people and shape public opinion. Much of the editorial opinion and commentary that is printed is that of syndicated columnists distributed nationwide and, as a result, we are told, on national and world issues there tends to be a homogeneity of editorial opinion, commentary, and interpretative analysis. The abuses of bias and manipulative reportage are, likewise, said to be the result of the vast accumulations of unreviewable power in the modern media empires. In effect, it is claimed, the public has lost any ability to respond or to contribute in a meaningful way to the debate on issues. The monopoly of the means of communication allows for little or no critical analysis of the media except in professional journals of very limited readership. . . .

. . . [I]t is reasoned that the only effective way to insure fairness and accuracy and to provide for some accountability is for government to take affirmative action. The First Amendment interest of the public in being informed is said to be in peril because the "marketplace of ideas" is today a monopoly controlled by the owners of the market.

Proponents of enforced access to the press take comfort from language in several of this Court's decisions which suggests that the First Amendment acts as a sword as well as a shield, that it imposes obligations on the owners of the press in addition to protecting the press from government regulation. . . .

In *New York Times Co. v. Sullivan,* the Court spoke of "a profound national commitment to the principle that debate on public issues should be uninhibited, robust, and wide-open." It is argued that the "uninhibited, robust" debate is not "wide-open" but open only to a monopoly in control of the press. Appellee cites the plurality opinion in *Rosenbloom v. Metromedia, Inc.,* which he suggests seemed to invite experimentation by the States in right to access regulation of the press.[18]

. . . They also claim the qualified support of Professor Thomas I. Emerson, who has written that "[a] limited right of access to the press can be safely enforced," although he believes that "[g]overnment measures to encourage a multiplicity of outlets, rather than compelling a few outlets to represent everybody, seems a preferable course of action." T. Emerson, The System of Freedom of Expression 671 (1970).

However much validity may be found in these arguments, at each point the implementation of a remedy such as an enforceable right of access necessarily calls for some mechanism, either governmental or consensual. If it is governmental coercion, this at once brings about a confrontation with the express provisions of the First Amendment and the judicial gloss on that amendment developed over the years.

. . . .

. . . [T]he Court has expressed sensitivity as to whether a restriction or requirement constituted the compulsion exerted by government on a newspaper to print that which it would not otherwise print. The clear implication has been that any such a compulsion to publish that which " 'reason' tells them should not be published" is unconstitutional. A responsible press is an

---

[18] "If the States fear that private citizens will not be able to respond adequately to publicity involving them, the solution lies in the direction of ensuring their ability to respond, rather than in stifling public discussion of matters of public concern.[15] . . .

"[15] Some states have adopted retraction statutes or right-of-reply statutes. . . .

"One writer, in arguing that the First Amendment itself should be read to guarantee a right of access to the media not limited to a right to respond to defamatory falsehoods, has suggested several ways the law might encourage public discussion. Barron, Access to the Press—A New First Amendment Right, 80 Harv. L. Rev. 1641, 1666-1678 (1967). It is important to recognize that the private individual often desires press exposure either for himself, his ideas, or his causes. Constitutional adjudication must take into account the individual's interest in access to the press as well as the individual's interest in preserving his reputation, even though libel actions by their nature encourage a narrow view of the individual's interest since they focus only on situations where the individual has been harmed by undesired press attention. A constitutional rule that deters the press from covering the ideas or activities of the private individual thus conceives the individual's interest too narrowly."

undoubtedly desirable goal, but press responsibility is not mandated by the Constitution and like many other virtues it cannot be legislated.

Appellee's argument that the Florida statute does not amount to a restriction of appellant's right to speak because "the statute in question here has not prevented the *Miami Herald* from saying anything it wished" begs the core question. Compelling editors or publishers to publish that which " 'reason' tells them should not be published" is what is at issue in this case. The Florida statute operates as a command in the same sense as a statute or regulation forbidding appellant from publishing specified matter. Governmental restraint on publishing need not fall into familiar or traditional patterns to be subject to constitutional limitations on governmental powers. The Florida statute exacts a penalty on the basis of the content of a newspaper. The first phase of the penalty resulting from the compelled printing of a reply is exacted in terms of the cost in printing and composing time and materials and in taking up space that could be devoted to other material the newspapers may have preferred to print. It is correct, as appellee contends, that a newspaper is not subject to the finite technological limitations of time that confront a broadcaster but it is not correct to say that, as an economic reality, a newspaper can proceed to infinite expansion of its column space to accommodate the replies that a government agency determines or a statute commands the readers should have available.

Faced with the penalties that would accrue to any newspaper that published news or commentary arguably within the reach of the right of access statute, editors might well conclude that the safe course is to avoid controversy and that, under the operation of the Florida statute, political and electoral coverage would be blunted or reduced. Government enforced right of access inescapably "dampens the vigor and limits the variety of public debate," *New York Times Co. v. Sullivan.* . . .

Even if a newspaper would face no additional costs to comply with a compulsory access law and would not be forced to forego publication of news or opinion by the inclusion of a reply, the Florida statute fails to clear the barriers of the First Amendment because of its intrusion into the function of editors. A newspaper is more than a passive receptacle or conduit for news, comment, and advertising. The choice of material to go into a newspaper, and the decisions made as to limitations on the size of the paper, and content, and treatment of public issues and public officials— whether fair or unfair—constitutes the exercise of editorial control and judgment. It has yet to be demonstrated how governmental regulation of this crucial process can be exercised consistent with First Amendment guarantees of a free press as they have evolved to this time. Accordingly, the judgment of the Supreme Court of Florida is reversed.

*It is so ordered.*

Justice BRENNAN, with whom Justice REHNQUIST joins, concurring.

I join the Court's opinion which, as I understand it, addresses only "right of reply" statutes and implies no view upon the constitutionality of "retraction" statutes affording plaintiffs able to prove defamatory falsehoods a statutory action to require publication of a retraction. See generally Note, Vindication of the Reputation of a Public Official, 80 Harv. L. Rev. 1730, 1739-1747 (1967).

---

## NOTES

1.   The first part of the decision in *Tornillo* recites the arguments for state right of reply legislation found in the opinion for the court in Rosenbloom v. Metromedia, 403 U.S. 29 (1971). Certainly *Rosenbloom* had to be faced up to by the court in *Tornillo*. The powerful endorsement in *Rosenbloom* of right of reply as an antidote to the decline of the libel remedy for damages as a consequence of *New York Times v. Sullivan* was a major factor in persuading the Florida Supreme Court to sustain the state's right of reply statute. But although *Rosenbloom* is acknowledged in *Tornillo,* it is hardly distinguished. There is nothing in *Tornillo* to explain why right of reply which in theory in Justice Brennan's opinion in *Rosenbloom* had seemed the answer to implementing that concern for debate in the press which was a major force in creating the new public law of libel was in the reality to be set aside.

2.   Justice Brennan said nothing in *Tornillo* to explain his surprising willingness to invalidate right of reply legislation. But in his dissent in *Gertz v. Welch,* text, p. 865, he did cite with continuing approval, the text and footnote from his plurality opinion for the court in *Rosenbloom* which was so heavily relied on by counsel for *Tornillo* in the courts. Moreover, he makes it clear in *Gertz* that in his view a libel plaintiff of whom something is printed that is in fact false will not be without a statutory remedy to correct the falsity. In this regard, Brennan suggests enactment of compulsory statutes not requiring proof of fault which would provide for retraction. He also suggests enactment of statutes which would compel publication of a court's determination of

falsity if the plaintiff can show the false statement was in fact made.

Since *Gertz* and *Tornillo* were decided the same day, these remarkable observations do prompt a question: Why aren't statutes such as Brennan proposes which compel newspapers to print that which they may not wish to print a violation of the first amendment a-la-*Tornillo*?

The only reference, and that oblique, in Brennan's dissent in *Gertz* to the fact that *Tornillo* was decided on the same day is a cautious confession that some questions "could be raised concerning the constitutionality of such statutes."

3. A thoughtful paper about the issues involved in *Tornillo* delivered before the rendition of the court's decision is Traynor, *Speech Impediments and Hurricane Flo: The Implications of a Right of Reply to Newspapers*, 43 U. CINN. L. REV. 247 (1974). Judge Traynor discussed the issue of whether retraction statutes are unconstitutional:

> . . . Retraction has served newspapers well, enabling them at their own volition to head off punitive damages without opening up their pages to complainants. . . . Now even that remedy has been vitiated by the declaration in the *Times* case of a constitutional freedom to publish even a falsehood without risk of liability for damages, so long as there is no actual malice. Significantly, the *Times* case held that the failure to make a retraction upon the Police Commissioner's demand was not "adequate evidence of malice for constitutional purposes."

What is the status of retraction statutes *after Tornillo?*

4. After *CBS,* was the result in *Tornillo* inevitable? The Miami Herald in its brief and oral argument so contended. Appellee Tornillo, however, distinguished *CBS* and other pre-*Tornillo* access cases in its brief as follows: "In the CBS case, at least as the FCC and the Supreme Court viewed the issues, nothing in the federal statutes or in FCC decision or regulations justified the recognition of a limited right of access to public television time. In other words, the access to editorial advertising claim was grounded on the First Amendment itself, there was no statute providing access rights." *Tornillo* was distinguishable because in *Tornillo,* unlike *CBS,* there was a statutory basis for the access claim. Why wasn't *Red Lion* the relevant precedent for the disposition of the *Tornillo* case?

5. The student should re-read *Gertz v. Welch,* text, p. 858, in connection with *Tornillo.* Is it fair to conclude that the unanimity of the court in *Tornillo* does not, as a matter of first

amendment philosophy, run very deep? That which appears to be irrevocably fixed in *Tornillo* appears to become unraveled all over again in *Gertz.*

How significant was it that the Florida right of reply statute, and the facts of *Tornillo,* were not limited to a defamation context? Would a statutory right of reply remedy made available to a person, not a political candidate, permitting him to respond to an editorial attack which constituted a defamation be constitutional?

The court says in *Tornillo* newspapers may not constitutionally be compelled to publish that which " 'reason' tells them should not be published."

Who determines whether in "reason" something should be published? If in "reason" something should be published, may the state enact legislation refusing publication? The decision in *Tornillo* suggests that editorial discretion is absolute. If it is absolute, does it make any sense to talk about whether something in "reason" should or should not be published?

6.   In a scholarly analysis of the case law involving an access-oriented approach to the first amendment, the following observation is made: "While there is no precedent for [the Florida Supreme Court's decision in] *Tornillo,* there is also very little authority opposed to it." *See* Lange, *The Role of the Access Doctrine in the Regulation of the Mass Media: A Critical Review and Assessment,* 52 N. CAR. L. REV. 1, 67 (1973). Does the court in *Tornillo* respond to this point?

For a critical commentary on the court's opinion in *Tornillo,* see *The Supreme Court, 1973 Term,* 88 HARV. L. REV. 174, 177 (1974):

> Had the Chief Justice relied principally on the burden which a right of reply imposes on a newspaper's decision in regard to printing an editorial, *Miami Herald* would be more closely analogous to existing precedent. By finding the statute's infirmity in its compulsion that newspapers print what they otherwise would not, Chief Justice Burger inescapably, if unwittingly, formulated new first amendment doctrine.

The same comment concluded that "*Miami Herald* does not, however, foreclose all methods of expanding access to the press." Do you agree?

---

Harry Lehman, candidate for state representative in Ohio, sought to purchase car card space on the publicly-owned Shaker Heights rapid transit system. The proferred advertising was refused because the city had a policy of not permitting political advertising. The rapid transit system, however, did accept ads for cigarettes, banks, liquor, retail and service establishments as well as church and public service groups. The Ohio state courts sustained the city's refusal. The Supreme Court granted certiorari and affirmed the Ohio Supreme Court. Lehman v. Shaker Heights, 418 U.S. 298 (1974).

Justice Blackmun, joined by Burger, White and Rehnquist delivered the opinion of the court:

". . . It is urged that the car cards here constitute a public forum protected by the First Amendment, and there is a guarantee of nondiscriminatory access to such publicly owned and controlled arenas of communication 'regardless of the primary purpose for which the area is dedicated.'

"We disagree.

"Because state action exists, however, the policies and practices governing access to the transit system's advertising space must not be arbitrary, capricious, or invidious. . . . Revenue from long-term commercial advertising could be jeopardized by a requirement that short-term candidacy or issue-oriented advertisements be displayed on car cards. Users would be subjected to the blare of political propaganda. There could be lurking doubts about favoritism, and sticky administrative problems might arise in parcelling out limited space to eager politicians. In these circumstances, the managerial decision to limit car card space to innocuous and less controversial commercial and service oriented advertising does not rise to the dignity of a First Amendment violation. Were we to hold otherwise to the contrary, display cases in public hospitals, libraries, military compounds, and other public facilities immediately would become Hyde Parks open to every would-be pamphleteer and politician. This the Constitution does not require.

"No First Amendment forum is here to be found. The city consciously has limited access to its transit system advertising space in order to minimize chances of abuse, the appearances of favoritism, and the risk of imposing upon a captive audience. These are reasonable legislative objectives advanced by the city in a proprietary capacity. In these circumstances, there is no First or Fourteenth Amendment violation."

Justice Douglas wrote a concurring opinion in the *Shaker Heights* case which particularly emphasized the captive audience point:

. . . In my view, the right of the commuters to be free from forced intrusions on their privacy precludes the city from transforming its vehicles of public transportation into forums for the dissemination of ideas upon this captive audience.

. . . .

Commercial advertisements may be as offensive and intrusive to captive audiences as any political message. But the validity of the commercial advertising program is not before us since we are not faced with one complaining of an invasion of privacy through forced exposure to commercial ads. Since I do not believe that petitioner has any constitutional right to spread his message before this captive audience, I concur in the Court's judgment.

Justice Brennan, with whom Justices Stewart, Marshall, and Powell join, dissenting:

. . . .

"The plurality opinion, . . . contends that as long as the city limits its advertising space to 'innocuous and less controversial commercial and service oriented advertising,' no First Amendment forum is created. I find no merit in that position.

. . . .

"There can be no question that commercial advertisements, when skillfully employed, are powerful vehicles for the exaltation of commercial values. Once such messages have been accepted and displayed, the existence of a forum for communication cannot be gainsaid. To hold otherwise, and thus sanction the city's preference for bland commercialism and noncontroversial public service messages over 'uninhibited, robust, and wide-open debate' on public issues, would reverse the traditional priorities of the First and Fourteenth Amendments.

"Once a public forum for communication has been established, both free speech and equal protection principles prohibit discrimination based *solely* upon subject matter or content."

---

## NOTES

1. Brennan concluded his dissent by saying that it was impossible to draw a line between ideological and nonideological speech. He pointed out that for some passengers commercial messages were as "profoundly disturbing" as political ones might be to other passengers. In the absence of evidence that political messages would impair the rapid transit system's primary mission of transportation, Brennan said that "the city's selective exclusion of political advertising constitutes an invidious discrimination on the basis of subject matter, in violation of the First and Fourteenth Amendments."

Brennan did not think much of Justice Douglas' argument that the "city's practice of censorship" was justified in the case of a "captive audience." He rejected the analogy to the problem of the transit passenger compelled to listen to broadcasts transmitted over loudspeakers in transit cars as illustrated by Public Utilities Comm. v. Pollack, 343 U.S. 451 (1952): "Should passengers chance to glance at advertisements they find offensive, they can 'effectively avoid further bombardment of their sensibilities simply by averting their eyes.' *Cohen v. California.* . . . Surely that minor inconvenience is a small price to pay for the continued preservation of so precious a liberty as free speech."

2.   The case law in the state and federal courts prior to the decision in *Shaker Heights* appeared to be establishing a right of access to both public and private non-communications facilities which were obvious places in which to seek an audience such as bus terminals, subway stations, and shopping centers. For a summary of these cases, see J. BARRON, FREEDOM OF THE PRESS FOR WHOM? 94-116 (1973). This summary concluded with the following comment: "To constitutionalize the gatekeeper's function does not mean that a right of entry for any idea or any group is or should be guaranteed to any forum. . . . Constitutionalizing the function of the gatekeeper demands merely that he articulate the standards for admission to his forum and that he fairly apply them."

3.   Isn't it Brennan's point in *Shaker Heights* that the transit authority has not banned all ads but rather has banned some and not others? It is that discrimination which Brennan considers to constitute both first amendment and equal protection violations.

The court's response to this in *Shaker Heights* appears to be that equal protection standards must only be respected with regard to political speech and not commercial speech. Is one of the consequences of the reasoning of the plurality opinion in *Shaker Heights* to so inflate the commercial speech doctrine as to destroy the use of the public facility as a forum?

In CBS v. Democratic Nat'l Comm., 412 U.S. 94 (1973) the ban on editorial advertising was imposed by "private broadcasters." In *Shaker Heights,* the ban on political ads was imposed by government itself. For Justice Brennan in dissent in *Shaker Heights,* a government imposed ban on public or political speech was an impermissible transvaluation of constitutional values.

Burger, in the plurality opinion for the court in *CBS* hinted that a different result might have been obtained if the ban on editorial advertising in broadcasting had been commanded by the FCC rather than the private broadcasters. Why then did

Burger who had written in the plurality opinion in *CBS* join in the plurality opinion for the court in *Shaker Heights?* The student should note that Justice Stewart who had joined with Burger in *CBS* joined Brennan and the other dissenters in *Shaker Heights.*

## ACCESS FOR THE PRESS AND ACCESS TO THE PRISONS

1. In Pell v. Procunier, 417 U.S. 817 (1974), inmates and journalists challenged the constitutionality of a regulation of the California prison system which prohibits interviews with specific individual inmates by members of the press, alleging that it violated their rights under the first and fourteenth amendments. The Supreme Court, per Justice Stewart, held, 5-4 that where there is a rational basis for the regulation, and other avenues of communication are available, the state may restrict the mode of communication between an inmate and members of the general public, including the press.

> . . . [N]ewsmen have no constitutional right of access to prisons or their inmates beyond that afforded to the general public. . . .

> . . . It is one thing to say that a journalist is free to seek out sources of information not available to members of the general public, . . . [I]t is quite another to suggest that the Constitution imposes upon government the affirmative duty to make available to journalists sources of information not available to members of the public generally.

2. In Saxbe v. The Washington Post Co., 417 U.S. 843 (1974), the constitutionality of a federal regulation prohibiting all personal interviews between representatives of the media and individual inmates was challenged on the ground that it infringed the rights of free press protected by the first amendment. The District Court held that the blanket prohibition, which did not take into consideration the inmate's behavior, the current condition of the institution, or any other administrative problems, precluded effective press reporting in the prison context and so violated the first amendment guarantees. The Court of Appeals affirmed. The Supreme Court, per Justice Stewart, held the case to be constitutionally indistinguishable from *Pell v. Procunier,* and so reversed the judgment of the lower courts. *See also* Procunier v. Martinez, 416 U.S. 396 (1974).

## 3. A First Amendment Basis for Newsman's Privilege?

If a reporter in pursuit of a story uncovers information which the law enforcement arm of the state cannot easily acquire, may the state secure access to this information by the issuance by a grand jury of a subpoena to the newsman to testify? Does such a subpoena violate the first amendment? Does the first amendment merely prohibit restraints on expression itself as distinguished from restraints on the information-gathering process? In 1972, three cases came before the Supreme Court for review of the question as to whether the first amendment provided a privilege to newsmen to refuse to testify in circumstances where the press is unwillingly being made an arm of government. The Supreme Court held that the first amendment gave journalists no privilege, qualified or absolute, to refuse to testify before a grand jury. Branzburg v. Hayes, 408 U.S. 665 (1972).

The most celebrated of the three newsman's privilege cases reviewed by the Supreme Court at the same time in *Branzburg* was Caldwell v. United States, 434 F.2d 1081 (9th Cir. 1970). The Ninth Circuit had rendered a ground breaking opinion holding that the first amendment conferred on newsmen a qualified first amendment privilege not to testify. Earl Caldwell was a black news reporter for the *New York Times* who covered the Black Panthers in California. Slowly Caldwell won the confidence of the Panthers, a confidence which provided him with a fund of information concerning the Panthers and denied to most other journalists. The result was two-fold: (1) a series of unusually informed articles about the Panthers in the *Times* and (2) the issuance of subpoenas to Caldwell to testify before a federal grand jury.

The basic constitutional question presented in the newsman's privilege cases was squarely put by Justice White, writing for the majority in *Branzburg v. Hayes:* "The issue in these cases is whether requiring newsmen to appear and testify before state or federal grand juries abridges the freedom of speech and press guaranteed by the First Amendment. We hold that it does not."

Justice White said: "The heart of the claim is that the burden on news gathering from compelling reporters to disclose confidential information outweighs any public interest in obtaining this information." The court agreed that the public has a right to every man's evidence and said further: "Until now the only testimonial privilege for unofficial witnesses that is rooted in the Federal Constitution is the Fifth Amendment privilege against compelling self-incrimination. We are asked to create another by interpreting the First Amendment to grant newsmen testimonial privilege that other students do not enjoy. This we decline to do."

The court in the newsman's privilege cases had three options to choose from in deciding whether the first amendment granted newsmen a right to refuse to testify in grand jury proceedings. The first option would have conferred an absolute privilege to refuse to testify. The second option would have conferred a qualified privilege on journalists. The third option, the one adopted by the court, was that the first amendment granted no privilege at all to journalists.

In Caldwell v. United States, 434 F.2d 1081 (9th Cir. 1970), the Ninth Circuit had of course elected the qualified privilege approach. But the Supreme Court refused to follow this path.

The Supreme Court emphasized the practical obstacles in the way of administering a judicially created newsman's privilege grounded in the first amendment. The court pointed to the difficulties that a qualified privilege would produce for a trial court: "In each instance where a reporter is subpoenaed to testify, the courts would also be embroiled in preliminary factual and legal determinations with respect to whether the proper predicate cause had been laid for the reporter's appearance: Is there probable cause to believe a crime has been committed? Is it likely that the reporter has useful information gained in confidence? Could the grand jury obtain the information elsewhere? Is the official interest sufficient to outweigh the claimed privilege?"

Also, the court was troubled about awarding a special privilege to journalists: "Almost any author may quite accurately assert that he is contributing to the flow of information to the public, that he relies on confidential sources of information, and these sources will be silenced if he is forced to make disclosures before a grand jury."

The court took a very stern view with regard to crimes that the journalist has witnessed as distinguished from sources that he does not wish to identify, stating: "Insofar as any reporter in these cases undertook not to reveal or testify about the crime he witnessed, his claim of privilege under the First Amendment presents no substantial question. The crimes of news sources are no less reprehensible and threatening to the public interest when witnessed by a reporter than when they are not."

Justice Powell in a separate concurrence stated that "state and federal authorities are not free to 'annex' the news media as 'an investigative arm of government.' " If a newsman is asked questions in a grand jury proceeding which are not asked in good faith, the journalist may secure the protection of the court "on a motion to quash and an appropriate protective order may be entered."

Justice Stewart, joined by Justices Brennan and Marshall, dissented in *Branzburg,* arguing for the recognition of a qualified privilege based on the first amendment. The dissenters described the approach they would have taken as follows: "Governmental officials, must, therefore, demonstrate that the information sought is *clearly* relevant to a precisely defined subject of governmental inquiry. And they must show that there is not any means of obtaining the information less destructive of First Amendment liberties."

Justice Stewart described the procedure by which a qualified privilege could be administered:

> I would hold that the government must (1) show that there is probable cause to believe that the newsman has information which is clearly relevant to a specific probable violation of law; (2) demonstrate that the information sought cannot be obtained by alternative means less destructive of First Amendment rights; (3) demonstrate a compelling and overriding interest in the information.
>
> This is not to say that a grand jury could not issue its subpoena until such a showing were made, and it is not to say that a newsman would in any way be privileged to ignore any subpoena that was issued. Obviously, before the government's burden to make such a showing were triggered, the reporter would have to move to quash the subpoena, asserting the basis on which he considered the particular relationship a confidential one.

In dissent, Douglas argued that the first amendment conferred an absolute privilege on the newsman to refuse to divulge news sources. Douglas criticized the qualified privilege view and the New York Times for supporting that view in *Caldwell:* "The New York Times, whose reporting functions are at issue here, takes the amazing position that First Amendment rights are to be balanced against other needs of convenience of government."

Douglas observed that "Caldwell's status as a reporter was less relevant than was his status as a student who affirmatively pursued empirical research to enlarge his own intellectual viewpoint." Would this mean that material accumulated by anyone in the furtherance of knowledge, whether the investigator be a professor, journalist, or scientist, has a first amendment privilege?

Douglas said that requiring a reporter to testify before a grand jury would have two harmful consequences: "Fear of exposure will cause dissidents to communicate less openly to trusted reporters. And, fear of accountability will cause editors and critics to write with more restrained pens."

---

## NOTES

1. Powell's concurring opinion, providing the crucial fifth vote in *Branzburg*, has been called "pivotal" and "the governing standard for future press-subpoena disputes." *See* Blasi, *The Justice & The Journalist*, THE NATION, September 18, 1972, p. 198. Blasi interprets Powell's separate views as providing a vitally significant qualification to the force of the court's decision in *Branzburg*. Though the outlines of Powell's protective-order procedure are unclear, his opinion does suggest that the *Branzburg* doctrine of no first amendment-based judicially created newsman's privilege might be subject to some amendment in the future. Blasi suggests that the news media keep this potential flexibility in mind instead of indulging in "an orgy of selfpity and an apocalyptic account of the Court's holding that can only exacerbate the apprehension of news sources."

Justice Powell was concerned with situations where the questions put to the journalist-witness bore only a tenuous relationship to the subject of investigation. But suppose the question is directly in the center of the subject matter of the proceeding? Further, the issuance of a protective order once the newsman is before the grand jury would not solve Earl Caldwell's problem. Caldwell had argued that his mere presence in the grand jury room would suffice to destroy his working relationship with the Panthers.

2. Do you think Justice Stewart's suggestion as to how a judicially-created privilege would operate successfully rebuts the concerns expressed in Justice White's opinion for the court about the difficulties inherent in the judicial administration of a qualified newsman's privilege?

The court expressed concern that the recognition of a newsman's privilege would stimulate the establishment of "sham" newspapers which would be set up to engage in criminal activity and "therefore be insulated from grand jury inquiry, regardless of fifth amendment grants of immunity." What protections could be employed to prevent this? Does the need for protection argue for the development of newsman's privilege by way of statutory enactment rather than by constitutional interpretation?

3. Both White, for the *Branzburg* majority, and Douglas, in dissent, recognized that the principle behind the constitutional claim for newsman's privilege might well apply to persons other

than professional journalists. For White, this fact militated in favor of denying a newsman's privilege altogether. For Douglas, as we have seen, the prospect of wider application for the first amendment privilege posed no difficulty.

Justice White states that the court's decision in *Branzburg* leaves statutory attempts such as the "shield" laws designed to provide some measure of newsman's privilege unaffected. But if there are constitutional difficulties in permitting the courts to define who is a journalist, are there not similar problems if the legislatures are permitted to define who is a newsman and what newsman's privilege means?

4.  What protection exists for the newsman or his sources if the real motive of the investigation is to censure or harass the group or cause which may have been written about even though they may have committed no crime? The majority in *Branzburg* placed great emphasis on the historical role of the grand jury as "protecting citizens against unfounded criminal prosecutions." Compare this view with the dissenting opinions. Justice Stewart pointedly reminded the court that the United States had stated in its *Caldwell* brief that the grand jury "need establish no factual basis for commencing an investigation, and can pursue rumors which further investigation may prove groundless."

Justice Douglas argued that the protective function of the grand jury could give way under political pressure to repressive "fishing expeditions" designed to harass and disable dissident groups. The subpoena which was served on Earl Caldwell, after the FBI had tried unsuccessfully to interview him six times, demanded not only a personal appearance by the reporter but also production of his notes and tapes from a year's relationship with the Panthers. The sole justification for such a sweeping order was that Caldwell's contacts with the Panthers appeared "relevant" to the grand jury's investigation.

5.  One critic of a constitutionally based newsman's privilege observes that "the right to gather news, unlike the right to disseminate, is not expressly granted by the First Amendment." *See* Beaver, *The Newsman's Code, The Claim of Privilege and Everyman's Right to Evidence*, 47 ORE. L. REV. 243 (1968).

6.  At least 24 states have "shield laws" which grant varying degrees of protection to members of the press against forced disclosure of confidential sources and/or information. *See* GILLMOR & BARRON, MASS COMMUNICATION, LAW, CASES AND COMMENT 492-498 (2d ed. 1974). A very recent enactment is New York's new shield statute. FREEDOM OF INFORMATION ACT FOR NEWSMEN, N.Y. CIVIL RIGHTS LAW, Ch. 615, § 79-h (McKinney 1970). Unlike some earlier newsman's privilege statutes, the New York law was

drafted to afford protection to broadcast journalists as well as to newspaper and magazine reporters and editors. The drafting problems attending "shield laws" and a comparison of various state provisions, *circa* 1969, are discussed in D'Alemberte, *Journalists Under the Axe,* 6 HARV. J. LEGIS. 307 (1969).

Federal legislation to establish newsman's privilege has been introduced in Congress many times but never enacted. *See, e.g.,* THE NEWSMAN'S PRIVILEGE ACT OF 1970, 91ST CONG. 2D SESS., S. 3552, which proposed a qualified privilege against disclosure of confidential information or the identity of confidential sources, whether before "any court, grand jury, agency, department, or commission of the United States or by either House of or any committee of Congress."

**7.** The movement for recognition of a first amendment based newsman's privilege may be seen as an example of the affirmative thrust of the first amendment. The Ninth Circuit, by process of constitutional interpretation, extended to newsmen a protection which the Constitution implied rather than commands. Such an approach recognized an implied first amendment mandate that the information process as a whole must be protected and encouraged.

The Supreme Court itself has noted that the first amendment may in some contexts demand affirmative encouragement of a more open exchange of ideas and information through the news media. Red Lion v. FCC, 395 U.S. 367 (1969), text, p. 869.

The news media argued in the newsman's privilege cases that affirmative action—judicial establishment of a constitutional doctrine of newsman's privilege—was required to avert a drying-up of news sources which would lead to less information flowing to the public. Doesn't the underlying theory of both *Red Lion* and *New York Times* support the news media argument? Are *Branzburg* and *Red Lion* and *New York Times* therefore inconsistent? Note that Justice White wrote the majority opinion in both *Red Lion* and *Branzburg.*

Is it possible that Justice White and his colleagues simply were not convinced that denial of privilege would automatically result in a drying-up of news souces and a consequent diminishing of information open to the public? If the court had accepted the cause-and-effect argument proposed by the newsmen in *Branzburg* would the result necessarily have been different? Would this explain the superficial inconsistency between *Red Lion* and *Branzburg?* Or does the inconsistency run deeper? Has the court adopted a less sympathetic approach or an affirmative approach to first amendment protection since the *Red Lion* decision?

4.  Obscenity: A Constitutional Concept?

### ROTH v. UNITED STATES
### ALBERTS v. CALIFORNIA
Supreme Court of the United States
354 U.S. 476, 1 L. Ed. 2d 1498, 77 S. Ct. 1304 (1957)

Justice BRENNAN delivered the opinion of the Court.

. . . .

The dispositive question is whether obscenity is utterance within the area of protected speech and press. Although this is the first time the question has been squarely presented to this Court, either under the First Amendment or under the Fourteenth Amendment, expressions found in numerous opinions indicate that this Court has always assumed that obscenity is not protected by the freedoms of speech and press. . . .

. . . .

In light of this history, it is apparent that the unconditional phrasing of the First Amendment was not intended to protect every utterance. This phrasing did not prevent this Court from concluding that libelous utterances are not within the area of constitutionally protected speech. Beauharnais v. People of State of Illinois, 343 U.S. 250, 266. At the time of the adoption of the First Amendment, obscenity law was not as fully developed as libel law, but there is sufficiently contemporaneous evidence to show that obscenity, too, was outside the protection intended for speech and press.

The protection given speech and press was fashioned to assure unfettered interchange of ideas for the bringing about of political and social changes desired by the people. . . .

All ideas having even the slightest redeeming social importance —unorthodox ideas, controversial ideas, even ideas hateful to the prevailing climate of opinion—have the full protection of the guaranties, unless excludable because they encroach upon the limited area of more important interests. But implicit in the history of the First Amendment is the rejection of obscenity as utterly without redeeming social importance. This rejection for that reason is mirrored in the universal judgment that obscenity should be restrained, reflected in the international agreement of over 50 nations, in the obscenity laws of all of the 48 States, and in the 20 obscenity laws enacted by the Congress from 1842 to 1956. . . . We hold that obscenity is not within the area of constitutionally protected speech or press.

It is strenuously urged that these obscenity statutes offend the constitutional guaranties because they punish incitation to impure sexual *thoughts,* not shown to be related to any overt antisocial conduct which is or may be incited in the persons stimulated to such *thoughts*. . . . It is insisted that the constitutional guaranties are violated because convictions may be had without proof either that obscene material will perceptibly create a clear and present danger of antisocial conduct, or will probably induce its recipients to such conduct. But, in light of our holding that obscenity is not protected speech, the complete answer to this argument is in the holding of this Court in *Beauharnais v. Illinois.*

However, sex and obscenity are not synonymous. Obscene material is material which deals with sex in a manner appealing to prurient interest. The portrayal of sex, *e.g.,* in art, literature and scientific works, is not itself sufficient reason to deny material the constitutional protection of freedom of speech and press. Sex, a great and mysterious motive force in human life, has indisputably been a subject of absorbing interest to mankind through the ages; it is one of the vital problems of human interest and public concern. . . .

. . . .

The early leading standard of obscenity allowed material to be judged merely by the effect of an isolated excerpt upon particularly susceptible persons. Regina v. Hicklin, [1868] L.R. 3 Q.B. 360. Some American courts adopted this standard but later decisions have rejected it and substituted this test: whether to the average person, applying contemporary community standards, the dominant theme of the material taken as a whole appeals to prurient interest. The *Hicklin* test, judging obscenity by the effect of isolated passages upon the most susceptible persons, might well encompass material legitimately treating with sex, and so it must be rejected as unconstitutionally restrictive of the freedoms of speech and press. On the other hand, the substituted standard provides safeguards adequate to withstand the charge of constitutional infirmity.

Both trial courts below sufficiently followed the proper standard. Both courts used the proper definition of obscenity. . . .

It is argued that the statutes do not provide reasonably ascertainable standards of guilt and therefore violate the constitutional requirements of due process. . . . The federal obscenity statute makes punishable the mailing of material that is "obscene, lewd, lascivious, or filthy . . . or other publication of an indecent character." The California statute makes punishable, *inter alia,* the keeping for sale or advertising material that is "obscene or indecent." The thrust of the argument is that these words are not sufficiently precise because they do not mean the same thing to all people, all the time, everywhere.

Many decisions have recognized that these terms of obscenity statutes are not precise. This Court, however, has consistently held that lack of precision is not itself offensive to the requirements of due process. . . .

In summary, then, we hold that these statutes, applied according to the proper standard for judging obscenity, do not offend constitutional safeguards against convictions based upon protected material, or fail to give men in acting adequate notice of what is prohibited.

. . . .

Affirmed.

Chief Justice WARREN, concurring in the result.

. . . .

. . . The line dividing the salacious or pornographic from literature or science is not straight and unwavering. Present laws depend largely upon the effect that the materials may have upon those who receive them. It is manifest that the same object may have a different impact, varying according to the part of the community it reached. But there is more to these cases. It is not the book that is on trial; it is a person. The conduct of the defendant is the central issue, not the obscenity of a book or picture. The nature of the materials is, of course, relevant as an attribute of the defendant's conduct, but the materials are thus placed in context from which they draw color and character. A wholly different result might be reached in a different setting.

. . . The defendants in both these cases were engaged in the business of purveying textual or graphic matter openly advertised to appeal to the erotic interest of their customers. They were plainly engaged in the commercial exploitation of the morbid and shameful craving for materials with prurient effect. I believe that the State and Federal Governments can constitutionally punish such conduct. . . .

. . . .

Justice HARLAN, concurring in the result in No. 61, and dissenting in No. 582. . . .

I concur in . . . *Alberts v. California.*

. . . .

In judging the constitutionality of this conviction, we should remember that our function in reviewing state judgments under the Fourteenth Amendment is a narrow one. We do not decide whether the policy of the State is wise, or whether it is based on assumptions scientifically substantiated. We can inquire only whether the state action so subverts the fundamental liberties implicit in the Due Process Clause that it cannot be sustained as a rational exercise of power. . . .

What, then, is the purpose of this California statute? Clearly the state legislature has made the judgment that printed words *can* "deprave or corrupt" the reader—that words can incite to antisocial or immoral action. The assumption seems to be that the distribution of certain types of literature will induce criminal or immoral sexual conduct. It is well known, of course, that the validity of this assumption is a matter of dispute among critics, sociologists, psychiatrists, and penologists. There is a large school of thought, particularly in the scientific community, which denies any causal connection between the reading of pornography and immorality, crime, or delinquency. Others disagree. Clearly it is not our function to decide this question. That function belongs to the state legislature. Nothing in the Constitution requires California to accept as truth the most advanced and sophisticated psychiatric opinion. It seems to me clear that it is not irrational, in our present state of knowledge, to consider that pornography can induce a type of sexual conduct which a State may deem obnoxious to the moral fabric of society. In fact the very division of opinion on the subject counsels us to respect the choice made by the State.

. . . .

What has been said, however, does not dispose of the case. It still remains for us to decide whether the state court's determination that this material should be suppressed is consistent with the Fourteenth Amendment; and that, of course, presents a federal question as to which we, and not the state court, have the ultimate responsibility. And so, in the final analysis, I concur in the judgment because, upon an independent perusal of the material involved, and in light of the considerations discussed above, I cannot say that its suppression would so interfere with the communication of "ideas" in any proper sense of that term that it would offend the Due Process Clause. I therefore agree with the Court that appellant's conviction must be affirmed.

I dissent in . . . *Roth v. United States.*

We are faced here with the question whether the federal obscenity statute, as construed and applied in this case, violates the First Amendment to the Constitution. To me, this question is of quite a different order than one where we are dealing with state legislation under the Fourteenth Amendment. I do not think it follows that state and federal powers in this area are the same, and that just because the State may suppress a particular utterance, it is automatically permissible for the Federal Government to do the same. . . .

. . . .

. . . [T]he interests which obscenity statutes purportedly protect are primarily entrusted to the care, not of the Federal Government, but of the States. Congress has no substantive power over sexual morality. Such powers as the Federal Government has in this field are but incidental to its other powers, here the postal power, and are not of the same nature as those possessed by the States, which bear direct responsibility for the protection of the local moral fabric. . . .

Justice DOUGLAS, with whom Justice BLACK concurs, dissenting.

When we sustain these convictions, we make the legality of a publication turn on the purity of thought which a book or tract instills in the mind of the reader. I do not think we can approve that standard and be faithful to the command of the First Amendment, which by its terms is a restraint on Congress and which by the Fourteenth is a restraint on the States.

. . . .

By these standards punishment is inflicted for thoughts provoked, not for overt acts nor antisocial conduct. This test cannot be squared with our decisions under the First Amendment. . . . This issue cannot be avoided by saying that obscenity is not protected by the First Amendment. The question remains, what is the constitutional test of obscenity?

. . . .

The test of obscenity the Court endorses today gives the censor free range over a vast domain. To allow the State to step in and punish mere speech or publication that the judge or the jury thinks has an *undesirable* impact on thoughts but that is not shown to be a part of unlawful action is drastically to curtail the First Amendment. . . .

If we were certain that impurity of sexual thoughts impelled to action, we would be on less dangerous ground in punishing the distributors of this sex literature. But it is by no means clear that obscene literature, as so defined, is a significant factor in influencing substantial deviations from the community standards.

. . . .

The absence of dependable information on the effect of obscene literature on human conduct should make us wary. It should put us on the side of protecting society's interest in literature, except and unless it can be said that the particular publication has an impact on action that the government can control.

. . . .

## NOTES

1. Obscenity under *Roth* is material which is (1) without redeeming social importance, and which (2) to the average person, applying contemporary community standards, (3) appeals to the prurient interest in its dominant theme taken as a whole.

Why did the Supreme Court fail to utilize the English test for obscenity, the *Hicklin* test, which made the standard for obscenity the effect of an isolated passage among the most susceptible persons? *See* Regina v. Hicklin (1868) L.R. 3 Q.B. 360. Is it because the English do not operate under a written constitutional command such as the first amendment? The American test obviously gives more latitude to freedom of expression. The definition of obscenity will clearly be narrower if the arbiter of what is obscene is the average rather than the susceptible person. Notice the *Roth* test rejects *Hicklin* in another way. The dominant theme of the material must appeal to the prurient interest. An isolated passage, unlike the case under *Hicklin,* would be insufficient to support a judgment that particular printed material is obscene.

2. Notice that the state statute in *Alberts v. California* made punishable the keeping for sale or advertising of material which had a "tendency to deprave or corrupt its readers." The federal statute made punishable the actual mailing of material that tended "to stir sexual impulses and lead to sexually impure thoughts." From a first amendment point of view, which statute, the state or the federal, was the most clearly defective? Was it not the federal statute which presents the greater problem? After all, the California statute could be read to involve action or speech "plus" but the federal statute appears to proscribe thought itself or pure expression.

3. Justice Harlan took the position that the state's power to "make printed words criminal" was greater than that of the federal government. The federal interest in protecting against pornography, says Justice Harlan, is more abbreviated than the state interest. The constitutional authorization for the federal obscenity statute is Art. I, § 8, cl. 7, which gives Congress the power to "establish Post Offices and Post Roads." What is Justice Harlan's constitutional argument on this point? The state's police power, on the other hand, is what makes obscenity legislation, in Justice Harlan's view, more fundamentally a state legislative prerogative.

In addition, as a matter of constitutional text, the first amendment speaks directly to congressional prohibitions on freedom of speech and press but only by implication, through the due process clause of the fourteenth amendment, are the states so prohibited.

What rebuttal, if any, is there available to Justice Harlan's argument that the Supreme Court should distinguish between "the power of a state against the restrictions of the Fourteenth Amendment" and the "power of the Federal government against the limitations of the First Amendment"?

4. The struggle for a fair and realistic definition of obscenity in the wake of *Roth* has been greatly influenced by the work of Dean William B. Lockhart and Professor Robert C. McClure of the University of Minnesota Law School. (Dean Lockhart later headed the United States Commission on Obscenity and Pornography.) *See Censorship of Obscenity: The Developing Constitutional Standards,* 45 MINN. L. REV. 5 (1960) and a summary piece, *Obscenity Censorship: The Core Constitutional Issue— What Is Obscene?,* 7 UTAH L. REV. 289 (1961). Lockhart and McClure stress that in *Roth,* the Supreme Court was interested in making "two, and only two" points: (1) the material accused of being obscene must be judged as a whole, not on the basis of isolated passages. And (2) it must be judged by its impact upon average or normal people, not on the particularly weak or susceptible members of the population. Beyond those rules, Lockhart and McClure argue, the Supreme Court intended to make no definitive statement on obscenity. To those seeking a coherent, comprehensive court policy on obscenity, Lockhart and McClure counseled patience. In the meantime, they put forward a proposal of their own for consideration: The "obscenity" that was denied constitutional protection was "hard-core" pornography.

5. A second theory espoused by Dean Lockhart and Professor McClure was the concept of "variable obscenity." In this view, the method of marketing and impact of the material on its primary audience are factors in the determination of obscenity. If a "variable obscenity" theory is applied, no publication is inherently obscene but may be deemed so in a certain context when directed at a certain audience. Under a "variable obscenity" approach, the social value test of *Roth* would afford constitutional protection only when the primary audience got some social value out of the work. Lockhart and McClure thus assumed that social value would be weighed against prurient appeal, and that both would be considered in relation to the primary audience rather than to an average citizen standard. Compare this approach with Professor Haimbaugh's discussion in *Obscenity—An End to Weighing?,* 21 S.C.L. REV. 357 (1969).

The concept of variable obscenity was a "sleeper." It appeared in *Roth,* in Chief Justice Warren's concurring opinion, but was almost totally unnoticed at the time. Much of what Lockhart and McClure proposed turned up later in Ginzburg v. United States, 383 U.S. 463 (1966), and Ginsberg v. New York, 390 U.S. 629 (1968).

Dean Lockhart made the following explanatory remarks about "variable obscenity" in Lockhart & McClure, *Obscenity Censorship: The Core Constitutional Issue—What Is Obscene?*, 7 UTAH L. REV. 289 (1961):

> The variable obscenity approved requires that in each instance the finding of obscenity depends upon the nature of the primary audience to which the sales appeal is made and the nature of the material's appeal to that audience.

6. Is there an element of elitism in the variable obscenity approach? In defining obscenity as "hard-core pornography"? Professor Monaghan hails *Roth* for its libertarian protection of "significant" literature but criticizes the variable obscenity approach for the encouragement it lends to prosecutorial harassment of less lofty pornography. Monaghan, *Obscenity 1966: The Marriage of Obscenity Per Se and Obscenity Per Quod*, 76 YALE L.J. 127 (1966). Without minimizing the importance of *Roth* as a decision which helped kill censorship of literature, Monaghan suggests that adoption of Lockhart and McClure's proposal would be regressive. In this view, many people would prefer a "girlie" magazine to *Fanny Hill* or *Tropic of Cancer*. They might prefer "skin flicks" to "mature audience" films, photographs of deviant sexual behavior to their local museum of art. Is a difficulty with variable obscenity that it tends to sanction suppression of ordinary people's interests while protecting the social value of what an elite considers to be art and literature?

7. One immediate issue in the wake of *Roth* was whether the "redeeming social importance" test and the "prurient interest" test were independent measurements of obscenity, *each* of which must be satisfied before a publication can be defined as "obscene." The alternate interpretation of *Roth* was that a finding of "obscenity" should hinge on a weighing of a publication's social value against its appeal to prurient interest. One advocate of the first approach was Charles Rembar, an attorney who coordinated the multi-state defense of *Fanny Hill* against obscenity proceedings in the early 1960's. Rembar's thesis was that *Roth* opened up a complete defense against obscenity prosecution for any work which could demonstrate a shred of social value. *See* REMBAR, THE END OF OBSCENITY (1968).

Rembar's theory, which found support with Justice Brennan and other members of the Court (though never an explicit majority), offered one answer to the "central" constitutional question concerning obscenity: "Is the pornographic matter complained of obscene because it is utterly without redeeming social importance, or is it utterly without redeeming social importance because it is obscene?" Haimbaugh, *Obscenity—An End to Weighing?*, 21 S.C.L. REV. 357 (1969). Professor Haimbaugh suggested that Rembar's interpretation of *Roth* was enjoying "current but possibly temporary ascendancy" as of 1969. Take a second glance at the "central question" posed by Professor Haimbaugh. Do you see the constitutional implications of the alternatives he describes?

**8.** In Professor Henkin's view, the standard free speech theory is tied to the legislative rationale that pornography, if freely available, would corrupt the minds of citizens and encourage criminal sexual depravity. Thus, the clear-and-present danger test asked whether the obscene material were so likely to lead to anti-social behavior that the government's interest in crime-prevention outweighed the purveyor's right to disseminate his "message" of obscenity.

Professor Henkin says the anti-social behavior rationale disguises what the legislature is really trying to do, *i.e.*, impose its moral standards on society. In effect, the legislature is proscribing sin. Obscenity legislation, in such a view, might even be a violation of the first amendment prohibition against the establishment of religion. Henkin, *Morals and the Constitution: The Sin of Obscenity*, 63 COLUM. L. REV. 391 (1963).

But doesn't the Constitution give the legislatures the right to regulate morality? On a due process challenge, governmental interests can be identified to validate obscenity legislation.

Is the *Roth* test for obscenity unacceptably vague? Is it true that the Supreme Court would not tolerate, let alone propound, such vague rules of constitutionality in any context but the obscenity cases? Consider the following statement by Justice Stewart in his concurring opinion in Jacobellis v. Ohio, 378 U.S. 184, 197 (1964): "I have reached the conclusion that under the First and Fourteenth Amendments criminal laws in this area [of obscenity] are constitutionally limited to hard-core pornography. I shall not attempt today further to define the kinds of material I understand to be embraced within that shorthand description, and perhaps I could never succeed in intelligibly doing so. But I know it when I see it."

Does this test of constitutionality meet the standards of specificity, certainty, and notice which we have seen applied in other areas of constitutional law? What suggestions would you make to establish coherent and predictable, *i.e.*, working standards for the constitutional definition of obscenity?

### A BOOK NAMED "JOHN CLELAND'S MEMOIRS OF A WOMAN OF PLEASURE" v. ATTORNEY GENERAL OF MASSACHUSETTS
Supreme Court of the United States
383 U.S. 413, 16 L. Ed. 2d 221, 86 S. Ct. 975 (1966)

[This case arose from a Massachusetts obscenity prosecution against an eighteenth century literary item popularly known as "Fanny Hill," the heroine of a book named "John Cleland's Memoirs of a Woman of Pleasure." The book was represented by attorney Charles Rembar who recorded his legal battles on behalf of "Fanny Hill" in his book. *See* Rembar, THE END OF OBSCENITY (1968). Note that under the Massachusetts procedure the book itself rather than the publisher or distributor can be a party-defendant.

[Rembar indicates in his book that he sought to make "social value" rather than "social importance" the focal point for separating that which is obscene and constitutionally unprotected from that which is not obscene and is, therefore, constitutionally protected. What difference would such a distinction make? As you read the Court's opinion, ask yourself whether Rembar was successful in getting the Court to make this referent of the *Roth* test.]

Justice BRENNAN announced the judgment of the Court and delivered an opinion in which the CHIEF JUSTICE and Justice FORTAS join.

. . . .

. . . The trial justice . . . adjudged *Memoirs* obscene and declared that the book "is not entitled to the protection of the First and Fourteenth Amendments. . . ." The Massachusetts Supreme Judicial Court affirmed the decree. . . . We reverse.

. . . [T]he sole question before the state courts was whether *Memoirs* satisfies the test of obscenity established in *Roth v. United States.*

We defined obscenity in *Roth* in the following terms: "[W]hether to the average person, applying contemporary community standards, the dominant theme of the material taken as a whole appeals to prurient interest." Under this definition, as elaborated in subsequent cases, three elements must coalesce: it must be established that (a) the dominant theme of the material taken as a whole appeals to a prurient interest in sex; (b) the material is patently offensive because it affronts contemporary community standards relating to the description or representation of sexual matters; and (c) the material is utterly without redeeming social value.

The Supreme Judicial Court purported to apply the *Roth* definition of obscenity and held all three criteria satisfied. We need not consider the claim that the court erred in concluding that *Memoirs* satisfied the prurient appeal and patent offensiveness criteria; for reversal is required because the court misinterpreted the social value criterion. . . .

The Supreme Judicial Court erred in holding that a book need not be "unqualifiedly worthless before it can be deemed obscene." A book cannot be proscribed unless it is found to be *utterly* without redeeming social value. This is so even though the book is found to possess the requisite prurient appeal and to be patently offensive. Each of the three federal constitutional criteria is to be applied independently; the social value of the book can neither be weighed against nor canceled by its prurient appeal or patent offensiveness. Hence, even on the view of the court below that *Memoirs* possessed only a modicum of social value, its judgment must be reversed as being founded on an erroneous interpretation of a federal constitutional standard.

. . . .

Reversed.

---

### NOTES

In the Massachusetts trial court conflicting expert testimony was introduced on the literary and educational character of the book. What consequence does Rembar's insistence on "social value" rather than "social importance" have in evaluating such testimony? Notice that the Supreme Court in *Memoirs* said that the test was whether the offending matter was "*utterly* without redeeming social value." Under such a test, does an expert literateur's comment that the book was without "literary merit" *fail* to establish that the book was obscene?

### GINZBURG v. UNITED STATES
Supreme Court of the United States
383 U.S. 463, 16 L. Ed. 2d 31, 86 S. Ct. 942 (1966)

Justice BRENNAN delivered the opinion of the Court.

. . . .

. . . In the cases in which this Court has decided obscenity questions since *Roth*, it has regarded the materials as sufficient in themselves for the determination of the question. In the present case, however, the prosecution charged the offense in the context of the circumstances of production, sale, and publicity and assumed that, standing alone, the publications themselves might not be obscene. We agree that the question of obscenity may include consideration of the setting in which the publications were presented as an aid to determining the question of obscenity, and assume without deciding that the prosecution could not have succeeded otherwise. . . . [W]e view the publications against a background of commercial exploitation of erotica solely for the sake of their prurient appeal. The record in that regard amply supports the decision of the trial judge that the mailing of all three publications offended the statute.

The three publications were EROS, a hard-cover magazine of expensive format; Liaison, a bi-weekly newsletter; and *The Housewife's Handbook on Selective Promiscuity* (hereinafter the *Handbook*), a short book. The issue of EROS specified in the indictment, . . . contains 15 articles and photo-essays on the subject of love, sex, and sexual relations. The specified issue of Liaison, . . . , contains a prefatory "Letter from the Editors" announcing its dedication to "keeping sex an art and preventing it from becoming a science." The remainder of the issue consists of digests of two articles concerning sex and sexual relations which had earlier appeared in professional journals and a report of an interview with a psychotherapist who favors the broadest license in sexual relationships. . . . The *Handbook* purports to be a sexual autobiography detailing with complete candor the author's sexual experiences from age 3 to age 36. The text includes, and prefatory and concluding sections of the book elaborate, her views on such subjects as sex education of children, laws regulating private consensual adult sexual practices, and the equality of women in sexual relationships. It was claimed at trial that women would find the book valuable, for example as a marriage manual or as an aid to the sex education of their children.

Besides testimony as to the merit of the material, there was abundant evidence to show that each of the accused publications was originated or sold as stock in trade of the sordid business of pandering—"the business of purveying textual or graphic matter openly advertised to appeal to the erotic interest of their customers." EROS early sought mailing privileges from the postmasters of Intercourse and Blue Ball, Pennsylvania. The trial court found the obvious, that these hamlets were chosen only for the value their names would have in furthering petitioners' efforts to sell their publications on the basis of salacious appeal; the facilities of the post offices were inadequate to handle the anticipated volume of mail, and the privileges were denied. Mailing privileges were then obtained from the postmaster of Middlesex, New Jersey.

EROS and Liaison thereafter mailed several million circulars soliciting subscriptions from that post office; over 5,500 copies of the *Handbook* were mailed.

The "leer of the sensualist" also permeates the advertising for the three publications. The circulars sent for EROS and Liaison stressed the sexual candor of the respective publications, and openly boasted that the publishers would take full advantage of what they regarded an unrestricted license allowed by law in the expression of sex and sexual matters. The advertising for the *Handbook,* apparently mailed from New York, consisted almost entirely of a reproduction of the introduction of the book, written by one Dr. Albert Ellis. Although he alludes to the book's informational value and its putative therapeutic usefulness, his remarks are preoccupied with the book's sexual imagery. The solicitation was indiscriminate, not limited to those, such as physicians or psychiatrists, who might independently discern the book's therapeutic worth. Inserted in each advertisement was a slip labeled "GUARANTEE" and reading, "Documentary Books, Inc. unconditionally guarantees full refund on the price of THE HOUSEWIFE'S HANDBOOK ON SELECTIVE PROMISCUITY if the book fails to reach you because of U. S. Post Office censorship interference." Similar slips appeared in the advertising for EROS and Liaison; they highlighted the gloss petitioners put on the publications, eliminating any doubt what the purchaser was being asked to buy.

This evidence, in our view, was relevant in determining the ultimate question of obscenity and, in the context of this record, serves to resolve all ambiguity and doubt. The deliberate representation of petitioners' publications as erotically arousing, for example, stimulated the reader to accept them as prurient; he looks for titillation, not for saving intellectual content. Similarly, such representation would tend to force public confrontation with the potentially offensive aspects of the work; the brazenness of such an appeal heightens the offensiveness of the publications to those who are offended by such material. And the circumstances of presentation and dissemination of material are equally relevant to determining whether social importance claimed for material in the courtroom was, in the circumstances, pretense or reality—whether it was the basis upon which it was traded in the market place or a spurious claim for litigation purposes. Where the purveyor's sole emphasis is on the sexually provocative aspects of his publications, that fact may be decisive in the determination of obscenity. Certainly in a prosecution which, as here, does not necessarily imply suppression of the materials involved, the fact that they originate or are used as a subject of pandering is relevant to the application of the *Roth* test.

. . . .

We perceive no threat to First Amendment guarantees in thus holding that in close cases evidence of pandering may be probative with respect to the nature of the material in question and thus satisfy the *Roth* test. . . .

. . . .

Affirmed.

Justice BLACK, dissenting.

. . . Since, as I have said many times, I believe the Federal Government is without any power whatever under the Constitution to put any type of burden on speech and expression of ideas of any kind (as distinguished from conduct), . . . I would reverse Ginzburg's conviction on this ground alone.

. . . .

. . . I agree with my Brother HARLAN that the Court has in effect rewritten the federal obscenity statute and thereby imposed on Ginzburg standards and criteria that Congress never thought about; or if it did think about them, certainly it did not adopt them. Consequently, Ginzburg is, as I see it, having his conviction and sentence affirmed upon the basis of a statute amended by this Court for violation of which amended statute he was not charged in the courts below. . . . Quite apart from this vice in the affirmance, however, I think that the criteria declared by a majority of the Court today as guidelines for a court or jury to determine whether Ginzburg or anyone else can be punished as a common criminal for publishing or circulating obscene material are so vague and meaningless that they practically leave the fate of a person charged with violating censorship statutes to the unbridled discretion, whim and caprice of the judge or jury which tries him. . . .

. . . .

[The dissenting opinions of Justices DOUGLAS, HARLAN and STEWART, are omitted.]

---

## NOTES

1. The dissenting Justices in *Ginzburg* were troubled by the new direction in the law of obscenity marked by that decision. Justice Stewart called Ginzburg's conviction a denial of due process of law. Justice Harlan termed the majority's treatment of the federal obscenity statute, 18 U.S.C. § 1641, "an astonishing piece of judicial improvisation." Does the advent of the "pandering" concept mean that the sender of constitutionally-protected

materials can be convicted of criminal offense because of the subjective reactions of judge and jury?

The court seemed truly offended by Ginzburg's attempt to secure mailing privileges from sexy-sounding post offices like Intercourse, Pennsylvania and Middlesex, New Jersey. Was the court so personally offended by Ginzburg's cheeky attitude that it fashioned a new rule to uphold his conviction?

Justice Black, true to his absolutist, "plain meaning" view of the first amendment, vigorously criticized the subjectivity of the majority approach. Under the *Ginzburg* formulation, Black said, "the law becomes certain for the first and last time."

2. For the view that the *Ginzburg* decision represents "a radical departure" from the post-*Roth* cases, see Silber, *The Supreme Court and Obscenity: The Ginzburg Test—Restriction of First Amendment Freedoms Through Loss of Predictability,* 21 RUT-GERS L. REV. 56, 70 (1966). Silber believes that the confusion in obscenity regulation, after *Ginzburg,* should prompt a re-appraisal of the *Roth* rule that obscenity (once defined) is outside first amendment protection.

Does the *Ginzburg* rule apply only to publishers? Why not to book distributors and street-corner druggists who stock borderline obscene magazines?

### A Special Obscenity Standard for Children?

1. In Ginsberg v. New York, 390 U.S. 629 (1968), the Supreme Court upheld the constitutionality of a state law prohibiting distribution to minors of materials deemed to be obscene as to minors—whether or not the materials were constitutionally protected (*i.e.,* not obscene) as to adults. The court expressly embraced the notion of "variable obscenity" propounded by Lockhart and McClure in their influential article, *Censorship of Obscenity: The Developing Constitutional Standards,* 45 MINN. L. REV. 5 (1960). By distinguishing the target audience and its particular susceptibilities, the New York legislature in *Ginsberg* successfully walked the tightrope between overbroad obscenity regulation and no regulation at all. In *Ginsberg,* the court held that a properly-drafted anti-obscenity statute addressed to distribution to minors would pass muster. What is crucial for the court in *Ginsberg* is the intent of the distributor and the way the material is treated by the intended audience.

However, the court did not explicitly face a crucial question in *Ginsberg.* Although the court upheld the constitutionality of the variable obscenity concept the court did not resolve the vagueness problems raised by the concept. Perhaps the New York statute was validated because the state's power to regulate the conduct of children is greater than its power over adults.

2.   Given the evident legislative commitment to obscenity regulation, might *Ginsberg* offer a safety valve of sorts to satisfy the majority's apparent wish to regulate and restrict pornography? Would law-makers be willing to give up extensive regulation of obscenity for adults, in exchange for a system of regulation for the protection of children?

One commentator contends that obscenity regulation for children would tend to satisfy the general public and avert private vigilantism which was particularly rampant before the Supreme Court stepped into the fray in *Roth* (1957). *See* Dibble, *Obscenity: A State Quarantine to Protect Children,* 39 S. CALIF. L. REV. 345, 346 (1966).

Professor Samuel Krislov agrees with this analysis, suggesting that enforcement of obscenity regulations to protect children would "relieve community tensions and anxieties. . . ." Krislov, *From Ginzburg to Ginsberg: The Unhurried Children's Hour in Obscenity Litigation,* 1968 SUP. CT. REV. 153, 196.

3.   The line of Supreme Court decisions from *Roth* to *Ginzburg* to *Ginsberg* struck many commentators as more than slightly erratic. Obscenity law, in one writer's view, was "a constitutional disaster area." Magrath, *The Obscenity Cases: Grapes of Roth,* 1966 SUP. CT. REV. 7, 57, 77. Professor Krislov, however, is convinced, while the court has not trod a single path, it has successfully retained a good deal of desirable flexibility on the issue of obscenity.

4.   The REPORT OF THE PRESIDENT'S COMMISSION ON OBSCENITY AND PORNOGRAPHY (1970) recommended repeal of all obscenity laws regulating private adult use and possession of obscene materials, including commercial distribution. However, the Report recommended a statute regulating the distribution of obscene materials to minors. This may well have been the Commission's attempt to build a half-way house between a general system of regulation and no regulation at all. If this was a strategy of the Commission, it failed. A vocal minority of Commission members filed a stinging dissent claiming that the Report was a Magna Carta for pornographers. The United States Senate voted overwhelmingly to *reject* the Report's recommendations. President Nixon gave the Report an unqualified rejection.

## STANLEY v. GEORGIA
Supreme Court of the United States
394 U.S. 557, 22 L. Ed. 2d 542, 89 S. Ct. 1243 (1969)

Justice MARSHALL delivered the opinion of the Court.

An investigation of appellant's alleged bookmaking activities led to the issuance of a search warrant for appellant's home. Under authority of this warrant, federal and state agents secured entrance. They found very little evidence of bookmaking activity, but while looking through a desk drawer in an upstairs bedroom, one of the federal agents, accompanied by a state officer, found three reels of eight-millimeter film. Using a projector and screen found in an upstairs living room, they viewed the films. The state officer concluded that they were obscene and seized them. Since a further examination of the bedroom indicated that appellant occupied it, he was charged with possession of obscene matter and placed under arrest. He was later indicted for "knowingly hav[ing] possession of obscene matter" in violation of Georgia law. Appellant was tried before a jury and convicted. The Supreme Court of Georgia affirmed. . . .

Appellant raises several challenges to the validity of his conviction. We find it necessary to consider only one. Appellant argues here, and argued below, that the Georgia obscenity statute, insofar as it punishes mere private possession of obscene matter, violates the First Amendment, as made applicable to the States by the Fourteenth Amendment. For reasons set forth below, we agree that the mere private possession of obscene matter cannot constitutionally be made a crime.

. . . In this context, Georgia concedes that the present case appears to be one of "first impression . . . on this exact point," but contends that since "obscenity is not within the area of constitutionally protected speech or press," the States are free, subject to the limits of other provisions of the Constitution, to deal with it any way deemed necessary, just as they may deal with possession of other things thought to be detrimental to the welfare of their citizens. If the State can protect the body of a citizen, may it not, argues Georgia, protect his mind?

It is true that *Roth* does declare, seemingly without qualification, that obscenity is not protected by the First Amendment. That statement has been repeated in various forms in subsequent cases. . . . None of the statements . . . were made in the context of a statute punishing mere private possession of obscene material; the cases cited deal for the most part with use of the mails to distribute objectionable material or with some form of public distribution or dissemination. . . .

. . . *Roth* and its progeny certainly do mean that the First and Fourteenth Amendments recognize a valid governmental interest in dealing with the problem of obscenity. But the assertion of that interest cannot, in every context, be insulated from all constitutional protections. Neither *Roth* nor any other decision of this Court reaches that far. . . .

It is now well established that the Constitution protects the right to receive information and ideas. "This freedom [of speech and press] . . . necessarily protects the right to receive. . . ." This right to receive information and ideas, regardless of their social worth, is fundamental to our free society. Moreover, in the context of this case—a prosecution for mere possession of printed or filmed matter in the privacy of a person's own home—that right takes on an added dimension. For also fundamental is the right to be free, except in very limited circumstances, from unwanted governmental intrusions into one's privacy. . . .

These are the rights that appellant is asserting in the case before us. He is asserting the right to read or observe what he pleases—the right to satisfy his intellectual and emotional needs in the privacy of his own home. He is asserting the right to be free from state inquiry into the contents of his library. Georgia contends that appellant does not have these rights, that there are certain types of materials that the individual may not read or even possess. Georgia justifies this assertion by arguing that the films in the present case are obscene. But we think that mere categorization of these films as "obscene" is insufficient justification for such a drastic invasion of personal liberties guaranteed by the First and Fourteenth Amendments. Whatever may be the justifications for other statutes regulating obscenity, we do not think they reach into the privacy of one's own home. If the First Amendment means anything, it means that a State has no business telling a man, sitting alone in his own house, what books he may read or what films he may watch. Our whole constitutional heritage rebels at the thought of giving government the power to control men's minds.

And yet, in the face of these traditional notions of individual liberty, Georgia asserts the right to protect the individual's mind from the effects of obscenity. We are not certain that this argument amounts to anything more than the assertion that the State has the right to control the moral content of a person's thoughts. To some, this may be a noble purpose, but it is wholly inconsistent with the philosophy of the First Amendment. . . . Nor is it relevant that obscenity in general, or the particular films before the Court, are arguably devoid of any ideological content. The line between the transmission of ideas and mere entertainment is much too elusive for this Court to draw, if indeed such a line can be drawn at all. Whatever the power of the state to control public dissemination of ideas inimical to the public morality, it cannot constitutionally premise legislation on the desirability of controlling a person's private thoughts.

Perhaps recognizing this, Georgia asserts that exposure to obscenity may lead to deviant sexual behavior or crimes of sexual violence. There appears to be little empirical basis for that assertion. But more importantly, if the State is only concerned about literature inducing antisocial conduct, we believe that in the context of private consumption of ideas and information we should adhere to the view that "[a]mong free men, the deterrents ordinarily to be applied to prevent crime are education and punishment for violations of the law. . . ." Whitney v. California, 274 U.S. 357, 378 (Brandeis, J., concurring). Given the present state of knowledge, the State may no more prohibit mere possession of obscenity on the ground that it may lead to antisocial conduct than it may prohibit possession of chemistry books on the ground that they may lead to the manufacture of homemade spirits.

It is true that in *Roth* this Court rejected the necessity of proving that exposure to obscene material would create a clear and present danger of antisocial conduct or would probably induce its recipients to such conduct. But that case dealt with public distribution of obscene materials and such distribution is subject to different objections. For example, there is always the danger that obscene material might fall into the hands of children, or that it might intrude upon the sensibilities or privacy of the general public. No such dangers are present in this case.

Finally, we are faced with the argument that prohibition of possession of obscenity is a necessary incident to statutory schemes prohibiting distribution. That argument is based on alleged difficulties of proving an intent to distribute or in producing evidence of actual distribution. We are not convinced that such difficulties exist, but even if they did we do not think that they would justify infringement of the individual's right to read or observe what he pleases. Because that right is so fundamental to our scheme of individual liberty, its restriction may not be justified by the need to ease the administration of otherwise valid criminal laws.

We hold that the First and Fourteenth Amendments prohibit making mere private possession of obscene material a crime. *Roth* and the cases following that decision are not impaired by today's holding. As we have said, the States retain broad power to regulate obscenity; that power simply does not extend to mere possession by the individual in the privacy of his own home. Accordingly, the judgment of the court below is reversed and the case is remanded for proceedings not inconsistent with this opinion.

It is so ordered.

Justice STEWART, with whom Justice BRENNAN and Justice WHITE join, concurring in the result.

Before the commencement of the trial in this case, the appellant filed a motion to suppress the films as evidence upon the ground that they had been seized in violation of the Fourth and Fourteenth Amendments. The motion was denied, and the films were admitted in evidence at the trial. In affirming the appellant's conviction, the Georgia Supreme Court specifically determined that the films had been lawfully seized. The appellant correctly contends that this determination was clearly wrong under established principles of constitutional law. But the Court today disregards this preliminary issue in its hurry to move on to newer constitutional frontiers. I cannot so readily overlook the serious inroads upon Fourth Amendment guarantees countenanced in this case by the Georgia courts.

. . . For what happened here was that a search that began as perfectly lawful became the occasion for an unwarranted and unconstitutional seizure of the films.

. . . .

---

## NOTES

1. After *Stanley*, what is the status of *Roth*? The Supreme Court, having branded obscenity as a constitutional outlaw in *Roth*, in *Stanley* prohibited a state from interfering with the right of a citizen to possess obscene materials in the privacy of his home. Although Justice Marshall, speaking for the court in *Stanley*, took pains to emphasize that the decision in that case left *Roth* undisturbed, the language of *Stanley* invoked the first amendment in rousing fashion: "If the First Amendment means anything, it means that a State has no business telling a man, sitting alone in his own house, what books he may read or what films he may watch. Our whole constitutional heritage rebels at the thought of giving government the power to control men's minds."

But if obscenity is "utterly without redeeming social importance" and therefore merits no constitutional protection whatsoever, why can't the state proscribe private possession of obscene materials? Is the court's answer to this question that the difference between *Roth* and *Stanley* is fully understandable because a competing constitutional value was at stake in *Stanley* which was not present in *Roth, i.e.* a first amendment-based right of privacy?

**2.** Some commentators viewed *Stanley* as a silent departure from the fundamental holding of *Roth* that obscenity is not constitutionally protected speech. *See, e.g.,* Engdahl, *Requiem for Roth: Obscenity Doctrine is Changing,* 68 MICH. L. REV. 185 (1969). Professor Engdahl argued that by insulating a person's private possession of obscene materials from criminal penalty, the Court had, silently perhaps, erected a constitutional shield for obscenity which overturns the basic premise of *Roth.*

### UNITED STATES v. REIDEL
Supreme Court of the United States
402 U.S. 351, 28 L. Ed. 2d 813, 91 S. Ct. 1410 (1971)

Justice WHITE delivered the opinion of the Court.

Section 1461 of Title 18, U.S.C., prohibits the knowing use of the mails for the delivery of obscene matter. The issue presented by the jurisdictional statement in this case is whether § 1461 is constitutional as applied to the distribution of obscene materials to willing recipients who state that they are adults. The District Court held that it was not. We disagree and reverse the judgment.

. . . .

*Stanley v. Georgia* . . . compels no different result. . . .

. . . .

The right Stanley asserted was "the right to read or observe what he pleases—the right to satisfy his intellectual and emotional needs in the privacy of his own home." The Court's response was that "a State has no business telling a man, sitting alone in his own house, what books he may read or what films he may watch. Our whole constitutional heritage rebels at the thoughts of giving government the power to control men's minds." The focus of this language was on freedom of mind and thought and on the privacy of one's home. It does not require that we fashion or recognize a constitutional right in people like Reidel to distribute or sell obscene materials. The personal constitutional rights of those like Stanley to possess and read obscenity in their homes and their freedom of mind and thought do not depend on whether the materials are obscene or whether obscenity is constitutionally protected. Their rights to have and view that material in private are independently saved by the Constitution.

Reidel is in a wholly different position. He has no complaints about governmental violations of his private thoughts or fantasies, but stands squarely on a claimed First Amendment right to do business in obscenity and use the mails in the process. But *Roth* has squarely placed obscenity and its distribution outside the reach of the First Amendment and they remain there today. *Stanley* did not overrule *Roth* and we decline to do so now.

. . . .

[Justices BLACK and DOUGLAS dissented.]

---

## NOTES

1. If material otherwise obscene were found in the home, Stanley v. Georgia, 394 U.S. 557 (1969), would prevent prosecution: possession in the home of obscene matter cannot constitutionally be made a crime. But if there is a constitutional right to keep obscene material in the home, was there not, in common sense, a corresponding right to acquire it? Had *Stanley* fatally undermined *Roth*? *Roth*, said Justice White, permitted the legislature to proscribe doing business in obscenity and using the mails to accomplish the same. *Stanley* left this proscription untouched.

2. If we put *Reidel* together with *Stanley*, is a fair statement of the law that the distributor of obscenity may be jailed but the willing recipient will be immune from legal sanction? Once the offending material is brought into his home, is the reason for this double standard related to the variable obscenity concept? The adult may consent to be confronted with obscene material at his home but the distributor may be punished for distributing it to him. Would it make more sense to punish the distributor only if the recipient was a minor? Or are other values served by punishing the distributor for distribution to consenting adults?

3. Considering the court's response in *Reidel*, would you agree with Professor Katz (*Privacy and Pornography: Stanley v. Georgia*, 1969 SUP. CT. REV. 203) that *Stanley v. Georgia* was a case in which "a per curiam reversal without opinion would have been most welcome"? In other words, did the court's privacy rationale in *Stanley* create more of a red herring than a solid new approach to obscenity law? Or should *Stanley* be viewed as a building block in the protection of private, consensual activities, relating perhaps to sexual conduct and other life style choices as well as to possession of obscene materials? *See* Laughlin, *A Requiem for Requiems: The Supreme Court at the Bar of Reality*, 68 MICH. L. REV. 1389, 1391 (1970).

4. United States v. Thirty-Seven Photographs, 402 U.S. 363 (1971), was another case which tested the meaning of Stanley v. Georgia, 394 U.S. 557 (1969). A tourist returning to the United States was carrying in his luggage 37 allegedly obscene photographs. The materials were being brought into the country for purely private use. Did *Stanley v. Georgia* forbid their seizure? The Supreme Court, per Justice White, held that it did not but did construe the federal law involved to require a time limit (14 days) for application of the law as required by Freedman v. Maryland, 380 U.S. 51 (1965).

### *New Developments: The Burger Court, Federalism and Obscenity*

### MILLER v. CALIFORNIA
Supreme Court of the United States
413 U.S. 15, 37 L. Ed. 2d 419, 93 S. Ct. 2607 (1973)

Chief Justice BURGER delivered the opinion of the Court.

. . . .

This case involves the application of a state's criminal obscenity statute to a situation in which sexually explicit materials have been thrust by aggressive sales action upon unwilling recipients who had in no way indicated any desire to receive such materials. This Court has recognized that the States have a legitimate interest in prohibiting dissemination or exhibition of obscene material when the mode of dissemination carries with it a significant danger of offending the sensibilities of unwilling recipients or of exposure to juveniles. It is in this context that we are called on to define the standards which must be used to identify obscene material that a State may regulate without infringing the First Amendment as applicable to the States through the Fourteenth Amendment.

. . . .

While *Roth* presumed "obscenity" to be "utterly without redeeming social value," *Memoirs* required that to prove obscenity it must be affirmatively established that the material is *"utterly without redeeming social value."* Thus, even as they repeated the words of *Roth,* the *Memoirs* plurality produced a drastically altered test that called on the prosecution to prove a negative, *i.e.,* that the material was *"utterly* without redeeming social value"— a burden virtually impossible to discharge under our criminal standards of proof. Such considerations caused Justice Harlan to wonder if the *"utterly* without redeeming social value" test had any meaning at all.

Apart from the initial formulation in the *Roth* case, no majority of the Court has at any given time been able to agree on a standard to determine what constitutes obscene, porno-graphic material subject to regulation under the States' police power. We have seen "a variety of views among the members of the Court unmatched in any other course of constitutional ad-judication." This is not remarkable, for in the area of freedom of speech and press the courts must always remain sensitive to any infringement on genuinely serious literary, artistic, political, or scientific expression. This is an area in which there are few eternal verities.

The case we now review was tried on the theory that the California Penal Code § 311 approximately incorporates the three-stage *Memoirs* test, *supra.* But now *the Memoirs test has been abandoned as unworkable by its author*[4] *and no member of the Court today supports the Memoirs formulation.* (Emphasis added.)

This much has been categorically settled by the Court, that obscene material is unprotected by the First Amendment. "The First and Fourteenth Amendments have never been treated as absolutes." We acknowledge, however, the inherent dangers of undertaking to regulate any form of expression. State statutes designed to regulate obscene materials must be carefully limited. As a result, we now confine the permissible scope of such regula-tion to works which depict or describe sexual conduct. That con-duct must be specifically defined by the applicable state law, as written or authoritatively construed. A state offense must also be limited to works which, taken as a whole, appeal to the prurient interest in sex, which portray sexual conduct in a patently offen-sive way, and which, taken as a whole, do not have serious literary, artistic, political, or scientific value.

The basic guidelines for the trier of fact must be: (a) whether "the average person, applying contemporary community stand-ards" would find that the work, taken as a whole, appeals to the prurient interest, (b) whether the work depicts or describes, in a patently offensive way, sexual conduct specifically defined by the applicable state law, and (c) whether the work, taken as a whole, lacks serious literary, artistic, political, or scientific value. We do not adopt as a constitutional standard the *"utterly* without re-deeming social value" test of *Memoirs v. Massachusetts;* that con-cept has never commanded the adherence of more than three Justices at one time. If a state law that regulates obscene ma-terial is thus limited, as written or construed, the First Amend-ment values applicable to the States through the Fourteenth

---

[4] See the dissenting opinion of Justice Brennan in Paris Adult Theatre I v. Slaton, 413 U.S. 49 (1973) [text, p. 927].

Amendment are adequately protected by the ultimate power of appellate courts to conduct an independent review of constitutional claims when necessary.

We emphasize that it is not our function to propose regulatory schemes for the States. That must await their concrete legislative efforts. It is possible, however, to give a few plain examples of what a state statute could define for regulation under the second part (b) of the standard announced in this opinion, *supra:*

(a) Patently offensive representations or descriptions of ultimate sexual acts, normal or perverted, actual or simulated.

(b) Patently offensive representations or descriptions of masturbation, excretory functions and lewd exhibition of the genitals.

Sex and nudity may not be exploited without limit by films or pictures exhibited or sold in places of public accommodation any more than live sex and nudity can be exhibited or sold without limit in such public places. At a minimum, prurient, patently offensive depiction or description of sexual conduct must have serious literary, artistic, political, or scientific value to merit First Amendment protection. For example, medical books for the education of physicians and related personnel necessarily use graphic illustrations and descriptions of human anatomy. In resolving the inevitably sensitive questions of fact and law, we must continue to rely on the jury system, accompanied by the safeguards that judges, rules of evidence, presumption of innocence and other protective features provide, as we do with rape, murder and a host of other offenses against society and its individual members.

. . . .

Under the holdings announced today, no one will be subject to prosecution for the sale or exposure of obscene materials unless these materials depict or describe patently offensive "hard core" sexual conduct specifically defined by the regulating state law, as written or construed. We are satisfied that these specific prerequisites will provide fair notice to a dealer in such materials that his public and commercial activities may bring prosecution.

. . .

. . . .

It is certainly true that the absence, since *Roth,* of a single majority view of this Court as to proper standards for testing obscenity has placed a strain on both state and federal courts. But today, for the first time since *Roth* was decided in 1957, a majority of this Court has agreed on concrete guidelines to isolate "hard core" pornography from expression protected by the First Amendment. Now we may abandon the casual practice of Redrup v.

New York, 386 U.S. 767 (1967), and attempt to provide positive guidance to the federal and state courts alike.

This may not be an easy road, free from difficulty. But no amount of "fatigue" should lead us to adopt a convenient "institutional" rationale—an absolutist, "anything goes" view of the First Amendment—because it will lighten our burdens. "Such an abnegation of judicial supervision in this field would be inconsistent with our duty to uphold the constitutional guarantees." Nor should we remedy "tension between state and federal courts" by arbitrarily depriving the States of a power reserved to them under the Constitution, a power which they have enjoyed and exercised continuously from before the adoption of the First Amendment to this day. "Our duty admits of no 'substitute for facing up to the tough individual problems of constitutional judgment involved in every obscenity case.' "

Under a national Constitution, fundamental First Amendment limitations on the powers of the States do not vary from community to community, but this does not mean that there are, or should or can be, fixed, uniform national standards of precisely what appeals to the "prurient interest" or is "patently offensive." These are essentially questions of fact, and our nation is simply too big and too diverse for this Court to reasonably expect that such standards could be articulated for all 50 States in a single formulation, even assuming the prerequisite consensus exists. When triers of fact are asked to decide whether "the average person, applying contemporary community standards" would consider certain materials "prurient," it would be unrealistic to require that the answer be based on some abstract formulation. The adversary system, with lay jurors as the usual ultimate fact-finders in criminal prosecutions, has historically permitted triers-of-fact to draw on the standards of their community, guided always by limiting instructions on the law. To require a State to structure obscenity proceedings around evidence of a *national* "community standard" would be an exercise in futility.

. . . .

We conclude that neither the State's alleged failure to offer evidence of "national standards," nor the trial court's charge that the jury consider state community standards, were constitutional errors.* Nothing in the First Amendment requires that a jury must consider hypothetical and unascertainable "national stand-

---

* Chief Justice Burger indicates in a footnote that community standards in the *Miller* case were ascertained by a police officer with many years of specialization in obscenity offenses. He had conducted an extensive statewide survey—the Chief Justice says nothing more specific about the survey—and had given expert evidence on 26 occasions in the year prior to the Miller trial.

ards" when attempting to determine whether certain materials are obscene as a matter of fact. . . .

It is neither realistic nor constitutionally sound to read the First Amendment as requiring that the people of Maine or Mississippi accept public depiction of conduct found tolerable in Las Vegas, or New York City. People in different States vary in their tastes and attitudes, and this diversity is not to be strangled by the absolutism of imposed uniformity. . . . We hold the requirement that the jury evaluate the materials with reference to "contemporary standards of the State of California" serves this protective purpose and is constitutionally adequate.

. . . .

In sum we (a) reaffirm the *Roth* holding that obscene material is not protected by the First Amendment, (b) hold that such material can be regulated by the States, subject to the specific safeguards enunciated above, without a showing that the material is *"utterly* without redeeming social value," and (c) hold that obscenity is to be determined by applying "contemporary community standards," . . . not "national standards." . . .

Vacated and remanded.

---

## NOTES

1. What are the major aspects of the court's opinion in *Miller*? Certainly, the most celebrated and publicized aspect of the case is the rejection of the idea formerly endorsed in Jacobellis v. Ohio, 378 U.S. 184 (1964), that what offends contemporary community standards is to be judged by a national standard. The court denied that "there are, or should or can be, fixed, uniform national standards of precisely what appeals to the 'prurient interest' or is 'patently offensive.'"

2. Who should determine what appeals to the "prurient interest of a community"? According to Burger, speaking for the court in *Miller,* the jury should make this determination. If these determinations should be left to the jury, then is it not possible that "Deep Throat" may be held to appeal to the prurient interest of Xenia, Ohio but not to the prurient interest of Shaker Heights, Ohio? If this is true, is it also true as Chief Justice Burger says in *Miller* that "fundamental First Amendment limitations on the powers of the States do not vary from community to community"?

3. Another idea in *Miller,* equally as important perhaps as the court's new resolution of the local versus national community standard issue is the court's reformulation of the *Roth* definition

of obscenity. Permitting a local jury to define contemporary community standards in effect constitutionalizes parochialism and provincialism. Yet, *Miller* wielded *Roth* still another body blow. The scope of the definition of obscenity is greatly expanded in *Miller* by substituting for an inquiry of "utterly without redeeming social importance" an inquiry which asks whether the "work, taken as a whole, lacks serious literary, artistic, political or scientific value."

By removing the protection provided by the "utterly without redeeming social importance" test, doesn't the court make it easier for the state to cast an obscenity net beyond the limits of "hard-core" pornography? This is an important issue because it has been urged that one of the functions of that part of the *Roth* definition of obscenity which required that the material in question be "utterly without redeeming social importance" was designed to constitutionally proscribe "hard-core" pornography and nothing else. It is interesting to note that Burger apparently believed that the *Miller* definition of obscenity will reach only "hard-core" pornography. The difficulty, of course, is that under the *Roth* test the perimeters of "hard-core" pornography were perhaps more secure than is now the case. After all, is it not far easier to say that a book lacks "serious . . . value" than it is to say that it is "utterly without redeeming social importance"?

## PARIS ADULT THEATRE I v. SLATON
### Supreme Court of the United States
### 413 U.S. 49, 37 L. Ed. 2d 446, 93 S. Ct. 2628 (1973)

[On the same day as *Miller,* the Court, per Chief Justice Burger, affirmed 5-4 a Georgia Supreme Court holding that two "adult" movies were constitutionally unprotected. The decision was notable because it held that courts were not obliged to require "expert" affirmative evidence that the materials were obscene. Further, the Court held that the state could validly regulate use of obscene material in local commerce and in places of public accommodation even if those using such materials voluntarily sought them out.]

Chief Justice BURGER delivered the opinion of the Court.
. . . .

. . . [W]e hold that there are legitimate state interests at stake in stemming the tide of commercialized obscenity, even assuming it is feasible to enforce effective safeguards against exposure to juveniles and to passersby. . . . These include the interest of the public in the quality of life and the total com-

munity environment, the tone of commerce in the great city
centers, and, possibly, the public safety itself. . . .

. . . .

. . . The idea of a "privacy" right and a place of public accommodation are, in this context, mutually exclusive. Conduct
or depictions of conduct that the state police power can prohibit
on a public street does not become automatically protected by
the Constitution merely because the conduct is moved to a
bar or a "live" theatre stage, any more than a "live" performance
of a man and woman locked in a sexual embrace at high noon
in Times Square is protected by the Constitution because they
simultaneously engage in a valid political dialogue.

. . . .

. . . [W]e reject the claim that the State of Georgia is here
attempting to control the minds or thoughts of those who patro-
nize theatres. Preventing unlimited display or distribution of
obscene material, which by definition lacks any serious literary,
artistic, political or scientific value as communication, is distinct
from a control of reason and the intellect. Where communication
of ideas, protected by the First Amendment, is not involved, nor
the particular privacy of the home protected by *Stanley*, nor any
of the other "areas or zones" of constitutionally protected privacy,
the mere fact that, as a consequence, some human "utterances"
or "thoughts" may be incidentally affected does not bar the
State from acting to protect legitimate state interests.

. . . .

Justice BRENNAN, dissenting.

. . . .

I am convinced that the approach initiated 15 years ago in
*Roth v. United States,* and culminating in the Court's decision
today, cannot bring stability to this area of the law without
jeopardizing fundamental First Amendment values, and I have
concluded that the time has come to make a significant departure
from that approach.

. . . .

. . . The essence of our problem in the obscenity area is that
we have been unable to provide "sensitive tools" to separate
obscenity from other sexually oriented but constitutionally protected speech, so that efforts to suppress the former do not spill
over into the suppression of the latter. . . .

. . . .

Our experience with the *Roth* approach has certainly taught
us that the outright suppression of obscenity cannot be reconciled
with the fundamental principles of the First and Fourteenth
Amendments. For we have failed to formulate a standard that

sharply distinguishes protected from unprotected speech, and out of necessity, we have resorted to the *Redrup* approach, which resolves cases as between the parties, but offers only the most obscure guidance to legislation, adjudication by other courts, and primary conduct. By disposing of cases through summary reversal or denial of certiorari we have deliberately and effectively obscured the rationale underlying the decision. It comes as no surprise that judicial attempts to follow our lead conscientiously have often ended in hopeless confusion.

Of course, the vagueness problem would be largely of our own creation if it stemmed primarily from our failure to reach a consensus on any one standard. But after 16 years of experimentation and debate I am reluctantly forced to the conclusion that none of the available formulas, including the one announced today, can reduce the vagueness to a tolerable level while at the same time striking an acceptable balance between the protections of the First and Fourteenth Amendments, on the one hand, and on the other the asserted state interest in regulating the dissemination of certain sexually oriented materials. Any effort to draw a constitutionally acceptable boundary on state power must resort to such indefinite concepts as "prurient interest," "patent offensiveness," "serious literary value," and the like. The meaning of these concepts necessarily varies with the experience, outlook, and even idiosyncracies of the person defining them. . . .

. . . .

. . . [T]he uncertainty of the standards creates a continuing source of tension between state and federal courts, since the need for an independent determination by this Court seems to render superfluous even the most conscientious analysis by state tribunals. And our inability to justify our decisions with a persuasive rationale—or indeed, any rationale at all—necessarily creates the impression that we are merely second-guessing state court judges.

The severe problems arising from the lack of fair notice, from the chill on protected expression, and from the stress imposed on the state and federal judicial machinery persuade me that a significant change in direction is urgently required. I turn, therefore, to the alternatives that are now open.

1. The approach requiring the smallest deviation from our present course would be to draw a new line between protected and unprotected speech, still permitting the States to suppress all material on the unprotected side of the line. In my view, clarity cannot be obtained pursuant to this approach except by drawing a line that resolves all doubts in favor of state power and

against the guarantees of the First Amendment. We could hold, for example, that any depiction or description of human sexual organs, irrespective of the manner or purpose of the portrayal, is outside the protection of the First Amendment and therefore open to suppression by the States. That formula would, no doubt, offer much fairer notice of the reach of any state statute drawn at the boundary of the State's constitutional power. And it would also, in all likelihood, give rise to a substantial probability of regularity in most judicial determinations under the standard. But such a standard would be appallingly overbroad, permitting the suppression of a vast range of literary, scientific, and artistic masterpieces. Neither the First Amendment nor any free community could possibly tolerate such a standard. Yet short of that extreme it is hard to see how any choice of words could reduce the vagueness problem to tolerable proportions, so long as we remain committed to the view that some class of materials is subject to outright suppression by the State.

2. The alternative adopted by the Court today recognizes that a prohibition against any depiction or description of human sexual organs could not be reconciled with the guarantees of the First Amendment. But the Court does retain the view that certain sexually oriented material can be considered obscene and therefore unprotected by the First and Fourteenth Amendments. To describe that unprotected class of expression, the Court adopts a restatement of the *Roth-Memoirs* definition of obscenity....

The differences between this formulation and the three-pronged *Memoirs* test are, for the most part, academic. . . .

The Court evidently recognizes that difficulties with the *Roth* approach necessitate a significant change of direction. But the Court does not describe its understanding of those difficulties, nor does it indicate how the restatement of the *Memoirs* test is in any way responsive to the problems that have arisen. In my view, the restatement leaves unresolved the very difficulties that compel our rejection of the underlying *Roth* approach, while at the same time contributing substantial difficulties of its own. The modification of the *Memoirs* test may prove sufficient to jeopardize the analytic underpinnings of the entire scheme. And today's restatement will likely have the effect, whether or not intended, of permitting far more sweeping suppression of sexually oriented expression, including expression that would almost surely be held protected under our current formulation.

Although the Court's restatement substantially tracks the three-part test announced in *Memoirs v. Massachusetts,* it does purport to modify the "social value" component of the test. Instead of requiring, as did *Roth* and *Memoirs,* that state suppression be limited to materials utterly lacking in social value, the Court today permits suppression if the government can prove that the materials lack "*serious* literary, artistic, political or scientific value." But the definition of "obscenity" as expression utterly lacking in social importance is the key to the conceptual basis of *Roth* and our subsequent opinions. In *Roth* we held that certain expression is obscene, and thus outside the protection of the First Amendment, precisely *because* it lacks even the slightest redeeming social value. The Court's approach necessarily assumes that some works will be deemed obscene—even though they clearly have *some* social value—because the State was able to prove that the value, measured by some unspecified standard, was not sufficiently "serious" to warrant constitutional protection. That result is not merely inconsistent with our holding in *Roth;* it is nothing less than a rejection of the fundamental First Amendment premises and rationale of the *Roth* opinion and an invitation to widespread suppression of sexually oriented speech. Before today, the protections of the First Amendment have never been thought limited to expressions of *serious* literary or political value.

Although the Court concedes that "*Roth* presumed 'obscenity' to be 'utterly without redeeming social value,' " it argues that *Memoirs* produced "a drastically altered test that called on the prosecution to prove a negative, *i.e.,* that the material was 'utterly without redeeming social value'—a burden virtually impossible to discharge under our criminal standards of proof." One should hardly need to point out that under the third component of the Court's test the prosecution is still required to "prove a negative"—*i.e.,* that the material lacks serious literary, artistic, political, or scientific value. Whether it will be easier to prove that material lacks "serious" value than to prove that it lacks any value at all remains, of course, to be seen.

In any case, even if the Court's approach left undamaged the conceptual framework of *Roth,* and even if it clearly barred the suppression of works with at least some social value, I would nevertheless be compelled to reject it. For it is beyond dispute that the approach can have no ameliorative impact on the cluster of problems that grow out of the vagueness of our current standards. Indeed, even the Court makes no argument that the reformulation will provide fairer notice to booksellers, theatre owners, and the reading and viewing public. Nor does the Court contend that the approach will provide clearer guidance to law enforcement officials or reduce the chill on protected expression. Nor, finally, does the Court suggest that the approach will mitigate to the slightest degree the institutional problems that have plagued this Court and the State and Federal Judiciary as a direct result of the uncertainty inherent in any definition of obscenity.

. . . The Court surely demonstrates little sensitivity to our own institutional problems, much less the other vagueness-related difficulties, in establishing a system that requires us to consider whether a description of human genitals is sufficiently "lewd" to deprive it of constitutional protection; whether a sexual act is "ultimate"; whether the conduct depicted in materials before us fits within one of the categories of conduct whose depiction the state or federal governments have attempted to suppress; and a host of equally pointless inquiries. In addition, adoption of such a test does not, presumably, obviate the need for consideration of the nuances of presentation of sexually oriented material, yet it hardly clarifies the application of those opaque but important factors.

If the application of the "physical conduct" test to pictorial material is fraught with difficulty, its application to textual material carries the potential for extraordinary abuse. Surely we have passed the point where the mere written description of sexual conduct is deprived of First Amendment protection. Yet the test offers no guidance to us, or anyone else, in determining which written descriptions of sexual conduct are protected, and which are not.

Ultimately, the reformulation must fail because it still leaves in this Court the responsibility of determining in each case whether the materials are protected by the First Amendment. . . .

3. I have also considered the possibility of reducing our own role, and the role of appellate courts generally, in determining whether particular matter is obscene. Thus, we might conclude that juries are best suited to determine obscenity *vel non* and that jury verdicts in this area should not be set aside except in cases of extreme departure from prevailing standards. Or, more generally, we might adopt the position that where a lower federal or state court has conscientiously applied the constitutional standard, its finding of obscenity will be no more vulnerable to reversal by this Court than any finding of fact. While the point was not clearly resolved prior to our decision in *Redrup v. New York,* it is implicit in that decision that the First Amendment requires an independent review by appellate courts of the constitutional fact of obscenity. That result is required by principles applicable to the obscenity issue no less than to any other area involving free expression, or other consti-

tutional right. In any event, even if the Constitution would permit us to refrain from judging for ourselves the alleged obscenity of particular materials, that approach would solve at best only a small part of our problem. For while it would mitigate the institutional stress produced by the *Roth* approach, it would neither offer nor produce any cure for the other vices of vagueness. Far from providing a clearer guide to permissible primary conduct, the approach would inevitably lead to even greater uncertainty and the consequent due process problems of fair notice. And the approach would expose much protected sexually oriented expression to the vagaries of jury determinations. Plainly, the institutional gain would be more than offset by the unprecedented infringement of First Amendment rights.

4.   Finally, I have considered the view, urged so forcefully since 1957 by our Brothers Black and Douglas, that the First Amendment bars the suppression of any sexually oriented expression. That position would effect a sharp reduction, although perhaps not a total elimination, of the uncertainty that surrounds our current approach. Nevertheless, I am convinced that it would achieve that desirable goal only by stripping the States of power to an extent that cannot be justified by the commands of the Constitution, at least so long as there is available an alternative approach that strikes a better balance between the guarantee of free expression and the States' legitimate interests.

Our experience since *Roth* requires us not only to abandon the effort to pick out obscene materials on a case-by-case basis, but also to reconsider a fundamental postulate of *Roth:* that there exists a definable class of sexually oriented expression that may be totally suppressed by the Federal and State Governments. Assuming that such a class of expression does in fact exist, I am forced to conclude that the concept of "obscenity" cannot be defined with sufficient specificity and clarity to provide fair notice to persons who create and distribute sexually oriented materials, to prevent substantial erosion of protected speech as a by-product of the attempt to suppress unprotected speech, and to avoid very costly institutional harms. Given these inevitable side-effects of state efforts to suppress what is assumed to be *unprotected* speech, we must scrutinize with care the state interest that is asserted to justify the suppression. For in the absence of some very substantial interest in suppressing such speech, we can hardly condone the ill-effects that seem to flow inevitably from the effort.

.   .   .   .

In short, while I cannot say that the interests of the State—apart from the question of juveniles and unconsenting adults—are trivial or nonexistent, I am compelled to conclude that these interests cannot justify the substantial damage to constitutional rights and to this Nation's judicial machinery that inevitably results from state efforts to bar the distribution even of unprotected material to consenting adults. I would hold, therefore, that at least in the absence of distribution to juveniles or obtrusive exposure to unconsenting adults, the First and Fourteenth Amendments prohibit the state and federal governments from attempting wholly to suppress sexually oriented materials on the basis of their allegedly "obscene" contents. Nothing in this approach precludes those governments from taking action to serve what may be strong and legitimate interests through regulation of the manner of distribution of sexually oriented material.

. . . .

---

## NOTES

1. Brennan says: "Today a majority of the Court offers a slightly altered formulation of the basic *Roth* test, while leaving entirely unchanged the underlying approach." Do you agree that the alteration of *Roth* is slight?

Is Justice Brennan saying it is impossible to define "hardcore pornography"? Justice Brennan says that *Miller-Paris Theatres* will have the effect "whether or not intended, of permitting far more sweeping suppression of sexually oriented expression, including expression that would almost surely be held protected under our current formulation." Brennan suggests that the majority in *Miller* may not have intended to curtail the "sexually oriented expression." Was the purpose of *Miller* then to provide a clear standard in the obscenity field?

2. In an obscenity case involving the sale of an unillustrated plain cover book, the court applied the *Miller* standard to "expression by words alone." *See* Kaplan v. California, 413 U.S. 115 (1973).

3. How is the *Miller* standard to be applied in a federal obscenity prosecution? The court answered that question as follows in Hamling v. United States, — U.S. — (1974):

Since this case was tried in the Southern District of California, and presumably jurors from throughout that judicial district were available to serve on the panel which tried petitioners, it would be the standards of that "community" upon which the jurors would draw. But this is not to say that a District Court would not be at liberty to admit evidence of standards existing in some place outside of this particular district, if it felt such evidence would assist the jury in the resolution of the issues which they were to decide.

### The "Carnal Knowledge" Case

*Miller v. California* was greeted with considerable criticism in the press and the arts and with a new, if sporadic, wave of censorious obscenity prosecutions in some localities throughout the country. Did *Miller* really mean that the new definition of "unprotected speech" had been indefinably broadened? Was the definition of obscenity now to be at the totally unstandardized mercy of the local jury?

Toward the end of term in 1974, the court faced these questions in Jenkins v. Georgia, 418 U.S. 153 (1974). In *Jenkins,* the manager of a movie theatre in Albany, Georgia had been convicted under the Georgia state obscenity statute for showing the film "Carnal Knowledge." The jury had convicted prior to the announcement of *Miller.* The Georgia Supreme Court affirmed after the announcement of *Miller.*

The court in *Jenkins,* per Justice Rehnquist, first declared that it intended to apply in *Miller* its holding announced the same day in Hamling v. United States, 418 U.S. 87 (1974): "[D]efendants convicted prior to the announcement of our *Miller* decisions but whose convictions were on direct appeal at that time should receive any benefit available to them from those decisions."

The *Jenkins,* or "Carnal Knowledge" case, was important for what it said on the role of the jury and the local versus national standard controversy:

"We agree with the Supreme Court of Georgia's implicit ruling that the Constitution does not require that juries be instructed in state obscenity cases to apply the standards of a hypothetical statewide community. *Miller* approved the use of such instructions; it did not mandate their use. What *Miller* makes clear is that state juries need not be instructed to apply 'national standards.' We also agree with the Supreme Court of Georgia's implicit approval of the trial court's instructions directing juries to apply 'community standards' without specifying what 'community.' *Miller* held that it was constitutionally permissible to permit juries to rely on the understanding of the community from which they came as to contemporary community standards, and the States have considerable latitude in

framing statutes under this element of the *Miller* decision. A
state may choose to define an obscenity offense in terms of 'contemporary community standards' as defined in *Miller* without
further specification, as was done here, or it may choose to
define the standards in more precise geographic terms, as was
done by California in *Miller*."

After sanctifying the darkness which surrounds the meaning
of the "contemporary community standards" which a jury is
obliged to apply, the court in *Jenkins* then subtracted some of
the new found dominance implicitly conferred on the jury in
the obscenity field by *Miller*.

The state had urged to the Court in *Jenkins* that one of
the purposes of *Miller* was to make the determination of whether
a particular work offended contemporary community standards
a jury question for ultimate factual determination by the Supreme Court. Since the jury had, with some evidence to justify
it, determined "Carnal Knowledge" to be obscene, the jury
determination should not be disturbed.

The court disagreed:

> Even though questions of appeal to the "prurient in-
> terest" or of patent offensiveness are "essentially questions
> of fact," it would be a serious misreading of *Miller* to
> conclude that juries have unbridled discretion in de-
> termining what is "patently offensive."

The court reminded the state that in *Miller* it had said that in
First Amendment cases it still retained its power to conduct
an "independent review of constitutional claims when necessary." The court pointed out that there were substantive constitutional limitations on what a jury could hold to be obscene.
In the court's view, the jury was limited to a narrow area by
*Miller*: "materials (which) depict or describe patently offensive
'hard core' sexual conduct. . . ."

What was "hard core" conduct? The Court thought that it
had explained that too in *Miller*. Examples of "hard core" conduct included "representations or descriptions of ultimate sexual
acts, normal or perverted, actual or simulated" and "representations or descriptions of masturbation, excretory functions, and
lewd exhibition of the genitals."

The court tried to clarify the substantive first amendment
limitations on jury discretion in the "obscenity" field by giving
an example of what could *not* be the depiction of "hard core"
sexual conduct, *i.e.,* "a defendant's depiction of a woman with
a bare midriff."

The abiding question, of course, was whether the court's attempt to give such a sufficient definition to "hard core" conduct to in effect leave the case-by-case determination of "obscenity" to juries could possibly work. The court concluded that "Carnal Knowledge" was not obscene because nudity alone was not obscene and there was "no exhibition of the actor's genitals, lewd or otherwise" during the nude scenes in "Carnal Knowledge."

But in the last analysis, wasn't the ultimate determination of obscenity back on a case-by-case basis to the court itself? Bare female midriffs were permissible; "lewd exhibitions of actor's genitals" were not. Did the "Carnal Knowledge" case clarification of the function of the jury in the obscenity field take us any further than the pre-*Miller* understanding of obscenity? Justice Brennan, concurring, joined by Stewart and Marshall thought it did not: "[T]he Court's new formulation does not extricate us from the mire of case-by-case determination of obscenity."

Brennan justified this conclusion as follows:

"After the Court's decision today, there can be no doubt that *Miller* requires appellate courts—including this Court—to review independently the constitutional fact of obscenity. Moreover, the Court's task is not limited to reviewing a jury finding under part (c) of the *Miller* test that the work, taken as a whole, lack[ed] serious literary, artistic, political or scientific value. *Miller* also requires independent review of a jury's determination under part (b) of the *Miller* test that the work depicts or describes in a patently offensive way, sexual conduct specifically defined by the applicable state law.

. . . .

"In order to make the review mandated by *Miller,* the Court was required to screen the film 'Carnal Knowledge' and make an independent determination of obscenity *vel non.*"

Brennan said that as long as the *Miller* test prevailed, no one could really know whether material is obscene until five members of the Supreme Court have said so.

### Obscenity and Prior Restraint

1.  In Freedman v. Maryland, 380 U.S. 51 (1965), the court imposed procedural requirements on censorship boards: (1) The board has the burden of showing that a film is unprotected expression.

(2)  Only a judicial proceeding will suffice to impose a valid final restraint on a film's exhibition.

(3) The state, either by statute, or by "authoritative judicial construction," must afford the exhibitor a procedure under which he is either issued a license or the censorship board is required to go to court to restrain the showing of the film in controversy.

2. The court in *Freedman* made it very clear that this decision by a movie censorship board to license or to enjoin must occur within a brief and specified period of time. Why this emphasis on time? Why this preference for judicial rather than administrative determinations of obscenity? Is it for the same reason the issue of obscenity is an issue of law for the judge rather than of fact for the jury? *Cf.* Jacobellis v. Ohio, 378 U.S. 184 (1964).

In a jurisdiction where judges are elected rather than appointed as are members of censorship boards, is it clear that the judges will have the "necessary sensitivity to freedom of expression"?

# Chapter 11

# FREEDOM OF RELIGION

---

## A. WHAT IS THE "FREE EXERCISE" OF RELIGION?

1. An early free exercise case decided by the Supreme Court was Reynolds v. United States, 98 U.S. 145 (1878). In that case a Mormon was charged with violating a federal law prohibiting polygamy in the federal territories. Reynolds defended against the charge on the ground that he, as a Mormon was obliged to practice polygamy as part of his faith. Did the federal statute prohibiting polygamy violate the free exercise of religion? The Court held it did not. The free exercise clause protected against restrictions on belief not on action.

In *Reynolds*, Chief Justice Waite, for the Court which affirmed the conviction, approached the problem by making a distinction between "beliefs" which he considered to be constitutionally protected and "practices" which he considered unprotected:

> . . . Congress was deprived of all legislative power over mere opinion, but was left free to reach actions which were in violation of social duties or subversive of good order. . . . Laws are made for the government of actions, and while they cannot interfere with mere religious beliefs and opinions, they may with practices. . . . Can a man excuse his practices to the contrary because of his religious belief? To permit this would be to make the professed doctrines of religious belief superior to the law of the land, and in effect to permit every citizen to become a law unto himself. Government could exist only in name under such circumstances.

2. Chief Justice Waite's hypothetical questions in *Reynolds* were brought to life in a federal prosecution, United States v. Ballard, 322 U.S. 78 (1944). Ballard had been indicted for using the mails to obtain funds by false representation. In soliciting funds for the "I AM" movement, Ballard claimed he had talked with Jesus, that he could cure the sick, and that he had been delegated by St. Germain to serve as a divine messenger.

The Supreme Court reversed and remanded, holding that Court of Appeals was in error in requiring that the issue of whether Ballard's religious beliefs were true or false should have gone to the jury. The court, per Justice Douglas, stated:

The religious views espoused by respondents might seem incredible, if not preposterous, to most people. But if those doctrines are subject to trial before a jury charged with finding their truth or falsity, then the same can be done with the religious beliefs of any sect. When the triers of fact undertake that task, they enter a forbidden domain.

3. Professor Kurland says the free exercise and establishment clauses formulate "a single precept: that government cannot utilize religion as a standard for action or inaction because these clauses, read together as they should be, prohibit classification in terms of religion either to confer a benefit or to impose a burden." P. KURLAND, RELIGION AND THE LAW 112 (1962).

Kurland points out that the *Reynolds* case can be read as applying this standard as well as the speech-action approach. How could the anti-polygamy statute in *Reynolds* be validated under the Kurland analysis?

Professor Kurland finds his mode of analysis more helpful than asking whether legislation trespasses on belief rather than action. His position is that legislation which is otherwise constitutional is still valid even if it conflicts with the commands of religious faith so long as the legislation, in inspiration and general application, is indifferent to religion. Professor Kurland says that the speech-action dichotomy is an illusory aid to solution of religious freedom problems. Under this approach, he argues, government could conceivably prohibit religious meetings. Why? Does Professor Kurland's approach protect the essence of religious freedom—at least insofar as judicial review in our system can protect religious freedom? What difficulties do you have with his analysis?

### FREE EXERCISE: A DEFENSE TO LEGAL OBLIGATION?

#### WISCONSIN v. YODER
Supreme Court of the United States
406 U.S. 205, 32 L. Ed. 2d 15, 92 S. Ct. 1526 (1972)

Chief Justice BURGER delivered the opinion of the Court.

. . . .

Respondents Jonas Yoder and Adin Yutzy are members of the Old Order Amish Religion, and respondent Wallace Miller is a member of the Conservative Amish Mennonite Church. They and their families are residents of Green County, Wisconsin. Wisconsin's compulsory school attendance law required them to cause their children to attend public or private school until reaching age 16 but the respondents declined to send their children, ages 14 and 15, to public school after completing the eighth grade. The children were not enrolled in any private school, or within any recognized exception to the compulsory attendance law, and they are conceded to be subject to the Wisconsin statute.

On complaint of the school district administrator for the public schools, respondents were charged, tried, and convicted of violating the compulsory attendance law in Green County Court and were fined the sum of $5 each. Respondents defended on the ground that the application of the compulsory attendance law violated their rights under the First and Fourteenth Amendments. The trial testimony showed that respondents believed, in accordance with the tenets of Old Order Amish communities generally, that their children's attendance at high school, public or private, was contrary to the Amish religion and way of life. They believed that by sending their children to high school, they would not only expose themselves to the danger of the censure of the church community, but, as found by the county court, endanger their own salvation and that of their children. The State stipulated that respondents' religious beliefs were sincere.

. . . .

There is no doubt as to the power of a State, having a high responsibility for education of its citizens, to impose reasonable regulations for the control and duration of basic education. See, *e.g.,* Pierce v. Society of Sisters, 268 U.S. 510, 534 (1925). Providing public schools ranks at the very apex of the function of a State. Yet even this paramount responsibility was, in *Pierce*, made to yield to the right of parents to provide an equivalent education in a privately operated system. There the Court held that Oregon's statute compelling attendance in a public school from age eight to age 16 unreasonably interfered with the interest of parents in directing the rearing of their offspring including their education in church-operated schools. . . .

. . . [I]n order for Wisconsin to compel school attendance beyond the eighth grade against a claim that such attendance interferes with the practice of a legitimate religious belief, it must appear either that the State does not deny the free exercise of religious belief by its requirement, or that there is a state interest of sufficient magnitude to override the interest claiming protection under the Free Exercise Clause. . . .

. . . .

. . . [T]he record in this case abundantly supports the claim that the traditional way of life of the Amish is not merely a matter of personal preference, but one of deep religious conviction, shared by an organized group, and intimately related to daily living. . . .

. . . .

The impact of the compulsory attendance law on respondents' practice of the Amish religion is not only severe, but inescapable, for the Wisconsin law affirmatively compels them, under threat of criminal sanction, to perform acts undeniably at odds with fundamental tenets of their religious beliefs. Nor is the impact of the compulsory attendance law confined to grave interference with important Amish religious tenets from a subjective point of view. It carries with it precisely the kind of objective danger to the free exercise of religion which the First Amendment was designed to prevent. As the record shows, compulsory school attendance to age 16 for Amish children carries with it a very real threat of undermining the Amish community and religious practice as it exists today; they must either abandon belief and be assimilated into society at large, or be forced to migrate to some other and more tolerant region.

. . . .

. . . The Court must not ignore the danger that an exception from a general obligation of citizenship on religious grounds may run afoul of the Establishment Clause, but that danger cannot be allowed to prevent any exception no matter how vital it may be to the protection of values promoted by the right of free exercise. . . .

. . . .

The State advances two primary arguments in support of its system of compulsory education. It notes, as Thomas Jefferson pointed out early in our history, that some degree of education is necessary to prepare citizens to participate effectively and intelligently in our open political system if we are to preserve freedom and independence. Further, education prepares individuals to be self-reliant and self-sufficient participants in society. We accept these propositions.

. . . .

. . . Whatever their idiosyncrasies as seen by the majority, this record strongly shows that the Amish community has been a highly successful social unit within our society even if apart from the conventional "mainstream." Its members are productive and very law-abiding members of society; they reject public welfare in any of its usual modern forms. The Congress itself recognized their self-sufficiency by authorizing exemption of such groups as the Amish from the obligation to pay social security taxes.

. . . .

The State, however, supports its interest in providing an additional one or two years of compulsory high school education to Amish children because of the possibility that some such children will choose to leave the Amish community, and that if this occurs they will be ill-equipped for life. The State argues that if Amish children leave their church they should not be in the position of making their way in the world without the education available in the one or two additional years the State requires. However, on this record, that argument is highly speculative. There is no specific evidence of the loss of Amish adherents by attrition, nor is there any showing that upon leaving the Amish community Amish children, with their practical agricultural training and habits of industry and self-reliance would become burdens on society because of educational shortcomings. . . .

. . . .

. . . The independence and successful social functioning of the Amish community for a period approaching almost three centuries and more than 200 years in this country is strong evidence that there is at best a speculative gain, in terms of meeting the duties of citizenship, from an additional one or two years of compulsory formal education. Against this background it would require a more particularized showing from the State on this point to justify the severe interference with religious freedom such additional compulsory attendance would entail.

. . . .

The requirement of compulsory schooling to age 16 must therefore be viewed as aimed not merely at providing educational opportunities for children, but as an alternative to the equally undesirable consequence of unhealthful child labor displacing adult workers, or, on the other hand, forced idleness. The two kinds of statutes—compulsory school attendance and child labor laws—tend to keep children of certain ages off the labor market and in school; this in turn provides opportunity to prepare for a livelihood of a higher order than that children could perform without education and protects their health in adolescence.

In these terms, Wisconsin's interest in compelling the school attendance of Amish children to age 16 emerges as somewhat less substantial than requiring such attendance for children generally. For, while agricultural employment is not totally outside the legitimate concerns of the child labor laws, employment of children under parental guidance and on the family farm from age 14 to age 16 is an ancient tradition which lies at the periphery of the objectives of such laws. . . .

Finally, the State . . . argues that a decision exempting Amish children from the State's requirement fails to recognize the substantive right of the Amish child to a secondary education, and fails to give due regard to the power of the State as *parens patriae* to extend the benefit of secondary education to children regardless of the wishes of their parents. . . .

. . . .

Contrary to the suggestion of the dissenting opinion of Mr. Justice DOUGLAS, our holding today in no degree depends on the assertion of the religious interest of the child as contrasted with that of the parents. It is the parents who are subject to prosecution here for failing to cause their children to attend school, and it is their right of free exercise, not that of their children, that must determine Wisconsin's power to impose criminal penalties on the parent. The dissent argues that a child who expresses a desire to attend public high school in conflict with the wishes of his parents should not be prevented from doing so. There is no reason for the Court to consider that point since it is not an issue in the case. The children are not parties to this litigation. The State has at no point tried this case on the theory that respondents were preventing their children from attending school against their expressed desires, and indeed the record is to the contrary. . . .

. . . .

. . . Our disposition of this case, however, in no way alters our recognition of the obvious fact that courts are not school boards or legislatures, and are ill-equipped to determine the "necessity" of discrete aspects of a State's program of compulsory education. This should suggest that courts must move with great circumspection in performing the sensitive and delicate task of weighing a State's legitimate social concern when faced with religious claims for exemption from generally applicable educational requirements. It cannot be over-emphasized that we are not dealing with a way of life and mode of education by a group claiming to have recently discovered some "progressive" or more enlightened process for rearing children for modern life.

. . . .

Affirmed.

Justice POWELL and Justice REHNQUIST took no part in the consideration or decision of this case.

Justice DOUGLAS, dissenting in part.

. . . The Court's analysis assumes that the only interests at stake in the case are those of the Amish parents on the one hand, and those of the State on the other. The difficulty with this approach is that, despite the Court's claim, the parents are seeking to vindicate not only their own free exercise claims, but also those of their high-school-age children.

. . . .

. . . Where the child is mature enough to express potentially conflicting desires, it would be an invasion of the child's rights to permit such an imposition without canvassing his views. . . . As the child has no other effective forum, it is in this litigation that his rights should be considered. And if an Amish child desires to attend high school, and is mature enough to have that desire respected, the State may well be able to override the parents' religiously motivated objections.

. . . .

---

## NOTES ON THE EXEMPTION THEORY OF THE *YODER* CASE

1. Burger's theory in *Wisconsin v. Yoder* is really an exemption theory. He disagrees with the Kurland-type analysis that the touchstone of violation of the religion clause is lack of neutrality. Burger holds for the court that sometimes an exemption must be made "from a general obligation." The danger of violating the establishment clause is, in this view, less than the reality of violating the free exercise clause.

2. Justice Douglas states that the "law and order" record of the Amish should be irrelevant. As a constitutional matter, the no-establishment principle probably demands that it be irrelevant. The question whether exemption from a general obligation can ever be anything less than an establishment certainly comes to the fore if the reason for the exemption is that the Amish have been in America for a long time, or that they are exceptionally law abiding, or industrious. If the Amish are granted an exemption because of these qualities, the government is susceptible to the charge of preferring one faith to another. The implication of the exemption theory of *Wisconsin v. Yoder* is that other faiths with less virtuous images than the Amish but with a similar aversion to compulsory secondary school education might not be granted an exemption. If that is so, did *Yoder* make an accommodation for free exercise or did it create an invalid establishment?

3. Is *Yoder* a case where the interests of child and parent are primarily in conflict? Was the solution to have their interests raised and considered by the court as argued by Justice Douglas or was the solution to appoint counsel to represent the absent children? Chief Justice Burger's approach of course was to observe that when a child raised the issue it would be time

enough to consider it. But how likely is it that an Amish child of 13 will bring a suit against the state or his parents? Yet the question of allowing a child the exercise of choice, either of occupation or of faith, is certainly immeasurably altered by state toleration of exemption of Amish children from the general obligation to attend school until 16.

4. In an article in *Harper's* in 1972, significantly entitled *The Importance of Being Amish,* Professor Walter Berns described the holding in *Yoder* as stating "one's religious conviction" entitled one "to an exemption from the requirements of a *valid* criminal statute." In Berns' view, this holding constituted "dangerous new law." He speculated that if a citizen is entitled to disobey law which conflicts with one's religious beliefs "the proliferation of sects and of forms of worship will be wonderful to behold: drug cultists, snake worshippers, income tax haters. . . ."

Is the rule of *Yoder* a rule of general application or an ad hoc example of preferential treatment? If the former, Berns says that judges will have to "do precisely what the Supreme Court has insisted that they may not do, namely, get in the business of distinguishing the honest profession of faith from the dishonest."

## B. WHAT IS THE MEANING OF THE ESTABLISHMENT CLAUSE?

### EVERSON v. BOARD OF EDUCATION
Supreme Court of the United States
330 U.S. 1, 91 L. Ed. 711, 67 S. Ct. 504 (1947)

Justice BLACK delivered the opinion of the Court.

A New Jersey statute authorizes its local school districts to make rules and contracts for the transportation of children to and from schools. The appellee, a township board of education, acting pursuant to this statute authorized reimbursement to parents of money expended by them for the bus transportation of their children on regular buses operated by the public transportation system. Part of this money was for the payment of transportation of some children in the community to Catholic parochial schools. These church schools give their students, in addition to secular education, regular religious instruction conforming to the religious tenets and modes of worship in the Catholic faith. The superintendent of these schools is a Catholic priest.

The appellant, in his capacity as a district taxpayer, filed suit in a State court challenging the right of the Board to reim-

burse parents of parochial school students. He contended that
the statute and the resolution passed pursuant to it violated
both the State and the Federal Constitutions. That court held
that the legislature was without power to authorize such payment
under the State constitution. The New Jersey Court of Errors
and Appeals reversed, holding that neither the statute nor the
resolution passed pursuant to it was in conflict with the State
constitution or the provisions of the Federal Constitution in
issue. . . .

. . . .

. . . The New Jersey statute is challenged as a "law respecting an establishment of religion." . . . Whether this New
Jersey law is one respecting the "establishment of religion" requires an understanding of the meaning of that language, particularly with respect to the imposition of taxes. Once again,
therefore, it is not inappropriate briefly to review the background
and environment of the period in which that constitutional
language was fashioned and adopted.

A large proportion of the early settlers of this country came
here from Europe to escape the bondage of laws which compelled
them to support and attend government favored churches. . . .

. . . .

. . . The imposition of taxes to pay ministers' salaries and
to build and maintain churches and church property aroused
indignation. It was these feelings which found expression in the
First Amendment. No one locality and no one group throughout
the Colonies can rightly be given entire credit for having aroused
the sentiment that culminated in adoption of the Bill of Rights'
provisions embracing religious liberty. But Virginia, where the
established church had achieved a dominant influence in political affairs and where many excesses attracted wide public attention, provided a great stimulus and able leadership for the
movement. The people there, as elsewhere, reached the conviction that individual religious liberty could be achieved best
under a government which was stripped of all power to tax, to
support, or otherwise to assist any or all religions, or to interfere
with the beliefs of any religious individual or group.

The movement toward this end reached its dramatic climax
in Virginia in 1785-86 when the Virginia legislative body was
about to renew Virginia's tax levy for the support of the established church. Thomas Jefferson and James Madison led the
fight against this tax. Madison wrote his great Memorial and
Remonstrance against the law. In it, he eloquently argued that
a true religion did not need the support of law; that no person,
either believer or non-believer, should be taxed to support a

religious institution of any kind; that the best interest of a society required that the minds of men always be wholly free; and that cruel persecutions were the inevitable result of government-established religions. Madison's Remonstrance received strong support throughout Virginia. And the Assembly postponed consideration of the proposed tax measure until its next session. When the proposal came up for consideration at that session, it not only died in committee, but the Assembly enacted the famous "Virginia Bill for Religious Liberty" originally written by Thomas Jefferson. . . .

This Court has previously recognized that the provisions of the First Amendment, in the drafting and adoption of which Madison and Jefferson played such leading roles, had the same objective and were intended to provide the same protection against governmental intrusion on religious liberty as the Virginia statute. . . .

. . . .

The "establishment of religion" clause of the First Amendment means at least this: Neither a state nor the Federal Government can set up a church. Neither can pass laws which aid one religion, aid all religions, or prefer one religion over another. Neither can force nor influence a person to go to or to remain away from church against his will or force him to profess a belief or disbelief in any religion. No person can be punished for entertaining or professing religious beliefs or disbeliefs, for church attendance or non-attendance. No tax in any amount, large or small, can be levied to support any religious activities or institutions, whatever they may be called, or whatever form they may adopt to teach or practice religion. Neither a state nor the Federal Government can, openly or secretly, participate in the affairs of any religious organizations or groups and vice versa. In the words of Jefferson, the clause against establishment of religion by law was intended to erect "a wall of separation between Church and State."

We must consider the New Jersey statute in accordance with the foregoing limitations imposed by the First Amendment. But we must not strike that state statute down if it is within the state's constitutional power even though it approaches the verge of that power. New Jersey cannot consistently with the "establishment of religion" clause of the First Amendment contribute tax-raised funds to the support of an institution which teaches the tenets and faith of any church. On the other hand, other language of the amendment commands that New Jersey cannot hamper its citizens in the free exercise of their own religion. . . .

Measured by these standards we cannot say that the First Amendment prohibits New Jersey from spending tax-raised funds to pay the bus fares of parochial school pupils as a part of a general program under which it pays the fares of pupils attending public and other schools. It is undoubtedly true that children are helped to get to church schools. There is even a possibility that some of the children might not be sent to the church schools if the parents were compelled to pay their children's bus fares out of their own pockets when transportation to a public school would have been paid for by the State. . . . Similarly, parents might be reluctant to permit their children to attend schools which the state had cut off from such general government services as ordinary police and fire protection, connections for sewage disposal, public highways and sidewalks. Of course cutting off church schools from these services, so separate and so indisputably marked off from the religious function, would make it far more difficult for the schools to operate. But such is obviously not the purpose of the First Amendment. That Amendment requires the state to be a neutral in its relations with groups of religious believers and non-believers; it does not require the state to be their adversary. State power is no more to be used so as to handicap religions, than it is to favor them.

This Court has said that parents may, in the discharge of their duty under state compulsory education laws, send their children to a religious rather than a public school if the school meets the secular educational requirements which the state has power to impose. See Pierce v. Society of Sisters, 268 U. S. 510. It appears that these parochial schools meet New Jersey's requirements. The State contributes no money to the schools. It does not support them. Its legislation, as applied, does no more than provide a general program to help parents get their children, regardless of their religion, safely and expeditiously to and from accredited schools.

The First Amendment has erected a wall between church and state. That wall must be kept high and impregnable. We could not approve the slightest breach. New Jersey has not breached it here.

Affirmed.

Justice RUTLEDGE, with whom Justice FRANKFURTER, Justice JACKSON and Justice BURTON agree, dissenting.

. . . .

This case forces us to determine squarely for the first time what was "an establishment of religion" in the First Amendment's conception; and by that measure to decide whether New Jersey's action violates its command. . . .

. . . .

Not simply an established church, but any law respecting an establishment of religion is forbidden. The Amendment was broadly but not loosely phrased. It is the compact and exact summation of its author's views formed during his long struggle for religious freedom. In Madison's own words characterizing Jefferson's Bill for Establishing Religious Freedom, the guaranty he put in our national charter, like the bill he piloted through the Virginia Assembly, was "a Model of technical precision, and perspicuous brevity." Madison could not have confused "church" and "religion" or "an establishment of religion."

The Amendment's purpose was not to strike merely at the official establishment of a single sect, creed or religion, outlawing only a formal relation such as had prevailed in England and some of the colonies. Necessarily it was to uproot all such relationships. But the object was broader than separating church and state in this narrow sense. It was to create a complete and permanent separation of the spheres of religious activity and civil authority by comprehensively forbidding every form of public aid or support for religion. In proof the Amendment's wording and history unite with this Court's consistent utterances whenever attention has been fixed directly upon the question.

. . . .

No provision of the Constitution is more closely tied to or given content by its generating history than the religious clause of the First Amendment. It is at once the refined product and the terse summation of that history. The history includes not only Madison's authorship and the proceedings before the First Congress, but also the long and intensive struggle for religious freedom in America, more especially in Virginia, of which the Amendment was the direct culmination. In the documents of the times, particularly of Madison, who was leader in the Virginia struggle before he became the Amendment's sponsor, but also in the writings of Jefferson and others and in the issues which engendered them is to be found irrefutable confirmation of the Amendment's sweeping content.

. . . .

In view of this history no further proof is needed that the Amendment forbids any appropriation, large or small, from public funds to aid or support any and all religious exercises. But if more were called for, the debates in the First Congress and this Court's consistent expressions, whenever it has touched on the matter directly, supply it.

By contrast with the Virginia history, the congressional debates on consideration of the Amendment reveal only sparse discussion, reflecting the fact that the essential issues had been settled. Indeed the matter had become so well understood as to have been taken for granted in all but formal phrasing. Hence, the only enlightening reference shows concern, not to preserve any power to use public funds in aid of religion, but to prevent the Amendment from outlawing private gifts inadvertently by virtue of the breadth of its wording. . . .

. . . .

Does New Jersey's action furnish support for religion by use of the taxing power? Certainly it does, if the test remains undiluted as Jefferson and Madison made it, that money taken by taxation from one is not to be used or given to support another's religious training or belief, or indeed one's own. Today as then the furnishing of "contributions of money for the propagation of opinions which he disbelieves" is the forbidden exaction; and the prohibition is absolute for whatever measure brings that consequence and whatever amount may be sought or given to that end.

The funds used here were raised by taxation. The Court does not dispute nor could it that their use does in fact give aid and encouragement to religious instruction. It only concludes that this aid is not "support" in law. But Madison and Jefferson were concerned with aid and support in fact, not as a legal conclusion "entangled in precedents." Here parents pay money to send their children to parochial schools and funds raised by taxation are used to reimburse them. This not only helps the children to get to school and the parents to send them. It aids them in a substantial way to get the very thing they are sent to the particular school to secure, namely, religious training and teaching.

Believers of all faiths, and others who do not express their feeling toward ultimate issues of existence in any creedal form, pay the New Jersey tax. When the money so raised is used to pay for transportation to religious schools the Catholic taxpayer to the extent of his proportionate share pays for the transportation of Lutheran, Jewish and otherwise religiously affiliated children to receive their non-Catholic religious instruction. Their parents likewise pay proportionately for the transportation of Catholic children to receive Catholic instruction. Each thus contributes to "the propagation of opinions which he disbelieves" in so far as their religions differ, as do others who accept no creed without regard to those differences. . . .

. . . .

No one conscious of religious values can be unsympathetic toward the burden which our constitutional separation puts on parents who desire religious instruction mixed with secular for their children. They pay taxes for others' children's education, at the same time the added cost of instruction for their own. Nor can one happily see benefits denied to children which others receive, because in conscience they or their parents for them desire a different kind of training others do not demand.

But if these feelings should prevail, there would be an end to our historic constitutional policy and command. No more unjust or discriminatory in fact is it to deny attendants at religious schools the cost of their transportation than it is to deny them tuitions, sustenance for their teachers, or any other educational expense which others receive at public cost. Hardship in fact there is which none can blink. But, for assuring to those who undergo it the greater, the most comprehensive freedom, it is one written by design and firm intent into our basic law.

. . . .

Two great drives are constantly in motion to abridge, in the name of education, the complete division of religion and civil authority which our forefathers made. One is to introduce religious education and observances into the public schools. The other, to obtain public funds for the aid and support of various private religious schools. . . . In my opinion both avenues were closed by the Constitution. Neither should be opened by this Court. The matter is not one of quantity, to be measured by the amount of money expended. Now as in Madison's day it is one of principle, to keep separate the separate spheres as the First Amendment drew them; to prevent the first experiment upon our liberties; and to keep the question from becoming entangled in corrosive precedents. We should not be less strict to keep strong and untarnished the one side of the shield of religious freedom than we have been of the other.

The judgment should be reversed.

---

## NOTES

Justice Black condemned in *Everson* government "aid to religion" as an invalid establishment. Professor Kauper, among others, has suggested that the unsatisfactory quality of the Black definition of what constitutes government establishment of religion is that the definition could certainly include that which Black put outside it (school transportation for parochial school children). Professor Kauper lists the following items as examples of government aid to religion: 1. Tax exemption for religious property; 2. Chaplains' Corps in the Armed Services; 3. Compulsory chapel in the military academies; 4. Religious use of public parks and streets; 5. Tax deductions for religious contributions; 6. Special income tax treatment for clergymen. P. KAUPER, CIVIL LIBERTIES AND THE CONSTITUTION 13 (1962).

Black's theory, of course, is that government conferral of a public or social benefit is not an establishment despite the fact that it may incidentally aid religion. For this reason, school transportation for all children, public or parochial, fire protection and water services do not violate the establishment clause.

These services are not available as an aid to religion. To exempt religion from them, however, would be to discriminate against religion. Using this public benefit approach, which of the items in Professor Kauper's list should be considered "aids to religion" and which should be considered "public benefits"?

## C. BLUE LAWS AND SABBATARIANS: A COMPARATIVE PERSPECTIVE

### BRAUNFELD v. BROWN
Supreme Court of the United States
366 U.S. 599, 6 L. Ed. 2d 563, 81 S. Ct. 1144 (1961)

Chief Justice WARREN announced the judgment of the Court and an opinion in which Justice BLACK, Justice CLARK, and Justice WHITTAKER concur.

This case concerns the constitutional validity of the application to appellants of the Pennsylvania criminal statute, enacted in 1959, which proscribes the Sunday retail sale of certain enumerated commodities. . . .

Appellants are merchants in Philadelphia who engage in the retail sale of clothing and home furnishings within the proscription of the statute in issue. Each of the appellants is a member of the Orthodox Jewish faith, which requires the closing of their places of business and a total abstention from all manner of work from nightfall each Friday until nightfall each Saturday. They instituted a suit in the court below seeking a permanent injunction against the enforcement of the 1959 statute. . . .

A three-judge court was properly convened and it dismissed the complaint. . . .

Appellants contend that the enforcement against them of the Pennsylvania statute will prohibit the free exercise of their religion because, due to the statute's compulsion to close on Sunday, appellants will suffer substantial economic loss, to the benefit of their non-Sabbatarian competitors, if appellants also continue their Sabbath observance by closing their businesses on Saturday; that this result will either compel appellants to give up their Sabbath observance, a basic tenet of the Orthodox Jewish faith, or will put appellants at a serious economic disadvantage if they continue to adhere to their Sabbath. Appellants also assert that the statute will operate so as to hinder the Orthodox Jewish faith in gaining new adherents. And the corollary to these arguments is that if the free exercise of appellants' religion is impeded, that religion is being subjected to discriminatory treatment by the State. . . .

Certain aspects of religious exercise cannot, in any way, be restricted or burdened by either federal or state legislation. Compulsion by law of the acceptance of any creed or the practice of any form of worship is strictly forbidden. The freedom to hold religious beliefs and opinions is absolute. Cantwell v. Connecticut. . . . But this is not the case at bar; the statute before us does not make criminal the holding of any religious belief or opinion, nor does it force anyone to embrace any religious belief or to say or believe anything in conflict with his religious tenets.

However, the freedom to act, even when the action is in accord with one's religious convictions, is not totally free from legislative restrictions. . . .

. . . .

. . . [T]he statute at bar does not make unlawful any religious practices of appellants; the Sunday law simply regulates a secular activity and, as applied to appellants, operates so as to make the practice of their religious beliefs more expensive. Furthermore, the law's effect does not inconvenience all members of the Orthodox Jewish faith but only those who believe it necessary to work on Sunday. And even these are not faced with as serious a choice as forsaking their religious practices or subjecting themselves to criminal prosecution. Fully recognizing that the alternatives open to appellants and others similarly situated—retaining their present occupations and incurring economic disadvantage or engaging in some other commercial activity which does not call for either Saturday or Sunday labor—may well result in some financial sacrifice in order to observe their religious beliefs, still the option is wholly different than when the legislation attempts to make a religious practice itself unlawful.

To strike down, without the most critical scrutiny, legislation which imposes only an indirect burden on the exercise of religion, i.e., legislation which does not make unlawful the religious practice itself, would radically restrict the operating latitude of the legislature. Statutes which tax income and limit the amount which may be deducted for religious contributions impose an indirect economic burden on the observance of the religion of the citizen whose religion requires him to donate a greater amount to his church; statutes which require the courts to be closed on Saturday and Sunday impose a similar indirect burden on the observance of the religion of the trial lawyer whose religion requires him to rest on a weekday. The list of legislation of this nature is nearly limitless.

. . . .

Of course, to hold unassailable all legislation regulating conduct which imposes solely an indirect burden on the observance of religion would be a gross oversimplification. If the purpose or effect of a law is to impede the observance of one or all religions or is to discriminate invidiously between religions, that law is constitutionally invalid even though the burden may be characterized as being only indirect. But if the State regulates conduct by enacting a general law within its power, the purpose and effect of which is to advance the State's secular goals, the statute is valid despite its indirect burden on religious observance unless the State may accomplish its purpose by means which do not impose such a burden.

As we pointed out in *McGowan v. Maryland,* we cannot find a State without power to provide a weekly respite from all labor and, at the same time, to set one day of the week apart from the others as a day of rest, repose, recreation and tranquility. . . . This is particularly true in this day and age of increasing state concern with public welfare legislation.

Also, in *McGowan,* we examined several suggested alternative means by which it was argued that the State might accomplish its secular goals without even remotely or incidentally affecting religious freedom. We found there that a State might well find that those alternatives would not accomplish bringing about a general day of rest. . . .

However, appellants advance yet another means at the State's disposal which they would find unobjectionable. They contend that the State should cut an exception from the Sunday labor proscription for those people who, because of religious conviction, observe a day of rest other than Sunday. By such regulation, appellants contend, the economic disadvantages imposed by the present system would be removed and the State's interest in having all people rest one day would be satisfied.

A number of States provide such an exemption, and this may well be the wiser solution to the problem. But our concern is not with the wisdom of legislation but with its constitutional limitation. Thus, reason and experience teach that to permit the exemption might well undermine the State's goal of providing a day that, as best possible, eliminates the atmosphere of commercial noise and activity. Although not dispositive of the issue, enforcement problems would be more difficult since there would be two or more days to police rather than one and it would be more difficult to observe whether violations were occurring.

Additional problems might also be presented by a regulation of this sort. To allow only people who rest on a day other than Sunday to keep their businesses open on that day might well provide these people with an economic advantage over their competitors who must remain closed on that day; this might cause the Sunday-observers to complain that their religions are being discriminated against. With this competitive advantage existing, there could well be the temptation for some, in order to keep their businesses open on Sunday, to assert that they have religious convictions which compel them to close their businesses on what had formerly been their least profitable day. This might make necessary a state-conducted inquiry into the sincerity of the individual's religious beliefs, a practice which a State might believe would itself run afoul of the spirit of constitutionally protected religious guarantees. Finally, in order to keep the disruption of the day at a minimum, exempted employers would probably have to hire employees who themselves qualified for the exemption because of their own religious beliefs, a practice which a State might feel to be opposed to its general policy prohibiting religious discrimination in hiring. For all of these reasons, we cannot say that the Pennsylvania statute before us is invalid, either on its face or as applied.

Justice HARLAN concurs in the judgment. Justice BRENNAN and Justice STEWART concur in our disposition of appellants' claims under the Establishment Clause and the Equal Protection Clause. Justice FRANKFURTER and Justice HARLAN have rejected appellants' claim under the Free Exercise Clause in a separate opinion.

Accordingly, the decision is affirmed.

Justice BRENNAN, concurring and dissenting. . . .

. . . .

Admittedly, these laws do not compel overt affirmation of a repugnant belief, as in *Barnette,* nor do they prohibit outright any of appellants' religious practices, as did the federal law upheld in Reynolds v. United States, cited by the Court. That is, the laws do not say that appellants must work on Saturday. But their effect is that appellants may not simultaneously practice their religion and their trade, without being hampered by a substantial competitive disadvantage. Their effect is that no one may at one and the same time be an Orthodox Jew and compete effectively with his Sunday-observing fellow tradesmen. . . .

What, then, is the compelling state interest which impels the Commonwealth of Pennsylvania to impede appellants' freedom of worship? What overbalancing need is so weighty in the constitutional scale that it justifies this substantial, though indirect, limitation of appellants' freedom? It is not the desire to stamp out a practice deeply abhorred by society, such as polygamy, as in *Reynolds,* for the custom of resting one day a week is universally honored, as the Court has amply shown. Nor is it the State's traditional protection of children, for appellants are reasoning and fully autonomous adults. It is not even the interest in seeing that everyone rests one day a week, for appellants' religion requires that they take such a rest. It is the mere convenience of having everyone rest on the same day. It is to defend this interest that the Court holds that a State need not follow the alternative route of granting an exemption for those who in good faith observe a day of rest other than Sunday.

. . . .

[Justice STEWART's dissenting opinion is omitted.]

---

### SHERBERT v. VERNER
Supreme Court of the United States
374 U.S. 398, 10 L. Ed. 2d 965, 83 S. Ct. 1790 (1963)

Justice BRENNAN delivered the opinion of the Court.

Appellant, a member of the Seventh-day Adventist Church was discharged by her South Carolina employer because she would not work on Saturday, the Sabbath Day of her faith. When she was unable to obtain other employment because from conscientious scruples she would not take Saturday work, she filed a claim for unemployment compensation benefits under the South Carolina Unemployment Compensation Act. . . . The . . . Employment Security Commission . . . found that appellant's restriction upon her availability for Saturday work brought her within the provision disqualifying for benefits insured workers who fail, without good cause, to accept "suitable work when offered . . . by the employment office or the employer. . . ." The Commission's finding was sustained . . . by the South Carolina Supreme Court. . . .

. . . .

We turn first to the question whether the disqualification for benefits imposes any burden on the free exercise of appellant's religion. We think it is clear that it does. In a sense the consequences of such a disqualification to religious principles and practices may be only an indirect result of welfare legislation within the State's general competence to enact; it is true that no criminal sanctions directly compel appellant to work a six-day week. But this is only the beginning, not the end of our inquiry. For "[i]f the purpose or effect of a law is to impede the observance of one or all religions or is to discriminate invidiously between religions, that law is constitutionally invalid even though the burden may be characterized as being only indirect." *Braunfeld v. Brown.* Here not only is it apparent that appellant's declared ineligibility for benefits derives solely from the practice of her religion, but the pressure upon her to forego that practice is unmistakable. The ruling forces her to choose between following the precepts of her religion and forfeiting benefits, on the one hand, and abandoning one of the precepts of her religion in order to accept work, on the other hand. Governmental imposition of such a choice puts the same kind of burden upon the free exercise of religion as would a fine imposed against appellant for her Saturday worship.

Nor may the South Carolina court's construction of the statute be saved from constitutional infirmity on the ground that unemployment compensation benefits are not appellant's "right" but merely a "privilege." It is too late in the day to doubt that the liberties of religion and expression may be infringed by the denial or placing of conditions upon a benefit or privilege. . . . [T]o condition the availability of benefits upon this appellant's willingness to violate a cardinal principle of her religious faith effectively penalizes the free exercise of her constitutional liberties.

. . . .

We must next consider whether some compelling state interest enforced in the eligibility provisions of the South Carolina statute justifies the substantial infringement of appellant's First Amendment right. . . . The appellees suggest no more than a possibility that the filing of fraudulent claims by unscrupulous claimants feigning religious objections to Saturday work might not only dilute the unemployment compensation fund but also hinder the scheduling by employers of necessary Saturday work. . . . [T]here is no proof whatever to warrant such fears of malingering or deceit as those which the respondents now advance. Even if consideration of such evidence is not foreclosed by the prohibition against judicial inquiry into the truth or falsity of religious beliefs, a question as to which we intimate no view since it is

not before us—it is highly doubtful whether such evidence would
be sufficient to warrant a substantial infringement of religious
liberties. For even if the possibility of spurious claims did threaten
to dilute the fund and disrupt the scheduling of work, it would
plainly be incumbent upon the appellees to demonstrate that no
alternative forms of regulation would combat such abuses without infringing First Amendment rights.

In these respects, then, the state interest asserted in the present
case is wholly dissimilar to the interests which were found to justify
the less direct burden upon religious practices in *Braunfeld.* . . .
That secular objective could be achieved, the Court found, only
by declaring Sunday to be that day of rest. Requiring exemptions
for Sabbatarians, while theoretically possible, appeared to present
an administrative problem of such magnitude, or afford the
exempted class so great a competitive advantage that such a
requirement would have rendered the entire statutory scheme
unworkable. In the present case no such justifications underlie
the determination of the state court that appellant's religion
makes her ineligible to receive benefits.

In holding as we do, plainly we are not fostering the "establishment" of the Seventh-day Adventist religion in South Carolina, for the extension of unemployment benefits to Sabbatarians
in common with Sunday worshippers reflects nothing more than
the governmental obligation of neutrality in the face of religious
differences, and does not represent that involvement of religious
with secular institutions which it is the object of the Establishment Clause to forestall. . . . Nor do we, by our decision today,
declare the existence of a constitutional right to unemployment
benefits on the part of all persons whose religious convictions
are the cause of their unemployment. This is not a case in which
an employee's religious convictions serve to make him a non-
productive member of society. . . .

. . . .

[Reversed and remanded.]

Justice Stewart, concurring.

. . . .

. . . I cannot agree that today's decision can stand consistently
with *Braunfeld v. Brown.* The Court says that there was a
"less direct burden upon religious practices" in that case than in
this. With all respect, I think the Court is mistaken, simply as a
matter of fact. The *Braunfeld* case involved a state *criminal*
statute. The undisputed effect of that statute, as pointed out by
Mr. Justice Brennan in his dissenting opinion in that case, was
that " 'Plaintiff . . . will be unable to continue in his business if
he may not stay open on Sunday and he will thereby lose his

capital investment.' In other words, the issue in this case . . . is whether a State may put an individual to a choice between his business and his religion." . . .

The impact upon the appellant's religious freedom in the present case is considerably less onerous. We deal here not with a criminal statute . . . Even upon the unlikely assumption that the appellant could not find suitable non-Saturday employment, the appellant at the worst would be denied a maximum of 22 weeks of compensation payments. I agree with the Court that the possibility of that denial is enough to infringe upon the appellant's constitutional right to the free exercise of her religion. But it is clear to me that in order to reach this conclusion the court must explicitly reject the reasoning of *Braunfeld*. . . .

Justice HARLAN, whom Justice WHITE joins, dissenting.

. . . .

. . . [T]his Court's decision . . . has particular significance in two respects.

*First,* despite the Court's protestations to the contrary, the decision necessarily overrules *Braunfeld v. Brown.* . . . [J]ust as in *Braunfeld*—where exceptions to the Sunday closing laws for Sabbatarians . . . would have required case-by-case inquiry into religious beliefs—so here, an exception to the rules of eligibility based on religious convictions would necessitate judicial examination of those convictions. . . .

*Second,* . . . [T]he meaning of today's holding . . . is that the State must furnish unemployment benefits to one who is unavailable for work if the unavailability stems from the exercise of religious convictions. The State, in other words, must *single out* for financial assistance those whose behavior is religiously motivated, even though it denies such assistance to others whose identical behavior (in this case, inability to work on Saturdays) is not religiously motivated.

It has been suggested that such singling out of religious conduct for special treatment may violate the constitutional limitations on state action. See Kurland, Of Church and State and The Supreme Court, 29 U. of Chi.L.Rev. 1; . . . My own view, however, is that at least under the circumstances of this case it would be a permissible accommodation of religion for the State, if it *chose* to do so, to create an exception to its eligibility requirements for persons like the appellant. . . .

. . . I cannot subscribe to the conclusion that the State is constitutionally *compelled* to carve out an exception to its general rule of eligibility in the present case. Those situations in which the Constitution may require special treatment on account of religion are, in my view, few and far between, and this view is amply supported by the course of constitutional litigation in this area. Such compulsion in the present case is particularly inappropriate in light of the indirect, remote, and insubstantial effect of the decision below on the exercise of appellant's religion and in light of the direct financial assistance to religion that today's decision requires.

. . . .

## NOTES

1.  The Supreme Court in *In re* Jenison, 375 U.S. 14 (1963), vacated for reconsideration, in light of Sherbert v. Verner, 374 U.S. 398 (1963), the judgment of the Minnesota court which held a woman in contempt because she refused to serve as a juror on religious grounds. The Supreme Court of Minnesota then reversed the conviction, 276 Minn. 136, 125 N.W. 2d 588 (1963). Professor Kurland had advocated a constitutional test for deciding when the freedom of religion clauses have been violated. Professor Kurland says "religion may not be used as a basis for classification for purposes of governmental action, whether that action be the conferring of rights or privileges or the imposition of duties or obligations." *See* P. KURLAND, RELIGION AND THE LAW 18 (1962). Is *Sherbert* consistent with this standard? Is *Jenison*?

2.  Doesn't Stewart score a good point in *Sherbert* when he emphasized that *Braunfeld* involved a state criminal statute? The coercive effect of fear of criminal punishment if the Sabbatarian breaks the blue law should loom much greater, at least from a legal point of view, then if someone like the Seventh Day Adventist should refuse to work on Saturday, and, therefore, loses a government benefit. The necessity for a comparative coercive effect analysis is, of course, avoided by the court in *Sherbert* because the court finds that the governmental burden on the Seventh Day Adventist's free exercise rights was direct but only indirect with respect to the Orthodox Jew's free exercise rights.

Do you think the direct-indirect burden approach to free exercise problems is more meaningful or helpful than the roughly analogous direct-indirect burden test that was once dominant in commerce clause adjudication? *See* text, pp. 188-90, 257-58.

3.  An exception to the law on behalf of free exercise is permitted in *Sherbert* and denied in *Braunfeld*. In *Braunfeld*, Chief Justice Warren did not pass on the validity of state statutes which create an exception to Sunday blue laws in order to permit Sabbatarians to work on Sunday. But he did suggest that such

statutes raised difficult problems involving unwelcome governmental evaluation of the sincerity of those who invoked Sabbatarian statutes: how was one to distinguish the Sabbatarian who worked on Sunday and rested on Saturday from religious conviction from the Sabbatarian who did the same to secure a competitive advantage?

Professor Galanter has written in favor of exemptions in behalf of free exercise: " . . . whatever the majority considers necessary for its religious practice is quite unlikely to be prohibited by law. And whatever the majority finds religiously objectionable is unlikely to become a legal requirement — for example, medical practices which substantial groups find abhorrent, like contraception, sterilization, euthanasia, or abortion. Exceptions then, give to minorities what majorities have by virtue of suffrage and representative government. The question is not whether the state may prefer these minorities, but whether it may counterbalance the natural advantages of majorities." Galanter, *Religious Freedoms in the United States: A Turning Point?*, 1966 WIS. L. REV. 215, 291 (1966). On the basis of *Sherbert* and *Braunfeld,* do you think Sabbatarian exemption statutes are constitutional?

4. McGowan v. Maryland, 366 U.S. 420 (1961), was approached by the Supreme Court on establishment rather than free exercise grounds. *McGowan* involved discount house employees who were indicted for violating the Maryland Sunday blue laws. They attempted to assert an infringement of their free exercise rights but the court rejected this contention:

> But appellants allege only economic injury to themselves; they do not allege any infringement of their own religious freedom due to Sunday closing. In fact, the record is silent as to what appellants' religious beliefs are. Since the general rule is that "a litigant may only assert his own constitutional rights or immunities," we hold that appellants have no standing to raise this contention.

The employees also made an establishment attack on the Maryland Sunday closing law. The court held that they had standing to raise the establishment issue:

> Appellants here concededly have suffered direct economic injury, allegedly due to the imposition on them of the tenets of the Christian religion.

A portion of Chief Justice Warren's opinion in *McGowan* responded to an equal protection attack by the discount house employees against some exemptions to the Maryland Sunday closing law which did permit the operation on Sunday of various amusements such as slot machines, pinball machines and bingo. Since many state blue laws present a crazy-quilt of prohibition and exemption, the court's disinclination in *McGowan* to open this route of constitutional attack on Sunday closing legislation is significant. Chief Justice Warren justified the statutory exemptions to the Maryland Sunday closing laws using the traditional doctrinal approach that equal protection was not violated when the state had made a reasonable classification:

> It would seem that a legislature could reasonably find that the Sunday sale of the exempted commodities was necessary either for the health of the populace or the enhancement of the recreational atmosphere of the day—that a family which takes a Sunday ride into the country will need gasoline for the automobile and may find pleasant a soft drink or fresh fruit; and those who go to the beach may wish ice cream or some other item normally sold there; that some people will prefer alcoholic beverages or games of chance to add to their relaxation; that newspapers and drug products should always be available to the public.

## A Comparative Perspective

The three American Sabbatarian cases discussed above, *Braunfeld, Sherbert,* and *McGowan,* make an interesting contrast when compared with the Canadian Sunday Closing case, *Robertson and Rosetanni v. The Queen,* [1963] Can. Sup. Ct. 651 [1964] 41 D.L.R. (2d) 485 (1963).

As you read the material which follows, reflect on the extent to which constitutional text and doctrine restrains or mirrors a society's dominant social forces.

## BARRON, SUNDAY IN NORTH AMERICA, 79 Harv. L. Rev. 42 (1965)*

. . . .

From a comparative point of view, the astonishing fact about the decisions involving Sunday legislation in the United States and Canada is the extent to which disparate doctrine has been used by two Supreme Courts to reach an identical result: affirmation of the validity of the legislation. Canada, unlike the United States, has no written constitutional guarantees assuring the free exercise of religion and prohibiting the establishment thereof. In 1960, however, the Federal Parliament of Canada enacted the

---

Canadian Bill of Rights, which provides essentially that legislation inconsistent with freedom of religion is invalid. In Canada, Sunday legislation is frankly conceded to be religious in purpose; indeed, if it were otherwise the basis for federal jurisdiction would be questionable. But the Supreme Court of Canada claims purpose can be separated from effect, and the effect of the Canadian Sunday legislation is said to be entirely secular.

In the United States, the religious purpose of Sunday legislation is denied as sternly as it is insisted upon in Canada. The legislation is declared to be today entirely secular in purpose, providing the citizenry with a uniform day of rest and recreation. If the United States Supreme Court had found a continuing religious purpose behind the Sunday legislation, the no-establishment principle would have commanded invalidation. It is interesting and odd that legislation, similar in intent and origin, is characterized as religious in Canada and secular in the United States, the characterizations thus coinciding with doctrinal necessity in the two countries. . . .

. . . .

A comparison of *Robertson v. The Queen* with the American *Sunday Closing Law Cases* is striking not only because of the similarity of the results in the cases, but also because of the similarity in doctrinal approach. One can take the view that this unity in method and result indicates that American constitutionalism is having a very great impact on the Supreme Court of Canada. This impact would be remarkable in view of the great structural differences in the constitutionalisms of the two countries. A more intriguing, although unprovable, conclusion would be to say simply that, in an area such as Sunday legislation, commonly shared social attitudes are more important than constitutional principles.

A further observation that can be drawn from this short study is that judicial analysis in both countries rejects an interpretation conceding religious motivation for Sunday legislation at the precise point at which acceptance would require invalidation of the legislation. In Canada we are told purpose and effect must be distinguished. The purpose of the Lord's Day Act is concededly religious, but we are assured the effect is entirely secular. In the United States, rejection of a theory of religious motivation begins at an earlier stage and both purpose and effect are held to be predominantly secular. The similarity in result reached suggests that the prevailing judicial tests for measuring whether Sunday legislation offends religious freedom are rather clearly expeditious.

Disparities in legal doctrine, it appears, are trivial in comparison to the overriding realities of social fact; and the dominant social fact is apparently that Sunday laws are a desired breed of legislation on this continent, with the two Supreme Courts being responsive to that reality. . . .

. . . .

## D.  RELIGIOUS NEUTRALITY IN A PLURALIST SOCIETY: SCHOOLS AND TAX EXEMPTIONS

### ENGEL v. VITALE
Supreme Court of the United States
370 U.S. 421, 8 L. Ed. 2d 601, 82 S. Ct. 1261 (1962)

Justice BLACK delivered the opinion of the Court.

The respondent Board of Education of Union Free School District No. 9, New Hyde Park, New York, acting in its official capacity under state law, directed the School District's principal to cause the following prayer to be said aloud by each class in the presence of a teacher at the beginning of each school day:

"Almighty God, we acknowledge our dependence upon Thee, and we beg Thy blessings upon us, our parents, our teachers and our country."

This daily procedure was adopted on the recommendation of the State Board of Regents, a governmental agency. . . . These state officials composed the prayer which they recommended and published as a part of their "Statement on Moral and Spiritual Training in the Schools," . . .

[T]he parents of ten pupils brought this action in a New York State Court insisting that use of this official prayer in the public schools was contrary to the beliefs, religions, or religious practices of both themselves and their children. . . . The New York Court of Appeals, . . . sustained an order of the lower state courts which had upheld the power of New York to use the Regents' prayer as a part of the daily procedures of its public schools so long as the schools did not compel any pupil to join in the prayer over his or his parents' objection. . . .

The petitioners contend among other things that the state laws requiring or permitting use of the Regents' prayer must be struck down as a violation of the Establishment Clause. . . . We agree with that contention since we think that the constitutional prohibition against laws respecting an establishment of religion must at least mean that in this country it is no part of the business of government to compose official prayers for any group of the American people to recite as a part of a religious program carried on by government.

. . . .

There can be no doubt that New York's state prayer program officially establishes the religious beliefs embodied in the Regents' prayer. . . . Neither the fact that the prayer may be denominationally neutral, nor the fact that its observance on the part of the students is voluntary can serve to free it from the limitations of the Establishment Clause, as it might from the Free Exercise Clause, of the First Amendment, both of which are operative against the States by virtue of the Fourteenth Amendment. Although these two clauses may in certain instances overlap, they forbid two quite different kinds of governmental encroachment upon religious freedom. The Establishment Clause, unlike the Free Exercise Clause, does not depend upon any showing of direct governmental compulsion and is violated by the enactment of laws which establish an official religion whether those laws operate directly to coerce nonobserving individuals or not. This is not to say, of course, that laws officially prescribing a particular form of religious worship do not involve coercion of such individuals. When the power, prestige and financial support of government is placed behind a particular religious belief, the indirect coercive pressure upon religious minorities to conform to the prevailing officially approved religion is plain. But the purposes underlying the Establishment Clause go much further than that. Its first and most immediate purpose rested on the belief that a union of government and religion tends to destroy government and to degrade religion. . . . Another purpose of the Establishment Clause rested upon an awareness of the historical fact that governmentally established religions and religious persecutions go hand in hand. . . . It was in large part to get completely away from this sort of systematic religious persecution that the Founders brought into being our Nation, our Constitution, and our Bill of Rights with its prohibition against any governmental establishment of religion. The New York laws officially prescribing the Regents' prayer are inconsistent with both the purposes of the Establishment Clause and with the Establishment Clause itself.

Justice FRANKFURTER took no part in the decision of this case.

Justice WHITE took no part in the consideration or decision of this case.

[Justice STEWART's dissenting opinion is omitted.]

## NOTES

1. Professor Milton Konvitz has summarized the *Engel* case as holding, among other things, that it makes no difference how innocuous a religious act is: if it is sponsored by government for essentially religious reasons, it constitutes an establishment. *See* M. KONVITZ, EXPANDING LIBERTIES: FREEDOM'S GAINS IN POST-WAR AMERICA 25 (1966).

Justice Douglas, somewhat mischievously, exploited this dimension of *Engel* when he suggested, in a concurring opinion, that even the announcement of the bailiff and the opening of the Supreme Court—"God Save the United States and this Honorable Court"—might be unconstitutional. In the *Schempp* case, which followed *Engel* by a year, the Supreme Court went out of its way to rebut Douglas' effort to put any reference to God outside of the constitutional pale. What difference can you see between forcing everyone to stand in the Supreme Court as the bailiff asks for God's blessing on the United States and the Supreme Court and a compulsory school prayer from which school children can be excused at their request?

2. One thing about *Engel* that should be stressed was the intense unpopularity that greeted it. Critics of the decision included such disparate types as Billy Graham, Cardinal Spellman, and President Eisenhower. Congressional reaction was extremely critical although few criticisms were as harsh as that made by Congressman Andrews of Alabama that the Supreme Court had "put the Negroes in the schools and now they've driven God out." *See* R. TRESOLINI, THESE LIBERTIES: CASE STUDIES IN CIVIL RIGHTS 216-217 (1968).

As you read the report of the *Schempp* case, try to identify those portions of *Schempp* where the Justices seems anxious to explain away portions of *Engel*.

### SCHOOL DIST. OF ABINGTON TOWNSHIP v. SCHEMPP, NO. 142

#### MURRAY v. CURLETT, NO. 119
Supreme Court of the United States
374 U.S. 203, 10 L. Ed. 2d 844, 83 S. Ct. 1560 (1963)

[In the *Schempp* case, the Court held that the first amendment's freedom of religion guarantee banned state ordained prayer even if the prayers involved were not state composed. Pennsylvania law had required that ten verses from the Bible should be read at the beginning of the day in every public school. The Pennsylvania law provided that a child could be excused from the Bible reading upon the "written request of his parent on each school day." The Supreme Court held that the establishment clause invalidated the Pennsylvania statute. A companion case held invalid a Baltimore school rule which provides for the reading without comment of either a chapter from the Bible or the Lord's Prayer. Murray v. Curlett, 374 U.S. 203 (1963).

[The student reading the *Schempp* case should watch for signs to see if the Court is in any way trying to retreat in *Schempp* from the rigor of its anti-establishment position in *Engel*. Is there any significance in the fact that in *Schempp* the majority decision was written by Justice Clark, a Protestant, with supporting concurring opinions by Justice Brennan, a Roman Catholic, and Justice Goldberg, a Jew? Besides the political significance of this batting line-up, are there not indications in the opinion that the Court is anxious to soften the criticisms that greeted *Engel* that the Court was making a religion of secularism and Godlessness?]

Justice CLARK delivered the opinion of the Court.

. . . .

The wholesome "neutrality" of which this Court's cases speak . . . stems from a recognition of the teachings of history that powerful sects or groups might bring about a fusion of governmental and religious functions or a concert or dependency of one upon the other to the end that official support of the State or Federal Government would be placed behind the tenets of one or of all orthodoxies. This the Establishment Clause prohibits. And a further reason for neutrality is found in the Free Exercise Clause, which recognizes the value of religious training, teaching and observance and, more particularly, the right of every person to freely choose his own course with reference thereto, free of any compulsion from the state. This the Free Exercise Clause guarantees. Thus, as we have seen, the two clauses may overlap. . . . [T]he Establishment Clause has been directly considered by this Court eight times in the past score of years and, with only one Justice dissenting on the point, it has consistently held that the clause withdrew all legislative power respecting religious belief or the expression thereof. The test may be stated as follows: what are the purpose and the primary effect of the enactment? If either is the advancement or inhibition of religion then the enactment exceeds the scope of legislative power as circumscribed by the Constitution. That is to say that to withstand the strictures of the Establishment Clause there must be a secular legislative purpose and a primary effect that neither advances nor inhibits religion. *Everson v. Board of Education; McGowan v. Maryland*. The Free Exercise Clause, likewise considered many times here, withdraws from legislative power, state and federal, the exertion of any restraint on the free exercise of religion. Its purpose is to secure religious liberty in the individual by prohibiting any invasions thereof by civil authority. Hence it is necessary in a free exercise case for one to show the coercive effect of the enactment as it operates against him in the practice of his religion. The distinction between the two clauses is apparent—a violation of the Free Exercise Clause is predicated on coercion while the Establishment Clause violation need not be so attended.

Applying the Establishment Clause principles to the cases at bar we find that the States are requiring the selection and reading at the opening of the school day of verses from the Holy Bible and the recitation of the Lord's Prayer by the students in unison. These exercises are prescribed as part of the curricular activities of students who are required by law to attend school. They are held in the school buildings under the supervision and with the participation of teachers employed in those schools. None of these factors, other than compulsory school attendance, was present in the program upheld in *Zorach v. Clauson.* The trial court in No. 142 has found that such an opening exercise is a religious ceremony and was intended by the State to be so. We agree with the trial court's finding as to the religious character of the exercises. Given that finding the exercises and the law requiring them are in violation of the Establishment Clause.

There is no such specific finding as to the religious character of the exercises in No. 119, and the State contends (as does the State in No. 142) that the program is an effort to extend its benefits to all public school children without regard to their religious belief. Included within its secular purposes, it says, are the promotion of moral values, the contradiction to the materialistic trends of our times, the perpetuation of our institutions and the teaching of literature. The case came up on demurrer, of course, to a petition which alleged that the uniform practice under the rule had been to read from the King James version of the Bible and that the exercise was sectarian. The short answer, therefore, is that the religious character of the exercise was admitted by the State. But even if its purpose is not strictly religious, it is sought to be accomplished through readings, without comment, from the Bible. Surely the place of the Bible as an instrument of religion cannot be gainsaid, and the State's recognition of the pervading religious character of the ceremony is evident from the rule's specific permission of the alternative use of the Catholic Douay version as well as the recent amendment permitting nonattendance at the exercises. None of these factors is consistent with the contention that the Bible is here used either as an instrument for nonreligious moral inspiration or as a reference for the teaching of secular subjects.

The conclusion follows that in both cases the laws require religious exercises and such exercises are being conducted in direct violation of the rights of the appellees and petitioners. Nor are these required exercises mitigated by the fact that individual students may absent themselves upon parental request, for that fact furnishes no defense to a claim of unconstitutionality under the Establishment Clause. See *Engel v. Vitale.* Further, it is no defense to urge that the religious practices here may be relatively minor encroachments on the First Amendment. The breach of neutrality that is today a trickling stream may all too soon become a raging torrent and, in the words of Madison, "it is proper to take alarm at the first experiment on our liberties." Memorial and Remonstrance Against Religious Assessments.

It is insisted that unless these religious exercises are permitted a "religion of secularism" is established in the schools. We agree of course that the State may not establish a "religion of secularism" in the sense of affirmatively opposing or showing hostility to religion, thus "preferring those who believe in no religion over those who do believe." We do not agree, however, that this decision in any sense has that effect. In addition, it might well be said that one's education is not complete without a study of comparative religion or the history of religion and its relationship to the advancement of civilization. It certainly may be said that the Bible is worthy of study for its literary and historic qualities. Nothing we have said here indicates that such study of the Bible or of religion, when presented objectively as part of a secular program of education, may not be effected consistent with the First Amendment. But the exercises here do not fall into those categories. They are religious exercises, required by the States in violation of the command of the First Amendment that the Government maintain strict neutrality, neither aiding nor opposing religion.

Finally, we cannot accept that the concept of neutrality, which does not permit a State to require a religious exercise even with the consent of the majority of those affected, collides with the majority's right to free exercise of religion. While the Free Exercise Clause clearly prohibits the use of state action to deny the rights of free exercise to *anyone,* it has never meant that a majority could use the machinery of the State to practice its beliefs. . . .

. . . .

Judgment in No. 142 affirmed; judgment in No. 119 reversed and cause remanded with directions.

[Justice STEWART dissenting.]

. . . .

To be specific, it seems to me clear that certain types of exercises would present situations in which no possibility of coercion on the part of secular officials could be claimed to exist. Thus, if such exercises were held either before or after the official school day, or if the school schedule were such that participation were merely one among a number of desirable alternatives, it could hardly be contended that the exercises did anything more than to provide an opportunity for the voluntary expression of religious belief. On the other hand, a law which provided for religious exercises during the school day and which contained no excusal provision would obviously be unconstitutionally coercive upon those who did not wish to participate. And even under a law containing an excusal provision, if the exercises were held during the school day, and no equally desirable alternative were provided by the school authorities, the likelihood that children might be under at least some psychological compulsion to participate would be great. In a case such as the latter, however, I think we would err if we *assumed* such coercion in the absence of any evidence.

Viewed in this light, it seems to me clear that the records in both of the cases before us are wholly inadequate to support an informed or responsible decision. . . . There is no evidence in either case as to whether there would exist any coercion of any kind upon a student who did not want to participate. No evidence at all was adduced in the *Murray* case, because it was decided upon a demurrer. . . . In the *Schempp* case the record shows no more than a subjective prophecy by a parent of what he thought would happen if a request were made to be excused from participation in the exercises under the amended statute. No such request was ever made, and there is no evidence whatever as to what might or would actually happen, nor of what administrative arrangements the school actually might or could make to free from pressure of any kind those who do not want to participate in the exercises. . . .

. . . It is conceivable that these school boards, or even all school boards, might eventually find it impossible to administer a system of religious exercises during school hours in such a way as to meet this constitutional standard—in such a way as completely to free from any kind of official coercion those who do not affirmatively want to participate. But I think we must not assume that school boards so lack the qualities of inventiveness and good will as to make impossible the achievement of that goal.

I would remand both cases for further hearing.

## NOTES

1. Isn't Justice Brennan right when he says in a concurring opinion that excusal or exemption has no relevance to the establishment question? If the state is giving aid or encouragement to religion, the establishment clause is violated per se whether or not the state permits objecting students to excuse themselves from having to participate in that aid and encouragement.

2. Does the court say flatly in *Schempp* that a procedure for excusal of the dissenting child will be unavailing to free a school system from a free exercise violation charge as a matter of *free exercise* doctrine? Justice Stewart thought that group pressure to participate on the nonconforming child could amount to coercion but thought the records were too inadequate in both *Murray* and *Schempp* to pass on the question of coercion. Dean Erwin Griswold has suggested that for a "minority" child to participate in religious exercise desired by the majority may not involve anything more than a decent respect for the sensibilities of the majority. *See* Griswold, *Absolute is in the Dark: A Discussion of the Approach of the Supreme Court to Constitutional Questions,* 8 UTAH L. REV. 167 (1963): "When the prayer (in a public school) is recited, if the (minority) child or his parents feel that he cannot participate, he may stand or sit, in respectful attention, while the other children take part in the ceremony. Or he may leave the room. It is said this . . . sets him apart . . . (and involves) an element of compulsion. . . ." But Griswold asks: "Is this the way it should be looked at? The child of nonconforming or minority group is, to be sure, different in his beliefs. That is what it means to be a member of a minority. Is it not desirable . . . for him to learn . . . not so much that he is different, as that other children are different from him? . . . No compulsion is put upon him. He need not participate. But he, too, has the opportunity to be tolerant. He allows the majority of the group to follow their own tradition, perhaps coming to understand and to respect what they feel is significant to them."

Justice Stewart speaks of the free exercise rights of the majority in *Schempp* as being worthy of protection. Is Dean Griswold sounding a similar theme in the above-quoted excerpt? But isn't the point of the establishment clause to forbid exactly that kind of government protection for the free exercise rights of the majority of which Griswold and Justice Stewart are speaking?

Of course, it may be said, as Justice Stewart argues, that if government may do nothing to make free exercise possible in public institutions such as the public schools then we have a governmentally-ordained "religion of secularism." But is the establishment clause the constitutional provision which would prohibit a "religion of secularism"? If it is not, does it make any sense to say, as Justice Stewart does, that the rule in *Schempp* creates a religion of secularism. If a religion of secularism were in fact affirmatively encouraged by government, as, say, atheism has been encouraged in the Soviet Union, it is the free speech and free press clauses which government would have infringed rather than the establishment clause.

3.  Professor Dixon in a thorough article which comprehensively analyzes American constitutional doctrine on church state relations says that the theme which emerges from *Schempp* is "a principle of 'neutrality' in regard to governmental relationships with religion." Dixon, *Religion, Schools, and the Open Society: A Socio-Constitutional Issue*, 13 J. PUB. L. 247, 297 (1964). But Dixon suggests that the "neutrality" principle of *Schempp* is overly simple: "There is no indication that Mr. Justice Clark or the majority (in *Schempp*) intended by their 'neutrality' concept to endorse inclusion of religious institutions in programs of general aid to education. Mr. Justice Douglas' concurrence contained an explicit and strong warning against using public funds to promote religious exercises and seemed to confine his *Engel* dictum that he would vote 'no' on *Everson* today. And yet a simple 'neutrality' principle would seem to leave no basis for objecting to such an inclusion, because to consider the religious character of an institution as a basis for confining the aid program would be a nonneutral act."

Dixon offers the following critique of the court's "secular purpose" and "primary effect" test for legislation: "It would seem, however, that the text . . . would raise serious doubts regarding monetary aid and many varieties of nonmonetary aid to parochial schools. The aids most frequently discussed do advance the parochial school program, and hence religion, else they would not be demanded in the first instance. It would be anomalous to use a concededly religious instrument as a means of achieving a 'secular legislative purpose.' And starting from a premise of an open society and tolerance promoted by frequent contact, it is doubtful that the major trend to segregate many children into parochial schools, if further encouraged by public aid, could be classified as a 'primary effect' that does not advance religion."

4.  What has the impact of *Engel* and *Schempp* actually been? Reich, *Schoolhouse Religion and the Supreme Court: A Report On Attitudes of Teachers and Principals on School Practices In Wisconsin and Ohio*, 23 J. LEGAL ED. 1 (1971), reports on his findings on compliance with respect to school prayer and Bible

reading as obtained from a questionnaire sent to public school teachers and principals in Ohio and Wisconsin. Illustrative are Reich's findings with respect to the prevalence of school prayer *after Engel:* "Prescribed prayer falls within the Court's ban. Its incidence in Wisconsin is small, but not negligible; three per-cent of the Wisconsin respondents (11 persons) report that it is required or permitted and done. The number of Wisconsin re-spondents who report a prohibition is slightly lower than in the cases of Bible reading and the Lord's Prayer. In Ohio prescribed prayer is reported considerably less frequently than Bible read-ing or the Lord's Prayer and more respondents say it is pro-hibited. Slightly over 15 percent of the Ohio respondents say it is permitted and done and about 42 percent report a prohibition on it."

Reich concludes: "The changes that have occurred, in very large part, have been changes in practices rather than changes in formal policy. In Ohio schools, where the potential impact of the decisions was high, the burden of the decision about classroom practices and the interpretation of the mood of the community apparently have been left in most cases to the classroom teacher. Given that pattern of decision making, there very probably will be a history of compliance following the school-prayer decisions similar to that for the released-time decisions. . . . Given the strong capacity for persistence that inheres in traditional forms of social behavior, there probably is an irreducible minimum of religious practices in the public schools. The social and po-litical costs of achieving full compliance undoubtedly would far outweigh any benefits that might be supposed to accrue." *See* S. WASBY, THE IMPACT OF THE UNITED STATES SUPREME COURT: SOME PERSPECTIVES 126-35 (1970); Birkby, *The Supreme Court and the Bible Belt: Tennessee Reaction to the "Schempp" Decision,* in THE IMPACT OF SUPREME COURT DECISIONS 110 (2d ed.; Becker & Feeley eds., 1973).

### LEMON v. KURTZMAN
Supreme Court of the United States
403 U.S. 602, 29 L. Ed. 2d 745, 91 S. Ct. 2105 (1971)

Chief Justice BURGER delivered the opinion of the Court.

These two appeals raise questions as to Pennsylvania and Rhode Island statutes providing state aid to church-related ele-mentary and secondary schools. . . .

. . . .

## The Rhode Island Statute

The Rhode Island Salary Supplement Act . . . authorizes state officials to supplement the salaries of teachers of secular subjects in nonpublic elementary schools by paying directly to a teacher an amount not in excess of 15% of his current annual salary. As supplemented, however, a nonpublic school teacher's salary cannot exceed the maximum paid to teachers in the State's public schools, and the recipient must be certified by the state board of education in substantially the same manner as public school teachers.

. . . .

The Act also requires that teachers eligible for salary supplement must teach only those subjects that are offered in the State's public schools. They must use "only teaching materials which are used in the public schools." Finally, any teacher applying for a salary supplement must first agree in writing "not to teach a course in religion for so long as or during such time as he or she receives any salary supplements" under the Act.

. . . .

The District Court concluded that the Act violated the Establishment Clause, holding that it fostered "excessive entanglement" between government and religion. In addition two judges thought that the Act had the impermissible effect of giving "significant aid to a religious enterprise." We affirm.

## The Pennsylvania Statute

. . . .

[The Pennsylvania Nonpublic Elementary and Secondary Education Act] authorizes appellee state Superintendent of Public Instruction to "purchase" specified "secular educational services" from nonpublic schools. Under the "contracts" authorized by the statute, the State directly reimburses nonpublic schools solely for their actual expenditures for teachers' salaries, textbooks, and instructional materials. A school seeking reimbursement must maintain prescribed accounting procedures that identify the "separate" cost of the "secular educational service."

. . .

There are several significant statutory restrictions on state aid. Reimbursement is limited to courses "presented in the curricula of the public schools." It is further limited "solely" to courses in the following "secular" subjects: mathematics, modern foreign languages, physical science, and physical education. Textbooks and instructional materials included in the program must be approved by the state Superintendent of Public Instruction.

Finally, the statute prohibits reimbursement for any course that contains "any subject matter expressing religious teaching, or the morals or forms of worship of any sect."

. . . .

[A three-judge federal court] held that the Act violated neither the Establishment nor the Free Exercise Clauses. . . . We reverse.

. . . .

Every analysis in this area must begin with consideration of the cumulative criteria developed by the Court over many years. Three such tests may be gleaned from our cases. First, the statute must have a secular legislative purpose; second, its principal or primary effect must be one that neither advances nor inhibits religion, finally, the statute must not foster "an excessive government entanglement with religion."

Inquiry into the legislative purposes of the Pennsylvania and Rhode Island statutes affords no basis for a conclusion that the legislative intent was to advance religion. . . .

. . . .

The two legislatures, however, have . . . recognized that church-related elementary and secondary schools have a significant religious mission and that a substantial portion of their activities are religiously oriented. They have therefore sought to create statutory restrictions designed to guarantee the separation between secular and religious educational functions and to ensure that State financial aid supports only the former. All these provisions are precautions taken in candid recognition that these programs approached, even if they did not intrude upon the forbidden areas under the Religion Clauses. We need not decide whether these legislative precautions restrict the principal or primary effect of the programs to the point where they do not offend the Religion Clauses, for we conclude that the cumulative impact of the entire relationship arising under the statutes in each State involves excessive entanglement between government and religion.

. . . .

The District Court made extensive findings on the grave potential for excessive entanglement that inheres in the religious character and purpose of the Roman Catholic elementary schools of Rhode Island, to date the sole beneficiaries of the Rhode Island Salary Supplement Act.

. . . .

. . . [T]he District Court concluded that the parochial schools constituted "an integral part of the religious mission of the

Catholic Church." This process of inculcating religious doctrine is, of course, enhanced by the impressionable age of the pupils, in primary schools particularly. In short, parochial schools involve substantial religious activity and purpose.

. . . .

In [Board of Educ. v. Allen, 392 U.S. 236 (1968)] the Court refused to make assumptions, on a meager record, about the religious content of the textbooks that the State would be asked to provide. We cannot, however, refuse here to recognize that teachers have a substantially different ideological character than books. In terms of potential for involving some aspect of faith or morals in secular subjects, a textbook's content is ascertainable, but a teacher's handling of a subject is not. We cannot ignore the dangers that a teacher under religious control and discipline poses to the separation of the religious from the purely secular aspects of precollege education. The conflict of functions inheres in the situation

In our view the record shows these dangers are present to a substantial degree. . . . With only two exceptions, school principals are nuns appointed either by the Superintendent or the Mother Provincial of the order whose members staff the school. By 1969 lay teachers constituted more than a third of all teachers in the parochial elementary schools, and their number is growing. . . .

. . . .

Several teachers testified, however, that they did not inject religion into their secular classes. And the District Court found that religious values did not necessarily affect the content of the secular instruction. But what has been recounted suggests the potential if not actual hazards of this form of state aid. . . .

We need not and do not assume that teachers in parochial schools will be guilty of bad faith or any conscious design to evade the limitations imposed by the statute and the First Amendment. We simply recognize that a dedicated religious person, teaching in a school affiliated with his or her faith and operated to inculcate its tenets, will inevitably experience great difficulty in remaining religiously neutral. . . . What would appear to some to be essential to good citizenship might well for others border on or constitute instruction in religion. . . .

. . . But the potential for impermissible fostering of religion is present. The Rhode Island Legislature has not, and could not, provide state aid on the basis of a mere assumption that secular teachers under religious discipline can avoid conflicts. The State must be certain, given the Religion Clauses, that subsidized teachers do not inculcate religion—indeed the State here has undertaken to do so. . . .

A comprehensive, discriminating, and continuing state surveillance will inevitably be required to ensure that these restrictions are obeyed and the First Amendment otherwise respected. Unlike a book, a teacher cannot be inspected once so as to determine the extent and intent of his or her personal beliefs and subjective acceptance of the limitations imposed by the First Amendment. These prophylactic contacts will involve excessive and enduring entanglement between state and church.

There is another area of entanglement in the Rhode Island program that gives concern. The statute excludes teachers employed by nonpublic schools whose average per-pupil expenditures on secular education exceed the comparable figures for public schools. In the event that the total expenditures of an otherwise eligible school exceed this norm, the program requires the government to examine the school's records in order to determine how much of the total expenditures are attributable to secular education and how much to religious activity. This kind of state inspection and evaluation of the religious content of a religious organization is fraught with the sort of entanglement that the Constitution forbids. It is a relationship pregnant with dangers of excessive government direction of church schools and hence of churches. . . .

The Pennsylvania statute also provides state aid to church-related schools for teachers' salaries. The complaint describes an educational system that is very similar to the one existing in Rhode Island. . . .

. . . .

The Pennsylvania statute, moreover, has the further defect of providing state financial aid directly to the church-related schools. This factor distinguishes both *Everson* and *Allen,* for in both those cases the Court was careful to point out that state aid was provided to the student and his parents—not to the church-related school. . . . The history of government grants of a continuing cash subsidy indicates that such programs have almost always been accompanied by varying measures of control and surveillance. The government cash grants before us now provide no basis for predicting that comprehensive measures of surveillance and controls will not follow. In particular the government's post-audit power to inspect and evaluate a church-related school's financial records and to determine which expenditures are religious and which are secular creates an intimate and continuing relationship between church and state.

A broader base of entanglement of yet a different character is presented by the devisive political potential of these state programs. In a community where such a large number of pupils are served by church-related schools, it can be assumed that state assistance will entail considerable political activity. Partisans of parochial schools, understandably concerned with rising costs and sincerely dedicated to both the religious and secular educational missions of their schools, will inevitably champion this cause and promote political action to achieve their goals. Those who oppose state aid, whether for constitutional, religious, or fiscal reasons, will inevitably respond and employ all of the usual political campaign techniques to prevail.

Ordinarily political debate and division, however vigorous or even partisan, are normal and healthy manifestations of our democratic system of government, but political division along religious lines was one of the principal evils against which the First Amendment was intended to protect. . . .

. . . .

In [Walz v. Tax Comm'n, 397 U.S. 664 (1970)] it was argued that a tax exemption for places of religious worship would prove to be the first step in an inevitable progression leading to the establishment of state churches and state religion. That claim could not stand up against more than 200 years of virtually universal practice imbedded in our colonial experience and continuing into the present.

The progression argument, however, is more persuasive here. We have no long history of state aid to church-related educational institutions comparable to 200 years of tax exemption for churches. Indeed, the state programs before us today represent something of an innovation. We have already noted that modern governmental programs have self-perpetuating and self-expanding propensities. . . . The dangers are increased by the difficulty of perceiving in advance exactly where the "verge" of the precipice lies. As well as constituting an independent evil against which the Religion Clauses were intended to protect, involvement or entanglement between government and religion serves as a warning signal.

. . . .

The decision of the Rhode Island District Court is affirmed. The decision of the Pennsylvania District Court is reversed. . . .

[Justice WHITE's dissent in the Rhode Island case is noted below.]

---

In Tilton v. Richardson, 403 U.S. 672 (1971), decided at the same time as *Lemon,* the court considered the constitutionality of Title I of the Higher Education Facilities Act of 1963, 20 U.S.C. §§ 701-758, "which provides construction grants for buildings and facilities used exclusively for secular educational purposes." Under the statute no facility constructed by funds allocated under it could be used for "sectarian worship," or for activities "primarily in connection with any part of the program of a school or department of divinity," or for "religious worship."

The fundamental constitutional question raised by the statute was whether church-related colleges and universities could constitutionally receive federal construction grants under Title I. Connecticut taxpayers brought suit in federal district court against the federal officials who administered the statute as well as four church-related colleges and universities receiving funds under Title I. The three-judge court sustained the statute on the ground that it promoted religion neither in purpose nor in effect. In an opinion for the court joined by Justices Harlan, Stewart, and Blackmun, Chief Justice Burger concluded that "the Act does not violate the Religion Clauses of the First Amendment except that part of § 754 (b) (2) providing a 20-year limitation on the religious use restrictions contained in § 751 (a) (2)."

With the exception of the 20-year provision, the court held that federal aid to church-related colleges and universities under the Higher Education Act of 1963 was constitutional. The court used four tests to decide the validity of the application of the statute to church-related institutions:

> First, does the Act reflect a secular legislative purpose? Second, is the primary effect of the Act to advance or inhibit religion? Third, does the administration of the Act foster an excessive government entanglement with religion? Fourth, does the implementation of the Act inhibit the free exercise of religion?

The court found, applying each one of these tests, that the statute did not violate the religion clauses.

The court distinguished Lemon v. Kurtzman, 403 U.S. 602 (1971), on these grounds. First, impressionable children in primary and secondary schools were more likely to be permeated by religion. The court reasoned that religious indoctrination was a less substantial purpose of church-related colleges than was the case with religiously sponsored primary and secondary schools. Second, the court reasoned that the facilities provided under the statute in *Tilton* were religiously neutral and therefore government surveillance was less necessary. Third, the federal aid here was dispensed on a one-shot basis greatly reducing the need for continuing federal inspection. (Obviously, in the court's judgment, these factors helped to reduce the potentialities for government entanglement with religion.)

The provision in the Act that a facility constructed under the Act could be used for religious purposes after the 20-year period was held to trespass on the religious clauses. If, after 20 years, a college building used for secular instruction could be converted into a chapel, "the original federal grant will in part have the effect of advancing religion." By invalidating just one provision of the Higher Education Facilities Act of 1963, the Court gave an illustration of its so-called "savings" construction approach, *i.e.,* saving as much of the challenged statute as possible. The circumstances of the invalidity of the reversion provision did not require the invalidity of the whole statute. This was so, said the court, even though there was no express severability provision in the Act. (In what circumstances would a court be *required* to invalidate a whole statute because of the invalidity of a single provision in it? *See* Champlin Ref. Co. v. Corporation Comm'n of Oklahoma, 286 U.S. 210, 234 (1932).)

Justice WHITE, concurring in part and dissenting in part stated in *Tilton:*

. . . .

It is enough for me that the States are financing a separable secular function of overriding importance in order to sustain the legislation here challenged. That religion and private interests other than education may substantially benefit does not convert these laws into impermissible establishments of religion.

It is unnecessary, therefore, to urge that the Free Exercise Clause of the First Amendment at least permits government in some respects to modify and mould its secular programs out of express concern for free exercise values. . . . The Establishment Clause, however, coexists in the First Amendment with the Free Exercise Clause and the latter is surely relevant in cases such as these. Where a state program seeks to ensure the proper education of its young, in private as well as public schools, free exercise considerations at least counsel against refusing support for students attending parochial schools simply because in that setting they are also being instructed in the tenets of the faith they are constitutionally free to practice.

I would sustain both the federal and the Rhode Island programs at issue in these cases. Although I would also reject the facial challenge to the Pennsylvania statute, I concur in the judgment for the reasons given below.

The Court strikes down the Rhode Island statute on its face.
. . .

. . . .

. . . The Court points to nothing in this record indicating that any participating teacher had inserted religion into his secular teaching or had had any difficulty in avoiding doing so. The testimony of the teachers was quite the contrary. . . .

Secondly, the Court accepts the model for the Catholic elementary and secondary schools that it rejected for the Catholic universities or colleges in the *Tilton* case. There it was urged that the Catholic condition of higher learning was an integral part of the religious mission of the church and that these institutions did everything they could to foster the faith. The Court's response was that on the record before it none of the involved institutions was shown to have complied with the model and that it would not purport to pass on cases not before it. Here, however, the Court strikes down this Rhode Island statute based primarily on its own model and its own suppositions and unsupported views of what is likely to happen in Rhode Island parochial school classrooms, although on this record there is no indication that entanglement difficulties will accompany the salary supplement program.

The Court thus creates an insoluble paradox for the State and the parochial schools. The State cannot finance secular instruction if it permits religion to be taught in the same classroom; but if it exacts a promise that religion not be so taught—a promise the school and its teachers are quite willing and on this record able to give—and enforces it, it is then entangled in the "no entanglement" aspect of the Court's Establishment Clause jurisprudence.

Why the federal program in the *Tilton* case is not embroiled with the same difficulties is never adequately explained. Surely the notion that college students are more mature and resistant to indoctrination is a make-weight, for the Court in *Tilton* is careful to note the federal condition on funding and the enforcement mechanism available. If religious teaching in federally financed buildings was permitted, the powers of resistance of college students would in no way save the federal scheme. Nor can I imagine on what basis the Court finds college clerics more reliable in keeping promises than their counterparts in elementary and secondary schools—particularly those in the Rhode Island case, since within five years the majority of teachers in Rhode Island parochial schools will be lay persons, with many of them being non-Catholic.

. . . .

The District Court also focused on the recurring nature of state payments; salaries must be supplemented and money appropriated every year and hence the opportunity for controversy and friction over state aid to religious schools will constantly remain before the State. The majority adopts this theme and makes much of the fact that under the federal scheme the grant to a religious institution is a one-time matter. But this argument is without real force. It is apparent that federal interest in any grant will be a continuing one since the conditions attached to the grant must be enforced. More important, the federal grant program is an ongoing one. The same grant will not be repeated, but new ones to the same or different schools will be made year after year. Thus the same potential for recurring political controversy accompanies the federal program. . . .

With respect to Pennsylvania, the Court, accepting as true the factual allegations of the complaint, as it must for purposes of a motion to dismiss, would reverse the dismissal of the complaint and invalidate the legislation. . . . From these allegations the Court concludes that forbidden entanglements would follow from enforcing compliance with the secular purpose for which the state money is being paid.

. . . I would no more here than in the Rhode Island case substitute presumption for proof that religion is or would be taught in state financed secular courses or assume that enforcement measures would be so extensive as to border on a free exercise violation. We should not forget that the Pennsylvania statute does not compel church schools to accept state funds. I cannot hold that the First Amendment forbids an agreement between the school and the State that the state funds would be used only to teach secular subjects.

I do agree, however, that the complaint should not have been dismissed for failure to state a cause of action. Although it did not specifically allege that the schools involved mixed religious teaching with secular subjects, the complaint did allege that the schools were operated to fulfill religious purposes and one of the legal theories stated in the complaint was that the Pennsylvania Act "finances and participates in the blending of sectarian and secular instruction." At trial under this complaint, evidence showing such a blend in a course supported by state funds would appear to be admissible and if credited would establish financing of religious instruction by the State. . . .

Justice DOUGLAS, joined by BLACK and MARSHALL dissented. Agreeing that the reversion provision was properly held unconstitutional, the dissenters argued that government will have to watch over a building for its useful life if the Court's mandate is to be observed. This surveillance will violate the Free Exercise clause: "Could a course in the History of Methodism be taught in a federally financed building? . . . How can the Government know what is taught in the federally financed building without a continuing auditing of classroom instruction?"

Beyond the possibly fatal consequences of the reversion provision, the dissenters thought that it was impossible to distinguish between sectarian and secular instruction in a church-related institution. Federal aid to such an institution violates the Establishment clause:

> Money saved from one item in the budget is free to be used elsewhere. By conducting religious services in another building, the school has—rent free—a building for nonsectarian use. . . .

Justice BRENNAN concurred in the Rhode Island case, believed that the judgment in the Pennsylvania case should be reversed outright and dissented in *Tilton*.

---

## NOTES

1. In Hunt v. McNair, 413 U.S. 734 (1973), the court relying on *Tilton*, upheld a South Carolina statute which authorized aid to higher educational institutions in the state through the use of tax exempt bonds. The statute precluded a grant of aid to a project which included buildings used for religious purposes. The case arose out of a taxpayer suit challenging the constitutionality of the statute insofar as it authorized the issuance of bonds for the benefit of the Baptist College of Charleston. The Supreme Court sustained the statute and held that the taxpayer had failed to show that the college was "an instrument of religious indoctrination." The court pointed out that only 60 per cent of the student body was Baptist and there were no religious qualifications for faculty membership or student admission.

2. In 1973, the court invalidated three New York laws which provided financial assistance to *nonpublic* elementary and secondary schools. Committee for Public Educ. v. Nyquist, 413 U.S. 756 (1973). One statutory program gave grants to nonprofit schools primarily serving low income families for the maintenance and repair of school facilities and equipment in the interest of health, welfare, and safety of the pupils. There was a requirement in the program that the money grants to nonpublic qualifying schools could not exceed 50 per cent of the comparable expenses in the public school system.

The court, per Justice Powell, held the program invalid.
There was no attempt, the court objected, to restrict the payments to "those expenditures related to the upkeep of facilities
used exclusively for secular purposes, nor do we think it possible
within the context of these religion oriented institutions to impose such restrictions." Powell concluded that the New York
law, described above, has a "primary effect that advances religion." The court declared that "a mere statistical judgment
would not suffice as a guarantee that state funds will not be
used to finance religious education." Powell speculated that
under such a "loose standard of scrutiny" a state might "openly
subsidize parochial schools."

A second state program which would have permitted "direct,
unrestricted grants of $50.00 to $100 per child (but not more
than 50 per cent of tuition actually paid) as reimbursement to
parents in low-income brackets who send their children to nonpublic schools" was also invalidated. The court held that these
grants failed to give any assurance that state financial aid would
support only secular as opposed to religious educational functions.

The state argued that the program should be held valid
because it is designed to promote the free exercise of religion
without state assistance. New York argued that the right of "low
income" parents to have their children "educated in a religious
environment 'is diminished or even denied.'" The court rejected the argument, on the ground that the tuition grants to
low income parents could only be regarded as having a primary
effect that advanced religion.

The third statutory program under review in *Nyquist* granted
state income tax relief to parents of nonpublic school children.
The court held that there was no difference between the tax
benefit and the tuition grant. In the court's view, by either
device the state was giving an encouragement to parents to send
their children to nonpublic schools.

The court in *Nyquist* tried to distinguish the legislative
programs under review in *Allen* and *Everson* as programs which
benefitted public school children as well as private school children. The court relied on this distinction to invalidate New
York legislative programs designed to aid nonpublic elementary
and secondary school children. The court held the latter grants
invalid as having a primary effect that advances religion: "The
grants to parents of private school children are given in addition to the right that they have to send their children to public
schools 'totally at state expense.'"

Chief Justice Burger and Justice Rehnquist dissented as to
the tuition grant and tax benefit programs. They rejected the

court's attempt to distinguish *Everson* and *Allen*. Chief Justice Burger stated: "It is beyond dispute that the parents of public school children in New York and Pennsylvania presently receive the 'benefits' of having their children educated totally at state expense; the statutes enacted in those states and at issue here merely attempt to equalize that 'benefit'. . . ."

Justice White also dissented with respect to the court's invalidation of the tuition grant and tax credit laws. White reasoned that New York and Pennsylvania had attempted to bail out the economically jeopardized parochial schools. It is true, said White, if the parochial schools were kept alive these schools would be able "to continue whatever religious functions they perform." But, said White, "preserving the secular functions of these schools is the overriding consequence of these laws and the resulting but incidental benefit to religion should not invalidate them."

3. In Sloan v. Lemon, 413 U.S. 825 (1973), a companion case to *Nyquist,* the court held unconstitutional a Pennsylvania law which would have defrayed some of the tuition expenses incurred by parents who sent their children to nonpublic schools. The Pennsylvania program would not have related tuition reimbursement to parental income. Justice Powell said for the court in *Sloan:*

" . . . The State has singled out a class of its citizens for a special economic benefit. Whether that benefit be viewed as a simple tuition subsidy, as an incentive to parents to send their children to sectarian schools, or as a reward for having done so, at bottom its intended consequences is to preserve and support religion-oriented institutions. We think it plain that this is quite unlike the sort of 'indirect' and 'incidental' benefits that flowed to sectarian schools from programs aiding *all* parents by supplying bus transportation and secular textbooks for their children. Such benefits were carefully restricted to the purely secular side of church-affiliated institutions and provided no special aid for those who had chosen to support religious schools. Yet such aid approached the 'verge' of the constitutionally impermissible. In *Lemon,* we declined to allow *Everson* to be used as the 'platform for yet further steps' in granting assistance to 'institutions whose legitimate needs are growing and whose interests have substantial political support.' Again today we decline to approach or overstep the 'precipice' of establishment against which the Religion Clauses protect. We hold that Pennsylvania's tuition grant scheme violates the constitutional mandate against the

'sponsorship' or 'financial support' of religion or religious institutions."

The effort in *Nyquist* to distinguish that case from *Everson*
and *Allen* because "the bus rides in *Everson* had no inherent
religious significance, and the state in *Allen* did not authorize
the loan of religious books" has been attacked as follows: "While,
(in *Brown* and *Allen*) the functions aided were superficially,
separate from the sectarian functions of church schools, economic
realities make the distinction meaningless. The tax money that
paid for bus fares and textbooks necessarily freed money that
would otherwise have been spent for those monies. This money
would now be spent on other, more religious oriented aspects
of the children's education." *See* Note, *Voucher Systems Of Public Education After Nyquist And Sloan: Can A Constitutional
System Be Devised?*, 72 MICH. L. REV. 895, 902 (1974).

The same Note argues that a full voucher system available
to all parents, not just to parents of children attending public
schools, would be constitutional: "A full voucher system will be
able to avoid the special treatment pitfall if the monetary value
of the voucher is high enough. If it is, parents who do not belong
to a religious denomination that already supports a system of
sectarian schools or who do not choose to send their children to
sectarian schools may want to use the vouchers at nonsectarian
private schools and, in response to this demand, many new private schools may be able to come into existence. In that case, the
state voucher system would not benefit a predominately religious
class but would offer realistic private educational alternatives
to all its citizens." Note, 72 MICH. L. REV., at 904. Do you
think Justice Powell would agree with this analysis? Why?

# Chapter 12

## STATE ACTION: A CYCLICAL CONCEPT?

---

### A. THE BEGINNINGS OF THE STATE ACTION LIMITATION ON FOURTEENTH AMENDMENT PROTECTION

The Federal Civil Rights Act of 1875 made criminal racial discrimination in "inns, public conveyances on land or water, theatres, and other places of public amusement." The issue the statute raised was whether Congress had constitutional power to enact such legislation. The Supreme Court in a landmark decision held that the Congress had no such constitutional power. Congress had no power under the Fourteenth Amendment to enact such legislation because Congress could legislate only with regard to state action.

### CIVIL RIGHTS CASES
#### Supreme Court of the United States
#### 109 U.S. 3, 27 L. Ed. 835, 3 S. Ct. 18 (1883)

Justice BRADLEY delivered the opinion of the Court.

. . . .

Has Congress constitutional power to make such a law? Of course, no one will contend that the power to pass it was contained in the Constitution before the adoption of the last three amendments. The power is sought, first, in the Fourteenth Amendment, and the views and arguments of distinguished senators, advanced whilst the law was under consideration, claiming authority to pass it by virtue of that amendment, are the principal arguments adduced in favor of the power. We have carefully considered those arguments, as was due to the eminent ability of those who put them forward, and have felt, in all its force, the weight of authority which always invests a law that Congress deems itself competent to pass. But the responsibility of an independent judgment is now thrown upon this court; and we are bound to exercise it according to the best lights we have.

The first section of the Fourteenth Amendment (which is the one relied on), after declaring who shall be citizens of the United States, and of the several States, is prohibitory in its character, and prohibitory upon the states. . . . It is state action of a particular character that is prohibited. Individual invasion of individual rights is not the subject-matter of the Amendment. It has a deeper and broader scope. It nullifies and makes void all state legislation, and state action of every kind, which impairs the privileges and immunities of citizens of the United States, or which injures them in life, liberty or property without due process of law, or which denies to any of them the equal protection of the laws. It not only does this, but, in order that the national will, thus declared, may not be a mere *brutum fulmen*, the last section of the Amendment invests Congress with power to enforce it by appropriate legislation. To enforce what? To enforce the prohibition. To adopt appropriate legislation for correcting the effects of such prohibited state laws and state acts, and thus to render them effectually null, void, and innocuous. This is the legislative power conferred upon Congress, and this is the whole of it. It does not invest Congress with power to legislate upon subjects which are within the domain of state legislation; but to provide modes of relief against state legislation, or state action, of the kind referred to. It does not authorize Congress to create a code of municipal law for the regulation of private rights; but to provide modes of redress against the operation of state laws, and the action of state officers executive or judicial, when these are subversive of the fundamental rights specified in the Amendment. Positive rights and privileges are undoubtedly secured by the Fourteenth Amendment; but they are secured by way of prohibition against state laws and state proceedings affecting those rights and privileges, and by power given to Congress to legislate for the purpose of carrying such prohibition into effect: and such legislation must necessarily be predicated upon such supposed state laws or state proceedings, and be directed to the correction of their operation and effect. . . .

　　. . . .

　　. . . Of course, legislation may, and should be, provided in advance to meet the exigency when it arises; but it should be adapted to the mischief and wrong which the Amendment was intended to provide against; and that is, state laws, or state action of some kind, adverse to the rights of the citizen secured by the Amendment. Such legislation cannot properly cover the whole domain of rights appertaining to life, liberty and property, defining them and providing for their vindication. That would be to establish a code of municipal law regulative of all private rights between man and man in society. It would be to make Congress take the place of the state legislatures and to supersede them. . . . In fine, the legislation which Congress is authorized to adopt in this behalf is not general legislation upon

the rights of the citizen, but corrective legislation, that is, such
as may be necessary and proper for counteracting such laws as
the states may adopt or enforce, and which, by the amendment,
they are prohibited from making or enforcing, or such acts and
proceedings as the states may commit or take, and which, by the
amendment, they are prohibited from committing or taking. It
is not necessary for us to state, if we could, what legislation would
be proper for Congress to adopt. It is sufficient for us to examine
whether the law in question is of that character.

An inspection of the law shows that it makes no reference
whatever to any supposed or apprehended violation of the
Fourteenth Amendment on the part of the states. It is not predicated on any such view. It proceeds *ex directo* to declare that
certain acts committed by individuals shall be deemed offences,
and shall be prosecuted and punished by proceedings in the
courts of the United States. It does not profess to be corrective
of any constitutional wrong committed by the states; it does not
make its operation to depend upon any such wrong committed.
It applies equally to cases arising in states which have the justest
laws respecting the personal rights of citizens, and whose authorities are ever ready to enforce such laws, as to those which
arise in states that may have violated the prohibition of the
amendment. In other words, it steps into the domain of local
jurisprudence, and lays down rules for the conduct of individuals
in society towards each other, and imposes sanctions for the
enforcement of those rules, without referring in any manner to
any supposed action of the state or its authorities.

If this legislation is appropriate for enforcing the prohibitions
of the amendment, it is difficult to see where it is to stop. . . .
The truth is, that the implication of a power to legislate in this
manner is based upon the assumption that if the states are forbidden to legislate or act in a particular way on a particular subject, and power is conferred upon Congress to enforce the
prohibition, this gives Congress power to legislate generally upon
that subject, and not merely power to provide modes of redress
against such state legislation or action. The assumption is certainly unsound. It is repugnant to the Tenth Amendment of the
Constitution, which declares that powers not delegated to the
United States by the Constitution, nor prohibited by it to the
states, are reserved to the states respectively or to the people.
. . . .

. . . [C]ivil rights, such as are guaranteed by the Constitution
against state aggression, cannot be impaired by the wrongful
acts of individuals, unsupported by state authority in the shape
of laws, customs, or judicial or executive proceedings. The wrong-

ful act of an individual, unsupported by any such authority, is simply a private wrong, or a crime of that individual; an invasion of the rights of the injured party, it is true, whether they affect his person, his property, or his reputation; but if not sanctioned in some way by the state, or not done under state authority, his rights remain in full force, and may presumably be vindicated by resort to the laws of the state for redress. . . . This abrogation and denial of rights, for which the states alone were or could be responsible, was the great seminal and fundamental wrong which was intended to be remedied. And the remedy to be provided must necessarily be predicated upon that wrong. It must assume that in the cases provided for, the evil or wrong actually committed rests upon some state law or state authority for its excuse and perpetration.

. . . But where a subject is not submitted to the general legislative power of Congress, but is only submitted thereto for the purpose of rendering effective some prohibition against particular state legislation or state action in reference to that subject, the power given is limited by its object, and any legislation by Congress in the matter must necessarily be corrective in its character, adapted to counteract and redress the operation of such prohibited state laws or proceedings of state officers.

. . . .

Justice HARLAN dissenting:

[The portion of Justice Harlan's opinion dealing with the Thirteenth Amendment has been omitted but is summarized and discussed in the notes.]

It remains now to consider these cases with reference to the power congress has possessed since the adoption of the fourteenth amendment. . . .

. . . .

. . . The first clause of the first section—"all persons born or naturalized in the United States, and subject to the jurisdiction thereof, are citizens of the United States, and of the state wherein they reside"—is of a distinctly affirmative character. In its application to the colored race, previously liberated, it created and granted, as well citizenship of the United States, as citizenship of the state in which they respectively resided. . . . Further, they were brought, by this supreme act of the nation, within the direct operation of that provision of the constitution which declares that "the citizens of each state shall be entitled to all privileges and immunities of citizens in the several states." Article 4, § 2.

The citizenship thus acquired by that race, in virtue of an affirmative grant by the nation, may be protected, not alone by the judicial branch of the government, but by congressional legislation of a primary direct character; this, because the power of congress is not restricted to the enforcement of prohibitions upon state laws or state action. It is, in terms distinct and positive, to enforce "the *provisions* of *this article*" of amendment; not simply those of a prohibitive character, but the provisions,—*all* of the provisions,—affirmative and prohibitive, of the amendment. . . .

. . . .

But what was secured to colored citizens of the United States —as between them and their respective states—by the grant to them of state citizenship? With what rights, privileges, or immunities did this grant from the nation invest them? There is one, if there be no others—exemption from race discrimination in respect of any civil right belonging to citizens of the white race in the same state. . . . It is fundamental in American citizenship that, in respect of such rights, there shall be no discrimination by the state, or its officers, or by individuals, of corporations exercising public functions or authority, against any citizen because of his race or previous condition of servitude. [T]o hold that the amendment remits that right to the states for their protection, primarily, and stays the hand of the nation, until it is assailed by state laws or state proceedings, is to adjudge that the amendment, so far from enlarging the powers of congress,— as we have heretofore said it did,—not only curtails them, but reverses the policy which the general government has pursued from its very organization. Such an interpretation of the amendment is a denial to congress of the power, by appropriate legislation to enforce one of its provisions. In view of the circumstances under which the recent amendments were incorporated into the constitution, and especially in view of the peculiar character of the new rights they created and secured, it ought not to be presumed that the general government has abdicated its authority, by national legislation, direct and primary in its character, to guard and protect privileges and immunities secured by that instrument. . . . It was perfectly well known that the great danger to the equal enjoyment by citizens of their rights, as citizens, was to be apprehended, not altogether from unfriendly state legislation, but from the hostile action of corporations and individuals in the states. And it is to be presumed that it was intended, by [the fifth section of the fourteenth amendment] to clothe congress with power and authority to meet that danger. . . .

. . . .

It is said that any interpretation of the fourteenth amendment different from that adopted by the court, would authorize congress to enact a municipal code for all the states, covering every matter affecting the life, liberty, and property of the citizens of the several states. Not so. Prior to the adoption of that amendment the constitutions of the several states, without, perhaps, an exception, secured all *persons* against deprivation of life, liberty, or property, otherwise than by due process of law, and, in some form, recognized the right of all *persons* to the equal protection of the laws. These rights, therefore, existed before that amendment was proposed or adopted. If, by reason of that fact, it be assumed that protection in these rights of persons still rests, primarily, with the states, and that congress may not interfere except to enforce, by means of corrective legislation, the prohibitions upon state laws or state proceedings inconsistent with those rights, it does not at all follow that privileges which have been *granted by the nation* may not be protected by primary legislation upon the part of congress. . . . That exemption of citizens from discrimination based on race or color, in respect of civil rights, is one of those privileges or immunities, can no longer be deemed an open question in this court. . . .

. . . .

But if it were conceded that the power of congress could not be brought into activity until the rights specified in the act of 1875 had been abridged or denied by some state law or state action, I maintain that the decision of the court is erroneous. . . .

In every material sense applicable to the practical enforcement of the fourteenth amendment, railroad corporations, keepers of inns, and managers of places of public amusement are agents of the state, because amenable, in respect of their public duties and functions, to public regulation. It seems to me that a denial by these instrumentalities of the state to the citizen, because of his race, of that equality of civil rights secured to him by law, is a denial by the state within the meaning of the fourteenth amendment. If it be not, then that race is left, in respect of the civil rights under discussion, practically at the mercy of corporations and individuals wielding power under the states.

. . . I agree that if one citizen chooses not to hold social intercourse with another, he is not and cannot be made amenable to the law for his conduct in that regard; for no legal right of a citizen is violated by the refusal of others to maintain merely social relations with him. . . . The rights which congress, by the act of 1875, endeavored to secure and protect are legal, not social, rights. The right, for instance, of a colored citizen to use the accommodations of a public highway upon the same

terms as are permitted to white citizens is no more a social right
than his right, under the law, to use the public streets of a city,
or a town, or a turnpike road, or a public market, or a post-
office, or his right to sit in a public building with others, of
whatever race, for the purpose of hearing the political questions
of the day discussed. . . .

. . . .

---

## NOTES

1.  According to Justice Bradley, Congress can only prohibit
*state* action which is contrary to the provisions of the fourteenth
amendment. But doesn't this interpretation make the congressional role superfluous? Subsequently, the federal courts were
permitted to restrain state action which violated the fourteenth
amendment. *See Ex parte* Young, 209 U.S. 123 (1908), text, p.
49, treating state action as individual action in order to avoid
the effect of the eleventh amendment. The case is an illustration
of the fact that judicial inventiveness concerning what is and
what is not state action has been a rather consistent phenomenon
of fourteenth amendment interpretation.

2.  Notice that Justice Bradley does not pass on the question
of whether Congress may enforce civil rights legislation under
the federal commerce clause. Reservation of decision on this
issue helped make possible the congressional decision reflected
in the Civil Rights Act of 1964 to base that statute on the federal
commerce clause rather than the fourteenth amendment, text,
pp. 195-215.

3.  Justice Bradley's decision in the *Civil Rights Cases* was
the formative element in creating an interpretation of the fourteenth amendment which limited its scope to state or public
action rather than individual or private action. As a result of
the limiting function of the state action concept, the necessity
to show state action became the engine without which the
promises and prohibitions of the fourteenth amendment were not
operative. The effort to extend the promise of the due process
and equal protection clauses of the fourteenth amendment to the
American Negro whom these clauses were intended to benefit
has been a major theme of mid-twentieth century constitutional
litigation. The thrust of this litigation has been to escape the
rigid confines of Justice Bradley's views.

4.  The petitioners in the *Civil Rights Cases* argued that if
the fourteenth amendment was unavailable to justify the federal
legislation at issue, then the thirteenth amendment authorized

the legislation. The argument was that the thirteenth amendment gave Congress the power to enact "direct and primary, as distinguished from corrective legislation." The plaintiffs contended that the thirteenth amendment was not "a mere prohibition of state laws establishing or upholding slavery, but an absolute declaration that slavery or involuntary servitude shall not exist in any part of the United States."

The proponents of the legislation under attack in the *Civil Rights Cases* contended that under the thirteenth amendment, legislation designed to eliminate all forms of slavery and involuntary servitude may regulate individual action whether state action was "sanctioned by state legislation or not." Under the fourteenth amendment, on the other hand, legislation corrective of state action was permissible. Justice Bradley rejected the attempt to rely on the thirteenth amendment in order to avoid the state action problem of the fourteenth amendment. The thirteenth amendment, he said, was concerned with slavery and not distinctions of race, class or color: "It would be running the slavery argument into the ground to make it apply to every act of discrimination which a person may see fit to make as to the guests he will entertain, or as to the people he will take into his coach or cab or car, or admit to his concert or theatre, or deal with in other matters of intercourse or business. Innkeepers and public carriers, by the laws of all states, so far as we are aware, are bound, to the extent of their facilities, to furnish proper accommodation to all unobjectionable persons who in good faith apply for them."

In dissent, the first Justice Harlan contended that the thirteenth amendment gave Congress express power to enact laws to protect the emancipated slaves "against the deprivation, on account of their race, of any civil rights enjoyed by other freemen in the same state." Harlan, in taking this approach, expressed a view very close to what became the public function theory of state action about three quarters of a century later. (*See* Evans v. Newton, 380 U.S. 971 (1965) text, p. 1012). Thus, Harlan stated that federal civil rights legislation enacted under the thirteenth amendment "may be of a direct and primary character, operating upon states, their officers and agents, and also upon at least, such individuals and corporations as exercise public functions and wield power and authority under the state." Elsewhere in his dissent in the *Civil Rights Cases,* Justice Harlan enlarged on his view of the thirteenth amendment:

> I am of opinion that . . . discrimination practiced by corporations and individuals in the exercise of their public or quasi-public function is a badge of servitude, the imposition

of which congress may prevent under its power, through appropriate legislation, to enforce the Thirteenth Amendment. . . .

If Harlan's approach to the thirteenth amendment had been accepted, it would have made that amendment a far more formidable and generative source of constitutional law and doctrine than in fact it has been. Additionally, Harlan's view of the thirteenth amendment would have diminished the importance of the state action requirement of the fourteenth amendment as a barrier to federal civil rights legislation. Do you see why?

KINOY, THE CONSTITUTIONAL RIGHT OF NEGRO FREEDOM, 21 Rutgers L. Rev. 387 (1967)*

### THE HERITAGE OF THE CIVIL RIGHTS CASES: THE ELUSIVE STATE ACTION CONCEPT

The legal rationale which the Bradley majority developed in 1883 to justify the abdication of primary national responsibility for the protection of Negro rights contains certain concepts which were . . . essential to the analysis of the secondary and corrective nature of national power. Central among these was the concept of "state action." Under the Bradley thesis of limited national responsibility the presence of "state action" was a critical ingredient in indicating the propriety of the invocation of federal power. It was designed to be and functioned primarily as a limiting, narrowing control.

Over the years, as the Bradley thesis remained unchallenged, the concepts it advanced became rigidified, almost constitutional postulates, unrelated to the context out of which they emerged. Thus the requirement of "state action" in the Fourteenth Amendment area as a precondition for the exercise of national power became an unquestioned axiom of constitutional law. Its origin, its purpose, its function, were forgotten. It emerged as an automatic requirement, like "consideration" in a contract. . . .

. . . In delineating the secondary or corrective role of the national government under the Fourteenth Amendment, the Bradley majority carefully indicated that the national power there authorized could come into play either where state action affirmatively deprived citizens of the equal protection of the laws *or* where the state had failed to protect the equal exercise of rights guaranteed by the Constitution. This was fully in accordance with the basic theory of the Bradley opinion. There was nothing mystical or sacrosanct about a requirement of *affirmative* state action prior to the exercise of national power. The Bradley hypothesis rested upon the theory discussed at some length above—that the *primary* responsibility for protecting Negro rights lay with the states. Once an opportunity was offered for the exercise of that responsibility, and the state failed to respond, even under the original Bradley formulation the corrective power of the Fourteenth Amendment could come into play. In an interesting series of letters written prior to the 1883 opinion, Bradley made it quite clear that he meant that if a state *failed* to enact laws to provide for equal accommodations, power resided in the national government to pass such direct legislation. This idea of state inaction as a condition precedent to the exercise of federal power would appear to be far closer to Bradley's original understanding of the purpose of the doctrine than most contemporary commentators would seem to concede. In any event, it serves to highlight the fact that the function of the concept as first contemplated was not to provide a boundary line delineating the outer reaches of national power, but rather to serve as a useful *indicium* of what was to the Bradley Court the main question: had the state failed to exercise its primary responsibility for protecting the rights involved? If the state itself was engaged in the denial of equal protection of its laws the answer to the question was obvious. But to pose the question was to infer, as Bradley himself suggested, that there were other ways of indicating the failure of the state to exercise its primary responsibility.

It is only when the concept has become removed from the context within which it was created that it becomes an end in itself in which the feverish search for some shred of affirmative state action becomes the *sine qua non* of the exercise of federal power. It becomes clear, therefore, that even if the Court continues to live within the four corners of the Bradley rationale, the presence or absence of "state action" ought not be permitted to be the decisive determinant but should be merely one indication of whether the state has failed to meet its primary responsibility for the protection of the rights involved. In any event, so long as the Court continues to utilize concepts which were originally fashioned to achieve an objective now discarded in life—the expectation that the states would assume primary responsibility for the protection of Negro rights—conflicts will continue to occur between the techniques of analysis upon which the Court relies and the rights it seeks to enforce.

. . . .

## Shelley v. Kraemer and the Broadening of the State Action Concept

A decision by the Vinson Court shortly after World War II might have hastened the expansion of the state action concept to the point where the fourteenth amendment would have easily reached private discrimination. In Shelley v. Kraemer, 334 U.S. 1 (1948), the Supreme Court held that racially discriminatory restrictive covenants in deeds were not judicially enforceable. Since the restrictive covenants involved in *Shelley* had been entered into by private persons, *Shelley* made it possible to conclude that the death knell had been sounded for an approach to the question of the scope of the fourteenth amendment which was exclusively dependent on the presence of state action. After all, it was private persons who had placed restrictive covenants in deeds under the fact pattern of the *Shelley* case. Legislative enactment had not decreed the presence of restrictive covenants in the deeds.

### SHELLEY v. KRAEMER
Supreme Court of the United States
334 U.S. 1, 92 L. Ed. 1161, 68 S. Ct. 836 (1948)

Chief Justice VINSON delivered the opinion of the Court.

These cases present for our consideration questions concerning the validity of court enforcement of private agreements, generally described as restrictive covenants, which have as their purpose the exclusion of persons of designated race or color from the ownership or occupancy of real property. Basic constitutional issues of obvious importance have been raised.

. . . .

Since the decision of this Court in the Civil Rights Cases, 109 U.S. 3, the principle has become firmly embedded in our constitutional law that the action inhibited by the first section of the Fourteenth Amendment is only such action as may fairly be said to be that of the States. That Amendment erects no shield against merely private conduct, however discriminatory or wrongful.

We conclude, therefore, that the restrictive agreements standing alone cannot be regarded as a violation of any rights guaranteed to petitioners by the Fourteenth Amendment. So long as the purposes of those agreements are effectuated by voluntary adherence to their terms, it would appear clear that there has been no action by the State and the provisions of the Amendment have not been violated.

But here there was more. These are cases in which the purposes of the agreements were secured only by judicial enforcement by state courts of the restrictive terms of the agreements. The respondents urge that judicial enforcement of private agreements does not amount to state action; or, in any event, the participation of the State is so attenuated in character as not to amount to state action within the meaning of the Fourteenth Amendment. Finally, it is suggested, even if the States in these cases may be deemed to have acted in the constitutional sense, their action did not deprive petitioners of rights guaranteed by the Fourteenth Amendment. We move to a consideration of these matters.

. . . .

We have no doubt that there has been state action in these cases in the full and complete sense of the phrase. The undisputed facts disclose that petitioners were willing purchasers of properties upon which they desired to establish homes. The owners of the properties were willing sellers; and contracts of sale were accordingly consummated. It is clear that but for the active intervention of the state courts, supported by the full panoply of state power, petitioners would have been free to occupy the properties in question without restraint.

These are not cases, as has been suggested, in which the States have merely abstained from action, leaving private individuals free to impose such discriminations as they see fit. Rather, these are cases in which the States have made available to such individuals the full coercive power of government to deny to petitioners, on the grounds of race or color, the enjoyment of property rights in premises which petitioners are willing and financially able to acquire and which the grantors are willing to sell. The difference between judicial enforcement and non-enforcement of the restrictive covenants is the difference to petitioners between being denied rights of property available to other members of the community and being accorded full enjoyment of those rights on an equal footing.

The enforcement of the restrictive agreements by the state courts in these cases was directed pursuant to the common-law policy of the States as formulated by those courts in earlier decisions. . . . The judicial action in each case bears the clear and unmistakable imprimatur of the State. We have noted that previous decisions of this Court have established the proposition that judicial action is not immunized from the operation of the Fourteenth Amendment simply because it is taken pursuant to the state's common-law policy. Nor is the Amendment ineffective simply because the particular pattern of discrimination, which the State has enforced, was defined initially by the terms of a private agreement. State action, as that phrase is understood for the purpose of the Fourteenth Amendment, refers to exertions of state power in all forms. And when the effect of that action is to deny rights subject to the protection of the Fourteenth Amendment, it is the obligation of this Court to enforce the constitutional commands.

We hold that in granting judicial enforcement of the restrictive agreements in these cases, the States have denied petitioners the equal protection of the laws and that, therefore, the action of the state courts cannot stand. We have noted that freedom from discrimination by the States in the enjoyment of property rights was among the basic objectives sought to be effectuated by the framers of the Fourteenth Amendment. That such discrimination has occurred in these cases is clear. Because of the race or color of these petitioners they have been denied rights of ownership or occupancy enjoyed as a matter of course by other citizens of different race or color. . . .

. . . .

The historical context in which the Fourteenth Amendment became a part of the Constitution should not be forgotten. Whatever else the framers sought to achieve, it is clear that the matter of primary concern was the establishment of equality in the enjoyment of basic civil and political rights and the preservation of those rights from discriminatory action on the part of the States based on considerations of race or color. Seventy-five years ago this Court announced that the provisions of the Amendment are to be construed with this fundamental purpose in mind. Upon full consideration, we have concluded that in these cases the States have acted to deny petitioners the equal protection of the laws guaranteed by the Fourteenth Amendment. Having so decided, we find it unnecessary to consider whether petitioners have also been deprived of property without due process of law or denied privileges and immunities of citizens of the United States.

For the reasons stated, the judgment of the Supreme Court of Missouri and the judgment of the Supreme Court of Michigan must be reversed.

Reversed.

Justice REED, Justice JACKSON, and Justice RUTLEDGE took no part in the consideration or decision of these cases.

## NOTES

1. A broad reading of *Shelley* did not transpire. Judicial adherence to traditional state action concepts proved to be quite stubborn and *Shelley* did not have the larger impact that some of its assumptions might have been expected to yield. There is little doubt that the court in *Shelley* did not intend to accomplish a revolution in the approach to state action. Chief Justice Vinson did not declare that restrictive covenants requiring racial discrimination were in themselves invalid. Professor Bernard Schwartz has pointed out that in a Canadian case, decided about the same time as *Shelley,* the Ontario High Court held that these restrictive covenants were themselves void because they were contrary to public policy: "If the common law of treason encompasses the stirring up of hatred between different classes of his majesty's subjects, . . . 'the common law of public policy is surely adequate to void the restrictive covenants which is here attached.' " *In re* Drummond Wren (1945), 4 D.L.R. 674, 679. Professor Schwartz emphasized that Chief Justice Vinson, on the contrary, tried to underscore the fact that the restrictive covenants were in themselves valid. *See* B. SCHWARTZ, AMERICAN CONSTITUTIONAL LAW 232 (1955).

2. If restrictive covenants were in themselves still valid, then private discrimination was still valid. Professor Louis Pollak set himself to the task of trying to extract a satisfactory doctrine from *Shelley,* a doctrine that would give the fourteenth amendment a greater scope but yet leave room for private discrimination. Why did *Shelley* need such an analysis? Presumably, because the case presented the courts with a dramatic choice between competing constitutional ideas: liberty (the right of private persons to discriminate among themselves for whatever reason) versus equality (the right of persons to have access to the ordinary activities and opportunities of life without regard to race, color or creed).

The conflict between these warring constitutional values raised questions which would prove to be one of the major themes of the constitutional litigation of the 50's and 60's. If a country club by virtue of a provision in its by-laws excludes members of minority groups, does *Shelley* mean that if members of such groups insist on using the club's facilities the club would not be able to use the courts to eject those whom it deemed unwelcome on racial or religious grounds?

If a restaurant refused to serve blacks, did the *Shelley* case mean that the state trespass laws could not be used to remove and prosecute blacks who demanded service against the will of the ownership? If the answer to the last question is in the affirmative, then the Civil Rights Act of 1964 would have been unnecessary. If legal or judicial process could not be used to enforce discrimination then all racially discriminatory private action has been constitutionalized. So far as legal sanction is concerned, under the broadest reading of *Shelley* private action which implements racial discrimination may not be enforced in the courts.

Professor Pollak contended that *Shelley* prevented the use of judicial process to enforce private discrimination among parties who do not wish to discriminate. *Shelley*, after all, involved a desire by a willing buyer to purchase a house from a willing seller. Professor Pollak, however, interprets *Shelley* to permit the use of judicial process to enforce private discrimination. *See* Pollak, *Racial Discrimination and Judicial Integrity: A Reply To Professor Wechsler*, 108 U. Pa. L. Rev. 1, 13 (1959).

Does this distinction help to answer the question raised above with respect to the scope of *Shelley*? Is Pollak's a distinction one which fourteenth amendment analysis demands? Is it a distinction which Vinson's opinion in *Shelley* will support?

## B. THE MOVEMENT TOWARD EXPANSION OF STATE ACTION

1. An early expansion of the state action concept occurred in Terry v. Adams, 345 U.S. 461 (1953). In that case, the question was whether the activities of a "private and voluntary" political organization, the Jaybird Democratic Association which held primaries prior to the Democratic primary and where nomination by the Jaybirds was tantamount to victory in both the Democratic primary and the general election, amounted to state action. The Supreme Court ruled the activity of the Jaybirds was prohibited as invalid state action under the fifteenth amendment. Justice Black said for the court in an opinion in which two other Justices joined:

> For a state to permit such a duplication of its election processes is to permit a flagrant abuse of those processes to defeat the purposes of the Fifteenth Amendment. The use of the county-operated primary to ratify the result of the prohibited election merely compounds the offense. It violates the Fifteenth Amendment for a state, by such circumstances, to permit within its borders the use of any device that produces an equivalent of the prohibited election.

2. Perhaps, the formative case in the push toward expanding private action is Burton v. Wilmington Parking Authority, 365 U.S. 715 (1961).

A restaurant located within an off-street automobile parking building in Wilmington, Delaware, refused to serve Burton food or drink solely because he was a Negro. The building was owned and operated by the Wilmington Parking Authority which is a Delaware state agency. The restaurant, Eagle Coffee Shoppe, Inc., was a lessee of the Parking Authority. Burton sought declaratory and injunctive relief against the Parking Authority. The Delaware Supreme Court held that the coffee shop was acting in a private capacity and that its action was not that of the Authority and that therefore the fourteenth amendment had not been violated. Eagle's action was not considered to constitute state action according to the Delaware Supreme Court.

The Wilmington Parking Authority made long-term leases with tenants for commercial use of some of the space available. The Parking Authority did this in order to obtain the capital necessary to service its indebtedness. Eagle's lease with the Authority did not require that its restaurant services be made available to the general public on a non-discriminatory basis.

In the *Burton* case, a private restaurateur was in effect brought under the fourteenth amendment's command to the states that they shall not engage in racial discrimination. (Is this a fair statement of Justice Bradley's view of the fourteenth amendment as expressed in his decision in the *Civil Rights Cases*?) The student should read the decision which follows and try to develop in greater detail each of the three strands of the state action theory employed by the court in *Burton*. Do you agree that the state admitted that it was benefiting from the racial discrimination practiced by the restaurant?

### BURTON v. WILMINGTON PARKING AUTHORITY
Supreme Court of the United States
365 U.S. 715, 6 L. Ed. 2d 45, 81 S. Ct. 856 (1961)

Justice CLARK delivered the opinion of the Court.

. . . .

. . . It is clear, as it always has been since the *Civil Rights Cases,* that "individual invasion of individual rights is not the subject matter of the amendment," and that private conduct abridging individual rights does no violence to the Equal Protection Clause unless to some significant extent the State in any of its manifestations has been found to have become involved in it. Because the virtue of the right to equal protection of the laws could lie only in the breadth of its application, its constitutional assurance was reserved in terms whose imprecision was necessary if the right were to be enjoyed in the variety of individual-state relationships which the Amendment was designed to embrace.

For the same reason, to fashion and apply a precise formula for
recognition of state responsibility under the Equal Protection
Clause is "an impossible task" which "this Court has never attempted." Only by sifting facts and weighing circumstances can
the nonobvious involvement of the State in private conduct be
attributed its true significance.

. . . [T]he Delaware Supreme Court seems to have placed
controlling emphasis on its conclusion, as to the accuracy of which
there is doubt, that only some 15% of the total cost of the facility
was "advanced" from public funds; that the cost of the entire
facility was allocated three-fifths to the space for commercial leasing and two-fifths to parking space; that anticipated revenue from
parking was only some 30.5% of the total income, the balance of
which was expected to be earned by the leasing; that the Authority had no original intent to place a restaurant in the building,
it being only a happenstance resulting from the bidding; that
Eagle expended considerable moneys on furnishings; that the
restaurant's main and marked public entrance is on Ninth Street
without any public entrance direct from the parking area; and
that "the only connection Eagle has with the public facility . . .
is the furnishing of the sum of $28,700 annually in the form of
rent which is used by the Authority to defray a portion of the
operating expense of an otherwise unprofitable enterprise."
While these factual considerations are indeed validly accountable aspects of the enterprise upon which the State has em-
barked, we cannot say that they lead inescapably to the conclusion that state action is not present. Their persuasiveness is
diminished when evaluated in the context of other factors which
must be acknowledged.

The land and building were publicly owned. As an entity, the
building was dedicated to "public uses" in performance of the
Authority's "essential governmental functions." 22 Del.Code, c.
5, §§ 501, 514. The costs of land acquisition, construction, and
maintenance are defrayed entirely from donations by the City
of Wilmington, from loans and revenue bonds and from the
proceeds of rentals and parking services out of which the loans
and bonds were payable. Assuming that the distinction would be
significant, the commercially leased areas were not surplus state
property, but constituted a physically and financially integral and,
indeed, indispensable part of the State's plan to operate its
project as a self-sustaining unit. Upkeep and maintenance of the
building, including necessary repairs, were responsibilities of the
Authority and were payable out of public funds. It cannot be
doubted that the peculiar relationship of the restaurant to the
parking facility in which it is located confers on each an inci-

dental variety of mutual benefits. Guests of the restaurant are afforded a convenient place to park their automobiles, even if they cannot enter the restaurant directly from the parking area. Similarly, its convenience for diners may well provide additional demand for the Authority's parking facilities. Should any improvements effected in the leasehold by Eagle become part of the realty, there is no possibility of increased taxes being passed on to it since the fee is held by a tax-exempt government agency. Neither can it be ignored, especially in view of Eagle's affirmative allegation that for it to serve Negroes would injure its business, that profits earned by discrimination not only contribute to, but are indispensable elements in the financial success of a governmental agency.

Addition of all these activities, obligations and responsibilities of the Authority, the benefits mutually conferred, together with the obvious fact that the restaurant is operated as an integral part of a public building devoted to a public parking service, indicates that degree of state participation and involvement in discriminatory action which it was the design of the Fourteenth Amendment to condemn. It is irony amounting to grave injustice that in one part of a single building, erected and maintained with public funds by an agency of the State to serve a public purpose, all persons have equal rights, while in another portion, also serving the public, a Negro is a second-class citizen, offensive because of his race, without rights and unentitled to service, but at the same time fully enjoys equal access to nearby restaurants in wholly privately owned buildings. As the Chancellor pointed out, in its lease with Eagle the Authority could have affirmatively required Eagle to discharge the responsibilities under the Fourteenth Amendment imposed upon the private enterprise as a consequence of state participation. But no State may effectively abdicate its responsibilities by either ignoring them or by merely failing to discharge them whatever the motive may be. It is of no consolation to an individual denied the equal protection of the laws that it was done in good faith. Certainly the conclusions drawn in similar cases by the various Courts of Appeals do not depend upon such a distinction. By its inaction, the Authority, and through it the State, has not only made itself a party to the refusal of service, but has elected to place its power, property and prestige behind the admitted discrimination. The State has so far insinuated itself into a position of interdependence with Eagle that it must be recognized as a joint participant in the challenged activity, which, on that account, cannot be considered to have been so "purely private" as to fall without the scope of the Fourteenth Amendment.

Because readily applicable formulae may not be fashioned, the conclusions drawn from the facts and circumstances of this record are by no means declared as universal truths on the basis of which every state leasing agreement is to be tested. Owing to the very "largeness" of government, a multitude of relationships might appear to some to fall within the Amendment's embrace, but that, it must be remembered, can be determined only in the framework of the peculiar facts or circumstances present. Therefore respondents' prophecy of nigh universal application of a constitutional precept so peculiarly dependent for its invocation upon appropriate facts fails to take into account "Differences in circumstances [which] beget appropriate differences in law." Specifically defining the limits of our inquiry, what we hold today is that when a State leases public property in the manner and for the purpose shown to have been the case here, the proscriptions of the Fourteenth Amendment must be complied with by the lessee as certainly as though they were binding covenants written into the agreement itself.

The judgment of the Supreme Court of Delaware is reversed and the cause remanded for further proceedings consistent with this opinion.

Reversed and remanded.

. . . .

[Justice HARLAN, Justice FRANKFURTER, and Justice WHIT-TAKER, dissented.]

---

## NOTES

1.  Justice Clark's opinion makes clear that the Wilmington Parking Authority had power to adopt rules and regulations respecting the use of the facilities. Should the failure of the Parking Authority to require that its lessees refrain from discriminating have been considered to furnish the requisite state action?

2.  State failure to act to implement fourteenth amendment objectives was only one element of decision in *Burton.* Subsequently, such inaction has been held by the court to constitute state action. The court in Griffin v. County School Bd., 377 U.S. 218 (1964), showed remarkable adeptness at checkmating the ingenuity of state legislators who were intent on exploiting the state action requirement of the fourteenth amendment in order to defeat the larger purposes of the amendment. In 1959, five years after the school desegregation case, the public schools in Prince Edward County, Virginia were closed. In 1960-1961,

the Virginia legislature established a program of tuition grants to be used by children attending private schools. At the same time, the Prince Edward County Board of Supervisors provided for property tax credits for contributions to any nonprofit, non-sectarian private schools in the county. The public schools elsewhere in Virginia were open.

The school officials in Prince Edward County had read the *School Desegregation Case* closely: The enforcement of segregation in the public schools through law was forbidden. Suppose there were no public schools at all? Would the *School Desegregation Case* then have no subject upon which its hated command could work? The Supreme Court pierced the subterfuge. Virginia had permitted Prince Edward County to abandon public schools and to operate private schools with state and county assistance for the sole reason of ensuring that white and colored school children in Prince Edward County would not go to the same school. Such state permission, the court, per Justice Black, held, amounted to state action prohibited under the fourteenth amendment. In *Griffin,* the court managed to bring nominally private action—theoretically outside the fourteenth amendment —within the prohibitions of the fourteenth amendment.

## "SIT-INS," LICENSING AND THE SEARCH FOR CONVENTIONAL STATE ACTION

One of the foremost battlegrounds of the sixties was the use of the "sit-in" to open up segregated lunch counters and restaurants. This occasion for wrestling with the state action problem arose within the very center of fourteenth amendment protection, the securement of legal equality for American Negroes. During the "sit-in" of the 1960's, Negro protestors throughout the South took seats at "whites-only" restaurants and lunch counters and remained in their seats until arrested. The demonstrators were arrested because the owners of lunch counters called the police to remove the protestors. Arrest and prosecution of the demonstrators was based on violation of state trespass laws. Fundamental constitutional questions soon arose: Could the state convict "sit-in" demonstrators consistent with the fourteenth amendment?

Could state courts enforce criminal trespass laws designed to protect against breach of the peace when the consequences of the state enforcement of the trespass laws led to perpetuation of a social system based on racial segregation? Arguably, the state courts were only enforcing the trespass laws rather than racial discrimination.

Was prosecution under the trespass laws permitted by *Shelley*? Under Professor Pollak's theory, would enforcement by the courts of such laws in such circumstances be unconstitutional state action under the fourteenth amendment? The *Shelley* doctrine was not resorted to by the Supreme Court to resolve the question.

Discrimination in privately-owned facilities, the argument ran, was the act of private persons and therefore as private action it was beyond the reach of constitutional command. The Supreme Court skillfully sought to avoid the issue of whether a pattern of private racial discrimination was to be permitted to rely for its sanction on judicial enforcement of the trespass laws. Perhaps, *Shelley* should or could have been expanded to prohibit judicial enforcement of the trespass laws in these circumstances. The court declined to move in that direction. Instead, it struggled to find state action in the classic sense.

In Peterson v. Greenville, 373 U.S. 244 (1963), a "sit-in" conviction was reversed on the ground that a city ordinance required separation of the races in restaurants. Therefore, the requisite state involvement was present. There was no need to inquire whether discriminatory motives by private parties could still warrant prosecution of state trespass laws. In Lombard v. Louisiana, 373 U.S. 267 (1963), another "sit-in" conviction was reversed but the court virtually ransacked the fact pattern of the case in order to find the state action as conventionally understood. The Supreme Court held in *Lombard* that the separation of the races in that case was instigated by the oral command of city officials. Justice Harlan dissented in *Lombard* objecting that "announcements of the Police Superintendent and the Mayor cannot well be compared with a city ordinance commanding segregated eating facilities." What is the difference between a Mayor's announcement and a city ordinance in terms of state action analysis?

In a concurring opinion in *Lombard v. Louisiana,* Justice Douglas made it clear that he was far more eager than his colleagues to face the state action problem head on. He made it clear that even if the state had not ordained segregation in some respect a constitutional barrier to inhibit restaurants and lunch counters from using the state trespass laws to enforce segregation might still be present. Justice Douglas wrote:

> Business, such as this restaurant, is still private property. Yet there is hardly any private enterprise that does not feel the pinch of some public regulation—from price control, to health and fire inspections to zoning, to safety measures, to minimum wages and working conditions, to unemployment insurance.

The hunt for a state action concept which would reach racially discriminatory private action revived interest in the first Justice Harlan's view that licensing was a basis for a broader state action concept. The first Justice Harlan, in his dissent in the *Civil Rights Cases,* had recognized that the fact that an enterprise was licensed provided a rationale for bringing a large sector of activity within the state action concept. Justice Douglas made a similar argument 80 years later in *Lombard v. Louisiana.*

In Garner v. Louisiana, 368 U.S. 157, 184 (1961), where a "sit-in" conviction was over-turned on the ground that the Louisiana breach of the peace statute did not cover peaceful protest, Justice Douglas, again in a separate concurrence, developed a similar thesis:

> The authority to license a business for public use is derived from the public. Negroes are as much a part of that public as are whites. A municipality granting a license to operate a business for the public represents Negroes as well as other races who live there. A license to establish a restaurant is a license to establish a public facility and necessarily imports, in law, equality of use for all members of the public.

Is there not a sense in which Douglas' licensing theory may also be used as an argument against broadening the definition of state action?

In Bell v. Maryland, 378 U.S. 226 (1964), the decision by a restaurant owner not to serve Negroes was in no sense state compelled. The case looked like an appropriate one for consideration of whether enforcement of state trespass laws would constitute sufficient state action to invalidate "sit-in" convictions when the participants in the "sit-in" were protesting racial discrimination in facilities which were open to all members of the public except blacks. But intervening state legislation prohibiting discrimination in public accommodations again made it possible for the court as a whole to dodge the question of whether private activity should be constitutionalized. Several opinions filed in the *Bell* case dealt with the constitutional issues. Certainly one of the most interesting opinions, since it re-opened the Bradley-Harlan debate concerning the purpose of the fourteenth amendment, was a long concurring opinion filed by Justice Goldberg in which Warren and Douglas joined. The court as a whole had agreed, with Justices Black, Harlan, and White dissenting, to vacate the judgment of the Maryland Court of Appeals and to remand the case to that court in light of the fact that the conduct punished was no longer illegal under Maryland law. Justice Goldberg, however, preferred to make a more frontal assault on the state action problem.

Justice Goldberg pointed out that the congressional debates on the fourteenth amendment illustrated a congressional desire to grant "civil rights" to the emancipated Negroes. He contended that civil rights "certainly included the right of access to places of public accommodation for these were most clearly places and areas of life where the relations of men were traditionally regulated by governments." Goldberg believed that it was an implied assumption of Justice Bradley's opinion in the *Civil Rights Cases* that a state could not apply its statutes or common law "to deny rather than to protect the right of access to public accommodations."

Justice Goldberg pointed out that Justice Bradley's private correspondence revealed that in his opinion a violation of the equal protection of the laws could flow from "omission to protect, as well as the omission to pass laws for protection."

How authoritative is it that Justice Bradley in private correspondence implied that state failure to act to correct private discrimination must be considered state action? With some impatience in his famous concurring opinion in Adamson v. California, 332 U.S. 46 (1947), Justice Frankfurter attacked Justice Black's reliance on congressional debates to show that the Bill of Rights were incorporated in the fourteenth amendment. Frankfurter rejected this use of extra-precedential material: "Remarks of a particular proponent of the Amendment, no matter how influential, are not to be deemed part of the Amendment. What was submitted for ratification was his proposal, not his speech." Is this objection even stronger with regard to private correspondence?

The enactment of the Civil Rights Act of 1964, 42 U.S.C. §§ 2000a-2000h (1964), mooted the controversy over the use of state trespass laws to enforce racial discrimination in public accommodations involved in interstate commerce as defined by the Act. The constitutional basis of the Civil Rights Act of 1964 was predicated on the federal commerce power rather than under § 5 of the fourteenth amendment. Did Justice Bradley's opinion in the *Civil Rights Cases* preclude basing the statute on the fourteenth amendment? The Civil Rights Act of 1964 was held to be a constitutional exercise of congressional power under the federal commerce power in the Heart of Atlanta Motel, Inc. v. United States, 379 U.S. 241 (1964), text, p. 200. *See also* text, p. 204.

2.    Another major effort to extend the frontiers of the state action concept in the direction of Harlan's opinion in the *Civil Rights Cases* while employing the doctrinal fabric spun by Bradley, arose out of a Georgia case decided by the Supreme Court in 1966.

In Evans v. Newton, 380 U.S. 971 (1965), the city of Macon, Georgia became trustee under a will which provided that certain land was to be used as a park for white people only. The park was maintained for many years by the city. The city was granted a tax exemption for the park and it was considered a part of the municipal establishment. Eventually, the city permitted Negroes to use the park. At that point, members of the all-white Board of Managers of the park brought suit in the state court asking that the city be removed as trustee and that private trustees be appointed. The Georgia state court appointed three individual trustees. An appeal was sought by Negro intervenors since the Georgia Supreme Court held that the testator, Senator Bacon, had the right to bequeath his property to a limited class (whites). The Supreme Court of Georgia held that charitable trusts are subject to supervision of a court of equity, and that the equity court has the power to approve new trustees so that the purpose of the trust will not fail. The Supreme Court granted certiorari.

In an opinion for the court, Justice Douglas, building on decisions like *Terry v. Adams,* enunciated a public function theory of state action. Under this theory, the decisive factor in determining whether the requisite state action was present was the public character of the activity involved rather than the nominal identity of the actor.

## EVANS v. NEWTON
Supreme Court of the United States
382 U.S. 296, 15 L. Ed. 2d 373, 86 S. Ct. 486 (1966)

Justice DOUGLAS delivered the opinion of the Court.
. . . .

There are two complementary principles to be reconciled in this case. One is the right of the individual to pick his own associates so as to express his preferences and dislikes, and to fashion his private life by joining such clubs and groups as he chooses. The other is the constitutional ban in the Equal Protection Clause of the Fourteenth Amendment against state-sponsored racial inequality, which of course bars a city from acting as trustee under a private will that serves the racial segregation cause. A private golf club, however, restricted to either Negro or white membership is one expression of freedom of association. But a municipal golf course that serves only one race is state activity indicating a preference on a matter as to which the State must be neutral. . . .

If a testator wanted to leave a school or center for the use of one race only and in no way implicated the State in the supervision, control, or management of that facility, we assume *arguendo* that no constitutional difficulty would be encountered.

This park, however, is in a different posture. For years it was an integral part of the City of Macon's activities. From the pleadings we assume it was swept, manicured, watered, patrolled, and maintained by the city as a public facility for whites only, as well as granted tax exemption under Ga. Code Ann. § 92-201. The momentum it acquired as a public facility is certainly not dissipated *ipso facto* by the appointment of "private" trustees. So far as this record shows, there has been no change in municipal maintenance and concern over this facility. Whether these public characteristics will in time be dissipated is wholly conjectural. If the municipality remains entwined in the management or control of the park, it remains subject to the restraints of the Fourteenth Amendment . . . We only hold that where the tradition of municipal control had become firmly established, we cannot take judicial notice that the mere substitution of trustees instantly transferred this park from the public to the private sector.

This conclusion is buttressed by the nature of the service rendered the community by a park. The service rendered even by a private park of this character is municipal in nature. It is open to every white person, there being no selective element other than race. Golf clubs, social centers, luncheon clubs, schools such as Tuskegee was at least in origin, and other like organizations in the private sector are often racially oriented. A park on the other hand, is more like a fire department or police department that traditionally serves the community. Mass recreation through the use of parks is plainly in the public domain, and state courts that aid private parties to perform that public function on a segregated basis implicate the State in conduct proscribed by the Fourteenth Amendment. Like the streets of the company town in *Marsh v. State of Alabama,* the elective process of *Terry v. Adams,* and the transit system of *Public Utilities Commission of District of Columbia v. Pollak,* the predominant character and purpose of this park is municipal.

Under the circumstances of this case, we cannot but conclude that the public character of this park requires that it be treated as a public institution subject to the command of the Fourteenth Amendment, regardless of who now has title under state law. We may fairly assume that had the Georgia courts been of the view that even in private hands the park may not be operated for the public on a segregated basis, the resignation would not have been approved and private trustees appointed. We put the matter that way because on this record we cannot say that the transfer of title *per se* disentangled the park from segregation under the municipal regime that long controlled it.

Since the judgment below gives effect to that purpose, it must be and is

Reversed.

---

## NOTES

1. Justice Black dissented on the ground that it was not appropriate to decide the constitutional questions yet since it was entirely possible, in his view, that successor trustees might not bar Negroes from the park.

2. Judge Harlan, joined by Justice Stewart, dissented because he did not think "the fourteenth amendment permits this Court in effect to frustrate the terms of Senator Bacon's will, now that the City of Macon is no longer connected, so far as the record shows, with the administration of Baconsfield." Justice Harlan made clear his distaste for Justice Douglas' "public function" theory:

"More serious than the absence of any firm doctrinal support for this theory of state action are its potentialities for the future. Its failing as a principle of decision in the realm of Fourteenth Amendment concerns can be shown by comparing—among other examples that might be drawn from the still unfolding sweep of governmental functions—the 'public function' of privately established schools with that of privately owned parks. Like parks, the purpose schools serve is important to the public. Like parks, private control exists, but there is also a very strong tradition of public control in this field. Like parks, schools may be available to almost anyone of one race or religion but to no others. Like parks, there are normally alternatives for those shut out but there may also be inconveniences and disadvantages caused by the restriction. Like parks, the extent of school intimacy varies greatly depending on the size and character of the institution.

"For all the resemblance, the majority assumes that its decision leaves unaffected the traditional view that the Fourteenth Amendment does not compel private schools to adapt their admission policies to its requirements, but that such matters are left to the States acting within constitutional bounds. I find it difficult, however, to avoid the conclusion that this decision opens the door to reversal of these basic constitutional concepts, and, at least in logic, jeopardizes the existence of denominationally restricted schools while making of every college entrance rejection letter a potential Fourteenth Amendment question.

"While this process of analogy might be spun out to reach privately owned orphanages, libraries, garbage collection companies, detective agencies, and a host of other functions commonly regarded as nongovernmental though paralleling fields of governmental activity, the example of schools is, I think, sufficient to indicate the pervasive potentialities of this 'public function' theory of state action. It substitutes for the comparatively clear and concrete tests of state action a catch-phrase approach as vague and amorphous as it is far-reaching. It dispenses with the sound and careful principles of past decisions in this realm. And it carries the seeds of transferring to federal authority vast areas of concerns whose regulation has wisely been left by the Constitution to the States."

## REITMAN v. MULKEY
Supreme Court of the United States
387 U.S. 369, 18 L. Ed. 2d 830, 87 S. Ct. 1627 (1967)

Justice WHITE delivered the opinion of the Court.

The question here is whether Art. I, § 26 of the California Constitution denies "to any person . . . the equal protection of the laws" within the meaning of the Fourteenth Amendment of the Constitution of the United States. Section 26 of Art. I, an initiated measure submitted to the people as Proposition 14 in a statewide ballot in 1964, provides in part as follows:

"Neither the State nor any subdivision or agency thereof shall deny, limit or abridge, directly or indirectly, the right of any person, who is willing or desires to sell, lease or rent any part or all of his real property, to decline to sell, lease or rent such property to such person or persons as he, in his absolute discretion, chooses."

The real property covered by § 26 is limited to residential property and contains an exception for state-owned real estate.
. . . .

[. . . The California Supreme Court] held that Art. I, § 26, was invalid as denying the equal protection of the laws guaranteed by the Fourteenth Amendment. . . .

We affirm the judgment of the California Supreme Court. We first turn to the opinion of that court, which quite properly undertook to examine the constitutionality of § 26 in terms of its "immediate objective," its "ultimate impact" and its "historical context and the condition existing prior to its enactment." Judgments such as these we have frequently undertaken ourselves. But here the California Supreme Court has addressed itself to these matters and we should give careful consideration to its views because they concern the purpose, scope, and operative effect of a provision of the California Constitution.

First, the court considered whether § 26 was concerned at all with private discriminations in residential housing. This involved a review of past efforts by the California Legislature to regulate such discriminations. The Unruh Act, Civ. Code §§ 51-52, on which respondents based their cases, was passed in 1959. . . . Finally, in 1963, came the Rumford Fair Housing Act, Health & Saf. Code . . . prohibiting racial discrimination in the sale or rental of any private dwelling containing more than four units. That act was enforceable by the State Fair Employment Practice Commission.

It was against this background that Proposition 14 was enacted. Its immediate design and intent, the California court said, was "to overturn state laws that bore on the right of private sellers and lessors to discriminate," the Unruh and Rumford Acts, and "to forestall future state action that might circumscribe this right." . . .

Second, the court conceded that the State was permitted a neutral position with respect to private racial discriminations and that the State was not bound by the Federal Constitution to forbid them. But, because a significant state involvement in private discriminations could amount to unconstitutional state action, the court deemed it necessary to determine whether Proposition 14 invalidly involved the State in racial discriminations in the housing market. Its conclusion was that it did.

To reach this result, the state court examined certain prior decisions in this Court in which discriminatory state action was identified. Based on these cases, it concluded that a prohibited state involvement could be found "even where the state can be charged with only encouraging," rather than commanding discrimination. . . .

. . . Petitioners contend that the California court has misconstrued the Fourteenth Amendment since the repeal of any statute prohibiting racial discrimination, which is constitutionally permissible, may be said to "authorize" and "encourage" discrimination because it makes legally permissible that which was formerly proscribed. But as we understand the California court, it did not posit a constitutional violation on the mere repeal of the Unruh and Rumford Acts. It did not read either our cases or the Fourteenth Amendment as establishing an automatic constitutional barrier to the repeal of an existing law prohibiting racial discriminations in housing; nor did the court rule that a State may never put in statutory form an existing policy of neutrality with respect to private discriminations. What the court below did was first to reject the notion that the State was required to have a statute prohibiting racial discriminations in housing. Second, it held the purpose and intent of § 26 was to authorize private racial discriminations in the housing market, to repeal the Unruh and Rumford Acts and to create a constitutional right to discriminate on racial grounds in the sale and leasing of real property. Hence, the court dealt with § 26 as though it expressly authorized and constitutionalized the private right to discriminate. Third, the court assessed the ultimate impact of § 26 in the California environment and concluded that the section would encourage and significantly involve the State in private racial discrimination contrary to the Fourteenth Amendment.

The California court could very reasonably conclude that § 26 would and did have wider impact than a mere repeal of existing statutes. . . . Private discriminations in housing were now not only free from Rumford and Unruh but they also enjoyed a far different status than was true before the passage of those statutes. The right to discriminate, including the right to discriminate on racial grounds, was now embodied in the State's basic charter, immune from legislative, executive, or judicial regulation at any level of the state government. Those practicing racial discriminations need no longer rely solely on their personal choice. They could now invoke express constitutional authority, free from censure or interference of any kind from official sources. . . .

This Court has never attempted the "impossible task" of formulating an infallible test for determining whether the State "in any of its manifestations" has become significantly involved in private discriminations. "Only by sifting the facts and weighing the circumstances" on a case-to-case basis can a "nonobvious involvement of the State in private conduct be attributed its true significance." Here the California court, armed as it was with the knowledge of the facts and circumstances concerning the passage and potential impact of § 26, and familiar with the milieu in which that provision would operate, has determined that the provision would involve the State in private racial discriminations to an unconstitutional degree. We accept this holding of the California court.

. . . .

[No precedent] squarely controls the case we now have before us. But [prior cases] do illustrate the range of situations in which discriminatory state action has been identified. They do exemplify the necessity for a court to assess the potential impact of official action in determining whether the State has significantly involved itself with invidious discriminations. Here we are dealing with a provision which does not just repeal an existing law forbidding private racial discriminations. Section 26 was intended to authorize, and does authorize, racial discrimination in the housing market. The right to discriminate is now one of the basic policies of the State. The California Supreme Court believes that the section will significantly encourage and involve the State in private discriminations. We have been presented with no persuasive considerations indicating that this judgment should be overturned.

Affirmed.

Justice DOUGLAS, concurring.

While I join the opinion of the Court, I add a word to indicate the dimensions of our problem.

. . . We deal here with a problem in the realm of zoning, similar to the one we had in *Shelley v. Kraemer.* . . .

Those covenants are one device whereby a neighborhood is kept "white" or "Caucasian" as the dominant interests desire. Proposition 14 in the setting of our modern housing problem is only another device of the same character.

Real estate brokers and mortgage lenders are largely dedicated to the maintenance of segregated communities. Realtors commonly believe it is unethical to sell or rent to a Negro in a predominantly or all-white neighborhood, and mortgage lenders throw their weight alongside segregated communities, rejecting applications by a member of a minority group who tries to break the white phalanx save and unless the neighborhood is in process of conversion into a mixed or a Negro community. . . .

The builders join in the same scheme. . . .

Proposition 14 is a form of sophisticated discrimination whereby the people of California harness the energies of private groups to do indirectly what they cannot under our decisions allow their government to do.

. . . .

Zoning is a state and municipal function. When the State leaves that function to private agencies or institutions who are licensees and who practice racial discrimination and zone our cities into white and black belts or white and black ghettoes, it suffers a governmental function to be performed under private auspices in a way the State itself may not act. . . .

. . . .

If we were in a domain exclusively private, we would have different problems. But urban housing is in the public domain as evidenced not only by the zoning problems presented but by the vast schemes of public financing with which the States and the Nation have been extensively involved in recent years. Urban housing is clearly marked with the public interest. . . .

. . . .

Since the real estate brokerage business is one that can be and is state regulated and since it is state licensed, it must be dedicated, like the telephone companies and the carriers and the hotels and motels to the requirements of service to all without discrimination—a standard that in its modern setting is conditioned by the demands of the Equal Protection Clause of the Fourteenth Amendment.

. . . .

Justice HARLAN, whom Justice BLACK, Justice CLARK, and Justice STEWART join, dissenting.

. . . .

The Court attempts to fit § 26 within the coverage of the Equal Protection Clause by characterizing it as in effect an affirmative call to residents of California to discriminate. The main difficulty with this viewpoint is that it depends upon a characterization of § 26 that cannot fairly be made. The provision is neutral on its face, and it is only by in effect asserting that this requirement of passive official neutrality is camouflage that the Court is able to reach its conclusion. In depicting the provision as tantamount to active state encouragement of discrimination the Court essentially relies on the fact that the California Supreme Court so concluded. It is said that the findings of the highest court of California as to the meaning and impact of the enactment are entitled to great weight. I agree, of course, that *findings of fact* by a state court should be given great weight, but this familiar proposition hardly aids the Court's holding in this case.

There is no disagreement whatever but that § 26 was meant to nullify California's fair-housing legislation and thus to remove from private residential property transactions the state-created impediment upon freedom of choice. There were no disputed issues of fact at all, and indeed the California Supreme Court noted at the outset of its opinion that "[i]n the trial court proceedings allegations of the complaint were not factually challenged, no evidence was introduced, and the only matter placed in issue was the legal sufficiency of the allegations." There was no finding, for example, that the defendants' actions were anything but the product of their own private choice. Indeed, since the alleged racial discrimination that forms the basis for the *Reitman* refusal to rent on racial grounds occurred in 1963, it is not possible to contend that § 26 in any way influenced this particular act. There were no findings as to the general effect of § 26.

The Court declares that the California court "held the purpose and intent of § 26 was to authorize private racial discriminations in the housing market . . . ," ante, p. 1631, but there is no supporting fact in the record for this characterization. Moreover, the grounds which prompt legislators or state voters to repeal a law do not determine its constitutional validity. That question is decided by what the law does, not by what those who voted for it wanted it to do, and it must not be forgotten that the Fourteenth Amendment does not compel a State to put or keep any particular law about race on its books. The Amendment forbids only a State to pass or keep in effect laws discriminating on account of race. California has not done this.

A state enactment, particularly one that is simply permissive of private decision-making rather than coercive and one that has been adopted in this most democratic of processes, should not be struck down by the judiciary under the Equal Protection Clause without persuasive evidence of an invidious purpose or effect. The only "factual" matter relied on by the majority of the California Supreme Court was the context in which Proposition 14 was adopted, namely, that several strong antidiscrimination acts had been passed by the legislature and opposed by many of those who successfully led the movement for adoption of Proposition 14 by popular referendum. These circumstances, and these alone, the California court held, made § 26 unlawful under this Court's cases interpreting the Equal Protection Clause. This, of course, is nothing but a legal conclusion as to federal constitutional law, the California Supreme Court not having relied in any way upon the State Constitution. Accepting all the suppositions under which the state court acted, I cannot see that its conclusion is entitled to any special weight in the discharge of our own responsibilities. Put in another way, I cannot transform the California court's conclusion of law into a finding of fact that the State through the adoption of § 26 is actively promoting racial discrimination. It seems to me manifest that the state court decision rested entirely on what that court conceived to be the compulsion of the Fourteenth Amendment, not on any fact-finding by the state courts.

. . . .

. . . The core of the Court's opinion is that § 26 is offensive to the Fourteenth Amendment because it effectively *encourages* private discrimination. By focusing on "encouragement" the Court, I fear, is forging a slippery and unfortunate criterion by which to measure the constitutionality of a statute simply permissive in purpose and effect, and inoffensive on its face.

It is true that standards in this area have not been definitely formulated, and that acts of discrimination have been included within the compass of the Equal Protection Clause not merely when they were compelled by a state statute or other governmental pressures, but also when they were said to be "induced" or "authorized" by the State. Most of these cases, however, can be approached in terms of the impact and extent of affirmative state governmental activities, *e.g.,* the action of a sheriff, *Lombard v. Louisiana;* the official supervision over a park, *Evans v. Newton;* a joint venture with a lessee in a municipally owned building, *Burton v. Wilmington Parking Authority.* In situations such as these the focus has been on positive state cooperation or partnership in affirmatively promoted activities, an involvement that could have been avoided. Here, in contrast, we have only the straight-forward adoption of a neutral provision restoring to the sphere of free choice, left untouched by the Fourteenth Amendment, private behavior within a limited area of the racial problem. The denial of equal protection emerges only from the conclusion reached by the Court that the implementation of a new policy of governmental neutrality, embodied in a constitutional provision and replacing a former policy of antidiscrimination, has the effect of lending encouragement to those who wish to discriminate. In the context of the actual facts of the case, this conclusion appears to me to state only a truism: people who want to discriminate but were previously forbidden to do so by state law are now left free because the State has chosen to have no law on the subject at all. Obviously whenever there is a change in the law it will have resulted from the concerted activity of those who desire the change, and its enactment will allow those supporting the legislation to pursue their private goals.

A moment of thought will reveal the far-reaching possibilities of the Court's new doctrine, which I am sure the Court does not intend. Every act of private discrimination is either forbidden by state law or permitted by it. There can be little doubt that such permissiveness—whether by express constitutional or statutory provision, or implicit in the common law—to some extent "encourages" those who wish to discriminate to do so. Under this theory "state action" in the form of laws that do nothing more than passively permit private discrimination could be said to tinge *all* private discrimination with the taint of unconstitutional state encouragement.

This type of alleged state involvement, simply evincing a refusal to involve itself at all, is of course very different from that illustrated in such cases as *Lombard, Peterson, Evans* and *Burton,* where the Court found active involvement of state agencies and officials in specific acts of discrimination. It is also quite different from cases in which a state enactment could be said to have the obvious purpose of fostering discrimination. I believe the state action required to bring the Fourteenth Amendment into operation must be affirmative and purposeful, actively fostering discrimination. Only in such a case is ostensibly "private" action more properly labeled "official." I do not believe that the mere enactment of § 26, on the showing made here, falls within this class of cases.

. . . Opponents of state antidiscrimination statutes are now in a position to argue that such legislation should be defeated because, if enacted, it may be unrepealable. More fundamentally, the doctrine underlying this decision may hamper, if not preclude, attempts to deal with the delicate and troublesome problems of race relations through the legislative process. . . .

. . . .

## NOTES

1.  One writer poses a challenging hypothetical on the basis of the *Mulkey* decision: "Suppose the state of California were to pass a statute which provided specifically that homeowners had the right to discriminate on racial and other bases as to persons whom they invited into their own houses as guests." *See* Williams, *Mulkey v. Reitman and State Action*, 14 U.C.L.A. L. REV. 26 (1966).

Would such a statute be constitutional under *Mulkey*? Or does the statute merely publicize the "law which already exists"? Or is there a major constitutional distinction between the right to discriminate on the basis of race with respect to an invitation to one's house which is quite different than the right to discriminate on the basis of race in the sale and rental of property?

2.  Two other writers, although agreeing with the result in *Mulkey*, profess to find the court's opinion doctrinally unsatisfying. *See* Horowitz & Karst, *The Proposition Fourteen Cases: Justice In Search of a Justification*, 14 U.C.L.A. L. REV. 37 (1966). Professors Horowitz and Karst reprimand the Supreme Court for failing to "examine the values represented by the state action requirement. . .". They suggest an alternative approach to the decision in *Mulkey*:*

. . . .

"A respectable opinion in these cases would take seriously the statement quoted by the court in *Mulkey:* 'Only by sifting facts and weighing circumstances can the nonobvious involvement of the State in private conduct be attributed its true significance.' The facts and circumstances would be measured against the reasons which have supported making a distinction between private conduct and state action: (a) individuals have important interests in freedom of choice—the state does not; (b) when the state acts to discriminate on the basis of race or otherwise to impair a constitutionally protected value, its impact on that value is normally far greater than would be the impact of a similar private act; (c) the state action requirement promotes the decentralization of both administrative and policy-making functions within the federal system. 'Significant involvement' by the state in private discriminatory conduct is a concept that is meaningful only in relation to these considerations. If the reasons for the state action requirement are ignored, then 'significant involvement' is nothing but a label to paste over a court's decision.

. . . .

"In the Proposition Fourteen cases, this approach would have required at least some inquiry into the nature and extent of the impact of discrimination on the would-be tenants, along with the extent of the individual, personal, or economic interests of the discriminating landlords, or any other justifications for the state's preference for the landlords' freedom of choice over the tenants' interest in housing. The court's bare citation of cases is not responsive to this need for inquiry. In the white primary cases the fourteenth amendment certainly did not restrict the actions of the private groups just because the state made their discrimination 'legally possible.' Rather, the private discriminatory conduct effectively nullified Negro participation in the electoral process—a vital impairment of the interests of the excluded Negroes. In *Marsh v. Alabama* private conduct effectively barred the excluded distributor of religious pamphlets from reaching an entire community. These serious invasions of important interests were what lent 'significance'—in the constitutional sense—to the state's 'authorization' of private discriminatory conduct. Presumably state law may authorize some kinds of private racial discrimination without violating the fourteenth amendment; to the extent that the court's opinion in the Proposition Fourteen cases suggests otherwise, it will be overruled or ignored."

Horowitz and Karst are trying to construct even-handed and meaningful criteria for identifying when a situation presents significant state involvement and when it does not. Do you think their effort succeeds? Is their approach an improvement over the rationale for decision in *Mulkey* offered by Justice White?

## EVANS v. ABNEY
Supreme Court of the United States
396 U.S. 435, 24 L. Ed. 2d 634, 90 S. Ct. 628 (1970)

Justice BLACK delivered the opinion of the Court.

. . . .

. . . [T]he action of the Georgia Supreme Court declaring the Baconsfield trust terminated presents no violation of constitutionally protected rights, and any harshness that may have resulted from the State court's decision can be attributed solely to its intention to effectuate as nearly as possible the explicit terms of Senator Bacon's will.

Petitioners first argue that the action of the Georgia court violates the United States Constitution in that it imposes a drastic "penalty," the "forfeiture" of the park, merely because of the city's compliance with the constitutional mandate expressed by this Court in *Evans v. Newton*. Of course, *Evans v. Newton* did not speak to the problem of whether Baconsfield should or could continue to operate as a park; it held only that its continued operation as a park had to be without racial discrimination. But petitioners now want to extend that holding to forbid the Georgia courts from closing Baconsfield on the ground that such a closing would penalize the city and its citizens for complying with the Constitution. We think, however, that the will of Senator Bacon and Georgia law provide all the justification necessary for imposing such a "penalty." The construction of wills is essentially a state-law question, and in this case the Georgia Supreme Court, as we read its opinion, interpreted Senator Bacon's will as embodying a preference for termination of the park rather than its integration. Given this, the Georgia court had no alternative under its relevant trust laws, which are long standing and neutral with regard to race, but to end the Baconsfield trust and return the property to the Senator's heirs.

. . . In the case at bar there is not the slightest indication that any of the Georgia judges involved were motivated by racial animus or discriminatory intent of any sort in construing and enforcing Senator Bacon's will. Nor is there any indication that Senator Bacon in drawing up his will was persuaded or induced to include racial restrictions by the fact that such restrictions were permitted by the Georgia trust statutes. . . .

. . . .

. . . It bears repeating that our holding today reaffirms the traditional role of the States in determining whether or not to apply their *cy pres* doctrines to particular trusts. Nothing we have said here prevents a state court from applying its *cy pres* rule in a case where the Georgia court, for example, might not apply its rule. More fundamentally, however, the loss of charitable trusts such as Baconsfield is part of the price we pay for permitting deceased persons to exercise a continuing control over assets owned by them at death. This aspect of freedom of testation, like most things, has its advantages and disadvantages. The responsibility of this Court, however, is to construe and enforce the Constitution and laws of the land as they are and not to legislate social policy on the basis of our own personal inclinations.

. . . .

The judgment is

Affirmed.

Justice MARSHALL took no part in the consideration or decision of this case.

Justice BRENNAN, dissenting.

. . . .

. . . When it is as starkly clear as it is in this case that a public facility would remain open but for the constitutional command that it be operated on a non-segregated basis, the closing of that facility conveys an unambiguous message of community involvement in racial discrimination. . . .

. . . .

First, there is state action whenever a State enters into an arrangement which creates a private right to compel or enforce the reversion of a public facility. . . .

Moreover, a State cannot divest itself by contract of the power to perform essential governmental functions. . . . The decision whether or not a public facility shall be operated in compliance with the Constitution is an essential *governmental* decision. . . .

. . . The resolution of the Mayor and Council upon their resignation as trustees makes it very clear that the probability of a reversion had induced them to abandon desegregation. Private interests of the sort asserted by the respondents here cannot constitutionally be allowed to control the conduct of public affairs in that manner.

A finding of discriminatory state action is required here on a second ground. Shelley v. Kraemer, 334 U.S. 1 (1948), stands at least for the proposition that where parties of different races are willing to deal with one another a state court cannot keep them from doing so by enforcing a privately authored racial restriction. Nothing in the record suggests that after our decision in *Evans v. Newton* the City of Macon retracted its previous willingness to manage Baconsfield on a nonsegregated basis, or that the white beneficiaries of Senator Bacon's generosity were unwilling to share it with Negroes, rather than have the park revert to his heirs. . . . Thus, so far as the record shows, this is a case of a state court's enforcement of a racial restriction to prevent willing parties from dealing with one another. The decision of the Georgia courts thus, under *Shelley v. Kraemer*, constitutes state action denying equal protection.

Finally, a finding of discriminatory state action is required on a third ground. . . .

. . . This state-encouraged testamentary provision is the sole basis for the Georgia courts' holding that Baconsfield must revert to Senator Bacon's heirs. The Court's finding that it is not the State of Georgia but "a private party which is injecting the racially discriminatory motivation" inexcusably disregards the State's role in enacting the statute [of 1905] without which Senator Bacon could not have written the discriminatory provision.

. . . .

I would reverse the judgment of the Supreme Court of Georgia.

[Justice DOUGLAS' dissent is omitted.]

---

## NOTES

1. The editors of the HARVARD LAW REVIEW make a distinction between *Evans I* and *Evans II* insofar as the state action point in it is concerned. A few years before Senator Bacon wrote his will the Georgia legislature enacted a statute which "explicitly authorized the establishment of charitable trusts with racially restrictive conditions." Justice White had argued in his concurrence in *Evans I* that there was sufficient state involvement in the discriminatory restrictions of the Senator's will to render those provisions state action. But the argument continues: "In *Evans II*, by contrast, the private act to which the state offered its support was not the drafting of the will by Senator Bacon, but rather the decision by his heirs to secure a reversion once the condition had failed." *See The Supreme Court, 1969 Term*, 84 HARV. L. REV. 1, 57-58 (1970).

The same law review editors raise some interesting questions on the relationship *Evans v. Abney* bears to previous state action cases in the Supreme Court:

In Griffin v. County School Bd., 377 U.S. 218 (1964), closing a public school system to avoid integration was declared unconstitutional. Should *Griffin* therefore have caused the Supreme Court to refuse to permit the reverter to the heirs in *Evans v. Abney*? Why or why not?

Public action, it might be argued, closed the public schools in Prince Edward County, Virginia but a private law suit to enforce the terms of a will closed the park in Macon, Georgia. If that analysis distinguished *Griffin*, should Shelley v. Kraemer, 334 U.S. 1 (1948), come into play? Does *Shelley* prohibit the use of courts to effect a result which has the consequence of avoiding compliance with the fourteenth amendment mandate against state-sponsored racial discrimination?

2. Dean Louis Pollak reads *Shelley* to proscribe judicial intervention where there has been state interference when the parties are otherwise willing to deal and not to discriminate on the basis of race. *See* Pollak, *Racial Discrimination and Judicial Integrity: A Reply to Professor Wechsler*, 108 U. PA. L. REV. 1, 13 (1959). Under Dean Pollak's analysis, is *Shelley* relevant to a fact pattern such as that of *Evans v. Abney*? Can you think of a construction of *Shelley v. Kraemer* which would prohibit the reverter under the facts of *Evans v. Abney*?

3. Does *Evans v. Abney* represent a retreat from *Reitman v. Mulkey*?

## State Action and Access to Private Property

A Supreme Court case which for a time appeared to mark a sharp turn-around in the traditional conception of state action was Marsh v. Alabama, 326 U.S. 501 (1946). There a company-owned town refused to permit a Jehovah's Witness to distribute religious literature on the main street of the town. The Supreme Court did not permit the private ownership of the town to place a whole community outside the bounds of constitutional obligation. An important aspect of the case was that no alternative forum was available to the Jehovah's Witness in the *Marsh* case. The court held that a company-owned town was still sufficiently public so that the exercise of first amendment rights could not be abridged, despite the claim of private ownership. Justice Black said for the court: "Whether a corporation or a municipality owns or possesses the town the public in either case has an identical interest in the functioning of the community in such manner that the channels of communications remain free."

Justice Reed dissented: "A state does not have the moral duty of furnishing the opportunity for information, education and religious enlightenment to its inhabitants, including those who live in company towns, but it has not heretofore been adjudged that it must commandeer, without compensation, the private property of other citizens to carry out that obligation."

The *Marsh* case did not revolutionize the state action concept. The potential for submitting private property to constitutional duty represented by the case was not realized and the more traditional approach reflected by Justice Reed's observations continued to reflect the basic judicial approach attitude to the state action problem. Yet the question raised by the case became increasingly important. To what extent, if any, should the private sector be subject to constitutional commands?

## AMALGAMATED FOOD EMPLOYEES UNION LOCAL 590 v. LOGAN VALLEY PLAZA, INC.

Supreme Court of the United States
391 U.S. 308, 20 L. Ed. 2d 603, 88 S. Ct. 1601 (1968)

[A case which revived the more sophisticated approach to the state action problem found in *Marsh* was *Amalgamated Food Employees Local 590 v. Logan Valley Plaza, Inc.*, where the Supreme Court held that informational picketing in a privately-owned shopping center could not be enjoined. The state court had enjoined the picketing on the ground that private property could not be used for such purposes if its owners did not so desire. The Supreme Court refused to allow private ownership to overrule the first amendment claims of the picketers. The Court was not impressed by the argument that since those restraining expression were private parties the first amendment claims were not relevant. The Court emphasized the quasi-public aspect of the shopping center and held that considering the role of the shopping center in the life of the community, the banishment of ideas and protest from a shopping center was action sufficiently quasi-public in effect to satisfy the state action requirement of the fourteenth amendment.]

Justice MARSHALL delivered the opinion of the Court.

. . . .

This Court has . . . held, in *Marsh v. State of Alabama*, that under some circumstances property that is privately owned may, at least for First Amendment purposes, be treated as though it were publicly held. . . .

. . . .

The similarities between the business block in *Marsh* and the shopping center in the present case are striking. . . . The general public has unrestricted access to the mall property. The shopping center here is clearly the functional equivalent to the business district of Chickasaw involved in *Marsh*.

It is true that, unlike the corporation in *Marsh* the respondents here do not own the surrounding residential property and do not provide municipal services therefore. Presumably, petitioners are free to canvass the neighborhood with their message about the nonunion status of Weis Market, just as they have been permitted by the state courts to picket on the berms outside the mall. Thus, unlike the situation in *Marsh*, there is no power on respondents' part to have petitioners totally denied access to the community for which the mall serves as a business district. This fact, however, is not determinative. . . .

We see no reason why access to a business district in a company town for the purpose of exercising First Amendment rights should be constitutionally required, while access for the same purpose to property functioning as a business district should be limited simply because the property surrounding the "business district" is not under the same ownership. Here the roadways provided for vehicular movement within the mall and the sidewalks leading from building to building are the functional equivalent of the streets and sidewalks of a normal municipal business district. The shopping center premises are open to the public to the same extent as the commercial center of a normal town. So far as can be determined, the main distinction in practice between use by the public of the Logan Valley Mall and of any other business district, were the decisions of the state courts to stand, would be that those members of the general public who sought to use the mall premises in a manner contrary to the wishes of the respondents could be prevented from so doing.

Such a power on the part of respondents would be, of course, part and parcel of the rights traditionally associated with ownership of private property. And it may well be that respondents' ownership of the property here in question gives them various rights, under the laws of Pennsylvania, to limit the use of that property by members of the public in a manner that would not be permissible were the property owned by a municipality. All we decide here is that because the shopping center serves as the community business block "and is freely accessible and open to the people in the area and those passing through," *Marsh v. State of Alabama*, the State may not delegate the power, through the use of its trespass laws, wholly to exclude those members of the public wishing to exercise their First Amendment rights on the premises in a manner and for a purpose generally consonant with the use to which the property is actually put.

We do not hold that respondents, and at their behest the State, are without power to make reasonable regulations governing the exercise of First Amendment rights on their property. Certainly their rights to make such regulations are at the very least co-extensive with the powers possessed by States and municipalities, and recognized in many opinions of this Court, to control the use of public property. Thus where property is not ordinarily open to the public, this Court has held that access to it for the purpose of exercising First Amendment rights may be denied altogether. See *Adderley v. State of Florida* [text, p. 808]. . . .

. . . .

It is therefore clear that the restraints on picketing and trespassing approved by the Pennsylvania courts here substantially hinder the communication of the ideas which petitioners seek to express to the patrons of Weis. . . .

The sole justification offered for the substantial interference with the effectiveness of petitioners' exercise of their First Amendment rights to promulgate their views through handbilling and picketing is respondents' claimed absolute right under state law to prohibit any use of their property by others without their consent. However, unlike a situation involving a person's home, no meaningful claim to protection of a right of privacy can be advanced by respondents here. Nor on the facts of the case can any significant claim to protection of the normal business operation of the property be raised. Naked title is essentially all that is at issue.

The economic development of the United States in the last 20 years reinforces our opinion of the correctness of the approach taken in *Marsh*. The large-scale movement of this country's population from the cities to the suburbs has been accompanied by the advent of the suburban shopping center, typically a cluster of individual retail units on a single large privately owned tract. It has been estimated that by the end of 1966 there were between 10,000 and 11,000 shopping centers in the United States and Canada, accounting for approximately 37% of the total retail sales in those two countries.

These figures illustrate the substantial consequences for workers seeking to challenge substandard working conditions, consumers protesting shoddy or overpriced merchandise, and minority groups seeking nondiscriminatory hiring policies that a contrary decision here would have. Business enterprises located in downtown areas would be subject to on-the-spot public criticism for their practices, but businesses situated in the suburbs could largely immunize themselves from similar criticism by creating a *cordon sanitaire* of parking lots around their stores. Neither precedent nor policy compels a result so at variance with the goal of free expression and communication that is the heart of the First Amendment.

Therefore, as to the sufficiency of respondents' ownership of the Logan Valley Mall premises as the sole support of the injunction issued against petitioners, we simply repeat what was said in *Marsh v. State of Alabama,* "Ownership does not always mean absolute dominion. The more an owner, for his advantage, opens up his property for use by the public in general, the more do his rights become circumscribed by the statutory and constitutional rights of those who use it." Logan Valley Mall is the functional equivalent of a "business block" and for First Amendment purposes must be treated in substantially the same manner.

The judgment of the Supreme Court of Pennsylvania is reversed and the case is remanded for further proceedings not inconsistent with this opinion. It is so ordered.

Justice BLACK, dissenting.

. . . .

. . . The question is under what circumstances can private property be treated as though it were public? The answer that *Marsh* gives is when that property has taken on *all* the attributes of a town, *i.e.,* "residential buildings, streets, a system of sewers, a sewage disposal plant and a 'business block' on which business places are situated." I can find nothing in *Marsh* which indicates that if one of these features is present, *e.g.,* a business district, this is sufficient for the Court to confiscate a part of an owner's private property and give its use to people who want to picket on it.

In allowing the trespass here, the majority opinion indicates that Weis and Logan invited the public to the shopping center's parking lot. This statement is contrary to common sense. Of course there was an implicit invitation for customers of the adjacent stores to come and use the marked off places for cars. But the whole public was no more wanted there than they would be invited to park free at a pay parking lot. Is a store owner or several of them together less entitled to have a parking lot set aside for customers than other property owners? To hold that store owners are compelled by law to supply picketing areas for pickets to drive store customers away is to create a court-made law wholly disregarding the constitutional basis on which private ownership of property rests in this country. And of course picketing, that is patroling, is not free speech and not protected as such. . . . These pickets do have a constitutional right to speak about Weis' refusal to hire union labor, but they do not have a constitutional right to compel Weis to furnish them a place to do so on his property.

. . . .

[The dissenting opinions of Justices HARLAN and WHITE are omitted.]

---

BARRON, AN EMERGING FIRST AMENDMENT RIGHT OF ACCESS TO THE MEDIA?, 37 Geo. Wash. L. Rev. 487 (1969)*

. . . .

What is truly significant about *Logan Valley* is that it represents a confrontation between modern land use and the first amendment. The Court states its awareness of the historic role that access to public places such as sidewalks, streets and parks has played in the enjoyment of freedom of expression in the United States. Moreover, we have examined the manner in which the lower federal courts have broadened the kinds of public facilities where such access must be permitted. What *Logan Valley* does is to forge a similar extension at the Supreme Court level as a result of the Court's awareness of changes in residential patterns. . . . [I]n *Logan Valley* the Court attempts to point out the significance which the shopping center has acquired in American life. The Court reasoned that in the automobile-centered suburb, the shopping center is a focal point for the community, so that access to its parking lot may be indispensable to secure access to that community. The Court qualified the sweep of this observation, however, by remarking that the store being picketed was located in the shopping center at issue and that the message in controversy was related to the operations of that particular store. The Court said it was not necessary to decide whether the shopping center's property rights could, under the first amendment, prevent picketing unrelated to the uses of the shopping center. But the implication seems clear that even unrelated picketing would be viewed sympathetically by the *Logan Valley* majority when conducted in a shopping center which is the only quasi-public facility in a community.

Particularly intriguing, and signifying a major step in the development of an access-oriented approach to the first amendment, is the Court's comparative indifference to whether the facilities in question are publicly or privately owned. Mr. Justice Marshall's somewhat deprecatory remark on this point was that "Naked title is essentially all that is at issue." The rise of a first amendment perspective indifferent to whether the source of restraint on freedom of expression is public or private is of course what rouses Mr. Justice Black to dissent. In retrospect, his dissent is rather ironic, in that the majority in *Logan Valley*

---

relied so heavily on *Marsh,* an opinion written by Mr. Justice Black. For him, however, *Marsh* is really a sport among the cases for it is that rare case where all the attributes of a town are in private hands. It appears that so long as anything less than a total deprivation of first amendment rights is involved, Mr. Justice Black would not make any new inroads on property rights. But whatever the misgivings of Mr. Justice Black and the other dissenters on the point, the majority of the Court now appears ready to expand the opportunities for access to a wider class of forums than ever before. The test of such access, however, apparently is not going to proceed on any simplistic private-public dichotomy but rather on the following inquiry: how crucial to the communication at issue is access to the forum in question?

A vital question is whether or not the protest must be somewhat related to the function of the public facility which is being used. In [Wolin v. Port of New York Authority, 392 F.2d 83 (2d Cir. 1968)] the fact that the bus terminal was primarily designed for large crowds was, in the court's view, just what made it an appropriate place for communicating political views. Apparently the court held that wherever there are public facilities through which large numbers of people can be easily reached, there is a right of access to those facilities by groups interested in using them for purposes of political expression. This is not true, of course, where the expression might injure the primary purpose for which the facility exists. This approach may well become, if in view of *Logan Valley* it is not already, the constitutional law of access to public facilities for purposes of political and social protest.

The implications of these developments are quite significant. If public use of government facilities imposes on government a duty to permit use of the facilities for the communication of ideas, the significance of this development for privately-run facilities is fairly clear. If such facilities, even though privately sponsored, are also "dedicated to a public use," then presumably the same affirmative obligations are placed on those facilities. The blurring of what is "private" and what is "public," which has come to characterize so much of our life, eventually may create an access-oriented approach to first amendment values which will endow any natural or obvious forum in our society with responsibilities for stimulating the communication of ideas. To be sure, the new concern with the public forum is a form of judicial response to the constitutionally sanctioned irresponsibility of the privately controlled mass communication system. To the extent that responsibilities are placed on the latter, and to the extent that they are voluntarily assumed, the pressure on the public facility to serve as an arena for protest in default may be lessened, but it should not be relieved entirely. An access-oriented approach to the first amendment implies affirmative obligation on government as well as the private sector and its concerns.

. . . .

_____

### Other Developments in State Action

1.   In Marjorie Webster Junior College, Inc. v. Middle States Ass'n of Colleges & Secondary Schools, Inc., 302 F. Supp. 459 (D.D.C. 1969), an incorporated proprietary college sought to enjoin a regional college accreditation association from refusing to evaluate or to accredit, if qualified, any but nonprofit schools. The federal district court gave judgment for the college on the ground that the accrediting association's action violated the antitrust laws and constituted arbitrary and unreasonable action in violation of the due process clause. The language of the court on whether the action of a private accrediting association should be considered sufficiently quasi-public to subject the association to constitutional limitation is illustrative of recent efforts to broaden the reach of state action:

"Much of the evidence adduced in connection with the first count of the complaint applies also to count two. As previously indicated, identical injury is alleged and the relief requested is the same. Plaintiff contends that although the Constitution of the United States normally limits only action by the government, a private association performing a state function or exercising delegated powers of a governmental nature becomes subject to the restraints of the Constitution, including the due process clause. Plaintiff further insists that when a private organization becomes so powerful that membership in that association is an economic necessity, the power must be exercised in a reasonable manner. Defendant, on the other hand, denies that membership is an economic necessity and that its refusal to make an exception to its rules for plaintiff is arbitrary and unreasonable. Middle States further denies that its activities are of a quasi-governmental nature and contends that the internal administration of a private association is beyond the reach of judicial review. . . . As a general rule, courts adhere to a policy of noninterference with the internal affairs of private voluntary associations. Membership in such a group is considered a privilege and not a right. However, there is an exception when the association enjoys monopoly power in an area of vital public concern. If the power, because of public reliance upon it, is great enough to make membership a necessity for successful operation, judicial intervention may be justified.

"Evidence has been presented that accreditation by Middle States is necessary for plaintiff to continue operating successfully as a junior college. Prominent educators appearing as witnesses in this proceeding expressed divergent views. However, some who are members of the defendant association testified that regional accreditation is more important today than ever before and that lack of it would be harmful to any institution. Accreditation has become the symbol of academic acceptability, and many states measure the educational excellence of their public institutions by the standards of the regional associations. Furthermore, defendant acts in a quasi-governmental capacity by virtue of its role in the distribution of Federal funds under the 'aid to education statutes.' Selection of the recipient schools is frequently dependent upon the accredited status of the applicant. Middle States and the other regionals are officially recognized by the United States Commissioner of Education who publishes a list of nationally recognized accrediting agencies and associations which he determines to be reliable authority as to the quality of training offered by an educational institution. 38 U.S.C. § 1653(a).

"In addition, the evidence discloses an arrangement between the United States Office of Education and the regional associations relative to the eligibility of institutions which are candidates for but have yet to achieve final accreditation. In 1967 Middle States' practice of attesting to the quality of these institutions through 'letters of reasonable assurance' of accreditation was discontinued when the Office of Education agreed to accept in lieu thereof 'Correspondent Status' listing as evidence of eligibility for assistance. Mr. John Proffitt, Director of the Accreditation and Institutional Eligibility Staff of the Office of Education testified: 'Accreditation has become, fundamentally speaking, a service aspect to the Federal Government in determining eligibility for funding. This has arisen as a result of the language written into Federal funding assistance legislation by Congress.'

"Over the years Middle States has achieved a position of great influence in American education. It has elevated the quality of education and has become a powerful instrumentality which sets policies in an area of vital concern to the public. Accreditation has been established in the public mind as a mark of distinction and quality. It confers a significant competitive advantage on defendant's members as distinguished from non-members. In view of the great reliance placed on accreditation by the public and the government, these associations must assume responsibility not only to their membership but also to society. There is need for the application of sound standards in the evaluation of all schools and for increased coordination and understanding throughout the educational world. The regional accrediting associations and the Federation have an opportunity to provide new leadership in orienting their policies toward the broader welfare of society and the public interest."

**2.** Willingness to find state action present where a powerful private actor such as a "private" accrediting association exercises "delegated powers of a governmental nature" made the federal district court decision in *Marjorie Webster* a pioneering decision and a prime example of a *continuing* movement to submit the corporation to constitutional standards. However, the court of appeals, per Judge Bazelon, reversed the district court on a non-constitutional ground: the deprivation suffered by the Marjorie Webster Jr. College was insufficient to justify judicial intervention. Marjorie Webster Junior College, Inc. v. Middle States Ass'n of Colleges & Secondary Schools, Inc., 432 F.2d 650 (D.C. Cir. 1969), *cert. denied* 400 U.S. 965 (1970). On the question whether state action would encompass private action such as the activity of the accrediting association, Judge Bazelon, citing Marsh v. Alabama, 326 U.S. 501 (1946) and Terry v. Adams, 345 U.S. 461 (1953), made the following comments:

> We may assume, without deciding, that either the nature of appellant's activities or the federal recognition which they are awarded renders them state action subject to the limitations of the Fifth Amendment. If so, however, the burden remains with appellee to show the unreasonableness of the restriction, not simply in the abstract but as applied specifically to it. We need not decide here the precise limits of those circumstances under which governmental action may restrict or injure the activities of proprietary educational institutions. For the reasons already discussed, we conclude that appellee has failed to show that the present restriction was without reasonable basis. Accordingly, it must be upheld.

**3.** Some constitutional law scholars have pointed out the anachronistic element in applying the state action concept in an era when so much power is exercised not by individuals but by corporations. Miller, *Toward the "Techno-Corporate" State?— An Essay in American Constitutionalism*, 14 VILL. L. REV. 1 (1968):*

. . . .

---

"With respect to the national government, the 'corporate states' are of far greater importance than are the 50 geographical entities. The latter are significant mainly as administrative districts for centrally established policies; they are, in large part, anachronisms in the body politic. Writing in 1908, Woodrow Wilson asserted that 'the question of the relation of the states to the federal government is the cardinal question of our constitutional system.' That may have been accurate when Wilson wrote, but if so, it no longer is. The marriage of science and technology to entrepreneurship has created the far more important question of the relation of the supercorporations to the federal government, even though Justice Frankfurter once observed, somewhat testily, that the 'unifying forces of modern technology' have not wiped out State lines. The learned Justice was accurate so far as formal federalism is concerned, but quite mistaken with respect to functional or economic federalism. . . . Functional federalism is a way of describing nongeographical private governments which operate within the American polity. The power of the units of functional federalism is far greater than that of the units of formal federalism.

· · · ·

"However, if due process of law is to become the way in which a measure of accountability is brought to the corporate enterprise, one major constitutional leap must be taken, namely, the concept of 'state action' will have to be dropped by the Supreme Court, at least in part. The Constitution has since the *Civil Rights Cases* of 1883 been said to run against governments only. The need is to recognize that governments can be both official *and* private. . . .

"It should not be inferred that corporate due process has proceeded very far or has even been recognized as valid by many commentators. For that matter, for much of public government that process which is 'due' is notably absent, as witness, for example, federal contract awards and the distribution of federal largesse. Despite *Marsh* and other judicial decisions and the actions by Congress and the President, the concept has far more potentiality as a means of effecting corporate accountability than it has actuality. However, it may be an idea 'whose time has come', as Alexander Pekelis predicted 20 years ago. The next generation of constitutional lawyers, he said, would ever increasingly be concerned with private governments. Corporate due process, within a broadly defined corporate community, will be a major part of that concern."

· · · ·

**4.** The court has held that a city, under an order to desegregate public recreational facilities, violates equal protection when it permits exclusive use of recreational facilities, however temporary, by segregated private schools since it enhances the attractiveness of such schools. Gilmore v. Montgomery, 417 U.S. 556 (1974). Justice Blackmun for the majority remanded the case, however, on the question of nonexclusive access to such facilities by segregated schools and, by segregated nonschool groups, in common or exclusively, in order to determine, under *Burton*, text, p. 1004, if it would involve the government so directly in the actions of such users "as to warrant court intervention on constitutional grounds," *e.g.*, "direct impairment of a school segregation order," use which "constitutes a vestige" of state-sponsored segregation in recreational facilities, and government rationing of the facilities. The court did emphasize, however, that exclusion from state facilities "infringes upon the freedom of the individual to associate as he chooses."

## C. THE BURGER COURT: THE NARROWING OF THE STATE ACTION CONCEPT?

### LLOYD CORP. v. TANNER
Supreme Court of the United States
407 U.S. 551, 33 L. Ed. 2d 131, 92 S. Ct. 2219 (1972)

Justice POWELL delivered the opinion of the Court.

This case presents the question reserved by the Court in Amalgamated Food Employees Union Local 590 v. Logan Valley Plaza, Inc., 391 U.S. 308 (1968), as to the right of a privately owned shopping center to prohibit the distribution of handbills on its property when the handbilling is unrelated to the shopping center's operations. . . .

Lloyd Corporation, Ltd. (Lloyd), owns a large, modern retail shopping center in Portland, Oregon. . . .

. . . .

On November 14, 1968, the respondents in this case distributed within the Center handbill invitations to a meeting of the "Resistance Community" to protest the draft and the Vietnam War. The distribution, made in several different places on the mall walkways by five young people, was quiet and orderly, and there was no littering. There was a complaint from one customer. Security guards informed the respondents that they were trespassing and would be arrested unless they stopped distributing the handbills within the Center. The guards suggested that respondents distribute their literature on the public streets and sidewalks adjacent to but outside of the Center complex. Respondents left the premises as requested "to avoid arrest" and continued the handbilling outside. Subsequently this suit was instituted in the District Court seeking declaratory and injunctive relief.

. . . .

The courts below considered the critical inquiry to be whether Lloyd Center was "the functional equivalent of a public business district." This phrase was first used in *Logan Valley,* but its genesis was in *Marsh.* It is well to consider what *Marsh* actually decided. . . . The Court simply held that where private interests were substituting for and performing the customary functions of government, First Amendment freedoms could not be denied where exercised in the customary manner on the town's sidewalks and streets. Indeed, as title to the entire town was held privately, there were no publicly owned streets, sidewalks or parks where such rights could be exercised.

*Logan Valley* extended *Marsh* to a shopping center situation in a different context from the company town setting, but it did so only in a context where the First Amendment activity was related to the shopping center's operations. There is some language in *Logan Valley,* unnecessary to the decision, suggesting that the key focus of *Marsh* was upon the "business district," and that whenever a privately owned business district serves the public generally its sidewalks and streets become the functional equivalents of similar public facilities. As Mr. Justice Black's dissent in *Logan Valley* emphasized, this would be an incorrect interpretation of the Court's decision in *Marsh.* . . .

The holding in *Logan Valley* was not dependent upon the suggestion that the privately owned streets and sidewalks of a business district or a shopping center are the equivalent, for First Amendment purposes, of municipally owned streets and sidewalks. No such expansive reading of the opinion for the Court is necessary or appropriate. The opinion was carefully phrased to limit its holding to the picketing involved, where the picketing was "directly related in its purpose to the use to which the shopping center property was being put," and where the store was located in the center of a large private enclave with the consequence that no other reasonable opportunities for the pickets to convey their message to their intended audience were available.

Neither of these elements is present in the case now before the Court.

The handbilling by respondents in the malls of Lloyd Center had no relation to any purpose for which the center was built and being used. It is nevertheless argued by respondents that since the Center is open to the public the private owner cannot enforce a restriction against handbilling on the premises. The thrust of this argument is considerably broader than the rationale of *Logan Valley*. It requires no relationship, direct or indirect, between the purpose of the expressive activity and the business of the shopping center. The message sought to be conveyed by respondents was directed to all members of the public, not solely to patrons of Lloyd Center or of any of its operations. Respondents could have distributed these handbills on any public street, on any public sidewalk, in any public park, or in any public building in the city of Portland.

Respondents' argument, even if otherwise meritorious, misapprehends the scope of the invitation extended to the public. The invitation is to come to the Center to do business with the tenants. It is true that facilities at the Center are used for certain meetings and for various promotional activities. The obvious purpose, recognized widely as legitimate and responsible business activity, is to bring potential shoppers to the Center, to create a favorable impression, and to generate goodwill. There is no open-ended invitation to the public to use the Center for any and all purposes, however incompatible with the interests of both the stores and the shoppers whom they serve.

. . . .

A further fact, distinguishing the present case from *Logan Valley*, is that the Union picketers in that case would have been deprived of all reasonable opportunity to convey their message to patrons of the Weis store had they been denied access to the shopping center. . . .

. . . .

Respondents contend, however, that the property of a large shopping center is "open to the public," serves the same purposes as a "business district" of a municipality, and therefore has been dedicated to certain types of public use. The argument is that such a center has sidewalks, streets, and parking areas which are functionally similar to facilities customarily provided by municipalities. It is then asserted that all members of the public, whether invited as customers or not, have the same right of free speech as they would have on the similar public facilities in the streets of a city or town.

The argument reaches too far. The Constitution by no means requires such an attenuated doctrine of dedication of private property to public use. The closest decision in theory, *Marsh v. Alabama*, involved the assumption by a private enterprise of all of the attributes of a state-created municipality and the exercise by that enterprise of semi-official municipal functions as a delegate of the State. In effect, the owner of the company town was performing the full spectrum of municipal powers and stood in the shoes of the State. In the instant case there is no comparable assumption or exercise of municipal functions or power.

Nor does property lose its private character merely because the public is generally invited to use it for designated purposes. Few would argue that a free standing store, with abutting parking space for customers, assumes significant public attributes merely because the public is invited to shop. Nor is size alone the controlling factor. The essentially private character of a store and its privately owned abutting property does not change by virtue of being large or clustered with other stores in a modern shopping center. This is not to say that no differences may exist with respect to government regulation or rights of citizens arising by virtue of the size and diversity of activities carried on within a privately owned facility serving the public. . . .

We hold that there has been no such dedication of Lloyd's privately owned and operated shopping center to public use as to entitle respondents to exercise therein the asserted First Amendment rights. Accordingly, we reverse the judgment and remand the case to the Court of Appeals with directions to vacate the injunction.

It is so ordered.

. . . .

Justice MARSHALL, with whom Justice DOUGLAS, Justice BRENNAN, and Justice STEWART join, dissenting.

. . . .

## NOTES

1. *Logan Valley* applied a "dedication to public" use concept to a privately owned shopping center.

2. Did the court in *Lloyd* put brakes on any further application of the dedication to public use doctrine as far as private premises are concerned? Certainly, under *Lloyd*, dedication to public use of a shopping center for free expression purpose is halted at the facts of *Logan Valley*. Exercise of the first amendment rights of the public is conditioned on a showing of a relationship between the site of the protest and the object of the protest. This doctrine makes the content of the communication the touchstone for the exercise of first amendment rights on private premises. In dissent, in *Lloyd*, Marshall argued that *Logan*

*Valley* had made the touchstone whether private premises are actually functioning like a city business district. Obviously, the effect of the "site of the protest-object of the protest test" is to tighten the state action requirement and therefore to limit the extent to which private entities are subject to first amendment obligation. But is there anything in the logic of the "object of the protest-site of the protest" idea that justifies such a distinction in terms of state action theory?

Is the distinction rooted in an idea that if a shopping center, or a unit within it, is involved in a dispute, it has somehow given consent to be involved in controversy, and, therefore, should be subject to suffer the promulgation of the views of its adversaries on its premises? In other words, in *Logan Valley*, the dedication to public use was, arguably, due to the acts of the Weis Market. Since Lloyd Corp. had presumably no connection with the Vietnam war one way or the other, Lloyd could not be said to have consented to a dedication of a public use of its property for purposes of promulgating the views of the anti-war protesters in *Lloyd v. Tanner*.

Notice that in *Lloyd* the state action concept is used to resolve a dispute between the claims of property and the assertion of rights under the first amendment. In a sense, the tougher the state action concept applied by the courts the greater the protection granted to property but the more limited the capacity of picketers and pamphleteers to be able to communicate or protest.

### MOOSE LODGE NO. 107 v. IRVIS
Supreme Court of the United States
407 U.S. 163, 32 L. Ed. 2d 627, 92 S. Ct. 1965 (1972)

Justice REHNQUIST delivered the opinion of the Court.

Appellee Irvis, a Negro, was refused service by appellant Moose Lodge, a local branch of the national fraternal organization located in Harrisburg, Pennsylvania. Appellee then brought this action under 42 U.S.C. § 1983 for injunctive relief in the United States District Court for the Middle District of Pennsylvania. He claimed that because the Pennsylvania liquor board had issued appellant Moose Lodge a private club license that authorized the sale of alcoholic beverages on its premises, the refusal of service to him was "state action" for the purposes of the Equal Protection Clause of the Fourteenth Amendment. . . .

A three-judge district court, convened at appellee's request, upheld his contention on the merits, and entered a decree declaring invalid the liquor license issued to Moose Lodge "as long as it follows a policy of racial discrimination in its membership or operating policies or practices." . . .

. . . .

Moose Lodge is a private club in the ordinary meaning of that term. It is a local chapter of a national fraternal organization having well defined requirements for membership. It conducts all of its activities in a building that is owned by it. It is not publicly funded. Only members and guests are permitted in any lodge of the order; one may become a guest only by invitation of a member or upon invitation of the house committee.

Appellee, while conceding the right of private clubs to choose members upon a discriminatory basis, asserts that the licensing of Moose Lodge to serve liquor by the Pennsylvania Liquor Control Board amounts to such State involvement with the club's activities as to make its discriminatory practices forbidden by the Equal Protection Clause of the Fourteenth Amendment. . . .

. . . .

The Court has never held, of course, that discrimination by an otherwise private entity would be violative of the Equal Protection Clause if the private entity receives any sort of benefit or service at all from the State, or if it is subject to state regulation in any degree whatever. Since state-furnished services include such necessities of life as electricity, water, and police and fire protection, such a holding would utterly emasculate the distinction between private as distinguished from State conduct set forth in *The Civil Rights Cases,* and adhered to in subsequent decisions. Our holdings indicate that where the impetus for the discrimination is private, the State must have "significantly involved itself with invidious discriminations," in order for the discriminatory action to fall within the ambit of the constitutional prohibition.

. . . With one exception, which is discussed *infra,* there is no suggestion in this record that the Pennsylvania statutes and regulations governing the sale of liquor are intended either overtly or covertly to encourage discrimination.

. . . .

Here there is nothing approaching the symbiotic relationship between lessor and lessee that was present in *Burton.* . . . Unlike *Burton,* the Moose Lodge building is located on land owned by it, not by any public authority. Far from apparently holding itself out as a place of public accommodation. Moose Lodge quite ostentatiously proclaims the fact that it is not open to the public at large. Nor is it located and operated in such surroundings that although private in name, it discharges a function or performs a service that would otherwise in all likelihood be performed by the State. In short, while Eagle was a public restaurant in a public building, Moose Lodge is a private social club in a private building.

With the exception hereafter noted, the Pennsylvania Liquor Control Board plays absolutely no part in establishing or enforcing the membership or guest policies of the club which it licenses to serve liquor. There is no suggestion in this record that the Pennsylvania Act, either as written or as applied, discriminates against minority groups either in their right to apply for club licenses themselves or in their right to purchase and be served liquor in places of public accommodation. The only effect that the state licensing of Moose Lodge to serve liquor can be said to have on the right of any other Pennsylvanian to buy or be served liquor on premises other than those of Moose Lodge is that for some purposes club licenses are counted in the maximum number of licenses which may be issued in a given municipality. Basically each municipality has a quota of one retail license for each 1,500 inhabitants. Licenses issued to hotels, municipal golf courses and airport restaurants are not counted in this quota, nor are club licenses until the maximum number of retail licenses is reached. Beyond that point, neither additional retail licenses nor additional club licenses may be issued so long as the number of issued and outstanding retail licenses remains above the statutory maximum.

The District Court was at pains to point out in its opinion what it considered to be the "pervasive" nature of the regulation of private clubs by the Pennsylvania Liquor Control Board. As that court noted, an applicant for a club license must make such physical alterations in its premises as the board may require, must file a list of the names and addresses of its members and employees, and must keep extensive financial records. The board is granted the right to inspect the licensed premises at any time when patrons, guests or members are present.

However detailed this type of regulation may be in some particulars, it cannot be said to in any way foster or encourage racial discrimination. Nor can it be said to make the State in any realistic sense a partner or even a joint venturer in the club's enterprise. The limited effect of the prohibition against obtaining additional club licenses when the maximum number of retail licenses allotted to a municipality has been issued, when considered together with the availability of liquor from hotel, restaurant, and retail licensees falls far short of conferring upon club licensees a monopoly in the dispensing of liquor in any given municipality or in the State as a whole. We therefore hold that, with the exception hereafter noted, the operation of the regulatory scheme enforced by the Pennsylvania Liquor Control Board does not sufficiently implicate the State in the discriminatory guest policies of Moose Lodge so as to make the latter "State action" within the ambit of the Equal Protection Clause of the Fourteenth Amendment.

The District Court found that the regulations of the Liquor Control Board adopted pursuant to statute affirmatively require that "every club licensee shall adhere to all the provisions of its constitution and by-laws." Appellant argues that the purpose of this provision "is purely and simply and plainly the prevention of subterfuge," pointing out that the *bona fides* of a private club, as opposed to a place of public accommodation masquerading as a private club, is a matter with which the State Liquor Control Board may legitimately concern itself. Appellee concedes this to be the case, and expresses disagreement with the District Court on this point. There can be no doubt that the label "private club" can and has been used to evade both regulations of State and local liquor authorities, and statutes requiring places of public accommodation to serve all persons without regard to race, color, religion, or national origin. . . .

The effect of this particular regulation on Moose Lodge under the provisions of the constitution placed in the record in the court below would be to place State sanctions behind its discriminatory membership rules, but not behind its guest practices, which were not embodied in the constitution of the lodge. Had there been no change in the relevant circumstances since the making of the record in the District Court, our holding . . . that appellee has standing to challenge only the guest practices of Moose Lodge would have a bearing on our disposition of this issue. Appellee stated upon oral argument, though, and Moose Lodge conceded in its Brief that the bylaws of the Supreme Lodge have been altered since the lower court decision to make applicable to guests the same sort of racial restrictions as are presently applicable to members.

Even though the Liquor Control Board regulation in question is neutral in its terms, the result of its application in a case where the constitution and bylaws of a club required racial discrimination would be to invoke the sanctions of the State to enforce a concededly discriminatory private rule. . . . *Shelley v. Kraemer,* makes it clear that the application of state sanctions to enforce such a rule would violate the Fourteenth Amendment. Although the record before us is not as clear as one would like, appellant has not persuaded us that the District Court should have denied any and all relief.

Appellee was entitled to a decree enjoining the enforcement of § 113.09 of the regulations promulgated by the Pennsylvania Liquor Control Board insofar as that regulation requires compliance by Moose Lodge with provisions of its constitution and by-laws containing racially discriminatory provisions. He was entitled to no more. The judgment of the District Court is reversed, and the cause remanded with instructions to enter a decree in conformity with this opinion.

Reversed and remanded.

Justice DOUGLAS, with whom Justice MARSHALL joins, dissenting.

. . . .

. . . [T]he fact that a private club gets some kind of permit from the State or municipality does not make it *ipso facto* a public enterprise or undertaking, any more than the grant to a householder of a permit to operate an incinerator puts the householder in the public domain. We must therefore examine whether there are special circumstances involved in the Pennsylvania scheme which differentiate the liquor license possessed by Moose Lodge from the incinerator permit.

Pennsylvania has a state store system of alcohol distribution. Resale is permitted by hotels, restaurants, and private clubs which all must obtain licenses from the Liquor Control Board. . . . Once a license is issued the licensee must comply with many detailed requirements or risk suspension or revocation of the license. Among these requirements is Regulation No. 113.09 which says "Every club licensee shall adhere to all the provisions of its Constitution and By-laws." This regulation means, as applied to Moose Lodge, that it must adhere to the racially discriminatory provision of the Constitution of its Supreme Lodge. . . .

. . . .

. . . The result, as I see it, is the same as though Pennsylvania had put into its liquor licenses a provision that the license may not be used to dispense liquor to Blacks, Browns, Yellows—or atheists or agnostics. Regulation No. 113.09 is thus an invidious form of state action.

Were this regulation the only infirmity in Pennsylvania's licensing scheme, I would perhaps agree with the majority that the appropriate relief would be a decree enjoining its enforcement. But there is another flaw in the scheme not so easily cured. Liquor licenses in Pennsylvania, unlike driver's licenses, or marriage licenses, are not freely available to those who meet racially neutral qualifications. There is a complex quota system, which the majority accurately describes. What the majority neglects to say is that the Harrisburg quota, where Moose Lodge No. 107 is located, has been full for many years. No more club licenses may be issued in that city.

This state-enforced scarcity of licenses restricts the ability of blacks to obtain liquor, for liquor is commercially available *only* at private clubs for a significant portion of each week. Access by blacks to places that serve liquor is further limited by the fact that the state quota is filled. A group desiring to form a nondiscriminatory club which would serve blacks must purchase a license held by an existing club, which can exact a monopoly price for the transfer. The availability of such a license is speculative at best, however, for, as Moose Lodge itself concedes, without a liquor license a fraternal organization would be hard-pressed to survive.

Thus, the State of Pennsylvania is putting the weight of its liquor license, concededly a valued and important adjunct to a private club, behind racial discrimination.

. . . .

Justice BRENNAN, with whom Justice MARSHALL joins, dissenting.

When Moose Lodge obtained its liquor license, the State of Pennsylvania became an active participant in the operation of the Lodge bar. Liquor licensing laws are only incidentally revenue measures; they are primarily pervasive regulatory schemes under which the State dictates and continually supervises virtually every detail of the operation of the licensee's business. Very few, if any, other licensed businesses experience such complete state involvement. . . .

Plainly, the State of Pennsylvania's liquor regulations intertwine the State with the operation of the Lodge bar in a "significant way [and] lend [the State's] authority to the sordid business of racial discrimination." . . .

. . . .

## NOTES

1. The approach to state action in *Moose Lodge* was hardly an inevitable one. In Seidenberg v. McSorley's Old Ale House, Inc., 317 F. Supp. 593 (S.D. N.Y. 1970), the National Organization for Women (NOW) succeeded in obtaining a ruling from a federal court that a well-known men's bar in New York City, McSorley's Old Ale House, violated the equal protection clause

of the fourteenth amendment by refusing to serve women. Mc-Sorley's defended by arguing that as a private business McSorley's was not bound by the equal protection clause of the fourteenth amendment. The federal district court, however, held that state action was present. The court used a "pervasive regulation" theory of state action. The following excerpt from Judge Mansfield's decision states the court's position:

> We believe that the present case is distinguishable from those licensing cases where courts have shied away from finding state action, because here we are not dealing merely with a bare state licensor-licensee relationship. In addition we are faced with a pervasive regulation by the state of the activities of the defendant, a commercial enterprise engaged in voluntarily serving the public except for women.

*McSorley's* case holds that where an industry is usually subject to a "pervasive scheme" of governmental regulation, that business should be viewed as essentially quasi-governmental. Should we conclude that in both the *CBS* case text, p. 1049, and the *Moose Lodge* case the Supreme Court has rejected the pervasive regulation theory? After *Moose Lodge,* is *McSorley's* case reversed *sub silentio*? Or can *McSorley's* be distinguished from *Moose Lodge*?

2. In *Moose Lodge* the court emphasized that the Pennsylvania Liquor Control Board played "absolutely no part in establishing or enforcing the membership or guest policies of the club which it licenses to serve liquor. In a footnote in *Moose Lodge,* the court said this was "unlike the situation in *Public Utilities Commission v. Pollak* where the regulatory agency had affirmatively approved the practice of the regulated entity after full investigation. . . ."

However, in *CBS,* hadn't the FCC "approved" the network practice of refusing to sell time for the editorial advertising? *See* text, p. 872.

In *CBS,* a no state action theory appears to be predicated on the fact that the FCC had not compelled the networks to abandon their policy of refusal to sell time for editorial advertising. But in *Moose Lodge,* a no-state action conclusion is reached on the ground that the state had taken no part in the club's "membership or guest policies." In *CBS,* on the other hand, the FCC held that the network policy of refusal to sell time to editorial advertising was as a matter of communications law and policy entirely permissible.

In other words, if the "regulatory approval" theory of *Moose Lodge* was the true touchstone of state action for the Burger

Court, shouldn't the court have concluded there was state action in *CBS*?

3. In CBS, a majority of the court held that a broadcasting policy of refusal to sell time to groups like the Democratic National Committee for purposes of editorial advertising did not offend the first amendment. First amendment and state action problems are closely intertwined in *CBS*. The case is reported and discussed from a first amendment perspective in the text on p. 872.

Chief Justice Burger, joined by Justices Stewart and Rehnquist, found that the network ban on selling editorial advertising to citizens and groups should not be considered "governmental action" for purposes of the first amendment. The Chief Justice analyzed broadcast legislation and found that it revealed a congressional intention "to maintain a substantial measure of journalistic independence for the broadcast licensee." Furthermore, Burger considered it crucial that the Federal Communications Commission, *i.e.,* the government, "has not fostered the licensee policy challenged here; it has simply declined to command particular action because it fell within the area of journalistic discretion."

Burger distinguished state action cases like *Burton v. Wilmington Parking Authority,* see text, p. 1004, on the ground that the government was not a partner with or engaged in a "symbiotic relationship" with the broadcasters in *CBS* as the state was with the Parking Authority in *Burton* because the government did not profit "from the invidious discrimination of its proxy" as it had in *Burton.*

The court in *CBS* went to considerable trouble to distinguish Public Utilities Comm'n v. Pollak, 343 U.S. 451 (1952). *Pollak* had held that a publicly owned bus company which had installed radio receivers in its buses was still subject to first amendment obligation. In *Pollak,* the District of Columbia Public Utilities Commission had approved the practice of equipping the buses with radio receivers and this was deemed sufficient to enable the court in *Pollak,* as Burger phrased it in *CBS,* "to trigger first amendment protections in a record involving agency approval of the conduct of a public utility."

Chief Justice Burger distinguished *Pollak* as follows:

Here, Congress had not established a regulatory scheme for broadcast licensees as pervasive as the regulation of public transportation in *Pollak.* More important, as we have noted, Congress has affirmatively indicated in the Communications Act that certain journalistic decisions are for the licensee, subject only to the restrictions imposed by evaluation of its overall performance under the public interest standard. In *Pollak* there was no suggestion that Congress had considered worthy of protection the carrier's interest in exercising discretion over the content of communications forced on passengers. A more basic distinction, between *Pollak* and this case is that *Pollak* was concerned with a transportation utility that itself derives no benefit from the First Amendment.

Burger reasoned in *CBS* that if the network ban on editorial advertising were deemed the equivalent of governmental action, few licensee decisions involving broadcast content "would escape constitutional scrutiny." Furthermore, Burger stated that treating network policies such as the one in controversy in *CBS* as governmental action would contradict a clear congressional purpose to legislate in behalf of "essentially private broadcast journalism held only broadly accountable to public interest standards."

Justice Brennan, joined by Justice Marshall, dissented in *CBS*. They took exception to the view that the network ban on editorial advertising was not governmental action. The dissenters took particular exception to the court's view that broadcasting was, unlike the buses in the District of Columbia in *Pollak*, not *subject* to the kind of pervasive regulation which should make industry policies like the no-editorial advertising ban be regarded as governmental action. Brennan stated:

> As the Court of Appeals recognized, "the general characteristics of the broadcast industry reveal an extraordinary relationship between the broadcasters and the federal government—a relationship which puts that industry in a class with few others." More specifically, the public nature of the airwaves, the governmentally created preferred status of broadcast licensees, the pervasive federal regulation of broadcast programming, and the Commission's specific approval of the challenged broadcaster policy combine in this case to bring the promulgation and enforcement of that policy within the orbit of constitutional imperatives.

4. Burger's principal argument that *Pollak* should be distinguished from *CBS* was that a transportation utility, unlike the broadcasting industry, derives no benefit from the first amendment. But how does that distinction, even if valid, serve to distinguish *Pollak* from *CBS* in terms of a state action analysis?

What response, if any, is available to the following argument? If the presence or absence of "regulatory approval" is still a decisive test for determining whether governmental action exists, as was recently declared to be the case by the Supreme Court in *Moose Lodge,* then FCC regulatory approval of the ban on editorial advertising policy should have been sufficient to show governmental action in *CBS.* The FCC approved the no-editorial advertising policy just as the Public Utilities Commission in *Pollak* approved equipping D.C. buses with radio receivers.

Is the key difference between *Pollak* and *CBS* that in *CBS,* in the court's view, Congress has manifested a policy of neither approving or disapproving broadcaster programming decisions. In *Pollak,* on the other hand, there was no manifest legislative intention to leave matters such as putting radios on buses to the bus company.

But can it be persuasively argued that when Congress *requires* licensee discretion, licensee compliance with that requirement is no longer governmental action?

After *CBS* and *Moose Lodge,* should we conclude that the "pervasive regulation" theory of state action has been abandoned by the Supreme Court?

5.   Adickes v. S. H. Kress & Co., 398 U.S. 144 (1970), a case which arose before the enactment of the Civil Rights Act of 1964, involved a white woman who had been denied service in defendant's restaurant because she was in the company of Negroes. The Supreme Court held that a case under 42 U.S.C.A. § 1983 could be made out if the plaintiff could prove that the employee of the restaurant and a city policeman joined in an understanding to deny plaintiff service or to cause her arrest because she was in the company of Negroes. What was essential for state action, using 42 U.S.C.A. § 1983, said Justice Harlan, for the court, was the involvement of the city policeman. This involvement would show the state action necessary to establish a denial of fourteenth amendment rights of equal protection.

Justice Brennan concurring in part and dissenting in part in *Adickes* said that in his view, three cases, Peterson v. Greenville, 373 U.S. 244 (1963), Lombard v. Louisiana, 373 U.S. 267 (1963), and Robinson v. Florida, 378 U.S. 153 (1964), established the following principle:

[A] state policy of discouraging privately chosen integration or encouraging privately chosen segregation, even though the policy is expressed in a form non-discriminating on its face, is unconstitutional and taints the privately chosen segregation it seeks to bring about.

Since under a Mississippi statute a restaurateur could discriminate for any reason, Brennan believed the statute violated the fourteenth amendment. This was so, in his view, because a private restaurateur, under such a state statute, was permitted to discriminate on the basis of race.

Under Brennan's theory in *Adickes,* can it be argued that the government cannot have a policy of encouraging the networks to ban the sale of broadcast time for editorial advertising any more than the government could directly forbid the networks to sell editorial advertising?

Is the difficulty with pressing this reasoning too far on the *CBS* facts that in *CBS* there was a government policy already operative in broadcasting which did encourage the free interchange of ideas, *i.e.,* the fairness doctrine? There was no equivalent state policy furthering integration in restaurants in Mississippi at the time the *Adickes* case arose.

*CBS* and *Adickes* together suggest that whether state action is found to exist or not often depends on the court's reaction to the merits of the substantive constitutional issue presented by a case. What the Democratic National Committee considered to be private censorship in *CBS,* a majority of the court considered to be editorial discretion.

### State Action and Privately-Owned Public Utilities

The definition of state action continues to be a source of constitutional litigation. Illustrative is a case involving shut-off of services by a public utility company.

The issue of whether the cut-off of electric utility service by a privately-owned utility company during a dispute over nonpayment constituted state action violative of the fourteenth amendment under 42 U.S.C. § 1983 came before the Supreme Court in Jackson v. Metropolitan Edison Co., — U.S. — (1975). The court, per Rehnquist, J., described the facts of the case as follows:

> Petitioner then filed suit against Metropolitan Edison in the United States District for the Middle District of Pennsylvania under the Civil Rights Act, 42 U.S.C. § 1983, seeking damages for the termination and an injunction requiring Metropolitan to continue providing power to her residence until she had been afforded notice, hearing, and an opportunity to pay any amounts found due. She urged that under state law she had an entitlement to reasonably continuous electrical service to her home and that Metropolitan's termination of her service for alleged nonpayment, action allowed by a provision of its general tariff filed with the Commission, constituted "state action: depriving her of property in vio-

lation of the Fourteenth Amendment's guarantee of due process of law."

The court held that the state was not sufficiently involved with the utility company's action terminating service to render that conduct "attributable to the state for the purposes of the Fourteenth Amendment." Although the court conceded that public utility regulation was extensive and detailed, the court held there was not a sufficiently close nexus between the state and the challenged action of the utility company. The monopoly status of a utility was declared to be not determinative of the issue of whether the utility's termination of service was "state action." In *Metropolitan Edison,* it was argued that the state Public Utilities Commission had approved a general tariff, a provision of which allowed discontinuance of service without notice or hearing by the utility company. The court held, however, that state action still had not occurred because the PUC had never really considered or authorized the tariff provision.

In *Metropolitan Edison,* Justice Douglas, dissenting, said in part:

> The particular regulations at issue, promulgated by the monopolist, were authorized by state law and were made enforceable by the weight and authority of the State. Moreover, the State retains the power of oversight to review and amend the regulations if the public interest so requires. Respondent's actions are sufficiently intertwined with those of the State, and its termination-of-service provisions are sufficiently buttressed by state law, to warrant a holding that respondent's actions in terminating this householder's service were "state action" for the purpose of giving federal jurisdiction over respondent under 42 U.S.C. § 1983. . . . [W]hat the Court does today is to make a significant departure from our previous treatment of state action issues.

---

Is *Metropolitan Edison* a departure from previous treatment of "state action" issues? It would appear to be consistent with *CBS,* text, p. 1049, but is it consistent with *Burton v. Wilmington Parking Authority,* text, p. 1004?

Are Justice Douglas' separate opinions in *CBS* and *Metropolitan Edison* consistent?

Chapter 13

CONGRESSIONAL LEGISLATION IN AID
OF CIVIL RIGHTS AND LIBERTIES

Throughout the text, reference has been made to congressional legislation in aid of civil rights, *e.g.*, Congress's use of its commerce powers to remedy discrimination in public accommodations (text, pp. 195-213), use of Title VI of the 1964 Civil Rights Act to cut off federal funds to grantees who discriminate (text, p. 243). In the present chapter, the focus will be on congressional power under the thirteenth, fourteenth and fifteenth amendments. In two reconstruction periods, separated by some 75 years, Congress fashioned a sword to implement the shield provided by the constitutional guarantees. Specific rights were defined and criminal and civil remedies were created.

After a general overview of the two reconstruction periods, the chapter will turn to the criminal and civil remedies available for denial of the constitutional guarantees. Attention will be given to the constitutional authority for enacting the particular remedial provisions. Questions that will concern us include whether the vague, nebulous guarantees of the fourteenth amendment, § 1, can be enforced through criminal sanctions consistent with the due process requirement that fair warning be given regarding what behavior is proscribed, the specific rights which are protected and the obstacles which exist to effective use of the remedial tools.

The focus will then turn to the respective roles of court and Congress in defining the substantive content of the guarantees. Can Congress interpret the constitutional provisions to provide more protection than afforded by judicial interpretation? Can it dilute judicially-recognized rights? The chapter ends with the question raised in *Marbury v. Madison:* What are the roles of the respective branches in interpreting the Constitution?

## A. TWO ERAS OF RECONSTRUCTION: SHIELD AND SWORD

### 1. The First Reconstruction

The Civil War left some four million newly-freed Blacks with little security in a hostile environment. State Black Codes, severely restricting the new freedmen's mobility, employment, and civil status, promised to replace the formal institution of slavery with a new form of subjugation. Prior to the war, constitutional protections were available, with few exceptions, only against the federal government, and federal protection of fundamental rights was generally nonexistent. The aftermath of that conflict, however, produced a rash of constitutional amendments and implementing legislation against state and even private denial of civil rights. Between 1866 and 1875, three amendments and seven civil rights statutes were enacted providing both a shield and a sword for individual security. If these tools had been reasonably implemented, a second reconstruction period may never have been necessary. As Robert K. Carr noted in his work FEDERAL PROTECTION OF CIVIL RIGHTS: QUEST FOR A SWORD 36 (1947): "The meaning and purpose of these Civil War Amendments has been the subject of much controversy. But one can build a strong case contending that their congressional framers meant them to serve as a basis for a positive, comprehensive federal program—a program defining fundamental civil rights protected by federal machinery against both state and private encroachment."

But such was not to be the fate of the first reconstruction. Judicial invalidation, legislative repeal and administrative nullification undermined the effectiveness of the legislative program. *See Slaughterhouse Cases,* text, p. 402; *Civil Rights Cases,* text, p. 989; *Plessy v. Ferguson,* text, p. 593. *See generally* M. BERGER, EQUALITY BY STATUTE (1967); Gressman, *The Unhappy History of Civil Rights Legislation,* 50 MICH. L. REV. 1323 (1952); Maslow & Robison, *Civil Rights Legislation and the Fight for Equality, 1862-1952,* 20 U. CHI. L. REV. 363 (1953). For a history of the debate on these measures, see STATUTORY HISTORY OF THE UNITED STATES: CIVIL RIGHTS, PART I (B. Schwartz ed. 1970). Nevertheless, some of the early legislation remains available, providing potential protection of individual rights against official and private misconduct.

1. The first assault of the reconstruction period came with the ratification of the thirteenth amendment, abolishing slavery and involuntary servitude in December, 1865. While the amendment was self-executing, § 2 gave Congress power "to enact all necessary and proper laws for the obliteration and prevention of slavery with all its badges and incidents." In *Civil Rights Cases,* 109 U.S. 3 (1883) (text, p. 989), the court stated that while the Amendment was self-executing, § 2 legislation could be "direct and primary," reaching governmental and private abuses alike. The question remains, of course, what actions are encompassed within the § 1 prohibition. *See Jones v. Mayer,* text, p. 1102. *See*

text, pp. 412-14, on the original understanding of the amendment's meaning.

2. The need for implementing legislation became immediately apparent. Southern Black Codes promised to undermine the new amendment. Congress responded in 1866 by enacting, over President Johnson's veto challenging the measure's constitutionality, a sweeping civil rights act. Section 1 declared that all persons born in the United States are citizens thereof and that all such citizens, with a few designated exceptions, "shall have the same right . . . to make and enforce contracts, to sue, be parties, give evidence, to inherit, purchase, lease, sell, hold and convey real and personal property, and to full and equal benefit of all laws and proceedings for the security of person and property, as is enjoyed by white citizens, and shall be subject to like punishment, pains, and penalties, and to none other, any law, statute, ordinance, regulation, or custom to the contrary notwithstanding." Although broad, this specification represented a compromise with the original draft bill providing "there shall be no discrimination in civil rights." The guarantees are presently embodied in 42 U.S.C. §§ 1981, 1982. *See Jones v. Mayer,* text, p. 1102. A Slave Kidnapping Act and a Peonage Abolition Act grounded on the thirteenth amendment were also passed in 1866 and 1867 respectively.

The 1866 Civil Rights Act went on to define appropriate remedies for effectuating these guarantees. As now embodied in 18 U.S.C. § 242, it provides: "Whoever, under color of any law, statute, ordinance, regulation, or custom, willfully subjects any inhabitant of any State, Territory, or District to the deprivation of any rights, privileges, or immunities secured or protected by the Constitution or laws of the United States, or to different punishments, pains or penalties on account of such inhabitant being an alien, or by reason of his color, or race, than are prescribed for the punishment of citizens, shall be fined not more than $1,000 or imprisoned not more than one year, or both; and if death results shall be subject to imprisonment for any term of years or for life." *See Screws v. United States,* text, p. 1062; *United States v. Price,* text, p. 1065.

3. Doubt concerning the adequacy of the thirteenth amendment to support this legislation and the desire to assure against the repeal of its safeguards by a less demanding Congress led to the adoption of the fourteenth amendment on July 9, 1868. In § 5, Congress was again empowered "to enforce, by appropriate legislation the provisions of this article." See text, pp. 1085-1101, on the scope of congressional power under this provision. Two years later, on March 30, 1870, the fifteenth amendment was ratified.

Whatever doubt might have existed as to Negro suffrage under the fourteenth, was removed by the guarantee of the franchise without regard to "race, color, or previous condition of servitude," applicable against both the state and the national government. In § 2, Congress was empowered to enact implementing legislation.

4. On May 31, 1870, Congress passed the first of three enforcement acts. The first two measures re-enacted the Civil Rights Act of 1866, extended federal protection for the franchise (see United States v. Reese, 92 U.S. 214 (1876), holding provisions unconstitutional because they were not limited to denials based upon race; see also James v. Bowman, 190 U.S. 127 (1903)), and introduced what is now 18 U.S.C. § 241. In its modern form, § 241 provides: "If two or more persons conspire to injure, oppress, threaten, or intimidate any citizen in the free exercise or enjoyment of any right or privilege secured to him by the Constitution or laws of the United States, or because of his having so exercised the same; or

"If two or more persons go in disguise on the highway, or on the premises of another, with intent to prevent or hinder his free exercise or enjoyment of any right or privilege so secured—

"They shall be fined not more than $10,000 or imprisoned not more than ten years or both; and if death results, they shall be subject to imprisonment for any term of years or for life." See United States v. Guest and United States v. Price, text, pp. 1066 and 1065.

5. The most sweeping of the Enforcement Acts, the Ku Klux Klan Act, was enacted on April 20, 1871, in response to the wave of violence against blacks throughout the South by organizations such as the K.K.K. Section 1 of the act, now 42 U.S.C. § 1983, gave a civil cause of action against those who, acting under color of law, denied a person's civil rights. In its modern form, it provides: "Every person who, under color of any statute, ordinance, regulation, custom, or usage, of any State or Territory, subjects, or causes to be subjected, any citizen of the United States or other persons within the jurisdiction thereof to the deprivation of any rights, privileges or immunities secured by the Constitution and laws, shall be liable to the person injured in action of law, suit in equity, or other proper proceedings for redress." See Monroe v. Pape, text, p. 1078.

In § 2 of the act, Congress, omitting the "under color of law" language, made it an offense to conspire or go in disguise for the purpose of depriving a person of the equal protection of the laws. While a criminal remedy was invalidated in United States

v. Harris, 106 U.S. 629 (1883), because of the absence of a state action limitation (*see also* United States v. Cruikshank, 92 U.S. 542 (1876); Virginia v. Rives, 100 U.S. 313 (1880), employing the same limitation in limiting enforcement of civil rights provisions), a civil remedy survived in what is now 42 U.S.C. § 1985(3): "If two or more persons in any State or Territory conspire to go in disguise on the highway or on the premises of another, for the purpose of depriving, either directly or indirectly, any person or class of persons of the equal protection of the laws, or of equal privileges or immunities under the laws; or for the purpose of preventing or hindering the constituted authorities of any State or Territory from giving or securing to all persons within such State or Territory the equal protection of the laws; [or] in any case of conspiracy set forth in this section, if one or more persons engaged therein do, or cause to be done, any act in furtherance of the object of such conspiracy, whereby another is injured in his person or property, or deprived of having and exercising any right or privilege of a citizen of the United States, the party so injured or deprived may have an action for the recovery of damages, occasioned by such injury or deprivation, against any one or more of the conspirators." *See Griffin v. Breckenridge,* text, p. 1081. These two provisions presently constitute two of the most important weapons in the arsenal available for individual protection of civil rights.

6. The final congressional blow of the first reconstruction came with the passage of the Civil Rights Act of 1875. In what was a precursor of Title II of the 1964 Civil Rights Act, Congress, using criminal sanctions, sought to open places of public accommodation without regard to race, color, or previous condition of servitude. However, the courts through the *Civil Rights Cases* text, p. 989, once again undermined the congressional program.

7. Eugene Gressman provides one perspective on the potential impact of the first reconstruction: "The changes made by this series of enactments and constitutional additions were of a most significant nature, altering substantially the balance between state and federal power. Civil rights were conceived of as inherent ingredients of national citizenship and as such were entitled to federal protection. And that protection was to be accorded in an affirmative fashion. Congress made what 'was probably the first attempt in the history of mankind to destroy the branches of slavery after its root had been destroyed.' The federal government was given effective weapons to combat and defend against all who would deprive inhabitants of the United States of their rights to be free of inequalities and distinctions based on race,

color and previous condition of servitude. These weapons were usable against both private individuals and those acting under color of state law." Gressman, *The Unhappy History of Civil Rights Legislation,* 50 Mich. L. Rev. 1323, 1336 (1952). The failure to realize these goals ultimately made a second recon- struction necessary.

### 2. The Second Reconstruction

1.  The initial congressional assault in the second recon- struction came with passage of the Civil Rights Act of 1957 and 1960 both of which were directed at expanding and protecting the franchise. While avoiding broader recommendations, such as those of the Civil Rights Commission, created under the 1957 Act, urging use of federal registrars to register qualified voters in the South, the legislation did extend district court jurisdiction in civil rights suits, provide for civil actions under designated con- ditions by the attorney general and for court certification of voters. *See* 42 U.S.C. § 1971.

2.  But the primary breakthrough came with passage of the Civil Rights Act of 1964. Consisting of eleven titles, it is a pan- oply of provisions recognizing civil rights and liberties and pro- viding for their enforcement. Title I, while still avoiding full fed- eral intervention in the voter registration process, did limit the use of exclusionary voter tests and strengthened the enforcement provisions of the 1957 and 1960 Acts by expediting voter suits. 42 U.S.C. § 1971. In Title II, the Act resurrected some of the principles of the 1875 Civil Rights Act, in providing injunctive relief for discrimination in places of public accommodation. 42 U.S.C. § 2000a. *See Heart of Atlanta Motel, Inc. v. United States* and *Katzenbach v. McClung,* text, pp. 200, 204. Title III provided for suits by the Attorney General to desegregate public facilities other than public schools when private suits could not be brought by the aggrieved parties. 42 U.S.C. § 2000b. Title IV provided for desegregation of public educational facilities through tech- nical assistance, training aid, and civil suits by the Attorney General when the private parties required such assistance. 42 U.S.C. § 2000c. As previously indicated (text, p. 243), Title VI of the 1964 Act provided the potentially potent weapon of cutting off federal funds to grantees who discriminate on the basis of race, color, or national origin. 42 U.S.C. § 2000d. The equal em- ployment opportunity provisions of Title VII, as amended in 1972 (42 U.S.C. § 2000e), prohibiting discrimination by employers, employment agencies or labor unions based on the individual's race, color, religion, sex or national origin have been previously noted. Text, p. 214. Titles VIII through XI (42 U.S.C. § 2000f-h

and 28 U.S.C. § 1447 (d)) deal with other provisions of less immediate interest.

3.  The failure of the southern states to take action to remedy voting discrimination coupled with Selma, Alabama when state troopers used extreme force to disperse a peaceful march to protest voting discrimination and the Democratic Party's need to enfranchise southern Blacks led to the 1965 Voting Rights Act (42 U.S.C. § 1973), *inter alia,* prohibiting the use of registration tests or procedures to discriminate racially and poll taxes, and providing for suspension of discriminatory tests or devices, for federal voting examiners, for review by the Attorney General or a three-judge court of the District of Columbia of changes in voting laws of states subject to the Act, and prohibiting interference with qualified voters or those seeking to aid them. *See South Carolina v. Katzenbach,* text, p. 1083, on the constitutionality of the Act.

4.  The 1968 Fair Housing Act prohibits discrimination based on race, color, religion or national origin, in the sale or rental of about 80 per cent of all housing as well as discrimination in financing or brokerage services. 42 U.S.C. § 3601 *et seq.* But as will be indicated below, the informal methods provided for enforcing the act have seriously limited its effectiveness. Text, pp. 1101-02. The 1968 Civil Rights Act also contained broad remedial provisions for denial of civil rights (text, p. 1076), an Indian Bill of Rights (25 U.S.C. § 1301 *et seq.*), and provisions setting criminal penalties for the use of interstate commerce to promote riots (18 U.S.C. § 2101).

5.  In 1970, Congress amended the 1965 Voting Rights Act, lowering the voting age to 18 in all elections and prohibiting the use of literacy tests and the use of state durational residency requirements for presidential and vice-presidential elections. On the constitutionality of these provisions, *see Oregon v. Mitchell,* text, p. 1095.

## B.  SECURING RIGHTS AGAINST OFFICIAL AND PRIVATE DISCRIMINATION

The first reconstruction provided a variety of general remedial provisions for protecting civil rights and liberties which are being used even today. While the criminal remedies in 18 U.S.C. §§ 241 and 242 have not lived up to their original promise, and 42 U.S.C. § 1985(3) is only presently recovering from an earlier adverse precedent, 42 U.S.C. § 1983 has become a vital tool in the arsenal of the civil rights attorney. In the present section, the focus will be on the statutory requirements and the constitutional problems these provisions raise. Under what circumstances can the statutes be used against official misconduct? Can private wrongs be constitutionally reached? What rights are secured by the statutes? Consider the respective strengths and weaknesses of civil versus criminal remedies for protecting civil rights, the need for effective federal intervention and the competing demands of federalism and the need for and desirability of formal legal sanctions as opposed to nonformal, nonlegal means of overcoming deprivations of civil rights, *e.g.*, alternative means of redressing grievances produced by police misconduct.

## 1. Criminal Remedies

*Statutory Requirements: Under Color of Law and Specific Intent*

1. An initial requirement of 18 U.S.C. § 242 (and its civil counterpart, 42 U.S.C. § 1983) is that the offensive action be done "under color of law." Is this the equivalent of "state action?" When, if at all, can private individuals be reached under this clause? Must private actors be motivated by state action? If state officials act contrary to state law can they nevertheless be acting under color of law?

2. During the course of an arrest, three local Georgia law enforcement officials beat and killed Hall, a young black man. Screws v. United States, 325 U.S. 91 (1945), involved a charge under 18 U.S.C. § 242 that the officers, acting under color of law, had willfully deprived Hall of his fourteenth amendment due process right to life, of his due process right to a trial, and if convicted, of his right to punishment according to law. A conspiracy count was also included.

A question on appeal was whether the defendants' conduct satisfied the statutory requirement that the action be done "under color of law." Justice Douglas's opinion for the court, joined by the Chief Justice and Justices Black and Reed, rejected the defendants' contention that state officers acting contrary to state law could not be said to be acting under color of state law. It was officers of the law, Justice Douglas reasoned, who made the arrest, and they were authorized to make an effective arrest. "It is clear that under 'color' of law means under 'pretense' of law. Thus acts of officers in the ambit of their personal pursuits are plainly excluded. Acts of officers who undertake to perform their official duties are included whether they hew to the line of their authority or overstep it." Justice Douglas cited the holding in United States v. Classic, 313 U.S. 299 (1941): "Misuse of power, possessed by virtue of state law and made possible only because the wrongdoer is clothed with the authority of state law, is action taken 'under color of' state law."

Responding to this interpretation of the statute, Justice Roberts joined by Frankfurter and Jackson, dissenting, argued that the only issue was "whether Georgia alone has the power and duty to punish, or whether this patently local crime can be made the basis of a federal prosecution. The practical question is whether the States should be relieved from responsibility to bring their law officers to book for homicide, by allowing prosecutions in the federal courts for a relatively minor offense carrying a short sentence. . . ." It followed that "[i]n the absence of clear direction by Congress we should leave to the States the enforcement of their criminal law, and not relieve States of the responsibility for vindicating wrongdoing that is essentially local or weaken the habits of local law enforcement by tempting reliance on federal authority for an occasional unpleasant task of local enforcement."

The defendants in *Screws* further argued that if the statute applied to their acts, it was unconstitutional since it made criminal acts violative of due process. It was contended that this would provide no ascertainable standard of guilt given the varying content of due process. Justice Douglas construed the statute to avoid this result.

The statuory requirement that the act be done "willfully," which Justice Douglas variously interpreted to mean with "bad purpose," or "an evil motive," or "reckless disregard," provided the saving feature. He claimed that "where the punishment imposed is only for an act knowingly done with the purpose of doing that which the statute prohibits, the accused cannot be said to suffer from lack of warning or knowledge that the act which he does is a violation of law." However, since the question of intent had not been properly submitted to the jury, the case had to be reversed and remanded for a new trial.

Responding favorably to the defendants' vagueness argument, Justice Roberts, joined by Frankfurter and Jackson, in dissent, warned that "[a]s misuse of the criminal machinery is one of the most potent and familiar instruments of arbitrary government, proper regard for the rational requirement of definiteness in criminal statutes is basic to civil liberties." Justice Roberts contended that this "intrinsic vagueness" could not be removed by requiring specific intent. "Does that not amount to saying that the black heart of the defendant enables him to know what are the constitutional rights deprivation of which the statute forbids, although we as judges are not prepared to state what they are unless it be to say that [§ 242] protects whatever rights the Constitution protects?"

See Alfange, "*Under Color of Law*": *Classic and Screws Revisited*, 47 CORNELL L.Q. 395 (1962); Shapiro, *Limitations in Prosecuting Civil Rights Violations*, 46 CORNELL L.Q. 532 (1961).

**3.** The *Screws* interpretation of the "under color of law" clause in § 242 was reaffirmed in Williams v. United States, 341 U.S. 97 (1951). Williams, a private detective, holding a special officer's card from the city, aided by two of his employees and a regular police officer detailed to aid in the investigation, successfully obtained confessions of theft by physical force. Justice Douglas, writing for the court, affirmed a conviction charging a violation of § 242, since the jury could properly find Williams was acting "under color of law." "[P]etitioner was no mere interloper but had a semblance of policeman's power from Florida."

## Secured Rights

**1.** *Screws* indicates that § 242 can be used to enforce fourteenth amendment due process rights and suggests that it is equally available for other fourteenth amendment, § 1, rights. But what of 18 U.S.C. § 241 which is not limited to actions done under color of law? Can it be used to enforce the fourteenth amendment, § 1, rights which refer to state action?

**2.** In a companion case to *Williams v. United States,* the court in United States v. Williams, 341 U.S. 70 (1951), provided a negative answer. The indictment charged that the private detective, his employees and the police officer had conspired to deprive citizens of their fourteenth amendment rights in violation of § 241. The petitioners were convicted, but the Court of Appeals reversed and the Supreme Court affirmed in a 5-4 decision.

Justice Frankfurter's opinion for the court, joined by Vinson, Jackson, and Minton, held that "§ 241 only covers conduct which interferes with rights arising from substantive powers of the Federal Government." It followed "that the rights which [§ 241] protects are those which Congress can beyond a doubt constitutionally secure against interference by private individuals. Decisions of this Court have established that this category includes rights which arise from the relationship of the individual and the Federal Government." *See* text, pp. 1073-74.

Justice Douglas, dissenting, adopted the position of Justice Rutledge in *Screws* that "in spite of the difference in wording of [§§ 241 and 242] there are 'no differences in the basic rights guarded. Each protects in a different way the rights and privileges secured to individuals by the Constitution.' " Justice Douglas reasoned that if Congress had desired to draw the distinction made by Justice Frankfurter "[t]he division of powers between State and Nation is so inherent in our republican form of government and so well established throughout our history that . . . it is hard to imagine that it would not have made its purpose clear in the language used."

3. In United States v. Price, 383 U.S. 787 (1966), the problems raised in the above cases were again considered. Three Mississippi law officers were accused of having taken three civil rights workers, Schwerner, Chaney, and Goodman from their cells at night, and transporting them to a place where 15 private persons were waiting. The indictments charged that the 18 defendants had "punished" the three men by willfully assaulting and killing them thus depriving them of their right "not to be summarily punished without due process of law."

The district court had sustained an indictment charging a conspiracy among the 18 defendants violative of 18 U.S.C. § 371, making it a crime to conspire to commit any offense against the United States (here § 242)—there was no appeal. While the lower court upheld counts charging a substantive violation of § 242 against the three law officers, it dismissed as to the 15 private individuals finding they were not acting under color of law.

While affirming the holding regarding the officers on the authority of Screws, the Supreme Court, per Justice Fortas, reversed the dismissal. "To act 'under color' of law," said Justice Fortas, "does not require that the accused be an officer of the State. It is enough that he is a willful participant in joint activity with the State or its agents." In this case, the indictment charged "joint activity, from start to finish. Those who took advantage of participation by state officers in accomplishment of the foul purpose alleged must suffer the consequences of the participation. In effect, if the allegations are true, they were participants in official lawlessness, acting in willful concert with state officers, and hence under color of law." In a footnote, Justice Fortas cited Burton v. Wilmington Parking Authority, text, p. 1004, in holding that the "conduct on the part of the private defendants . . . constitut[ed] 'state action,' and hence action 'under color' of law with section 242."

The court then considered an indictment charging each of the 18 defendants with a violation of § 241 which the district court had dismissed on the authority of United States v. Williams. Treating the problem as statutory rather than constitutional and noting the division of the court in Williams, the Supreme Court reversed. Justice Fortas concluded that the language of

§ 241 "includes rights or privileges protected by the Fourteenth Amendment; that whatever the ultimate coverage of the section may be, it extends to conspiracies otherwise within the scope of the section participated in by officials alone or in collaboration with private persons; and that the indictment . . . properly charges such a conspiracy in violation of § 241." Justice Fortas stressed that the language of the statute was "plain and unlimited" and that "it embraces *all* of the rights and privileges secured to citizens by all of the Constitution and *all* of the laws of the United States." In this case, there was no question of federal-state relations since there was "an allegation of state action which, beyond dispute, brings the conspiracy within the ambit of the Fourteenth Amendment."

## UNITED STATES v. GUEST
Supreme Court of the United States
383 U.S. 745, 16 L. Ed. 2d 239, 86 S. Ct. 1170 (1966)

Justice STEWART delivered the opinion of the Court.

The six defendants in this case were indicted . . . for criminal conspiracy in violation of 18 U.S.C. § 241 (1964 ed.). . . .

In five numbered paragraphs, the indictment alleged a single conspiracy by the defendants to deprive Negro citizens of the free exercise and enjoyment of several specified rights secured by the Constitution and laws of the United States. The defendants moved to dismiss the indictment on the ground that it did not charge an offense under the laws of the United States. The District Court sustained the motion and dismissed the indictment as to all defendants and all numbered paragraphs of the indictment.

. . . [W]e reverse the judgment of the District Court. As in *United States v. Price,* we deal here with issues of statutory construction, not with issues of constitutional power.

[Review of the first paragraph of the indictment was not available under the Criminal Appeals Act.]

The second numbered paragraph of the indictment alleged that the defendants conspired to injure, oppress, threaten, and intimidate Negro citizens of the United States in the free exercise and enjoyment of:

"The right to the equal utilization, without discrimination upon the basis of race, of public facilities in the vicinity of Athens, Georgia, owned, operated or managed by or on behalf of the State of Georgia or any subdivision thereof."

Correctly characterizing this paragraph as embracing rights protected by the Equal Protection Clause of the Fourteenth

Amendment, the District Court held as a matter of statutory construction that 18 USC § 241 does not encompass any Fourteenth Amendment rights, and further held as a matter of constitutional law that "any broader construction of § 241 . . . would render it void for indefiniteness." In so holding, the District Court was in error, as our opinion in *United States v. Price* . . . makes abundantly clear.

To be sure, *Price* involves rights under the Due Process Clause, whereas the present case involves rights under the Equal Protection Clause. But no possible reason suggests itself for concluding that § 241—if it protects Fourteenth Amendment rights—protects rights secured by the one Clause but not those secured by the other. We have made clear in *Price* that when § 241 speaks of "any right or privilege secured . . . by the Constitution or laws of the United States," it means precisely that.

Moreover, inclusion of Fourteenth Amendment rights within the compass of 18 USC § 241 does not render the statute unconstitutionally vague. Since the gravamen of the offense is conspiracy, the requirement that the offender must act with a specific intent to interfere with the federal rights in question is satisfied. Screws v. United States, 325 U.S. 91. And the rights under the Equal Protection Clause described by this paragraph of the indictment have been so firmly and precisely established by a consistent line of decisions in this Court, that the lack of specification of these rights in the language of § 241 itself can raise no serious constitutional question on the ground of vagueness or indefiniteness.

Unlike the indictment in *Price*, however, the indictment in the present case names no person alleged to have acted in any way under the color of state law. The argument is therefore made that, since there exist no Equal Protection Clause rights against wholly private action, the judgment of the District Court on this branch of the case must be affirmed. On its face, the argument is unexceptionable. The Equal Protection Clause speaks to the State or to those acting under the color of its authority.

In this connection, we emphasize that § 241 by its clear language incorporates no more than the Equal Protection Clause itself; the statute does not purport to give substantive, as opposed to remedial, implementation to any rights secured by that Clause. Since we therefore deal here only with the bare terms of the Equal Protection Clause itself, nothing said in this opinion goes to the question of what kinds of other and broader legislation Congress might constitutionally enact under § 5 of the Fourteenth

Amendment to implement that Clause or any other provision of the Amendment.

. . . .

This case . . . requires no determination of the threshold level that state action must attain in order to create rights under the Equal Protection Clause. This is so because, contrary to the argument of the litigants, the indictment in fact contains an express allegation of state involvement sufficient at least to require the denial of a motion to dismiss. One of the means of accomplishing the object of the conspiracy, according to the indictment, was "By causing the arrest of Negroes by means of false reports that such Negroes had committed criminal acts." . . . Although it is possible that a bill of particulars, or the proof if the case goes to trial, would disclose no co-operative action . . . by officials of the State, the allegation is enough to prevent dismissal of this branch of the indictment.

The fourth numbered paragraph of the indictment alleged that the defendants conspired to injure, oppress, threaten, and intimidate Negro citizens of the United States in the free exercise and enjoyment of:

"The right to travel freely to and from the State of Georgia and to use highway facilities and other instrumentalities of interstate commerce within the State of Georgia."

The District Court was in error in dismissing the indictment as to this paragraph. The constitutional right to travel from one State to another, and necessarily to use the highways and other instrumentalities of interstate commerce in doing so, occupies a position fundamental to the concept of our Federal Union. . . .

. . . .

. . . [I]f the predominant purpose of the conspiracy is to impede or prevent the exercise of the right of interstate travel, or to oppress a person because of his exercise of that right, then, whether or not motivated by racial discrimination, the conspiracy becomes a proper object of the federal law under which the indictment in this case was brought. . . .

. . . .

[Reversed and remanded.]

Justice CLARK, with whom Justice BLACK and Justice FORTAS join, concurring.

. . . .

. . . Although the Court specifically rejects any such connotation, it is, I believe, both appropriate and necessary under the circumstances here to say that there now can be no doubt that the specific language of § 5 empowers the Congress to enact laws punishing all conspiracies—with or without state action—that interfere with Fourteenth Amendment rights.

Justice HARLAN, concurring in part and dissenting in part.
. . . To the extent that . . . [the Court holds] that 18 USC § 241 (1964 ed.) reaches conspiracies, embracing only the action of private persons, to obstruct or otherwise interfere with the right of citizens freely to engage in interstate travel, I am constrained to dissent. On the other hand, I agree that § 241 does embrace state interference with such interstate travel, and I therefore consider that this aspect of the indictment is sustainable. . . .

This right to travel must be found in the Constitution itself.
. . . My disagreement with this phase of the Court's opinion lies in this: While past cases do indeed establish that there is a constitutional "right to travel" between States free from unreasonable *governmental* interference, today's decision is the first to hold that such movement is also protected against *private* interference, and, depending on the constitutional source of the right, I think it either unwise or impermissible so to read the Constitution.

. . . .

I would sustain this aspect of the indictment only on the premise that it sufficiently alleges state interference with interstate travel, and on no other ground.

Justice BRENNAN, with whom The CHIEF JUSTICE and Justice DOUGLAS join, concurring in part and dissenting in part.

. . . .

. . . I am of the opinion that a conspiracy to interfere with the right to equal utilization of state facilities described in the second numbered paragraph of the indictment is a conspiracy to interfere with a "right . . . secured . . . by the Constitution" within the meaning of § 241—without regard to whether state officers participated in the alleged conspiracy. I believe that § 241 reaches such a private conspiracy, not because the Fourteenth Amendment of its own force prohibits such a conspiracy, but because § 241, as an exercise of congressional power under § 5 of that Amendment, prohibits *all* conspiracies to interfere with the exercise of a "right . . . secured . . . by the Constitution" and because the right to equal utilization of state facilities is a "right . . . secured . . . by the Constitution" within the meaning of that phrase as used in § 241.[3]

_____

[3] Similarly, I believe that § 241 reaches a private conspiracy to interfere with the right to travel from State to State. I therefore need not reach the question whether the Constitution of its own force prohibits private interferences with that right; for I construe § 241 to prohibit such interferences, and as so construed I am of the opinion that § 241 is a valid exercise of congressional power.

My difference with the Court stems from its construction of the term "secured" as used in § 241 in the phrase a "right . . . secured . . . by the Constitution or laws of the United States." The Court tacitly construes the term "secured" so as to restrict the coverage of § 241 to those rights that are "fully protected" by the Constitution or another federal law. Unless private interferences with the exercise of the right in question are prohibited by the Constitution itself or another federal law, the right cannot, in the Court's view, be deemed "secured . . . by the Constitution or laws of the United States" so as to make § 241 applicable to a private conspiracy to interfere with the exercise of that right. The Court then premises that neither the Fourteenth Amendment nor any other federal law prohibits private interferences with the exercise of the right to equal utilization of state facilities.

In my view, however, a right can be deemed "secured . . . by the Constitution or laws of the United States," within the meaning of § 241, even though only governmental interferences with the exercise of the right are prohibited by the Constitution itself (or another federal law). The term "secured" means "created by, arising under or dependent upon," rather than "fully protected." A right is "secured . . . by the Constitution" within the meaning of § 241 if it emanates from the Constitution, if it finds its source in the Constitution. Section 241 must thus be viewed, in this context, as an exercise of congressional power to amplify prohibitions of the Constitution addressed, as is invariably the case, to government officers; contrary to the view of the Court, I think we are dealing here with a statute that seeks to implement the Constitution, not with the "bare terms" of the Constitution. Section 241 is not confined to protecting rights against private conspiracies that the Constitution or another federal law also protects against private interferences. No such duplicative function was envisioned in its enactment. Nor has this Court construed § 241 in such a restrictive manner in other contexts. Many of the rights that have been held to be encompassed within § 241 are not additionally the subject of protection of specific federal legislation or of any provision of the Constitution addressed to private individuals. For example, the prohibitions and remedies of § 241 have been declared to apply, without regard to whether the alleged violator was a government officer. . . . [Cases cited in text, pp. 1073-74, note 1.] The full import of our decision in United States v. Price, 383 U.S. 787, regarding § 241 is to treat the rights purportedly arising from the Fourteenth Amendment in parity with those rights just enumerated, arising from other constitution-

al provisions. The reach of § 241 should not vary with the particular constitutional provision that is the source of the right.
. . .

For me, the right to use state facilities without discrimination on the basis of race is, within the meaning of § 241, a right created by, arising under and dependent upon the Fourteenth Amendment and hence is a right "secured" by that Amendment. It finds its source in that Amendment. . . . The Fourteenth Amendment commands the State to provide the members of all races with equal access to the public facilities it owns or manages, and the right of a citizen to use those facilities without discrimination on the basis of race is a basic corollary of this command. Cf. Brewer v. Hoxie School District No. 46, 238 F.2d 91 (C.A. 8th Cir. 1956). Whatever may be the status of the right to equal utilization of *privately owned facilities,* it must be emphasized that we are here concerned with the right to equal utilization of *public facilities owned or operated by or on behalf of the State.* To deny the existence of this right or its constitutional stature is to deny the history of the last decade, or to ignore the role of federal power, predicated on the Fourteenth Amendment, in obtaining nondiscriminatory access to such facilities. It is to do violence to the common understanding, an understanding that found expression in Titles III and IV of the Civil Rights Act of 1964 dealing with state facilities. Those provisions reflect the view that the Fourteenth Amendment creates the right to equal utilization of state facilities. Congress did not preface those titles with a provision comparable to that in Title II explicitly creating the right to equal utilization of certain privately owned facilities. Congress rightly assumed that a specific legislative declaration of the right was unnecessary, that the right arose from the Fourteenth Amendment itself.

In reversing the District Court's dismissal of the second numbered paragraph, I would therefore hold that proof at the trial of the conspiracy charged to the defendants in that paragraph will establish a violation of § 241 without regard to whether there is also proof that state law enforcement officers actively connived in causing the arrests of Negroes by means of false reports.

My view as to the scope of § 241 requires that I reach the question of constitutional power—whether § 241 or legislation indubitably designed to punish entirely private conspiracies to interfere with the exercise of Fourteenth Amendment rights constitutes a permissible exercise of the power granted to Congress by § 5 of the Fourteenth Amendment "to enforce, by appropriate legislation, the provisions of" the Amendment.

A majority of the members of the Court[6] expresses the view today that § 5 empowers Congress to enact laws punishing *all* conspiracies to interfere with the exercise of Fourteenth Amendment rights, whether or not state officers or others acting under the color of state law are implicated in the conspiracy. Although the Fourteenth Amendment itself, according to established doctrine, "speaks to the State or to those acting under the color of its authority," legislation protecting rights created by that Amendment, such as the right to equal utilization of state facilities, need not be confined to punishing conspiracies in which state officers participate. Rather, § 5 authorizes Congress to make laws that it concludes are reasonably necessary to protect a right created by and arising under that Amendment; and Congress is thus fully empowered to determine that punishment of private conspiracies interfering with the exercise of such a right is necessary to its full protection. It made that determination in enacting § 241 and, therefore § 241 is constitutional legislation as applied to reach the private conspiracy alleged in the second numbered paragraph of the indictment.

I acknowledge that some of the decisions of this Court, most notably an aspect of the *Civil Rights Cases,* have declared that Congress' power under § 5 is confined to the adoption of "appropriate legislation for correcting the effects of . . . prohibited State laws and State acts, and thus to render them effectually null, void, and innocuous." I do not accept—and a majority of the Court today rejects—this interpretation of § 5. It reduces the legislative power to enforce the provisions of the Amendment to that of the judiciary;[7] and it attributes a far too limited objective to the Amendment's sponsors.[8] Moreover, the language of § 5 of the Fourteenth Amendment and § 2 of the Fifteenth Amendment are virtually the same, and we recently held in *South Carolina v. Katzenbach* [text, p. 1083], that "[t]he

[6] The majority consists of the Justices joining my Brother Clark's opinion and the Justices joining this opinion. The opinion of Mr. Justice Stewart construes § 241 as applied to the second numbered paragraph to require proof of active participation by state officers in the alleged conspiracy and that opinion does not purport to deal with this question.

[7] Congress, not the judiciary, was viewed as the more likely agency to implement fully the guarantees of equality, and thus it could be presumed the primary purpose of the Amendment was to augment the power of Congress, not the judiciary.

[8] As the first Mr. Justice Harlan said in dissent in the Civil Rights Cases, 109 U.S., at 54: "It was perfectly well known that the great danger to the equal enjoyment by citizens of their rights, as citizens, was to be apprehended not altogether from unfriendly State legislation, but from the hostile action of corporations and individuals in the States. And it is to be presumed that it was intended, by that section [§ 5], to clothe Congress with power and authority to meet that danger."

basic test to be applied in a case involving § 2 of the Fifteenth Amendment is the same as in all cases concerning the express powers of Congress with relation to the reserved powers of the States." The classic formulation of that test by Chief Justice Marshall in *McCulloch v. Maryland*, was there adopted:

"Let the end be legitimate, let it be within the scope of the constitution, and all means which are appropriate, which are plainly adapted to that end, which are not prohibited, but consist with the letter and spirit of the constitution, are constitutional."

It seems to me that this is also the standard that defines the scope of congressional authority under § 5 of the Fourteenth Amendment. . . .

Viewed in its proper perspective, § 5 of the Fourteenth Amendment appears as a positive grant of legislative power, authorizing Congress to exercise its discretion in fashioning remedies to achieve civil and political equality for all citizens. No one would deny that Congress could enact legislation directing state officials to provide Negroes with equal access to state schools, parks and other facilities owned or operated by the State. Nor could it be denied that Congress has the power to punish state officers who, in excess of their authority and in violation of state law, conspire to threaten, harass and murder Negroes for attempting to use these facilities. And I can find no principle of federalism nor word of the Constitution that denies Congress power to determine that in order adequately to protect the right to equal utilization of state facilities, it is also appropriate to punish other individuals—not state officers themselves and not acting in concert with state officers—who engage in the same brutal conduct for the same misguided purpose.

. . . .

---

## NOTES

1.  As indicated above (text, pp. 195-213), Congress can legislate under its plenary commerce powers against even private discrimination. Further, the thirteenth amendment, § 2, can be used to legislate remedies for private action violating the rights therein guaranteed since the amendment proscribes *all* slavery and involuntary servitude, not merely that imposed by government. Finally, it is established that Congress can legislate against official or private action violative of "federal rights" arising from the relation of the citizen to the national government. *See, e.g.,* United States v. Classic, 313 U.S. 299 (1941) (the right to vote in con-

gressional primaries secured by Art. I, § 2, as modified by Art. I, § 4, and Art. I, § 18, cl. 18); *In re* Quarles, 158 U.S. 532 (1895) (right of informer under federal custody to protection); *Ex parte* Yarbrough, 110 U.S. 651 (1884) (right to vote in federal elections); United States v. Cruikshank, 92 U.S. 542 (1876) (right to assemble and petition government). *See Griffin v. Breckenridge*, text, p. 1081, on the right of interstate movement. Rights secured by federal statute against private action can also be effectuated by congressional action.

Consider the statement of Justice Story in rejecting a constitutional challenge to the fugitive slave legislation in Prigg v. Pennsylvania, 41 U.S. (16 Peters) 539, 615 (1842): "If indeed, the Constitution guarantees the right . . . the natural inference is, that the national government is clothed with the appropriate authority and functions to enforce it. The fundamental principle applicable to all cases of this sort, would seem to be, that where the end is required, the means are given. . . ."

**2.** If Justice Stewart adds the right of interstate movement to these federal rights, what is its source? If it is a privilege or immunity of national citizenship or a due process guarantee it could be argued that state action was still required. It has been said that "[t]he difficulty with the majority's analysis [in *Guest*] is that all but one of the cases cited in the opinion dealt with state interference with interstate travel. . . . [T]he majority in *Guest* was able to cite no authority clearly supporting its holding that the right to travel is protected against private interference." Feuerstein, *Civil Rights Crimes and the Federal Power to Punish Private Individuals for Interference with Federally Secured Rights*, 19 VAND. L. REV. 641, 662-63 (1966). Consider Justice Stewart's assertion in *Griffin v. Breckenridge*, text, p. 1082, that the right of interstate travel is not necessarily dependent on the fourteenth amendment.

**3.** In Katzenbach v. Morgan, 384 U.S. 641 (1966), text, p. 1085, the court stated: "By including § 5 the draftsmen sought to grant to Congress, by a specific provision applicable to the Fourteenth Amendment, the same broad powers expressed in the Necessary and Proper Clause, Art. I, § 8, cl. 18. . . . Correctly viewed, § 5 is a positive grant of legislative power authorizing Congress to exercise its discretion in determining whether and what legislation is needed to secure the guarantees of the Fourteenth Amendment." Citing this decision and his decision in *Guest*, Justice Brennan in Adickes v. S. H. Kress & Co., 398 U.S. 144 (1970), stated that the rule established in the *Civil Rights Cases* "that Congress cannot under § 5 protect the exercise of Fourteenth Amendment rights from private interference has been overruled." Do you agree?

4. Professor Harris identifies three primary views among the framers of the enforcement legislation. At one extreme were legislators who "embraced a construction of the amendment which sustained almost unlimited congressional power to protect constitutional rights against both official and private action, to the point of displacing state authority altogether without awaiting abridgements of constitutional rights." At the opposite extreme were those who took what has become the traditional view "that congressional power was limited to the elimination of unequal laws and the correction of official or state action alone." Finally there was a middle ground suggesting that "Congress had the responsibility to protect constitutional rights in the event of failure of the states to do so, but only after the states had failed or refused to do their duty." R. HARRIS, THE QUEST FOR EQUALITY 45 (1960).

Which view does Justice Brennan take? *Compare* J. TENBROEK, EQUAL UNDER LAW (1951), who argues for the congressional supremacy position, with McKenney, *An Argument in Favor of Strict Adherence to the "State Action" Requirement,* 5 WM. & MARY L. REV. 213 (1964) and Avins, *Federal Power to Punish Individual Crimes Under the Fourteenth Amendment: The Original Understanding,* 43 NOTRE DAME LAW. 317 (1968). For the view that the moderate approach was adopted by the reconstruction Congress, see Frantz, *Congressional Power to Enforce the Fourteenth Amendment Against Private Acts,* 73 YALE L.J. 1353 (1964).

5. Assume equal access to public facilities is the right secured by the equal protection clause according to Justice Brennan. There are three possibilities for characterizing such a right: a right to a racially neutral state policy in admitting persons to public facilities; a right to be free from interference with the states' duty to provide equal protection of the laws; or a right to affirmative state action in protecting the person's nondiscriminatory access to public places. *See* Buchanan, *Federal Regulation of Private Racial Prejudice: A Study of Law in Search of Morality,* 56 IOWA L. REV. 473, 496-503 (1971).

Do the rights in the fourteenth amendment, § 1, change depending on whether they are enforced directly by a court or through congressional legislation? Does the state owe a similar duty for access to privately-owned places of public accommodation? To public facilities generally? To private facilities generally? How do you determine the scope of the state's duty under the fourteenth amendment, § 1? Does it extend to state protection of all "fundamental rights"? *See* Feuerstein, *Civil Rights Crimes,* 19 VAND. L. REV., at 665-67.

**6.** Justice Brennan in *Guest* recognizes congressional power to define the substantive rights provided by the fourteenth amendment, § 1. Consider the point made by Professor Cox that "to speak of 'Fourteenth Amendment rights' *simpliciter* suggests that they are rights in rem, good against all the world regardless of the limited nature of the duties from which they are derived. The only rights exactly correlative to the duties imposed by the Fourteenth Amendment are rights against the state, not against private individuals." He adds: "[I]f crossing over the conceptual distinction between securing rights against a state and protecting their exercise against private interference means that Congress may also deal with all other forms of private racial discrimination and even take any action against private individuals which it judges appropriate to secure full enjoyment of the rights to life, liberty, and property, then *United States v. Guest* opens the road to a much larger addition to federal regulation which might well be thought to unbalance the long range structure of government. It was the fear of this consequence that Justice Bradley cited in the *Civil Rights Cases* to support the declaration that the power of Congress under Section 5 is limited to correcting the effect of unconstitutional state laws in rendering them innocuous." *Foreword: Constitutional Adjudication and the Promotion of Human Rights,* 80 HARV. L. REV. 91, 110, 115 (1966).

**7.** In 1968, Congress provided a new criminal law remedy for denial of constitutional rights. The key provisions are:

**Sec. 245.   Federally protected activities.**
. . . .
"(b)   Whoever, whether or not acting under color of law, by force or threat of force willfully injures, intimidates or interferes with, or attempts to injure, intimidate or interfere with—
"(1)   any person because he is or has been, or in order to intimidate such person or any other person or any class of persons from—
   "(A)   voting or qualifying to vote, qualifying or campaigning as a candidate for elective office, or qualifying or acting as a poll watcher, or any legally authorized election official, in any primary, special, or general election;
   "(B)   participating in or enjoying any benefit, service, privilege, program, facility, or activity provided or administered by the United States;
   "(C)   applying for or enjoying employment, or any perquisite thereof, by any agency of the United States;
   "(D)   serving, or attending upon any court in connection with possible service, as a grand or petit juror in any court of the United States;

"(E)   participating in or enjoying the benefits of any program or activity receiving Federal financial assistance; or

"(2)   any person because of his race, color, religion or national origin and because he is or has been—

"(A)   enrolling in or attending any public school or public college;

"(B)   participating in or enjoying any benefit, service, privilege, program, facility or activity provided or administered by any State or subdivision thereof;

"(C)   applying for or enjoying employment, or any perquisite thereof, by any private employer or any agency of any State or subdivision thereof, or joining or using the services or advantages of any labor organization, hiring hall, or employment agency;

"(D)   serving, or attending upon any court of any State in connection with possible service, as a grand or petit juror;

"(E)   traveling in or using any facility of interstate commerce, or using any vehicle, terminal, or facility of any common carrier by motor, rail, water, or air;

"(F)   enjoying the goods, services, facilities, privileges, advantages, or accommodations of any inn, hotel, motel, or other establishment which provides lodging to transient guests, or of any restaurant, cafeteria, lunchroom, lunch counter, soda fountain, or other facility which serves the public and which is principally engaged in selling food or beverages for consumption on the premises, or of any gasoline station, or of any motion picture house, theater, concert hall, sports arena, stadium, or any other place of exhibition or entertainment which serves the public, or of any other establishment which serves the public and (i) which is located within the premises of any of the aforesaid establishments or within the premises of which is physically located any of the aforesaid establishments, and (ii) which holds itself out as serving patrons of such establishments; or

"(3)   during or incident to a riot or civil disorder, any person engaged in a business in commerce or affecting commerce, including, but not limited to, any person engaged in a business which sells or offers for sale to interstate travelers a substantial portion of the articles, commodities, or services which it sells or where a substantial portion of the articles or commodities which it sells or offers for sale have moved in commerce; or

"(4)   any person because he is or has been, or in order to intimidate such person or any other person or any class of persons from—

"(A)   participating, without discrimination on account of race, color, religion or national origin, in any of the benefits or activities described in subparagraphs (1) (A) through (1) (E) or subparagraphs (2) (A) through (2) (F); or

"(B)   affording another person or class of persons opportunity or protection to so participate; or

"(5)   any citizen because he is or has been, or in order to intimidate such citizen or any other citizen from lawfully aiding or encouraging other persons to participate, without discrimination on

account of race, color, religion or national origin, in any of the
benefits or activities described in subparagraphs (1)(A) through (1)
(E) or subparagraphs (2)(A) through (2)(F), or participating lawfully
in speech or peaceful assembly opposing any denial of the opportunity to so participate—

shall be fined not more than $1,000, or imprisoned not more than one
year, or both; and if bodily injury results shall be fined not more than
$10,000, or imprisoned not more than ten years, or both; and if death
results shall be subject to imprisonment for any term of years or for
life."

How does § 245 compare with §§ 241 and 242 as a tool for
protecting constitutional rights? It has been suggested that the
compromises reflected in § 245 which were designed to mitigate
potential federal-state friction resulting from civil rights prosecutions have limited the section's effectiveness as a source of protection. D. BELL, RACE, RACISM AND AMERICAN LAW 881-83 (1973).
With few exceptions (see, e.g., United States v. Price, 464 F.2d
1217 (8th Cir. 1972) affirming defendant's conviction for abusive
treatment of a Black citizen), attempts to use § 245 have been
unsuccessful.

### 2. Civil Remedies

1.   Monroe v. Pape, 365 U.S. 167 (1961), considered many
of the same issues raised in the criminal civil rights cases in the
context of a civil suit for damages under 42 U.S.C. § 1983. The
complaint, against the city of Chicago and 13 police officers
alleged an illegal search and arrest constituting a deprivation
of the plaintiff's constitutional rights, privileges, or immunities.
The district court dismissed the claim and the court of appeals
affirmed.

Justice Douglas, for the court, rejected any suggestion that
§ 1983 could not be used to enforce fourteenth amendment rights
or that the action alleged was not done under color of law.
Citing the history of § 1983 and his opinion in Screws, Douglas
concluded that the "under color of law" clause should have the
same construction as it does in 18 U.S.C. § 242, including acts of
state officials contrary to state law. It was immaterial that the state
afforded a remedy for the wrong. "The federal remedy is supplementary to the state remedy and the latter need not be first
sought and refused before the federal one is invoked." Justice
Douglas further determined that § 1983 does not require a showing of specific intent, noting that the word "wilfully" is not in the
statute and that § 1983 deals with civil rather than criminal
remedies. It followed that the section "should be read against the
background of tort liability that makes a man responsible for the
natural consequences of his actions." He did hold, however, that

Congress had not intended to include municipalities as a "person" in § 1983.

Feeling bound by *Classic* and *Screws,* Justice Harlan, joined by Justice Stewart, concurred. Justice Frankfurter, in dissent, examined the text and history of § 1983, concluding that it "created a civil liability enforceable in the federal courts only in instances of injury for which redress was barred in the state courts because some 'statute, ordinance, regulation, custom, or usage' sanctioned the grievance complained of."

2.    The meaning of the reference to "custom" in the "under color of law" clause of § 1983 was dealt with in Adickes v. S. H. Kress & Co., 398 U.S. 144 (1970), text, p. 1051. Justice Harlan, for the court, after examining the history of § 1983 concluded that "[a]lthough not authorized by written law, . . . practices of state officials could well be so permanent and well settled as to constitute a 'custom or usage' with the force of law." Whether enforced against black or white such settled practices of officials "may, by imposing sanctions or withholding benefits, transform private predilections into compulsory rules of behavior no less than legislative pronouncement."

Justice Brennan, concurring in part and dissenting in part, concluded that "a person acts under color of a custom or usage of a State when there is among the people of a State or subdivision of a State a wide spread and long-standing practice regarded as prescribing norms for conduct and supported by community sentiment or sanctions and a person acts in accordance with this custom either from a belief that the norms it prescribes authorize or require his conduct or from a belief that the community at large regards it as authorizing or requiring his conduct." Justice Douglas, dissenting in part, similarly read custom to include "the unwritten commitment, stronger than ordinances, statutes, and regulations, by which men live and arrange their lives." It was not merely a reflection of "the prejudices of a few" but instead "it must reflect the dominant communal sentiment."

3.  *Immunities.*

a.  *Sovereign Immunity.* In damage actions under the civil rights statutes, individual defendants, especially low echelon officers, frequently lack the means to satisfy a judgment even if the plaintiff is successful. Litigants, therefore, often attempt to secure a remedy against the government-employer either for primary wrong-doing or under the doctrine of *respondeat superior.* States, however, are protected from suit under the eleventh amendment (*see* text, pp. 48-50) and the court, in *Monroe v. Pape* held that a municipality is not a "person" for § 1983 purposes. Lower courts have applied this bar to actions against public agencies generally. While commentators have criticized the Supreme Court's reading of statutory history (see, e.g., Kates, *Liability of Public Entities Under § 1983 of the Civil Rights Act*, 45 S. CALIF. L. REV. 131 (1972)) the court has refused to revise its determination. Further, in Moor v. County of Alameda, 411 U.S. 693 (1973), the court rejected an argument that if the local governmental unit is not immune under state law it would not be immune in a federal civil rights action. Such a holding, the court determined, would undermine congressional intent as construed in *Monroe v. Pape*. Still another impediment to relief against the governmental actor came in Kenosha v. Bruno, 412 U.S. 507 (1973), a non-racial case, holding that a city is not a person for purposes of § 1983 even if the request is for equitable relief. *See The Supreme Court 1972 Term*, 87 HARV. L. REV. 1, 252 (1973).

b. *Official Immunity*. The Supreme Court has held that judges (Pierson v. Ray, 386 U.S. 547 (1967)) and state legislators (Tenney v. Brandhove, 341 U.S. 367 (1951), but see Nelson v. Knox, 256 F.2d 312 (6th Cir. 1958) holding that municipal legislators have only a qualified immunity for acts done in good faith), are immune from § 1983 damage actions even when they are alleged to have acted maliciously. A number of other officials, when performing "quasi-judicial" or "quasi-legislative" functions, have been said to share in this immunity. What is the justification for immunity from civil rights damage claims? Does the rationale support absolute immunity? *See* Kates, *Immunity of State Judges Under the Federal Civil Rights Acts: Pierson v. Ray Reconsidered*, 65 Nw. U.L. REV. 615 (1970); Note, *Liability of Judicial Officers Under Section 1983*, 79 YALE L.J. 322 (1969).

While some courts have questioned whether state executive and administrative officers have any immunity in § 1983 suits (see Carter v. Carlson, 447 F.2d 358, 365 (D.C. Cir. 1971), *rev'd on other grounds sub. nom* District of Columbia v. Carter, 409 U.S. 418 (1973); Sostre v. McGinnis, 442 F.2d 178, 205 (2d Cir. 1971) (en banc)), the statement of Chief Justice Burger in Scheuer v. Rhodes, 416 U.S. 232 (1974), recognizing the possible liability of high state officials individually for the Kent State killings, seems to be generally accepted: "[I]n varying scope, a qualified immunity is available to officers of the executive branch of Government, the variation dependent upon the scope of discretion and responsibilities of the office and all the circumstances as they reasonably appeared at the time of the action on which liability is sought to be based. It is the existence of reasonable grounds for the belief formed at the time and in light of all the circumstances, coupled with good faith belief, that affords the basis for qualified immunity of executive officers for acts performed in the course of official conduct." State officials not acting in the performance of discretionary functions may defend against damage suits on the basis that the acts were done in "good faith." *See* Pierson v. Ray, 386 U.S. 547 (1967). *See generally* C. ANTIEAU, FEDERAL CIVIL RIGHTS ACTS—CIVIL PRACTICE 67-75 (1971), as supplemented.

4.   Federal officials are not amenable to § 1983 suits. However, in Bivens v. Six Unknown Named Narcotics Agents, 403 U.S. 388 (1971), the court, per Justice Brennan, held that a damage claim for violation of fourth amendment rights was available—the district court has ordinary federal question jurisdiction under 28 U.S.C. § 1331(a). The case was remanded on the question of immunity. On remand, the court of appeals indicated that the same immunity governing liability of state officials should apply. 456 F.2d 1339 (2d Cir. 1972).

In District of Columbia v. Carter, 409 U.S. 418, 432 (1973), the court, while holding that the District of Columbia is not a "State or Territory" within the meaning of § 1983, did indicate that this would not foreclose a suit in federal courts using *Bivens.* Could municipalities, nonpersons under § 1983, be sued for violation of the Constitution using the federal courts' ordinary federal question jurisdiction? *See* Kenosha v. Bruno, 412 U.S. 507 (1973), where the case was remanded to determine if the jurisdictional requirements of § 1331(a) were satisfied.

5.   42 U.S.C. § 1985(3) (see text, p. 1059), has no "under color of law" provision. To what extent can it be used to reach private conspiracies? What rights does it protect? *See generally* Schwartz, *Expanding the Fourteenth Amendment Through the Federal Civil Rights Act,* 5 CLEARINGHOUSE REV. 567 (1972).

In Griffin v. Breckenridge, 403 U.S. 88 (1971), the court recognized a § 1985(3) action brought by blacks for compensatory and punitive damages against white persons who, mistaking them for civil rights workers, stopped them on the highway, detained, assaulted, and beat them. The complaint alleged a conspiracy to prevent the plaintiffs from seeking equal protection of the laws and from enjoying the equal rights, privileges and immunities of citizens, including but not limited to freedom of speech, movement, association, and assembly, the right to petition their government for redress of grievances, security in their homes, their right not to be enslaved nor be deprived of life and liberty without due process of law.

Justice Stewart, for the court, examining the language of § 1985(3), its companion provisions and its history, concluded that they "point unwaveringly to § 1985(3)'s coverage of private conspiracies." This did not mean that the provision was a general federal tort law since Congress intended that "there must be some racial, or perhaps otherwise class-based, invidiously discriminatory animus behind the conspirators' action. The conspiracy, in other words, must aim at a deprivation of the equal enjoyment of rights secured by the law to all." Justice Stewart noted that the court was not deciding whether some other "invidiously discriminatory intent" other than race might suffice. He claimed further that the requirement of "animus" was not equivalent to the specific intent required in *Screws*. Since the complaint set forth all of the elements of a § 1985(3) action, it was necessary to determine if Congress could constitutionally reach such action.

Justice Stewart found the requisite constitutional support for such an application of § 1985(3) in the thirteenth amendment: "Congress was wholly within its powers under § 2 of the 13th Amendment in creating a statutory cause of action for Negro citizens who have been the victims of conspiratorial, racially discriminatory private action aimed at depriving them of the basic rights that the law secures to all free men."

Further support was found in cases, including *Guest*, which "have firmly established that the right of interstate travel is constitutionally protected, does not necessarily rest on the Fourteenth Amendment, and is assertable against private as well as governmental interference." This right of interstate travel "like other rights of national citizenship, is within the power of Congress to protect by appropriate action."

Justice Stewart concluded with the following comment: "In identifying these two constitutional sources of congressional power, we do not imply the absence of any other. More specifically, the allegations of the complaint in this case have not required consideration of the scope of the power of Congress under § 5 of the Fourteenth Amendment. By the same token, since the allegations of the complaint bring this cause of action so close to the constitutionally authorized core of the statute, there has been no occasion here to trace out its constitutionally permissible periphery." In a footnote, Justice Stewart cited *Guest, Katzenbach v. Morgan*, text, p. 1085, and *Oregon v. Mitchell*, text, p. 1095.

On the meaning of the thirteenth amendment, see text, pp. 412-14 and 1102-10. How does "animus" differ from "specific intent"? Perhaps nonracial discriminatory animus suffices. The historical pre-occupation with the needs of blacks for protection in framing the 1871 KKK Act may impose such a limitation. *See* Schwartz, *Expanding the Fourteenth Amendment*, 5 CLEARINGHOUSE REV. at 569. If the right of interstate travel is to be used as a constitutional nexus, must there be a showing that the right is somehow burdened? Can private interference with other fourteenth amendment rights be reached? *See The Supreme Court, 1970 Term*, 85 HARV. L. REV. 3, 95-100 (1971).

## C. DEFINING THE SUBSTANTIVE RIGHTS: LEGISLATING AGAINST DISCRIMINATION IN VOTING AND HOUSING

### 1. Discrimination in Voting

1. As indicated above (text, p. 1060), the initial thrust of congressional legislation in the second reconstruction was in the area of voting rights. But the results of the 1957, 1960 and 1964 [Title I] acts were generally disappointing. The legislation provided only weak remedies which were procedurally difficult to invoke. Government enforcement tended to be slow and limited. Reform proceeded on a case by case basis with complainants forced to overcome litigation difficulties as well as local defiance. Even when a case was won, the local jurisdiction would often only replace the condemned restrictive voting device with another device, equally as restrictive. *See* U.S. COMM'N ON CIVIL RIGHTS, POLITICAL PARTICIPATION (1968); U.S. COMM'N ON CIVIL RIGHTS, THE VOTING RIGHTS ACT (1965); U.S. COMM'N ON CIVIL RIGHTS, VOTING (1961).

2. Congress tried a new tack with the Voting Rights Act of 1965, 42 U.S.C. § 1973, prohibiting the use of voter registration requirements to abridge the right to vote on account of race or color. In addition to providing for federal voting examiners (§ 1973(a)), the Act automatically suspends the use of voting tests to disqualify potential voters in states where the Attorney General finds that a test has been used and where less than 50 per cent of the persons of voting age are registered to vote. Coverage can be removed if the District Court for the District of Columbia determines that no test has been used for five years to discriminate on account of race (§ 1973(b)) (see Gaston County v. United States, 395 U.S. 285 (1969), barring reinstitution of literacy tests because of prior de jure segregation in education). When a state subject to the act attempts to add new voting qualifications, they must be approved by the Attorney General of the United States or by a three-judge court of the District of Columbia. (§ 1973(c)) (see, *e.g.*, Perkins v. Matthews, 400 U.S. 379 (1971); Allen v. State Bd. of Elections, 393 U.S. 544 (1969)).

3. The constitutionality of these provisions was upheld by the court, per Chief Justice Warren, in South Carolina v. Katzenbach, 383 U.S. 301 (1966), an original suit by six southern states subject to the Act. Authority for the legislation was found in

the fifteenth amendment, § 2, which, Warren stated, uses the same basic test "as in all cases concerning the express powers of Congress with relation to the reserve powers of the states: 'Let the end be legitimate, let it be within the scope of the Constitution, and all means which are appropriate, which are plainly adapted to that end, which are not prohibited, but consist with the letter and spirit of the Constitution, are constitutional.' *McCulloch v. Maryland.*" *See Ex parte* Virginia, 100 U.S. (10 Otto) 339 (1880), applying this principle to the fourteenth amendment. In exercising its power, "[a]s against the reserved powers of the States, Congress may use any rational means to effectuate the constitutional prohibition of racial discrimination in voting." Warren rejected South Carolina's contention "that Congress may appropriately do no more than to forbid violations of the Fifteenth Amendment in general terms—that the task of fashioning specific remedies or of applying them to particular localities must necessarily be left entirely to the courts." Instead, Congress's power under § 2 "is complete in itself, may be exercised to its utmost extent, and acknowledges no limitations, other than are prescribed in the constitution. *Gibbons v. Ogden.*"

Applying these standards, Warren found that elimination of case by case adjudication was a legitimate response to the problem of voting discrimination: "Congress had found that case-by-case litigation was inadequate to combat wide-spread and persistent discrimination in voting, because of the inordinate amount of time and energy required to overcome the obstructionist tactics invariably encountered in these lawsuits. After enduring nearly a century of systematic resistance to the Fifteenth Amendment, Congress might well decide to shift the advantage of time and inertia from the perpetrators of the evil to its victims."

Turning to the remedial provisions, Warren noted that "[t]he record shows that in most of the States covered by the Act, including South Carolina, various tests and devices have been instituted with the purpose of disenfranchising Negroes, have been framed in such a way as to facilitate this aim, and have been administered in a discriminatory fashion for many years. Under these circumstances, the Fifteenth Amendment has clearly been violated." The suspension of tests was a legitimate response to this problem since "Congress knew that continuance of the tests and devices in use at the present time, no matter how fairly administered in the future, would freeze the effect of past discrimination in favor of unqualified white registrants. Congress permissibly rejected the alternative of requiring a complete re-registration of all voters, believing that this would be too harsh on many whites who had enjoyed the franchise for their entire adult lives." Requiring approval of new state voting regulations in § 1973(c) was similarly permissible. "Congress knew that some of the States covered . . . had resorted to the extra-ordinary stratagem of contriving new rules of various kinds for the sole purpose of perpetuating voting discrimination in the face of adverse federal court decrees. Congress had reason to suppose that these States might try similar maneuvers in the future in order to evade the remedies for voting discrimination contained in the Act itself. Under the compulsion of these unique circumstances, Congress responded in a permissibly decisive manner." Finally, provisions for appointment of federal examiners was "clearly an appropriate response to the problem."

Warren concluded: "After enduring nearly a century of widespread resistance to the Fifteenth Amendment, Congress has marshalled an array of potent weapons against the evil, with authority in the Attorney General to employ them effectively. . . . We here hold that the portions of the Voting Rights Act properly before us are a valid means for carrying out the commands of the Fifteenth Amendment. Hopefully, millions of non-white Americans will now be able to participate for the first time on an equal basis in the government under which they live."

Justice Black dissented from the court's holding on § 1973(c), which, he argued, distorted the constitutional structure of government. "Certainly if all the provisions of our Constitution which limit the power of the Federal Government and reserve other power to the States are to mean anything, they mean at least that the States have power to pass laws and amend their constitutions without first sending their officials hundreds of miles away to beg federal authorities to approve them."

## KATZENBACH v. MORGAN
Supreme Court of the United States
384 U.S. 641, 16 L. Ed. 2d 828, 86 S. Ct. 1717 (1966)

Justice BRENNAN delivered the opinion of the Court.

These cases concern the constitutionality of § 4(e) of the Voting Rights Act of 1965. That law, in the respects pertinent in these cases, provides that no person who has successfully completed the sixth primary grade in a public school in, or a private school accredited by, the Commonwealth of Puerto Rico in which the language of instruction was other than English shall be denied the right to vote in any election because of his inability to read or write English. Appellees, registered voters in New York City, brought this suit to challenge the constitutionality of § 4(e) insofar as it pro tanto prohibits the enforcement of the election laws of New York requiring an ability to read and write English as a condition of voting. Under these laws many of the several hundred thousand New York City residents who have migrated there from the Commonwealth of Puerto Rico had previously been denied the right to vote, and appellees attack § 4(e) insofar as it would enable many of these citizens to vote. . . . A three-judge district court . . . granted the declaratory and injunctive relief appellees sought. . . . We reverse. We hold that, in the application challenged in these cases, § 4(e) is a proper exercise of the powers granted to Congress by § 5 of the Fourteenth Amendment and that by force of the Supremacy Clause, Article VI, the New York English literacy requirement cannot be enforced to the extent that it is inconsistent with § 4(e).

Under the distribution of powers effected by the Constitution, the States establish qualifications for voting for state officers, and the qualifications established by the States for voting for members of the most numerous branch of the state legislature also determine who may vote for United States Representatives and Senators, Art. I, § 2; Seventeenth Amendment. But, of course, the States have no power to grant or withhold the franchise on conditions that are forbidden by the Fourteenth Amendment, or any other provision of the Constitution. . . .

The Attorney General of the State of New York . . . urges that § 4(e) cannot be sustained as appropriate legislation to enforce the Equal Protection Clause unless the judiciary decides —even with the guidance of a congressional judgment—that the application of the English literacy requirement prohibited by § 4(e) is forbidden by the Equal Protection Clause itself. We disagree. Neither the language nor history of § 5 supports such a construction. As was said with regard to § 5 in *Ex parte* Virginia, 100 U.S. 339, 345, "It is the power of Congress which has been enlarged. Congress is authorized to *enforce* the prohibitions by appropriate legislation. Some legislation is contemplated to make the amendments fully effective." A construction of § 5 that would require a judicial determination that the enforcement of the state law precluded by Congress violated the Amendment, as a condition of sustaining the congressional enactment, would depreciate both congressional resourcefulness and congressional responsibility for implementing the Amendment. It would confine the legislative power in this context to. the insignificant role of abrogating only those state laws that the judicial branch was prepared to adjudge unconstitutional, or of merely informing the judgment of the judiciary by particularizing the "majestic generalities" of § 1 of the Amendment.

. . . [O]ur decision in Lassiter v. Northampton Election Bd., 360 U.S. 45, sustaining the North Carolina English literacy requirement as not in all circumstances prohibited by the first sections of the Fourteenth and Fifteenth Amendments, is inapposite. *Lassiter* did not present the question before us here: Without regard to whether the judiciary would find that the Equal Protection Clause itself nullifies New York's English literacy requirement as so applied, could Congress prohibit the enforcement of the state law by legislating under § 5 of the Fourteenth Amendment? In answering this question, our task is limited to determining whether such legislation is, as required by § 5, appropriate legislation to enforce the Equal Protection Clause.

By including § 5 the draftsmen sought to grant to Congress . . . the same broad powers expressed in the Necessary and Proper Clause. The classic formulation of the reach of those two powers was established by Chief Justice Marshall in *M'Culloch v. Maryland*.

"Let the end be legitimate, let it be within the scope of the constitution, and all means which are appropriate, which are plainly adapted to that end, which are not prohibited, but consist with the letter and spirit of the constitution, are constitutional."

. . . Correctly viewed, § 5 is a positive grant of legislative power authorizing Congress to exercise its discretion in determining whether and what legislation is needed to secure the guarantees of the Fourteenth Amendment.

We therefore proceed to the consideration whether § 4(e) is "appropriate legislation" to enforce the Equal Protection Clause, that is, under the *M'Culloch v. Maryland* standard, whether § 4(e) may be regarded as an enactment to enforce the Equal Protection Clause, whether it is "plainly adapted to that end" and whether it is not prohibited by but is consistent with "the letter and spirit of the constitution."[10]

There can be no doubt that § 4(e) may be regarded as an enactment to enforce the Equal Protection Clause. . . . More specifically, § 4(e) may be viewed as a measure to secure for the

---

[10] Contrary to the suggestion of the dissent, § 5 does not grant Congress power to exercise discretion in the other direction and to enact "statutes so as in effect to dilute equal protection and due process decisions of this Court." We emphasize that Congress' power under § 5 is limited to adopting measures to enforce the guarantees of the Amendment; § 5 grants Congress no power to restrict, abrogate, or dilute these guarantees. Thus, for example, an enactment authorizing the States to establish racially segregated systems of education would not be—as required by § 5—a measure "to enforce" the Equal Protection Clause since that clause of its own force prohibits such state laws.

Puerto Rican community residing in New York nondiscriminatory treatment by government—both in the imposition of voting
qualifications and the provision or administration of governmental services, such as public schools, public housing and law
enforcement.

Section 4(e) may be readily seen as "plainly adapted" to
furthering these aims of the Equal Protection Clause. The practical effect of § 4(e) is to prohibit New York from denying the
right to vote to large segments of its Puerto Rican community.
Congress has thus prohibited the State from denying to that
community the right that is "preservative of all rights." This
enhanced political power will be helpful in gaining nondiscriminatory treatment in public services for the entire Puerto
Rican community. Section 4(e) thereby enables the Puerto Rican
minority better to obtain "perfect equality of civil rights and
the equal protection of the laws." It was well within congressional
authority to say that this need of the Puerto Rican minority for
the vote warranted federal intrusion upon any state interests
served by the English literacy requirement. It was for Congress,
as the branch that made this judgment, to assess and weigh the
various conflicting considerations—the risk or pervasiveness of
the discrimination in governmental services, the effectiveness of
eliminating the state restriction on the right to vote as a means
of dealing with the evil, the adequacy or availability of alternative remedies, and the nature and significance of the state interests
that would be affected by the nullification of the English literacy
requirement as applied to residents who have successfully completed the sixth grade in a Puerto Rican school. It is not for
us to review the congressional resolution of these factors. It is
enough that we be able to perceive a basis upon which the
Congress might resolve the conflict as it did. There plainly was
such a basis to support § 4(e) in the application in question in
this case. Any contrary conclusion would require us to be blind
to the realities familiar to the legislators.

The result is no different if we confine our inquiry to the
question whether § 4(e) was merely legislation aimed at the
elimination of an invidious discrimination in establishing voter
qualifications. We are told that New York's English literacy
requirement originated in the desire to provide an incentive for
non-English speaking immigrants to learn the English language
and in order to assure the intelligent exercise of the franchise.
Yet Congress might well have questioned, in light of the many
exemptions provided, and some evidence suggesting that prejudice played a prominent role in the enactment of the requirement, whether these were actually the interests being served.

Congress might have also questioned whether denial of a right deemed so precious and fundamental in our society was a necessary or appropriate means of encouraging persons to learn English, or of furthering the goal of an intelligent exercise of the franchise. Finally, Congress might well have concluded that as a means of furthering the intelligent exercise of the franchise, an ability to read or understand Spanish is as effective as ability to read English for those to whom Spanish-language newspapers and Spanish-language radio and television programs are available to inform them of election issues and governmental affairs. Since Congress undertook to legislate so as to preclude the enforcement of the state law, and did so in the context of a general appraisal of literacy requirements for voting, see *South Carolina v. Katzenbach,* to which it brought a specially informed legislative competence, it was Congress' prerogative to weigh these competing considerations. Here again, it is enough that we perceive a basis upon which Congress might predicate a judgment that the application of New York's English literacy requirement to deny the right to vote to a person with a sixth grade education in Puerto Rican schools in which the language of instruction was other than English constituted an invidious discrimination in violation of the Equal Protection Clause.

There remains the question whether the congressional remedies adopted in § 4(e) constitute means which are not prohibited by, but are consistent "with the letter and spirit of the constitution." [The Court held that the limitation of relief to American-flag schools in a reform measure does not constitute invidious discrimination.]

Reversed.

Justice HARLAN, whom Justice STEWART joins, dissenting.

. . . .

. . . Although § 5 most certainly does give to the Congress wide powers in the field of devising remedial legislation to effectuate the Amendment's prohibition on arbitrary state action, I believe the Court has confused the issue of how much enforcement power Congress possesses under § 5 with the distinct issue of what questions are appropriate for congressional determination and what questions are essentially judicial in nature.

When recognized state violations of federal constitutional standards have occurred, Congress is of course empowered by § 5 to take appropriate remedial measures to redress and prevent the wrongs. But it is a judicial question whether the condition with which Congress has thus sought to deal is in truth an infringement of the Constitution, something that is the necessary prerequisite to bringing the § 5 power into play at all. . . .

. . . .

. . . The question here is not whether the statute is appropriate remedial legislation to cure an established violation of a constitutional command, but whether there has in fact been an infringement of that constitutional command, that is, whether a particular state practice or, as here, a statute is so arbitrary or irrational as to offend the command of the Equal Protection Clause of the Fourteenth Amendment. That question is one for the judicial branch ultimately to determine. Were the rule otherwise, Congress would be able to qualify this Court's constitutional decisions under the Fourteenth and Fifteenth Amendments, let alone those under other provisions of the Constitution, by resorting to congressional power under the Necessary and Proper Clause. In view of this Court's holding in *Lassiter* that an English literacy test is a permissible exercise of state supervision over its franchise, I do not think it is open to Congress to limit the effect of that decision as it has undertaken to do by § 4(e). In effect the Court reads § 5 of the Fourteenth Amendment as giving Congress the power to define the *substantive* scope of the Amendment. If that indeed be the true reach of § 5, then I do not see why Congress should not be able as well to exercise its § 5 "discretion" by enacting statutes so as in effect to dilute equal protection and due process decisions of this Court. In all such cases there is room for reasonable men to differ as to whether or not a denial of equal protection or due process has occurred, and the final decision is one of judgment. Until today this judgment has always been one for the judiciary to resolve.

I do not mean to suggest in what has been said that a legislative judgment of the type incorporated in § 4(e) is without any force whatsoever. Decisions on questions of equal protection and due process are based not on abstract logic, but on empirical foundations. To the extent "legislative facts" are relevant to a judicial determination, Congress is well equipped to investigate them, and such determinations are of course entitled to due respect. . . .

But no such factual data provide a legislative record supporting § 4(e) by way of showing that Spanish-speaking citizens are fully as capable of making informed decisions in a New York election as are English-speaking citizens. Nor was there any showing whatever to support the Court's alternative argument that § 4(e) should be viewed as but a remedial measure designed to cure or assure against unconstitutional discrimination of other varieties, *e.g.*, in "public schools, public housing and law enforcement" to which Puerto Rican minorities might be subject in such communities as New York. There is simply no legislative record supporting such hypothesized discrimination of the sort we have hitherto insisted upon when congressional power is brought to bear on constitutionally reserved state concerns. See *Heart of Atlanta Motel*, [text, p. 200]; *South Carolina v. Katzenbach* [text, p. 1083].

. . . .

In assessing the deference we should give to this kind of congressional expression of policy, it is relevant that the judiciary has always given to congressional enactments a presumption of validity. However, it is also a canon of judicial review that state statutes are given a similar presumption. Whichever way this case is decided, one statute will be rendered inoperative in whole or in part, and although it has been suggested that this Court should give somewhat more deference to Congress than to a state legislature, such a simple weighing of presumptions is hardly a satisfying way of resolving a matter that touches the distribution of state and federal power in an area so sensitive as that of the regulation of the franchise. . . . At least in the area of primary state concern a state statute that passes constitutional muster under the judicial standard of rationality should not be permitted to be set at naught by a mere contrary congressional pronouncement unsupported by a legislative record justifying that conclusion.

. . . To hold, on this record, that § 4(e) overrides the New York literacy requirement seems to me tantamount to allowing the Fourteenth Amendment to swallow the State's constitutionally ordained primary authority in this field. For if Congress by what, as here, amounts to mere ipse dixit can set that otherwise permissible requirement partially at naught I see no reason why it could not also substitute its judgment for that of the States in other fields of their exclusive primary competence as well.

. . . .

## NOTES

### Congressional Means to a Judicially Defined End

1. The initial part of Justice Brennan's opinion argues that elimination of the state's literacy requirement was a proper means to promote nondiscriminatory treatment by government in providing and administering public services. How was this done in the public accommodation cases decided under the commerce clause? *See* text, pp. 195-213. In *South Carolina v. Katzenbach?* Professor Cox notes: "[T]he *Morgan* case left no doubt that Sec-

tion 5 of the fourteenth amendment gives Congress power to deal with conduct outside the scope of Section 1 and within the reserved powers of the states where the measurement is a means of securing the state's performance of its fourteenth amendment duties, regardless of its past compliance or violations." *Foreword: Constitutional Adjudication and the Promotion of Human Rights,* 80 HARV. L. REV. 91, 103 (1966).

**2.** But Justice Harlan, dissenting, argues that there is no data establishing a legislative record supportive of such a means-end relationship. Similarly, Professor Engdahl contends that "the legislative history fails to disclose any evil clearly offensive to the fourteenth amendment and independent of higher age restrictions themselves, which the voting age provision was intended to eliminate." *Constitutionality of the Voting Age Statute,* 39 GEO. WASH. L. REV. 1, 12 (1970). Must Congress build a legislative record? Can the presumption of constitutionality substitute for a lack of empirical support? Professor Engdahl appears to suggest that the court should independently review a congressional judgment that a measure is a proper means for furthering a recognized constitutional right.

**3.** In this instance, Congress' fact-finding was arguably inconsistent with that of the state. Was it proper for the court under these circumstances to defer to congressional fact-finding? Why is a congressional finding of fact to be preferred to that of the states? Given the strong state interest in defining the qualifications for the franchise under Art. I, should deference be accorded the congressional judgement? *See* Burt, *Miranda and Title II: A Morganatic Marriage,* 1969 SUP. CT. REV. 81, 105-10.

**4.** Professor Bickel posed the following hypothetical: "[S]uppose Congress decided that aliens or eighteen-year-olds or residents of New Jersey are being discriminated against in New York. The decision would be as plausible as the one concerning Spanish-speaking Puerto Ricans. Could Congress give these groups the vote?" He argued that "[i]f Congress may freely bestow the vote as a means of curing other discriminations, which it fears may be practiced against groups deprived of the vote, essentially because of this deprivation and on the basis of no other evidence, then there is nothing left of state autonomy in setting qualifications for voting. The argument proves too much." Professor Bickel claimed that while the court properly emphasized the need that the means be appropriate and adapted to the given end, "it de-emphasized altogether too much Marshall's caveat that the means chosen must also not be prohibited, and must 'consist with the letter and spirit of the Constitution.'" *The Voting Rights Cases,* 1966 SUP. CT. REV. 79, 101.

## Congressional Definition of Ends

1. Justice Brennan also argued that Congress could determine that the literacy requirements themselves violate the equal protection guarantee even though the court had held to the contrary. The court makes no independent assessment of whether Congress' possible evaluation of the state interests was accurate.

2. Consider the following critique of the majority opinion: "The *Morgan* decision embodies revolutionary constitutional doctrine, for it overturns the relationship between Congress and the Court. Under American constitutional theory, it is for the Court to say what constitutional commands mean and to what situations they apply. Congress may implement the Court's interpretation, as it is specifically empowered to do by Section 5 of the Fourteenth Amendment. But Section 5 was intended as a power to deal with implementations only. *Morgan* would also overturn the relationship between federal and state governments. Once Congress is conceded the power to determine what degree of equality is required by the equal protection clause, it can strike down any state law on the ground that its classifications deny the requisite degree of equality. *Morgan* thus improperly converts Section 5, which is a power to deal with remedies, into a general police power for the nation." R. Bork, Constitutionality of the President's Busing Proposals 10 (1972). *See* Bickel, *The Voting Rights Cases,* 1966 Sup. Ct. Rev. 79, 97; Engdahl, *Constitutionality of the Voting Age Statute,* 39 Geo. Wash. L. Rev. 1, 15-25 (1970). On the other hand, Professor Cox argued: "Congressional supremacy, over the judiciary in the areas of legislative factfinding and evaluation and over the state legislatures under the supremacy clause in any area within the federal power, would seem to be a wiser touchstone, more consonant with the predominant themes of our constitutional history, than judicially-defined areas of primary and secondary state and federal competence." *Foreword,* 80 Harv. L. Rev., at 107. *See* Cox, *The Role of Congress in Constitutional Determinations,* 40 U. Cin. L. Rev. 199, 228-29 (1971).

Who decides what is interstate commerce—Congress or the court? Which branch has plenary power in defining the taxing and spending powers? Are the answers to these questions determinative of the allocation of roles in defining fourteenth amendment rights? *Compare* Engdahl, *Constitutionality of the Voting Age Statute,* 39 Geo. Wash. L. Rev., at 17-19, Cox, *Foreword,* 80 Harv. L. Rev., at 106-07, and Bickel, *The Voting Rights Cases,* 1966 Sup. Ct. Rev., at 97-98.

**3.** There are many grounds for judicial deference to the legislative holding on the substantive meaning of a constitutional right such as fact-finding capabilities, Congress' position as the people's representative in policymaking as well as the respective position of the court and Congress in relation to the states. Professor Cox emphasizes the importance of the fact-finding element in *Morgan*. But consider the view of Professor Engdahl: "[T]he question whether a particular state practice violates the equal protection clause, just like the question whether a particular activity is interstate commerce, had always—until *Morgan*—been reserved for ultimate judicial determination, not because it is a question which requires skills and procedures which Congress does not have, but simply because that is where generations of experience indicate the line separating the powers of legislature and judiciary should be drawn. Wisdom does dictate that matters of ultimate constitutional construction be left to final decision by a body disciplined in the reasoning process of the law and remote from gross political influences, rather than by Congress, whose very nature is to respond expediently to the political pressures of the moment." *Constitutionality of the Voting Age Statute*, 39 GEO. WASH. L. REV., at 20. *See Developments*, 25 STAN. L. REV. 885, 892-93 (1973).

**4.** Are there any limits to Congress's power to legislate under § 5 under the majority rationale? Could Congress strike down de facto segregation in education? Read the "state action" requirement out of the fourteenth amendment, § 1? Enact broad open housing legislation? *See* text, pp. 1101-10. Does *Morgan* logically lead "to the conclusion that Congress can constitutionally adopt a comprehensive code of criminal procedure applicable to prosecutions in state courts"? Cox, *Foreword*, 80 HARV. L. REV., at 108.

### Restricting Constitutional Rights

**1.** Justice Brennan, in footnote 10, rejects Justice Harlan's contention that, under the majority holding, Congress would necessarily have the power to restrict fourteenth amendment, § 1, rights. The same rationale that supports deference may support restrictive legislation. What justification is there for limiting the congressional power to define the right? *See* R. BORK, CONSTITUTIONALITY OF THE PRESIDENT'S BUSING PROPOSALS 8 (1972); Engdahl, *Constitutionality of the Voting Age Statute*, 39 GEO. WASH. L. REV., at 22. Professor Cox asserts: "There is no a priori reason for linking power to expand constitutional safeguards with power to dilute them. One can assert without logical fallacy that, since the chief function of the Supreme Court is to protect human rights, it should never defer to any legislative determination which restricts those rights without making its own investigation and characterization of the interests affected, even though it welcomes any legislative determination that extends human rights and is subject to challenge only as an unconstitutional extension of federal power at the expense of the States." *The Role of Congress in Constitutional Determinations,* 40 U. CIN. L. REV., at 253.

2.   Does Congress have power to restrict court-ordered remedies for desegregating formerly de jure segregated schools, *i.e.,* can the 1974 anti-busing legislation (text, p. 621) be based on Congress' § 5 powers? *Compare* R. BORK, CONSTITUTIONALITY OF THE PRESIDENT'S BUSING PROPOSALS (1972), with Goldberg, *The Administration's Anti-Busing Proposals—Politics Makes Bad Law,* 67 NW. U.L. REV. 319 (1972). Can *Morgan* be used to support Title II of the Omnibus Crime Control Act of 1968 which attempts to limit *Miranda? See* Burt, *Miranda and Title II: A Morganatic Marriage,* 1969 SUP. CT. REV. 81 (1969); Blackmar, *The Legislative Challenge to the Judiciary,* 14 ST. LOUIS U. L.J. 24 (1969).

### Limiting the § 5 Power: The Voting Rights Act of 1970

In the 1970 Voting Rights Act, Congress sought to lower the voting age from 21 to 18 in federal and state elections, to prohibit the use of literacy tests in state and national elections for five years, and to eliminate the use of state residency requirements in presidential and vice-presidential elections. The constitutionality of these provisions came before the court in Oregon v. Mitchell, 400 U.S. 112 (1970).

1.   *Age Requirements in State Elections.* In *Oregon v. Mitchell,* the court struck down the provisions of the Act lowering the voting age to 18 in state elections. Justice Black, announcing the judgment of the court in a separate opinion, argued that Art. I, § 2, was "a clear indication that the Framers intended the States to determine the qualifications of their own voters for state offices, because those qualifications were adopted for federal offices unless Congress directs otherwise under Art. I, § 4." The Constitution, he contended, was intended to preserve the independence of the states and "[n]o function is more essential to the separate and independent existence of the States and their governments than the power to determine within the limits of the Constitution the qualifications of their own voters for state, county, and municipal offices and the nature of their own machinery for filling local public offices." *Morgan,* where the court recognized congressional power to upset state voting qual-

ifications, was inapposite since "division of power between state and national governments, like every provision of the Constitution was expressly qualified by the Civil War Amendments' ban on racial discrimination."

Justice Stewart, in an opinion joined by Burger and Blackmun, concurred in Black's approach. But Stewart also considered the constitutionality of such age restrictions under the equal protection clause. The states, he argued, have "a constitutionally unimpeachable interest in establishing some age qualification as such. . . . Obviously, the power to establish an age qualification must carry with it the power to choose 21 as a reasonable voting age, as the vast majority of the States have done." He rejected application of the "compelling interest" standard since this would really "deny a State any choice at all, because no state could demonstrate a 'compelling interest' in drawing the line with respect to age at one point rather than another."

Turning to the effect of *Morgan,* he argued that it did not hold that Congress has power to determine what are and what are not compelling state interests. "The Court upheld the statute on two grounds: that Congress could conclude that enhancing the political power of the Puerto Rican community by conferring the right to vote was an appropriate means of remedying discriminatory treatment in public services; and that Congress could conclude that the New York statute was tainted by the impermissible purpose of denying the right to vote to Puerto Ricans, an undoubted invidious discrimination under the Equal Protection Clause." (Is this a correct statement of the holding in *Morgan?*) It would be necessary to go further to uphold the 1970 voting age provision since "[t]he state laws which it invalidates do not invidiously discriminate against any discrete and insular minority." Justice Stewart reasoned that the provisions would be constitutional only if Congress had power "to determine as a matter of substantive constitutional law what situations fall within the ambit of the [equal protection] clause, and what state interests are 'compelling.' " But, he concluded, *Morgan* gave § 5 its "furthest possible reach" and to sustain the present provisions "would require an enormous extension of that decision's rationale."

Justice Harlan, concurred separately, since a lengthy exegesis on the history of the fourteenth amendment led him to conclude that "[s]ection 1 must have been seen as little more than a constitutionalization of the 1866 Civil Rights Act"; it was not meant to deal with "rights arising from governmental organization, which were political in character." It was not intended to confer Negro suffrage since the fourteenth amendment, § 2, provided the remedy for franchise discrimination and the fifteenth amendment extended the suffrage.

Turning to the bearing of this historical understanding on present constitutional interpretation, Harlan asserted that judicial deference is not based on "relative fact-finding competence, but on due regard for the decision of the body constitutionally appointed to decide." In this case, "[e]stablishment of voting qualifications is a matter for state legislatures. Assuming any authority at all, only when the Court can say with some confidence that the legislature has demonstrably erred in adjusting the competing interests is it justified in striking down the legislative judgment." And the same principles apply to Congress's ability to displace state decisions. When policy perspectives and values differ between national and state legislators, "[t]he Supremacy Clause does not, as my colleagues seem to argue, represent a judgment that federal decisions are superior to those of the States whenever the two may differ." In any case, whether the state "has so exceeded the bounds of reason as to authorize federal intervention is not a matter as to which the political process is intrinsically likely to produce a sounder or more acceptable result. It is a matter of the adjustment of the federal system. In this area, to rely on Congress would make that body a judge of its own cause. The role of final arbiter belongs to this Court."

In considering the constitutionality of the age limitation, Justice Harlan concluded "that the suggestion that members of the age group between 18 and 21 are threatened with unconstitutional discrimination, or that any hypothetical discrimination is likely to be affected by lowering the voting age, is little short of fanciful. I see no justification for stretching to find any such possibility when all the evidence indicates that Congress—led on by recent decisions of this Court—thought simply that 18-year-olds were fairly entitled to the vote and that Congress could give it to them by legislation."

Justice Brennan, joined by Justices White and Marshall, dissented. First, he found that there was "serious question" whether the state age restriction could withstand scrutiny under the equal protection clause. Since the state restricted the franchise, the law was to be judged by the "compelling interest" standard. *See* text, pp. 665-75. While the state had a legislative interest in "promoting intelligent and responsible exercise of the franchise," there were only "bare assertions and long practice" supporting the exclusion of those under 18 as "less able." Forty-nine of 50 states hold 18-year-olds to adult criminal standards; every state permits them to marry; attendance at school is nowhere required beyond age 18;

and, there is no evidence that intelligence increases between age 18 and 21. Finally, there was no evidence that 18-year-old voters in Georgia and Kentucky, which had lowered the voting age, are any less interested, able or responsible.

In any case, the provision was a proper exercise of Congress' power under the fourteenth amendment, § 5. Justice Brennan noted that when state laws challenged as violating equal protection come before the court, they are cloaked with a presumption of constitutionality. But this limitation on review "is a limitation stemming not from the Fourteenth Amendment itself, but from the nature of judicial review. . . . The nature of the judicial process makes it an inappropriate forum for the determination of complex factual questions of the kind so often involved in constitutional adjudication." But this has no application to Congress. "Should Congress . . . undertake an investigation in order to determine whether the factual basis necessary to support a state legislative discrimination actually exists, it need not stop once it determines that some reasonable men could believe the factual basis exists. Section 5 empowers Congress to make its own determination on the matter."

In the present case, "[t]he core of dispute . . . is a conflict between state and federal legislative determinations of the factual issues upon which depends decision of a federal constitutional question—the legitimacy, under the Equal Protection Clause, of state discrimination against persons between the ages of 18 and 21. Our cases have repeatedly emphasized that, when state and federal claims come into conflict, the primacy of federal power requires that the federal finding of fact control."

Justice Brennan also responded to Justice Harlan's historical thesis that the fourteenth amendment was not intended to limit state power to set voter qualifications. After an extensive review of the historical evidence, he concluded "that the Amendment was framed by men who possessed differing views on the great question of the suffrage and who, partly in order to formulate some program of government and partly out of political expediency, papered over their differences with the broad, elastic language of § 1 and left to future interpreters of their Amendment the task of resolving in accordance with future vision and future needs the issues which they left unresolved." The historical record, "a product of differing and conflicting political pressures and conceptions of federalism" was simply "too vague and imprecise to provide . . . sure guidance in deciding the pending cases."

Justice Douglas also dissented on the basis of *Morgan*.

2. *Age Requirements in Federal Elections.* The provisions of the 1970 Act lowering the voting age to 18 in federal elections

were upheld 5-4. Justice Black joined the judgment of Justices Brennan, White, Marshall and Douglas who relied on the reasoning set forth above to sustain the federal age provisions under the fourteenth amendment, § 5. Justice Black, however, had a completely different reason. He asserted that Art. I, § 2 granting power to the states to set voter qualifications, was limited by Art. I, § 4, recognizing congressional power to "alter such Regulations." What are the "such Regulations" referred to in Art. I, § 4? Justice Black concluded "that Congress has ultimate supervisory power over congressional elections."

The Stewart group dissented since they rejected Justice Black's contention that Art. I, § 4, in any way limited state power to determine voter qualifications under Art. I, § 2. Justice Harlan similarly dissented for the reasons indicated in note 1.

**3.  Literacy Tests.** The court unanimously upheld the provisions of the Act proscribing literacy tests as a proper means of implementing the fifteenth amendment, § 2. Justice Black's opinion noted that in enacting the legislation, "Congress had before it a long history of the discriminatory use of literacy tests to disenfranchise voters on account of their race" and "striking evidence" of the impact of the 1965 voting act on minority registration.

Justice Stewart agreed and noted that nationwide application of the ban "reduces the danger that federal intervention will be perceived as unreasonable discrimination against particular States or particular regions of the country"; that it "facilitates the free movement of citizens from one State to another, since it eliminates the prospect that a change in residence will mean the loss of a federally protected right"; that it eliminates the difficult task of selecting states requiring federal intervention and lessens the burden on administrative and judicial machinery. Finally, such nationwide application was reasonable "when Congress acts against an evil such as racial discrimination which in varying degrees manifests itself in every part of the country." Congress was not required to make state by state findings. "In the interests of uniformity, Congress may paint with a much broader brush than may this Court, which must confine itself to the judicial function of deciding individual cases and controversies upon individual records."

Even Justice Harlan, while admitting difficulty, concluded that "[d]espite the lack of evidence of specific instances of discriminatory application or effect, Congress could have determined that racial prejudice is prevalent throughout the Nation, and that literacy tests unduly lend themselves to discriminatory application, either conscious or unconscious."

At least five Justices also concluded that the provision was constitutional under the fourteenth amendment, § 5, since, as Justice Black stated, "[t]here is substantial, if not overwhelming, evidence from which Congress could have concluded that it is a denial of equal protection to condition the political participation of children educated in a dual school system upon their educational achievement."

4. *Residency Tests.* Eight Justices held the residency provisions of the 1970 Act constitutional. The Brennan group relied on the fourteenth amendment, § 5, as enforcing "the constitutional right of all citizens to unhindered interstate travel and settlement" which could be burdened only when necessary to a compelling state interest. While not specifying the locus of the asserted right, Justice Brennan concluded that "Congress has explicitly found both that the imposition of durational residence requirements abridges the right of free interstate migration and that such requirements are not reasonably related to any compelling state interests."

Justice Stewart's opinion similarly held that "Congress could rationally conclude that the imposition of durational residency requirements unreasonably burdens and sanctions the privilege of taking up residence in another State." However, while noting the availability of § 5, he argued that the "Court has sustained the power of Congress to protect and facilitate the exercise of privileges of United States citizenship without reference to § 5. . . . These cases and others establish that Congress brings to the protection and facilitation of the exercise of privileges of United States citizenship all of its power under the Necessary and Proper Clause." He concluded: "Congress has acted to protect a constitutional privilege which finds its protection in the Federal Government and is national in character."

Justice Douglas argued that the provision rested on Congress's power under the fourteenth amendment, § 5, to enforce the privileges and immunities clause—"[t]he right to vote for national officers is a privilege and immunity of national citizenship."

Justice Black joined in the judgment based on his determination that "[i]n enacting these regulations for national elections Congress was attempting to insure a fully effective voice to all citizens in national elections. . . . Acting under its broad authority to create and maintain a national government, Congress unquestionably has power under the Constitution to regulate federal elections."

Only Justice Harlan dissented since he found "no specific clause of the Constitution empowering Congress to enact [the provision]," and was unable to see "how that nebulous construct, the right to travel can do so."

## 2. Discrimination in Housing

There have been numerous instances in this text of litigation designed to eliminate residential segregation. In north and south, decent, low-income housing is scarce and the problem is exacerbated when the individuals seeking a home are members of a racial minority. There are simply fewer markets open to them. The Kerner Commission Report in citing housing segregation as a major cause of disorders, noted that a "major factor condemning vast numbers of Negroes to urban slums is racial discrimination in the housing market. Discrimination prevents access to many non-slum areas, particularly the suburbs, and has a detrimental effect on ghetto housing itself." With discrimination in housing comes the concomitant problems of segregation in education and employment. REPORT OF THE NATIONAL ADVISORY COMM'N ON CIVIL DISORDERS 259 (1968). Nor is the housing problem simply a matter of economics. Black and white residential segregation exists regardless of the economic status of the residents.

In 1968, two major blows were struck against maintenance of housing discrimination. The first was enactment of the 1968 Open Housing Act, 42 U.S.C. § 3601 et seq., prohibiting discrimination in the sale or rental of housing on the basis of race, color, religion or national origin. The Act also reaches discrimination in financing, real estate brokerage and advertising for the sale or rental of property. Owners who sell their own dwellings, owners who lease three units or less in a building they occupy (Ms. Murphy's Boarding House), private clubs which provide housing incident to their primary purpose and religious organizations which sell to members of their own sects are exempt from coverage. Nevertheless, it has been estimated that as of 1970 over 80 per cent of the nation's housing was covered. U.S. COMM'N ON CIVIL RIGHTS, FEDERAL CIVIL RIGHTS ENFORCEMENT 142 (1970).

While the coverage of the legislation is fairly broad, enforcement provisions leave much to be desired. The Secretary of the Department of Housing and Urban Development is only entitled to receive complaints, not initiate them. In seeking resolution, the Secretary is required to use informal methods of conference, conciliation, and persuasion, deferring where possible to state authorities. Only when the Secretary determines that there is a "pattern or plan of resistance" may he refer the matter to the

Attorney General for prosecution. The individual can file a civil suit, but again, the difficulties of private litigation limit the effectiveness of this remedy. Further, Congress has been reluctant to appropriate funds to administer the Act resulting in inadequate staffing. Finally, HUD itself has tended to emphasize processing of individual complaints rather than broader compliance reviews (to determine the extent to which discriminatory housing practices are occurring within a community) and affirmative action programs. "The enforcement priorities that have been developed have placed primary emphasis on the processing of individual complaints. This, in the Commission's view, makes it unlikely that significant changes in the policies and practices in the housing industry can be brought about in the reasonably foreseeable future or that the growing trend towards racial residential segregation can be reversed." U.S. COMM'N ON CIVIL RIGHTS, FEDERAL CIVIL RIGHTS ENFORCEMENT EFFORT 145 (1970).

The second major effort against residential segregation came from the court in *Jones v. Alfred H. Mayer Co.*

### JONES v. ALFRED H. MAYER CO.
Supreme Court of the United States
392 U.S. 409, 20 L. Ed. 2d 1189, 88 S. Ct. 2186 (1968)

Justice STEWART delivered the opinion of the Court.

In this case we are called upon to determine the scope and constitutionality of an Act of Congress, 42 U.S.C. § 1982, which provides that:

> "All citizens of the United States shall have the same right, in every State and Territory, as is enjoyed by white citizens thereof to inherit, purchase, lease, sell, hold, and convey real and personal property."

On September 2, 1965, the petitioners filed a complaint in the District Court . . . alleging that the respondents had refused to sell them a home in the Paddock Woods community of St. Louis County for the sole reason that petitioner Joseph Lee Jones is a Negro. Relying in part upon § 1982, the petitioners sought injunctive and other relief. The District Court sustained the respondents' motion to dismiss the complaint, and the Court of Appeals for the Eighth Circuit affirmed, concluding that § 1982 applies only to state action and does not reach private refusals to sell. . . . [W]e reverse the judgment of the Court of Appeals. We hold that § 1982 bars *all* racial discrimination, private as well as public, in the sale or rental of property, and that the statute, thus construed, is a valid exercise of the power of Congress to enforce the Thirteenth Amendment.[5]

At the outset, it is important to make clear precisely what this case does *not* involve. Whatever else it may be, 42 U.S.C. § 1982 is not a comprehensive open housing law. In sharp contrast to the Fair Housing Title (Title VIII) of the Civil Rights Act of 1968, . . . the statute in this case deals only with racial discrimination and does not address itself to discrimination on grounds of religion or national origin. It does not deal specifically with discrimination in the provision of services or facilities in connection with the sale or rental of a dwelling. It does not prohibit advertising or other representations that indicate discriminatory preferences. It does not refer explicitly to discrimination in financing arrangements or in the provision of brokerage services.[10] It does not empower a federal administrative agency to assist aggrieved parties. It makes no provision for intervention by the Attorney General. And, although it can be enforced by injunction, it contains no provision expressly authorizing a federal court to order the payment of damages.

Thus, although § 1982 contains none of the exemptions that Congress included in the Civil Rights Act of 1968, it would be a serious mistake to suppose that § 1982 in any way diminishes the significance of the law recently enacted by Congress. . . .

. . . .

On its face, . . . § 1982 appears to prohibit *all* discrimination against Negroes in the sale or rental of property—discrimination by private owners as well as discrimination by public authorities. . . . Stressing what they consider to be the revolutionary implications of so literal a reading of § 1982, the respondents argue that Congress cannot possibly have intended any such result. Our examination of the relevant history, however, persuades us that Congress meant exactly what it said.

[Justice STEWART's lengthy review of legislative history is omitted. He concluded:]

---

[5] Because we have concluded that the discrimination alleged in the petitioners' complaint violated a federal statute that Congress had the power to enact under the Thirteenth Amendment, we find it unnecessary to decide whether that discrimination also violated the Equal Protection Clause of the Fourteenth Amendment.

[10] In noting that 42 U.S.C. § 1982 differs from the Civil Rights Act of 1968 in not dealing explicitly and exhaustively with such matters, we intimate no view upon the question whether ancillary services, or facilities of this sort might in some situations constitute "property" as that term is employed in § 1982. Nor do we intimate any view upon the extent to which discrimination in the provision of such services might be barred by 42 U.S.C. § 1981. . . .

In light of the concerns that led Congress to adopt it and the contents of the debates that preceded its passage, it is clear that the Act was designed to do just what its terms suggest: to prohibit all racial discrimination, whether or not under color of law, with respect to the rights enumerated therein—including the right to purchase or lease property.

. . . .

As we said in a somewhat different setting two Terms ago, "We think that history leaves no doubt that, if we are to give [the law] the scope that its origins dictate, we must accord it a sweep as broad as its language." United States v. Price, 383 U.S. 787. "We are not at liberty to seek ingenious analytical instruments," to carve from § 1982 an exception for private conduct— even though its application to such conduct in the present context is without established precedent. . . .

The remaining question is whether Congress has power under the Constitution to do what § 1982 purports to do: to prohibit all racial discrimination, private and public, in the sale and rental of property. Our starting point is the Thirteenth Amendment, for it was pursuant to that constitutional provision that Congress originally enacted what is now § 1982. . . .

As its text reveals, the Thirteenth Amendment "is not a mere prohibition of state laws establishing or upholding slavery, but an absolute declaration that slavery or involuntary servitude shall not exist in any part of the United States." Civil Rights Cases, 109 U.S. 3, 20. It has never been doubted, therefore, "that the power vested in Congress to enforce the article by appropriate legislation," includes the power to enact laws "direct and primary, operating upon the acts of individuals, whether sanctioned by state legislation or not."

. . . The constitutional question in this case, therefore, comes to this: Does the authority of Congress to enforce the Thirteenth Amendment "by appropriate legislation" include the power to eliminate all racial barriers to the acquisition of real and personal property? We think the answer to that question is plainly yes.

"By its own unaided force and effect," the Thirteenth Amendment "abolished slavery, and established universal freedom." Civil Rights Cases, 109 U.S. 3, 20. Whether or not the Amendment *itself* did any more than that—a question not involved in this case—it is at least clear that the Enabling Clause of that Amendment empowered Congress to do much more. For that clause clothed "Congress with power to pass *all laws neces-*

*sary and proper for abolishing all badges and incidents of slavery
in the United States." Ibid.* (Emphasis added.)

. . . .

. . . Surely Congress has the power under the Thirteenth
Amendment rationally to determine what are the badges and
the incidents of slavery, and the authority to translate that
determination into effective legislation. Nor can we say that the
determination Congress has made is an irrational one. For this
Court recognized long ago that, whatever else they may have
encompassed, the badges and incidents of slavery—its "burdens
and disabilities"—included restraints upon "those fundamental
rights which are the essence of civil freedom, namely, the same
right . . . to inherit, purchase, lease, sell and convey property,
as is enjoyed by white citizens." Civil Rights Cases, 109 U.S. 3,
22. Just as the Black Codes, enacted after the Civil War to restrict the free exercise of those rights, were substitutes for the
slave system, so the exclusion of Negroes from white communities became a substitute for the Black Codes. And when racial
discrimination herds men into ghettos and makes their ability to
buy property turn on the color of their skin, then it too is a
relic of slavery.

. . . .

Reversed.

Justice HARLAN, whom Justice WHITE joins, dissenting.

. . . .

. . . I believe that the Court's construction of § 1982 as applying to purely private action is almost surely wrong, and at the
least is open to serious doubt. The issue of the constitutionality of
§ 1982, as construed by the Court, and of liability under the
Fourteenth Amendment alone, also present formidable difficulties. Moreover, the political processes of our own era have, since
the date of oral argument in this case, given birth to a civil rights
statute embodying "fair housing" provisions which would at the
end of this year make available to others, though apparently not
to the petitioners themselves, the type of relief which the petitioners now seek. It seems to me that this latter factor so diminishes the public importance of this case that by far the wisest
course would be for this Court to refrain from decision and to
dismiss the writ as improvidently granted.

. . . .

Like the Court, I began analysis of § 1982 by examining its
language. . . . For me, there is an inherent ambiguity in the
term "right," as used in § 1982. The "right" referred to may

either be a right to equal status under the law, in which case the statute operates only against state-sanctioned discrimination, or it may be an "absolute" right enforceable against private individuals. To me, the words of the statute, taken alone, suggest the former interpretation, not the latter.

[Justice Harlan's counter-legislative history and comments on the ethics of the Reconstruction period is omitted. He concluded:]

In sum, the most which can be said with assurance about the intended impact of the 1866 Civil Rights Act upon purely private discrimination is that the Act probably was envisioned by most members of Congress as prohibiting official, community-sanctioned discrimination in the South, engaged in pursuant to local "customs" which in the recent time of slavery probably were embodied in laws or regulations. . . .

. . . .

. . . I think it particularly unfortunate for the Court to persist in deciding this case on the basis of a highly questionable interpretation of a sweeping, century-old statute which, as the Court acknowledges, contains none of the exemptions which the Congress of our own time found it necessary to include in a statute regulating relationships so personal in nature. In effect, this Court, by its construction of § 1982, has extended the coverage of federal "fair housing" laws far beyond that which Congress in its wisdom chose to provide in the Civil Rights Act of 1968. . . .

. . . .

---

## NOTES

### The Statutory Issues

1. *The Language of § 1982: Rights and Duties.* Does § 1982 have a "plain meaning?" It has been argued: "If one reads the plain words of § 1982, with one's mind swept clear of the encrustations of interpretation of the past century, it is hard to see how the English language could be more explicit. . . . Picture a situation in which a seller has placed property on the market for sale at a particular price, with the reservation that purchase is open to whites only. Freeze the situation at that instance in time, and then ask whether black citizens in that situation have the same right to purchase real property as white citizens. Plainly they do not, if the words have any meaning at all." Larson, *The New Law of Race Relations,* 1969 Wis. L. Rev. 470, 487. But does the recognition of a "right" of a prospective purchaser necessarily imply a "duty" to sell? It has been argued that "[t]he

'same rights' to purchase property could simply mean the same legal competence, that is, the same immunity from state-imposed disabilities." *The Supreme Court, 1967 Term,* 82 HARV. L. REV., 63, 96 (1968). Consider the other "rights" recognized in § 1982— do they help in clarifying the meaning of the term? Perhaps "right" could mean "liberty" or "privilege." *See* Casper, *Jones v. Mayer: Clio, Bemused and Confused Muse,* 1968 SUP. CT. REV. 89, 96-99.

   2. *Legislative History.* A principal point of contention among commentators has been whether the majority's or Justice Harlan's historical exegesis was correct. Did the reconstruction Congress intend § 1982 to reach private action, particularly discrimination in the sale or rental of property? Professor Casper argues that its purpose "was to give practical effect to the repeal of discrimination laws and customs in the South." *Jones v. Mayer,* 1968 SUP. CT. REV., at 99. *See* C. FAIRMAN, HISTORY OF THE SUPREME COURT OF THE UNITED STATES, VOL. V: RECONSTRUCTION AND REUNION, 1864-1888, Part I 1207-59 (1971). Others argue that *Jones* did not even go as far as intended by the reconstruction Congress. *See* Kohl, *The Civil Rights Act of 1866, Its Hour Come Round at Last: Jones v. Alfred H. Mayer Co.,* 55 VA. L. REV. 272 (1969); Note, *Jones v. Mayer: The Thirteenth Amendment and the Federal Anti-Discrimination Law,* 69 COLUM. L. REV. 1019, 1023 (1969). Consider again Chief Justice Warren's commentary on the value of the legislative history of the reconstruction Congresses as a guide to decision in *Brown v. Board of Education,* text, pp. 595-96. *See* Larson, *The New Law of Race Relations,* 1969 WIS. L. REV. 470, 488-90, who is critical of the attempt to rest the decision in *Jones* on the ambiguous historical record.

## The Constitutional Issues

   1. *Alternative Constitutional Rationale.* Section 1982 was reenacted in the 1870 Civil Rights Act, following passage of the fourteenth amendment. The petitioners in *Jones* also argued a fourteenth amendment violation. What are the obstacles to successfully maintaining such a claim? Is it relevant that the respondent was a housing developer exercising continuing authority over a surburban housing complex having about 1,000 inhabitants? Is there any theory for overcoming the "state action" obstacle?

   2. *A New Thirteenth Amendment?* Prior to *Jones,* the thirteenth amendment had been construed narrowly, limited primarily to federal legislation proscribing peonage and enforced

labor. *See* Shapiro, *Involuntary Servitude: The Need for a More Flexible Approach,* 19 RUTGERS L. REV. 65 (1964). What is the rationale for reading "badges of slavery" into the thirteenth amendment, § 1? Is it a matter of historical interpretation? *See* text, pp. 412-14. It has been argued: "Perhaps due to their misunderstanding of the institution [of slavery], the framers did not write their oratory concerning natural rights into the Constitution. Neither, however, did they specify that henceforth one man could not own another. The language they did choose may at least be seen as lying in a middle range between 'specific' and 'great' concepts. Although seemingly narrow, it appears to have been designed as a full response to the evil perceived. As modern perceptions of that evil grow, the response may take on increasingly broader scope." Note, *The "New" Thirteenth Amendment: A Preliminary Analysis,* 82 HARV. L. REV. 1294, 1302 (1969). In the absence of congressional enforcement legislation, does the thirteenth amendment, § 1, bar all "badges of slavery?" *See* Henkin, *Foreword: On Drawing Lines,* 82 HARV. L. REV. 63, 87 (1968). Has the court adopted the senior Justice Harlan's interpretation of the thirteenth amendment in his dissent in the *Civil Rights Cases,* text, p. 992?

3.  Does the thirteenth amendment impose affirmative duties on government to eliminate "badges of slavery"? Perhaps it is a command to promote "freedom" or "liberty," the converse of slavery. *See* text, p. 414. Or, perhaps it is a command to eliminate, root and branch, the "relics of slavery" (whatever that may mean). Or, finally, it may be a protection of all "fundamental rights." *See* Notes, *The New Thirteenth Amendment,* 82 HARV. L. REV., at 1306-12.

4.  What are the implications of *Jones* regarding congressional power? Does it open the door to broad congressional legislation against private racial discrimination? Professor Larson contends: "One certainly gets the impression from the opinion as a whole that, under the rubric of abolishing the badges and incidents of slavery, Congress would be within its constitutional rights in passing legislation striking down almost any conceivable kind of action, public or private, characterized by racial discrimination." Larson, *The New Law of Race Relations,* 1969 WIS. L. REV. 470, 504. Must such legislation be limited to blacks or can other minorities be protected? *See* Note, *Jones v. Mayer,* 69 COLUM. L. REV., at 1026.

5.  42 U.S.C. § 1981, which was also part of the 1866 Civil Rights Act, reenacted in the 1870 legislation, seems even broader than § 1982: "All persons . . . shall have the same rights . . . to make and enforce contracts, to sue, be parties, give evidence,

and to the full and equal benefit of all laws and proceedings as is enjoyed by white citizens, and shall be subject to like punishment, pains, penalties, taxes, licenses, and exactions of every kind and to no other."

The principle of *Jones* has been said to apply to the provision: "At least since Jones v. Mayer, a strictly private right, be it in the property field as such, or the contract field, is within the protection of the Civil Rights Act of 1866 against interference by a private citizen or a group of citizens. Governmental sanction or participation is no longer a necessary factor in the assertion of a § 1981 action." Dobbins v. International Bhd. of Elec. Workers, 292 F. Supp. 413 (S.D. Ohio 1968). What is included in the term "contract"? Employment? Admission to public places? Education? Access to hospitals? *See* C. ANTIEAU, FEDERAL CIVIL RIGHTS ACT—CIVIL PRACTICE 27-29 (1971), as supplemented.

6.  Are there any viable limits on the potential of the *Jones* rationale? Instead of looking at the values furthered by the thirteenth amendment's expansion, the question can be approached by looking at the competing values such as the rights of privacy, freedom of expression and freedom of association. A balancing of values may be required. Should a distinction be drawn between discrimination by a developer and that of a private individual? *See* Notes, *The New Thirteenth Amendment*, 82 HARV. L. REV., at 1312-15. Professor G. Buchanan suggests:

"Implicitly, this broader definition of the badge of slavery prohibited by Sections 1981 and 1982 should require that the contractual relationship be sought in a setting where nonpersonal, economic factors predominate. Although the Court in *Jones* does not expressly impose this requirement, the Court's emphasis on economic equality suggests the requirement exists as a tacit assumption. Without this requirement the *Jones* badge of slavery concept would sweep too broadly. For example, marriage is in many respects a contractual relationship. . . . Nevertheless, the mind rebels at a governmental attempt to prohibit a refusal to marry based on race. Clearly, in a marriage setting, the factor of personal choice predominates. The same should be true where a person is seeking to establish a contractual relationship with a genuinely private club. Here, as in marriage, the dominant motive on both sides for entering into the relationship is personal and associational rather than economic. In such relationships, the legal system can justly place a higher premium on preserving an unfettered right of personal choice." Buchanan, *Federal Regulation of Private Racial Prejudice: A Study of Law in Search of Morality*, 56 IOWA L. REV. 473, 507 (1971).

   **7.** In Sullivan v. Little Hunting Park, Inc., 396 U.S. 229
(1969), the court, per Justice Douglas, held that refusal by the
board of a community recreation facility to approve assignment
of membership by the owner to a lessee of his house fell within
the term "lease" in § 1982 giving rise to action for damages on
behalf of both the white owner and black lessee. This was reaffirmed, and an attempt to claim exemption as a private club
rejected, in Tillman v. Wheaton-Haven Recreational Ass'n,
Inc., 410 U.S. 431 (1973), where Justice Blackmun for the court
stated: "When an organization links membership benefits to residency in a narrow geographical area, that decision infuses those
benefits into the bundle of rights for which an individual pays
when buying or leasing within the area. The mandate of 42
U.S.C. § 1982 then operates to guarantee a non-white resident,
who purchases, leases, or holds this property, the same rights as
are enjoyed by a white resident."

# Index

References are to page numbers